Poetry Criticism

Guide to Gale Literary Criticism Series

For criticism on	Consult these Gale series
Authors now living or who died after December 31, 1999	*CONTEMPORARY LITERARY CRITICISM (CLC)*
Authors who died between 1900 and 1999	*TWENTIETH-CENTURY LITERARY CRITICISM (TCLC)*
Authors who died between 1800 and 1899	*NINETEENTH-CENTURY LITERATURE CRITICISM (NCLC)*
Authors who died between 1400 and 1799	*LITERATURE CRITICISM FROM 1400 TO 1800 (LC)* *SHAKESPEAREAN CRITICISM (SC)*
Authors who died before 1400	*CLASSICAL AND MEDIEVAL LITERATURE CRITICISM (CMLC)*
Authors of books for children and young adults	*CHILDREN'S LITERATURE REVIEW (CLR)*
Dramatists	*DRAMA CRITICISM (DC)*
Poets	*POETRY CRITICISM (PC)*
Short story writers	*SHORT STORY CRITICISM (SSC)*
Literary topics and movements	*HARLEM RENAISSANCE: A GALE CRITICAL COMPANION (HR)* *THE BEAT GENERATION: A GALE CRITICAL COMPANION (BG)*
Asian American writers of the last two hundred years	*ASIAN AMERICAN LITERATURE (AAL)*
Black writers of the past two hundred years	*BLACK LITERATURE CRITICISM (BLC)* *BLACK LITERATURE CRITICISM SUPPLEMENT (BLCS)*
Hispanic writers of the late nineteenth and twentieth centuries	*HISPANIC LITERATURE CRITICISM (HLC)* *HISPANIC LITERATURE CRITICISM SUPPLEMENT (HLCS)*
Native North American writers and orators of the eighteenth, nineteenth, and twentieth centuries	*NATIVE NORTH AMERICAN LITERATURE (NNAL)*
Major authors from the Renaissance to the present	*WORLD LITERATURE CRITICISM, 1500 TO THE PRESENT (WLC)* *WORLD LITERATURE CRITICISM SUPPLEMENT (WLCS)*

ISSN 1052-4851

Poetry Criticism

Excerpts from Criticism of the Works of the Most Significant and Widely Studied Poets of World Literature

Volume 58

Lawrence J. Trudeau
Project Editor

THOMSON
GALE

Detroit • New York • San Francisco • San Diego • New Haven, Conn. • Waterville, Maine • London • Munich

Poetry Criticism, Vol. 58

Project Editor
Lawrence J. Trudeau

Editorial
Jessica Bomarito, Kathy D. Darrow, Jeffrey Hunter, Jelena O. Krstović, Michelle Lee, Ellen McGeagh, Joseph Palmisano, Linda Pavlovski, Thomas J. Schoenberg, Russel Whitaker

Data Capture
Francis Monroe, Gwen Tucker

Indexing Services
Synapse, the Knowledge Link Corporation

Rights and Acquisitions

Imaging and Multimedia
Dean Dauphinais, Leitha Etheridge-Sims, Lezlie Light, Dan Newell

Composition and Electronic Capture
Kathy Sauer

Manufacturing
Rhonda Williams

Product Manager
Janet Witalec

LIBRARY OF CONGRESS CATALOG CARD NUMBER 91-118494

ISBN 0-7876-8692-1
ISSN 1052-4851

Printed in the United States of America
10 9 8 7 6 5 4 3 2 1

Contents

Preface

*P*oetry Criticism (PC) presents significant criticism of the world's greatest poets and provides supplementary biographical and bibliographical material to guide the interested reader to a greater understanding of the genre and its creators. Although major poets and literary movements are covered in such Gale Literary Criticism series as *Contemporary Literary Criticism (CLC), Twentieth-Century Literary Criticism (TCLC), Nineteenth-Century Literature Criticism (NCLC), Literature Criticism from 1400 to 1800 (LC),* and *Classical and Medieval Literature Criticism (CMLC),* PC offers more focused attention on poetry than is possible in the broader, survey-oriented entries on writers in these Thomson Gale series. Students, teachers, librarians, and researchers will find that the generous excerpts and supplementary material provided by PC supply them with the vital information needed to write a term paper on poetic technique, to examine a poet's most prominent themes, or to lead a poetry discussion group.

Scope of the Series

PC is designed to serve as an introduction to major poets of all eras and nationalities. Since these authors have inspired a great deal of relevant critical material, PC is necessarily selective, and the editors have chosen the most important published criticism to aid readers and students in their research. Each author entry presents a historical survey of the critical response to that author's work. The length of an entry is intended to reflect the amount of critical attention the author has received from critics writing in English and from foreign critics in translation. Every attempt has been made to identify and include the most significant essays on each author's work. In order to provide these important critical pieces, the editors sometimes reprint essays that have appeared elsewhere in Thomson Gale's Literary Criticism Series. Such duplication, however, never exceeds twenty percent of a PC volume.

Organization of the Book

Each PC entry consists of the following elements:

- The **Author Heading** cites the name under which the author most commonly wrote, followed by birth and death dates. Also located here are any name variations under which an author wrote, including transliterated forms for authors whose native languages use nonroman alphabets. If the author wrote consistently under a pseudonym, the pseudonym will be listed in the author heading and the author's actual name given in parenthesis on the first line of the biographical and critical introduction. Uncertain birth or death dates are indicated by question marks. Single-work entries are preceded by the title of the work and its date of publication.

- The **Introduction** contains background information that introduces the reader to the author and the critical debates surrounding his or her work.

- A **Portrait of the Author** is included when available.

- The list of **Principal Works** is ordered chronologically by date of first publication and lists the most important works by the author. The first section comprises poetry collections and book-length poems. The second section gives information on other major works by the author. For foreign authors, the editors have provided original foreign-language publication information and have selected what are considered the best and most complete English-language editions of their works.

- Reprinted **Criticism** is arranged chronologically in each entry to provide a useful perspective on changes in critical evaluation over time. All individual titles of poems and poetry collections by the author featured in the entry are printed in boldface type. The critic's name and the date of composition or publication of the critical work are given at the beginning of each piece of criticism. Unsigned criticism is preceded by the title of the source in which it appeared. Footnotes are reprinted at the end of each essay or excerpt. In the case of excerpted criticism, only those footnotes that pertain to the excerpted texts are included.

- Critical essays are prefaced by brief **Annotations** explicating each piece.

- A complete **Bibliographical Citation** of the original essay or book precedes each piece of criticism.

- An annotated bibliography of **Further Reading** appears at the end of each entry and suggests resources for additional study. In some cases, significant essays for which the editors could not obtain reprint rights are included here. Boxed material following the further reading list provides references to other biographical and critical sources on the author in series published by Thomson Gale.

Cumulative Indexes

A **Cumulative Author Index** lists all of the authors that appear in a wide variety of reference sources published by Thomson Gale, including *PC*. A complete list of these sources is found facing the first page of the Author Index. The index also includes birth and death dates and cross references between pseudonyms and actual names.

A **Cumulative Nationality Index** lists all authors featured in *PC* by nationality, followed by the number of the *PC* volume in which their entry appears.

A **Cumulative Title Index** lists in alphabetical order all individual poems, book-length poems, and collection titles contained in the *PC* series. Titles of poetry collections and separately published poems are printed in italics, while titles of individual poems are printed in roman type with quotation marks. Each title is followed by the author's last name and corresponding volume and page numbers where commentary on the work is located. English-language translations of original foreign-language titles are cross-referenced to the foreign titles so that all references to discussion of a work are combined in one listing.

Citing *Poetry Criticism*

When writing papers, students who quote directly from any volume in the Literary Criticism Series may use the following general format to footnote reprinted criticism. The first example pertains to material drawn from periodicals, the second to material reprinted from books.

Sylvia Kasey Marks, "A Brief Glance at George Eliot's *The Spanish Gypsy,*" *Victorian Poetry* 20, no. 2 (Summer 1983), 184-90; reprinted in *Poetry Criticism,* vol. 20, ed. Ellen McGeagh (Detroit: The Gale Group), 128-31.

Linden Peach, "Man, Nature and Wordsworth: American Versions," *British Influence on the Birth of American Literature,* (Macmillan Press Ltd., 1982), 29-57; reprinted in *Poetry Criticism,* vol. 20, ed. Ellen McGeagh (Detroit: The Gale Group), 37-40.

Suggestions are Welcome

Readers who wish to suggest new features, topics, or authors to appear in future volumes, or who have other suggestions or comments are cordially invited to call, write, or fax the Product Manager:

Product Manager, Literary Criticism Series
Thomson Gale
27500 Drake Road
Farmington Hills, MI 48331-3535
1-800-347-4253 (GALE)
Fax: 248-699-8054

Acknowledgments

The editors wish to thank the copyright holders of the criticism included in this volume and the permissions managers of many book and magazine publishing companies for assisting us in securing reproduction rights. We are also grateful to the staffs of the Detroit Public Library, the Library of Congress, the University of Detroit Mercy Library, Wayne State University Purdy/Kresge Library Complex, and the University of Michigan Libraries for making their resources available to us. Following is a list of the copyright holders who have granted us permission to reproduce material in this volume of *PC*. Every effort has been made to trace copyright, but if omissions have been made, please let us know.

COPYRIGHTED MATERIAL IN *PC*, VOLUME 58, WAS REPRODUCED FROM THE FOLLOWING PERIODICALS:

Bucknell Review, v. XXXVIII, 1994 for "'An Origin Like Water': The Poetry of Eavan Boland and Modernist Critiques of Irish Literature" by Ann Owens Weekes. Edited by John S. Rickard. Copyright © 1994 by Associated University Presses, Inc. Reproduced by permission.—*Chaucer Review,* v. 4, 1970; v. 13, summer, 1978; v. 14, spring, 1980; v. 31, 1997; v. 32, 1997. Copyright © 1970, 1978, 1980, 1997 by The Pennsylvania State University. All reproduced by permission of the publisher.—*Chicago Review,* v. 17, 1964. Copyright © 1964 by *Chicago Review.* Reproduced by permission.—*Colby Quarterly,* v. XXXII, June, 1996; v. XXIII, December, 1997; v. XXXV, December, 1999; v. XXXVI, September, 2000; . XXXVII, December, 2001. Copyright © 1996, 1997, 1999, 2000, 2001 by *Colby Quarterly.* All reproduced by permission.—*English Language Notes,* v. 22, 1985; v. 25, March, 1988. Copyright © 1985, 1988 by Regents of the University of Colorado. All rights reserved. Both reproduced by permission.—*Exemplaria,* v. 5, March, 1993; v. 8, spring, 1996. Copyright © 1993, 1996 by Center for Medieval and Early Renaissance Studies, SUNY. Both reproduced by permission.—*French Forum,* v. 13, January, 1988. Copyright © The University of Nebraska Press, 1988./ v. 19, May, 1994. Copyright © 1994 by *French Forum.* Both reproduced by permission of the University of Nebraska Press.—*Explicator,* v. 60, winter, 2002. Copyright © 2002 by Helen Dwight Reid Educational Foundation. Reproduced with permission of the Helen Dwight Reid Educational Foundation, published by Heldref Publications, 1319 18th Street, NW, Washington, DC 20036-1802.—*L'Esprit Créateur,* v. XXXII, summer, 1992; v. XXXVI, fall, 1996. Copyright © 1992, 1996 by L'Esprit Créateur. Both reproduced by permission.—*Medium Aevum,* v. 58, 1989. Copyright © 1989 by Society for the Study of Mediaeval Languages and Literature. All rights reserved. Reproduced by permission.—*Mosaic,* v. 33, September, 2000. Copyright © *Mosaic* 2000. Acknowledgment of previous publication is herewith made.—*Neophilologus,* v. 75, January, 1991 for "'A Coverchief or a Calle': The Ultimate End of the Wife of Bath's Search for Sovereignty" by Colin A. Ireland. Reproduced by permission of the author. / v. 85, January, 2001. Copyright © 2001 by Kluwer Academic Publishers. Reproduced by permission of Kluwer Academic Publishers.—*Orbis Litterarum,* v. 41, 1986. Copyright © 1986 Munksgaard International Publishers, Ltd. Reproduced by permission of Blackwell Publishers.—*P.N. Review,* v. 18, January-February, 1992 for "Inside and Outside History" by Anne Stevenson; Copyright © 1992 by *Poetry Nation Review.* All rights reserved. Reproduced by permission of the author. / v. 25, January-February, 1999 for "A Certain Slant of Light" by David Ward. Copyright © 1999 by *Poetry National Review.* All rights reserved. Reproduced by permission of the author.—*PMLA,* v. 102, January, 1987. Copyright © 1987 by the Modern Language Association of America. Reproduced by permission of the *Modern Language Association of America.*—*Poetry,* v. CXXVIII, June, 1976 for "Stances on Love" by David Mus. Copyright © 1976 by the Modern Poetry Association. Reprinted in *Mus, The Essays,* Ateneo Roma, 1988. Reproduced by permission of the Editor of Poetry and the author.—*Romance Notes,* v. XIX, fall, 1978. Copyright © 1978 by *Romance Notes.* Reproduced by permission.—*Southern Review,* Louisiana State University, v. 35, spring, 1999 for "Ireland's Best" by Kate Daniels. Copyright © 1999 by Kate Daniels. Reproduced by permission of the author.—*Studies in 20th Century Literature,* v. 13, winter, 1989. Copyright © 1989 by Studies in 20th Century Literature. Reproduced by permission.—*TriQuarterly,* v. 54, spring, 1982 for "Talking about Writings through Finnegan's Wake" by John Cage and Richard Cory Kostelanetz. Copyright © 1982 by *TriQuarterly,* Northwestern University. Reproduced by permission of the respective authors.—*Twentieth Century Literature,* v. 37, winter, 1991. Copyright © 1992 by Hofstra University. Reproduced by permission.—*Women: A Cultural Review,* v. 8, spring, 1997. Copyright © 1997 by Oxford University Press. Reproduced by permission of Routledge, Taylor & Francis Group at http://www.tandf.co.uk/journals.—*Women's Studies,* v. 11, 1984. Copyright © 1984 by H. Marshall Leicester, Jr. / v. 15, 1988. Copyright © 1988 by Gordon and Breach, Science Publishers, Inc. Both reproduced by permission.

Thomson Gale Literature Product Advisory Board

The members of the Thomson Gale Literature Product Advisory Board—reference librarians from public and academic library systems—represent a cross-section of our customer base and offer a variety of informed perspectives on both the presentation and content of our literature products. Advisory board members assess and define such quality issues as the relevance, currency, and usefulness of the author coverage, critical content, and literary topics included in our series; evaluate the layout, presentation, and general quality of our printed volumes; provide feedback on the criteria used for selecting authors and topics covered in our series; provide suggestions for potential enhancements to our series; identify any gaps in our coverage of authors or literary topics, recommending authors or topics for inclusion; analyze the appropriateness of our content and presentation for various user audiences, such as high school students, undergraduates, graduate students, librarians, and educators; and offer feedback on any proposed changes/enhancements to our series. We wish to thank the following advisors for their advice throughout the year.

Eavan Boland
1944-

(Full name Eavan Aisling Boland) Irish poet and critic.

INTRODUCTION

Boland is viewed as one of the most important poets in contemporary Irish literature. Critics commend her exploration of feminist issues in her work, particularly the role of women in Irish literature and society. In her poetry she has also subverted traditional Irish mythology and concepts of female identity in order to express a more accurate perspective on the contributions and achievements of women in Irish history, politics, and culture.

BIOGRAPHICAL INFORMATION

Boland was born on September 24, 1944, in Dublin. Her father, the Irish diplomat Frederick H. Boland, was posted in 1950 as the Irish Ambassador to the Court of St. James in London, and then in 1956 as the President of the United Nations General Assembly. Growing up in London and New York City, Boland felt alienated from her Irish heritage, particularly in London, where she encountered prejudice against the Irish. As a teenager she returned to Ireland and attended the Holy Child Convent in Killiny, County Dublin. She immersed herself in Irish culture and began to write poetry. In 1962 she attended Trinity College in Dublin and published her first collection of verse, *23 Poems*. In 1966 she received degrees in English and Latin from Trinity and was hired by the English department as a lecturer. In a short time, however, she left Trinity and became a full-time literary critic and poet. Much of her early poetry focused on domestic concerns, such as marriage, children, and her home in a suburb of Dublin. Yet with the publication of *In Her Own Image* (1980), critics began to take notice of her exploration of feminist issues, particularly the role of female poets within the patriarchal literary establishment in Ireland. Her work generated much controversy and brought her international recognition as a feminist literary figure. She has taught at several universities, including University College, Dublin; Bowdoin College; the University of Utah; and Stanford University. In addition, she has received several awards for her work, such as the Lannan Award for Poetry in 1994, the Bucknell Medal of Merit in 2000, and the Frederick Nims Memorial Prize in 2002.

MAJOR WORKS

Boland's early poems were conventional in style, centered on a celebration of domestic issues such as marriage and children, and were heavily influenced by the work of William Butler Yeats. Yet even at this early stage she demonstrated a recurring interest in the role of women in Irish literature and society, which later became a central thematic concern of her poetry and essays. In *In Her Own Image,* Boland explores such topics as domestic abuse, anorexia, breast cancer, and infanticide. She also addresses the lack of real women in Irish myths and national history and announces her suspicion of the male literary tradition and its portrayal of women. *Night Feed* (1982) considers the concept of female identity through an examination of ordinary women as well as female figures who have been marginalized in Irish mythology. Through these depictions of regular women, she celebrates the complexity of women's lives. In *Outside History* (1990) she continues her exploration of female identity, and strives to uncover the silence of generations of women whose lives and contributions to history and culture have been largely ignored. For example, "The Achill Woman" portrays Boland's encounter, during a stay in Achill, with an old woman, who discusses of the Irish Famine and the people's struggle to survive such difficult times. The poet relates this woman's story to her own life and realizes her own failure in recognizing the importance of this woman's voice and her own connection to women throughout Irish history. In these collections, Boland also rejects the notion that women who live in suburbia and raise families are unworthy of attention. Her poetry celebrates the beauty in these lives and the importance of family, marriage, and domestic responsibilities. *The Lost Land* (1998) returns to the dynamics of family, as Boland reflects on her children growing up and leaving home and the ways in which this process affects her sense of identity. In *Against Love Poetry* (2001), Boland once again finds value and beauty in everyday existence and explores the tension between marriage and independence.

CRITICAL RECEPTION

Boland has emerged as one of the most important female voices in Irish poetry. Feminist critics have applauded her attempts to locate herself within the Irish poetic tradition by rejecting and reexamining the limited, traditional role of women in Irish mythology and history. By subverting these myths and history, they contend, she succeeds in repossessing her identity as an Irish woman and poet. In a broader sense, critics maintain, Boland's poetic development reflects the dramatic political and cultural shifts in Ireland in the past several decades. Commentators have noted the exploration of such controversial themes as child abuse, violence against women, self-esteem, and eating disorders in her verse. She also touches on issues of alienation, assimilation, identification, and exile. Critics praise her painterly consciousness, poignant lyrics, keen sense of poetic ethics, and use of the concrete to reveal hidden stories in Irish histories. A few critics caution against a strict feminist reading of her poems, contending that this minimizes her work and her contribution to modern poetry. Others have derided her verse as strident and accuse her of mythologizing the domestic sphere and the suburban life. Yeats and Adrienne Rich are regarded as profound influences on Boland's poetry, and commentators have found affinities between the poetry of Boland and Seamus Heaney.

PRINCIPAL WORKS

Poetry

23 Poems 1962
New Territory 1967

In Her Own Image 1980
The War Horse 1980
Introducing Eavan Boland 1981
Night Feed 1982
The Journey 1983
Selected Poems 1990
Outside History: Selected Poems, 1980-90 1990
In a Time of Violence 1994
Collected Poems 1995
An Origin Like Water: Collected Poems, 1967-1987 1996
Anna Liffey 1997
The Lost Land 1998
Limitations 2000
Against Love Poetry 2001
Journey with Two Maps: An Anthology 2002
Three Irish Poets, An Anthology: Eavan Boland, Paula Meehan, Mary O'Malley [edited by Boland] 2003

Other Major Works

W. B. Yeats and His World [with Michael MacLiammoir] (nonfiction) 1970
A Kind of Scar: The Woman Poet in National Tradition (nonfiction) 1989
Object Lessons: The Life of the Woman and the Poet in Our Time (nonfiction) 1995

CRITICISM

Patricia L. Hagen and Thomas W. Zelman (essay date winter 1991)

SOURCE: Hagen, Patricia L., and Thomas W. Zelman. "'We Were Never on the Scene of the Crime': Eavan Boland's Repossession of History." *Twentieth Century Literature* 37, no. 4 (winter 1991): 442-53.

[*In the following essay, Hagen and Zelman assert that Boland aims to "repossess" her place within the Irish literary tradition.*]

From Yeats and the Celtic Revival onward, Irish poets have recorded, shaped, and criticized their nation's emerging independent identity. In the process, of course, they also attempted to reforge links to the past by creating for Ireland a literary tradition incorporating the myths, folklore, and symbols of a long-suppressed Gaelic heritage. Now, at the end of the twentieth century, the literary tradition wished into existence by Yeats has been expanded, modified, complicated, and virtually completed: it has become, so the argument goes, a "given" in Irish literature, a dead issue. Thus in *Modern Irish Poetry*, Robert Garratt "assumes a change among a younger generation of writers in their attitude toward tradition" (5). For today's poets, Garratt argues, the "need to create and establish a tradition in literature no longer appears foremost in their thoughts" (5); contemporary poets no longer feel compelled to write the "definitions" and "apologetics" that so obsessed their poetic forefathers.

Although Garratt does not use the word, *forefathers* is by implication a key concept in his formulation; the tradition Garratt traces ("from Yeats to Heaney") is exclusively male. For women, who until recently have appeared only as subjects and objects of poems, not as their authors, the matter of tradition carries considerably more urgency than it does for their male counterparts. Indeed, just as the early Revivalists sought reconnection with a Gaelic heritage suppressed by centuries of English domination, so Irish women poets seek reconnection with a female heritage suppressed by centuries of male domination. Eavan Boland, a major figure in the current generation of Irish poets, is vitally concerned with the "ethics" underlying the Irish poetic tradition, most notably the ethical choices involved in a writer's selection of themes worth exploring in poetry, for these themes will naturally reveal the writer's—and, collectively, the tradition's—ability to bear witness to the truth of experience.

As a poet and a critic, Eavan Boland displays a painterly consciousness, a keen, painful awareness of the shaping power of language, and a fundamental sense of poetic ethics, three strands that merge into a vital concern with the artistic image and its relationship to truth. Art—poetry, painting, history—outlasts human lives; its images offer us a sense of the past which allows us to view and situate ourselves, individually and collectively, as heirs to tradition. As Boland notes, "we ourselves are constructed by our constructs" (*Kind of Scar* 20). Given the relation between image and selfhood, the poet—especially the woman poet—has an ethical obligation to de- and re-construct those constructs that shape literary tradition, bearing witness to the truths of experience suppressed, simplified, falsified by the "official" record.

In their broad strokes these issues are not, of course, uniquely Irish; as Boland acknowledges, "poetic ethics are evident and urgent in any culture where tensions between a poet and her or his birthplace are inherited and established" (*Kind of Scar* 7)—a view suggesting the difficulty women poets encounter as they approach a sanctioned national myth. Nevertheless, it is within the Irish poetic tradition that, by both birth and choice, Eavan Boland locates herself. Indeed, because of her upbringing, as she describes in **"Irish Childhood in England,"** issues of assimilation and estrangement, identification and exile—issues themselves central to an Irish tradition in literature—became significant for her at an early age. She arrived in England, a "freckled six year old"

overdressed and sick on the plane
when all of England to an Irish child
was nothing more than what you'd lost and how. . . .

                                          (*Journey* 50-51)

For this child in exile, "filled with some malaise / of love for what [she'd] never known [she] had" (50), educated in English schools, the songs and poems of her birth-country—the Irish poetic tradition—in many ways created Ireland for her. **"Fond Memory"** (*Journey* 52) juxtaposes her early sense of identification with the Ireland of song and poem against her adult sense of estrangement from that construction. Evoking her disturbingly peaceful childhood in postwar England, one in which she "wore darned worsted" and

    . . . learned
how wise the Magna Carta was, how hard the Ha-
    noverians
had tried . . .

Boland moves from her primary-school experience in the first half of the poem to her home in the second, where her father plays the "slow / lilts of Tom Moore" at the piano. She is affected strongly by the music and

        . . . as much as I could think—
I thought this is my country, was, will be again,
this upward-straining song made to be
our safe inventory of pain. And I was wrong.

                                          (52)

As an adult, she rejects the "safe inventory of pain," with its manifold falsifications and simplifications, but nonetheless retains a fundamental sense of identity as an Irish poet. "I didn't know what to hold, to keep" (*Journey* 50), the speaker claims in **"An Irish Childhood in England: 1951."**

"On the one hand," Boland writes, "I knew that as a poet, I could not easily do without the idea of a nation. . . . On the other, I could not as a woman accept the nation formulated for me by Irish poetry and its traditions" (*Kind of Scar* 8). The only reconciliation possible for her was to "repossess" that tradition. By affirming herself as an Irish poet, and thus rejecting the common notion that women's poetry should be quarantined from mainstream literature, Boland is in essence claiming her birthright, her say in that tradition, her right to "establish a discourse with the idea of a nation" (*Kind of Scar* 20).

As Boland cautions, such "repossession" is neither a single nor a static act, but a fluid process of de- and reconstruction. It is as if she has been presented with a seemingly completed jigsaw puzzle, but herself holds a series of additional pieces. In defiance of those who suggest she create a nice border around the original, Boland would break apart the completed picture and reconstruct a new image. In this model, the first part of the tradition to be shattered must be its alienating "fusion of the national and the feminine which seemed to simplify both" (*Kind of Scar* 7). Instead of real lives, the tradition offers Dark Rosaleen, the Old Woman of the Roads, and Cathleen Ni Houlihan, images that by their mythic and ornamental nature necessarily reduce the complex feelings, aspirations, and lives of real women—but not only of women. Boland views these emblematic women, "passive projection[s] of a national idea" (*Kind of Scar* 13), as "an underlying fault in Irish poetry; almost a geological weakness" because "all good poetry depends on an ethical relation between imagination and image. Images are not ornaments; they are truths" (*Kind of Scar* 23). By recasting a defeated nation into a triumphant woman, the Irish literary tradition may have gained aesthetically, but it lost ethically: gone were the "human truths of survival and humiliation" and in their place were the "hollow victories . . . the rhyming queens" (*Kind of Scar* 13).

Boland's poems, then, attempt to unseat the rhyming queens and reinscribe the human truths they have suppressed, to "repossess" those portions of history ignored by the Irish canon and to reassess the truth of the national identity. In this task, her starting point is frequently the driving of a wedge into the "almost geological weakness" of the Irish poetic tradition. In its simplest terms, the resulting division is the distance between male and female—the split, in Boland's terms, between "hearth and history," *her hearth* and *his story*. *Her* world, if seen at all, is confined to the margins of *his* story, the celebration of the grand sweep of Irish heroism. As Boland notes, while the nation's "flags and battle-cries, even its poetry" at times use feminine imagery, "the true voice and vision of women are routinely excluded" (*Kind of Scar* 19). "It's our alibi / for all time," she writes in **"It's a Woman's World,"** "that as far as history goes / we were never / on the scene of the crime" (357). In the official records—the history books, battle-cries, songs, and poems—women exist largely as lamenting voices, mouthpieces, ornaments: the Young Queen, the Old Mother, the Poor Old Woman. "So when the king's head / gored its basket," the speaker notes, "we were gristing bread"

> or getting the recipe
> for a good soup
> to appetize
> our gossip.

(357)

"Like most historic peoples," women are "defined / by what we forget, by what we never will be: / star-gazers, / fire-eaters" (357). The unsensational and therefore unwritten sufferings of ordinary women, ordinary people, are doomed to become unhistory: "And still no page / scores the low music / of our outrage" (358). Within *his story,* gristing bread is of no consequence, despite its overwhelming importance in sustaining life; *her hearth* (a precondition of the "heroics" celebrated

by *his story*), trivialized into recipes and gossip, is beneath notice in the records of mythic "big events." History rests, that is, on the assumption that the ordinary and the important are mutually exclusive categories, an assumption that justifies omitting women's experience from the records even today; women's aspirations, sufferings, and unglamorous heroics are rendered invisible by their ordinariness:

> . . . appearances
> still reassure.
> That woman there,
> craned to the starry mystery
>
> is merely getting a breath
> of evening air,
> while this one here—
> her mouth
>
> a burning plume—
> she's no fire-eater,
> just my frosty neighbor
> coming home.

(358)

The "reassuring" qualifiers *merely* and *just* are instructive, marking the boundaries between the traditional reading of women's lives and the speaker's reinscription of them. While the "historian" may dismiss one woman as "merely" getting a breath of air, the other as "just" a neighbor, the speaker subverts these tidy reductions by allowing us to see the star-gazer in the woman taking the air, the fire-eater in the "frosty neighbor." Both are still "ordinary women," but *ordinary* is no longer pejorative, no longer synonymous with *simple* and *unimportant.*

Although real women are "never on the scene of the crime" in the Irish literary tradition, their mythic counterparts appear with predictable regularity. The reductive force of the fusion of the feminine and the national, with its corollary invisibility of real, complex women, makes the subversion of this image a natural starting point in Boland's act of repossession. This subversion permeates such divergent poems as the **"Tirade for the Mimic Muse," "Envoi," "Making Up,"** and **"Mise Eire."**

The title of the latter poem (rendered into English as **"I Am Ireland"**) is particularly evocative, for it echoes both *Cathleen Ni Houlihan* and Patrick Pearse's poem "I Am Ireland," two prototypical examples of the "Ireland is a woman" tradition. Boland's title, however, also suggests, at least visually, both mise en scène (pointing up the staginess of the typical nationalist poem) and the misery of that stock figure, Mother Ireland, who, in Pearse's poem, expresses a conventional pride in the heroics of "Cuchulain the valiant" and an equally conventional shame at bearing "children that sold their mother" (*Irish Verse* 295). Boland's poem begins by destabilizing the conventional evocation of the passive, all-patient, all-sorrowful woman-who-is-Ireland; suddenly the woman is digging in her heels, demanding a divorce from the mystic: "I won't go back to it," she insists,

> my nation displaced
> into old dactyls,
> oaths made
> by the animal tallows
> of the candle—
>
> (***Journey*** 11)

Dissociating herself from the canonical tendency to venerate the heroism of Cuchulain and Finn, she divorces herself as well from

> the songs
> that bandage up the history
> the words
> that make a rhythm of the crime
>
> where time is time past.
>
> (11)

Finally, she rejects the bloodless, abstract portrait typically presented of her, insisting on her right to appear in less idealized roles: as the camp follower who trades sex for cambric and rice-colored silks, or as the emigrant woman with her half-dead baby,

> mingling the immigrant
> guttural with the vowels
> of homesickness who neither
> knows nor cares that
>
> a new language
> is a kind of scar
> and heals after a while
> into a passable imitation
> of what went before.
>
> (11)

For these women, whose "roots are brutal," defeat is not transmuted into victory, not even into myth. The image of Cathleen protected by Cuchulain does nothing to soothe their anger and suffering.

"Mise Eire" shatters the poetic idea of defeated nation reborn as triumphant woman, insisting instead on bearing witness to the real defeats of Irish history, the real sufferings of Irish women. In *A Kind of Scar* Boland writes,

> The wrath and grief of Irish history seemed to me—as it did to many—one of our true possessions. Women were part of that wrath, had endured that grief. It seemed to me a species of human insult that at the end of all, in certain Irish poems, they should become elements of style rather than aspects of truth.
>
> (12)

"Mise Eire" redresses that insult and thrusts before the reader images of Irish women to take the place of stylized, falsified ones.

As the title of her collection ***In Her Own Image*** suggests, the poems in this volume comprise a subversive, repossessive discourse. In the first poem in the collection, **"Tirade for the Mimic Muse,"** Boland blasts the whorish muse who parades for men but refuses to involve herself in real households where real families live. The speaker begins by holding up a mirror to force the aged and ugly muse to confront herself: "I've caught you out. You fat trout" (9). Yeats may have been inspired, like Aengus, by this trout-cum-beautiful-girl, this piece of silvery Celtic twilight, the speaker implies, but "I know you for the ruthless bitch you are":

> Eye-shadow, swivel brushes, blushers,
> Hot pinks, rouge pots, sticks,
> Ice for the pores, a mud mask—
> All the latest tricks.
> Not one of them disguise
> That there's a dead millennium in your eyes.
> You try to lamp the sockets of your loss:
> The lives that famished for your look of love.
> Your time is up. There's not a stroke, a flick
> Can make your crime cosmetic.
>
> (10)

The speaker, of course a woman, sees through the seductress's tricks of ornamentation and make-up, the cosmetics of language that allow us to "make an ornament of the past; to turn the losses to victories and to restate humiliations as triumphs" (*Kind of Scar* 24); her "tirade" lays bare the Muse's aesthetic that favors the mythic and the fraudulent:

> With what drums and dances, what deceits,
> Rituals and flatteries of war,
> Chants and pipes and witless empty rites
> And war-like men
> And wet-eyed patient women
> You did protect yourself from horrors. . . .
>
> (***Image*** 10)

In this catalogue of the stock elements of the Irish poetic tradition, the speaker reviles the Muse for inspiring celebrations of martial splendor and female passivity, thus turning "a terrible witness into an empty decoration" (*Kind of Scar* 24). Had poets taken as their muse a real woman, not merely a male construct, she could have turned them to face the real conditions of life:

> The kitchen screw and the rack of labour,
> The wash thumbed and the dish cracked,
> The scream of beaten women,
> The crime of babies battered,
> The hubbub and the shriek of daily grief. . . .
>
> (***Image*** 11)

Indeed, this is a world the Muse "could have sheltered in [her] skirts," but instead she primly "latched [her] belt and itched [her] hem / And shook it off like dirt" (*Image* 11).

The speaker's rage is compounded by her recognition that she too was once implicated in this crime, once constructed by this construct: I "mazed my way to womanhood," she tells us, "Through all your halls of mirrors, making faces." But "in a nappy stink, by a soaking wash / Among stacked dishes"—that is, in the details of her own life, the truth of her own experience—"Your glass cracked," she tells the Muse.

> Your luck ran out. Look. My words leap
> Among your pinks, your stench pots and sticks,
> They scatter shadow, swivel brushes, blushers.
> Make your face naked,
> Strip your mind naked,
> Drench your skin in a woman's tears.
>
> (11)

The ordinary details of experience create an upheaval, causing an earthquake along the "almost geological fault" in the Irish tradition. In an act of repossession, the poet strips off the Muse's makeup and forces upon her an aesthetic of inclusiveness: "You are the Muse of all our mirrors. / Look in them and weep" (11). With the *all* of this announcement, Boland is ready to inaugurate her own aesthetic, one that truly bears witness.

"Envoi," a companion piece, affirms the speaker's belief that "My muse must be better than those of men / who made theirs in the image of their myth" (*Journey* 43). Boland's homely (but not conventional) images contrast sharply with the "chants and pipes and witless empty rites" inspired by the Mimic Muse of the Irish poetic tradition:

> Under the street-lamps the dustbins brighten.
> The winter flowering jasmine casts a shadow
> outside my window in my neighbor's garden.
> These are the things that my muse must know.
>
> (*Journey* 43)

The final quatrain of the poem establishes Boland's aesthetic—and her poetic ethics—with great clarity:

> If she will not bless the ordinary,
> if she will not sanctify the common,
> then here I am and here I stay and then am I
> the most miserable of women.
>
> (43)

This artistic restructuring of given myths Boland extends to another art form—painting. Inspired by works of Renoir, Canaletto, and Chardin, among other artists, she problematizes what she sees, extending the

two-dimensional canvas in a further dimension to include that which the artist simplifies away, i.e., the subject's interior complexity. For example, **"Self-Portrait on a Summer Evening"** imagines how Jean-Baptiste Chardin, in "painting a woman," diminishes her:

> All summer long
> he has been slighting her
> in botched blues, tints,
> half-tones, rinsed neutrals.
>
> (*Journey* 12)

The faint colors, the suggestive forms—"the sky that odd shape of apron"—encroach upon the woman to seal off her possibilities, to "shrink" and "reduce" her realm of experience, and, by extension, that of the viewer, Boland herself. Stepping into the portrait, Boland sees herself

> crossing between
> the garden and the house,
> under the whitebeam trees,
> keeping an eye on
> the length of the grass,
> the height of the hedge,
> the distance of the children
> I am Chardin's woman
>
> edged in reflected light,
> hardened by
> the need to be ordinary.
>
> (12)

In this painting "the common" is present, but not "sanctified"; the woman is "edged in *reflected* light," reduced by the painter's vision to a collection of "tints / half-tones," and "neutrals," a nonentity. In the painter's view, she is "hardened by / the need to be ordinary" and therefore can be no fire-eater or star-gazer. Implicit here is a critique of the tradition in which one can be either ordinary *or* heroic, common *or* complex, a male aesthetic that "hardens" the woman in the portrait and the one viewing her. In **"The Journey"** the poet's guide, Sappho, shows her women and children and cautions her, "be careful. / Do not define these women by their work" (*Journey* 41); these women are not to be simplified into laundresses, court ladies, and washerwomen, as Chardin's woman is reduced to a mere housewife. By adopting the perspective of Chardin's woman, Boland destabilizes the neat category, the exclusionary aesthetic that denies both the woman-as-subject and the woman-as-viewer their complexity, their potential to be fire-eaters *and* housewives, star-gazers *and* women, indeed poets *and* mothers.

Although Boland is deeply concerned with the way in which the grand, mythic tradition of Irish poetry has silenced and trivialized women, she implies as well that it has also silenced many of the *genuine* voices of men; the distance between male and female, while real enough, is subsumed by the more critical distance between the official image and the human truth. Poetic renderings of Irish heroism, with their seductive assurances about Irish history and Irish womanhood, are, Boland claims, narcotic and amnesiac (or, in Joycean terms, "paralytic"), seducing female *and* male readers to embrace a collective fantasy, to pursue an unreal self-image, both personally and nationally. **"The Glass King"** illustrates the destructive power of this tradition. In this poem Boland explores the misery King Charles VI inflicts upon himself and his queen Isabella in his belief that he is made of glass. Isabella, "an ordinary honest woman" perplexed by the King's madness, remembers the marital pleasure they once took in each other:

> They were each other's fantasy in youth.
> No splintering at all about that mouth
> when they were flesh and muscle, woman and man,
> fire and kindling. See that silk divan!
>
> Enough said. . . .
>
> (*Journey* 59)

Yet the sensuality and intimacy of their former relationship has been sacrificed to Charles's distorted perceptions, a madness suggesting the narcissism and insularity that result from a preoccupation with *his*tory and its corollary rejection of the quotidian. The speaker, "wanting nothing more than the man / she married," thinks, "I need his hand now."

> Outside my window October soaks the stone;
> you can hear it; you'd almost think
> the brick was drinking it; the rowan drips
>
> and history waits. Let it wait. I want
> no elsewheres. . . .
>
> (59)

History, an abstract composite of flags and battle-cries and momentary deeds, denies the value of what, to Isabella, are the truly important matters: the rain, the rowan, the silk divan, the flesh and blood, the "ordinary," the "common," the real. By contrast, Charles, more fully constructed by the constructs of history, is "demented in a crystal past," capable of seeing himself only "in mirrors, self-deceptions, self-regardings" (60). The idealized images in the glass quite literally define him; he turns himself into an abstraction.

The destructive power of the Irish poetic tradition is explicit as the poet "elect[s]" Charles, in his madness, "emblem / and ancestor of our lyric:"

> it fits you like a glove—
> doesn't it?—the part; untouchable, outlandish,

> esoteric, inarticulate and out of reach
>
> of human love. . . .
>
> (60)

Such a lyric, in Boland's schema, is a kind of scar, the aftermath of something genuine and powerful, or, as she says in **"The Women"** (*Journey* 27), the wound of a real event "heal[ed] into myth" and become inert. Charles's myth has placed at a distance—has marginalized—the love of his wife, who wants "nothing more than the man / she married, all her sorrows in her stolid face" (*Journey* 60). It has also, of course, isolated him, hardened him by the need to be un-ordinary, and driven him mad, completely destroying him. The consequences of *his story* have been reaped not only by women.

Through her "dialogue with the idea of a nation," Eavan Boland destabilizes the "emblems and enchantments" of the Irish poetic tradition, exposing ways in which the "exhausted fictions of the nation" have "edit[ed] ideas of womanhood and modes of remembrance," leaving Irish poetry informed "not [by] the harsh awakenings, but the old dreams" (*Kind of Scar* 13). By working to "repossess" Ireland, she points toward a new ethic for Irish poetry, one that reinscribes the ordinary and restores its complexity, recognizing that everyday experience is always intricate, frequently harsh and disappointing, yet extremely fragile, vulnerable to "the grace music gives to flattery / and language borrows from ambition" (**"The Achill Woman,"** *Kind of Scar* 4). Thus Boland's poetry is microcosmic and keenly observant; her interest in the meaning of Ireland is an interest in houses, flowers, blackbirds, and children, in the "great people" who suffered the famine, in the "teddy bears and rag dolls and tricycles and buckets" that constitute "love's archaeology" (**"The Journey,"** *Journey* 41). It is as if by particularizing, Boland will avoid "the harmonies of servitude," the soothing rhetoric of generalization. Committed to the keen scrutiny that "witness-bearing" entails, Eavan Boland reintroduces to public discourse the perspectives that run counter to the demands of Irish myth, to lead away from the safety of amnesia and toward the risky complexity of life.

Works Cited

Boland, Eavan. *In Her Own Image*. Dublin: Arlen House, 1980.

———. "It's a Woman's World." *Contemporary Irish Poetry*. Ed. Anthony Bradley. Berkeley: U of California P, 1988. 357-58.

———. *A Kind of Scar: The Woman Poet in a National Tradition*. Dublin: Attic Press, 1989.

———. *The Journey and Other Poems*. Dublin: Arlen House, 1986.

Garratt, Robert, ed. *Modern Irish Poetry: Tradition and Continuity from Yeats to Heaney.* Berkeley: U of California P, 1986.

Pearse, Patrick. "I Am Ireland." *The Penguin Book of Irish Verse.* Ed. Brendan Kennelly. 2nd ed. New York: Viking-Penguin, 1981. 295.

Anne Stevenson (essay date January-February 1992)

SOURCE: Stevenson, Anne. "Inside and Outside History." *P.N. Review* 18, no. 3 (January-February 1992): 34-5.

[*In the following essay, Stevenson regards Boland's encounter with the Achill woman, chronicled in her verse and her essay "Outside History," as an important moment in her life and work.*]

As will be evident to anyone who has followed Eavan Boland's purgatorial journey into self-placement, the story of her meeting with the Achill woman occurs at least twice in her published work: once in the verse sequence of *Outside History* (Carcanet, 1990), and again as a prologue to her essay of the same title (*P.N.R.* 75). Boland, then a student at Trinity College, had borrowed a friend's cottage on Achill Island for a week at Easter, bringing with her, for study, a volume of the Court poets of the Silver Age, 'those 16th century song-writers like Wyatt and Raleigh, whose lines appear so elegant . . . yet whose poems smell of the gallows'. Since the cottage was without water, an old woman carried it up every evening in a bucket.

> I remember the cold rosiness of her hands.
> She bent down and blew on them like broth.
> And round her waist, on a white background,
> in coarse, woven letters, the words 'glass cloth'.
> And she was nearly finished for the day.
> And I was all talk, raw from college— . . .

Both poem and essay mark the occasion as an epiphany, an incident that affected the direction of the poet's life and thinking. 'She was the first person to talk to me about the famine. The first person, in fact, to speak to me with any force about the terrible parish of survival and death which the event had been in those regions.' When the young poet turned her back on the woman and re-entered the cottage to light a fire and memorize lines from the Court Poets, she was ignorantly turning, she says, away from her own history, away from the Achill woman and what she represented of Ireland's past in order 'to commit to memory the songs and artifices of the very power system which had made [the old woman's] own memory such an archive of loss'.

In her poetry, Eavan Boland raises the problem of her Irish identity in the context of that 'archive of loss'. At the same time, her concerns are much broader. Memory,

change, loss, the irrecoverable past—such are the shared conditions of humankind with which she scrupulously engages. Her poems give an impression of a grave, even solemn intelligence, very little ruffled by the politics of nationalism, or, for that matter, of the women's movement. A sensitive poet, then, a poet unafraid of thought, rarely thrown off balance by anger; a poet willing to brave current fashions by freely advancing ideas—though she works, usually, with concrete images. Daringly, she calls a poem **'We are Human History. We are not Natural History'**, placing her children in a 'short-lived' and 'elegiac' light of a particular encounter with nature (a wild bees nest) so as to explore, in tentative yet exact language, her sense of the uniquely *human* experience of time, which is selective memory. 'And this— / this I thought, is *how it will have been / chosen* from those summer evenings / which under the leaves of the poplars— / striped dun and ochre, simmering over / the stashed-up debris of old seasons— / a swarm of wild bees is making use of.' (My italics).

Given the distinction Boland makes between human history and the natural world, one might expect an essay entitled 'Outside History' to point to an area of release. Human history, seen as a record of power struggle, war and wastage, is indeed a horror story; the whole of it (and natural history, too) could be described as 'a parish of survival and death'. But to see *around* 'history' into the filtering byways of individual creation and discovery can liberate the mind from useless self-laceration. I opened the essay, 'Outside History', with an expectation, founded on the poems, of engaging with a personal philosophy of survival. To my surprise, the essay, though very personal, turned out to be a polemic: a disquisition on the 'virulence and necessity of the idea of a nation', and especially on how the poetic inheritance of Ireland has cut across the poet's identity as a woman.

Though Eavan Boland as an Irishwoman and I as an American are separated by very different historical experiences, the undergraduate encounter with the Achill woman is easy enough to share. The title **'Outside History'** perhaps points to that silent majority excluded from the history books whom the practitioners of 'total history' have sought to bring inside history (as, for example, with Peter Laslett's *The World We Have Lost*). For most of us probably, who seek to identify with the past but who feel excluded by gender or class or much else from the conventional national pasts of the history books, it is through these silent majorities that we must make our connections. Yet, is it only my American background that makes me pause before the 'virulence and necessity of the idea of a nation'? For a Serbian or Croatian poet entering new nightmares after the long Ottoman centuries the language fits well enough. But for an Irish poet in a republic secure in the

Economic Community, whose changing mood is now reflected in the election of a woman president? I'm not sure.

History, perhaps, should also be brought to bear on Boland's central premise: 'that over a relatively short time—certainly no more than a generation or so—women have moved from being the subjects and objects of Irish poems to being the authors of them.' That almost all the Irish poets of the modern period have been male, and that women, by and large, have been motifs in their love poems and songs—yes, that no one could deny. Forget for a moment Yeats's complicated admiration for powerful political women: Maude Gonne, Constance Markowitz, Lady Gregory. Forget Joyce's warm and ebullient Molly Bloom (surely the character most likely to survive in *Ulysses*) and turn instead to the contents page of John Montague's *Faber Book of Irish Verse* (1978). Chronologically, after Thomas Moore (1779-1852) only two women's names appear: Eavan Boland herself, with one poem, and Eiléan Ní Chuilleanáin, with two. The list might well be extended to include Máire Mhac an tSaoi, Nuala Ní Dhomhnaill and Medbh Mc Guckian; perhaps to one or two others. Still, that shows a proportion of, say, six women to over sixty men. The anxieties, the bafflements, the evident distress Eavan Boland experienced, given her contemporary social conscience and highly developed self-consciousness, look to be real enough.

I still recall my fury, one evening during the 1970s, after Montague himself, with James Simmons, had performed in the Old Fire Station, Oxford. Over drinks, insulted to be treated as an object of gallantry rather than a poet in my own right, I spoke rather hotly, I believe, to John Montague on the subject of women poets. Why could not (male) Irish poets take us seriously? Montague, to my surprise, laughed at my ignorance, maintaining that, on the contrary, women poets had never been discriminated against in Ireland. Many of the greatest poets in Irish had been women. I disbelieved him.

Many years later I came across a copy of *The Faber Book of Irish Verse* that John Montague must have been editing at that time. The introduction, dwelling on the oral tradition of early Irish literature, has a good deal to say about the loss, to Anglicized Irish poets, of their national language. The rediscovery of ancient Irish literature was spurred on by the Celtic revival of Yeats's time, a movement which continues into the present. Most Irish poets, at some time in their lives, turn their talents to translating from the ancient Irish epics. Pagan classics like *The Great Tain* and *Cúchulain* survived, ironically enough, in the monasteries. One paragraph in Montague's introduction struck me forcibly.

> And here we should remark another aspect of early Irish poetry: it is the only literature in Europe, and perhaps in the world, where one finds a succession of

women poets. Psychologically, a female poet has always seemed an absurdity, because of the necessarily intense relationship between the poet and the Muse. [I doubt that Montague would risk such a chauvinist speculation today.] Why then did poetry always seem a natural mode of expression for gifted Irish women? I think this was because there was no discrimination against them; the first woman poet of whom we hear, Liadan of Corcaguiney, was a fully-qualified member of the poets' guild, which could mean as much as twelve years of study. It was as an equal that the poet Cuirithir wooed her, and though she drove him off, for religious reasons, her lament rings in our ears to this day.

A section of Montague's anthology is devoted to Women and Love in the 9th century—much of it love poetry written by women, passionately to their men. The women's verse Montague represents in translation includes a famous prototype of Villon's 'Belle Heaulmière' called 'The Hag of Bere', Liadan's 'Lament for Cuirithir', and, from the 18th century, Eibhlin Dubh O'Connell's 'Lament for Art O'Leary'—the culmination, Montague writes, of 'a long line of such poems'.

Ann Owens Weekes (essay date 1994)

SOURCE: Weekes, Ann Owens. "'An Origin like Water': The Poetry of Eavan Boland and Modernist Critiques of Irish Literature." *Bucknell Review* 38, no. 1 (1994): 159-76.

[*In the following essay, Weekes applies Richard Kearney's theory about the connection between Irish Revivalism and modernism to Boland's poetry.*]

In his excellent study, *Transitions* (1988), Richard Kearney explores the tensions between Revivalism and modernism in twentieth-century Irish narratives. Revivalism is associated with Yeats's attempt to present a unity of culture by privileging "primordial images of ancient Celtic mythology which predated all subsequent historical divisions into different religious (Catholic/Protestant) or political (Nationalist/Unionist) beliefs."[1] Modernism, on the other hand, is associated with Joyce and Beckett's denial of "the possibility of sustaining a continuous link between past and present," and "is essentially a 'critical' movement in the philosophical sense of questioning the very notion of *origins*" (*T*, 12). Thus the modernist rejects unifying images: "The modes of communication are more significant than the message communicated, since there no longer exists any inherited reservoir of meaning which can be taken for granted. Not surprisingly then, the very notion of culture as a transmission of collective experience is itself at issue" (*T*, 13). Contemporary texts, Kearney notes, attracted at times to both arguments, gravitate between these opposite poles.

Kearney's thoughtful and rich analysis is based on his perception of Irish culture "as a complex web of interweaving narratives which refuse the facility of an homogeneous totality" (*T,* 17). He approves inclusive work which embraces different religious and political views and disapproves the ideological and particular. The study lends itself to generalizations about contemporary Irish narrative. I am interested in the extent to which it applies to Irish women poets and propose to examine this relevance by analyzing the poetry of Eavan Boland—a poet who frequently speaks of the intersections of womanhood and Irish nationalism—through the lens of Kearney's conclusions about Joyce and modernism.

Speaking of several modern writers, but particularly of Joyce, Kearney suggests three closely related points: 1) the refusal to acknowledge a continuous tradition of literary experience based on a continuous, homogenous heritage; 2) the dominance of language as the site of meaning; and 3) the multipossibilities of myth. In regard to literary and cultural traditions, Kearney notes that Joyce "was no less sceptical of the allurements of imperial British culture than he was of national Irish culture. This resistance to all forms of cultural hegemony was best expressed at the level of *language*" (*T,* 32). Kearney cites the incident of Stephen Dedalus's recognition of his alien status in the English language as evidence of Joyce's awareness of the revealing and concealing tendencies of language.[2] Joyce "worked inside the language as an outsider, forever mindful of the confusions, ambiguities and discontinuities which this language of Empire—like most hegemonic languages of the European nation-states—sought to conceal in order to preserve the veneer of a pure homogeneous identity" (*T,* 32). Joyce's deconstructive approach to the literary tradition was not motivated solely by postcolonial resentment, however; Joyce believed with his modernist associates that "the real metaphysical problem today is the *word*" (*T,* 33). Writing became for him "a sort of linguistic psychoanalysis of the repressed genesis of western culture. In the *Wake* he proposes to 'psoakoonaloose' the multi-voiced unconscious of language" (*T,* 34).

Moving to myth, Kearney sees Joyce as "one of the first" to oppose "the *multi-minded* logic of utopian myth to the *one-minded* logic of ideological myth" (*T,* 279). Mythology, Kearney notes, "implies a *conflict of interpretations.* And this conflict is, in the final analysis, an ethical one" (*T,* 276). Used for ideological purposes, myth excludes and perpetrates a single ideal of nationalism, for example, but myth also has utopian possibilities which allow it to reach beyond the national to universal aspirations. "The positive universality of myth—which enables it to migrate beyond national boundaries and translate into other cultures—resides, paradoxically, in its very multiplicity. . . . A postmod-

ern approach to myth construes it as a two-way traffic between tradition and modernity, rewriting the old as a project of the new" (*T,* 278). Joyce, "in defiance of chauvinistic stereotypes of the motherland . . . reinterpreted the ancient Celtic heroine, Anna, as Anna Livia Plurabelle—the 'Everliving Bringer of Plurabilities'" (*T,* 279).

Kearney's use of the work of postmodernist critics to examine Joyce's linguistic play is appropriate, as the following introduction to the texts of four renowned postmodernists, Jacques Lacan, Roland Barthes, Michel Foucault, and Jacques Derrida, shows: "They force the reader to consider them as objects in their own right. They are designed to prevent the reader from looking *through* them at some external referent; they are designed to make the reader look *at* them and to work at them, actively involving him in their construction or recreation."[3] Beckett's comment on Joyce, which Kearney quotes approvingly, makes the same point: "his writing is not *about* something, it *is* that something" (*T,* 13).

In her pamphlet, *A Kind of Scar: The Woman Poet in a National Tradition,* Eavan Boland admires Joyce's ability to deconstruct the myth of mother Ireland in the opening pages of *Ulysses,* yet I suggest that the postmodernist impulse, with its emphasis on the play of language, is different in kind from Boland's poetic endeavor. Joyce rejects the myth of mother Ireland as simplification and hypocrisy and seeks to *uncover* the multi and contradictory mothers concealed by the image; Boland rejects it because by its very pervasiveness it *excludes* actual women and their situations from Irish narratives, and because it substitutes a false relationship between the image in poetry and the imagination.

Women in Irish poems, Boland notes, are "often passive, decorative, raised to emblematic status. This was especially true where the woman and the idea of the nation were mixed: where the nation became a woman and the woman took on a national posture. . . . Dark Rosaleen. Cathleen Ni Houlihan."[4] Even after Irish poets "rejected the politics of nationalism, they continued to deploy the emblems and enchantments of its culture" (*KS,* 13). The result of seeing women through myths of Ireland, as Boland shows through her analysis of Francis Ledwidge's "The Blackbirds" and Patrick Kavanagh's "Pygmalion," is the exclusion of the realities of women.[5] "The wrath and grief of Irish history seemed to me—as it did to many—one of our true possessions. Women were part of that wrath, had endured that grief. It seemed to me a species of human insult that at the end of all, in certain Irish poems, they should become elements of style rather than aspects of truth" (*KS,* 12). She continues, "something was gained by poems which used the imagery and emblem of the national muse . . . but only at an aesthetic level. While what was lost occurred at the deepest, most ethical level; and what was lost was what I valued. Not just the details of a past. Not just the hungers, the angers. These, however terrible, remain local. But the truth these details witness— human truths of survival and humiliation—these also were suppressed along with the details. Gone was the suggestion of any complicated human suffering. Instead, you had the hollow victories, the passive images, the rhyming queens" (*KS,* 13). Later she notes that these simplifications produced "a geological weakness" in Irish poetry. "All good poetry depends on an ethical relation between imagination and image. Images are not ornaments; they are truths" (*KS,* 23). Boland's insistence on this ethical relationship between the image of poetry and the imagination differs from postmodernism's involvement with language: although it is never simple, Boland's poetry directs the reader outward, toward the object of the imagination, not inward, toward linguistic ambiguity and contradiction. I shall return to this point at the end of this essay.

For Joyce and Beckett, Kearney notes, "It is not what one writes about that is of primary importance but the process of writing itself" (*T,* 13). In this process, Joyce attempts to reach the "repressed genesis of western culture" (*T,* 34). For Joyce, then, the language itself carries the trace of the buried, of what has been concealed in order to promote cultural hegemony. Through psychoanalysis of the "nightmare of history," he hopes to recover the repressed. This is not Boland's enterprise. Although women's experiences have been partially expressed by male poets, she notes:

> It is difficult, if not impossible, to explain to men who are poets—writing as they are with centuries of expression behind them—how emblematic is the unexpressed life of other women to the woman poet, how intimately it is her own. And how, in many ways that silence is as much part of her tradition as the Troubadours are of theirs.[6]

Boland cannot play with or psychoanalyze language in an attempt to uncover women's experience because this experience has never been part of the written narrative. Thus Boland's project is by nature different from that of Joyce and the postmoderns: as she notes in "It's a Woman's World," "as far as history goes / we were never / on the scene of the crime."[7]

For many years now, Boland has called attention to the absence of women from Irish poetry and to the impossibility of breaking that past silence, of recovering that lost history. In the title poem in the 1986 volume, *The Journey,* Sappho conducts the persona, here as often a poet/mother/housewife, on a journey to the underworld, where "children of the plague" suckle weary women, while others make "terrible pietas." Sappho warns the watcher not to "define these women by their work," for

> ". . . these are women who went out like you
> when dusk became a dark sweet with leaves,

> recovering the day, stooping, picking up
> teddy bears and rag dolls and tricycles and buckets—

> "love's archaeology—and they too like you
> stood boot deep in flowers once in summer
> or saw winter come in with a single magpie
> in a caul of haws, a solo harlequin."

Unable to reach the women across "the narcotic crossing," the persona begs Sappho to let her "be their witness." But their experiences, Sappho warns, are "beyond speech, / beyond song, only not beyond love."[8] They are unrecoverable because they have never been recorded, have never entered the unconscious of language. Sappho, the mother poet, wishes her daughter to "know forever"—and honor—"the silences in which are our beginnings, / in which we have an origin like water." The male poet may plumb the language to release the submerged, subversive bodies, the "hitherto concealed, possibilities" (*T,* 272), but the woman poet exploring the same heritage finds no evidence of her existence.

Believing that silence is part of her tradition, Boland attempts to find ways to reveal this silence. Fever, a word whose etymology is obscure, is linked in the poem of that title to an unseen power which authorities feared in women, a power which provoked irrational acts of injustice against them. Fever

> is what they tried to shake out of
> the crush and dimple of cotton,
> the shy dust of a bridal skirt;
> is what they beat, hurt, lashed like

> flesh as if it were a lack of virtue
> in a young girl sobbing her heart out
> in a small town for having been seen
> kissing by the river; is what they burned

> alive in their own back gardens
> as if it were a witch.

(*OH,* 87)

The persona's grandmother died in a fever ward, the poem notes, leaving only "a half-sense of half-lives." Nothing else, unless:

> I reconstruct the soaked-through midnights;
> brokenhearted vigils; the histories I never learned
> to predict the lyric of; and reconstruct
> risk: as if silence could become rage,

> as if what we lost is a contagion
> that breaks out in what cannot be
> shaken out from words or beaten out
> from meaning and survives to weaken

> what is given, what is certain
> and burns away everything but this
> exact moment of delirium when
> someone cries out someone's name.

(*OH,* 87-88)

If the stories were recoverable, the poem hints, they would weaken the "given" story, the accepted histories (and nationalist literary canons). But the effort to recreate women's experiences is also linked to the irrational attempts to beat the elusive power out of women throughout centuries. The stories cannot be retrieved because they were never written: "no page / scores the low music / of our outrage" (**"It's a Woman's World,"** *Night Feed,* 52). The silence cannot become rage: today's writers can no more beat the unwritten stories they seek from the past than could yesterday's authorities beat the "fever" they feared from women's bodies.

Throughout her work Boland continues to "unveil the silence" of women's lives.[9] Ironically, while she suggests that writers cannot reconstruct the stories, hopes, ideas of past women, her work also implies—in contrast to that studied by Kearney—that women share a collective past which the poet can evoke—the experience of loss. The experience is invoked, not in the interest of revivalism, but to expose and destroy its persistence in the present. In the most recent volume, *Outside History,* **"The Photograph on My Father's Desk"** and **"What We Lost"** uncover the silence of the persona's mother and grandmother. Wound becomes an appropriate metaphor in this volume for the silence of women: as the poet writes in **"The Making of an Irish Goddess,"** "Myth is the wound we leave / in the time we have" (*OH,* 39).

If postmodern means beating or coaxing repressed meanings from language, Boland—whose major subject is contemporary women's lives and the loss of women's history—could not be classed as such. But Boland also interrogates the myths that pattern women's lives. In **"Tirade for the Mimic Muse,"** she tracks down the muse who deceives poets into accepting the faded images of traditional myths: the Muse of Mimic Art, the "fat trout," "fumed in candle-stink," who uses all the "latest tricks" of makeup but can't disguise the "dead millennium" in her eyes. "Trout" recalls the "silver trout" of "Song of Wandering Aengus," Yeats's tribute to the god of love and to the pursuit of romantic love:

> With what drums and dances, what deceits,
> Rituals and flatteries of war,
> Chants and pipes and witless empty rites
> And war-like men
> And wet-eyed patient women
> You did protect yourself from horrors.

> (*In Her Own Image,* 31, 32)

The muse protects herself (and by extension the poet and readers) from the aging of women, the drudgery of domestic routine, the sorrow of "beaten women," the "crime of babies battered," and all the sorrow that hides "behind suburb walls," by focusing on traditional images of active warriors and passive women. Ignoring

realities that should appear in literature, the muse insists—much as would Aengus, god of love—that women "needed nothing else to know / But love and again love and again love." The "trout," the traditional male and female images, and the muse's advice to the young woman all suggest that those who follow the Muse of Mimic Art attempt to follow the early Yeats, to see and depict the world as did the obvious model, the famous Irish poet.

The authentic muse, however, is difficult to reach. Watching a woman tending her child, her busy, cleaning hand "making light and rain, / smiles and a frown" across his face, the persona of "the Muse Mother" reflects:

> If I could only decline her—
> lost noun
> out of context,
> stray figure of speech—
> from this rainy street
>
> again to her roots,
> she might teach me
> a new language:
>
> to be a sibyl,
> able to sing the past
> in pure syllables,
> limning hymns sung
> to belly wheat or a woman
> able to speak at last
> my mother tongue.

> (*OH,* 134-35)

The 1982 volume, *Night Feed,* focuses on the extraordinary side of the lives of ordinary women, as if the Muse mother had responded to the poet's call. Indeed, Boland turned to suburbia as early as her second volume, *The War Horse* (1975), as she courageously mined the battleground inhabited by many women, ignored or ridiculed by many poets. One thinks of Eliot's satire of suburban women in **"Prufrock,"** for example. Boland frequently remarks the "restrictive programme" of Irish poetry, nurtured presumably on traditional subjects: "You could have a political murder in the Irish poem but not a baby. You could have the Dublin hills but not the suburbs."[10] Contemporary poets do not castigate suburbia in Eliot's manner, but they ignore it entirely, believing perhaps that nothing of interest could dwell there, or subordinate it to the public life.

Discussing Pat Murphy's film *Maeve* in *Transitions,* Kearney notes that "the solution [to the problem of identity in Northern Ireland] lies not in some escapist return to the haven of family domesticity—for this would simply be to reinforce the traditional gender stereotypes which oppose the public world of male action to the private world of female passivity" (*T,* 188).

Although Kearney's oppositions are accurate in the context of *Maeve,* I question the assumptions that underlie them as well as the selection of *Maeve.* The easy traditional opposition begs for analysis. If the domestic is dismissed as passive, uninteresting, the majority of women's lives are so defined and dismissed. The assumption here is that domestic lives consist only of the routines and pettiness of domestic labor. Kearney neither sees the violence of the domestic world which Boland exposes in poems such as **"Suburban Woman"** and **"In Her Own Image,"** nor comprehends the imaginative and intellectual reaches of the inhabitants of this world as Boland reveals them in many poems, including **"In the Garden," "We Are Human History. We Are Not Natural History."** Limiting domestic to passive, he falls into the trap Sappho warned of and defines the lives of women by their work.

The choice of *Maeve* as the single work by a woman in a study of twelve writers also invites questions.[11] The self-reflexive nature of *Maeve* aligns it with postmodernist works, but self-reflexive is the norm rather than the exception today. Is Kearney comfortable with *Maeve* because the discussion here is of the public (male? universal?) world? I am not suggesting that Kearney approves of that world; indeed he praises Maeve's resolve "to liberate Republicanism from its male-dominated mythology" (*T,* 188). I am reminded, however, of Frank O'Connor's 1963 argument that men rather than women are the authors of Irish Renaissance literature because politics is the material of literature. The Irishman, O'Connor continued, is lost in Mary Lavin's work because the revolution "practically disappears" to be replaced by a "sensual richness" quite foreign to him.[12] Kearney selects Seamus Heaney as contemporary poet, he tells us, rather than "Mahon, Montague, Longley and Kinsella," or "Durcan and Bolger" (*T,* 101). Why not consider Eithne Strong, Eiléan Ní Chuilleanáin, Boland, or Medbh McGuckian? Whether by accident or choice Kearney in selecting *Maeve* continues the tradition that celebrates the public and dismisses the private—ironic in a writer who lauds Joyce's celebration of Molly and Anna Livia as "Bringers of plurabilities" (*T,* 40).

As she explores and reveals contemporary suburbia, Boland also exposes dangers in traditional interpretations of the myths of Ceres and Persephone and Daphne and Apollo. These myths of loss evoke women's collective experience of the lost past, but Boland also uses them to warn of continued loss if contemporary women's lives, so many lived in suburbia, are deemed unworthy of narrative. Boland is more suspicious of myth than is Joyce. Rather than uncovering liberating possibilities, she discloses confining restrictions. Ceres is introduced in the early poem, **"Suburban Woman."** The goddess who loses her daughter Persephone to Pluto the god of the underworld, Ceres punishes with

sterility the earth which has closed over her daughter. But when Zeus, in response to her plea, forces Pluto to restore Persephone to Ceres for half of each year, she withdraws her curse and the earth is fruitful for the duration of Persephone's visit. Ceres appears in **"Suburban Woman"** as poet whose sacrifice of her life as poet is weighed against the advent of her daughter:

> The chairs dusted and the morning
> coffee break behind, she starts pawning
>
> her day again to the curtains, the red
> carpets, the stair rods, at last to the bed,
>
> the unmade bed where once in an underworld
> of limbs, her eyes freckling the night like jewelled
>
> lights on a cave wall, she, crying, stilled,
> bargained out of nothingness her child,
>
> bartered from the dark her only daughter.
> Waking, her cheeks dried, to a brighter
>
> dawn she sensed in her as in April earth
> a seed, a life ransoming her death.
>
> (*The War Horse,* 28-29)

The emphasis here is not on the blessings of fruitfulness produced by Ceres' compromise, but on the sacrifice of Ceres, on woman's surrender of her talent, of her individuality, to promote the general welfare. The day's work over, poet and mother meet, "veterans of a defeat / no truce will heal."

"Night Feed" shows Ceres in another mood:

> This is dawn.
> Believe me
> This is your season, little daughter.
> . . .
> I tiptoe in.
> I lift you up
> Wriggling
> In your rosy, zipped sleeper.
> Yes, this is the hour
> For the early bird and me
> When finder is keeper.
>
> I crook the bottle.
> How you suckle!
> This is the best I can be,
> Housewife
> To this nursery
> Where you hold on,
> Dear life.
>
> (*OH,* 139)

As the child ends the feed, day breaks, and the persona notes, "we begin / The long fall from grace." The light of day is associated with the light of reason, and the mother's response to her child is seen here as instinctive and positive. Instinct is also celebrated as "brute grace" in **"In the Garden"**; in **"Monotony,"** however, "brute routines" are contrasted to "our gleams," illustrating the complex, contradictory responses of women to motherhood, and of all human beings to the routines of nature. The self-reflexive nature of many of the poems in *Night Feed* illustrates the constant interaction of thought and instinct. The persona is never an unquestioning advocate of domesticity or traditional motherhood, but a woman who finds in the basic patterns of life material for philosophical reflection.

The Ceres myth reappears to be rejected in the most recent volume, *Outside History*, in **"The Making of an Irish Goddess."** Ceres went to hell unchanged, forever young, but the contemporary woman asserts,

> But I need time—
> my flesh and that history—
> to make the same descent.
>
> (*OH,* 38)

In the woman's face and body, the persona reads the signs of time, the evidence of what she has been, of her history. To reject and devalue these signs is to reject one's history, to place value on only one portion, youth, of a woman's life. The lines quoted earlier from this poem, "Myth is the wound we leave / in the time we have," act as a sharp reminder that contemporary women's lives are—like those of their mothers—in danger of being lost, becoming wound, if women accept traditional mythic and literary concepts of female value and of domesticity.

Focusing on Ceres herself rather than on the results of Ceres' compromise, Boland presents a more complex and less positive aspect of the myth. Daphne—changed into a laurel tree by her father, the river god Peneus, to escape the pursuit and love of Apollo—is also a myth of loss of self and history, as the woman is transformed into the unchanging, ever-green laurel. Daphne becomes for Boland an image of the routines of housework, the housewife as remote sexually as the nymph. In **"Daphne with Her Thighs in Bark,"** the persona/housewife offers advice, so that her sister "in the next myth / will be wiser." "The opposite of passion / is not virtue / but routine," she warns and encourages her sister to go for the exotic, the strange, the passionate: "Save face sister. / Fall. Stumble. / Rut with him." Those who take chances will have memories, or imaginative life, but those who do not "shall be here forever, / setting out the tea" (*OH,* 128-29).

While the Daphne myth is an obvious and appropriate myth of loss, Boland's use also highlights Yeats's approval of Daphne as model in his poem "A Prayer for My Daughter." Delineating the ideal woman, Yeats prays:

> May she become a flourishing hidden tree
> That all her thoughts may like the linnet be,

> And have no business but dispensing round
> Their magnanimities of sound,
> Nor but in merriment begin a chase,
> Nor but in merriment a quarrel.
> O may she live like some green laurel
> Rooted in one dear perpetual place.[13]

Yeats is reacting to what he sees as the inappropriate political and public behavior of Maud Gonne, but his allusion to Daphne's rootedness, her captivity, his wish for his daughter as married woman, is shocking. **"Daphne Heard with Horror the Addresses of the God"** (*OH,* 41-42) seems prompted by Yeats's "Prayer." Boland's four-stanza poem establishes no definite connection, but moves by suggestive association. The first stanza places the persona in the garden with another person who tells of "the wedding of a local girl, / long ago, and a merchant from Argyll." In the second stanza the persona looks to the garden: "The laurel hedge was nothing but itself, / and all of it so free of any need / for nymphs, goddesses, wounded presences." The third stanza returns to the story: "By the time / I paid attention they were well married: / The bridegroom had his bride on the ship." In the fourth stanza, the persona and the storyteller clear up; the storyteller goes inside while the persona remains looking at the garden: "freshening and stirring. A suggestion, / behind it all, of darkness: in the shadow, / beside the laurel hedge, its gesture." The ceremonial nature of the wedding suggests the ceremonial and ritual ordering that Yeats desires. Although physical nature is seen in the second stanza as distinct from and unaffected by human concerns— "nothing but itself," the "darkness" appears "beside the laurel tree"—Daphne's shadow—at the conclusion of the story of the wedding. Human reason, then, is unable to restrict perception to physical fact, and human perception is molded by an almost unconscious association of the facts of the story with the nonverbalized understanding of a meaning of the myth. Daphne's "horror" arises again as the contemporary persona hears a story remote chronologically from, but somehow frighteningly similar to, that of Daphne.

Boland's revision of myth, then, is quite different from the moderns Kearney discusses: while they unfold new utopian possibilities, she reveals hidden, negative depths. This difference may spring from Boland's idea of history. Like Kearney's writers, she sees that history is a human construct. It is not the sum of human and animal actions, but the human perception and record of these acts, as she notes in **"We Are Human History. We Are Not Natural History"** (*OH,* 44). The problem is that "we are ourselves constructed by our constructs"—constructs which, for women, include myths of limitation (*KS,* 19). Boland seems to doubt our ability to free ourselves by reshaping the constructs, and fears instead that human beings are in danger of being trapped by myth, their individuality annihilated beneath its molding pressure. This fear is not groundless, as Yeats's "Prayer" and the continuation of the emblem women in contemporary poetry suggest. As Boland sees it, the shaping mythic force intrudes uninvited, dangerous. In **"The Women,"** the persona talks of the hour "of metamorphosis," when she moves from being mother/housewife to poet:

> My time of sixth sense and second sight
> when in the words I choose, the lines I write,
> they rise like visions and appear to me:
>
> women of work, of leisure, of the night,
> in stove-coloured silks, in lace, in nothing,
> with crewel needles, with books, with wide open legs,
>
> who fled the hot breath of the god pursuing,
> who ran from the split hoof and the thick lips
> and fell and grieved and healed into myth,
>
> into me in the evening at my desk
> testing the water with a sweet quartet, . . .

> (*OH,* 84)

These lines suggest a causal relationship between the "emblematic nature" of women's unspoken lives, of their loss, and the shaping of the contemporary poet by the stories or myths of the past. The persona understands those lost lives because she and the life she lives is the fruit of their loss. The women have healed into her, as a new language heals "into a passable imitation / of what went before" (**"Mise Eire,"** *The Journey,* 72). Although the poet calls up the images deliberately, and can retreat from them to the world of order, "light, linear, precisely planned, / a hemisphere of tiered, aired cotton," she cannot cut herself off completely. As she moves between the two worlds, she brings something with her that she "should have left behind."

In **"Suburban Woman: A Detail,"** mythic pressure lies in wait, hidden, threatening and transforming the individual. Leaving her house in the evening, the woman notes:

> I am definite
> to start with
> but the light is lessening,
> the hedge losing its detail,
> the path its edge.
>
> Look at me, says the tree.
> I was a woman once like you,
> full-skirted, human.
>
> Suddenly I am not certain
> of the way I came
> or the way I will return,
> only that something
> which may be nothing
> more than darkness has begun
> softening the definitions of my body, leaving

> the fears
> and all the terrors of the flesh,
> shifting the airs and forms
> of the autumn quiet,
>
> crying "remember us."

> (*OH,* 99)

To sum up: Boland—unlike Joyce—rejects myths because they offer women only limitations, and because they threaten to obscure consciousness and conscious choice. There are two possible avenues, she suggests, myth *or* history; we cannot have both. "Out of myth into history I move to be," she notes, as she chooses existence, becoming rather than the stasis of myth. A second difference is her belief in her ability to evoke women's collective experience of loss, the "unexpressed life of other women" (*KS,* 44). Finally, by bringing to poetry the contemporary experience of real women—their intellectual and philosophical reflections as well as their actions, emotions, and instinctive responses—Boland illustrates their richness and variety. To neglect or dismiss suburbia because of the routine dullness of domestic tasks is to see women as synonymous with the tasks. This attitude is satirized in **"It's Woman's World."** "Appearances reassure" the viewer that:

> that woman there,
> craned to
> the starry mystery,
>
> is merely getting a breath
> of evening air.
> While this one here,
> her mouth a burning plume—
>
> she's no fire-eater,
> just my frosty neighbour
> coming home.

> (*Night Feed,* 52)

Whether she writes of the women of the past or of the present, this is Boland's point: it is not just the record of women's work that is lost, it is the record of their lives, thoughts, reflections, fears. This is **"What We Lost."** And this is what we will continue to lose if we are foolish enough to "define these women by their work"; to celebrate only women's achievements in the "public" world, to believe that action alone defines life. An Irish woman who "could not easily do without the idea of a nation" (*KS,* 8), Boland valorizes the hitherto excluded and helps to transform Irish poetry from a set of "predictable component parts" into "a changing interior space" (**"Symposium,"** 9).[14] Now it's time for critics to catch up and to introduce gender, not just token women, as a site of critical analysis.

I would like to conclude by referring to **"The Achill Woman,"** a poem which underscores the need for an ethical relationship between image and imagination, and one which has been misread. The student narrator of the poem describes a woman carrying a bucket of water up the hill, wearing "a half-buttoned, wool cardigan, / a tea-towel round her waist." The woman puts her bucket down; its "zinc-music . . . tuned the evening" into a series of conventional poetic images. The persona is "all talk, raw from college," the evening cools, the woman goes back down the hill, and the persona turns to "the set text / of the Court poets of the Silver Age." The conclusion of the poem is heavy with regret:

> but nothing now can change the way I went
> indoors, chilled by the wind
> and made a fire
> and took down my book
> and opened it and failed to comprehend
> the harmonies of servitude,
> the grace music gives to flattery
> and language borrows from ambition—
>
> and how I fell asleep
> oblivious to
>
> the planets clouding over in the skies,
> the slow decline of the spring moon,
> the songs crying out their ironies.

(*OH,* 35-36)

Like the persona in the poem, Boland vacationed in Achill while at college and talked each night with a local woman. This woman on Achill, Boland notes, was the first person to speak to her about the famine. "She kept repeating to me that they were great people, the people in the famine. Great people. I had never heard that before" (*KS,* 5). Through the years the woman's image remained with Boland, and while she could not articulate the experience at the time, she realized that "the anguish and power of that woman's gesture on Achill, with its suggestive hinterland of pain, was not something I could predict or rely on in Irish poetry" (*KS,* 7). Appropriately, **"The Achill Woman"** is the first poem in *Outside History,* a sequence which takes us from the "False Spring" of a young poet's career, through her recognition that myth and superstition entail limitation and loss of history for women, to her rejection of myth for history. Trained on the poetry of the past, the young poet is trained to perceive certain images and stories as poetic, others as ordinary and non-poetic. Human perception, as noted earlier, is shaped not only by acts, but by the words of stories and poets. This is where the tone of regret enters the poem: the poet turned from her real experience with the Achill woman to accounts of experience foreign to her own. She sought poetry not in the actual world of anguish and sorrow but in the world of artifice, from whence she might hope to write "derivative, formalist, gesturing poems," works inspired by the Muse of Mimic Art (*KS,* 10).

Ignoring Boland's insistence on **"The Achill Woman"** as the first poem of a sequence, Edna Longley suggests that Boland "feels unnecessarily guilty for (as an apprentice poet) having read 'English court poetry' on Achill, and having imitated the English 'Movement' mode of the early sixties." "To whom," Longley asks, "to what avatar, to what icon is she apologizing?" She answers, "it is to Mother Ireland herself." Longley further argues that "Boland's new Muse, supposedly based on the varied historical experience of Irish women, looks remarkably like the Sean Bhean Bhocht. . . . The 'real women of an actual past,'" she accuses, "are subsumed into a single emblematic victim-figure."[15] It is inaccurate to suggest that the nationality alone of the poets prompted Boland's apology—it is her own conditioning she regrets, her own training which causes her to look to conventions of the past rather than to the actual figure of the woman; Boland is in fact condemning the young poet she was for "wasting / his [her] sweet uncluttered metres on the obvious / emblem instead of the real thing" (*The Journey,* 87).

It is true that Boland does not allow the figure of the Achill Woman to speak in her poem. To do so would have been easy, but inaccurate and a contradiction of the argument, the self-condemnation of the poem. The ethical relationship of image to experience demands this representation. Indeed, it is instructive to compare **"The Achill Woman"** with Yeats's "The Fisherman." Yeats's fisherman,

> The freckled man who goes
> To a grey place on a hill
> In grey Connemara clothes
> At dawn to cast his flies,

is not distinct from, but ironically, has no counterpart *in,* nature. He is "A man who does not exist, / A man who is but a dream" (Yeats, 61-62). Yeats's image corresponds to a mental composition, created in opposition to, not in harmony with, the reality around him. Yeats castigates those who do not appreciate his poetry; Boland castigates herself for not appreciating the woman's world. Just as Boland refused in earlier poems to give voice to the silent, to allow "silence . . . [to] become rage," she refuses to give voice to the Achill woman. The silence of women of the past in history is an "aspect" of their truth, and the silence of the Achill woman is the truth of the young "gesturing" poet's response; to presume to break this silence is an insult, not unlike the earlier "human insult" of silencing them by making them "elements of style rather than aspects of truth" (*KS,* 12). Here we have a difference from both Yeats and the modern poets: while Yeats would present a tradition, largely self-created, as a unifying concept, and Joyce and Beckett would reject such a concept, immersing themselves instead in the indeterminate play of signifiers, one suggesting multimeanings, one suggesting none, Boland still believes in a relationship between image and experience that the ethical poet must not distort or defer.

Notes

1. Richard Kearney, *Transitions: Narratives in Modern Irish Culture* (Manchester: Manchester University Press, 1988), 25; hereafter *T,* with page references cited in the text.

2. See James Joyce, *Portrait of the Artist as a Young Man* (1916; reprint, Harmondsworth: Penguin, 1983), 189.

3. Eve Tavor Bannet, "Introduction," in *Structuralism and the Logic of Dissent* (Urbana: University of Illinois Press, 1989), 8.

4. Eavan Boland, *A Kind of Scar: The Woman Poet in a National Tradition* (Dublin: Attic Press, 1989), 12, 13; hereafter *KS,* with page references cited in the text.

5. Eavan Boland, "The Woman Poet in a National Tradition," *Studies* 6 (Summer 1987): 148-58.

6. Eavan Boland, "The Woman Poet: Her Dilemma," *Midland Review* 3 (Winter 1986): 44.

7. *Eavan Boland: Selected Poems* (Manchester: Carcanet, 1989), 51. This selection features poems from five volumes: *New Territory* (1967), *The War Horse* (1975), *In Her Own Image* (1980), *Night Feed* (1982), and *The Journey* (1986). Hereafter, poems from these volumes will be cited in the text by volume title, with page references to *Selected Poems.*

8. Eavan Boland, *Outside History* (New York: Norton, 1990), 95, 96. This edition features poems from three volumes: *Outside History* (1990), *The Journey* (1986), and *Night Feed* (1982, listed as *Domestic Interiors*). Hereafter, poems from this edition will be cited as *OH,* with page references to this 1990 edition.

9. Nancy Kelleher, a student in my "Irish Revolutionary Literature" class, University of Arizona, Fall 1992, coined this phrase for Boland's endeavor.

10. "Eavan Boland at the Symposium," *James Joyce Newestlatter* (November 1992), 8; hereafter "Symposium," with page references cited in the text.

11. Kearney devotes six of 282 pages of text to an analysis of *Maeve,* plus a little over one page to a concluding analysis of *Maeve* and Neil Jordan's *Angel.*

12. Frank O'Connor, *The Lonely Voice: A Study of the Short Story* (Cleveland: World Publishing Co., 1963), 203-4.

13. *Selected Poems and Three Plays of William Butler Yeats,* ed. M. L. Rosenthal, 3d ed. (New York: Macmillan, 1986), 91; hereafter Yeats, with page references cited in the text.

14. Marilyn Reizbaum speaks of Boland's "valorizing" that which has been excluded in "Canonical Double Cross," in *Decolonizing Tradition,* ed. Karen R. Lawrence (Urbana: University of Illinois Press, 1992).

15. Edna Longley, *From Cathleen to Anorexia: The Breakdown of Irelands* (Dublin: Attic Press, 1990), 17.

Debrah Raschke (essay date June 1996)

SOURCE: Raschke, Debrah. "Eavan Boland's *Outside History* and *In a Time of Violence*: Rescuing Women, the Concrete, and Other Things Physical from the Dung Heap." *Colby Quarterly* 32, no. 2 (June 1996): 135-42.

[*In the following essay, Raschke asserts that "Boland's* Outside History *and* In a Time of Violence *use the concrete, physical world to revise notions of what sustains, to query historiography, and to expose the dangers of mythology."*]

Eavan Boland's poetry has been described as "impeccably scornful," as "denunciatory," as too "strident" and too "vehement" (Henigan 110), and as justification for "her dangerous attachment to bringing up babies" (Reizbaum 472). She has been accused of unduly elevating the domestic, of mythologizing the suburbs, and of betraying an Irish literary tradition, which, in emphasizing Gaelic roots, relies heavily on mythical images.[1] Such claims relegate Boland to a preoccupation with trivia, to plebeian tastes. Yet Boland's two latest works, **Outside History** and **In a Time of Violence,** contain some of the most poignant lyrics written within the Irish and British traditions in the last half of this century.[2] Her poetry and her criticism, as Hagen and Zelman note, display "a painterly consciousness, a keen, painful awareness of the shaping power of language, and a fundamental sense of poetic ethics" (443). Take, for example, the conclusion of **"Outside History"** for which her penultimate collection is named:

Out of myth into history I move to be
part of the ordeal
whose darkness is

only now reaching me from those fields,
those rivers, those roads clotted as
firmament with the dead.

How slowly they die
as we kneel beside them, whisper in their ear.
And we are too late. We are always too late.

Here and elsewhere within her last two collections there is a haunting lyricism, which, nonetheless, does not back down from conviction. Rescuing the physical world from the dung heap, Boland's *Outside History* and *In a Time of Violence* use the concrete, physical world to revise notions of what sustains, to query historiography, and to expose the dangers of mythology.

Like many contemporary women poets and novelists, Boland uses the concrete to create spiritual sustenance. In the first chapter of *Outside History,* entitled "Object Lessons," simple things (objects to which we become attached)—a black lace fan given to her by her mother, the empty chair of another woman poet, her lover's mug "with a hunting scene on the side"—take on a heightened significance. These images and the scenes created within this first section of poems become "object lessons" necessary for memory and for life—how barren our memories would be without their physical referents. How barren poetry would be without the concrete. The concrete in **"The Room of Other Women Poets"** becomes a statement of Boland's poetics and, too frequently, "what we lost."[3] Likewise, in *In a Time of Violence,* the individual moments sustain and heal, as in **"This Moment,"** where the instant in which a "woman leans down to catch a child" juxtaposes stars rising, moths fluttering, apples sweetening in the dark.

More radical, however, is Boland's use of the concrete to reveal missing stories and missing histories. In *Outside History,* Boland claims history should be personal and ordinary lest it shift truth, a theme that emerges even more strongly in *Violence.* Like much current fiction (Penelope Lively's *Moon Tiger,* Graham Swift's *Waterland,* and Margaret Atwood's *The Handmaid's Tale*), the first section of *Violence,* **"Writing in a Time of Violence,"** ponders the problems of historiography— the inefficiencies of empirical recording, the failures of reason, the missing suppressed stories. Boland uses these insufficiencies to unveil the hidden stories in Irish history. In the opening poem, **"That the Science of Cartography Is Limited,"** maps fail. They cannot relay the "shading of / forest." They "cannot show the fragrance of the balsam," or "the gloom of the cypresses." These gaps are what Boland wishes to "prove" as she peers over a map of Connacht, which does not tell the history of the famine road or the hunger cries of 1847 during which approximately one million Irish died. The map, metonymic for a silenced Irish history, distorts the story—an "apt rendering of / the spherical as flat." Similarly, in **"Death of Reason"** the Peep-O-Day Boys lay "fires down in / the hayricks," igniting the "fleshsmell of hatred." The history of the Peep-O-Day Boys, an Irish Protestant sect active in the 1780's who raided Catholic villages under the guise of righting the wrongs of the Protestant peasantry, remains a buried history in this poem, an untold story. All we can see is the fire. This untold story juxtaposes another buried history—

that which eighteenth-century portrait painting masks. Here eighteenth-century portrait painting is a disingenuous empiricism. It renders a century's apparent calm and control through the perfected face in the portrait: "the painter tints alizerine crimson with a mite of yellow" and finds "how difficult it is to make the skin / blush outside the skin." The face in the portrait, supposedly an accurate facsimile, conceals an underlying violence:

> The easel waits for her
> and the age is ready to resemble her and
> the small breeze cannot touch that powdered hair.
> That elegance.
> But I smell fire.

Portrait painting, and all with which it is associated, disguises the real face. The portrait lies. Paired with a poetics of control and elision and with histories that gloss, it is ultimately doomed.

"The Dolls Museum in Dublin" suggests another silenced event in Irish history. Like the map of Connacht, the Dublin dolls enshrined in a glass museum case do not give the full story. "Cradled and clean," the dolls are a re-creation of Easter in Dublin. "Their faces memorized like perfect manners," the dolls are what is left of the past and the present, who "infer the difference / with a terrible stare." They, however, do "not feel" the difference and do not "know it." One senses, though, it is not just the dolls who do not know the history they represent, that those who look upon the dolls also see nothing of the underlying history. Doubly mirrored, the "terrible stare" is not just the stare of the dolls, but the look of one who remembers what is generally forgotten and who knows that others have forgotten.

Once again, there is a cryptic history. **"The Dolls Museum in Dublin"** depicts Easter in Dublin—a seemingly innocuous subject—but if one remembers the history, one recalls one specific Easter in Dublin, Easter 1916, when rebellion erupted in an attempt to overthrow British rule. Recalling also the imagery of Yeats's "Dolls" (which Boland having written on Yeats would know), Boland's **"The Dolls Museum in Dublin"** extends Yeats's theme. Yeats's demonic dolls rail against their dollmaker and his wife for their new infant, which currently occupies the cradle, seeing it as an "insult" and a "disgrace" to their more perfected, inhuman state. Boland changes Yeats's story, revealing the old paint on the dolls' faces, the "cracks along the lips and on the cheeks" that "cannot be fixed," silencing the dolls' protest to a stare; for Boland, an aesthetic that ignores the human and a political stance that ignores the particulars fail.

"Writing in a Time of Violence" concludes this first section and extends Boland's critique to the concealment embedded in language. Ostensibly about an essay the persona wrote in college on Aristotle's *Art of Rhetoric* (a paradigm of the rhetorical refinements of concealment), the critique of glossed histories here extends to glossed language. Going beyond the particular commentary on Aristotle's rhetoric, this critique extends to all language: all poetry and all history that conceal and all mythology that hides under the camouflage of beauty are guilty. Such camouflage yields a fallacious and perilous picture:

> we are stepping into where we never
>
> imagine words such as *hate*
> and *territory* and the like—unbanished still
> as they always would be—wait
> and are waiting under
> beautiful speech. To strike.

As Boland notes: "In Ireland, we've always had this terrible gap between rhetoric and reality. In the void between those two things some of the worst parts of our history have happened" (Consalvo 96). Boland wants the gaps unveiled. Language is clearly a means for control. Avoiding the hard pictures, the abstract may temporarily provide respite, but such camouflage breeds a violence that will eventually erupt. Even pleasurable camouflage is rejected, as seen in an earlier poem **"Fond Memory"** in *Outside History*. **"Fond Memory"** tells of playing English games in school, of trying hard to learn lessons in English history—the value of the Magna Carta (and the unspoken divine right of kings to exploit Ireland). She looks forward to a different refuge, to coming home to the solace of her father playing the "slow / lilts of Tom Moore" on the piano. The song for her was a "safe inventory of pain." The poem, however, concludes with: "And I was wrong." There is no safety. In Stephen Dedalus' words, there is no "breakwater of order and elegance against the sordid tide of life" (*Portrait* 98).

Boland's use of the concrete does not stop at disclosing hidden Irish history and camouflaged language; she extends this critique to mythology and particularly mythology about women. For clearly, one of the missing histories to which Boland alludes is the presence of women. Traditionally, women have been captured by myth. Myth elevates and, in elevating, it frequently runs from life and, in running from life, it distorts and kills. The nymph Daphne in Ovid's *Metamorphoses* chooses to become a tree rather than succumb to Apollo's pursuits. Boland in *Outside History* asks us to query this choice. What a horrible fate to be stuck forever with one's "thighs in bark." Boland, using Daphne's voice in **"'Daphne with Her Thighs in Bark,'"** has a better solution. Instead of running from sexuality, Daphne urges her later sister:

> Save face, sister.
> Fall. Stumble.

> Rut with him.
> His rough heat will keep you warm.
>
> You will be better off than me[.]

Myths, inescapably, are part of our ordinary lives—they enrich the intensity, depth, and mystery of ordinary experiences. In *Violence*'s **"The Pomegranate,"** the myth of Ceres and Persephone becomes metaphor for the love and feared loss the mother feels for her child. The myth intensifies an ordinary moment of the mother watching the daughter with a "can of Coke" and a "plate of uncut fruit."

But myths are also the catalyst for doom, particularly when we attempt to live our lives as if they were myth. In **"Love,"** myths collide—one of grand passion, which features its participants in some heroic epic script, one of an ordinary existence, which pales before the former. **"Moths"** ups the ante. First, there are the legends of moths: "Ghost-swift moths with their dancing assemblies at dusk. / Their courtship swarms." Some "steer by / the moon." And then there are real moths, drawn by the light and heat, who will crackle, burn, and perish on that summer night. That "stealing of the light"—of myth—(for the moths and for the persona, who also is threatened with this "perishing") is alluring and deadly, an "Ingenious facsimile" that deceives and distorts. The dangers of myth are not, however, isolated to the personal and the romantic. In **"In Which the Ancient History I Learn Is Not My Own,"** history becomes conflated with the oracular, with divine myth. In this poem there is another map laying out a vision of the world, this time of the English occupation of Northern Ireland where "the red of Empire" and "the stain of absolute possession" were clear. The persona becomes almost convinced, becomes "nearly an English child." She could "list the English kings," "name the famous battles," and "was learning to recognize / God's grace in history." In this history lesson, the Roman Empire, the "*greatest Empire / ever known—*" (until, of course, the emergence of the British Empire), juxtaposes the Delphic oracle, the imagined "*exact centre / of the earth.*" Greece, and by extrapolation, Rome and Great Britain, seemingly have some special connection with the gods. Occupied Ireland becomes more distant, the blue-green of the Irish Sea giving way to "the pale gaze / of a doll's china eyes— / a stare without recognition or memory." Recalling the **"Dolls Museum in Dublin"** in which the dolls "infer the difference / with a terrible stare," but do not "feel it" or "know it," the "pale gaze / of a doll's china eyes" suggests the stupor that ensues from digesting a history and identity that is not one's own, of believing that erasure of one's own identity stems from the "grace" of God.

Myth, as well as history conflated with myth (legendary oracles and divine rights), is dangerous. It blinds, consumes, and kills. It is a particular problem for women, who are too frequently seen as myth—as not real—what Jacques Lacan suggests when he says that "Woman" does not exist. Myth is a way of distancing that avoids human relations, that, in essence, avoids life—the Platonic ascent, the forever unconsummated romance. In *Outside History*'s **"Listen: This Is the Noise of Myth,"** myth and legend deceptively keep human touch at a distance:

> Consider
>
> legend, self-deception, sin, the sum
> of human purpose and its end; remember
> how our poetry depends on distance[.]

"Gravity," however, "will bend starlight," will bring us down to earth.

In **"Anna Liffey,"** which begins the last section of *Violence,* "Life," the "daughter of Cannan," who comes to the "plain of Kildare," asks that the land be named after her. And so:

> The river took its name from the land.
> The land took its name from a woman.

But a "river is not a woman." Nor is the river Liffey a woman, as it is for Joyce who makes it analogous to Anna Livia Plurabelle in *Finnegans Wake* and to a lesser extent to Molly in *Ulysses*[4] (Ellmann 550). In **"Lestrygonians,"** the river Liffey is a sewage-filled river, which provides the wheeling gulls with "grub," their bread of life, the Anna Liffey, on which swans preen themselves (*Ulysses* 125-26), and the metaphoric referent for Molly's fluidity and sexuality in **"Penelope."** In the *Wake,* the river literally becomes a woman. As Margot Norris notes, the heroine Anna Livia Plurabelle not only has the river's name, but she "both *looks* and *acts* like the river Liffey." She is the "Everywoman, Everygoddess, Everyriver" (Glasheen 10), whose "human activities coincide with river functions: bathing, laundering, baptizing, running errands, bringing things, carrying refuse, tempting, giving life and pleasure, wrecking and destroying" (Norris 198). More generally, women in Joyce become (as they do for Yeats) mythologized—a river, a country, a muse, a siren.

A river, however, is not a woman; nor is Ireland. And it is precisely this mythologizing of woman that Boland writes against. In an interview in the Spring issue of *Poetry Book Society Bulletin,* Boland writes:

> The poem **"Anna Liffey"** is drawn from the centre of that life I led, and continue to live. The front door is my front door. The hills I see are the ones I have seen from that doorway for twenty-two years. The Liffey rises there as it always has. All that has changed is that I feel more confident that the private, downright vision is the guarantor of the political poem.
>
> (PBSB 2)

Boland, in describing the hills outside Dublin, does present a sacrality of place, but it is a sacrality imbued with the particulars—with the bend of Islandbridge, swans, neons, thirteen bridges to the sea. Although the Liffey in *Ulysses* is also something we can see as the gulls swoop and the swans preen on its waters, the Liffey becomes something else: the "flow of language," the "stream of life" (125-26), Molly's sexuality; it becomes something "outside history."

The first section of **In a Time of Violence** opens with the following epigraph from Book X of Plato's *Republic:*

> As in a city where the evil are permitted to have authority and the good are put out of the way, so in the soul of man, as we maintain, the imitative poet implants an evil constitution, for he indulges the irrational nature which has no discernment of greater or less.

It is a telling beginning. At first glance, it seems merely to call attention to Plato's banning poets from his ideal State and to the continually precarious position of the poet. However, like the many poems in this collection, this epigraph functions as palimpsest. As the epigraph indicates, Plato, in part, bans poets from his ideal State because the poet indulges the "irrational nature," but closer examination reveals that the excluded "irrational nature" is also associated with the feminine. Socrates tells Glaucon that the "best of us" when "we listen to a passage of Homer, or one of the tragedians, in which he represents some pitiful hero who is drawling out his sorrows in a long oration, or weeping, and smiting his breast," take "delight in giving way to sympathy" and "are in raptures, at the excellence of the poet who stirs our feelings most" (*The Republic* 535). Such delight, Socrates warns, is, nevertheless, dangerous:

> But when any sorrow of our own happens to us, then you may observe that we pride ourselves on the opposite quality—we would fain be quiet and patient; this is the manly part, and the other which delighted us in the recitation is now deemed to be the part of a woman.
>
> (335)

Thus, this epigraph, which immediately precedes Socrates' commentary on the poet's indulging the "irrational nature" and his subsequent identifying the irrational with feminine, underscores not only the exclusion of poets, but also the exclusion of the feminine from the ideal State.[5] And by extrapolation it accentuates Boland's challenging, within several interviews, the exclusion of the female voice from Irish poetry (from the ideal Irish tradition), where the prevailing voice has emerged from an exclusionary bardic tradition that relegates women to myth and muse (Consalvo 92-93, Reizbaum 479, Wright 10).

Book X of *The Republic* also dismisses poets because, as "imitators," they are "thrice removed" from "the truth" (*The Republic*). Socrates posits that since "God, whether from choice or from necessity, made one bed in nature and one only," the particular beds created by a bedmaker are imitations of a more perfected form. Thus, when a poet attempts to create an imitation of a particular bed, he is creating an imitation of an imitation (522-25). What is being dismissed here are the particularities, the "object lessons," which for Boland are essential. Thus, the epigraph that initiates this collection also functions as protest against a conception of truth that is distant, mythic, and abstract.

Outside History and *In a Time of Violence* both are testimony to Boland's desire to resurrect the concrete in history and aesthetics—in essence, to rescue the physical world from the dung heap. Throughout, Boland combines the sublime with the ordinary and critiques the suppression of the ordinary that frequently occurs in art—in sculpture, in writing. *Violence*'s **"We Are the Only Animals Who Do This"** conjoins "the grey / undertips of the mulberry leaves" that melds into a "translucence which is all darkness" with the particularities of nature and the world of the ordinary—car keys, traffic, aging, the sobbing of her mother. Thinking of her mother weeping, the persona comments that "weeping itself has no cadence." Looking at a statue, a "veiled woman," she comments: "all / had been chiselled out with the veil in / the same, indivisible act of definition / which had silenced her." Perhaps what is so disquieting to some about Boland is her ability to conjoin these.

Notes

1. Boland, in response to some of this criticism in an interview with Wright and Hannan in July 1990, states: "Yes, there are all these code words like 'domestic,' which imply a restrictive practice within the poem itself. A woman said to me of a male editor, 'He said the best poems I wrote were the least female—' instead of looking at the thing the right way around, which is to look at the work of young women, and asking, 'How are they putting together the Irish poem differently?' That is the real question" (10).

2. *Outside History* collects poems (many revised and reordered) from two previous volumes, *The Journey* and *Night Feed.*

3. Hagen and Zelman note that "what we lost" is also the "unwritten sufferings of ordinary women, ordinary people" who "are doomed to become unhistory" (445). Their discussion of some of Boland's earlier works, *In Her Own Image, A Kind of a Scar,* and *The Journey and Other Poems,* establishes a thematic consistency in which the "repossession of history" emerges as central to her poetry (444).

4. Richard Ellmann notes that "Molly Bloom, once Marie Tallon, Amalia Popper, and Nora Joyce, became the river Liffey" (550). Of the river Liffey,

Don Gifford notes that "'Anna' is close to the Irish for river" and that "Anna Liffey" is usually "applied to the attractive upper reaches of the river west and south of Dublin" (159). Adaline Glasheen calls the Anna Liffey "Dublin's little winding, brown, polluted river" (10).

5. Several revisionary studies in philosophy address the exclusion of the feminine from conceptions of Truth in Western metaphysics. For further commentary on how Plato excludes the feminine, see, for example, Irigaray's *Speculum.*

Works Cited

Boland, Eavan. *In a Time of Violence.* New York: Norton, 1994.

———. *Outside History.* New York: Norton, 1990.

The Collected Poems of W. B. Yeats. 1956 ed. New York: Macmillan, 1965.

Consalvo, Deborah McWilliams. "An Interview with Eavan Boland." *Studies: An Irish Quarterly Review* 81 (1992): 89-100.

Ellmann, Richard. *James Joyce.* Rev. ed. Oxford: Oxford UP, 1982.

Gifford, Don, and Robert J. Seidman. Ulysses *Annotated.* 2nd ed. Berkeley: U of California P, 1989.

Glasheen, Adaline. *Third Census of* Finnegans Wake. Berkeley: U of California P, 1977.

Hagen, Patricia L., and Thomas W. Zelman. "'We Were Never on the Scene of the Crime': Eavan Boland's Repossession of History." *Twentieth Century Literature* 37 (1991): 442-53.

Henigan, Robert H. "Contemporary Women Poets in Ireland." *Concerning Poetry* 18 (1985): 103-15.

Irigaray, Luce. *Speculum of the Other Woman.* Trans. Gillian G. Gill. Ithaca: Cornell UP, 1985.

Joyce, James. *A Portrait of the Artist as a Young Man.* New York: Viking, 1964.

———. *Ulysses.* Gabler ed. New York: Random, 1986.

Norris, Margot. "Anna Livia Plurabelle: The Dream Woman." *Women in Joyce.* Ed. Suzette Henke and Elaine Unkeless. Urbana: U of Illinois P, 1982, 197-213.

Plato. *The Republic.* Trans. Benjamin Jowett. New York: Heritage Press, 1944.

Poetry Book Society Bulletin. No. 160 (Spring 1994): 1-2.

Reizbaum, Marilyn. "An Interview with Eavan Boland." *Contemporary Literature* 30 (1989): 471-79.

Wright, Nancy Means, and Dennis J. Hannan. "Q. & A. with Eavan Boland." *Irish Literary Supplement* 10 (Spring 1991): 10-11.

Rose Atfield (essay date spring 1997)

SOURCE: Atfield, Rose. "Postcolonialism in the Poetry and Essays of Eavan Boland." *Women: A Cultural Review* 8, no. 2 (spring 1997): 168-82.

[*In the following essay, Atfield considers the issue of postcolonialism in Boland's verse.*]

Postcolonialism in the poetry of Eavan Boland is a process of the recognition and exposure of colonialism: its denial and repression of identity, and the restoration and reconstruction of that identity in terms of place, history and literary tradition. Boland established a sense of dual postcolonialism when, in the Ronald Duncan lecture for the Poetry Book Society, she referred to 'two identities' which 'shape and reshape what I have to say'. 'I am an Irish poet and a woman poet. In the first category I enter the tradition of the English language at an angle. In the second, I enter my own tradition at an even more oblique angle' (Boland 1994b).

Boland employs a traditional representation of colonialism of place as physical location, in the reading of maps, in the poem **'In Which the Ancient History I Learn Is Not My Own'** (Boland 1994a). Here she recalls 'The Linen map' on which

> The colours
> were faded out
> so the red of Empire—
> the stain of absolute possession—
>   . . . was
> underwater coral.

The rebellious emphasis of the connotations of corruption in the choice of the word 'stain' recreates her feeling of exile; although born in Dublin she lived with her parents in London in her childhood. Later verses of the poem explore the associated sense of displacement and loss of identity the experience created in her, through a wry irony:

> Ireland was far away . . .
>
> I was nearly an English child.
> I could list the English kings.
> I could name the famous battles.
> I was learning to recognise
> God's grace in history.

Boland suggested in an essay, 'The Woman, The Place, The Poet', that 'what we call place is really only that detail of it which we understand to be ourselves', and

continued: 'I learned quickly, by inference at school and reference at home, that the Irish were unwelcome in London . . . All I knew, all I needed to know, was that none of this was mine' (Boland 1990c). This reaction and the teacher's insensitivity to it is dramatized in the poetic recreation of the lesson:

> The teacher's voice had a London accent.
> This was London. 1952.
> It was Ancient History Class . . .
>
> *Remember this, children,*
>
> *The Roman Empire was*
> *the greatest Empire*
> *ever known—*
> *until our time of course—*

Later in the poem the memory of restoration and reconstruction of identity in terms of place indicates an early apprehension of the poet's postcolonial stance:

> . . . Suddenly
> I wanted
> to stand in front of it.
> I wanted to trace over
> and over the weave of my own country.
> To read out names
> I was close to forgetting.
> Wicklow. Kilruddery. Dublin.

The sense of being one of the colonized, despite her father's diplomatic status as a Southern Ireland representative in London and living in the Irish embassy, is further underlined in another recollection of this time. 'I made a distinction between a city one loved and a city one submitted to. I had not loved London, for instance, where I had spent the greater part of my childhood. The iron and gutted stone of its postwar prospect had seemed to me merely hostile . . .' (Boland 1990c). The terms 'submitted' and 'hostile' give this personal reminiscence a wider political significance and extend it into an examination of the effect of such displacement on Boland's creative identity, as implied in another essay, 'A Kind of Scar': 'My image-makers as a child, therefore, were refractions of my exile . . . For me, as for many another exile, Ireland was my nation long before it was once again my country' (Boland 1989).

One of those 'image-makers' may well have been the legend of the naming of Dublin's river Liffey which Boland would have clung to, like all the names of the places recalled, as a comforting litany. In the poem **'Anna Liffey'** she continues the postcolonial restoration and reconstruction of identity in terms of place:

> *Life,* the story goes,
> Was the daughter of Canaan,
> And came to the plain of Kildare . . .

The river took its name from the land.
The land took its name from a woman . . .

Maker of
Places, remembrances,
Narrate such fragments for me:

One body. One Spirit.
One place. One name.
The city where I was born.
The river that runs through it.
The nation which eludes me.

Fractions of a life
It has taken me a lifetime
To claim.

(Boland 1994a)

The personal and national claim are integrated in the poem which directly reflects a further expression of the underlying concern in a later part of the essay:

Who the poet is, what she or he nominates as a proper theme for poetry, what self they discover and confirm through this subject matter—all of this involves an ethical choice. Poetic ethics are evident and urgent in any culture where tensions between a poet and her or his birthplace are inherited and established.

(Boland 1989)

This 'ethical choice' and the 'inherited tensions' are particularly evident in the exploration of the 'second category' of identity established by Boland in my opening quotation, 'a woman poet'. In Irish cultural convention, woman's place has been colonized, subjected to restricted and marginalized interpretation and representation. Nationalism has led to the placing of an idealized, simplified, passive image of woman on a pedestal. Boland has examined this aspect of colonialism in a number of essays, explaining in 'A Kind of Scar':

When a people have been so dispossessed by events as the Irish in the eighteenth and nineteenth centuries an extra burden falls on the very idea of a nation . . . The majority of Irish male poets depended on women as motifs in their poetry . . . images of women in which I did not believe and of which I could not approve . . . these passive and simplified women seemed a corruption . . . a species of human insult that . . . they should become elements of style rather than aspects of truth . . . Once the idea of a nation influences the perception of a woman . . . She becomes the passive projection of a national idea.

(Boland 1989)

In the poem **'Time and Violence'**, Boland dramatizes an imaginative confrontation with such 'passive projections', in the form of typically idealized motifs, 'a shepherdess . . . her arm injured from . . . the pastorals where she posed . . . Cassiopeia trapped . . . a mermaid with invented tresses . . .'. Having recognized and exposed such colonialism, Boland begins the

restoration and reconstruction of female identity in terms of a more realistic concept of woman's place. As she said in her essay 'Outside History':

In any new dispensation the idea of a nation must seem an expendable construct . . . it has never admitted of women. Its flags and songs and battle-cries, even its poetry . . . make use of feminine imagery . . . the true voice and vision of women are routinely excluded. In such poems, the real woman behind the image was not only not explored, she was never even seen.

(Boland 1990b)

The challenge the poet imagines issuing from idealized national icons is a desperate plea for release into true identity, humanity rather than the fallacious immortality of artifice:

We cannot sweat. Our skin is icy.
We cannot breed here. Our wombs are empty.
Help us to escape youth and beauty.

Write us out of the poem. Make us human
in cadences of change and mortal pain
and words we can grow old and die in.

(Boland 1994a)

Boland recognized the challenge in comments published in 1989:

I could not as a woman accept the nation formulated for me by Irish poetry and its traditions . . . it seemed to me that I was likely to remain an outsider in my own national literature, cut off from its archive, at a distance from its energy. Unless, that is, I could repossess it.

(Reizbaum 1989)

At that time, however, the poetic strategies necessary to achieve this repossession had not been realized; a year later Edna Longley suggested that the postcolonial restoration and reconstruction of identity had not been achieved: 'By not questioning the nation, Boland recycles the literary cliché from which she desires to escape . . . without considering how that construct itself, both inside and outside poetry, has marginalised and scarred many Irish women and men' (Longley 1990). However, in the essay 'Outside History' in 1990, Boland had established the approach of the poem published in 1994: 'my own discourse must be subversive . . . must be vigilant to write of my own womanhood . . . in such a way that I never colluded with the simplified images of women in Irish poetry' (Boland 1990b).

By 1994 the 'subversive discourse' had been explored in a number of poems described in an interview: 'Writing about the lost, the voiceless, the silent . . . exploring my relation to them . . . more dangerous still—feeling my ways into the powerlessness of an experience through the power of expressing it' (Allen-Randolph 1994). In **'Story'** the powerlessness of the experience into which she feels her way is that of the traditional legend of threatened lovers. She imaginatively enters the restrictive and prescriptive idealized representation of the character of the woman and the powerlessness of her colonized place:

> They do not know. They have no idea
> how much of this: the ocean-coloured peace
>
> of the dusk, and the way legend stresses it,
> depend on her to be young and beautiful.

As the poem progresses Boland moves with it, into the real world of a real woman, not colluding 'with the simplified images' but presenting a post-colonial restoration of female identity in the everyday details of a lived domestic life:

> . . . suddenly what is happening is not
> what happens to the lovers in the wood
>
> . . . But what is whispering out of sycamores . . .
>
> . . . And is travelling to enter a suburb
> at the foothills of the mountains in Dublin.
>
> And a garden with jasmine and poplars. And
> a table at which I am writing. I am writing
>
> a woman out of legend. I am thinking
> how new it is—this story. How hard it will be to tell.

(Boland 1994a)

The 'new story' which is so hard to tell is not only that of real women but of the woman poet telling the story, for another kind of colonialism exposed by Boland is that of the literary and cultural establishment in Ireland and the consequent denial of the female voice. As colonialism can generally be defined as the establishment of ruling power systems by imposition, Eavan Boland remarked: 'power has just as much to do with a poetic sphere of operation as any other . . . power has operated in the making of canons, the making of taste, the nominating of what poems should represent the age and so on' (Allen-Randolph 1994).

She talked in an interview in 1991 of the difficulty of establishing any place for women writers in the cultural milieu:

> the ugly part is the intimidation for a woman to write a poem, get a book together, wonder where it's going to be published, how it will be received. In other words: the ugly part in every single minority in a writing culture is, Where does the power lie? Who has the power? . . . the contemporary poetry course in Trinity this year carried not one woman poet! . . . The male Irish poets have treated exclusion as invention but there is absolutely no doubt that that exists. There is no give

on this issue. It is a matter of fact . . . If you look back at *Eire Ireland* for example, there are almost no references to women's writing.

(Means Wright and Hannan 1991)

This denial and repression of female identity has been counteracted to some extent by Boland's own provision of poetry workshops for women writers but the cultural imposition—or what she has called 'the weight of the feminine convention on the individual woman' ('Nationalism' 1979)—has exacerbated this colonial exclusivity. As she recalled:

> There is not an equal societal commission here for people to explore their individuality in an expressive way—for a woman to cross the distance in writing poetry to becoming a poet. 'If I called myself a poet,' a young woman in one of my workshops told me, 'people would think I didn't wash my windows' . . . this community nominates women as the receptors of other people's creativity and not as the initiators of their own.

(Means Wright and Hannan 1991)

In **'Bright Cut Irish Silver'** Boland resists the concept of poetic art as a male birthright; she uses the correlative of silver mining, restoring female identity in terms of women's place in creative artistry by advocating usurpation of poetic tradition:

> This gift for wounding an artery of rock
> was passed on from father to son, to the father
> of the next son;
>
> is an aptitude
> for injuring earth while inferring it in curves and
>   surfaces;
>
> is this cold potency which has come,
> by time and chance,
>
> into my hands.

(Boland 1990a)

The postcolonial stance is emphasized by the references to previous 'wounding . . . injuring . . . cold potency', implying the aggressive imposition of creative skill which will now be transformed to a more positive collaboration.

In 1991 Boland commented: 'the critique in this country remains obdurately male and patriarchal . . . Although a great deal of vital work by women has been done, the critique is really sitting on top of it. It's made up of an older writing culture which is predominantly male' (Means Wright and Hannan 1991). And still in 1994 she emphasized the colonialism of the literary-critical establishment in Ireland: 'there won't be good or valuable criticism of this whole area until it's understood that the issues raised by the woman poet are the issues central to poetry now . . . questions about voice and the self . . . not to mention the crucial relation of the poet to the act of power' (Allen-Randolph 1994). However she has opened the way for other women poets to move in from the outskirts and find their place, as she positively asserts: 'Poetry is not a fiefdom or a private domain. It is a city whose gates stand wide' (Boland 1994b).

A colonized people's identity is often denied in the suppression of its history. Where Irish experience has been marginalized Boland restores significance; as she said in an interview:

> You can accept the history on face value and write out of that but I don't want to. I feel a great need to somehow get behind that history as a woman and as a poet to the great source out of which the history comes and of which it is only a fragment.
>
> (Tall 1988)

One of the most appalling eras of loss in Irish history, notoriously mismanaged by the governmental relief organization, was the famine, evidence of which still scars the landscape although it is literally obliterated in terms of cartographical record. In the poem **'That the Science of Cartography Is Limited'**, Boland reclaims the human aspect of the basic facts of dates and death:

> this was once a famine road.
>
> 1847, when the crop had failed twice,
> Relief Committees gave
> the starving Irish such roads to build.
>
> Where they died, there the road ended . . .
>
> and ends still and when I take down
> the map of this island, it is . . .
>
> . . . to tell myself again that
>
> the line which says woodland and cries hunger
> and gives out among sweet pine and cypress,
> and finds no horizon
>
> will not be there.
>
> (Boland 1994a)

The poet's imaginative empathy crosses the generations and breaks through the barrier of signs and symbols to the reality of individual suffering. The starkness of the final line exposes and challenges the colonial perspective of denial, which is satirically exposed in another poem, the title of which relates the personae directly to the same historical situation, **'March 1 1847. By the First Post'**. Here the insensitive arrogance of the colonial presence in Ireland is also individualized in the self-centred concerns of society ladies; the imaginative recreation of the circumstances in epistolary form ef-

fectively dramatizes the contrasting perspective. The English woman denies any sense of identity to the Irish by concentrating only on her own inconvenience, ignoring the desperate plight of another woman who, but for an accident of history, might have been in her place:

> A woman lying
> across the Kells Road with her baby—
> in full view. We had to go
> out of our way
> to get home & we were late
> & poor Mama was not herself all day.
>
> (Boland 1994a)

It is the personalization of history which brings it to life and restores the identity of those whose past has shaped the Irish present; this is demonstrated in Boland's awareness of its repression in official record in which previously she has colluded, unwittingly, as she suggests in **'Inscriptions'** in which her frame of reference is particularized by focusing her imaginative attention on a specific item, a child's cot painted with his name, Peter:

> Someone knew
> the importance of giving him a name.
>
> For years I have known
> how important it is
> not to name
> the coffins, the murdered in them,
> the deaths in alleyways and on doorsteps—
>
> in case they rise out of their names
> and I recognise
>
> the child who slept peacefully
> and the girl who guessed at her future.
>
> (Boland 1994a)

It is the recognition of her own denial which endorses Boland's exposure of the colonial repression of Irish identity in the nation's history; naming individuals evokes a more uncomfortable reality which cannot so easily be ignored. This colonialism imbued the literature she studied and thus influenced her own early work, as she acknowledged in a lecture:

> The poem I wrote was nominally called Irish, yet it was blemished by the music of drawing rooms and light tenor voices . . . it averted its eyes from the harsh facts of the loss of a language and the abandonment of history . . . A darker nineteenth century, a more bitter eighteenth century demanded to be acknowledged.
>
> (Boland 1994b)

This same 'abandonment of history' is recognized in another example of the poet's particular facility for imaginative empathy, developed as a postcolonial strategy counteracting earlier denial, in the poem **'In a Bad Light'**. In this poem she moves from the contemplation of an item, this time a doll clothed in period costume, to full identification with the colonized peoples who would have sewn the fabric for the woman who had the resources and influence to travel to the New World of St Louis in 1860.

From her privileged position in her own time, 'I stand in a room in the museum', she reads: 'A notice says no comforts were spared. The silk is French. The seamstresses are Irish.' She then becomes one with those whose history has been abandoned, restoring their identity in reclaiming their part in this history:

> I am in the gas-lit backrooms.
>
> . . . We are sewing
>
> coffin ships, and the salt of exile. And our own death in it. For history's abandonment we are doing this . . .

The ironic contrast, of the seamstresses' suffering with the ignorant pleasure of the woman, is underlined in the presentation of the dress as a symbol of exploitation:

> We dream a woman on a steamboat parading in sunshine in a dress we know we made. She laughs off rumours of war. She turns and traps light on the skirt. It is, for that moment, beautiful.
>
> (Boland 1994a)

In this recreation of women's experience, both colonizers and colonized, Boland again confirms the second of her declared identities, also emphasized in an interview: 'I think it's important that Irish poets have a discourse with the idea of Irishness and I think it's probably very important that an Irish woman poet doesn't shirk that discourse because there have been gaps, vacancies or silences in the literature' (Tall 1988). In her recognition and exposure of a dual colonialism Boland vocalizes such silences, embodies the gaps and vacancies by reconstructing *her* story in history, restoring the identity of women in the Irish past. In an introduction to her collection *Outside History,* for the Poetry Book Society, she commented:

> I think a good few poems in the book are anchored in the conflict between the received version and the unofficial one . . . So much that matters, so much that is powerful and frail in human affairs seems to me, increasingly, to happen outside history: away from the texts and symmetries of an accepted expression . . . for that very reason, at risk of being edited out of the final account.
>
> (Boland 1990a)

As Margaret Ward suggested in *The Missing Sex,* 'despite all our efforts, our foremothers remain in the margins, unknown to most' (Ward 1991). Eavan Boland went on a personal pilgrimage to recover one of hers, as she records in her essay 'The Woman, The Place,

The Poet'. She bears witness to the identity denied one of the typical inmates of the workhouse her great-grandfather ran:

> I refused to imagine him—my ancestor . . . Instead, I imagined a woman . . . There were several reasons why she might have been there. The most obvious—unmarried motherhood—remains the most likely. She could as easily have been a survivor of an eviction—hundreds of them, complete with bailiff and battering ram, took place in Ireland every year . . . was this where my great-grandfather had lived? At least, by these visible survivals, I could guess at his existence. There was no trace of hers . . . She is part of all our histories. . . .
>
> (Boland 1990c)

Boland restores the woman's identity through imaginative recreation; a similar witness is borne to her grandmother, for whom she also creates a story and thus reconstructs a silent history, defending this imaginative process as a validation of the life lived but only remembered through 'something thrown out once in a random conversation; / a hint merely.' The history is derived from the 'Lava Cameo' of the poem's title, the static artefact which has been handed down and must be used as the catalyst for revitalization:

> . . . there is a way of making free with the past,
> a pastiche of what is
> real and what is
> not, which can only be
> justified if you think of it
>
> not as sculpture but syntax:
>
> a structure extrinsic to meaning which uncovers
> the inner secret of it.
>
> (Boland 1994a)

By 'making free' with the past, rather than being casually irresponsible to the facts of the lives lived, Boland releases them from the restrictions, simplifications and marginalization of colonialism; the static 'sculpture' gives way to the fluid 'syntax', the dead stone to the living word.

Boland expresses the disregard of women's contribution to Irish history, such as the suffrage movement, noted by Margaret Ward as being reduced to marginalia in even fairly recent standard textbooks: 'The professional historian's level of awareness concerning women's contribution to politics and society can only be described as abysmal . . . the effects of this blinkered vision are not confined within the walls of academia' (Ward 1991).

Boland recognizes this ubiquitous 'blinkered vision', referring to Irish popular culture and literary expression reflecting an internal colonialism; 'it has never admitted of women. Its flags and songs and battle-cries, even its poetry . . . make use of feminine imagery . . . the true voice and vision of women are routinely excluded' (Boland March/April 1990). This remark is made in the essay 'Outside History', and in the poem of the same title Boland offers a way forward, exposing the idealized mythical representation of women and reconstructing a more realistic identity:

> I have chosen:
>
> out of myth into history I move to be
> part of that ordeal . . .
>
>> How slowly they die
>> as we kneel beside them, whisper in their ear.
>> And we are too late. We are always too late.

> (Boland 1990a)

Boland rejects the traditional concept of women as merely carers, the comforters after the battle, at the edges, on the periphery of history. 'too late' to have any significant effect. She challenges the sanitization of women in myth, the decorative adjuncts of the real action in the male world; 'in using and re-using women as icons and figments, Irish poets were not just dealing with emblems. They were also evading the real women of an actual past: women whose silence their poetry should have broken' (Boland 1990b).

The postcolonial response to this challenge comes in restoration of these women's identities through reclaiming the history previously unrecognized and unregarded. It has been the journey of Boland's professional writing life to do this, a counterpart to the physical pilgrimage she made to the site of her ancestor's workhouse. At first she despaired the lack of matrilineal poetic foremothers, commenting:

> I did not feel in possession of a tradition. I simply felt that I could not record the life I lived in the poem I wrote, unless I could find my name in the poetic past . . . when I turned to the tradition to find support for that visionary claim, I could not find it. The name of my life was missing in the history of my form.

> (Boland 1990b)

In **'The Achill Woman'**, she records a confrontation with a real woman whom she could not write into her poem without betraying the history the woman represented; the poem is a searingly honest indictment of her failure yet in itself it establishes a great distance travelled from the position described:

> She came up the hill carrying water . . .
>
> . . . I was all talk, raw from college—
> week-ending at a friend's cottage
> with one suitcase and the set text
> of the court poets of the Silver Age.

> We stayed putting down time until
> the evening turned cold without warning.
>
> . . . but nothing now can change the way I went
> indoors . . .
>
> took down my book
> and opened it and failed to comprehend.
>
> the harmonies of servitude . . .

> (Boland 1990a)

In a prose version of this incident, from her essay 'A Kind of Scar', Boland again castigates herself but also recognizes the responsibility of the colonized literary-historical tradition in which she was brought up:

> I knew, without having words for it, that she came from a past which affected me . . . I went in, lit a fire, took out my book of English court poetry and memorised all over again—with no sense of irony or omission—the cadences of power and despair . . . nothing that I understood about poetry enabled me to understand her better . . . I turned my back on her in that cold twilight and went to commit to memory the songs and artifices of the very power systems which had made her own memory such an archive of loss.

> (Boland 1989)

She exposes the falsification of the record produced by such 'songs and artifices': 'How had the women of our past . . . suffered Irish history and inscribed themselves in the speech and memory of the Achill woman, only to re-emerge in the Irish poetry as fictive queens and national sibyls?' (Boland 1989). Her answer is to produce a postcolonial history through an alternative poetic representation, as she described in interviews, 'For a poet like myself, who comes into the tradition at an oblique angle, experiments of usurpation can be . . . exciting and rewarding. Turning the poem inside out. Taking the nature poem, the dream-poem, the love poem and subverting them' (Allen-Randolph 1994). 'I don't have a desire to separate myself from the body politic of poetry. I have a great desire to subvert what is there. In this sense, the invention of a male muse would have been a separatist initiative. The holding to a female one would be a subversive one' (Means Wright and Hannan 1991).

In the poem **'Time and Violence'**, Boland exposes colonialism in the literary tradition of 'fictive queens and national sibyls'; its denial and repression of the true identity of Irish women, by subverting the aisling or vision-poem and offering a postcolonial representation of the female muse:

>> . . . a voice was saying:

> This is what language did to us. Here
> is the wound, the silence, the wretchedness

of tides and hillsides and stars where

we languish in a grammar of sighs,
in the high-minded search for euphony,
in the midnight rhetoric of poesie.

(Boland 1994a)

In this poem published in 1994 Boland offers an answer
to the question with which she challenged herself in her
1989 essay, 'A Kind of Scar': 'Why do you . . . write
in forms explored and sealed by English men hundreds
of years ago? You are Irish. You are a woman. Why do
you keep these things at the periphery of the poem?
Why do you not move them to the centre, where they
belong?' (Boland 1989). Once again the 'two identities'
and her sense of dual colonialism are clearly apparent.

In another remark from Boland's essay 'A Kind of
Scar', she celebrates the fact that

women have moved from being the subjects and objects
of Irish poems to being the authors of them. It is a
momentous transit. It is also a disruptive one. It raises
questions of identity . . . it changes our idea of the
Irish poem; of its composition and authority, of its right
to appropriate certain themes and make certain fiats.

(Boland 1994b)

In recognizing an insidious colonialism of poetic authority and theme through 'exclusions and erasures' denying the identity of women in literary tradition, Boland
prepares the way for its restoration. She recalls her
early uncertainties in the traditional female, domestic
role:

I now inhabited the lyric moment itself but with no
signposts, no directions . . . in that kitchen, I felt more
like the object of a poem than its author. I felt part of
the visionary absences I seemed unable to change . . .
What would it take I wondered to confer on these, not
simply a visionary reality but a visionary permission as
well? . . . To be able to create it, endow it, argue for
it seemed to me where the true authority of the poet
lay.

(Boland 1994b)

By the time she came through to the elegant simplicity
of the poem **'Anna Liffey'** the confidence of having
found that authority and claimed it for herself and others is celebrated:

Make of a nation what you will
Make of the past
What you can—

There is now
A woman in a doorway.

It has taken me
All my strength to do this.

Becoming a figure in a poem.

Usurping a name and a theme.

(Boland 1994a)

The same confidence in this postcolonial restoration of
her woman's identity in literary tradition underlies her
comment on her latest work; 'I knew this world was
worthy of poetry. I knew it deserved the visionary claim
I wished to make on its behalf. I knew that I was Irish;
I knew I was a woman; that these categories of identity
made a duality of reference' (Boland 1989).

To return to the image of map-making at the beginning
of this paper, Boland's final words in an interview after
the publication of her latest volume seem to sum up her
achievement and the concept of postcolonialism in her
work:

When the history of poetry in our time is written—I
have no doubt about this—women poets will be seen to
have re-written not just the poem, not just the image.
They won't just have re-balanced elements within the
poem. They will have altered the cartography of the
poem. The map will look different.

(Boland 1994b)

Works Cited

Allen-Randolph, J. (autumn 1994), 'An Interview with
Eavan Boland', *Irish University Review.*

Boland, Eavan (1989), *A Kind of Scar: The Woman
Poet in a National Tradition,* Dublin: Attic Press.

———(1990a), *Outside History,* Manchester: Carcanet.

———(March/April 1990b), 'Outside History', *American Poetry Review.*

———(spring/summer 1990c), 'The Woman, The Place,
The Poet', *Georgia Review* 44/1-2.

———(1994a), *In a Time of Violence,* Manchester: Carcanet.

———(October 1994b), 'Gods Make Their Own
Importance: On the Authority of the Poet in Our Time',
The Ronald Duncan Lecture, Poetry Book Society.

Longley, Edna (1990), *From Cathleen to Anorexia: The
Breakdown of Irelands,* Dublin: Attic Press.

Means Wright, N. and D. J. Hannan (spring 1991),
'Question & Answer with Eavan Boland', *ILS.*

'Nationalism and Obsession in Irish Poetry: Interview
with Eavan Boland' (winter 1979), *Literary Review* 22.

Reizbaum, Marilyn (winter 1989), 'An Interview with
Eavan Boland', *Contemporary Literature.*

Tall, Deborah (autumn 1988), 'Question & Answer with
Eavan Boland', *ILS.*

Ward, Margaret (1991), *The Missing Sex: Putting Women into Irish History,* Dublin: Attic Press.

Nell Sullivan (essay date December 1997)

SOURCE: Sullivan, Nell. "Righting Irish Poetry: Eavan Boland's Revisionary Struggle." *Colby Quarterly* 23, no. 4 (December 1997): 334-48.

[*In the following essay, Sullivan perceives Boland's "revisionary struggle" with Irish mythology, which depicts women in subordinate and passive roles as an attempt to "repossess" Irish poetry for women.*]

> My muse must be better than those of men
> who made theirs in the image of their myth.
>
> —Boland, **"Envoi"**

Traditionally, the envoi sends the poet's work out into the world with modest hopes, anxious disclaimers, and humble apologies. But in her poem **"Envoi"** from *Outside History,* Evan Boland unabashedly announces her agenda: "My muse must be better than those of men / who made theirs in the image of their myth." She must exceed the male poetics of Ireland to correct the mythology inherited from the male tradition because its dangerous appropriation of the female image estranges women from their own bodies and abets the exclusion of women's experience from both literature and history. Discussing her dilemma as an Irish woman poet, Boland states that given a tradition that depicts women as merely "passive, decorative," or "emblematic," "it seemed to me that I was likely to remain an outsider in my own national literature, cut off from its archives, at a distance from its energy. Unless, that is, I could repossess it" (*Am. Poetry Rev.* 32-33).[1] In order to "repossess" Irish poetry for dispossessed women, Boland engages in what Sandra Gilbert and Susan Gubar call a "revisionary struggle" with the myths of the male tradition (*Madwoman* 49), speaking from both the female body and female experience to authorize her own creativity.

Boland first articulated her nascent suspicion of the male tradition in the collection *In Her Own Image,* published in the United States within the volume *Introducing Eavan Boland.* The title of *In Her Own Image* suggests Boland's usurpation of the Romantics' prerogative of God-like creation. In the poem **"Making Up,"** Boland toys in particular with the Coleridgian notion of the infinite *I-am,* the God-like imagination. The poem plays with the connotations of the phrase "making up," for as Boland's speaker describes her *toilette,* she makes it clear as she "raddles" and "prinks" that she is also talking about the "making up" of poetic truths:

> I look
> in the glass.
> My face is made,
> it says:
> Take nothing, nothing
> at its face value
> . . .
> it's a trick.
> Myths
> are made by men.
>
> (ll. 29-40)

Boland's speaker implicitly critiques the male versions of femininity (inscribed in the poem as "thigh and buttock / that they prayed to") by creating a "false" version of herself in a morning ritual, by *redefining* the lines of her face with cosmetics in the image of ideal women who have been themselves defined in the lines of poetry "made by men." At the end of the poem, the speaker seizes the symbolic tools of artifice: "Mine are the rouge pots / . . . out of which / I dawn" (ll. 53-59). This gesture is ambivalent, however, since the tools of creativity she seizes are used to inscribe "made up" (that is, false) versions of womanhood.[2]

In **"Tirade for the Mimic Muse"** from the same collection, Boland comes closer to finding a poetry free from masculine inscriptions of femininity. Here, Boland's speaker rebukes the muse erroneously adopted by some women poets (even the very young Boland), the muse that encourages women to "mimic" male poetry and thus leads them astray. For women poets, this muse is "Our criminal, our tricoteuse, our Muse— / Our muse of mimic art" (ll. 9-10). She is a traitor to her sex, a whore luxuriating in (and spawned by) male myths. But if it is "before the glass" that Boland's speaker recognizes the dangerous lies of traditional poetry in **"Making Up,"** it is also before a mirror, ironically, that Boland's speaker will show the "mimic muse" the treachery of her failure to reproduce faithfully the truth of women's experience:

> I will wake you from your sluttish sleep.
> I will show you true reflections, terrors.
> You are the Muse of all our mirrors.
> Look in them and weep.
>
> (ll. 57-60)

Reforming this fallen muse becomes Boland's first step in her search for the "better muse" she later invokes in **"Envoi."**

The rage that pervades *In Her Own Image* is quieted in Boland's later poetry collected in *Outside History.* As Patricia Hagen and Thomas Zelman note, Boland moves from the belligerent "announcement" of *In Her Own Image* to an active "inauguration" of "her own aesthetic, one that bears witness" in her later poetry (449). This inauguration, however, requires her acknowledgment of her previous unconscious complicity with the mimic muse. In the confessional **"The Achill Woman,"** for example, Boland admits her own failure to recognize "true reflections." The poem recounts an encounter the young Boland had with a serving woman in Achill, an encounter whose significance became clear only years later. According to Boland, "When I met the Achill woman I was already a poet, I thought of myself as a poet. Yet nothing that I understood about poetry enabled me to understand her better" (*Am. Poetry Rev.* 33). Under the tutelage of the mimic muse, the young Boland fails to comprehend the implications of the woman's servitude, for Boland is immersed in the study of her male precursors:

> And she was nearly finished for the day.
> And I was all talk, raw from college—
> weekending at a friend's cottage
> with one suitcase and the set text
> of the Court poets of the Silver Age.
>
>   (ll. 14-18)

Boland and the woman part with the growing chill of evening, and Boland begins to study the verses commended to her by the canonical curriculum of her college. Yet she "fail[s] to comprehend" both in the existence of the woman and in the lines she reads "harmonies of servitude." The "raw" Boland does not yet understand that the Court poetry both inscribes and obscures the power structure that oppressed women and helped to defeat the Irish nation, nor does she understand that as a student of those very lines, she is a servant bound by defeat just as surely as the Achill woman is. **"The Achill Woman"** is Boland's confession of her apprenticeship to the mimic muse, for she falls "asleep," like the muse of that earlier poem, "oblivious to / . . . the songs crying out their ironies" (ll. 33-37).

In rejecting the mimic muse (and hence challenging her male precursors), Boland wins her first battle with what Gilbert and Gubar have called "the female affiliation complex"(*No Man's Land* 168). As Gilbert and Gubar note, Bloom's "anxiety of influence" does not explain female poetics and thus "must give way to a paradigm of ambivalent affiliation, a construct which dramatizes women's intertwined attitudes of anxiety and exuberance about creativity" (170). According to Bloom's paradigm, the male poetic tradition endlessly repeats the Freudian family romance as male poets struggle with their literary fathers for possession of their mother-muse. Since the female poetic tradition is one marked by silences, women poets suffer from an anxiety about their creativity (the "anxiety of authorship," discussed in *Madwoman*); instead of engaging in agonistic struggles with literary mothers, then, women poets actively seek these mothers as proof that women can write.[3]

Boland herself has expressed a desire for a poetic matrilineage, for when she discovered that the predominantly male tradition excluded women's truth, she regretted "the absence of an expressed poetic life" dignifying and authorizing her own (*Am. Poetry Rev.* 33). In **"The Rooms of Other Women Poets"** (a title recalling Virginia Woolf's anxiety of authorship in *A Room of One's Own*), the speaker "wonders" about other women at their writing. She wonders if they reject, as she does, the relegation of women's creative expression to dried flowers arranged on the "rims" of saucers (or other such *marginal* art) as "a savage, old calligraphy" (l. 8), if they write prolifically instead, "bearing up unmarked, steel-cut foolscap / a whole quire of it" (ll. 13-14). By an act of imagination, Boland creates her mothers and sisters, affirming by the end of the poem that she is not alone: "Somewhere you are writing or have written in / a room you came to as I come to this" (ll. 19-20).

In *Outside History*'s **"The Journey,"** Boland chooses to affiliate with Sappho, an historical (rather than imaginary) literary mother. Even given the historical distance of some 2500 years, this choice is appropriate. As Gilbert and Gubar note, "female genealogy does not have an inexorable logic because the literary matrilineage has been repeatedly erased, obscured, or fragmented" (*No Man's Land* 199). Perhaps in choosing Sappho as her guide to the underworld in "The Journey," Boland recalls Sappho as a symbol of the silencing of women's writing throughout history, for Sappho's poems have only been handed down to modernity in fragmented form; some of them were recovered when archaeologists discovered them written on strips of papyrus gracing the remains of mummified bodies in Egypt (Wilkie and Hurt 574). The silence enshrouding her writing enables Sappho to reveal to Boland's pilgrim the "real terrors" Boland herself shows the mimic muse of *In Her Own Image.*

In writing **"The Journey,"** Boland wanted to "invert" the male tradition (Klauke 61), purposely using the mythic journey to the underworld that has come to us via the literary patriarchs Homer, Virgil, and Dante. In all three of the male journeys, men seek the wisdom of other men: Odysseus seeks Teiresias, Aeneas seeks his father Anchises, and Dante seeks Virgil as the personification of Reason itself. Tellingly, Sappho has no place in the literary lineage Dante forges for himself in *Inferno,* an exclusive group called the "Six Intelligences." In **"The Journey,"** Boland creates an alternative to the patriarchal line of descent for truth and wisdom by inserting women's experience, as she says, "in one of the elite conventions of poetry which had turned its back on experience of that sort" (Reizbaum 473). As Alicia Ostriker has argued, women poets who opt to use myths must alter them "by female knowledge of female experience, so that they [myths] can no longer stand as foundations of collective male fantasy. . . . They are retrieved images of what women have collectively and historically suffered" (Ostriker 318):

Before the pilgrim Boland falls asleep in the poem, she bemoans the fact that "somewhere a poet is wasting / *his* sweet uncluttered meters on the obvious / emblem instead of the real thing" (ll. 7-9, emphasis mine). Boland's choice of pronouns shows it is a male poet who thus misses the truth, but Boland's journey reclaims the truth of women's suffering by pulling to the center that which traditional (male) poetry marginalizes or simply dismisses as "private." In this poem, Boland seeks wisdom not only from women, but in the silences of women, specifically of mothers.

According to Boland, the genesis of **"The Journey"** was the experience of nearly losing her own infant daughter to meningitis. After the ordeal, she felt moved to voice the pain of mothers who had not been spared such terrible losses (Houston MFA, March 1991). At first it may seem unclear why Boland chooses Sappho, who wrote sensual love lyrics, to guide her to the underworld of bereaved mothers. But the poem the pilgrim Boland is reading before she dozes is "Aphrodite comforts Sappho in her love's duress," a poem that proves Sappho is also a poet of inconsolable loss. Her lyrics often entail an elision of maternal and sexual love in a prototype of Adrienne Rich's "lesbian continuum" in which diverse kinds of love forge "woman-identification" (Rich 159). In Boland's poem, the pilgrim is "calm and unsurprised" when Sappho appears beside her: "and I would have known her anywhere / and I would have gone with her anywhere" (ll. 29-30). This moment of spontaneous bonding reveals the reason Sappho is an appropriate guide to the world of grieving mothers: the relationship that the literary mother Sappho shares with the daughter Boland.[4] In a move akin to Dante's making of himself one of the six immortal poets, Boland has Sappho place her firmly in the literary matrilineage: "there are not many of us; you are dear / and stand beside me as my own daughter" (ll. 84-85). This gesture of inclusion ironically underscores women's exclusion from the patriarchal canon, for Sappho admits, "there are not many of us."

"The Journey" reiterates the traditional patriarchal silence about the suffering of women with its own poignant silences. Sappho comes to Boland "wordlessly" and Boland's pilgrim follows her "without a word" (ll. 31-32). The dead children, victims of "Cholera, typhus, croup, diptheria," are "suckling darknesses" and their mothers who hold them create "terrible pietas." The pilgrim, who has herself been saved from this terrible fate, cannot "reach or speak to them." She "whispers" her desire to "at least be their witness" in the world above, but her guide insists on the impossibility of breaking this silence: "what you have seen is beyond speech / beyond song, only not beyond love" (ll. 79-80). Finally, the ironic "witnessing of silence" is the purpose of Sappho's journey, for as she tells the pilgrim, "I have brought you here so you will know

forever / the silences in which are our beginnings" (ll. 86-87). The tradition with which Boland chooses to align herself, then, is born of the silences in which women have suffered.

Women across all social and historical boundaries are united in maternal suffering and "love's archaeology" in **"The Journey."** However, it is particularly the silences about women's suffering in Irish history that prove the most fertile space for Boland's myth-making. For Boland, poetry *is* "where myth touches history" (*Ga. Rev.* 104), and in a "defeated" history such as Ireland's, the defeated sex is enveloped in the greatest silence. The poet is then much freer to create the myths that explain history, freer to "make up" details (108). Boland, of course, became thoroughly dissatisfied with Irish poetry the way she found it; with its "Cathleen ni Houlihan or the Old Woman of the Roads or Dark Rosaleen," Irish poetry doubled the defeat of Irish women by refusing to portray them honestly (*Am. Poetry Rev.* 38, 34). Boland evoked instead the real, suffering women, "the paragons of dispossession" (*Ga. Rev.* 107), women whom Swift acknowledged, but Yeats did not. To repossess Irish poetry for these dispossessed women, Boland is bound to engage in what Gilbert and Gubar refer to as the "revisionary struggle" with the myths of the male tradition (*Madwoman* 49).

The Irish poetic tradition, as Boland inherited it, was concerned with "public" issues such as nationalism and politics rather than "private" matters such as the fate of individual women during the famine years. Women's experience everywhere has been relegated to the "private" sphere, and as Iris Marion Young has noted, modern political philosophy exacerbates this split between the feminine/private and the masculine/public by characterizing the difference between public and private as "an opposition between reason, on the one hand, and the body, affectivity and desire on the other" (Young 59). As Alicia Ostriker suggests, myth-making is one alternative available to women writers who, like Boland, want to break down the public-private barrier. Myth has "double power":

> It exists or appears to exist objectively, in the public sphere, and consequently confers on the writer the sort of authority unavailable to someone who writes "merely" of the private self. Myth belongs to "high" culture and is handed "down" through the ages by religious, literary, and educational authority. At the same time, myth is quintessentially intimate material, the stuff of dream life, forbidden desire, inexplicable motivation.
>
> (Ostriker 317)

"The Making of an Irish Goddess," an overtly revisionist poem, calls attention to Boland's conscious effort to make up, in her own image, a mythology that breaks down the rigid distinctions between the "public" history and "private" stories of women's experiences. In fact, Boland makes herself the Irish goddess, revising the myth of Demeter and Persephone to establish a connection between individual moments of universally suffered maternal pain. In the classical myth, Demeter goes to the underworld to retrieve her daughter, whom the rapacious Pluto has abducted. The loss of the child shatters the prelapsarian world where there is "no sense of time" and the "wheat at one height" covers "a seasonless, unscarred earth" (ll. 2, 7, 10). Demeter's grief fragments this timelessness and pristine plenitude into seasons—the cycle of birth, death, rebirth all stemming from a mother's sorrow. To make her own myth, Boland says, "I need time— / my flesh and that history" (ll. 11-12). "That history" refers to Demeter's original sorrowing, but it also looks forward to "that agony" (l. 23) later in the poem, the "private" history of Irish mothers in the time of famine. The famine itself seems to reenact the blight imposed by Demeter's cyclical grieving. Here, however, "the failed harvests" and "the fields rotting to the horizon" become the causes of the grief rather than its effects. Moreover, the descent these famine mothers make to the underworld is one-way, and the despair unconditional:

> the children devoured by their mothers
> whose souls, they would have said,
> went straight to hell,
> followed by their own.

(ll. 26-29)

In fact, these mothers, driven by hunger, seem to dispatch their children to hell rather than redeem them from it. Yet, the ambiguity of the pronouns "they" and "their" causes confusion, if not elision, of identity. "They" in line 27 could even refer to an outsider passing judgment on these women, the "they-would-have-said" of a *public* authority that fails to comprehend that life itself was hell for these women and children. In **"The Journey,"** the "terrible pietas" seemed to be "shadows" (l. 46), but in **"The Making of an Irish Goddess,"** Boland insists on the reality of these ironic versions of Demeter: "There is no other way" (l. 30).

In her essay "The Woman the Place the Poet,"[5] Boland discusses her inspiration for **"The Making of an Irish Goddess"**: the Clonmel Workhouse where her great-grandfather had been Master. Boland imagined, in the absence of surviving accounts, a history for a Clonmel inmate, "a woman like myself, with two small children" who is destined to "a final and, almost certainly fatal, homelessness" (102). This woman would haunt Boland in the most mundane moments, particularly when she was safe in her Dublin suburb, calling her children home at sunset. In these moments, Boland recalls, she felt an almost mystical connection with that famine-ridden past (105-06). Thus, in **"The Making of an Irish Goddess,"** the "gesture" of calling in her daughter

unites myth and history. The gesture that inscribes the "agony" of motherhood is Boland's:

> holding up my hand
> sickle-shaped, to my eyes
> to pick out
> my own daughter from
> all the other children in the distance.

(ll. 37-41)

The "sickle-shaped" cupping of her hand recalls Demeter as the goddess of harvests, and the anxious peering through the twilight recalls Demeter's search for Persephone. The poem ends with the recognition of her daughter's "back turned to me," a milder, transitory version of the loss that the Demeter myth describes and Irish history bears out. In the anxiety of finding her child before nightfall, Boland becomes part of the continuum of irremediable loss and suffering experienced by the "defeated" mothers. Elsewhere Boland has said, "In myth there are healing repetitions" (*Ga. Rev.* 108), but in **"The Making of an Irish Goddess"** Boland seems to deny the healing properties of myth: "Myth is the wound we leave / in the time we have" (ll. 31-32). This apparent contradiction resolves when we realize that Boland is invoking once again what Alicia Ostriker calls the "double power" of myth. Women's voices and stories have been consistently silenced and marginalized in historical discourse, but as the inscription of unutterable loss, myth disrupts the fabric of those literal (male) chronicles of "time" by interjecting women's pain (just as Demeter's grief wounds her time with seasons). A wound is, after all, the visible sign of pain; a scar, its artifact. Because, as Ostriker says, myth sanctions the "private," it serves Boland as a way to leave a visible sign of the unchronicled suffering during the famine. But since myth further serves to voice and thus to externalize suffering in this poem, it also "heals" by diffusing "private" pain in a public ritual.

These defeated Irish mothers form links in the chain that binds Boland herself to the Demeter myth in **"The Making of an Irish Goddess."** From the suffering of these women, she devises her own deification. "In my body . . . in my gestures . . . must be / an accurate inscription / of that agony" (ll. 14, 18, 21-23). That is, Boland becomes the goddess by embodying the myth, literally giving it a body, her own. Boland needs her "flesh" to make the journey that deifies her (l. 12). "Neither young now nor fertile," her body bears "the marks of childbirth" and a "stitched, healed blemish a scar" (ll. 15-16, 20). Her body is not that of the eternally beautiful goddesses of classical myths, but the body of an historical female subject who has suffered and still does.

Boland's revision of myth in this poem resembles what Hélène Cixous called "a new resurgent writing" (284), or *feminine écriture*. According to Cixous, this form of writing allows woman to "carry out the indispensable ruptures and transformations in her history" and "return to the body which has been more than confiscated from her, which has been turned into the uncanny stranger on display" (284). Only by this kind of writing can a woman put herself "into the world and into history" (279). As Jody Allen-Randolph argues, Boland's earlier volume *In Her Own Image* answers Cixous' call with "a writing practice grounded in female experience, a practice which uses the female body as both vehicle and cipher, as both the site of female knowledge and writing and the interpreter of the knowledge unearthed" (53). However, writing the body is not enough; "I need time," the would-be Irish Goddess says, "my flesh and that history." It is by extending the female body and experience diachronically, across time, that Boland fully establishes them in **"The Making of an Irish Goddess"** and throughout *Outside History* as bases of authority in her revisionary struggle.

Another implication of Cixous' call to repossess the female body and text is that Gilbert and Gubar's paradigm might be extended to describe the true anxiety women poets feel in relation to their poetic fathers. Far from suffering merely from the pen envy suggested by Gilbert and Gubar's early formulation of "anxiety of authorship," these daughters must eventually do battle with their poetic fathers for possession of *themselves.* Male precursors "must be annihilated" not only because male *authority* undermines a woman poet's faith in her ability to write, as Gilbert and Gubar suggest (*No Man's Land* 214), but because male appropriation of the imaginary female body seems to violate the woman poet physically, as well. I would suggest that the "revisionary struggle," especially in the case of Eavan Boland's attempt to "repossess" Irish poetry, is a struggle for *self-possession.* In an interview with Amy Klauke, Boland insists that a woman poet can be her own muse and, by implication, that a woman can possess herself (58). But this literary self-possession requires the overthrow of the usurping male authority. To repossess the imaginary female body from the Irish tradition, Boland must therefore contend with Yeats. Because he was, according to Boland, the first Irish poet to make "poetry a great construct of reality" (Klauke 58), rewriting Yeats's limiting version of Irish womanhood is a prerequisite for writing women into the Irish tradition.

In 1971, Boland, along with Michael MacLiammoir, co-authored *W. B. Yeats and His World,* a rather uncritical biography possibly intended for coffee tables and high-school libraries. Boland was still then a dutiful daughter, but over the next twenty years, particularly the ten years between the publication of *In Her Own Image* and *Outside History,* her rebellion against her literary father surfaced in her own lyrics. In **"Daphne Heard with Horror the Addresses of the God,"** which is both a

revision of and an answer to Yeats's "A Prayer for My Daughter," Boland directly confronts the specter of Yeats in the Irish tradition. In her poem, Boland rebukes Yeats for the threat he poses to his daughter Anne, whom he manages to delimit in a prayer proclaiming his daughter as a possession to be exchanged with another man. Clearly, Boland, the literary daughter, views the encroachment on the biological daughter as a threat to herself.

As Harold Bloom (among others) has pointed out, baby Anne is merely a *pretext* for Yeats's poem; the true subject is Maud Gonne (Bloom 326, Perloff 29-33).[6] Other critics have attempted to redeem the poem as the poignant wish of an anxious father. Douglas Archibald, for example, does a careful reading of Yeats's poem in relation to Coleridge's "Frost at Midnight" (Archibald 1-12), but fails to note one crucial difference—while Coleridge opens up possibilities for his son, Yeats in effect limits them for Anne:

> May she be granted beauty and yet not
> Beauty to make a stranger's eye distraught
> . . .
> An intellectual hatred is the worst,
> So let her think opinions are accursed.
>
> (ll. 17-18, 57-58)

Yeats's poem becomes a prescription for appropriate feminine behavior, with Maud Gonne—thinly veiled as Helen and Aphrodite—as the negative example. By refusing his many marriage proposals, Maud failed to "choose right" (l. 24). The poem thus becomes a celebration of the marriage that Maud refused. By the end of the poem, Yeats has Anne safely married off (although she is still ostensibly asleep in her crib) with a "bridegroom" who brings "her to a house / Where all's accustomed, ceremonious" (ll. 73-74). But as Bloom has noted, Yeats makes himself the bridegroom (Bloom 326), since Anne the daughter is merely a supplément for Maud. This implicitly incestuous possession of the daughter (which Bloom fails to acknowledge as such) is supported by Yeats's casual use of the Daphne myth in the sixth stanza:

> May she become a flourishing hidden tree
> That all her thoughts may like the linnet be,
> And have no business but dispensing round
> Their magnanimities of sound,
> Nor but in merriment begin a chase,
> Nor but in merriment a quarrel.
> O may she live like some green laurel
> Rooted in one dear perpetual place.

Here, Yeats prays for the same transformation for his daughter that Daphne beseeches of her own father. In the myth, Apollo pursues Daphne, who resists his advances. When rape seems imminent, Daphne prays for the assistance of her father Peneus, a river god, who transforms her into a laurel tree. Since Apollo's mind dwells more on the woman lost, he promptly makes the laurel sacred to himself and, as the god of poetry, possesses Daphne by appropriating her transformed body as the emblem of poetry, his domain. As Boland would point out, behind this myth lies the silence of a woman as well as the scene of rape, another confiscation of a woman's body by a man. In Yeats's poem, his desire that Anne be "rooted" in one place is really just the translation of his daughter into the kind of emblem of art that Boland so detests in Irish poetry. Thus Yeats plays the roles of Peneus *and* Apollo, both father and possessor.

By invoking the Daphne myth, Yeats eroticizes his daughter's body in what Luce Irigaray calls "the double movement of exhibition and chaste retreat" (Irigaray 25-26). Anne, "rooted in one place," is thus objectified, and throughout the poem Yeats will insist upon her "stillness" as an image. He desires for his daughter "radical innocence," which, as Douglas Archibald notes, means "rooted"—hence "immobile"—innocence (9). In his lines recalling Keats's "Ode on a Grecian Urn," Yeats says, "She can, though every face should scowl, / And every windy quarter howl / Or every bellows burst, be happy *still*" (ll. 70-72, emphasis mine). It is after the establishment of this happy stillness that the bridegroom (who, like Apollo, is another figure for Yeats in the poem) takes possession of the daughter, who can acquiesce since this chase begins not in terror but "in merriment" (l. 45).

The title of Boland's **"Daphne Heard with Horror the Addresses of the God"** denies the "merriment" of the chase. Boland adopts an eight-line stanza that mimics Yeats's ottava rima, but she dispenses with the rhyme and meter of "custom" and "ceremony." Boland begins her poem in the deceptively tranquil "early summer," a setting quite different from Yeats's symbolic storm. The sinister element introduced with the "cutthroat sweetness" of the stephanotis disturbs this peace. The "you" of the poem tells a story very much like the scenario Yeats imagines for Anne, "a story . . . about the wedding of a local girl, / long ago, and a merchant from Argyll" (ll. 6-8). Hardly enthralled by her male companion's story,[7] the speaker's thoughts wander to the garden, which she "*thought* . . . looked so at ease":

> The laurel hedge was nothing but itself,
> and all of it so free of any need
> for nymphs, goddesses, wounded presences—
> the fleet river daughters who took root
> and can be seen in the woods in
> unmistakable shapes of weeping.

> (ll. 11-16)

As yet unaffected by the tale she is hearing, the speaker thinks of the garden as only "itself" rather than as an emblem. The laurel does not recall to her poetry, nor does she think the garden needs explanatory myth, tellingly figured here as the "wounded presences," which recall Boland's statement in **"The Making of an Irish Goddess"**: "Myth is the wound we leave in the time we have." Of course, Daphne, whose horror the title proclaims, is evoked as "a fleet river-daughter who took root," yet in this stanza, Boland seems to dismiss the need to voice suffering as she does in **"The Making of an Irish Goddess."** If there really is no "need" here for the wounded presences, why does she name them? Boland has adopted nicely a Sapphic strategy of letting her title stand apart from the poem as a sort of gloss on the poem, so that Daphne is always already in the poem even before the male authority describes his version of the Argyll wedding. The invocation of Daphne is crucial to Boland's revision of Yeats, since as Alicia Ostriker suggests, altering myths "by female knowledge of female experience" ensures that these myths "can no longer stand as foundations of collective male fantasy. . . . They are retrieved images of what women have collectively and historically suffered" (318).

Boland's poem builds a connection between the wounded presence of Daphne in "unmistakable shapes of weeping" and the local girl who is married off in the story within the poem. This unnamed girl becomes—like Daphne, the Irish mothers, and the emblematized Anne Yeats—a "paragon of dispossession"; she doesn't even have a name. Boland begins paying attention to the story only after "they were well married." "The bridegroom *had* his bride on the ship" (ll. 17-19, emphasis mine). "Had" suggests not only location, but possession, specifically the threatening corporal possession that Apollo sought of Daphne and perhaps Yeats of Maud Gonne. Certainly, this is a bride with neither voice nor agency, and she is caught up in the "accustomed, ceremonious" (**"Prayer"** l. 74) as the "well-wishers / took in armfuls, handfuls, from the boats / white roses and threw them on the water" (**"Daphne"** ll. 22-24).

In fact, the story that Boland listens to does need "wounded presences." For though the "wounded presences" are absent from this tale of marriage, the garden evokes them after the speaker begins to "pay attention":

> the garden in its last definition,
> freshening and stirring. A suggestion,
> behind it all, of darkness: in the shadow,
> behind the laurel hedge, its gesture.

> (ll. 29-32)

Syntactically, the "suggestion" first seems to arise from the garden, but the phrase "behind it all" indicates that the story of the girl's ceremonious dispossession, and not the garden, suggests Daphne and "darkness." The "gesture" of the laurel is "weeping," and by restoring the laurel's ability to "gesture"—a form of agency—

Boland reembodies the woman behind the myth, returns to Daphne, and all the emblematized women whom she represents, the bodies that have been confiscated from them in life and art.

Moreover, because the title stands apart from the rest of the poem, it may refer just as easily to Boland the listener as to the girl who marries the merchant of Argyll. Obviously, the "you" shares a domestic relationship with the speaker of the poem, for they drink tea and discuss "how / the greenfly needed spraying" (ll. 25-26). And the teller is obviously a male authority like Yeats, invoking another emblematic image of womanhood, this time the blushing bride. Since Boland's speaker is the listener here, perhaps she also "hears with horror" yet another story that fails to represent women as they are. There is a sort of "cutthroat sweetness" about the story similar to the "radical innocence" of Yeats's prayer for his daughter's future. Certainly by the end of the poem, the speaker's mood has darkened as she perceives the "gesture" of the laurel, implicitly the expression of Daphne's horror in the title. With both the title and the final stanza, Boland evinces that which is suppressed in and by the "sweet" traditional view, thereby revising, in effect, the story the male authorities (both Yeats and the unnamed "you") tell her.

"Daphne Heard with Horror the Addresses of the God" therefore shares the same agenda as **"Making Up," "The Journey," "The Making of an Irish Goddess,"** and many other Boland poems: the struggle to move the marginalized experiences of women to the center of poetry, a struggle entailing the revision of both myth and *his*tory, and the "repossession" of Irish poetry and the female body. Boland recognizes the formidable nature of her undertaking; the fear of failure she expresses in **"Envoi"** reveals how much is at stake personally for her. As she says of her muse in **"Envoi,"**

> If she will not bless the ordinary,
> if she will not sanctify the common,
> then here I am and here I stay and then am I
> the most miserable of women.
>
> (ll. 25-28)

Yet her tenacious assertion of "I" in line 27 suggests that in spite of any anxiety, Boland will not retreat. By such a contest with the male tradition, Hélène Cixous says, woman will make "her shattering entry into history" (284). In her revisionary struggle, Boland forges a female voice from the "silences which are our beginnings," a voice forceful enough to tumble the walls of an official history which has for too long refused women entry.

Notes

1. A version of the essay "Eavan Boland: Outside History" also appears in Boland's *Object Lessons: The Life of the Woman and the Poet in Our Time*

(123-53). In this collection (published after I completed the present essay), Boland discusses her project at length, within the context of personal, literary, and political history. In "Turning Away," for example, Boland discusses her retrospective recognition of even the poems she wrote as a teenager as "radical acts" that began a "series of engagements and assessments with the place and the time and the poem" (94). After reading Sylvia Plath's *Ariel,* a more mature Boland would "see increasingly the stresses and fractures between a poet's life and a woman's. And how—alone, at a heartbroken moment—they might become fatal"(113). However, the recognition of these "fractures" did not oblige her to abandon poetry or its forms, for as she explains in "The Woman Poet: Her Dilemma":

> Artistic forms are not static. . . . They are changed, shifted, detonated into deeper patterns only by the sufferings and self-deceptions of those who use them. By this equation, women should break down barriers in poetry in the same way that poetry will break the silence of women.
>
> (254)

The "equation" Boland discusses in this passage precisely describes her revisionary struggle in the collection *Outside History.*

2. In her insightful article on Boland's poetry. Jody Allen-Randolph similarly reads "Making Up" as a critique of "a patriarchal discourse which constructs feminine identity in its own image" (59). Allen-Randolph, however, does not note the ambivalence involved in Boland's choosing cosmetics as a metaphor for female creativity. See "Ecriture Feminine and the Authorship of Self in Eavan Boland's *In Her Own Image,*" cited below.

3. In "Anxiety, Influence, Tradition, and Subversion in the Poetry of Eavan Boland," Kerry E. Robertson notes the double nature of the anxiety experienced by Irish women poets who write in English: "First, not only are they forced to write in a language that is in many ways antagonistic to their gender, they also must write in one that is at odds with their national and cultural heritage" (267).

4. Ellen M. Mahon reads Boland's 1987 volume, *"The Journey" and Other Poems* (in which "The Journey" was originally collected), as a collection of woman-centered poems in which Boland eventually recognizes Sappho as "Mother." See "Eavan Boland's Journey with the Muse," cited below.

5. A version of "The Woman the Place the Poet" also appears in *Object Lessons* (154-74).

6. For a thorough reading of Yeats's attempted appropriation, see Marjorie Perloff's "Between

Hatred and Desire: Sexuality and Subterfuge in 'A Prayer for My Daughter,'" cited below.

7. Here I disagree with Mary Kinzie, who interprets the teller as a commiserating female. According to Kinzie, [the speaker] and the companion who pours the tea are also mentally turning and touching again in the homely anecdote the ageless mystery of money (the merchant) and rapine (the innocent local girl bartered against her future), responding in a subtly *womanly* way to what Philip Larkin too neatly labeled the 'religious wounding' at the wedding night. (12, emphasis mine)

Although it is true the speaker of the poem recognizes the import of the story, I do not read any sympathy in the teller's version of the wedding; he seems oblivious to the fact that something is amiss in the wedding tale. Further, the teller's action in the final stanza negates the possibility of a "womanly response": "and you went inside. I / stayed in the heat looking at / the garden" (ll. 27-29). Boland here reasserts the inside/outside dichotomy permeating *Outside History*. The male authority retreats, tellingly, *inside* the tradition, while Boland's speaker remains *outside*. This spatial arrangement underscores the absence of female bonding between the speaker and her companion, an absence further suggested by the speaker's admission in line 18 that she hadn't been paying attention to the tale. See Kinzie, "Meaning in Place: A Moral Essay," cited below.

Works Cited

Abel, Elizabeth, and Emily Abel, eds. *The "Signs" Reader: Women, Gender, and Scholarship.* Chicago: U Chicago P, 1983.

Allen-Randolph, Jody. "Ecriture Feminine and the Authorship of Self in Eavan Boland's *In Her Own Image.*" *Colby Quarterly* 27 (1991): 48-59.

Archibald, Douglas. *Yeats.* Syracuse: Syracuse UP, 1983.

Bloom, Harold. *Yeats.* New York: Oxford UP, 1970.

Boland, Eavan. "Eavan Boland: Outside History." *American Poetry Review* 19 (1990): 32-38.

———. *Introducing Eavan Boland.* Princeton: Ontario Review P, 1981.

———. *Object Lessons: The Life of the Woman and the Poet in Our Time.* New York: Norton, 1995.

———. *Outside History: Selected Poems 1980-1990.* New York: Norton, 1990.

———. Poetry Reading. Museum of Fine Arts, Houston, Texas. March 1991.

———. "The Woman the Place the Poet." *Georgia Review* 44 (1990): 97-109.

———, and Michael MacLiammoir. *W. B. Yeats and His World.* London: Thames and Hudson, 1971.

Cixous, Hélène. "The Laugh of the Medusa." Trans. Keith Cohen and Paul Cohen. Abel and Abel 279-97.

Gilbert, Sandra M., and Susan Gubar. *Madwoman in the Attic.* New Haven: Yale UP, 1979.

———. *No Man's Land.* Vol. 1: *The War of the Words.* New Haven: Yale UP, 1988.

Hagen, Patricia L., and Thomas W. Zelman. "'We Were Never on the Scene of the Crime': Eavan Boland's Repossession of History." *Twentieth Century Literature* 37 (1991): 442-53.

Irigaray, Luce. "This Sex Which Is Not One." *The Sex Which Is Not One.* Ithaca: Cornell UP, 1985, 23-34.

Kinzie, Mary. "Meaning in Place: A Moral Essay." *American Poetry Review* 21.1 (1992): 7-14.

Klauke, Amy. "An Interview with Eavan Boland." *Northwest Review* 25.3 (1987): 55-61.

Mahon, Ellen M. "Eavan Boland's Journey with the Muse." *Learning the Trade: Essays on W. B. Yeats and Contemporary Poetry.* Ed. Deborah Fleming. West Cornwall, Conn.: Locust Hill Press, 1993, 179-94.

Ostriker, Alicia. "The Thieves of Language: Women Poets and Revisionist Myth Making." *The New Feminist Criticism.* Ed. Elaine Showalter. New York: Pantheon, 1985, 314-38.

Perloff, Marjorie. "Between Hatred and Desire: Sexuality and Subterfuge in 'A Prayer for My Daughter.'" *Yeats Annual* 7 (1989): 29-50.

Reizbaum, Marilyn. "An Interview with Eavan Boland." *Contemporary Literature* 30 (1989): 471-79.

Rich, Adrienne. "Compulsory Heterosexuality and Lesbian Existence." Abel and Abel 139-68.

Robertson, Kerry E. "Anxiety, Influence, Tradition, and Subversion in the Poetry of Eavan Boland." *Colby Quarterly* 30 (1994): 264-78.

Wilkie, Brian, and James Hurt. *Literature of the Western World.* Vol. 1. New York: Macmillan, 1988.

Yeats, W. B. *Selected Poems and Three Plays of William Butler Yeats.* Ed. M. L. Rosenthal. New York: Macmillan, 1986.

Young, Iris Marion. "Impartiality and the Civic Public: Some Implications of Feminist Critiques of Moral and Political Theory." *Feminism as Critique.* Ed. Seyla Benhabib and Drucilla Cornell. Minneapolis: U Minnesota P, 1987, 56-76.

David C. Ward (review date January-February 1999)

SOURCE: Ward, David C. "A Certain Slant of Light." *P.N. Review* 25, no. 3 (January-February 1999): 66-8.

[*In the following review, Ward considers the place of* The Lost Land *within Boland's poetic oeuvre and deems the collection to be Boland's return to political concerns.*]

'My passport is green,' was Seamus Heaney's defiant assertion of his poetic patrimony. Heaney's confident nationalism has never been shared by his compatriot Eavan Boland. Boland's poetic career began conventionally enough with her writing nicey-nice lyric poems about Ireland; in one she describes Yeats as the 'sum' of all she could learn. But writing poems called **'Elegy for a Youth Changed to a Swan'** soon palled for a poet as preternaturally aware as Eavan Boland and, at least in retrospect, they must seem to her like the poetic equivalent of foot binding. Growingly conscious of her double colonization as both Irish and a woman, Boland used her marginality as a powerful salient from which to scour both the lyric and its subjects. Too urban and modern to ever be seriously interested in pastorals or landscapes, at first, in poems such as **'Famine Road'**, Boland simply grafted the 'old' lyric to a political and aesthetic recovery of the voices of lost Irish men and women. This was partial progress but Boland, doubly subjected as both Irish and an Irishwoman, was cognizant that she was still following an agenda set by others. Her own felt-life as a woman, the heir to the history she wrote about, was severed from any emotional or even actual links to the past by an Irish history and mythology which was, as written, largely aggressively masculine. Despite its daunting architectural facade, that history turned out to be so full of exclusions, elisions, suppressions, and bad faith that to continue to pull in its traces would be to compound Boland's subjection with self-betrayal. What makes Boland such an original and brilliant poet is that she was able to write herself out of her dilemma the hard way: not by acquiescence but by internalizing everything—personal, stylistic, historical—acting upon her and reshaping them into weapons of her own devising. While most poets choose either self or subject, Boland contrived to do both, combining an almost third-person awareness of her own state-of-mind even as she surveyed the terrain around her; her *Object Lessons* is, among its other strengths, an object lesson in combining memoir and history, illuminating both by the light of the other in its connection of the past with the present, history with the individual. It's as if her own doubly-colonized status permitted her to work from a double consciousness of both strength and weakness, both actor and acted upon. A master of negative capability, in Boland's writing the parts and the whole are always visible even as they combine in her poems. Boland's continual risk-taking makes her exhilarating.

Boland realized that if she was going to change the subject she would have to change the language. Poems she wrote about suburbia were blocked by the lyric just as its music had obfuscated the past into comfortable pieties. In **'Mise Eire'** she cut the cord, declaring independence: 'I won't go back to it— // my nation displaced into old dactyls . . . the words / that make a rhythm of the crime // where time is time past.' (Interesting that Larkin should slur Heaney as a 'gombeen man' or usurer / leech while Boland pays her mise for autonomy from the auld community.) Boland sharpened her focus right down to essence: 'My roots are brutal: I am the woman—'. Getting down to roots was a journey to self-knowledge. In a series of poems published in *In Her Own Image* (1980)—the title turns out to be not quite as ironic as it first appears—Boland stripped her lines down to barely a heartbeat; from **'Menses'**, 'I am sick of it / filled with it / dulled by it, / thick with it' and from **'Witching,'** 'and smell / how well / a woman's / flesh / can burn.' On one level (the tiny lines and stanzas, the elemental subjects) these poems seem part of an 'anorexic aesthetic' in which a woman internalizes her oppression, at times wasting away to less than skin and bones in a misplaced self-hatred; **'Anorexic'** begins 'Flesh is heretic. / My body is a witch. / I am burning it.' But these poems are not quite as stark or as deterministic as they first appear. For one thing, their structure is Boland's choice and she delivers a tour-de-force performance in showing how much rhythm and meaning can be hung on a poem's narrow spine; from **'Mastectomy'**, for instance, 'the specialist / freshing death / across his desk.' And as the women in her poems are not without means of resistance, neither was Eavan Boland. If in these poems 'the personal was political' it was in the original meaning of that now corrupted slogan, that both worlds—public and private—would dialectically combine. Boland did not devolve into either victim's art or narcissism and having shriven her poetry she then had a platform from which to re-emerge, writing her way back to the world in a literal widening to an expansive verse written on her own terms. There were, in a triumph of humanism over determinism, other narratives besides the body; **'Anna Liffey'** concludes, 'The body is a source. Nothing more.' The Liffey, Boland reminds us, is the river of life.

A river is a particularly apt simile for Boland's verse because both are always in process. But rivers have a conclusion to which Boland can only aspire: 'They are always en route to / Their own nothingness. From the first moment / They are going home.' Home is always problematic, contingent, elusive and probably unattainable for Boland; even with the Good Friday accords instituting a kind of post-modern nation (Ireland as a state of mind) it is doubtful that Boland will ever be less than wary of 'home's embrace. Formed by colonization and exile, *The Lost Land* suggests not pessimism but a fatalistic acceptance that consciousness will never find a home, that the rivers of the body and the mind will never find completion in the oceans; from **'The Lost Land'**: 'and memory itself / has become an emigrant, / wandering in a place / where love dissembles itself as landscape . . .' Process, the wandering flow of words is all and Boland ends *The Lost Land,* with **'Whose',** a poem which ends like **'Anna Liffey'** ('I was a voice.'):

> But the roads
> stayed put. Stars froze over the suburb.
> Shadows iced up. Nothing moved.
> Except my hand across the page. And
> these words.

Dedicated to Mary Robinson, *The Lost Land* marks Boland's return to politics. Some of it reads like a holding action, a circling around topics and themes she has explored before. Here the river analogy breaks down because gravity gives rivers a watercourse while Boland has to make her own way which sometimes means doubling back or even stalling. The stifling reifications of History appear again as does the necessity to bear witness:

> I am your citizen: composed of
> your fictions, your compromise, I am
> a part of your story and its outcome.
> And ready to record its contradictions.

That 'I am / a part' (and the double meaning of 'a part' when read again as 'apart'), where autonomy falls after the line-break into implication, evokes the teetering doubleness which always characterizes Boland's bifurcated point of view; the push-pull of separation and completion. From **'The Mother Tongue'**:

> I was born on this side of the Pale
> I speak with the forked tongue of colony.
> But I stand in the first dark and frost
> of a winter night in Dublin and imagine
>
> my pure sound, my undivided speech
> travelling to the edge of this silence.
> As if to find me. And I listen: I hear
> what I am safe from. What I have lost.

The Lost Land suggests the family as a haven of wholeness in a world of division and Boland is slightly sentimental about her daughters leaving home, playing on this as a kind of reverse exile and rebuking herself for picking over styles 'with my child, / with my back turned to her, / searching—oh irony!—for beautiful things.' Not to downplay the importance of family in both life and art, I suspect that these domestic poems are a convention (the ones about her parents are pretty

slight) that Boland is working through or even discarding by publishing. The poems in *The Lost Land* seem to me to be Boland's warming up for a full throated spate of poems centered on the dark and bloody ground of politics, Irish or otherwise. The tip-off is the diction. Like the 'body poems', although not as spare, many of these poems are terse, flat, declarative, bitten off; **'Unheroic'** starts, 'It was an Irish summer. It was wet. / It was a job. I was seventeen.' Or **'Imago'**:

> Head of a woman. Half-life of a nation.
> Coarsely-cut blackthorn walking stick.
> Old Tara brooch.
> And bog oak.
> A harp and a wolfhound on an ashtray.

This is a morse-code evocation of the Ireland that Boland, however many times she pays her mise, cannot get away from and from which she will never be finished. Having made the initial cut in *The Lost Land* I expect the watercourse to deepen in her next book just as the roots of her 'woman' poems gave forth blossoms. (Remember that the book ends with the poet in a frozen world, starting to write, starting the flow from ice to water.) At least as Boland travels, wherever she goes next, she won't have to worry about her passport: she's always written her own.

Kate Daniels (essay date spring 1999)

SOURCE: Daniels, Kate. "Ireland's Best." *Southern Review* 35, no. 2 (spring 1999): 387-93.

[*In the following excerpt, Daniels finds similarities between the poetry of Boland and Medbh McGuckian and differentiates the poetry of* The Lost Land *from Boland's earlier poetic work.*]

If one were to compose a scale of oppositions upon which to consider contemporary poetry by Irish women, the Dublin poet Eavan Boland (b. 1944) would appear at one end, and Medbh McGuckian (b. 1951), from Belfast, at the other. Although their work is fundamentally different—Boland the mistress of a highly cadenced, formalistic verse that favors "a lyric speech, a civil tone" (to use her own words), and McGuckian the wielder of nonlinear, surrealistic pieces—both women share a preoccupation with the liberation of Irish poetry from the historical grip of male readers and writers. As well, their work assaults on many levels the patriarchal assumptions engendered by the history of the Irish nation, its state religion, and its literature, all of which—until recently—have fairly successfully inhibited female literary expression. Boland, of course, has written at length, in poetry and in prose, of her intense struggle with this:

> By luck, or by its absence, I had been born in a country
> where and at a time when the word *woman* and the
> word *poet* inhabited two separate kingdoms of experi-

ence and expression. I could not, it seemed, live in both. As the author of poems I was an equal partner in Irish poetry. As a woman—about to set out on the life which was the passive object of many of those poems—I had no voice. It had been silenced, ironically enough, by the very powers of language I aspired to and honored. By the elements of form I had worked hard to learn.

(Object Lessons)

McGuckian has spoken more informally of the deeply ingrained, gender-specific assumptions of Irish poetry, characterizing its exclusively male environment in the 1960s as a "closed shop" and "like a secret-society meeting." She first came to public recognition when she was awarded a major poetry prize in the '70s. Her winning composition was quite calculated. Having determined that previous winners had tended toward "narrative poems of about forty lines," she scribbled three in this mode and invented an androgynous pseudonym for herself. The trouble began when it was discovered that McGuckian was not only female but six months pregnant as well. Eventually, the contest sponsors reallocated the prize money so that McGuckian received *less* than the second-place winner, who was a "well-known [male] literary figure." McGuckian says: "I didn't care. I was pregnant and I had won this. But *TLS* cared. They created a huge fuss for weeks, wanting to know whether my prize money had been cut from £1,000 to £500 because I was Irish, or Catholic, or a woman" (*Southern Review,* "Comhrá").

For readers on this side of the Atlantic, Boland's and McGuckian's plaints are recognizable versions of the dilemma Adrienne Rich found herself in as a young American poet struggling to emerge from the grip of New Criticism in the self-satisfied, narcoleptic culture of the '50s. Rich was a bit more assertive and hard-edged than the Irish women in pointing out the deficiencies of the inherited tradition for the female poet:

> I had been born a woman, and I was trying to think and act as if poetry—and the possibility of making poems—were a universal—a gender-neutral—realm. In the universe of the masculine paradigm, I naturally absorbed ideas about women, sexuality, power from the subjectivity of male poets—Yeats not least among them. The dissonance between these images and the daily events of my own life demanded a constant footwork of imagination, a kind of perpetual translation, and an unconscious fragmentation of identity. Every group that lives under the naming and image-making power of a dominant culture is at risk from this mental fragmentation and needs an art which can resist it.

(Blood, Bread, and Poetry)

A young mother of three and the wife of a Harvard professor, Rich wheeled her baby carriages right to the edge of madness before she discovered the way out.

Her engagement with the civil rights and antiwar protests of the '60s led her directly into the women's movement and a new woman-centered poetry—from separatist lesbian poet, to feminist reclaimer, to post-feminist matriarch. Though she has not vanquished what she calls the male-inscribed "oppressor's language," she has certainly reconfigured a huge portion of our poetic discourse to make a place for female voices and experience.

One might think that today's Irish women poets could draw inspiration from Rich's example. Hampered by the virtual absence of women poets in Irish literary history, and hobbled by the culture's profoundly masculinist bent, which has been so powerfully reinforced by Catholicism, Irish women poets are sorely in need of models and heroines. Yet though Boland often quotes Rich, there is almost always an edge—if not an outright challenge—in the invocation:

> What is [the female writer] to make of the suggestion by a poet like Adrienne Rich that "to be a female human being, trying to fulfil female functions in a traditional way, is in direct conflict with the subversive function of the imagination?" . . . Separatist thinking is a persuasive and dangerous influence on any woman poet writing today. It tempts her to disregard the whole poetic past as patriarchal betrayal. It pleads with her to discard the complexities of true feeling for the relative simplicity of anger. It promises to ease her technical problems with the solvent of polemic. It whispers to her that to be feminine in poetry is easier, quicker and more eloquent than the infinitely more difficult task of being human. Above all, it encourages her to feminize her perceptions rather than humanize her femininity.

(Object Lessons)

Tangled lines connect but obfuscate the similar struggles of Irish and American women poets. *Separatism,* in the context of American history, connotes our most deeply impressed national image: our Revolutionary War for freedom from Britain. Most American liberation movements—for example the utopian colonies of the nineteenth century; the Black Panthers in the 1960s; Adrienne Rich during the 1970s, as she sought to bring to prominence images of women and minority peoples that had long been submerged—have, early on in their development, utilized the techniques of separatism. The indelible connection between individualism and separatism—the individual's *right* to separate—is perhaps the most vital aspect of our collective democratic consciousness.

But in Irish history, *separatism* suggests the opposite of our American ideas: partition, the Troubles, the presence—rather than the absence—of British rule. Whereas American women poets have had the great fortune of claiming as their original Muse an eccentric female unencumbered with (shall we say) "issues around separation," Irish women are only now beginning to ponder the image of themselves removed from the context of patriarchal history. The struggle of Irish women writers to define themselves both individually and collectively without disowning their extraordinary national literary history is what connects the wildly different poetries of Eavan Boland and Medbh McGuckian.

Two prominent American poets, both male, have confessed to me that they do not care for Eavan Boland's poetry. "Frankly," said one, "I don't see what all the excitement is about—it's so quiet, so flat." Yet Boland's poetry has garnered both critical respect and a large readership in the United States. As far as such things go, she is one of the most celebrated poets writing today.

Her work is, as our anonymous poet suggested, somewhat "flat." She has always preferred a short, strongly end-stopped line highly dependent on monosyllabic words. She favors midline caesuras created by periods or dashes. She is partial to free verse. If her voice is flat, it is the flatness of authority—no nonsense, take-no-prisoners. It is a voice that must be reckoned with, that will not shrivel up and disappear in the face of disagreement or disapproval. On the surface, then, with its unadorned lineation, its well-modulated voice, and its simple, dignified vocabulary, it might appear "quiet." And yet Boland's poetry is a classic example of that which walks quietly but carries a big stick. Two sticks, in fact: an extraordinary gift for large metaphor, and a deeply historical, but revisionary, consciousness. Paired, these features identify one of the most important bodies of poetic work presently being created.

Boland has again and again, in prose and poetry, made her case for the emerging work of Irish women poets. Indeed—although a certain kind of reader may not realize it—that is her central subject. And in *The Lost Land,* her new collection of twenty-nine poems, she brings together two narrative strands she has not heretofore connected by performing a paradoxical task—inserting women into the predominantly male cast of recorded history and myth, and removing herself from the autobiographical script of her life as a mother. This is the "lost land" of the title, what Boland calls a "ghostly territory" where "human experience [—lived, but lost; lived, but unrecorded—] comes to be stored." Thus the book is a kind of celebratory dirge about both loss and gain, exile and residence—the loss of motherhood through the agency of daughters grown to womanhood, the gain of historical representation through an investigation of historicized images of absence and loss.

> What is a colony
> if not the brutal truth
> that when we speak

> the graves open.

> And the dead walk?

> ("Witness")

> Daughters of parsons and of army men.
> Daughters of younger sons of younger sons.
> Who left for London from Kingstown harbour—
> . . .
> Who took their journals and their steamer trunks.
> Who took their sketching books.
> . . .
> I see the darkness coming.
> The absurd smallness of the handkerchiefs
> they are waving
> as the shore recedes.

> I put my words between them
> and the silence
> the failing light has consigned them to:

> I also am a daughter of the colony.
> I share their broken speech, their other-whereness.

> No testament or craft of mine can hide
> our presence
> on the distaff side of history.

> ("Daughters of Colony")

In **"Colony,"** the long, twelve-section poem that composes the book's first half, Boland explores the related ideas of colonization and exile. The narrative persona here is aware that the psychic territory possesses public as well as personal resonance, and so the voice—perhaps the voice that has turned away some male readers—has shed some of the cozy, homemaking tone that characterized earlier volumes. Gone are the tea cozies and pram sheets. In this book there is less visual detail emanating from the domestic and maternal worlds; there are fewer characters claustrophobically sealed into small environments—cottages, gardens, nurseries—with demanding young children. Within the more abstract dimensions of this new world, the settings are primarily metaphorical, so when Boland allows herself the embellishment of concrete details, the effect can be breathtaking:

> Head of a woman. Half-life of a nation.
> Coarsely-cut blackthorn walking stick.
> Old Tara brooch.
> And bog oak.
> A harp and a wolfhound on an ashtray.

> ("Imago")

One of the book's best poems, **"Unheroic,"** appears in this first section. Here Boland recounts the story of an ordinary Irishman, a resident manager in a hotel where the narrator has a summer job. This man suffers from a highly metaphoric medical condition: a wound that refuses to heal. Each day, in private and without speaking of it to anyone, he cleans and re-bandages his injury:

How do I know my country? Let me tell you
it has been hard to do. And when I do
go back to difficult knowledge it is not
to that street or those men raised
high above the certainties they stood on—
Ireland hero history—but how

I went behind the linen room and up
the stone stairs and climbed to the top.
And stood for a moment there, concealed
by shadows. In a hiding place.
Waiting to see.
Waiting to look again.
Into the patient face of the unhealed.

The counterpart to this poem, **"Heroic,"** appears in the second half of the book.

The patriot was made of drenched stone.
His lips were still speaking. The gun
he held had just killed someone.

I looked up. And looked at him again.
He stared past me without recognition.

I moved my lips and wondered how the rain
would taste if my tongue were made of stone.
And wished it was. And whispered so that no one
could hear it but him: *make me a heroine.*

In the figure these two poems make, we see the full sweep of Boland's challenge to Irish history. By animating the symbolic stone statuary of the conventionally heroic and by restoring stature to the wounded, disenfranchised people the history books have effaced, she goes about creating the "undivided speech" of an undivided land and a fully participatory citizenry that her work has called for. In the book's penultimate poem, **"Formal Feeling,"** Eavan Boland's "quiet," "flat" style affords her an authority rarely achieved by any poet, man or woman:

Eros look down.
See as a god sees
what a myth says: how a woman still
addresses the work of man in the dark of the night:

The power of a form. The plain
evidence that strength descended here once.
And mortal pain. And even sexual glory.

And see the difference.
This time—and this you did not ordain—
I am changing the story.

Albert Gelpi (essay date December 1999)

SOURCE: Gelpi, Albert. "'Hazard and Death': The Poetry of Eavan Boland." *Colby Quarterly* 35, no. 4 (December 1999): 210-28.

[*In the following essay, Gelpi investigates the influence of the American poet Adrienne Rich on Boland's poetry.*]

Eavan Boland's growing international reputation is grounded in the recognition that she is the first great woman poet in the history of Irish poetry. Her success is yet another validation of William Carlos Williams' observation that the local is the universal. That very American conviction, which runs from Thoreau through Whitman and Dickinson to Frost and Robinson Jeffers on to Robert Lowell and Elizabeth Bishop and Denise Levertov, is perhaps one reason why Boland, despite or perhaps because of the Irishness of her work, has found a reciprocated affinity with American poets. She has acknowledged the particular example of women poets, especially poets of the immediately previous generation like Bishop and Levertov, Sylvia Plath and Adrienne Rich, as she struggled to establish herself in a tradition that, for all its length and distinction, included no Dickinson, no H. D., no Marianne Moore.

On a number of occasions, for example in her 1996 "Introduction" to an Irish edition of Adrienne Rich's *Selected Poems,* Boland has singled Rich out for special notice as an empowering forebear. There she reports that she began reading Rich "in my early thirties" (i)—that is to say, in the mid 1970s, when, after *New Territory* (1967) and *The War Horse* (1975), Boland was in the travail of defining her own voice. *Diving into the Wreck* (1973), Rich's first overtly feminist volume, became "a cornerstone volume" (v), and she had also read *The Dream of a Common Language* (1978) before her own breakthrough book *In Her Own Image* (1980). Not surprisingly, then, a number of critics have taken the Rich connection as a defining point for Boland's development. Jody Allen-Randolph draws the parallels:

Born half a generation apart, Rich in 1929 and Boland in 1944, both came from upper middle class backgrounds, began writing poems in childhood, received privileged educations, and were much praised for the technical preciosity of their early first books. Beginning as conservative young formalists, both would reform themselves radically as poets, partly in response to the political upheavals of the 1960s and 1970s—the Anti-War Movement in the US, the Civil Rights Movements in both countries, the Troubles in Ireland, and the first surge of the contemporary Women's Movement.

(Allen-Randolph, "The New Critics" 15)

Victor Luftig sums up their "similar trajectories" in similar terms:

very early first books that proved remarkable formal gifts; dramatic turning points signalled by poems of intense self-examination and feminist emphases; then strikingly ambitious and historically-engaged works, increasingly broad and explicit in their feminist politics, still all the more impressive in formal expertness and powerful in their troubled self-scrutiny.

(Luftig 58)

There are obviously important parallels between the two careers, as Rich's example served to sustain

Boland's efforts to enter and transform the Irish tradition. At the same time, when acknowledging Rich's importance to her emergence as a poet, Boland has almost always gone on to point out how different their poetry and poetics actually are. In her "Introduction," Boland commends Rich's poems: "They are fiercely questioning, deeply political, continuously subversive. They celebrate the lives of women and the sexual and comradely love between them. They contest the structure of the poetic tradition. They interrogate language itself." But she immediately adds: "In all of this, they describe a struggle and record a moment that was not my struggle and would never be my moment. Nor my country, nor my companionship. Nor even my aesthetic" (i).

Moreover, when we examine the poems themselves, we quickly begin to see that the differences are more defining than the parallels. Boland's "Introduction" makes an observation that illuminates why this is so: "A truly important poet changes two things and never one without the other: the interior of the poem and external perceptions of the identity of the poet. By so doing, they prove that the two are inseparable. That these radicalisms not only connect, they actually have their source in each other" (i-ii). Boland is here speaking of Rich as a poet whose greatness resides in her having redefined, simultaneously and inseparably, the substance of her poetry and the public identity of the poet. But I want to extend her point to Boland's own development to examine how she, committed as she also was to comprehending the intersections of personal and national identity, forged a different poetry and a different image of the poet. My focus in what follows will be on Boland with Rich as counterpoint, and my other point of departure is Boland's equally incisive remark: "I felt that the life I lived was not the one these poems [i.e., Rich's] commended. It was too far from the tumult, too deep in the past. And yet these poems helped me live it" (i).

Both Rich and Boland won the praise of male poets and critics for the technical (and, implicitly, emotional) control of their first two books, yet in retrospect these early books foreshadow the divergent courses they would take. "Aunt Jennifer's Tigers," "Afterward," and "An Unsaid Word" from Rich's *A Change of World* (1951)—a book that W. H. Auden condescendingly praised for its "modesty" and "detachment from the self" (Gelpi 278)—are now clearly seen to anticipate Rich's political radicalism in the 1960s and her feminism in the 1970s. Similarly, Boland's *New Territory* (1967)—Yeatsian in its evocation of Celtic myth, Larkinesque in its prosodic nimbleness—adumbrates her constellating concerns: life as a chancy exploration of a world of violence and mortality and death (**"New Territory," "The Pilgrim," "Migration"**); and the necessary and compensatory function of the poet in

negotiating those chances. As Derek Mahon has indicated (Mahon 27-28), the crucial poem in the collection is **"Athene's Song,"** which Boland placed first in her collected poems, *An Origin Like Water* (1996). Athene—daughter of patriarchy, "goddess of the war" sprung "from my father's head"—becomes a poet, learning on her pipe to make "a new music," so that, even on the battlefield, far from the woods where she played her musical instrument, her "mind" follows not her father's dictates but "my heart" and "holds its own" (17; unless otherwise indicated, page numbers to Boland's poems refer to *An Origin Like Water*). In **"Yeats in Civil War"** the poet has "exchanged the sandals / Of a pilgrim" for "escape" into a "fantasy of honey" (24), but elsewhere the imagination is given a tougher task. **"The Poets"** begins:

> They like all creatures, being made
> For the shovel and worm,
> Ransacked their perishable minds and found
> Pattern and form
> And with their own hands quarried from hard words
> A figure in which secret things confide.
>
> (25)

At times Boland too feels "Ready for Flight" with her beloved, as one poem puts it, into an idealized realm "of butterfly and swan and turtle dove" (84). But *The War Horse* (1975) begins to define the poet's task in tougher, less escapist terms: "And what perspective / on this sudden Irish fury / can solve it to a folk memory?" (79). Athene's pastoral nostalgia and Yeats's "fantasy of honey" give way to a realistic acknowledgement of the precariousness of the poet's public and private situation. **"The Famine Road," "Child of Our Time,"** and **"The Soldier's Son"** all deal with the tragedy of history, specifically Irish history. But **"The War Horse,"** perhaps Boland's first fully mature poem, confronts the vulnerability of the home, marriage, and family to hostile forces. This poem introduces what will become Boland's characteristic way of setting up a poem: a domestic or familial incident is localized by a speaker, almost always the poet herself, and by time, year or season or hour, and by place, most often her house and garden, and the reflection on the incident reveals its "secret things" and invests it with figurative significance, at once personal and historic. Here the woman in the domestic shelter observes, through her window, a horse from the tinkers' nearby camp as it moves down her narrow lane, "huge / Threatening" in "his" indifference to the damage his brute bulk wreaks in his passage. Emblematic of the forces of nature and history, "the war horse" passes by undeterred, leaving her and her loved ones "safe" this time behind the stone wall of their "line of defense," with only minor damage to hedge and path. Nonetheless, his passage recalls "a cause ruined before, a world betrayed" (49). Always already betrayed.

The poet here is the urban or suburban married woman, as in Rich's early books, and in a similarly alien world. In "A Marriage in the 'Sixties," Rich writes:

> Two strangers, thrust for life upon a rock,
> may have at last the perfect hour of talk
> that language aches for; still—
> two minds, two messages.
>
>   (Gelpi 15)

In **"The Botanic Gardens,"** Boland, addressing her husband, the novelist Kevin Casey, writes: "Now you have overstepped / My reach"; "I watch and love you in your mystery" (82). But we can begin to hear the poets' different sensibilities in the contrast between Rich's sense of dramatized extremity and Boland's sense of comfort in the mutual companionship of marriage:

> Still at night our selves reach to join.
> To twine like trees in peace and stress
> Before the peril of unconsciousness.
>
>   (82)

"Like This Together" is dedicated to Rich's husband, the economist Alfred Conrad, but, in contrast to Boland's lines, the poem describes the demolition of the domestic refuge by outside forces, and describes with such vehement comprehension of the debacle as almost to anticipate it:

> They're tearing down, tearing up
> this city, block by block.
> Rooms cut in half
> hang like flayed carcasses,
> their old roses in rags,
> famous streets have forgotten
> where they are going. Only
> a fact could be so dreamlike.
> They're tearing down the houses
> we met and lived in,
> soon our two bodies will be all
> left standing from that era.
>
>   (Gelpi 22-23)

With poems like **"Ode to Suburbia"** and **"Suburban Woman"** in *The War Horse,* Boland began to ground herself in the house and garden in Dundrum that she shares with husband and daughters. Her purpose became thereafter to write of "the life of a woman in a Dublin suburb with small children" and to make "a visionary claim . . . for that life" (Allen-Randolph, "Interview" 119). The move was at once literary and political: to enter "the tradition at an oblique angle" (*Lannan Literary Videos, #42: Eavan Boland*), and thereby alter the tradition henceforth. Her intention, as she put it in the Lannan interview, was to prove that "the issues raised in the poetry of women are issues that pertain to all poetry. They are issues that have relevance and concern to the health and the dignity and the expansion of all poetry."

In the process, however, Boland's literary politics took the opposite direction from Rich's. After her husband's death and in the momentum of the Women's Movement, Rich moved in the early 1970s to the margins of patriarchy as a feminist and then lesbian poet in order to subvert the established structures, social and political as well as literary. But where Rich's politics were revolutionary, Boland's were evolutionary. She even made a distinction between being a feminist and being a poet that Rich would unhesitatingly reject. After interviewing Rich for the *Irish Times* in 1984, Boland articulated Rich's position sympathetically and then demurred: "But there are some like me, who deeply admire Adrienne Rich's poetry, and who consider themselves feminist, who are yet uneasy about her political and radical commitments." In Boland's view, "feminism is a collective politic" in which she can participate to change policy and structures, but "poetry is . . . executed by individuals from complex and difficult resources of humanity, from solitary depths" ("Path to Self Discovery" 10). This is not the place to argue out these conflicting positions, but to acknowledge the different consequences for the poetry of these two women. Rich's position is fully delineated in her three prose books: *On Lies, Secrets, and Silence* (1979); *Blood, Bread, and Poetry* (1986); and *What Is Found There* (1993). But Boland has been equally clear about her position, as in this 1993 interview:

> Feminism is an enabling perception but it is not an aesthetic one. The poem is a place—at least for me—where all kinds of certainties stop. All sorts of beliefs, convictions, certainties get left at that threshold. I couldn't be a feminist poet. Simply because the poem is a place of experience and not a place of convictions—there is nothing so illuminated and certain as that sort of perspective in the poems I write. My poems have nothing to do with perspective; they have to do with the unfinished business of feeling and obsession. But outside the poem feminism has been a vital, enabling way of seeing the climate in which I write the poem.
>
>   (Allen-Randolph, "Interview" 125)

Both moved to the clarity of their positions haltingly and painfully through the dangers and ambivalences of challenging patriarchy. Irony and self-irony was a double blade that cut both ways. Rich's initial call for *A Change of World* went through the questioning and self-questioning of "Snapshots of a Daughter-in-Law" before attaining *The Will to Change*. In staking out her own *New Territory,* Boland first described poets as lions: "Their spirits like a pride / Of lions circulate" (25). But the irony evident in raising an **"Ode to Suburbia"** turns on its domesticating "compromises"; the proud lion seemed reduced to pussycat: "The same lion who tore stripes / Once off zebras. Who now sleeps, / Small beside the coals" (**"Ode to Suburbia"** 77); "The irony / of finding him here in the one habitat / I never expected" (**"Prisoners"** 83); "Like a pride / of lions toiled for booty" (**"Suburban Woman"** 87). Is the home, then, a cage, keeping the poet prisoner? William Logan was not alone in relishing his self-satisfied male judgment: "For Ms. Boland, the kitchen is a mortuary, but in poem after poem the kitchen and the garden remain scenes of her bloodless anger" (Logan 22).

"Suburban Woman," the last poem in *The War Horse,* bears comparison to Rich's "Snapshots of a Daughter-in-Law," the title poem in Rich's 1963 volume, as responses to the dilemma of the woman poet in the home. The poems share a mordant self-stinging wit: "*Dulce ridens, dulce loquens,* / she shaves her legs until they gleam / like petrified mammoth-tusk" ("Snapshots"; Gelpi 10); ". . . courtesan to the lethal / rapine of routine. The room invites. / She reaches to fluoresce the dawn. / The kitchen lights like a brothel" (**"Suburban Woman"** 86-87). But the poems' outcomes are tellingly different. The climactic section of "Snapshots" describes a dramatic swan dive out of the daughter-in-law's trap into liberation, rendered in the present tense and in verse much freer than in the preceding nine sections:

> Well,
> she's long about her coming, who must be
> more merciless to herself than history.
> Her mind full to the wind, I see her plunge
> breasted and glancing through the currents
> . . .
>   poised, still coming,
> her fine blades making the air wince
>
> but her cargo
> no promise then:
> delivered
> palpable
> ours.

>   (Gelpi 12-13)

"Suburban Woman" was written a decade later, but in a different culture. In contrast to Rich's kinetic and ecstatic "ours," the rhymed couplets of the final section of **"Suburban Woman"** belatedly elide the suburban woman's ironized and objectified "she" and the speaker's "I" into a "we" with a shared fate:

> Defeated we survive, we two, housed
>
> together in my compromise, my craft—
> who are of one another the first draft.

>   (88)

Where Rich envisions the woman sprung from the constraints imposed by patriarchy, Boland sets out to work from within to redefine the domestic world on her own affirming terms. The housewife can turn apparent defeat into survival, housed in "my craft," the poem; for the cunning of the poet's craft is the discipline to rewrite her life beyond the first draft. The turnabout is

enacted in the elision of "compromise," "craft," and then "craft," "draft": "one" can write one's self into "another." *In Her Own Image* (1980) and *Night Feed* (1982) are the second and third drafts of **"Suburban Woman."** Boland has said that she was writing the poems in these two books more or less alternately during these tumultuous transitional years of self-definition, and the disposition of the poems into two complementary books marks the phases in moving beyond the dark and damaging self-image of woman in patriarchy to the dawning of a new and creative identity.

Much has been written about *In Her Own Image* as a pivotal book in Boland's career, but, significantly, it is mediated not by Rich but by Sylvia Plath's *Ariel* (1965). After the silken cadences of Boland's early poems, the lines here are deliberately short, jagged, emphatic: compacted by alliteration and rhyme and grouped into a staccato succession of tercets. The shift in verse technique matches the Plathian subject matter, as the poems dramatize a series of suppressed, forbidden female topics: battering, anorexia, menstruation, alienation, and self-destruction. Equally significant, however, is the fact that Boland's poems are not "confessional," as are Plath's and Anne Sexton's, but rather dramatic soliloquies by a series of personae. If, on the one hand, she wanted to avoid what seemed to her the "separatist" tendency of Rich's feminist course (Wright, "Q. and A. with Eavan Boland" 11), she was also, on the other hand, determined to avoid the suicidal drive of Plath and Sexton.

Moreover, Boland's positive and creative intentions are built into the structure of the book. The dramatic soliloquies of *In Her Own Image* are framed by a pair of poems, **"Tirade for a Mimic Muse"** and **"Making Up,"** both of which appropriate the trope of women's make-up work to redefine the woman's identity from "his" cosmetically falsified image of her to an image of her own composition. "Made up" can mean "self-made." The poet-speaker of **"Tirade"** excoriates the male-fashioned Muse with the promise that these "words" will "make your face naked," will "wake you from your sluttish sleep" and "show you true reflections, terrors" (92). The earlier self-alienation—"She is not myself"; "I / am not myself" (93)—becomes in the course of the sequence "I dawn" (111). **"Making Up"** begins with "My naked face; / I wake to it," but reaches the conclusion that this newly "made-up / tale // of a face" is "my own" (111).

"I dawn"; yet "I wake to dark" (107). The final waking of this new-made "I" only follows and is earned by two night poems, **"Witching"** and **"Exhibitionist."** The personae in both poems are poets, women of words. The witch's "craft" is "nightly, shifty, bookish" as she writes "a page of history for those my sisters // for those kin / they kindled" (104,106); the woman-exhibitionist exults: "What an artist am I!" "working / from the text, / making // . . . my aesthetic" (107). *In Her Own Image* is, then, Boland's most explicitly feminist volume, as the dramatic poems about living in the female body begin to write the image of woman out of patriarchy. But she saw this book and its sequel, *Night Feed,* as presenting the two sides of her dilemma, "the shadow-side" and "the brighter": "*In Her Own Image* allowed me to experiment with the anti-lyric which I saw as proving or guaranteeing the lyricism of *Night Feed*" (Allen-Randolph, "Interview" 122-23). And Jody Allen-Randolph is surely right in judging *Night Feed* "one of the most important volumes of Irish poetry produced by her generation" because in it Boland finally "hit her stride as a poet, found her voice, and harnessed a poetic self to a powerful private vision" (Allen-Randolph, "Finding a Voice" 14). For though written simultaneously with *In Her Own Image, Night Feed* is constructed to build to "**Domestic Interior,**" a sequence written again in her own voice, and it is here, rather than in "**Witching**" or "**Exhibitionist**" or any of the poems of *In Her Own Image,* that Boland actually works the dialectic through to the ethical and aesthetic mode that will govern the rest of her work.

Thus *Night Feed* begins: "You rise, you dawn," but the poems actually negotiate the dialectic between night and day, light and dark. The polar terms recur in the alternation of poems of stasis and metamorphosis resolved in "**Domestic Interior.**" For example, "You rise, you dawn" is the first line of "**Degas's Laundresses,**" but turns out to be ironic as the poem describes the women arrested in their domestic labors in the deadly fixity of the male artist's gaze and his painting: the "twists" of his mind and art are the "winding sheet" that binds them (115-16). Poems about the stasis of women's inculturated role ("**Woman in Kitchen,**" "**It's a Woman's World**") and about the male myths that bind them ("**Degas's Laundresses,**" "**A Ballad of Beauty and Time,**" "**The New Pastoral,**" "**Pose [After the painting *Mrs. Badham* by Ingres]**") alternate with poems offering new myths in which the woman speaker enacts a metamorphosis which frees her from domestic routine and procreative sexuality ("**Daphne with Her Thighs in Bark,**" "**The Woman Turns Herself into a Fish,**" "**The Woman Changes Her Skin**"). These last three poems speak in the Plathian manner of *In Her Own Image,* but neither Plath nor Rich, however therapeutic and liberatory Boland found their violational boldness, provides the basis for her own position as a woman poet in a world of chance and a nation of violence; she would do that in the concluding poems of *Night Feed.* "**Patchwork**" and "**Lights**" lead immediately into "**Domestic Interior**" and begin to work out the psychological, ethical,

even metaphysical terms for her dawning sense of identity as wife and mother: what we heard her call "a visionary claim for that life."

"**Patchwork**" contrasts the lighted interior of the house with the nighttime infinity of the universe flecked with scattered stars:

> My back is to the dark.
> Somewhere out there
> Are stars and bits of stars
> And little bits of bits.

> (131)

The speaker's existential strategy is to employ her "craft or art" to give the domestic interior a semblance of order against the external void. The scraps in the patchwork rug make "a night-sky spread" that, "laid / right across the floor," will "in a good light" help to create a space and shelter for the family against the surrounding dark: "Those are not bits. They are pieces. // And the pieces fit" (132). In "**Lights**" the poet remembers herself as a twelve-year-old, shipboard on a homeward voyage, seeing the northern seas under the Aurora Borealis as an "Arctic garden," a "hard, sharkless Eden." But even so young, the poem tells us, she "was a child of the Fall" rather than of unfallen Eden: she knew the "python waves" were the "phosphor graves" of hapless sailors. In the second six stanzas of the poem the speaker, now "three times twelve" in age, with her own "child asleep beside me," gazes now out of the window at her own garden and sees it as the sinister simulacrum of the ruined, alien world:

> Doubt still sharks
> the close suburban night.
> And all the lights I love
> Leave me in the dark.

> (134)

Then the sequence "**Domestic Interior**" continues to explore the trope of the garden and the fall, the founding myth of the Judeo-Christian tradition. We have heard Boland insist that for her "the poem is a place . . . where all kinds of certainties stop. All sort of beliefs, convictions, certainties get left at that threshold." Genesis originates human history in the fall, but in Boland's poetry Catholicism does not enter directly to offer religious comprehension and spiritual consolation any more than the Judaism of Rich's heritage does in her poetry. Both are writing of the chances and possibilities of temporal, embodied experience. Indeed, for Boland, "unless poetry is part of a human rather than an ideal struggle—unless it redeems that struggle with meaning—I cannot think of any reason why we should continue trying—in Beckett's great phrase—'to leave a stain upon the silence'" ("Religion and Poetry"). Thus "**Hymn,**" the third poem in Boland's sequence, invokes the Nativity to elevate and sacralize the immediate domestic situation: "Here is the star / of my nativity / a nursery lamp / in a suburban window." And the final lines adapt the opening of John's Gospel—the Word made flesh—to the dawning of a new day: "And in the dark / as we slept / the world / was made flesh" (139). Nevertheless, the poems never blink away the sad fact that the new day dies each night. Years before in **"The War Horse"** she had acknowledged the risks of mortality. Now **"Night Feed,"** the first poem in the sequence, acknowledges the limits of maternal providence in a nursery world already fallen: at the "last suck" the nursing infant opens her eyes "birth-colored and offended" that the milk is exhausted, and "we begin the long fall from grace." The mother's gesture is protective but futile: "I tuck you in" (135-36).

"The Muse Mother," placed at the center of **"Domestic Interior,"** focuses on the image of a mother and child—a workaday, suburban variant of the Madonna and Child—and dedicates the poet to finding the language to write their myth:

> If I could decline her—
> lost noun
> out of context,
> stray figure of speech—
> from this rainy street
> again to her roots,
> she might teach me
> a new language:
>
> to be a sibyl
> able to sing the past
> in pure syllables,
> limning hymns sung
> to belly wheat or a woman—
>
> able to speak at last
> my mother tongue.
>
> (142-43)

The last and title poem of the sequence moves from the finished composure of Van Eyck's painting of the married couple in the "Arnolfini Portrait" to a more female conception of art attendant on life's process. The closing lines address the husband:

> But there's a way of life
> that is its own witness:
> put the kettle on, shut the blind.
> Home is a sleeping child,
> an open mind
>
> and our effects,
> shrugged and settled
> in the sort of light
> jugs and kettles
> grow important by.
>
> (150-51)

The very fixity of art educes a bogus satisfaction by removing its subjects from the vicissitudes of temporal existence. Even as early as **"From the Painting *Back from Market* by Chardin"** in *New Territory,* Boland has worried about the falsity of aesthetic completion: "I think of what great art removes: hazard and death" (18). So now **"Domestic Interior"** sets art to the paradoxical task of following from and following out "a way of life / that is its own witness": a poetry that discloses moment by ordinary moment the luminous essentiality of all that is dear and doomed by "hazard and death."

Boland has spoken of Rich's poetry as "a work of personal witness" and called "Diving into the Wreck" "prophetic" in its concluding line about women's unwritten "book of myth" ("Path to Self Discovery" 10; Wright, "Q. and A. with Eavan Boland" 11). But how different in fact the poets' "witness" is, how opposite the locus and focus of their myths of woman's lives. As early as "Shooting Script (11/69-7/70)" Rich had taken as her purpose a radical change in the life she had been living in patriarchy:

> To read there the map of the future, the roads radiat-
>   ing from the initial
> split, the filaments thrown out from that impasse.
> . . .
> To pull yourself up by your own roots; to eat the last
>   meal in the old
> neighborhood.
>
> (Gelpi 47)

In the long sequence "Sources" (1981-82) Rich writes: "I stare anew at things / . . . / —into that dangerous place / the family home"; and the next section asks:

> And if my look becomes the bomb that rips
> the family home apart
>
> is this betrayal, that the walls
> slice off, the staircase shows
>
> torn-away above the street
> that the closets where the clothes hung
>
> hang naked . . . ?
>
> (Gelpi 107-08)

The only answer to the question is "I can't stop seeing like this." Where in "Like This Together" Rich spoke of the anonymous "they" as destroying her domestic world, her "prophetic" words here are the force destroying the family home as constructed in patriarchy.

Nothing could be farther from Boland's own "witness" as aggrieved and grieving guardian of the family home. We have heard Boland say that "the interior of the poem" and "the identity of the poet" are "inseparable" functions of each other. Rich's poetry compassionates the victims of oppression and injustice, but is capable, as here, of presenting images of violence not just inflicted and suffered but resisted and returned. Boland's poetry, by contrast, speaks again and again of healing the inescapable and fatal wounds of time and history. In one interview Boland even agreed with Auden's anti-revolutionary comment, famous or infamous depending on one's politics, that "poetry makes nothing happen" and noted that, while Rich has spoken "of the traditional roles of women being oppressive to the imaginative function," she wanted instead to submit those roles to imaginative realization because they "have a strong, tribal relation to the past" with which she seeks "continuity" (Auden 242; Somerville-Arjat, *Sleeping with Monsters* 85, 83). Both Rich and Boland work towards a new language, are sustained by a "dream of a common language." But where Rich speaks from a conviction of *Time's Power,* the title of her 1989 volume, Boland speaks from an equally deep conviction of time's losses. Where Rich's new language aims at change, Boland's aims at recovery: "to sing the past / in pure syllables" means that "language is a kind of scar / and heals after a while / into a passable imitation / of what went before" (143, 157).

Boland was correct in calling Rich a prophet. Etymologically, the prophet "speaks for" a transforming vision, and if Rich makes no claim to divine inspiration, as do the Hebrew prophets, nevertheless she does, like them, invoke her powers of speech to denounce her nation's failings and call for a changed "way of life." But if Rich is an instance of the woman poet as prophet, Boland is the woman poet as elegist. Her time of day is not really dawn but dusk; her season, autumn rather than spring. Poetry does not change the "way of life" but laments its passing. So vulnerable is she to time's losses that in **"Suburban Woman: A Detail,"** "the last light" at dusk in the open space between a neighbor's house and her own presages imminent dissolution and summons her to the elegist's task of remembrance:

> I am definite
> to start with
> but the light is lessening,
> the hedge losing its detail,
> the path its edge.
> . . .
> Suddenly I am not certain
> of the way I came
> or the way I will return,
> only that something
> which may be nothing
> more than darkness has begun
> softening the definitions
> of my body, leaving
>
> the fears and all the terrors
> of the flesh shifting the airs
> and forms of the autumn quiet
>
> crying "remember us."

(171)

The focus of this essay has prevented much comment on Boland's technical development as she moved (as did Rich) from early reliance on meter and rhyme to more flexible and open verses like these. But, as she remarked, the poem's interior is an extension and expression of the poet's stance in the world. Boland has not remarked at length on her prosody, but one glancing comment is relevant here. In response to a question about her tendency to use long sentences that unfold and unfold, enjambing lines and even stanzas, Boland said that she wanted to slow down the pace from the characteristically brisk clip of Irish verse (*Lannan Literary Videos, # 42: Eavan Boland*). So in verses like those above and others cited from the later poems the unwinding, devolving movement from line to line down the page measures out the elegist's act of grave and quiet remembrance.

The first poem in the next volume is called, emblematically, **"I Remember,"** and in fact the volumes in the fifteen years since *Night Feed—The Journey* (1987), *Outside History* (1990), *In a Time of Violence* (1994), and *The Lost Land* (1998)—have consolidated and elaborated Boland's elegiac perspective. The title poem of *The Journey* has been one of her most frequently cited poems and occupies a special place in her work because it gathers in so many central concerns. Like "Diving into the Wreck," **"The Journey"** is a dream vision of a descent into an underworld that sets the poet's mission, but where "Diving into the Wreck" leaves the future open, **"The Journey"** turns back. Boland's classical epigraph comes from Book VI of the *Aeneid,* Aeneas' descent into the underworld and his encounter with the wretched but voiceless shades there; this passage had always struck her, even as a schoolgirl, with particular poignancy as **"The Latin Lesson"** (in *Outside History*) recounts. But since her myth is not a male myth but the myth of mothers, her psychopomp to the world of the dead is not Virgil, Dante's guide, but Sappho, the archetypal woman poet. Across the uncrossable banks of the Styx, the river of forgetfulness cutting off the world of the dead, Sappho reveals a vision of bereaved mothers suckling and cradling infants killed by the various diseases and plagues that through history have ravaged "old Europe."

Yet these "terrible pietàs" come to exemplify and to arouse in the poet "the grace of love" that transfigures the doom it can neither escape nor defer. When the poet beseeches, "Let me at least be their witness," Sappho consecrates her as "my own daughter" with these oracular words about the limits and responsibilities of the poet:

> What you have seen is beyond speech,
> beyond song, only not beyond love;
> remember it, you will remember it
> . . .

I have brought you here so you will know forever
the silences in which are our beginnings,
in which we have an origin like water. . . .

(184)

By titling the American edition of her Collected Poems
An Origin Like Water, Boland indicated the originary
importance of this passage. The well-spring of her
words of remembrance is the worldlessness of the lost:
mother and child, generation after generation "beyond
speech, / beyond song." Poetry therein finds its sacred
mission as remembrance recovers and extends "the
grace of love." When the poet awakes in the suburban
house where her two daughters lie asleep, she realizes
that that "grace" is not a supernatural gift but a human
bond in the face of ineluctable destiny:

Nothing was changed; nothing was more clear
but it was wet and the year was late.
The rain was grief in arrears; my children
Slept the last dark out safely and I wept.

(185)

Nothing was changed except her deeper realization of
human responsibility, one to another, mother to child,
generation after generation. The poem's speech and
song generates its own witness. The **"Envoi"** to **"The
Journey"** is a poem of "Easter in the suburb," but the
poet awaits not the risen Savior but the empowering
"muse mother" of home and garden:

I have the truth and I need the faith.
It is time I put my hand in her side.

If she will not bless the ordinary,
if she will not sanctify the common,
then here I am and here I stay and then am I
the most miserable of women.

(186)

A number of poems in *The Journey* examine the pos-
sibilities of a "new language" of women's elegy: **"Mise
Eire," "The Oral Tradition," "The Unlived Life,"
"Listen. This Is the Noise of Myth," "Tirade for a
Lyric Muse."**

The titles of the recent books—*Outside History, In a
Time of Violence, The Lost Land,* as well as the
pamphlet *A Kind of Scar: The Woman Poet in a
National Tradition* (1989) and the prose *Object Lessons: The Life of the Woman and the Poet in Our Time*
(1995)—indicate a more deliberate effort on Boland's
part to make the connection between the woman poet
and the national poet, and most commentary on these
volumes has concerned Boland's writing of the excluded
woman into the national history and the literary canon
of Ireland. Her presence (along with that of the other
women poets of her generation) has already made and
will continue to mark a decisive shift in the scope of

Irish literary endeavor and the conception of nation in
the past and present. What has gone almost completely
unobserved, however, is the distinctive and defining
note of Boland's particular achievement: namely, the
elegiac cast of her presentation of women's experience
and of Irish history.

The sequence **"Outside History,"** a series of autobiographical reminiscences, illustrates Boland's characteristic note. In **"We Are Human History. We Are Not
Natural History,"** she locates the distinction in the human consciousness of its fate as she watches her
children, heedless in their innocence, cross the grass in
a light that she sees as "short-lived and elegiac as / the
view from a train window of / a station parting, all
tears" (*Outside History* 44). **"We Are Always Too
Late"** identifies the human sense of nature's enduring
comfort with "our need for these / beautiful upstagings
of / what we suffer by / what survives" (47). In the title
poem of the sequence, the stars in the firmament, light
years away in the universe, are "outside history," but
within history we travel rivers and roads "clotted as /
firmaments with the dead": "we kneel beside them,
whisper in their ear. / And we are too late. We are
always too late" (50). Words, as consciousness' necessary but unavailing effort to signify the absent, record
"possibilities and disappointments" in saving **"What
We Lost"** (49). No wonder Boland identified as "a
theme which always has come back to trouble me" the
unavoidable question of "how much right we have to
return to the past, to that place of complex feeling, and
reconstruct it to our own purposes" (*Lannan Literary
Videos, #42: Eavan Boland*).

"The Making of an Irish Goddess," from the **"Outside
History"** sequence, recalls **"The Journey"** as a poem
of descent to the underworld, and its invocation of the
Ceres myth links it with the middle section of **"Suburban Woman: A Detail"** (from *The Journey*) and with
"The Pomegranate" (from *In a Time of Violence*:
"The only legend I have ever loved is / The story of a
daughter lost in hell" 26). This poem, however, makes a
point of rewriting the story of Ceres, who "went to hell
/ with no sense of time":

But I need time—
my flesh and that history—
to make the same descent.

In my body,
neither young now nor fertile,
and with the marks of childbirth
still on it,

in my gestures—
the way I pin my hair to hide
the stitched healed blemish of a scar—
must be

an accurate inscription
of that agony. . . .

                                        (38)

The word "inscription," of course, makes the correlation between the mortal descent and the poem moving down the page. Both here and in the concluding lines below, parataxis and apposition and qualifying modifiers spin out the sentence as though she cannot bear for it to end, turning remembered details to elegy through the slow-paced, heavily enjambed verses:

> Myth is the wound we leave
> in the time we have—
> which in my case is this
> March evening
> at the foothills of the Dublin mountains,
> across which the lights have changed all day,
> holding up my hand
> sickle-shaped, to my eyes
> to pick out
> my own daughter from
> all the other children in the distance;
>
> her back turned to me.
>
>   (39)

Myth is the wound and, as we heard in **"Mise Eire,"** language is the scar that heals and seals but thereby marks the indelible wound of mortality. "Sickle-shaped" identifies the mother, willy-nilly, as Mother Time, the grim reaper.

"What Love Intended" is to my mind so much the paradigmatic Boland poem, both metrically and thematically, that I want to quote it in full and let it stand on its own. The middle sentence, beginning "I will be its ghost," is eighteen-plus lines long.

> I can imagine if;
> I came back again,
> looking through windows at
>
> broken mirrors, pictures,
> and, in the cracked upstairs,
> the beds where it all began.
>
> The suburb in the rain
> this October morning
> full of food and children
>
> and animals, will be—
> when I come back again—
> gone to rack and ruin.
>
> I will be its ghost,
> its revenant, discovering
> again in one place
>
> the history of my pain,
> my ordeal, my grace,
> unable to resist

> seeing what is past,
> judging what has ended
> and whether, first to last,
>
> from then to now and even
> here, ruined, this
> is what love intended—
>
> finding even the yellow
> jasmine in the dusk,
> the smell of early dinners,
>
> the voices of our children
> taking turns and quarreling,
> burned on the distance,
>
> gone. And the small square
> where under cropped lime
> and poplar, on bicycles
>
> and skates in the summer,
> they played until dark;
> propitiating time.
>
> And even the two whitebeams
> outside the house gone,
> with the next-door neighbor
>
> who used to say in April—
> when one was slow to bloom—
> they were a man and a woman.
>
>   (*Outside History* 67-68)

Writing in and of the present but in the past tense: "they were a man and a woman." The poem, like others, recalls Frederic Jameson's phrase "nostalgia for the present" (though utterly, of course, without his Marxist inflection of the phrase). The "October morning" of the opening becomes "dark" by the end, as the sense of the past makes the present moment already past. In the dusk the suburb of children and neighbors is an underworld of shades.

"Love," from *In a Time of Violence,* has become a signature poem, which Boland almost always includes in readings. Writing to her husband in the present ("I am your wife. . . . We love each other still") about the crisis years before when their infant daughter nearly died of meningitis, the two of them in her recollection become voiceless shades in Virgil's underworld, so that when she asks, "Will we ever live so intensely again," "the words are shadows and you cannot hear me. / You walk away and I cannot follow" (24-25). Poem after poem moves to desolation. In **"Moths"** "the kitchen bulb . . . makes / my child's shadow longer than my own" (29). **"The Parcel"** describes in loving detail Boland's mother's skill in wrapping packages for mailing but then watches it get lost and break apart:

> See it disappear. Say
> this is how it died

out: among doomed steamships and outdated trains,
the tracks for them disappearing before our eyes,
next to station names we can't remember
on a continent we no longer
recognize. The sealing wax cracking.
The twine unravelling. The destination illegible.

(In a Time of Violence 45)

The last section of *In a Time of Violence* contains a cluster of poems about the function of language in conveying and resisting the passing present. **"Anna Liffey"** invokes the time-honored connection between river and woman in male myth and amends Joyce's celebration of Dublin's river Liffey as the feminine principle eternal in its cycles. Boland's poem, her longest, concludes: "In the end / Everything that burdened and distinguished me / Will be lost in this: / I was a voice" (60). The past tense and the future are linked in the present of the poem, yet the poem's very voice laments the "loss" of the poet. **"What Language Did"** reiterates that her kind of poem rejects the male effort to fix woman in "terrible / suspension of life" (69) but instead seeks to "*make us human / in cadences of change and mortal pain / and words we can grow old and die in*" (65). And again, in **"A Woman Painted on a Leaf,"** "I want a poem / I can grow old in. I want a poem I can die in" (69-70).

Rich's recent books—*Your Native Land, Your* Life (1986), *An Atlas of the Difficult World* (1991), *Dark Fields of the Republic* (1995)—indicate her own increasing engagement with national destiny. But a juxtaposition of *Atlas* and Boland's *The Lost Land* (1998) underscores the two poets' different responses to history and the very different courses their poetry has taken. Part of the reason can no doubt be attributed to the different circumstances of the American experience and the Irish experience, but perhaps even more important are the personal differences in temperament and assumption and outlook. In "Atlas" there is no question that the difficult world Rich is addressing is the dark field of her native land. The first twelve sections of the sequence intersperse personal and political reflections to map out the territory, and the concluding section, called "(Dedications)," undertakes performatively to create a new community by summoning the readers of the poem. The long lines, threaded on the repeated and incantatory phrase "I know you are reading this poem . . . ," gather momentum with a Whitmanesque immediacy and inclusiveness as the litany draws the readers, scattered and alienated, to the poet and to each other. Here are a few lines from the concluding section:

I know you are reading this poem in a waiting-room
of eyes met and unmeeting, of identity with strangers.
I know you are reading this poem by fluorescent light
in the boredom and fatigue of the young who are
   counted out,
count themselves out, at too young an age. I know

you are reading this poem through your failing sight,
   the thick
lens enlarging these letters beyond all meaning yet
   you read on
because even the alphabet is precious.

(Gelpi 158)

Boland has remarked that her life and poetry would probably seem, in Rich's judgment, "too far from the tumult," "too deep in the past" ("Introduction" i). The two closely related halves of Boland's most recent collection—**"Colony"** and **"The Lost Land"**—also mingle personal and national history, like "Atlas," but they confirm her as elegist rather than prophet. She is quoted on the dust jacket as indicating that the lost land is "not exactly a country and not exactly a state of mind. . . . The lost land is not a place that can be subdivided into history, or love, or memory. It is the poet's own, single, and private account of the ghostly territory where so much human experience comes to be stored." Storied and stored. Stored and restored. She has resolutely rejected the "bardic stance" of male Irish poets and has expressly shied away from any suggestion of special inspiration: "I have never been sympathetic to the idea of inspiration" (Wright, "Q. and A. with Eavan Boland" 10; Somerville-Arjat, *Sleeping with Monsters* 80). Yet her elegiac stance expresses what she herself has suggested is the religious impulse behind poetry like hers.

Not the nineteenth-century notion of a religion of poetry, poetry as a substitute for religion: she views that falsifying notion with "a mix of familiarity and contempt." Her conviction, "which I have over the years come to believe more and more," inverts the terms: "poetry—the very act—has a separate force within it which could very nearly be called a religious momentum." Poetry, in her experience, arises out of the realization "that man is flawed, that he has been tampered with, fractured," and its consequent impulse is paradoxical: "even as it gives the most obvious witness to the truth that man is not perfect, it suggests through its music the possibility that he might once have been and—through its offices—might momentarily be again." By "drawing its deepest energies from trying to restore these harmonies," poetry "sets out to heal a wound, to make peace between man's fallen and unfallen nature." "Fallen," "unfallen," "wound," "heal," "witness": these key words in Boland's poetic testimony here take on deeper resonance from the Christian myth of human imperfection and redemption. (All quotations are from her essay "Religion and Poetry.")

Eavan Boland's exploration of what it is to be a woman poet and an Irish poet in our time is thus informed by her conviction that the "best poetry" deals with "death and limitation and time": an effort in which "the sources and restrictions of the creative gift" can be "openly faced and . . . frankly lamented and . . . lovingly accepted" ("Religion and Poetry"). Therein lies the elegist's power of healing. The world that the poet knows and addresses is a world of "hazard and death," and the lost land is paradise lost but yearned for. And perhaps glimpsed in the yearning; perhaps even in a sense regained, at least temporarily, in the crafted closure, the harmonies and silences of poetic time. The "momentum" of her poetry is the quest for that lost land, and its enduring claim on readers around the world is the chance of sighting it in the poems time and again.

Works Cited

Allen-Randolph, Jody. "Finding a Voice Where She Found a Vision." *P. N. Review* 22.1 (Sept.-Oct. 1994): 13-17.

———. "An Interview with Eavan Boland." *Special Issue: Eavan Boland. Irish University Review* 23.1 (Spring/Summer 1993): 117-30.

———. "The New Critics: Adrienne Rich and Eavan Boland." *P. N. Review* 22.2 (Nov.-Dec. 1995): 15-17.

Auden, W. H. *The English Auden: Poems, Essays and Dramatic Writings 1927-1939.* Ed. Edward Mendelson. New York: Random House, 1977.

Boland, Eavan. *In a Time of Violence.* New York: W. W. Norton, 1994.

———. Introduction. *Adrienne Rich: Selected Poems.* Knockeven, Ireland: Salmon Press, 1996.

———. *The Lost Land.* New York: W. W. Norton, 1998.

———. *An Origin Like Water: Collected Poems 1967-1987.* New York: W. W. Norton, 1996.

———. *Outside History: Selected Poems 1980-1990.* New York: W. W. Norton, 1990.

———. "Path to Self Discovery." *The Irish Times* 21 June 1984: 10.

———. "Religion and Poetry." *The Furrow* 33.12 (Dec. 1982).

Gelpi, Barbara Charlesworth, and Albert Gelpi, eds. *Adrienne Rich's Poetry and Prose.* New York: W. W. Norton, 1993.

Jameson, Frederic. *Postmodernism, or the Cultural Logic of Late Capitalism.* Durham: Duke UP, 1991.

Lannan Literary Videos, #42: Eavan Boland. Los Angeles: Lannan Foundation, 1994.

Logan, William. "Animal Instincts and Natural Powers." *New York Times Book Review* 21 April 1991: 22.

Luftig, Victor. "Something Will Happen to You Who Read": Adrienne Rich, Eavan Boland." *Special Issue: Eavan Boland. Irish University Review* 23.1 (Spring/Summer 1993): 57-66.

Mahon, Derek. "Young Eavan and Early Boland." *Special Issue: Eavan Boland. Irish University Review* 23.1 (Spring/Summer 1993): 23-28.

Somerville-Arjat, Gillean, and Rebecca E. Wilson, eds. *Sleeping with Monsters: Conversations with Scottish and Irish Women Poets.* Edinburgh: Polygon, 1990.

Wright, Nancy Means, and Dennis J. Hannan. "Q. and A. with Eavan Boland." *Irish Literary Supplement* 10.1 (Spring 1991): 10-11.

Michael Thurston (essay date December 1999)

SOURCE: Thurston, Michael. "'A Deliberate Collection of Cross Purposes': Eavan Boland's Poetic Sequences." *Colby Quarterly* 35, no. 4 (December 1999): 229-51.

[*In the following essay, Thurston offers a thematic and stylistic examination of Boland's longer poetic works.*]

Beginning in the early 1980s, Eavan Boland began to work not only in individual lyrics but in slightly longer poems (**"The Journey"**) and sequences of lyrics (including the poems gathered in *In Her Own Image*). Indeed, since the 1990 American appearance of *Outside History: Selected Poems 1980-1990,* each of Boland's books has included at least one such sequence (*Outside History* included two, the title sequence and also **"Domestic Interior,"** which consisted of poems originally published as free-standing lyrics, first gathered into a titled sequence in this American publication). While they share the central concerns that have structured Boland's career, each sequence focuses its meditation through a different thematic lens. **"Domestic Interior"** elaborates and problematizes its titular familial spaces as a haven from history; **"Outside History"** develops, questions, and finally rejects the possibility of finding and inhabiting any space "outside history" and explores the kinds of spaces available within the history the poet ultimately chooses; **"Writing in a Time of Violence"** takes up language itself and the role of representation in the construction of history and the subject's response to it; and **"Colony,"** from Boland's most recent collection, *The Lost Land,* meditates on such public repositories of historic residues as cityscapes and monuments. As this description indicates, I find something of a suggested teleological narrative in Boland's sequence of sequences. I want to emphasize, however, that these extended attempts to comprehend history are, like the individual poems of which they are made up, "a deliberate collection of cross purposes," for each sequence both touches on the concerns central to the others and proceeds through nonlinear and self-questioning methods. Taken individually and as a group, Boland's poetic sequences instantiate a political and ethical poetry whose end is neither exhortation nor confirmation in a predetermined agenda, but is rather the formation of a tentative, cautious, self-doubting and highly aware subjectivity whose very weakness is at once the core of its ethics and politics and the basis of its strength.[1] Boland's sequences constitute a determined effort not to *solve* historical problems or to resolve the tensions they construct, but instead precisely to *resist* solutions and resolutions and to hold open and demand continued attention to the problems posed by public history, private life, and the problematic mediations of memory, myth and language.

"Domestic Interior," whose poems were all first published in *Night Feed* (1982), dwells on and makes symbolic a set of common household objects (teakettles, baby bottles, blankets, flowers) and tasks (sewing, cleaning, cooking). On this much, critics have tended to agree, though some jeer while others applaud the poems' rich and careful re-creation of the domestic. Interestingly, both attacks and encomiums depend upon the critic's sense of Boland's stance toward the home spaces in which she situates the poems. William Logan, for example, finds that "the kitchen and the garden remain scenes of [Boland's] bloodless anger" and argues that "when a poet is so self-divided, so drawn to realms she despises, it should not be surprising if her poetry suffers division too, here between prose and the poetic" (22). And on the plus side, Arthur MacGuinness praises the poems of *Night Feed,* writing that the book

> for the most part treats suburban woman and chronicles the daily routines of a Dublin housewife in a quite positive way. The book has poems about baby's diapers, about washing machines, about feeding babies. The cover has a very idyllic drawing of a mother feeding a child.

(202)

Both of these readings suffer from a strange myopia, an inability or unwillingness to register the complexity of Boland's attitude toward the domestic and the lives women live in its spaces. Logan misses the quite tender evocations of home life in many poems, and MacGuinness, though he notes that Boland "seems conflicted" about the meanings of home and housework, ultimately argues that "many poems in *Night Feed* accept [women's] lesser destiny" (203). Each critic seems to find what he expects in the poems, and each seems to base his expectations on Boland's perceived hatred for or love of her poems' "homes."

But Boland neither wholly loves nor wholly hates, entirely praises nor completely criticizes, the domestic she renders in these poems. Rather, she values domestic spaces, objects, tasks and relationships by examining them honestly and rigorously. Most importantly, she situates these in a network of other concerns, especially art and the land, in an effort to locate the "domestic interior" in history; in so doing, Boland forcefully locates history, especially as mediated by mythic and

literary languages, in the poems' domestic spaces. The divisions traditionally erected between home and history, in other words, come under intense scrutiny here, come to seem imposed and arbitrary and ultimately false. The poems work musically, through the repeated deployment and development of images, allusions and leitmotifs, the sounding of ideas and affects in varied contexts and combinations to elaborate and finally produce a rich and complex understanding of history at home.

But to describe the sequence's method in this way is not to deny the integrity and importance of the individual poems that comprise it. Indeed, Boland's musical elaboration of her themes' significances depends upon the provisionally complete understandings achieved poem by poem. "Night Feed," the sequence's first poem, not only introduces such motifs as flowers, children, and times of day, but reaches a resolution (however tentative and open to complication) of its themes. "This is dawn," the poem begins, and the opening gesture at once establishes the moment on which the poem meditates, a time of transition, wakening, and newness, and also the rhetorical mode (the deictic) by which this meditation will proceed. We learn from the first stanza's images that sunrise promises change and provides the opportunity for reflection linked somehow to that change. At this key moment, "daisies open" and gathered rainwater, itself changeable and "mercurial," "makes a mirror for sparrows." The dawn enacts and enables. Its arrival causes (or accompanies) the quiet flurry of activity the speaker narrates: "I tiptoe in. / I lift you up," and, later, "I crook the bottle." But amidst this activity we find a resistance to it, a desire for stasis manifest in the speaker's very syntax, for Boland consociates dawn and daughter, daylight and nourishment, sunrise and the speaker's sense of renewal and value in a series of "this" phrases: "This is your season, little daughter," "this is the hour / For the early bird and me," "This is the best I can be," "this nursery" (139). Even the most domestic interior, the poem goes on to illustrate, even the apogee of unity (between mother and child, between child and earth) from which any change is a descent, bears in its figuration into language its own dissolution into distances.

As much as it is "about" anything, "Domestic Interior" is about precisely this problem, the gaps between the elements that make up the very homes we hope to protect from history—domestic objects and relationships. Boland sets this as the problem we must confront and think through as we make sense of the sequence's poems on their own and in relation to each other. Through its individual poems, the sequence continually draws us out to face its problems; it maintains its thematic forces in precarious balance, repeatedly allowing provisional resolutions which unravel even as they are made and keep important questions open. Stepping back from the local suspensions, we can read these moments as changes Boland rings on the cluster of images that recur throughout the sequence. The stars that fade in **"Night Feed"** and reappear as constelled simulacra in **"Monotony,"** for example, modulate in **"Hymn"** both into "the cutlery glitter" of the winter sky and "the star / of my nativity," which is actually a "nursery lamp / in that suburb window," and which brings a strangely enabling darkness when it "goes out." They assert, in **"Patchwork,"** both the apparent randomness of the universe and the sense of pattern and design achieved by perspective and will. Daisies, opening in the dawn of **"Night Feed,"** evince an accumulative energy and startle with "economies of light" in **"Energies,"** and the flowers they exemplify shimmer in the weird light of **"Endings"** to reveal "what it is the branches end in." The baby bottle of **"Night Feed"** and the altars of **"Monotony"** combine in **"Hymn"** to sacralize a winter dawn and realize the world anew as human flesh, while the domestic space they metonymize resounds in **"Energies"** and in **"After a Childhood Away from Ireland"** as "the dissonances // of the summer's day ending." Boland stages her themes and variations in new combinations, drawing out their changeable significances, inviting us along to contemplate homes and the ways we make them, "home" and the ways we construct the concept.

The sequence's poems explicitly about art make this especially plain, for in these poems Boland draws our attention to constructedness itself, to how meaning depends not only upon perspective or standpoint but also on active involvement, interpretation, and making. **"Patchwork,"** in which the speaker narrates her work on a quilt, her effort to impose order and harmony on a "trash bag of colors" and a roomful of "triangles and diamonds," associates the fabric cuttings with those recurrent stars:

> My back is to the dark.
> Somewhere out there
> are stars and bits of stars
> and little bits of bits,
> and swiftnesses and brightnesses and drift—
> but is it craft or art?

(145)

The stanza's closing question echoes often around "folk art" forms like quilting, and the answer to it is much less important in this context than the way it links quilting and the cosmos; both involve "bits," and even "bits of bits," which yield order and utility and significance only when we put them together. And the act of making meaning, of imposing through imagination and the effort of "aligning," enables the speaker to realize that "these"—stars and fabric scraps alike—"are not bits / they are pieces / and the pieces fit."

But the pieces fit because the artist (quilter or astronomer or poet) makes them fit. They yield their significance not through their own shapes but, as Boland writes in **"Fruit on a Straight-Sided Tray,"** through "the space between them." Art manifests "the geometry of the visible" (a locution that recalls the squares, circles, and triangles of **"Patchwork"**), but it does so on the signifying ground of that which we do not see; it is "the science of relationships," a means with which we might explore the mechanisms that enable us to make sense of what surrounds us. But that science's substratum is that which is not there. The poem continually, almost obsessively, reminds us of this in its repetition of "space" and "between," in its return to "absence" and "distances" (specifically between mother and child, so close in the sequence's opening poem) and in its devastating conclusion that those distances are "growing to infinities" (148).

Distances, physical and temporal but also intellectual and affective, provide the background against which things represented or remembered signify, but they ensure that the significances themselves are limited, partial, blurry, and deceptive. Distances suggest resemblances, seduce with sentiment, refine and process places, people, objects and relationships because their spaces are not empty. Distances fill, the moment we create them, with desire—to go back, to get back, to return, retrieve, regain what we have moved from, what has been removed from us. Moreover, distances' desires are not, themselves, fluid and fungible. Distances, at least in Boland's poetic vocabulary, bear within them the accumulated desires that make up histories and traditions, the culturally repeated desires borne in **"Night Feed"** by the effort to "hold on / [for] Dear Life," and in **"After a Childhood Away from Ireland"** by land and by "the habit of land." They are the shared, the social, and, therefore, the necessarily historical spaces in which objects, actions, and relationships exist, occur, and take on their significances. This awareness is one of the key competences Boland's work demands that we develop and deploy.

The "true subject is the space between." Not emptiness but the significant distances that surround objects, surround us. These enable objects not only to mean but to be, for without separation there can exist no distinction, no identifiable individuality. But such spaces are not simply absences. They are painting's negative space, the figure's ground, room occupied not by nothing but by the something, rendered conventionally invisible, which enables us to see something else against it. We might as easily call such spaces the left out, the unattended to, the unnoticed, the assumed. And Boland's emphasis on this as "the true subject" in a painter's composition, an emphasis situated in the context of her meditations on the domestic and its construction in language, suggests something she will treat at length in later sequences—this taken for granted background plays a crucial role in history, for by its absence or its firm location as the ground against which figures take their shape it shapes the history we have come to know. And it is when pictorial polarities reverse, when the ground becomes the figure, that history becomes unknowable to us as we have known it before, invisible to us as we grasp the new figures emerging from "the space between."

Those figures, Boland has often argued in her prose writings, are women, whose lives occur, too often, outside history and as the silent background for men's more important actions.[2] **"Domestic Interior,"** this sequence's title poem and conclusion, focuses on just such a figure—a bride painted by Van Eyck. But any easy promise for political change wrought simply through a shift in our attention from the figure to the ground (in painting or in history) is questioned here.[3] Boland makes clear the painter's control over the represented woman's shape and significance:

> The oils,
> the varnishes,
> the cracked light,
> the worm of permanence—
> all of them supplied by Van Eyck—
>
> by whose edict she will stay
> burnished, fertile
> on her wedding day,
> interred in her joy.

(151)

We find no surprises here. Caught by the painter's gaze and the application of his craft, the woman is silent and powerless. She cannot help but signify the painter's sense of her; she cannot help but symbolize the quiescent fertility Van Eyck bestows upon her. And she cannot escape interment in the oils and varnishes that transform her from living woman to polished artifact.

We might expect the poem's speaker, the woman as author instead of object, as priestess and not sacrifice, to articulate, through her revelation of man's hand in this construction, a means of resistance. We might expect that a new way of seeing will somehow release the woman's energy, revise the symbolic vocabulary that imprisons her. But even the most well-intentioned eye, Boland writes, "so loving, bright / and constant," must reflect the woman as she appears "in her varnishes." Instead of a revisionary way of *seeing* (an epistemology), which would liberate the woman from the limits of her representation, Boland offers a praxis, a *lived knowledge*: a "way of life / that is its own witness." That way of life, as Patricia Hagen and Thomas Zelman have written, depends more than anything else upon particularity:

> Boland's poetry is microcosmic and keenly observant; her interest in the meaning of Ireland is an interest in houses, flowers, blackbirds, and children, in the "great

people" who suffered the famine, in the "teddy bears and rag dolls and tricycles and buckets" that constitute "love's archaeology." It is as if by particularizing, Boland will avoid the "harmonies of servitude," the soothing rhetoric of generalization.

(452)

Concluding the sequence, Boland gets particular; she names what throughout the sequence she has modeled, a way of inhabiting domestic spaces, of handling domestic objects, of living domestic relationships in full awareness of their constructedness in (and in relation to) history. This way of life consists of everyday actions—"put the kettle on, shut the blind"—neither mindlessly repeated as bits of routine nor cast into fixed relationships as background to a more important life outside, but carried out as self-consciously as artistic composition or religious ritual.

The result of Boland's self-witnessing way of life is a sense of home enriched by the situation of the "domestic interior" in the web of discourses the sequence has spun out, the multiple contexts that enable it to mean:

> Home is a sleeping child,
> an open mind
> and our effects,
> shrugged and settled
> in the sort of light
> jugs and kettles
> grow important by.

(152)

A space valued for its living inhabitants and their "effects" (at once their property and their impacts) viewed from the perspective Boland has developed over the course of the sequence, home is a fragile haven continually threatened but constantly enabled by its constitution through absence, its composition through historically tainted language, and its construction out of "bits" transformed by light and unceasing effort into "pieces" that fit into usable wholes. More than this, "home" in **"Domestic Interior"** is a space whose contours we must map, through our deployment of linguistic, rhetorical, and literary competences in the verbal space of these poems. And when we work through Boland's vision to comprehend home as she finally defines it, we have done more than interpret and understand. We have experienced the constant dissolution of that safe and comfortable space, the continual need to reconstitute it. By entering, through the cognitive and affective commitments entailed by our interpretation, the synthetic consciousness that struggles to protect unity against distance even as it recognizes that unity is constituted by distance, to protect the home against history even as it recognizes the home's interdependence with history, we take up and work through the same struggles. We at once see by and become the "sort of light / jugs and kettles / grow important by."

The history that comes to visit and ends up making itself at home in **"Domestic Interior"** is a vague presence, less like a threatening constable or terrorist than like a doddering relative or neighbor whose stories meander associatively and never reach their point. Inhering in the distances and gaps and silences, this history lacks, for the most part, compelling specificity. While I would not ascribe the claim to Boland, this sequence explores and establishes in a preliminary way a set of notions about lived history in the abstract(able) home that the later sequences will concretize and specify.

"Outside History" opens with just such a specifying gesture; its first poem, **"The Achill Woman,"** locates its speaker and its action on an island off the northwest coast of Ireland, in a region hit hardest by the depredations of the 1840s Famine and still largely impoverished. On Easter vacation, "raw from college," the poem's speaker spends a twilight talking with an old woman who has brought water to her borrowed cottage. The poem tells us nothing of that conversation's content. "We stayed," Boland writes, "putting down time until / the evening turned cold without warning." The woman heads for home, the speaker goes inside and tries to study "the set text / of the Court poets of the Silver Age." Boland's prose account of her encounter with the old woman on Achill, in her essay "A Kind of Scar: The Woman Poet in a National Tradition," is worth glancing at before going further with the poem:

> She was the first person to talk to me about the famine. The first person, in fact, to speak to me with any force about the terrible parish of survival and death which the event had been in those regions. She kept repeating to me that they were great people, the people in the famine. Great people. I had never heard that before. She pointed out the beauties of the place. But they themselves, I see now, were a sub-text. On the eastern side of Keel, the cliffs of Menawn rose sheer out of the water. And here was Keel itself, with its blonde strand and broken stone, where the villagers in the famine, she told me, had moved closer to the shore, the better to eat the seaweed.
>
> (5)[4]

Here we see what the poem does not show: that the two women talked, there in the chilly and changeable twilight, about the single most important catastrophe in modern Irish history, about that catastrophe's remnants on the land and in memory. The caretaker helps Boland, in the prose version, to read not only the "sub-text" of the landscape's natural beauty but also the "text" a lived past has written on the land, a text of need and suffering spelled out in bodies and their works, or what remains of them.

But the lesson Boland recounts in her essay, she tells us, she learned only much later. At the time, she writes, she only knew in a way she could not name that the

woman "came from a past which affected me" (6). The poem explores the distance between the remembered moment and what the poet later finds the moment to mean. The women talk, we know not what about, the caretaker leaves and the speaker goes inside to make a fire and study unsuccessfully "the Court poets of the Silver Age." A range of complex texts confronts the speaker: a woman wearing words (her tea-towel apron woven with the words "glass cloth"), an evening "tuned" by the metallic sound the caretaker's bucket makes when she sets it down, a sky and landscape linked by a stream's reflection of the rising "Easter moon" and stars, and a book of sixteenth-century English lyrics composed in their own tangle of political alliances and agendas. But she fails in her effort to read any of these adequately or to note the similarities beneath their superficial differences. She fails even to register the land and the woman *as* texts, with their own histories and meanings. The poem ends in regretted ("nothing now can change") ignorance; the poet recalls how she fell asleep oblivious to

> the planets clouding over in the skies,
> the slow decline of the spring moon,
> the songs crying out their ironies.
>
> (36)

This is the province of **"Outside History,"** the texts unrecognized as texts, the ways they jostle against culturally recognized and valued signs and their significances, the ways in which change clouds or clarifies what we remember and how we can act on our memories. To put it another way, the sequence explores the space between (with all the weight that phrase carries over from **"Domestic Interior"**) Boland's conversation with the caretaker as remembered in the poem and the same conversation as remembered in her prose account. Moreover, as the opening poem's strong sense of location shows, **"Outside History"** takes as its province the specific non-texts of Irish and women's and Irish women's non-history. Reworking some of the same images and allusions Boland explored in **"Domestic Interior,"** the sequence charts an elliptical and recursive course from the speaker's failure to comprehend in **"The Achill Woman"** to an understanding and strategic resolve twelve poems later in **"Outside History."** More than this, though, the sequence requires that we learn the lesson with the poet, that we traverse with her the distance between oblivion and awareness. The reason for this is simple. No amount of telling us will ever let us know what it means to be outside history, what is at stake in entering it. No speech the caretaker might give would enable the college student on vacation to sense her situation's ironies. But living the experience, by assuming the lyrically assembled mind that limns it, can bring us to understand. In this sequence Boland asks us once again to bring to bear our own affect, our own weighted networks of memory, our own cultural knowledges, to follow the poet's modelled subjectivity and make sense of historically burdened languages and myths and narratives and memories, and to work our way in from the place where she makes us begin: on Achill, in the twilight, outside history.

As Terry Eagleton has written, the Famine "strains at the limits of the articulable, and is truly in this sense the Irish Auschwitz" (11)[5]:

> On the very threshold of modernity, Ireland experienced in the Famine all the blind, primeval force of the pre-modern, of a history as apparently remorseless as Nature itself, a history not *naturalized* but natural, a matter of blight and typhus and men and women crawling into the churchyard to die on sacred soil.
>
> (11)

The combination of utter dependence upon the potato and consecutive years of failure in the Irish crop due to the fungus *Phytophthora infestans,* exacerbated by the British Treasury's religious devotion to laissez-faire economic philosophies and the government's consequent refusal to provide comprehensive relief to the starving, with the additional scourges of typhus and relapsing fever running unchecked through crowded and squalid workhouses as well as the weakened peasants outside, reduced Ireland's population by at least 2 1/2 million or roughly 25% (Woodham-Smith 411-12).[6] Such terms and statistics, though, obscure the human suffering that ravaged Ireland for almost five years. Contemporary witnesses and chroniclers left shocked and still-shocking accounts of skeletally emaciated crowds clamoring for food, of villages entirely wiped out by starvation and disease, of families subsisting in ditches, eating grass and roots, clothed in rags after selling all their property for food, of half-covered mass graves rotting in the summer heat, of corpses left in the open by survivors too weak to move or bury them, of desperate and isolated cases of cannibalism. In Eagleton's trenchant summation, "part of the horror of the Famine is its atavistic nature—the mind-shaking fact that an event with all the premodern character of a medieval pestilence happened in Ireland with frightening recentness" (14).

The Famine provides a specific locus for one route through Boland's second sequence. A number of thematic or symbolic continuities or recurrences shoot through the twelve poems of **"Outside History"**: stars, flowers, talk between women, sewing or things sewn, climatic changes, the look of objects in the distance. We could trace any of them to see how Boland draws us to weigh the sense we make of what we confront. But the trajectory perhaps most central to Boland's exploration of lived history is the one readers will recognize from **"Domestic Interior,"** the one that follows Boland's considerations of myth and literature. In

this sequence, that way leads from **"A False Spring"** and **"The Making of an Irish Goddess"** to the sequence's concluding poem, **"Outside History."** Our way through is a *via dolorosa,* a way that leads to loss and wounds and scars, a way that culminates in a transfiguration not from mortality to eternal life but from all fantasies of immortality to the certainty of death. Along this way, the words become flesh.

I choose this phrase in part because the first two of these poems, **"False Spring"** and **"The Making of an Irish Goddess,"** thematize precisely this embodiment of some disembodied past. The two, appearing back to back in **"Outside History,"** seem, more than is usually the case in Boland's sequences, a matched set, a pair of poems that elaborate historic embodiment in almost dialogic fashion through the central conceit of visits to the underworld. In **"False Spring,"** the speaker (or a younger version of her) has herself endured a sort of epic *nekuia,* immersing herself in the study of Latin, and specifically in the sixth book of Virgil's *Aeneid,* in which Aeneas descends into hell. Looking back from a present moment distant from her school days, the speaker recalls emerging from her work into the college gardens and the cold of January. She wants "to find her, / the woman [she] once was," to recover this student (or to help her recover herself). Exhausted by "the topsy-turvy seasons of hell," the young woman emerges from the dual underworlds of the *Aeneid* and the reading room with "her mind so frail her body was its ghost." This condition calls forth the speaker's expressed wish to meet her old self and to reassure her, to "tell her she can rest, she is embodied now." An older self, a stronger mind, a wealth of experience, a life have given to her wearied intelligence a physical presence, a greater durability. But the desire to reassure her former self is, of course, impossible to realize. In the college garden upon which she now looks out, after looking into her past and looking for the woman she once was, the speaker finds only "narcissi / opening too early." The flower is an accurate emblem for the speaker's own activity throughout the poem, her staring at or searching for only herself. And it is doomed, for hell is not the only place whose seasons have gone "topsy-turvy." South winds raise their "bad sound" in the poem's final strophe, threatening rain "from some region which has lost sight of / our futures." The winter will return after this false spring, bringing with it death for the narcissi and the irises, the crocuses and plum blossoms. Aeneas' descent reverses here; hell rises and enters the college garden. The speaker's backward glance, like Orpheus', dooms her younger self's Eurydice to nothing but "what one serious frost can accomplish" (37-38).

Those garden references, though, and the object of the speaker's search—a younger version of herself—suggest another classical resonance, the goddess Ceres' search for her lost daughter, Proserpine. Ceres, of course, was the goddess of agriculture; all the vegetation on view in **"A False Spring"** falls under her mythological mandate. And Ceres famously goes out to find what we might think of as her younger self, her daughter (who has been out gathering the flowers with which the college garden here is filled). Even Proserpine's fate is echoed by the speaker's student-self; kidnapped by Pluto, she is borne off to the underworld, as is the young scholar, consigned to the Dis of a dim reading room and travelling through her set text to hell itself. Like her goddess model, Boland's speaker seems to find the girl she seeks, but, also like Ceres, she cannot ultimately bring her back. The spring is false; Proserpine has always to return to Pluto and her mother annually withdraws and renders the earth barren once again.[7] Likewise, the speaker cannot find or reassure her former self. She seems, indeed, to know this. "I want to find," she says, "I want to tell"; this diction recognizes the prospect of failure. Both losses seem to follow from inefficacious speech. The spring falters because the crocuses "stammer" and the storm's "bad sound" rises.

Indeed, at the heart of this poem, which immediately follows **"The Achill Woman,"** is precisely the ironic crying out of songs with which that poem ends. The remembered student-self has been at work specifically on the Greek shades' reaction to their living enemy's appearance in the underworld:

> how his old battle-foes spotted him there—
>
> how they called and called and called
> only to have it be
> a yell of shadows, an O vanishing in
> the polished waters. . . .

(37)

Boland's language succeeds here in doing what the Greek shades cannot do. It speaks, clothing their calls in sensible sound. And this gives substance to the speaker's wish to tell her earlier self, discorporated by her scholarly labor and the intervening years, "she is embodied now." The poem's words carry the student's frail mind and flesh out her ghostly body, keeping them present in palpable form. So speech and its failure wrestle each other, the fact of words upon the page refuting what the words themselves combine to mean, the language's materiality opposing its meaning. Even as the poem treats this Ceres' inability to rescue her Proserpine, its words—especially in their sounds—strangely succeed.

"The Making of an Irish Goddess" more explicitly imagines its speaker's search for her daughter in terms of Ceres' mythic descent into the underworld.[8] Unlike the earlier poem's speaker, Ceres makes her journey "with no sense of time," and when she looks back she sees only "a seasonless, unscarred earth." But this poem's speaker cannot share the goddess' perspective. Her descent requires the sense of time that yields a sense of history: "I need time— / my flesh and that history— / to make the same descent." Time as experienced by a mortal woman, time as change wrought upon a body, time figured as seasons evolving into one another and as man-made scars stiffening in the earth enables the speaker's vision of what this goddess of agriculture cannot see: "the failed harvests, / the fields rotting to the horizon" (38-39). Time as experienced by a mortal woman and a mother yields a memory the god's-eye view eliminates, the crucial memory of modern Ireland's defining agricultural and historical moment, the Great Famine of the 1840s. The making of an Irish goddess, then, is a quite different thing from the old stories of the Greek and Roman immortals, for it demands a location in the body marked by childbirth, the body stitched, blemished, and scarred. Only out of these traces, in these embodiments of human life and suffering, Boland suggests, can we make "an accurate inscription" of the nation's constitutive trauma.

Boland casts that national trauma, or its recovery in the speaker's present, in the specific bodily terms of the same mother-child relationship that propels Ceres into hell (and that we ought to recognize from **"Night Feed"**). The Famine's most horrific consequence, Boland writes, was mothers devouring their children, dooming the children's souls to hell and following shortly after with their own. The embodied memory of this horror is the "accurate inscription," and it is to be read not in poetic mythologizing or in historical narrative, but on the speaker's own maternal body and in that body's self-protective but revealing gestures:

> In my body,
> neither young now nor fertile,
> and with the marks of childbirth
> still on it,
>
> in my gestures—
> the way I pin my hair to hide
> the stitched, healed blemish of a scar—
> must be
>
> an accurate inscription
> of that agony.

(38)

Like the past self sought by the speaker of **"A False Spring,"** the starving mothers of the Famine are embodied in a contemporary Irish woman.

Where **"A False Spring"** zeroes in on the cries of Aeneas' enemies in the underworld, **"The Making of an Irish Goddess"** enacts not only a Cerean search for her daughter but also an epic echo of Aeneas' descent to confer with the shade of Anchises and to recapitulate, in that moment, the classical figure of *pietas,* the hero leading his son by the hand and carrying his father on his shoulder as Troy burns behind them (*Aeneid,* Book II, lines 920-41).[9] Boland's speaker carries her national/ historical Mother on/in her body and for her daughter. The poem's conclusion aligns the patchwork bits of Ceres and Aeneas to show how the pieces fit:

> holding up my hand
> sickle-shaped, to my eyes
> to pick out
> my own daughter from
> all the other children in the distance;
>
> her back turned to me.
>
> (38)

Patricia Haberstroh reads this image as an oblique reference to Father Time, which, though it picks up on the poem's concern with time and life in it, seems not quite warranted (82).[10] The handier reference, of course, is Ceres, against whom the speaker has identified herself anyway; the goddess of agriculture and the harvest as well as a searcher for her abducted daughter, Ceres is fairly directly indicated by the sickle shape of the speaker's hand. She is the model that myth provides this mother who seeks her own daughter in the distance. But Ceres is an insufficient model, ultimately, which is why an Irish goddess must be made. And the Irish goddess is made, in part, through the experience of time and loss (and the anticipation of loss that follows from her sense of time). More importantly, though, the Irish goddess is fashioned from events that have unfolded over time in Ireland, and from the Famine most of all. The mother here, shading her eyes against the changing light over Dublin foothills, seeks the future (her daughter) like Ceres and finds the past (Famine-era mothers) like Aeneas. Living in time and bearing that past within herself, she finally harvests (with the "sickle-shaped" hand that "picks") her daughter from the present's underworld.

Or does she? The fact of the child's turned back, her failure to return her mother's gaze, grows in light of the poems that follow and make up the spatial, if not the thematic, heart of the sequence. These poems emphasize the ephemeral and the fleeting, the uncontainable lost in the flux of time. **"White Hawthorn in the West of Ireland"** and **"Daphne Heard with Horror the Addresses of the God"** cast doubt on the possibility of capturing natural beauty and the beautified nature of story, and also on the morality of any attempt to preserve these. (That "the god" in the latter poem's title is Apollo, associated through his lyre with lyric poetry, implicates the poet's own practice in this ethical questioning.) Even when significant moments *are* captured, as in **"The Photograph on My Father's Desk"** and **"An Old Steel Engraving,"** Boland focuses attention on these efforts' failures to catch or communicate the living essence of what they depict.

Photographed lavender bears no fragrance and the engraved river neither flashes nor wanders. Moreover, the representations perpetrate a kind of violence; the photographed couple are robbed of breath, while the engraved figure, in strangely Keatsian fashion, forever falls but cannot finally die. At best, Boland suggests in **"An Old Steel Engraving,"** the "spaces on the page . . . widen to include us." At best, in other words, we might inhabit the gaps and margins that surround and separate. These spaces carry the same significance with which Boland imbues negative space in **"Fruit on a Straight-Sided Tray."** They are the "in-between" or distances that shimmer with potential meanings, that structure the relationships between things, people, moments, images, or poetic lines and stanzas.

It is tempting to read the gestures of **"The Making of an Irish Goddess"** in terms famously suggested by Walter Benjamin in his "Theses on the Philosophy of History," to read Boland's imagined simultaneity of contemporary suburban woman and Famine-era mother as the sort of "unique experience with the past" that Benjamin credits the historical materialist with supplying (262). The mother's experience in the poem's evocative moment might, in this light, "blast open the continuum of time" and drag a specific episode from the past into the arrested moment of the present (262-63). But the attention to space urged and enacted in **"An Old Steel Engraving"** resonates much more strongly with Mikhail Bakhtin's notion of *vzhivanie,* or "projection," the intense engagement with an other that at once seeks identification with the other and requires the retention of one's own position in order to set that identification against a broader horizon (25).[11] When we enter the "spaces" around our standard histories' representation and causal linking of individuals and events, we confront others like the nameless and multiple mothers who suffered their children's deaths during the Famine. We descend, motivated by our own needs, by the pressures of our own moment, and confront an other, a host of others, with whom we might identify and empathize even as we hold on to our selves.

To do otherwise, to rest securely in the present and to trust complacently our distance from the history frozen in photographs, engravings, and narratives, to identify with the goddesses and heroes of myth and imagine ourselves like Ceres, with "no sense of time," is to elect myth over history. Or to return, as Boland does, to something like our starting point, such an attitude is the decision to remain, as the speaker of **"The Achill Woman"** remains, "oblivious." Boland's sequence concludes with an affirmation of knowledge over ignorance, of time over oblivion. While the stars remain forever "outside history," while they "keep their distance," the world beneath them offers "a place where you found / you were human, and // a landscape in which you know you are mortal" (50). The stars write mythic figures in the sky's eternity. They provide a means by which we might console ourselves by divining cozy, or at least familiar, futures and assuring ourselves of permanence. The earth, on the other hand, offers death now and in all times, deaths past constructing the deaths of present and future. Boland concludes her sequence with a choice and, appropriately, a gesture:

Out of myth into history I move to be
part of that ordeal
whose darkness is

only now reaching me from those fields,
those rivers clotted as
firmaments with the dead.

(50)

From myth into history. From the light into the dark, where we must feel our way, bereft of heavenly illumination. Such a movement forces us to confront what has happened, is happening, in its concrete particularity. Ireland's fields, rivers, and roads, for one who has let go Ceres, cycles, and the consolations they provide, make up a grisly mirror image of the star-filled sky; they remain full of corpses numerous as the stars, a heaven on earth, as tourist board advertisements might have it, though shot through with the cruel irony history guarantees.

While the Famine is clearly a fundamental reference point for Boland's meditations in **"Outside History,"** it remains unnamed in the sequence itself. Indeed, that sequence's vital work consists, in part, of leaving readers to discover the Famine through the network of associations and elisions Boland fashions from fragments of myth and memory, the bits and pieces she fits together like patchwork (or like **"Patchwork"**). **"Writing in a Time of Violence"** (1994), in contrast, opens with an explicit invocation of the Famine (or its trace in the landscape of Irish history) and clearly establishes the Famine as a key to the sequence. On one hand, Boland's direct exploration of the Famine realizes the resolve with which **"Outside History"** closes; moving "out of myth into history," Boland leaves behind the likes of Ceres and Aeneas and addresses herself to the marks left on the land by a specific and cataclysmic historical event. At the same time, though, Boland's introduction of the Famine through its near invisibility foregrounds the questions of representation and escape that play in counterpoint to the themes announced in the sequence's title. Where **"Outside History"** addressed the textuality of texts not recognized as such, **"Writing in a Time of Violence"** works through the failures and inadequacies of textual representations and, especially, the escapes that they allow. The sequence confronts, and asks us to confront, the problems of writing in a time of violence so as not to write escapes or evasions. Taken as a whole—theme and harmonic background together—**"Writing in a Time of Violence"**

makes clear how hard it is to keep the concluding promise of **"Outside History."**

Boland begins this sequence with an assertion, a bare and bold claim she explicitly sets out to substantiate. **"That the Science of Cartography is Limited"** is at once the title and first line of the sequence's first poem:

That the science of cartography is limited
—and not simply by the fact that this shading of
forest cannot show the fragrance of balsam,
the gloom of cypresses,
is what I wish to prove.

(7)

As evidence in support of her contention, Boland adduces a moment when, early in their relationship, her speaker's lover or husband took her to "the borders of Connacht" and pointed out a "famine road":

I looked down at ivy and the scutch grass
rough-cast stone had
disappeared into as you told me
in the second winter of their ordeal, in

1847, when the crop had failed twice,
Relief Committees gave
the starving Irish such roads to build.

Where they died the road ended.

(7)

All maps are incomplete. Though they might indicate woods with shading or crosshatching, they cannot include the data of our senses on the spot, the rich atmosphere created by our emotional engagement with a place. What remains unrepresented, then, even on the best maps, is history—the marks left on the land by human subjects under a specific set of conditions, circumstances, and constraints. And without their presence on a map, such traces go mostly unnoticed by contemporary travelers and residents. The science of cartography's great flaw is that it cannot indicate change over time, or, more importantly, marks left in time, wounds made by men on earth in time as time ran out. For all that it can do to render three dimensions on a map's flat page (and Boland lists the science's representational advances), cartography cannot, in Pound's famous phrase, "include history." But map making is not alone in this. At the end of this poem, Boland turns her critique of cartographic science against her own representational endeavors:

the line which says woodland and cries hunger
and gives out among sweet pine and cypress,
and finds no horizon

will not be there.

(8)

"The line" refers, of course, to the road's remnant and to its imagined rendering upon a map. But poetry is also made of lines, and Boland knows that in her poem, as much as on a map, the line that she describes, the line that speaks physical details and exclaims the body's sensations of need, "will not be there."

I began this essay claiming that Boland's poems invite us to inhabit a problem, and that if we accept their invitation we work through a problem with some social and political significance. While the poems might not proffer a political solution—and one of Boland's strengths, especially in the sequences I've been discussing, is that she insistently leaves questions unanswered and problems unresolved—the experience of the poem trains us to see the left out, the spaces in between that grant objects and events their meanings. Entering the sequences, we see that the scattered and apparently random bits are pieces, and that the pieces fit (or can be made to fit). We test the continuities and consolations offered by myth and feel the atmospheric change when we move in from outside history. What, though, must we reflect on as we work out **"That the Science of Cartography is Limited"**? That maps leave out landmarks? That poems, too, are always incomplete? Few readers will resist these conclusions. Few need to work through these matters.

The specific event (or set of events) of the Famine, however, reinflects these questions and sharpens their political edge, for what's missing from Boland's maps and poems is what Cormac O'Grada has called "the main event in modern Irish history, as important to Ireland as, say, the French Revolution to France or the Industrial Revolution to England" (*Ireland Before and After the Famine* 174). We might, therefore, encapsulate the problem as Michael Harper does in his devastating treatment of a similar blind spot in "American History": "Can't find what you can't see, / can you?" (196). But wait. We *can* see the Famine (or the road). The line Boland knows "will not be there" *is* there, right in the words that claim its absence. As she does in **"A False Spring,"** Boland plays in this passage with the disjunction between what language says and what it does. The line that "will not be there" occurs three lines above this predicate, occurs as this predicate's subject, as the line which says "the line which says woodland and cries hunger." So the problem hovers around the next step: in her typical fashion, Boland asks us to confront the costs entailed *even* in those acts of seeing which she seems to call for, the costs concomitant with sketching in the missing line, the costs that come with writing in a time of violence.

The sequence's third poem, **"March 1, 1847: By the First Post,"** draws us into writing directly. Cast as a letter from an English (or, perhaps, but less likely, aristocratically Anglo-Irish) woman to "Etty," a friend or relative back in London, the poem's chatty rehearsal of upper-class country life—flowers observed and dresses

sewn—is interrupted by unceasing conversation about the very catastrophe unrecognized by the science of cartography. Not only is the famine noticed here: "*Noone talks of anything but famine*" (11). Boland's imagined correspondent, pining for the pleasures even a dull London season would offer, certainly seems to see the line the map leaves out. And, more importantly, she speaks the line Boland finds missing even in poems. But the young woman's act of writing in a time of famine, rather than confronting and comprehending the event she cannot help but notice, turns immediately to evasion:

> I go nowhere—
> not from door to carriage—but a cloth
> sprinkled with bay rum & rose attar
> is pressed against my mouth.

(11)

Boland's speaker (or writer) says nothing about the causes of the land's unpleasant smell, reporting only on the measures she takes to protect herself from it. More telling even than her described prophylaxis is the offhand phrase that introduces it: "*not from door to carriage.*" Her forays into starved and stinking Ireland begin in shelter and conclude in closed conveyance, each pole locating her firmly outside the affliction (outside history?) and inside spaces closed off from the sufferers.

Two details link **"March 1"** to the poems around it in less than obvious but ultimately revealing ways. The letter's writer mentions, first of all, Etty's "copper silk," a nice bit of characterization and verisimilitude. But the reference also reaches out to the preceding poem, **"The Death of Reason,"** whose central subject, a painter's model, wears "gun-colored silks / To set a seal on Augustan London" even as the flames of Rebellion rage "From Antrim to the Boyne." And to the sequence's next poem, **"In a Bad Light,"** whose speaker comes upon a dress while wandering in a St. Louis museum. Fabrics, then, provide the thread that runs from poem to poem. The Irish seamstresses here also specify the likely agents behind "your copper silk is sewn." Most importantly, the figures Boland binds with "silk" share a position vis-à-vis a history made up of "Peep-O-Day Boys," famine, and "rumours of war." Though none of these women opt for the mythological, though none try to escape into the safety of "domestic interiors," though all stand in historical moments Boland sketches with some specificity and, presumably, notice what goes on around them (one, at least, writes of what she notices), each of the women in silk remains "outside history." Each remains immune from national catastrophe. Each writes off her "time of violence" and bequeaths a document of civilization—portrait, letter, and dress—that conceals its origins in barbarism.

As if to don the silk herself (something her speaker literally does in **"Inscriptions,"** the sequence's sixth poem), Boland sets **"The Dolls Museum in Dublin"** in rhymed (or, more often, slant-rhymed) quatrains:

> The wounds are terrible. The paint is old.
> The cracks along the lips and on the cheeks
> cannot be fixed. The cotton lawn is soiled.
> The arms are ivory dissolved to wax.
>
> (14)

The formal poise and polish of this poem make it stand out in the sequence. While the other poems are built on patterns of image, figure, and sound, only **"The Dolls Museum"** employs the meter and rhyme that, more than anything, define and demarcate the traditional English lyric. Boland's quatrains raise the question of poetic form's preservative and ordering capacities and the relationship between these and the fleeting messiness of history. Form here, in fact, goes beyond raising the question; the quatrains act the problem out by dressing the poem's thematics in something quite like silk.

Throughout the early stanzas, the poem's glossy finish suits the scene it sets, the Anglo-Irish upper classes of Dublin celebrating Easter. Quadrilles, waltzes, promenades, and carriages (an echo from **"March 1"**) conjure the Dublin of over eighty years ago, and the dolls are back in the hands of their young owners. Boland sumptuously describes the city streets, the church's sanctuary, the spring, interrupting only briefly to let history in. While the terraces are filled with "Laughter and gossip," "Rumour and alarm" strike at the barracks. The darkness drops again, or, at least, "Twilight falls," and the shadow of events chills children as they are "cossetting their dolls." Back in the present, the shadows remain; they "are bruises on the [dolls'] stitched cotton clothes." The children are gone, aged into adulthood and, eventually, death, but, protected in their museum display cases, the dolls stand as mute witnesses. Though decaying, they have survived. But their survival comes only at a great cost:

> To have been stronger than
>
> a moment. To be the hostages ignorance
> takes from time and ornament from destiny. Both.
> To be the present of the past. To infer the difference
> with a terrible stare. But not to feel it. And not know
>   it.
>
> (15)

The dolls are versions of the portrait model, Etty's correspondent, and the St. Louis plastic woman. They function as a metonym for the children who carry and fondle them and as a synecdoche for the society that thinks itself immune while it wears seams stitched by the suffering. And we who read the poem are positioned by its form and its thematic handling of stasis and mutability

and by the imperatives of its second stanza—"Recall," "Hum," "Promenade," "Put back"—to act the dolls' part, to inhabit as we "re-create" our own private Dublin. The dolls stare, terribly, but cannot see. They withstand history but cannot witness it. Insentient and inert, they can "infer" the impact of events (in the long tertiary usage of that word to mean something like "suggest," if not in its primary meaning of "to conclude by reasoning") but they can "not feel it. And not know it."

"The Dolls Museum in Dublin" serves a vital function in the sequence, for while readers can easily dismiss or distance themselves from the letter writer of **"March 1,"** they are drawn by form to follow Boland into a position ultimately not all that different from the nameless, inconvenienced young woman's. And the poem's key recognition about the dolls—that they do in fact perform a kind of witness by becoming, like the poem, legible signs in which we can read insights the dolls' own blind eyes and "terrible stares" must miss—tracks back to **"March 1"** as well. In her intent focus on herself and how her path is altered by obstructions the Famine creates, that poem's speaker/writer misses the enormous human tragedy, the historic cataclysm, that surrounds her. But in writing even of her attempts at evasion, she names that history and makes it manifest in her own sentences. The dolls in the museum, or better, **"The Dolls Museum"** partly redeems the figures of the earlier poems by showing that any writing in a time of violence includes the history that it might well seek to set aside, close off, or step over.

This realization has a flip side, though. If we take it seriously, we must apply it to Boland's writing too, and to any writing that, like Boland's, seeks not to escape history but to engage it. Even the best-intentioned acts of literary witness carry unintended significances. But Boland keeps trying to find and draw the lines missing from maps and poems. She keeps trying, however, with a full awareness of the treachery (a loaded word in any context and one even more severely burdened in the case of this Irish poet writing in English words and prosodies, but one I mean with all its heft and harshness) inherent in her project.

That effort continues in Boland's most recent sequence, **"Colony"** (in her 1998 collection, *The Lost Land*). **"Colony"** extends the trajectory I have traced through Boland's earlier sequences, from the intensely personal spaces of **"Domestic Interior"** through the play of national myth and memory of **"Outside History"** to the explicit thematizing of Irish history in **"Writing in a Time of Violence."** The newest sequence, consisting of twelve obliquely linked lyrics, reworks some of the images so crucial in the earlier work: darkness, Dublin, water, and, especially, wounds and scars. Any of these provides a way through the sequence. Darkness falls on a latter-day Irish bard at the end of **"My Country in**

Darkness," approaches again as émigrés leave Dublin in the middle of **"Daughters of Colony,"** looms over Boland's father in **"City of Shadows,"** creeps up from the river on "an ordinary evening" in **"The Colonists,"** and surrounds the speaker as she contemplates a boundary ditch and its dually Irish nomenclature in **"The Mother Tongue."** Scars appear midway through the sequence in **"The Scar,"** where Boland recalls the way her "skin felt different" after she was cut by glass as a child and then asks, "If colony is a wound what will heal it? / After such injuries / what difference do we feel?" (23). Two poems later, **"Unheroic"** wonders about a mysterious hotel guest's unhealing wound and contrasts it with the "unbroken skin" of Dublin's monuments. Finally, Boland knits a whole set of significances into the skillful cicatrix of **"A Habitable Grief":**

> This is what language is:
> a habitable grief. A turn of speech
> for the everyday and ordinary abrasion
> of losses such as this:
>
> which hurts
> just enough to be a scar.
>
> And heals just enough to be a nation.
>
> (32)

I could go on. Water (from the Irish Sea, the River Liffey, and the sky), language itself (most nicely through an allusion to Brendan Behan's Irish-speaking Prisoner C), memory, maps, and Dublin landmarks all recur in various contexts and accumulate symbolic heft and richness both over the course of this sequence and in light of their appearance in Boland's earlier sequences. In **"Colony,"** though, Boland adds to this repertoire the monument, the solid state to which history aspires. Throughout the sequence, she explores through a suggestive set of antitheses the dangers posed by too, too solid stone even as it helps us hold on to what water and darkness threaten, as it helps us read what grows illegible in lost languages, lost lands.

"Unheroic" makes the contrast clearest, when Boland recalls her summer hotel job and the reclusive, rumored-to-be-wounded guest:

> How do I know my country? Let me tell you
> it has been hard to do. And when I do
> go back to difficult knowledge it is not
> to that street or those men raised
> high above the certainties they stood on—
> *Ireland hero history*—but how
>
> I went behind the linen room and up
> the stone stairs and climbed to the top.
> And stood for a moment there, concealed
> by shadows. In a hiding place.
> Waiting to see.

> Waiting to look again.
> Into the patient face of the unhealed.
>
> (27)

In the wounded, fragile living people we encounter, not the dead on pedestals, begin responsibilities. The sequence as a whole serves as a rehearsal of those responsibilities, and I mean that word, *rehearsal,* not only in the sense of ticking off for quick reference but also in the more dramatic sense: Boland invites us, here as throughout the sequences that punctuate her recent career, to work through the specific set of ethical problems posed by Ireland's relatively new nationhood, by its continuing struggle with an old colonial identity.

Notes

1. By "ethical" here I do not mean a prescriptive set of rules but rather what Adam Zachary Newton describes as "recursive, contingent, and interactive dramas of encounter and recognition" crystallized and recirculated "in acts of interpretive engagement" (12). While Newton is specifically interested in narrative fictions, his claim that "certain kinds of textuality parallel this description of the ethical encounter" applies, with some modification, to lyric as well:

   > Cutting athwart the mediating role of reason, narrative [and lyric] situations create an immediacy and force, framing relations of provocation, call, and response that bind . . . reader and text. . . . [T]hese relations will often precede decision and understanding, with consciousness arriving late, after the assumption or imposition of intersubjective ties.
   >
   > (13)

2. See, for example, the 1986 essay, "The Woman Poet: Her Dilemma," in which Boland writes:

   > The more I looked at these images [of women] in Irish poetry, the more uneasy I became. I did not recognize these women. These images could never be a starting point for mine. There was no connection between them and my own poems. How could there be? I was a woman. I stood in an immediate and unambiguous relation to human existences which were only metaphors for male poets. As far as I was concerned, it was the absence of women in the poetic tradition which allowed women in the poems to be simplified. The voice of a woman poet would, I was sure, have precluded such distortion.
   >
   > ("The Woman Poet: Her Dilemma" 43)

3. Though Boland, as the passage quoted in note 2 shows, sometimes makes it seem this simple in her prose. The greater problem with this too-easy resolution is that, while Boland's poetry rarely assumes it, some critics, following the lead of Boland's prose, read her according to this logic, oversimplifying both the poetry and their own critical arguments. See, for example, Conboy,

"'What You Have Seen is Beyond Speech,'" Henigan, "Contemporary Women Poets in Ireland," Cannon, "The Extraordinary Within the Ordinary," and Consalvo, "In Common Usage."

4. Also, as "Outside History," in *Object Lessons: The Life of the Woman and the Poet in Our Time* (123-53).

5. I quote Eagleton here and below because his discussion of the Famine, though brief, is typically pithy and trenchant. The classic historical treatment of the Famine is Cecil Woodham-Smith's *The Great Hunger: Ireland, 1845-1849.* More recent and specialized scholarly work on the Famine includes Cormac O'Grada's *Ireland Before and After the Famine: Explorations in Economic History, 1800-1925,* and his *The Great Irish Famine,* Donal A. Kerr's *'A Nation of Beggars?' Priests, People, and Politics in Famine Ireland, 1845-46,* Austin Bourke's erudite *'The Visitation of God?' The Potato and the Great Irish Famine,* Christine Kinealy's *This Great Calamity: The Irish Famine, 1845-52.*

6. I take this overview from Woodham-Smith, who gives the 2 1/2 million and 25% figures (411-12). For her thorough discussion of the Irish dependence upon the potato and of the land occupation practices and policies that exacerbated the Famine's impact, see 28-37. For her horticulturally informed account of the blight itself, see 38-43. See also Bourke, *'The Visitation of God?' The Potato and the Great Irish Famine.* Woodham-Smith's treatment of British Government policies, centering on Charles Trevelyan and the Treasury, is exhaustive and even-handed; while it extends throughout the book as a whole, its central conclusions are reprised on 407-11. On the fever that followed famine between 1846 and 1849, see Woodham-Smith, 188-205.

7. Ovid, Boland's likely source for her retellings of the Ceres myth, includes a passage quite in line with "Outside History"'s Famine background. Upon first finding that her daughter is missing, Ceres

> reproached all the lands of the earth, calling them ungrateful, undeserving of the gift of corn. . . . She broke with cruel hands the ploughs which turned up the earth, and in her anger condemned the farmers and the oxen which worked their fields to perish alike by plague. She ordered the fields to betray their trust, and caused seed to be diseased. The land whose fertility had been vaunted throughout the whole world lay barren, treacherously disappointing men's hopes. Crops perished as soon as their first shoots appeared. They were destroyed, now by too much sun, now by torrential rain: winds and stormy seasons harmed them,

> and greedy birds pecked up the seeds as they were sown. Tares and thistles and grass, which could not be kept down, ruined the corn harvest.

(*Metamorphoses* 128-29)

8. The trip with which Boland begins the poem is, of course, a trip the goddess does not make in classical sources. In Ovid's version, quite probably the one with which Boland is most familiar and on which she draws, Ceres hears of Proserpine's fate from the nymph Arethusa in Book V of the *Metamorphoses*:

> suffice it now, that the earth opened up a way for me and, after passing deep down through its lowest caverns, I lifted up my head again in these regions, and saw the stars which had grown strange to me. So it happened that, while I was gliding through the Stygian pool beneath the earth, there I saw your Proserpine, with my own eyes.

(*Metamorphoses* 129)

9.
> 'Then come, dear father, Arms around my neck:
> I'll take you on my shoulders, no great weight.
> Whatever happens, both will face the danger,
> Find one safety. Iulus will come with me,
> My wife a good interval behind.[']
> . . .
> When I had said this, over my breadth of shoulder
> And bent neck, I spread out a lion skin
> For tawny cloak and stooped to take [Anchises']
> weight.
> Then little Iulus put his hand in mine
> And came with shorter steps beside his father.

(*Aeneid* 58; lines 921-25; 936-41)

Incidentally, Creusa, Aeneas' wife, is lost in that "good interval," left behind in the confusion of Aeneas' flight from Troy.

10. I concur, however, with the sentences that frame Haberstroh's gloss: "Transferring Ceres' suffering over the loss of her daughter to a Dublin mother who anticipates such a loss, the speaker links her own feelings to those of the mythic woman. But she also identifies with Father Time, for the hand shading her eyes is shaped like his sickle. The Irish goddess, seeking an 'accurate inscription' of her fear and loss, sets it within history" (82).

11. Bakhtin, in *Art and Answerability,* elaborates this concept, which he describes as an intense engagement with an other that at once seeks identification with the other and requires the retention of one's own position in order to set that identification against a broader horizon. Bakhtin uses the example of a suffering person to clarify the concept ("Let us say that there is a human being before me who is suffering"). The sufferer "does not see the agonizing tension of his own muscles, does not see the entire, plastically consummated posture of his own body or the expression of suf-

fering on his own face. He does not see the clear blue sky against the background of which his suffering outward image is delineated for me. . . . I must put myself in his place and then, after returning to my own place, 'fill in' his horizon through that excess of seeing which opens out from this, my own, place outside him" (*Art and Answerability* 25). See also Newton's discussion (85-86).

Works Cited

Bakhtin, Mikhail. *Art and Answerability: Early Philosophical Essays.* Ed. Michael Holquist and Vladimir Liapunov. Austin: U of Texas P, 1990.

Benjamin, Walter. "Theses on the Philosophy of History." *Illuminations.* Ed. Hannah Arendt. New York: Schocken, 1968.

Boland, Eavan. *In a Time of Violence.* New York: W. W. Norton, 1994.

———. *A Kind of Scar: The Woman Poet in a National Tradition.* Dublin: Attic, 1989.

———. *The Lost Land.* New York: W. W. Norton, 1998.

———. *Object Lessons: The Life of the Woman and the Poet in Our Time.* New York: W. W. Norton, 1995.

———. *Outside History: Selected Poems 1980-1990.* New York: W. W. Norton, 1990.

———. "The Woman Poet: Her Dilemma." *Midland Review* 3 (1986): 40-47.

Bourke, Austin. *'The Visitation of God?' The Potato and the Great Irish Famine.* Dublin: Lilliput, 1993.

Cannon, M. Louise. "The Extraordinary Within the Ordinary: The Poetry of Eavan Boland and Nuala Ni Dhomhnaill." *South Atlantic Review* 60.2 (1995): 31-46.

Conboy, Sheila. "'What You Have Seen is Beyond Speech': Female Journeys in the Poetry of Eavan Boland and Eilean Ni Chuilleanain." *Canadian Journal of Irish Studies* 16 (1990):65-71.

Consalvo, Deborah McWilliams. "In Common Usage: Eavan Boland's Poetic Voice." *Eire-Ireland* 28.2 (1993): 100-15.

Eagleton, Terry. *Heathcliff and the Great Hunger: Studies in Irish Culture.* London: Verso, 1995.

Haberstroh, Patricia. *Women Creating Women: Contemporary Irish Women Poets.* Syracuse: Syracuse UP, 1996.

Hagen, Patricia L., and Thomas W. Zelman. "'We Were Never on the Scene of the Crime': Eavan Boland's Repossession of History." *Twentieth-Century Literature* 37.4 (1991): 442-53.

Harper, Michael. *Images of Kin: New and Selected Poems.* Urbana: U of Illinois P, 1977.

Henigan, Robert. "Contemporary Women Poets in Ireland." *Concerning Poetry* 18.1-2 (1985): 103-15.

Kerr, Donal A. *'A Nation of Beggars?' Priests, People, and Politics in Famine Ireland, 1845-46.* Oxford: Oxford UP, 1994.

Kinealy, Christine. *This Great Calamity: The Irish Famine, 1845-52.* Dublin: Gill and MacMillan, 1994.

Logan, William. Review of *Outside History: Selected Poems 1980-1990. New York Times Book Review* 21 April 1991: 22.

MacGuinness, Arthur E. "Hearth and History: Poetry by Contemporary Irish Women." *Cultural Contexts and Literary Idioms in Contemporary Irish Literature.* Ed. Michael Kenneally. Gerrards Cross: Colin Smythe, 1988. 197-220.

Newton, Adam Zachary. *Narrative Ethics.* Cambridge: Harvard UP, 1995.

O'Grada, Cormac. *The Great Irish Famine.* London: Economic History Society (MacMillan), 1989.

———. *Ireland Before and After the Famine: Explorations in Economic History, 1800-1925.* Manchester: Manchester UP, 1988.

Ovid. *Metamorphoses.* Trans. Mary M. Innes. London: Penguin, 1955.

Virgil. *Aeneid.* Trans. Robert Fitzgerald. New York: Random House, 1983.

Woodham-Smith, Cecil. *The Great Hunger: Ireland, 1845-1849.* New York: Harper and Row, 1962.

Catriona Clutterbuck (essay date December 1999)

SOURCE: Clutterbuck, Catriona. "Irish Critical Responses to Self-Representation in Eavan Boland." *Colby Quarterly* 35, no. 4 (December 1999): 275-87.

[*In the following essay, Clutterbuck addresses the critical reaction to issues of feminism and nationalism in Boland's verse.*]

This article examines Irish critical responses to a central issue in Eavan Boland's work, responses which were published during eight years of vital development, not only in her own aesthetic, but in her reputation as an artist and in the wider position of women in Irish cultural and political life. In 1987, the results of abortion and divorce referenda in the Republic had consolidated restrictive socio-sexual ideologies; access to contraception was legally restricted; the country was in the grip of recession, large-scale emigration and (though unrecognized at the time) widespread institutionalized corruption in its economic affairs; and the level of publication of Irish women's poetry, though noticeably on the increase, had not affected general debate on Irish poetry. By 1995, divorce was legalized and open access to contraception and abortion information and the right to travel abroad for an abortion had been legally safeguarded in the South; the Republic was accustomed to the new communitarian energies of a highly successful woman Head of State; and women representatives North and South in community groups, the media, and local and national politics were successfully challenging traditional approaches to public policy. Such change elicited the optimistic claim in a recent mapping of the Irish women's movement that "[f]eminism has become a transformational politics and a comprehensive ideology that encompasses every level of Irish society".[1] The exponential increase in the publication of Irish women's poetry between 1987 and 1995 is both catalyst and effect of this larger change.[2] The period is bracketed by Eavan Boland's publication of the first and the final versions of what would become one of the most important essays in Irish literary culture, titled "The Woman Poet in a National Tradition" in 1987, "A Kind of Scar" in 1989, and by 1995, when collected in Boland's volume of prose, retitled again as "Outside History".[3] This essay, as we will see, makes a statement about the relations between Irish women past and present, Boland herself as poet, and the Irish nation, which has focused response to this writer around the issue of self-representation ever since.

This article examines and responds to these trends, many of which were operative in Boland criticism before 1987 and are still operative at the time of writing. But the eight-year slot under examination here—in which these currents in the criticism of one woman poet found most direct expression—coincides with a period of great controversy in gender politics in Irish literary culture, exemplified for most witnesses by the acrimonious and still-resonating 1992 debate over equity of representation of male and female authors and editors in *The Field Day Anthology of Irish Writing*. That coincidence is not accidental: Boland criticism helps reveal the larger debate and vice versa. The following discussion does not claim comprehensiveness, either with regard to the quantity of Irish critics dealt with in the field of Boland studies, or the full extent of each of their engagements with the poet's work. Neither does it claim that the trends it identifies are exclusive to Irish sources working on Boland. Its aim is to illuminate the manner in which poetry's force field becomes active through the critical environment in which poems are embedded, as seen with reference to one poet, in an Irish context at a particular point in history.

The three developments named above—of Boland's poetry, of that poetry's reputation, and of Irish feminism—can each be said to be partly facilitated by the peculiarly complementary relationship which Eavan Boland effected in the late eighties and early nineties between the mediums of poetry and prose. Many critics of Boland (of all nationalities) assumed an unproblematic continuity between these two genres in her work at this time.[4] This assumption underwrote responses to Boland, responses which in Ireland tended to be based on her reputation as much as on her poetry. This is perhaps an inevitable feature of local reaction to a poet in the period of major expansion of her international reputation, but in the case of Eavan Boland, another factor came into play. The issue of her reputation was brought to the fore by Irish and non-Irish criticism alike as a result of the habit of reading her poems as being, first and foremost, disguised political tracts. Boland has been both praised and condemned under this apprehension for many years, and a recent consequence among Irish critics is a particularly outspoken brand of negative criticism of the quality of form in Boland's 1998 volume *The Lost Land.*[5] This latest focus of critique is a product of a longer-seeded underlying suspicion that a Boland industry prompting mimetic criticism is flourishing:[6] that is, that the poet's own carefully planted commentary on her poetic practice may be surfacing as other critics' "autonomously" developed critical insight on the poems themselves.[7]

However, the anxiety that Boland effects ventriloquism through the voices of acolytes does not arise solely through reaction to "less astute" criticism of Boland, it also arises through a serious, but, I would argue, incomplete, reading of her poetry. It is both ironic and, perhaps, predictable, that a suspected condition of the expansion of Boland's reputation—her control of ventriloquism—is an actual condition of her development as a poet. In Boland's acts of ventriloquism in her poems, a double substitution is registered. First, there is the substitution of the macrocosm of a generalized multiple subjecthood for the microcosm of her personal sense of identity;[8] second is found her substitution of a philosophy of positivism, whereby historical loss can be retrieved, for a philosophy of negativism—whereby that loss can only be exposed. (In Boland's negativism she seems to castigate politics' and culture's culpability in destructing individual identity, especially that of the female; in her positivism she calls for the return of that self.) The most notable incidence of this complex ventriloquism, and hence the keynote for the following discussion, is, appropriately, itself structured upon an interchange—that between the two categories Boland most intimately associates with realized identity: womanhood and nationhood. Boland's famous statement in the essay "Outside History" glosses both the rendering universal of her own personal context and the rendering positive of the profoundly negative conditions described:

> The truths of womanhood and the defeats of a nation?
> An improbable intersection? At first sight perhaps. Yet
> the idea of it opened doors in my mind which had

hitherto been closed fast. I began to think that there was indeed a connection; that my womanhood and my nationhood were meshed and linked at some root. . . . I was excited by the idea that if there really was an emblematic relation between the defeats of woman-hood and the suffering of a nation, I need only prove the first in order to reveal the second. If so, then Irish-ness and womanhood, those tormenting fragments of my youth, could at last stand in for one another. Out of a painful apprenticeship and an ethical dusk, the laws of metaphor beckoned me.[9]

Here, an implied positivism succeeds a definite negativ-ism *because* the hinge between them is definable as literary form—"the laws of metaphor". Boland's aesthetic is based on an ideology of estrangement—a negativism both caused and made dynamic by its as-sociation with linguistic representation.

However, the prominent position of language in Boland tended to be neglected in the many critical interpreta-tions of her aesthetic by Irish critics in the period under review, which rejected its basis in negativism. These analyses concerned themselves with the poet's direct political relevance and tended to overlook her poetry's aesthetic impact, which is alone what enables any poetry's larger engagement with systems of representa-tion. Jennifer Fitzgerald, in a review of the above-quoted essay redeveloped as the pamphlet *A Kind of Scar,* argued that "[Boland's] identification throughout of women with suffering, and therefore with passivity, does nothing to nurture their power".[10] Terence Brown, in his approval of Boland, also pinned her to an overt political standard: "The sovereign self finds itself in redundancy and loss, and discovers, even, a community of loss in which forgotten forms of solidarity can be as-sumed and built upon."[11] Brown's use of the terms "sovereign self" and "building upon solidarity", in its advocacy of an unproblematically coherent replacement identity, contradicts his earlier statement of acceptance of Boland's ideology of estrangement here. This may happen because in this review of *The Journey and Other Poems,* Brown has responded to the active, engaged and affirmative tone of the poems' speakers without fully noticing that Boland's ideology of estrangement is paradoxically present *in* the very language of "solidarity" that is used by the poems' politically capable speakers, a language which is itself under interrogation in the texts. That didacticism in the voice of her speakers is the essential feature of Boland's radical act of ventriloquism. Through it she makes overt the principles on which the authority of the poet rests. Critics, neglecting this reflexive aspect of the voices, found the authoritarianism which this overtness gives rise to, either inspiring or misguidedly arrogant. Both of these positions under-read Boland through their assump-tion that her didacticism can only be outward-directed, away from her own role as writer, functioning solely to support her theme of the political visibility of the

subject in iconic and verbal representation (**"Mise Eire"**[12] and **"The Achill Woman"** [*C.P.* 148] in particular providing apparently quintessential evidence).

This self-reflexivity in her work, when noted, was often regarded as a problem. For example, Gerald Dawe in a 1992 essay questioned many of the poems of *Night Feed* because "their design upon us becomes transpar-ent and the guiding light of subjectivity is overshadowed by Boland's critical intelligence . . . while the medita-tions on language which characterize Eavan Boland's more recent work provide her poetry with an intellectual order, they also threaten to distract rather than strengthen the imaginative focus on her 'self'".[13] This argument valuably supports focus on the subjective in the poem but limits its terms by suggesting that self-reflexivity should apply only to the authorial, representative self and not to the text's complementary role in interrogat-ing the position of the poet in that controlling role. The fact of Boland's focus on linguistic self-reflexivity at-tracted censure from many such critics who otherwise celebrate her focus on the private zone. Lachlann MacKinnon, in his review of *The Journey,* protested: "When she conceals her art, Eavan Boland can be memorable and unnervingly honed, but when she does not she is hardly an artist at all."[14] But Catherine By-ron's similar reservations regarding *The Journey and Other Poems* unwittingly pinpointed the rationale behind Boland's position, suggesting that textual self-reflexivity does indeed problematize the traditional status and function of content in the poem: "More and more the poetry seems purely self-reflexive. Beneath the make-up and the dimity, behind all those sketched-in apparent portraits, is—Eavan Boland, with a pen in her hand and a mirror before her. . . . In all the beauty of Boland's pictures it is the substantiality of [the] truth beneath that I begin to miss. She is superb at presenting us with the wrappings, the bandages, the face-paint of her women. . . . But what of substance, of 'truth', lies beneath her obsessive fabrics?"[15] What may be opera-tive in the criticism I am discussing here, is a blind spot regarding the invigilation conducted by the formal, *of* the biographical form of self-reflexivity, in Boland's work.

This feature of response to Boland is not, of course, confined to Irish critics in this period, and must be seen within its historical context. Jody Allen-Randolph's doubts about the element of textual self-reflexivity in Boland are related to the impetus, particularly urgent in the late 1980s and early 1990s and shared by many Irish critics, to celebrate in Boland's poems the recovery of an unproblematically representative subject-position for Irish women. Allen-Randolph argued in a 1993 es-say: "It was in *Night Feed* (1982) that Boland . . . harnessed a poetic self to a powerful private vision. By moving the lyrical persona closer to the material, she achieved the radiantly unified sensibility that would carry her forward into the impressive technical advances of *The Journey* (1987) and *Outside History* (1990)."[16] Allen-Randolph is correct in that Boland did move her lyrical persona closer to her material in *Night Feed* (by opting finally for her own life-experience as primary subject matter) and that this is a major enabling tool in her later work (and indeed most obviously distinguishes the later from her earlier work). The problem here, however, is the assumption that the achievement of a "radiantly unified sensibility" is what makes possible the technical advances of the later volumes. Instead I would argue that it is the poet's developing insight into, and power to foreground within the texts, the *disunified* sensibility which bears on the poems, which leads to their effect.

An important result of this blind spot regarding the link between subjectivity and form, is the particular kind of attention devoted to the issue of gender in Boland in these years. Both positive and negative commentary on Boland which did *not* take this self-reflexive capacity into account, responded to what was interpreted as her single-minded ambassadorship for women and women poets. For Edna Longley in 1995, Boland's work loads the scales by which she is assessed through her production of poetry "that underlines its own feminist credentials".[17] Anne Fogarty's 1994 assessment of Boland counters this by arguing for the *absence* of a specifically feminist aesthetic in the poet's output and rejecting the tendency to automatically associate gender as subject matter with Boland's (and Medbh McGuckian's) poetic achievement: "They stress their difference of perspective as women but refuse the suggestion that their writing is on these grounds alone radical or other."[18] Whether under challenge or not, such intense attention paid to a narrowly defined category of politicized feminist consciousness for the source of Boland's emblematic status resulted in these years in critics' neglect of a proper assessment of the wider effect of the role of gender in her aesthetic—namely, its impact on her prevailing thematic and textual concern with subjectivity.

Barra O'Seaghdha and Ann Owens Weekes, for example, took up opposed positions on the question of the relevance of the overtly political theme of women in Boland, while respectively discounting or not attending to the equally important politics of the gendered *textual* self in the poet's work. Barra O'Seaghdha's 1990 comment on Boland's pamphlet *A Kind of Scar* suggests that the problem of gender-discrimination in Irish writing may have already been solved, thus he said: "The linguistic gestures are those of someone handling volatile material, moving it with the greatest care, explaining every precaution. In the absence of actual explosive, these measures come across as over-cautious, almost fussy."[19] Ann Owens Weekes, in opposition, argued for the continuing relevance of an overtly

politicized support for women in Boland's work. For her (speaking in 1994), the poems offer "a sharp reminder that contemporary women's lives are—like those of their mothers—in danger of being lost, becoming wound, if women accept traditional mythic and literary concepts of female value and domesticity".[20]

In the late 1990s, at a remove from the fraught Irish literary-political wars that centred on gender in the early 1990s in which oppositional and monodimensional critical positions became entrenched, it has become clearer that Boland's intention as a poet is to investigate and subvert systems of authority implicit in women's (mis)representation, and that only by raising representation over women in the order of her concern as poet can she truly engage with this vital feminist concern. Peter Sirr, in his review of *The Journey and Other Poems,* suggests this priority:

> We are aware . . . of a combination of willed identification and forceful intellect as submerged lives are invoked. . . . The presence of the poetic self, the consciousness of the thing being made are characteristically overt: this is a poetry determined always to define its own terms. . . . With other poets this kind of editorial tight rein is a liability, but here the impression is of an intelligence pushing itself surely and moving outwards rather than disappearing in its own self-consciousness.[21]

Gender is not a subordinate issue to that of textuality in Boland; rather, it cannot be fully recognized without attending to the question of representation. Boland's work suggests that the impact of gender as focused through textuality can only be registered by *inverting* this equation and first concentrating on the impact of textuality as focused through gender.

Not only is the artistic act Boland's primary theme, but that theme is presented using herself as exemplar of the potential for creation and abuse in the poet's role. Critics who acknowledged Boland's exposure of the devices of image-making,[22] in general paid insufficient attention to the formal potential of Boland exposing her *own* use of these devices.[23] Boland throughout this period was gradually opening up for inspection within her own poems the basis of power in the creative act, and the in-built capacity of art to abuse that power.[24] She became more and more aware of her own complicity in the cultural constructing of identity on trial in her poetry. Her poetry's assured voice is a mask she wears to be reflected in the mirror of critical response to her work, a mirror obliquely angled both at herself and at the authoritarian society ironically but aptly symbolized by the literary critic whom she also represents.

This focus by Boland in her texts on her own complicity with what she condemns, her own questioning of the representative function of the authorial self, was generally under-read by Irish critics at this time. For Denis Donoghue, Boland's manner of centring themes via the self is problematic. Reviewing **In a Time of Violence,** he said: "Her themes issue from her personal life or from other lives she draws into her own. . . . [I]f her tenderness takes the form of brooding on those lives, she rarely imagines them apart from her brooding."[25] Donoghue resisted Boland's personalization of poetic material because of his objection to her option for the representative self: "She tends to see herself in a dramatic and representative light, such that her censoriousness is to be understood as exemplary, her moods as universally significant. Her representative 'suburban' woman has only to stand in a garden in Dundrum to feel the whole natural world ministering to her disposition as if the fate of nations hung upon it. . . . She evidently assumes that the natural world and the elements it contains have nothing better to do than to sustain her allegories."[26] This critique, ironically, bears close resemblances to Boland's own oft-stated aversion to the figure of the self-conscious Romantic poet.[27] If we accept that for Boland the role of the poet is to confront the representation of the self by exploring the *processes* of both representing herself and representing through herself, then it follows that Donoghue is likely to be under-reading Boland here. His negative reaction to her work may have arisen through a distaste for the element of theatricality which is essential to the play of "self" in poems as above described. The subtext of Donoghue's critique suggests that it is not the poet's representativeness that is at stake so much as her public consciousness, acceptance and assertion of it.

The unsuitability of the representative self for Gerardine Meaney centred, not on the infringement of ego-taboos as a result of claiming representativeness, but on the problems raised by casting the net too wide. In a 1993 essay, Meaney questioned Boland's "insistence on women's 'experience' as having, in every place and every time, some common factor".[28] Speaking of the poet's linking of her student self with the old woman in **"The Achill Woman",** Meaney says: "The extent to which nationality, gender or even womanhood can have the same meaning for these two women is occluded . . . the poet's right to be witness, the spokesperson for the other woman's recollections, and to make an 'emblem' of that woman are unquestioned."[29] But if the differences between the two women are not occluded so much as being allowed to become indistinct in a process of empathizing which is also watched by its own active agent (the mature poet), then we see a writer who is not ignoring but highlighting and investigating the processes of takeover of identity through simultaneous cultural and textual ventriloquism.

The Achill woman also became the focus of Edna Longley's 1990 LIP pamphlet critique of Boland. Longley, like Donoghue and Meaney, objected to Boland's drive towards cohesion. For her, this meant neither the fact of Boland's *self*-appointment as representative, which Donoghue censured, nor the fact of the poet's claim to *widely* represent, as queried by Meaney. Instead Longley questioned Boland's "unitary assumptions" about the *fact* of the nation in relation to which the poet works out her identity in the essay and poem from which the Achill woman figure is derived.[30] Longley considered that Boland may have checkmated any critique she makes of the false construction of female identity by Irish culture because the poet has opted to negotiate with the idea of nation: "Because she does not blame Nationalism, her alternative Muse turns out to be the twin sister of Dark Rosaleen. . . . Boland's new muse . . . looks remarkably like the Sean Bhean Bhocht."[31] Longley—in suggesting that Boland was unaware of her own continuing slavishness to the ideology of nation—like Donoghue and Meaney was neglecting the self-reflexive basis of Boland's work upon which the poet's sharp critique of nation is founded.

Ann Owens Weekes suggested this self-reflexive basis in her response to Edna Longley's disapproval of Boland: "Boland is in fact condemning the young poet she was. . . . It is true that Boland does not allow the figure of the Achill woman to speak in her poem. To do so would have been easy, but inaccurate and a contradiction of the argument, the self-condemnation of the poem. The ethical relationship of image to experience demands this relationship."[32] However, this self-condemnation (that is, personal self-reflexivity) should itself be viewed through the lens of textual self-reflexivity in order to realize its radical potential. Edna Longley's commentary focuses on the former in its reaction to a Boland preconditioned by (positive) critical commentary: for her, Jody Allen-Randolph's commentary on **"The Journey"** "accurately summarizes the poem's ambition",[33] though not, Longley argued, its success in fulfilling it. In the context of her premise that "Boland has been too easily allowed to set the terms of her own agenda",[34] it can be said that Longley was reading Boland via the criticism rather than reading the criticism via Boland. The terms which Longley used for what is missing in **"The Journey"** are revealing: "No interior dialogue or psycho-drama connects 'Sappho', the speaker's poetry books and sleeping children, and a female underworld of cholera and typhus victims."[35] Longley here called for an unforced "interior dialogue" between the speaker and the subjects of the poem, but overlooked the poem's attempt to initiate a *self-reflexive* dialogue between that speaker and the *failure* of the poetic process that this text is specifically witness to, which is also the poem's subject. In other words, the poem needs to be read in the broader context of its own production. Therefore, when Longley found fault with **"The Journey"** for being "a programmatic inversion rather than a creative subversion of male poetic myth-making", she ironically touched on the actual risky strategy which Boland was in the early stages of developing in this 1987 volume—a creative direction based on Boland's literary as well as socio-political critical impulse.

The criticism dealt with so far, finds its focus through an examination of the *nature* of the representative link between private and public spheres in Eavan Boland's aesthetic; however, a more radical critique arises when the very *fact* of that link is called into question. Such criticism was offered by Clair Wills in a 1991 essay on Irish women's poetry. Like Edna Longley, Wills's argument was concerned with the issue of Boland's use of nation, but, whereas Longley disapproved of Boland's choice of nation as the public sphere which must be related to, Wills objected to Boland's assumption that *any* public construct (which in Boland's case happens to be nation) could be guaranteed by a separable private sphere called "self".

Wills criticised the idea of a public/private symbiosis in Irish poetry through an interrogation of the actual concept of witnessing or representation. For Wills, "The nationalist poet's role is to bear witness, thus enabling 'a restoration of the culture to itself', a restoration which like all restorations opposes itself to modernity, losing itself in a nostalgic celebration of a pure, organic and monocultural society."[36] Wills associated Boland with this nationalist agenda because of the poet's custodial concern with the metaphorical link between nation and gender: "the writer who rejects the association of woman and land thereby questions the relationship between poet and community".[37] Wills diagnosed Boland, however, as being so intent on carving out a place for the woman poet in the public sphere of "nation"—by means of the "personal dimension"—that she as poet does not question whether the very nature of the link between public and private can even be called "representational":

> To gain a place in the construction of the idea of a nation Boland turns to experiential testimony. The linkage of femininity and the idea of nation is accepted, and her objections turn on the simplifications which both have undergone in male writing. . . . Her argument could be summed up as a version of 'No taxation without representation'; Boland is, in effect, a suffragette. She seeks not to challenge the basis of the poet's authority, but to widen the political constituency, adding women to the electoral rolls.[38]

For Wills, however, the private cannot *represent* the public because the private *is* public already. Wills established this theory in the context of the debate on women and nation in Irish poetry, specifically in relation to Eavan Boland's poem, **"Mise Eire"**:

> Privacy, defined as the domestic, is not the residence of the unique and individual, the non-communicable. It is a social institution with genres, codes and a semantics.

Moreover 'Mise Eire' knows this. For all that we seem to be offered a woman's 'private' thoughts on her 'personal' situation, what the poem in fact stresses is that her sexuality is publicly owned (through prostitution), her personal story *is* a public narrative. So even though one might want to reject the symbolization of the dispossession of the nation through a woman's rape, any attempt to be possessive in one's turn, even self-possessed, is doomed to failure.[39]

For Wills, as a result, "Boland herself does not so much represent female experience as trope it"[40] in service to the power-politics of poetry: "A trope of privacy appears . . . the function of which is to allow women to accede to the role of poet."[41] Anne Fogarty suggests the same ultimate reason for the poetics used by Boland and McGuckian which—in contrast to Wills's idea of the troping of privacy—she names as "a shadowplay of feint and counterfeit . . . [a] denial of all positionality [as] the only means by which they can licence their creativity".[42] Fogarty assigns this practice of "feint and counterfeit" by Boland and McGuckian to the poets' awareness of the pitfalls of feminist essentialism rather than those of individualist essentialism which Wills warns against. Fogarty states: "Because of the way in which patriarchy controls literary structures they are both painfully aware of the fact that the incorporation of women's experience into poetry may be as much a betrayal and a distortion as a triumphant breakthrough."[43] Clair Wills made a sharp distinction between Boland and McGuckian in her assessment of the degree of awareness which Fogarty here credits to both women poets. Wills's is a severe critique because it accuses Boland, using the principle tenet—if not the name—of what is Boland's own principled rejection of a romantic tradition which she sees operating within Irish poetry to guarantee problematically the power of the poet. Wills's assessment that Boland tropes privacy is accurate, but as I have argued, Boland's poetry, particularly her later work, specifically uses the poet-speaker's complicity here identified by Wills, as an essential part of its effect.

During the period under review, the status of language in Boland's work became increasingly recognized by her critics as vital to her effect. It is the heightened profile of language which is at the heart of Boland's defence of a state of loss, exile or lack as the basis of identity inside the poem. However, a positivist impulse in Irish criticism asserts that Boland's aesthetic, in Lacanian terms, resists the symbolic domain predicated as it is upon loss, and posits as ideal a return to the Imaginary (linked to the Kristevean semiotic). Gerardine Meaney worked within the terms of this tendency in her 1993 argument that for Boland: "Language and reality, particularly women's reality, cannot be rejoined",[44] but that this is something which Boland regrets: "the scar left by violent incorporation into the symbolic is also the mark of resistance to that economy of separation".[45] **"The Journey"**, she argued, "is haunted by a sense of the inevitability of the loss of the mother, and of the accession to language as separation from that mother. It posits poetry as a reversal of this process."[46] For Meaney, therefore, although Boland accepts the symbolic she resists it: "Despite its resistance to exile in language, Boland's poetry is eventually forced to recognize that it is only really at home in that strange place."[47] Anne Fogarty similarly claimed that Boland resists the symbolic domain, through a recognition of Boland's and McGuckian's consciousness of the gap between written and writing selves: "Through their insistence on a distinction between their real-life identities and their fictional personae they indicate that there is a gap between the materiality of women's existences and literature which their poetry cannot close. Both poets . . . fear a dissolution of experience into language. Often, indeed, the female subjectivity which they describe finds no accommodation in language."[48] For Fogarty, as for Meaney (though less regretfully), Boland's language cannot thereby be assumed to have entered the semiotic realm: "Boland recognizes that the simple insistence on the tangible immediacy of historical experience is not in itself sufficient for the creation of a new language. . . . Despite its feminism, [her] work cannot readily be aligned with any preconceived belief in a hidden, radical dynamic in women's language."[49]

One could argue, however, that the challenge of Boland lies in her demonstration that subjectivity *per se* does not find accommodation in language, rather, that language, specifically the language of poetry, finds its accommodation in subjectivity. If language and reality *could* be rejoined, there would be no need for the poem—or for the self as poet—and Boland recognizes this at a fundamental level of her aesthetic. In fact, I would argue, Boland *embraces* the symbolic and the power that comes with it; she does not posit poetry as a reversal of the separation from the mother because this would suggest that she required poetry—which is of the symbolic realm—to reverse the action of its own zone of operation. This would demand that poetry annihilate itself. While a poet like Derek Mahon, whose aesthetic links itself closely with Boland's in its sensitivity to the voices of the silent, was once drawn to this option,[50] Eavan Boland has never been. There is a positive undercurrent of celebration in the states of exile Eavan Boland declares, for these bring about the "new language" that is poetry—a "passable imitation"[51] of what it recognizes—and approves—as lost to it in "reality". In her most recent volumes which deal with the experience of ageing, the speaker is finally her own embodiment of the state of loss of self that brings about the presence of the "self" within the poem, and so the tracing of that destruction is firmer than ever before.

Irish criticism of Eavan Boland varies from the defensive to the accusatory, from the reverent to the irritated, from the coolly observant to the mystified, from the celebratory to the outrightly dismissive. These divisions too often function as ammunition for a wearying internecine literary warfare through which an impotence symptomized by lack of contextualization incubates under cover of the country's reputation for robust literary critical life. Critics' differences could instead testify to shared principles with regard to literature's potential to intervene critically in the projects of self-recognition and development of Irish peoples. These principles are more likely to be active when a critic's approach to the primary text involves viewing comparatively and situating historically the body of criticism it has generated, of which their own work forms a part. In adopting this approach, it is important to remember that good criticism generates real engagement with texts and cultural contexts, as much for the individual who actively disagrees with it, as it does for those who find themselves in inspired consensus with it. Bad criticism, on the other hand, is more concerned to establish the impact of the critic than that of either the literature under examination or the aspiration to self-critical growth in Irish life which that literature could facilitate. There is thus a concordance between the kind of vigilant focus on egotism which I have argued is central to the complex self-representation in Boland's work, and that which might be explored in the criticism framing it and other Irish writing. It is in this way that the status of the critic may be said to be interchangeable with that of the artist, and Boland's complementary relationship between prose and poetry comes to make sense.

Notes

1. Linda Connolly, "From Revolution to Devolution: Mapping the Contemporary Women's Movement in Ireland", Anne Byrne and Madeleine Leonard, eds., *Women and Irish Society: A Sociological Reader* (Belfast: Beyond the Pale Publications, 1997), 566.

2. Roughly the same number of women (about fifty) began publishing poetry in book format in Ireland between 1987 and 1995 as had begun publishing in that format during the previous fifty years. For statistical details and analysis see Joan McBreen, *The White Page/An Bhileog Bhán:Twentieth Century Irish Women Poets* (Cliffs of Moher: Salmon Press, 1999), and Catriona Clutterbuck, "Irish Women's Poetry and the Republic of Ireland: Formalism as Form", *Writing in the Republic: Literature, Culture Politics in the Republic of Ireland, 1949-1999,* ed. Ray Ryan (Basingstoke: Macmillan Press), forthcoming in 2000.

3. Eavan Boland, "The Woman Poet in a National Tradition", *Studies* 76.302 (Summer 1987): 148-

58; *A Kind of Scar: The Woman Poet in a National Tradition,* LIP Pamphlet (Dublin: Attic Press, 1989); "Outside History", *Object Lessons: The Life of the Woman and the Poet in Our Time* (Manchester: Carcanet Press, 1995), 123-53.

4. See, for example, Edna Longley's reaction to Boland's poem "The Journey", which responded to Jody Allen-Randolph's article and interview with Boland, both published in the 1993 *Irish University Review Special Issue* on Boland, in which Longley concludes: "there seems to be convergence between the language of the poem, the interview and the critical article". "Irish Bards and American Audiences", *The Southern Review* 31.3 (Summer 1995): 765.

5. See, for example, Peter McDonald, "Extreme Prejudice" (review of Eavan Boland, *The Lost Land*), *Metre* 6 (Summer 1999): 85-89.

6. See, for example, Peter Sirr's comment, "It shouldn't be necessary to praise everything [about Boland's work] simply because the work fits into a particular political perspective, or to create the kind of critical atmosphere around the work where to question any aspect of it is to be consigned to a doghouse for the unreconstructed." 'The Figures in the Tablecloth" (review of Anthony Roche and Jody Allen-Randolph, eds., *Irish University Review* 23.1 *Special Issue: Eavan Boland*), *Irish Times* 26 June 1993: 8.

7. See Edna Longley's critique of Boland in particular, especially that in "Irish Bards and American Audiences" (op. cit.).

8. Sean Dunne's approving comment on Boland suggests this position, "by finding a voice for herself she has found a voice for us all". "Tugged Thread" (review of Eavan Boland, *In a Time of Violence*), *Irish Times* 26 March 1994: 9.

9. Boland, "Outside History", *Object Lessons,* 148.

10. Jennifer Fitzgerald, "No Glorious Inheritance" (review of Eavan Boland, *A Kind of Scar: The Woman Poet in a National Tradition*), *The Honest Ulsterman* 91:84.

11. Terence Brown, "The In-Betweens" (review of Eavan Boland, *The Journey and Other Poems*), *Graph* 2 (Spring 1987): 7.

12. Eavan Boland, *Collected Poems* (Manchester: Carcanet Press, 1995), 102.

13. Gerald Dawe, "The Suburban Night", *Against Piety: Essays in Irish Poetry* (Belfast: Lagan Press, 1995), 179, 182.

14. Lachlann MacKinnon, "A Material Fascination" (review of Eavan Boland, *The Journey and Other Poems*), *Times Literary Supplement* 4.403 (21 Aug. 1987): 904.

15. Catherine Byron, "Bandaged but Unhealed" (review of Eavan Boland, *The Journey and Other Poems*), *Poetry Review* 77.4 (Winter 1987/88): 50.

16. Jody Allen-Randolph, "Private Worlds, Public Realities: Eavan Boland's Poetry 1967-1990", *Irish University Review* 23.1 (Spring/Summer 1993): 13.

17. Edna Longley, "Irish Bards and American Audiences", 764.

18. Anne Fogarty, "A Noise of Myth", *Paragraph* 17.1 (1994): 93.

19. Barra O'Seaghdha, "Journeywomen" (review of Eavan Boland, *A Kind of Scar: The Woman Poet in a National Tradition*), *Graph* 8 (Summer 1990): 6.

20. Ann Owens Weekes, "An Origin Like Water: The Poetry of Eavan Boland and Modernist Critiques of Irish Literature", *Irishness and Postmodernism,* ed. John S. Rickard (Lewisburg: Bucknell UP, 1994), 169.

21. Peter Sirr, "The Muse in the Psychic Suburb" (review of Eavan Boland, *The Journey and Other Poems*), *Irish Times* 31 Jan. 1987: 5.

22. See, for example, Sylvia Kelly, who praises *In Her Own Image* because "[r]ead as a whole these poems become a narrative of despair and hope, informing the reader of both the devices which create an icon and the poet's knowledge of female suffering". "The Silent Cage and Female Creativity in *In Her Own Image*", *Irish University Review* 23.1 (Spring/Summer 1993): 47.

23. Anne Fogarty, however, clearly highlights Boland's focus on narrative subjectivity. Of the poem "Anorexic" Fogarty remarks: "The security blanket of disengagement is removed. The lyric 'I' is no longer male, transcendent and universalizing, rather it is female, specific and self-critical." "A Noise of Myth", 98.

24. For analyses of this feature in Boland, see Margaret Mills Harper, "First Principles and Last Things: Death and the Poetry of Eavan Boland and Audre Lorde", *Representing Ireland: Gender, Class, Nationality,* ed. Susan Shaw Sailer (Gainesville: UP of Florida, 1997), 181-93, and Catriona Clutterbuck, "Irish Women's Poetry and the Republic of Ireland: Formalism as Form" (op. cit.).

25. Denis Donoghue, "The Delirium of the Brave" (review of Eavan Boland, *In a Time of Violence*), *The New York Review of Books* 41.10 (26 May 1994): 26.

26. Ibid. The tone of Donoghue's critique was anticipated in reviews such as John Jordon's, which praised *The Journey* as illustrating Boland

at her "least affectedly winsome to date". "A Worthy Quarter" (review of Eavan Boland, *The Journey and Other Poems*), *Poetry Ireland Review* 20 (1987): 62.

27. See Boland's essay, "The Woman Poet: Her Dilemma", *Object Lessons,* 239-54.

28. Gerardine Meaney, "Myth, History and the Politics of Subjectivity: Eavan Boland and Irish Women's Writing", *Women: A Cultural Review* 4.2 (Autumn 1993): 142. For similarly based critiques, see Fitzgerald, "No Glorious Inheritance", 83, and Augustine Martin, "Quest and Vision: *The Journey*", *Irish University Review* 23.1 (Spring/Summer 1993): 82, 83.

29. Meaney, "Myth, History and the Politics of Subjectivity", 140.

30. Edna Longley, "From Cathleen to Anorexia", *The Living Stream: Literature and Revisionism in Ireland* (Newcastle-Upon-Tyne: Bloodaxe Books, 1994), 187.

31. Ibid., 188.

32. Weekes, "An Origin Like Water", 175.

33. Longley, "Irish Bards and American Audiences", 765.

34. Ibid., 764.

35. Ibid., 765.

36. Clair Wills, "Contemporary Irish Women Poets: The Privatization of Myth", *Diverse Voices: Essays on Twentieth Century Women Writers in English,* ed. Harriet Devine Jump (Hemel Hempstead: Harvester Wheatsheaf, 1991), 255.

37. Ibid.

38. Ibid., 256, 257.

39. Ibid., 258, 259.

40. Ibid., 258.

41. Ibid., 259.

42. Fogarty, "A Noise of Myth", 97.

43. Ibid.

44. Meaney, "Myth, History and the Politics of Subjectivity", 151.

45. Ibid., 152.

46. Ibid., 151. See also Ann Owens Weekes, who similarly rejects the symbolic on Boland's behalf. "An Origin Like Water", 162.

47. Meaney, "Myth, History and the Politics of Subjectivity", 152.

48. Anne Fogarty, "A Noise of Myth", 93.

49. Ibid., 98, 94.

50. See, for example, Derek Mahon, "Ovid in Tomis", *The Hunt by Night* (Oxford: Oxford UP, 1982), 37.

51. Eavan Boland, "Mise Eire", *Collected Poems,* 102.

Jacqueline Belanger (essay date September 2000)

SOURCE: Belanger, Jacqueline. "'The Laws of Metaphor': Reading Eavan Boland's 'Anorexic' in an Irish Context." *Colby Quarterly* 36, no. 3 (September 2000): 242-51.

[*In the following essay, Belanger maintains that Boland's poem "Anorexic" "best illustrates her attempts to reinsert excluded realities of female experience into an Irish poetic tradition and to explore the implications of the allegorisation of nation as woman."*]

In her 1989 pamphlet, *A Kind of Scar: The Woman Poet in a National Tradition,* Dublin poet Eavan Boland describes her search for a way to locate herself in an Irish poetic tradition and for ways to render her experiences of being an Irish woman into poetry; what she found in this search, however, was what she terms "a rhetoric of imagery which alienated me: a fusion of the national and the feminine which seemed to simplify both" (76). She found a tradition dominated by representations of Ireland as woman, a tradition which elided the real human suffering women had experienced throughout Irish history. It became her determination, she says in this pamphlet, to repossess Irish poetry by undoing the simplifications in its use of women as passive, emblematic, decorative and mythic figures. Throughout her poetry, Boland attempts to expand the parameters of what is deemed acceptable subject matter for Irish poetry by inserting female experiences of their bodies into her work and by problematising the intersection between womanhood and nation.

Nine years before this pamphlet was written, Boland had begun this project of repossession and reinscription with her collection of poems entitled *In Her Own Image,* and it is this collection, and one poem in particular, entitled **"Anorexic",** on which I will be focusing my attention. The overall project of this volume of poems is to explore women's experiences of their own bodies; Boland locates these experiences in poems dealing with domestic violence, anorexia, mastectomy, masturbation and menstruation. In taking these as her subjects, Boland is using arguably some of the most taboo of female experiences in order to broaden a poetic tradition which had hitherto only admitted women in spiritualised and sanitised form. In using the extremes of female bodily experience, Boland illustrates exactly how far the image of Ireland as woman is from Irish women's experiences with and within their own bodies. However, Boland is ultimately still seeking an emblematic relationship between Irish women and Ireland:

> The truths of womanhood and the defeats of a nation? An improbable intersection? At first sight perhaps. Yet the idea of it opened doors in my mind which had hitherto been closed fast. . . . I was excited by the idea that if there really was an emblematic relation between the defeats of womanhood and the suffering of a nation, I need only prove the first in order to reveal the second. If so, then Irishness and womanhood, those tormenting fragments of my youth, could at last stand in for one another. Out of a painful apprenticeship and an ethical dusk, the laws of metaphor beckoned me.

> (*A Kind of Scar* 89)

It is exactly these "laws of metaphor" which will be explored here. While a metaphorical reading of anorexia is possible for this poem, as a metaphorical reading is for many, if not all, of the poems in this collection, reading anorexia in this way not only obscures the actuality of physical pain but also continues to mystify the issue of hunger and starvation in an Irish context—a mystification which becomes even more problematic in the context of political hunger strikes.

Susie Orbach is one of the first feminist scholars to have read anorexia as a metaphor for contemporary Western life: "The starvation amidst plenty, the denial set against the desire, the striving for invisibility versus the wish to be seen—these key features of anorexia—are metaphors for our age" (24). Orbach, in attempting to read anorexia in this way, runs the risk of denying the physical experience of the illness itself. Jody Allen-Randolph suggests in her reading of this poem that "[u]sing anorexia as both an illness and as a metaphor for culture, Boland probes the relationship between anorexia and myths of human origin which fashion women as virgins or whores" (52). Allen-Randolph does not, however, problematise this reading of anorexia as both experience and metaphor. This issue does need to be explored in terms of the specific possibilities for reading anorexia as metaphor in an Irish post-colonial context, and in terms of the problems this reading might present in light of the explicit use of starvation for political ends both in Irish history and in contemporary Northern Ireland.

In using these "laws of metaphor" for issues such as anorexia, Boland does indeed call into question rhetoric which excludes women's bodily experiences; but, in using anorexia in this way, she also obscures the bodily suffering she sought to make visible in the first place. This article will first present a reading of this poem in

terms of its connections to representations of women and Ireland, and will question the extent to which Boland problematises issues surrounding self-mutilation and self-sacrifice in the Irish context. The various ways in which we may read Boland's poem as simply reinstating the metaphorical parameters in which Ireland is constructed as woman will be examined, using the issue of Irish hunger strikes to attempt to explore some of the tensions which these metaphorical connections introduce when read in a specific context.

While many of Boland's poems—particularly those contained in the volume *In Her Own Image*—have been read in terms of *ecriture feminine,* this is not the project of this particular paper. While reading these poems in this way is useful and illuminating, the critics who have done so have not engaged with the specifically Irish context in which Boland so explicitly situates herself. This is to obscure the fact that Boland is seeking not so much to explode tradition, but to expand it and situate a variety of female experiences within it. Furthermore, critics who have sought to read this volume in terms of "a writing which flows from the experience of the body" (Allen-Randolph 55) perhaps ignore that this way of writing is problematised in these poems because they ultimately deny the very physical actuality they seek to reinstate.

The tradition which Boland sees herself as confronting is one in which Ireland has often been allegorised as female. Irish representations of their own nation, as C. L. Innes has pointed out, have tended to fall into two categories: Ireland represented as either the maiden or the mother figure. At various points these constructions of Ireland as woman intersect with Christian iconography surrounding the Virgin Mary and with notions of the female muse acting as inspiration to the male poet. Indeed, these constructions converge in the Irish aisling poem, a genre in which Ireland appears in a vision to the poet as a suffering maiden calling for rescue from colonial invaders. The result of these representations is the construction of woman in Irish discourse as a spiritualised, suffering and ultimately disempowered figure.

So entrenched has this figure become in Irish discourse, that even those writers such as Seamus Heaney, in poems such as "Act of Union" and "Ocean's Love to Ireland", who would not necessarily endorse the nationalist rhetoric linked with the trope of Ireland as woman, continue to use this construction in their poetry in order to comment on Ireland's postcolonial status. In the collection *In Her Own Image,* Boland is engaging both with allegorical representations of Irish womanhood and with the nationalist ideologies which inform and are reinforced by them.[1]

It is Boland's poem **"Anorexic"** which best illustrates her attempts to reinsert excluded realities of female experience into an Irish poetic tradition and to explore the implications of the allegorisation of nation as woman. **"Anorexic"** enacts and describes the separation of the female "self" from the body. The woman speaker sees her body as an "it", an alien "other"—a point emphasised by the speaker referring to her body as "she", "her", and "the bitch".[2] The speaker's body is an "other" with whom she is engaged in an adversarial struggle to the death. According to Susan Bordo, a critic who has examined anorexia as the locus of various cultural pressures, anorexics "experience hunger as an alien invader, marching to the tune of its own seemingly arbitrary whims, disconnected from any normal self-regulating mechanisms. Indeed, it could not possibly be so connected, for it is experienced as coming from an area outside the self" (25).

In seeing her identity as severed from her bodily "other", the woman speaker re-enacts the splitting of self from other which occurs in discourses of colonial encounters; in the Irish context, the severing of the woman from her body acts to interrogate the impact on Irish women of a poetic tradition which requires the woman to be disembodied in order to stand for Ireland. The Irish anorexic is represented by Boland as a figure attempting to come to terms with a discourse which denies her own bodily self in its common everyday experiences of hunger and sexual desire. In this context, Boland's representation of the anorexic woman in this poem is the extreme example of a tradition which continuously requires women to be spiritualised and separated from the material body. The speaker of the poem starves her body into a form "thin as a rib", and it is this image of the phallic rib which carries the speaker through the rest of the poem. She imagines starving herself back into a male body in a reversal of Eve's creation from Adam's rib, eventually starving herself into her "original" existence as Adam's rib itself:

How warm it was and wide

once by a warm drum,
once by the song of his breath
and in his sleeping side.

Only a little more,
only a few more days
sinless, foodless.

I will slip
back into him again
as if I had never been away.

Starving herself becomes a means of spiritual purification, a state in which she becomes "sinless", rid of the "heretic" flesh, the body which she describes as a "witch". This notion of holiness and starvation is continued in the next lines of the poem, when the speaker imagines herself pre-Fall, before woman's physical desires came to symbolise all that is base:

Caged so
I will grow
angular and holy

past pain
keeping his heart
such company

as will make me forget
in a small space
the fall

into forked dark,
into python needs
heaving to hips and breasts
and lips and heat
and sweat and fat and greed.

The woman wishes to starve herself into a time before the association of "sweat and fat and greed" with woman's "curves and paps and wiles", as it is articulated in the poem. The speaker explicitly associates the physical reality of her existence, her body, with "greed", with insatiable desire which comes from her body—and which results in "sweat" from the sexual act—and with fat from attempting to satisfy her hunger for food. She wishes to do away with any curves on her body at all: "I am starved and curveless. / I am skin and bone." She starves herself in order to do away with all that represents her desire and female body. She attempts to spiritualise herself, make herself "holy", in a re-enactment of the way in which she has been spiritualised in Irish poetic and political rhetoric. This is the impact of the collision of the rhetoric of woman as Ireland with the body of an Irish woman: the speaker talks of her "self-denials" which scorch her body (perhaps even purifying it), and this can be read as the actual denial of food, the denial of the desire for food, as well as the speaker's literally denying her *self* an existence.

In representing the desire on the part of the anorexic Irish woman to return to a state of pre-Fall innocence, to a time when she was not faced with the contradictions inherent in possessing a body which poetic discourse virtually denies her, Boland is also engaging with a specifically Irish reconstruction of the Fall. In doing this, Boland explores the implications of the fusion of the national with the feminine for contemporary attempts to come to terms with historical suffering in the process of creating the Irish nation. In the Irish reworking of the story of Adam and Eve's fall and expulsion from paradise, the first Norman conquerors are brought into Ireland as a result of a woman's infidelity—thus the history of Ireland's status as a colonised nation is constructed as having a woman's desire as its cause. It is the anorexic's desire to efface her sexual, desiring self in this specifically Irish context that represents the attempt to return to a pre-Fall, pre-colonised notion of Ireland—a desire frequently expressed in nationalist rhetoric. It is this construction of the woman's role in Irish colonisation that has led in some ways to the continuing need for the representation of Irish womanhood as suffering for the nationalist cause. As a result of her sexual transgression, and of her role as catalyst to Irish colonisation, Irish womanhood is appropriated and represented as both betrayer and betrayed. In the construction of colonial and nationalist discourse, she is made to give up her children in the struggle for independence and is used as an empty emblem to inspire Irish men to fight for Ireland-as-woman.

However, it can be argued that Boland is using the anorexic speaker of her poem to undermine the notion of redemption through female suffering which underlies many of the representations of Ireland as woman. In discussing the novels of two Francophone Caribbean writers, Myriam Warner-Vieyra and Suzanne Dracius-Pinalie, the critic Françoise Lionnet argues that "the physical suffering of the main female characters functions as a code for denouncing an unsettling situation: the ambiguous status, the legacy of a colonial past. . . . The suffering is the consequence of a spiritual quest that drives the heroines to exile in their search for lost origins" (89). The use of the illness anorexia allows Boland to point out in its most extreme form "the illusion through which the return to the past and physical suffering can play a mediating role in the search for authenticity" (Lionnet 91).

These observations are illuminating for Boland's work in that they point to an interrogation not only of a legacy of the colonial past in Ireland, but also of the nationalist rhetorics used in anti-colonial and postcolonial discourse. In this poem, Boland is questioning whether what is in reality disempowering self-mutilation can really be equated with an heroic and spiritualised idea of self-sacrifice—a question which becomes even more important in terms of the overtly political uses of starvation in hunger strikes. In the poem **"Anorexic"** Boland sees as fruitless the disembodiment of woman into pure emblem, specifically in terms of the notion that through this disembodiment Ireland can return to a mythic, pre-colonial state of unitary and authentic Irishness. This disembodiment is ultimately a sterile, unproductive rhetorical gesture. The anorexic starving herself to death comes to stand not only for the suffering of women who have traditionally been excluded from an Irish poetic tradition, but also for the literally self-defeating gesture of using suffering to return to an idealised past. In describing the self-mutilation of the anorexic in terms associated with (religious) self-sacrifice (holy, sinless—purified, spiritualised, and literally disembodied), Boland shows Irish poetic rhetoric for what it really is—ultimately disempowering and alienating for Irish women.

However, the intersection of metaphor and illness in this poem is such that, even while using the suffering represented by anorexia as a way to undermine a search for one type of "authenticity"—that of the nationalism posited by some Irish male poets—the poem reinstates another metaphorical connection between woman and nation in its place. The issue for Boland seems to be not so much the intersection of nation and woman, but the complete omission of human pain in the process of allegorisation. In locating these poems in such visceral forms of female bodily suffering, Boland is attempting to describe real women's suffering at its most tangible level. However, the reading of anorexia as metaphor enacts and in many ways continues to mystify the ways in which women's experience of their own bodies becomes metaphor for a contemporary woman poet's place in the Irish Republic.

Northern Irish poet Paul Muldoon explicitly makes the connection between the sterility of Irish nationalist rhetoric and the representation of Ireland as woman in his poem "Aisling", written at the time of nationalist hunger strikes in Northern Ireland in 1981. As I mentioned earlier, the "aisling" is a particular type of Irish poem in which Ireland is allegorised as female, and in his version, Muldoon sardonically substitutes the figure "Anorexia" for the traditional suffering maiden:

> Was she Aurora, or the goddess Flora,
> Artemidora, or Venus bright,
> or Anorexia, who left
> a lemon stain on my flannel sheet?

> *(New Selected Poems* 79)

Hunger strikers, in consciously using starvation for political ends, are in some ways conflating notions of wilful starvation as self-mutilation with notions of self-sacrifice. How, then, is one to separate readings of hunger in the Irish context as unconscious acts expressing individual psychological issues and conscious acts of political protests, when writers such as Boland use anorexia as a metaphor for women's place within the contemporary Irish Republic?[3] In using the figure of "Anorexia" in this way, Muldoon points up the contradictions inherent in the glorification of self-mutilation as heroic sacrifice. In conflating "Anorexia" with female figures both actual and mythological, Muldoon makes "Anorexia" the very real woman who left a "lemon stain on my flannel sheet[s]", and possibly deflates the idea of starvation as somehow heroic, as above the reality of bodily experience. That the hunger striker in this poem has called off his strike also acts to deflate these notions of a heroic aspect to self-inflicted pain.

The connection between anorexia and a political hunger strike is made by Orbach, and her theorising can be useful in attempting to understand some of the problems of reading anorexia as metaphor in an Irish context. Orbach sees anorexia as in some ways protest against demands placed on Western women's desires:

> A woman who overrides her hunger and systematically refuses to eat is in effect on a hunger strike. Like the hunger striker, the anorectic is starving, she is longing to eat, she is desperate for food. Like the hunger striker, she is in protest at her conditions. Like the hunger striker, she has taken as her weapon a refusal to eat. Like the suffragettes at the turn of the century in the United Kingdom or the political prisoners in the contemporary world, she is giving urgent voice to her protest. . . . She is driven to act in a dramatic and seemingly self-punishing way through the conviction that she jeopardises her cause if she eats, just like the explicitly political prisoner. But unlike her fellow hunger strikers, she may not be able to articulate the basis of her cause. The hunger strike may be her only form of protest. To situate the act of not eating in the realm of the political is to shed a new light on both the activity and the plight of the anorectic woman. We begin to see anorexia as an attempt at empowering, and the food refusal as the action of one whose cause has been derogated, dismissed, or denied.
>
> (101-02)

The key here is that while the hunger strikers articulate their cause explicitly—they are using their bodies as a metaphor for larger political issues—in Orbach's understanding it is the doctor's or the psychiatrist's (or, perhaps in this case, the literary critic's) ability to read and interpret the metaphor of the woman's body which allows one to understand the "reality" behind the physical illness:

> While she may not be able to talk directly about her cause, we can begin to decipher her language. The text we read is the transformation of her body and her activity of food refusal. A seemingly incoherent set of actions and activities begins to display the outlines of something quite purposeful. She expresses with her body what she cannot tell us with words.
>
> (102)

Even though the anorectic is not actually conscious of her "cause" of self-assertion, one is able to read it as being so—to "translate" and "decode" the meanings she herself cannot express. In this reading, the woman's body literally becomes a sign with which she expresses herself, it is the tool which she has available.

As Irish critic Edna Longley observes, "in blaming the hunger-strikers' emaciation on their idealised cause . . . [Muldoon] equates that cause with a form of physical and psychic breakdown. 'Anorexia' is thus Cathleen Ni Houlihan [one of the many allegorisations of Ireland as woman] in a terminal condition. Anorexic patients pursue an unreal self-image—in practice, a death-wish. Similarly, the nationalist dream may have declined into a destructive neurosis" (162). Ultimately the question must be asked, is the anorexic of Boland's poem, like

that of Muldoon's "Aisling", yet another construction of the woman-as-Ireland trope? Is Boland appropriating the painful experience of a woman's struggle with anorexia in her attempts to "repossess" Irish tradition?

As Orbach's formulations suggest, there are many problems in reading anorexia as a form of the overtly political protest of the hunger strike; for example, would it be valid to say that, much as in the case of the political prisoner in Northern Ireland, whose only weapon might be his or her body, Boland is asserting that a woman's body as represented in poetry is the most important weapon to fight the aestheticisation of women that has occurred in Irish poetry? These slippage seem problematic on a number of levels. What Orbach's, Muldoon's, and, ultimately, Boland's use of the anorexic have in common is the denial of the specificity of the bodily and psychological experience of anorexia. While Boland herself does not equate anorexia with an overtly political hunger strike, and indeed undermines in many ways the rhetoric of female self-sacrifice which legitimates the ability to read starvation as somehow heroic, she is using anorexia to make a larger political point, and in this way is indeed on a continuum with Longley's formulation of "Anorexia" as yet another woman-as-Ireland figure. Boland's poems, while expanding the parameters of female experience admitted into the "canon" of Irish poetry, do not ultimately take apart the limits of these parameters which insist on woman, and women's bodies, as being read metaphorically.

Boland's poem suggests a reading of illness as metaphor which ultimately defies the ostensible project of this poem, and of the whole volume in general: that is, in setting up her project specifically as reinstating the actualities of female bodily experience back into Irish poetry, of defying the sanitised images of woman as muse and woman as nation, Boland situates her poems in actual female experience. However, from the very first poem, it is established that these poems are responses to images of Ireland as woman, which immediately enables a reading of these poems in terms of women's place in postcolonial Ireland. In doing this, illness can be read metaphorically, and in this way defies the project of representing the actuality of women's experience. Her two projects—representing Irish women's "complicated human suffering" and reconnecting the "intersection" of womanhood and nationhood (*A Kind of Scar* 89)—would perhaps seem to be, if not mutually exclusive, at least fraught with contradictions. In attempting to link the personal and the political in a new way, Boland has subverted the very project she has set for herself. In attempting to reinstate new metaphorical connections between woman and Ireland, Boland has reinstated a reading of woman's bodily experience which ultimately denies the actual painful reality of its existence. In attempting to construct metaphors for her own experience as an Irish woman poet, Boland actually obscures the ways in which metaphors of woman as nation are constructed in the first place.

Reading anorexia as metaphor in an Irish context has disturbing implications for readings of self-starvation across a range of experiences in both the Republic and Northern Ireland. However, it would perhaps be incorrect to say that anorexia should never be read in terms of metaphor, as it could be said that reading illness as metaphor in a postcolonial context could be productive of meaning both for the ways in which illness is viewed across a range of cultures and for the ways in which women in postcolonial societies have experienced colonisation and decolonisation.[4] As the body has been the site and subject of both colonial and postcolonial representations, the use of the physical body as an emblem and means of protest against colonial (and, in the case of anorexia in women, patriarchal) domination generates and allows for readings of illness as a metaphor for the impacts of colonial and postcolonial experiences on colonised peoples. What must be reinstated, however—and this has not always been the case in readings of **"Anorexic"** in terms of *ecriture feminine*—is an acknowledgement of the Irish postcolonial context in which ***In Her Own Image*** was produced, as this context opens up important and problematic issues otherwise obscured.

Notes

1. When I speak of nationalist discourse, I am referring both to that deployed in the Irish struggle for independence in the nineteenth and early twentieth centuries and also to that in contemporary Northern Ireland.

2. All quotations taken from Eavan Boland, *In Her Own Image.*

3. Hunger strikes had long been used in Ireland and in Catholicism as a means of protest: "The Brehon Laws allowed a creditor to hungerstrike at his debtor's door until terms of repayment could be agreed upon. In Roman Catholic tradition, St. Eusabius [sic] had fasted for ten days rather than take food from a heretic" (75). Used by Irish suffragettes such as Hannah Sheehy-Skeffington, it was during the Irish Civil War in 1922-23 that female Republicans began to use hunger strikes to protest against the Free State government. It is in one of these protesters that representations of Ireland as woman and the political use of the starving body come together most powerfully: Maud Gonne-MacBride, the actress and activist, began a hunger strike in Kilmainham Prison in 1923 after being detained for Republican activities. She had previously played Cathleen Ni Hou-lihan, one of the many representations of Ireland as woman, onstage, and cultivated this image for herself in her own political activities. Here was the powerful Yeatsian embodiment of Ireland starving herself to death for the Republican cause (Fallon, "Civil War Hunger Strikes").

4. See, for example, the use of eating disorders in Caribbean author Suzanne Dracius-Pinalie's novel *L'autre qui danse* and in Zimbabwean author Tsitsi Dangarembga's *Nervous Conditions*. See also Derek Wright's "Illness as Metaphor in Nuruddin Farah's Novels" in *New Literatures Review.*

Works Cited

Allen-Randolph, Jody. "Ecriture Feminine and the Authorship of the Self in Eavan Boland's *In Her Own Image.*" *Colby Quarterly* 27.1 (1991): 48-59.

Boland, Eavan. *In Her Own Image.* Dublin: Arlen, 1980.

———. *A Kind of Scar: The Woman Poet in a National Tradition.* LIP Pamphlet. Dublin: Attic, 1989.

Bordo, Susan. *Unbearable Weight: Feminism, Western Culture, and the Body.* Berkeley: U of California P, 1993.

Dangarembga, Tsitsi. *Nervous Conditions.* Seattle: Seal Press, 1989.

Dracius-Pinalie, Suzanne. *L'autre qui danse.* Paris: Seghers, 1989.

Fallon, Charlotte. "Civil War Hungerstrikes: Women and Men." *Éire-Ireland* 22.3 (1987): 75-91.

Innes, C. L. *Woman and Nation in Irish Literature and Society, 1880-1935.* New York. Harvester Wheatsheaf. 1933.

Lionnet, Françoise. *Postcolonial Representations: Women, Literature, Identity.* Ithaca: Cornell UP, 1995.

Longley, Edna. *From Cathleen to Anorexia: The Breakdown of Irelands.* LIP Pamphlet. Dublin: Arlen, 1990.

Muldoon, Paul. *New Selected Poems 1968-1994.* London: Faber, 1996.

Orbach, Susie. *Hunger Strike: The Anorectic's Struggle as a Metaphor for Our Age.* London: Faber, 1986.

Wright, Derek. "Illness as Metaphor in Nuruddin Farah's Novels." *New Literatures Review* 30 (1995): 31-45.

Paul Keen (essay date September 2000)

SOURCE: Keen, Paul. "The Doubled Edge: Identity and Alterity in the Poetry of Eavan Boland and Nuala Ní Dhomhnaill." *Mosaic* 33, no. 3 (September 2000): 19-34.

[In the following essay, Keen places the poetry of Boland and Nuala Ní Dhomhnaill in relation to their writings on gender, nationalism, and history.]

In November 1994, the Irish government collapsed. Its disintegration was all the more dramatic because the Taoiseach, Albert Reynolds, was enjoying unprecedented popularity for his role in brokering an IRA cease-fire and securing the prospect of peace negotiations. Within weeks he had resigned in disgrace over his promotion of Harry Whelehan to president of the high court after it emerged that Whelehan, while serving as attorney-general, had delayed for seven months a warrant for the extradition of a paedophilic priest, Father Brendan Smyth. Reflecting on these events, the Irish columnist Fintan O'Toole suggested that like the surreal Irish novel *At Swim-Two-Birds,* the debacle had not one but several beginnings. One was the news in 1992 that the Bishop of Galway had fathered a son and used Church funds to pay for his upbringing. A second was the Beef Tribunal's final report, which provided "tangible, if complicated evidence of a murky relationship between politics, business, and the administration of the state," an impression that was reinforced by the fact that Whelehan, acting as Reynolds's attorney-general, had taken legal action barring the Tribunal from inquiring into cabinet decisions. A third was the infamous "X" case, in which Whelehan, again acting as attorney-general, took out a High Court injunction to prevent a fourteen-year-old girl, pregnant as a result of rape, from leaving Ireland to have an abortion in England. The speed with which the attorney-general's office had acted to prevent the girl's abortion highlighted the gravity of its seven-month delay in dealing with the warrant for the extradition of Father Smyth.

The irony of Reynolds's fall from grace, O'Toole suggested, was that despite Reynolds's insistence on the importance of his continuing role in securing peace in Northern Ireland, the cease-fire was itself evidence that Sinn Fein had recognized the force of a growing spirit of liberalization, which both Fianna Fáil and the Church failed to grasp. Behind the resignation of Albert Reynolds and the IRA cease-fire was a momentum "towards democracy, and away from all forms of private power, whether it be the brute force of private armies, the subtle hints of senior churchmen, or the discreet intimacies of the cabinet room" (O'Toole).

One could multiply the beginnings to this story, all of which reinforce O'Toole's impression of a gathering momentum of popular expectations about the accountability of different forms of power. One could point to the Field Day controversy as yet another beginning. Seamus Deane, the general editor of the Field Day anthology, envisioned the project as one that would emphasize both the continuities and the contingencies of Ireland's overlapping traditions. It would highlight the authenticating power of these various—sometimes competing, sometimes complementary—claims to historical continuity, and stress their necessarily constructed nature (24). Unfortunately for Field Day,

the anthology's cultural revisionism was turned back against it by critics who saw the under-representation of women writers as symptomatic of the exclusionary nature of the deeply masculinist narratives of Irish culture.

Faced with the broader asymmetries that the Field Day fiasco suggests, many women writers have engaged with Irish history by inhabiting these cultural contradictions rather than by attempting to respond from some originary position outside of history. In doing so, their poetry becomes a kind of critical performativity that highlights the extent to which entrenched narratives are products of often invisible, always highly complex, social relations. Whatever the Field Day anthology's success in this regard, Deane's comment that "there should perhaps be a moratorium on words like 'tradition', 'identity', their plurals and all their associated cohorts," serves as an even more fitting description of the work of many Irish women writing poetry today (23-24). To the extent that they have performed Deane's reconsideration of Irish culture by levering gender and nationalist issues against each other in ways that unsettle the hegemonic weight of entrenched assumptions, their task is the double one of creating a discursive space in which women's voices might be heard, and—what is perhaps more difficult—understanding *how* these voices might be represented without collapsing back into a newly essentialized femininity. I want to explore the nature of these complications in the work of Eavan Boland and Nuala Ní Dhomhnaill, perhaps the two women poets who, in different but overlapping ways, are most explicit about their relationship to Ireland's cultural traditions. Both have been eloquent participants in the struggle to challenge in traditional Irish poetry "an ideological superficiality [. . .] that disproportionately projects a masculine perception and imagination" (McWilliams Consalvo 103). Their work exposes what Jody Allen-Randolph describes as an "ethical fault-line in Irish poetry" that locates women as ornaments rather than producers of literature (15).

The Field Day controversy underlined the fact that the achievement of these women writers was not simply a comforting celebration of an apolitical pluralism, but an intervention into a deeply rooted system of value judgements and sanctions on the limits of poetic utterance and personal agency. Brendan Kennelly's lament that, "for such a rebel race, eloquently so, Irish poets can be comically, sadly conservative," might be extended to those editors, publishers, and teachers who, through their selection of anthologies, course lists, and publications, have traditionally reinforced these assumptions (57). Together, however, these various beginnings, which converged in the reaction against the costly political arrogance of Albert Reynolds, suggest the existence of a sea change in attitudes towards undemocratic power structures: the coercive force of alienating representations of femininity as much as that of "the brute force of private armies, the subtle hints of senior churchmen, or the discreet intimacies of the cabinet room" (O'Toole).

These different strands of cultural change and contradiction suggest the profound interpenetration of the issues of gender and nationalism which must be confronted by any effort to come to terms with the historically rooted network of problems and opportunities, obstacles and transformations, within contemporary Irish culture. If the fight against British imperialism embraced the ideal of Irishness as a metonym for national liberation, that same vision has itself become the site of a new postcolonial recognition that "the political necessity of creating as rapidly as possible a fully independent and sovereign state with a unique and separate identity, was only possible by obeying a political imperative hostile to pluralism" (McCartney 8). Because it depended on a strong sense of cultural homogeneity, the achievement of sovereignty has in turn generated a second wave of liberation directed against entrenched assumptions (sometimes codified into law) within the nationalist tradition.

Nuala Ní Dhomhnaill's poem sequence, *Immram,* translated by Paul Muldoon as *The Voyage*—a high-spirited version of an old Irish literary form—does not so much disqualify the imaginative appeal of an ahistorical Irish identity steeped in mystical powers and dependent on certain images of femininity, as shed light on the complicated networks of belief systems which underlie the fundamentalist impulse of romantic nationalism. Like the traditional form, Ní Dhomhnaill's poem centres on the adventures of a ship and its crew as they visit mysterious Atlantic islands. But Ní Dhomhnaill exploits the spiritual and imaginary dimensions of the form, as well as the plurality of these islands, to simultaneously celebrate and dislodge the authenticating promise of nationalist discourse. The first poem in the sequence, "The City of God," rehearses the attraction, but also the dangers of some national essence capable of smoothing out the rough edges of history. The poem's scepticism does not lessen its sense of the allure of such a promise of cultural purity free from contradictions:

> Sometimes I glimpse it, though, that heavenly city,
> however evanescently, there, at the very horizon,
> like an island where no one has ever set
> foot: sometimes it appears to me in the middle of the
>   desert;
> on top of a sandstone chimney-pipe or column
> somewhere in South Dakota or Nevada or Wyoming
>
> (*Astrakhan* 73)

The vision appears, but only with a tantalizing unsteadiness. The phrase, "there, at the very horizon," conveys a sense of immediacy (there it is!!) but also detachment

(over there, rather than here). The idea of an island on which no one sets foot is appropriate to the promise of this vision, which is only as alluring as it is impossible, but the elevated tone is undermined, sent off balance by the paradoxical location of this island in a desert, a kind of mirage that is dangerously tempting but destined to disappear. The mystical jostles with the mundane, the comical rubs elbows with the deadly serious; a single image conjures up both the biblical and the quotidian, the great events of history and whimsical moments of personal distraction—the City of God discovered "on top of a sandstone chimney-pipe," not in the Holy Lands of the Middle East, but in the American West.

The other thirteen poems which comprise *The Voyage* locate the island somewhat closer to home for a poem written in Irish: "sometimes it lies within a mile and a half / of the Great Blasket, sometimes in the middle of the bay" (82-83). In another poem it "appeared out of nowhere / like that half-rainbow that sometimes appears south-west of Slea Head" (83). The island's appearances as poetic image are as inconsistent as the geographical sightings themselves: the island emerges out of the shreds and patches of different conversations and anecdotes, works its way into folklore; it is described in the cadences of various discourses that rehearse the heteroglossia rather than the homogeneity of the national community. In one instance the vision occurs while the narrator is "lying in a hospital bed spaced out on Valium" (79). In another, the sight of it becomes so popular that guards have to be dispatched to get the situation back under control, "though not before / the ice-cream and fish-and-chip vendors / had made a killing" (81).

The final lines of *The Voyage* record the island's complete disappearance, but it is not at all clear from this that the rumours are to be dismissed as a nonsense. Like so much of Ní Dhomhnaill's work, *The Voyage* is dialogical rather than dialectical, its different voices fragment and interact without any orientation towards the promise of some future synthesis. Referring to the work of Mikhail Bakhtin, Mary O'Connor argues that the "sheer vitality" of Ní Dhomhnaill's "radical comic vision" works "to cut through the iconic and stylized use of the folk tradition that supported a certain romanticized native identity and to reimagine and authenticate a wider range of roles for Irish women" (149-51). This extension of women's social roles is reflected in *The Voyage* in Ní Dhomhnaill's anti-foundationalist sense of cultural identity. The heterogeneous nature of the references to the island runs against the grain of "the City of God" as a mystical vision or transcendent essence. Yet this in no way lessens the appeal of the island as vision any more than the romantic nationalist appeal of a common identity has ever been diminished by the fact that it is at odds with the differences within any community. Instead of simply dismissing the historical mutations of nationalism, the poem embodies the tension between this impulse to harmonization and the historical fact of the irreducible complexities that make this impulse appealing.

The tension is reinforced by the linguistic element of the poem: written in Irish and translated into English by another poet whose translation is often a fairly free adaptation of the original text. Patricia Boyle Haberstroh emphasizes that the effects of appearing in translation are double-edged. On the one hand, it has helped to extend Ní Dhomhnaill's audience, and in doing so, has encouraged a much wider awareness of Irish poetry. On the other hand, "[a]nyone who reads the poems in Irish, or has ever heard Ní Dhomhnaill read her poems in Irish (for she is quite a good reader), appreciates that much is lost in translation" (162). But given Ní Dhomhnaill's insistence on the spiritual dimension of the Irish language, of which we shall see more in the next section, the juxtaposition of the (original or authentic) Irish version with the (revised) English version also rehearses the tension evoked in *The Voyage* between the lure of a transcendent national identity and the contingencies of history informing this desire. For the English reader, the true poem always remains at one remove, in a language that Ní Dhomhnaill herself associates very explicitly with the genius of a nation.

Eavan Boland's poetry is more personally reflective than the carnivalesque spirit that animates Ní Dhomhnaill's, an archive of loss rather than the scene of riotous laughter. Its affirmations are domestic, even suburban. As such, it provoked the resistence of both the literary establishment, who dismissed her subject matter as marginal, and of many feminist critics who argued that it celebrated "the traditional female roles and values" in a way that seemed "emphatically regressive" (Allen-Randolph 14). As Kerry E. Robertson puts it, "Boland's muse must come to her exactly where she is, in the suburbs among the dustbins and street lamps, among the 'ordinary' and 'common things' that make up her world" (276). Boland's focus on "traditional female role and values" had a polemical force precisely because these concerns had been so rigorously excluded from the traditional themes of Irish poetry. Levering one tradition against the other enabled Boland to begin "to recover the experiences of lost Irish women whose real historical presence has been shrouded by romanticized representations of 'Mother Ireland' in literature and song" (Conboy 65).

Boland's literary achievement is greater than this restitution of the forgotten voices and experiences of Ireland's history though. Her poetry also operates, on a self-reflexive level, as a meditation on the ways that these forms of cultural amnesia are perpetuated and the difficulties that are inherent in any attempt to reverse them. As her poem **"The Women"** suggests, her work is characterized by a profound sense of an enabling ambivalence:

> This is the hour I love: the in-between,
> neither here-nor-there hour of evening.
> The air is tea-coloured in the garden.
> The briar rose is spilled crepe-de-Chine.
>
> This is the time I do my work best,
> going up the stairs in two minds,
> in two worlds, carrying cloth or glass,
> leaving something behind, bringing
> something with me I should have left behind.
>
> The hour of change, of metamorphosis,
> of shape-shifting instabilities.
> My time of sixth sense and second sight
> when in the words I choose, the lines I write,
> they rise like visions and appear to me

(*The Journey* 27)

Like many of Boland's poems, **"The Women"** is situated along the edges of the narratives of dispossession, in the half-light of myths that are a product of Ireland's colonial history, and which, because they trade so heavily on simplistic images of femininity, are an active force in the perpetuation of similar processes of displacement *within* the nationalist tradition. It is a cultural location that she identifies with in her own role as a writer: "there was a point when I realized that, as a woman poet, within the tradition of Irish poetry, I was at best marginal, and at worst, threatened by it" (*Sleeping* 88). Faced with these contradictions, Boland situates her writing in the ambivalent space between the images that tradition sustains and the absences that are its price, alive to the possibilities "of metamorphosis / of shape-shifting instabilities." Her vocation is an absent-minded one, both in the sense that she conjures up of her forgetfulness during an evening, and more urgently, because her writing represents a commitment to a renewal of histories that have been edited out of the dominant narratives of the nation:

> women of work, of leisure, of the night,
> in stove-coloured silks, in lace, in nothing,
> with crewel needles, with books, with wide open legs
>
> who fled the hot breath of the god pursuing,
> who ran from the split hoof and the thick lips
> and fell and grieved and healed into myth

(27)

It is a critical perspective that remains in the "neither here-nor-there" of what is remembered by history and what is forgotten, the "two worlds" of lived experience and the narratives which are inevitably a distortion of those experiences. As Deborah Sarbin suggests, this involves two distinct but related projects: "on the one hand, a rejection of the idealized, dichotomized versions of women that appear so frequently in western, and particularly Irish, poetry. On the other hand, the reconstructive component [which] seeks to restore women into historical vision and to reintroduce the previously silenced voices of women" (86).

Rather than attempting to exempt herself from the deformations of history in any absolute way, Boland more frequently highlights the alienating effects that selective historical memory had in the development of her own critical consciousness, "leaving something behind, bringing / something with me that I should have left behind." In *A Kind of Scar*, Boland offers her own much earlier encounter with a woman on Achill Island as an example of her complicity with the alienating effects of the dominant cultural traditions. The erasure of the histories which this woman from Achill is able to share with her is redoubled in Boland's own turn away from this woman in order to apply herself, as the dutiful college student, to her book of English court poetry, memorizing "all over again—with no sense of irony or omission, the cadences of power and despair" (6).

Whatever difficulties these exclusionary dynamics may have created for her, the mature Boland turns these issues to her own advantage, exploring the selective historical processes that blinded her to the experiences represented by the Achill woman. If the colonization of Ireland is redoubled by a colonization of women that is effected by the circulation of simplified images of femininity within nationalist discourses, Boland would refigure nationalism in the image of women, not as ornaments but as particularized individuals experiencing poignantly realized desires and struggles. Boland now possesses considerable influence within the Irish literary community as a result of her achievements, but any opportunity that this may create to retreat to the relative safety of an authoritarian voice is undermined by her insistence that the political authority of any poem "grows the more the speaker is weakened and made vulnerable by the tensions he or she creates" ("Writing" 497). Instead of seeking this sort of ideological refuge, her poetry remains situated in the "neither here-nor-there" world where different, and often antagonistic, cultural pressures intersect.

Eavan Boland's and Nuala Ní Dhomhnaill's poems testify to the fact that the subversion of those partitions generated by a tangle of ideas about masculinity, femininity, national identity, "and all their associated cohorts," is a matter of playfulness *and* politics, a revelry that is rooted in, rather than balanced against, an oppositional politics, even though its effect is frequently to unsettle any easy oppositions. Making these claims raises important questions, though, about tensions which are inherent in any attempt to work

within and against a tradition in order to develop alternative, forgotten histories without merely reduplicating the essentializing moves that are being rewritten. And it raises questions about how we as critics attempt to recognize the emergence of a group of Irish women poets as part of broader cultural changes without reimposing the sort of homogeneity on them—as "women writers," an identifiable group of authors working from a highly determined position—that they are writing against.

One answer is that it is a very different thing to talk about "women poets" in ways which highlight the persistent invisibility of gender within a masculinist literary tradition, than it is to talk about "women writers" in ways which continue to insist on their supplementarity to that tradition. The "very stubborn and privileged perspective" that Boland has identified, "which would see male poets as Irish poets and women poets as women poets," is the formalization of the masculinist nature of this tradition ("Interview with Jody Allen-Randolph" 124). Boland's response to this cultural "quarantine" is not to seek to transcend the issue of gender by extending the invisibility claimed by "Irish [i.e., male] poets" to women, but to insist on the informing nature of gender in the work of *all* writers. As Terry Eagleton argues, gendered identity structures, like nationalism, "involve an impossible irony": a series of alienating contradictions that have to be embraced before they can be ended, worked through rather than merely transcended, but always with the hope of reemerging in a less polarized context which makes an appreciation of the heterogeneity of lived experience possible (23).

All of this becomes more complicated when these sorts of negotiations are set within the terms provided by the received assumptions of any tradition. For both Ní Dhomhnaill and Boland, the contingency of history is balanced against a continuity between gender and nation that echoes the discursive connections they would displace. Ní Dhomhnaill's insistence on the distinct poetic concerns of women reveals some of the pressures inherent in re-imagining the historical relationship between gender, language, and nation:

> What women find when they go [into the deeper levels of the psyche] is very different from what men have written about. That's the really exciting thing. Lots of women's poetry has so much to reclaim: there's so much psychic land, a whole continent, a whole Atlantis under the water to reclaim. It's like this island, again in Irish folklore, which surfaces from under the water every seven years, and if somebody can go out to it and light a fire, or do something, it will stay up for ever."

> (*Sleeping* 152)

This concept of a lost island highlights the importance of the efforts of women writers to come to terms with the internalized effects of their historical predicament, but it also implies that this psychic land, because it can be retrieved "whole," needs less to be reconstructed as the product of shifting and unstable psychic economies, than rediscovered, still in some original—and therefore ahistorical—condition.

This same distinction between the promise of authenticity suggested by efforts to reclaim lost worlds and the interpretive ambiguities involved in rewriting them is reflected in Ní Dhomhnaill's discussion of male muses: "the male muse is ferociously dangerous. Number one, being a man, he's inclined to all or nothing action: killing yourself, walking out of a relationship, black or white, right or wrong. Number two, he's allied with society against you, against your deeper levels of subjectivity, because he's male" (*Sleeping* 150). To be a man is to be an action man, "ferociously dangerous," given to all or nothing behaviour like "walking out of a relationship." He is "allied with society against [women's] deeper levels of subjectivity," not because of choice or historical pressures but "because he's male." "He's a dangerous fucking bugger, that fellow, I can tell you!" (151). Many would argue that it is precisely this image of masculinity, sublimated here into a discussion of muses rather than of actual individuals, which must be recognized as a distortion if the corresponding cluster of ideas about femininity, including the issue of female agency, is to be re-imagined. Carol S. Vance has rejected this sort of equation between male and abusive as a "rag-bag of myths and folk knowledge" that undermines the very possibility of male responsibility. "Trafficking in these stereotypes of male aggression lets men off the hook since, according to the implications of this image, in abusing women, men are only living up to their inherently violent nature" (3).

In using these images Ní Dhomhnaill reinforces rather than re-imagines the stereotypes about gender that she elsewhere attempts to unsettle. But as with her sense of the sunken island of unique female experiences, Ní Dhomhnaill's sense of her muse is not without its own feminist logic: it is intended to reverse the projection by male creators of their "inner woman" onto women, revealing a displaced history of the male muses of women writers that echoes the subordinate history of women writers (*Sleeping* 150). Her sense of the "inner woman" of male creators may forestall any more complex notions of the historical constitution of gender identity, but Ní Dhomhnaill is insistent that the evocation of the female muse by male poets has tended to ignore the more heterogeneous, and often more monstrous, nature of these female muses: "when you set out on the journey towards your Mother's, you think you're going to meet the Great Mother, the Good Mother, the Ecstatic Mother, but what do you do when you meet the Teeth Mother?" (153).

This sense of the dynamics of a male tradition, within which the female muse is more "like the distant Beatrice" than "this negative femininity, this Hag Energy, which is so painful to mankind," converges with Boland's sense of the selective processes of traditional narratives (153). But the recourse to the muse as archetypal presence is less easily reconciled with Boland's emphasis on the development of identity structures in terms of the complex intersection of the various discourses within which individual experience is inevitably inscribed. You may not find the Mother that you're planning on, but whichever one you do find, she is there waiting for you like an Atlantis, a lost continent that needs only to be discovered for its nature, in all of its self-presence, to be recognized.

Compared with the scepticism of Boland's more theoretically informed commitment to the subordination of myth to history, Ní Dhomhnaill's emphasis on muses and sunken worlds remains a mystification of creativity that partially reinforces the hegemonic weight of gender constructions within Ireland's cultural traditions. And yet Boland's views converge with Ní Dhomhnaill's in her emphasis that differences between women are contained within a larger sense of "womanhood" (*Sleeping* 81). Like Ní Dhomhnaill though, Boland's essentialism is part of a more radically revisionary feminist strategy. She insists that "a lot of what we now call 'feminine experiences', or 'women's experiences', or 'women's issues', within poetry, are in fact, if people would only look at them more closely, powerful metaphors for types of humiliation, types of silence, that are there throughout human experience" (81). This posture enables Boland to reverse the symbolic force of the narratives of Irish nationalism, organizing these narratives into "an emblematic relation between the defeats of womanhood and the suffering of the nation" so that "Irishness and womanhood, those tormenting fragments of my youth, could at last stand in for one another" (*A Kind of Scar* 20-21).

Boland's project is less one of subverting the symbolic equation between women and Ireland ("Mother Ireland") than of rewriting it in ways that foreground some new fusion of these concepts based on a more "real" sense of women's experiences. To the extent that this project hinges on an equation between "Irishness and womanhood," however, Boland's work is recontained within the very processes of abstraction that she attempts to undermine; it is less about representations of particular women than the *idea* of particular women, an argument that repeats the mythologizing effects that she would seek to undo by moving out of "myth" into "history." Boland's differentiation between myth and history, perhaps most explicit in the poem **"Outside History,"** ultimately blurs rather than enforces the distinction between these two ideas, simultaneously historicizing the development of the dominant cultural narratives or "myths," and mythologizing her own revisionary historical speculations. Rather than resolving any differences between these two ideas, Boland's poetry remains rooted in "the untidy clash between myth and history—

where they soak into one another" ("Interview with Jody Allen-Randolph" 128).

Boland situates herself as a writer within a nationalist tradition whose window onto the world is "womanhood"; Ní Dhomhnaill formulates a similar relationship between women and the nation in her reflections on the Irish language: "Irish in the Irish context is the language of the Mothers, because everything that has been done to women has been done to Irish. It has been marginalised, its status has been taken from it, it has been reduced to the language of small farmers and fishermen, and yet it has survived and survived in extraordinary richness" (*Sleeping* 154). Because of "the Irish context," there is a congruity between the experiences of women (Mothers) and the history of the Irish language, which is also bound up with a history of the Irish people—the historical "context" in which these duplications are possible. What is perhaps most remarkable about Ní Dhomhnaill's sense of this convergence is the implicit equation of the history of Irish with the fate of *the Irish,* the fluidity with which a language can "stand in for," to use Boland's phrase, the condition a people, both of which find their further representation in the fate of women.

The Irish language is able to serve as an emblem of Irish history, not only because it has suffered a fate that mirrors the fate of the Irish in general and Irish women in particular, but also because it failed to evolve in ways that absorbed the major historical developments of the modern era: "the Reformation, the Renaissance, the Enlightenment, Romanticism and Victorian prudery" (27). Such a vision situates Irish as an exciting antithesis to the evils of modernity, but as Mary O'Connor suggests, Ní Dhomhnaill's "enthusiasm sometimes paints her into corners" (151). The problem with Ní Dhomhnaill's historical account is that it promotes a spiritual equation between Irish and the identity of the Irish that is sometimes impossible to reconcile with changing social realities. Ní Dhomhnaill depicts herself:

> writing my journal in Irish in a modern shopping mall in a Dublin suburb. Not a single word of Irish in sight on sign or advertisement, nor a single sound of it in earshot. All around me are well-dressed and articulate women. I am intrigued by snatches of animated conversation, yet I am conscious of a sense of overwhelming loss [. . .].
>
> At some level, it doesn't seem too bad. People are warm and not hungry. They are expressing themselves without difficulty in English. They seem happy [. . .].
>
> Any yet, and yet . . . I know this will sound ridiculously romantic and sentimental. Yet not by bread alone . . . We raise our eyes to the hills . . . We throw our bread upon the waters. There are mythical precedents. Take for instance Moses' mother, consider her predicament.
>
> ("Why" 28)

Faced with a "global pop-monoculture that reduces everything to the level of the most stupendous boredom," in this case "a modern shopping mall in a Dublin suburb" (28), Ní Dhomhnaill's yearnings for a lost order are perhaps appealing, but the cost of this nostalgia is registered in Boland's sense of the difficulty of her own struggle to insist on her domestic, suburban experiences as the legitimate subjects of poetic utterance against the pressures of an entrenched and alienating tradition steeped in the myths of heroic resistance.

The extent to which a politics of difference is intermingled with organicist assumptions about interrelationships between language, gender and nation which implicitly reject the contingencies of history in favor of ideals of community based on notions of "womanhood" or "Irishness," manifests itself in Ní Dhomhnaill's and Boland's distinct but related belief in certain continuities within the complex relationship between the author and her nation. Ní Dhomhnaill's suggestion that poetry comes from "the *lios* or 'faery fort,'" which is neither a Middle Age settlement nor a place "where the fairies live," but "a deeper level of the psyche," implies a continuity between artist and "the people" based on a connection between the "otherworlds" of a lost epoch and an alienated "subconscious" (*Sleeping* 149). As Deborah McWilliams Consalvo puts it, "Ní Dhomhnaill's use of the Irish vernacular [. . .] allows her poetry to become a textual 'projectile' capable of evoking the powerful, vivid images of the Irish past," a time when women enjoyed far more importance and freedom, but which is now only available to the poet (148).

Boland, who has "never been sympathetic to the idea of inspiration," is more sceptical about the organicist claims of national identity, and more wary of the sometimes deeply alienating ways that narratives of belonging are internalized within the individual psyche (*Sleeping* 80). "Let us be rid at last," she has argued, "of any longing for cultural unity, in a country whose most precious contribution may be precisely its insight into the anguish of disunity; let us be rid of any longing for imaginative collective dignity in a land whose final and only dignity is individuality" ("Weasel's" 322-23). And yet, despite her emphasis on banishing the myth of cultural unity, and however blatantly oppressive the traditional roles of women may have been in Ireland, Boland elsewhere suggests that she shares an equally organicist sense of women's "strong, tribal relationship to the past [. . .]. Wonderful tribal echoes [that] come in when you are raising a family." Nor are these connections vulnerable to the caprices of history: "Nothing has changed in them. No industrial revolution has wiped them out. The advent of the washing machine doesn't change certain things that are constant and enduring and simple. By doing them you restore your continuity with those feelings, those emotions. You can't participate in them and not have a wider sense of connection with the whole human experience" (*Sleeping* 83). To be a woman within a masculinist tradition is, for Boland, to live with the consequences of entrenched assumptions about gender identity, but her rejection of unchanging identities is mitigated by her sense that these connections are unaffected by changing social conditions. Such a position would seem to be at odds with her insistence, in the title to one of the poems in the *Outside History* sequence, that **"We are Human History. / We are not Natural History"** (*Outside* 38). The essentialized categories of the latter version of history are bound up with the sort of rigid identity politics that her work has consistently challenged. Yet even for a sceptic such as Boland, the appeal of these transhistorical "echoes" remains compelling.

The defensive tone of Ní Dhomhnaill's comment that "I am not constructing an essentialist argument here, though I do think that" suggests the extent to which her sense of the relationship between language, gender, and national identity also participates in a set of myths about collective identity that are increasingly perceived as oppressive ("Why" 28). But the too-easy subordination of these myths of belonging to an alternative emphasis on historical discontinuities is less an attempt to wrestle with, than simply to wish away, the coercive force of cultural traditions. Instead, Eavan Boland and Nuala Ní Dhomhnaill, amongst a growing number of Irish women writers, are gathering critical acclaim for work which unsettles the hegemonic weight of entrenched traditions by occupying, ironizing, sometimes trashing, sometimes rehearsing the temptations of the contradictory beliefs that they have themselves been formed by. In doing so they have brought together and redefined the formerly quarantined phrases, "Irish poet" and "woman poet," and have helped to sustain an ongoing interrogation of the many different partitions, the zones of distrust which for a long time inhered in this separation.

In *Ireland: A Social and Cultural History, 1922-1985,* Terence Brown suggests that the sorts of cultural transitions which O'Toole highlights, and which Brown traces back over the previous two or three decades, have deprived Irish writers of the older, monolithic order that generated forms of meaningful dissent, and which provided their work with a socially rooted vision. However welcome the dawning of this sense of heterogeneity might be, though, the Field Day fiasco, particularly when it is thought through in the context of the recent events such as the "X" case and the 1992 abortion referendum, highlighted a continuing, masculinist homogeneity that has left a growing number of women writers in little doubt about their cultural role, even if the only certainty is that this role can never be reduced to any single manifesto. Neither Eavan Boland nor Nuala Ní Dhomhnaill were amongst the delegates involved in the recent peace process. But as the editors of the Field Day anthology and Albert Reynolds can testify, political leaders who ignore the social dynamics

that are given voice to in the work of these poets do so at the peril of any agreement that may have been forged between them.

Works Cited

Allen-Randolph, Jody. "Finding a Voice where She Found a Vision." *PN Review* 21 (1994-95): 13-17.

Boland, Eavan. *A Kind of Scar: The Woman Poet in a National Tradition.* Dublin: Attic P Pamphlet, 1989.

———. "Interview with Jody Allen-Randolph." *Irish University Review* 23.1 (1993): 117-30.

———. *The Journey.* Manchester: Carcanet P, 1987.

———. *Outside History.* Manchester: Carcanet P, 1990.

———. "Interview." *Sleeping with Monsters: Conversations with Scottish and Irish Women Poets.* Ed. Gillean Somerville-Arjat and Rebecca E. Wilson. Dublin: Wolfhound P, 1990. 79-90.

———. "The Weasel's Tooth." *Irish Times* 7 June 1974.

———. "Writing the Political Poem in Ireland." *The Southern Review* 31.3 (1995): 485-98.

Boyle Haberstroh, Patricia. *Women Creating Women: Contemporary Irish Women Poets.* Syracuse, NY: Syracuse UP, 1996.

Brown, Terence. *Ireland: A Social and Cultural History, 1922-1985.* London: Fontana P, 1985.

Conboy, Sheila C. "'What You Have Seen Is Beyond Speech': Female Journeys in the Poetry of Eavan Boland and Eiléan Ní Chuilleanáin." *Canadian Journal of Irish Studies* 16.1 (1990): 65-72.

Deane, Seamus. "Canon Fodder: Literary Mythologies in Ireland." *Styles of Belonging: The Cultural Identities of Ulster.* Ed. Jean Lundy and Aodán Mac Póilin. Belfast: Lagan P, 1992. 22-32.

Eagleton, Terry. "Nationalism: Irony and Commitment." *Nationalism, Colonialism, and Literature.* Minneapolis: U of Minnesota P, 1990. 23-39.

Kennelly, Brendan. "Irish Poetry Since Yeats." *Journey Into Joy.* Ed. Åke Persson. Newcastle upon Tyne: Bloodaxe Books, 1994. 55-71.

McCartney, R. L. M. *Literature and Authority in Ireland.* Derry: Field Day Theatre Company, 1985.

McWilliams Consalvo, Deborah. "The Lingual Ideal in the Poetry of Nuala Ní Dhomhnaill." *Éire-Ireland* 30.2 (1995): 148-61.

Ní Dhomhnaill, Nuala. *The Astrakhan Cloak.* Trans. Paul Muldoon. Loughcrew: Gallery Books, 1992.

———. "Why I Choose to Write in Irish: The Corpse That Sits Up and Talks Back." *New York Times Book Review* Jan. 1995: 3-28.

———. *Selected Poems: Rogha Dánta.* Trans. Michael Hartnett. Dublin: The Raven Arts P, 1988.

———. "Interview." *Sleeping with Monsters: Conversations with Scottish and Irish Women Poets.* Ed. Gillean Somerville-Arjat and Rebecca E. Wilson. Dublin: Wolfhound P, 1990. 148-57.

O'Connor, Mary. "Lashings of the Mother Tongue: Nuala Ní Dhomhnaill's Anarchic Laughter." *The Comic Tradition in Irish Women Writers.* Ed. Theresa O'Connor. Gainesville, FL: UP of Florida, 1996.

O'Toole, Fintan. "Ould Ireland's Gone Forever." *The Guardian* 19 Nov. 1994: 27.

Robertson, Kerry E. "Anxiety, Influence, Tradition and Subversion in the Poetry of Eavan Boland." *Colby Quarterly* 30 (1994): 264-78.

Sarbin, Deborah. "'Out of Myth into History': The Poetry of Eavan Boland and Eiléan Ní Chuilleanáin." *Canadian Journal of Irish Studies* 19.1 (1993): 86-96.

Vance, Carole S. "Pleasure and Danger: Towards a Politics of Sexuality." *Pleasure and Danger: Exploring Female Sexuality.* Ed. Carole S. Vance. Boston: Routledge, 1984.

Katie Conboy (essay date 2000)

SOURCE: Conboy, Katie. "Revisionist Cartography: The Politics of Place in Boland and Heaney." In *Border Crossings: Irish Women Writers and National Identities,* edited by Kathryn Kirkpatrick, pp. 190-203. Tuscaloosa: The University of Alabama Press, 2000.

[*In the following essay, Conboy investigates the connection between poet and place in the work of Boland and Seamus Heaney.*]

> . . . and when I take down
> the map of this island, it is never so
> I can say here is
> the masterful, the apt rendering of
> the spherical as flat, nor
> an ingenious design which persuades a curve
> into a plane,
> but to tell myself again that
>
> the line which says woodland and cries hunger
> and gives out among sweet pine and cypress,
> and finds no horizon
> will not be there.
>
> —Boland, *ITV* 7-8

Eavan Boland's most recent volume of poems, *In a Time of Violence* (1994), and her collection of essays, *Object Lessons: The Life of the Woman and the Poet in Our Time* (1995), extend her preoccupation with woman's place in Irish life and in the landscape of Irish writing. Indeed, many of the concerns that characterize Boland's new work emanate from the central questions in her earliest attempts to theorize the gender politics of Irish literature: How does a locality influence an individual writer? What is the relationship of woman to nation in Ireland? What is the place of women's writing in Irish literary history?

Clearly, Boland had already responded to such questions in her poetry. Even a poem like **"An Old Steel Engraving,"** from her volume *Outside History* (1990), can be read as an oblique commentary on women's "place" in a larger historical and cultural picture. In mapping history—both general and literary—as landscape, she laments that

> we have found
> the country of our malediction where
> nothing can move until we find the word,
> nothing can stir until we say this is
> what happened and is happening and history
> is one of us who turns away
> while the other is
> turning the page.
>
> (*OH* 45)

The past, Boland suggests, is as fixed as a steel engraving unless the poet can "find the word" that will make the "unfinished action" of the picture "widen to include us," to include those unrepresented in the tableau, those who remain "outside history."

Indeed, **"Outside History,"** the title poem of the title sequence of that collection, confirms the political correction toward which Boland—writing self-consciously as an Irish woman—strives: "I have chosen: / Out of myth into history I move to be / part of that ordeal" (*OH* 50). Her recent poetry, such as the first poem in her new collection (quoted in the epigraph), continues to reconsider Ireland's topography—both literal and poetic. The speaker announces at the outset: "That the science of cartography is limited / . . . Is what I wish to prove" (*ITV* 7). And while she seeks to re-sketch the actual famine roads, all but obliterated by time and memory, those obscure paths can also be read as analogues for other kinds of erasure and that historical great hunger for other unrecorded desires.[1]

By investigating links between poetry and place, Boland's prose, now collected in *Object Lessons,* explores similar ground to that charted by Seamus Heaney in his 1987 talks for the Richard Ellmann Lectures in Modern Literature, printed in 1989 in a volume called *The Place of Writing.* In these essays, Heaney expands his long-standing interest in place to discuss not only how the writer "becomes a voice of the spirit of the region" (20), but also how the poet both writes place into existence and then unwrites it.

Additionally, he considers not only a writer's relationship to a specific locality—such as Yeats's to his imaginatively creative (and created) Thoor Ballylee—but also a writer's awareness of the place of poetry in his specific literary tradition and political milieu. Revisiting poets' places, tracing lines of influence, demarcating the terrain of contemporary Irish poetry—in short, mapping his territory with the sureness of an experienced cartographer—Heaney uses only male poets as landmarks. As if in response, Boland moves backward in a more cautious pursuit—recovering the places of the dispossessed, reading the blank pages of history, staking out the borderlands.

Indeed, Boland's prose provides a subtle revision of the literary geography set forth by Heaney. Heaney's second lecture in *The Place of Writing* investigates (among other issues) both how poetry is related to political debate and what "status we are to assign to such symbolic utterance within the historical circumstances where we live our lives" (*PW* 36). Although Heaney acknowledges that art may be "a means to redress or affront public and historical conditions"—a topic he expands considerably in his Oxford lectures, published as *The Redress of Poetry* (1995)—here he confines his political questions to the context of the British/Irish troubles, cautioning against "poetry as a self-conscious function of the national culture" and yet celebrating those contemporary poets who are "resourceful in changing the demands and pointing to a new agenda for Irish poetry."[2] He appears as the "objective" narrator, the contemporary literary historian, the mapmaker.

Boland's prose, however, exposes a different "vexed question" in Irish political debate, a question that falls outside Heaney's circumscribed territory of interest: the place of women in Irish culture. In two essays in particular, *A Kind of Scar: The Woman Poet in a National Tradition* (first published as a LIP pamphlet in Ireland and republished as "Outside History" in *The American Poetry Review* and in *Object Lessons*) and "The Woman The Place The Poet" (first published in 1990 in *The Georgia Review*) Boland takes up these "other troubles" with a perspective quite different from Heaney's. She is the implicated narrator—part sojourner, part sleuth—scrutinizing literary history and reading the map to reveal a topography of displacement.

Because he belongs to a poetic tradition that so easily links poetic vision and national identity, Heaney is in a position to criticize the dangers of such connections. Citing a range of possible misuses of nationalism—from the local "campaign of violence mounted in the name of Ireland by the provisional IRA" (*PW* 37) to the more far-reaching and repugnant "stain of Nazi ideology and Aryan racism" (*PW* 42)—Heaney explains that "even to canvas the idea of a connection between a founded nation and a founded poetic voice is in danger of being judged old-fashioned, if not downright retrograde" (*PW* 39). Nevertheless, Heaney himself admits that the old questions about the relationship of the poet to the idea of a nation can be refigured, though poets are required to address them "in an imaginatively rewarding way" (*PW* 43). However, Boland, exiled from the very tradition that Heaney is able to contextualize, attempts to recover or to reconstruct exactly that connection that Heaney renders suspect: to "repossess" her nation from a hollow rhetoric that makes her, as a woman, "an outsider in my own national literature, cut off from its archive, at a distance from its energy" (*OL* 128).

Tracing in Irish poetry "the tendency to fuse the national and the feminine, to make the image of the woman the pretext of a romantic nationalism" (*OL* 151), Boland explores the difficulty of forging identity and "ethical direction" for women who "have moved from being the objects of Irish poems to being the authors of them" (*OL* 126).[3] To some extent, women writers have been paralyzed by a tradition of imagery that, in Boland's words, created "an association of the feminine and the national—and the consequent simplification of both" (*OL* 135). Women have, in other words, been put in their place and kept there, and theirs has not been the "place of writing," but rather the place of the written—the defined, the fixed, and the permanent.

Thus, Boland laments her displacement from that predominantly male tradition that Heaney comfortably finds a place in. Heaney's collection of essays explores, implicitly at least, the influence of two modern poets, Yeats and MacNeice, on a generation of contemporary poets, and he has little trouble finding glances toward those two figures in recent poetry by Michael Longley, Derek Mahon, and Paul Muldoon. His own poetry, though rarely discussed in detail in his prose, also contributes to an ongoing dialogue with poets past and present, thus establishing a place in both filial and fraternal communities. Boland, in contrast, looks to literary history for continuity, but discovers no matrilineage. Indeed, even for sorority she must travel east to Anna Akhmatova or west to Adrienne Rich and Elizabeth Bishop, and a great deal of support for her argument comes, ironically, from male writers of other nations or from Irish writers like Padraic Colum, whose status as a "peasant poet" made him, too, into "a cipher of the national cause" (*OL* 140).

If Boland and Heaney have any common ground, it may be their shared interest in the idea of exile, a concept that both writers turn into a positive force. Heaney's second essay in *The Place of Writing,* "The Pre-Natal Mountain: Vision and Irony in Recent Irish Poetry" (an astonishing title for a chapter that discusses no women poets), proposes that "MacNeice provides an example of how distance, either of the actual, exilic, cross-channel variety or the imaginary, self-renewing, trans-historical and transcultural sort, can be used as an enabling factor in the work of art in Ulster" (*PW* 46). Boland's sense of exile is less voluntary, yet no less powerful in its effects: she never has to leave the country, or even to quarrel with it, to achieve her marginalized status.

Still, this marginality also confers "certain advantages" (*OL* 147) on the female outsider who, because "invisible," is "able to move, with almost surreal inevitability, from being within the poem to being its maker" (*OL* 151). Boland explains that

> A woman poet . . . is too deeply woven into the passive texture of that tradition, too intimate a part of its imagery to be allowed her freedom.
>
> . . . I thought it vital that women poets such as myself should establish a discourse with the idea of a nation. I felt sure that the most effective way to do this was by subverting the previous terms of that discourse. Rather than accept the nation as it appeared in Irish poetry, with its queens and muses, I felt the time had come to rework those images by exploring the emblematic relationship between my own feminine experience and a national past.

> (*OL* 148)

Thus, one might say that Heaney, to borrow a phrase from Hamlet, must "by indirection find direction out," that is, must gain an aesthetic distance from both contemporary Ulster and Irish poetic history, in order to recognize his relationship to each, whereas Boland must "by indirection find direction in," that is, gain entry into a poetic tradition from which she, like other women writers whom she represents, has been excluded. Yet their relationship does not end with this opposing movement. While Heaney is in no way immediately responsible for Boland's exiled position—in fact his poems do not, in general, make political stereotypes of female figures—he is at least incidentally responsible for perpetuating a tradition to which women writers have little or no access.[4] In mapping new ground in his prose, he, like his literary forefathers, excludes women, displacing them anew.

Boland boldly responds to exclusion as she struggles to make her own experience representative and to embody in her work those disembodied and silenced women, "the real women of an actual past" (*OL* 153). *A Kind of Scar,* the original pamphlet version of the essay "Outside History," borrows its title from **"Mise Eire,"** the second poem in Boland's 1986 collection, *The Journey.* Claiming in the poem's title that she too is "of Ireland," she refuses to "go back to it," that place with "the songs / that bandage up the history, / the words / that make a rhythm of the crime / where time is time past" (*OH* 78). Aligning herself with stereotypes of womanhood—the prostitute or the immigrant

mother—she ultimately claims that "a new language / is a kind of scar / and heals after a while / into a passable imitation / of what went before" (*OH* 79). Both her prose and her poetry elaborate the images of wounding and scarring, implying that the wound of exile, while it heals, leaves its mark on the injured party.

Yet in another sense, Boland also displays the desire to perpetrate the injury: to violate the terms of an exclusive literary tradition. In **"Outside History,"** a sequence of poetry in her 1990 collection, and in the essay "The Woman The Place The Poet" (which is to some extent a prose background to these poems), Boland moves beyond recording the hurt of women's historical exclusion to seizing the weapon—language—and wielding it to inflict pain. These works carve out a place in the canon for the woman writer in general and for Boland in particular; they assault the apparently intact body of Irish literary history and, if they do not leave it "split to the knob of its gullet" (to revise Synge's Christy Mahon), they certainly make incisions large enough to leave permanent scars.

In "The Woman The Place The Poet," Boland's personal history becomes the vehicle for her reinvention of Irish history and for her insistence that the lost voices of history be recovered in the literary tradition. Tracing her ancestor who had been appointed master of the Irish workhouse at Clonmel, she becomes painfully aware of what has been excised from his history and hers—the fates of those multitudes of faceless, nameless victims of the workhouse. She conjures up one,

> A woman like myself, with two small children, who must have come to this place as I came to the suburb. She would have come here in her twenties or thirties. But whereas my arrival in the suburb marked a homecoming, hers in the workhouse would have initiated a final and almost certainly fatal homelessness. At an age when I was observing the healings of place, she would have been a scholar of its violations.

> (*OL* 163)

Boland's essay makes audible what for this woman remained silent, yet she also expands the significance of the woman's terrible sufferings: the essay laments not only the history of her losses but also, even more important, the loss of her history. Recognizing that "poets have been free to invoke place as a territory between invention and creation"—and admitting that she herself has taken such liberties—she insists that writers must also see place as "what it has been for so many: brute, choiceless fact" (*OL* 163). In this sense, she questions the comfort inherent in the supposedly restorative function of myth: "Is there something about the repeated action—about lifting a child, clearing a dish, watching the seasons return to a tree and depart from a vista—which reveals a deeper meaning to existence and heals some of the worst abrasions of time?" (*OL* 169).

While Boland is certain that her own life provides a contrast to the workhouse woman's experience, the reader understands that in literary history, Boland is threatened with the same displacement, silence, and disembodiment: she, too, could disappear without a trace, as many women writers already have.[5] However, Boland's poetry, probing even deeper into the metaphors of wounding and scarring, intimates that a quick healing is not always desirable; indeed, she asks her own body to reflect (like her poetry) the history of defeated womanhood in Ireland. In **"The Making of an Irish Goddess,"** she mentions "the way I pin my hair to hide / the stitched, healed, blemish of a scar," but by writing her poem, she opens another sore. Describing the famine facts of

> the failed harvests,
> the fields rotting to the horizon,
> the children devoured by their mothers
> whose souls, they would have said,
> went straight to hell,
> followed by their own,

Boland compares such experiences to her own life, to the safety of a March evening when she looks into the suburban neighborhood distance for her own daughter. She claims that "Myth is the wound we leave / in the time we have" (*OH* 38-39) and thus reinflicts the pain of the past on the reader's present life as she invokes the spirits of the buried mothers and children of famine (**"The Making of an Irish Goddess"**), the figures of myth transformed into landscape (**"Daphne Heard with Horror the Addresses of the God"**), the exiled German *au pair* girls of her childhood (**"In Exile"**), her own mother and grandmother (**"What We Lost"**): the dead.

Further, when her poems stop short of clarifying the role of the dead, her prose elaborates. In imagination, she can become these past lives; she can become not her ancestor, whose history is at least partially recorded, but the workhouse woman whose past has been erased. She can take that woman's place. For while Boland acknowledges that in real life such surrogacy is impossible, "yet even as a figment this woman was important":

> She cast her shadow across the suburb. She made me doubt the pastoral renewals of day-to-day life. And whenever I tried to find the quick meanings of my day in the deeper ones of the past, she interposed a fierce presence in case the transaction should be too comfortable, too lyric.
>
> (*OL* 171)

Boland continually rejects that comfort; she refuses to hide the wound. In her poem **"In Exile,"** she hears again the hurt of the German *au pair* girls' voices "forty years on and far from where / I heard it first." She identifies with that painful "music" from her own exiled

position in a "New England town at the start of winter" and insists "my speech will not heal. I do not want it to heal" (*OH* 46).

Ultimately re-mapping Heaney's "exclusive" landscape, then, Boland, in both her prose and her poetry, begins to record women's history and to renovate Irish poetic tradition by giving a written place to her personal and personalized experience. Indeed, contrary to Edna Longley's assertion that Boland must still adopt a more critical perspective on the idea of Ireland—a perspective that would emphasize "the extent to which the North has destabilised the 'nation'" and which would question "unitary assumptions about 'a society, a nation, a literary heritage' [Boland's own terms]" (16)— Boland's prose writings have long revealed a sensitivity to the complex nature of Irish culture. Failing to acknowledge that Boland's *A Kind of Scar* even moves in the right direction, Longley complains that

> Boland's new Muse, supposedly based on the varied historical experience of Irish women, looks remarkably like the Sean Bhean Bhocht. Her pamphlet begins by invoking an old Achill woman who speaks of the Famine. The "real women of an actual past" are subsumed into a single emblematic victim-figure: "the women of a long struggle and a terrible survival," "the wrath and grief of Irish history."
>
> (17)

As early as 1974, however, Boland recognized that Irish writers must "be rid at last of any longing for cultural unity, in a country whose most precious contribution may be precisely its insight into the anguish of disunity" ("Weasel's Tooth"). Here, Boland actually seems to anticipate one of Longley's models for Irish people's own "salvation"—the model borrowed from women's groups. Longley suggests a celebration of the "web" of relationships among Irish people, which Boland has also supported:

> The image of the web is female, feminist, "connective" as contrasted with male polarisation. So is the ability to inhabit a range of relations rather than a single allegiance. The term "identity" has been coarsened in Ulster politics to signify two ideological package-deals immemorially in offer. To admit to more varied, mixed, fluid and relational kinds of identity would advance nobody's territorial claim. It would undermine cultural defenses.
>
> (Longley 23)

In fact, at the same time that Longley's pamphlet was published, Boland's **"The Woman The Place The Poet"** and ***Outside History*** appeared, testifying to Boland's many different cultural identifications.

Moreover, if Boland's writing through 1990 seems to have searched primarily in the past for its relationships, a more recent interview indicates that her current thoughts are quite aligned with Longley's. Criticizing a narrowly nationalist conception of "united Ireland," Boland reminds her readers that

> Irish nationhood—for more than a century—has been a constellation of tensions and fragmentations. If we want that nation then we have to respect the different cultures within it. As poets and writers we ought to understand those cultures.
>
> (Consalvo 96)

Clearly, she has no simplistic conception of an Irish culture, and her latest writing attempts to explore not only her sense of personal and national history, but also the voices still unheard in contemporary Irish life and letters.

Boland urges women to bond together in their shared exile. Unlike Heaney's picture of a self-willed and stoic isolation that feeds the genius of his male contemporaries, Boland's portrait of female marginalization is unwilled, but potentially powerfully communal. Whereas Heaney argues both "that the poetic imagination in its strongest manifestation imposes its vision upon place rather than accepts a vision from it" and "that this visionary imposition is never exempt from the imagination's antithetical ability to subvert its own creation" (*PW* 20)—thus making the poet the ultimately powerful individual seer—Boland instead exposes how much historical "unwriting" and rewriting must be done before women can discover and trust their own visions and their own voices. Boland personally desires to "compel . . . some recognitions" from the predominantly male "authoritarian literary community" (Consalvo 97), and she seems to hope that Irish women writers will collectively rechart the literary maps that have been consigned to them.

Heaney's recent prose, whether in response to Boland or not, has, in fact, validated feminist claims for some territorial rights. In his most recent volume of essays, *The Redress of Poetry,* he directly acknowledges both the need to reconsider the writer's "place" and the complications attending any political "redress":

> Writers have to start out as readers, and before they put pen to paper, even the most disaffected of them will have internalized the norms and forms of the tradition from which they wish to secede. Whether they are feminists rebelling against the patriarchy of language or nativists in full cry with the local accents of their vernacular . . . [t]hey will have been predisposed to accommodate themselves to the consciousness which subjugated them.
>
> (*RP* 6-7)

Such a comment is clearly grounded in an affirmation of the liberating possibilities of poetry itself or in a humanist desire for inclusiveness—for "a new com-

monwealth of art, one wrested out of the old dramas of conquest and liberation, of annexation and independence" (*RP* 201). Boland cannot yet dream of that commonwealth. She is too much aware, as she puts it, of "the distance between my own life, my lived experience, and conventional interpretations of both poetry and the poet's life. . . . It was that being a woman, I had entered into a life for which poetry has no name" (*OL* 18). For Boland, then, "naming" compels recognition, and she underscores that we must mark differences before we can erase them with commonalties.

All the essays in Boland's *Object Lessons* trace the personal implications of being a woman and a poet in contemporary Ireland. Boland asserts that these reflections are constructed "as a poem might be: in turnings and returnings" (xiii). Heaney, too, has certain "preoccupations" that shape his prose works. However, Heaney's recent work begins to show a change, as if his poetic decision, in *Seeing Things,* to "credit marvels"—extended in his Nobel lecture to "crediting poetry"—has allowed him to consider with generosity perspectives he had never fully taken into account. Heaney's narrative of the place of poetry—especially of Irish poetry—has suffered from omissions, but Boland's has languished in repetitions. *Object Lessons* recounts the same story too many times, ultimately flattening out the map Boland wants to show in sharp relief.

Nevertheless, it is a story that needs telling, and without definitively speaking for women with experiences other than her own, Boland has at least put a new territory on the literary map: women's exclusion and its representative images of wounding and scarring. She has made the picture "widen to include us." In seeking to embody the homeless, placeless women of history—to give voice to their real sufferings—she must open old wounds; she must stall the healing; she must point to the scars. She must refuse to "[turn] away / while the other is / turning the page" (*OH* 45). She must expose the limits of cartography by pointing to the map and re-marking the famine roads.

Notes

1. A famine road is a literal "trace" of the starving nineteenth-century Irish who were given make-work jobs building roads. Where the workers died, the roads end; they are literally dead ends.

2. Heaney appears to have recognized the social responsibility of the poet in *The Place of Writing*:

> All of these [poets from different subjugated countries] have been caught at a crossroads where the essentially aesthetic demand of their vocation encountered the different demand that their work participate in a general debate which preoccupies their societies. The topic of this debate typically concerns the political rights and cultural loyalties of different social or racial groups

resulting from separate heritages, affronts and identities; and even if individual poets have been spared direct pressure to address those concerns in their work, they would need to have been insensitive in a disqualifying way not to feel the prevalent expectation—if only as an anxiety about their creative purposes.

(PW 36-37)

Yet, as the best-known poet and perhaps the best-known literary essayist in Ireland today, Heaney has not yet displayed much interest in those female writers who attempt to express women's experience or to critique the patriarchal structure of language.

3. For a discussion of Boland's sense of "poetic ethics," see Hagen and Zelman, who look at Boland's earlier work in light of her sense of exile.

4. In his silence about women poets' accomplishments, Heaney is in the company of many contemporary critics and anthologists. The noisy controversy over the exclusion of many women writers (and Irish-language writers) from *The Field Day Anthology of Irish Writing* merely underscores a tradition of such omissions. Robert Garratt's *Modern Irish Poetry* (1989), for example, purports to trace "tradition and continuity from Yeats to Heaney," but his book gives no space to women poets, even in his chapter on "The Tradition of Discontinuity." In addition, Dillon Johnston, who quite unabashedly titles the first chapter of his 1985 *Irish Poetry after Joyce* "The Irish Poet and *His* Society" (my emphasis), gives a scant three pages to the "three younger women poets"—Boland, McGuckian, and Ní Chuilleanáin—whom he finds "invite serious attention." Indeed, his remarks about these are, at best, cursory. Several anthologists, too, seem to discount women poets: Anthony Bradley's "new and revised" edition of *Contemporary Irish Poetry* (1988) finds room for only five women among forty-nine contributors; Fallon and Mahon's *The Penguin Book of Contemporary Irish Poetry* (1990) includes only four women of thirty-five poets represented; Paul Muldoon's *The Faber Book of Contemporary Irish Poetry* (1989) places only Medbh McGuckian among the ten poets who constitute his curiously narrow pantheon; and Thomas Kinsella's *The New Oxford Book of Irish Verse* (1989) names *no* women in its section on the nineteenth and twentieth centuries. Ostensibly inclusive in their representation of relatively unknown male writers, each of these volumes excludes female writers of at least equal merit.

5. Recently, several individual anthologists and publishing projects have begun to discover some "lost" women writers as well as "lost" texts by even writers who are well known. A. A. Kelly's

Pillars of the House (1987), though perhaps suffering from inclusion of an overabundance of poets at the expense of truly introducing any of them, displays a long-standing tradition of women's poetry in Ireland that has been unacknowledged in most anthologies. In fiction, Pandora Press's Mothers of the Novel series has made available novels long out of print, such as Lady Morgan's *The Wild Irish Girl* and Maria Edgeworth's *Belinda*. Feminist presses like Attic Press have also made a major contribution to the ongoing, if somewhat marginalized, dialogue about women's issues.

Works Cited

Boland, Eavan. *In a Time of Violence*. New York: W. W. Norton, 1994.

———. *A Kind of Scar: The Woman Poet in a National Tradition*. Dublin: Attic, 1989.

———. *Object Lessons: The Life of the Woman and the Poet in Our Time*. New York: W. W. Norton, 1995.

———. *Outside History: Selected Poems 1980-1990*. New York: W. W. Norton, 1990.

———. "The Weasel's Tooth." *Irish Times* June 7, 1974: 7.

———. "The Woman The Place The Poet." *Georgia Review* 44 (1990): 97-109.

Bradley, Anthony, ed. *Contemporary Irish Poetry*. Berkeley: Univ. of California Press, 1988.

Consalvo, Deborah McWilliams. "An Interview with Eavan Boland." *Studies* 81 (1992): 89-100.

Deane, Seamus. ed. *The Field Day Anthology of Irish Writing*. Derry, Northern Ireland: Field Day, 1991.

Fallon, Peter, and Derek Mahon, eds. *The Penguin Book of Contemporary Irish Poetry*. London: Penguin, 1990.

Garratt, Robert F. *Modern Irish Poetry: Tradition and Continuity from Yeats to Heaney*. Berkeley: Univ. of California Press, 1989.

Hagen, Patricia, and Thomas W. Zelman. "'We Were Never on the Scene of the Crime': Eavan Boland's Repossession of History." *Twentieth Century Literature* 37 (1991): 442-53.

Heaney, Seamus. *Crediting Poetry: The Nobel Lecture*. New York: Farrar Straus Giroux, 1996.

———. *The Place of Writing*. Athens, Ga.: Scholars, 1989.

———. *The Redress of Poetry*. New York: Farrar Straus Giroux, 1995.

———. *Seeing Things*. London: Faber, 1991.

Johnston, Dillon. *Irish Poetry after Joyce.* Notre Dame, Ind.: Univ. of Notre Dame Press, 1985.

Kelly, A. A., ed. *Pillars of the House: An Anthology of Verse by Irish Women from 1690 to the Present.* Dublin: Wolfhound, 1987.

Kinsella, Thomas, ed. *The New Oxford Book of Irish Verse.* Oxford: Oxford UP, 1989.

Longley, Edna. *From Cathleen to Anorexia: The Breakdown of Irelands.* Dublin: Attic, 1990.

Muldoon, Paul, ed. *The Faber Book of Contemporary Irish Poetry.* London: Faber, 1989.

Anne Shifrer (essay date December 2001)

SOURCE: Shifrer, Anne. "The Fabrics and Erotics of Eavan Boland's Poetry." *Colby Quarterly* 37, no. 4 (December 2001): 309-42.

[In the following essay, Shifrer examines the role of fabrics in Boland's poetry.]

By focusing on the role of fabrics in Eavan Boland's poetry, I hope to provide readers with a better key to reading Boland's domestic world, one which reveals her demolition of the aesthetic—and its aftermath, in which Boland recuperates the aesthetic for feminine pleasure. There's a logic, I believe, in reading Boland's poems, at first, autoerotically, reveling in the fabrics, the flowers, the colors of twilight. In moving to a deeper understanding, we then can better see how our pleasure arises out of both beauty and barbarism. As we learn to read the language of Boland's fabrics, we discover that the very clothes we wear on our backs point outward to the field of social relations and backwards to history. Fabric in Boland's poetry is an honored token of exchange between women and an emblem of their connectedness; but it also signifies the troubled entanglements of human relationships, the trouble of class, for instance, and oppressive economic and sexual relations.

The site of many Boland poems—her house and garden in a suburb south of Dublin—may initially seem Edenic: she writes predominantly of a vespers setting when light is fading and the world seems quiet and closing. Her signature palette—the family of lavender, lilac, mauve, plum, all tinted with evening—is lavish and suggests almost a Celtic twilight with faeries in the wing. At first her world seems remote from social commentary, but closer reading—of worn linens and muslin aged to amber—reveals a penetrating critique of "the woman's sphere." As Michael Thurston suggests, Boland uses domestic spaces not exclusively to legitimate these as sites of discourse but also to examine the domestic interior in history: "the divisions tradition-

ally erected between home and history" are intensely scrutinized and revealed as "arbitrary and ultimately false" (230). While her poems often evoke "the domestic sublime," her treatment of the home and "feminine things" is scrutinizing and ultimately subversive. For a full understanding of how Boland's use of the domestic and its appurtenances is related to her larger critique of the aesthetic, some background in the critical reception to date and the publication history of her work is helpful.

In her essays, collected in 1995 under the title *Object Lessons: The Life of the Woman and the Poet in Our Time,* Boland recurrently describes the exclusionary force of the heroic traditions of Irish poetry. Real women, Boland suggests, have been written out of Irish history in favor of idealized figures that serve Ireland's nationalist agenda and a male erotic economy. Boland contends that woman as subject and voice must be created against Irish poetic tradition. This aspect of Boland's project has been often discussed in the critical literature. However, the particular ways in which Boland's poetry refashions the aesthetic, the erotic, and the sensual is less thoroughly discussed. The publication history of Boland's work accounts, I believe, for some misreadings of her work, both readings that focus on domesticity and the feminine prettiness of Boland's poetry (e.g., the male reviewer who dismissed Boland as "the bard of fabrics") and those that turn Boland's essays into polemics (rather than personal essays that include cultural critique) and then read the poetry in terms of the polemic.

Boland became widely known with the publication of *Outside History: Selected Poems, 1980-1990,* which came out in 1990. In 1996, her collected works appeared under the title *An Origin Like Water: Collected Poems, 1967-1987,* which includes more compendious selections from Boland's early volumes, titled *New Territory, The War Horse, In Her Own Image.* It doesn't include any of the poems of *Outside History,* Part 1, which, we gather, were written after 1987. The selected and collected volumes create quite different pictures of how Boland came to be a poet noted for the distinctive way in which she writes women and the domestic realm into history. The poems of *Outside History* seem to be a serene company, serenely achieved in comparison to the more troubled genealogy we see in the collected poems. While most of the poems in *Outside History* seem to celebrate the domestic realm as a site for poetry, *An Origin Like Water* contains more poems about the bondage and occlusion of the home. It also contains more poems about the problematic nature of being a woman, in particular a number of disturbing poems about cosmetic surgery and makeup. *An Origin Like Water* also shows us Boland's apprenticeship, which was very Yeatsian in its immersion in Irish legend and its craft-consciousness. One can note, for instance,

Boland's studious molding of assonance and her symmetries of slant rhyme and stanza form, formal skills that she later relaxes but hasn't abandoned. One can also note that Boland's apprenticeship occurred primarily in relation to male predecessors, something she herself notes and laments.

An Origin Like Water reveals a much more painful process of becoming than does *Outside History.* This pain casts a great shadow on the sensual opulence of *Outside History.* The release of a collection that includes these darker poems and in some ways supplants the exquisiteness of *Outside History* suggests the need for a different reading of Boland's work to date. In her essay "Death and the Poetry of Eavan Boland and Audre Lorde," Margaret Mills Harper remarks upon this need in her discussion of how *In a Time of Violence* and *Object Lessons* invited her to revisit and consolidate her first, tentative readings of earlier material:

> Boland's recent work clarifies for me the issues I felt but could not articulate on the evidence of her previous volumes. *Object Lessons,* in particular, in reconstructing the paths that led Boland to her present convictions, draws together themes about which she has written persuasively for years and makes them into a bold and complete aesthetic. She has made herself in her writing by finding a way to age and move toward death there, remaking the lyric subject into an approximation of a time-bound, disappearing body and thus revising the idea of art in the process. (182)

The stateside publication *An Origin Like Water* had, I believe, a similar impact for studious readers of Boland's work. Enchanted by our first readings of *Outside History,* we only became able to see the scope and deliberateness of Boland's project when the collected poems appeared. The following analysis of poems relevant to this reappraisal will give first place to the erotics of Boland's fabrics and gradually yield to its darker significations.

"The Briar Rose" employs many of Boland's key motifs—fabrics, flowers, the transposition of light as it fades. It also has a shadowy instability that evokes eros while also pointing to its complications:

> Intimate as underthings
> beside the matronly damasks—
>
> the last thing
> to go out at night
> is the lanternlike, white insistence
> of these small flowers;
> their camisole glow.

(Outside History 86)

(All following quotations are from this volume unless otherwise indicated.)

The pale colors of damasks and briar roses are both luminescence and interior, the underneath of nature. This delicate undressing of nature, the lovely aptness

and innocence of the briar roses glowing like a camisole alongside the properness of the matronly damask roses subtly prepare for the overt sexuality of the second part of the poem. Here, the speaker remembers herself as a child inadvertently happening upon a scene of adult sexuality. As she stands looking inside the mysterious armoire of nature, she recollects herself as a child, catching an illicit glimpse of an erotic scene:

> I could be
> the child I was, opening
>
> a bedroom door
> on Irish whiskey, lipstick
> an empty glass,
> oyster crepe de Chine
>
> and closing it without knowing why.

(86)

The bedroom fabric, like the lantern light of the roses, has its oyster-like, interior luminescence and additionally its adult clutter of sexual paraphernalia—whisky, lipstick, empty glass, discarded clothing. The implied removal of clothes which reveals underclothes and sexuality evokes a tender vulnerability, at once innocent and stained. The poem seems to allude to the fairy tale "Little Briar-Rose," with its princess who pricks herself, thereby falling into a one hundred-year sleep, as the curse required. In Boland's poem, the prick of sexuality similarly induces a closing of the door, "a sleep," which the camisole glow of small flowers later penetrates.

The bivalve construction of **"The Briar Rose,"** in which the view of the garden and the view of the bedroom conflate and close together, leaving the alliance of sensuality and sexuality mysteriously unphrased, suggests the delicate way in which Boland studies female sensuality. The poem also begins to reveal the alliance Boland creates between fabric and the textures of the erotic and emotional lives of women. While "the language of fabrics" in Boland's poetry is thusly allied with a study of pleasure, its significations are not limited to this. The centrality and variety of the language of fabrics as it speaks in Boland's poetry will become evident as we look at four poems: **"What We Lost"** (48-49), **"The Women"** (84-85), **"In the Rooms of Other Women Poets"** (20-21), and **"The Oral Tradition"** (75-77).

"What We Lost" is about the hidden records of women and the fragmentary state of their personal histories. The poem is also deeply concerned with connections between women, with fabric serving as a metaphor for both intimacy between women and the stories that might weave their intimacy closer. Boland, as it were, attempts to pick up lost threads of the story so that an alternative lineage, one that is passed through women, can be discovered. She also creates a vision of the past in which the common life becomes the center rather than the periphery of history. Fabric appears in the poem on several occasions. We have linen, muslin, satin, gaberdine, worsted, cambric, tobacco silk, "the sugar-feel of flax," "traveled silks," and "tones of cottons," as well as much touching of clothes, either in sewing or against the body.

The poem begins with a re-created scene, in which the speaker imagines her mother as a child listening to stories told by her mother, the speaker's grandmother. The imagined scene takes place in one of Boland's favored sites, a kitchen, and at her favored time, the approach of dusk. Sewing, specifically mending, is linked to the storytelling of the grandmother. The poem creates a strong sense of the undisclosed and of words drifting into silence, making story, and thus history, perilous structures:

> She is a countrywoman.
> Behind her cupboard doors she hangs sprigged,
> stove-dried lavender in muslin.
> Her letters and mementos and memories
>
> are packeted in satin at the back with
> gaberdine and worsted and
> the cambric she has made into bodices;
> the good tobacco silk for Sunday Mass.
>
> She is sewing in the kitchen.
> The sugar-feel of flax is in her hands.
> Dusk. And the candles brought in then.
> One by one. And the quiet sweat of wax.

> (48)

Words and other symbolic tokens are revered. The grandmother has wrapped these in satin. But the poem suggests that there's a rupture between words and their reception. Indeed, Boland seems to suggest that words, stories, histories dissolve into the physics of their happening in spite of attempts to preserve them:

> There is a child at her side.
> The tea is poured, the stitching put down.
> The child grows still, sensing something of importance.
> The woman settles and begins her story.
>
> Believe it, what we lost is here in this room
> on this veiled evening.
> The woman finishes. The story ends.
> The child, who is my mother, gets up, moves away.
> [. . .]
> The light will fail and the room darken,
> the child fall asleep and the story be forgotten.

> (48-49)

The child forgets the story in sleep; legend becomes language, becomes silence. The treasured words hidden in the scented closet become almost woven into the fabric, leaving texture as their last expressive gesture.

An additional poignancy comes to this poem when we learn from Boland's autobiographical prose in *Object Lessons* that her grandmother died at thirty-one, before either daughter or granddaughter could really know her. She left behind five children and "died alone, in pain, away from her children and her husband and in a public ward" (30). "Lava Cameo," the first chapter in *Object Lessons,* is an attempt to re-create this woman's story from the handful of details left to the family

"What We Lost" begins to reveal Boland's deep concern with the connections and disconnections that exist between women and the frailty of the thread that might ally women through history, enabling them to envision their circumstances within a historical perspective. This is not, in other words, a sentimental poem about lost family stories. It also makes a forceful ontological point: The erasure of mundane chronicle disables individual women's ability "to see" and "to think" themselves, for a historical-social sense of "woman" can only arise in the collective.

In introducing the impressive set of ethnographic essays titled *Cloth and Human Experience,* the editors of this collection discuss the great importance of cloth in human culture:

> Another characteristic of cloth, which enhances its social and political roles, is how readily its appearance and that of its constituent fibers can evoke ideas of connectedness or tying. . . . Social scientists and lay persons regularly describe society as a fabric, woven or knit together. Cloth as a metaphor for society, thread for social relations, express more than connectedness, however. The softness and ultimate fragility of these materials capture the vulnerability of humans.

> (2)

Boland's fabric imagery intimates all of these social meanings and links them specifically to the society of women. The fragility of connectedness is, of course, one of the central demonstrations of **"What We Lost."**

While **"What We Lost"** focuses on family and personal history, **"The Women"** extends these concerns to the community of women. The personal life, for Boland, is finally understood and resolved, even healed, in terms of the collective life, those experiences that become legendary or mythic—in Boland's own unforgettable words, "Myth is the wound we leave in the time we have" (**"The Making of an Irish Goddess"** 39). Myth is comprised of repeated injury. It is the fit between our pain and the pain of others.

Fabric, once again, becomes the major vehicle for conveying these ideas:

> This is the hour I love: the in-between
> neither here-nor-there hour of evening.

The air is tea-colored in the garden.
The briar rose is spilled crepe de Chine,

This is the time I do my work best,
going up the stairs in two minds,
in two worlds, carrying cloth or glass,
leaving something behind, bringing
something with me I should have left behind.

(84)

One could linger long over the beauty of these lines
and their graceful craft, the gentle iambic pentameter,
the carefully slanted rhymes. The exquisite imagery of
in-betweenness—the garden at its evening hour, the
pause on the stairway—forecasts a larger in-
betweenness, the in-betweenness of poetry itself, which
is for Boland a negotiation between herself and other
women. She calls evening her time of "sixth sense and
second sight":

when in the words I choose, the lines I write,
they rise like visions and appear to me:

women of work, of leisure, of the night,
in stove-colored silks, in lace, in nothing,
with crewel needles, with books, with wide-open legs,

who fled the hot breath of the god pursuing,
who ran from the split hoof and the thick lips
and fell and grieved and healed into myth,

into me in the evening at my desk
testing the water with a sweet quartet,
the physical force of a dissonance—

the fission of music into syllabic heat—

(84)

In these lines, Boland seems to experience writing as a
transfusion of herself into the lives of other women.
Writing is becoming or, more precisely, writing moves
her into the space that myth makes for women of the
present, past, and future. Myth for Boland is not an
abstracted space or a story; it rather occurs in congruent
styles of ordeal and suffering.

The movement at the end of the poem is utterly surprising; one expects that this poem about writing poetry
will lead us through the speaker's creative process.
Instead, she breaks it off in the middle of the heat and
goes downstairs. The poem ends in an almost celestial
display of fabric imagery:

. . . getting sick of it and standing up
and going downstairs in the last brightness

into a landscape without emphasis,
light, linear, precisely planned,
a hemisphere of tiered, aired cotton,

a hot terrain of linen from the iron,
folded in and over, stacked high,
neatened flat, stoving heat and white.

(84-85)

One adores Boland for this deeply human gesture—for
getting sick of her work, admitting it, and then turning
to a more mundane but satisfying task. Ironing has its
own kind of heat. In the delicate crafting of this final
image, Boland manages to suggest that ironing can be
aesthetically gratifying. It can culminate in a finished
work of neatly folded, fragrant linens. The world of
ironing can be its own little world—"a landscape," "a
hemisphere," "a hot terrain." The interior logic of this
world also links Boland to other women; the cloth of
women in silks, lace, or nothing is different from the
cotton and linen cloth of home, but both have their
heat, their eros.

This poem, one of Boland's finest, says much about her
peculiar form of daring. To funnel the creative energy
of writing into ironing is a wonderful elevation of
domestic ritual. Ironing also comments on writing a
poem, suggesting that it is a provisional, do-it-again
task rather than a consummation.

"The Women" naturally links with another poem about
writing as a metaphorical weaving of herself into the
lives of other women. In **"The Rooms of Other
Women Poets,"** Boland presents Woolf's proverbial
"room of one's own" as being conjoint with the rooms
of other women writers:

I wonder about you: whether the blue abrasions
of daylight, falling as dusk across your page,
make you reach for the lamp. I sometimes think
I see that gesture in the way you use language.

(20)

Boland then imagines the other poet's chair and
desk—Is the chair cane or iron mesh?—and how she
might feel when she leaves her writing room:

. . . when you leave I know

you look at them and you love their air of
unaggressive silence as you close the door.

The early summer, its covenant, its grace,
is everywhere: even shadows have leaves.

Somewhere you are writing or have written in
a room you came to as I come to this

room with honeyed corners, the interior sunless,
the windows shut but clear so I can see

the bay windbreak, the laburnum hang fire, feel
the ache of things ending in the jasmine darkening
  early.

(20-21)

The ardor of this poem is remarkable, remarkable in the love it expresses for writing, the spaces of writing, and the page itself, the remote silence of which asks for nothing but invites everything. Anyone who has written with intense focus knows the insular and fecund atmosphere that writing can generate. The ardent and yet slyly worked consanguinity between the poem's speaker and her imagined sister in writing is equally remarkable. The poem superimposes one absolute privacy upon another, without diminishing either, and yet communion occurs as if by the miracle of holding still on an early summer evening.

In this and other poems, Boland spins a delicate web of relations between herself and other women. **"The Oral Tradition,"** one of Boland's most majestic poems, explores the interwovenness of women's lives with a somewhat different emphasis. Here, Boland explores her alliance with the common woman and her oral traditions. As in **"The Rooms of Other Women Poets,"** Boland captures an eerie sense of absolute intimacy and absolute privacy as she overhears two women talking about another woman who gave birth in an open meadow. The poem is deeply textured by Boland's distinctive alchemy: the fall of night with its shadowed colors and two signal allusions to fabric. Gazing out a window is the circumstance that frames many of Boland's deepest perceptions. In this poem, the gazing trance of the speaker makes her into a vessel, almost a spirit medium, for the conversation of two women in the room.

> One moment I was standing
> not seeing out,
> only half-listening
>
> staring at the night; the next
> without warning
> I was caught by it:
> the bruised summer light
> the musical subtext
>
> of mauve eaves on lilac
> and the laburnum past
> and shadows where the lime
> tree dropped its bracts
> in frills of contrast
>
> where she lay down
> in vetch and linen
> and lifted up her son
> to the archive
> they would shelter in:
>
> the oral song
> avid as superstition,
> layered like an amber in
> the wreck of language
> and the remnants of a nation.

(76-77)

One could labor the details of this poem to loving infinity, but since the poem is much commented upon, I'll content myself with marking a few grace notes that might go unplayed. The golds and yellows of the poem are complications to Boland's customary colors. The yellow of laburnum's pendulous flower clusters, the pale yellow-green of lime-tree bracts when they fall, and finally the brown-gold of resin amber seem to be the golden undersong of the miraculous in the poem. The lush colors of this middle section of the poem are transformations of the more Rembrandt-like atmosphere and colors of the poem's opening:

> We were left behind
> in a firelit room
> in which the color scheme
> crouched well down—
> golds, a sort of dun
>
> a distressed ocher—
> and the sole richness was
> in the suggestion of a texture
> like the low flax gleam
> that comes off polished leather.

(75)

In a lavish transposition, the subdued colors of this scene become the dramatically golden, almost oneiric coloration of the speaker's vision out the window. In this sensory heightening, the speaker not only sees more vividly but also hears more acutely. The story of the boy born in a field is the story of a common boy, but it seems in this opulent twilight almost the story of a god. One of the women exclaims: "What a child that was / to be born without a blemish!" The phrase "bruised summer light" is an important contrast to the perfection of the boy. It's notable too that the shadowy purples of bruises might be seen as twilight-colored, and we remember the "blue abrasions" that begin the dusk in **"The Rooms of Other Women Poets."** Though usually used to suggest time's abundance and transformative possibilities, Boland's emblematic colors suggest in these phrases the injuries done by time. Alongside these symbolic transmutations of color, fabric, specifically the textural qualities of linen, fabric reverberates through the poem, from the "low flax gleam / that comes off polished leather" to the "skirt of cross-woven linen" to the final, "She lay down in vetch and linen."

The miraculous story is like a thread that aurally weaves storyteller and auditor into a common fabric. The music of other women's voices becomes woven into the speaker's own experience. "[T]he oral song," those bits and pieces of melody suspended in the archive of our wrecked common tongues, becomes the abiding residue of the experience. It is this lingering music that penetrates the departure of the speaker and ends the poem:

> . . . I had distances

ahead of me: iron miles
in trains, iron rails
repeating instances
and reasons; the wheels

singing innuendos, hints,
outlines underneath
the surface, a sense
suddenly of truth,
its resonance.

(77)

I've emphasized to this point the commonality of women in Boland's poetry and suggested that this is an incipient form of her social and historical vision. Boland, however, also discerns a perfidious union of women in which women are bound exploitatively and in mutual subjugation to an iconic image of woman. Of the latter, Boland has written most passionately and poignantly, focusing on the ways in which her own elected medium, poetry, and her own Irish poetic tradition disinvite the aging woman. Boland describes her own intense commitment to writing a poetry in which women can grow old with integrity and passion, a poetry that would countervail dominant traditions and ready molds of male perception and poetry. Her essay "Making the Difference: Eroticism and Aging in the Work of the Woman Poet" is devoted to analyzing the erotic nexus of the male poetic tradition and her own stumbling efforts to revise and rewrite this tradition so that pleasure is available to woman as subject, as mortal subject:

> It stands to reason that the project of the woman poet—connected as it is by dark bonds to the object she once was—cannot make a continuum with the sexualized erotic of the male poem. The true difference women poets make as authors of the poem is in sharp contrast to the part they were assigned as objects in it. . . . It has been my argument that in a real and immediate sense, when she does enter upon this old territory, where the erotic and sexual came together to inscribe the tradition, the woman poet is in that poignant place I spoke of: where the subject cannot forget her previous existence as object.

(31)

"A Woman Painted on a Leaf," the last poem of *In a Time of Violence,* movingly echoes and instantiates the critical project of "Making the Difference: Eroticism and Aging in the Work of the Woman Poet":

> I found it among curios and silver
> in the pureness of wintry light.
>
> A woman painted on a leaf.
> [. . .]
> This is not death. It is the terrible
> suspension of life.
>
> I want a poem
> I can grow old in. I want a poem I can die in.

(69)

Changing the space occupied by woman in the lyric poem depends not so much on men altering their representations of women but on women coming to accept the altering of their mortal bodies.

Boland is not blind to the odds against this, to the historically tenacious ways in which women cooperate in their own oppression. The internalization of the cultural erotic script that fashions women as beautiful objects is almost cellular in its deepness. Boland's dark poems acknowledge this, and while she celebrates the sustaining and utopic possibilities of women's interconnectedness, she also examines the sinister ways in which women are bound together.

To explore what might be called "the infernal union of women," Boland makes extensive use of textile imagery. These poems range from ones in which Boland looks at the history of a fabric or lace, to poems about cosmetic surgery in which cutting and stitching become ways in which women attempt to remake their bodies. A poem in *Outside History* called **"Lace,"** first published in an early volume called *Journey,* and two poems from *In a Time of Violence,* **"In a Bad Light"** and **"The Dolls Museum in Dublin,"** are especially revealing of Boland's sense that textiles can signify, in figure and fact, networks of oppression.

Clothing can be looked at as a kind of map to women's oppression, often the ways in which women facilitate this oppression. Boland, as will be seen, primarily cites examples from the historical record but her critique has absolute applicability to our present day. Our complicity sometimes makes news. In 1996, for instance, newspapers around the country reported that two major mass-produced clothing lines of the United States—both named after and promoted by glamorous women, the Kathie Lee line and the Jacqueline Smith line—were heavily reliant on sweat shops and child labor to produce their clothing. Kathie Lee—penitent, indignant, and cosmetically perfect—appears on television to denounce the practice and deny her complicity. She didn't know?

Boland, however, is greatly concerned about the provenance of textiles, using them as subtle ways in which to trace the undersides of history. **"Lace,"** a much admired Boland poem, alludes to the terrible social history of lace-making. Lace worn at "the wrist / of a prince / in a petty court" is the extravagance that caused women laborers to lose their eyesight. Lace, however beautiful,

> . . . is still
> what someone
> in the corner
> of a room,
> in the dusk,
> bent over

as the light was fading

lost their sight for.

(90-91)

Boland's poem correctly portrays the early conditions of lace-making. Women often had to work in dark and dank spaces because some threads were so delicate that a moist environment was required to keep them flexible. They worked around a central candle, ranked according to ability; women in the corners would have but scant light to work by.

Interestingly, Boland connects herself to the lace-makers and to the disturbing relation between a privileged class and human laborers. The poem begins with the speaker writing—again at dusk. Her language is likened to lace:

> Bent over
> the open notebook—
>
> light fades out
> making the trees stand out
> and my room
> at the back
> of the house, dark.
>
> In the dusk
> I am still
> looking for it—
> the language that is
>
> lace . . .

(89)

The unspoken anxiety of this poem is that her own work may be an ornate luxury for a social elite. The poem does not assert this but its hidden shame is that the poet, like the lace-makers, may be in the business of adorning privilege. Through the suggestive history of lace and its aptness as an image of complexity, Boland suggests the ways in which a woman's labor might be invisibly allied to elaborate systems of oppression. As Michael Thurston notes, the poetic sequence **"In a Time of Violence"** is linked by fabric imagery: "Fabrics, then, provide the thread that runs from poem to poem" (247). He also suggests that each of the women in the sequence "bequeaths a document of civilization—portrait, letter, dress—that conceals its origins in barbarism" (247). Thurston's allusion to Walter Benjamin's famous statement in "Theses on the Philosophy of History"—"There is no document of civilization which is not at the same time a document of barbarism" (256)—has an entire aptness in relation to **"Lace"**; indeed, when Boland uses artifacts from women's history, these are often called up in terrible duality as representations of both civilization and barbarity.

"In a Bad Light" and **"The Dolls Museum in Dublin"**—like the poem **"Lace"**—also use textiles to explore barbarous networks of exploitative labor. Here,

though, Boland more clearly demonstrates the profound ways in which women are complicitous with the subordination of other women. Both poems deal with dolls—the first, in a museum in St. Louis, a replica of a woman bound for New Orleans; the second, dolls from the children of officers in the service of the British Empire. Both poems belong within the literature of dolls—for instance, the essays of Baudelaire and Rilke on dolls—which remarks the uncanny ability of the doll to peer, somehow threateningly, into our human condition.

"In a Bad Light" is the more straightforward poem, one that shares concerns with "Lace" but which makes the topic pointedly Irish and pointedly addressed to the historically tenacious fact that women oppress other women in the interests of their own beauty and adornment:

> I stand in a room in the Museum.
>   In one glass case a plastic figure
> represents a woman in a dress,
>   with crepe sleeves and a satin apron.
> And feet laced neatly into suede.
>
>   She stands in a replica of a cabin
> on a steamboat bound for New Orleans.
>   The year is 1860. Nearly war.
> A notice says no comforts were spared. The silk
>   is French. The seamstresses are Irish.
>
> I see them in the oil-lit parlours.
>   I am in the gas-lit backrooms.
> We make in the apron front and from
>   the papery appearance and crushable
> look of crepe, a sign. We are bent over
>
>   in a bad light. We are sewing a last
> sight of shore. We are sewing coffin ships.
>   And the salt of exile. And our own
> death in it. For history's abandonment
>   we are doing this. And this. And
>
> this is a button hole. This is a stitch.
>   Fury enters them as frost follows
> every arabesque and curl of a fern: this is
>   the nightmare. See how you perceive it.
> We sleep the sleep of exhaustion.
>
>   We dream a woman on a steamboat
> parading in sunshine in a dress we know
>   we made. She laughs off rumours of war.
> She turns and traps light on the skirt.
>   It is, for that moment, beautiful.

(*In a Time of Violence* 12-13)

While well we know that the unparalleled affluence of the United States is grounded in African slavery, we are less aware of other oppressions, such as the fact that colonial women's wear was got at the cost of Irish labor. Boland reminds us that feminine beauty has its terrifying costs. She also points to a curious circumlocution in oppression. She, as Irish speaker of the poem, joins the "we" of the historically prior Irish seamstresses. At the end of the poem, however, it becomes clear that she joins these women because she, in her own way as a modern woman, is a victim of the culture of beauty. The Irish seamstresses may be furious about the estranged uses to which their labor is put, but they are also seduced by imagery of feminine beauty. It infests their dreams.

"The Dolls Museum in Dublin" is a further demonstration of the abject and terrifying role that women play in the history of oppression. Like dolls, they are fully and finely accoutered, but they are stupidified, living in the squalor of their narcissism. After recreating the waltz-time of officers and their women before war and the nervous promenading of the privileged and their children "walking with governesses" and "cossetting their dolls," the speaker views time's distillate, these dolls in a museum:

> It is twilight in the dolls' museum. Shadows
> remain on the parchment-coloured waists,
> are bruises on the stitched cotton clothes,
> are hidden in the dimples on the wrists.
>
> The eyes are wide. They cannot address
> the helplessness which has lingered in
> the airless peace of each glass case:
> To have survived. To have been stronger than
>
> a moment. To be the hostages ignorance
> takes from time and ornament from destiny. Both.
> To be the present of the past. To infer the difference
> with a terrible stare. But not feel it. And not know it.

> (*In a Time of Violence* 15)

Like Yeats's dolls, these dolls press themselves mockingly on humanity. The female reader must feel especially indicted. Our historical ignorance and our efforts to preserve the face of youth are sadly kin to the impassive stares of the dolls.

The dolls in Boland's poems are intimately linked to female practices of making-up, the attempt to create a perfect and ageless face. The horror of this is the subject of some of Boland's less well-known poems. Readers who loved the selected poems in Boland's *Outside History* will be surprised by some of the poems restored to her corpus in *An Origin Like Water.* These are raw, unhouseled, almost brutal poems that deal with making-up, cosmetic surgery, and the exhibitionism implicit in the feminine cult of appearance. In these poems, painting one's face, clothes, and cutting and sewing become the diabolical tools of femininity.

Only one of these poems, **"A Ballad of Beauty and Time,"** appears in *Outside History,* giving this volume a softer more affirmative feel. The black poems of *An*

Origin Like Water—notable among them are **"Exhibitionist"** (107), **"Making Up"** (110), **"The Woman Changes Her Skin"** (128), and **"Tirade for the Lyric Muse"** (195)—importantly condition and frame Boland's treatment of fabric and fabrications. Woman as maker, as artificer of fabric or poem, has a deeply disturbing and ironic underside, for women are still what one might call "the cosmetic sex." Fashion and fabrics with their global network of oppressed labor are largely devoted to women, and the cosmetic industry (which fills a good aisle in every grocery store of the United States) serves, almost exclusively, our notions of feminine beauty.

In his essay "'Hazard and Death:' The Poetry of Eavan Boland," Albert Gelpi calls *In Her Own Image* "Boland's most explicitly feminist volume" and asserts that these poems "about living in the female body begin to write the image of woman out of patriarchy" (216). Absolutely, but this softens, I think, Boland's critique of feminine complicity. These poems are less about liberation than they are about women's collusion with patriarchal ideals of beauty. All of the poems I mention above show us a feminine humanity still deeply lodged in narcissistic self-fashioning. Rather than poems, women make their faces. The stripping woman that Boland imagines in **"Exhibitionist"** regards her body as the very foundation of aesthetics. She is, in an important sense, Everywoman. And so are the women in **"Making Up"** and **"The Woman Who Changes Her Skin."** In these poems, Boland presents us with Everywoman's bleak and lurid morning ritual. I quote from the beginning and the end of the poem:

> My naked face;
> I wake to it.
> How it's dulsed and shrouded!
> It's a cloud,
>
> a dull pre-dawn.
> But I'll soon
> see to that.
> I push the blusher up,
>
> I raddle
> and I prink,
> pinking bone
> till my eyes
>
> are
> a rouge-washed
> flush on water.
> [. . .]
> Myths
> are made by men.
> The truth of this
>
> wave-raiding
> sea-heaving
> made-up
> tale

of a face
from the source
of the morning
is my own:

Mine are the rouge pots,
the hot pinks,
the fledged
and edgy mix
of light and water
out of which
I dawn.

(An Origin Like Water 110-111)

This poem offers a brutal contrast between men and women as makers: Men make myths, and women make the fictions of their faces, the lie of beauty upon which men base their grandest myths. Boland makes it painfully clear that Western culture produces woman as an incoherency of self-love and self-loathing.

In her poems about cosmetic surgery, Boland converts her treasured imagery of cutting and stitching into a hellish communion of women:

The room was full of masks:
lines of grins gaping,
a wall of skin stretching,
a chin he had reworked,
a face he had remade.
He slit and tucked and cut,
then straightened from his blade.

"A tuck, a hem" he said—
"I only seam the line.
I only mend the dress.
It wouldn't do for you:
your quarrel's with the weave.
The best I achieve
is just a stitch in time."

("A Ballad of Beauty and Time" 123)

Woman's necessarily troubled relation to "the aesthetic" is made abundantly clear in this poem:

"See the last of youth
slumming in my skin,
my sham pink mouth.
Here behold your critic—
the threat to your aesthetic.
I am the brute proof:
beauty is not truth."

(123-24)

The terse, poisoned tone of this poem and the black comedy of its rhymes in some ways belie the poem's poignancy. "Beauty," the archetypal figure of the ballad, is an aging woman. She delves into the black arts of beauty in an attempt to save her currency. But fury at her own abasement becomes the energy of her life. Her last and slender gratification is the hope that her unbeautiful old age will confute masculine aesthetics.

If Boland can write the poems she has committed herself to, poems in which a woman can grow old, she will be the aesthetician of the next millennium. The work is a daunting one. The multifaceted way in which she uses the symbolism of textiles reflects this complexity. The first part of this essay has considered how Boland uses traditional symbolism and values of fabric to express a reweaving of the society of women, and how she seeks to reconstitute the erotic and erotic objects for the pleasure of women. We cannot be blithe about our proximity to the goals Boland sets. Her dark inversion of the imagery that is foundational to her poetry reminds us of the distance.

Works Cited

Benjamin, Walter. *Illuminations.* New York: Schocken Books, 1969.

Boland, Eavan. *An Origin Like Water: Collected Poems, 1967-1987.* New York: W. W. Norton, 1996.

———. *In a Time of Violence.* New York: W. W. Norton, 1994.

———. "Making the Difference: Eroticism and Aging in the Work of the Woman Poet." *America Poetry Review* 23, no. 2 (March/April) 1994: 27-32.

———. *Object Lessons: The Life of the Woman and the Poet in Our Time.* New York: W. W. Norton, 1995.

———. *Outside History: Selected Poems, 1980-1990.* New York: W. W. Norton, 1990.

Gelpi, Albert. "'Hazard and Death:' The Poetry of Eavan Boland." *Colby Quarterly* 35, no. 4 (December 1999): 210-28.

Harper, Margaret Mills. "Death and the Poetry of Eavan Boland and Audre Lorde." *Representing Ireland: Gender, Class, Nationality.* Edited by Susan Shaw Sailer. Gainesville: UP of Florida, 1997.

Thurston, Michael. "'A Deliberate Collection of Cross Purposes:' Eavan Boland's Poetic Sequences." *Colby Quarterly* 35, no. 4 (December 1999): 229-51.

Weiner, Annette B. and Jane Schneider, eds. *Cloth and Human Experience.* Washington, D.C.: Smithsonian Institution P, 1989.

Richard Rankin Russell (essay date winter 2002)

SOURCE: Russell, Richard Rankin. "Boland's 'Lava Cameo.'" *The Explicator* 60, no. 2 (winter 2002): 114-17.

[In the following essay, Russell argues that a close reading of Boland's "Lava Cameo" "illustrates how its subject, tone, sentence structure, and diction enable

Boland to imagine this scene, sympathetically write herself into it, and establish a new relationship with her grandparents and her own personal history."]

Eavan Boland's 1995 volume of poetry, **In a Time of Violence,** explores her imaginative re-creations of history. The middle section of that volume, "Legends," contains a remarkable poem entitled **"Lava Cameo,"** which depicts a moment when her grandmother met her grandfather disembarking in Cork. A close reading of this poem illustrates how its subject, tone, sentence structure, and diction enable Boland to imagine this scene, sympathetically write herself into it, and establish a new relationship with her grandparents and her own personal history.

In "Lava Cameo," the opening essay of her memoir, *Object Lessons,* Boland relates her inspiration for her poem:

> I found an emblem for her [Boland's grandmother, the subject of the essay] before I even realized I would find it difficult to name her life. Or my own. It happened one Sunday afternoon when I was married with young children. I went to an antiques fair [. . .] in a hotel in south Dublin [. . .]. I wish now that I had looked closely at one item. I remember the dealer pointing and talking. This, she told me, was a lava cameo. An unusual brooch and once fashionable. Unlike the ordinary Victorian cameos, which were carved on shells, this one was cut into volcanic rock. The brooch was a small oval. The face was carved into stone the color of spoiled cream. I looked at it quickly and moved on.

> (*OL* 32-33)

The information about the brooch is reduced to a parenthetical phrase preceding the poem, almost as if to downplay its importance for Boland: "(*A brooch carved on volcanic rock*)" (**Collected Poems** 195). This aside establishes the poem's musing tone. Boland languidly remarks in the first line: "I like this story." She further qualifies her tale in the second stanza, noting,

> except that it is not a story,
> more a rumour or a folk memory,
> something thrown out once in a random conversation;
> a hint merely.

> (5-8)

In her essay "Lava Cameo," Boland describes the "hint" in some detail: "I left school when I was seventeen. A rainy summer intervened before I began my courses at Trinity College. Sometime during these months my mother showed me the only piece of paper—a letter from her father to her mother—in her possession" (*OL* 14). Boland recalls being struck by the intimacy and yearning in the letter, as well as by her grandfather's anxious tone and fear of the future. Another detail about her grandparents' marriage, repeated to her by her

mother, has also colored her view of their relationship: "Whenever my grandfather's ship docked, often at Cork Harbour, Mary Ann would go and meet him. She did this because she feared the women at the ports" (*OL* 16).

One of these meetings between her grandparents is the subject of Boland's poem **"Lava Cameo."** In lines 2 through 4, she quickly sketches in the details:

> My grandfather was a sea-captain.
> My grandmother always met him when his ship docked.
> She feared the women at the ports—

> (2-4)

In her essay "Lava Cameo," she laments the fact that her grandmother died alone in a maternity hospital in Dublin. She turns to musing upon her own imagined relationship to her grandmother and then, swiftly, to her own struggles as a woman and a poet. The poem follows this same general pattern.

Two conditional clauses enforce the relaxed opening tone, but they also prepare the reader for a conclusion of more force, which follows in line 16. The first conditional clause adheres to an opening common in logical reasoning and is typical of Boland's remarkable evocation of feminine apparel:

> If I say wool and lace for her skirt and
> crepe for her blouse
> in the neck of which is pinned a cameo.
> carved out of black volcanic rock;

> (9-12)

In these lines she is literally dressing up the memory of her grandmother. After this conditional comes the second:

> if I make her pace the Cork docks, stopping
> to take down her parasol as a gust catches
> the silk tassels of it—

> (13-15)

Boland adds motion to her memory in these lines, infusing it with a dream-like, near-ethereal quality.

These two conditionals and the conversational tone of the speaker, however, are swiftly answered with the entrance of a new, academic voice, which adds, "then consider this:" (196). This line is both a quasi conclusion to the previous section and the beginning of a proposal about history that Boland the academic poses to herself and her audience:

> there is a way of making free with the past,
> a pastiche of what is
> real and what is
> not, which can only be

justified if you think of it

not as sculpture but syntax:

a structure extrinsic to meaning which uncovers
the inner secret of it.

(17-24)

Her own construction of history as justified by "syntax" is echoed by her diction in these lines: Words such as "pastiche" and the Latinate word "extrinsic" reflect the distantiation of Boland the academic poet from her family history. Her evocation of history as a syntactical construction runs counter to the claims of postmodernism: She is not claiming that history or meaning do not exist but that their recovery is fraught with difficulty.

This detached tone is broken by two lines of declarative sentences in which Boland relates what she does know: "She will die at thirty-one in a fever ward. / He will drown nine years later in the Bay of Biscay" (25-26). What follows constitutes a final break in the poem and is another device typical of Boland: She inserts herself into the poem, and as she does so, the distinctions between her grandmother and her poetic muse blur:

They will never even be
Sepia, and so I put down

The gangplank now between the ship and the ground.
In the story, late afternoon has become evening.
They kiss once, their hands touch briefly.
Please.

Look at me. I want to say to her; show me
The obduracy of an art which can
arrest a profile in the flux of hell.

Inscribe catastrophe.

(27-36)

In the absence of her grandparents, Boland builds a bridge to their past, inserting herself as "I" into the poem and seemingly pleading with her grandmother to look at her. The evocative, near-keening quality of "Please" is emphasized by its placement as a separate line and by the full stop that follows it. She urges her grandmother to slow down the moment and fix it like the lava cameo that represents her. Additionally, she pleads with her grandmother to give her the ability to freeze moments like this with her poetry. The "profile" of the penultimate line refers to both the actual cameo drawing and the picture of her grandparents that the poet has developed. The final line also has a double meaning: it refers both to the actual construction of the lava cameo, something inscribed on a product of catastrophe—a volcano—and to Boland's own inscription of the catastrophe looming over her grandparents' heads.

In the essay "Lava Cameo," Boland relates her growing fixation with the cameo: "The more I thought about it, the more the lava cameo seemed an emblem of something desperate. If it was a witticism in the face of terror, if it made an ornament of it, what else was memory? Yet in the end, in my need to make a construct of that past, it came down to a simple fact. I had no choice" (*OL* 34). Her absorption with the cameo illustrates her own need to write a history upon the flux of her family's past, one that she was largely locked out of. It typifies Boland's poetry, representing both her search for her feminine, Irish past and her attempts to insert herself into that past through poetry.

Works Cited

Boland, Eavan. "Lava Cameo." *Collected Poems.* Manchester, England: Carcanet, 1995.

———. "Lava Cameo." *Object Lessons: The Life of the Woman and the Poet in Our Time.* New York: Norton, 1995.

FURTHER READING

Criticism

Burns, Christy. "Beautiful Labors: Lyricism and Feminist Revisions in Eavan Boland's Poetry." *Tulsa Studies in Women's Literature* 20, no. 2 (fall 2001): 217-36.
> Explores "the tension in Boland's work between her political investment in representing women—especially the laboring poor—and her attraction to beautiful images and seductive, lyrical language."

Consalvo, Deborah McWilliams. "In Common Usage: Eavan Boland's Poetic Voice." *Éire-Ireland* 28, no. 2 (summer 1993): 98-115.
> Examines the range of Boland's craft as a poet and assesses her poetic contribution.

Fogarty, Anne. "'A Noise of Myth': Speaking (as) Woman in the Poetry of Eavan Boland and Medbh McGuckian." *Paragraph* 17, no. 1 (March 1994): 92-102.
> Notes affinities between the work of Boland and Medbh McGuckian.

———. "'The Influence of Absences': Eavan Boland and the Silenced History of Irish Women's Poetry." *Colby Quarterly* 35, no. 4 (December 1999): 256-74.
> Juxtaposes the work of Temple Lane and Rhoda Lane with Boland's poetry in order to discuss the concept of the invisible female poet within the Irish literary tradition.

Foster, Thomas C. "In from the Margin: Eavan Boland's 'Outside History' Sequence." In *Contemporary Irish Women Poets: Some Male Perspectives,* edited by Alexander G. Gonzalez, pp. 1-12. Westport, Conn.: Greenwood Press, 1999.

Considers Boland's struggle to define and repossess her identity as a woman poet through an examination of the poems in *Outside History.*

Harper, Margaret Mills. "First Principles and Last Things: Death and the Poetry of Eavan Boland and Audre Lorde." In *Representing Ireland: Gender, Class, Nationality,* edited by Susan Shaw Sailer, pp. 181-93. Gainesville: University Press of Florida, 1997.

Addresses the relationship of dying and writing in the work of Boland and Audre Lorde.

Kupillas, Peter. "Bringing It All Back Home: Unity and Meaning in Eavan Boland's 'Domestic Interior' Sequence." In *Contemporary Irish Women Poets: Some Male Perspectives,* edited by Alexander G. Gonzalez, pp. 13-32. Westport, Conn.: Greenwood Press, 1999.

Explores the placement and unity of the poems in the "Domestic Interior" sequence in *Outside History.*

Riley, Jeannette E. "'Becoming an Agent of Change': Eavan Boland's 'Outside History' and 'In a Time of Violence.'" *Irish Studies Review,* no. 20 (autumn 1997): 23-9.

Contends that Boland explores the tension between national and feminine identities in *Outside History* and *In a Time of Violence.*

Russell, Richard Rankin. "W. B. Yeats and Eavan Boland: Postcolonial Poets?" In *W. B. Yeats and Postcolonialism,* edited by Deborah Fleming, pp. 101-32. West Cornwall, Conn.: Locust Hill Press, 2001.

Considers the influence of W. B. Yeats on Boland's verse.

Additional coverage of Boland's life and career is contained in the following sources published by Thomson Gale: *British Writers Supplement,* **Vol. 5;** *Contemporary Authors,* **Vols. 143, 207;** *Contemporary Authors New Revision Series,* **Vol. 61;** *Contemporary Literature Criticism,* **Vols. 40, 67, 113;** *Contemporary Poets,* **Ed. 7;** *Contemporary Women Poets; Dictionary of Literary Biography,* **Vol. 40;** *DISCovering Authors Modules: Poets; Feminist Writers; Literature Resource Center; Major 20th-Century Writers,* **Ed. 2; and** *Poetry for Students,* **Vol. 12.**

Yves Bonnefoy
1923-

French poet, essayist, critic, fabulist, editor, and translator.

INTRODUCTION

Bonnefoy is viewed as one of the finest poets and most
influential figures in contemporary French poetry. A
prolific critic, editor, translator, and poet, he has written
several collections of poetry and long poems that have
received much critical acclaim. Commentators commend Bonnefoy's verse for its range of imagery and its
exploration of profound philosophical and spiritual matters. His emphasis on the omnipresence of death in
everyday life has led many commentators to consider
him as the first true existential poet.

BIOGRAPHICAL INFORMATION

Bonnefoy was born on June 24, 1923, in Tours, France.
As a child, he spent his summers at his grandfather's
house in Toirac; many images from his later poetry
were derived from these idyllic experiences. When he
was thirteen years old his father died, which had a
profound impact on him. Many critics note that the
recurring sense of loss in his poetry may be traced back
to this tragic event. In 1941 he graduated with honors
from the Lycée Descartes and then went on to study
mathematics, science, and philosophy at the Université
de Poitiers and the Sorbonne. In 1944, while living in
Paris, Bonnefoy began to write poetry. Critics contend
that this early verse was heavily influenced by such
prominent Surrealist poets as Victor Brauner and André
Breton. Bonnefoy became so interested in poetry and
literary theory that he put aside his advanced studies in
philosophy to study literary theory at the Centre
National de la Recherché Scientifique. Bonnefoy's first
major collection of poetry, *Du Mouvement et de
l'immobilité de Douve* [*On the Motion and Immobility
of Douve*], was published in 1953 to critical acclaim. In
1967 he co-founded the prestigious art and literary
review *L'Ephéme,* acting as co-editor until 1972, when
the periodical folded. He has been a professor at several
academic institutions, including Centre Universitaire de
Vincennes, the Université de Nice, the Université d'Aix-
en-Provence, and the Collège de France. In addition, he
has taught literature at various universities, including
Brandeis, the City University of New York, Johns Hop-

kins University, Princeton University, Yale University,
and Geneva University. He is regarded as a respected
critic and scholar, as well as a poet, and has written essays on literature, art, and architecture. He is also
praised for his translations of Shakespeare. He has
received several awards for his work, including the Prix
Montaigne in 1978, the Prix Goncourt in 1987, and the
Grand Prix Nationale de Poèsie in 1993.

MAJOR WORKS

In Bonnefoy's first major collection of poetry, *On the
Motion and Immobility of Douve,* the poet reflects on
his capacity to fully express the essence of being, which
he calls "presence," a concept central to his work. The
poems of the collection focus on the death, decomposition, and rebirth of the enigmatic female figure, Douve,
who has been interpreted alternatively as the poet's
lover, a mythological representation of all women,
nature, or the poem itself. Critics note his use of

metonymy and other devices to circumvent the logic of ordinary discourse. In his next collection, *Hier régnant désert* (1958), Bonnefoy expresses dissatisfaction with his previous poetry. Instead, he utilizes stark imagery, such as that of an iron bridge or black clay, to explore such thematic concerns as death, survival, and redemption. In *Pierre écrite* [1958; *Words in Stone*), Bonnefoy turns to the fertile imagery of a garden to express ideas about presence and to impart a fuller and more accurate perception of reality. Commentators assert that this rich garden imagery and the more optimistic tone of the poetry in this collection can be traced to his experiences with his wife at his country home at Valsaintes in Provence. *Dans le leurre du seuil* (1975), his next major collection, utilizes the same affirmative vision and garden imagery as *Words in Stone*. Yet critics maintain that it is a more ambitious work, in that it is a long poem divided into seven sections and explores Plato's theory of ideas, which Bonnefoy initially discussed in *L'Anti-Platon* (1947). The verses describe the journey through stages of self-doubt, revision, regeneration, and affirmation. His 1987 collection *Ce qui fut sans lumière* touches on themes of abandonment, love, and mortality. The poems also underscore another recurring thematic concern of Bonnefoy's poetry: the connection between art and poetry. In his critical and poetic work, he has frequently discussed the unique ability of art and the act of painting to express presence.

CRITICAL RECEPTION

Bonnefoy is regarded as a talented, experimental poet whose work is committed to expressing truth. Commentators have traced the develop ent of his work, particularly in light of his claim that each of his poetry collections has been built on the one before it. Therefore, stylistic and thematic progressions from volume to volume have been central to examinations of his poetry, and critics praise his ability to experiment with different forms, imagery, and themes. Connections between his theory of language and his poetry have been a recurrent topic of critical discussion. The thematic concerns of his verse—mortality, absence and presence, excarnation and incarnation, redemption, the power of love, and the experience of transcendence—have been investigated and traced back to such philosophers as Georg Wilhelm Friedrich Hegel, Soren Kierkegaard, and Martin Heidegger. In fact, his emphasis on death and the transience of all earthly things has led many critics to call him the first existential poet. Others detect the influence of classical materialism on his work and underscore his affinities with the metaphysical poets of the seventeenth century, the tradition of nineteenth-century French poets Charles Baudelaire and Arthur Rimbaud, and the Surrealists of the twentieth century. His interest in painting, particularly fifteenth-century Italian art, has also been examined. Stylistically, reviewers have discussed Bon-

nefoy's grandiloquent language, his use of metonymy and metaphor, and his tendency toward abstractions. His detractors maintain that his verse is difficult and can be viewed mainly as an offshoot of his philosophical ideas. His innovative and distinctive approach to poetics has made him one of the most significant and influential French poets in contemporary literature.

PRINCIPAL WORKS

Poetry

L'Anti-Platon 1947
Du Mouvement et de l'immobilité de Douve [*On the Motion and Immobility of Douve*] 1953
Hier régnant désert 1958
Pierre écrite [*Words in Stone*] 1958
Dans le leurre du seuil 1975
Poèmes: Yves Bonnefoy 1978
Ce qui fut sans lumière 1987
Début et fin de la neige 1989
Early Poems, 1947-1959 1990
New and Selected Poems: Yves Bonnefoy 1995
Les Planches courbes 2001

Other Major Works

L'Improbable (essays) 1959
La Seconde simplicité (essays) 1961
Rimbaud par luimême [*Rimbaud*] (criticism) 1961
Miró (criticism) 1964
Un rêve fait à Mantoue (essays) 1967
Rome 1630: L'Horizon due premier baroque (criticism) 1970
L'Arrièrepays (autobiography) 1972
Le Nuage rouge: essays sur la poétique (essays) 1977
Rue traversière (essays) 1977
Entretiens sur la poésie (essays) 1981
The Grapes of Zeuxis and Other Fables/Les Raisons de Zeuxis et d'autres fables (fables) 1987
La Vérité de parole (essays) 1988
The Act and Place of Poetry: Selected Essays (essays) 1989
Alberto Giacometti: Biographie d'une oeuvre [*Alberto Giacometti: A Biography of His Work*] (criticism) 1991
Remarques sur le dessin (essays) 1993
The Lure and the Truth of Painting: Selected Essays on Art (essays) 1995
Théâtre et poésie: Shakespeare et Yeats (criticism) 1998
Baudelaire: La Tentation de l'oubli (criticism) 2000
Keats et Leopardi: Quelques traductions nouvelles (criticism) 2000

CRITICISM

F. C. St. Aubyn (essay date 1964)

SOURCE: St. Aubyn, F. C. "Yves Bonnefoy: First Existentialist Poet." *Chicago Review* 17, no. 1 (1964): 118-29.

[*In the following essay, St. Aubyn discusses "similarities between Bonnefoy's approach to poetry and the existentialist approach to being."*]

Since 1953 Yves Bonnefoy has published, in addition to an earlier work he has subsequently preferred to forget, three volumes of poetry, a book on French gothic art, a critical biography of Rimbaud, two volumes of essays, and translations of at least three of Shakespeare's plays. His first significant volume of poetry appeared when Bonnefoy was thirty. His development would thus seem to have been a slow maturation which burst into full and prolific bloom. His poetry is serious, not to say somber, and evidences the obscurity and hermeticism of much of recent French literature. The study of Bonnefoy's poetry has been facilitated, however, by the publication of the two volumes of his essays, above all by the earlier entitled *L'Improbable* [abbreviated *I*] which constitutes his *ars poetica*, and to a lesser extent by the later volume, *La seconde simplicité*.

L'Improbable[1] has indeed already been called the "Art poétique le plus important et le plus personnel qui se soit exprimé depuis les grands textes didactiques de Reverdy, de Breton et de Jouve."[2] Even the dedication cannot be overlooked since it announces many of the themes of Bonnefoy's poetry and provides a brief outline of his poetic theory. At first glance the essays themselves would seem to be extremely heterogeneous, for the subjects include the tombs of Ravenna, fifteenth century Italian art, the contemporary artists Balthus and Raoul Ubas, the writers Baudelaire, Gilbert Lely, and Valéry, as well as a chapter on poetic theory entitled "L'Acte et lieu de la poésie" and one entitled "Dévotion" which again announces many of the themes of Bonnefoy's poetry. Upon closer inspection, however, one finds that they all treat of artistic creation and provide important insights into Bonnefoy's own poetic creation.

The basic premise of Bonnefoy's theory is the desire to identify poetry and hope: "Je voudrais réunir, je voudrais identifier presque la poésie et l'espoir" (*I*, 149). Even Bonnefoy cannot tell us for sure, however, precisely for what poetry is a hope: "Il se peut que la poésie ne soit qu'espoir sans issue" (*I*, 47). He can only tell us that we owe to Rimbaud the sure knowledge that poetry is a means and not an end. Hope nevertheless has its reasons and means their ultimate ends. Poetry is after all something.

In revealing to us his theory of poetry Bonnefoy also reveals himself to be the most existentialist of poets, perhaps even the first true existentialist poet. Not only are many of his intellectual sources, Hegel, Kierkegaard, Heidegger, frequently the same as those of Sartrian existentialism, but his poetic gods so to speak, Baudelaire, Rimbaud, Mallarmé, are also those of existentialism. Even Bonnefoy's interest in fifteenth century Italian art parallels in a way Sartre's interest in sixteenth century Venetian art.[3]

Much more important however are the similarities between Bonnefoy's approach to poetry and the existentialist approach to being. Indeed the two approaches lead to the same thing. The shock of recognition that being exists outside consciousness is the same for Bonnefoy as for Sartre's Roquentin: "la surprise de l'homme devant le monde abandonné à lui-même, devant l'object réel apparu dans l'énigme d'une muette présence" (*I*, 169). For Bonnefoy as well as for Sartre no god sanctifies the created thing, no faith, no formula, no myth sustains it, it is but pure matter and pure chance. Even Bonnefoy's concept of time seems existential. Being is its past only in the mode of no longer being it and its future only in the mode of not yet being it, that is, it is nothing but its present: "l'acte de la présence, où le avenir qui vaille est ce présent absolu où se défait notre temps, tout le réel est *à être*, et aussi bien son 'passé'" (*I*, 179). Bonnefoy along with the existentialists cannot agree with Plotinus who maintained that consciousness, far from being the essential foundation of being, is an accident, a diminution. For Bonnefoy "ce fond de l'être est intelligence et regard" (*I*, 71). For Bonnefoy as for Sartre in this world where all being is object for the look, "C'est comme si la vue était devenue substance. Et le savoir un avoir" (*I*, 173). There is no other way of knowing and this is as close to possession as we come. Both Bonnefoy and Sartre declare simply that being is, that being is in appearance, that the material object is nothing other than presence, and that presence is an act, the act of manifestation. As Bonnefoy puts it: "le monde sensible n'est qu'une action en puissance" (*I*, 28).

Bonnefoy shares the existentialist disdain for metaphysics. Bonnefoy, like Sartre, does not attempt to prove the existence of being. Neither writer is interested in useless conjectures on the possible source or sources of the phenomenon. Bonnefoy wants merely to name. He is interested only in concrete existence, "la description de ce monde que l'on pressent" (*I*, 27). The young creative writers in France today, the immediate heirs of existentialism, thus find themselves caught between two possibilities, two desires, "entre l'espirit de poésie et l'esprit de l'enquête méthodique, entre la frénésie, l'amour aventureux de certaines choses sensibles et la volonté de patience et de rigueur" (*I*, 119). Michel Butor has demonstrated that his attempts to reconcile these opposites led him naturally to the novel.[4] To date the most obvious heirs to existentialism have indeed been the so-called "New Novelists" or "New Realists." Bonnefoy is quick to disassociate himself, however, from this group. Their realism is not his. He feels that poetry is returning to "un réalisme profond. Lequel n'est pas—est-il besoin de le dire?—l'inventaire précis, 'objectif' nous assure-t-on, de ces romans nouveaux où celui qui parle s'efface" (*I*, 168-9). Bonnefoy is thus attempting to arrive at reality through his poetic creation just as Sartre attempts to arrive at it through his phenomenological ontology.

The reality of being has its necessary concomitant for Bonnefoy as well as for Sartre: "Le néant consume l'object" (*I*, 172). Being does not exist, only being and nothingness exist. Life is not simply life but life and death, and for Bonnefoy this fact is the true threshold, "le lieu d'accueil de ce qui est substantiel" (*I*, 165). This nothingness, this death is also a sign to man of his exile. To penetrate "le difficile réel" (*I*, 21), the young French poets have had to invent anew "les quelques gestes élémentaires qui nous unissent aux choses" (*I*, 168). They have had to create a poetry which effects "la transmutation de l'abouti en possible, du souvenir en attente, de l'espace désert en cheminement, en espoir. Et je pourrais dire qu'elle est un *réalisme initiatique* si elle nous donnait, au denouement, le réel" (*I*, 184). This "if" of reality is perhaps as close as poetry will ever come to reality, "if" indeed reality exists.

Bonnefoy analyzes at great length the means available to the poet for the expression of this reality. His condemnation of the concept as a vehicle for poetic expression is total. For him the concept is both a profound refusal of death and a flight. In company with Kierkegaard and most contemporary existentialists Bonnefoy condemns all static systems and lays their blame at Hegel's feet. He recognizes that there is a conceptual truth, but he also maintains that the concept in general separates man from the things of this world and in so doing lies: "On sait depuis Hegel quelle est la force de sommeil, quelle est l'insinuation d'un système" (*I*, 13) Any system which isolates man from his situation in the world which treats man in a vacuum, is a false system. Kierkegaard recognized the inadequacy of the system but took refuge from reality in his belief in God. Even Heidegger does not always escape the conceptual trap. If Bonnefoy admires in his writings "cette mort décisive, qui vivifie le temps, oriente l'être" (*I*, 12), Bonnefoy can give to Heidegger only an aesthetic or intellectual adherence since Heidegger uses death as a final resolution. The concept, since it attempts to found truth without death, denies poetry its true subject. The concept, far from being a means of revelation, is a means of concealment, an illusion. Discourse is linked to the concept and both lie in their attempts to produce an essence which is stable and sure and purified of all nothingness. For Bonnefoy, "Rien n'est que par la mort. Et rien n'est vrai qui ne se prouve par la mort" (*I*, 40). True discourse comes about only through poetry as a meditation on death: "Au moins la mort en acte fonde-t-elle le *vrai discours*" (*I*, 43). The concept as system is thus of no use to Bonnefoy in the creation of his poetry amidst the fleeting events and the eternal things of the world: "Y a-t-il un concept d'un pas venant dans la nuit, d'un cri, de l'éboulement d'une pierre dans les broussailles? De l'impression que fait une maison vide?" (*I*, 13). One might argue that the very word is concept, that image and metaphor are concept, in the end that poetry is nothing but concept. Bonnefoy is thinking primarily, however, of concept as system. Poetry, to express the true nature of being in the world, must go beyond the static system.

The Platonic idea or essence comes closer to capturing the reality of Bonnefoy's world. Bonnefoy is sure that the Platonic world of ideas exists, that there is to be found in all being "la substantielle immortalité" (*I*, 31) whose expression is the idea. For Bonnefoy Mallarmé was the first in French literature to attempt to capture this essence, this kernel of being. Mallarmé's faith lay ultimately in the word. He equated the word and the idea but his attempt was a partial failure: "Ce n'est pas l'Idée qui apparait dans la phrase, ce n'est que notre éloignement de la parole facile, notre réflexion si l'on veut, confirmation de l'exil" (*I*, 153). There remains the inevitable gap, the irremediable distance "du mot et de *cette* chose réele" (*I*, 139). Mallarmé however, unlike Valéry, demanded of poetry a future salvation and in his poetry he made a step towards being of which the Platonic idea is incapable since it rejects most of what Sartre would call the ontological structures of being: "la matiére, le lieu, le temps" (*I*, 139). The Platonic idea is in its way as deceiving as the concept since what it reveals is of a stable nature while the correlative of being is nothingness. Thus the idea is also inadequate for Bonnefoy's purposes.

For the concept and the idea Bonnefoy would substitute intuition. In place of a system Bonnefoy formulates what he calls a negative theology, negative because, just as Sartre bases much of his ideology on negation, so Bonnefoy does not reject that part of being which is "la négation où fonder" (*I*, 57). Bonnefoy hopes to capture all of this in what he terms "la vérité de parole, forme supérieure du vrai . . . La vérité de parole est au delá de toute formule. Elle est la vie de l'esprit, et non plus dècrite mais en acte. Originelle, issue du logis de l'âme, distincte du sens des mots et plus forte que les mots" (*I*, 37). The word is for Bonnefoy "la part intemporelle de la chose" (*I*, 121), "l'âme de ce qu'il nomme" (*I*, 149), "ce qui demeure de ce qui a disparu" (*I*, 180). Words are the substance of intelligence, our knowledge of reality: "de notre rapport avec ce qui est, la parole est-elle l'intelligence" (*I*, 183). Bonnefoy, like Sartre, makes such extensive use of religious terminology, God, conversion, sacrifice, spirit, salvation, grace, sacred, soul, that one is not surprised to find him, after Mallarmé, making a religion of poetry and constructing his own theology: "*Théologie négative,* elle substitute à toute divinité conceptuele cette présence de la réalité, sensible dans ce qui va se perdre."[5] In Bonnefoy's own words: "Une 'théologie' négative. La seule universalité que je reconnaisse à la poésie. Un savoir, tout négatif et instable qu'il soit, que je puis peut-être nommer la *vérité de parole.* Tout le contraire d'une formule. Une intuition, entière dans chaque mot. Et un 'amer savoir,' certes, puisqu'il confirme la mort" (*I*, 178). Poetry assumes the religious rites of salvation and redemption. The poetry of Lely, for example, is "la rédemption de ce qui se ruine" (*I*, 121). As the title of the final chapter of *L'Improbable* indicates, poetry is a "Dévotion" to the evanescent things of the world. Poetry is the religion of the finite: "Ce que nous aimions et qui meurt a sa place dans le sacré" (*I*, 151). To capture the reality of this passing but permanent being intuition must become the act of poetry, must become poetry.

As might have been foreseen from what has been said, Bonnefoy's fundamental intuition associates poetry and death: "La matière de la poésie après tant d'errances recommencéies est la méditation de la mort" (*I*, 139). To express it another way: "La mort dans son lieu d'élection et la parole attentive composent la voix profonde capable de la poésie" (*I*, 44). All three volumes of Bonnefoy's poetry are a monument to this dictum. Poetry is for Bonnefoy a combat, in Hegel's terms, "du médiat et de l'immédiat, du langage et de l'être, de la civilisation et de l'existence" (*I*, 52), "une incessante bataille, un théâtre oú l'être et l'essence, la forme et le non-formel se combattront durement" (*I*, 176). Poetry is the theatre for all essential action. The romantics had thought to fill their poetry with the whole world. Baudelaire was the first to change all that. Baudelaire replaced the theatre of the world in which a Hugo convoked the shadows of Napoleon and Canute by another theatre, "celui de l'évidence, le corps humain" (*I*, 43). With Baudelaire poetry came back to its true source, to the human body in a perceptible world. Baudelaire was the

first to express this poetic and verbal truth in *Les Fleurs du mal*: "La vérité de parole est directement issue de cette rencontre . . . du corps blessé et du langage immortel" (*I*, 44). This is the theatre, the true place where another religious rite occurs: "Le vrai lieu est celui d'une conversion profonde" (*I*, 23). The true place is a threshold, a frontier. The true place is not an unforgettable yesterday nor an impossible tomorrow, the true place is this burning present, this here and now: "Le vrai lieu est un fragment de durée consumé par l'eternel" (*I*, 181). The true place is given by chance but here chance loses its enigmatic character. The anguish of the true place expresses itself in poetry: "l'angoisse du vrai lieu est le serment de la poésie" (*I*, 182). Again Baudelaire was the first in French poetry to invent death, "un aspect profound de la présence des êtres, en un sens leur seule réalité" (*I*, 162). Baudelaire did more than invent death, "il a inventé, lorsque Dieu pour beaucoup avai cessé d'être, que la mort peut être efficace" (*I*, 48). Baudelaire did more than describe the here and now in poetry, "le seul bien concevable, le seul lieu qui mérite le nom de lieu" (*I*, 175). He was the here and now. Only in the here and now of fleeting time where the act of poetry takes place can we go beyond time. Only by words do we arrive at the threshold of the true place. Only through poetry can we hope to arrive at reality.

Even the elements of Bonnefoy's reality are existentialist. One has only to remember Roquentin's "galet" to know that stone will be for Bonnefoy "le réel exemplairement" (*I*, 18). Sartre has suggested that he would like to establish a lapidary for Rimbaud.[6] Bonnefoy's prose as well as his poetry offer an equally rich quarry. Roquentin's anguish in the face of the existence of the stone is Bonnefoy's: "De quelle gêne pour l'esprit peut être une pierre nue, soigeusement refermée, lavée par le soleil de toute idée de la mort" (*I*, 13). In speaking of the stones of Egypt Bonnefoy says "la vie massive de la pierre se conjoint dans ce miracle d'un présent où la mort n'est plus" (*I*, 20). He would even maintain that Egypt affirms through stone that the only future possible is in this physical world. The being of stone becomes for Bonnefoy the equivalent of the concept: "Que tel morceau d'une pierre morte, posée ici, dans son irréfragable présence, soit le plus strict équivalent de la généralité du concept" (*I*, 22). In speaking of the landscape of Raoul Ubac Bonnefoy says: "l'élément qui domine est une pierre cendreuse. Elle n'est pas le modèle . . . mais la chose méditée. . . . La pierre que dit Ubac est une métaphore de l'être" (*I*, 80). The stone is thus the first element of reality, one of "les objets les plus vifs de cette terre—l'arbre, un visage, une pierre" (*I*, 175), which assures man that in its present there is a future.

Again like Roquentin Bonnefoy remarks the being of the tree, "l'arbre qui meurt sans savoir la mort" (*I*,

113). In the tree, in the ivy, in the leaf, Bonnefoy finds salvation: "Je dirai par allégorie: c'est ce fragment de l'arbre sombre, cette feuille cassée du lierre. La feuille entière, bâtissant son essence immuable de toutes ses nervures, serait déjà le concept. Mais cette feuille brisée, verte et noire, salie, cette feuille qui montre dans sa blessure toute la profondeur de ce qui est, cette feuille infinie est présence pure, et par conséquent mon salut" (*I*, 29). Bonnefoy finds immortality in ivy: "L'immortalité qu'il y a dans la présence du lierre, bien qu'elle ruine le temps n'en est pas moins dans son cours. Conjonction d'une immortalité impossible et d'une immortalité sentie, elle est l'éternel que l'on goûte, elle n'est pas la guérison de la mort" (*I*, 30). All truth becomes possible "dans ce débris de lierre que j'ai tenu, dans le passage et l'écume" (*I*, 32). Another sign to be deciphered is the being of water, "l'énigme de la présence de l'eau" (*I*, 141). Eternity awaits us here also: "Il y a de l'éternté dans la vague. Fabuleusement, concrètement, dans le jeu de l'écume au sommet de la vague" (*I*, 31). He who attempts to join the things of this world, "Qui tente la traversée de l'espace sensible rejoint une eau sacrée qui coule dans toute chose. Et pour peu qu'il y touche, il se sent immortel" (*I*, 31). There is the cry of the bird, the passing of the wind, the gesture which is eternal: "Qui n'est pas fasciné par ce temps physique où bat, comme la sève universelle dans chaque plante, l'intemporel dans le geste humain?" (*I*, 90). This vision of the world, this attempt to arrive at reality can only be called love: "L'affrontement de la connaissance intellectuelle et de cette invention de l'objet qu'on peut certest nommer l'amour" (*I*, 139). Thus for Bonnefoy the act of poetry becomes an act of love, love of this world which is all we have and which suffices to tell us that in "cette obscurité d'un instant qui est l'appréhension de la mort" (*I*, 15), if we look closely enough we will find eternity: "Un possible apparaît sur la ruine de totu possible" (*I*, 172).

One of Bonnefoy's most important symbols is the orangery which he uses to designate seventeenth century French classicism and more specifically Racine. Because the figure appears frequently in Bonnefoy's poetry, we must quote at length:

> Et ainsi, je suppose, s'approchait-on, dans ce siècle qu'on dit solaire et sur le sable qui crisse, des orangeries fermèes. Car je les tiens pour la clef eblématique, la conscience latente de cette époque, elles que leurs grands fenêtres, sous l'admirable plein cintre, ouvrent au soleil de l'être, elles qui n'ont pas de parties sombres, elles qui préfigurent, par ces fleurs et ces plantes exmplaires qu'elles accueillent, le jardin mallarméen à venir—mais que la nuit, ou le souvenir de la nuit, emplit d'un léger goûte de sang, sacrificiel, comme si un acte profond devait une fois y avoir lieu. L'orangerie française est l'index de nuit, l'un des "mille chemins ouverts" que Racine avoue, et plus encore ce *moi vacant,* cette poésie classique elle-même, qui se connaît presque mais sans agir, qui attend qu'une intuition l'accomplisse, et qui va exercer pour cette raison sans doute, sur la poésie ultérieure, une irréductible fascination. Il faudra venir à l'orangerie, appuyer son front à ses vitres noires. Je vois un Baudelaire enfant dans le jardin essentiel.

> (*I,* 159)

The hothouse with its windows which are so many thresholds, so many frontiers, remains a place of symbolic growth where death is conceived only as the invisible, as an absence. Bonnefoy's task, the "acte profond," is to make of this "essential garden" of classicism an existential garden. As one critic put it: "On voit bien que c'est le poète qui porte aujourd'hui l'avenir du réel comme du sacré, qu'il est le véritable interrogateur d'un nouveau classicisme alliant le spirituel, la présence et la lumière."[7] Bonnefoy's problem is to bring death into the orangery while maintaining the life of its fragile inhabitants. This he succeeds admirably in doing in his poetry.

To follow the development of these existentialist elements poem by poem would necessitate another article. We can, however, see how they help give form to each individual volume. The problem on Bonnefoy's first volume, *Du mouvement et de l'immobilité de Douve* [abbreviated *D*], is who or what is Douve. One of the earliest critics was also one of the most accurate when he stated that Douve is precisely what it is indicated to be throughout the poem.[8] Another poet-critic whose knowledge of the Bible sometimes gets in the way of his better judgment, suggested somewhat peevishly that Douve was Abishag, the young and beautiful Shunammite who ministered to the aging King David with so little success.[9] A third critic wondered whether, since Bonnefoy knows English so well, "the author has not been attracted by the linguistic and thematic proximity of the emblem of the Holy Grail, the Dove."[10] A glance at the table of contents resolves much of the mystery. The sub-titles come directly from Bonnefoy's poetic theory which was not available to the early critics. The first sub-title is the scene of all symbolic action, "Théâtre" (19 poems), the theatre we have already encountered where being and essence, the form and the formless will struggle so valiantly. Next come the two necessary concomitants of all theatre, the gesture, "Derniers gestes" (14 poems), those gestures which unite us with reality, and the word, "Douve parle" (14 poems), the fundamental intuition, "la vérité de parole" which expresses reality. The fourth section is again a place, this time the place of symbolic being and growth mentioned above, "L'Orangerie" (14 poems). Finally we arrive at *the* place, "Vrai lieu" (7 poems). The movement is clear: the long struggle, the attempt to find those gestures which will unite us with the reality of this world, the words which will express that reality, the passage through the orangery, a sort of purification in order to arrive at last at the true place. All that transpires in these various places reveals the geography of a state of mind, or better of a state of being which alone renders the creation of poetry possible for Bonnefoy.

The long title of the poem reminds one immediately of the fundamental idea of Valéry's *Le Cimetière marin* while Douve herself reminds one of Valéry's *La Jeune Parque.*[11] Bonnefoy has somewhat grudgingly acknowledged his debt to Valéry but he also states: "Nous avon à oublier Valéry" (*I*, 145). Bonnefoy's attitude towards Hegel is equally ambiguous. The epigraph from Hegel at the head of his poem is both a help and a hindrance. A hindrance because a reading of the poem reveals it to be at least non-Hegelian in import while in *L'Improbable* Bonnefoy has revealed himself to be positively anti-Hegelian. The poem would seem to be much more existential than Hegelian but like the existentialists, Bonnefoy has perhaps taken almost as much from Hegel as he has refused. The epigraph reads: "Mais la vie de l'esprit ne s'effraie point devant la mort et n'est pas celle qui s'en garde pure. Elle est la vie qui la supporte et se maintient en elle" (*D*, 7).[12] If Bonnefoy's method is not Hegelian, the quotation does nevertheless reveal to us the subject of the poem, does help to situate the poem. Not only does the life of the spirit contemplate death, it also maintains itself in and through death, the very crux of Bonnefoy's poetic theory. The movement and immobility of Douve is but another way of stating this passage back and forth between life and death, being and nothingness, being-for-itself and being-in-itself, to use the existentialist terminology.

The title of Bonnefoy's second volume of verse, ***Hier régnant désert*** [abbreviated ***H***], also lends itself to an existentialist interpretation. Yesterday reigns because we are our past, but it is empty because we are our past only in the mode of no longer being it. Again the epigraph is a quotation from a German author. This time the idea: "Tu veux un monde, dit Diotima. C'est pourquoi tu as tout, et tu n'as rien" is attributed to "Hypérion" (***H***, 7). The quotation would seem to be a somewhat free adaptation from two paragraphs in the first part of Hölderlin's philosophical novel *Hyperion* of 1797 in which the hero in a letter to his friend Bellarmin quotes his beloved Diotima: "du wolltest eine Welt . . . Darum, weil du alles hast und nichts . . ."[13] The world includes nothingness as well as being. In wanting both one may end up with all or nothing. In this volume we are still in the true place of the conclusion of ***Douve*** where the poet seems to be reaffirming all his gains up to this point.

The volume is divided into four sections. The first, "Menaces du témoin" (13 poems), recalls the many witnesses of ***Douve.*** The second, "Le Visage mortel" (19 poems), reminds us of the mortality of being, while the third section, "Le Chant de sauvegarde" (13 poems), offers some hope. The final section, "A une terre d'aube" (11 poems), is again the true place.

Bonnefoy's third book, ***Pierre écrite,*** is a much shorter volume with only nineteen poems, the same number of poems as found in the two longest sections of his first two books. The epigraph this time: "O Charidas, que sont les choses d'en bas?—Obscurité profonde" is a quotation from an epitaph by Callimachus the Alexandrian written for Charidas of Cyrene who was probably a Pythagorean philosopher. Bonnefoy had already quoted this epitaph at greater length in *L'Improbable* (*I*, 91). An epitaph as epigraph is peculiarly suited to this volume since its ambiguous title means both the carved rock of the tombstone and the "ardoises taillées" of the illustrating artist Raoul Ubac. In ***Pierre écrite*** Bonnefoy has brought us to the very door of the tomb. His cemetery is not, however, a mournful and lugubrious place but again the true place where the instant finds its eternity, where death finds its life, where poetry finds its source.

From what has been said it can be seen that Bonnefoy has to date contributed to French literature a poetic theory which is at the same time highly personal and profoundly spiritual as well as soundly realistic and gravely compelling. In it he dares to explore the single greatest problem of life which is death and to find in his explorations a reason for an enduring hope. His knowledge of literature, philosophy, and art, his familiarity with the ancients and the moderns, give his theory an authority which is rare in contemporary letters. His manipulation of the existentialist concepts of consciousness, being, nothingness, negation, and time, his use of phenomenological description, his rejection of the Hagelian synthesis and the Platonic essence, his emphasis on the being-in-itself of the stone and the tree and the role their being plays in being-for-itself, mark Bonnefoy as a man of today. From this general analysis of the existentialist elements of Bonnefoy's poetic theory we can proceed to the careful consideration of his poetic creation which it so richly deserves.

Notes

1. To simplify notation the initial followed by the page number or numbers of those works of Bonnefoy which interest us here will be given in parentheses after quotations. All of his works with the exception indicted were published in Paris by Mercure de France:

   Du mouvement et de l'immobilité de Douve (1953): *D*

   Hier régnant désert (1958): *H*

   Pierre écrite, ardoises taillées par Raoul Ubac (Paris, Galerie Maeght, 1958): (I should like to express my appreciation to the Galerie Maeght for allowing me to consult a copy of this rare and beautiful book.)

L'Improbable (1959): I

La seconde simplicité (1961)

2. O (livier de). M(agny)., in *Ecrivains d'aujourd'hui 1940-1960,* Dictionnaire anthologique et critique, ed. Bernard Pingaud (Paris, Grasset, 1960), p. 128.

3. Jean-Paul Sartre, "From a Study on Tintoretto," trans. Richard Howard, in *New French Writing,* ed. Georges Borchardt (New York, Grove Press, Inc., 1961), pp. 9-54.

4. Michel Butor, "L'Ecriture, pour moi, est une vertébrale," *Les Nouvelles Littéraires,* 5 février 1959, pp. 1, 7.

5. Olivier de Magny, *Ecrivains d'aujourd'hui,* p. 131.

6. Jean-Paul Sartre, *L'Etre et le néant,* Essai d'ontologie phénoménologique (Paris, Gallimard, 1943), p. 692.

7. Manuel de Diéguez, "Yves Bonnefoy et la critique de style," *Esprit,* XXVIII (décembre, 1960), 2128.

8. Maurice Saillet, *Sur la route de Narcisse* (Paris, Mercure de France, 1958), pp. 191-192. Article dated November 1953.

9. Jean Grosjean, "La Poésie. Yves Bonnefoy: *Du Mouvement et de l'immobilité de Douve,*" *Nouvelle Revue Française,* II (1er septembre 1954), 511.

10. Mario Maurin, "On Bonnefoy's Poetry," *Yale French Studies,* No. 21 (Spring-Summer 1958), p. 19.

11. Pierre de Boisdeffre, "Résurrection d'une Parque: La Poésie d'Yves Bonnefoy," in *Une Histoire vivante de la littérature d'aujourd'hui* (Paris, Librairie Académique Perrin, 1962), pp. 606-608.

12. The quotation in English translation reads: "But the life of mind is not one that shuns death, and keeps clear of destruction; it endures death and in death maintains its being." G. W. F. Hegel, *The Phenomenology of Mind,* trans. J. B. Baillie (New York, Macmillan, 1931), p. 93.

13. Friedrich Höderlin, *Sämtliche Werke*: III *Hyperion* (Stuttgart, W. Kohlhammer Verlag, 1958), p. 70.

David Mus (review date June 1976)

SOURCE: Mus, David. "Stances on Love." *Poetry* 128, no. 3 (June 1976): 163-77.

[In the following review, Mus provides a stylistic analysis of Dans le leurre du seuil, *asserting that Bonnefoy's verse is grandiloquent and difficult for English-speaking readers.]*

"*Je veux que la fréquentation d'un maître me rende à moi-même; toutes les fois que je sors de chez Poussin, je sais mieux qui je suis.*" I would love to apply this *mot* of Cézanne's to my reading of Yves Bonnefoy's new book [**Dans le leurre du seuil**]. If only I knew more about myself, or about him for that matter, as I put it down . . . But the élan with which I enter the experience is broken page by page. I am put off, simply, by the grand language—by the persistent abstractions, the rarefied metaphorical cast, the lofty tone and the difficulty of knowing, in such staginess, what at any moment is going on. In short, very much the difficulties I experience before one of those passionately rhetorical paintings of Poussin, apropos of which after all Cézanne was speaking. Painting, poem—it is all about something else than him and me; it deals resolutely with what I have to guess at, of which "we" are scarcely even aspects.

The rest of Cézanne's judgment gives me a way out: "*Imaginez Poussin refait entièrement sur nature, voilà le classique que j'entends. Ce que je n'admets pas, c'est le classique qui vous borne. Je veux que la fréquentation d'un maître . . . etc.*" Should I in order to make contact with this artist imagine him "*refait entièrement sur nature*"? Will it only be at the price of this distortion that I enter his work? The poet is not limiting me by interposing rhetoric between me and his experience, rather I feel *borné* as it is, my limits are being, from the first words—"*Mais non*", already a rhetorical gesture—both challenged and confirmed. What I come to know better through this rendezvous manqué, however I take it, is not what I think I am but what I might become through the poem if only I could get past its language. Maybe that is just what Cézanne meant?

This experience, of being routed into a poem through an elaborately contrived defeat of immediacy, has a flavor of *déjà vu*. Have I ever read a French poem which did not produce it? Not to draw you in at once with the communication of an experience, but to circle off into weighty words and constructions, wheel and posture as in a tedious gavotte—a certain grandiloquence is the hallmark of *la poésie,* its claim to fame or at the least to a *mystique.*

> *Mais non, toujours*
> *D'un déploiement de l'aile de l'impossible*
> *Tu t'éveilles, avec un cri,*
> *Du lieu, qui n'est qu'un rêve . . .*

My reaction to such prancing is equally familiar: we are all, we moderns, leery of what we call with a grimace "rhetoric" because it smacks of posturing and calculation. We wince before statements of general truth in starched language as surely as we shrink from a touch of simple sentiment. We are nervous in fact about saying anything, hearing anything, about life, or truth, or the world, or ourselves, that does not spring from someone's irrefutable experience. Whatever you say about me without knowing me reeks of arrogance, parental, pedagogical, or patrician. Individual experience—*le vécu*—must guarantee all plausible speech: that is, as we cogently put it, our "outlook".

There are good reasons why such views should prevail. "Poetry" sounded at the beginning of this century much more like *"poésie"*; the two terms carried a similar prestige. There are equally good reasons why *la poésie* should have retained its highfalutin cast, despite valiant tries at making it racy, direct, and concrete. Usually we allege the advent of Malherbe, as it was put even then (poor old bogeyman, always cited, never read). But Malherbe's was a conservative intelligence; medieval French poetry, even at its most pithy and spare, even Rutebeuf, even Villon, is steeped in rhetoric and bound to a stringently erudite versification. *La poésie française* remains today an abstruse craft to a degree we English-speakers can hardly conceive.

I am deliberately blurring distinctions drawn by words like "grandiloquent", "rhetorical", "classical", "erudite", "craft", so as to point out the one direction we have to face when we read French poetry, any French poetry, even that which has strained for something else. Does the picture we get, which can so easily put us off, only confirm the *lapalissade* that French is French and English, English? No, these languages are today not only versions of their own past, forging ahead, but great partners and rivals, dialectical views of the virtualities of language itself. The relation has been explicit in the law courts since 1066; and in poetry, since Chaucer and Deschamps made the bond one of friendship. French had much to give us then, and notably abstractions in their relation to substance. If a pig was stuck in the barnyard, pork was served at table. Written French has never stopped cultivating its classy side, drawing steadily away from the wide-ranging, tolerant, popular bent of English as well as from its own colloquial temptations.

Take the words of the title before us. *"Leurre"* has no remote connection with the bit of bright red leather tossed in the air to lure the falcon down. I even doubt if we can catch in the word a hint of the glittering fly arching into the trout stream. The word cannot be used metaphorically, it has withered to an abstraction, and yet . . . and yet from its fastness in the mind, the word can be made as here to turn back into the out-of-doors, through its power to name the ineffable yet deeply familiar force which draws us out to hunt and fish. Similarly, what we cross, rod in hand, is not this stone slab under door-posts, worn smooth and hollow, solid and homely beyond thought; but a threshold hung as by magic somewhere in the world of Being. Like *"le leurre"*, *"le seuil"* brings us back to the specific and

concrete through its links with art and artifacts, with images and substance, perfectly matched by the spell the word itself casts as sight and sound.

When we say "threshold", this stone is here. We move past its hard and fast singular densities, reach towards its specialized figured uses and arrive, if ever, at pure meaning. English looks out along the myriad aspects of a foreground into the distant prospect of significance. French has long since retired to its room with its bag of choice meanings to pore over them into the wee hours. Such vignettes are our way of putting it; a Frenchman would talk of mirrors and spheres, of acceptance and exclusion, of presence and purity and the sacred. In what other language could the theater of essences be the work of a man named *Racine*? or the founder of theatrical eloquence bear the name *Corneille*? These are differences in metaphysical bias; they have fascinated us from the start. To the question, Why read French poetry? we could answer, Because we always have; which solves a great deal, but not the more urgent problem, What have I to learn from French? and more pointedly, Why should I read or try to read Yves Bonnefoy?

All the more trying in that M. Bonnefoy has not made things easy for his English-speaking friends. He has not taken in his new book, the first in ten years, any of the currently favored avenues of escape from eloquence. He has found rather an old entry into the place where the search for "one's own voice" lights on that of language and exults. This exultation, the tone of the explorer and adventurer of an *ancien régime,* is what we hear as grandiloquence. Its resemblance to the traditional edifice of rhetoric, or to our own version of the high-flown (the far-fetched) is only apparent, though the appearance counts. Grandiloquence seems to us superadded, fulsome, dispensable—scaffolding you clear away, Latin magnificence you edit out in order to get down to bedrock, the simple telling Anglo-Saxon roots, the way people really speak. There is not such an alternative for French. True, *siroter* moves no one while *boire* is busy making its point. Yet the decision to be made line by line is not at all stylistic, between plain words simply arranged and the recherché terms welded into complex constructions. Rather the French poet has the choice between words and word-orders which convey a notion, or else those which carry conviction. An impersonal conviction: words like *fleur, mur, vin, épaule*—or *énigme, présence, absolu,* for that matter— can be made to clang like a buoy when lifted by the swell of verse. This magisterial clamor is like that of the sea: not always joyous, never without grandeur. It is a grandiloquence at the heart of a language, which one reaches by a sedulous, a strenuous attending to the power of words to mean more than they either name or suggest, and by setting aside both the sensual and the conceptual with their claim to a monopoly of valid signification. The word *fleur* brings us into the presence of something which noting the delightful aspects of a hollyhock can blind us to, and which vanishes without a trace when we set on it with a pack of concepts. The "place" of presence and of conviction, *ce lieu,* can open to us before any object; it is the unmistakably meaningful clearing this poetry invites us into.

We imagine rhetorical language to be justified only by the other acts of language it permits—the way we used to think Metaphysical poetry was saved from its rhetorical character by its sensuous imagery—the way we assume a course of purposeful action is only redeemed from insincerity by specific acts of purpose. The concentration on meaningfulness alone may seem to reduce much poetry in English to catalogues, anecdotes, legal briefs, chiding and rapture. But to speak such lofty speech, pursuing as a purpose an intensely articulated, restricted vision, is already to have meaning, is someone meaning, meaning towards, thrusting out, *vers,* "*plus avant*". The hard-headed English stylist may only hear from across the water *l'art pour l'art* or else that intellectualizing pretension known, after its unwitting American parent, as *la Poësie.* The fact remains, putting meaningfulness before meaning, mindfulness before concepts: these thrusts define a poetic which side-steps critical categories and contemporary viewpoints. Hence the peculiarly patrician tone of its authority, the elusive nature of its claim on our attention, the anachronistic not to say archaic bent of its shameless eloquence.

What is it then, this poetry, about?—not, What does it mean? since *le sens* is subordinated to a purpose, but, What is it up to? What I called the rarefied metaphorical cast of Yves Bonnefoy's language makes it hard to say, yet gives us a clue. In French poetry there is no such thing as literalism, not even the fiction of literalism which even the most sustained directness, in Spenser or in Whitman, comes down to. Instead French has an immediacy of figure and a complication of mediating voice which English cannot match. All naming in a French poem stands for the act of naming. To say "*une fleur*" is to say "*Je dis: 'une fleur'*". There have been voices which broke on the silence where literalism lives, unappeased by eloquence; we hear no authentically broken, inelegant voices . . . At the same time, placed on a page the word flowers into metaphorical bloom, into essential significance, *le sens,* arch-traitor to the cause of immediacy. Between the "*Je dis*" and the outrageous blossoming of meaning, this pink hollyhock, here and now, mine and yours, is effaced—in the worst of cases is vanished, as the magicians say, by an astonishing and sometimes irresponsible legerdemain. This middle kingdom of the *hic et nunc* Yves Bonnefoy has set out to explore and conquer for poetry.

For French poetry, because he writes not just in French but in that high dialect called *la parole poétique.*

Inescapably, in such a self-conscious medium, an affirmation of the here and now takes the form of a "*Je dis*" and becomes matter for a meaning. An old dialectic reaffirms itself. The art of Yves Bonnefoy in his new book is to have let it do so, within his own focus and intent, while respecting the build and bearing of the ancient French poetical act—while making what we recognize as a true French poem. In it, words come to have all they can of the literal: the immediacy of grand scenes made of close-knit, humble things, *la table, l'éponge, l'enfant*—a cuisine of representative items having abundant meaningfulness but no single reference, something like the Passion instruments, borne by angels in thin air. Up until five or six years ago, each day placed a stunning example of such language before every generation of French poets: the Latin liturgy, an ancestral accomplice as telling, as immediate as the famous Anglo-Saxon roots. Yves Bonnefoy's poetry means to recreate, *réinventer,* a secular liturgy. What is celebrates is not just the here and now, but *le lieu, l'heure,* the substance of the *substantif,* which the French definite article keeps indicating; not the, nor yet this here and now, but—how should I say?—"the this here", "the this now".

Substance, presence, the here and now: these realities are always on the tip of our tongue. If we cannot quite speak them, it is because of the dead space, the dark flaw, unutterable, which the thing itself opposes to the light of speech. Can we somehow celebrate that too? Celebration is a mystery; the word *pain* names not this bread I break, but the humble thing dignified by its otherness, by its inscrutable reserve. The word takes me into the secret of the loaf, which is not its essence, elsewhere, but the reason why this or any such thing has value, "value" to which both concepts and objects are to be referred in weighing their truth, "truth" which is not primarily an attribute either of postulates ("*Je dis*") or of things ("*une fleur*"). Extend this vision of their strength to all words, not just to the venerable dignitaries of the language but also to upstart parvenus like *la télévision* or *la fourgonnette,* and the whole language wheels round, brings us back toward objects on a new slant. In the same way the generalizing of the trope "*une fleur = 'Je dis: "une fleur"'*" makes over the page of poetry, which becomes itself a metaphor for speech, "*feuillage*", an allegory or extended metaphor condoning each failure of literalism and charging with the significance of the act of utterance everything on it.

If in this poetry the language gives us the meaningfulness and value of particular objects; if the page gives us in advance the act of utterance—where then should we find the poet and his experience? the story, the history, of his encounter with what is not himself? Someone is there, rising before dawn with a cry from his dream, leaving a rumpled bed, going to the window, getting a glass of water, tepid in the heat, grappling with first words, first sights and sounds, on the very edge of language . . . But his person is dissolved in the consciousness of the terrifying, austere conditions of even these simplest acts. This intimate *mise en scène* is itself a mock-up, a tableau vivant; the person is a figure, who can only speak of himself, precisely, in the second person:

> Et tu te lèves une éternelle fois
> Dans cet été qui t'obsède . . .

Such a figure questions the objects which insist on seeming to surround and include him, he gathers their message and speaks for them: not "*Je dis*" like himself, but "*Je consens*". Their consent is not to a beneficent order, merely to a living totality of which his language gives the image, to an appertaining of each to each and to the conditions of being there—*appartenance, tutoiement* which are those of the articulate questioner as well.

Question and answer are always rhetorical, what the objects say standing for what this object might have said if as in English the poet had, at a particular moment, met it within a mood, interrogated it through his senses, then let it speak as if for itself on the page. *L'eau,* this tepid water in the cracked jelly-glass this morning, is also *l'eau* the elemental, one of the four ancients, worthy to be interviewed on the great questions, noble enough to reply through our voice. As for the object itself, it never has to appear in court: French poetry has for long been burdened by that vaguely patronizing wonder, when "objects" or the out-of-doors come into view, which we associate with the classically-educated intellectual and the inveterate city-dweller. As for the poet's own experience, it goes without saying: hence that authority, that sureness of touch and mastery of purpose—that high hand, so often galling—which we associate with the artist who never leaves his studio to work *sur le motif.* Both these sumptuous contributions to eloquence should be seen as the outcome of the Frenchman's experience of his own experience: a most poignant *pudeur.*

In English, for a long time—perhaps since Sir Thomas Wyatt, the first whose experience matters to us even at all?—any particular has been able to act as a figure for our experience of it. To place the word "daffodils" on a bare page would be to say, Here are daffodils, or, I saw daffodils, while recalling the poem which sums up for us the encounter of the roaming mind with anchored particulars. This is still the way our poetry works. One thinks for example of Richard Eberhart's remarkable meeting with a dead groundhog . . . Take though a similarly remarkable passage from **Dans le leurre du seuil,** where the poet recounts the death of a dear friend, the musicologist Boris de Schloezer. It is an achievement of his art, not a failure, that you do not know

finally whether the poet was present. The language does not give us his experience and is not meant to. It moves us rather from its own realm, an exalted *ouï-dire,* a surmise, towards what might be experienced. The language, that is to say, is tendentious; the words have a dynamism, a direction, they exert a pressure. To find common ground, the translator has to push an equal distance the opposite way:

> Aujourd'hui le passeur
> N'a d'autre rive que bruyante, noire
> Et Boris de Schloezer, quand il est mort
> Entendant sur l'appontement une musique
> Dont ses proches ne savaient rien (était-elle, déjà,
> La flûte de la délivrance révélée
> Ou un ultime bien de la terre perdue,
> "Oeuvre", transfigurée?)—derrière soi
> N'a laissé que ces eaux brûlées d'énigme.
> Ô terre,
> Étoiles plus violentes n'ont jamais
> Scellé l'orée du ciel de feux plus fixes,
> Appel plus dévorant de berger dans l'arbre
> N'a jamais ravagé été plus obscur.
> . . .

> Terre,
> Qu'avait-il aperçu, que comprenait-il,
> Qu'accepta-t-il?
> Il écouta, longtemps,
> Puis il se redressa, le feu
> De cette oeuvre qui atteignait,
> Qui sait, à une cime
> De déliements, de retrouvailles, de joie
> Illumina son visage.

> Bruit, clos,
> De la perche qui heurte le flot boueux,
> Nuit
> De la chaîne qui glisse au fond du fleuve.
> Ailleurs,
> Là où j'ignorais tout, où j'écrivais,
> Un chien peut-être empoisonné griffait
> L'amère terre nocturne.
> Nowadays the ferryman
> Must ply a dark, and chattering shore . . .
> And Boris de Schloezer, as he was dying,
> Hearing from the jetty music
> Those who loved him best could not make out (was it,
> So soon, a piping from across the waters?
> Or a last gift from the departed shores,
> Life-work transfigured?)—behind him left
> His passage, these waters charred inscrutable.
> Oh earth—
> Never has a crueller race of stars
> Sealed heaven's lid with flames more fixed;
> No all-consuming cry of shepherd from his tree
> Has ever ravaged summer so obscure.
> . . .

> Earth, what had he glimpsed, what grasped
> And what accepted?
> He listened, for a long time,
> Then he drew himself up, the flame
> Of that work reaching to
> A summit, who can say,

Of deliverance, reconciliation, joy,
Lit up his face.

Brief sound, blind;
Pole striking into the muddy stream,
Night
Of that chain which drags along the bottom.
Elsewhere,
Where I knew nothing of it, where I wrote,
A dog, perhaps he was poisoned, clawed
At the bitter, benighted earth.

What, or where, is the common ground? The poet is not alienated from what we call "his own" experience—"*Je consens*" is his watchword—neither cut off nor brutally present as the modern poet in English is likely to be; but eternally detached, at a precise distance, *un écart*; eternally elsewhere, *ailleurs,* in a world of images which are not appearance nor illusion nor mere dream, rather the substance of all three. A language of images which precede and determine experience, where things and their meaning maintain an easy commerce, where "rhetoric" is a natural employment of logic: such a language is familiar to us through the tradition of thought and writing which modern (romantic) poetry renounced, that of the Elizabethans. A language determined to come to grips, from its stronghold in the universals, with the starkly or the joyously singular; a language of place, where the grievances which rule our lives can play themselves out dialectically: this is the language of the theater. Yves Bonnefoy has translated half a dozen of Shakespeare's plays and written of the translator's problems. His new book, like his last, bears an epigraph from *The Winter's Tale,* in which we watch the two aging kings discover the miracle of Perdita's rebirth: "They look'd as if they had heard of a world ransom'd, or one destroyed". ***Dans le leurre du seuil*** is written as an homage to this play, to its author, and to its promise of a possible, a here-and-now redemption.

The faces of the royal friends confronting this unmerited, unexpected, unbelievably joyous new lease on life, as acutely seen by the anonymous courtier, express an equivocation: "A notable passion of wonder appeared in them. But the wisest beholder, that knew no more but seeing, could not say if the importance were joy or sorrow . . ." What do we know in the theater that redeems seeing from equivocation? We know, beyond the speeches of any one character, the set of the whole play's imagery, which sustains its dialectic. Lunacy and reason, cruel jealousy and burning love—these can be arbitrated by a single language which affirms them all. It does so by composing once for all with the grief and hazard of unreasonable circumstance, disorder, bafflement, surprise, and death. A love of the creature world, in its place among over-mastering stars, has staged our crazy tale.

This love, this eagerness of our language to conjure with broken and imperfect destinies, gives today's poet in French an example, with paradigmatic value, of one thing which can be done. Shakespeare to the French has never been a *fait accompli* as in the famous German translations, but a renewed discovery, an élan of the whole sensibility of the language. Voltaire, Stendhal, Mallarmé each tried to make this thrust explicit; Victor Hugo and Claudel tried to reproduce it in the theater, from the distance of their own tradition. Such is this distance in time, in life, and in art, that the approach to Shakespeare could never be other than an attitude. Yet such is the central place of attitudes in French literary life that to take one up—even to strike one—is to commit yourself on principle to a way of life and to defending your choice with statements about what is fitting. To take up Shakespeare, thus, is to commit yourself, intellectually, to his affirmation of love and to its language.

One might put it, for Yves Bonnefoy, that *l'amour des êtres passe par une prise de position, c'est-à-dire par une image.* The yearning thrust into life is a movement of art, words and their patterns, a *projet,* a *recherche,* an *expérience*; in sum, an *oeuvre.* While in English we think no art truly important which does not proceed from that thrust and affirm it! That in French the image itself should precede the affirmation, an image through which consciousness enters the world, this further complication of awareness and intent gives its intellectualizing twist to what familiars of art know as *l'art.* That the élan towards living particulars—broken, imperfect, ephemeral—should require statement to goad it on and complete its *geste*—apostrophe, prosopopoeia, tableaux vivants, all the rhetorical finery of an appeal, *un appel,* self-addressed first of all—this most unhappy bind is now, openly, in this volume, the poet's drama.

The poet takes a stance on love: this is the awkward posture of those who feel the weight of an inheritance, that of a literary language, as a responsibility to take up, an opportunity to seize and a debt to pay. This paradox, which the notion "a literary language" already embodies, has been for the most responsible a living dialectic, as best expounded by that most aware of French poets in poems he called *Les Fleurs du mal.* Since, the emphasis but not the burden has shifted, as the titles indicate, from the person to the place where pain is transcended. (***Dans le leurre du seuil*** rings as an affectionate echo of, and reply to, André du Bouchet's *Dans la chaleur vacante.*) The page has become an opening before which one stands, that pre-dawn window through which, in the early parts of the book, the poet can peer past the walls of his dark image-haunted house. For this stance on love does not go without saying. There are other attitudes to acknowledge, or to combat, and first of all in oneself. There is coldness, amour-propre, fear; further on, here come denials, refusals, aloofness; and even further, lying in ambush, the whole troop of previous commitments, and ambition, disdain, indifference. Each of these must be given its place and its voice in the total drama to which the poet has said *"Oui!"* and *"Je consens!"* The grand language which stymied us at first is not thus oratory; but an authentic theatrical eloquence.

It takes an expert reader to know at any point who is speaking and in what voice. Beneath the dialogue, however, within the imagery, a dialectic unfolds which most of us are better equipped to follow. The opposing thrusts of English and French, for example: *The Winter's Tale* deals differently with the theme of redemption which is also Poussin's in his three versions of *Moïse sauvé des eaux,* whose imagery the poem also studies and expands. Thus our century, when the 17th asks it to stand and deliver, distinguishes, compares, synthesizes in its own untrained but generous fashion. Thus too, within what has come to be known as *l'écriture,* a dialectic of modes: the word, *le verbe,* saying itself, *la parole* flogging itself on towards an acceptance of experience—this painful spectacle of wanderings, survivals, and recognitions vies as illumination with the hieratic simplicities, with the composure, the bright elegance of the pastoral and the pictorial. Writing as a continuing discovery, a progressive revelation; *l'oeuvre* as it becomes itself and then *le livre,* an organic whole built on growth and whole parts—these indulgences of process war with an Apollonian temptation to conceive it all in advance, make it perfect, impose a polished conceptual order on inert materials which can't talk back, achieve *l'Oeuvre* in *le Livre,* the complete world-grammar or book of spells, *grimoire* supposedly so dear to Mallarmé.

We take it for granted that the page of poetry should reconcile conflicting strains in a new music. Black and white harmonize there without exciting the wonder with which the gourmet discovers Port and Stilton, or should I say *chambolle-musigny* and *brie*? Connoisseurs will find in Yves Bonnefoy's versification delight enough and wonder, page by page, to smooth down any number of feathers ruffled by his grandeur. He is a conscientious craftsman, the prosody of his new book flows from the dialectical situations we have just been examining. They can in fact only be disjoined by a critical artifice, drama and imagery owing their existence to arrangements on a printed page. This page, in this book, has become the formal unit of poetry. We take it for granted also that some kind of mediating form should stand on the page between it and the verse—even if only a form of regularity or consistent irregularity—subtly controlling our attention. Here the disorder of the lines, like the seemingly haphazard leafage of a tree, alternately masks and reveals the framework on which it has grown. This framework, which we divine before we see it, evinces on close scrutiny the functional intelligence of a system without a system's rigidity.

Nothing more modern than to set aside the classic mediations; nothing more contemporary than to pretend to eliminate formal mediation itself. Nothing more artful than to have picked up the discarded fragments and rearranged them in a mocking collage or a deceitful appliqué—but the arch and the cunning are not, mercifully, elements of this very earnest book. The traditional versification has been shattered, yes; but only to permit a reassessment of its strengths and a rehabilitation, not of its appearance but of its original bias. There is, the poet is telling us, no such thing as a "personal" versification, for this would be a conscientious failure to versify. Verse means belonging to a tradition—in one's own way, yet this way is authenticated by the rites of belonging, is no more "mine" than the language I speak. That language has its rules. To use it is to respect them freely, not to kowtow. Yves Bonnefoy has rethought syllabic versification, the French rules, even the perfectly traditional breaking of them.

The basic unit here is the broken *alexandrin,* the hemistich of six syllables (the title is a good example) which can become the old lofty line when occasion demands a lofty emphasis; which more often, with four syllables added, turns into a reversed or else a disjointed decasyllable; and which sometimes takes on five syllables more to make up the rare hendecasyllable, the verse of the Absolute, of the One. Each of these lines, even the incompleted gesture towards them, even their perversions, permutations and approximations, has its rôle in the dramatic pattern of the page. Each contributes a tone, largely traditional; each also comments in its own voice on what is being said by the dramatic voice which uses it and the kind of imagery it supports. For number, the poet is telling us, lives everywhere in our world, in all its forms, to which as to all else we may cry *"Je consens!"* Like the past, like redemption, like perfection and eternity, number does not vanish from our horizon merely because we have ceased to believe in it. Rather it endures, curiously strengthened, as an image, *un leurre,* called still to play its part in the drama of the human mind. Number is everywhere: on each different page of virtually 26 lines; in the pagination, so carefully arranged, the prime numbers insistent; even down to the 19 points which mark the gaps between speech and silence.

Number as presence, then, on the page; number also as image of what is absent, as *leurre*: this dialectic takes us into the most important dimension of the prosody. The tradition of syllabic verse, I have said, is one of rules kept and of rules broken. There is no adhering to a tradition except from outside, just as there is no breaking with it until its rules and their spirit have been so exteriorized as to seem no longer yourself, but something a self can renounce. The "number" that is everywhere is not the same "number" that those knew, in Poussin's time, say, who belonged to it. That number—those syllables or those proportions, like the other classic mediations, ode, altar-piece, architected nave—defined a community of belief. What is the number that remains with us—a mocking sign of our community of unbelief? Or something more? To use an *alexandrin* now is both to raise and to answer this question. Shakespeare, Poussin, Malherbe: the past has come and gone leaving on the mind's retina a burning image. And not just "an image" nor yet "the image", but *l'image*. The page as a form of consciousness stands over number as presence, number as absence, and creates from their deadlock, from the desuetude of their promise of order and community, a new promise, *un seuil*. The *leurre* may be only a mirage; it can also be a "*nuée*"—a radiant elemental form, imaginative entry into the meaningful. The image may be a cruel reiterating deception; or else a *revenant* with news from the past or the beyond. And our belief that we have a say in where such figures lead us may illustrate our credulousness, or else the ultimate bad faith of art. These dilemmas, at any event, define the place where we stand; our good faith will sanction no other.

The tradition has been there. We are released now even from the choice of adhering to it or renouncing it from outside. To use its terms is to name literally our consciousness of this freedom—or else the unaccountable ways we have yet to find we are still part of it. *Le leurre* is that of which *l'art* now gives a literal rendering, expounding its grammar, researching its provenance, guiding its growth, highlighting its truth. Poetry having been essentially a use of language, then a form of language, then for long a quality of language, looks now, in these pages, like a responsibility of speech to its better self: the conscience of language. Not, I should say, a responsibility to one's better self, at least not oneself as we know it, the individual, personal experience hedging our approach to knowledge. "Self", "individual", "personal", "experience", even "knowledge", even "tradition"—these are the old terms. They provide us with an image, not of what we have lost—vain nostalgia—but of what we might become if only we could get past their grandiloquence. Faced with the claims of scientific discourse to deal with generalizable fact, poetry takes responsibility for universalizable insight, what we used to identify with knowledge of truths, or with the moral sense, or, more baldly, with wisdom. These are long-accepted commonplaces, yet they locate in our current prose the far more precise and interesting imperative to which the poem alone can bring us. Here is no wisdom—thank heaven! sighs modern taste—but the struggle of a man to make his peace with the claim on him of his own inmost speech. He does it by adding to poetic language a new layer of consciousness.

Yet another layer . . . Is such a thing possible after the work of Paul Valéry? Eliot thought not, and claimed in his essay *From Poe to Valéry* that a return to some form of naïvety was more likely. Yet naïvety in another sense may be just what we have yet to transcend. The possible degrees of heightened awareness are after all infinite; there is no reason why, like the individual, poetry may not keep on climbing and cultivating them. All it risks is a further narrowing of its audience, a risk to be taken with full knowledge of poetry's powers to educate and persuade. The natural capacities of a language may be no more natural than the artful uses we put them to. The recent advances in the recording of personal experience, in the capturing of precise sense impressions, in the skilled use of the Anglo-Saxon roots, may be leading us to the end of the era when such choices had meaning. "In general terms, we may have reached that point in Western history when the major languages have to emerge from their naïvety and break with their instinctive assumptions, so as to establish themselves in a different kind of truth, with all its contradictions and difficulties." (This is from Yves Bonnefoy's essay, *Shakespeare et le poète français,* which I quote in the curiously Englished version published by *Encounter,* June 1962.)

Yet another layer? It may look as if Yves Bonnefoy were trying instead, not quite single-handed, to turn the French language around, to face it out towards experience and the source of experience; away from intellect and its props and its narcissism, back towards that tense enigmatic life among objects whence words ultimately draw their power. *Imaginez la langue française refaite entièrement sur nature* . . . Can French seize that otherness and account for it, move out from behind its own wise abstractions and, armed with a few elemental terms, approach those singular experiences of what there is, that can perfectly well do without words, if not without us, altogether? Is such a project *outré*? its formulation arrogant? the summons to it an unacceptable didacticism?

Certainly nothing, unless it be grandiloquence, makes us bristle quicker than didacticism. And there are dramatic passages on this theme in this new book whose fervor reaches into the hortatory and the polemical. Since the poet's consciousness is of that rare practical turn which makes over every anguished question of, What is to be done? into another, What is to be done next? his fervor speaks for an attitude unleashed, optimism becoming the self-conscious power to move. The question remains, is this *parti pris* what we would call an axe to grind? Is the capacity for profound mutation, and for this particular mutation, a genuine gift of the language that the author has seen and brings us to acknowledge? Or else a quirk of his own mind and style, even a delusion, like Leontes' jealous lunacy in *Le Conte d'hiver*? If the odds at the end, as at the end of the play, are on the side of a genuine intuition, that is because the voice which gives it most cogency is not, by gum! the one which proclaims, expounds and defends it. This fervor speaks equally for despair and defeat, *"le mauvais désir de l'infini"*, for mere meaning, abstraction, and aloofness, speaks from that winter of the heart where this *conte d'été* was written. It speaks within a dramatic poem where voices and attitudes balance and strain: "a world ransom'd, or one destroyed". Conversely, to address oneself to the problems of the hour is another way of affirming one's presence in a world of ephemera. The stance on love, in other words, remains a stance, and a stance taken also on the matter of taking stances. The dialectic is intact. It includes the urge to persuade and instruct within another kind of persuasion. The poem and its attitudes imply each other mutually.

What we are called to by this very drama is not a partial betrayal of language in lieu of an impossible affirmation; but a heightened awareness of all it offers, a more complex relation even to the classic notions of self and experience. The poet sets the example: he and his experience are not here, as we have seen, and the *ailleurs* of the images where we find him is our place as well:

> Tu fus jeté sanglant
> Dans la lumière,
> Tu as ouvert les yeux, criant,
> Pour nommer le jour,
> Mais le jour n'est pas dit
> Que déjà retombe
> La draperie du sang, à grand bruit sourd,
> Sur la lumière.

The *"draperie du sang"* is authentically Shakespearian, precise yet polyvalent, telling, irreplaceable. Yet the rest, the *"grand bruit sourd"* carries toward the figure that peculiarly sonorous, *disert* eloquence which makes the *"draperie"* a plush proscenium curtain and the image an unmistakably French one—unmistakably Yves Bonnefoy's meld of innocence and experience, of loftiness and stern perspicuity, recalling the early-Baroque achievement of disciplined compassion. The foibles of this poet, or any other who speaks with such authority and such moving restraint, are not mere accident. They make and then become the history of the language.

The summons, in fine, sounds a challenge. Whose stance on love? Whose love? Can this poet yet know? "Who's there!" cries the sentry twice on the opening page of *Hamlet,* peering into the ghost-ridden, pre-dawn dark, on the high stone parapet. In his translation Yves Bonnefoy renders this desperate appeal with both of the possible French versions. At first, *"Qui va là?"* a simple question of presence; but then, in the other, the grand direction, subjunctive, the question of allegiance: *"Qui vive?"*

Marc Hofstadter (essay date fall 1978)

SOURCE: Hofstadter, Marc. "The Search for Transcendence in Yves Bonnefoy's *Un feu va devant nous.*" *Romance Notes* 19, no. 1 (fall 1978): 4-9.

[*In the following essay, Hofstadter examines "experiences of transcendence" in "Un feu va devant nous," the third section of* Pierre écrite.]

Death is an almost overwhelming reality in Yves Bonnefoy's poetry. In his vision of things, death undermines all happiness and all permanence. Not something we encounter at the end of life only, it is indistinguishable from the actual world around us. Pervading all things, it often causes reality to become silent and barren for us, alien in its otherness. It may seem to be the prime force in existence, to dominate our lives.

But there are times when reality turns and reveals another face. Such occasions are described in a number of places in Bonnefoy's prose. The world turns slowly within the moment, leaving time and space behind. All that we had seemed to lose, through death, is returned to us. Nothingness is replaced by a fullness of being, and we begin to live the "vraie vie" which Rimbaud, one of Bonnefoy's masters, sought. Bonnefoy calls what happens in these moments "présence," a condition in which all seems part of an illuminated, vital unity. It is because of such experiences that life is worth living after all; they give us hope and a possibility of fulfillment. Presence, not death, though he writes of death so much, is the goal and heart of Bonnefoy's efforts.

We can come near to such presence or illumination, though, only through mortal things, through the things of our world. Since finitude is the only realm we live in, *it* must be the object of transformation if we are to attain to a sacred condition. Bonnefoy therefore writes a great deal of things of the earth: stones, birds, stars, leaves, water, blood—and of humble, domestic objects: tables, lamps, hearths. However, it is not particular, concrete things in which he is interested—this red porcelain cup in front of me, that stained window-shade. It is generalized, elemental presences—L'eau, La pierre, L'étoile, La table. These are not abstract universals, though—not concepts. Concepts are not adequate to the experiences he reveals, and Bonnefoy believes in general that they turn us away from reality, are set apart from the world. Instead of showing us sensuous particulars, or ideas, Bonnefoy reveals the mythic and permanent aspects of objects, the region in which they take on shape as elemental presences. We are transported to worlds of significance and resonance beyond our normal perceptions. All being suffused with a hushed, other-worldly beauty, we are spoken to, a truth fills us with its being. The world becomes thoroughly meaningful, with a meaning beyond mere reference, and we feel liberated and transformed. Such a moment passes, and we are returned to our world of limitation and death, but poetry can keep awake the moment's memory. Poetry is of the past—of those images that have retained their significance for us—and of the future—of a possibility hovering over the horizon. But it helps us wait for the decisive moment. It is a proximity and a hope of things to come.

One section of Bonnefoy's book *Pierre écrite* is pervaded more perhaps than any other with the revelation of a sacredness: "Un feu va devant nous." The third of four sections of which the volume is composed, "Un feu va devant nous" follows on a division, "Pierre écrite," which has at its core death and suffering. Many of the poems in that part bear the title "Une pierre," and most of these are desolate or sad. To Bonnefoy stones suggest impenetrability, the impossibility of the entry or embrace of thought. In this sense they resemble death, which too is impenetrable, unthinkable. However, "Un feu va devant nous" shifts the focus of the book. While containing such poems of dark waiting as **"La patience, Le ciel"** and **"Le jour au fond du jour sauvera-t-il . . . ,"** its main thrust is the nearness of a plenitude. Poems like **"La chambre," "L'epaule," "L'arbre, La lampe," "Les chemins," "Le myrte," "La lumière, changée," "Le cœur, L'eau non troublée"** and the culminating **"Le livre, pour vieillir"** convey us to realms characterized by silence, immobility and a suffusing light, qualities central for Bonnefoy, I will try to show, to experiences of transcendence. The poems embody faithfully in their structures Bonnefoy's descriptions of the coming of presence, which involves a *slow turning within the moment*—a gliding, gradual transition that takes place almost outside of time, in an expanded instant, as though in a dream. This kind of experience is repeated, in differing ways, in many of the poems of "Un feu va devant nous." Each constitutes a moment of special insight and revelation.

A careful though necessarily brief study of a few of these poems will suggest the essential nature of Bonnefoy's vision of the proximity of presence. One may well start with the first poem of the section, **"La chambre."** The poem's scene is a mythic bedroom at morning. An endless ebb and flow as of waves in the sea prevails, "Toujours se reformant, toujours brisé," a movement resembling the ebb and flow of sleep. Everything dozes and perhaps dreams, or else is in a state between sleep and waking. Like the mirror and the overflowing river, which call to each other across the room and merge their lights in the darkness, the speaker and the being he addresses (a lover?) communicate within sleep through solid stone steps whose density normally would prevent such interchange. The elements of the scene are transparent; there is an endless flow of light, a clear, dreamlike interpenetration of beings and objects. All lives and has meaning, even sleeping and

inanimate things. The "main pure" comforts and protects the "main soucieuse," and the red robe, like a holy object, is magically radiant in its sleep. Filled with peace, the poem gives a sense of a world made finally real and significant.

The world of **"La chambre"** is characterized by immobility, silence and light. It is full of activity and communication but these take place as though in a dream, enclosed within the slow stillness of a single moment. The qualities of the earth are there, but they exist on a new plane. Moving slowly in a duration that unfolds within a timeless instant, we virtually turn away from the domain of time to approach a condition of permanence. We are in a visionary state in which stillness dominates despite movement, silence prevails in spite of speech, and light renders everything transparent. With a slow turning we move away from the ordinary, mortal world to live in radiance and serenity.

A great many of the poems in "Un feu va devant nous," in their various ways, embody similar types of experience. Described in **"L'arbre, La lampe"** is a summer dawn or sunset—the poem is ambiguous as to time—that lasts an almost eternal second, perhaps the seemingly limitless duration of the sun's rising or falling. Light disperses grief and the darkness is healed, while all is virtually still with a stillness of dream. Drowsiness dominates: sleep comes on "dans la sève du monde" (suggesting sunset) and "la lumière des lampes . . . rêve dans le jour" (implying it is dawn). Is the morning sun bringing a growing brightness, or is this red robe's light that of the end of day? As at twilight, the birds cease their singing; nothing in the scene disturbs the silence. The poem's movement is that of a very slow change of light and wakefulness, a barely perceptible growth or fading away. Vulnerable and delicate, the moment is "Comme la flamme d'une lampe que l'on porte." With light glowing and the soul throbbing with feeling, the sickness of mortality that assails us is made well. "La barque . . . rejoint le rivage et tombe" into a peacefulness at the end, as back into sleep. Like **"La chambre," "L'arbre, La lampe"** demonstrates a gradual turning from duration towards a condition of timelessness, a turning enclosed within a moment.

"L'epaule," "Le myrte," and **"La lumière, changée,"** among other poems in "Un feu va devant nous," display the same slow shifting within the instant, the same silence, stillness and light. The structure of **"L'epaule"** expresses a gradual and continuous progression from a hope (first stanza) to a sparkling dream (stanza two) to the beginning of an actual merging with eternity (third stanza). Having endured his "obscur déchirement de nuit" the speaker in the end comes near to a transcendent "gave Qui s'apaise, ou se perd, dans notre éternité." There is no sound or motion but the gliding of "L'eau d'un rêve" and the "bruissement du feuillage." Light grows from the dawn of the first line through the mirroring dazzle of the waters' afflux in stanza two to the putting down of the light-excluding mask in stanza three. We move closer and closer to a new source of breath and illumination with a slow-gliding opening up to being. Like **"L'epaule," "Le myrte"** describes an approach to an eternity—a seemingly endless summer, "un grand été." The speaker's contact with a loved one becomes in stanza two a purgative transformation which leads to the state of ecstasy of the third strophe. There the bed, turning slowly, gains the freedom and majesty of the high seas. The scene is permeated by light—the summer sun, the flashes from the burning of the tree—and by the miraculous lingering continuation of the summer. In **"La lumière, changée,"** too, one finds a gradual motion away from everyday life—this time a seeking for something primal, sacred: "L'arbre est plus proche et la voix des sources plus vive." The participants move by tiny, unseen steps towards this "Dieu qui n'est[t] pas." There is no sound except for the mysterious "voix des sources" and the "cris d'oiseaux." The poem has little light—like some other poems in "Un feu va devant nous" such as **"Une voix"** and **"Un feu va devant nous"** itself—for it is an enigmatic presence that is nearby. But like the other poems we have been discussing, it embodies a dreamlike, hushed, visionary state.

In the transcendently moving **"Le livre, pour vieillir,"** more than in the other poems, Bonnefoy seems to have actually found what he has been seeking. The stars—transhumant like sheep—and the shepherd bend protectively over earthly happiness. There is "tant de paix," a peace which is great in its very, irregular, earthliness and humanness. Instead of words, it is silence that rises from the book towards the heart; no words are needed for this communication. A wind stirs, also silently, at the center of the meaningless sounds of the world. Time smiles willingly at its own end and the orchard's simplicity of fruition caps the fulfillment that the speaker feels. "Tu vieilliras," yes, time still exists. You will be, finally, "la terre menacée," like it, threatened by death. But "Tu reprendras le livre à la page laissée, Tu diras, C'étaient donc les derniers mots obscurs": you will pick up the book again, you and it continuing to exist in time, but now able to say that all is clear, that you understand, that you can face this death that will come. The poem conveys an absolute serenity in which one sees into the heart of things. Set within a perfect moment which is wholly silent and suffused with light, it offers a glimpse of something that makes our life completely peaceful.

These poems, and many others in "Un feu va devant nous," display a common type of transcendence. Time slows down, space expands, everything seems to glide motionlessly and silently, bathed in light. Instead of be-

ing opaque, dark, dominated by death, the world becomes transparent, illuminated, alive. Solid objects swell with the presence of something divine and become permeated with meaning. We ourselves lose some portion of our mortality and live in what for a moment seems permanence. Eventually we fall back into time and finitude. However, we have the memory of our experience, and the hope that it will come again. We can wait with patience, and in this, poetry can help. Poetry is a metaphor for transcendence, and aids us in preparing for its coming.

Mary Ann Caws (essay date 1984)

SOURCE: Caws, Mary Ann. "The Poet and the Voice." In *Yves Bonnefoy*, pp. 4-20. Boston: Twayne Publishers, 1984.

[*In the following essay, Caws explores the major themes and images of* On the Motion and Immobility of Douve *and* Hier régnant désert.]

L'Anti-Platon (*The Anti-Plato* [abbreviated *AP*]), an odd series of nine brief prose poems published in 1947, opens with a call to human specificity, in opposition to the realm of vague Platonic Ideas. Bonnefoy will never relax his concern with the particular, and even in moments of his greatest temptation toward another land, a crossroads to another life, he maintains his visible loyalty to the here and now, to this land and the range of things which are its furnishings, seen in detail or in a wider perspective.

"And now this object: a horse's head larger than life, containing a whole town, with its streets and its ramparts running along between the eyes, wedding the winding path to the length of the nose" (*AP*, 11). Like a contemporary *vanitas,* the object here is a stark reminder of mortality or *memento mori,* including a death skull, a candle, and a glass; a meaningful and typical assortment of symbols of everyday living and its necessary end, this vision is all the more terrible in that a horse's head replaces the ordinary human skull, as if in mockery. Moreover, the everydayness is intensified; the tiny model town is more "civilized" and organized than the usual assortment of miscellaneous things which would be placed upon the vanity table by the skull, while its insertion into the animal head sets up an anamorphic play between two ways of seeing, between the animal and the cultural. As for the balance between and real and the artificial, the town is constructed of wood and cardboard, but illuminated, on the bias (still the unsettling angle of "this thing"), by the real moon. Then suddenly the anamorphic play is accentuated by the skull's turning into a woman's head, turning on the disc of a phonograph. Multiple forms of intensification are used here: surprise, aggrandization (of the head by the town inside it), substitution (of the animal for the human), and then resubstitution (of the human construction for the animal). When a woman's head replaces the horse's head, more horrible still in its chaotic appearance with the hair streaming about the wildly turning head upon the phonograph, the music of harmony is replaced by this melodramatic disharmony.

The presentation is deliberately shocking in its offsets and contrasts: this initial image is followed by the peace of the reeds, the stone, and the water of the countryside, the calm suddenly interrupted by the last images: "robes tachées" ("spotted dresses"), blood-covered laughter, and the absence of any gaze whatsoever. Such a horrible absence and equally horrible presence provide an unequaled combination of "choses d'ici," or earthly things, weighing in the long run more than the perfection of Ideas. The anti-Platonic theme initiates a violence full of uneasy and monstrous forms: a hatchet falls, the woman's head is thrown into flames, and a statue of blood is sacrificed by knife edge to a "funereal dialectic" or rebirth and division (13). The country, once seen with its water and stones, is now composed of blood, blackened flesh and death: death as the illuminating wound, which, by the certainty of suffering, clarifies all about it, including the subjective and occasionally ambivalent world of poetry. Here it provides also a theater for the struggle of love and death, a dramatic *liebestod* to be taken up again in a broader sweep, within the nineteen parts of the **Mouvement et immobilité de Douve,** for which this earlier poem is in some sense a preparation—a few images recur: the penetration of the body into summer, the black grass "like a funereal cloak," a cry, the fissure in the earth. Illumination also, because, surrounded by a set of teeth buried in the earth, this stone at the middle of it all, this touchstone of sacrifice, lies at the very center of the turning world: "From having touched this stone the lamps of the world spin, the secret lighting circulates" (19).

The theater of the death of Douve, the name signifying at once a depression in the ground and woman's proper name, is sketched in the opening section of **Du Mouvement et de l'Immobilité de Douve** (**Of the Movement and the Immobility of Douve,** 1953), which enlarges upon the nine sections of the poem just mentioned. Douve is surely one of the most haunting of contemporary literary creations, for she takes shape all at once in an unforgettable scene of violence and pathos and love. She is seen running, battling the wind, and being torn apart by the forces of death. It is once again summer, and the sun and wind spotlight specific gestures, as the ivy, this simple image torn and bruised, appearing in the essays as the very signal of presence itself, is chosen over any vague Idea: ("rather the ivy"). We remember from the preceding volume that Platonic Ideas cannot

approach the strength of the specific object, either for violence or for affection, and can "only tinge the lips." It is only in the small details—a sunny patch left on a windowpane at the coming of night, a spot of light upon a mountain, or a single leaf of an unnamed tree or its accompanying ivy—that life is felt as something beyond a generality, and as the transcendence, already, of the death to come. And yet the specificity is accompanied by the very incompletion of such statements as "Rather the ivy. . . . Rather the wind. . . . Rather, on some mountainside. . . ." They are left open to all possible comparisons. Rather than what?—the choice may be made elsewhere, but it need not be specified here, and the preference seems all the stronger for the incompletion.

The poem is anything but gentle: the wind is stronger than any memory, so that the present occupies the entire scene. The dress blows about, in tongues of flames, until the beating wings of wind and their exultation are perceived as celebrating both death and life. But directly after this violent "beating" wind, the poet describes the rain beating down, as the heart beat before. Wind and rain, dream and vision mix in a natural metaphor and a human reaction. Douve's gestures, immemorial and luminous, those of deathless beauty and ceaseless birth, then slow down: "Gestures of Douve, already slower, black gestures" (27). In seeking death, she somehow clarifies life. For the opposites will always meet within Bonnefoy's vision, especially in this period: with rain and a subterranean river there mixes the "fire" of her gestures; this arm inflames, is raised, and falls; the shadow and the mist cover over the gaze shared by the woman and the poet.

Now the pounding of the arteries, within which are felt the beating down of rain and the roll of drums, is replaced by a terrible and disintegrating music in her hands, knees, head, as the facial muscles dislocate, the eyes are ripped out, and the body is extended horribly under a swarm of insects. Even the dress, once pure and flaming, is now soiled from the oil of the lamp: the morbidity of the imagery prepares the rôle of the poet as watcher, as the observer of her secret knowledge—of the ceaseless corruption of her eyes, now clouding over. The strident "exultation" of insects is now heard in an atrocious music, displacing all images to leave behind only an imageless truth, as the insects advance in an endless pitiless assault upon the body. Resplendent with a somber fire, she has access to regions lower and lower as the violence and the horror subside.

Solemnly and not without grandeur, an incantation in the form of a hymn to death now rises, marked by anaphoric final repetition: *now, now, now,* drawing attention to the vividness of the moment, this "présence exacte":

Le ravin pénètre dans la bouche maintenant,
Les cinq doigts se dispersent en hasards de forêts
　maintenant,
La tête première coule entre les herbes maintenant
. . . et c'est nous dans ce vent dans cette eau dans ce
　froid maintenant.

(39)

(The ravine penetrates the mouth now,
The five fingers are dispersed in forest random now,
The head first of all slips among the grass now,
. . . and we are in this wind in this water in this cold
　now.)

The observer and the reader are drawn into the saluta-
tion of earth, which appears to have neither sadness nor
resignation to it. The blood, appearing exactly where
the poem is said to tear apart, renders the poem living,
and in the intensely oxymoronic atmosphere already
pointed out—flame/cold, birth/death—tension marks the
fitting site for trial. As if the poem were some matter to
be rent asunder, on which to inflict damage and thus
prove the vitality of the stuff inside: "You had to appear
at the secret border of a funereal place where your light
dims; you had to submit to trial" (40). Along with the
dying figure in the poem, the poem undergoes the trial
of death, in order to live. Even the death "infused in her
laughter" only contributes to the dazzle and brilliance
of her theatrical gestures: she, and the poem, pass the
test.

Finally, this Douve is seen as an aperture, cut into the
world, and into its thickness, an opening through which
we learn to perceive. She is the first figure loved and
lost as the drama opens, always, through her presence
even at her most faraway instants, denying absence and
unfeeling in the world about her, forcing awareness
upon an erstwhile numbness: thus her description as an
"ouverture dans l'épaisseur du monde" ("opening in the
thickness of the world"). Nevertheless, the tragedy of
this poem is essential: a nineteenth part, coming directly
after the concluding encounter of poet and the dazzling
vision, and written in two stanzas of free verse instead
of the prose of the preceding eighteen parts, contains
the history of an attempt at our own evasion of the
everyday into another zone: breathing the initial cold,
perceiving afresh, we rise into another atmosphere, but
are only momentarily able to imitate a figure's flight,
falling back again upon the ground like a wounded bird
or an arrow whose feathers break at a touch, like some
lesser Icarus or some Phoenix in utter failure.

The passing of the world's opacity into perception was,
after all, only attempted through the gesture of another,
and we cannot possibly imitate or reincarnate another's
triumphant bareness; if, then, the final test of perception
is to be identification with the flight and fate of another
figure, no matter how close, we are to fail. Imagination,

admiration, even union, are not the genuine mutual
interpenetration of that denseness of the phenomenal
world which we most passionately desired. Myths are
not so easily transformed into realization: the essential
solitude of this poem gives to the title its fullest
poignancy: in a theater, one observes, identifies in
imagination, but remains an observer. Poetic perception
is not necessarily, at least not so far, action.

Of course, the volume does not end there, neither with
the theater nor in the observer's failure as actor. The
voice of the poet will from now on address itself to
other things than to the failure of identification: the
gestures of dying, once so dazzling to the onlooker, are
now echoed in a section of "Derniers gestes" ("Last
Gestures"). The travel of Douve beyond death on a path
of trees, these closing after her in order to guarantee her
continued brightness even as she becomes nothing,
across the river Lethe of forgetfulness along the path
she only can take, "this going / Along so much night
and in spite of all this river" (43), links her fate to that
of the narrator, through the mediation of nature and the
word.

For these gestures of crossing and those made by the
poet, like some ancient rite of passage, and the gestures
of linking already signaled by the image of the
threshold, which will be all-important in Bonnefoy's
work and to which the last chapter of this book refers,
are like the *gesta* of the medieval *chanson de geste*:
deeds recounted, lending dignity to the telling word and
guaranteeing both to teller and listener emotional
participation. The brief verses following the grave salute
to the parting gesture of Douve are eloquent:

Que saisir sinon qui s'échappe,
Que voir sinon qui s'obscurcit,
Que désirer sinon qui meurt,
Sinon qui parle et se déchire?

(44)

(What to seize but what is escaping,
What to see but what is darkening
What to desire but what is dying
Speaking and tearing itself apart?)

Silence is above all the object of desire, the word heard
and seen as departing always. What is not repeated and
not glimpsed again beyond its own temporary moment
is infused with nostalgia and longing, as in Baudelaire's
sonnet to the passerby, to which Bonnefoy so often
refers: "Ô toi que j'eusse aimée / Ô toi qui le savais!"
("You whom I would have loved / You who knew it!")

The single possible offering acceptable to the person
departing forever, as to the dead, would be a speech
cast in its very materiality like a blanket "over origin
and night." A Maenad consumed by fire in her dancing,

Douve disappears by her name into her action to which the poet is the only witness, as she hurls herself into the flames of the sea. This clash of elements is responsible for her intense verticality lit from above, as if we were seeing the dance from some terrace or parapet far above the water where she is hurled. So contemplated, she is at once fleeting, as in a game, and in an attitude of supplication, as in the ancient representations of Maenads. The somber light and the flickering fire place her desolation in a still theatrical setting: "Tout se défait, pensai-je, tout s'éloigne" ("Everything is undone, I thought, everything takes its distance," 50).

And then it is a question of nomination: "Vrai nom" ("True Name"). The True Name given to the dead reminds us of the true place spoken of elsewhere, and leads to the "Vrai Corps" ("True Body"): the act of naming is the essential act of this poetry, and only the poet can effectively name. As a double act of love and hostility, of spirituality and materiality, of freeing and of tying down, the poet opposes her even as he names her: "I am your enemy who will show no pity" (51). Through interdependence of contraries, even the purest words depend upon matter, as spirit depends upon body, meaning upon naming, poetry upon presence and upon the acknowledgment of death inserted in life: "Il te faudra franchir la mort pour que tu vives, / La plus pure présence est un sang répandu" ("In order to live you must traverse death, / The purest presence is a blood spilled forth," 52). The full sense of the epigraph from Hegel at the outset of the volume is understood at present: "But the life of the spirit is not frightened before death and does not keep itself pure of it. It is bearing death and maintaining itself within it" (21). In the privileged or true place of poetry for the accomplishment of the sacrificial ritual, the true act, preparatory to the successful flight of the Phoenix, is joyous, all-powerful and self-perpetuating as the Phoenix is self-resurrecting. With the bird, the poet's song endures, and the voices echo, one against the other: that of Douve, of the bird, of death and life. The meditation on naming implies in the same speaking voice the poet, the listener, and the respondent. Each is called upon to recognize this death or "lowest marriage," which buries the bright destiny in the earth, Douve in death, and the poet in her knowledge and in her name: "Douve, je parle en toi; et je t'enserre / Dans l'acte de connaître et de nommer" ("Douve, I speak in you; and I hold you close / In the act of knowing and of naming," 55). Douve answers, in self-containment, within her own silence and lack of sight: "Pourtant ce cri sur moi vient de moi, / Je suis muré dans mon extravagance" ("Yet this cry upon me comes from my own self, / I am walled in my own extravagance," 57).

But against the charged dialogue of poet and victim—whether a victim of destiny or of self or of the act of poetry itself—other voices are raised. Unspecified except as "a voice, another voice," they serve at once as parts of a tragic chorus, representing outside and in, exteriorising Douve's point of view upon herself, the poet's other aspects, and, perhaps above all, a questioning of the gestural and verbal *signs* uttered so far. "Long have I retreated before you, signs," says one voice, and another: "What sign are you bringing on your black lips?" I shall inhabit you, it continues, lifting you to yet another emptiness. But these are not negative cries of death and distress, rather, "distant beneficent voices" of dawn and rain, waking the clay figures along the longing earth, expressing fruitfulness even in the act of dying.

Douve, waking from her hypnotic state as stone, having shared its blindness, now sees her own drama clarified in the dying and suffering which is the sure way to the mind. Reassured by day, by the summer and the naked earth, she calls upon silence once more after these voices are heard, forged as they are in the hearth of contraries. Her invocation to cold and death is ardent in its tone, made with "reddening words":

> Que le verbe s'éteigne
> Dans cette pièce basse où tu me rejoins,
> Que l'âtre du cri se resserre
> Sur nos mots rougeoyants.
>
> Que le froid par ma mort se lève et prenne un sens.
>
> (63)
>
> (Let the word die out
> In this low room where you join me,
> Let the hearth of the cry narrow in
> Upon our reddening words.
>
> Let cold through my death rise up and take on
>   meaning.)

The imploration gathers up all the strength of the preceding voices, and is answered by a further sign of the interdependence of perception and of speech (64). The watcher keeps vigil in the speaker, as death in life and life in death. He implores for Douve the destruction she has already invoiced, echoing her speech act: "Demande pour tes yeux que les rompe la nuit" ("Ask, for your eyes, that night shall break them," 66). But the verbal command is followed by a doubt as to the efficacy of the word, expressed by one of the voices: "Oui, c'est bientôt périr de n'être que parole, / Et c'est tâche fatale et vain couronnement" ("Yes, being but word means to perish soon, / And is a fatal task and vain coronation").

And yet this doubt is itself balanced by one of the most celebrated images recurring in Bonnefoy's work, that of the orangerie, that "site far off" where the salamander acts as Phoenix, assuring presence and resurrection, living through the fire. It is appropriate that after the ways of death and their insertion into life, the place of poetry should appear again. The orangerie is allied, as both contrary and complement, to the Ordalie or medieval trial. This ritual and the orangerie itself allow easy access: the latter is marked by a vase on its threshold, placed in welcome to the wanderer as to the reader, for whom, also, "words of healing" will be recited: "Let a place be made for the one approaching, / A person cold and deprived of a dwelling" (85). The place is a true place, "un vrai lieu," but also a place of combat: in its perfect form, the orangerie invites a meditation of the mythical. The salamander desired by Douve is celebrated in a luminously erotic series of prose statements. She desires penetration by the narrow animal, desires both blindness and possession; but at the same time she is herself the salamander, immobile and knowing. The single vigil kept over the dead and through the dying ("I keep watch in you") leads to a double vigil at the summit of the winter's night. The wound (of knowledge, of love, and of their penetration by each other) marks the moment of sacrifice, and the woman as well as the hollow which she also signifies, receive once more their identical name: "Et maintenant tu es Douve" ("And now you are Douve," 74); "Douve sera ton nom" ("Douve will be your name," 82). "Justice" and "Truth" precede a poem called **"True Place",** and in that truest place of the orangerie now named, Douve will be laid.

So the true place "where everything is unveiled" or disclosed (as in the Heideggerian sense of being made apparent or "called into disclosedness") contains war and repose, specificity and abstraction. The orangerie can be represented anywhere, and it then becomes the true place; for instance, the Chapel Brancacci suggests the powerful image of "vigil-lamp of January," casting its light upon the tiled floor, as the shadow all about and the dark frescoes provide a place suited to the search for eternity within what can be grasped here and now, in one of the privileged sites for the imagination: "Ce que je tiens serré n'est peut-être qu'une ombre, / Mais sache y distinguer un visage éternel" ("What I hold tight is perhaps only a shadow, / But discern in it an eternal face," 86). The play of light and shadow here leads to the final poems of "lieu" or place concluding the volume: **"Lieu du combat" ("Place of Combat")**, where the knight of sorrow becomes the brother "whose face is sought near all fountains," whose death is equivalent to nocturnal shadow, and against whose suffering the truth of dawn and day must be measured. And this is now the **"Lieu de la Salamandre" ("Place of the Salamander")**, whose awareness traverses fire and with whose purity and silence the poet is intimate, calling it his accomplice and his own thought, wedded to the flame in an allegory of risk and joy beyond wordlessness itself.

Finally, the **"Vrai lieu du cerf" ("True Place of the Deer")** is charged with the weight of religious myth, recalling the medieval allegory of Christ as the deer pursued by hunters, and escaping. All that is implied in this ending of a volume on death and what traverses it in a deeply poetic consciousness: "Ô notre force et notre gloire, pourrez-vous / Trouer la muraille des morts?" ("Oh our strength and our glory, shall you / Pierce the wall of the dead?" 91).

Much of the strength and carrying power of Bonnefoy's work lies in its intense emphasis on polar opposites: for example, the movement and immobility in Douve's title, or the rest and combat visible in the poems, or the purity and the eroticism of the salamander, which are then absorbed each into the other. The poetic process is similar to the one by which the poet has his vision *through* Douve or speaks within her, or even lives in her ("I shall find out how to dwell in you," 59); and yet the ambiguities remain. For instance, from Douve: "If this night is other than the night" (60), implying a tension between specificity and generality, and nevertheless also the common ground between them, that undeniably links night to night, beyond any specificity or distinction.

The ambiguous relation of the other and the same is stressed by Douve's question as to what voice is speaking near her or against her, naming her, and by her subsequent claim about being the origin of all she hears; "Yet this cry upon me comes from myself." Furthermore, the words said by one of the unidentified voices could be said of this poem as a whole, and its coherence as an inseparable unit, for the voices are, all of them, part of the rhapsody. The volume, rewritten with several linking passages for its final form in 1978 after its initial publication in 1953, makes now a complete narration whose harmonies are complex, moving, and ardent: "I have borne my word within you as a flame" (67). The very speaking and narrating of the Death and poetry of Douve into the arduous shadows, like consciousness into dark, compose this elegy, like the name Virginia Woolf was tempted to give to her novels, which sets ablaze by its spirit the silence before and after.

Readers tend to be greatly divided as to their opinions of the successive volumes of Bonnefoy's poetry, some preferring *Douve* for its incantatory power and dramatic sequence, some preferring the condensed inscriptions of *Pierre écrite* (*Written Stone*), **some the continuities and imagery of the massive *Dans le Leurre du seuil*** (In the lure of the threshold), Bonnefoy's most recent long poetic work at the time of this writing. The brief volume about to be discussed, *Hier Régnant Désert* (Yesterday the desert reigning, 1958), might, on the other hand, appeal to the reader who would choose brevity, depth of feeling, and an indescribable tone of melancholy conveyed by an essential understatement. The poem of yesterday never leads to a statement entire, but only to the threshold of a place where it might have been made.

The title of the initial poem here, called **"Menaces du témoin,"** places the reader immediately at risk, for the observation itself leaves no place for uninvolvement. The fear and blindness within the poem as stated come to paralyze the watcher also, even the one who would by choice remain upon the sidelines. In this text, destruction is paired with the cessation of combat, age with immobility and loneliness, made parallel to the retraction of mental and physical warmth by the image of the fire receding. The withdrawal of the flame, but also of such strength as the emotion of fright might itself bring, enables the growth of the person, and implicitly, the deepening of the poem equated with the interior experience of language at its most profound. But the static menace hangs heavy in the cessation of all things, in the decrescendo of the dying down in word and wind: "Puis j'ai vieilli. Dehors, vérité de parole / Et vérité de vent ont cessé leur combat" ("Then have I aged. Outside, truth of word / And truth of wind have ceased their battle," 95).

After the first-person lamentation, the narrator addresses a second bystander implied in the battle with questions as to motivation and identity and place: ("Où es-tu, qui es-tu?") associated with the garden of memory and the shadow included in the shadow, presumably within the watching self. The notion enframed in the poem comes to a halt abruptly, as the poem is haunted by its own closure, encapsulated in the repetition of "même . . . même":

> Vois, déjà tous chemins que tu suivais se ferment,
> Il ne t'es plus donné même ce répit
> D'aller même perdu. Terre qui se dérobe
> Est le bruit de tes pas qui ne progressent plus.
> . . .
>
> Tu cesses de venir dans ce jardin,
> Les chemins de souffrir et d'être seul s'effacent. . . .
>
> (96-97)
>
> (See, already all the paths you took are closing,
> You are no longer given even this respite
> Of going even lost. Earth which slips away
> Is the sound of your steps which go on no longer.
> . . .
>
> You stop coming in this garden,
> The paths of suffering and of loneliness fade out. . . .)

The gradual slowing down, the closing off of possibilities, the blinding of paths and former illuminations and revelations: "Il te suffit / De mourir longuement comme en sommeil" ("It is enough / For you to die slowly as in sleep," 97), all these elements which could, from any traditional perspective, be seen as negative, are here transmuted by the tone itself, noble, resigned, but remarkably strong in the telling and narrating voice. Quite unlike the tone of the words addressed to Douve in her pilgrimage to a land beyond death and her laying-to-rest in the orangerie, the elegy—if it can be called that—to and of a lost being here includes an interrogation new in this poetry: "Es-tu celui qui meurt, toi qui n'as plus d'angoisse, / Es-tu même perdu, toi qui ne cherches pas?" ("Are you the one who dies, anguished no more, / Are you even lost, who do not seek?" 98).

The loss is far from certain, and there are no dramatic gestures, no disintegration such as is evident in **Douve**: only question and quiet, as the wind falls still and the fire of the word is laid. This is the continuation of Kierkegaard's "Knight of Sorrow," whose premonition we heard already in **Douve.** The rod or the arm is and will remain the surest weapon for vanquishing in both the fields of erotic love and combat, and for the construction of a timeless, spaceless, limitless warmth and radiance, in the dwelling of poetry.

In the next poems, the solitude remains, together with the silence; yet the oath of construction, recently sworn, is not undone. The knight renounces glory, fame, distinction, to choose obscurity and another kind of song, as yet unheard. The grey waters on the shifting earth match his renunciation, paralleled by the demythification of the Phoenix, who himself tires of being the self-resurrecting bird and gives in to his age-old wound, thus undoing himself and his legend as well as his lie, accepting in their place silence, age, and death: "L'oiseau se défera par misère profonde . . . / Il vieillira . . . / Il se taira . . . / Il saura bien mourir . . ." ("The bird will undo himself in deepest misery . . . / He will grow old . . . / He will fall silent . . . / He will know how to die . . . ," 102).

But renunciation by the bird of his myth, by the knight of his renown, do not rule out remorse: rather they increase it. The light of summer in its mingled sweetness and fear has left its radiant mark upon the poem and upon all it surrounds and contains: regret, remorse, and the deepest longing for what is no more. The summer is wounded in the greyest of its dawns, and the poetry, grave:

> Ce fut un bel été, fade, brisant et sombre,
> Tu aimas la douceur de la pluie en été.
> . . .
>
> Et ton orgueil aima cette lumière neuve,
> L'ivresse d'avoir peur sur la terre d'été.
>
> (105)
>
> (The summer was lovely, pale, somber in its shattering,
> You loved the softness of the summer rain.
> . . .

And your spirit loved this novel light,
The excitement of fearing upon the summer earth.)

In the final invocation, a poverty contrary to all the former pride in poetry and in things previously loved brings about a difference. As bareness breaks and remakes the spirit, this voluntary renunciation in flames within the desert tables of writing, sets them afire with an inalienable loneliness: alone, the knight finds no appeasement (107).

The title **"Le visage mortel"** (**"The Mortal Face"**) designates death already inscribed upon the visage of being; by the poem, the flame is returned to the somber daylight, as if its ardor were to be undone by the light of day. Beauty is here dishonored and dispossessed as it ruins being and undoes the joy of the daily. All things are changed and oddly opposed in preparation for the Ordalie, that medieval trial (already compared to the *other* of the orangerie) where the voice falls into contradiction with itself, and then into the silence seen as the ultimate grandeur; so is belief to be tested. The sword is pulled from the stone, in a simple statement of a renewed Arthurian gesture. In the poetic universe where the interchanges of word and self are heightened, the essential "grayness of the word" is to be penetrated only by the ardent "red iron of being" for hospitality and communion: "Nous venions de toujours . . ." ("We were coming from always . . . ," 103); "Et j'ai rompu ce pain où l'eau lointaine coule" ("And I broke this bread where the distant water runs," 116). The other surrounding gestures are simple, solitary, and therefore honored: praying, keeping the fire, standing guard, or waiting, gestures of the beseeching *orante,* the weeping *pleureuse,* the faithful *veilleur* watching, the dutiful *servante,* the mysterious Parque who controls our fate. The very simplicity of the tasks is moving: watching the fire and sweeping the hearth are the duties of a vestal virgin; just so, the protective gestures of the figure of large stature who comes to participate "in the stone," holding the lamp and leaning over. Gray stones and cold trees surround these acts in which the observer shares also, as he too sleeps, trusts, ages, and dies, watching always.

Upon rereading these texts, old and new, as they are inserted now in this present edition, one cannot help being conscious of the relationship of the figures in some composite imaginary picture, distant and yet intimate, unsentimental and yet of distinctly emotional affective power. The gray stone surrounding the scene is the background and yet is at the same time the stuff of which the figures are composed, legendary and yet actual, dead and yet living, suffering and imploring: the stone, by its wounding, offers its own cry of anguish. The night of imagination and dread is long and tormented, and the path seems interminable; the poems of this section end quietly, in separation, bareness, and indeterminate time, as the figures withdraw into loneliness.

"Le Chant de sauvegarde" (**"The Song of Safe Conduct"**) returns to the figure of the Phoenix, to the scene of this death and shipwreck and passage by fire. Called by some bird cruel and of a black voice, the narrator enters, speaks, ages, and is silent, before hearing another song; as if an entire story were to have been absorbed in this short stanza. On a page alone we read or hear a song made of brief lines, telling both of destruction and salvation: "Que l'oiseau se déchire en sables, disais-tu, / Qu'il soit, haut dans son ciel de l'aube, notre rive" ("Let the bird tear apart in sand, you were saying / Let him be, high in his dawning sky, our shore," 129).

"Le Feuillage éclairé" (**"The Foliage Lit"**), which begins by an interrogation, is strengthened in this recent edition by the doubling of the question, "Dis-tu? Dis-tu?", conveying perfectly the feeling of legend, of vague mystery and certain sadness. It opens thus, after the initial questions in their echoing repetition, leading into a simplicity of statement consonant with the birdsong:

> Dis-tu qu'il se tenait sur l'autre rive,
> Dis-tu qu'il te guettait à la fin du jour?
>
> L'oiseau dans l'arbre de silence avait saisi
> De son chant vaste et simple et avide nos coeurs,
> Il conduisait
> Toutes voix dans la nuit où les voix se perdent
>
> (131)

> (Are you saying he stayed on the other shore,
> Are you saying he watched you closely at day's end?
>
> The bird in the tree of silence had seized our hearts
> With his vast, simple, and avid song
> He was leading
> All the voices in the night where voices are lost)

What we call after, as the bird well knows, is what is lost and is to be found no more. Such a song is never unmixed with pain; again we think of Rilke's bird song, joining inner and outer worlds, and again of Baudelaire's Passerby, loved and lost, loved because lost. The setting is full of memories, although bare of detail. With the bird as guide, the wanderer in the lofty and tragic "boat laden with grief" devotes himself to the task: "L'oiseau m'a appelé, je suis venu" ("The bird called me, and I came," 130), and leaves what is most familiar and homelike, the earth of lamplight and hearth, for the night. The song was simple: presently it takes on a tone of irony and a threat of death, while the vocabulary increasingly stresses distance, refusal, blackness, poverty, and hardship; the bare moment in the harsh work of earth.

The very harshness of the setting, while it sets the task and the calling apart from the everyday, intensifies the solitude about the one who, like Siegfried, will have now to seize the sword, bright-colored with red and with blue, like a red sun against an azure sky, or within the flame of some brightly colored fruits. For even in the land of exile, the obscure land of shadow and yet of dawn, where "une ombre essentielle / voile toute lumière et toute vérité" ("an essential shadow / veils all light and all truth," 134), the love of earth remains strong, and the love of love. The sun, rising only to age and to sink, shares man's pattern. Each text will elaborate—although keeping the same simplicity—upon the hero's call, task, and knowledge. You (for the second-person form is retained) will hear the bird call, "like a sword in the distance," cutting through all the shadow and fear and despair, will see "shining the naked blade you must seize" (136), and this will be the end of waiting.

The task is legendary: the sword is cold, its handle rusty, and its flame now grown dark. It is inscribed in the stone, which bleeds from its wound, and on which the lessons of moving and dying are traced. The task is, as we might have expected, eternal, and endless. As other trees closed off the path after Douve's death and departure, these on the contrary open a path, which must be taken.

The concluding section, **"À une Terre d'aube" ("To an Earth of Dawn")** is brief. Its form is that of dedication, of a devotion as in the prose poem called by that name, at the end of the volume and already referred to: in this edition it has become a separate item, standing, as indeed it should, apart. Dawn, daughter of tears and suffering, is to rearrange and reshape the room of rest, and the heart to begin again and take on color, after that colorless face, in another brightness. Life will return afresh. "Écoute-moi revivre, je te conduis Au jardin de présence . . ." ("Hear me reliving, I lead you / To the garden of presence . . . ," 144). Each of a number of privileged images—the dawn coming, like the red wound of a sun against a sky, or water making a hollow in the stone of day, or fire and spirit seen in the broken bread, or the conflagration of every dead branch—discovers or uncovers a country. Again we think of the Heideggerian call and disclosure, in this "pays découvert" ("land discovered"). A star marks the threshold, and the ardor within is perhaps only what we call time. This is at last, then, the place, sought, toward which all steps were leading. "Le pas dans son vrai lieu" ("The step in its true place," 149). The voice after its unrest is happy in these rocks of silence, and will continue to sound within the stone of the tree, recalling another legendary task: Oedipus saved as well as sacrificed, about to do battle. For this voice: "The same voice, always," traverses all pain and anguish and all time, emanating from the bird of ruins.

Here, at the end of this yesterday which was deserted and was a desert *Hier régnant désert,* is the true, clear place, no longer dawn but now day, no longer the

mirage of a song, but the certainty of the task chosen alone, in this place built from memory and from stone. "Ici, dans le lieu clair. . . . Ici, et jusqu'au soir. . . . Ici, toujours ici" ("Here, in the clear place. . . . Here, and until evening. . . . Here, always here" 150).

The poetic path has not led far off, but only to a song of the here and now, of a presence recaptured in full clarity.

Alex Argyros (essay date 1986)

SOURCE: Argyros, Alex. "The Topography of Presence: Bonnefoy and the Spatialization of Poetry." *Orbis Litterarum* 41, no. 3 (1986): 244-64.

[*In the following essay, Argyros considers the complex relationship between critical interpretations of Bonnefoy's verse, his own theoretical writings, and his long poem,* On the Motion and Immobility of Douve.]

For the most part, the poetry of Yves Bonnefoy has been read as an expression or application of Bonnefoy's numerous theoretical statements concerning the function of poetry. In other words, Bonnefoy's poetry has been understood as the practical materialization of his esthetic speculations. Critical work on Bonnefoy, consequently, has operated within the horizon of one of the fundamental binary oppositions of Western esthetics: pure idea/its reification. A variant of the mind/body dichotomy, the theory/application couplet is not a neutral concept, but participates in specific ways in the historical development of Western philosophy. As Derrida has frequently argued, the Western metaphysical tradition has tended to create its edifice by deploying a series of privileged binary oppositions. Specifically, the theory/application couplet makes a number of implicit assumptions. It assumes the possibility of a clear demarcation between two identifiable realms: the realm of theoretical prose and that of its realization in verse. Furthermore, it assumes that poetry can incarnate a content which is not essentially poetic. If it is possible to conceive of a transference of sense from prose to poetry, then sense must be in principle independent of the medium of its expression. Even in the extreme case where poetry is not understood as a vehicle for the conveyance of a message, but as the creation of a content, if that content is legitimized by its mimetic relation to a preexisting canon, then even its self-actualizing performance is derivative of a conceptual apparatus that has ontological precedence.

Such, then, is the broad theoretical structure underpinning much of the critical work on Bonnefoy. My contribution to that corpus, this paper, has two goals. Firstly, to analyze certain dominant interpretations of

Bonnefoy's poetry (including his own); and secondly, to related this analysis to a specific poetical work of Bonnefoy, *Du mouvement et de l'immobilité de Douve* (henceforth to be designated as *Douve*). I will seek to focus neither on Bonnefoy criticism, nor on *Douve,* but on the complex interaction between them. Ultimately, I think, the relation between theory and praxis will both help to illuminate the encounter among Bonnefoy's theoretical work, his poetry, and the analyses of certain powerful critics, and to suggest that it is precisely the difficult burden of this enormously idealistic dialectic that has prevented another kind of reading of Bonnefoy to emerge.

I. Presence and Contingency

Most critics have understood Bonnefoy's esthetic position as the impassioned championing of material presence.[1] Before proceeding to an investigation of what, according to Bonnefoy, presence is, let us begin by asking what it is not. In a relatively recent text, "Sur La Fonction Du Poème," originally a paper read to the Académie de Belgique in 1972, Bonnefoy defends his notion of poetry against what he perceives to be the dominant critical perspective of the day:

> Evoquez-vous un homme, une pierre, un arbre, ou même tel être bien précis, tel fait de la société ou de la culture connus de tous, et voici qu'aussitôt ces références sont prises dans la continuité de l'écrit, modifiées par les apports du contexte, suspendues par son devenir—, et donc arrachées à toute authenticité d'échange au niveau du simple et dans l'instant. L'écrit transpose l'intention, défait la voix transitive.[2]

According to Bonnefoy, because writing resists the possibility of immediacy it is inimical to the production of effects of presence. And, inasmuch as poetry is a linguistic act, it must paradoxically buy its authenticity at the cost of abandoning writing:

> De la trace que laisse en moi le texte que j'ai refusé de poursuivre, une intimation me vient donc, de toute façon, déjà, qui n'est pas de recommencer à écrire, sur de nouvelles bases métaphoriques, mais de quitter l'écriture, pour pratiquer, hors texte, les situations de la vie: un dehors où se reforme, en somme, la dimension d'expérience et de vérité qui manquent aux langues, quand elles s'enchantent de soi.[3]

Bonnefoy would be the poet of the *hors texte,* a writer whose language is endlessly engaged in self-annihilation and self transcendence towards unmediated experience. Clearly, the conceptual framework at work here is massively Hegelian, so it is not surprising that Bonnefoy suggests that it is only in a dialectical movement that writing and presence might coexist:

> Mais que, par une décision de la même sorte, soit dénoncée cette primauté du poème, et l'écriture pourra se révéler le creuset où, par une dialectique de l'exister et du livre—l'action et le rêve réconciliés!—la présence va, non seulement advenir, mais approfondir son rapport à soi.[4]

Poetry, then, is the site of the "vrai lieu," wherein presence is reconciled with its opposite—writing. And yet, those who reject the possibility of such a resolution obsess Bonnefoy: "En fait, si j'ai évoqué d'emblée ceux qui dénoncent dans le poème ce qu'on pourrait appeler *l'effet de présence,* simple mirage, c'est que leur pensée m'obsède."[5]

Why do the thinkers of the logic of writing (can the name Jacques Derrida be avoided here?) impose themselves on Bonnefoy's vision of presence? Can writing, in fact, allow itself to be recruited into the service of presence by the expedient of passing it through the sieve of poetry? The answer to these questions, beyond any doubt the central ones as far as Bonnefoy's esthetics are concerned, requires a twofold consideration. We must interrogate the status of writing and presence in Bonnefoy's dialectical conceptual schema. In doing so, moreover, we must be sensitive to the powerful and unavoidable marks recent French critical theory (especially Deconstruction) has etched on these seminal concepts.

Bonnefoy clearly understands writing literally, as speech transcribed into a permanent form through the agency of conventional signs. Derrida, on the contrary, does not intend to limit his concept of writing to its phenomenal face: "Il s'agit de produire un nouveau concept d'écriture. On peut l'appeler *gramme* ou *différance.*"[6] Writing is not simply institutionalized marks on a page, but that fabric of spacing, differentiation and deferment which first produces the possibility of conceptualizing the writing/speech opposition:

> Le gramme comme différance, c'est alors une structure et un mouvement qui ne se laissent plus penser à partir de l'opposition présence/absence. La différance, c'est le jeu systématique des différences, des traces de différences, de l'*espacement* par lequel les éléments se rapportent les uns aux autres. Cet espacement est la production, à la fois active et passive (le *a* de la *différance* indique cette indécision par rapport à l'activité et à la passivité, ce qui ne se laisse pas encore commander et distribuer par cette opposition), des intervalles sans lesquels les termes "pleins" ne signifieraient pas, ne fonctionneraient pas.[7]

In other words, writing is the constitution of an opening which, because it is internally articulated, is separated from itself by the distance of the space it both creates and is created by. Only after the temporal and spatial movement of "espacement" has hewn an opening for writing/speech to appear can the phenomenal form of writing be decried as inimical to presence.

For Derrida, presence is that product of *différance* that has come to function as the structuring concept of Western Metaphysics. Simply, following Husserl, and his famous principle of principles,[8] Derrida defines the meaning of Being as the temporal and spatial immediacy of evidence unveiling itself in the present. Presence is the possibility of integrity, of propriety (the proper, property—a "vrai lieu"—etc.) and of access which allows for the erection of truth as a normative principle. And, regardless of the modality of its constitution, that is, whether presence announces itself as such or after a detour through its other, presence has functioned as the ground for thought in the Western philosophical tradition.

Things are no different for Bonnefoy. Describing "l'acte de la présence," he says:

> S'il est vrai que la question reste entière de savoir ce que serait un salut, si nous avons eu à douter dans la mesure même, presque dans l'instant même où nous avons eu à croire, nous avons reçu malgré tout le bien d'une certitude, nous savons quelle est l'origine, au-delà d'une révision des fins humaines, qu'il nous restera pour fonder. Désormais nous avons une raison d'être, qui est cet acte soudain. Et un devoir et une morale, au moins *par provision,* qui sera de le retrouver.[9]

Presence is an origin and it is a destination. Poetry, for Bonnefoy, participates in a circular teleological movement which will be completed when language expends itself in the face of presence. Presence, therefore, funds poetry inasmuch as it both precedes it and serves as its goal. Presence is a here and now to which a poem points while remaining exterior to it: "Et Baudelaire va chercher à faire dire au poème cet extérieur absolu, ce grand vent aux vitres de la parole, l'*ici* et le *maintenant* qu'a sacralisés toute mort."[10] Poetry, then, is a means, a bridge to the pre- or post-linguistic bed of presence. Furthermore, since this bed is constituted by its contingent character, it would seem to be essentially finite. And yet, during certain privileged moments, in certain "actes de présence," the here and now sheds its veil of contingency to reveal its infinite and eternal essence: "Ici—c'est toujours le même ici—et dans cet instant, toujours le même, nous avons quitté tout espace, nous avons glissé hors du temps.[11]

How can a here and now be stripped of the particularity of a specific context? In other words, what conceptual presuppositions are at play in Bonnefoy's desire to postulate the possibility of a universal experience of the contingent? Let us turn to one of Bonnefoy's favorite images, the salamander. In "La poésie française et le principe d'identité," Bonnefoy subjects a remembered or imagined perception to a phenomenological interrogation: "Et j'imaginerai, ou me rappellerai—on verra peut-être plus tard que les deux notions s'équivalent—que j'entre un jour d'été dans une maison en ruine et vois soudain, sur le mur, une salamandre."[12] Having "encountered" the salamander, Bonnefoy wonders what options are available to him. One is to classify it:

> Eh bien, plusieurs chemins se sont ouverts devant moi. Je puis analyser ce que m'apporte ma perception, et ainsi, profitant de l'expérience des autres hommes, séparer en esprit cette petite vie des autres données du monde, et la classer, comme ferait le mot de la prose, et me dire: *"Une* salamandre", puis poursuivre ma promenade, toujours distrait, demeuré comme à la surface de la rencontre.[13]

However, another approach is possible:

> Mais d'autres mouvements, plus en profondeur, sont possibles. Car, par exemple, je puis garder les yeux sur la salamandre, m'attacher aux détails qui m'avaient suffi pour la reconnaître, croire continuer l'analyse qui en fait de plus en plus *une* salamandre, c'est-à-dire un objet de science, une réalité structurée par ma raison et pénétrée de langage—mais tout cela, soudain, pour ne plus rien percevoir, dans ces aspects brusquement comme dissociés l'un de l'autre, dans ce contour d'une patte absolu, irréfutable, désert, qu'un faisceau effrayant d'énigmes. Ces choses ont un nom, mais se sont faites soudain comme étrangères au nom.[14]

In a moment of felicity, the surface incrustations of logic and language are transcended, and the depth ("plus en profondeur" not "à la surface de la recontre") of the salamander reveals itself. Freed from the limitations of language's conceptual structure, the salamander unveils itself as pure presence. So striking is this moment of epiphany, that it is impossible to distinguish the salamander from other objects: "Ce que j'ai essayé de montrer, en somme, c'est que dans l'unité, ou en tout cas sous son signe, il n'y a plus *une* salamandre par opposition à un âtre ou deux ou cent hirondelles, mais *la* salamandre présente au coeur des autres présences."[15] The salamander gives way to a salamander, a thing which exists in much the same way that all other things exist. The thing-in-itself is, for Bonnefoy, no longer a particular thing, since the experience which yields access to it moves through the conceptual distinctions of language to a realm of absolutely undifferentiated existence: "L'idée d'un être, sur ce plan—illusion ou non, peu importe—implique son existence, et cela détruit le concept, qui divise pour signifier. Dans l'espérance de la venue, on ne signifie pas, on laisse une lumière se désenchevêtrer des significations qui l'occulte."[16] If writing is not simply marks on paper, but the ontologically primordial movement of spacing and differentiation, then Bonnefoy's desire for presence, or for one of its synonyms, light, can be understood as the desire to erase writing. In fact, Bonnefoy's entire project is perhaps best situated within what Derrida describes as the dominant thrust of the Western philosophical tradition—the desire to eradicate, or at least obscure, the immemorial filiation between perception and articulation.

Presence, then, has two components for Bonnefoy. Firstly, it is the experience of what lies beneath the surface of a thing. And secondly, it is the experience of homogeneity. In other words, for Bonnefoy, the eternity promised by the revelatory act of presence is defined by two fundamental hierarchical binary relations: surface/depth and articulation/undifferentiation. Beneath surface articulations—the world of appearances, and significantly, the world of language—lies a depth which, because it is foreign to the difference essential to identity,[17] is fundamentally unqualifiable.[18] Bonnefoy's goal, then, is a glimpse into a world without difference. Ultimately, the destination of his textual trajectory is identical to its imagined origin: the world before the Fall. That is why his text would be a "théologie négative," an instant of presence, an eternal instant, an instance of fusion between the subject and the world ("Ici la réalité muette ou distante et mon existence se rejoignent, se convertissent, s'exaltent dans la suffisance de l'être."[19]), ultimately, a kind of salvation. Bonnefoy's notion of the sensible is in principle little else than inverted Hegelianism or inverted Christianity.[20] It may be negative, but Bonnefoy's theology is nevertheless in the service of the divine:

> C'est que, dans la difficulté de notre approche, il y a ce pressentiment que, nous retournant par un impossible mouvement pour voir face à face ce que nous ne sommes autorisés à regarder qu'en nous en détournant, ce que nous verrons, ce qu'en vérité toujours déjà nous avons vu, c'est—l'appellerions-nous le sensible ou le corps terrestre,—c'est le divin même, ce que toujours les hommes ont visé indistinctement par ce nom.[21]

What has always been called the divine, what salvation has always offered, is existence prior to the fall into difference. Difference, as Derrida has argued so powerfully, is the taboo of Onto-theology because it suggests the absence of an integral and homogeneous origin. For Bonnefoy, who rejects the primacy of writing, even though he is haunted by it, such an origin is precisely that which guarantees the *correct* use of poetry as an avenue in the circular trajectory back to the beginning. I emphasize "correct" because, as Bonnefoy often suggests, poetry is constantly threatened with disintegration into an auto-referential sign system.

In order for it to fulfill its mission, poetry must struggle against writing's obstinate refusal to negate itself in the name of transitivity: "L'écrit transpose l'intention, défait la voix transitive."[22] Poetry is authentic only to the extent that it enters into a dialectical relation with presence thereby becoming a *place* receptive to the unveiling of being: "J'ai retrouvé ce point où, par grâce de l'avenir, réalité et langage ont rassemblé leurs pouvoirs. Et je dis que le désir du vrai lieu est le serment de la poésie."[23] A negative dialectic will make writing into a crucible in which presence can appear. Otherwise, poetry is in danger of reassuming the intransitive function its status as linguistic artifact invites: "La parole est déjà l'oubli, il se peut bien qu'elle ait été notre chute, la voici en tout cas privée de la rencontre de

l'être, ne faut-il pas condamner, une fois de plus, la prétention de la poésie?"[24] Although Bonnefoy will answer his rhetorical question with a qualified "no," it is only if poetry recognizes the imperative that it be a vehicle and not a goal, that is, if it is ready to annihilate itself, that it is salvageable. If poetry will not (or can not) be its own disappearance, then the logic of Bonnefoy's conceptual system compels him to make a *de jure* equation between the untranscendable materiality of language and the notion of a fall.

Poetry is a site, a "vrai lieu," only to the extent that it does not fall by announcing itself as matter. To do so would be to suggest the possibility that articulation is not a provisional incarnation of presence in language, but the essential pre-condition for presence. The difference between a "vrai lieu" and the poem as text, what Bonnefoy calls a "poème achevé," is that while the former is a window to absolute plenitude, the latter does not serve as a sign announcing the extra-linguistic; it simply is: "le poème achevé, ne parle pas, il *est* . . ."[25] The autonomy of its formal structure vitiates both the purity of the presence it should represent and the presence of the author who would inscribe himself in his work so that, in the wake of dialectical mediation, he may remain face to face with the universal concrete:

> Je sais, d'expérience dûment et bien des fois vérifiée, que le poème achevé—j'insiste sur ce mot—a le caractère d'une forme, qui a son autonomie, et non seulement par rapprt à beaucoup d'intentions qu'elle méconnaît chex les autres hommes, mais même par rapport à moi, qui ai décidé de chacun des mots. Suisje "présent" dans le livre que je publie?[26]

If the poem is a "vrai lieu" it is a sign system whose function is to insure the integrity of the undifferentiated by the promise it makes to limit its own articulated incarnation to a provisional and erasable moment in a speculative development. If the poem is a "poème achevé," it is another kind of site, a site resistant to that bracketing of materiality that has made of theology and idealism historical allies.

I return, therefore, to the problem that opened this essay. How does Bonnefoy's theoretical position on the function of poetry affect the reader's critical reaction to his poetry? As I have already suggested, and as I will shortly attempt to demonstrate, critics of Bonnefoy have tended to read his poetry as the successful application of his esthetics. In the light of the preceding analysis of Bonnefoy's conceptual system, I think it is possible to begin to re-evaluate this relation between theory and practice. The desire to see Bonnefoy's poetry as the materialization of the views expressed in his essays is composed of two other wishes: the wish to salvage a nucleus of sense able to survive the passage from prose to poetry and the wish to see poetry as the bearer of the message of its own disposability. Both of these desires,

I would argue, are versions of the historically determined desire to dissociate sense from the body which is purported to be the medium of its transmission. As long as poetry can dissolve before the radically a-textual depth of presence, then its necessity is at best strategic and provisional. And as long as Bonnefoy's poetry is interpreted as the performance of such an act of self-transcendence, then criticism can continue to represent itself as the defender of what it assumes to be both its source and its destination—the truth of a pre-predicative place.

II. THE SITE OF POETRY

For the most part, critics have read *Douve* as a long invocation to presence. In other words, they have assumed the success of Bonnefoy's project. Whether, as does Mary Ann Caws, *Douve* is read as a moment in a dialectic composed of Bonnefoy's entire corpus: "In the final act, a sense of individual presence ('this tree') is perceived as one with the universal, in a place at once interior and exterior, where all elements reveal a unique coincidence of essence and existence: 'true name,' 'true place,' 'true body.'";[27] or whether it is read in the manner of John E. Jackson, for whom *Douve* is capable of its own dialectical accomplishment: "Ce n'est qu'avec 'Vrai lieu' que s'accomplira l'intégration, une intégration qu'il faut comprendre au sens hegelien de la 'Aufhebung', du dépassement qui maintient.";[28] the ultimate result is the same: *Douve* is a poem bearing the message of its own transcendence.

Although I do not deny that there is clear evidence in the poem of Bonnefoy's desire to incorporate his esthetic views in verse, I will attempt to approach *Douve* from a different perspective. My goal is not to disprove the traditional readings of the poem, nor to suggest that I am offering a more correct one. In fact, it is the notion of a correct reading, of an interpretation founded on evidence which is itself not already interpreted, that I will be contesting. My analysis of *Douve* will simply seek to argue that the dialectical approach to the poem is not exhaustive, but on the contrary leaves out a margin that is perhaps resistant to that kind of critical husbandry fundamental to negative theology.

Of the many critics who have read *Douve* from Bonnefoy's dialectical perspective, I think that Jean-Pierre Richard offers the most nuanced and supple analysis.[29] For example, despite his desire to see Bonnefoy's work as a series of syntheses, Richard is nevertheless sensitive to junctures in *Douve* where that totalizing tendency is disrupted. Commenting on the poem **"Aux Arbres,"** Richard says:

> D'insignifiants, de totalement imperméables à la pensée, voici donc les éléments devenus *médiateurs*: en eux nous atteindrons désormais à autre chose qu'eux; leur ascétisme même développe et trahit une qualité de l'être; tout en restant pure matière, ils sont devenus langage.[30]

There are at least two ways to understand Richard's statement. The traditional interpretation would maintain that the trees function as an image of matter transcending its frustratingly material impermeability towards a final revelation of the unity of being. It is possible, however, to adopt a different posture towards Richard's reading. It is possible to take him literally. That is, when he observes that the trees function as matter which has been made to signify, as matter behaving semiotically, we are in a position to interrogate the referential nature of matter, and, perhaps more importantly, the materiality of language. By taking Richard at his word, the dialectical progression of *Douve* can be disrupted precisely at the moment when an intriguing affiliation between language and matter is announced.

It is, of course, insufficient to merely claim that matter signifies in *Douve.* As I suggested earlier, for Bonnefoy presence is never the simple experience of unadorned matter, but the recruitment of that experience into the service of the revelation of a concrete universal. Even in Bonnefoy's teleological historical synthesis, things signify, if only their own potential eclipse. What is lost, however, in matter's dash towards universality, is its particularity. In other words, although it is perfectly congruent with Bonnefoy's teleological ontology to conceive of matter as semiotic, it is far less manageable to posit the possibility that it is precisely the irrefragable finitude of both language and matter which makes them irremediably polysemous.

At the same time that *Douve* is a poem invoking its own annihilation in the face of unarticulated presence, it is a poem playing out the drama of the materiality of its own inscription. By far the dominant trope in the poem is that of *place.* From **"Théâtre,"** to the various "vrai lieu,"'s to **"Orangerie,"** to **"Chapelle Brancacci,"** to **"His Est Locus Patriae,"** the poems which comprise *Douve* are repeatedly concerned with the question of a finite location. As with the case of language, it is possible to interpret Bonnefoy's use of space dialectically. Richard, for example, argues that the spatial metaphors strewn throughout *Douve* are a poly, a kind of trap to capture and unveil being:

> Au lieu de crever éperdument l'écran des choses, il s'agira, un peu comme un Mallarmé renonçant à l'azur pour s'enfermer entre les parois nocturnes d'une chambre, de construire soi-même cet écran, d'aménager au sein du paysage un creux sensible, d'édifier en somme une sorte de piège naturel où viendrait, littéralement, se prendre l'être.[31]

Richard contrasts those spatial tropes that are of human origin with those that are presumably natural, although, in the end, the dialectical machine is capable of negating and incorporating even this difference:

> instrument d'évidement et de clôture, le décor est en somme au paysage vrai ce que le concept est à la réalité, mais son mensonge se destine désormais non à

éluder, bien plutôt à capter le vrai; il est comme un concept qui se condamnerait lui-même à l'illusion, qui s'affirmerait ouvertement tricheur afin de permettre en lui un possible dévoilement de l'être.[32]

Structures of human origin (Orangerie, Théâtre, etc.) offer, for Richard, access to the true space ("le paysage vrai," "le vrai lieu", etc.) where presence is unveiled. Consequently, space, understood as the institution of finite differences, disappears. All that remains is the indefinite revelation of the oxymoron, *pure space.* For things to be otherwise, for the procession of interioriz-ation and sublation to be disrupted, the poem must be subjected to another kind of reading. Specifically, the relation between language and space needs to be examined in a way that does not presuppose the eventual transcendence of matter.

To this end, I propose to analyze the representation of the materiality of both space and language in *Douve.* Let us begin with the poem described by Richard as suggesting a filiation between language and matter—**"Aux Arbres."** The poem does not immediately sug-gest space as such. Except for that space which trees must be presumed to occupy, the trope of site or loca-tion is not thematized by the poem. Instead, it describes the self-effacing materiality of trees: "Vous qui vous êtes effacés sur son passage," and "Vous fibreuse mat-ière et densité".[33] The trees erase themselves because they are mediators, yet their essence is to be fibrous and dense. If, as Richard claims, the trees are a kind of language, they are language as excipient, as the conveyor of a message in principle separable from it:

> Le tonnerre profond qui roule sur vos branches,
> Les fêtes qu'il enflamme au sommet de l'été
> Signifient qu'elle lie sa fortune à la mienne
> Dans la médiation de votre austérité.

> (33)

Such, at any rate, is the conventional reading of the poem. And, indeed, it is a correct one as long as the poem is assumed to be referential in nature. In other words, to the extent that the signifier *trees* is read as a poetic representation of the referent tree, the poem does in fact fit into the dialectic mold. But such is not the case, at least not simply.

Richard asserts that the trees are language. What, then, is language in the poem? How is the linguistic sign represented in a poem which is ostensibly a paean to presence? Although language can take many forms in *Douve,* it is possible to isolate a crucial quality of language, of the sign in general, that informs the vari-ous modalities of its appearance in the poem. In the only poem in which writing is mentioned, **"Une Voix,"** the narrator describes his fear of signs as the fear of exile from density: "J'ai reculé longtemps devant tes signes, / Tu m'as chassée de toute densité." (50) A sign,

therefore, is threatening because it is somehow inimical to the kind of fibrous density associated with matter. To the extent that, as Derrida argues, a sign is constituted by arbitrariness and iterability, a sign is not a thing because it cannot be dismembered to reveal presence.[34] Not a thing in the conventional sense, a sign is neverthe-less a place: "Quelle maison veux-tu dresser pour moi, / Quelle écriture noire quand vient le feu?" (50) **"Une Voix"** identifies the process of writing (or the produc-tion of signs) with the erection of a house. Writing is a house, but a hollow one. Resistant to the rebirth promised by fire, foreign to the density of matter, the network *writing-sign-house* is out of place in a poem ruled by the logic of dialectical teleology. If we add the trees of **"Aux Arbres"** to the equation, a series of terms is beginning to emerge whose dynamic structure is incompatible with the kind of reading of *Douve* that extols presence.

In fact, along with the familiar set of images associated with the poetry of Bonnefoy (fire, cries, wind, stone, blood, etc.), it is possible to adduce a second type of imagistic web revolving around the relation between the various incarnations of the *sign* and the numerous metaphoric resonances of *house* or *abode.* The poem is studded with references to things or figures that signify (parler, parole, nommer, le verbe, écriture, signe, mots, chant, etc.) and to structures that create space by demarcating it from what it isn't (site, âtre, maison, cathédrale, théâtre, lieu, locus patriae, orangerie, Chapelle Brancacci, etc.). It would appear, at first sight, that the connection between these two series of images is easily established. Both involve culturally determined structures and can therefore be contrasted to those phenomena of nature which are presumed to be alien to culture. Furthermore, both language and architecture function by articulation. It is only by assuming the ontological priority of difference (between one sign and another, between signifier and signified, between signi-fied and referent, between one space and another, etc.) that it is possible to even posit the identity of a sign or house. As opposed to the supposed natural homogeneity of presence, signs and buildings are conventional, hence constituted by difference. And yet, there is one element in *Douve* that refuses to fit into either side of this formula. How are we to insert the trees of **"Aux Ar-bres,"** with which, after all, this part of our analysis began, into our two series of images? If, as Richard suggests, trees are a kind of language, they are signs. But they are not conventional. And if their organization suggests structure, its texture is radically different from the culturally determined division of space implied by the notion of architecture.

Is it possible, then, to understand this aporia without resorting to dialectical legerdemain? As I suggested earlier, it would be impossible to extricate **"Aux Ar-bres"** from the teleological perspective if the signifier *arbres* is read in a mimetic fashion. Instead, I will argue that although it is impossible to divorce a signifier from its stock of usual signifieds, it is equally impossible to limit it to them. Specifically, although *arbres* certainly does refer to trees, it would be myopic to restrict its semiotic resources to one kind of meaning. In fact, I will attempt to demonstrate that the standard signified of *arbres* is troped in **Douve** in such a way as to disrupt the sublation of the signifier that the poem is presumed to effect.

Let us first return to a poem whose title suggests the centrality of site: **"His Est Locus Patriae."** The poem begins with a description of trees as an invading force: "Le ciel trop bas pour toi se déchirait, les arbres / Envahissaient l'espace de ton sang." (66) Of course, it is possible to interpret this invasion of the body's space by vegetal matter in much the same way that Roquentin interprets the chestnut tree in *La Nausée*. Such is Richard's approach:

> Quand Yves Bonnefoy entreprend, à l'inverse de l'ordre regroupé que nous impose le concept, d'imaginer l'infinie dispersion où nous jette toute saisie un peu sincère de l'objet, sa pensée s'arrête de préférence dans l'ordre où la rupture semble se faire naturellement proliférante: l'ordre brut mais vivant du végétal.[35]

This tack, however, becomes impossible in the light of the poem's second quatrain, which begins: "Un vase décorait le seuil. Contre son marbre / Celui qui revenait sourit en s'appuyant." (66) A vase decorated the threshold (the imperfect tense is significant. I will consider the importance of verbal tenses in **Douve** presently.) Leaning against a vase, a returning figure smiled. The image of someone approaching or returning recurs frequently in the poem, especially towards the end. Usually, the figure of a wanderer in **Douve** is associated with the notion of homelessness. For example, the first verse of **"Voix basses et Phénix"** is: "Tu fus sage d'ouvrir, il vint à la nuit," (60) and an unnamed poem, the first one in **"Vrai Lieu,"** begins: "Qu'une place soit faite à celui qui approche, / Personnage ayant froid et privé de maison." (81) A wanderer was returning, then, to a threshold adorned with a vase. Although he did not enter, the threshold was clearly promising access to a seminal site. The poem's title, loosely translated as "Here is the location of the fatherland," implies that the "here" it designates is one of the poem's organizing centers. The site of the father, it is the locus of a stable and founding base. One expects this to be the "vrai lieu," the clearing in which presence is unveiled. It is nothing of the kind.

The here (hic), the source to which a homeless wayfarer was returning, is nothing other than a poem: "Ainsi le jour baissait sur le lieudit *Aux Arbres*. / C'était jour de parole et ce fut nuit de vent." (66) The site of ancestral authority is not an image of material density or even of vegetal proliferation. The "locus patriae" to which one who has been exiled returns is radically devoid of the kind of presence extolled by both Bonnefoy and his sympathetic readers. It is to an earlier poem, to the poem which Richard claims makes matter into language, that the exiled figure returns.

In **Douve,** therefore, a later poem refers to an earlier poem as a place. **"Aux Arbres"** is not simply a set of signs expending themselves in the service of a the pre- or post-semiotic, it is also, and perhaps foremost, a destination. In other words, we are in a position to do two things. Firstly, the role of **"Aux Arbres"** in Bonnefoy's catalog of artificial structures has been clarified. We are conjoined by the poem **"Hic Est Locus Patriae"** to think of trees not as natural objects beyond the sway of convention, but as images of the poem within the poem. Secondly, Richard's analysis of the poem **"Aux Arbres"** can now be read in the strongest possible manner. Trees are language, yes, but they are not language in search of a non-linguistic foundation. Trees are language inasmuch as trees are a poem. Ultimately, it is impossible to distinguish clearly between "les arbres" and **"Aux Arbres."** The trees invading Douve's blood are both trees as a natural image and trees as a metaphor for the semiotic resources inherent in the poetic act. In the end, even the classic opposition between image and metaphor, or between writing as a transitive act and writing as an intransitive act, is rendered indistinct by **Douve's** retranscription of the notion of place.

The central concern in **Douve** is the constitution of a site in which poetry can house itself. The images of articulated space abounding in the poem, consequently, are in fact metaphors for the poem itself. However, even if we shift our focus from the revelation of an extra-poetic presence to the creation of a seam capable of housing poetry, one major problem remains. In a poem about poetry, **"Art Poétique,"** Bonnefoy asks the perhaps rhetorical question: "En quel âtre dresser le feu de ton visage / O Ménade saisie jetée la tête en bas?" (46) The art of poetry is to incorporate. However, even if the locus of a poem's concern is actually an image of the poem as place, it is still possible, especially in the light of a poem such as **"Art Poétique,"** to conceive of the poem's architecture as a body housing a non-poetic core of meaning. It appears that although much has been gained, I am in fact not far from the dialectical style of interpretation I am seeking to disturb. For although I am claiming that **Douve** is an investigation into the various modalities of its own spatialization, my reading seems to allow for the possibility of an extrasemiotic existence. The very notion of incorporation, or of return, implies the conceivability of an unarticulated site, of what Bonnefoy calls presence. **"His Est Locus Patriae"** does end, after all, with a reference to the wind, to that wind described in "III" of **"Théâtre"** as stronger than memory: "Il s'agissait d'un vent plus fort que nos mémoires." (13) It can be demonstrated, in fact, that in general the necessity of a site is described in *Douve* in past tenses, while the possibility of rupture and transgression is described in the present or future (for example, "Demande pour tes yeux que les rompe la nuit, / Rien ne commencera qu'au delà de ce voile," [58]). Consequently, the "nuit de vent" closing **"His Est Locus Patriae"** must be read as an allusion to a cleansing wind, a harbinger of transcendence towards regenerated presence.

We must therefore not evade the possibility that, despite *Douve's* inscription of its own articulated texture as the site wherein presence is smitten with finitude in order that it may announce itself, it may still be possible to think of the poem's architecture as the provisional incarnation of a content which can, in principle, exist without a body. During those moments in the poem when a site is understood as a stopover (for example, "L'orangerie, / Nécessaire repos qu'il rejoignait," [67]), *Douve* appears to make the classic metaphysical assumption that it is possible to distinguish between two realms—pure presence and the location it sometimes adopts. If I am to offer a genuinely un-Hegelian reading of *Douve,* it is essential to engage the poem at precisely those junctures where a radically un-poetic experience appears to be suggested. To this end, I will consider certain of those metaphors for the meta-poetic that for many critics of *Douve* (and arguably for Bonnefoy himself) have come to characterize the poem's ultimate message.

In order to overcome the fundamental contradiction of attempting to say the unsayable, Bonnefoy resorts to what Richard would call a trap or subterfuge—a number of images of that ineffable presence presumed to lie outside the poem. There is the salamander. And, of course, there is Douve. First, however, let us consider the stag. Although critics often designate "Lieu de la salamandre" as the climax of *Douve,* it is interesting to note that the next poem, the last titled poem in the collection, is **"Vrai lieu du cerf."** As such, the reader is led to expect that this poem will in some way designate the "true place" for which he assumes *Douve* has all the while been searching. The stag is distinguished from the salamander by its affinity for the forest. Whereas the salamander tends to merge with the rock upon which it crawls, the stag is more likely to lose itself among trees. And, since we have established a connection between trees and **"Aux Arbres,"** that is, between the tree as a symbol of nature and the tree as a metaphor for the sparse, articulated space of the poem, the stag is somehow implicated in the poem's self-representation. And yet, the stag is not the poem, at least not simply.

Let us begin with **"Le seul témoin,"** the next titled poem after **"Aux Arbres."** To the extent that it describes the redemptive potential of death by fire, **"Le seul témoin"** is a typical Bonnefoy poem. It is, however, far more complex than just a mere hymn to resurrection. Towards the end of the poem, the narrator addresses the Douve-Phoenix figure:

> ô je fus,
> Ménade consumée, dure joie mais perfide,
> Le seul témoin, la seule bête prise
> Dans ces rets de ta mort que furent sables
> Ou rochers ou chaleur, ton signe disais-tu.
>
> (35)

The poetic persona who speaks in the first person refers to himself as a witness and a sign. A witness is one who describes an event he observed in the past, or who observes an event so that he may describe it in the future. In either case, the notion of a witness is essentially wed to a futural representation of a past experience. In other words, a witness is one for whom the future is constituted by the potential recreation of the past. Consequently, rather than perceiving the future as the possible revelation of undifferentiated presence, the future exists for a witness as a story to be retold.

The sole witness, the narrator, is also a sign. He is a sign for Douve. Or perhaps he is Douve's sign, a sign belonging to Douve. In any case, as both sign and witness, the voice which says "I" is structured by flatness, articulation and representation. It is therefore not surprising that the next poem, "II," has Douve fleeing into trees that are endowed with the potential for simulation: "Elle fuit vers les saules; le sourire / Des arbres l'enveloppe, simulant / La joie simple d'un jeu." (36), and that "IV" suggests that Douve herself might be capable of deception: "Est-tu vraiment morte ou joues-tu / Encore à simuler la paleur et le sang, . . . Es-tu vraiment morte ou joues-tu / Encore en tout miroir" (38). To be a sign for something else, to be a witness remembering the future, or to be a tree whose branches are the mark of an immemorial fissure is also, and perhaps primarily, to be impregnated with the instability of the simulacrum. The narrator, while looking for a way to sublate his essentially intersubjective relation with Douve, discovers that he is a witness to a possible act of deception. And, to the extent that Douve is also a tree, insofar as both are capable of presenting themselves as other than they are, the witness who says "I" is ultimately deprived of a fixed standard by which to distinguish between presence and representation.

The stag returns in the next poem, "V." With tree-like antlers on its head, the decidedly male stag is one of a host of masculine figures in the poem (le Phénix, le chevalier de deuil, various unnamed "il"s, the narrator, etc.) contrasting with the feminine Douve and salamander. The stag is missing. Furthermore, the missing stag is the one who gave testimony (in the passé simple) concerning Douve's death and silence:

Où maintenant est le cerf qui témoigna
Sous ces arbres de justice,
Qu'une route de sang par elle fut ouverte,
Un silence nouveau par elle inventé.

(39)

Like the "je," who is also a witness, the stag is a male observer of a feminine artifact. In addition, the stag and the narrator both speak in the place of Douve, who for the part remains silent (except, perhaps, in the section named "Douve Parle," and even there Douve's central concern is to be named). If Douve is, as the poem certainly suggests, a metaphor for the experience of presence, then that experience appears to exist only as the result, not as the cause, of an essentially belated testimony. Underneath the trees of justice, the stag reported that Douve blazed a new path of silence. The stag itself is absent in the present of the narration, and Douve, the object of his testimony, can, like the site of his testimony (the trees), prove to be a fruitless detour. Far from a simple metaphor for the annihilation and regeneration of something like a "concrete universal," Douve appears to be strangely similar to the house that bears her.

Much later in *Douve,* in **"Lieu de la salamandre,"** the salamander, previously described as a kind of future promised land ("Le pays le plus beau longtemps cherché / S'étendra devant nous terre des salamandres." (65), returns to its proper site. The sluggish, stone-like salamander, which Mary Ann Caws, following Bonnefoy's own analysis, characterizes as the dialectical resolution of the binary opposition between the particular and the universal: "the specific image in its universal essence ("la salamandre") includes at once the salamander on this wall and all others."[36], is clearly intended to be a symbol of universal material presence: "Que j'aime qui s'accorde aux astres par l'inerte / Masse de tout son corps," (85). As such, it is reminiscent of Douve, who is, among other things, a river and a heath. And, like Douve, it is capable of subterfuge: "La salamandre surprise s'immobilise / Et feint la mort" (85). Of course, the salamander's dissimulation is intended as a provisional gesture ("Tel est le premier pas de la conscience dans les pierres," [85]), yet the fact that the voice which refers to itself as "I" can even think the possibility of deception implies that, like Douve, the salamander may be a kind of particular staunchly resistant to assimilation into the universal homogeneity of presence.

Just as the salamander can merge with stone, the stag is capable of becoming a forest. **"Vrai lieu du Cerf"** begins:

Un dernier cerf se perdant
Parmi les arbres,
Le sable retentira
Du pas d'obscurs arrivants.

(86)

With the verb a present participle, a last stag is losing itself among the trees. While he is entering into their texture, the auditory trace of dark arriving figures (can writing—"quelle écriture noire"—be far away?) echoes in the sand. A stag, then, who earlier testified under the trees, is now escaping into them just as unknown wanderers return to a house reminiscent of the Chapelle Brancacci (if only because of the repetition of "dalles"). The stag escapes into the sound of obscure footsteps, into the house that he carries on his head, ultimately into that dark writing that is the fabric of the poem:

Dans la maison traversée
Du bruit des voix,
L'alcool du jour déclinant
Se répandra sur les dalles.
Le cerf qu'on a cru retrait
Soudain s'évade.
Je pressens que ce jour a fait
Votre poursuite inutile.

(86)

The chase is futile because the threshold which constitutes the stag's space leads to no clearing. Dashing into that forest that Richard sees as bridge to presence, the stag finds himself in his true place, in the poem that produced him, in the trees. Ultimately, critics of *Douve* are correct. Douve is the salamander, and both are the stuff about which the stag testifies. However, the poem does not choreograph a rhythmic retreat into something like a "universal concrete." There is no salvation here. There is just Douve.

In "XIII" of **"Théâtre,"** the first person narrator addresses Douve:

Ton visage ce soir éclairé par la terre
Mais je vois tes yeux se corrompre
Et le mot visage n'a plus de sens.

(23)

In the presence of Douve's face, the word *face* loses its meaning. This seminal metaphysical opposition, contrasting sign and referent, is the condition of possibility of the thinkability of the desire to escape into a depth beyond poetry. And yet, like the stag whose true place is the frustratingly flat "lieudit *Aux Arbres,"* the "je" cannot extricate himself from his role as witness:

La mer intérieure éclairée d'aigles tournants,
Ceci est une image.
Je te détiens froide à une profondeur où les images
ne prennent plus.

(23)

"La mer intérieure" is an image, certainly. And the narrator desires to tear it apart so as to descend into a depth whose very density is a hostile environment for poetry. But it is not only "la mer intérieure" that is an image. The verse "Ceci est une image" is itself an image. In fact, to the extent that the signifier *image* is a catachresis (an essentially metaphoric term, since the object it would designate lacks a proper name), the verse is an infinitely regressive abyss. Despite the narrator's desire to transcend the poetic image, the word *ceci* cannot help but testify to the flat intransitivity of his language. If he knew where to look, the narrator imagines he could see beyond the realm of images into the heart of things. Using *ceci* as a pointer, he would designate the depth of presence and then cast his tool aside. Unfortunately, as he knows when he is the stag, the place to which he aspires has never existed as such; it only exists as the product of the vehicle he would use to reach it. Throw that away, and there is nothing. Even the "profondeur où les images ne prennent plus" is an image.

In the end, all the narrator's efforts to break through poetry into presence are frustrated not simply because the language he must adopt as an instrument with which to effect his transgression is itself haunted by the memory of its own semiotic dispersion; it is not simply that he constantly finds himself in a flat house trying to peer into what is not a house; the ultimate failure to attain a depth beyond poetry is that the depth is itself profoundly poetic. Like the stag who can only escape into the poem that created him, the narrator seeks to find in Douve the solace of pure presence only to discover that Douve is absolutely nothing beyond the long and taunting place called **Douve.**

Notes

1. See, for example, Jackson, John E., *La question du moi* (Neuchatel: Baconnière, 1978); Richard, Jean-Pierre, *Onze études sur la poésie moderne* (Paris; Seuil, 1964); Winspur, Steven, "The Poetic Significance of the Thing-in-Itself" (*Sub Stance*, Vol. XII, No. 4, 1983); Arndt, Beatrice, *La quête poétique d'Yves Bonnefoy* (Zurich: Juris Druck et Verlag Zurich, 1970); and Caws, Mary Ann, *The Inner Theatre of Recent French Poetry* (New Jersey: Princeton University Press, 1972).

2. Bonnefoy, "Sur la fonction du poème," in *Le nuage rouge* (Paris: Mercure de France, 1977), p. 268.

3. "Sur la fonction du poème," p. 278.

4. "Sur la fonction du poème," p. 280.

5. "Sur la fonction du poème," p. 270.

6. Derrida, Jacques, *Positions* (Paris: Les Editions de Minuit, 1972), p. 37.

7. *Positions*, pp. 38-9.

8. "But enough of such topsy-turvy theories: No theory we can conceive can mislead us in regard to the *principle of all principles*: that the *very primordial dator Intuition is a source of authority* (Rechtsquelle) *for knowledge, that whatever presents itself in 'intuition' in primordial form* (as it were in its bodily reality), *is simply to be accepted as it gives itself to be, though only within the limits in which it then presents itself.*" (Husserl, Edmund, *Ideas* [New York: Collier-Macmillan, 1931], no. 24.

9. Bonnefoy, "L'acte et le lieu de la poésie," reprinted in *Du mouvement et de l'immobilité de Douve* (Paris: Gallimard, 1970), pp. 204-5.

10. "L'acte et le lieu de la poésie," p. 195.

11. "L'acte et le lieu de la poésie," p. 204.

12. Bonnefoy, "La poésie française et le principe d'identité,"in *Un rêve fait à Mantou* (Paris: Mercure de France, 1968), p. 95.

13. "La poésie française et le principe d'identité," pp. 95-6.

14. "La poésie française et le principe d'identité," p. 96.

15. "La poésie française et le principe d'identité," p. 98.

16. "La poésie française et le principe d'identité," p. 98-9.

17. According to Heidegger, identify is the product of difference. See *Identity and Difference* (New York, Harper and Row, 1974).

18. Cf. Roquentin's experience of the chestnut tree in *La Nausée* (Paris: Gallimard, 1938): "Ou plutôt la racine, les grilles du jardin, le banc, le gazon rare de la pelouse, tout ça s'était évanoui; la diversité des choses, leur individualité n'était qu'une apparence, un verni. Ce verni avait fondu, il restait des masses monstrueuses et molles, en désordre—nues, d'une effrayante et obscène nudité." (p. 180).

19. Bonnefoy, *L'Improbable* (Paris: Mercure de France, 1959), p. 23.

20. For the relation between the negative forms of Hegelianism and Christianity, as it pertains to the work of Bonnefoy, see Blanchot, Maurice, "Le Grand Refus," (*La Nouvelle Revue Française,* No. 82, October, 1959).

21. "Le Grand Refus," p. 685.

22. "Sur la fonction du poème," p. 268.

23. "L'acte et le lieu de la poésie," p. 211.

24. "L'acte et le lieu de la poésie," p. 206.

25. "Sur la fonction du poème," p. 271.

26. "Sur la fonction du poème," p. 270.

27. *The Inner Theatre of Recent French Poetry*, p. 150.

28. *La question du moi*, p. 251.

29. In *Onze études sur la poésie moderne.*

30. *Onze études sur la poésie moderne*, p. 227.

31. *Onze études sur la poésie moderne*, p. 229.

32. *Onze études sur la poésie moderne*, p. 229.

33. *Bonnefoy, Du mouvement et de l'immobilité de Douve* (Paris: Mercure de France, 1967), p. 33. All future references to *Douve* will be to this edition and will be indicated by a page reference following a citation.

34. See Derrida, "Signature Evénement Contexte," in *Marges de la philosophie* (Paris: Minuit, 1972).

35. "Onze études sur la poésie moderne," p. 217.

36. *The Inner Theatre of Recent French Poetry*, p. 143.

Richard Stamelman (essay date January 1988)

SOURCE: Stamelman, Richard. "The Crack in the Mirror: The Subversion of Image and Representation in the Poetry of Yves Bonnefoy."[1] *French Forum* 13, no. 1 (January 1988): 69-81.

[*In the following essay, Stamelman explores the dimensions of "Bonnefoy's subversion of representation in his poetry and writings on art."*]

"C'est simple," Yves Bonnefoy writes in **"L'Entaille,"** a recent poem in prose:

> On trempe un doigt dans la gouache bleue, on le fait glisser sur les mots à peine tracés dans l'encre noire, et du mélange de l'encre et de la couleur monte, marée, algues qui remuent dans l'eau trouble, ce qui n'est plus le signe, n'est plus l'image,—nos deux passions, nos deux leurres. On a ouvert les yeux, on avance, dans la lumière de l'aube.
>
> Mais je m'éveille. Devant moi sur le mur aux couleurs superposées qui s'écaillent, il y a cette forme qui fut gravée dans leur profondeur, avec un clou, jusqu'au plâtre. Est-ce l'évocation d'un agneau qu'un dieu porte sur ses épaules? Est-ce une figure obscène? En fait l'entaille va si avant dans la nuit du plâtre que c'est son rebord désert qui compte seul, déchirure qu'il est de toute quête d'image, dissipation de tout signe.[2]

Image and sign are undone by the mixing of color and ink, subverted by a combination that has neither the visual form of painting nor the lexical structure of writing. Rather, a blurring, an amorphous intermingling, of elements normally used to create a representation has

occurred. But this is only the first failure or subversion of mimesis in the poem. For the groove etched in the wall and penetrating through several coats of paint—like the tear that death cuts into the night of human existence or the zigzag that a flash of lightning engraves momentarily on a black sky—opens the closed world of the image to the reality of finite being. It breaks the prisonhouse of poetic and artistic form; it interrupts a representation's confident but deceptive will-to-meaning, to perfect imitation, invading its illusory dream-world of completeness and immobility with the ambiguity (is it a lamb? is it an obscene figure?), the barrenness (the plaster has become night) and the loss (image and sign are dispersed) that are associated with mortal existence. In Yves Bonnefoy's poetic and critical writings the mirror of representation is cracked. Through the fractured image enter the pain and joy, the darkness and light, the being and nothingness of a perpetually open, changing and immediate world which the closure of form, sign and image could never fully apprehend or express. In what follows I would like to discuss three dimensions of Yves Bonnefoy's subversion of representation in his poetry and writings on art: first, his questioning of the authority of the image and of mimesis; second, his fascination with the nonrepresentational powers of color and light; and third, his insistence on the drift away from imitation, the swerving toward what is unintended and other, that is inherent in all representations.

"AN ART FREED FROM MIMESIS" (*NR* 131)

Bonnefoy observes that, from the Greeks to the beginning of the twentieth century, mimesis has coincided with the development and dominance of conceptual thought and with the formation of language as a system. As a result, the painted and poetic image has arrogated to itself the name and authority of reality ("Héritier" 8). But the image cannot authentically represent the world of things. It is a deceit, a lie, an evasion. It symbolizes the desire to construct a perfect, transcendent and self-enclosed world, so narcissistically preoccupied with its own system and structure that the finitude, mortality and fragmentary nature of temporal existence are masked. It is the hubris of representation, Bonnefoy argues, that seeks to triumph over what is most menacing in the world, to master the incoherence of being, to order the chaos of fragmentary events and to signify an inexpressible plenitude. The image needs to be in harmony with temporal rhythms of living and dying. It should express the inaccessibility of presence; it should insist on the primacy of being over representation. Representations in poetry and art need to be traversed by fissures, fragmented by cuts, effaced by erosion, their forms and letters rendered indecipherable by the passage of time, their sealed world made porous to finite being, their will-to-perfection disrupted.

This explains, for example, Bonnefoy's fascination with the final scene of *The Winter's Tale,* redramatized in his long poem **Dans le leurre du seuil.** At the end of Shakespeare's play love magically dissolves the bonds of art that have kept Hermione entrapped in a sublime, cold perfection that, while giving the illusion of beauty and lifelikeness—"we are mocked with art" (V, iii, 67), Leontes says—envelops her in death. Love, the relation of one being to another, awakens the representation to life, for the statue's mimetic perfection is an invitation to the world, a self-defeating lure, that will eventually destroy the very art of the image: "Good my lord, forbear!" warns Paulina in order to keep Leontes from embracing the statue, "The ruddiness upon her lip is wet; / You'll mar it if you kiss it, stain your own / With oily painting" (V, iii, 80-83). But marring and staining are effects that art and poetry should strive for. Leontes moves to open the statue to the world of pain, absence and loss in which he has dwelled. His act is that of a poet:

> Et poésie, si ce mot est dicible,
> N'est-ce pas de savoir, là où l'étoile
> Parut conduire mais pour rien sinon la mort,
>
> Aimer cette lumière encore? Aimer ouvrir
> L'amande de l'absence dans la parole?

> *(CQFSL 42)*

Similarly, in a recent fable, appropriately entitled "Les Raisins de Zeuxis," Bonnefoy describes how mimetic representation contains the seeds of its own destruction. As the creation of a perfect copy the most sublime of representations contributes to its own undoing. Bonnefoy reaches back to the legendary sources of mimetic art in the West to reveal nature's antagonism to representation, offering an intriguing interpretation of the classic story of how Zeuxis, the great realist painter of antiquity, deceived the birds:

> Un sac de toile mouillée dans le caniveau, c'est le tableau de Zeuxis, les raisins, que les oiseaux furieux ont tellement désiré, ont si violemment percé de leurs becs rapaces, que les grappes ont disparu, puis la couleur, puis toute trace d'image en cette heure de crépuscule du monde où ils l'ont traîné sur les dalles.

> *(Raisins)*

As a representation perfect in its imitation of natural forms, Zeuxis's painting of grapes is attacked by the world, punctured, pierced and made imperfect. Attracted to the false lure of the image, the world takes its revenge. Forms, colors and figures disappear. The surface of the painting is wiped clean, until nothing remains but the wrinkled canvas itself. The representation is reduced to a piece of cloth, a discarded sack, a thing among things, lying wet, trampled and abandoned in a gutter. The painting is returned to the world, to a finite place of death and decomposition and to the substance and matter it has never really ceased to be. The painting has been picked clean of its images. In this effacing of the imaginary, this washing away of form and color, is found Bonnefoy's impossible longing for an image that is "purifiée, lavée, de son être—de sa différence—d'image . . . délivrée, en sa naissance même, en sa conception par l'artiste, de la boue de la rêverie" ("L'Artiste du dernier jour," *RR* 175-76).[3]

The opacity of the image is undone, its lines, colors, forms, structures and relationships effaced. The unsatisfiable desire for an art freed from mimesis comes perhaps a little closer to possible realization. This is to be welcomed because human dependence on representation has gotten out of hand, as Bonnefoy suggests in "L'Artiste du dernier jour," an extraordinary tale in which the world is about to end because the number of images that mankind has produced will shortly surpass the number of living creatures. Mimesis is the evil which "le péché de l'œil" (*RR* 177) has created. In his dealings with the finite world man cannot do without the mediation that the image affords. The world's only hope for salvation and rebirth at this twilight hour of doom is that some artist will be able to stop the proliferation of images by magically creating an imageless image, an "outre-image" (*NR* 362), a non-mimetic representation, wherein

> . . . cette figure ne montre plus, ne dise pas, ne suggère rien, ne soit plus la rivale illicite de ce qui est,— *soit,* elle-même et tout simplement, comme les images jamais ne furent, qui se dédoublent sans fin, se déchirent, renaissent, dans l'espace de la parole, *soit* comme l'arbre ou la pierre sont, dans l'ignorance d'eux-mêmes.

> ("L'Artiste du dernier jour," *RR* 176)

Only a representation of the unrepresentable, the expression of what Bonnefoy calls the "au-delà du représentable" ("Liberté" 11 and "Héritier" 8)—a different kind of representation, self-consciously aware of the limits and deficiencies of mimetic figuration—can initiate a new kind of art free from the tyranny of mimesis. The last chance "l'artiste du dernier jour" may possibly have—and it is not certain in Bonnefoy's story that he will undertake it—is to "copy" a child's face, that is, to draw the purity of "l'irreprésentable lumière" (*RR* 177), the unrepresentable light of joy emanating from that face. For Bonnefoy light is a phenomenon which, although it may be the essential concern and preoccupation of the painter, cannot ultimately be represented, and the child, "l'enfant / Qui porte le monde" (*DLS* 42), is the unifying force of hope, redemption, love and presence inhabiting the center of the world, the transparence of things (*I* 318). Light is a child "Qui joue, qui ne veut rien, qui rêve ou chante" (*CQFSL* 92). By incorporating the light of the child's joyful face into his drawing, the artist may possibly escape the immobility of figurative representation, for light is not a fixed image. The contact with the radiance of the child's innocent face may possibly "redeem" the drawing, removing it from the domain of mimesis and marking it with the trace of an unrepresentable plenitude that is not unlike the purity and wholeness of childhood itself. Similarly, in another enigmatic tale Bonnefoy describes the artist who creates an icon of the Virgin from paint that has been mixed with thousands of particles of ground glass. The resulting representation radiates with the reflected light of the sky, its thousands of shimmering sequins and dazzling facets replacing and blotting out the image itself ("La Mort du peintre d'icônes," *RR* 171). The encounter with light, therefore, can change the nature of representation because no strategy of mimetic recovery could ever capture the experience which light offers and which Bonnefoy calls "la présence," the enigmatic encounter with plenitude and oneness that happens in an instant so fleeting that neither meaning nor sign nor image has the time to coalesce, to "take," to *re*-present. Presence is the unrepresentable "clef de la vie" ("Liberté" 18).

Bonnefoy wages a war against the image not in order to do away with it, but rather to make it more expressive of realities of disintegration and effacement. A representation must always be corrected by the world: by the fading light of a setting sun, by the owl's cry, the cricket's chirp, the rustle of trees, a child's smile, a red cloth, a puddle of water, a stone, all of which must be allowed to "collaborate in our works" ("La Mort du peintre d'icônes," *RR* 172). Bonnefoy's denunciation of the Image (with a capital I) as a pure, transcendent and self-centered essence, hiding the fragmentary, divided condition of human existence, does not, however, compromise his love of images. He knows that in language, poetry and art images cannot be dispensed with. They translate human desire, even if they do tend to become part of the imaginary, idealized world he calls "le rêve." Images are signs of a longing for what is non-existent, unrealized, and they are obstinate acts of hope for future fulfillment (*NR* 163). They are expressions of the humanness of desire endlessly nourished by lack and absence.[4] Although we are, Bonnefoy remarks, "les prisonniers de l'image que nous substituons à ce monde" (*E* 143), and even though "l'Image est certainement le mensonge, aussi sincère soit l'imagier" (*PI* 34), this does not mean that the poet must renounce their use. Bonnefoy's assertion, "Je me refusais au culte des images" (*E* 16), is a refusal not of images in themselves, but of a reverence, an excessive worship or passion, for images. He rejects the kind of representation that privileges the image above everything else, life included. It is the "Image" as a Platonic Form that Bonnefoy rejects. Poetry, he writes, "a dénoncé l'Image mais pour aimer, de tout son cœur, les images" (*PI* 56). Where being and image coexist, where existence corrects and unsettles the figures of represented entities,

where unsatisfied desire thwarts the final saying of things, Bonnefoy finds representations, poetic or pictorial, that are very much open to the world. The true artist, the painter of finitude, is one who works to "accueillir comme et quand il vient le grand flux des choses fugaces" ("Cartier-Bresson" 7). As long as a representation does not lose sight of the object it *re*-presents, of the original for which it is the copy, of the fleeting perception it has immobilized, then Bonnefoy welcomes it. He desires a representation that, being open to the world, will present the pure and immediate evidence of the *here* and *now* as fleetingly, as minimally and as precariously as the Zen artist who paints a bird or a tree or a crab as it has never been seen before with one, just one, quickly executed brushstroke of color, explaining that this single line—this breath—of color expresses with haiku-like density all that need be expressed, and that it is the most beautiful representation only because it embodies the painter's close experience with the bird or the tree or the crab: his having become one with the physical time and place of its being in the world. The brushstroke, the trace of color on the canvas, is thus "une émanation du monde" ("Cartier-Bresson" 8).[5]

In several collections of poetry and in innumerable essays on painting, sculpture, drawing and architecture—from Byzantine art through the Quattrocento to Poussin and Rubens, down to Giacometti, Mondrian and Cartier-Bresson in our own day and age—Bonnefoy searches for an art delivered from the primacy of mimesis, an art sensitive to the otherness that lies behind every representation: the *other* words and images that could have been written in a poem, the *other* forms and shapes a painting could have displayed, the *other* world of death and suffering, which every immutable representation hides: "le temps de la douleur / Avant l'image" (*DLS* 34). Not only does a representation contain a will to perfection and to petrification that eventually contributes to its own downfall, as in Zeuxis's painting of the grapes, but it also conceals other, secret and dangerous images behind those painted or drawn on its surface: images of death, destruction and darkness, each capable, like the anamorphic skull in Holbein's *The Ambassadors,* of troubling the viewer's perception of the intersecting lines, the harmony of colors, the balance of forms that compose the work of art. In one of Bonnefoy's *récits*, for example, a painter describes the fresco of the Madonna and child on which he has been laboring for years. Behind the Virgin's hair, which falls in curls onto her shoulders, behind her crown sparkling with jewels and behind the beatific smile she directs at the radiant face of the child she holds in her arms, there appeared

> ". . . les ailes et les griffes, . . . le cou et le bec étrange d'un immense vautour totalement dégagé de la pénombre d'un arbre sur lequel il était perché, vers la cime, regardant fixement je ne sais quoi hors du monde. Je poussais un cri, de douleur. Il s'envola.

"Mais pendant toutes les années qui suivirent, mes amis, je ne cessai de pousser ce cri, ce fut ce que vous disiez mon silence."

("Le Vautour," *RR* 169)

This is a cry echoing the otherness, the shadowy alterity, the dark unconscious that every representation possesses, but also necessarily represses.

COLOR AND LIGHT: THE *BEYOND* OF REPRESENTATION

Bonnefoy's sensitivity to the otherness that representations hide has led him to write a poetry that in its fight against closure meanders, swerves, digresses, circles and turns away, as if an "esthetics of drift" might allow the poem to escape the immobilizing finality of form and meaning. In his long poems *Dans le leurre du seuil* and *Ce qui fut sans lumière* and in recent prose poems and stories, concerning the non-referentiality of color and the artist's problematic attitude toward the representability of the world, Bonnefoy actively questions and subverts the authority of representation. In *Dans le leurre du seuil,* for example, the textual field is transformed into an "interstitial space," recalling the world beyond the poem. Here a fragmented, irregular syntax, a decentered, digressive poetic discourse, a flow of disappearing and reappearing metaphors and a poetics of gathering and dispersion, all work to mar the so-called "beauty" of poetic speech, opening it to death and nothingness, darkening its transparence, cracking the mirror of its mimetic surface, thus causing the *cri,* the cry of pain and death, to pierce the mask of the *écrit,* the text.

Moreover, in several very recent prose poems and poetic fables and *récits* (*Remarques sur la couleur, L'Artiste du dernier jour*—both collected in *Récits en rêve*—and *Les Raisins de Zeuxis*) Bonnefoy suggests that color, through its immediacy, energy and vibrant physicality, opens representation to an encounter with the temporal world of mortal existence. Color is the "chiffre de la présence" (*I* 328), the light of being itself. Neither an abstract quality nor a formal concept, it is simple, elemental and rarely capturable. It is free of the imaginary. Color is not a representation, but a light; not an image or a copy, but a substance; not an imitation, but the direct apprehension of the real. Color undoes the image, for it establishes the presentness of a thing, the being-thereness (*Dasein*) of material reality; it has ontological presence. It does not copy a thing, it *is* a thing, "une présence de chose" ("Liberté" 17), in the fullness and immediacy of its corporeality. And this presentness of color is always new, always disruptive of form and image, which it pierces like Roland Barthes's *punctum*.[6] Color in a painting is not only seen, but lived. By means of reds, blues, yellows and greens a work of art is touched by the materiality and physicality of the

world and by its relativity as well, since colors are never perceived as they truly and physically are and since there are as many "blues," for example, as there are persons who hear the word and call the color to mind, as Joseph Albers, the painter and color theorist, has demonstrated.[7] Through color the world comes to inhabit, to participate in and to collaborate with the work of art. As a power, a mass of energies, "une densité de possibles (formes ou vies)" ("Héritier" 12), color has a life truly all its own; it has its own pulsation, its own vibration. It becomes a force of presencing, and what it makes present, especially in the enclosed pictorial space of the work of art, is the world. It is in revolt against representability because pure color is ultimately unrepresentable, uncopiable and unnameable. In its innumerable hues, tones, intensities and values, color defeats nomination; it announces an alterity and an indeterminacy that its name cannot signify or explain.[8] It thus affirms "un au-delà du représentable," that which is beyond or outside representation ("Héritier" 8). It is through color, Bonnefoy argues, that art seeks "la délivrance de l'être dans le dépassement de l'image" ("Héritier" 17).[9]

Bonnefoy's fascination with color translates a certain fascination with light, the very matter and medium of color. For Bonnefoy light is "le miracle d'ici" (*CQFSL* 23), something lived and felt, "une joie" (*CQSFL* 66). His poetry could be described as expressing a "poetics of light." He is conscious of the unseizability of light, its continuous passage; but he is also sensitive to the way it transfigures the world, opening it to sudden flashes, to epiphanic illuminations, to a "matière soudain lumière" (*NR* 115). Wherever it appears, light carries the authentic presence of the world: whether in a flash of the setting sun reflected in a windowpane or in a luminously red cloud or in an owl's cry "suddenly filling a sealed sign with light" (*NR* 326) or in "a moment of true radiance on some stony path" (*NR* 76) or in the way a painter "guides things toward their true place, / there enveloping them in light" (*CQFSL* 68) or in poetry through which we come to know, "there where the star / Appears to lead us toward nothing if not death, how, still, to love this light" (*CQFSL* 42). Through the heliotropic intensity of color and through the chromatic presence of light, physical reality in all its fundamental unrepresentability—"Qui a jamais pu *imiter* un rayon solaire?" (*NR* 128)—is momentarily brought into the framed, enclosed, artificial space of the work of art.[10] Light is "la tâche du peintre, et non le matériau de son entreprise" ("La Mort du peintre d'icônes," *RR* 170), as it is also the preoccupation of a poet concerned with the ephemeral visibility of things and with words "blessée[s] d'une lumière" (*DLS* 116). Thus, through light and through color the finite world in all its immediacy, vibrancy and presentness comes to dwell within a representation that it simultaneously creates and contests, that it fashions and fragments. A work of art for Bonnefoy is a mirror held up to the world of appearances. But it is also the crack the world opens in the smooth, reflecting surface of that mirror: the wound, tear, hole, cut, rupture—signs of death and loss, alterity and difference—which every representation possesses but labors to disguise. This is what Bonnefoy refers to as "le cri / Qui perce la musique" (*DLS* 85), "La tache noire dans l'image" (*DLS* 85), "[la] ronce dans les bouquets" (*RT* 52), "[le] cauchemar dans le plus beau rêve" (*E* 33)—each expressing the surge of mortality through perfect form; for Bonnefoy never forgets that while death is often a figure of speech, it is also, as the poet Joseph Brodsky writes, "a figure that leaves [us] speechless."[11]

THE "DRIFT" OF REPRESENTATION

Often in his poetry and criticism Bonnefoy uses the imagery of cloud and river to express the reality of writing, painting and being. Both images, as well as the natural phenomena they signify, are essential to his poetic and ontological response to the world. There can be no forgetting the lesson in movement taught by what he calls "La dérive majeure de la nuée" (*DLS* 116), poignantly incarnated, for example, in Mondrian's painting *The Red Cloud*, as there can be no closing one's ears to the sounds of a rushing river, sign of the perpetually disruptive flux of living. But in a deeper, more substantial way these images point to what one might call the "drift" (in the double sense of orientation and deviation) of representation: that is, the way a poem or a painting may errantly wander away from the object, event or subject the creator has in mind to copy, thus defeating mimetic intention by swerving in an unforeseen direction. In addition to this swerving away from intention in the artistic process, which establishes otherness, there is also the movement of representation away from the world of everyday reality, its enclosure within a haven of eternal, unchanging form. This *errancy* of representation is also its *error*, its falseness and illusion—the way it distorts reality by excluding the transitory and impermanent experience of being-in-the-world.

In *Dans le leurre du seuil* Bonnefoy makes his images resist their own will to closure and coherence; they function as forces of disintegration (*E* 140), breaking apart the poetic systems which they, along with words and sounds, construct. Self-consciously aware of their "fault," their "error," these images call themselves into question; they paradoxically affirm and deny their own reality as representations, for they are "written" according to "le vocabulaire et la syntaxe premiers du naître, du vivre, et du mourir" (*NR* 280). These images—as well as the long poetic sequences or "ensembles" of poem-fragments which constitute Bonnefoy's œuvre—focus attention on the contradictory, often discontinuous movements by which they move towards and then swerve away from the assertion of a meaning. In addition, they emphasize the dialectical nature of a poetry

where acts of gathering and dispersion have equal power. In their movements to and fro and in their contestative relations with each other, images in *Dans le leurre du seuil* resemble the restless, drifting, cloud-like words that give them expression, as the final verses of the poem affirm:

> Les mots comme le ciel
> Aujourd'hui,
> Quelque chose qui s'assemble, qui se disperse.
>
> Les mots comme le ciel
> Infini
> Mais tout entier soudain dans la flaque brève.

> (*DLS* 121)

This is an unsettled, changeable writing, a cloud-writing, but one that does not dwell only within airy, atmospheric spaces high above the earth, so to speak. Writing is reflected in the world, coming to dwell in the simplest and most fugitive of places: in a pool of rain water, the "flaque brève," that will soon evaporate. Words for Bonnefoy are like the sky, images like clouds, poetry like the river. A representation or a writing should suddenly be subject to change the way a summer sky can darken with clouds and then, following a torrential rain, become clear again, or it should swell and expire the way a wave gathers momentum, crests and then crashes onto shore. Both of these metaphors express a gathering of force and energy, an initial filling up and expansion, followed by an unleashing, an emptying, a depletion, of power. Cloud and wave lose their form, are hollowed out, "consumed," dissipated and exhausted into formlessness after they have, so to speak, *ex*-pressed themselves. They stand as models for the precarious reality that images should have in representations.

In *Dans le leurre du seuil* poetic representation is self-consciously dialectical. Acts of gathering, coalescence, assembling, knotting, concentration, linking, clustering and convergence are countered by powerful centrifugal motions of dissipation, errancy, unknotting, divergence, depletion, crumbling, fracturing and excavation. The acts of gathering and dispersion determine the swerving, drifting motion of the poem, which at various moments comes together in long verse formations not unlike massed clouds, and at others dissipates into the vacancy and the incompletion symbolized by dots of ellipsis and white space. We are given a vision of what the title of the final section of the poem calls "L'Epars, L'Indivisible." It is this dialectical pattern of dispersion and compaction, of depletion and accumulation—so vividly expressed in the images of cloud, river and wave—that characterizes what could be called the "drift" of images in Bonnefoy's work: what he identifies, in regard to the painting of Piero della Francesca, as "la dialectique du centre et de l'à-côté" (*RT* 33), the contest between the artistic work centered upon itself and the world of finitude lying to the side, beyond the protecting frame.[12]

CONCLUSION

The poet and the painter live, according to Bonnefoy, in a tentative world which, because it is buffeted by the realities of time and death, is continuously open; it is, in fact, that place of finitude and mutability that Rilke in the eighth of the *Duino Elegies* named the "Open." The artist is one who, "hardi autant que privé d'espoir, se risque un instant dans l'ouvert" (*NR* 142) and who seeks to "rétablir l'*ouvert*" (*PI* 51). Any representation that presents this place of being as closed, complete or permanent is a fiction, a dream. For the artist or writer who must work with forms that almost naturally and inherently tend toward closure and toward the illusion of achieved harmony, sublime perfection and esthetic plenitude, the only hope is to seek the unrepresentable: that light, those colors, those material forms that enter the enclosed spaces of a work of art or the ordered syntax of a poem, still steaming with the heat of the world, still moving unpredictably like a cloud, in other words, a light, a color, a physical presence that not only represent reality, but are the *real* itself. Addressing the painter—and, implicitly, the poet—in **"Dedham, vu de Langham"** (a poem inspired by the Constable painting), Bonnefoy calls on him or her to link image with world, representation with death, poetry with temporality, and to open mimesis to the disintegration and fragmentation of things as they truly and simply *are* in the physical and sensual *light* of being:

> Peintre,
> Dès que je t'ai connu je t'ai fait confiance,
> Car tu as beau rêver tes yeux sont ouverts
> Et risques-tu ta pensée dans l'image
> Comme on trempe la main dans l'eau, tu prends le
>   fruit
> De la couleur, de la forme brisées,
> Tu le poses réel parmi les choses dites.
> . . .
>   Elle, la mort,
> Elle défait le temps qui va le monde,
> Montre le mur qu'éclaire le couchant,
> Et mène autour de la maison vers la tonnelle
> Pour offrir, ô bonheur ici, dans l'heure brève,
> Les fruits, les voix, les reflets, les rumeurs,
> Le vin léger dans rien que la lumière.

> (*CQFSL* 67, 69)

Notes

1. This article is an expanded version of a paper delivered in December 1986 at a session on "Non-representational Strategies in Twentieth-Century Poetry" at a meeting of the Modern Language Association in New York City.

2. *Les Raisins de Zeuxis et d'autres fables/The Grapes of Zeuxis and Other Fables,* trans. Richard Stamelman, with etchings by George Nama (Montauk: Monument Press, 1987), n. pag. (hereafter cited as *Raisins*). Further references to Yves Bonnefoy's work will be indicated by the following abbreviations: "Cartier-Bresson": Introduction to *Henri Cartier-Bresson, photographe* (Paris: Delpire, 1979); *CQFSL: Ce qui fut sans lumière* (Paris: Mercure de France, 1987); *DLS: Dans le leurre du seuil* (Paris: Mercure de France, 1975); *E: Entretiens sur la poésie,* coll. Langages (Neuchâtel: Baconnière, 1981); "Héritier": "Un Héritier de Rimbaud," *Derrière le Miroir,* 279 (May 1978) (Paris: Maeght) 1-17 (exhibition catalogue of the works of Pablo Palazuelo); *I: L'Improbable et autres essais* (Paris: Mercure de France, 1980); "Liberté": "La Liberté de l'esprit," *Raymond Mason,* coll. Contemporains 6 (Paris: Centre Georges Pompidou, 1985) 9-33; *NR: Le Nuage rouge: Essais sur la poétique* (Paris: Mercure de France, 1977); *PI: La Présence et l'image* (Paris: Mercure de France, 1983); *RR: Récits en rêve* (Paris: Mercure de France, 1987); *RT: Rue Traversière* (Paris: Mercure de France, 1977).

3. A similar decomposition of the image is imagined by Bonnefoy in the fading away of a photograph, which over time becomes fused with the natural landscape it might have represented. The image is reintegrated into the "real." No longer are representation and world separate; they are joined through an experience of temporal loss, for this is a photograph of "quelques arbres sur une crête mais prise par accident, d'un déclic imprévu, inaperçu, de l'appareil, et jamais développée, puis jetée, et perdue, vraiment perdue, rendue aux dissolutions et transmutations de la matière sous un éboulement de décombres—l'humidité défaisant les sels, l'astre sans dimensions ni couleur se levant dans la couleur, dans la forme" ("L'Artiste du dernier jour," *RR* 176).

4. To give expression to a desire sustained and ultimately struck by loss is for Bonnefoy the goal of poetic writing: "On écrit pour ne pas oublier, non tant l'unité perdue, que le désir qu'on en a, et qui lui-même s'efface" ("Le Sommeil de personne," *Du romantisme au surnaturalisme: Hommage à Claude Pichois,* coll. Langages [Neuchâtel: Baconnière, 1985] 316).

5. Related to the Zen artist is the aged painter of washes in Bonnefoy's *récit* "Le Fou Rire." His speciality is tracing "d'un seul grand coup de pinceau—oui, des fous rires," with the result that the painted "image" coalesces with, becomes the phenomenon represented: "Et, sur la pointe des pieds, dans cette galerie du fond du jardin de bambous, on s'approchait de la porte de sa cellule. Ecoutez, chuchotait-on (et l'on riait, l'on riait!), écoutez le bruit du pinceau" (*RT* 113).

6. Color, writes Barthes in an essay on the artist Cy Twombly, is an intrusion, an invasion, a penetration, a piercing of the visual field in which it ap-

pears: "Qu'est-ce que la couleur? Une jouis-sance. . . . Il faut se rappeler que la couleur est *aussi* une idée (une idée sensuelle): pour qu'il y ait couleur (au sens jouissif du terme), il n'est pas nécessaire que la couleur soit soumise à des modes emphatiques d'existence; il n'est pas nécessaire qu'elle soit intense, violente, riche, ou même déli-cate, raffinée, rare, ou encore étale, pâteuse, fluide, etc.; bref il n'est pas nécessaire qu'il y ait affirma-tion, *installation* de la couleur. Il suffit qu'elle ap-paraisse, qu'elle soit là, qu'elle s'inscrive comme un trait d'épingle dans le coin de l'œil . . . il suf-fit qu'elle déchire quelque chose." Color does not express an effect, but "un geste, le plaisir d'un geste." It is something "à la fois attendu (ce crayon que je tiens, je sais qu'il est bleu) et inattendu (non seulement je ne sais quel bleu va sortir, mais encore le saurais-je, j'en serais toujours surpris, car la couleur, à l'instar de l'*événement,* est neuve à chaque coup; c'est précisément le *coup* qui fait la couleur, comme il fait la jouissance)" (*L'Obvie et l'obtus: Essais critiques III,* coll. Tel Quel [Paris: Seuil, 1982] 153).

7. *Interaction of Color* (rev. ed. New Haven: Yale UP, 1975).

8. Ludwig Wittgenstein observes that "When we're asked 'What do the words "red," "blue," "black," "white" mean?' we can, of course, immediately point to things which have these colours,—but our ability to explain the meanings of these words goes no further! For the rest, we have either no idea at all of their use, or a very rough and to some extent false one" (*Remarks on Colour,* ed. G. E. M. Anscombe, trans. Linda L. McAlister and Margarete Schättle [Oxford: Basil Blackwell, 1977] 11). And in a later passage he remarks that it is wrong to say "'Just look at the colours in nature and you will see that it is so.' For looking does not teach us anything about the concepts of colours" (12). This is true because "In any serious question uncertainty extends to the very roots of the problem" (23).

9. For a related discussion of the poetics of color in Bonnefoy's poetry and prose, see my "Transfigur-ings of Red: Color, Representation, and Being in Yves Bonnefoy and Claude Garache," *The Com-paratist* 10 (May 1986) 90-107.

10. In truth, light for Bonnefoy is ultimately not seiz-able, not possessable, because it is perpetually in passage. Unlike the image, it cannot be perma-nently fixed, pinned down, enclosed by forms. It resists incarnation. In its unseizability it resembles the past itself, the childhood that we, as adults, can do no more than nostalgically look back upon. The narrator of Bonnefoy's story "La Mort du peintre d'icônes" suggests this by describing how as a child he and his school friends would "play"

with light: "Quand l'heure avait trop duré, il y avait bien un garçon pour tirer de sa poche un de ces minces miroirs qui étaient en ce temps-là à la mode, ronds ou ovales, avec Greta Garbo im-primée sur le fer émaillé rose ou vert pomme de l'autre face. Il captait le soleil dans ce petit piège, il en faisait danser le reflet sur les murs ou le plafond de la salle, légère tache effrayée qui n'en finissait pas de bondir, de s'enfuir par la fenêtre, de revenir comme un oiseau aveuglé,—jusqu'à se prendre, tremblante, dans les cheveux de l'institutrice. Et là cette illusion s'attardait, toute une minute, sous l'ondée de nos rires mal réprimés; puis elle s'effaçait, dans la crue qui mon-tait de toute part, fleuve sans rives ni rides, de cette lumière d'alors, que nul n'a revue sur la terre" (*RR* 173). To think that the "lumière d'alors" can be captured is an illusion. For a brief moment the mirror does indeed contain and focus the light, does single out one ray to dance upon the face of things. In an instant radiance is given body, is concentrated in a concrete form. From it ephemeral icons of crystallized light can be fashioned, as the painter in the story, who has mixed particles of glass with his paint, learns. The appearance of light is more memory than presence, however. It is effaced quickly. Its capture is only momentary ("et là cette illusion s'attardait, *toute une minute*"), for it flees the space of its containment like a flow-ing, cresting river. Unlike the artistic representa-tion whose surface absorbs and contains an embodied light which, strictly speaking, since it is now "captured," ceases to be light, the mirror reflects only the *passage* of light, the movement from presence to absence. Such radiance is eventu-ally remembered as the light of childhood now lost, "cette lumière d'alors, que nul n'a revue sur la terre."

11. *Less Than One: Selected Essays* (New York: Far-rar Straus Giroux, 1986) 49.

12. For further discussion of the drift and otherness of representation in Bonnefoy's poetry, see my "'Le Cri qui perce la musique': Le surgissement de l'altérité dans l'œuvre d'Yves Bonnefoy," *Sud* 15 (1985) 171-210.

John T. Naughton (essay date winter 1989)

SOURCE: Naughton, John T. "The Notion of *Presence* in the Poetics of Yves Bonnefoy." *Studies in 20th Century Literature* 13, no. 1 (winter 1989): 43-60.

[*In the following essay, Naughton considers the notion of presence as a unifying element of Bonnefoy's poetry as well as a recurring topic of critical discussion.*]

The notion of presence is a common element, linking Yves Bonnefoy's earliest pronouncements about poetry to his latest. Just as the polarity between *incarnation* and *excarnation* has helped to clarify his poetics, so too the idea of presence, together with its opposite, absence, is useful for an understanding not only of Bonnefoy's conception of poetry, but also, to a certain extent, of the poetic texts themselves. The emergence of what Bonnefoy calls "presence" creates the "true place," as he says; providing centrality, it invests the world with irrefutable significance and coherence, although at the moment these certainties are lived outside the sphere of words. It is the experience of presence that convinces Bonnefoy that it is in this world that the poet must work, and it is the knowledge that any aspect of this life may suddenly become the pathway to essential being that leads him to refuse the worlds proposed by words, and indeed all modes of representation, since these may tend to become ends in themselves, and as such, forms of absence and excarnation. These notions are, by now, fairly evident to students of Bonnefoy. On the other hand, the insistence on presence has triggered something amounting to a critical debate about Bonnefoy's work, and this debate is a highly significant one, since the controversy over the nature and destiny of poetry is central to it.

Although the term "presence" occurs in a great variety of contexts in Bonnefoy's writings, both in the critical essays and in the poems themselves, and although the term is clearly the cornerstone of his entire poetics, the idea is never defined once and for all, and this is one reason why it has become the object of considerable discussion in analyses of his work. It seems to me, furthermore, that there is a certain evolution and development in Bonnefoy's own understanding and use of the term, and that this in part explains why there should be some confusion and disagreement about its meaning and validity. In a letter to the Swiss critic John E. Jackson, written in 1980 and published in the volume called *Entretiens sur la poésie* (*Interviews on Poetry*), Bonnefoy is very specific about the possibility of some change in his thought.[1] "I readily admit that what I say may seem to contradict this or that remark made earlier," he says, "although I do dream of understanding, some day, the reason for these shiftings, which sometimes are nothing more than differences in point of view brought on by the changes in priority—be these intellectual or emotional—that are a part of one's life" (*E*, p. 130). It is fair to say, furthermore, that it is part of the very nature of what Bonnefoy means by "presence" that it should be at once the simplest and the most ineffable of realities.

His first important essays—those from the early fifties, when one can sense quite clearly the influence of the "Philosophie de l'Existence" (Heidegger, Kierkegaard, Shestov)—would seem to suggest that Bonnefoy is not far from the *chosistes* and from the widespread intellectual tendency that was seeking at the time to free the object from the subjective, anthropocentric mists that had traditionally surrounded it. Thus, when Bonnefoy

writes in his essay "Les Tombeaux de Ravenne" (1953) that "l'objet sensible est présence," it is natural to assume that it is the presence of the concrete world that he is evoking, since the phrase seems to mean, at least on one level, that physical objects, or whatever makes its appeal to the senses, can be presences. "Whoever attempts the crossing of physical spaces (*l'espace sensible*)," he adds, "reconnects with a sacred water that flows through all things":

> And if he makes even the slightest contact with it, he feels himself immortal. . . . That this world exists, I am certain: it is, in the ivy and everywhere, the substantial immortality.

> (*I*, pp. 23, 26)

Similarly, in his essay on "Shakespeare and the French Poet" of 1959, Bonnefoy speaks of "the metaphysical *thereness* of things, most remote from verbalization." Poetry, he writes, "conceives of the Thing, the real object, in its separation from ourselves, its infinite otherness, as something which can give us an instantaneous glimpse of essential being, and thus be our salvation, if indeed we are able to tear the veil of universals, of the conceptual, to attain it."[2] In these essays, Bonnefoy initiates what will be an unflagging attack on the intellectual categories of language, which tend to replace the richer and more complicated world in which we live and make choices, and to smother those moments of mutuality and relation that sometimes mysteriously surge up in it. Although by "thing" and "real object" Bonnefoy means any of the "signs of being" apprehended by the speaking subject, it is nonetheless true that the early texts emphasize such "objects" as ivy leaves and stones, the one to suggest the "immortality" or continuity of being, the other to mark the unalterable limitations that impinge upon it. More recently, however, and doubtless in an effort to clarify misunderstandings, Bonnefoy has insisted that by "presence" he does not mean simply the "concrete," but rather the illumination that springs from "meetings," a kind of wordless epiphany experienced by consciousness in a wide range of circumstances, a *recognition*—filled with wonder and awe—of being. "What counts for me," he says in another interview, "is not simple appearance, or the texture of the world, but rather what escapes perception—although with the possibility of restoring to perception all its intensity and its seriousness. . . . It is . . . an experience of the present moment in all of its memoryless plenitude" (*E*, pp. 57-58).

It is in the very nature of the kind of "meeting" or relation that Bonnefoy means by *presence* that it should not be easily definable, that its power and its mystery should disappear in the words that seek to describe or to analyze it: "this experience," Bonnefoy says, "can hardly be spoken" (*I*, p. 248). To encounter a being as a presence is to come into contact with the unity of all being, for, as presence, any being, however seemingly insignificant, becomes central, becomes the gateway to being itself, since its essence can "spread into the essence of other beings, like the flow of an analogy by which I perceive everything in the continuity and sufficiency of a *place,* and in the transparency of *unity*" (*I,* p. 248). And as for words which would seek to account for the reality of presences, or to preserve something of their depth and their mystery in the poem, Bonnefoy reminds us that "in the hope of presence, one cannot 'signify'; one tries to free a light from the efforts to make sense of it that in fact cover and conceal it" (*I,* p. 249).

If the nature of presence cannot be reduced to a simple formula or a neat definition, if it is rather the cumulative resonance that must be discerned—the notion grown dense, rich with meaning through various evocations and applications—it is nonetheless unmistakably clear that the term is associated with poetry's positive, life-affirming mission, with its desire to align itself with hopefulness. Bonnefoy's emphasis on presence appears as the self-conscious determination to distinguish his idea of poetry from that of Mallarmé, Valéry, and their descendants. The encounter with presence is the guarantee that this world has meaning and coherence and that it can therefore be the proper home for man—a hearth even, providing light and warmth. Much of the emphasis of the French poetry inspired by Mallarmé has been on the idea of *absence*: the recognition of the fatal abolition of the signified by the signifier; the feeling that the "real life" is elsewhere and that society's use of language is a hopeless corruption; the conviction that the poet's mission is therefore to "give a purer meaning to the words of the tribe" and thus to establish, through a rarefied poetic speech, access to the true, to the ideal world compared to which the sorrowful world we languish in is an unfortunate impoverishment ruled by chaos and chance. Critics from Edmund Wilson to Jean-Paul Sartre have been quick to call into question the anti-social and world-denying implications of Symbolist poetics. Sartre, in fact, praises Bonnefoy himself in his book *What Is Literature?* for recognizing, even as a "young Surrealist," the fundamental difference between the exercise of words and the practice of living.[3]

Having once experienced presence, and despite its immediate disappearance, consciousness is, in Bonnefoy's view, changed, and hope arises. This hope is based, as I have tried to show, on a faith in the world we live in. It is built on a ready acceptance of all things, on an openness and a waiting. Any element of the creation, however simple and "impoverished," may become a presence, may become the lamp that beckons toward unity, toward the convinced intuition that the world has meaning. But this is not to say that such moments of being are other than fleeting and impermanent, for Bonnefoy knows how quickly they vanish and how rapidly

they are replaced by the more durable sense of futility and decline, by the awareness of limitation and death. And yet, it is the experience of these moments of presence that gives the sense of purpose and direction to Bonnefoy's poetic quest:

> Something has happened, something of infinite depth and gravity . . . but already the veil of time has wrapped us in its folds, and as the instant draws near we are exiled anew. Something was offered to us . . . but we were unable to grasp it. . . .
>
> And yet, in spite of this missed opportunity, we are no longer the same, we are no longer so poor, some hope remains. Although indeed the question of what might save us remains unanswered, although we have had to doubt in so far as, and almost at the very instant when, we were given to believe, nonetheless we have received the boon of certainty; we know on what basis . . . we can build. Henceforward, we have a reason for existence, which is that sudden act. And a duty and a moral goal—at any rate provisionally—which will be to recover it. And all our actions, lost, crippled creatures that we are, should be a call to this; or rather should recognize that this is what they have always been, in depth. . . .
>
> (*I,* pp. 122-23)

Still, all of Bonnefoy's work will insist that the presence of things is made bright against the backdrop of eventual disappearance and absence. It is this background that gives a certain urgency to the evocation of presence, especially in Bonnefoy's earlier work, since it is against the threat of nothingness that things "cry out" their being.

It is important to stress, I think, that when Bonnefoy speaks of presence, he is evoking what first of all occurs outside the world of language. Poetry does not begin as words. It begins as relation. And the world of presence is always abolished, or made absent, through writing and all forms of representation, even, though to a lesser degree, in the writing or painting most conscious of the problem. "We would have very little if we only had words," he says in his essay on *The Song of Roland.* "What we need are the presences that words leave in dotted lines in the mysterious spaces between them and that words in themselves will never know how to restore to life" (*NR,* p. 175). What is hoped for from words, from the "few," from the "deep" words, is that they might be able to commemorate the experience of unity, of plenitude, experienced in real time and space (*here and now,* as Bonnefoy loves to say), and that the encounter with the "place" of presence—be it the sudden intuition of finitude or the vaulted spaces provided by eroticism—shine forth in them. Readers of poems, especially professional readers, can of course reduce them to words, to an identifiable rhetorical strategy. They can, in fact, place even the idea of presence, which in Bonnefoy's work is so clearly opposed to the habitual response created by words, within the flow of language and make it recuperable as itself: a simple phenomenon of the language that invents and constitutes it. But when Bonnefoy speaks of presence, he asks the reader to find his or her own moments of special intensity that initially come to impose themselves before the words that later seek to give expression to them have come into being. (When he writes of presence, Bonnefoy will often evoke what "speaks" without language: the sound of a stone falling in a ravine; the cry of a bird; the movement of leaves against the darkness; the running of water. These are the elementary, "pre-theological" features of a language all men share, and Bonnefoy has said that the elements are the stuff of the only authentic poetic idiom, the "speech of being" that poetry tries to draw forth. [See *I*, pp. 125-26]). That all written language, even that most acutely conscious of the contradiction, should be estranged from the mutuality and transparency of presence, that all evocation of it should seem a part of the flow of intertextuality, is, I believe, rather perfectly obvious. Words can never really recreate the impression of presence, which is fatally absent in them. But what poetry can do is "tell of presence, 'cry out its name,'" thus helping the reader to rediscover the memory of it, and making of the confinements in which we are all caught, and of which one's writing is only one example, the occasion, at last fully apprehended and grasped, for a superior form of lucidity."[4]

Bonnefoy's notion of presence obviously has its affinities with the project of *voyance* announced in 1871 by Arthur Rimbaud—the French poetic ancestor who seems to have exercised the most lasting influence on Bonnefoy. On the other hand, one would not want to confuse Bonnefoy's idea of presence with the practice of "simple hallucination" experienced and then denounced by Rimbaud. Bonnefoy has repeatedly insisted that the experience of presence does not necessitate a complete repudiation of those faculties given us for discerning and deciphering the world, although of course the purely conceptual mediations proposed by these may in fact come to smother or replace the world of presences. In short, Bonnefoy has never sought to deny the contradictions of the Western person:

> But so that this movement of return be more than mere simulation, it is essential that the two terms of the contradiction be kept face to face, and that this separated and unhappy life of the mind, which would like to return to the substantiality that was lost, be itself affirmed to the very end in its profound difference. We are from the Western world, and this cannot be denied. We have eaten of the tree of knowledge, and this cannot be denied. And far from dreaming of a cure for what we are, it is through our irrevocable intellectuality that we must try to reinvent presence, which is salvation.
>
> (*I*, p. 40)

These statements may be said to constitute a response of sorts to the assertions sometimes made about the nature of Bonnefoy's nostalgia and quest for presence—namely, that it evokes what is outside the experience of language in a highly abstract mode of discourse which is easily recuperable within a recognizable philosophical tradition; that his work—both the poems and the prose—while ostensibly concerned with non-mediated immediacy, is in fact a meditation on historically canonized forms such as the plays of Shakespeare or the great works of Poussin, Tintoretto, and Constable. Steven Winspur, for one, has tried to show that even non-conceptual poetic speech "is itself a sign dependent on an underlying code for its meaning, and hence not a way out of the circle of signs."[5] Winspur points to the network of intertextual elements that flow through Bonnefoy's work and argues that "it is the institution of Western literature . . . that gives meaning to Bonnefoy's project of describing the human life that grounds, and yet is outside, all sign-systems" (pp. 161-162). I do not believe that Bonnefoy would attempt to say that his project seeks to establish itself entirely outside literary, artistic, or philosophical tradition. Rather, he would argue, I think, that the reason we love certain works and can have confidence in them and can "reflect" upon them is that they pursue the same dialectic we do: "sketching out intelligible worlds, personal languages, only in order to simplify them, to the point of seeing born in them, as it were, on its humble bed of straw, an absolute form, this time that of life itself" (*NR*, p. 280). In this way, not only one's own work, but also that of many other artists, who have similarly sought "that immanence in which the personal expression of the artist tends to dissipate" (*E*, p. 58), becomes dialectical: "the crucible in which, through a dialectic of our life and our book—action and dream reconciled!—presence will not only emerge, but deepen its relation to us" (*NR*, p. 280). Thus the evocations of Poussin's paintings on "The Finding of Moses" in Bonnefoy's long poem ***Dans le leurre du seuil*** (***In the Lure of the Threshold***, 1975) are evocations, it is true, of mediation, but of mediations that speak of the need to rid oneself of mediation, to banish the image that stifles the world. These works hint at the "even breathing" that says that world and spirit are in harmony. In this sense, these works of art are but "reflections" of the poet's desire: his longing for simplicity and transparency; his will to purify images of the unduly "imaginary"; his refusal of the false prestige assigned to a self that is merely contrived, to the purportedly special or privileged psychology called the poet; his affirmation of an earth of simple presences that all men share.

This embracing of contradiction and paradox—the insistence on reason *and* on its limitations; the love and yet the suspicion of the image, of representations—in part explains Bonnefoy's break with the Surrealists, whose project was based, in Bonnefoy's view, on an over-determined faith in "magic" and "occult powers." By focusing only on certain dimensions of the object, by evoking presence as a detached or arbitrary entity, isolated from coherence or meaningful context, the surrealist image achieves, from Bonnefoy's point of view, a kind of "negative intensity," becomes what he calls "la mauvaise présence," a terrifying or absurdist manifestation of presence. True, the surrealist image breaks free from the world of conditioned response and forces attention to the marvelous and improbable "being-there" of things. Still, the presence of which Bonnefoy speaks, and which is the object of a quest that is both artistic and lived, is revealed rather through all simple things whose very finitude allows them to participate in the greater unity of which they are a part. Of this unity Bonnefoy has said:

> It is what asks us to put our faith in finitude, since totality only exists through the mutual recognition of each part, which has limitation as its essence: but this is what grants us, in the very assumption of our nothingness, access to the universal. And here is what I would call the religious act, here is the potential sacred order—and enough for me to break with surrealism

> (*E*, pp. 123-24)

Bonnefoy's idea of presence has its parallels not only in Rimbaud, but also in the experiences of more modern, and even contemporary thinkers, as well. One thinks, in this connection, of Roland Barthes's encounters, while studying photographs, with what he calls the *punctum*— that moment of shock, of rupture in the known and the acquired, during which, as he says, "words fail."[6] It is in his *La Chambre claire* that Barthes begins, in Bonnefoy's view, to draw closer to the spirit of poetry than in any of his other books.[7] In his search for traces of presence left in the photographs of his dead mother (a search which leads him to examine the medium generally), Barthes contrasts the *punctum* to the *studium,* which he says is "ultimately always coded." What can be named, Barthes goes on to say, "cannot really prick me" (p. 51). I once maintained that the relation that Barthes establishes between the *punctum* and the Zen *satori* experience seems applicable to Bonnefoy's notion of presence as well, especially as the latter is presented in Bonnefoy's most recent work.[8] I still think that the parallel is worth exploring, since the Zen man's insistence on the transparency between subject and object in the *satori* experience, his idea that the simplest of realities may trigger the moment of wordless illumination, although no amount of effort or will may guarantee it, all have clear affinities with Bonnefoy's statements about presence. On this occasion, however, I would prefer to mention another possible connection: Martin Buber's "Thou."

Readers of Bonnefoy's work will have noticed the extraordinary predominance of the "Tu" or "Thou" form in his poetry.[9] Furthermore, the "I" of Bonnefoy's poems often addresses the "Thou" in such a way as to underscore the affinities with Buber. Both writers emphasize the boundlessness of *relation* and the capacity of whatever we relate to with the whole of our being to open into the eternal and the universal and thus to invest the world with a meaning and a coherence, the certainty of which, though ineffable, appears nonetheless irrefutable. It is a moment, as Bonnefoy says, that will vanish a thousand times, but which has the glory of a god. Buber insists just as strongly as Bonnefoy that the relation to the "Thou" in no way involves a repudiation of our normal, rational faculties, and like Bonnefoy, he maintains with emphatic conviction that the intuition of meaning, of unity, of eternity emerges from a relation to this world and to this life, and not another. Both writers evoke, furthermore, an experience of the "timeless present," and both stress *mutuality,* since, as Buber says, in "I-It" relations only the "I" is active and engaged. And yet, both are also aware that nothing in human will or effort can ever guarantee the emergence of presence, that the "Thou" always meets us as a kind of "grace." "How powerful is the unbroken world of *It*," writes Buber, "and how delicate are the appearances of the *Thou!*"[10] And Bonnefoy has said that "it is enough to hold onto anything—to 'no matter what,' be it only a stone," for the sense of meaninglessness to vanish and for loving mutuality to triumph. And yet, he adds, "however important this may be, one knows as well that it cannot be forced: there is no power for making sure of this power" (*I*, p. 324).

Bonnefoy, like Buber, has also said that we make contact with "essential being" by means of our relation to "unessential being," thus stressing the conviction that any dimension of our life, however seemingly banal or trivial, may become a presence. "In our contact with being," says Bonnefoy, "we cannot do without the mediation of specific beings" (*R*, p. 126). The "beings" on which Bonnefoy focuses, however (and hence the particular way in which he envisions presence) vary, as might be expected, over the years of his development. In lectures, Bonnefoy sometimes tries to evoke what he means by presence through the use of the philosophical distinction between *quiddité*—that is, what makes a thing what it is; its formal definition or essence—and *eccéité*—the sudden emergence of the thing from behind the veil of its definition; the bold imposition of its presence; the principle by means of which essences are made individual. And certainly one function of the poem is to try to bring a universal category into the realm of specific experience. On the other hand, the experience of presence is also an intuition of the universal in the particular, as I hope to show in a moment. I have suggested elsewhere that the distinction Bonnefoy establishes in Shakespeare's work between the "readiness" of Hamlet and the "ripeness" of Lear might be applied, cautiously, to his own development.[11] It does seem that the work before the sixties, and in particular the poems of *Douve* (1953) and *Hier régnant désert* (*Yesterday's Desert Dominion,* 1958), are marked by an iconoclastic violence, by the "negative theology" that aims at discovering the world of presence through the destruction of representations. Even this very destructiveness must be contested if the poet is to avoid some "fine art" of disillusionment. In a first phase of his development (which is not without its affinities with contemporary deconstructionist tendencies), Bonnefoy is trying to burn away the hard bark of mediation, to expose the illusory protection of the idea, in order to venture to a depth, to a calcinated earth where, though "images no longer work," a new departure might be envisioned. Presence is often evoked in poems that have an unmistakably allegorical quality, however. The salamander of *Douve,* Bonnefoy's first book of poems, for instance, becomes the symbol of a silent adherence to simple earth, and as such, assures a disillusioned resurrection from the world of the imaginary which has been put to the flames:

"Lieu de la salamandre"

La salamandre surprise s'immobilise
Et feint la mort.
Tel est le premier pas de la conscience dans les pierres,
Le mythe le plus pur,
Un grand feu traversé, qui est esprit.

La salamandre était à mi-hauteur
Du mur, dans la clarté de nos fenêtres.
Son regard n'était qu'une pierre,
Mais je voyais son coeur battre éternel.

O ma complice et ma pensée, allégorie
De tout ce qui est pur,
Que j'aime qui resserre ainsi dans son silence
La seule force de joie.

Que j'aime qui s'accorde aux astres par l'inerte
Masse de tout son corps,
Que j'aime qui attend l'heure de sa victoire,
Et qui retient son souffle et tient au sol.

(*P,* p. 89)

"Place of the Salamander"

The startled salamander freezes
And feigns death.
This is the first step of consciousness among the
   stones,
The purest myth,
A great fire passed through, which is spirit.

The salamander was halfway up
The wall, in the light from our windows.
Its look had turned to stone,
But I saw its heart beating eternal.

O my accomplice and my thought, allegory
Of all that is pure,
How I love what draws up thus in silence
The only force of joy.

How I love what is in harmony with the stars through
   the inert
Mass of its whole body,
How I love what awaits the hour of its victory,
And holds its breath and clings to the ground.

The poem is first of all located in a common experience: the spotting of a salamander frozen on a wall. This simple experience, which is described in lines 1 and 2, and 6 through 9, opens, however, into "thoughts" and "ideas" which connect the salamander to a "myth" and allow it to become "allegorical." Doubtless Bonnefoy is not unaware that the salamander has, through historical tradition, developed a symbolic identity: the creature who is able to pass through fire unscathed and who survives devastating floods is closely associated with the principle of resurrection. The power of this poem in part resides, therefore, in the co-existence of the banal and the profound; a moment of one's daily life merges with, but is not overwhelmed by, a long tradition of representation. The salamander stands for what survives in the iconoclastic fury of Bonnefoy's early tendencies toward deconstruction and disillusionment. Anticipating death with stony resignation, the salamander resides in silence and vigilant immobility. Its "mythic" or "allegorical" function, which is to symbolize spiritual wakefulness and persistence even in the face of death, is nonetheless seen as a "first step" of consciousness. Though clearly the pathway to more wide-ranging associations—with eternity and the immortal stars—its centrality is couched in the context of a characteristic "negativity," since it is silent, motionless, restrained, waiting.

It seems to me that by the mid-sixties, Bonnefoy's life and poetic emphasis clearly change. He comes to distance himself a bit from the earlier preoccupation with presence as revelation of human finitude and from the "words of war" raised against the world of the image. "I used to think," he says in an essay of 1967 called "Baudelaire Speaks to Mallarmé," "that words, desiccated by their conceptual use, failed to convey presence, were forever limited to a 'negative theology.' Now I sense that some sort of archaeology is possible, which would reveal, piece by piece, the essential elements of our form" (*E,* p. 91). "Fire and the name of fire *are,* so that life might have a center" (*E,* p. 90). The experiences of place, of shared love, of trust in another human being seem to have provided access to an apprehension of the unity of being, which the poet experiences, in this second phase, with a peaceful and radiant conviction. The theater of destruction and self-doubt, the evocations of terror and fragmentation yield to scenes of gentle, erotic binding and trustful participation in plenitude. (There is even an increasing confidence in the image itself, as a poem such as **"On a Pietà of Tintoretto"** from the book *Words in Stone* [1965] clearly shows.) A woman's red dress is now added to the stone as a source of illumination and guidance, and poems such as **"The Myrtle"** (*Words in Stone*) are richly suggestive of the entry, through eroticism, into what Georges Bataille has called "the continuity of being":

"Le Myrte"

Parfois je te savais la terre, je buvais
Sur tes lèvres l'angoisse des fontaines
Quand elle sourd des pierres chaudes, et l'été
Dominait haut la pierre heureuse et le buveur.

Parfois je te disais de myrte et nous brûlions
L'arbre de tous tes gestes tout un jour.
C'étaient de grands feux brefs de lumière vestale,
Ainsi je t'inventais parmi tes cheveux clairs.

Tout un grand été nul avait séché nos rêves,
Rouillé nos voix, accru nos corps, défait nos fers.
Parfois le lit tournait comme une barque libre
Qui gagne lentement le plus haut de la mer.

(P, p. 203)

"The Myrtle"

Sometimes I knew you as earth, and I would drink
From your lips the anguish of the fountains
When it wells up from the warm stones, and summer
Would loom high above the happy stone and the
    drinker.

Sometimes I would say you were myrtle and we would
    spend
A whole day burning the tree of all your gestures.
These were great brief fires of vestal light,
Thus I would invent you amid your bright hair.

A whole vast empty summer had dried out our dreams,
Rusted our voices, strengthened our bodies, loosened
    our chains.
Sometimes the bed would shift like a ship set free
And which slowly moves out to high sea.

Once again, the poem begins with the perfectly mundane: one drinks from a fountain, then builds and watches a fire. The text is in striking contrast to the poem on the salamander, however, through the absence this time of the overtly allegorical and mythic element that characterizes the earlier work. Furthermore, the emphasis in the earlier poem on restriction and wakefulness yields here to a sense of erotic expansiveness and repose, signaled in the last lines through the notion of the marriage bed "moving out to high sea." Here the poet abandons the impersonal and rather abstract formula of the poem on the salamander ("How I love what") and instead addresses a "Thou" which emerges intermittently and in different forms—Bonnefoy organizes the text around the repetition of the initiatory word "sometimes"—and these various manifestations of presence are represented by the elemental realities of earth, water, and fire which are evoked in succession.

Here again, there can be little doubt that Bonnefoy knows about the historical significance of myrtle—the fact that this evergreen shrub was sacred to Venus, the goddess of love, and that, while connected with resurrection and life-in-death, it is also closely associated with love, marriage, and bounty. That the myrtle in Bonnefoy's poem keeps some of its traditional erotic symbolism is confirmed by the fact that the gestures—of bending to drink, of watching the flash of fire—are nicely ambiguous and could be read as suggesting the fundamental physicality of the sexual act itself. But this is the richness of presence—and this time evoked on a much less allegorical and stylized level—that it lead from one thing to another, that it encourage the poet, as a part of his "inventiveness," to see hair in fire, or fire in hair, or to feel lips in earth's water, water in lips.

There are three common criticisms levelled against Bonnefoy's notion of presence. The first is that the affirmation of a world of presence is often presented in a highly abstract, even "conceptual" diction. The second is that Bonnefoy does not so much recreate the reality of presence in his poems as simply designate, or even list, its manifestations in the life of the poet. The third criticism is that Bonnefoy does not give the reader enough intimate detail about his personal experience, that the *specifically* human face is effaced or even obliterated in the highly "essentialized" landscape of his poetic world.

I have already spoken at length to the first criticism. There can be no doubt that there is a profoundly paradoxical dimension to Bonnefoy's work. As a product of history who speaks of the importance of moments outside time, and as a speaker in a personal, idiosyncratic tongue that nonetheless establishes a significant dialogue with the language that a tradition has erected and embellished, Yves Bonnefoy has elaborated a poetic speech that places itself both inside and outside a long line of Western representation. But all great poetry, it could be argued, is born from just such a fundamental contradiction, and we might profitably discuss this poet's work from the perspective of the way in which he confronts and seeks to come to terms with the contradictions that divide him. Clearly, the poet must at every moment both depart from the acquired and the known, thus venturing toward openness and renewal, and, at the same time, remain within a recognizable system of signs in order to communicate with others. If the poem were only the expression of what is initially experienced outside words, it would, presumably, be totally incomprehensible; if, on the other hand, it were only a description of this experience, it would become purely formulaic or conceptual, a kind of prose statement. Bonnefoy's poetry is neither of these things exclusively, and yet something of both worlds exists and may be discerned in it.

Two responses might be made to the charge—which was often levelled at T. S. Eliot as well—that, particularly in the later poetry, Bonnefoy tends to present the reader with an accumulation of lists, that he simply points to things, and that the evocation of presence is therefore insufficient: a kind of insistence rather than a rediscovery through words; an intellectual image which, through repetition, hardens into a verbal fetish. There is first of all, of course, Bonnefoy's own testimony that as his relation to language developed, as he attempted to "excavate" to the level of origins, to the place of absolute simplicity, he found the few, deep, elemental words that, in his view, are the "pillars upholding the vault of speech" (*E*, p. 90). For Bonnefoy, these words are so fully steeped in what they name as to become for the poet who uses them more signified than signifier. Thus the poem strives to designate and retain only the "simple abundance" of the earth all men share. And the poet therefore proposes "no longer to try to reabsorb what is in a formula, but, on the contrary, to reabsorb the formula in a participation in the real" (*I*, p. 250). Secondly, one might suggest that the "insufficiency" in the evocation of presence—the mere listing of things—is in part intentional, a deliberate effort to prevent the poem from becoming an end, a world, in itself. Shouldn't the reader *not* be absorbed in the glimpses of presence that the writing may vouchsafe, since these are only moments in a poem, and—Bonnefoy will never cease telling us this—the poem does not matter as much as life does? Doesn't he then deliberately send us away from the work and into our own life, giving us hints only, following—or leading us forth—with mere glimmers?

No human face in Yves Bonnefoy's world? It is certainly true that this poet tends to de-emphasize the particular differences that exist between people (and that are often explored by the artist who fusses over what he thinks sets him apart or makes him unique and superior) in favor of those experiences that are universal. His poetics aims at a pure ontology, through which words seek to elaborate a "common speech," so that "no longer being concerned with anything separated, closed off, they [words] dissipate the last enchantments of the mythical self, they speak of the simplest of human desires in the presence of the simplest of objects, which is being; they bring together the universal self" (*NR*, pp. 279-80). On the other hand, the many essays that Bonnefoy has written as homages to his friends— the pieces on Gaëton Picon, Paul Celan, Georges Seferis, and Paul de Man—all bear witness to the importance in his life of those he has loved. Evoking the blue gaze, the prominent forehead, the ready smile of Paul de Man, for instance, Bonnefoy says: "a presence began to make itself felt, with all the mystery that this word entails."[12] But if friendship is clearly the arena for presence, it is also true that Bonnefoy is the least sentimental of writers and one of the furthest removed from the cult of personality and the fascination with individuality as such. And the poems, it seems to me, by expanding

what is specific in personal experience, by disentangling the over-determined understanding of it, by muting the aspects of a particular destiny, open their richness to what everyone has lived or felt—they sketch out the face and the hands that are everyman's.

I imagine that future Bonnefoy studies will need to focus more on how specific poems function and less on statements made by Bonnefoy himself about his concept of poetry and about his intentions. The issue of presence, once decoded and placed within the body of intertexts that constitutes and sustains it, does however remain, it seems to me, the area where what readers have felt with particular intensity must come into play. Let me evoke Buber once again. Seeking in the postscript to the second edition of *I and Thou*, written in 1957, to explain the emergence of spirit that "has not yet entered the world but is ready to do so, and becomes present to us," Buber says that this he "cannot point out" but only "indicate indirectly" through "certain events in man's life which can scarcely be described," but which experience spirit "as meeting." These efforts at explanation may, however, prove futile, he tells us, and when all else fails, "there is nothing for me but to appeal, my reader, to the witness of your own mysteries—buried, perhaps, but still attainable" (p. 127).

Notes

1. *Entretiens sur la poésie* (Neuchâtel: Éditions de la Baconnière, 1981), p. 130. Hereafter I will be referring to this text in the body of my paper as *E*. To facilitate matters, I will refer to Bonnefoy's major works in the following way: *L'Improbable et autres essais* (Paris: Mercure de France, 1980) is *I; Le Nuage rouge: Essais sur la poétique* (Paris: Mercure de France, 1977) is *NR; Rome 1630; L'Horizon du premier Baroque* (Paris: Flammarion, 1970) is *R; Poèmes* (Paris: Mercure de France, 1978) is *P*.

2. The essay "Shakespeare et le poète français" was first published in the French review *Preuves,* 100 (June 1959), 42-48. An English translation of the piece appeared in *Encounter,* 105 (June 1962), 38-43.

3. Jean-Paul Sartre, *Situations II* (Paris: Gallimard, 1948), pp. 324-25.

4. Yves Bonnefoy, *Gilbert Lely* (Paris: Thierry Bouchard, 1979), p. 8.

5. Steven Winspur, "Yves Bonnefoy's Three Strikes Against the Sign," *Romanic Review,* 77, No. 2 (March, 1986), 160.

6. Roland Barthes, *Camera Lucida. Reflections on Photography,* trans. Richard Howard (New York: Hill and Wang, 1981), p. 109.

7. Yves Bonnefoy, *La Présence et l'Image* (Paris: Mercure de France, 1983), p. 12.

8. John T. Naughton, *The Poetics of Yves Bonnefoy* (Chicago: The University of Chicago Press, 1984), pp. 18, 164-66.

9. See, for instance, Jacques Gadeau, "La Question de l'autrui dans *Du Mouvement et de l'immobilité de Douve*" and Didier Coste, "La Deuxième Personne comme personne du lyrique chez Yves Bonnefoy," in *Poétique et Poésie d'Yves Bonnefoy*, Cahiers de l'Université de Pau et des Pays de l'Adour, No. 18 (Pau, 1983), pp. 3-9, 11-22, resp. For an exhaustive and compelling discussion of the general question of alterity in Bonnefoy's work, see Richard Stamelman, "'Le Cri qui perce la musique': Le Surgissement de l'altérité dans l'oeuvre d'Yves Bonnefoy," *Sud,* 15 (1985), 171-210.

10. Martin Buber, *I and Thou,* trans. Ronald Gregor Smith (New York: MacMillan Publishing Company, Collier Books, 1987), p. 98.

11. *The Poetics of Yves Bonnefoy,* pp. 107-108 and in my essay "L'Idée de l'Incarnation dans la poétique d'Yves Bonnefoy," *Sud,* 15 (1985), 68-80.

12. Yves Bonnefoy, "Paul de Man," in *The Lesson of Paul de Man, Yale French Studies,* 69 (1985), 18.

James Lawler (essay date summer 1992)

SOURCE: Lawler, James. "'La neige piétinée est la seule rose': Poetry and Truth in Yves Bonnefoy." *L'Esprit Créateur* 32, no. 2 (summer 1992): 43-54.

[*In the following essay, Lawler underscores the search for truth in the poetry of* Début et fin de la neige.]

Can poetry aspire to a kind of truth? Is it possible, two hundred years after Goethe, to think of a convergence? Do we not know that the gods have disappeared, that the myths have small virtue, that language is deceptive? Char calls poetry and truth "synonymous," but his vision is as unarguable as the Sorgue. On the other hand, Yves Bonnefoy, from as early as his *Traité du pianiste* (1946), plies the status of poetry with searching questions. He recognizes that he had to break his allegiance to Surrealism, for the Surrealists erred in confusing dream with illumination. Yet they were right in their pursuit of a *vraie vie.* Bonnefoy demands of himself a poetry that will advance, in the greatest openness of the sensibility, to an achieved perception. Dream is a necessary resource, but he will be alive to the lures of the seductive image, the facile rhythm. If the origin is desire, the end is awareness, each poem being qualified

by the next in the way that each of his collections takes up the earlier ones. Thus, when he describes the life of a writer, he does so in terms of an existential pursuit. "Il n'y a pas que des livres," he observes in his *Leçon inaugurale au Collège de France* (1982); "il y a des destinées littéraires, où chaque ouvrage marque une étape: ce qui semble indiquer un désir de mûrir à soi."[1]

To come to maturity: nothing shows this process more clearly than *Début et fin de la neige* which was published by the Mercure de France in the spring of 1991. It is the most recent of fourteen books of poetry, to which nineteen volumes of essays and narratives serve as complement. The mass of Bonnefoy's work is splendid, especially when one compares it with that of other French poets in the second half of the twentieth century. Yet I would wish to emphasize not only his productivity and formal breadth and reach, but his growth as artist and thinker. *La Vérité de parole* (1988) and *Entretiens sur la poésie* (1990) offer the most sustained discussion of poetry and poetics since Valéry; while the latest collection shows him writing at the peak of his art.

Début et fin de la neige comprises twenty-four poems arranged in five sections. (It is followed by a short piece, **"Là où retombe la flèche,"** linked to it by more than one trait but of a different inspiration; I shall therefore limit my remarks to the major work.) The title brings to mind Bonnefoy's use of oppositions in naming his books, whether these are explicit—*Anti-Platon, Du mouvement et de l'immobilité de Douve*—or implicit—*Hier régnant désert, Dans le leurre du seuil, Ce qui fut sans lumière.* Attention is directed to a division as fertile as a Claudelian "partage." Petrarch (the epigraph to *Début et fin de la neige* is taken from the *Canzoniere*), the Renaissance architects ("O mes amis"), the ancient philosophers (Aristotle, Lucretius) propose a balance like a childhood of the spirit. The poet, however, must live with other premises as he inscribes a ceaseless dialectic.

The intertext is obliquely suggested. Certainly Baudelaire is present in the course of a verse paragraph that refers to a train journey through a snowstorm, at one point of which the poet happens to see in the pages of a neighbor's newspaper a large portrait of Baudelaire— "Toute une page / Comme le ciel se vide à la fin d'un monde / Pour consentir au désordre des mots" (36). Disorder, not order, since the photograph is a manner of epiphany, or a Surrealist lucky chance. Baudelaire is a sign; but *Début et fin de la neige* seems to me to record the passage of another poet who left his mark. Saint-John Perse published *Neiges* in 1944, at a time when France was still occupied and the world at war.[2] Perse turns to snow to tell of patience and expectancy: "Epouse du monde notre patience, épouse du monde notre attente! . . ." We know that Bonnefoy considers

Perse to be one of the very few modern French poets who have found a truth in nature—"la réalité naturelle dans son évidence glorieuse," "une immédiateté, 'autrefois' donnée, aujourd'hui lointaine et comme interdite." The homage is significant. Bonnefoy, although not an "Atlantic man" as Perse called himself, could admire the solemn sweep of the Perse apostrophes, like those of *Neiges*:

> Et nous ravisse encore, ô monde! ta fraîche haleine de
> mensonge! . . .

The gravity, the self-awareness are close to Bonnefoy, even the ceremonial syntax of inversion, whose analogue occurs in **Début et fin de la neige**: "Te soit la grande neige le tout, le rien . . .", "Te soient ces branches qui scintillent la parole . . ." (43).

On the other hand, we can hardly be further from the central thrust of Perse. Bonnefoy does not seek Perse's hieratic grandeur but goes to the opposite extreme: not solemnity but intimacy, not incantation but reflexion, not the untrodden but the trodden snow that tells the tensions of reality and desire. It appears to me that **Début et fin de la neige** sublates *Neiges* in the way of a calling heard and answered in the most personal terms.

Bonnefoy gives us a sequence in which the lyrical élan is constantly surveyed by an exacting eye. We are held by a language alert to errors of commission or omission. The unit is not the well-made poem, the four-square piece, the text woven with an unbroken thread, but rather the total collection with its diverse moments of time, mood, thought. Poetry becomes a self-qualifying whole, free in form—unmetered, unrhymed—and composed in the way of a Symbolist book or a musical composition. So the fifteen sections of the long first part chronicle the day, from one dawn to the next, of the first snowfall of the season ("La grande neige"), like the successive strands of an ample movement in which "enchevêtrer," "se désenchevêtrer," "enchevêtrement" signal points of junction and disjunction; or the repetitions of "écharpe," "feuilles," "lumière"; or the gamut of colors—white, green, yellow, blue, red.

The opening lines have the brevity of a haiku in which the poet discovers the drama inherent in nature:

> Première neige tôt ce matin. L'ocre, le vent
> Se réfugient sous les arbres.
>
> (13)

Time writes an instant of vulnerability that is also perhaps an intimation of eternity, a flight that is also stillness, a shadow that is also dream. It is the meeting of two worlds:

> Un peu de vent
> Ecrit du bout du pied un mot hors du monde.
>
> (13)

The small ("un peu"), the tangential ("du bout du pied") are a deferred revelation. Words dissolve into the whiteness of the page before beginning again on a moment of reflexion—the poet recalls the day before—and retrospection—he looks at the mirror behind him. The world has become pale like a snow-charged sky or a glass that allows fresh perceptions:

> Neiger
> Se désenchevêtre du ciel.
>
> (14)

Snow untangles itself from the sky, the present from the past, thought from dream, image from mirror. The sound of voices, a plough transformed by snow, stir the house of memory in which the poet is a child again, enchanted by the play of his breath on the windowpane as he looks out on the features of nature. In a few lines he relives the wonder of infancy: "A ce flocon / Qui sur ma main se glisse . . ." A surge of emotion causes him to want to dedicate his life to the beauty of a snowflake. He would wish to be no less pure—"Un instant simplement: cet instantci, sans bornes"—so as to translate the welling heart. Yet the poem swerves on an adversative by which gain becomes loss like the melting flake:

> Mais déjà il n'est plus
> Qu'un peu d'eau qui se perd
> Dans la brume des corps qui vont dans la neige.
>
> (16)

The hendecasyllable has a Dantesque resonance: mortal forms vanish, gray on gray, snow to water. Whereas the poet could imagine, a few lines before, his happiness unlimited, he sees now the finitude of happiness.

The word "illusion" must be pronounced—*illusion* of this flake, *illusion* of the poppy growing last summer among dry stones. The lyrical moment has led to disappointment. Yet is there nothing left but illusion? If illusion there is, then there is also promise like that of the apples of the supreme enchantress:

> Circé
> Sous sa pergola d'ombres, l'illuminée,
> N'eut pas de fruits plus rouges.
>
> (17)

The injection of myth takes the poem to another register. We recognize the eternal drama of promise and reality, which the poet is called to live ever again. He finds in the snow not only a mythical aura but a properly religious one that leads him to a Christian frame of reference: "Madone de miséricorde de la neige" (18). Lightness, mist, embroidery: snow becomes the goddess of mercy in whose praise language echoes the return to a mother's breast:

> Contre ton corps
> Dorment nus

Les êtres et les choses, et les doigts
Violent de leur clarté ces paupières closes.

(18)

The divine figure is warmly consoling, discreetly sensual.

Is this ultimate reality? Can the poet enter the rose-garden? The medieval imagery evokes the quest for the paradisal gate and the lost mother:

Il neige.
Sous les flocons la porte
Ouvre enfin au jardin
De plus que le monde.

(19)

All seems to have come to ripeness since the gate is open. But at this very time the link is severed: a trivial happening interrupts the dream as the poet's scarf tears on some rusty metal; a fortuitous event is enough to destroy the exultant vision. He learns once more the irony indissociable from the world: "et se déchire / En moi l'étoffe du songe" (19).

However, the next poem (**"Les Pommes"**) does not give way to melancholy or regret. The laconic verse allows no indulgence in self-pity: the poet refuses to linger, resolutely begins again, asks himself a question which appears to be a non-sequitur but which in fact affirms anew his confidence in nature. Not by solipsism, but by a sensitive contact with the natural substance of things will a way be found:

Et que faut-il penser
De ces pommes jaunes?
Hier, elles étonnaient, d'attendre ainsi, nues
Après la chute des feuilles . . .

(20)

The religious apprehension is set aside for a lovely encounter with apples as crisp as Williams's wheelbarrow. They are women naked on the bare trees of winter, but the snow clothes them in delicate fashion:

Aujourd'hui elles charment
Tant leurs épaules
Sont, modestement, soulignées
D'un ourlet de neige.

(20)

"Charment" reminds us of Circe, yet establishes the difference: the image is no longer mythical but humanly close. The question asked—"What are we to make of these yellow apples?"—is not answered, though we know that the rift between poet and snow is healed, for "charment" calls as much on Greek *karis* as on Latin *carmen.*

"J'avance . . . je perçois . . . on ne comprend pas . . . l'on voit . . ."—the movement is toward the abstraction of a universal self. The poet's eyes, closed to apples and snow ("J'ai fermé les yeux . . ."), are open to the words he is using as if they were as random and as potentially fruitful as the snow, "Qui tourbillonne, se resserre, se déchire" (21). They speak to him with all the memory they contain like leaves beneath flakes, or earth beneath the winter cold, or a mind barely visible beneath the faded ink of an old letter. It is as if he were spoken to by a person he cannot name or explain. The language of this internalized snow has many mute e's—musical rests, mental pauses—like a poem in which the metaphors foreshadow rather than state a meeting. At the same time it bears the presentiment of fingers that touch:

On dirait,
Dès qu'il neige plus dru,
De ces mains qui refusent d'autres mains

Mais jouent avec les doigts qu'elles refusent.

(22)

The poet multiplies analogies in an effort to define a presence that teases, rejects, connects no less elusively than the snow.

Can there be a final sense? The fine tissue of familiar reality has disappeared in the snowfall. But the poet, this self-conscious user of language, refers to the *Poetics* to confirm the value of playfulness, the worth of clarity. For Aristotle language works to a purpose like snow or bees or water. "Comme" occurs three times (23), affirming by the emphatic use of simile that criticism reads Aristotle awry when it treats him as a mere rhetorician. The philosopher, like the poet, does not refuse the simple, which for him is not a pre-conceptual revelation, but the coincidence of language and being: "C'est la transparence qui vaut . . ." (23).

Another philosopher bears witness in the domain of words and things. Lucretius described the physical universe in a way suggestive of modern atomic theory:

Lucrèce le savait:
Ouvre le coffre,
Tu verras, il est plein de neige
Qui tourbillonne.

(24)

The Epicurean vision of atomic dynamism is put in the metaphorical frame of the modern poem; fusion and diffusion become the life and death of two words, two shadows, night and dream, white and red—carefree and joyful in the manner of flakes that melt in their "peu de mort" (24).

What anguish can resist such limpidity? In one of the most beautiful moments of the sequence, the poet sets aside philosophers and abstract thought to address his soul, for he is able to declare the existence of this *animula blandula*: "Ame, que voulais-tu / Que tu n'aies eu de naissance éternelle?" (25). The world, for the religious sensibility, is decked for a feast comparable to first love, when flowers, leaves and music hold the heart. The self believes itself to be born to happiness like snow-covered nature:

> Mais des corolles, des feuilles y sont brodées,
> Et déjà la musique se fait entendre
> Dans la salle voisine, illuminée.
> Une ardeur mystérieuse te prend la main.
>
> Tu vas, le cœur battant, dans la grande neige.
>
> (25)

The poet beckons to medieval lyric on the one hand, to Wordsworthian elegy on the other. Nature is the mistress of long desire.

The next poem, "Noli me tangere" (26), deepens emotion by a religious insight more poignant than that of "La vierge de miséricorde" (18). The words of the title are those of Jesus to Mary Magdalene after his resurrection, which designate in Latin as in the French form given in the ninth line ("'Non, ne me touche pas', lui dirait-il") a sacred inviolability. Yet the speaker is not the poet but a snowflake, the most holy being the most fragile. (I think again of Claudel in *Cent phrases pour éventails*: "Seule la rose est assez fragile pour exprimer l'Eternité."[3]) The imagery of the garden returns, and it seems that the soul can at last gain admission to a domain in which the past is without loss, the present without sadness, the future without grief:

> sans souvenir
> Du tombeau, sans pensée que le bonheur,
> Sans avenir
> Que sa dissipation dans le bleu du monde.
>
> (26)

Four conditionals ("entrerait," "pourrait," "dirait," "serait") propose a bounding hope, in relation to which refusal is tantamount to consent. "Mais même dire non serait de lumière": the adversative, the infinitive used nominally, the conditional designate an ideal resolution, although this dream is conscious of its own tenuousness.

Nevertheless the fifteen poems of **"La grande neige"** do not end on an imminent gnosis. The poet again finds real time ("Juste avant l'aube . . ."), real action ("Je sors . . ."), lucidity ("l'esprit . . . plus clair . . ."), but also new questions ("Dort-il . . . ?"). The snowfall has ended; the snow lies like a pool of blue water shining in the darkness. The poet goes down the stoop, feels the cold in his ankles, moves from speculation to sensation. But his night of poetry has not been lived in vain.

> Il semble que l'esprit en soit plus clair,
> Qui perçoit mieux le silence des choses.
>
> (27)

The discovery is not what he thought it might be a poem ago. Awareness is achieved, whose sense he takes into himself rather than enunciates. Not for now, then, any conclusion, but the evocation of an unseen chipmunk which may have already gone out into the snow from under its woodpile. It writes a sign whose formulation is left unspoken: "Je vois d'infimes marques devant la porte" (27). By this littleness the poet calls up all of concrete nature. Does it perhaps signify trust, or simplicity, or acceptance of the rhythms of the seasons like sleep and waking, death and life? For now, he has no compulsion to gloss the image.

The second half of the book is made up of four parts that comprise nine poems more expansive than before. Tone and mood are meditative as if this were the echo and deep amplification of the previous pieces in the manner of recitatives after brief measures, musing after experience. In the first of these, **"Les Flambeaux,"** the poet invokes the snow that lies on the ground, his voice weaving a sinuous way in sentences as long as twenty-two lines. The time is that of silence between one fall and the next; the space is that of light between the "embuement" on the windowpanes and the "étincellement" on the white ground which is now spread out like a table of plenty—"la grande table." The poet has seen torches burning beneath the snow-clad trees as for a banquet—lamps, mirrors—and he would wish his words to resemble them in brightness, freedom, sensibility. For a moment he thinks that a single word, like a whirling flake, might save the world. Can this possibly be? Is this what the snow *wants to say*? (I think of Mallarmé, who spoke of the *vouloir dire* of natural objects.):

> Et tel plus lent et comme égaré s'éloigne
> Et tournoie, puis revient. Et n'est-ce dire
> Qu'un mot, un autre mot encore, à inventer,
> Rédimerait le monde? Mais on ne sait
> Si on entend ce mot ou si on le rêve.
>
> (32)

Coming in the midst of simple words, "rédimerait" is as rare as the flake the poet imagines. The word refers to the payment of a debt, the repurchase of a privilege, but here it is also charged with the soteriological force of English "redemption." Hope is great, even if tempered by the conditional tense and the subsequent adversative and negative; dream may be only dream.

The chipmunk in **"La grande neige"** has already shown the scene to be American. Now the title "Hopkins Forest" makes the reference explicit as a series of recollections is strung together like a personal memoir. The ample movement begins in a casual way:

J'étais sorti
Prendre de l'eau au puits auprès des arbres . . .

(35)

The narrative mode is a prelude to the expression of wonder as a group of stars as red as a brazier appear on the horizon; and similar wonder comes when the poet returns inside to his book in which the words resemble the sky he has just seen, or an abyss with indecipherable constellations, or a portrait of Baudelaire. *Through a glass, darkly.* The poet remembers this and other signs which became his objects of reflexion during one past autumn when he walked in the New England forest. (May we not fancifully surmise the special congeniality of a name that recalls a poet who celebrated sacramental nature in its particularity?) He learned to know non-conflictual oppositions in the forest's large embrace of life and death, heard laughter like a resurrection, saw the simultaneity of white and color:

C'était encore la couleur, et mystérieuse
Comme un qui sortirait du sépulcre et, riant:
"Non, ne me touche pas", dirait-il au monde.

(37)

He learnt the continuousness of the visible and the invisible, present and past. Having lived by snow, he now can hear a whisper fertile in sense: "Et je revois alors tout l'autre ciel, / J'entre pour un instant dans la grande neige" (37).

"Hopkins Forest" is a moving testimony to past experience. The poet returns to the present in **"Le tout, le rien,"** whose title gives a philosophical bearing. The prosody finds the musical regularity of twelve quatrains arranged in three groups of four. Neither alexandrines nor decasyllables, the lines hover around the evasive hendecasyllable of Marceline Desbordes-Valmore, Verlaine, and Rimbaud. The poet speaks to the young child for whom this last snow of the season is the first snow of life. In the end is the beginning; in death are surprise, cry, laughter; the child is father to the man.

et l'enfant
Est le progéniteur de qui l'a pris
Un matin dans ses mains d'adulte et soulevée
Dans le consentement de la lumière.

(41)

Such happiness is not possession: the poet knows he must not try to hold the world or the child to himself, but rather to dispossess himself in the act of naming. Poetry is not seclusion but inclusion, and Bonnefoy's definition is memorable: "Une façon de dire, qui ferait / Qu'on ne serait plus seul dans le langage" (42). So the lesson, unarticulated before, can be drawn in the form of a blessing. May the child's desire be in the likeness of snow, encompassing everything, seizing nothing

("Les mains ne s'agrippant qu'à la lumière," 43); may its words be a way of glimpsing and not appropriating ("Sinon tu ne dénommerais qu'au risque de perdre," 43); may its values be light and shade and not any banal formula ("De la colline dans l'échancrure des arbres," 43); may almond blossom and water relay the snow so that the dream of joy does not end. The anaphoras ("Te soit. . . . Te soient . . . Te suffisent . . .") stylize the address like a litany.

The book concludes on the four sections of **"La seule rose,"** the title of which suggests a mystical finality. The poet has left the country for the city and, as he walks in empty streets still covered by snow, it is as if he himself were a child once more and the buildings around him worthy of the Italian Renaissance architects; as if man-made forms had become flowers—"D'un seul grand trait floral" (47)—and matter were free of gravity. To look at the city under snow is to experience hope like a growth of new grass ("regain"), to touch the snow is to discover oneself a child in an open field with the bees humming and the snowflakes changed to flowers or honey: "Ce que j'ai dans mes mains, ces fleurs, ces ombres, / Est-ce presque du miel, est-ce de la neige?" (48). Time disappears on this city threshold at which the poet stands, just as on a threshold linking memory and desire ("car peut-être / Je dors, et rêve, et vais par les chemins de l'enfance," 49).

Is this, then, the goal? Will the book end with a palimpsest on which the adult finds the child, the snow a summer meadow in the manner of a Proustian "peu de temps à l'état pur" or an ultimate epiphany? The last page does not transcend contradictions for it affirms the distance that separates the world from golden numbers. Perfection lies on the other shore which the poet sees but cannot reach; it fortifies him but gives no guarantee. Whatever his dream, he cannot forget that the snow is not untrodden. Yet it is precisely the awareness of such imperfection that allows him to summon his energies. "L'imperfection est la cime," he writes in *Hier régnant désert* (1958). The words on which his most recent book closes are analogous, but won in respect of this particular quest elaborated, this song-cycle completed:

La forme la plus pure reste celle
Qu'a pénétrée la brume qui s'efface.
La neige piétinée est la seule rose.

(49)

The virginal is not a place of refuge. Paradoxes encapsulate the tension by which the poet holds himself *ready* in mind and soul.

I take *Début et fin de la neige* to stand high in modern poetry for the purity of its commitment. Bonnefoy demonstrates an admirable poise that consistently chooses the lesser melody, the simpler word, the natural image—at once signified and signifier—of a rare measure. His poetry embodies a truth, which is alertness to the dual imperatives of lyricism and lucidity. As he asks in *Le Nuage rouge* (1977), in terms that underwrite his latest work: "Qu'est-ce qu'une foi qui doute de soi non par accident mais par essence?"

Notes

1. The following works of Yves Bonnefoy are cited in the text: *Du Mouvement et de l'immobilité de Douve* (Paris: Mercure de France, 1953); *Hier régnant désert* (Paris: Mercure de France, 1958); *Anti-Platon* (Paris: Galerie Maeght, 1962); *Dans le leurre du seuil* (Paris: Mercure de France, 1975); *Le Nuage rouge* (Paris: Mercure de France, 1977); *Leçon inaugurale de la chaire d'Etudes comparées de la fonction poétique* (Paris: Collège de France, 1982); *Ce qui fut sans lumière* (Paris: Mercure de France, 1987); *La Vérité de parole* (Paris: Mercure de France, 1988); *Entretiens sur la poésie* (Paris: Mercure de France, 1990); *Début et fin de la neige,* suivi de *Là où retombe la flèche* (Paris: Mercure de France, 1991).

2. Saint-John Perse, *Neiges. Œuvres complètes.* Bibliothèque de la Pléiade (Paris: Gallimard, 1972).

3. Paul Claudel, *Cent phrases pour éventails. Œuvre poétique.* Bibliothèque de la Pléiade (Paris: Gallimard, 1957).

James McAllister (essay date May 1994)

SOURCE: McAllister, James. "Metonymy and Metaphor in Yves Bonnefoy's Poetry." *French Forum* 19, no. 2 (May 1994): 149-60.

[*In the following essay, McAllister contends that Bonnefoy favors metonymy over metaphor in his verse.*]

Yves Bonnefoy's conception of writing as *un*-writing (*désécriture*) fosters poetic texts in which metonymy intertwines with metaphor so that metonymic processes both extend and subvert analogical associations. Denouncing metaphor as the stuff of esthetic lies, he turns to metonymy to tear through the opaque fabric of analogy for an authentic approach to reality. His comments on the genesis of **"A San Francesco le soir"** exemplify his antagonistic interpretation of the two rhetorical figures:

> Par exemple, j'ai intitulé un poème d'*Hier régnant désert,* jadis, **"A San Francesco le soir,"** sans dire qu'il s'agissait là d'une des églises de Ferrare. . . . Pourquoi cette forclusion, en l'occurence délibérée, d'un élément signifiant? . . . eussé-je nommé Ferrare, dans le poème, ce nom y eût assumé d'emblée la fonction d'un signifiant dans un texte, autant déterminé par

celui-ci, aux dépens de mon vrai rapport à Ferrare, qu'indicateur de cette expérience: alors qu'à ne pas l'évoquer c'est toute la réalité de Ferrare, avec son sens pour moi encore impénétré, inachevé, foisonnant, qui reste associée, métonymiquement, à l'écrit—et s'y maintient, comme une exigence. . . . Ces marges du poème sont pour elle [la prose] la dimension métonymique restée ouverte où elle pourra puiser de quoi briser les constructions fermées de la métaphore, qui n'est que la décision d'hier, en somme, la compréhension toujours trop hâtive qui risque de rester du passé et me garder séparé du monde, faisant de mon rapport à sa présence possible une ténèbre, un désert. La "métaphore," l'interprétation analogique, c'est elle qui nous bâtit une langue, nous voue aux illusions de l'image—il faut en chercher les failles, en sonder les fausses parois, et sans penser, pessimistement, que ce soit en vain.[1]

This deprecation of metaphor is to be read in the context of Yves Bonnefoy's ontological conception of poetics as a dialectic of *inscription* and *incarnation*: of the *fixity of the trace* as it founds esthetic propositions of permanence, on the one hand, and, on the other hand, "le temps et le lieu où autrui advient," the world of *finitude,* where we die.[2] If analogical interpretation "builds us a language" and "delivers us to the illusions of the image," it is because this root of mimesis has facilitated the development of conceptual categorization.[3] Based on abstract similarities of aspect, the concept underlies differential sign systems which imitate *what is.* Bonnefoy reproaches the images and word-worlds that such linguistic systems produce for their Mallarmean abolition of "hasard," for the closure of their *re*-presentation, which separates them from the reality of death and our approach to a radically different *other* in an "open" world of impermanence and change. The equivalences metaphors propose construct an eidetic "unity" which imprisons an *ego* (a concept of linguistic origin) in the false permanence of *inscription,* while excluding the enigma of the *other.* So the "closed constructions of metaphor" are separated from the finite world of interpersonal exchange that their fixed images counterfeit. Thus metaphoric invention cannot attain to the universal acceptance that could found "un réel pour la société"[4] and redeem the *wasteland* of the sign to recreate what Yves Bonnefoy calls "la terre-lieu."[5]

If metaphor is implicated in the closure of representation and the illusions of the image, metonymy is seen as breaking through the "faults" in analogical associations. This breakthrough implies a poetic approach to a presence that language obfuscates just as the translation of *what is* into differential sign systems gives way to the analytical classifications of the concept. Metonymy is based not on analogy but on associations of contiguity or concentricity. In the collaborative rhetorical research carried out in the seventies by the "Groupe μ," the analysis of metonymy was based on the *co-inclusion*[6] of its terms in a *place,* on their *juxtaposition,* as construed spatially, or, by extension, temporally, or logically: to include interdependent relationships of cause and effect, production and product, container and contained, etc. By this analysis, metonymy can be seen to depend not on similarity of terms but on the *collocation* or interaction of *unlike* terms. Such a definition corresponds to Yves Bonnefoy's interpretation of the metonymic dimensions of his poetry as they imply a transfer of contiguity into the continuity and simultaneity which correspond to our potential rediscovery of that *place* that conceptual language and indelible images have lost.[7]

Ce qui fut sans lumière[8] opens with a "memory" which seeks to establish a threshold between *inscription* and *incarnation,* between the image's autonomous permanence and the illegible place where we live and die. This "memory" inaugurates the *un*-writing of Yves Bonnefoy's previous poetic work as it begins unraveling the images which had built up a word-world around the house at Valsaintes. This house, discovered in 1963, and the poet's relation to it, his "dream" of living there, in the "vrai lieu" it seemed potentially to offer, had figured centrally in *Dans le leurre du seuil* and, already, if less obviously, in *Pierre écrite.*[9] *Ce qui fut sans lumière* reconsiders the *locus amoenus* the poetic imagery had invented for this country place,[10] while in life it slipped further and further out of reach. The poet attempts to free himself from the illusion of the image as he decries its failure in a metonymic context where "memory," "wind," and "farewell" conspire to refute the creations of metaphor, as their metonymic dimension opens the poems toward lived experience beyond the closed book. And the house at Valsaintes, as it had lent itself to the constructions of dream and a Gnostic longing for escape from *finitude,* as it had become the myth of a serene, timeless dwelling in mutual love, undisturbed by outside influences, is now reappraised in the light of its actual dilapidation. So the house as text is confronted with the real house which denies the text.

The remembered wind of **"Le Souvenir"** tatters a series of textual *mises en abyme* (analogous reflections of the whole poetic work in its individual images)[11] as it is metonymically echoed in the poem:

> Ce souvenir me hante, que le vent tourne
> D'un coup, là-bas, sur la maison fermée.
> C'est un grand bruit de toile par le monde,
> On dirait que l'étoffe de la couleur
> Vient de se déchirer jusqu'au fond des choses.
> Le souvenir s'éloigne mais il revient,
> C'est un homme et une femme masqués, on dirait
>   qu'ils tentent
> De mettre à flot une barque trop grande.
> Le vent rabat la voile sur leurs gestes,
> Le feu prend dans la voile, l'eau est noire,
> Que faire de tes dons, ô souvenir. . . .

                             (*SL* 11)

The closed house was the center of a fixed image-world. It is now abandoned to the uncontrollable wind of change. The autonomous order of the illusory creation is here revealed as a deceit by the illegible wind, the antithesis of order.[12] From the wind turning on the closed house, the poem pivots metonymically to the sound of the wind rending the great canvas ("C'est un grand bruit de toile par le monde . . ."). The canvas catching the wind to produce the sound is at once the metonymic evidence of the wind that causes the sound and the analogous reflection of the text (L. *textus* "textile" < *texere* "to weave"). The coarsely woven fabric of the torn canvas reflects the fabrication of the previous poetic text as its illusory serenity and sufficiency are exposed by the retrospective lucidity of *Ce qui fut sans lumière.*

The textual *mise en abyme* develops with "l'étoffe de la couleur," metonymically associated with the "toile" of the preceding verse to evoke the painter's canvas, while the ambiguous genetive also presents "l'étoffe" (Germ. *stopfôn* "stuff," "tissue," "material") as the substance of color. The canvas is now the painted fabric,[13] the surface on which the painter paints, and so, the metonymic support of color, while, at the same time, color has substance, it *is* material. The tearing of "l'étoffe de la couleur" coincides with the rending of the fabric of images that the previous poetic texts have woven as they correspond, *ut pictura poesis,* to the painted image. And, specifically, prospectively, the relationship between poem and painting is that pictorial intertextuality which *Ce qui fut sans lumière* will establish between the *locus amoenus* of Valsaintes in *Dans le leurre du seuil* and the works of two painters: John Constable's series of variant views of Dedham from Langham[14] and Claude Lorrain's *Psyche and the Palace of Amor.* The wind rips the canvas as the *memento mori,* the haunting "souvenir" of *finitude,* recalls the beloved house, around which the imagery of peaceful sufficiency had coagulated—now closed up, abandoned to the wind—"ce bruit d'un ailleurs": the metonymic, sonorous evidence of an *hors-texte,* an extralinguistic *elsewhere,* invisible, violent, ever undermining the autonomy of text. Like Psyche returning to weep before the Palace of Love, lost through her *hubris,* like John Constable repeatedly coming back to the subject of the distant Dedham, ever revealed as paint by the thick oils of his highly textured landscapes, the poet returns in memory to Valsaintes, to separate the fixity of the poetic image from the real place, now lost.

If the wind tears the stuff of color "to the very heart of things," it is because color, as the substance of the *trace* (the black of the ink, the pigment of the paint) constitutes a threshold between the sign and the heterogeneous world of things. As an event of light, color reifies inscription while defying the play of signifiers. Consubstantial with inscription, color brings the *trace* into the finite reality of fading, tearing. The sonorous interpretation of the memory implies a reality of color beyond mimesis, a presence beyond representation. The tearing of the painting exceeds the linguistic signs which compose it, to affect its "color" beyond the sign. Fissuring the mimetic substance in the world of finite things, the tearing affects both the image and its "real" counterpart. It is as though the torn landscape ruptures the very earth it represents, as though its poetic counterpart, repudiated as such, carries away the house at Valsaintes, now lost also in life.[15]

The sound of wind in canvas is taken up in a different register with the transformation of the memory. The metonymic wind now prevents the masked figures from raising the sail. Like the house where the dialogic lovers of *Dans le leurre du seuil* had dwelt in peaceful sufficiency, now abandoned to the wind, like the empty palace Amor and Psyche have gone from, like the torn canvas of the landscape, brought back to the destructive time from which the painted image would remove it, the boat that cannot be rigged is a variant textual *mise en abyme* implying the failure of the image. The wind hinders the raising of the sail. It fans the fire that burns it. So the "ship of words"[16] cannot carry the man and the woman on the dark water. The masks that hide their faces reveal them as actors, *personnages* (L. *persona* "rôle" < *per + sonare* "make sound [speak] through [the mask]"), in a drama, a play on reality, a fiction which is by definition *other than* "real." Imprisoned in solipsism, these masked egos are excluded from the face to face encounter that can occur only in life. Their pantomimed struggle cannot overcome the wind to make the wood and canvas object into a functional boat that could save them from the violence of the storm. Their struggle against the wind reflects the poet's abiding concern with the struggle between image and life. The wind impedes the launching of the concept "boat," since the object cannot attain to the function characteristic of *boatness*. And the would-be boat that cannot be sailed reflects the poetic image as it fails to be lived, as it falls short of *incarnation* and so remains unreal, unrealized. Another invention of the "ship of words," the boat-image corresponds to the image-house as it is overtaken by the tempestuous violence of the lucidity that disperses illusion and decries the failure of the image. The boat founders. The house is abandoned, ruined. The image's veil, impervious to destruction, is torn away.

The torn canvas, the unwieldy sail fulfill the omen of the rattling shutter as the world that *Dans le leurre du seuil* had "ransom'd" in calm words is "destroyed"[17] by the illegible wind that the painting, the sail and the shutter all metonymically attest to:

> Et tu te lèves une éternelle fois
> Dans cet été qui t'obsède.
> A nouveau ce bruit d'un ailleurs, proche, lointain;

> Tu vas à ce volet qui vibre. . . . Dehors, nul vent,
> Les choses de la nuit sont immobiles
> Comme une avancée d'eau dans la lumière.

> (*DLS* 231)

The intertextual retrospective here mirrors *en abyme* the *hors-texte* which refutes text. The textual lie ("Dehors, nul vent") is revealed from outside the text (*Dans le leurre du seuil*) in the new text (*Ce qui fut sans lumière*) which denounces text as darkness. The landscape and the sail are at once metaphorical representations of the poetic image and the metonymic textual manifestations of the extra-textual wind. Torn and buffeted, these causal representatives of the wind are thus metaphors subverted by metonymy. The interplay of the two rhetorical figures reflects the opposition of text and *hors-texte,* of image and mortality, as the forces of writing and *un*-writing collide in poetic images in search of their own refutation.

In order to profit from the memory, the poetic voice announces the return to the dream of the image-world:

> Que faire de tes dons, ô souvenir,
> Sinon recommencer le plus vieux rêve,
> Croire que je m'éveille? La nuit est calme,
> Sa lumière ruisselle sur les eaux,
> La voile des étoiles frémit à peine
> Dans la brise qui passe par les mondes.

> (*SL* 11)

Like the dreamer's belief in the reality of dream, the poet-reader's suspension of disbelief leads to the snare of illusion. The wind's violence is calmed as the battered canvas gives way to the "voile des étoiles," the starry canvas of night reflected on still waters. But the textile metaphor now echoes the metonymic wind. The torn painting and the buffeted sail conspire to undermine the acceptance of the peaceful equilibrium where the delicately trembling, sparkling "voile des étoiles" unfolds. And the "joys" of the image world are now reconsidered in the "light" of the wind waiting to blow them away: "O joies, comme un rameur au loin, qui bouge peu / Sur la nappe brillante . . ." (*SL* 12). The boat gliding effortlessly on the shining waters now recalls the other boat that could not be set afloat. The atemporal "joys" of the image-world are now deprived of their inaugural freshness as they are subjected to the corrosive time that memory's repetition implies. The temporal metaphor of the river flowing carries with it the metonymic mud to sully the serenity of fixed images, now remembered and re-considered as "what was dark": an insufficient, illusory approach to an elusive reality that esthetic images obscure.

> Joies, et le temps qui vint au travers, comme un fleuve
> En crue, de nuit, débouche dans le rêve,
> Et en blesse la rive, et en disperse
> Les images les plus sereines dans la boue.

> (*SL* 12)

The dreamer is reluctant to repudiate his dream world: "Je ne veux pas savoir la question qui monte / De cette terre en paix . . ." (*SL* 12). The refusal to question the habitable reality of the image-world immobilizes "cette terre en paix" in the darkness of the enduring night: "Et on ne sait, / Seuls à nouveau dans la nuit qui s'achève, / Si même on veut que reparaisse l'aube . . ." (*SL* 13). And, like the dawn, the moment of recognition and acquiescence is deferred: "L'heure n'est pas venue de porter la flamme / Dans le miroir qui nous parle dans l'ombre" (*SL* 13). The mirror in shadow is the metaphoric representative of the "memory" as recognition of what is lost. The deferred lighting of the mirror implies the eventual replication of the image as such, reflected in the mirror which will reduce it to the silent play of refracted light and provide the metonymic equivalent of the wind and the negative response to the rejected question: "is this real?"

But the poet-dreamer comes inevitably to the "adieu" that establishes a metonymic causal relationship with the "souvenir" as it elicits the farewell to what has slipped away. Intertwined with the figure of the companion identified with shadow and with the Earth, a complex series of metaphors is at once built up and torn down by the "adieu" that *un*-writes each new metaphoric dimension as it introduces it:

> Je vais,
> Et il me semble que quelqu'un marche près de moi,
> Ombre, qui sourirait bien que silencieuse
> Comme une jeune fille, pieds nus dans l'herbe,
> Accompagne un instant celui qui part.
> Et celui-ci s'arrête, il la regarde,
> Il prendrait volontiers dans ses mains ce visage
> Qui est la terre même. Adieu, dit-il,
> Présence qui ne fut que pressentie
> Bien que mystérieusement tant d'années si proche,
> Adieu, image impénétrable qui nous leurra
> D'être la vérité enfin presque dite,
> Certitude, là où tout n'a été que doute, et bien que
>   chimère
> Parole si ardente que réelle.

(SL 14-15)

The "presentiment of presence" is recognized as "impenetrable image," at once "threshold" and "lure," as *Dans le leurre du seuil* had affirmed. But if the "threshold" had weighed however slightly more in the balance of the previous work, *Ce qui fut sans lumière*'s reassessment tips the balance in favor of the "lure." So the "adieu," which is the negative side of memory, relinquishes the *locus amoenus,* now recognized as the illusion of metaphor. And the "truth finally almost spoken" is given up, however reluctantly, as "almost" takes on the negative connotation: but *not quite.* Thus the "souvenir" as an obsessive attempt to re-possess gives way to the "adieu" which abnegates possession at the "threshold" of the elusive reality of *finitude.* Like the wind tearing the canvas, the "adieu" unveils the

deceit of appearance. What had seemed to be the truth is decried as lies. Certainty is replaced by doubt.

The object of memory is necessarily image, a glimpse of a former, now vanished presence. If metaphors describe such an image, building up equivalences between face and earth, metonymy dismisses such comparisons, delivers them to the wind, then retrieves them as mere traces of what is lost. So the metonymic presence of the titular "souvenir" joins the wind of destruction and the "adieu" to unravel the textiles of metaphor. Like the metonymic Ferrare of **"A San Francesco le soir,"** the remembered wind of **"Le Souvenir"** opens the text to the reality of a specific place, Valsaintes, and to that tragic reality of place in general, which is erosion, ruin, collapse, and that elusiveness that escapes language's attempts to take possession of what slips away.

Yet the poem closes with a refusal of the "adieu": "Adieu? Non, ce n'est pas le mot que je sais dire" (*SL* 16). The fascinated poet-dreamer returns again and again to the empty house. And now the place is temporally expanded by the metonymic echo of a former occupant:

> Et mes rêves, serrés
> L'un contre l'autre et l'autre encore, ainsi
> La sortie des brebis dans le premier givre,
> Reprennent piétinant leurs plus vieux chemins.
> Je m'éveille nuit après nuit dans la maison vide,
> Il me semble qu'un pas m'y précède encore.

(SL 16)

The house becomes an historical monument to abandon, to the passing away of its inhabitants, as the dreamer harkens to the hallucinatory traces of a spectral predecessor,[18] a shepherd; the vestiges of his time in the house enrich the place with a rhythmic resonance of the coming and going of his sheep, as his footsteps lead the dreamer back to a different time: "the kind of natural, elementary time that is untouched by the degradation of the absolute clocks subject us to."[19] The recurring dreams dawn night after night in a frosty tapestry of white on white as repetition takes on the cyclic value of the sheep's daily going out to pasture along the same old trails. The comparison of the dreams to sheep is based on the metonymic association between path and movement, between the trails the sheep follow and the course of the dreams. The going out of the dream sheep accomplishes a blending of figure and ground, a visual blurring of contiguity into continuity as the flock moves over the frost covered ground. So the dreams are situated in the enduring continuity of place, now lost, that Valsaintes has come to signify.

As the sheep go out to pasture, the dreamer goes out behind the house, following the call of the shepherd of the past:

Je sors
Et m'étonne que l'ampoule soit allumée
Dans ce lieu déserté de tous, devant l'étable.
Je cours derrière la maison, parce que l'appel
Du berger d'autrefois retentit encore.
J'entends l'aboi qui précédait le jour,
Je vois l'étoile boire parmi les bêtes
Qui ne sont plus, à l'aube. Et résonne encore la flûte
Dans la fumée des choses transparentes.

(SL 16)

The perceived descent of the morning star setting low on the horizon coincides with the movement of the beasts leaning down to drink, as all this dream stuff dissipates at dawn. The alternation of the setting star and the rising sun corresponds to the alternation of the dream of what was and waking to what is gone. Thus the star shines in the dream with the light of difference, the harbinger of dawn signaling the end of dream and the disappearance of the illusory beasts as it seems, despite its distance, to come down among them. Opening the dream-text to what is other than dream, exploding the spatial context of "parmi," the star's incomprehensible distance obviates the image it produces, as the shepherd's call gives way to the flute sounding at the threshold between the disappearing images and the place they approached but could not contain. "par où la terre finit" will give the flute to the child of lost paths, whose playing recreates the world:

Chemins,
Non, ce n'est pas dans vos rumeurs que rien s'achève.
Vous êtes un enfant qui joue de la flûte
Et dont les doigts confiants recréent le monde
De rien qu'un peu de terre où se prend le souffle.

(SL 60)

Here the flute is the final metonymy of an other presence, recalling the sound of the wind in canvas, now transposed for flute, as the light child's[20] breath awakens an earthly presence yet to come—elsewhere, tomorrow, beyond the text disintegrating in the wake of becoming. Opening to the light already shining through the dream of language, this presence illuminates its transparent images as they vanish. If metaphors wove the text and its images, veiling Valsaintes in a *locus amoenus,* metonymy has torn them apart in the name of *what is,* to save the light of being from the dark of the word, to open the "garden"[21] to the wild. And the poem drifts away, trembling between memory and oblivion: "Quelques figures simples, quelques signes / Qui brillent au-delà des mots, indéchiffrables / Dans l'immobilité du souvenir" (*SL* 69).

Notes

1. Yves Bonnefoy, "Entretiens avec Bernard Falciola," *Entretiens sur la poésie* (Paris: Mercure de France, 1990) 50-53.

2. *Inscription* refers here to the manipulation of the sign as *trace* in the production of *text* and the esthetic image, as defined in "Entretiens avec Bernard Falciola," *Entretiens* 12: "le cadre, la page, la fixité du tracé, tout ce qui semble faire de la vision fugitive un fait malgré tout, un fait relevant d'un autre lieu que celui de notre vie, et témoignant même peut-être de l'existence d'un autre monde." *Incarnation* refers to an illegible *hors-texte,* an ineffable domain, heterogeneous to language: that extra-linguistic "time and place where others come to us" ("le temps et le lieu où autrui advient") (Yves Bonnefoy, *Le Nuage rouge* [Paris: Mercure de France, 1976] 77).

3. See Richard Stamelman, "The Crack in the Mirror: The Subversion of Image and Representation in the Poetry of Yves Bonnefoy," *French Forum* 13 (1988) 70: "Bonnefoy observes that, from the Greeks to the beginning of the twentieth century, mimesis has coincided with the development and dominance of conceptual thought and with the formation of language as a system. As a result, the painted and poetic image has arrogated to itself the name and authority of reality ('Héritier' 8). But the image cannot authentically represent the world of things. It is a deceit, a lie, an evasion."

4. "Poésie et vérité," *Entretiens* 267: "Sous le signe de l'unité . . . le rapport à autrui renaît, que la pensée conceptuelle brouille, et permet trop aisément de détruire. Et c'est dans cette dimension de l'altérité, aussi bien, que la pensée proprement poétique se développe. Sachant qu'il n'est d'expérience de la présence que si autrui est aussi rencontre pleine, il lui faut par nécessité rechercher les désirs, les biens, les impressions, les valeurs que les habitants de la terre peuvent chacun accepter sans avoir pour autant à se démettre. Pour dire la présence, la poésie doit élaborer un lieu qui vaudra pour tous. Voilà la sorte d'universel que sa vérité recherche. Et voilà ce que l'on peut dire la sorte de réalité qui se diversifie dans son dire, sans désormais se fragmenter, s'extérioriser: non la nature mais une terre; non la matière et ses lois mais un lieu et ses clefs de voûte dans la parole, ce qu'autrefois assuraient les mythes. Un réel pour la société, dont il est désastreux qu'on l'étudie aujourd'hui comme simplement un fait, aux limites de la matière, quand elle est d'abord cette instauration, au degré poétique de la parole. Quand elle n'a de santé possible que par la vérité de la poésie."

5. "Lettre à John E. Jackson," *Entretiens* 110: "La terre est l'avenir de l'écriture qui se refuse à l'image—l'image, cette vision qui n'est vraie que quand elle exprime le besoin frustré, la révolte, et ment si elle consent à sa cohérence trop courte, qui n'engendre bientôt que l'orgueil et la tyrannie. Et c'est la terre aussi bien, la terre non la nature,

la terre-lieu que je voyais poindre comme présence et finalité ultime dans les transgressions tentées ou rêvées dans le nom de Douve. . . ."

6. See Jacques Dubois et al., *Rhétorique générale* (Paris: Larousse, 1970), and *Rhétorique de la poésie* (Brussels: Complexe, 1977). On the analysis of metonymy, see esp. *Rhétorique générale* 91-144.

7. Yves Bonnefoy, *La Vérité de parole* (Paris: Mercure de France, 1988) 45: "Qu'est-ce qui se perd, quand on a recours à des mots? Le fait que ce que les mots différencient, cet arbre, disons, ce ravin, cette source au fond, cette colline au-delà, ce ciel, choses qu'ils vont entraîner chacune dans leur espace mental, pour un travail de pensée, qui les classera, les séparera—soient ensemble encore, soient dans une relation de contiguïté, de simultanéité, de continuité où nous-mêmes d'ailleurs nous sommes reçus: soient une seule présence. Cette contiguïté, ce *donné ensemble* de l'arbre, et du rocher près de lui, et de la source plus loin, la source qu'on entend au moment même où on la regarde, voilà bien, en effet, ce que le mot *arbre* va détruire, puisque le mot n'intervient que par référence à des arbres de toutes sortes, dont l'intrusion nous fait aussitôt quitter notre état premier d'implication pure et simple dans l'expérience du lieu."

8. Yves Bonnefoy, *Ce qui fut sans lumière* (Paris: Mercure de France, 1987). Subsequent citations from this work will be followed by the abbreviation *SL* and the appropriate page number.

9. References to Yves Bonnefoy's previous poetic works are to the volume *Poèmes: Du mouvement et de l'immobilité de Douve* (*Douve*), *Hier régnant désert* (*HRD*), *Pierre écrite* (*PE*), *Dans le leurre du seuil* (*DLS*) (Paris: Mercure de France, 1978).

10. On the *locus amoenus* and its vernacular avatar, the *loc aizi* of the troubadours, as "a hypothetical place-time suggestive of cosmic origins," see Charlotte Gross, "The Cosmology of Rhetoric in the Early Troubadour Lyric," *Rhetorica* 9.1 (1991) 41. On the development of the *loc aizi*, see Gross, "Studies in Lyric Time-Structure: Dream, Visions, and Reveries," *Tenso* 2.1 (1986) 21-36. Cf. Yves Bonnefoy's remarks on the role of his house at Valsaintes in his poetry, in the interview published with John Naughton's translation of *Ce qui fut sans lumière, In the Shadow's Light* (Chicago: U of Chicago P, 1991) 163: "I had made the place the material of a great dream, the dream of being able to live there, simply, in its atemporality and quiet transparency. . . ."

11. On the history and development of this term, see Lucien Dällenbach, *Le Récit spéculaire* (Paris: Seuil, 1977).

12. *Entretiens* 265: "On dira aussi, avec Rimbaud, que le vent est 'salubre,' ce qui peut sembler sans rigueur, mais c'est que le vent vient d'ailleurs, invisible autant que violent, et métaphorise ainsi la transgression de ce monde-image que la langue reclôt sur soi."

13. The painted fabric implied by "l'étoffe de la couleur" evokes the "étoffes peintes" and "les étoffes rouges" of *Pierre écrite* (164, 174, 185, 204), and "le rouge des lourdes / Etoffes peintes / Que lavait l'Egyptienne, l'irrévélée, / De nuit, dans l'eau du fleuve . . ." (*DLS* 259). This latter image constitutes another textual *mise en abyme,* through the reference to Poussin's *Moïse sauvé.* See Richard Vernier's discussion of Poussin in relation to *Dans le leurre du seuil* in "From Critical to Poetic Discourse: Bonnefoy and Poussin," *L'Esprit Créateur* 22 (1982) 26-36.

14. On Yves Bonnefoy's "reading" of John Constable's landscapes in the poem "Dedham, vu de Langham," see James McAllister, "Yves Bonnefoy and John Constable: 'la tâche terrestre délivrée,'" *Romance Notes* 32.3 (1992) 281-89.

15. Cf. Richard Stamelman's analysis of "Les Raisins de Zeuxis" in "The Crack in the Mirror" 71: "The representation is reduced to a piece of cloth, a discarded sack, a thing among things, lying wet, trampled and abandoned in a gutter. The painting is returned to the world, to a finite place of death and decomposition and to the substance and matter it never really ceased to be."

16. This boat is a complex and very ambiguous image. Yves Bonnefoy has written about it in response to John Naughton's question about how it is to be understood: "I too seek to know the meaning of that boat that came over from *Dans le leurre du seuil,* and thus I give movement to it: sometimes it is the barque of the dead of ancient cultures; sometimes it is a little boat stopped in the middle of the river under the sky and so an image of the peacefulness of mind in the sufficiency of the moment. But these are only some aspects among others, aspects I haven't controlled, and in order to know more, I have to write again and search . . ." (*In the Shadow's Light* 176). Earlier in the same interview, the poet had mentioned the "ship of words" in the context of certain narrative aspects of his poetry: "There are events, past or virtual, hidden in the depths of a poem, and even if they are not made explicit, many of their elements are nonetheless visible in brief evocations which provide writing with its

metaphors, or, through a fleeting metonymy, enrich the great symbols that are in all poetry and already active in the author's mind. And it is very fortunate that this is so, for now the ship of words, which is so apt to go off in any direction, is anchored in things, and facts, that exceed the imaginary" (*In the Shadow's Light* 170). There is, in fact, a relationship between the "ship of words" and this boat and the house at Valsaintes—and the "tempest" of lucidity that blows them all away.

17. The prefatory quotation from Shakespeare's *Winter's Tale* ("They look'd as they had heard of a world ransom'd, or one destroyed") describes the struggle between image and life as embodied in *Dans le leurre du seuil.*

18. *Dans le leurre du seuil* had quoted the inscription left by such a predecessor in the indeterminate past: "Et Jean Aubry, d'Orgon / Et ses fils Claude et Jean. / 'Nous avons fait ce jour / Appui de communion.' La date manque" (*DLS* 320).

19. This is Yves Bonnefoy's description of the temporal atmosphere of the house at Valsaintes, *In the Shadow's Light* 167.

20. "On dit que la lumière est un enfant / Qui joue, qui ne veut rien, qui rêve ou chante. / Si elle vient à nous c'est par jeu encore, / Touchant le sol d'un pied distrait, qui serait l'aube" (*SL* 92).

21. The rejected "farewell" will be encountered again in the poem "L'Adieu," where, like Adam and Eve hesitating at the edge of the archetypal *locus amoenus,* the dialogic couple question the value of *un*-writing, wondering if the "seed of light" can be taken out of the image and into the world: "Pourrons-nous recueillir de cette lumière / Qui a été le miracle d'ici / La semence dans nos mains sombres, pour d'autres flaques / Au secret d'autres champs 'barrés de pierres'?" (*SL* 23).

Mary Ann Caws (essay date fall 1996)

SOURCE: Caws, Mary Ann. "Yves Bonnefoy, *Sostenuto*: On Sustaining the Long Poem." *L'Esprit Créateur* 36, no. 3 (fall 1996): 84-93.

[*In the following essay, Caws maintains that Bonnefoy's moral concerns help to sustain his long poems.*]

Often, a general question apparently about form is not that only: it aims at something specific, and goes beyond form. The one I want to ask now, both generally and in a specific meditation on the work of Yves Bonnefoy—concerns the long poem, and so implies connectedness and interruption. In so doing, it concerns more than that: I take it as a question not only aesthetic, but moral.

What is it, then, that sustains the long poem? What kinds of joinings enable its articulation? What gives it breath? Whatever response we could give, which of course, as in all such cases, is individual and comes from our own perception, background, and judgement, may, because of that, matter more to our own sustenance than we might have thought. That figures among the many reasons why one should only write on writers and thinkers one cares deeply about: your response will affect you profoundly, perhaps irrevocably. From my point of view, the question is at its high point of interest for American poetry in the case of Wallace Stevens (for example, "The Rock") and, for French poetry, in the case of Yves Bonnefoy's *Douve* and especially his majestic *Dans le leurre du seuil.*

I will contend that for Bonnefoy a moral sustenance underpins the other more formal one. The same intensely moral concerns make themselves felt everywhere in his work, from his critical essays on literature and art to his translations of Shakespeare and Yeats, and, especially, his poems themselves. As in his great essays, such as "The Act and Place of Poetry," or in his briefer and apparently more informal ones, say, those included in his *Remarques sur le dessin,* the readers we are can sense an implicit ethical stance whose consistency sustains not just the work and the person but those acquainted with them, that is, ourselves.

We are all familiar, from our first readings in the field of French poetry, with the concept of the poem-as-passage and its close relative, the poem-voyage: Baudelaire's "Voyage," Rimbaud's "Bateau Ivre," Apollinaire's "Zone," Cendrars' "Prose du Transsibérien et de la Petite Jehanne de France."[1] These major poems have prepared us for the experience of the metaphysical and mental passage of the long poem from 1975 that I remain haunted by, Bonnefoy's **"Dans le leurre du seuil."** That an experience of passage should be architecturally marked as a poem of threshold by its title already suggests the necessarily interdependent complexities of the reading, for this voyage is—paradoxically and poetically—also a stance, as the threshold is already an invitation to passage. Clearly, any sort of moral stance that eschews complexity and to which paradox is foreign is unlikely to touch more than the skin of things. And here, as in one of André Breton's poems that Bonnefoy knows so well, "Je ne touche plus que le cœur des choses je tiens le fil" ("Vigilance").

In the poetics of voyage literature as I read it, there is above all a consciousness not only of motion, but more particularly of invitation and invocation, of description as of interrogation, in the realization of the lyric subject through space and time. Lyricism, narration, and cognition converge, marking the verbs of articulation upon which such poetry depends, imposing a particular tone. In a sense, all these voyages of self-realization and metaphoric development are composed of successive momentary views of the same lyric subject or object at once super-imposed in the reading memory and nevertheless ongoing simultaneously. These spatial and psychological movements find their articulation and nourishment in the silences between the verbal motions like so many sources of energy, forming the pulse of the passage, its characteristic rhythm. At the end, as the reader looks back, a retrospective patterning may be detected, or then reconstructed.[2]

Such a rhythm of movement and stasis, of stress and silence, of gesture and stillness, can be experienced as analogous to the breath, inhaling and exhaling, unconsciously. In the vivid terminology of the *expiration* of the breath, as in the *execution* of the musical effect of poetry performed, an inescapable sense of mortality penetrates this silence heard from moment to moment. These pauses in the long poem must be sensed, together with their moments of renascence. From these deaths and the positive physicality of "la petite mort érotique" the text takes its life. The convergence of expiration and execution, of desire and extinction within the lyric subject in its development only deepens our own identification with that subject: it becomes our own.

GESTURES OF PASSAGE

The voyaging verbs of Rimbaud's magnificently inebriated vessel, which is also and marvelously the poet, are framed between knowing and seeing: "Je sais . . . j'ai vu . . . j'ai rêvé . . . j'ai suivi . . . j'ai heurté, savezvous . . . j'ai vu." Realization, disappointment, exhaustion, excess: "Mais vrai, j'ai trop pleuré," before the return to the point of origin, now transfigured by perception, from which language is born. In *Dans le leurre du seuil,* a radically interiorized transposition of the voyage poem, everything happens with little material action: it is internalized, with very few gestures made, all the more significant for that. Among the more important, I would single out the invocation of sight, and its subsequent interrogation:

> Regarde! De tous tes yeux regarde! Rien d'ici,
> (. . .)
>   N'a plus cet à jamais de silencieuse
> Respiration nocturne qui mariait
> Dans l'antique sommeil
> Les bêtes et les choses anuitées
> A l'infini sous le manteau d'étoiles.

Vision and breath are linked here, as if unconsciously—and yet they are profoundly interwoven, as links between the body and the world, the physical and the mental. In its continued exclamations and interrogations—"O terre, terre / Pourquoi . . . / Et d'où / D'où / Et pourquoi . . . ?"—the poem exhales about itself the space necessary for definitive action.

In such a long poem, there is time, as here, to feel any distance as very near, as a familiar person who might arise in the summer night to throw open the blinds, and to whom one might say: "Look. . . ." Time to change your mind, the way you see things, or then, your life. You can hear the breath here inside, while out there, immobile, the night is unbreathing, windless. As if there were only this poem being born, in order to transfigure, to reassemble the things scattered about so silently:

> Je crie, Regarde,
> La lumière
> Vivait là, près de nous! Ici, sa provision
> D'eau, encore transfigurée. Ici le bois
> Dans la remise. Ici, les quelques fruits
> A sécher dans les vibrations du ciel de l'aube.
>
> Rien n'a changé,
> Ce sont les mêmes lieux et les mêmes choses,
> Presque les mêmes mots,
> Mais, vois, en toi, en moi
> L'indivis, l'invisible se rassemblent.

(59)

DIFFERENCE AND DISTANCE

The poem *Dans le leurre du seuil* concerns, among other things, the temptation to perfection, that specific and most terrible lure. One of the most powerful temptations in reading anything is a tendency to believe that "reality" is objective, and so, that we must feel our own subjectivity as being less true.[3] So we leave behind our own point of view, our own particularity, unable to resist the voracity of the objective appetite. Perhaps, says one American philosopher, we should no longer identify reality with objective reality. But then how do we know that the person desiring X now and the one desiring Y next is the same person we think we are? How recognize our own poetico-psychological impulses and their lyric continuity? Critics, says Harold Bloom, love continuities; poets detest them.

Among the meditations on interruptions and gaps, one of the most powerful is that of the surrealist André Breton, obsessed as he was with the lagging moments, the "moments nuls" he so roundly condemned in Dostoevski's descriptions. They were to be banished from his writing and thinking and seeing. Now of course, the vow to write or narrate or describe anything always in the same tone would be a self-condemnation to a closed system, where you could learn nothing. According to Bakhtin, it's only in the novel that you can have a heterology of different voices; so how shall the unique voice narrating or then simply speaking in a long poem find its sustenance in time? What kind of ongoing integrity can the subject find in all its irregularities?

The poem retrospectively constitutes the poet as lyric subject, communicating its enthusiasm and its intensity. We might want to think: Yves Bonnefoy is constituted a poet *also* by his figure and metaphor and creation Douve seen all at once in her motion and her immobility, as he is, for all time, in the photograph of him on the threshold stone in front of the closed wooden door of the great structure at Valsaintes, standing on tiptoe and holding the stone arch on either side.[4] *That too is Yves Bonnefoy, see, there.*

In any case, it is the effort that must precede the impression of unity: ". . . we project towards the center of the mind the very subject whose unity we are trying to explain: the individual person with all his complexities" (*N,* 164). We have to learn to experience the poem from the inside and outside at the same time, situated as it is nowhere and yet in our life, by means of this lyric behavior the surrealists liked to invoke: whereas the narrative disperses the subject's attention, the lyric's intensity tends to concentrate it. We must read them differently.

Now among the intensities opposed to those nul moments that Breton refused, which hold, I think, the key to the long poem's integrity, let me give place of privilege to the always nineteen points that punctuate now and again the density of the poem's verbal parts, like so many concentrations of silence. You might think them simple interruptions of the text; I think them the all-important ports of entry into the text itself. They open its density into space, I think, so that the distance beyond them can be seen, like another *Arrière-Pays,* situated further than the imagination of our own country. They are the ways that distance is brought into text.

John Rewald quotes a friend of Cézanne who recounts that painter of Aix telling how it was distance that counted in a picture: first, you had to paint the climactic point of the object as it appeared to you, the high point being always nearest your eyes, and then you had to "find the distance." That was what you had to express, had you any talent as a painter.[5] A long poem, then, must also hold distance, as well as a vivid consciousness of death. Distance, unlike absence, can be a profound part of presence. How present, for instance, just beyond those hills, is the country behind, distant yet so lit. I want to return later to that so-present distance, crucial to the long poem, and to us.

For the text to be full, for it to be entire, it must incorporate the consciousness of nothingness—for, otherwise, it results in a willed betrayal of truth. In the dialogue between plenitude and poverty, between speech and silence, control over a perfect universe will be abandoned. The text will not be closed to chaos—but what it opens upon is, also, presence.

Bonnefoy salutes Baudelaire who knew, precisely through his imperfections—that is, the padding of his verses (those "chevilles" for which critics so reproached him), and his excesses—how to crack apart the old

closed prosody and that stability of control. He brought mortality in. Among Bonnefoy's other salutes, I find most moving the one to Cézanne in a chapter of his *Remarques sur le dessin,* called simply: "Devant la Sainte-Victoire." The powerful equivalent of Rilke's celebrated letters to his wife on the subject of Cézanne's paintings of his mountain, Bonnefoy's remarks are eloquent on the relations between the white spaces and the forms sketched out, in the drawings and in the late paintings of the one we have learned to call simply "The Holy Man of Aix."

Rilke quotes a friend of Count Kessler saying those empty spaces in Cézanne's canvasses were "things he didn't know yet." For Bonnefoy, they are testimonies to the impossibility of representing any mountain ("S'il y a montagne pour nous . . . c'est parce que nous subissons une impression de présence").[6] The interruption of Cézanne's line in his representation of the summit, the break that indicates presence, is analogous to the poetic line that refuses to close upon itself (*RD,* 36). Nothing is closed here, or slickly finished, and the poem, like the drawings, will live through its irresolutions and instabilities, through its *points de suspension,* which open it out into the imperfect universe, with which it can maintain an impassioned relationship.

Fire and Water

Bonnefoy's epic poem draws to its end with a long conjunction of fire and water, situating itself thus in the long tradition of epic closing lines of this kind of elemental convergence. Like the end of Eliot's great *Waste Land,* like the end of Tzara's *Homme approximatif,* like the end of Breton's long incantation of his love called "Union libre" ("Ma femme . . . / Aux yeux de niveau d'eau de niveau d'air de terre et de feu") and the concluding line of his "Sur la route qui monte et qui descend" ("Flamme d'eau guide-moi jusqu'à la mer de feu"[7]), Bonnefoy's convergence begins:

　　Bois, je suis l'eau, brûlée

and continues then, at greater length:

　　Comme Dieu le soleil levant je suis voûté
　　Sur cette eau où fleurit notre ressemblance.
　　. . . Moi, le passeur,
　　Moi la barque de tout à travers tout,
　　Moi le soleil
　　Je m'arrête au faîte du monde dans les pierres.

Moi, la barque . . . the poet's identification with his sailing craft reminds us ineluctably again of Rimbaud's "Bateau ivre," one craft echoing the other in salute. Later, the elements recognize each other as the water in its "coupe fugitive" reflects the still more fleeting fire, "which is nothingness," and sends it into the light, so that earth and air and water and fire should finally meet:

Nuages,
Et un, le plus au loin, ou, à jamais
Rouge, l'eau et le feu
Dans le vase de terre . . .

Here, the enunciation is as modest as the container. This earthen vase holds everything, and in these few lines the oath is taken upon the same two elements of fire and water:

Oui, par ce feu,
Par son reflet de feu sur l'eau paisible,
Par notre lieu, qui va,
Par le chemin de feu sous le fruit mûr.

The fruit is ripe in its time, which is ours.

OPENING AND HOLDING

The invocation backwards, Bonnefoy's strong summoning of the Rimbaldian gesture and tone—from "J'ai heurté, savez-vous, d'incroyables Florides . . . ," when the poet speaks as his own inebriated vessel—works as a liminal action, the threshold to its own threshold. "Heurte," he cries: "Heurte à jamais. / Dans le leurre du seuil." This is the verbal equivalent of the material gesture of knocking against something: "Heurte, heurte à jamais . . ." It is a demand for contact, a dialogue with the other, preceding or following, writing or reading.

Paradoxically, in the space formed by this eternal gesture ("à jamais"), things are lit at once from close up and in the clarity of the infinite. In this space and in the smallest possible container you can gather the earth entire. And yet that statement with its immemorial tone is made without the slightest taint of narrational prosaics entering in. Each gesture, every moment is imbued with a simple luminosity:

Je t'écoute, je prends
Dans ton panier de corde
Toute la terre . . .

The universe can be held here in the humblest of things, in this slight rope basket. The image is strong as are all containing images.[8] The force of a containing poem is double, for it is holding that which holds.

At the conclusion of Rimbaud's voyage as and in poetic craft, closure in seeming reduction produces an effect as natural as convincing, as the drunken boat, then the boat adrift, becomes the frail toy of a saddened child, as the river and sea become a small puddle. Bonnefoy's great long poem will transform by memory Rimbaud's small puddle and toy boat, and with them, the entire experience. It will end—if such poems end—with the perception of an entire sky and all of poetry held, suddenly and forever, in a small pool like a painting. Like a haiku poem, its small size holds, along with the sky, its sustaining strength. Great poetry passes on its greatness.

The holding action of the final lines of the poem is prepared by another, earlier one, when the sky is caught in the disturbed water and in a personal context, framing the picture with its simple symbolic masses in intimacy:

Toi, tu es ce pays
Toi que j'éveille,
Comme dans l'eau qu'on trouble, même de nuit
Le ciel est autre.

At the conclusion of the threshold poem, the brief expanse of the pool will reflect the infinite, this "other" sky—the water can absorb the sky, just as the fruits of the earth can be held in the human hand:

Dans la main de dehors, fermée
a commencé à germer
Le blé des choses du monde.

All these things held and treasured: whether in a rope basket, or in a hand, or in some water, all these are vast things which continue giving life. The space is a generous one, in which nature and the lyric subject are met and awake each other, in a presence where container and contained converge.

THRESHOLD

The threshold must never be domesticated—it opens on more than a house. It is also the border between, say, the sea and the land. It is everything that joins and separates. And so this poem joins all the others of the same spirit, where nothingness can enter and ripen the fullness. As Harold Bloom puts it, "The meaning of a poem is another poem." Like a musical tone, it can be heard only in relation to another.

Finally, I want to speak of the musical term *ostinato,* where the bass repeats obstinately, while the other voices are modified.[9] Gérard Genette hears in the obligato the "tremblement, le bégaiement indéfini d'une création qui procède toujours, et partout . . ." I have used the term *sostenuto* instead because I have wanted to interpret not only the continuing *basso obligato,* but the moral respiration that sustains both tone and text in relation to the others, to the poet himself, and to us.

In those *points de suspension* that open the space of the text towards something else which might be the threshold of who knows what construction, whether of a house quite simply or a majestic abbey in ruins, it is a question of always renewing one's interior threshold, of keeping the most distant distances in what is nearby. For it is the mark of willed imperfection that brings us near the lyric dwelling. The lyric subject sustains itself both in the search for the developing self and in this creation proceeding always and everywhere. These holes tearing into the veil of the page are so many secret figures of this voyage, with their apparent negativity transformed into the positive, in this extraordinary and long *yea-saying* procession, this exploration of a promise and a path:

> Oui, par la main que je prends
> Sur cette terre.
> . . .
>
> Oui, par la mort,
> Oui, par la vie sans fin.
> . . .
>
> Oui, par même l'erreur,
> Qui va,
>
> Oui, par le bonheur simple, la voix brisée.

These simple words give way finally to a six-line ending, where three lines mirror the others, as the sky is mirrored in the small puddle. At last, the dispersal of sounds and signs and significance is reassembled, suddenly entire:

> Les mots comme le ciel
> Aujourd'hui,
> Quelque chose qui s'assemble, qui se disperse.
>
> Les mots comme le ciel,
> Infini
> Mais tout entier soudain dans la flaque brève.

> (*DL,* 121)

It is in its own and our own depths that all this long creation sustains, and will continue to sustain us.

Notes

1. For a discussion of the poem-as-passage, see my *Metapoetics of the Passage: Architextures in Surrealism and After* (Hanover: New England University Press, 1981).

2. For a discussion of this kind of retrospective patterning in the reader's mind, see Barbara Herrnstein Smith, *How Poems End* (Chicago: University of Chicago Press, 1968), 254.

3. Thomas Nagel, *Mortal Questions* (Cambridge: Cambridge University Press, 1979), 197.

4. In *Yves Bonnefoy: Livres et documents* (Paris: Bibliothèque nationale/Mercure de France, 1992), 130.

5. John Rewald, *Paul Cézanne* (New York: Shocken, 1968), 196.

6. "Devant la Sainte-Victoire," 27-42, *Remarques sur le dessin* (Paris: Mercure de France, 1993), 29. (Referred to hereafter as *RD.*)

7. André Breton, *Clair de terre* (Poésie/Gallimard, 1966), 113.

8. To feel its strength, take a similar image, although at the other pole of size and feeling, from René Char's "Compagne du vannier," where the container is no less humble: "Je t'aimais. J'aimais ton visage de source raviné par l'orage et le chiffre de ton domaine enserrant mon baiser. Certains se confient à une imagination toute ronde. Aller me suffit. J'ai rapporté du désespoir un panier si petit, mon amour, qu'on a pu le tresser en osier." *René Char: Selected Poems,* ed. Mary Ann Caws and Tina Jolas (New York: New Directions, 1992), 18.

9. I am at present translating Louis-René des Forêt's ongoing autobiography *Ostinato,* of which translation parts have been published in *Pequod* and *The Denver Quarterly.*

Emily Grosholz (essay date fall 1996)

SOURCE: Grosholz, Emily. "The *Valsaintes* Poems of Yves Bonnefoy." *L'Esprit Créateur* 36, no. 3 (fall 1996): 52-64.

[*In the following essay, Grosholz finds allusions to Bonnefoy's Valsaintes country home in his verse.*]

The shadow of an old house falls across the poems in Yves Bonnefoy's *Pierre écrite* (1965), *Dans le leurre du seuil* (1975) and *Ce qui fut sans lumière* (1987).[1] The house itself is never the topic of the poems, and is only fleetingly described in some of its details now and then. In general, the diction of Bonnefoy's poetry is quite abstract, and he pointedly excludes most references to particular places, occasions, or people. Yet the house is there, indefinite but inescapable, and at some level it must haunt the reader. Certainly it has haunted this reader, although I had been reading Bonnefoy's poetry for about a decade before the house occurred to me. When I began to discern the "ghostly demarcations" it lent to the poetry, the poetry changed and deepened in meaning. And indeed, Bonnefoy has written, "Pas un mot depuis *Pierre écrite* ne serait le même dans ces livres, en fait ils n'existeraient pas, j'aurais écrit tout autre chose, je ne sais quoi, s'il n'y avait un Valsaintes" (private letter).

Yves and Lucie Bonnefoy arrived at the old house in Valsaintes in the summer of 1963. Like all Parisians, they had wished for a house in the country, and finally a bit of extra grant money allowed them to purchase the partly intact, partly ruinous house that the inhabitants of the nearby village Valsaintes called the abbey or château de Bolinette or Boulinette. The history of the house is obscure, but it seems to have served as a summer retreat for the monks of an abbey in a larger town, and at some point in the more recent past its chapel served as a sheepfold. Whatever the details, its past is chequered.

For about a decade, the house provided the Bonnefoys with a refuge and solace. Part of a tiny settlement on the top of a rise overlooking steeply craggy, forested hills and valleys, the abbaye de Bolinette is protected from the mainstream of modern life. The region of Haute-Provence in which it is located, west of the river Durance and town of Manosque (about an hour north of Aix-en-Provence), is quite empty, partly because the terrain is so rugged, and partly because the region has been depopulated by the flight of the region's rural poor to the big cities. Thus, the Valsaintes poems in *Pierre écrite* and *Dans le leurre du seuil* are situated (in a sense that needs to be examined more closely) within the house; they were written by the poet when he was still truly its inhabitant, at least during the periods when he and his wife could escape from Paris. Precisely for that reason, the poems speak of the house very little; it was the condition for the possibility of their existence, not their theme.

But ownership of the house proved to be a mixed blessing. Trying to care for a house in which one is not living continuously is always difficult, but the house at Valsaintes presented special problems. First, parts of it were truly in a state of ruin. The house was at first almost uninhabitable, without a functioning kitchen or other amenities. And certain of the walls and roofs threatened to collapse. Second, it was difficult and expensive to find anyone in the region willing to carry out repairs, and then the labor, when secured, was intermittent and unreliable. Third, the neighbors, peasants who probably rather enjoyed quarreling with city-folk, invented an endless stream of petty quarrels, about right of way, contiguous buildings, access to water, and so forth.

These practical difficulties seemed trivial at first, but as they accumulated year after year they began to strangle the possibility of the Bonnefoys' life in Valsaintes. The work of reconstruction seemed endless, and the disputes irresolvable. These anxieties color the poems in *Dans le leurre du seuil.* As Bonnefoy writes, that book expresses "le souci créé par le lieu, devenu pour moi métaphore de tout désir, de toute illusion, de toute réflexion, de tout essai de lucidité, de sagesse" (private letter). What should have been the simplest thing in the world, to live comfortably and at peace in a lovely old house in the country, proved to be impossible. The Bonnefoys gave up their sojourns there in the mid-seventies, around the time of the birth of their daughter, who would then only encounter it via the memories of her parents.

The poems of *Ce qui fut sans lumière* which concern Valsaintes are thus written in a kind of exile. Indeed, when the book was published, the Bonnefoys were already trying to sell the abbaye de Bolinette. Lost in reality, the house enters these poems in a more urgent, insistent, explicit way, as the poet tries to recover it in art, knowing full well how ambiguous the recoveries of art (or dream) can be. Yet an object of reflection is still an object; and the house still stands. Instead of the poet inhabiting the house, one might say that the house inhabits the poet. Bonnefoy writes, "Avec le recul, Valsaintes est devenu objet de réflexion. J'en parle, au lieu de parler en elle" (private letter).

In the following sections, I will examine the way that the house at Valsaintes exists and is represented in the poems of these three books, by choosing a few exemplary poems for deeper analysis. My intentions are twofold. On the one hand, I am writing as a literary critic interested in finding for the work of Yves Bonnefoy a wider and more appreciative audience in the English-speaking world. Bonnefoy has served the English language so generously as a translator, that we owe his distinguished body of poems equally generous attention. I believe that setting Bonnefoy's poems in relation to a particular place and time may illuminate them for an audience accustomed to a more concrete level of diction and reference from its poets. I also believe in general that the circumstances of a poet's life are pertinent to the poetry, though knowledge of them is only a supplement to careful attention to the forms on the printed page, and each poem's relations to earlier poems.

On the other hand, I am writing as a philosopher. One of the issues Bonnefoy's poems raise for me is the nature of human consciousness, in particular, the way in which our awareness is constituted by a specific location in space and time, and yet always transcends that location. For our awareness is not limited to the here and now: it stretches indefinitely backwards in memory and forwards in expectation, as well as indefinitely outwards: the stars are just as present to it as the tree in the courtyard.

Indeed, our awareness is not limited to the perceptible, even granting the indefinite and perhaps infinite scope of human perception. The world of which we are aware is fraught with meaning. And meanings are constituted in part by loved things which existed but exist no longer except as they are alive in us; by possibilities once hoped for that will never be actualized; by the bright shadow of what we hope for still and await; and by the ideal things of mathematics and ethics which organize and regulate our life though they are never found within it. All these imperceptible dimensions of human life exist for us as surely as the tree in the courtyard, and demand expression. If we try to deny the imperceptible dimensions of our life, we impoverish life but we do not escape those dimensions: they return as tenacious ghosts instead of as angels. By contrast, if we acknowledge them through the expressive power of (for example) poetry, life is intensified and deepened; our understanding is increased and our emotions are purged or purified. The catharsis of art is at once a revisiting and a farewell.

I.

In the book *Pierre écrite,* certain poems in the section "Un feu va devant nous" are direct evocations of Valsaintes, according to the poet: **"L'Arbre, la lampe," "Les chemins," "Le Sang, la note si," "L'Abeille, la couleur," "Le Soir," "La Lumière du soir," "La Patience, le ciel," "Une voix," "Nous prenions par ces prés," "Le livre, pour vieillir."** At the risk of seeming literal-minded, I would like to suggest that if the reader imagines what life might have been like for Yves and Lucie Bonnefoy when they first arrived at Valsaintes, certain features of the poems are illuminated. In my own exercise of imagination, I make use of the brief sojourns in various places in the south of France that I've enjoyed, my memories of the landscape, of its scents, sounds, and colors, and indeed my memories of youth, of what a life of beginnings, of the repeated suspension of obligation, of pure discovery, was like.

One humble detail was that the house had no amenities: no kitchen, no bathroom, no electricity. At first the Bonnefoy's sojourns there were a bit like camping out. This meant, among other things, that the fire in the fireplace and the flame in the oil lamp assumed great importance, became visible as they rarely do for people who live in the city. Likewise, they must have noticed more acutely than usual the withdrawal of light at dusk and its return at dawn.

And this would have been all the more true because, as I imagine, the boundaries between inside and outside would have been more permeable than usual. In a derelict house, one must go outside all the time for various reasons. And in a summer house, surrounded by the quiet, wild, delicious hills of Haute Provence, one would constantly leave the windows open. Then the changing light of sun and moon, occasional bugs and butterflies and perhaps even birds, the edge of a sudden rainstorm, the pervasive smell of rosemary and thyme, and the shrill of cicadas would enter in.

And the Bonnefoys wouldn't have had much to distract them, far away from telephones and the crowded schedule of Parisian life. What would they have done with their days? Read, write, take long walks, amuse themselves as young people in love usually amuse themselves. So their sense of time was transformed. On the one hand, the excessive temporal structuring of each day by modern urban life was absent; and on the other hand, most of what surrounded them, the wild flora and fauna of the countryside, proceeded in its own inhuman temporality not along the line of history but round about in the cycles of nature.

The single flame of a lamp or a candle has such integrity of shape, such visual allure, such liveliness, that poets have often taken it as a metaphor for the human soul.

In **"L'Arbre, la lampe"** (*Pierre écrite,* 201), Bonnefoy writes about the soul-flame just at the moment of dawn, when it pales in the light of the sun, its great Original.

> L'arbre vieillit dans l'arbre, c'est l'été.
> L'oiseau franchit le chant de l'oiseau et s'évade.
> Le rouge de la robe illumine et disperse
> Loin, au ciel, le charroi de l'antique douleur.
>
> O fragile pays,
> Comme la flamme d'une lampe que l'on porte,
> Proche étant le sommeil dans la sève du monde,
> Simple le battement de l'ame partagée.
>
> Toi aussi tu aimes l'instant où la lumière des lampes
> Se décolore et rêve dans le jour.
> Tu sais que c'est l'obscur de ton cœur qui guérit,
> La barque qui rejoint le rivage et tombe.

The poem is located within the house, with the dreamers who have just woken up, or who sense the end of a long, wakeful night: the house is furnished with a lamp, a red dress perhaps cast carelessly over a chair or table, and perhaps also a bed, since Bonnefoy often uses the word "barque" as a figure that not only indicates some kind of journey or transition, but also stands for a bed. After all, the activities of passengers in a bed, dreaming and making love, often contribute to important spiritual voyages. Yet the walls of the house are porous: the tree and the sky are present, and birdsong enters as well. Indeed, the second stanza uses the flame of the lamp as a kind of middle term between the soul and the surrounding world, "l'âme partagée" and the "fragile pays."

This poem seems to be a poem of solace, of reconciliation and hope, especially when taken in contrast to his earlier poem **"Aube, fille des larmes, rétablis"** (*Hier régnant désert* [1958], 143). Though it uses many of the same images as **"L'Arbre, la lampe,"** it seems to be simply an expression of grief. The place of this earlier poem is an enclosed room, where a lamp goes out beside one who has died, and the poet can only ask, "Le navire des lampes / Entrera-t-il au port qu'il avait demandé, / Sur les tables d'ici la flamme faite cendre / Grandira-t-elle ailleurs dans une autre clarté?" And the dawn, whom the poet petitions as **"Aube, fille des larmes,"** has not yet come.

By contrast, the place of **"L'Arbre, la lampe"** integrates inner and outer with its suggestion of open windows. It integrates day and night by taking dawn as its moment. And the poem combines regret or grief with consolation because of the way its two implied protagonists, the speaker and the "tu," understand the dawn. Dawn is ambiguous for the soul; the lamp does not go out before dawn, nor does the light of dawn wholly overpower it: "Toi aussi tu aimes l'instant où la lumière des lampes / Se décolore et rêve dans le jour." Dawn makes possible alteration and creativity, the power of dream which draws as much upon darkness as upon the light. The very ambiguity of dawn is the source of the poem's hopefulness. Related imagery appears in the erotically charged poem, **"Le Sang, la note si"** (*Pierre écrite*, 204), where the last stanza begins, "Ainsi vieillit l'été. Ainsi la mort / Encercle le bonheur de la flamme qui bouge. / Et nous dormons un peu." Conversely, the poems **"L'Abeille, La Couleur," "Le Soir," "La Lumière du soir," "Une Voix,"** and **"Une Pierre,"** take the ambiguous moment of sunset, when day mingles with night, as their setting, to similar purpose (*Pierre écrite*, 205, 206, 207, 209, 213).

Yet though these poems are often given a quite explicit temporal tag, the poet also insists that something strange is happening to the time inhabited by the two implied protagonists. Their awareness of time is transformed in the moment of reconciliation or integration or revelation. One way of describing this transformation is that time becomes spatial: instead of a succession in which the to-come and the has-been are lost, time opens up sideways. The river becomes a lake. This odd damming of time is implicit in the poem **"L'Arbre, la lampe,"** which holds the passing moment of dawn suspended throughout the whole of the poem, but it is more explicitly carried out in other poems.

At the end of **"L'Abeille, la couleur"** (*Pierre écrite*, 205), Bonnefoy mentions one of the sounds of the Provençal countryside, the hum of bees: "Et tout ce bruit / D'abeilles de l'impure et douce éternité / Sur le si proche pré si brulant encore." Unlike the sound of human talk or a melody, which carries one forwards through time, the archaic, undifferentiated hum of bees seems to hold one suspended in time which pools and circles, as long as no distractions intervene. This is not the transcendent eternity of Christianity, but a more modest timelessness, "impure et douce." Similarly, in **"Le Soir"** (*Pierre écrite*, 206) the poet describes the way time slows as one gazes into a fire on the hearth at evening as "l'éternité de la sauge"; and in **"La Lumière du soir"** (*Pierre écrite*, 207) he describes the quietness of lovers this way: "Et le temps reste autour de nous comme des flaques de couleur." It is as if time extended outwards all around, like the hills of Haute Provence around the abbaye de Bolinette.

The poem **"Le Livre, pour vieillir"** (*Pierre écrite*, 217), the final poem in the section "Un feu va devant nous," has two stanzas. In the first, time opens out, extends itself, pauses. In the second, the soul surrounded by such pastures of time is itself transformed: like the flame of the lamp in **"L'Arbre, la lampe,"** it alters and dreams.

> Etoiles transhumantes; et le berger
> Voûté sur le bonheur terrestre; et tant de paix
> Comme ce cri d'insecte, irrégulier,
> Qu'un dieu pauvre façonne. Le silence

> Est monté de ton livre vers ton cœur.
> Un vent bouge sans bruit dans les bruits du monde.
> Le temps sourit au loin, de cesser d'être.
> Simples dans le verger sont les fruits murs.

> Tu vieilliras
> Et, te décolorant dans la couleur des arbres,
> Faisant ombre plus lente sur le mur,
> Etant, et d'âme enfin, la terre menacée,
> Tu reprendras le livre à la page laissée,
> Tu diras, C'étaient donc les derniers mots obscurs.

II.

The poems in **Dans le leurre du seuil** are each quite long, and yet without any obvious narrative framework. This makes them difficult to discuss in a few brief pages, since they resist summary. Nonetheless, the way in which the house at Valsaintes enters into **"Deux Barques," "La Terre," "Les Nuées,"** and **"L'Epars, l'indivisible"** provides a thematic focus for reflection. I'll limit my comments to **"La Terre,"** which in virtue of its important features may stand for the others.

When one has tried very hard to make something happen and then failed in the attempt, one must live through a process of renunciation. Like forgiving, renouncing is slow and difficult work for the spirit; one may forgive or renounce superficially and quickly, but the true act takes a long time to ripen. But it often then happens that a completed renunciation brings with it unexpected gifts or recompense. Something new comes to take the place of the thing renounced; and the thing renounced proves to exist still in a different mode, conferring on life greater richness of meaning.

In **"La Terre"** (*Dans le leurre du seuil*, 271-88), the house at Valsaintes is a great source of anxiety in so far as it is still in the poet's possession, but simultaneously it is a source of wisdom in so far as the poet comes to understand that it must be relinquished. The place is really falling apart; the vocabulary of the poem is permeated by words about decay, erosion, rust. There are also allusions to finally ineffective attempts at reconstruction, which seem rather to increase the material disorder of the house. As I read it, the poem begins with the return of the Bonnefoys to the house after a certain period to find it in disarray; perhaps the visit is one of their very last.

What greets them is the light of Provence, which has been watching over the house better than its human caretakers.

> Je crie, Regarde,
> La lumière
> Vivait là, près de nous! Ici, sa provision
> D'eau, encore transfigurée. Ici le bois
> Dans la remise. Ici, les quelques fruits
> A sécher dans les vibrations du ciel de l'aube.

They are also met by the spectacle of an almond tree in bloom, which the poet cannot fail to take as an intimation of immortality, a vision of transcendence: "l'à jamais de la fleur éphémère." And yet it must be the homely, terrestrial kind of transcendence, since a tree is a tree.

> Je crie, Regarde,
> L'amandier
> Se couvre brusquement de milliers de fleurs.
> Ici
> Le noueux, l'à jamais terrestre, le déchiré
> Entre au port. Moi la nuit
> Je consens. Moi l'amandier
> J'entre paré dans la chambre nuptiale.

The house is still porous; the tree enters inside, and the poet stands with the tree in the courtyard, arrayed in a different version of *primavera*.

Yet nonetheless the house is in terrible shape. The language of light and the whiteness of the almond tree changes into that of a sacrificial, consuming flame which plays upon the house and its disordered contents: "Flamme le verre / Sur la table de la cuisine abandonnée, / A V. / Dans les gravats. / Flamme, de salle en salle, / Le plâtre, / Toute une indifférence, illuminée." And a bit later in the poem, the flame of dispossession seems to consume the house itself, seen from without.

> Regarde,
> Ici, sur la lande du sens,
> A quelques mètres du sol,
> C'est comme si le feu avait pris feu,
> Et ce second brasier, dépossession,
> Comme s'il prenait feu encore, dans les hauts
> De l'étoffe de ce qui est, que le vent gonfle.
> Regarde,
> Le quatrième mur s'est descellé,
> Entre lui et ta pile du coté nord
> Il y a place pour la ronce
> Et les bêtes furtives de chaque nuit.

With the growing realization that the beloved house really can't be retrieved, the poem more and more moves towards images, not of nothingness exactly, but of the impalpable, invisible, and imponderable that accompanies our life, that completes it and gives it meaning. For this is the residue of the house, as it slips away.

> Aujourd'hui la distance entre les mailles
> Existe plus que les mailles,
> Nous jetons un filet qui ne retient pas.
> Achever, ordonner,
> Nous ne le savons plus.
> Entre l'œil qui s'accroît et le mot plus vrai
> Se déchire la taie de l'achevable.
> O ratures, o rouilles

In my ear, the last line echoes Rimbaud's "O saisons, o châteaux," but as an ironic inversion.

Nothingness is not an easy poetic subject. As the poem progresses, Bonnefoy tries again and again to articulate it using the vocabulary of flame, of light, of eros, even of godhead.

> Regarde,
> Ici fleurit le rien; et ses corolles,
> Ses couleurs d'aube et de crépuscule, ses apports
> De beauté mystérieuse au lieu terrestre
> Et son vert sombre aussi, et le vent dans ses branches,
> C'est l'or qui est en nous: or sans matière,
> Or de ne pas durer, de ne pas avoir,
> Or d'avoir consenti, unique flamme
> Au flanc transfiguré de l'alambic.

Instead of persisting in the illusion that the house can be saved, or of closing the door behind him and trying to forget, Bonnefoy here goes through a poetic process of renunciation that prepares the way for further grieving and for further imaginative recollection. The house will be built, or rebuilt, of poems.

But another kind of recuperation is at work in **"La Terre."** As the poet labors to give nothingness a habitation and a name, "le rien" attracts the word "dieu" and that word gives birth, as it were, to the word "enfant." The poem alludes at various points, always indirectly and inexplicitly, to the relationship between Yves and Lucie Bonnefoy, that persists in the midst of the dissolution of the house and in the face of their growing awareness of mortality, an awareness that suddenly deepens as one approaches the half-century mark.

> Et soyons l'un pour l'autre comme la flamme
> Quand elle se détache du flambeau,
> La phrase de fumée un instant lisible
> Avant de s'effacer dans l'air souverain.

Again, at the risk of seeming literal-minded, or of projecting my own experience on the poetry of Yves Bonnefoy, I see the child who appears so often in **"La Terre"** as a reference to or a premonition of the birth of their child, an event which roughly coincided with the completion of *Dans le leurre du seuil*. It often happens, who knows why, that when we give up something precious, consenting to the constraints of mortality and truly thinking, imagining, and feeling our way through the loss, that life suddenly offers us something unexpected. Reality is in many ways much larger and more imaginative than we are. In this case, as it seems to me, the life of the Bonnefoys offered them a child, and the child is in the poem.

It appears in the play of sunlight on water, upon the sacrificial stone, in the midst of the flowering almond tree.

> Et vois, l'enfant
> Est là, dans l'amandier,
> Debout
> Comme plusieurs vaisseaux arrivant en rêve.

And the poet is the pilgrim soul, in search of the god-child who naturally arrives in a stable.

> Je consens. Moi le berger,
> Je pousse la fatigue et l'espérance
> Sous l'arche de l'étoile vers l'étable.
> Moi la nuit d'août,
> Je fais le lit des bêtes dans l'étable.
> Moi le sommeil,
> Je prends le rêve dans mes barques, je consens.

III.

I conclude this essay with a consideration of the poem **"Les Arbres"** from the first section of *Ce qui fut sans lumière* (17-18); as Bonnefoy has noted, all the poems of this section were written directly apropos of the house at Valsaintes, as he tried to absorb its loss. On my sole visit there, I came to understand this poem in a new way simply by virtue of standing next to the old house. I saw with my own eyes the terrace and the trees, the steep slopes behind the house and the way the sunlight fell on the walls. "Oh," I said to myself, "that's what he meant about the long shadow of the trees."

> Nous regardions nos arbres, c'était du haut
> De la terrasse qui nous fut chère, le soleil
> Se tenait près de nous cette fois encore
> Mais en retrait, hôte silencieux
> Au seuil de la maison en ruines, que nous lassions
> A son pouvoir, immense, illuminée.

As in *Pierre Ecrite,* the hour of sunset attracts the poem; the poem both suspends itself in time and moves towards dusk. As in *Dans le leurre du seuil,* the sun is imagined as a kind of housekeeper in the Bonnefoys' absence. But by contrast here, their visit exists in the poem at three removes: it is about shadows, shadows remembered, and they seem to have been cast during a fleeting visit after the Bonnefoys had ceased to live in the house, perhaps while they were in the region, looking in on their property which had not yet been sold. The tone is fraught with nostalgia.

Look, says the poet, how the sun casting shadows appears to combine things that we know are spatially separate: the couple, the trees, the terrace wall.

> Vois, te disais-je, il fait glisser contre la pierre
> Inégale, incompréhensible, de notre appui
> L'ombre de nos épaules confondues,
> Celle des amandiers qui sont près de nous
> Et celle même du haut des murs qui se mêle aux au-
>   tres,
> Trouée, barque brûlée, proue qui dérive,
> Comme un surcroît de rêve ou de fumée.

As in the earlier two books, the image of a boat reenters. The conceit of the poem is that the terrace is the prow of a boat, drifting with its two voyagers on the currents of time. But the oak trees far away on the other side of the ravine seem motionless, as if they were the shores of eternity.

> Mais ces chênes là-bas sont immobiles,
> Même leur ombre ne bouge pas, dans la lumière,
> Ce sont les rives du temps qui coule ici où nous
>   sommes,
> Et leur sol est inabordable, tant est rapide
> Le courant de l'espoir gros de la mort.

Thus the poem poses various degrees of separation. The two people, and the two people and the house, are separate; but the sun as physical agent and the poet as artist each joins them, at least as shadows, and they sit quietly together on the terrace, content to be so joined. The more serious separation is that between time and eternity, "le sol inabordable," a separation which the vast landscape around the abbaye de Bolinette makes plausible. But finally the warm sun, "hôte silencieux," and the poet struggling to renounce what once offered him protection and solace, bridge the gap, at least for the moment of a stanza. After all, the moment of a stanza, artificial as it is, can always be revisited by the reader and thus has some aspect of timelessness.

> Nous regardâmes les arbres toute une heure.
> Le soleil attendait, parmi les pierres,
> Puis il eut compassion, il étendit
> Vers eux, en contrebas dans le ravin,
> Nos ombres qui parurent les atteindre
> Comme, avançant le bras, on peut toucher
> Parfois, dans la distance entre deux êtres,
> Un instant du rêve de l'autre, qui va sans fin.

The way the couple touches gently, sitting side by side, registers as well a harmony in their apprehension of the invisible, as the visible world of house, ravine, and forested slope registers the interplay of time and timelessness, the actual and the possible, the real and the ideal. And the reader too is included, for the poem also affirms the possibility of communication, not just about rocks and trees, but about the greater reality that despite our dissipation grants us meaning, and despite our separateness hold us, gently, together.

Note

1. *Pierre écrite* and *Dans le leurre du seuil* are included in *Poèmes* (Paris: Mercure de France, 1978); *Ce qui fut sans lumière* (Paris: Mercure de France, 1987).

Dimitrios Kargiotis (essay date January 2001)

SOURCE: Kargiotis, Dimitrios. "Death and the Problematics of Representation in Bonnefoy's *Du mouvement et de l'immobilité de Douve.*" *Neophilologus* 85, no. 1 (January 2001): 53-69.

[*In the following essay, Kargiotis analyzes the various modalities and functions of death in* On the Motion and Immobility of Douve.]

"L'esprit [. . .]," says Yves Bonnefoy in "Les tombeaux de Ravenne," "s'interroge sur l'être, mais rarement sur la pierre" (11). Neglecting the value of experience, humans struggle to master *concepts,* but we forget that concepts cannot embrace the totality of the real: "[y] a-t-il un concept d'un pas venant dans la nuit, d'un cri, de l'éboulement d'une pierre dans les broussailles? De l'impression que fait une maison vide?" (13). The endeavor to conceptualize stems, for Bonnefoy, from the desire for *permanence* and *identity,* a naive hope that life can overcome death. Such a desire, nevertheless, disregards that death is organically tied to life: "it provides that very point of anchorage, that totally irreversible attachment to the earth [. . .]," that allows for "continuity and cyclicalness" (Bishop 197). This paper will attempt to outline the problematics of representation of death in **Du mouvement et de l'immobilité de Douve.** The double character such a representation exhibits is particularly interesting, since there is a shift in the semantic field of death from a referential to a metalinguistic level. Accordingly, what the represented object that points to death will have accomplished is the transference of its reference to something extratextual: from images of death to the death of the image, the annulment of representation in order to capture the real.

Let us start, then, by attempting to outline Bonnefoy's understanding of images and concepts. "Il y a une vérité du concept [. . .]," Bonnefoy claims, "[m]ais il y a un mensonge [. . .] *en général,* qui donne à la pensée pour quitter la maison des choses le vaste pouvoir des mots" (*Tombeaux* 13). "Words put distance between [men] and things" (*Image and Presence* 168) because words are *representations* of things. For Saussure, for instance, "a linguistic sign is not a link between a thing and a name, but between a concept and a sound pattern [*image acoustique*]" (66); the sign is constituted of the interweaving of a *representation* of a conceptual image and an acoustic *im-pression* of an articulation which takes place in the mind. Rather than a particular referent, such a sign has a broad semantic field: to use the Saussurian example, the sign "tree" does not refer to any *specific* tree. Focusing his investigation on the signs themselves rather than examining how they relate to the world—the referents—, Saussure draws a distinction between "[. . .] *la langue,* which is to say the ensemble of linguistic possibilities or potentialities at any given moment, and *la parole,* or the individual act of speech, the individual and partial actualization of some of those potentialities" (Jameson 22). Attempting to analyze the way the former operates, Saussure does "[. . .] not so much describe how language works as wonder what, in language, guarantees that it *will* work" (Avni, *Reference* 40). The Saussurian *langue* is accordingly defined in a negative way: "*[I]n the language itself, there are only*

differences" (118). If there is *something* that the sign signifies, it is solely what is *not* signified by the totality of all other signs different from it.

Bonnefoy's emphasis on *objects* (*Interview* 146), however, entails a much more essentialist understanding. He is interested in the referent, in the thing itself rather than abstract representations of it. It is only inevitable, then, that in the beginning of his career he becomes associated with the Surrealists who proclaim another relation to things, a "more real" one. A "more real" understanding and, subsequently, creation, of reality takes place, among other ways, through a new conception of the notion of *image.* According to Breton's incorporation in the *Manifeste du Surréalisme* (324) of Reverdy's definition of an image,

> L'image est une création pure de l'esprit.
>   Elle ne peut naître d'une comparaison mais du rapprochement de deux réalités plus
> ou moins éloignées.
>   Plus les rapports des deux réalités rapprochées seront lointains et justes, plus l'image
> sera forte—plus elle aura de puissance émotive et de réalité poétique . . . etc.

Such a new perception involves, above all, a certain revolutionary magic. Indeed, Bonnefoy admits, "[. . .] the Surrealist image, especially when it is most arbitrary and most gratuitously provoking, never strikes me, not even now, without stirring up the beginnings of fascination; it is as though some mysteriously rooted hope were suddenly making itself known through a sign intended less to present me with some good than to call me to battle [. . .] The greatness of this movement—it is the only genuine poetic movement this century has had—was its effort to reanimate in secular times, and necessarily outside the perimeter of religion because of the times that are ours, the feeling of transcendancy" (*Transcendancy* 135, 137).

This "feeling of trancendancy" is enough for Bonnefoy to make him accept the Surrealist image, "[. . .] even if it is in fact a denial of coherent representation" (*Interview* 143). For within a conceptual framework that explicitly rejects concepts, it is not "even if," but rather "because of" the fact that such a denial takes place that an interest in Surrealism emerges: Bonnefoy sees in it a new force in accordance with many of his beliefs.

Breton's definition, however, is not unquestionably valid, despite the fact that, provocative as it is, it provides a new, revolutionary conception of the image. Its problematic nature was implicitly perceived even by Breton himself, (when talking, i.e., of "an aesthetics a posteriori" (324), or when examining the degree of intentionality (337-340)), and has been put into question[1] by scholars as well. Indeed, such a definition can be said to disregard the referential, cognitive and meta-lingual functions of language such as Jakobson defined them in "Linguistics and Poetics," and ignore the dimension of *motivation* in the image. Motivation is a crucial factor in the poetic process, because it plays a chief role regarding the way syntagms and paradigms (or else, word combinations and substitutions) will be not only understood, but, in the first place, constructed in the text. The concept of construction, on the other hand, implies a self-conscious process, and it would be unfair to criticize on such a basis a poetics that insists on the automatic character of creation. Post-surrealist poetry, however (and by this is meant poetry that creatively assimilates surrealist heritage, such as the poetry of Bonnefoy), does emphasize intentionality in the creative process. Consequently, the poem is no longer approached in terms of an addressor/addressee dialectic; a third term, that of the message, comes into play, a message that now requires decoding. And precisely in such poetry is the role of the image central.

The centrality of the image, on the one hand, but also the limitations of its surrealist definition, make the later Bonnefoy adopt a different position. For, in the end, even the surrealist image does not escape representability; on the contrary, it is susceptible to a double bind. Surrealist representations, so to speak, are "twice removed from truth," to use a vocabulary that Bonnefoy detests: on the one hand, they are images, which means that they are distanced from the world, since they represent it; on the other hand, these images are "surreal:" they represent a world which cannot objectively exist, to which there is no objective reference.

Bonnefoy, then, is caught in a dilemma. As John T. Naughton puts it, "[t]he paradoxical reality of images is that they give us our world [. . .]; but through providing us with an approach to the world, images do not, in themselves, have any being" (14). Or, to use Bonnefoy's new definition: "this impression of a reality at last fully incarnate, which comes to us, paradoxically, through words which have turned away from incarnation, I shall call *image*" (*Image and Presence* 164). The binary opposition *incarnation/excarnation*, central to Bonnefoy's poetics, reproduces the binaries we have mentioned and refers to the opposition between a seizure of materiality, a capturing of reality on the one hand, and its representation through the mediation of words, concepts or images on the other; in other words, the tension between what philosophy calls *le sensible* and *l'intelligible*,[2] codifying the paradigms of *feeling, affectivity, passibility,* on the one hand, and *cognition,* on the other. Considered within the framework of Lyotard's theory of *phrases*[3] according to which "phrases from heterogeneous regimens cannot be translated from one into the other" (xii), Bonnefoy's task may be described as an attempt to answer the question: how is it possible to translate (literally: transpose) an incarnate

(*sensible*) phrase into excarnate (*intelligible*) words without creating an excarnate image? How is it possible to reconcile phrases which, since they belong to the *sensible,* have no referent, with phrases which, cognitive as they are, since they use language, are characterized by reference? Or, to put the question in its most elementary formulation, how do we re-present the unrepresentable?

To present means, above all, *to make present.* Bonnefoy is against "the substitution of an image for the world—in favor of presence" (*Image and Presence* 171). His attempt is directed towards the domain of things, of the world, of *le sensible,* the domain of what Husserl calls *Gegenwärtigung* or *Präsentation* (which Derrida renders as *perception* or *présentation originaire*), while images partake of the world of concepts, *l'intelligible,* and, therefore, all they can do is only create an impression of presence, of *Vergegenwärtigung* (of *re-présentation* or *re-production représentative* or *présentification*) (Derrida 50).[4] Thus Bonnefoy now comes to define his poetry as a "war against the Image" (*Image and Presence* 170). From the surrealist quest to consider an imaginary, non-existent, hyper-real representation/image of an object as real, Bonnefoy now arrives at a poetics of an image of an object that questions its representational real-ness. A poetics of death is Bonnefoy's way of attaining such an image. Death is a major category in Bonnefoy for two reasons. On the one hand, because he explicitly, as we have seen, insists on the "idea" of death as a major parameter of incarnation; this insistence becomes poetically realized in representations ("images") of death. On a second plane, Bonnefoy's ingenuity consists in a masterful depiction of the death of language: death is *presented* as the annihilation of imagery and linguistic representability themselves. Consequently, Bonnefoy, in an indicative way, proclaims the death of representation by representing death in this double aspect.

Images of death are abundant throughout **Douve**, and they appear in a variety of ways:

a. As a dialectic play with life. Death and life are not to be understood as opposite or complementary, but rather as two faces of a being, of an existence that always is, in which death and life are only phases. Douve will always be alive and dead, continuously questioning the boundaries between the two: ". . . à chaque instant je te vois naître, Douve, / A chaque instant mourir" (48).[5]

A poem that expresses more obviously the problematics of such a dialectic, is no. IV from **"Derniers gestes"** (70):

> Es-tu vraiment morte ou joues-tu
> Encore à simuler la pâleur et le sang,
> O toi passionnément au sommeil qui te livres
> Comme on ne sait que mourir?

Es-tu vraiment morte ou joues-tu
Encore en tout miroir
A perdre ton reflet, ta chaleur et ton sang
Dans l'obscurcissement d'un visage immobile?

This life/death play is constructed on two planes; first, the very way of questioning ("vraiment," "ou joues-tu") shows that the poetic subject is ignorant of the truth, or might be suspicious: "are you dead or alive?" At the same time the poetic device of semantic inversions is functioning: complementary to the question "es-tu vraiment morte" we would expect "*dis*simuler le sang" and not "simuler," since if Douve were dead, she would not have any blood; the same way, in the second stanza, we do not expect her to "*perdre* son reflet dans l'obscurcissement," but rather to find it. These inversions undermine the conventional semantic fields of "life" and "death" and lead to their new understanding.

b. Death also appears in relation to the poetic subject, as a situ-ation that the poetic subject *discovers, reveals* or simply *sees*. For instance:

O plus noire et déserte! Enfin je te vis morte,
Inapaisable éclair que le néant supporte,
Vitre sitôt éteinte, et d'obscure maison.

(72)

Or the following:

[. . .] Présence ressaisie dans la torche du froid,
O guetteuse toujours je te découvre morte [. . .]

(53)

—here the play on vision is double: the "guetteuse" who sees and the poetic subject who sees her ("je te decouvre").

Images of death are operative on both rhetorical and semantic levels. Let us consider, for instance, the powerful description in **"Vrai Corps:"**

Close la bouche et lavé le visage,
Purifié le corps, enseveli
Ce destin éclairant dans la terre du verbe,
Et le mariage le plus bas s'est accompli.

(77)

Here, the three participles ("close," "lavé," "purifié") function on three planes: first, they refer to "Douve," whose "vrai corps" the reader is expecting to see; at the same time, the participles have their own subjects. This creates an impression of fragmentariness: the dead body, deprived of life, ceases to be an organic unity and is perceived as a sum-total of limbs. Nevertheless, the inability to tell whether the "destin" of line 3 is the grammatical subject or the object of "enseveli," along with the abstract signified of the subject/object signifier, resulting at an image of significant abstraction ("enseveli

ce destin éclairant dans la terre du verbe"), function in such a way as to provide a perception or impression of death, one which might not be fully understood at first, but which the reader comes to contact with despite the incapacity of language to express it.

But the very opening of the poem constitutes an image of death:

Je te voyais courir sur des terrasses,
Je te voyais lutter contre le vent,
Le froid saignait sur tes lèvres.

Et je t'ai vue te rompre et jouir d'être morte ô plus belle
Que la foudre, quand elle tache les vitres blanches de ton sang.

We are to discern two temporal moments in the poem: a past time of continuity and repetition versus a momentary, instant past. Life is, then, represented by three imperfects; the first two are verbs of energy, of power: "courir," "lutter." The third, "saigner," through a poetic inversion, (instead of "les lèvres," it is "le froid" that "saignait") connects the first part of the poem to the second: the image of red faces because of the cold is an indication of health; nevertheless it is blood, associated with death, that gives this color. Death, moreover, does not signify a negative moment: she (for we know that the "tu" is a "she" from line 4) enjoys ("jouir") death, being prettier than "le foudre . . .".

The imagery of the text is powerful. Not only is the poem itself constructed through images ending in a simile, but there is also a play on the actual reception of images: the poetic subject *watches* the "tu" rendering to the reader, through words, those images of "tu" in a section intituled "théâtre," whose Greek root contains the meaning of "watching" or "vision." But this vision ultimately leads to the vision of death, which, in this first poem, annuls temporality (the instant "passé composé"). To annul temporality is, of course, to cancel a fundamental linguistic operation and, create, therefore, a context of "incarnation" from the beginning.

c. Finally, death is also represented in the poem through a powerful textual voice. This voice can appear through the simple narration of an omniscient poetic subject. ***Douve*** is full of such descriptions: "Et des liasses de mort pavoisent ton sourire . . ." (63), or even more explicitly in **"Le seul témoin."** There the poetic subject sees Douve die, provides a description of the process and makes an authorial comment: "je fus . . . le seul témoin, la seul bête prise / dans ces rets de ta mort . . ." (67). In other words, the reader that sees this "theatre" is urged to accept those images that the only witness is able to provide. Thus, the act of vision provides death. "Regarde, diras-tu, cette pierre: / Elle porte la présence de la mort" (93).

This textual voice sometimes appears very authoritative, and this occurs when the power of the text gains authority even over that of the poetic subject. A central example of this constitutes the poem **"Hic est locus patriae"** (94). Here death is implied rather than explicitly described, the image of death is evoked for the reader of a text which is an account of the poetic subject "seeing" a place of death. The landscape (sky, trees) evokes the romantic topos of nature, and the use of the imperfect intensifies such an impression. But then, Cassandra appears, a silent figure associated with death. We will examine in a moment the figure whose silence is in accord with the silence of the place. The presence of silence becomes thus overwhelming, literally monumental; along with the sky, the trees, the marble and, of course, the latin inscription, an image of a place of death, of a cemetery, is made present. The ingenuity of the inscription/title is that the emphasis can be put on any word, not only without altering, but rather making more prominent the image of death: "*Hic* (here, in the cemetery) est locus partiae" or "hic *est* (in present/is present) locus patriae" or "hic est *locus* ("le lieu") patriae" or "hic est locus *patriae*" (our real country, our father-land).

To represent death, or better, to provide images of death, is only one way in which the text is structured. On the one hand, we have simultaneous images of life and death, images where life and death are either directly represented or implicitly expressed, juxtaposed or combined together; or we have a vision of images of death provided either through an omniscient narrator or through the text itself. We have seen such examples above. Finally, on another level of representation, it is metaphors or metonymies—double representations—, that take precedence: Douve being Phoenix/Salamander being death.

Douve is metonymically identified with Phoenix and the Salamander. Phoenix, a bird which, dying, at the same time "refuse toute mort," (**"Phénix,"** 75), whose "chevelure" is at the same time its "cendre," (**"Une autre voix,"** 81), always "se recompose" (**"Voix basses et Phénix,"** 90). The poem where the dialectical images of life/death and all their paradigms are more evident in their understanding not as opposite but as complementary, is **"Une voix"** (87):

> Souviens-toi de cette île où l'on bâtit le feu
> De tout olivier vif au flanc des crêtes,
> Et c'est pour que la nuit soit plus haute et qu'à l'aube
> Il n'y ait plus de vent que de stérilité.
> Tant de chemins noircis feront bien un royaume
> Où rétablir l'orgueil que nous avons été,
> Car rien ne peut grandir une éternelle force
> Qu'une éternelle flamme et que tout soit défait.
> Pour moi je rejoindrai cette terre cendreuse,
> Je coucherai mon coeur sur son corps dévasté.
> Ne suis-je pas ta vie aux profondes alarmes,
> Qui n'a de monument que Phénix au bûcher?

"Feu" as destructive is opposed to "vif olivier," but as a "non-tangible object" is combined with the constructive "bâtir;" then from the oppositions "nuit"/"aube" and "vent"/"stérilité" we pass to the subtlety of the indirect opposition "chemins noircis" (negative)/"royaume" (positive) that will "reestablish" (and we expect something concrete)/"l'orgueil" (an abstract notion). Also, the "éternelle force" will be "grandie" through a "flamme," which is normally a destructive (or purifying/ destructive) image, but also by a destruction proper: "que tout soit défait." The second appearance of the poetic subject is to declare that it will join the "terre" which is, however, "cendreuse;" but is it the ashes-remains of a destructive fire, or the ashes of the Phoenix which are about to be reborn? The same play takes place in the opposition "coeur"/"corps dévasté." Finally, the dialectic of the oppositions ends up in a triumphant way, when, at the end of the poem, both the rhetorical and semantic aspects of the line are together at play: on the one hand, "monument" (concreteness, stability, presence) is not only contrasted to "Phénix au bûcher" (in-concreteness, instability, destruction, annihilation of temporality/ presence), but rather *is* this Phoenix itself; the monument *is* nothingness, but one which is about to stop being one, which will again annihilate itself, and so on. On the other hand, to the *rhetorical* question "am I not your life . . ." the implied answer "yes, you are" is latent; but "yes, you are" means "you are nothing but a monument of nothingness," a present monument of absence.

The Salamander operates in a similar way. Its figure reconciles images of earth and spirit, life and death, presence and absence, purity and impurity, happiness and sadness. **"Lieu de la salamandre"** is one of the "salamander poems" where it is somewhat more transparent to discern the dialectic of this image:

> La salamandre surprise s'immobilise
> Et feint la mort.
> Tel est le premier pas de la conscience dans le pierres,
> Le mythe le plus pur,
> Un grand feu traversé, qui est esprit.
> . . .
>
> O ma complice et ma pensée, allégorie
> De tout ce qui est pur,
> Que j'aime qui resserre ainsi dans son silence
> La seule force de joie.
> . . .

(111)

Here the dialectic death/life is presented through the characteristics of the reptile. The salamander is able to stay so still as to appear dead because the temperature of its blood is very low; in fact, the mythological tradition presents the salamander with the power to put out fires with the coldness of its body. This simultaneous aspect of life and death is presented as the "first step" (movement) of "consciousness" (the extreme manifestation of life), in contrast to the image of death (immobility and death of consciousness). The play on such oppositions continues structured around the centrality of "pierres:" indeed, "pierres" as a concrete object is juxtaposed to "mythe" (abstract idea), to "feu" ("intangible" object which nevertheless exists, which nevertheless the salamander can annihilate) and finally to "esprit" ("spiritual" object). Like in the Phoenix poem above, the rhetorical and semantic aspects of the lines function harmoniously: on the one hand, "le premier pas" is an expression denoting beginning, but at the same time it contains "pas," actual movement, which is what the salamander annuls; on the other hand, the salamander is an "allegory of everything pure," a characteristic attributed to the animal, but at the same time an explicit depoetization of a literary device, allegory. Finally the characteristic of the salamander mentioned in the very first line of the poem, alludes to the title of the collection: "[la salamandre] est, en un mot, 'le mouvement' et 'l'immobilité' de Douve réunis" (Jackson 263).

Except for Phoenix and Salamander, there is a third figure that represents death in the poem: Cassandra. Cassandra's function is double. On the one hand, she operates in a direction similar to that of Phoenix and the Salamander in that she is a living presence who nevertheless carries in itself the message of death and perdition. On the other hand, Cassandra constitutes a third way in the representation of death we have insofar seen. Indeed, either as strict images of death, or as metonymies of a dialectic life/death, death is represented through images, that is, through signs. It is Cassandra who marks a passage from narrative to non-linguistic representation. A mythological figure who either does not speak, or, when she does, is not believed, Cassandra invalidates the function of speech as bearer of truth and presence. Her figure, above all, symbolizes the death of language and death as language.

> Lisse-moi, farde-moi. Colore mon absence.
> Désoeuvre ce regard qui méconnaît la nuit.
> Couche sur moi les plis d'un durable silence,
> Éteins avec la lampe une terre d'oubli.
>
> (101)

This third double presence of death (death of language/death as language) is more evident in the poems where the "image" of "Ménade" comes into being. It is not by chance that the first poem where Douve appears as a Maenad is **"Le seul témoin,"** a poem where death is present in a very direct way, as we have already observed. A multidimensional play on vision is the means of this presentation, and the figure of Maenad follows this direction. Maenad as a dionysiac figure refers to an archaic conception of the primordial drama: the act of worship. There representation (*l'intelligible*)

is constituted through an extreme favoring of divine delirium (*le sensible*) that posits even death as its telos (as becomes the case in later representations, i.e., Greek theater). In a similar way, Maenad, a figure who, through an act of extreme incarnation, love, nevertheless kills her victims in the end, appears in the poem "consumée" herself. In part III of the same poem, we have another appearance of her death and her reconciliation with nothingness, with an "ombre."

But more than a simple metonymy for death, the image of Maenad has an implication of another dimension. Her dionysiac character can also be seen as a return to a prelinguistic state of things, where pure presence was available since no language existed that could "put distance between men and things." As has been put, "le dionysisme est interprétable comme une lutte contre l'"aveuglement" du concept et comme un refus de l'autonomie du signe linguistique" (McAllister, *Ménadisme* 223). The only way that Douve herself, as Maenad, can be presented is through an expression of sublimity, of non-representability, an exclamation that means nothing because, at the same time, it comprises everything: "ô." We are reminded of the Kantian typology of the sublime, where pleasure and pain arise in the subject as a result of the violence done to the imagination by the unboundedness of the referent which awakens the desire for its representation (Kant 114-115). The Maenad is, accordingly, always introduced with the sublime "ô." And it seems that for Bonnefoy there is only one way that the unrepresentable can be represented:

> Art poétique
> Visage séparé de ses branches premières
> Beauté toute d'alarme par ciel bas,
>
> En quel âtre dresser le feu de ton visage
> O Ménade saisie jetée la tête en bas?
>
> (78)

Where are beauty and sublimity to be housed? The question is rhetorical, of course, since the title provides the answer: this "âtre" is poetry, in the shift in the status of representation the latter enacts. What is at stake here is the difference between poetic language and ordinary language: "[l]e langage poétique n'est pas la relation d'un signifié et d'un signifiant, mais l'acte qui fait passer du non-être qui précède l'oeuvre à l'être qu'elle sera" (qtd. in Fauskevåg 241). If "[the language of concepts] leads to the fragmentation of demonstration, the divisions and reifications of structure and reason, [the language of presence, on the other hand,] offers a totality, an identity, a destiny that eschew all sectioning and reduction" (Bishop 203). It is within the framework of a language of presence that "Ménade" is simultaneously what has created the poem and what is created by it. But precisely because of that every attempt to approach this figure in terms of language is doomed to fail, since ordinary language annuls presence. We cannot "explain" what the Maenad is, because she "is" herself the death of language but "she" also is death insofar as she is language.

Death, therefore, becomes "a category in this poem which involves not only inevitable physical decomposition but also the inertia and lifelessness of established representation, that paralysis of *la langue* and the ever renewed struggle of *la parole* to pass beyond, to resurrect from the ashes of a spiritless 'letter'" (Naughton 46). The undermining of "established representation" seems to be Bonnefoy's constant task throughout **Douve**: indeed, strange, unusual images can be found throughout the poem. But if the image of the Maenad symbolizes the death of language, there are poems where the death of image is also proclaimed. It is now a specific poetics which is the target, the poetics of image as conventional sign. It is not that various figures, for instance, are presented as whichever symbols, as is the case of Phoenix or the Salamander, but rather the specific annulment of the idea of the image itself, the death of the image, so to speak, and the *laying bare* of a poetic device.

> Ton visage ce soir éclairé par la terre,
> Mais je vois tes yeux se corrompre
> Et le mot visage n'a plus de sens.
>
> La mer intérieure éclairée d'aigles tournants,
> Ceci est une image.
> Je te détiens froide à une profondeur où les images ne
>   prennent plus.
>
> (57)

Here Douve's face, through a poetic inversion, will be illuminated by earth (instead of sun, for instance); but before the image becomes complete, the poetic subject sees her eyes fall apart and comments that the word "face" does not mean anything anymore. The poetic subject itself annuls the very image it has created, somewhat recognizing the impossibility of description. The description started in the second stanza is annulled in a similar way. After its beginning, the narrator intervenes to inform the reader that "this is an image." Finally, in the last line of the poem, we have an explicit invalidation of the idea of the image itself. As James McAllister puts it, the image "slip[s] away from the fixity of the trace, broken before it attains a monolithic association of signifier and signified, as successive detours inscribe their variant Douve figures in a complex network of reprises. [. . .] This unrepresented pretextual Douve is the icon that the text gradually elaborates as orientation, beyond the sign, toward an ineffable experience of being" (*Image* 100).

Another side of this second level of the representation of death as the "death of the image," is the annihilation of the "metrical image," of the "metrical frame" itself.

If we adopt John Hollander's differentiation between "rhythm" and "meter," according to which "rhythm" characterizes the series of actual effects upon our consciousness of a line or passage of verse," while "meter [. . .] appl[ies] to whatever it was that might constitute the framing, the isolating" (135-136), then Bonnefoy very often annuls the "image" of rhythm imprinted upon the reader's mind as a result of the poem's perfect alexandrins, for instance, by introducing a metrically disruptive line. This results in the *defamiliarization* of the reader who is following the path of the rhythm, and is inscribed into the same device of rendering poetics itself a literary device. Such a treatment of the "rhythmical image" is repeated throughout the poem.

To intermingle poetic material (in our case, various sorts and "levels" of images) with devices of poetics proper, or, in other words, to render the process of poetic creation into poetic myth itself, can only take place through the cancellation of conventional imagery. The poem that best captures the impossibility of images as an image itself is one from **"Derniers Gestes:"**

> Que saisir sinon qui s'échappe,
> Que voir sinon qui s'obscurcit,
> Que désirer sinon qui meurt,
> Sinon qui parle et se déchire?
>
> Parole proche de moi
> Que chercher sinon ton silence,
> Quelle lueur sinon profonde
> Ta conscience ensevelie,
>
> Parole jetée matérielle
> Sur l'origine et la nuit.
>
> (66)

This new image tries to realize the impossible in a seemingly contradictory and paradoxical endeavor. It seeks to represent the unrepresentable, by attempting to capture what cannot be captured, see the unseeable, desire the annulment of desire, look for the silence of speech. The "sinon" reveals the imperative of this attempt. Another poem that perhaps illustrates better this effort is the following:

> La lumière profonde a besoin pour paraître
> D'une terre rouée et craquante de la nuit.
> C'est d'un bois ténébreux que la flamme s'exalte.
> Il faut à la parole même une matière,
> Un inerte rivage au delà de tout chant.
>
> Il te faudra franchir la mort pour que tu vives,
> La plus pure présence est un sang répandu.
>
> (74)

What is explicitly at stake here is not only how to capture *le sensible,* but also the necessity of such an attempt (Naughton 59). To the difficulty of such a task, only faith can provide the force: "[o]n ne doit jamais abandonner tout espoir" (Bonnefoy, *Fonction* 273). "When words revealed death to men, when conceptual notions put distance between them and things [. . .] something in fact like faith was needed for us to carry on with words; and everything indicates that it is also in words themselves—but this time understood as *names,* cried or called out in the midst of absence—that this faith has sought its way" (Bonnefoy, *Image and Presence* 168) (emphasis added). Faith in words, accordingly, is the first step in capturing *le sensible.* And this operation will not take place in an abstract, conceptual way: "[j]e ne poserai pas de quelque façon philosophique le problème du sensible. Affirmer, tel est mon souci" (*Tombeaux* 24). The affirmation is realized through a poetic device: the creation of Douve, a sign which is, at the same time, a name, a referent, an image and a metonymy.

Carrie Jaurès Noland has codified the various levels of approaching this cryptic name. We would like to focus on Douve's double aspect. On the one hand, the word "douve" exists in French, and the *image* of its signification inevitably comes to mind: "douve" is a moat around a castle.

> Douve sera ton nom au loin parmi les pierres,
> Douve profonde et noire,
> Eau basse irréductible où l'effort se perdra.
>
> (104)

The castle is thus protected by the moat; the moat guarantees its safety through the perdition of the trespassers. In this aspect, the linguistic sign "douve" is itself an image of death. But what is this castle that the moat surrounds to protect?

> Je nommerai désert ce château que tu fus,
> Nuit cette voix, absence ton visage,
> Et quand tu tomberas dans la terre stérile
> Je nommerai néant l'éclair qui t'a porté.
>
> (73)

From death as an image ("douve"), we pass to the death of imagery as we saw it above. Things are renamed and a double image is at play, that of the previous referent and that of the new one. Thus "château" becomes "désert," "voix" becomes "nuit," "visage" becomes "absence," "éclair" becomes "néant." This is why the poem is called "vrai nom." Douve as a name, as a proper name, is inscribed in the same problematics. The poetic voice gives to the "castle" which Douve as moat is supposed to protect the name "désert." What is surrounded by the moat is nothingness; the very existence of the castle is undermined. But the disappearance of the castle entails a shift in emphasis. When both the moat and the castle are there, what is at stake is the safety of the castle; but if the castle does not exist, the focus is shifted from the surrounded to the surrounding, the moat itself.

The only thing we know about this moat is its name, Douve. But who or what is Douve? Bonnefoy talks about her: "[e]t si j'ai éprouvé si intensément pour ma part l'attrait d'un vocable qu'un moment de mon écriture avait vidé de tout sens, c'était certes d'abord parce que sa syncope dans l'énoncé avait incité, comme je l'ai dit, à la décoagulation, à l'espoir, mais aussi parce que "Douve", c'était déjà un nom, un nom propre, ce qui suggère sous son énigme une veille, qui nous concerne, et non un en-soi, une indifférence. Un visage, non une essence. En poésie il n'y a jamais que de noms propres" (*Entretiens* 141). Thus, what is functioning here is the double aspect of the sign "Douve." Douve the noun has a particular referent, but Douve the name comprises all the characteristics of proper names. As Lyotard puts it, "[n]ames transform *now* into a date, *here* into a place, *I, you, he* into Jean, Pierre, Louis. [. . .] Names grouped into calendars, cartographical systems, genealogies and civil statutes are *indicators of possible reality* (emphasis added). They present their referents, dates, places, and human beings as givens. A phrase, otherwise deprived of deictic marks, presents *Rome* instead of *over-there.* The name Rome acts like a deictic: the referent, the addressor, and the addressee are situated in relation to an "as-if right here [*comme-si ici*]" (Lyotard 39). "Reality is not expressed therefore by a phrase like: *x is such,* but by one like: *x is such and not such*" (45). Whereas the common name can have universal reference, the proper name refers, on the contrary, exclusively to one reality to whose uniqueness it responds.

To give a unique proper name means to baptize; to baptize alludes to a divine power, since, by naming, one creates a being. For Benjamin, for instance, "[t]he absolute relationship of name to knowledge exists only in God, only there is a name, because it is inwardly identical with the creative word, the pure medium of knowledge" (323). God/the poetic subject has brought Douve into existence in a process similar to the biblical "in the beginning was the Word." Douve comes into being because she is named.

The divine character of naming is evident in the implications of the "breath:"

> A peine si je sens ce souffle qui me nomme.
>
> (79)

In *Genesis,* chapter 2, we read: "then the Lord formed man out of the dust of the ground and breathed into his nostrils the breath of life, and man became a living being." In a similar operation, it is now Douve who, through a poetic breath, has acquired life. Once a living being, to question "who is Douve" is irrelevant. Douve is Douve, in a similar way that God is God: "I am the being" (or "I am the one who is") God replies when asked who he is. To a question of knowledge (*intelligible*) God answers with a verb of presence (*sensible*), in an apparently tautological sentence. In a similar way, then, "[. . .] Douve is absolutely nothing beyond the long and taunting place called **Douve**" (Argyros 263):

> [. . .] je t'enserre
> Dans l'acte de connaître et de nommer.
>
> (77)

What thus realizes a passage to incarnation is the name. Its unique referentiality captures the real, and is explicitly contrasted to the universal referentiality of the noun which creates distance from it. Since it is by nature an intelligible form, *the common noun* can be approached in terms of language; it can answer the question "what is it." But any attempt to explicate *a name* in intelligible terms is not simply doomed to fail; it is irrelevant altogether. This is why Bonnefoy insists: "je ne prétends que nommer. Voici le monde sensible. Il faut que la parole, ce sixième et ce plus haut sens, se porte à sa rencontre et en déchiffre les signes" (*Tombeaux* 25).

Thus "l' acte de saisie et de nomination de Douve se confond avec un acte de saisie et de nomination du réel" (Jackson 253). And this has to presuppose and proclaim the death of re-presentation in favor of presentation. The literary history of the poetics of such an impossibility comprises significant figures, and this paper has attempted to analyze one of the ways Bonnefoy is inscribed in it.

Notes

1. See Ora Avni, "Breton et l'idéologie . . .".

2. I shall henceforth be using the French term *sensible,* since the English "sensible" has different connotations.

3. Expressed at its best in *The Differend, Phrases in Dispute,* according to which a phrase is the only thing that is "indubitable [. . .], because it is immediately presupposed" (xi). There are phrases, therefore, *there are* to be understood in its most existential meaning. "There is no non-phrase" (xii). As opposed to "language," which is an articulate form of expression, "phrase" can be any semantic unit, articulate or not. There is neither a first nor a last phrase: silence and death are also phrases. Each phrase involves an addressor, an addressee and a meaning; whether there is a reference or not depends on whether the phrase is articulate or not. "A phrase, even the most ordinary one, is constituted according to a set of rules (its regimen)" (xii).

4. The etymology of the German words elucidates from another angle than that of Derrida's translation the poetics of Bonnefoy: "Gegen-wärtigung,"

literally "against waiting" explains this notion of im-mediate, atemporal, incarnate, *sensible* present, as opposed to the notion of "making it (as if) against waiting" of "Ver-gegen-wärtigung."

5. All page numbers refer to the Gallimard edition.

Works Cited

Argyros, Alex. "The Topography of Presence: Bonnefoy and the Spatialization of Poetry." *Orbis Litterarum* 41.3 (1986): 244-264.

Avni, Ora. "Breton et l'idéologie machine à coudre—parapluie." *Littérature* 51 (1983): 15-27.

Avni, Ora. *The Resistance of Reference.* Baltimore: The Johns Hopkins UP, 1990.

Benjamin, Walter. "On Language as Such and on the Language of Man." *Reflections.* Tr. Edmund Jephcott. New York: Schocken, 1978, 314-332.

Bishop, Michael. "An Infinity of Flashing Briefness: The Poetics of Yves Bonnefoy." *Neophilologus* LXX. 2 (1986): 194-207.

Bonnefoy, Yves. "Les tombeaux de Ravenne." *L'improbable.* Paris: Mercure de France, 1959, 9-34.

Bonnefoy, Yves. "The Feeling of Transcendancy." *Yale French Studies* 31 (1964): 135-137.

Bonnefoy, Yves. "The Origins and Development of my Concept of Poetry: An Interview with John E. Jackson (1976)." *The Act . . .* 143-155.

Bonnefoy, Yves. "Sur la fonction du poème." *Nuage rouge.* Paris: Mercure de France, 1977, 267-283.

Bonnefoy, Yves. *Entretiens sur la poésie,* Neuchâtel, Suisse: Éd. de la Baconnière, 1981.

Bonnefoy, Yves. *Poèmes.* Paris: Gallimard, 1982.

Bonnefoy, Yves. "'Image and Presence': Inaugural Address at the Collège de France." *The Act and the Place of Poetry, Selected Essays.* Ed John T. Naughton. Chicago: U of Chicago P, 1989, 156-172.

Breton, André. *Oeuvres complètes.* Paris: Pléiade, 1988.

Derrida, Jacques. *La voix et le phénomène.* Paris: PUF, 1967.

Fauskevåg, Svein Eirik. "Yves Bonnefoy et le réalisme poétique." *Orbis Litterarum* 41.3 (1986): 229-243.

Hollander, John. *Vision and Resonance: Two Senses of Poetic Form.* 2nd ed. New Haven: Yale UP, 1985.

Jackson, John E. *La question du sujet, un aspect de la modernité poétique européenne.* Neuchâtel, Suisse: Éd. de la Baconnière, 1978.

Jakobson, Roman. "Linguistics ans Poetics." *Language in Literature.* Ed. Krystyna Pomorska, Stephen Rudy. Cambridge: Harvard UP, 1987, 62-94.

Jameson, Fredric. *The Prison-House of Language: A Critical Account of Structuralism and Russian Formalism.* Princeton: Princeton UP, 1972.

Kant, Immanuel. *Critique of Judgment.* Tr. Werner S. Pluhar. Indianapolis: Hackett, 1987.

Lyotard, Jean-François. *The Differend: Phrases in Dispute.* Tr. G. Van Den Abbeele. Minneapolis: U of Minnesota P, 1988.

McAllister, James. "Le ménadisme de Douve." *Studia Neophilologica* 61.2 (1989): 221-231.

McAllister, James. "The Image and the Furrow: Yves Bonnefoy, Claude Garache." *Symposium* XLV. 2 (1991): 97-108.

Naughton, John T. *The Poetics of Yves Bonnefoy.* Chicago: U of Chicago P, 1984.

Noland, Carrie Jaurès. "What's in a Name? Yves Bonnefoy and the Creation of 'Douve'." *French Forum.* 17.3 (1992): 311-328.

Saussure, Ferdinand de. *Course in General Linguistics.* Tr. Roy Harris. La Salle, Illinois: Open Court, 1983.

FURTHER READING

Criticism

Bishop, Michael. "An Infinity of Flashing Briefness: The Poetics of Yves Bonnefoy." *Neophilologus* 70, no. 2 (April 1986): 194-207.

Articulates the principal features of Bonnefoy's poetics through an examination of his verse.

———. "Image, *Justesse,* and Love: Breton, Reverdy, and Bonnefoy." *Symposium* 42, no. 3 (fall 1988): 187-97.

Examines questions of love, being, and consciousness in the work of Andre Breton, Pierre Reverdy, and Yves Bonnefoy.

Bonnefoy, Yves. "Lifting Our Eyes from the Page." *Critical Inquiry* 16, no. 4 (summer 1990): 794-806.

Bonnefoy addresses the reading of poetry.

Caws, Mary Ann. *Yves Bonnefoy.* Boston: Twayne Publishers, 1984, 114 p.

Biographical and critical study.

Giskin, Howard. "Yves Bonnefoy's Conception of Poetry in *Pierre écrite.*" *Tropos* 13, no. 1 (spring 1986): 23-35.

Contends that Bonnefoy viewed his poetry in *Pierre écrite* as the highest expression of reality.

Hochman, Hugh. "Yves Bonnefoy's Materialist Words." *Dalhousie French Studies* 60 (fall 2002): 94-100.

Examines Bonnefoy's verse in light of the classical materialism of Epicurus and Lucretius.

Lawall, Sarah N., and Mary Ann Caws. "A Style of Silence: Two Readings of Yves Bonnefoy's Poetry." *Contemporary Literature* 16, no. 2 (spring 1975): 193-217.

Provides two readings on the theme of silence in Bonnefoy's poetry.

Lawall, Sarah. "Bonnefoy's *Pierre écrite*: Progressive Ambiguity as the Many in the One." In *The Ladder of High Designs: Structure and Interpretation of the French Lyric Sequence,* edited by Doranne Fenoaltea and David Lee Rubin, pp. 172-98. Charlottesville: University Press of Virginia, 1991.

Maintains that *Pierre écrite* "sets into play two complementary notions of unity: a formal unity that is demonstrated only to be denied, and the vision of a proximate One whose definition accumulates substance but not fixity throughout an expanding series of associations."

Maurin, Mario. "On Bonnefoy's Poetry." *Yale French Studies,* no. 21 (1958): 16-22.

Evaluates *On the Motion and Immobility of Douve* within the French poetic tradition.

McAllister, James. "The Image and the Furrow: Yves Bonnefoy, Claude Garache." *Symposium* 45, no. 2 (summer 1991): 97-108.

Investigates affinities between *On the Motion and Immobility of Douve* and the painted images of Claude Garache.

———. "Yves Bonnefoy and John Constable: 'La tâche terrestre, délivrée.'" *Romance Notes* 32, no. 3 (spring 1992): 281-89.

Considers the relationship between John Constable's series of sketches entitled *Dedham from Langham* and Bonnefoy's poem of the same name.

Naughton, John T. *The Poetics of Yves Bonnefoy,* Chicago: The University of Chicago Press, 1984, 209 p.

Full-length study of Bonnefoy's verse and poetic theory.

———, ed. *Yves Bonnefoy: The Act and the Place of Poetry.* Chicago: The University of Chicago Press, 1989, 172 p.

Collection of critical essays.

Noland, Carrie Jaurés. "Yves Bonnefoy and Julia Kristeva: The Poetics of Motherhood." *Poetry and Poetics* 18 (1991): 134-44.

Asserts that Bonnefoy and Julia Kristeva frequently refer to the maternal figure in their poetic theories.

Petterson, James. "Yves Bonnefoy and the Absence of Myth." In *Postwar Figures of* L'Ephémère: *Yves Bonnefoy, Louis-René des Forêts, Jacques Dupin, André du Bouchet*, pp. 21-62. Cranbury, N.J.: Associated University Presses, 2000.

Elucidates the role of mythology in Bonnefoy's verse.

Prothin, Annie. "The Substantive Language of Yves Bonnefoy." *Sub-Stance,* no. 20 (1978): 45-58.

Illustrates "how Bonnefoy's poetry incorporates into the text, by means of grammatical categories and a particular lexicon, an original poetics which is deeply embedded in his poetry."

Stamelman, Richard. "Landscape and Loss in Yves Bonnefoy and Philippe Jaccottet." *French Forum* 5, no. 1 (January 1980): 30-47.

Demonstrates "how the experience of loss and of death is supported and confirmed by the poet's experience of landscape" in the verse of Bonnefoy and Philippe Jaccottet.

————. "The 'Presence' of Memory." *L'Esprit Créateur* 36, no. 3 (fall 1996): 65-79.

Investigates the role of memory in Bonnefoy's work.

Vernier, Richard. "Yves Bonnefoy and the Conscience of Poetry." *Sub-Stance,* nos. 23-24 (1979): 149-56.

Surveys the defining characteristics of Bonnefoy's poetry.

————. "From Critical to Poetic Discourse: Bonnefoy and Poussin." *L'Esprit Créateur* 22, no. 4 (winter 1982): 37-46.

Analyzes Bonnefoy's theory of the relationship between painted and poetic images.

Winspur, Steven. "Yves Bonnefoy's Three Strikes against the Sign." *Romanic Review* 77, no. 2 (March 1986): 155-65.

Explicates Bonnefoy's theory of language and assesses its consequences for his poetry.

Additional coverage of Bonnefoy's life and career is contained in the following sources published by Thomson Gale: *Contemporary Authors,* **Vols. 85-88;** *Contemporary Authors New Revision Series,* **Vols. 33, 75, 97;** *Contemporary Literary Criticism,* **Vols. 9, 15, 58;** *Contemporary World Writers,* **Ed. 2;** *Dictionary of Literary Biography,* **Vol. 258;** *DISCovering Authors Modules: Most-studied Authors* **and** *Poets*; *Encyclopedia of World Literature in the 20th Century,* **Ed. 3;** *Guide to French Literature: 1789 to the Present*; *Literature Resource Center*; **and** *Major 20th-Century Writers,* **Eds. 1, 2.**

John Cage
1912-1992

(Full name John Milton Cage, Jr.) American poet, composer, essayist, and graphic artist.

INTRODUCTION

Inventive and experimental, Cage was an influential and controversial avant-garde composer of music and poetry. In his works, he relentlessly strove to enhance and perfect the visual and aural texture of music, language, and art. His innovative work with mesostics—poetry and prose arranged to spell out words and ideas vertically through the text—and creative use of punctuation reflected his belief that language is merely a tool of art and can be manipulated to provide the reader with multiple avenues of interpretation.

BIOGRAPHICAL INFORMATION

Cage was born on September 5, 1912, in Los Angeles, California, to John Cage, Sr., an inventor, and Lucretia Harvey Cage, a journalist. An exemplary student, he was the valedictorian of his class in high school. Upon graduation in 1928, he enrolled in Pomona College but left after two years. He then traveled through Europe and studied music composition, piano, painting, and poetry. He returned to the United States in the early 1930s, and in 1934 began three years of study with the composer Arnold Schoenberg in Los Angeles. In 1935 Cage married Xenia Andreyevna Kashevaroff, and two years later they moved to Seattle, where he took a teaching position at the Cornish School. While in Seattle, he met the dancer Merce Cunningham, with whom he later frequently collaborated, and he was introduced to the principles of Zen Buddhism. He relocated to New York in 1942 and became acquainted with the artists Jasper Johns, Robert Rauschenberg, and Marcel Duchamp, the composers David Tudor and Morton Feldman, and the Zen scholar Daisetz Teitaro Suzuki. Cage began in the early 1950s to read the *I Ching,* an ancient Chinese text used in a form of divination in which the results of the tossing of coins is related to specific passages. This reading led him to experiment with incorporating elements of chance into his musical and poetic compositions. In the 1960s he began using the *I Ching* to create poems, deriving them from the works of other writers, such as James Joyce's *Finnegans Wake* and Henry David Thoreau's *Journals.* He also developed his me-

sostics. Cage continued to experiment with sounds, silences, and languages, and to perform innovative "lectures" and readings until his death in 1992.

MAJOR POETIC WORKS

Cage's early career was primarily devoted to composing music, and his first experiments with nontraditional sounds were in this medium. He placed various objects on piano strings to change the tone of the instrument, used electronic sounds in his performances, and incorporated silence as an integral part of music. As he began to explore poetics and language, Cage blended musical qualities with the spoken word. *Silences* (1961), *A Year from Monday* (1967), and *Pour les ouiseaux* (1976; *For the Birds*) contain many of these performance pieces and innovative writings. Cage's mesostics, a type of visual and textual poetry that reflected Cage's appreciation for chance events, are included in *Sixty-Two Mesostics re: Merce Cunningham* (1971) and

M: Writings, '67-'72 (1973). He also created pieces that applied the principles of the *I Ching* to texts written by others. *Mureau* (1970; collected in *M*) was derived from Henry David Thoreau's *Journals* (the title comes from combining the words "music" and "Thoreau"); and *Writings through Finnegans Wake* (1978) was based on James Joyce's work. In *Empty Words: Writings, '73-'78* (1979), Cage continued to develop poems with freedom of form and innumerable possibilities of interpretation. He further investigated free form in *Themes & Variations* (1982) and *X: Writings '79-'82* (1983).

CRITICAL RECEPTION

Due to their iconoclastic nature, Cage's poetic works at first did not receive favorable mainstream criticism, and much of the commentary they did receive was uncomprehending, bemused, or indifferent. As Cage further developed his ideas and style, however, reviewers began to recognize the artistry of his poetics. Observers increasingly applauded Cage's attempts to free poetry from the constraints of language, incorporating a significant element of chance into his compositions while, in an apparent paradox, adhering to consistent forms and techniques. In the view of a number of critics, Cage's works derived from other's texts, such as *Mureau* and *Writings through Finnegans Wake,* enhance the understanding and appreciation of the originals. Many commentators now acknowledge his important contributions to music and poetry and consider Cage one of the most influential avant-garde artists of the twentieth century.

PRINCIPAL WORKS

Poetry

Sixty-Two Mesostics re: Merce Cunningham 1971
Writings through Finnegans Wake 1978
Empty Words: Writings, '73-'78 1979
Another Song 1981
Themes & Variations 1982
X: Writings '79-'82 1983

Other Major Works

Silence: Lectures and Writings (essays, poetry, and lectures) 1961
A Year from Monday: New Lectures and Writings (essays, poetry, and lectures) 1967

Diary: How to Improve the World (You Will Only Make Matters Worse) Continued, Part 3 (poetry and lectures) 1967
M: Writings, '67-'72 (poetry and lectures) 1973
Pour les ouiseaux: entretiens avec Daniel Charles [For the Birds] (lectures, poetry, and conversations) 1976
I-VI (lectures) 1990
John Cage, Writer: Previously Uncollected Pieces (poetry and prose) 1993

CRITICISM

John Cage and Richard Kostelanetz (interview date 1974-75)

SOURCE: Cage, John, and Richard Kostelanetz. "Empty Words (1974-1975)." In *John Cage (ex)plain(ed),* pp. 115-32. New York: Schirmer, 1996.

[*In the following interview, conducted in 1974-75, Cage discusses* Mureau, *his work on Thoreau's* Journal *and explains his experiments with the structure and sound of language in* Empty Words.]

> I was always impressed by John Cage's statement that when you build a structure that strong you can accept all sorts of things into it.
>
> —Robert Dunn, in an interview with Don McDonagh, *The Rise and Fall and Rise of Modern Dance* (1970)

Language was the base of much of John Cage's work in the 1970s and 1980s—language that is meant to be read and spoken without specific pitches (that would, by contrast, make the words song). These works are not essays, or even antiessays, like his earlier "Lecture on Nothing" (1959). As literary creations these later works are generically closer to poetry than to essays or fiction in that they represent compressions of language rather than extensions into narrative (fiction) or definitions of extrinsic reality (essays). Cage's first departure in this poetic direction was the essayistic **"Diaries,"** produced in the late sixties, which are, in essence, a formally rigorous and typographically various shorthand for miscellaneous remarks. Three of these **"Diaries"** appeared in *A Year from Monday* (1967), and in the course of reviewing this book I suggested that Cage's work with words had not been as radical as his work with sound. Rather than dispute me, Cage remembered my criticisms (and repeatedly reminded me that he had) and moved ahead. He made a sequence of cleverly structured visual poems in memory of his friend Marcel Duchamp, *Not Wanting To Say Anything About Marcel* (1969), and then *Sixty-two Mesostics re Merce Cun-*

ningham (1971), a series of vertically organized words that exploit the unique possibilities of rub-off lettering. He developed, in **Mureau** (1971), a nonsyntactic prose that was based not, like the **"Diaries,"** upon his own experience and his own language, but upon words drawn from Henry David Thoreau's *Journal*. He further extended this line of work in his 1979 book, **Empty Words.**

Empty Words contains expository essays on "The Future of Music" and "How the Piano Came to Be Prepared." Both of these are of interest to followers of Cage's musical thinking. Another section, ostensibly about both the choreographer Merce Cunningham and food, illustrates Cage's genius for storytelling. However, most of this book contains language constructions that must be called "poetry," partly because they are not prose but mostly because they cannot be persuasively classified as anything else. Because these poems are radically unlike everything else in American writing today, it is scarcely surprising that they are rarely discussed by "poetry critics" and never mentioned in the current surveys of American literature.

Notwithstanding his advocacy of "chance" and artistic freedom, Cage was a poetic formalist who invented alternative ways of *structuring* language. One device is the mesostic. Whereas the familiar acrostic has a word running down the left-hand margin of several lines, the mesostic has a recognizable word running down the middle. In Cagean practice, this vertical word is usually the name of a friend—Merce Cunningham, Jasper Johns, Norman O. Brown. Within this mesostic constraint, Cage makes concise statements:

```
        not Just
          gArdener
     morelS
          coPrini
       morEls
        cop Rini.
          not Just hunter:
     cutting dOwn
       ailan tHus
         cuttiNg down
     ailanthuS.
```

The title piece of **Empty Words** is a four-part poem drawn from Henry David Thoreau's remarks about music and sound. Cage copied relevant passages out of Thoreau's journals and then subjected them to *I Ching*-aided chance processes that, in effect, scrambled and combined them, eventually producing a nonsyntactic pastiche of Thoreau's language:

```
        speaksix round and longer than
   the shelloppressed and
   now ten feet high hero Theclosely isor
        have looked wellthat and spruces
   the and a darker line below it
```

This stanza comes from the first page of the first part, which contains phrases, words, syllables, and letters (characters) from Thoreau. The second part of **"Empty Words"** contains just his words, syllables, and letters; the third part just syllables and letters; and the fourth part just letters.

Cage's long poem **"Empty Words"** is less about Thoreau than about sound, or the sound of language about sound, compressed and recombined; reading it is not about assuaging our powers of literary understanding but about challenging and expanding them. This is rigorously Platonic poetry that takes initially spiritual literature and recomposes it into a yet more ethereal realm. In my opinion, **"Empty Words"** is better heard than read.

Scarcely contented with past poetic inventions, Cage developed a series of conceptually ambitious schemes for extracting language from James Joyce's multilingual masterpiece, *Finnegans Wake*. In the initial scheme, Cage worked from the beginning of Joyce's book to its end, extracting words that contain letters that fit into a mesostic structure based upon the name "James Joyce." Since the first *J* in *Finnegans Wake* appears in the word "nathandjoe," Cage took out that word and then, by a decision of taste, decided to take as well the three adjacent words to the left of it (ignoring those to the right). For the *a* of "James" he selected only the article (and implicitly decided against both sets of words adjacent to it). The next *m* appears in the word "malt"; the next *e* in "Jhem"; and the next *s* in "Shen." Thus, Cage's opening stanza reads:

```
   wroth with twone nathandJoe
              A
            Malt
            jhEm
            Shen
```

It is a simple measure of Cage's originality that nobody ever made poetry like this before—the method is, like so much of his work, at once sensible and nutty. To my mind, **Writing Through Finnegans Wake** is interesting in part because it is so audaciously innovative; it succeeds in part because it recycles James Joyce. Hearing Cage read it aloud, with sensitive precision, was a special pleasure.

Empty Words contains only the second of Cage's workings with the *Wake*; the first, longer Joyce piece appeared initially as a special issue of the *James Joyce Quarterly* and has since been reissued as a book, **Writing Through Finnegans Wake** (1978). Both Cage **Wake** pieces appear together in a third book, a large-format signed and limited edition titled **Writings Through Finnegans Wake** (1978) (note the plural in the first word). Reproducing Cage's manuscript in its original size, this sumptuously produced volume is superior to the reduced versions, even though its high price is amenable, alas, primarily to libraries and collectors of Cage's visual art.

Cage described **Empty Words** as progressing, over its four parts, from literature to music, and it seems to me that both this work and its Joycean successor finally realized an identity between the two traditional arts. *Text-sound* is the epithet I use to define language works that cohere primarily in terms of sound rather than syntax or semantics; and Cage, as a literary musician, was clearly a master of that domain. On the other hand, because both **Empty Words** and **Writings Through Finnegans Wake** are language-based, they fit snugly into the great American tradition of poetry that realizes an eccentric innovation in the machinery of the art—a radical change not in meaning or in sensibility but in the materials indigenous to poetry: language, line, syntax, and meter. (In this sense Cage's principal poetic precursors are Whitman, Cummings, and Gertrude Stein.) Considered in this way, Cage was not a literary curiosity but an exemplary American poet.

I spoke with Cage about how he created these unusual literary works, including **Mureau** and **Empty Words**; here's some of his thoughts.

[Cage]: Having agreed to write a text about electronic music, and having noticed that HDT—that's Thoreau— listened to sound as electronic composers listen to it, not just to musical sounds but to noises and ambient sound generally, it occurred to me that making a chance-determined mix of his remarks in the *Journal* about sound, silence, and music would make a text relevant to electronic music. Therefore, I gave it the title **Mu**(music)**reau**(Thoreau). I went through the index of the Dover edition of the *Journal,* and I noticed every occurrence in the index of anything that could be remotely thought to be connected with music, and then I listed all of those appearances; then I subjected it all to chance operations in terms of sentences, phrases, words, syllables, and letters. I made a permutation of those five possibilities, so that it could be each of the five alone, or in any groups of two, or any groups of three, or any groups of four, or finally all five.

[Kostelanetz]: *In gathering the original material for* **Mureau,** *you took phrases out of Thoreau and sentences out of Thoreau and words out of Thoreau.*

First I listed all the things having to do with sound. Then I asked, what it was of all those permuted possibilities I was looking for, whether I was looking for all five together or a group of four of them, or a group of three or a group of two or one. And when I knew what I was doing, my next question was for how many events was I doing it? And the answer could be

anywhere from one to sixty-four. Let's say I got twenty-three. Then if I knew that I was looking for twenty-three events which were any of these five, then I asked of this five which is the first one. Which is the second? Which is the third? So I knew finally what I was doing. And then when I knew what I was doing, I did it.

How did you decide to begin work, in the case of **Mureau***?*

I wanted to make a text that would have four parts, and it was written for a magazine in Minneapolis called *Synthesis*. And they were written to be columns. I was a columnist for the magazine. I don't think of these texts as lectures. They were conceived as columns, initially, and if you'll notice, the columns have different widths. I did that on purpose.

I was continuing **Mureau,** but extending it beyond Thoreau's remarks about sound and music to the whole of the *Journal*. To begin with, I omitted sentences, and I thought of **Empty Words** as a transition from literature to music.

In the first notebooks of **Empty Words,** each part is called a lecture. It was something to be read aloud, and therefore I made it a length that some people would consider excessive; I made a length of two hours and a half for each lecture.

How did you determine that?

Most people consider this excessive, and they don't want me to give it as a lecture. I think that's because the average lecture, say in a college, should be forty minutes.

Why did you make your own lectures nearly four times as long?

I had been very impressed by an experience I had in Japan, in 1964, of going to a Buddhist service. We went to an evening lecture there that went on for hours and hours, and we had been warned that it was going to be tiresome. I was with Merce Cunningham and the Dance Company. It was very cold, and we were not protected by any warmth. They had told us it would be uncomfortable and long, but we were told also that we didn't have the right to leave once we had decided that we wanted to stay. So we all suffered through it, and it went on and on, for something like six hours.

And then a few days later, or maybe it was on another trip to Japan, I was in a Zen temple in Kyoto. When I was invited to go to an early morning Buddhist service, I did. I noticed that after a lengthy service they opened the doors of the temple, and you heard the sounds coming in from the outside. So, putting these two things together, the long night business and then the dawn of the opening of the doors, I thought of the opening of the doors occurring at dawns and making four lectures and the fourth would begin at dawn with the opening of the doors to the outer world so that the sounds would come in—because you see it was a transition from literature to music, and my notion of music has always been ambient sound anyway, silence.

This was Thoreau's notion of music too, you see. Music is continual, he said; it's only listening which is intermittent. I can read to you from the *Journal* long passages written when he was twenty-one years old, if you please, or twenty-two at the most, on the subject of silence. He said silence was a sphere, and sounds were bubbles on its surface. Isn't that beautiful?

So your idea of **Empty Words** *was a lecture heard for ten hours. . . .*

And you'd have half-hour intermissions between the parts. So you'd first have to find out when dawn was coming, the way fishermen do, and then you'd figure back and you'd finally know when the lecture was to begin. So, with three half-hour intermissions, you'd therefore have to begin eleven and a half hours before dawn. I then thought, probably because of Margaret Mead, that those intermissions should include food, that people eating together is an important thing and that is basic to Margaret Mead's notion of ritual.

So that's how the record of **Empty Words** *should ideally be heard as well?*

Yes, during that length of time, if one does listen to it over that length of time, there should be periods when one stops listening and has something to eat.

Why does it have the title **Empty Words**?

It comes from a description of the Chinese language that was given to me by William McNaughton, who has made marvelous translations of both Japanese and Chinese texts. The Chinese language, he said, has "full words" and "empty words." Full words are words that are nouns or verbs or adjectives or adverbs. We don't know in Chinese which of these a full word is. The word is so full that it could be any of them. For instance, the word "red" is an adjective. It could be—I'm hypothesizing now—it could be the same as the verb to blush, to turn red. It could be the same as ruby or cherry, if those were names for red. It is a full word because it has several semantic possibilities. It can mean any one of those things. An empty word, by contrast, is a connective or a pronoun—a word that refers to something else. Or it has no meaning by itself. For example, if I say to you "it," that would be an empty word. But if I said "microphone," that would be a full word. I would

like with my title to suggest the emptiness of meaning that is characteristic of musical sounds. That is to say they exist by themselves—that when words are seen from a musical point of view, they are all empty.

You had this notion of **Empty Words** *in your mind at the beginning. You also had the notion of developing a piece that would be away from something that was just read on the page to something that would be performed, as it approaches music.*

The approach to music is made by steadily eliminating one of the aspects of language, so that as we start Lecture One of *Empty Words,* we have no sentences. Though they did exist in *Mureau,* now they're gone. In the second one, the phrases are gone, and in the third part the words are gone, except those that have only one syllable. And in the last one, everything is gone but letters and silences.

So you've had a further reduction within the piece. But let me go back a step. Were the same compositional methods used in manipulating the material from Thoreau in **Mureau** *as were used in* **Empty Words**?

Yes.

Then why is **Mureau** *generally written continuously, like prose?*

Mureau was a column to be printed in a magazine, and **Empty Words** is a lecture. In fact, the whole thing is, through chance operations, put in the form of stanzas. That is to say that one part of it is separated from another part. And the parts were determined by the appearance of a period following whatever word, syllable, or letters that were chance-obtained.

Let me go back to the question of the four major Sections, or "Lectures" as you call them. When did one of them end?

When there were 4,000 events at least. In the case of the First Lecture, there are 4,060, and the reason for that excessive number is this: when I got to making the 3,997th event, I threw a sixty-four, and it took me up to 4,060.

So you did the first 4,060 lines, and thereby finished Part One of **Empty Words.** *In Part Two, you continued with your method but you removed the possibility of phrases. And continued to do the same thing. And in* **Empty Words,** *Three, you removed the possibility of words, so you had just syllables and letters, and then in Four, just letters.*

I had one further idea, but I guess that it doesn't apply to the recording. That was to sit in profile for the first one. Then face the audience for the second one. To sit in profile again but on the other side for the third. And then with my back to the audience for the fourth. And it was actually at Naropa that I sat with my back to the audience, and they became infuriated.

Each of the four works comes with a preface—actually each section has a preface that incorporates the prefaces of its predecessor, until there is a four-part preface to the last one. What are they meant to do?

All the information, all the answers to all the questions, such as those you now are asking me, are given as conscientiously as I can in these introductions. I tried to imagine what it is anyone would want to know and then I give them that information in the introduction, but not in any logical sequence.

How were these prefaces written?

The first thing I did was find out how many words I had at my disposal for the first remark or for the first answer. One, two, three, plus two plus two plus one, eleven. I had eleven words. Now I thought, well, what shall I say. And it occurred to me to say at the beginning how it was that I came to be in connection with Thoreau. That seemed to be a reasonable beginning.

And it reads: "Wendell Berry: Passages outloud from Thoreau's Journal *(Port Royal, Kentucky, 1967)." That's eleven words.*

It was at that time and in that place that Wendell Berry picked up a copy of the *Journal*—we had just had dinner together; I was in his home. He read passages out loud to me. And the moment he did that was the next remark, which has thirty-four words: "Realized I was starved for Thoreau (just as in 1954 when I moved from New York City to Stony Point, I had realized I was starved for nature; took to walking in the woods)." I thought I should have said after that, but I didn't have room, that I took to reading Thoreau just as I had taken to walking in the woods; but I thought that once I'd said it in that way—that since I realized I was starved for Thoreau, I think you'd realize I started reading the *Journal*.

And then, "Agreed to write work for voices (Song books)" and so forth. The third line of the first preface seems like a very long statement, but then you have a very short statement about "Syntax: arrangement of the army," which is a reference to Norman O. Brown's sensitive remark that conventional syntax, in its lining up of words, represents the militarization of language.

These are answers to possible questions about *Empty Words.*

Admittedly in skeletal form. You also explain here how you use the I Ching *in this piece.*

And do you know what? I was able—you see, time passes and I get involved in different projects and I had forgotten—and I had for years been reading Part Three. Every time anyone asked me to give a lecture I would read that. And I forgot how I had read Part One. Or Part Two. And when I tried to do it for the record, I found I couldn't. I didn't know how. So I thought, how will I find out. Then I realized that I'd answered all these questions in the introduction. So I got out the Introduction to Part Three and it says there, "Searching (outloud) for a way to read. Changing frequency. Going up and then going down; going to extremes. Establish (I, II) stanza's time. That brings about a variety of tempi (short stanzas become slow; long become fast)." I counted the number of stanzas and divided the total length, two hours and one-half, by the number of stanzas and thus determined that most of the stanzas in Part One would be forty seconds long. Some, the longer ones, would be a little longer.

In your own score for your readings, what you've done is timed when you should begin each stanza, and beside you as you read is a stopwatch. You have other marks suggesting where words should be divided into syllables. Let's say you have a stanza, like the twenty-third, which has twelve lines. If you have only forty seconds, you'd have to speak quite quickly to get through that.

Right. A stanza that long has to be read very fast. See, it has forty-four seconds actually. In order to make the thing come out evenly with two hours and one-half, I made a complicated but symmetrical arrangement, and I gave a few more seconds to the longer stanzas so that reading them became more practical. Not a great many, but, like, four seconds. I was delighted to learn how to read this and to learn this from my introduction.

That is why those introductions are so important, not only to readers but to you.

There was a criticism of this text by our dear friend Jackson Mac Low in that interesting critical magazine called L=A=N=G=U=A=G=E. Jackson said that though he enjoyed hearing *Empty Words,* he had no interest in reading it. He found that he never picked it up to read. The only reason he doesn't pick up the text is that he doesn't know how to read it. If he knew how to read it, he would immediately become fascinated by it. I've shown that with the recording, and I've found it out from reading the introduction, that the moment you set up the stanza time and then follow that, timed with a stopwatch, then immediately you become fascinated with the whole problem of reading it. That's the musical problem.

Let's go back to the very beginning of Part One, "notAt evening." You have that section marked for forty seconds and the one after that for eighty seconds on the stopwatch and then for one hundred twenty seconds and then the one after that for two minutes. Is it your notion that one should read each part for forty seconds?

No. The forty seconds will include your reading of those lines. And anything else that's in those forty seconds is silence, which is to say ambient sounds.

Therefore, I look at those first three lines, and I have forty seconds to think about them, while I glance at the stopwatch to measure myself. When I look at the next two lines, I get forty more seconds to consider them.

No, no. You read them. You've been advised to do this by James Joyce in connection with *Finnegans Wake*. He says the book was not to be read silently, but should be read out loud.

Out loud to oneself?

Yes. Not just looked at but said out loud.

So just as a Bach score is meant to be taken to the piano to play, **Empty Words** *is meant to be taken with a stopwatch and read aloud to oneself. Or to one's friends, whoever's there. If someone asks you, as I had planned to do, what is the difference between hearing it and reading it, you would reply that there is no reading without hearing—you haven't read the text unless you've heard it.*

So, therefore, one can in eleven hours have the experience, the full experience, of **Empty Words** *entirely by oneself.*

It's conceivable, don't you think, that if someone initiated such a search as that, and such a discipline, that he might discover another way to read it.

I was going to ask about that. Once you've recorded it, haven't you prejudiced its sound, to most of us; and your answer would be, no, I've given you only my way to do it, but that's not necessarily going to be your way to do it.

What then do I hear when I hear you reading it, in performance or on the record? What would I hear when I hear myself reading it?

I think that this is a question that changes with each listener. There are people, as you know, who are color blind. So there must be people who just have no interest in sound whatsoever and who are insensitive to everything in language but "meaning."

And they would say that in **Empty Words** *they had heard nothing.*

And then there may be, on the other hand, people who are musically inclined who are not so oppressed by meaning. Or the need to have meaning. There are very many ways to hear something. I'll put it this other way: I think one should pay attention to everything when one does anything. And if one is listening one should be attentive to all the various characteristics of sound and language that there are, because we are dealing with a complex situation, a transition from language to music, or from literature to music.

Is it then comparable to the experience, which we've all had, of being in a room where everybody's talking in a language we don't know and we thus try to appreciate the music of the language itself?

Someone speaking a foreign language, except that the language here is not entirely foreign. It's from Thoreau. When it gets inscrutable, because it does with letters and syllables and so on, people remark to me frequently that it sounds like old English—something else they don't understand. What's interesting are all the variety of things that happen: the sounds, the rhythm, the inflections, the this, the that—all these things. You can never tell when something's going to set your faculties working.

So, indeed, it is meant to remind you of other things as well.

It's unavoidable, don't you think, Richard? Because the human mind is more complex than a computer; the moment something comes into it, it touches bells, it rings bells, with regard to the rest of the mind. And everybody's mind is like this, even the man in the street, who's not supposed to be bright. But he is very bright. He's brighter than a computer.

Now it seems to me that **Empty Words** *demands of us a kind of discipline in that, as it goes from Part One to Part Four, it does get harder and harder to listen to, as the intentional verbal or vocal content gets sparser and sparser.*

This varies with people. Very frequently someone gets up and leaves during the course of the reading, but at the same performance someone will come to me after the reading and say that I could have gone on forever. As far as he was concerned, it would have been a pleasure. And this is true of Part Three which I've been reading so frequently. Part Four, well, offered problems to the audience at Naropa. And part of it came, I think, from my sitting with my back to them, for I'd no sooner begun to read than they began an uproar. And I had to be protected physically by quite a redoubtable group of people, including Allen Ginsberg.

How large an audience was there?

Three thousand people, and they went into a state of disenchantment—complete disenchantment.

How many stayed until the end?

I would say at least three-quarters of the audience. And it went on for two hours and a half.

And you had your back turned. Were you amplified in any way?

Yes. Some of the silences were twelve and thirteen minutes long. After the performance I promised them that I would go through a period of self-examination, and I counseled them to do likewise, since we had gotten along so badly together that night.

I first heard you perform Part Four at St. Marks Church in the spring of 1975. Then you spoke it; since then, I've heard that you've developed a singing style for it.

A chanting, yes. Well, it was part of this reexamination that I counseled the audience at Naropa to do. And I decided to make this text more musical than I had.

And this decision came after your Naropa reading?

It was for the recording, actually. And now that I've made it, and now that I've done it, I enjoy it, and I will in the immediate future, when I'm asked to give a lecture, do this chant.

Just for Part Four. Does it bother you when people walk out?

No, it doesn't bother me because they are the ones who are walking out. I myself am staying.

Does it bother you when people heckle, as apparently they did at Naropa?

I can't say that it doesn't bother me, but I can say this: that it does not bother me to such an extent that I stop what I'm doing. What I'm doing is so exigent, so demanding, it requires me to pay attention to everything I am doing. I don't have much time to be bothered by the people who are walking out.

How many times have you performed **Empty Words** *around the United States? Twenty times? Forty times?*

More. I don't know. In Europe, too. You see it's a text that, since it doesn't mean anything, can be read in a foreign country. This is one of the advantages of non-syntactical writing.

That's an advantage of music as well.

That it moves toward a whole world.

Have you ever read it to an audience that has copies of the text in front of them, as people possessing the record will?

I think that will happen more, because **Empty Words** is my next book and the book will be included in the package with the recording [that has not yet appeared].

Does it help? Is it a good idea?

I think it will help, yes.

Do you recommend it?

It's according to whether you're the sort of person who likes to read the score while listening to the music.

On this projected recording, Maryanne Amacher is your collaborator. How did you conceive of her role and how would you describe what she is doing?

I've done a number of works involving environmental sound, ambient sound. One of them was *Score with Parts* (1974), which I did for the St. Paul Chamber Orchestra. I used the environmental sound of dawn at Stony Point, New York, where I had written the music, and David Behrman made that recording, and he made another recording for me for the piece called *Etcetera*. Again it was ambient sound not at dawn, just anytime during the day. It was composed for a dance that Merce did in Paris called *Un Jour ou Deux* [*One Day or Two*]. And when I was invited by the CBC to make a bicentennial piece called **Lecture on the Weather,** I thought also of asking David Behrman to make a recording of wind, rain, and thunder for the whole thing. Somehow he didn't receive the letter that I sent him. He was at York University in Toronto, and it went to the wrong part of the university. It just wasn't received. Finally I telephoned him, but he was then committed and couldn't do it and thought I should engage Maryanne Amacher, for, he said, she did the best recordings of ambient environmental sounds. I knew that her work was very beautiful. I had heard it, and I agreed with him immediately. So I engaged her to do that and her friend Luis Frangella, an Argentinian, to make a film of lightning with the drawings of Thoreau as the flashes of light. So that Thoreau himself became the thunder. And the speakers preferably would be people who had given up their American citizenship and were becoming Canadians, so it was a dark bicentennial piece. Like Thoreau, it criticized the government and its history. And the twelve speakers are speaking quotations from the "Essay on Civil Disobedience," the *Journal,* and *Walden,* according to chance operations.

Which are coherent quotations, or fragments, as in **Mureau** *or* **Empty Words***?*

They're coherent, but they're so superimposed that you can't understand anything. It's the same experience you would have if you had twelve radios going at once. Or if you had tuned between stations and could hear several going at once.

John Cage and Richard Kostelanetz (interview date spring 1982)

SOURCE: Cage, John, and Richard Kostelanetz. "Talking about *Writings through Finnegans Wake*." *TriQuarterly* 54 (spring 1982): 208-16.

[*In the following interview, Cage explains his use of mesostics (aligning letters within a text to spell out words vertically), clarifies the formulas for picking the words and letters in his mesostics, and discusses his decision to rework James Joyce's* Finnegans Wake *in this style.*]

In the 1960s, John Cage wrote poetry, initially in a series of notational "Diary" pieces that I regard as a rich extension of Black Mountain poetics. More recently, he has been rewriting poetry—to be precise, rewriting someone else's poetry. His principal literary project of the early 1970s was based upon the writings of Henry David Thoreau. Our conversation about it appeared first in the *New York Arts Journal,* 19 (November 1980) and then in the recent collection of my essays on poetry, *The Old Poetries and the New* (Ann Arbor: University of Michigan Press, 1981). More recently, Cage has been working with James Joyce's *Finnegans Wake.* When we met for the following conversation, for SoHo Television in the spring of 1978, he had already finished two of his *Writings through Finnegans Wake*; he was now beginning a third that, in fact, he subsequently put aside, so that the title *Writing for the Third Time through Finnegans Wake* went instead to a piece composed in a different way. At last report, the piece begun during the following conversation is titled . . . *for the Fifth Time.* At any rate, my 1979 review of Cage's *Wake* project appeared first in *The New York Times Book Review* (December 2, 1979) and then in *The Old Poetries and the New.*

As poetry radically unlike any written before, that is composed in ways original with Cage, it is, in the truest sense, avant-garde work that is important not only in itself but also for its status in Cage's continuing artistic adventure. It is not difficult poetry in the sense of something no one else can do. Rather, it is inventive poetry—better yet, audaciously inventive poetry. It was often said of Cage's music that no one else composes like this, because no one else would dare; the same might be said of his poetry. His *Writings through Finnegans Wake* exist outside not only the mainstream of contemporary American poetry but its tributaries as well. It is not reviewed in poetry magazines; it is not anthologized or mentioned in the literary histories of native work. Nonetheless, on several grounds, it connects to advanced tendencies both in the other arts and in literature around the world—to tendencies that to various degrees and in various ways reflect Cage's influence.

[*Kostelanetz*]: *I'm with John Cage. He is just beginning a new piece. What is it called, John?*

[Cage]: Just a second. 41, 42, 43, 44, 45, 46, 47, 48, 49, 50, 51, 52, 53, 54, 55, 56. I was counting the letters in this line of *Finnegans Wake.* The text will be called **Writing for the Third Time through Finnegans Wake.**

It follows, therefore, the pieces called **Writing for the Second Time through Finnegans Wake** *and* **for the First Time.**

Right. But the first time didn't have that in the title. It just said **Writing through Finnegans Wake.** Actually, the title of this third one may change because I'm not going through it. What I'm doing is, through chance operations, landing here and there in it: coming down on phrases, words, syllables and letters but not writing or riding or walking through it, but flying over it and landing here and there on it.

How did you do the first one?

For the first one I made mesostics. You know what an acrostic is, with the name down the edge. A mesostic is the name down the middle.

It's a form you have used before.

Right. I have made them for the names of Marcel Duchamp and Merce Cunningham and Mark Tobey and so on, but these are on the name James Joyce and this is the first page of them. The number 3 on the right refers to the opening page of *Finnegans Wake* which is page 3. It opens: "wroth with twone nathandJoe" which includes the words "wroth" and "joe." "Joe" has a "J" in it and that "J" doesn't have an "A" after it, because the "A" belongs to the second line.

Because the mesostic spine here is J-A-M-E-S.

This is the first "J" that doesn't have an "A" after it. I think it's actually the first "J" in the book.

It seems to be, yes.

You know how you can tell—you can turn the page upside down and then if you look for the dots you can catch the "I"s and the "J"s that way very easily because the "J"s dip below the line whereas the "I"s don't. I had a friend named Hazel Dreis who was a fantastic proofreader, and she proofread the *Leaves of Grass* of Walt Whitman which she had bound for the Grabhorn Press in San Francisco. She proofread it upside down and backwards. That means—and this is something I think of as very close to my work—that means that we do very good work when we don't know what we're doing.

That comes into a lot of your work, except that you're a very good proofreader too. I know because you proofread my own book about you, and you found mistakes that I missed.

No, we're all rather poor at proofreading. Anyway, here's "wroth with twone nathandJoe," and then my second line is "A" and I skip the word "rot" that lies between them. "A"—this is the first word that has an "A" that doesn't have an "M" after it. Then I leave out "peck of pa's" and here's the letter "M" in "malt." M-A-L-T doesn't have an "E" in it.

The "E" being the next letter in "James." The next "E" in the text appears in "Jhem."

And then "S" is in "Shen." Then we have the brothers Jhem and Shen.

Since brothers in various form are a continuing motif in Finnegans Wake, *you were lucky to get them into the opening mesostic of your own redoing of* Finnegans Wake.

Now we look for the next "J," and here's the first thunder-clap, by the way—the hundred-letter word.

Right, but there's no "J" there.

No, we don't get a "J" until we come to this marvelous word right here: "pftjschute."

Which sounds like air going down a chute.

Right, the falling of Humpty Dumpty—"the pftjschute of Finnegan." He fell off a ladder, you remember.

So it's a neologism for falling. But here you broke the phrase into two lines, putting "pftjschute" and only it with the "J" and then "Of Finnegans" for the "O." Why did you use "of Finnegan," rather than just "of" alone?

Because I was so delighted to get "Finnegan."

Ah, you made a decision of taste.

Well, you see, I'm not dealing with chance here, and I have the choice, I gave myself the liberty, of going up to forty-four characters to the left and forty-four to the right, so that the name would come down the middle.

Forty-four characters in measuring away from the letter on the mesostic axis.

Right, and sometimes I made a long line and kept quite a lot—except there was a tendency to omit and, in that way, to arrive at a different rhythm than was in the original, though all my words are words from the *Wake* itself. Anyway, for the next line I need a "Y": "that the humptYhillhead of humself." You see, we don't have any "C" there. Here we'll have it: "is at the knoCk out." You see I had to skip practically a whole line . . .

. . . to get the next "C."

Because the original reads this way: "that the humptyhillhead of humself promptly sends an unquiring one well to the west in quest of his tumptytumtoes: and their upturnpikepointandplace is at the knock out in the park. . . ."

So you take the "c" from "knock."

Right, and the "e" is in "in the park."

So, in effect, you've completed one mesostic there—one vertical "James Joyce."

And we leave out the rest of the sentence, which is: "where oranges have been laid to rust upon the green since devlinsfirst loved livvy."

So what you did, in **Writing through Finnegans Wake,** *is go through the entire* Wake, *writing up mesostics on the name "James Joyce."*

Then what I'm going to do, Richard, is distribute the punctuation by chance operations on the page like an explosion. Read just the text and you'll see the punctuation omitted. You can imagine it where you like. You can replace it where you wish. And I also have it oriented according to the twelve parts of the clock.

Which is to say that it isn't all horizontal—that the exclamation point on the first page, for instance, is tilted slightly like the tower of Pisa.

Right, and you know that the night hours are important in *Finnegans Wake*. So that's the first one. Anyway, my editor at the Wesleyan University Press found the text, which is about 125 pages, to be too long and boring, and he said I should make a shorter text and I didn't want to shorten that because that one is complete. It's like Schoenberg said: A long work can't be cut because if it is cut it would be a long work which was cut. So I wanted to make a new work which wasn't cut but which was shorter. And what I did was to make a further discipline, keeping the ones I had of J-A-M-E-S J-O-Y-C-E but keeping an index—I actually kept a card index. And once I used a syllable, I put it in the card index.

How did you measure a syllable?

Well, like in the word "nathandjoe," I assume that it's the syllable "joe" that has the "J" in it.

Why isn't "nath" the syllable?

Because it doesn't have the "J."

Oh, the only syllable you're counting is the syllable on the mesostic axis.

Right. So "joe," j-o-e, represents the "J" of James which I don't identify as the "J" of Joyce. I keep it as the "J" of James. "A" represents the "A" of James and "malt" represents the "M" and they never do it again in the entire work. So the result was, following that discipline, that something like 125 pages here became something like 39 pages there. You can see that the word "just," for instance, which recurs and recurs in the *Wake*, only gets used twice here, once for the "J" of James and once for the "J" of Joyce, because "just" has neither "A" nor "O" after it. I did one thing that was, again, a question of taste. I knew, from having written that, that the final mesostic could be this one:

> Just a whisk
> Of
> pitY
> a Cloud
> in pEace and silence

And I admit to being very fond of that. Somehow, it's very evocative. And so I saved the word "just," representing Joyce, for the end. And even though it could have come up earlier, I didn't let it.

It seems to me that, here and elsewhere, one characteristic of your work is always this: Yes, chance is a basic principle for doing things, but certain decisions of taste appear throughout. They govern quite a bit.

Well, they govern, for instance at the beginning, the decision to work with *Finnegans Wake*.

Which is a very key decision.

I'm actually glad that I made that decision, because I think that, living in this century, we live, in a very deep sense, in the time of *Finnegans Wake*. Don't you think so? And there I was, here I am rather, sixty-six years old almost, and I have never read *Finnegans Wake* through. I had read parts of it but this process of working with it and writing with it has gotten me deeply engaged in it and I've not only read it once, I've read it many times. And, as I pointed out to you, sometimes upside down.

And you're always discovering new things in Finnegans Wake, *as you're always going to discover new things in your own redoings of* Finnegans Wake, *because you've*

respected the basic richness and multiplicity of the text. Is your reworking of the Wake a work of literature or a work of music?

Well, this is whether we pay attention to it as literature or whether we pay attention to it as music, and we're capable—that's one of the lovely things about being a human being—we're capable of turning one way or another. We can turn ourselves toward literature or we could turn toward music. One could take, for instance, the text, and say I sang it to you. Then would you say, "Is that literature?" You would rather think that it was music, if I sang it. Actually, reading is the process that takes place in time so that literature has an affinity for music, because they both take place in time. If the literature sits, so to speak, on the page and waits for you to come to it and doesn't itself move, as some concrete poetry does, then we might say it is not having an affinity for music; it's having an affinity for painting.

Are you going to publish this?

Certainly. This little one is actually going to be in my next book from Wesleyan [*Empty Words,* 1979]. And the big one is going to be published by the *James Joyce Quarterly* [and the University of Tulsa Press]. The two of them, together, are being published in a limited edition printed by the Steinhour Press.

What will that edition look like? Will it be multi-colored like those special editions of your Diaries?

No, it's going to be black and white, but the punctuation, as I told you, is going to illustrate each page. It will be on fine paper. The Wesleyan edition and the *James Joyce Quarterly* edition will be reduced in size and not on fine paper.

Are you going to make a record of it as well?

I think that this is naturally something that one wants to do now, and Joyce himself wanted to do that and did—to make records of parts of *Finnegans Wake*, but we more and more like to hear something rather than just read it. On the other hand, the expenses of all our technologies, even though we have all their benefits, the expenses are still very great. And now that everything is so expensive, it's quite possible that we'll all eat dinner, rather than listen to records of my readings.

One question that constantly comes up with reference to your activity is whether you're now a composer who writes or, since you've done so much writing recently, a poet who also composes.

Well, this morning I was writing music and this afternoon I'm showing you how I'm starting *a Third Time.*

So you've set up an existence in which you can do one thing at one time and another thing at another time, for they are simply options in your own life.

Which seems reasonable. One can also go to sleep.

*Sure enough. Now that we know how the **Second Time** was done, let me ask about the new piece.*

The new one is not going through the book but, as I told you, landing on it, so it's a mix of phrases, words, syllables and letters, and I omit sentences. That's perhaps again a question of taste. And if I kept sentences I might come out with something like **Mureau,** which is music/Thoreau; and this, instead of coming from *Finnegans Wake*, comes from the *Journal* of Thoreau, and this includes sentences. So it has sentences, phrases, words, syllables and letters, and it produces a sound like this: "sparrowsita grosbeak betrays itself by that peculiar squeakarieffect of slightest tinkling measures soundness ingpleasa we hear!"

This is, in effect, a prose, as Finnegans Wake *is prose.*

A kind of prose, yes. Now **Empty Words** begins this way and it doesn't have any sentences and yet it comes from the same material that **Mureau** came from and it goes this way:

                notAt evening
                        right can see
                                suited to the morning hour

                        trucksrsq Measured tSee t A
                ys sfOi w dee e str oais

So by avoiding sentences you approach poetry.

That first section that I just read to you has phrases, words and letters. Now if you have just those things, one, two, three and four—phrases, words, syllables and letters—you can use them singly, one two three four, or in combinations of two, phrases and words . . .

Which is to say singly—only phrases, only words?

Right, or you can use phrases and words, or phrases and syllables, or phrases and letters, or you can use words and syllables or words and letters—this is the principle of permutation—or syllables and letters; or phrases, words and syllables; or phrases, words and letters; or words, syllables and letters, or all four, phrases, words, syllables and letters. That means you have fourteen possibilities. A little bit before we began talking, I began this. I found out what I was to write through the chance operation—and this beside me is the printout of the *I Ching*. I no longer toss the coins. A young man named Ed Kobrin at the University of Illinois pro-

grammed for *HPSCHD* (1967-69) a simulation of tossing three coins six times, and I use the printout now instead of the coins.

So that the I Ching *process is now all coded.*

Right. And then I form the questions. Now I have a question dealing with the number 14. Which of these permutations am I going to involve myself in? And then we got, as you recall, the answer that led to words and letters. And then our next question was how many words and letters are we looking for? And the answer was 28.

You made twenty-eight lines there, to be filled.

Twenty-eight places, yes. Then I had to find out which were words and which were letters and that's a question having to do with the number 2, so that the table of 2 in relation to 64 is one to 32 is *one* and 33 to 64 is *two.*

That means, in this either-or question, if you get any number between one and 32, it is one choice; if you get between 33 and 64, you have the other choice.

I pick a word and the other way get a letter, and so I've gone through here and I get W, W, W, W, W, letter, letter, word, word, letter, etc., and now I know what I'm doing. Then the next question is what part of *Finnegans Wake* am I looking in? And here are the parts of *Finnegans*. The first part about the father and mother has eight chapters and these are the page numbers and these are the numbers of pages. This is the second part about the children: 41, 49, 74, 17. This is the third part: 26, 45, 81, 36; and this is the last part which returns to the first: 36 . . . So there are 17 parts. And I ask that question, of course, in this case now for this first part of words and letters I asked it 28 times: which part are we in? And then which page of that part are we on? And then which line am I going to? And it turns out that the full pages have 36 lines.

And all these decisions are made by consulting the I Ching*?*

Right. And then I count the words or letters as the case may be, and I finally pinpoint a word.

Which you pull out or extract from the Wake*?*

Or I pinpoint a letter. And in this case I'm keeping a table of what pages and lines it comes from because the words in *Finnegans Wake* are so invented that there might come up later on some question as to their spelling. And I can refer back.

That is a very shrewd way of keeping track of Joyce's neologisms that are not only easy to misspell but easy to miscopy.

Right. Now when the program or when our conversation just now began—that's a question: is this a conversation or is it a program?—what do you think? It's according, as I said, don't you think, according to how we pay attention.

Or what you want it to be in your life?

Right. Anyway, I was looking for a letter which is on page 203; and when you asked me the first question, I was counting the letters and there are 56 letters in this line, and now I want to know which letter I've put in the text. So my next number here is the number 17. And I turn to the table for 56, because there are 56 letters, and 1 to 24 equals 1 to 24, so it will be the 17th letter: 1, 2, 3, 4, 5, 6, 7, 8, 9, 10, 11, 12, 13, 14, 15, 16, 17, which is an "I." And since it's surrounded by consonants, there's no question about it. I just plain take the "I."

If there were another vowel, you might take the other vowel?

If there were another vowel, I would then ask, shall I have them both or shall I have just one of them?

And what would govern your choice?

The *I Ching* again. The reason I did that was because of the vowels really more than the consonants, because of the diphthongs, which you know are important among vowels.

So what you've done here is develop a compositional method by which lots of choices are made by you by consulting the I Ching, *your chart there that you made before, the chart here, from which you thereby extract words from* Finnegans Wake, *a text by Joyce that you chose, just as you chose the* I Ching. *Now what is it going to look like in the end?*

Well, I don't know exactly.

How long will it take you to finish?

I have the habit, which I see no reason for breaking, of making a text of this kind until I have completed 4,000 events. And this first business of mine has 28 events; and I've now in an hour done eight of them. So you could divide eight into four thousand and could give me an estimate.

Five hundred hours.

But you see, I'm doing other things. Like this morning, I was writing music. So I don't know exactly when it would be through. But it's the sort of work that I can take with me; and when I'm waiting in line or riding in the bus or subway or plane or whatnot, I can continue this work.

If you can carry not only the Wake *but all your code-books with you.*

Right.

Marjorie Perloff (essay date 1982)

SOURCE: Perloff, Marjorie. "'Unimpededness and Interpenetration': The Poetic of John Cage." In *A John Cage Reader: In Celebration of His 70th Birthday*, edited by Peter Gena and Jonathan Brent, pp. 4-16. New York: C. F. Peters, 1982.

[*In the following essay, Perloff refutes John Hollander's negative assessment of the artistic merit of Cage's work and offers the explanation that Cage's writing—although it has a strict form—actually is about the freedom from conventional form and style.*]

> —One does not then make just any experiment but does what must be done.[1]

John Hollander, reviewing **Silence** for *Perspectives of New Music* in 1963, complained that, however amusing and inventive Cage's verbal and musical compositions may be, "something seems to be missing":

> Perhaps what Mr. Cage's career as a composer lacks is a certain kind of hard work. Not the unbelievably elaborate effort merely, of planning, arranging, constructing, rationalizing (however playfully or dubiously); not the great pains of carrying off a production, but something else. The difference between the most inspired amateur theatricals and the opera, between the conversation that one would like to record and the poem, between the practical joke and the great film, is not one of degree of effort or of conviction. It is that peculiar labor of art itself, the incredible agony of the real artist in his struggles with lethargy and with misplaced zeal, with despair and with the temptations of his recent successes, *to get better*. The dying writer in Henry James' "The Death of the Lion" puts it almost perfectly: "Our doubt is our passion and our passion is our task. The rest is the madness of art." The rest, to be sure; but Mr. Cage's sense of indeterminacy is not this profound doubt, and his métier is not task.[2]

The Romantic myth of the artist as suffering hero, as dying Lion undergoing the Agony (Hollander's own word) and the Ecstasy—it is ironic that the Cagean enterprise should be judged to be deficient by the very standard it has consistently and resolutely called into question. "The difference between the most inspired amateur theatricals and the opera"—a difference Hollander accepts as a given—is one that Cage has never recognized, committed as he is to the erasure of boundaries between genres, modes, and media—indeed, between what we call "art" and "life." Again, what Hollander calls the artist's "struggle with lethargy and misplaced zeal" seems curiously beside the point in the case of an artist like Cage, who, by his own account, refused to be psychoanalyzed when, at a preliminary meeting, the analyst told him: "I'll be able to fix you so that you'll write much more music than you do now." "I said, 'Good heavens!'" Cage recalls, "'I already write too much it seems to me'" (*S,* 127). As for the temptations of . . . recent successes," Cage has always gone by the precept that if something works once, you must not repeat it, that "Whenever I've found what I'm doing has become pleasing, even to one person, I have redoubled my efforts to find the next step."[3] "Doubt as our passion," "passion as our task," "the madness of art"—these are phrases not only alien to Cage's aesthetic; they represent, in terms of that aesthetic, a neo-Romantic self-centeredness to be resisted by all the discipline at one's command.

I mention discipline because readers of *Silence, A Year from Monday,* and the later writings are often misled by Cage's repeated insistence that "art is not an attempt to bring order out of chaos . . . but simply a way of waking up to the very life we're living, which is so excellent once one gets one's mind and one's desire out of its way and lets it act of its own accord" (*S,* 12). Isn't this to imply that anyone can be an artist, that all we have to do is to be *open* to the world around us and the rest will take care of itself?

In order to answer such questions, we must distinguish between what Hollander calls "the peculiar labor of art itself" and what Cage means by "true discipline" (*RK,* 13). A good place to begin is with a Cage interview of 1965, conducted by Richard Schechner and Michael Kirby and published in the *Tulane Drama Review.* The subject of discussion is the nature of theater and the theatrical. At one point, Cage becomes quite angry, recalling a symposium on the performing arts held at Wesleyan University, led by George Grizzard, then playing Hamlet at the Tyrone Guthrie, and the director Alan Schneider:

> I certainly wouldn't have gone had I known what was going to take place. It was a warm evening and they began by taking their coats off, and trying to give the feeling of informality, and they went so far as not to use the chairs but to sit on the table which had been placed in front of them. They proceeded to say that they had nothing to tell the audience, in other words they wanted to have a discussion. Of course there were no questions. So they had to chat and supplement one another's loss of knowledge of what to do next. The whole thing was absolutely disgusting: the kind of ideas and the kinds of objectives, the vulgarity of it, was almost incomprehensible.[4]

The irritation expressed here is at first quite puzzling to anyone familiar with Cage's usual equanimity, his belief that "rather than using your time to denounce what someone else has done, you should . . . if your feelings are critical, reply with a work of your own" (*RK,* 30). Why is Cage so annoyed by the behavior of Grizzard and Schneider? Hasn't he said, earlier in the same interview, that art is "setting a process going which has no necessary beginning, no middle, no end, and no sections"? Why then can't the director and actor sit silently on the platform, waiting to see what process will unfold? After all, if, as Cage says in *Silence,* "There is no such thing as an empty space or an empty time" (*S,* 8), isn't something interesting likely to happen?

The problem has to do with the authenticity—or lack thereof—of the situation. As Cage explains:

> I was quite heated. I normally don't like to talk against things, but I had been asked to [by the chairman of the meeting]. When we couldn't discuss Happenings because they had no knowledge nor interest and didn't think it was as serious as *Hamlet* and thought they were being virtuous, then I said, "Well, what do you think about TV?" They weren't interested in TV. And yet they're living in an electronic world where TV is of far more relevance than the legitimate theatre.

> (*TDR,* 71)

What Cage finds so irritating about this "performance" is that the speakers claim to have no ideas about theater, when the fact is that they conceive theater quite narrowly as what Cage calls "the *Hamlet* situation," with its accompanying rejection of "low" art forms like Happenings and "low" media like television. The audience, understanding that its response is not really being solicited, predictably says nothing; the two speakers just as predictably move to break the silence, a silence that has nothing to do with the natural "silence"—really full of sound-events—that is central to Cage's aesthetic, by engaging in chitchat. By this time, the symposium has become pure power play, defying Cage's aphorism, "We are involved not in ownership but in use" (*RK,* 10). Here the discussion leaders *are* involved in "ownership" and so nothing of artistic interest can possibly happen.

"True discipline," Cage tells Richard Kostelanetz in an interview of 1966, "is not learned in order to give it [self-expression] up, but rather in order to give oneself up. . . . It is precisely what the Lord meant when he said, give up your father and mother and follow me" (*RK,* 13). Such self-surrender has nothing in common with what John Hollander calls "the incredible agony of the real artist," an agony that Cage would surely associate with excessive ego. "When I say that anything can happen I don't mean anything that I *want* to have happen" (*TDR,* 70). Rather, as Cage puts it in "Happy New Ears!" (1965), "I have for many years accepted, and I still do, the doctrine about Art, occidental and oriental, set forth by Ananda K. Coomaraswamy in his book *The Transformation of Nature in Art,* that the function of

Art is to imitate Nature in her manner of operation"
(**YM,** 31). Here the phrase "manner of operation" is
tricky. Cage writes:

> Our understanding of "her manner of operation"
> changes according to advances in the sciences. These
> advances in this century have brought the term "space-
> time" into our vocabulary. Thus, the distinctions made
> . . . between the space and the time arts are at present
> an oversimplification.
>
> (**YM,** 31)

To put it another way, the scientific and technological
advances of our own time inevitably demand a reinterpretation of the very nature and role of art; the "Death
of the Lion" is, so to speak, no longer our "death." In
this context, an art that is to be genuinely avant-garde
must, first of all, acknowledge the present.[5]

This has been, from the start, one of Cage's central
themes. Consider the following exchange between Cage
and Richard Kostelanetz, prompted by Cage's complaint
that his work is too frequently interrupted by phone
calls, often from total strangers:

KOSTELANETZ:

Why do you keep your name in the phone book?

CAGE:

> I consider it a part of twentieth-century ethics, you
> might say. I think that this thing I speak of about flu-
> ency is implied by the telephone, and that is partly why
> I have these ideas I have. If I were to have a totally
> determined situation in my own conception, then of
> course I would be unlisted.

KOSTELANETZ:

Well, if you want to close yourself off, it is the easiest
way.

CAGE:

> Yes but it would fail. Morris Graves, an old friend of
> mine, is searching for a place to live that is removed
> from the twentieth century; but he can't find it, even in
> Ireland. The airplane flies overhead. If he finds a beauti-
> ful property, he has to bring a bulldozer in.

KOSTELANETZ:

You want very much yourself to live in the twentieth
century?

CAGE:

> I don't see that it would be reasonable in the twentieth
> century not to.
>
> (*RK,* 6)

We are now in a better position to understand the
famous Cage aphorism, "PERMISSION GRANTED,
BUT NOT TO DO WHATEVER YOU WANT" (**YM,**
28). To be false to one's art is to impose inappropriate
restraints that impede the process of creation—nostalgia
for the past, for example, or needless repetition of
oneself or of others, or the refusal to recognize what is
actually going on around us, as in the case of George
Grizzard's ignorance of television. But this is not to say
that one can make any experiment one pleases:

> Paraphrasing the question put to Sri Ramkrishna and
> the answer he gave, I would ask this: "Why, if
> everything is possible, do we concern ourselves with
> history (in other words with a sense of what is neces-
> sary to be done at a particular time)?" And I would
> answer, "In order to thicken the plot."
>
> (*S,* 68)

What does this mean in practice? In the Foreword to
Silence, Cage writes: "As I see it, poetry is not prose
simply because poetry is in one way or another formalized. It is not poetry by reason of its content or ambiguity but by reason of its allowing musical elements (time,
sound) to be introduced into the world of words" (*S,* x).
This distinction may strike us at first as decidedly un-
Cagean, for doesn't the composer-poet always argue
that "structure" must give way to "process," and that, as
he declares in the prefaces to such sound poems as
Mureau and *Writings through Finnegans Wake,* it is
essential to "demilitarize the language" by getting rid of
conventional syntax? Why, then, the concern for formal-
izing the language by means of sound repetition or, in
other cases, by means of visual patterning?

Here a Zen proverb is applicable: "To point at the moon
a finger is needed, but woe to those who take the finger
for the moon." To write a poem—say, a series of mesostics or a sound text like *Empty Words* or a prose
meditation on Jasper Johns—one submits oneself to a
particular rule, generated, in Cage's case, by an *I Ching*
"change" or chance operation, so as to free oneself
from one's habitual way of doing things, one's stock
responses to word and sentence formation. Once the
rule (for example, telling one story per minute as in
"Indeterminacy" [**S,** 260]) or using twelve typefaces
and forty-three characters per line without ever
hyphenating a word as in **"Diary: How to Improve the
World"** (**YM,** 3) has been established, it generates the
process of composition. What the rule is, in other words,
matters much less than the fact that one *uses* it.

Consider how this works in Cage's **"36 Mesostics Re
and not Re Duchamp"** (**M,** 26-34). The words "Marcel" or "Duchamp" form a vertical column of capital
letters down the middle of each stanza, which has, accordingly, either six or seven lines. The stated rule is
that "a given letter capitalized does not occur between
it and the preceding capitalized letter" (**M,** 1). Here is
the first stanza:

a utility aMong
swAllows

is theiR
musiC
thEy produce it mid-air
to avoid coLliding.

Our first reaction to this little mesostic is likely to be one of skepticism: isn't this merely game-playing? And if Cage wants to restrict his movements by imposing rule, why not use such traditional prosodic devices as a fixed stress or syllable count, the repetition of vowel and consonant sounds, rhyme?

The fact is that these devices *are* used. "Their" rhymes with "-air," and the first and last lines chime with the near-rhyme "Am*ong*" / "collid*ing*." The fifth line has another such near rhyme internally—"avoid" / "coLlid-," and there is marked assonance throughout of short, lightly stressed *a*'s ("*a*," "*a*void," "*a*Mong," "*a*ir") and *i*'s ("ut*i*lity," "*i*s," "mus*i*C," "*i*t," "m*i*d-air," "coLlid*i*ng"), as well as alliteration of laterals and nasals ("uti*l*ity," "sw*A*llows," "co*L*liding," "a*M*ong," "*m*usiC," "*m*id-air"). Further, the syllable count is 7-2-2-2-6-6—hardly an arbitrary pattern, the number of stresses remaining within the limit of one ("músiC") and three (thÉy prodúce it mîd-áir"). But because our usual way of processing poems today is to read them silently, Cage provides us with the column "MARCEL," a column designed for the eye only since it is obviously impossible to hear the embedded letters as forming the word "Marcel." One might thus say that Cage's lyric pays tribute to what he calls "twentieth-century ethics," to the world of typographic layout and print format in which we all live, at the same time as it slyly sneaks poetic conventions in by the back door. In this sense, the mesostics for Marcel Duchamp nicely exemplify Cage's "concern . . . with history in order to thicken the plot."

Cagean *plot* is generally characterized by what Jung, in his Foreword to the Bollingen edition of the *I Ching*, designates as "sychronicity":

> . . . the configuration formed by chance events in the moment of observation, and not at all the hypothetical reasons that seemingly account for the coincidence. While the Western mind carefully sifts, weighs, selects, classifies, isolates, the Chinese picture of the moment encompasses everything down to the minutest nonsensical detail, because all of the ingredients make up the observed moment.[6]

How such a "configuration" is created out of what seems to be "the minutest nonsensical detail" may be observed in Cage's longer lecture-poems or collage-essays, for example, the recent *Where Are We Eating? and What Are We Eating? (38 Variations on a Theme by Alison Knowles),* originally written for a collection of essays and photographs on Merce Cunningham (1975) and reprinted in *Empty Words* (1979).

The preface to the **"38 Variations"** begins with a neat distinction:

> No one need be alarmed by the exercises dancers give their stomachs. Dancers are furnaces. They burn up everything they eat. Musicians as furnaces are not efficient; they sit still too much.

> (*EW,* 79)

As such, Cage himself began in his late forties to suffer various aches and pains, for example, arthritis, for which the doctors prescribed huge doses of aspirin—a remedy that, so Cage tells us matter-of-factly, did no good at all. Finally, in 1977, on the advice of Shizuko Yamamoto, he adopted a macrobiotic diet and "For two days I lived in shock. I ate almost nothing. I couldn't imagine a kitchen without butter and cream, nor a dinner without wine." But as soon as the diet has gotten underway, "The pain behind the left eye went away. After a month the toes began to move. Now my wrists, though somewhat misshapen, are no longer swollen and inflamed. I've lost more than twenty-five pounds."

It all sounds very virtuous, rather like one of those ads for Granola or Raisin Bran. But Cage's account of his new cooking habits—his use of sesame oil and tamari to flavor mushrooms, of dill and parsley to flavor brown rice—is only the framework for his text, a framework that is wholly exploded by the outrageously funny food catalog contained in the "Variations" themselves. Eating miso soup and nuka pickles, the piece implies, is all very well—indeed essential if you are a musician rather than a dancer—but don't think it will make you forget the joys of *real food.* Or, in Cage's own words, "One does not seek by his actions to arrive at the establishment of a school (truth) but does what must be done. One does something else. What else?" (*S,* 68).

Where Are We Eating? and What Are We Eating? is thus the elaborate food fantasy (paradoxically straight fact) of the artist as macrobiotic dieter. The **"38 Variations"** range from 15 to 24 lines with irregular left and right margins, the lines themselves averaging around 10 syllables. This stanzaic structure is visual only, for the discourse is that of a diary, written in short sentences and sentence fragments that regularly override line endings. But not quite a diary either, for Cage's prose has no continuity: each variation catalogs items and incidents unconnected in time and space, the only point of reference being that everything mentioned refers to *where* and to *what* members of the Merce Cunningham troupe ("America's Best Fed Dance Company," as Cage calls it in **"Variation 31"**),[7] eat as they travel around the world. For example:

> We were invited to the Riboud's in
> Paris. They had just received a large
> box full of fresh mangoes from India. We
> kept on eating until they were finished.

> In a Buffalo hotel Sandra and Jim stayed on
> the eighth floor. They had a large can of
> sardines for breakfast. Five they didn't
> eat they flushed down the toilet.
> After paying the bill at the desk, Sandra
> went to the ladies' room. There in the
> bowl of the toilet were two of her five
> sardines. We stopped at a small
> crowded restaurant on the road between
> Delaware and Baltimore. After our orders
> were taken, we waited a long time.
> The waitress finally came with some of
> our food. Hastily, she said to Carolyn,
> "You're the fried chicken," and to
> Viola, "And you're the stuffed shrimp."
>
> (*EW*, 87)

The fresh mangoes from India eaten at the Riboud's in Paris have no connection to the sardines eaten for breakfast in a Buffalo hotel room (two of which turn up in the toilet downstairs) or with the crowded restaurant, somewhere between Delaware and Baltimore, where the waitress pronounces Carolyn a fried chicken and Viola a stuffed shrimp. But Cage's curious lamination has the effect of making the world quite literally the poet's oyster, for it is a world defined by only two or three things: the quality of the performance space ("Zellerbach, in Berkeley, / is one of the most comfortable theaters / we've ever performed in. Stage is / wide and deep, has big wings" [*EW*, 81]), the setting for food intake, and, most important, the 1001 attributes and species of the food itself.

Cage's settings are carefully chosen so as to take us around the world in "**38 Variations**" but we come back, again and again, to Joe's in Albany ("**Variations 1**," "**9**," "**21**," "**30**"), where one eats a "number 20 (Old English): Beef, / ham, tongue, lettuce, tomato, with / Russian dressing"; to the Moosewood Inn in Ithaca, New York ("**15**," "**21**," "**25**," "**26**," "**36**"), whose luncheon menu features "Spinach and mushroom soup," "asparagus soufflé," and "yoghurt cream cheese pie (nuts in the crust)" (*EW*, 91); and to the Sri Lanka in London ("**6**," "**32**," "**34**"), where dinners generally begin with egg hoppers: "An egg hopper is an / *iddiapam* made with rice flour and coconut / milk in the bottom of which fried egg / sunny-side up is placed. On top of / the egg your choice of condiments from a / tray of many" (*EW*, 95).

In between these points, the journey takes the Cunningham troupe to every conceivable variety of eating place: the Cafe de Tacuba in Mexico City (**4**), the Big Tree Inn in Geneseo, New York ("**7**"), a motel in Malibu, whose "miserable" Chinese restaurant is perceived as serving "delicious" food once the company is sufficiently "plastered" ("**7**"), a truck stop outside Chicago ("**12**"), a restaurant inside a gas station in Eau Claire, Wisconsin ("**16**"), a California bungalow Japanese

restaurant on the Sunset Strip ("**19**"), the lawn in front of Howard Johnson's ("**19**"), an Amish farm ("**22**"), a Durango whorehouse ("**26**"), a supermarket in Ljubljana, Yugoslavia ("**"29**), a Ceylonese restaurant in Boulder, Colorado ("**32**"), and the Whole Earth in Santa Cruz ("**36**")—not to mention private homes, hotels, open-air restaurants, and clubs in Paris, Warsaw, Grenoble, Amsterdam, St. Paul de Vence, Tennessee, Bremen, the Hague, Oklahoma City, and Delhi. There is even one dinner in "a lodge in a meadow surrounded by / a forest near the north rim of the Grand Canyon" (*EW*, 80).

The descriptions of food become more and more elaborate in the course of the "**Variations**." The poem begins on a low key: dancers need, Cage explains, a good steak restaurant with a liquor license so they can have some beer. But by the end of the first variation, we are already taken to Sofu Teshigahara's house: "room where we ate had two parts: one / Japanese; the other Western. Also, two / different dinners; we ate them both" (*EW*, 80). From here on out, we move into a world of "tequila sangrita" ("**4**," "**5**") and Pernod ("**10**"), of "risotto with truffles" ("**6**") and "*mousse au chocolat*" served with "a large pot of *crème fraiche*" ("**6**"), and then on to moments when food seems to come alive and take over the human scene:

> Picnic preparation in hotel room.
> Chicken, marinated in lemon and *sake,*
>   wrapped'n foil, left overnight, next day
> dipped in sesame oil and charcoal-broiled.
> Broccoli, sliced, was put in ginger in
>   twenty-five packages; corn, still in
>   husks, silk removed,
>   butter'n' wrapped. Noticing bathtub was
> full of salad, David said, "I don't want any
>   hairs in my food." In addition to the
>   roast beef and cheese on rye, Robert had
> triscuits, a sour orange from Jaffa, a
> banana, and some apple pie. David's sticky
> fermented Passion-fruit juice geysered on
>   the way to Grenoble. Bus floor and
>   handbags were cleaned and the windows
>   were opened. Then it geysered again.
>
> (*EW*, 87-88)

Here David (Tudor's) "Passion-fruit juice geyser[ing]" in the bus becomes a kind of fountain of love, the jet stream that keeps this wild group of people going.

But don't dancers do anything but eat? Cage's narrative playfully takes the great art of Merce Cunningham (to whom he has paid frequent tribute)[8] as a given, as if to say, "Well, of course the dancing is marvelous, so why say anything more about it?" Deflecting our expectations, his text presents, under the guise of simple record—a logbook in fact—a Gargantuan eating dream that outdoes Leopold Bloom's Lestrygonian fantasies. Cage's technique is to collage individual—and often quite unrelated—events (conscientiously providing every name and date—what Jung calls "the minutest nonsensical detail"), in keeping with the Zen belief that it is only the coincidence of events in space and time that reveals to us the "UNIMPEDEDNESS AND INTERPENETRATION" (*S*, 46) at the heart of the universe. The narrative is, moreover, entirely autobiographical ("this happened to me and then this and then that") without being in the least "confessional": we learn nothing whatever about Cage's personal life. The Zen precept followed is "Never explain, indicate," for there is no such thing as final understanding. Accordingly, everyone is called by name—Carolyn, Rick and Remy, Carroll Russell, Meg Harper, Kamalini—but the names are entirely opaque; they point to no hidden truth, no conceptual reality. Again, Cage's Orient is not the Exotic East, any more than his Paris is the City of Light; indeed, the Japanese restaurant on the Sunset Strip (where the waitress who brings Cage a pineapple ice, tells him, "Oh yes, that'll cut the grease in your stomach" (*EW*, 88]) might serve one's purpose just as well as the real thing, depending upon one's mood and what happens to be on the menu that night.

The Global Village presented in Cage's narrative has no center: the Ceylonese restaurant in Boulder is no more peripheral than the Swiss chalet in Ceylon; Jerusalem Artichoke may be ordered at the Moosewood Inn in Ithaca, and fresh mangoes from India are served in Paris. Indeed, one's dream recipe may turn up anywhere: in Cage's case, it makes its appearance in Room 135 of the Holiday Inn (city undesignated):

> Four
> cups of ground walnuts; 4 cups of
> flour; 12 tablespoons of sugar; 2 2/3
> cups of butter; 4 teaspoons of
> vanilla. Form into circa 125
> small balls. Bake at 350°
> in motel oven. Now back to Room 135.
> Roll in 1 pound of powdered sugar.
> Nut balls.

(*EW*, 91)

These nut balls keep reappearing (**"Variation 36"** begins, "After Jean'n' I'd rolled one hundred / balls, I remembered I'd forgotten the vanilla"), but fond as Cage is of this particular recipe, he is just as pleased to come across "Excellent *tempura* (not greasy; flaky, delicate batter)" or to take note of Cunningham's high-protein breakfast drink:

> two
> parts yeast, one part liver, one
> part wheat germ, one part sunflower-
> kernel meal, one part powdered milk (cold
> pressed), pinch of kelp, one part lecithin,
> one-half teaspoon powdered bone meal.
> At home, mixed with milk and banana in a
> blender. On tour USA, mixed with

> milk in portable blender. On tour
> elsewhere, mixed with yoghurt or
> what-have-you.

(*EW*, 95)

Rules, that is to say, are always useful but one must retain one's flexibility in applying them: "one does not seek by his actions to arrive at the establishing of a school (truth) but does what must be done. One does something else. What else?" (*S*, 68)

The final, or thirty-eighth, variation thickens the plot by a remarkable twist:

> "You go home now?" No; this ends the
> first of five weeks. Toward the
> end, Black Mountain didn't have a
> cent. The cattle were killed and the
> faculty were paid with beefsteaks. Chef
> in Kansas motel-restaurant cooked
> the mushrooms I'd collected. Enough
> for an army. They came to the table
> swimming in butter. Carolyn, who isn't
> wild about wild mushrooms, had seconds. I
> complimented the cook. How'd you know
> how to cook 'em? "We get them all
> the time: I'm from Oklahoma." There's a
> rumor Merce'll stop. Ten years ago, London
> critic said he was too old. He himself
> says he's just getting a running start.
> Annalie Newman says he's like wine:
> he improves with age.

(*EW*, 97)

The faculty at Black Mountain College are paid in beefsteaks because there is no money; the mushrooms Cage collects swim in butter; Cunningham is like wine: "he improves with age." How are we to interpret these overwhelming "what one eats is what one is" metaphors, when we remember that the man who is telling us this whole story is eating nothing but barley bread and brown rice?

A helpful perspective on this question is provided by the following exchange between Richard Kostelanetz and Cage:

KOSTELANETZ:

But why don't you go yourself to every happening?

CAGE:

I've been telling you how busy I am. I barely have time to do my own work.

KOSTELANETZ:

What I meant is, why do you go to one and not another? Because you happen to be in New York at that time?

CAGE:

Purely.

KOSTELANETZ:

> Do you walk out of one feeling happier that you went to that one rather than another?

CAGE:

> The big thing to do actually is to get yourself into a situation in which you use your experience no matter where you are, even if you are at a performance of a work of art which, if you were asked to criticize it, you would criticize out of existence. Nevertheless, you should get yourself into such a position that, were you present at it, you would somehow be able to use it.

KOSTELANETZ:

> But does that alter the fact that you might have preferred going to a different happening?

CAGE:

> That's not an interesting question; for you are actually at this one where you are. How are you going to use this situation if you are there? This is the big question.

> > (*RK,* 28)

Which is to say, with reference to our text, that when one is engaged in eating, one enjoys what one eats, and when one is dieting, one finds a way to use that particular experience so that it will yield positive results. Now that Cage is on his macrobiotic diet, does he hold forth on the horrors of slaughtering cattle? No more than he objected to a vegetarian dance or to Merce's yeast-and-liver drink during his feasting days with the Cunningham troupe.

Where Are We Eating? and What Are We Eating? is thus, in a curious sense, an exemplary tale. The narrative reveals no psychological complexities, whether Cage's or anyone else's; it has neither a climax nor a turning point; it does not, for that matter, move toward an epiphany because our attention has been carried, so to speak, "not to a center of interest but all over the canvas and not following a particular path" (*YM,* 31). Yet what seems to be a set of variations made up of "sheer multiplicity, unfocused attention, decentralization" (*RK,* 8) thickens the plot by layering its seemingly trivial data so as to arrest the attention, thus forcing us to rethink the meaning of its title. "EAT," we learn in **"Variation 34,"** is the acronym of an organization called "Experiments in Art and Technology." "Merce," Cage remarks, "never got involved in it. David Tudor and I did" (*EW,* 95). Was it then a good thing to be, so to speak, part of EAT? Or is Cage to be defined by his new role as consumer of brown rice and seaweed? "The situation," as Cage says in his collage-essay on Jasper Johns, "must be Yes-and-No not either-or. *Avoid a polar situation*" (*YM,* 79).

Notes

1. "History of Experimental Music in the United States" (1958), reprinted in *Silence,* p. 68. The following abbreviations are used for Cage's works throughout this essay:

   S: *Silence, Lectures and Writings* (Middletown, Conn.: Wesleyan University Press, 1961).

   YM: *A Year from Monday, New Lectures and Writings* (Middletown, Conn.: Wesleyan University Press, 1967).

   M M, Writings '67-'72 (Middletown, Conn.: Wesleyan University Press, 1973).

   EW: *Empty Words, Writings '73-'78* (Middletown, Conn.: Wesleyan University Press, 1979).

   RK: *John Cage,* ed. Richard Kostelanetz (1970; New York: Praeger Publishers, Inc., 1974).

2. *Perspectives of New Music,* I (Spring 1963), p. 141.

3. Cited by Calvin Tomkins, "John Cage," in *The Bride and the Bachelors, Five Masters of the Avant-Garde* (New York: Penguin Books, 1976), p. 107.

4. *Tulane Drama Review,* X:2 (Winter 1965), p. 71. Subsequently cited as *TDR.*

5. For a good discussion of the analogies between contemporary art and science, see Michael Kirby, "The Aesthetics of the Avant-Garde" (1969), in *Esthetics Contemporary,* ed. Richard Kostelanetz (Buffalo, N. Y.: Prometheus Books, 1978), pp. 36-70.

6. *The I Ching or Book of Changes,* the Richard Wilhelm translation from Chinese into German, rendered into English by Cary F. Baynes, Bollingen Series III (1950; Princeton: Princeton University Press, 1967), p. xxiii. I discuss the non-sensicality of Cage's Zen stories in the larger context of his performance aesthetic in my *The Poetics of Indeterminacy: Rimbaud to Cage* (Princeton: Princeton University Press, 1981), pp. 288-339.

7. For the sake of convenience, I have numbered the variations; similarly, in reproducing portions of the Kostelanetz interview, I normalize the format; Kostelanetz does not use names but italicizes his own questions, a device useful in a long interview but confusing in the case of brief quotations.

8. See, for example, "Four Statements on the Dance," in *Silence,* pp. 87-97.

Arthur J. Sabatini (essay date 1989)

SOURCE: Sabatini, Arthur J. "Silent Performances: On Reading John Cage." In *John Cage at Seventy-Five,* edited by Richard Fleming and William Duckworth, pp. 74-96. Lewisburg, Penn.: Bucknell University Press, 1989.

[*In the following essay, Sabatini describes the various media and genres of Cage's works, analyzes his experimental forms and styles, and attempts to explain his use of space and visuals to enhance poetic and artistic impact.*]

At any rate, my musical words, strictly speaking, have managed to arouse either indignation or sympathy—nothing compared to my books. You can't imagine how many people were touched by *Silence!* I received many letters, sometimes extremely lucid, always interesting. Next to that, the reactions to my music are predictable.

Cage to Daniel Charles

The writings of John Cage are destined to provoke more varied, and ultimately more enduring, responses than his music. This is no doubt a chancy proposition, but since Cage's aesthetic is most widely known because of theories founded upon his concept of "silence," it is not unreasonable to argue that his art and practice are most dramatically experienced in the context of that realm where silence has reigned most inviolable: reading. Moreover, because nearly everything in Cage's writings directs reading into performance, his texts have the potential to create increasingly unpredictable readerly responses and generate an abundance of "touched" and touchy reactions.

Each reading of Cage is, in effect, a silent performance. The silence associated with reading, however, differs from the silence, or nonsilence, of music. It is a self-induced, private silence, drawn between consciousness and the page. Though occurring over time, reading is not bound by time measured as in music; nor has anyone ever suggested that the silence that surrounds the trance of reading is pure. The French poet Stephen Mallarmé, who wrote about reading, elegantly described the silence "between the sheets and the eye" as "the condition and delight of reading," an authentic, luxurious state.[1]

But since Mallarmé, Joyce, and a long list of others, the art of reading has undergone a great transformation. As texts broke out of the cages of linear narrative, closed forms, generic definitions, typographic constraints and physical structure, readers assumed and were forced to adopt new roles. Reading evolved from a passive, reactive phenomena to an active, performative state. It also acquired its own elaborate poetics, theoretical formulations, and romance. "Let others boast of the pages they have written," Jorge Luis Borges announced in a poem titled "A Reader," "I take pride in those I've read."[2] John Cage has echoed that sentiment in practice by often referring to authors and books and by writing on names, in mesostics, and "through" the books of Thoreau, Joyce, Pound, and Merce Cunningham. Cage has even taken Borges a few steps further, for the next lines of the poem are

I may not have been a philologist,
or gone deeply into declensions or moods or those
            slow shifts of letter sounds—
the *d* that hardens into *t*.
the kinship of the *g* and *k*—
but through the years I have professed
a passion for language.

Since his days at Black Mountain, and perhaps before, Cage's attention to language, writing, and writing-as-process has set the stage for performative readings—by himself and others. He has written lectures and works that were specifically for performance. In numerous instances, he has "composed" texts as he composed music for use in performance situations. A 1979 work, *Circus On,* is a score "for translating a book into a performance without actors, a performance which is both literary and musical or one or the other." Finally, when compiling his books, Cage has given careful consideration to their style, structure, and the effect on the reader. In many ways, he has "prepared" readers and insured that whoever chooses one of his texts is never a mere page turner.

Cage has not only written, performed, composed, typed, copied, printed, Letrasetted, plexi-glassed, and framed his texts, but, in *Themes and Variations,* the mesostic **"Composition in Retrospect,"** and other pieces, he has subjected them to rereadings and rewritings. His more recent writings are, in fact, glosses and reductions of earlier work. Employing a surface of sounds and letters, in mesostics and the "writings through" (*Finnegans Wake*) Cage seems to be in search of an Ur-language, another form of silence, or not. And, with each new writing—which, of course, reflects off and through all previous writings—the reader warily accompanies Cage. Or not.

For, by now, to read Cage is to knowingly pass (kick, fall, run?) into a galaxy where performance is everywhere influenced by a physics that mixes aesthetics with psychology and politics. The features of Cage's universe are clearly documented. Philosophically and in practice, Cage is concerned with *indeterminancy, purposeful purposelessness, nonintention, uncertainty, anarchy, meaninglessness as ultimate meaning,* and various states of presence and absence (silence/nonsilence, mobility/immobility, art/life). These unsteady states (of mind and being) are plentiful and unavoidable because of the very structure, intention, and thematic interrelationships among all the writings. In order to pursue any vector within the Cagean system, a reader must negotiate Cage's thought and come to grips with his methods and directives. Where reading Cage was once a matter of "seeking" information or playing with a text's descriptions and formulas, the immensity of his oeuvre now seems to impose other considerations. There are simply too many demands, explicit and implicit, prompted by a Cagean text. The allusions, practices, and sheer density of meaning (encompassing, as it does, nonmeaning) that have accumulated around Cage's every gesture—at this point in his long career—transform reading into a self-conscious and reflexive performative behavior.

Inevitably the dynamics of Cage's discourse entangle and perhaps threaten the reader. Then, as Cage quotes Sri Ramakrishna, the plot thickens. For a reader's silence, though active, is above all circumscribed by the need for security and affirmation. Reading is a one-on-one game which flows toward resolution, order, and meaning. Yet, with Cage, reading becomes risky, unpredictable. Readers are confronted with the possibility of a reading/performance that results in the production of a text that is the very antithesis of the agenda of reading. Stated directly, reading Cage creates the conditions for the production of nonmeaning, purposeful purposelessness, uncertainty, etc.—and the reader is an adjunct to the process. As an aesthetic gesture—or a social one—conspiring to produce nonmeaning, even within the privacy of the readerly cocoon, is an act of some consequence. At the very least, nonmeaning is a noise neither desired nor easily accommodated in the silent orbit of a reader's journey and, at its farthest reaches, nonmeaning is a notion (Cagean, Zen-like, nature-like) that is problematic with regard to reading and consciousness.

Reading through the works of John Cage raises these and other issues. Cage's texts, and his performance theories (of music, writing, reading) are elaborate and complex. In this essay I want to wander/wonder through the near and far territories of Cage's writings. I will begin by surveying the multiplicity and character of Cage's texts, since the sheer quantity and variety of them poses questions for any would-be reader. (For the most part, I will focus on writings in books and collections.) The second matter I'll address is the physical structure and composition of the writings, with particular attention to Cage's use of mesostics and open formats. The third part of the essay is more speculative and referential, as I gauge Cage's work according to schemes of reading/writing that are simultaneously ancient and postmodern.

I believe Cage's writings will eventually gain more attention than his music because, McCluhan notwithstanding, we remain a culture of print and the book. The writings are, unarguably, stunning repositories of original insights, aesthetic theory, and poetries. They include valuable critical commentaries on musicians, composers, artists, dancers, and social theorists as well as an intriguing personal history of the avant-garde from the 1930s to the present. And they are plainly fun to read.

As an author, Cage has been prolific. He has written, coauthored or contributed to twelve published books under his own name. Several books are collections of previously published material; three (*For the Birds* and Kostelanetz's books) include extensive interviews and articles by others; a few books, usually collaborations (*Another Song, Mud Book*), are primarily photographic or graphic. In addition, he has written innumerable pieces for periodicals, catalogues, and other sources which have yet to be collected.

The most striking and obvious facts about Cage the writer is that he is stylistically consistent, ceaselessly inventive, and never at a loss to meet the demands of the occasion or the page. The hybrid quality of his writing—part essay, part narrative, part word/text play, part score—is always maintained. All of which poses the first question to any would-be reader: what, precisely, is a Cagean text? Is it to be read as diversion, as instructions, as a continuation or development of theses? Do the writings in a given collection add up to a "statement" or "position"?

Throughout his career, Cage's range has been astonishing. He has written reviews, program notes, essays, lectures, diaries, scripts, sound/text pieces, scores, mesostics, letters, books, and more. Scattered among the work are biographical notes, anecdotes, commentaries, dialogues, forewords, afterwords, and explanations concerning methods of composition or the circumstances that surrounded a particular writing. When editing collections, as he does periodically, Cage augments his books with fillers, minutiae, photographs, and etchings.

Amidst this plethora of texts, a reader's first questions echo titles of some of Cage's early lectures: where to begin? what order to follow? where to go next? how to read? and what am I reading for?

If one's impulse, or method, is to "read in order," a first question is what type of order? Cage's writings, it is true, are scrupulously identified chronologically, but reading pieces according to their dates quickly reveals little in the way of a systematic development of ideas. Cage often wrote essays or delivered lectures on specific subjects to fulfill commissions. On given occasions he repeated himself; or reused serviceable anecdotes or comments as a source for continuing a thought. In **"45' for a Speaker,"** for example, he notes that "the text itself was composed using previously written lectures together with new material."[3] After reading any number of pieces, the same material about his teachers reappears: D. T. Suzuki ("Before studying Zen, men are men and mountains are mountains"), Satie ("You'll see when you're fifty, I'm fifty and I've seen nothing"), Schoenberg ("The eraser is more important than the point of the pencil"). By the time Cage writes **Themes and Variations,** he acknowledges "fifteen men who have been important to me in my life and work" and "one hundred and ten ideas" he "listed in the course of a cursory examination of my books."[4] The repetitiousness of Cage's thoughts and sources in different types of texts thus belies reading in "order."

Nevertheless, it is possible to approach at least one of Cage's efforts chronologically. The **Diary: How to Improve the World (You Will Only Make Matters**

Worse) dates from 1965 and numbers eight sections (to 1982, as published in *X*). It is a remarkable documentation of Cage's interests, travels, readings, friendships, and enthusiasms. The nominal "theme" of the Diary is "improving the world." For Cage, this involves observations of daily events, incidental notes and remarks on the way things ought to be, according to his "teachers" (Norman O. Brown, McLuhan, et al.) and his own good uncommon sense.

Although wonderfully engaging and diligently kept, the Diary remains more of a listing than a reliable chronicle. It details Cage's activities but does not disclose a reasoned development of his thinking. Cage, for instance, often quotes Fuller or McCluhan, but (intentionally) refrains from analyzing or reviewing issues. He cites Mao Tse-tung, but never considers Mao in the context of the negative, often murderous circumstances of the Cultural Revolution. The chosen abbreviated form of the Diary, which Cage calls a "mosaic," prohibits elaboration on his part. Reading the Diary offers a chronological glimpse of Cage's life and times, if that, but little else.

Surveying Cage's entire output as a writer, any "order" for reading would be arbitrary. Cage's writings do not handily fall into genres or categories. Lectures are simultaneously performance works, essays are rewritten interviews or radio transcriptions; and what of the mesostics? They are at once formal structures and about a variety of subjects. As in the case of any number of Cage's compositions (*Fontana Mix* comes to mind), the materials for performance are available ultimately for the reader to select and define.

And the materials are abundant. But, even as one chooses, say, to proceed through the Diary, or only read lectures or mesostics, the complete contents and structurings that surround Cage's texts influence the readerly effort. In each of the books and collections, Cage is at pains to identify occasions, clarify his method for composition or otherwise append notes to the writings. The books are dense with prefaces, introductions, opening statements, afterwords, parenthetical notes, and interludes. Often italicized, this considerable body of information appears useful; but it subtly complicates matters.

These *italicizations,* to name this material, form something of a multitracked tape that loops around and through the Cagean galaxy. One track is inscribed with names: Merce Cunningham, Buckminster Fuller, Mother, Erik Satie, Jasper Johns; another with places and occasions: Juilliard, Emma Lake, a lecture series, Darmstadt, a birthday, New York City; another with tools and numbers: the I Ching, 100 words a day, two weeks, Letraset, 2 pages, forty-eight measures; and another is imprinted with quotations from letters and

comments by friends. In cases where published writings were first delivered as lectures or performances, Cage italicizes the precise requirements for reading: "Each line is to be read across the page from left to right, not down the columns in sequences."[5] "The following text was written to be spoken aloud. It consists of five sections, each to take twelve minutes. The fourth is the fastest and the last one is the slowest."[6] In a few instances, he notes that original versions of pieces, or small printings of special editions, differ or were printed with photographs or in colored ink.

To whom, even a slightly self-conscious reader must ask, are all these *italicizations* addressed? What are they about? Are they meant to be informative or directive? What is their cumulative effect? What value am I supposed to place on the fact that Cage completed this work in six days, or that it was done in script, or produced in Ann Arbor? If I choose to read at my own pace, am I missing something essential to Cage's meaning? How accurate is Cage's information? What relation does one set of descriptions bear to another? Do I have to read aloud?—knowing that Cage himself wonders about "Searching (outloud) for a way to read."[7]

I find the *italicizations* winding through Cage's writings to be functional yet unsettling. Functional in that they serve as a framing and a connecting device that locates both Cage and a reader in the scheme of a long, peripatetic life through the twentieth century's worldwide avant-garde. The frequent reappearance of friends, predictable allusions or ideas permits the unfolding of each new text against a familiar background, establishing something of a narrative structure for readers. There is a comforting quality to this, on the one hand, and, on the other, it affirms Cage's belief in the continuity of art and life.

Yet this persistent, detailed identification of times, dates, instructions, and notes on methodologies also instills a feeling of alienation (to borrow a notion from Brecht's theory of acting). Like an actor, according to Brecht, who does not intend to create "empathy" but to read his lines so as to show the nature of an incident or character, Cage's instructions turn a text into just such an "exemplification."[8] Each explanation over-explains and over-determines the text, like too many stage directions underscoring the action. The printed italics also serve as a reminder that reading is a partial act, a secondary performance that follows after the specific, recorded act of composition or life experience. Reading is only truly reading, the italics imply, when it follows Cage's rules (e.g., each story in **"How to Pass, Kick, Fall, and Run"** takes one minute to read).[9]

To a degree, Cage creates conditions which undermine, or challenge, the reader. As with the A-effect, the reader is poised not to rush into a pursuit of the text's meaning, but to cooly assess its declarations, possibilities, and technical requirements.

When there are extensive proscribed formulas for following a text, reading becomes more problematic. After being instructed that the text requires a reading of one line per second, what is the measure of a reading that lingers over a phrase or skips to the bottom of the page? Or, consider two other subtle forms of insistence by Cage. When a text—the essays on Jasper Johns or Morris Graves—is meant to "relate somehow to the canvases and personality of the painter" or "Graves in the act of painting,"[10] isn't a reader at a disadvantage without a clear image of the painter's work? Similarly, when Cage indicates that a given piece was written as he composed a musical work (in the above instance, the Johns essay followed the plan of *Cartridge Music*) or according to the pattern in a musical composition (the Graves essay derives from the "fourth movement of my *Quartet* for percussion (1935)"), isn't the reader meant to hear the work in the background?—in the silence?

Another complicating factor is the presence of Cage's italicized "voiceovers" incessantly pointing to this, emphasizing that. This voice, albeit a soft and friendly one, flows as metatext surrounding the reader at every step. (For many, this voice is potentially Cage's actual voice, remembered from conversations and performances: a factor that could enhance or detract from one's silence).

All of the *italicizations* in Cage's writings cause, however slight, an adjustment in any reading/performance. Reading according to the instructions of a text amounts to a form of readerly complicity that contradicts the unstated law which maintains that a reader determines the nature of the action. To have the space between the self and the page "directed," even if the directions aren't followed, establishes a set of relations between reader and writer that, as is the case with Cage's music, demands a rethinking of readerly postures, strategies, and ethics. This is the case for new readers as well as seasoned ones. Richard Kostelanetz, in an interview in 1979, seemed to be taken up short after Cage explains how he should read: "I'm sorry, John; do you want me to read **Empty Words** with a stopwatch?" And Cage replies, "Yes. Then immediately you become fascinated with the whole problem of reading it."[11]

Any event that follows a space is a new event. Making music by reading outloud. *To read.* To breathe. *IV: equation between letters and silence. Making language saying nothing at all. What's in mind is to stay up all night reading.* Time reading so that at dawn (IV) the sounds outside come in (not as before through closed doors and windows). Half-hour intermissions between any two parts. Something to eat. In I: use, say, one hundred and fifty slides (Thoreau drawings); in IV only

five. Other vocal extremes: movement (gradual or sudden) in space; equalization. (Electronics.) *Do without whatever's inflexible. Make a separate I Ching program for each aspect of a performance. Continue to search.*[12]

To this point (space?), I have been suggesting that the silence surrounding the reader of Cage's works is precarious. Cage's writings, a career-long commitment, are extensive and each piece inflects a reading of another. There is no order to speak of when attempting to read Cage, and what order there is—a chronological one—reveals but a vague biographical montage. Cage's writings also present a chorus of voicings, directives, instructions, and allusions that invoke a sense of an "other" hovering around and through each text. (Assessing a book by Derrida, the literary critic Geoffrey Hartman comments that for certain writers the "less ego the more echo seems to be the rule,"[13] which surely is apt in this context). Reading Cage, I find, cannot merely "proceed" because processions are predisposed by Cage's *italicizations* (never anything but helpful, nevertheless intrusive). Then there is Cage's explicit intention to remove intention, to replace meaning with meaninglessness, and to otherwise change minds. Thus the multitude of distractions, shifts, adjustments, queries, and modulations that comprise Cage's texts lead me uneasily toward fulfilling Cage's desiderata. This possibility is, I think, emphatically reinforced when I consider not only the words, but the pages and books.

But the reading I've been discussing so far pertains to the content, general outline, and order of the writings—the common ground of texts. A decidedly more complicating issue is Cage's conception of texts and books: lettering, shape, page formats, etc. Since his earliest lectures, Cage has toyed with typography, graphics, and the limitations of the white rectangle of the page. He has always expressed an awareness of the tools and conditions of writing; all of his collections are printed in different typefaces and some with drawings. "How is this text to be presented?" he notes at the beginning of **Empty Words,** "As a mix of handwriting, stamping, typing, printing, letraset?"[14] Cage answered this query in the 1958 "Composition as Process" lecture in **Silence.**

To cite another example, Cage's Diary was fastidiously planned with irregularities of type in mind. They were written, he notes, for Clark Coolidge's magazine *Joglars* and since it

was printed by photo-offset from typescripts, I used an IBM Selectric typewriter to print my text. I used twelve different type faces, letting chance operations determine which face would be used for which statements. So, too, the left marginations were determined, the right marginations being the result of not hyphenating words and at the same time keeping the number of characters per line forty-three or less.[15]

Cage regularly acknowledges such chance-determined, self-imposed word limits, or the printing formats of publications. A work for *Dance Magazine* is titled **"2 Pages, 122 Words on Music and Dance"** because of the number of "dummy pages" sent to Cage for a piece. After selecting the number of words by chance operations, Cage positioned them according to the "imperfections in the sheets of paper."[16] In *Music for Piano,* Cage placed notes on the score, in ink, according to the imperfections.[17] *Muoyce* is printed in columnar form

> bling fingers to Caer Fere rd'sc weyou king a of willy wooly woolf on ben aon watchbeupytamong Lugge-lawecurband that yrain may love that golden silence mud Cicely oshis agrammatical partsm typ d llbnf *o* b nds en'sgr t tk satw e o ci-d r ntpe ong le rwhoiIrchy ea erd a sj rby e ypsr lwhts o w a t ty were unde-cidedly attachedlifting upu in brother handhiswherever emanating deafdein the porchwaylonely one Maas*shows*eno sense-by memoryshall have beenbarcelonas *has* when the rothMutt for Felim in request how starringthetoller-might factionwith our obeisant servants was sitting even provisionally who red altfrumpishly OF THE PASTthenPap Ilhim Itand swarthythe ladwigs *babel* with any WiltAnd Kevwith the twirlers continuallyatloftaredon't Shoal effectand TROTH-BLOWERSand andis-bar TRADITIONor Meynhir-curfewhobblede-

in order to "facilitate the publishing in Japan."[18] Of the "Indeterminacy" lecture in **Silence,** Cage italicizes "The excessively small type in the following pages is an attempt to emphasize the intentionally pontifical character of this lecture."[19]

The adherence to chance operations and arbitrary limits reinforces Cage's belief that "Artists who use disciplines to free their work from their intentions start the flow moving in an outgoing direction."[20]

> Devote myself
> to askIng
> queStions
> Chance
> determIned
> answers'll oPen
> my mind to worLd around
> at the same tIme
> chaNging my music
> sElf-alteration not self-
> expression

[X, p. 132]

On another level, as Cage remarked to Daniel Charles, "Typographic changes, like the 'mosaic' form, are noises which erupt in the book! At one and the same time, the book is condemned to nonexistence and the book comes into being. It can welcome everything."[21]

For the reader, these pronouncements about the numbers of letters and words, and this consciously designated placement of graphic "noise" (?), is yet another challenge to the social and psychological contract of the readerly code which normally separates the writer's toil from the reader's pleasure. I may know that Hemingway woke up each morning and sharpened his pencils and when he finished writing he literally counted his word production. But I don't expect lead shavings to fall on my lap when I open *The Sun Also Rises.* Ezra Pound, Charles Olson (and before them Futurist poets, Apollinaire and others) all seized on the mechanics of lettering, typesetting, and the typewriter to visually engage readers and break down expectations of the printed text. But Pound and Olson measured lines according to breath and poetic beats, not by counting letters! (There are of course numbers of novelists, sound-text, and "concrete" poets who expose, and espouse, composition employing visual methods. Much of what Cage does easily fits into their contexts.)

As for certain techniques Cage selects, the utilization of common typographic materials serves to collapse the reading/writing process—by implying that the commercial intermediaries (editors, publishers, printers, distributors) between author and reader are nonexistent. But, ultimately, these meanings are part of the invisible operations that constitute the history of a book or inform that realm of "biographical" subtexts. (Though, again, postmodern writers often precisely incorporate this material as a way of emphasizing the performative role of the reader.)

Cage supplements the inherent significations of postmodern writing and extends them through the introduction of Duchampian aesthetics. Page measurements, type fonts, printing requirements, ink colors—and words themselves—all become found objects, fields upon which imaginations play. "My work was only sometimes that of identifying," he says in reference to his writings through *Finnegans Wake,* "as Duchamp had, found objects."[22] The physical fact of a page becomes a field of possible meanings not determined by the author—in the same way that Duchamp allowed the accidental breakage of "The Large Glass" to contribute to its history and mythology.

One of the questions raised by this process is how should a reader account for semantics or "meaning" of Cage's text knowing that, in many cases, the choice of language was the result of a purely visual requirement or numerical calculation? Readers, like mathematician Lewis Carroll's Alice, don't mind ambiguity, puns, and language play, but they expect authors to write with some precise meanings in mind.

Of course, Cage's "exemplifications" of ideas and meanings are resolved in the context of performance/readings, by himself or others. At least that was the case in writings included in books up to **A Year from Monday.** Through that collection Cage's pieces were essentially scores from lectures or reprints of introductions, statements, etc. Much of the work exhibited word and page play, but except for **"Talk 1,"** where phrases and words are splayed across the page in a representation of the seating pattern of the audience at a lecture in Ann Arbor, Cage still remained within the bounds of conventional linear form and the writings employ ordinary syntax. But with *M: Writings '67-'72,* everything changes.

The title of the work was chosen, Cage notes, by chance. Nevertheless, the letter M references

> many words and names that have concerned me for many years (music, mushrooms, Marcel Duchamp, M. C. Richards, Morris Graves, Mark Tobey, Merce Cunningham, Marshall McLuhan, my dear friends the Daniels—Minna, for twenty-three years the editor of *Modern Music,* and Mell, early in my life and now again in later life the painter)—and recently (mesostics, Mao Tse-tung).[23]

M, he adds, is also the first letter of *Mureau,* the first of Cage's "writings through" another text, in this case the remarks of Henry David Thoreau. M, it is worth noting, is the thirteenth letter of the alphabet; it is the favorite letter for characters in the works of that literary master of silence, Samuel Beckett (Murphy, Malloy, Malone); and it is that curious, universal nasal consonant that connotes primal soundings and the border between sound and silence: mama, mu, mute, om, mum, mmmmm . . .

With *M,* Cage's writings become more minimal, graphic, and harshly disciplined. *M* includes sixty-two Letraset mesostic constructions taken from syllables and words from Cunningham's *Changes: Notes on Choreography* and thirty-two other books used by Cunningham. Based on the name Merce Cunningham, Cage uses "seven hundred different typefaces" meant to ideographically image Cunningham the dancer. Other mesostics appear throughout the collection. Mesostics subsequently dominate Cage's next books, *Themes and Variations, Empty Words,* and *X.* Cage's mesostics and the "writings through" (*Finnegans Wake, The Cantos*) follow various rules established for each piece. Chance is of course essential to the process of composition.

This by now twenty-year-old practice of writing mesostic texts, writings without syntax, and syllable/sound-text constructions (from *Mureau* to *Muoyce*) marks a profound remaking for Cage—and any reader. For, although the early writings intimate radical possibilities, Cage's game changes substantially when he chooses to forgo logically developed texts, ignore ordinary syntactical relations, write almost exclusively in the mesostic form, and intentionally compose sound/text compositions. If reading Cage previously was fraught with self-consciousness, A-effects and an aura of

complexity, this turn toward letterism, vocables, and vertical schematics goes further in undermining thorough or nondiscursive readings.

There are several points to be made regarding the page, letters, and Cage's "rewritings" since *M.* The most obvious physical change in Cage's newer texts and books is the presence of the whiteness of the page. It dominates. Mesostics, like unattended scrabble games, lay on pages. The whiteness, with all its imperfections, wraps around the oddly constructed ideograms and thickset letters of the Cunningham mesostics. In the 8 ½" × 11" format of *Themes and Variations,* the text skitters up and down the center of each page like individually planted corn stalks. In *Empty Words* reproductions of Thoreau's drawings are scratched alongside the frail typeset lettering; and in **"Writing for the Second Time through *Finnegans Wake*"** punctuation, like small blemishes, are flecked through the pages. By contrast, *Mureau* and *Mouyce* are printed in dense, nonparagraphed, nonjustified form so that the white margins function as tailored borders around the formal rectangular blocks of letters.

In previous writings, blank spaces and whiteness were intended to signify pauses, breaths, or specific temporal divisons, as in **"Composition as Process—I. Changes."**[24] Concerning the layout of **"Lecture on Commitment,"** Cage indicates "The typography is an attempt to provide changes for the eye similar to the changes varying tempi in oral delivery give to the ear."[25] The earlier texts were, in effect, more like scores. But, after *M,* the whiteness is irregular and purely spatial. It is part of the aleatory numerical/geometric plan. (And oddly in accord with a theory of writing put forth in Borges's story "The Library of Babel." Borges's narrator conjectures that the reason for so many chaotic books in the "universe (which others call the Library)" is that the originators of writing merely endlessly manipulated twenty-five signs comprised of twenty-two letters, a period, a comma, and a space.[26]

Cage's writing after *M* is more for the eye and for the thought and pleasure of the reader. Stripped of its temporal requirements, the whiteness of the page accumulates other meanings and uses. The rectangular shape of the margins in ordinary books is a space where the reader can duplicate the text: marginalia is, in a sense, a scribbling that mimics the printed page. Cage thus opens up other possibilities for the reader, both physically and conceptually.

> turNing the paper
> intO
> a space of Time
> imperfections in the pAper upon which
> The

```
                        musIc is written
            the music is there befOre
                it is writteN
```

[X, p. 136]

Mallarmé, exquisitely, says something similar: "To seek support, according to the page, upon the blank space, which inaugurates it, upon oneself, for an ingenuousness . . . and, when, in a break—the slightest, disseminated—chance is aligned, conquered word by word, indefectibly the white blank returns, a moment ago gratuitous, certain now, to conclude that nothing beyond and to authenticate the silence—"[27]

In Cage's writings, the extensive whiteness is transformed simultaneously into background and covering, landscape and dreamscape, emptiness and plenitude, space and shape. And, most forcefully, the whiteness reveals the formal schematics of the texts (mesostics and "writings through") and thereby isolates the printed forms as what they are: lines, marks, patterns; mere movements of the hand, tool, and ink; writings as visual structures—signifiers cut loose from referents and, possibly, meaning. Writing as gesture, nothing more.

Visually, in most printings, the mesostic form focuses the eye on the word or name in the center of the image. It creates a readerly movement down the page, and, secondarily, from left to right. This movement of the eye vertically adds a hitherto unacknowledged geometry (for Western readers): the crease or fold in the middle of two pages is replicated by the spine of letters of the mesostics, which are echoed and enclosed by the edges of the pages on either side. There are thus five "lines" down the center of the pages of the open book (five is the number Cage, repeating Buckminster Fuller, feels is the number of ideas one should use to begin to solve problems).[28] The two strings of the mesostics figuratively double each other as well as the centerfold between pages. There are also four white spaces, two per page, surrounding the writing. The forms of the pages with centered mesostics increase the reader's awareness of Cage's process of doubling and repetition.

In practice, Cage's mesostics are nearly always extended compositions on names or concepts long familiar to him, and the repetition within the mesostic follows certain patterns. This persistence of doublings and repetitions in the (re) writings since *M,* along with the expansion of whiteness and the return to the letter, suggest that Cage's writings are actually readings, of himself, or of himself reading others (Joyce, etc.). These readings—silent performances—ultimately position Cage where readers of his works have been since the beginning: amidst uncertainty and self-referencing, yet surrounded by familiar names and recognizable ideas. In *Themes and Variations,* Cage cites as one of his themes, "Importance of being perplexed. Unpredictability" and also observes "Influence derives from one's own work (not from outside it)."[29]

But while Cage is reading/performing Cage, what of his readers? The "writings through" Pound and Joyce in recent mesostics border on cryptic indulgence and, with regard to conventional meaning, seem opaque. Reading Cage of late (since *M*) is more problematic than ever because none of the questions raised by earlier texts are resolved while others are being posed. And, to complicate matters, as he notes in **"Composition in Retrospect"** (1981):

```
                My
                mEmory
            of whaT
                    Happened
                is nOt
        what happeneD

                i aM struck
                by thE
                facT
                    tHat what happened
                is mOre conventional
        than what i remembereD
```

[X, p. 124]

Yet, curiously, there is a resonant quality about this work—something paradoxically evocative of ancient poetic impulses and postmodern mysteries. It is as if Cage's selfless, disciplined, thorough pursuits have resulted in the production of texts that so literally "exemplify" themselves as to create the extraordinary—purely Cagean—condition of reading that, like silence, is non-reading. Thus, Cage's "theme": "Problems of music (vision) only solved when silence (non-vision) is taken as the basis"[30] can be reformulated as: Problems of reading (meaning) only solved when nonreading (meaninglessness) is taken as the basis. Or, to say it another way: "Poetry is having nothing to say and saying it; we possess nothing."[31] Saying nothing is of course not simple, as attested to by many characters in the works of Samuel Beckett, one of whom, Malone, drily remarks "Nothing is more real than nothing."[32]

For readers of John Cage, nonreading is a consequence of reading, just as listeners to his music encounter silence. Cage's later writings distill and rarify the performance of writing/reading to a point of utter density: a black hole within which all the physics of the Cagean universe simultaneously hold true and are questionable. For both Cage and readers, nonreading is readings' dumb show: a performance that verges on meaning, where signs are ultimately themselves, isolated, yet as full as Cagean silence.

Cage insinuates the reader into nonreading by seizing on a writing process that identifies the atoms, the ABCs, of the writing system and reveals their negative charge. For Cage and readers, the letters of the alphabet literally become the formal units of practice/process/performance. Letters: a script in mime that is both a sign of itself and the source of other meanings.

The alphabet. Alphabets order sound and signs; they are social and intellectual tools that contribute to the possibilities of shared meaning. The use of an alphabet is, for Cage, a way of employing a system of notation not unlike musical notation—given that the vocalization of the sounds of letters have, of course, a different value and relationship than pitches. (The ancient Egyptian myth of the god Treuth, related by Socrates in Plato's *Philebus,* interrestingly relates how both the alphabet and musical intervals were selected and ordered from the sounds in nature.)

> To raise language's
> temperature we not only remove syntax:
> we
> give each letter undivided attention,
> setting it in unique face and size;
> to read becomes the verb to sing.
>
> [*M,* p. 107]

> The mechanism of the I Ching, on the other
> hand is utility.   Applied to
> letters and aggregates of letters, it
> brings about a language that can be
> enjoyed without being understood.
>
> [*M,* p. 215]

Cage's use of the alphabet assumes two forms, with many variations. In works such as ***Empty Words*** and the "writings through," he employs chance operations to select syllables and individual letters. In the mesostics, the letters of selected names, arranged vertically, become the structure for the text. In both cases, individual letters retain their visual and phonetic character.

Cage has written why he chose to write in the mesostic form, an alphabetic reduction: "Due to N. O. Brown's remark that syntax is the arrangement of the army, and Thoreau's that when he heard a sentence he heard feet marching, I became devoted to nonsyntactical "demilitarized" language."[33] Apparently he missed McLuhan's analysis of alphabets in *Understanding Media,* although he does note in **"Seriously Comma"**[34] that McLuhan says that the inflexibility of the order of the alphabet made the Renaissance inevitable. But McLuhan elaborates, arriving at the conclusion that the alphabet created a new literacy and a sense of individuality accessible to everyone. When the language of the tribe broke down, clans separated and travel between language-distinct regions was facilitated. This, he noted, enhanced those who sought power and the "freedom to shape an individual career manifested itself in the ancient world in military life."[35]

The alphabetic writings derive from names or other texts, and elusively refer to their predecessors. Cage ingeniously taunts readers with the possibility that his reductions offer yet another method for reading Joyce, Thoreau, or others. His processes, not far removed from certain computer analyses of linguistic structures in texts, raise questions about how we read and understand literary works.

Cage's alphabets are approaches to reading *and* writing. Like a minimalist Pierre Menard (a character in a Borges story who successfully "writes" *Don Quixote* in 1934 by writing the exact words from *Don Quixote*), Cage recycles all that he has read and written *by the letters,* as if they retained a mystical or coded meaning.

Perhaps they do. For the notion of the alphabet holds other significations for Cage. A longish lecture/performance mesostic titled "James Joyce, Marcel Duchamp, Erik Satie: An Alphabet" (1981) begins with Cage's comment that "It is possible to imagine that the artists whose work we live with constitute not a vocabulary but an alphabet by means of which we spell our lives."[36]

He amplifies this statement with references to the poetry of Jackson MacLow, whose work he has known for many years. MacLow, Cage remarks, has many vocabularies "restricting each to the letters to be found in the name of a particular friend."[37] Cage then recounts the effects of Joyce, Satie, and Duchamp on his life and work. He explains how he came to write their names as mesostics and, for this work, thematically bring them "on stage" as ghosts. He also quite pointedly states that he has never understood the work of Duchamp or Joyce.

Nonunderstanding is nearly a Cagean axiom, though it neither restricts him from thought or work. As a response to "not understanding" his teachers, Cage sets their names in mesostic form, as alphabets, and pursues "a way of writing which though coming from ideas is not about them; or is not about ideas but produces them."[38]

Cage's writing process is directed toward liberating him from conscious choice while imposing discipline. He has said as much and there is little to argue with in Cage's adoption of "Eastern" techniques for both "freeing the self" and not pursuing "self-expression." Cage's specific "alphabetic" method, however, not only reminds one of ancient disciplines but it is curiously postmodern. His practices are reminiscent of the mysteries of incantation and the decidedly conscious postmodern practice of writing intertextually.

Many of Cage's mesostics are based on the names of individuals. This form of "alphabeting" is analogous to the peculiar process of "anagramatic" writing explored by linguist and phoneticist Ferdinand de Saussure. This investigation, never published by Saussure, is recollected and enclosed within a commentary by Jean Starobinski in a small book titled *Words Upon Words.*

Briefly, while studying Saturnian Latin poetry, Saussure realized that each text seems to contain a "theme-word" which provides the poet with a phonemic source for the writing of the poem. Anagrams, as he designated these words, were generally names of gods, rulers, friends, or lovers. In effect, the letters of the poem's "theme-word" functioned as the structure for a given poem. This practice, Saussure notes, occurs in Vedic poetry where there is often a "reproduction in a hymn of the syllables of the sacred name which is the object of the hymn." He also conjectures that Indo-European poetry might have conformed to a process "invoked in relation to superstitious fixation on a letter."[39]

Saussure develops his theory by diligently counting (à la Cage) the repetition of syllables and letters of anagrams in poems. In the course of his work, he recognizes that it is possible that anagrams do exist, not only in the poems he analyzes but in all texts—simply by the chance occurrence of the letters and sounds of any given word or name. He is also troubled by the fact that he cannot locate any written rule that instructs poets to employ anagrams.

In Starobinski's reflections, he suggests, in accordance with Cage, that the strict adherence to a method leads to a condition not of self-expression but "literary production," as opposed to "literary creation." He comments further on the "inspiration" provided by "theme-words" or magic names. In concluding arguments, he addresses notions of nonintention, antecedent words, and the poet's silence: themes directly relevant to Cage's activities for decades.

Cage's alphabets—even those, as in **"Composition in Retrospect,"** that are based on words (discipline, method, etc.)—provide a contemporary exemplification for the theorizing of Saussure and Starobinski. Cage has always attempted to avoid self-expression and deliberation by the ego. His choice of influences both satisfies the dynamics in his personal pantheon and, subtly, inspires him to produce new work. The fact that Cage is absolutely overt about his practice, unlike the Latin poets, promotes it as an object lesson. This exposure and focused attention to the facts of his writerly performance also marks the postmodern direction of Cage's writing.

Several qualities identify postmodern texts: they are performative, self-conscious, open-ended, process-oriented, self-referential, polyvalent, combinatory, dialogic. Cage's texts, taken as a whole, fulfill all these criteria. The postmodern text also recognizes itself as one text among many, part of the circularity and intertextuality of all writing. Cage's Duchampian obviousness about his sources and references underscores this proclivity. Moreover, several of Cage's sources are themselves postmodern in their referentiality, notably

Joyce, Brown, McLuhan. And Cage, like Borges, Calvino, Raymond Federman, and so many others, rereads himself: a double performance for the reader who finds himself reading through Cage-reading-Cage.

Cage's writings, readings, performances—and silences—seem, finally, to curve back upon themselves. Letters, scattered or structured on the page, chance selections from other texts, the whitenesses and *italicizations* are warped and woven together as language to be "enjoyed without being understood":[40] readings for nonreading, texts for nothing, indeterminate, nonintentional performances of silence in silence.

What, then, can a reading of Cage be? Nothing but a ceaseless series of performances, perhaps in silence, bounded by uncertainty: nonreading without goals or meaning? Pure play!

For this reader/ing a response is embedded in an untitled poem in *X* (*X*, incidentally, was a letter picked by chance, but, no matter, its significations are enormous) and Starobinski's last two sentences in *Words Upon Words* (p. 123). The poem is about readers, as is the quotation.[41]

if you exi ted
~~becauSe~~
we mIght go on as before
but since you don't we ~~wi~~'Ll
mak
~~changE~~
our miNds
anar hic
~~so that we~~ Can
d to   let it be
convert~~Enjoy~~ the chaos / ~~that~~ you are /
stet

[*X*, p. 117]

"But the poet, having said all he has to say, remains strangely silent. One can produce any hypothesis about him: he neither accepts nor rejects it."

Notes

1. Jacques Derrida, *Dissemination,* trans. Barbara Johnson (Chicago: University of Chicago Press, 1981), p. 175.

2. Jorge Luis Borges, *In Praise of Darkness,* trans. Norman Thomas di Giovanni (London: Penguin Books, 1975), p. 121.

3. John Cage, *Silence: Lectures and Writings* (Middletown, Conn.: Wesleyan University Press, 1961), p. 146.

4. John Cage, *Themes and Variations* (Barrytown, N.Y.: Station Hill Press, 1982), introduction.

5. Cage, Lecture on Nothing," *Silence,* p. 109.

6. Cage, *Themes and Variations,* introduction.

7. John Cage, *Empty Words: Writings '73-'78* (Middletown, Conn.: Wesleyan University Press, 1979), p. 51.

8. *Brecht on Theater,* ed. and trans. John Willett (New York: Hill and Wang, 1957), p. 135; and *Silence,* p. ix.

9. John Cage, *A Year from Monday: New Lectures and Writings* (Middletown, Conn.: Wesleyan University Press, 1967), p. 133.

10. See Cage, *Year from Monday,* p. 73 and *Empty Words,* p. 99.

11. Richard Kostelanetz, *The Old Poetries and the New* (Ann Arbor: University of Michigan Press, 1981), p. 263.

12. Cage, *Empty Words,* p. 51.

13. Geoffrey Hartman, *Saving the Text* (Baltimore: The Johns Hopkins University Press, 1981), p. 9.

14. Cage, *Empty Words,* p. 33.

15. Cage, *Year from Monday,* p. 3.

16. Cage, *Silence,* p. 96.

17. Ibid., p. 26.

18. John Cage, *X: Writings '79-'82* (Middletown, Conn.: Wesleyan University Press, 1983), p. 173.

19. Cage, *Silence,* p. 35.

20. Cage, *Themes and Variations,* p. 5.

21. *For the Birds* (John Cage in Conversation with Daniel Charles), trans. Richard Gardner (Salem, N.H.: Boyars, 1981), p. 117.

22. Cage, *Empty Words,* p. 136.

23. John Cage, *M: Writings '67-'72* (Middletown, Conn.: Wesleyan University Press, 1973), foreword.

24. Cage, *Silence,* p. 18.

25. Cage, *Year from Monday,* p. 112.

26. Jorge Luis Borges, *Ficciones,* ed. and trans. Anthony Kerrigan (New York: Grove Press, 1962), pp. 79-80.

27. Derrida, *Dissemination,* p. 178.

28. Cage, *Themes and Variations,* introduction.

29. Ibid.

30. Ibid.

31. Ibid.

32. Samuel Beckett, *Three Novels: Molloy, Malone Dies, The Unnamable* (New York: Grove Press, 1955), p. 192.

33. Cage, *Empty Words,* p. 133.

34. Cage, *Year from Monday,* p. 26.

35. Marshall McLuhan, *Understanding Media: The Extensions of Man* (New York: New American Library, 1964), p. 90.

36. Cage, *X,* p. 53.

37. Ibid.

38. Cage, *Themes and Variations,* introduction.

39. Jean Starobinski, *Words Upon Words: The Anagrams of Ferdinand de Saussure,* trans. Olivia Emmet (New Haven: Yale University Press, 1979), pp. 22 and 24.

40. Cage, *M,* p. 215.

41. This paper was written with support from the Pennsylvania Council on the Arts (Visual Arts Panel) and I wish to express my thanks to the Council.

Daniel Herwitz (essay date 1994)

SOURCE: Herwitz, Daniel. "John Cage's Approach to the Global." In *John Cage: Composed in America,* edited by Marjorie Perloff and Charles Junkerman, pp. 188-205. Chicago: University of Chicago Press, 1994.

[*In the following essay, Herwitz views Cage's works as anarchic studies of humanity, politics, and language.*]

It was almost inevitable that John Cage would move from composing in music to composing in words. For Cage, music was never just music, it was always the occasion for reformation. When Cage set out in the early 1950s to reform music, to silence what he saw as its constricted practices, he was really aiming to free constricted human beings by freeing their ears. For Cage, music was to be an exemplar of how human beings relate to the world and to one another. Cage set out, in redefining our relation to sounds, in opening the ear to the full panoply of the acoustical, to free human beings from their encagements, thus allowing them to "be" in the world of whatever happened to happen. Cage's musical experiments were motivated by his belief that when we approach sound with ears informed by our concepts and expectations about musical structure and expression, we are precluding a deep and immediate acknowledgment of both sound and the world, opting instead for a kind of distorted attempt at control. Indeed, he believed that the very attempt to order sound in the mind's ear as coherent, complete, resolving, elaborative, and formal, is an act of manipulation or possession. In projecting through the ear our concepts of the musical, we are doing to sound what we do to other people when we try to recast them in our own images as opposed to letting them freely be themselves. To acknowledge sound, like acknowledging people, is for Cage to just let it be. Such a view goes beyond any mere plea for tolerance in music (or in ethics) for it identifies respect with noninterference. So long as we don't interfere, sound and life are fine.

Following suit on this belief, Cage's music has nearly from its inception been an art of disturbance, aimed at the breakdown of traditional musical commitments to structure and expression. Cage's ideas about human liberation, or restoration to the natural flow of life without interference, had in the 1950s and early 1960s been worked out through (1) his musical experiments in engaging new sounds and new silences, and (2) through his bricolage of writings. The writings had remained in some sense separate, with the focus of Cagean practice being the musical experiments. While not "purely musical," because defined by the force of the writings and rhetoric, Cage's musical past had focused on experiments in sound. This, I think, reflected his modernist optimism that changes in musical experience, hypercharged with a modernist rhetoric of ideas, could and would change the world. Experiments in sound, with ideas to back up their already suggestive powers, were the currency of liberation.

One found in the Cage of the 1950s and early 1960s an intoxication with the future of music, as if changes rung in musical concepts through formal sound experiments would bring about the full liberation of the human being, as if the dropping of discriminatory musical practices would liberate us from mind and desire, thus making our lives more natural and more beautiful. Rather than being strictly musical, Cage's battles over music optimistically extended to the center of the world.

Such an inflated belief in the power of an avant-garde artwork to ring changes in life as a whole may also be found in the rhetoric of the Bauhaus, of Constructivism, of Mondrian and De Stijl, of Le Corbusier, and even of André Breton. Mondrian wrote as if by calibrating his canvases into a mysterious harmonic balance, by freeing them from all but primary colors and rectangular shapes, he would succeed in bringing about a similar balance in the world as a whole; he wrote as if his announcement in paint of the coming of platonic truth would simply bring that truth about. Mondrian, writing such things in 1942, a bad year for Europe if ever there was one, can only in retrospect strike us as wild. Yet his grandiose belief in the capacity of art to change the world is in some sense a defining feature of the avant-garde. Which goes to show that Cage the reformer kept good spiritual company in those halcyon, Black Mountain days. And it also goes to show that Cage had drunk rather deep of avant-garde optimism.[1]

It takes more than the freeing of music from its dependence on harmonic hierarchy and melodic phrasing to change the world—which brings us to Cage's reconceptualization of the future of music, specifically of music's mode of address. Cage could not simply write essays and compose indefinitely as if changes in the structure of musical sounds would by themselves reform the world if he really took himself to be a reformer of life through the domain of art. What he subsequently added to the concept of the musical work is words, and my topic here is to describe how Cage's poetic mesostics reflect his attempt to address complex global issues while retaining his older ideas about musical liberation. By turning music into poetry Cage has, paradoxically, like Wagner, made the scope of music more referential and more global. Is this because, like Wagner, he believed that music is an event which, if big enough and overwhelming enough *can* bring about a redefinition of the world? I prefer to think that Cage's mesostics represent his way of acknowledging music's (or poetry's) dependence on the world as well as its independence from it. Not only is music literally nothing, without a form of life to give shape to its practices and force to the reception of its tonalities; but furthermore, a musical work cannot be a vehicle for the world's greening simply through its formal innovations, however fetishized such experimental gestures may be by an avant-garde utopian theory. The musical work must acknowledge the world and address it in order to make something happen. Silence may be golden, but the world will not change (either in four minutes and thirty-three seconds or in a lifetime) if the musical work remains silent. At least if it remains silent about the world.

We turn then to Cage's development of a global mode of address in the medium of words. How can his mesostics engage the world while retaining his commitment to the power of musical silence? The answer can only be: By chance. I will return to this point, but first, let me suggest that we think of Cage's mesostics as embodying a kind of soul-force, a mode of Satyagraha, of passive resistance to the world. This is not of course the only interpretive perspective one can have of Cage's poetry, which like all poetry is highly overdetermined; but it is a way of getting at the nature of his "poethics," of approaching the politics resident in the poetry. Through the imposition of chance operations onto language, specifically onto the source texts Cage uses in his poetic compositions, Cage symbolically aims to halt the march of language, meaning, and human control. Silence is preserved in the mode of passive resistance to meaning (by one who is implacable in the face of the onslaught of human language, certainty, and human omnipotence). As conceptual control and political imposition are silenced through Cage's fragmenting play with words, another silence opens up for the community of readers or listeners, a silence in which intimacy may be cultivated and communion between persons may occur. "The best communion between men happens in silence," Cage is fond of quoting Thoreau as saying.

In "The Future of Music," Cage asserts:

> more and more a concern with personal feelings of individuals, even the enlightenment of individuals, will be seen in the larger context of society. We know how to suffer and control our emotions. If not, advice is available, There is a cure for tragedy. The path to self-knowledge has been mapped out by psychiatry, by oriental philosophy, mythology, occult thought, anthroposophy and astrology . . . What we are learning is how to be convivial. "Here comes everybody." Though the doors will always remain open for the musical expression of personal feelings, what will more and more come through is the expression of the pleasures of conviviality . . . And beyond that a non-intentional expressivity, a being together of sounds and people . . . A walk, so to speak, in the woods of music, or in the world itself."[2]

This remark about conviviality brands Cage's new music as aiming to create what Kant calls a "sensus communis," a community of taste in which each shares the pleasures of all and takes pleasure in this sharing.[3] But unlike Kant's Enlightenment community, which is based on sameness of taste, morals, and rationality, Cage's is Thoreauvian. Cage's idea of a musical body is one in which the free play of differences are given vent and let be without interference. By extension the conviviality he wishes to engender is conviviality with a difference, that is, a form of communion in which each person acknowledges the differing presence of the others in quietude, toleration, and friendliness. Cage's is an anarchist homage to the politics of Thoreau, who said, as Cage is often fond of repeating, "the best form of government is none at all."

These differences between Cage and Kant are worth pursuing. Each founds his idea (ideal) of a community on the claim of shared reciprocity—each member of the community should treat the others in the manner in which the others should treat him or her. Yet the thrust of Kantian thought is in the direction of a community in which each person is conceptualized as the same as the others. For Kant, the cardinal moral rule is to act so that one's action might be willed as a universal law, which is to say a law which would produce good results were everyone else to do the same under the same circumstances. You cannot do anything (such as not voting or not keeping your promises) which, were everyone else to do the same, would produce infelicitous results. On Kantian lines, the deepest and most self-realizing form of freedom available to people is the freedom to set before themselves this moral law. Each person must judge his or her actions according to the rule of universalizability, a rule which, while unclear in its applications to practical moral decision making, has a clear intention behind it, namely to bind us together under the umbrella of a universal conception of humanity in which all rule their actions by the constraint of considering how things would be were everybody else to do the same (in the same circumstances).

For Cage, as an American freethinking maverick, it is not true that everybody does or should do the same under the same conditions. For him, the deepest freedom is the Thoreauvian freedom to be oneself, to listen to the differences between oneself and others without imposing an ethics of hierarchical evaluation or punishment, and to accept the flow of the world in its myriad incarnations of blossoming. We do not and need not be expected to act in the way in which everyone else would act in the same situation. People should be allowed to differ, just as sounds should be permitted to sound as they are. The kind of learning required for this exigency called "life" is a learning to hear mutually and accept mutually the differences as well as the similarities among our styles of feeling, response, action and reaction.

Since both Cage and Kant treat the work of art as a body symbolic of humanity, one can trace the differences in their conceptions of art to differences in how each imagines humanity to be. For Kant, the artwork—in Kant's well-known phrase the "symbol of Morality"—allows us to take pleasure in our capacity to set the moral law freely before us. Kant finds in the artwork a play of freedom, necessity, and purpose that allows us to treat it as symbolic of this capacity. Specifically, for Kant, the artwork is freely organized in that it is made in the absence of rules. (Kant refers to the capacity to make things in the absence of rules as "genius"). Yet it also suggests both formal necessity and formal finality. We feel that its parts fit together as if tending toward some ultimate goal, and we feel that the parts are so required by the setting of this goal that, were a single note in the Mozart sonata different, were a single chord or counter-rhythm in the Beethoven symphony other than it is, we would, according to Kant, fear that the entire work would collapse. Yet the Mozart sonata or Beethoven symphony is made, in Kant's view, in the absence of any rule that would justify our conviction about its finality and necessity. This Kantian urge to find in symbols the coordination of freedom, necessity, and finality—an urge aptly reflected by the classicized art and music of his time—is the urge to find traces both of human freedom and of the binding necessity of the moral law. We seek, according to Kant, inevitability in such symbols, a sense of their purpose, yet we also seek in them a compulsion which is paradoxically freely achieved by the genius of the work (in its creation and reception). It is this tripartite projection of freedom, necessity, and finality onto things, this reshaping of things in the name of humanity, that makes things beautiful according to Kant.

Rather than eliciting a feeling of formal necessity, structure, and finality, Cage's poems celebrate the spontaneous, the fortuitous, the incomplete, and the nonhierarchical concord and discord called "life." His music and poems evoke a humanity perfected through its spontaneity, shared contingency, and above all, its mutual capacity to listen to the voices of its differing members without judgment. Cage's music and poetry acknowledge a humanity whose bonds are established through the agreement to reject laws that impose sameness and by implication, necessary moral action. Thus Cage's music and poetry reject the Kantian approach of symbolizing a humanity defined by law and necessity, and equally the creation of art which imposes a sense of necessity onto its audience. For Cage, little pleasure is to be found in such a structured universe. Rather he uses form purely as a means of artificially organizing the free play of "whatever happens to happen," eschewing all further sense of formal necessity. And he uses chance operations to determine that form. Cage's poems try to force us to confront the contingencies of events and the play of relations among sounds—relations which exist in an anarchic space that discourages any urge to find a set of necessary connections or ultimate goals, but encourages a discipline of focused, nonhierarchical listening, and immersion into the play of the poem.

Cage's image of an anarchic body politic is therefore reflected in the structure and texture of his poetry. The anarchic play of linguistic particles and musical voices in his poems suggests that he identifies the human commitment to conceptual certainty (whether about conceptual truth or about the moral law) with the politics of human control. Cage identifies the claim of reason to order the world with the claim of desire to rule the world omnipotently. Where there is clear meaning, there is clear hierarchy, and where there is hierarchy, there is the master and the slave. In his suspicion of the urge toward conceptual control, Cage is like Derrida and certain feminist critics.[4] His aim is to diffuse the tendency toward political control by forcing us to give

up the conceptual claim of imposing interpretive hierarchies and interpretive certainties onto the world. The structure of Cage's mesostics aims to put what Wittgenstein would call a "full stop" (in the *Philosophical Investigations*) to meaning, textual imposition, and the desire for world control, thus freeing us to let the complexities of the world just be, and allowing us to bond in the midst of our various differences. About this Cage is quite serious.

In his preface to the **"Lecture on the Weather,"** his Bicentennial present to the United States, Cage states:

> It may seem to some that through the use of chance operations I run counter to the spirit of Thoreau (and '76, and revolution for that matter). The fifth paragraph of *Walden* speaks against blind obedience to a blundering oracle. However, chance operations are not mysterious sources of "the right answers." They are a means of locating a single one among a multiplicity of answers, and at the same time, of freeing the ego from its taste and memory, its concern for profit and power, of silencing the ego so that the rest of the world has a chance to enter into the ego's own experience whether that be outside or inside.

and,

> The desire for the best and the most effective in connection with the highest profits and the greatest power led to the fall of nations before us: Rome, Britain, Hitler's Germany. Those were not chance operations. We would do well to give up the notion that we alone can keep the world in line, that only we can solve its problems.

> *(EW, 5)*

Chance operations are meant to put a full stop to the imposition of the inexorable or determinate onto the recipient, be the recipient a nation or a listener. By silencing the politician's—or composer's—own desires for control, chance operations give the nation—or the listener—the chance to develop personality and conviviality on their own.

It is well known that the formal key to Cage's fragmentation of meaning is his use of chance operations. How do chance operations structure Cage's mesostics? In these poetic compositions Cage operates on tones, producing highly arbitrary strings of words which occupy a given time segment, for example the space of the six Norton Lectures delivered at Harvard during the academic year of 1988-89 (and published under the title *I-VI* by the Harvard University Press in 1990). Cage treats the occasion as an open time segment to be filled with his art, which is what the book is the text of, and one should understand the reasons for his choice. Like all of Cage's mesostics it has rules. In a brief introduction, Cage tells us he uses the *I Ching* plus a complex computer program (designed partly by Andrew Culver and partly by Jim Rosenberg) in order to subject a set of source texts to chance operations. Cage's sources (presented at the back of the book) are quotations from Wittgenstein, Thoreau, Emerson, Buckminster Fuller, McLuhan, Duchamp, himself, and others. He also uses *Finnegans Wake* and the daily newspaper. The computer program churns out from the source texts vertical strings of names in capital letters. The actual compositions proceed horizontally across the page, and there also the words used are generated by chance. Cage then subjects himself to the following rule. Using the vertical string as the central axis of the horizontal composition, he disallows the use in the intervening horizontal small-case string of the letter that forms the second capital of any successive pair of capital letters.

Cage's technique turns language into a game, into a form of activity that renders ordinary words into syntactically and semantically arbitrary patterns, whose sense or nonsense is a matter of the accidental, and whose parts seek and implicate various semantic configurations. Cage also aims to homogenize the parts of language (particles, connectives, nouns, verbs, etc.) as if they were twelve tones of equal value. The technique makes music by imposing rhythmical continuity much in the manner of twelve-tone composition, through restrictions on the stock of words (confined to the source texts) and restrictions on which letters can be used when. It is marvellous to hear Cage himself reading these lectures.[5] In his calming voice, the repetitions of words from his sources at odd, fortuitous places, combined with the continuity imposed by his compositional form, gradually soothes one's ears and opens them to the play of conceptual suggestions that wind in and out of each other in a diffuse, amniotic ambience. The feeling is one of a forest of signs in a montage without master-editing that includes world events, information circuits, philosophical snippets, modernist jokes, the blooming, buzzing ecologues of Joyce, and the ecologies of philosopher/naturalists. This vale of immersion is akin to the philosophical skeptic's picture of perception as a flow of information and feeling whose dimensions exceed conceptualization and our ability to determine what our role in their phenomenological fabrication is. Yet we do not fear this apparent defeat of perceptual knowledge but rather welcome it as the relinquishment of an impossible, horrendous perceptual task: that of finding knowledge in the endless play of forms or imposing domination onto it, thus closing ourselves off and making ourselves crazy.

I have suggested that this diffusion of meaning in an ambience of sound through chance operations is Cage's act of passive resistance to the domain of meaning, interventionist desire, and aggression. Yet we should not go too far in agreeing with the claim that meaning has been disarmed in these poetic texts. The poetry must have meaning in order to live as an act of passive resistance, for all passive resistance is resistance to *something,* and the choice of what to resist must be made by somebody, presumably by the author. Then Cage cannot have abolished his tastes and his ego in these works because, if I am right, they are directed to the world and are thus part of the politics of his art. Anarchy is after all a political choice.

As are the targets of Cage's practice, and as are Cage's specific choice of source texts. The source texts or prefaces Cage provides in his Norton Lectures or his **"Lecture on the Weather"** make very clear what his political likes and dislikes are, which brings us to the central paradox of Cage's poetry, namely how the poetry both fragments the meanings of the texts Cage chooses while at the same time making present for the listener the true meaning of the very texts which Cage's poetry fragments. This paradox demands elaboration. Cage's utopian ideas of resistance are given by the source texts he chooses in the Norton Lectures: texts by Thoreau, Wittgenstein, Fuller, from the daily newspaper, and so on. They are texts which are to his taste (for example he chooses very little Emerson even though Emerson is in many ways like Thoreau, because he detests Emerson), and they are texts whose politics he admires. When one hears the mesostics of the Norton Lectures it is crucial to one's experience of them that one knows what these source texts are, otherwise one loses the full scope of the vision of the world which Cage's poetic satyagraha is at the service of bringing about. To insure familiarity with that vision, he begins his Norton Lectures by describing which texts he has used. Then paradoxically—and wonderfully—Cage's poetry becomes a politics *precisely by fragmenting the meanings of those texts whose meanings the listener must know and keep in mind,* into a whirl of chance configurations—nearly. I say "nearly" because were they completely obliterated, the very point of the fragmentation would be lost, namely that the truth of these texts is proved, inculcated, or intimated into the listeners through the listeners' experience of the fragmentation of what they know these texts to be.

For the listener who already has the source texts in mind, their meanings are preserved in the mesostic through the associations between words and linguistic fragments that continuously emerge from the mesostic's play on word and sound association. In particular, associations emerge through Cage's own choice of the mesostic's wing words, which reverberate with textual resonance. The informed listener will feel this resonance of the source texts in Cage's vocabulary, rhythm, and phrasing. Composing in the wake of *Finnegans Wake,* Cage's brilliance in word and phrase juxtaposition offers an abundance of intimations—including associations to the source texts. It is crucial to listen through these poems, to find a path generated by the aural and auratic cast of their vocabulary, to find their rhythmic pulse and phrase structure. The listener can easily fail to do this. Indeed the work involved in hearing these through represents just that disciplined form of engagement, just that kind of care and attentiveness, that Cage demands of living in general. (It is worth noting in this regard that Cage could be very critical of his own performances of the mesostics.)

An illustration is in order. In the **"Fourth Mesostic"** of the Norton Lectures, one finds the following passage (like any such passage it is partly generated by chance operations and partly by Cage's own choice of the wing words):

> the Dance
> the magIc
>   in Some way
> the Contours'
>   I was standing quite close to
> Process'
> mind to worLd around'
>   I
> suddeNly
> thE
> two worLds
> envIronment'
> the divinity and Still the trembling
> Covers' the
> studyIng'
> the contours and Postures of
> why shouLd we be
> varIous
> THE' eNglish
> THE'
> swamps anD
> searchIng
> juSt
> beComes
> In other
> Port'
> fossiL fuels
> I said'
> weather at aNy hour'
> wE
> of peace anD
> goIng in by
> haSte to
> whiCh of
> IN is
> Pointing'
> schooLs
> If we could grasp the whole'

(***I-VI***, 220)

The play of semantic hits and misses is nicely illustrated in this passage where we are encouraged by the Cageian ambience to find deeper and deeper levels of association in the language, while also being encouraged simply to let the words lie where they are—as if the world of the poem, like the world as a whole, were

nothing but nature. Let us briefly consider it, beginning with the line: "mind to WorLd around'." The line carries the global reference of "world," and leads us to focus on the idea of connection between mind and world, an idea which is not defined but rather left for concentration and imagination. This phrase also plays semantically on the word "mind," which can be heard as both a noun and a verb, the verb being "to mind" or "to listen, think, and take care in approaching," suggesting a moral duty. But the line is also simply a piece of language which plays around the letter "L," as if that were its home, the location these words happened to have found to romp around in. "To worLd around" does not quite make sense, in spite of its suggestions of minding the world, of world travel, and of playing around, even, in the light of what has preceded this line two lines back, of "dancing around." Paradoxically this whirl of language is ecstatically suggestive, it stimulates the imaginative sensorium, because of its ultimate ungrammaticality. The words stimulate because they miss.

The next line of the mesostic is simply the word "I" (or is it simply the letter "I"?). Well, one hears it as the word "I"; one hears it as a stand-in for the poet himself, who appears to be on the verge of pronouncement or self-description. But his pronouncement or description never occurs (or does it?), because the "I" is dropped in the next phrase: "suddeNly / thE / two worLds / envIronment." That is, the "I" is dropped unless the readers hears "the . . . worLds envIronment" as the domain of the "I," say of a global "I" whose existence is the terrain of the world itself. At any rate the entrance of "suddeNly" after "I" is a surprise, one heard as an event. As such, the reader expects a description or narration of the event to follow, and does not get it. For what follows after "suddeNly" is a noun phrase ("the . . . worLds envIronment"), not an action or event sentence. The noun phrase which follows both resists and absorbs the narrative expectation given by "suddeNly." On the one hand, the reader feels, when he or she hears "the . . . worLds envIronment" following "suddeNly," a kind of letdown. The reader hears: "suddeNly . . . nothing." On the other hand, the expectation of an action or event given by "suddeNly" is transposed onto "the . . . worLds envIronment," vivifying it with the pulsation of activity. It is as if the mere fact of the world were itself an event—say an event of recognition, opening, or elaboration. The reader is brought to see the worlds environment as an event, to face it freshly. Resonance from the source texts occurs at just this point, for "the . . . worLds envIronment" is a major player in those texts, and by extension in Cage's global concerns and his global politics. The informed reader will pick up this resonance by being brought face to face with the thought of the worlds environment. Therefore it is through the semantic clashes and "infelicities," in

Cage's words, that the resonance of the source texts occurs. The source texts are preserved by means of fragmentation.

"[S]uddeNly / thE . . . worlDs / envIronment" is matched in rhythm by two other phrases in the selection quoted: "weather at aNy hour'"; and "If we could grasp the whole'." Both of these phrases are emphasized by their placement in the text as relatively long single lines. "[W]eather at aNy hour" makes one stand by and be ready for whatever happens to happen. I personally hear in it both "weather at any hour" and "whether at any hour." "Whether at any hour" ("Whether at any hour?") suggests a question asked about what might happen when. The question is of course not answered. Moreover I cannot help but hear Cage's **"Lecture on the Weather"** in these words—his lecture composed out of Thoreau's words in a storm of weather and its clearing, a storm of communion, peace, and communication. Thus I cannot help but hear the trace of Cage's Preface to that work in this line, which means I cannot help but hear a plea about our preparedness, say for the world's weather, behind the question of "whether at any hour." These layers of resonance will not occur to everyone, nor need they. My point is that the poem invites this play of texture, which is how its source texts reside in it by association.

What follows "wE / of peace" is the phrase "anD / go-Ing in by / haSte." Haste is the opposite of peace—both of world peace and peace of mind. When I play with these lines, I hear that when minding a world one must be at peace; I hear that minding a world requires that form of care (of *minding*) which is the opposite of haste, superficiality, or inattentiveness. This Cageian language of hasting and wasting, language also so congenial to a Protestant genius like Thoreau who is among the sources of the language, leads to a final plea: "If we could grasp the whole." "If we could grasp the whole" is the only grammatically correct and complete sentence in this selection. If we could grasp the whole . . . then what? What would we be able to do or be? The desire for such grasping rings deep, but the thought behind it lacks ultimate coherence, for we do not know what the whole is. The poem does not tell us. Shall we call the whole "weather at any hour"? Does all the weather of all the hours comprise a whole, say the whole of what happens in the world? Or is the whole some further and more portentous dimension of things, say the interconnectedness of all things? Then are all things interconnected in any single or fathomable way?

Consider how the fabric of the mesostic itself comprises a whole. It is a kind of weather at any hour, an ongoing pattern of unique linguistic events and associations, defined partly by regularity, partly by design and partly generated chaotically (by chance).[6] It cannot be grasped as a whole if by that one means computed into an

overall theory. Yet the urge to grasp the whole remains insistent. In its classically philosophical formulation, the urge to grasp the whole is precisely the urge to find an account of the poem or the world which will fully conceptualize all of its parts into a determinate relation. This is the urge for a philosopher like Hegel. Cage, again in a spirit akin to Derrida's, wishes to diffuse that urge and replace it by the urge for a kind of holistic thinking, a self-recognition of one's dwelling within a whole which resists overall determination, a holistic caring or minding. The urge to grasp the whole may be called the urge to acknowledge that interpenetration of people and things called "nature." This acknowledgment of the holistic, this address to the incomplete, this attentiveness to everything that happens and to one's place in this majesty called "everything," this care for the unknown and knowledge of its unknownness, is imbricated by the poem, and left unanalyzed. Grasping is, to use a phrase of Stanley Cavell's, "acknowledgment," not "*begriff*."[7] Shall we call the satisfaction of this urge the condition of being at peace with things? Then we must correspondingly say that the condition of being at peace with the world is a condition which both is and can never be completed, because being at peace with the world is also *minding* it: being at peace always carries the requirement of discipline and "minding."

What Cage's mesostic then allows—or requires—the listeners to do in working through its fragmented associations is to evolve for themselves its underlying meanings. The listener must mind the mesostic to uncover or attend to its play of concepts. And that is just the work of grasping the whole, in whatever sense it is possible to do this. Grasping and letting go, desiring to grasp and being at peace, finding and letting go, these are redefined as interconnected activities through the very work of listening. We then know the inner meanings of the source texts by being forced to live their meanings in the life of the poem. We are taught or occasioned. Only then can we understand what its associations intimate. Only then will the work of association be free, for only then will we learn to live its paths of connection. Then freedom and discipline—the discipline of attention—are in the end the same.

Meaning paradoxically shines through in Cage's mesostics through fragmentation and chance. The listener is afforded an experience of diffusion and attention; one's need to project meaning and to control the flow of one's perceptions is diffused. One is free to move about in the body of the poem (or world) without imposition, and in the mutual state of everybody else's being there in the same state, for this language is shared.

Cage calls that the recovery of the listener's natural state. I would call it the recovery of the listener's state of free association.[8] It is an enlightened state without the universalizing theory of the Enlightenment (Kant's) to back up its formulation. It is the state of inhabiting oneself. Therefore Cage's mesostics show us something philosophical about the nature of human dwelling. How much one should expect such a cultivated state of dwelling to carry over into political decisions is another story. Freud, ever skeptical of rosy views of what is natural to the political animal would be chary about proposing politics on the basis of such an optimistic conception of the power of enlightened experiences. It was Freud's concern in *Civilization and Its Discontents* to unmask those who make such optimistic proposals about human possibilities as persons who are displaced from their own aggression and thus refuse to acknowledge the full power of aggression in others. Whether this is true in the present case I leave to others. At any event, in partial defense of Cage's address to the world as opposed to Freud's suspicions, Cage's practice is not necessarily a denial of aggression, but a forceful, even, dare one say it, aggressively structured attempt, to make us recall our forgotten spirit of communion: to fight aggression with the force of communion. Is that crazy? No more so than the ideas of the transcendentalists, whom it ought to be the duty of communities to remember.[9]

Cage's claim that the point of his poetry is to remove his own ego, his own likes and dislikes from the music, therefore cannot be right. Rather Cage's poetry is meant to be an act of passive resistance to global facts about which Cage emphatically disapproves. As I said, Cage's beliefs and preferences, his ego if you will, is present in his work through the lingering presence of the meanings of his source texts. Meaning is dropped, but also retained. What is right is that Cage's mesostics aim to soften the brutality of the ego, to silence or deflate its claims to total conceptual and political control. This is right and it is powerful. Is it not enough? Does one need, for the purposes of life or philosophy, to do more to the ego than that? Can one impose more silence on its powers of operation than that, short of terrorizing it?[10]

I wish to make one final remark about the philosophical character of Cage's mesostics. They do not simply show us something about the conditions of human freedom and dwelling, they also reveal something about the nature of human identity. This is made clear through the relation between Cage's mesostics and their source texts. The game in the Norton Lectures is not for Cage to rid himself of Thoreau, Wittgenstein, or Fuller, but to identify himself with Thoreau and the rest in a way that is both direct and obscure.[11] The identification is obscure because Thoreau's words are present in Cage's work in indirect and scrambled ways, as an overall presence, roughly in the way my father is present in me, or my mother, or my history as an American. It is direct because the route from the source texts to their place in the poetry is clearly delineated by the structure of the chance operations, roughly in the way the route from

my parents to me is clearly marked by the history of my conception, gestation, and birth, and by my DNA. The presence of my parents, or more vaguely, of America, can be located in me precisely everywhere—in all the regions of my thoughts, attitudes, habits, and personality, and nowhere in particular—which is to say the mode of presence of my parents and my history in me is diffuse, obscure, and hard to unravel. This complex place occupied by facts of lineage in me reveals something philosophically deep about the opacity of my identity. By extension it reveals something about human identity generally. My identity is established vis-à-vis my genealogy out of a thousand similarities and differences between myself and my sources, one of which is the empirical world itself (in Cage's Norton Lectures the relation between the poetry and the empirical world is signified by the fragmented presence of the daily newspaper as a source). My identity depends on those sources while requiring separation from them, as does Cage's poetic work, as does all art require separation from the strands of real life which remain nevertheless strangely present in the artwork. My genealogy is present in me, one might say, silently, like a set of source texts. There is probably no clear and characterizing criterion of human identity for this reason. Nor for art. Cage's poetry then reveals something about the structure of its own identity as art, and about human identity.

There is therefore no clear and characterizing criterion for the identity of Cage's mesostics. Cage's poetic events can be approached from a number of different perspectives, mine being, at best, only one. Do they then invite the same kind of interpretive anarchy which they politically prescribe? Can one say anything about them and get away with it? If not, if some interpretations of them are better than others, how does that fact speak to the prospects for a noninterfering anarchy? And conversely, how much interpretive control is one entitled to assume in approaching the mesostics? At what point in the act of interpretation will these Cageian objects bristle? At what point should they bristle? All heady questions, again philosophical, which I leave for the heads of others.

Notes

1. For an extended discussion of the optimism of the avant-garde, of the way in which that utopian optimism requires theory, and of the inheritance of such theoretical stances by the contemporary world of art, see my *Making Theory/Constructing Art: On the Authority of the Avant-Garde* (Chicago: University of Chicago Press, 1993).

2. John Cage, "The Future of Music," in *Empty Words, Writings '73-'78* (Middletown, CT: Wesleyan University Press, 1979), p. 179. Hereafter cited as *EW.*

3. Immanuel Kant, *Critique of Judgement* (trans. J. Meredith (Oxford: Clarendon Press, 1973).

4. See Jacques Derrida, *Of Grammatology,* trans. G. C. Spivak (Baltimore: Johns Hopkins University Press, 1976); and Luce Irigaray, *Speculum of the other Woman,* trans. Gillian Gill, (Ithaca: Cornell University Press, 1985).

5. Selections from Cage's reading of the Norton Lectures can be heard on the tape which accompanies *I-VI* (Cambridge and London: Harvard University Press, 1990).

6. For discussions of the role of the chaotic in Cage's mesostics, see the essays by Joan Retallack and by N. Kathrine Hayles in this volume.

7. The replacement of the classical concept of *begriff* (the concept of a concept as a fully determinate interpretation) by a concept of knowing as acknowledging, is a central theme of Stanley Cavell's philosophy, one which he finds in the philosophy of the later Wittgenstein. I take it to have its place here. See Cavell, "Knowing and Acknowledging," in *Must We Mean What We Say?* (Cambridge: Cambridge University Press, 1976), pp. 238-66).

8. I take this capacious free association to be Cage's way of recovering a dimension of human freedom in his mesostics. The mesostics are textual bodies whose paths into association ring with amazement, amazement because one feels that the works have no bottom, no place at which one could say: there is no further semantic resonance, semantic firing, and semantic primary process to be found here. It is in this respect that Cage's mesostics are representations of the very idea of freedom, an idea now removed from its Enlightenment definition in terms of free obedience to the moral law, and redefined as the freedom to turn oneself into a field of play in which all the parts of oneself, from the most conscious to the least, are brought into the train of association. One is then free to inhabit oneself, to live in the depth of connection that is one's person. I take it that in a very different context, psychoanalysis aims for a similar capaciousness in the freedom to associate all the parts of one's self, and that the freedom to inhabit oneself is partly to be defined in terms of this capacity.

9. I refer to Stanley Cavell's insistence that American philosophy and letters has repressed the thought of the transcendentalists, who ought to be made part of the conversation of letters. In this sense Cage at Stanford is especially germane to the present time.

10. See my *Making Theory/Constructing Art,* chap. 5, where I explore this question in detail as part of a general discussion of how to address Cage's philosophical skepticism about the limits of our musical minds and musical practices.

11. I am here influenced by remarks of Marjorie Perloff in her essay, "Music for Words Perhaps: Reading/Hearing/Seeing John Cage's Roaratorio," in Perloff, ed., *Postmodern Genres* (Norman: University of Oklahoma Press, 1989), pp. 193-228.

Marjorie Perloff (essay date 1997)

SOURCE: Perloff, Marjorie. "The Music of Verbal Space: John Cage's 'What You Say . . . .'" In *Sound States: Innovative Poetics and Acoustical Technologies,* edited by Adalaide Morris, pp. 129-48. Chapel Hill: University of North Carolina Press, 1997.

[*In the following essay, Perloff examines the form and content of Cage's mesostic endeavors, arguing that in his mesostic poems, Cage adds musical texture and deeper meaning to the texts he uses for his poems, therefore enhancing the original texts and creating new poetic interpretations.*]

> Syntax, like
> government, can only be obeyed. It is
> therefore of no use except when you
> have something particular to command
> such as: Go buy me a bunch of carrots.
>
> (Cage *M* 215)

As early as 1939, when he was in residence at the Cornish School of Music in Seattle, John Cage investigated the application of electrical technology to music. His first (perhaps *the* first) electroacoustic composition was *Imaginary Landscape No. 1,* a six-minute radio piece for muted piano, cymbal, and two variable-speed record turntables, designed to accompany the production of Jean Cocteau's play *Marriage at the Eiffel Tower.* The piece was performed by Cage, his wife Xenia, and two friends in two separate studios, mixed in the control room, and beamed the short distance to the theatre.[1] *Imaginary Landscape No. 1* looks ahead to any number of Cage compositions involving radio, magnetic tape, and computer technologies. And yet the irony is that, having produced so many complex intermedia works using the most varied acoustic materials, by 1970 or so, Cage started to write a series of "mesostics," performance works that made use of only a single instrument—the human voice—and a single medium—language.

"My first mesostic," Cage writes in the Foreword to *M,* "was written as prose to celebrate one of Edwin Denby's birthdays. The following ones, each letter of the name being on its own line, were written as poetry. *A given letter capitalized does not occur between* it and the preceding capitalized letter. I thought I was writing acrostics, but Norman O. Brown pointed out that they could properly be called 'mesostics' (row not down the edge but down the middle)" (*M* 1).

Here is the Edwin Denby mesostic of 1970 called **"Present"**:

> rEmembering a Day i visited you—seems noW
> as I write that the weather theN was warm—i
> recall nothing we saiD, nothing wE did; eveN so
> (perhaps Because of that) that visit staYs.

This first attempt, as Cage suggests, was clearly not quite satisfactory. The four-line text, with its justified left and right margins, doesn't have much visual interest, the capital letters merely appearing in a linear sequence. More important, the Denby mesostic doesn't have much aural or musical complexity, its prose format being that of normal writing of the sort we all do when we write a note to a friend on an occasion like a birthday. True, the mesostic rule (Cage was later to call this a 50% mesostic since the given letter capitalized can occur between it and the *following* capitalized letter, whereas a 100% mesostic doesn't allow for occurence of the letter either preceding or following its appearance) is observed, but hearing this particular text read, one would not especially notice the structuration of language by the EDWIN DENBY string, although—a harbinger of things to come—the "Y" word, "staYs," rhymes with the "D" word, "Day."

The difficulty at this stage was that Cage was still using normal syntax. In another early mesostic, entitled **"On the windshield of a new Fiat for James K[losty] (who had not made up his mind where to go) and Carolyn Brown,"** we read:

> asK
> Little
> autO
> Where it wantS
> To take
> You.

(M 94)

Unlike the Denby mesostic, this one is "written as poetry," in that each capital letter gets a line to itself (and as a 100% mesostic, its wing words are of necessity very short), but again, the poem's syntax and sound are almost those of ordinary conversation. Thus, although the Klosty mesostic is visually more of a "poem" than is the Edwin Denby one, the poetic problem has not yet been resolved.

Cage was quite aware of this quandary. When, in the early seventies, the French philosopher Daniel Charles posed the question, "*Aren't your lectures, for examples,*

musical works in the manner of the different chapters of *Walden?*", Cage replied, "They are when sounds are words. But I must say that I have not yet carried language to the point to which I have taken musical sounds. . . . I hope to make something other than language from it." And he adds, "It is that aspect, the *impossibility of language,* that interests me at present." Again, in a later exchange, when Charles remarks, "*You* propose to musicate language; you want language to be heard as *music,*" Cage responds, "I hope to let words exist, as I have tried to let sounds exist" (*For the Birds* 113, 151).[2]

Making language as interesting as music, Cage was to learn, depended on the dismantling of "normal" *syntax.* Much as he loved Joyce, Cage felt that even *Finnegans Wake* was conventional in this respect:

> Reading *Finnegans Wake* I notice that though Joyce's subjects, verbs, and objects are unconventional, their relationships are the ordinary ones. With the exception of the Ten Thunderclaps and rumblings here and there, *Finnegans Wake* employs syntax. Syntax gives it a rigidity from which classical Chinese and Japanese were free. A poem by Basho, for instance, floats in space. . . . Only the imagination of the reader limits the number of the poem's possible meanings.

("Foreword," M 2)

In the former case, the words themselves are made strange, Joyce being, of course, a master of word formation, punning, metaphor, and allusion, but the syntax is left intact; "Joyce," Cage remarks elsewhere, "seemed to me to have kept the old structures ("sintalks") in which he put the new words he had made" (**"Writing"** 133). The alternative (Basho's) is to use "ordinary" language but to explode the syntax, a process Cage regularly referred to as the "demilitarization of the language." "Speaking without syntax," he explains in a note on **"Sixty-Two Mesostics Re Merce Cunningham,"** "we notice that cadence, Dublinese or ministerial, takes over. (Looking out the rear-window.) Therefore we tried whispering. Encouraged we began to chant. . . . To raise language's temperature we not only remove syntax: we give each letter undivided attention setting it in unique face and size; *to read* becomes the verb *to sing*" ("Notes" 97). But he admits in the "Foreword" to *M* that "My work in this field is tardy. It follows the poetry of Jackson MacLow and Clark Coolidge, my analogous work in the field of music, and my first experiments, texts for *Song Books.* . . . Concrete and sound poets have also worked in this field for many years, though many, it seems to me, have substituted graphic or musical structures for syntactical ones" (2).

Cage is quite right to refer to his "work in this field" as "tardy." As early as 1960, Jackson Mac Low had written a sequence called *Stanzas for Iris Lezak* based on chance operations. **"Call me Ishmael,"** for example, takes the first three words of *Moby Dick* as its acrostic string, and finds the words that begin with the thirteen consecutive letters *C-A-L-L-M-E-I-S-H-M-A-E-L* in the novel's first few pages, as determined by *I Ching* chance operations.[3] The *I Ching* also determined their lineation, so that we have five three-line stanzas, with the pattern 4-2-7 words per line respectively:

Circulation. And long long
Mind every
Interest Some how mind and every long

Coffin about little little
Money especially
I shore, having money about especially little

Cato a little little
Me extreme
I sail have me an extreme little

Cherish and left, left,
Myself extremest
It see hypos myself and extremest left,

City a land. Land.
Mouth; east,
Is spleen, hand, mouth; an east, land.

(89)

When Cage began to write mesostics, he adopted Mac Low's acrostic procedures, but with an important difference. Whereas in the example above, Mac Low lets chance operations generate the entire text, Cage, as we shall see, uses these operations to generate the word pool to be used and the rules to be followed, but he then fills in lines with "wing words," generated, as he repeatedly put it, "according to taste."[4] The result is an idiom markedly different from Mac Low's, especially in its vocal quality, Cage preferring softer, blending sounds to the harshly stressed monosyllabic nouns, separated by strong caesurae, that we find in **"Call me Ishmael."** A similar difference may be observed between Cage and such concrete poets as the Brazilian *Noigandres* group (Augusto de Campos, Haroldo de Campos, and Decio Pignatari), with whom he shared many aesthetic principles and who have assiduously translated and disseminated his writings. In concrete poetry—say Augusto de Campos's *Luxo* or Pignatari's *Beba coca cola*—the visual image predominates, the actualization of performance not giving the listener the full effect of the figure the poem makes, a figure depending on complex patterns of typography, spacing, color contrasts, and so on. In Cage, by contrast, it is the aural that dominates. Indeed, however visually striking Cage's verbal scores may be, the mesostic column creating an interesting pattern and the punctuation marks of the original often strewn around the page, as in *Roaratorio,* poetic density depends primarily on sound, as actualized in performance. Cage was, after all, a composer even when the materials he worked with were linguistic rather than musical.

The influences Cage cites in *M* could thus take him only so far. A decade of experimentation followed. While the earliest mesostics, like the **"25 Mesostics Re and not Re Mark Tobey"** (*M*186-94) were written in Cage's own words (the first "MARK" mesostic reads "it was iMpossible / to do Anything: / the dooR / was locKed"), and while what we might call the middle ones were "writings through" such great literary texts as *Finnegans Wake* or Ezra Pound's *Cantos,*[5] in his last years, Cage turned increasingly to making mesostics out of texts not in themselves consciously "poetic." In Tokyo in 1986, for example, Cage performed a mesostic piece called **"Sculpture Musicale,"** which used as its source text for the mesostic string only that title and the following words of Duchamp's: "sons durant et partant de differents points et formant une sculpture sonore qui dure." A second Tokyo piece submitted to "writing through" Cage's own **"Lecture on Nothing,"** even as his **"Rhythm, etc."** (1988) takes a passage from *A Year from Monday* ("There's virtually nothing to say about rhythm . . .") and uses the four sentences of this passage as the mesostic string.

Discussions of Cagean mesostic have usually ignored this evolution from mesostic strings based on single proper names, repeated throughout (as in the case of the name "JAMES JOYCE" in the *Roaratorio*), to strings derived from larger statements or paragraphs, whose individual words are part of the standard lexicon. The turning point from the "proper name" string to what we might call the "sentence" string may well have come with the writing, in the early eighties, of the performance piece *Marcel Duchamp, James Joyce, Erik Satie: An Alphabet.* In this complex work, the hypothetical "conversation" between the three artists is presented, partly by means of found text, artfully collaged from their writings, partly by Cage's own discourse, structured by the proper names of the three artists, repeated as mesostic strings according to chance operations. In "A Conversation about Radio in Twelve Parts" with Richard Kostelanetz, conducted a few years later, Cage expressed dissatisfaction with *Alphabet* because its "scenes [are] in a very simple way differentiated from one another. They don't overlap so that it's as simple as a work by Stravinsky, but within each part there's a great disparateness with the next part; so that the act of listening is very uncomfortable." "All those scenes," he explained, "have beginnings and endings. It's a multiplicity of beginnings and endings. That's what annoys me. I don't mind it as something to read; but as something to hear" (293-94).

What Cage means, I think, is that proper-name mesostics, derived, not from a "writing through" but from sentences made up for the occasion, have a tendency to form independent strophes of four to six lines, strophes divided by a sharp pause and hence not sufficiently "interpenetrating" phonemically. For example:

> from his Jumping
> the older one is Erik SAtie
> he never stops sMiling
> and thE younger one
> iS joyce, thirty-nine
>
> he Jumps
> with his back tO the audience
> for all we know he maY be quietly weeping
> or silently laughing or both you just Can't
> tEll[6]

Here the syntactically straightforward narrative perhaps too easily yields the requisite mesostic letters: J-A-M-E-S and J-O-Y-C-E; if, say, an "O" were needed as the final mesostic letter, Cage could substitute "knOw" for "tEll" without it making much difference. Then, too, the stanza break follows the normal syntactic break: "the younger one is Joyce, thirty-nine. // He jumps . . . ," thus producing the "differentiat[ion] from one another" Cage criticizes.

> The solution was to use a seemingly inconsequential prose text as the source, not only for his own "writing through" but for the mesostic string as well. There would be, in other words, a rule to follow, but that rule would be so hidden that "beginnings and endings" would not call attention to themselves. Moreover, the discourse of ordinary prose—a passage from an interview, a newspaper paragraph, a statement from a lecture—could now be decomposed and recharged so as to uncover the mysteries of language. "You see," Cage told Niksa Gligo in an interview, "language controls our thinking; and if we change our language, it is conceivable that our thinking would change" (Kostelanetz 149). For this purpose, "empty words" are more useful than "full" ones. "Full words," Cage explains to Richard Kostelanetz, "are words that are nouns *or* verbs *or* adjectives *or* adverbs," whereas "empty words" (what we call function words or deictics) are "connective[s] or pronoun[s]—word[s] that refer to something else"
>
> (141).

As an example of such an "empty word" mesostic, I have chosen a short piece called **"What you say . . ."** from 1987, a "writing through" of an informal statement on aesthetic made by Jasper Johns in an interview with Christian Geelhaar. This is the first of two companion texts based on John's commentary on his work, the second being **"Art Is Either A Complaint Or Do Something Else,"** which is taken from a series of statements cited by Mark Rosenthal in his *Jasper Johns: Work Since 1974* (Philadelphia Museum of Art, 1988). Cage discusses this mesostic piece with Joan Retallack, in an interview originally published in *Aerial* (1991), together with **"Art Is Either A Complaint."** As Cage explains the piece:

> . . . it's all from words of Jasper Johns, but they're used with chance operations in such a way that they make different connections than they did when he said them. On the other hand, they seem to reinforce what he was saying . . . almost in his way. And why that should surprise me I don't know because all of the words are his. (*laughs*) But they make different connections.
>
> (Retallack 107)[7]

Consider the "different connections" in **"What You Say . . ."**, which draws on a statement Johns makes at the very end of the Geelhaar interview:

> What you say about my tendency to add things is correct. But, how
> does one make a painting? How does one deal with the space? Does
>   one have something and then proceed to add another thing or does
>   one have something; move into it; occupy it; divide it; make the
>   best one can of it? I think I do different things at different
> times and perhaps at the same time. It interests me that a part can
> function as a whole or that a whole can be thrown into a situation
>   in which it is only a part. It interests me that what one takes to
> be a whole subject can suddenly be miniaturized, or something, and
>   then be inserted into another world, as it were.

Notice that Cage's reproduction of Johns's response is already a kind of writing through, the sentences being arranged as line lengths and centered so as to give the whole an accordion-like visual shape. At the Los Angeles performance I attended (at UCLA, 4 September 1987, in conjunction with the opening of the exhibition of the Samuel Beckett-Jasper Johns collaboration *Fizzles*), **"What you say . . ."** was preceded by the reading of three short mesostics on the name JASPER JOHNS, one of them having appeared in *Empty Words* (1979) under the title **"Song"**:

> not Just
>   gArdener
> morelS
>   coPrini,
>   morEls,
>   copRini.
>
>   not Just hunter:
> cutting dOwn
>   ailantHus,
>   cuttiNg down
> ailanthuS.
>
> (10)

Notice that this mesostic belongs to Cage's earlier "concrete poetry" phase, the lines built primarily on catalogues of nouns, and the game being that each of two words (or phrases) per stanza can supply the poet with the necessary capital letters (e.g., the "S" and "E" of "morels"). These are primarily eye devices. By the time Cage wrote **"What you say . . ."**, his aim was to "musicate" the language, letting it do the sorts of things he had hitherto done with musical sounds. Indeed, at the UCLA performance, the piece was performed by a dozen or so readers, according to the following program notes:

> For any number of readers able to read in one breath any of the 124 "stanzas" (a "stanza" is a line or lines preceded and followed by a space).

> Each reader, equipped with a chronometer, and without intentionally changing the pitch or loudness of the voice quietly reads any 4 "stanzas" at any 4 times in each minute of the agreed-upon performance time.

> The readers are seated or stand around the audience or both within and outside it.[8]

Whether performed chorally or by Cage himself (and I have heard it done both ways), the "frame" is now no longer the decision how many times to repeat a given proper name like JAMES JOYCE but the "agreed-upon performance time." Cage's initial experiments with magnetic tape in the late forties and early fifties, Margaret Leng Tan has pointed out, "emphasized the fact that duration (time length) is synonymous with tape length (space) and it is the application of this principle which forms the basis for the space-time proportional notation used in the *Music of Changes* and the *Two Pastorales* of 1951" (51). The same principle, Cage came to see, could be applied to language texts. In the case of **"What You Say . . ."**, duration would seem to be determined by the need to provide one line for each of the 512 letters in Johns's paragraph. But in fact **"What You Say . . ."** is much longer than 512 "lines" because of the spacing (silence) Cage introduces between word groups, with extra rests replacing the missing letters. Missing because "For several letters there were no words: the v of have (twice); the v of move; the j of subject; and the z of miniaturized. Spaces between lines take the place of the missing letters" (*F* [*Formations*] 53).

The selection of words from the source pool, Cage explains in his note to **"What you say . . ."** (*F* 53), is based on MESOLIST, "a program by Jim Rosenberg," extended for this particular piece by a second program made by Andrew Culver, which extended the number of characters in a search string . . . to any length; this extended MESOLIST was used to list the available words which were then subjected to IC (a program by Andrew Culver simulating the coin oracle of the *I Ching*)." Although I have not seen this program, it seems clear that even though the MESOLIST-derived "chance operations" do govern the sequencing of the words that contain the requisite letters for the mesostic

string, the variable length of the search string made it possible for Cage to create precisely the semantic and phonemic juxtapositions that suited him. In this particular case, he had to begin with a line containing the "W" of the first word "What," followed by the "h," the "a," and so on, and the first "W" word designated by Mesolist is the last word of Johns's statement—"were." But although chance operations dictated the selection of "were" as the first capitalized word to be used in **"What you say . . ."**, it was Cage's own choice to place, in the opening line, the whole phrase, "as it Were." Indeed, as we shall see, in this instance as elsewhere, Cage's poetic composition is nothing if not *designed*. As he put it in the Foreword to *Silence*: "As I see it, poetry is not prose simply because poetry is in one way or another formalized. It is not poetry by reason of its content or ambiguity but by reason of its allowing musical elements (time, sound) to be introduced into the world of words" (x).

The world of words, in this case, consists of seven "ordinary" sentences (three of them questions), containing 127 words, 99 of them monosyllables. This is already an unusual linguistic situation but what's even odder: there are only seven words in the entire passage that have more than two syllables.[9] And further: the majority of monosyllables and disyllables are deictics or function words: "it" appears seven times, "thing" six times, "one" five times, "something" three times, "how," "what" and "whole" twice each. In this context, the word that stands out is the five-syllable "miniaturized" in the next to last line.[10]

The sentence structure is as elementary as is the word pool. "How does one" with the variant "does one" appears four times; "it interests me that" twice, and simple parallel structure occurs in "move into it; occupy it; divide it; make the best one can of it." Johns's statement, at least as lineated here, thus has a naive or child-like sound structure, especially since the artist hesitates or withdraws statements, as in "I think I do different things at different times and perhaps at the same time," or when he declares that "a whole subject can suddenly be miniaturized, or something." Finally, the paragraph concludes with the qualifier, "as it were."

Why would Cage, who has previously written through the incredibly rich word pool of *Finnegans Wake* or the hieratic rhythms of Pound's *Cantos,* select such an ordinary flat discourse to "write through"? After all Johns's statement is just an unrehearsed response to a question from an interviewer. This is of course Cage's point. "There is no such thing as an empty space or an empty time. There is always something to see, something to hear" (*Silence* 8). Even in his off-the-cuff remarks about his art-making, Johns, so Cage posits, is saying something significant, is posing basic questions about painting. And moreover, Johns's own vocal patterns, with which Cage was of course deeply familiar, produce a sound curve to which Cage's own sound curve is designed to respond. Indeed, the composer-poet's role, in this scheme of things, is to bring Johns's "something," his particular signature—the visual made verbal and vocal—out into the open, by "demilitarizing" the syntax so as to controvert the chosen statement's linearity and permit its components to realign themselves. Let me try to elaborate.

"What you say . . ." opens with the final "as it Were" of Johns's paragraph and comes full circle to "wEre" on its last page. Here is the beginning:

> as it Were
> anotHer world
>   A whole or
>   The best one can of it
>
> suddenlY
>   sOmething
>   move
> miniatUrized

Perhaps the first thing to notice here is the elaborate sound structure, a structure especially notable in Cage's own reading of the text in which each line, spoken slowly, is followed by a silence the length of a short syllable.[11] The first three lines are linked by stress pattern (two stresses per line), anaphora of short "a"s and internal rhyme ("Were" / "world"" "or"). In line 4, the sound shifts to short vowels, embedded in "t"s and "th's; the lightly stressed monosyllabic line "The best one can of it," being related to the first three by the repetition of "it", the internal rhyme of "an" (in "another") and "can", and of "-tHer" and "The." ("t"s and "th"s, incidentally, constitute 52 or roughly one tenth of the poem's phonemes.) Lines 5 and 6—"suddenlY / sOmething"—are again related by stress pattern and alliteration, and "move," with its open vowel followed by a voiced spirant opens the way for the alliterating "m" of the passage's longest (and perhaps least musical) word, "miniatUrized," a word that appears again and again, furnishing the different letters of the **"What you say . . ."** string.

But there is also a curious clinamen in this passage. Line 7, "move" is not part of the mesostic string at all, "WHAT YOU" being complete without it. The source text reads: "does one have to do something; move into it." Cage might have put "move" on line 6 along with the semi-colon, or he might have left the word out completely since the search string can be, as Cage points out, of any length. Yet "move," physically moved over to the right here, has an important effect. The domain of art, the text suggests, is "as it Were / anotHer world / A whole or / The best one can of it." This other

world is "suddenlY / sOmething," and it is, in Cage's elliptical construction, "move"—which is to say, moving, on the move, in movement, in a move toward, the "miniaturization" of "subject" which is art.

But of course the text itself we are reading (or hearing) is precisely this miniaturization, this creation of "suddenlY / sOmething." Lift the ordinary out of the zone of saying, Cage seems to say ("The best one can of it") and "it" will become "something." Just as Johns would paint ordinary numbers (0 to 9) or the letters of the alphabet (A to Z), or a clothes hanger or beer can, so Cage will take words as uninteresting as "as," "it," "or," "of," and "a," place those words in particular spatial configurations, white space (silence) being at least as prominent as the spoken and written language itself," and create a minimalist ars poetica.

That Cage's work continues to go unrecognized as poetry by those who produce books like the *Norton Anthology of Poetry* as well as those who read and review them, has to do with our general inability to dissociate "poetry" from the twin norms of self-expression and figuration. **"What you say . . .",** it is argued by Cage's detractors (and they are legion) is, after all, no more than a reproduction of someone else's text: the "I" is not Cage's and, in any case, there is no psychological revelation of a personal sort. Moreover, in the passage we have just read there isn't a single metaphor (except for that dead metaphor "world") or arresting visual image. Indeed, Cage's diction, so this line of reasoning goes, is merely trivial, isn't it?

This is to ignore the crucial role played by the context in which words occur, by their temporal and spatial arrangement, and especially by their sound. Take, for example, the common phrase "make the best one can of it" in Johns's paragraph. Eliminate the initial "make" and the phrase becomes the strange "The best one can of it," made even stranger by its insertion in the text between "A whole or" and "suddenlY." Yet the realignment produces a new meaning: "a whole or / the best" may now be read as adjectives modifying "world," and "the best one can" may be construed as a noun phrase. Certainly a "can" is a kind of whole. Aural performance, in any case, activates any number of meanings, especially since the spacing (the visual equivalence of silence) ensures very slow reading, whether one or more persons are reading simultaneously. "SuddenlY / sOmething / move / miniatUrized"—one word per line, a rest between lines: the audience is forced to listen carefully, to pay attention to the sound of each unit.

The strategy of **"What you say . . ."**—and this is where the mesostic mode, with its dependence on a fixed word pool, can work so effectively—is to recharge individual words by consistently shifting their context and hence their use. Take the word "whole," used three times in Johns's statement: "It interests me that a part can function as a WHOLE or that a WHOLE can be thrown into a situation in which it is only a part. It interests me that what one takes to be a WHOLE subject can suddenly be miniaturized . . ." (my emphasis). In Cage, this "normal" syntax gives way to astonishing variations. "Whole" appears twenty-eight times, each of its letters appearing in the mesostic string of the text. Along the way it yields such stanzas as:

> oF it
> a whole sUbject
> aNd then
> a whole Can be
> whaT you say about
> It
>
> Occupy it
>
> a whole caN
> hAve
> different timeS and
> tAkes
> can be throWn
> and perHaps at the same time
>
> Or
> how does one deaL with
> diffErent times and
>
> (*F* 62)

Here the mesostic string is "FUNCTION AS A WHOLE." But the poem itself questions this "function"; the "whole sUbject" is in apposition to a mere "it"; "a whole Can be" "whaT you say about / It," "a whole caN / hAve / different timeS and / takes," it can be "throWn / and perHaps at the same time." On the next page "wHole" furnishes Cage with the "H" mesostic letter and thus becomes a "hole."

Now let us look again at the source text which reads: "What one takes to be a whole subject can suddenly be miniaturized." Cage's own text enacts precisely this statement: what we "take to be a whole" dissolves into a number of possibilities. Not only can this "whole" be "miniaturized" but it "caN / hAve / different timeS and / tAkes"; there is no essential truth behind the word: "a whole Can be / whaT you say about it." A neat illustration, as it were, of Wittgenstein's proposition that "the meaning of a word is its use in the language."

Again, consider the couplings and uncouplings given to the word "tendency," which appears only once in Johns's statement, in the opening sentence: "What you say about my tendency to add things is correct":

> hoW
> about my tenDency
> thrOwn into a
> thEn
> and then be inSerted
> my tendency tO
> move iNto it

What tendency, we wonder, is this? ThrOwn into a / thEn? "My tendency tO / move iNto it"? It sounds risky. Two pages later, we read:

> How does one
> It
> my teNdency to
> have somethinG
> deAl

where "deal" may be either noun or verb, either indicative or imperative, the "tendency to / have somethinG" therefore being quite mysterious. Further down on the same page, the plot thickens:

> i Think
> a situatiOn in which
> you sAy about
> one Deal with
> tenDency
> As it were

Let's make a deal and take care of the situation in which the tendency in question arises, as it were. Two pages later, we find the stanza:

> moVe
> It
>   make
> i Do
> movE
> whIch
>   Tendency
>   My
> situAtion in which
> i thinK
> onE
> can funcTion as

The instructions are to "moVe it" (reenforced by the verb "make," another one of what we might call outriders in the text, "make" not being part of the mesostic chain, which here is "[DI]VIDE IT MAKE T[HE BEST OF IT]"), to which the response is "i Do movE," and now "tendency" is explicitly linked to "situation," a "situAtion in which / i thinK / one can funcTion as." Function as what? Johns's "tendency to add things" now takes on a darker cast, his tendency producing a situation in which the artist only thinks he can function." When "tendency" reappears some time later in the performance, it is "thAt / teNdency to / oF it," where the "tendency" can be interpreted in a variety of ways.

Or again, it becomes a whoLe / tendencY to / whAt one / occuPy." The last three pages of **"What you say . . ."** accelerates the repetition, "tendency" appearing six more times:

> to bE
> my tendenCy
>   That
>   spaCe
>
> doeS one
>   fUnction as a
> tenDency
>
>   mY tendency
>   is correct
>
>   it intErests me
>   tenDency
>   it
>
>   anD perhaps
>   whaT one takes to be
> tendency to add tHings is
>   havE
>
>   caN
>   One
>   Tendency to
>   sometHing

This is Cage at his most Steinian, charging language by means of permutation, words like "tendency" taking on a different aura with every repetition. What makes these pieces so remarkable is that they are, to use Joyce's term, "verbivocovisual." Visual, to take it backwards, in that the spacing and mesostic chain produces its own meanings, so that "tenDency," with that "ten" separating out, is not the same as "tendenCy," and the construction of larger units will depend upon word placement and spacing. "Verbi," in that Cage is always constructing new meanings, in this case giving new connotations to a "tendency" Johns mentions only casually. But it is the "voco" ("musical") element which perhaps dominates here. For given the nature of the writing-through process, there are only so many words at the composer's disposal, and these words—"what," "world," "perhaps," "another," "something," "interest," "function"—appear again and again, becoming familiar counters. "Miniaturized," for example, has nine lives, supplying the mesostic string with necessary letters (aurally phonemes) at frequent intervals, even as its "z," as Cage notes, cannot be used.

As such, Cage's sound structure has a decisive semantic import. Unlike most actual art discourse, the mesostic "written through" lecture or essay cannot just continue, cannot move from point to point, from thesis statement to exemplification or analogy, in a logical way. Rather, the discourse must "say something" about aesthetic, using no more than its baseline of 127 words, whose rule-governed permutations take us from "as it Were" to "a wholE can / peRhaps / wEre."

That it does "say something" is, of course, the work's great feat. **"What you say . . .",** what Cage's work "says" takes us back to the famous (perhaps too famous) theorem of "Experimental Music" that the "purposeless play" of art means "waking up to the very life we're living, which is so excellent once one gets one's mind and one's desires out of its way" (**Silence** 12). Purposeless play is not a matter of making "just any experiment." It does not mean that anything goes, that anyone can be an artist, that any random conjunction of words or sounds or visual images becomes art. What it does mean, as a reading of **"What you say . . ."** teaches us, is that the ordinary (in this case, Jasper Johns's not terribly edifying comment about his painting habits) can provide all that the artist needs to make "something else." Indeed, the challenge is to take the ordinary—words like "it" and "one" and "function" and "situation"—and "miniaturize" it into "something."

And that is of course what Johns himself does in his paintings. When he remarks, "Does one have something and then proceed to add another thing OR does one have something; move into it; occupy it; divide it; make the best one can of it?", we should note the allusion to his own famous warning to "Avoid a polar situation." For of course there is no meaningful opposition between "add[ing] another thing" or "hav[ing] something [and] mov[ing] into it"; the either-or proposition is falsely posed. Johns is playing similar games when he says, "I think I do different things at different times and perhaps at the same time." At one level, the tautology is absurd. But as we learn from Cage's **"What you say . . .",** such tautologies are integral to the process whereby we learn that there *is* no essential truth about art making, no way of saying for sure what art is or what the artist does.

"I think," Cage remarked a few months before his death, "a very impressive quality [of Johns's painting] is the absence of space. Something has been done almost everywhere. So it leads very much to the complexity of life."[12] The verbal equivalent of this "absence of space" can be seen in a passage like the following:

>   Or does one
>   function As
> another WorlD
>
>   Do
>   Time
>   and tHen proceed to
>   dIvide it
>
>   oNe
>   a paintinG
>
>   (*F* 54)

In the source-text interview, Johns speculates on the ways "a whole subject" might "be inserted into another world." Cage shows how such insertion is performed by presenting himself as "one" who can actually "function As / another WorlD." And just as Johns's painting is characterized by an "absence of space" (which is to say, unused space), so Cage's performance poem is characterized by an absence of time, in that each word, each morpheme, each phoneme must do double duty: look, for example, at the way "d"s "o," and "n"s are modulated in the "miniaturizing" sequence "Or—does—one—function—another—world—do—proceed—to—divide—one—painting."

When Cage began to experiment with mesostics, he worried that he had not yet hit upon a way of "carry-[ing] language to the point to which I have taken musical sounds." The solution, it seems, was to learn to "Do / Time / and tHen proceed to / dIvide it." But even this stanza, taken out of context, may seem too assertive, too dogmatic to suit those like Cage and Johns who want to avoid polar situations. And so the poem makes a tentative circle back to the "as it Were" of the opening:

> a wholE can
>   peRhaps
>   wEre

where the last two lines introduce internal rhyme—"peR" / "wEre"—only to qualify repetition by the intrusion of that little particle "haps," which repeats the "p" sound but combines it with a prominent spirant so as to produce dissonance. A wholE can / peRhaps / wEre": the difference, as Gertrude Stein would put it, is spreading.

Notes

1. In *The Roaring Silence,* David Revill notes that "It was also in the *Imaginary Landscape* that Cage first employed his system of rhythmic structure. The simple figures that constitute the piece fit into a scheme of four sections consisting of three times five measures which are separated by interludes which increase in length additively from one to three measures; the piece ends with a four-measure coda (65-66).

2. The English version, *For the Birds, John Cage in conversation with Daniel Charles,* was published by Marion Boyars (Boston and London) in 1981. The actual interviews were begun in 1968 but were submitted by Charles to Cage for revision and commentary and not published until 1976 under the title *Pour les oiseaux.*

3. The *I Ching or Book or Book of Changes* has, of course, been a source book for many poets and artists. Cage's own use of the *I Ching* began in 1950, when Christian Wolff gave him the new Bollingen (Princeton) two-volume edition of the English translation by Cary F. Baynes of Richard Wilhelm's German translation with the introduction by C. G. Jung. The magic square of 64 hexagrams, Cage explains in "Tokyo Lecture,"

transferred to the computer, "works musically to tell me for instance how many sound events take place in what length of time, at what points in time, on which instruments, having what loudnesses, etc. And in my writing it lets me continue, in a variety of ways, my search for a means which comes from ideas but is not about them but nevertheless produces them free of my intentions" (pp. 178-79). Mac Low has used similar techniques, first by throwing coins and dice, later with the computer, to determine factors of 64 that govern individual lineation and stanzaic structure.

4. See, for example, John Cage, *Roaratorio, An Irish Circus on Finnegans Wake,* p. 173.

5. Cage was not satisfied with his "writing through" of Pound's *Cantos.* "Now that I've done so [i.e., "written through" them]," he remarks in an interview, "I must say that I don't regard them as highly as I do the *Wake.* The reason is that there are about four or five ideas that keep reappearing in the *Cantos,* so that in the end the form resembles something done with stencils, where the color doesn't really change. There's not that kind of complexity, or attention to detail, as there is in Joyce"; see Richard Kostelanetz, *Conversing with Cage,* p. 152.

No doubt, Cage also objected to Pound's studious elimination of the very words Cage himself liked best—prepositions, conjunctions, articles, pronouns—and that Pound's parataxis of nouns and noun phrases made any "writing through" extremely difficult. Much more suitable for his purposes was Allen Ginsberg's "Howl"; I have written of Cage's brilliant deconstruction of that poem in "A Lion in Our Living Room: Reading Allen Ginsberg in the Eighties," *Poetic License: Essays in Modernist and Postmodernist Lyric,* pp. 219-22.

6. On the piece as a whole, see my "'A Duchamp Unto Myself': Writing Through Marcel," in *John Cage: Composed in America.*

7. For Cage's account of the evolution and design of "Art Is Either a Complaint or Do Something Else," see Retallack, pp. 109-114. Unlike "What You Say . . .", this piece is based on separate statements made by Johns, appearing in different contexts.

8. These program notes were not included in the printed version in *Formations,* evidently because there is no way the instructions could be followed during a silent reading of the text. What status, then, does the printed text have? It is, we might say, a score that must be activated, an incomplete verbal-visual construct that needs to be "audiated."

9. I am not counting "different" or "interests" because in standard American speech (and certainly in Jasper Johns's Southern idolect) both

words are pronounced as having only two syllables: "dif-rent," "in-trests." The seven words are "another" (used twice), "tendency," "occupy," "suddenly," "inserted," "situation," and "miniaturized."

10. Again, syllable count is not the same in the oral performance as in the written. When spoken, "miniaturized" usually has four syllables: "min-ya-tyuw-riyzd."

11. Cage's reading of this and related mesostics is, in many ways, inimitable, his soft, neutral California speech rhythms giving the pattern of sounds and silences of the lineated text an edge not quite duplicatable when anyone else (myself included) reads the "score."

12. John Cage, "Second Conversation with Joan Retallack," *Conversations with John Cage,* Wesleyan University Press, 1996.

FURTHER READING

Biography

Revill, David. *The Roaring Silence: John Cage, A Life.* New York: Arcade Publishing, 1992, 375 p.
  Biography that seeks to demonstrate the interrelation of Cage's life with his work and thought.

Criticism

Bruns, Gerald L. "Poethics: John Cage and Stanley Cavell at the Cross Roads of Ethical Theory." In *John Cage: Composed in America,* edited by Marjorie Perloff and Charles Junkerman, pp. 206-25. Chicago: University of Chicago Press, 1994.
  Explores the works and ideas of Cage and philosopher Stanley Cavell to illustrate the link between artistic expression and ethical considerations.

Cushing, James. "Zarathustra over America: Nietzschean Return, Self-Overcoming, and John Cage." *Denver Quarterly* 29, no. 3 (winter 1995): 98-117.
  Draws parallels between Friedrich Nietzsche's tale of Zarathustra and Cage's self-exploration and artistic endeavors.

Mac Low, Jackson. "Cage's Writing up to the Late 1980s." In *Writings through John Cage's Music, Poetry, and Art,* edited by David W. Bernstein and Christopher Hatch, pp. 210-33. Chicago: University of Chicago Press, 2001.
  Provides an overview of the structure and formulation of Cage's poems.

Pasler, Jann. "Inventing a Tradition: Cage's 'Composition in Retrospect.'" In *John Cage: Composed in America,* edited by Marjorie Perloff and Charles Junkerman, pp. 125-43. Chicago: University of Chicago Press, 1994.
  Analyzes Cage's mesostics and regards them as developing elements of Cage's innovative work in poetry.

Pritchett, James. "'Joy and Bewilderment' (1969-1992)." In *The Music of John Cage,* pp. 175-214. Cambridge: Cambridge University Press, 1993.
  Examines the connection between Cage's musical compositions, his poetic writings, and his attention to visual representation.

Retallack, Joan. "High Adventures of Indeterminacy." *Parnassus: Poetry in Review* 11, no. 1 (spring-summer 1983): 253-63.
  Examines Cage's views on the importance of sounds and nature in *For the Birds,* explores his experiments with Eastern philosophy and poetics, and analyzes the mesostics in *Themes & Variations.*

Richards, M. C. "John Cage and the Way of the Ear." *TriQuarterly* 54 (spring 1982): 110-21.
  Stresses the role of sound, silence, and musicality in Cage's works.

Ulmer, Gregory L. "The Objects of Post-Criticism." In *The Anti-Aesthetic: Essays on Postmodern Culture,* edited by Hal Foster, pp. 83-110. Port Townsend, Wash.: Bay Press, 1983.
  Investigates the performative aspects of Cage's poetics and discerns in Cage's writings the postmodernist blending and layering of various forms of artistic styles and media.

The Wife of Bath's Prologue and Tale

Geoffrey Chaucer

The following entry presents criticism on Chaucer's *The Wife of Bath's Prologue* and *Tale* (circa 1386-1400). For further information on Chaucer's life and career, see *Poetry Criticism,* Volume 19.

INTRODUCTION

The Wife of Bath's Prologue and *Tale* from Chaucer's *Canterbury Tales* contain, in the character Alisoun, the Wife of Bath, one of the most fully developed and discussed women in medieval literature. Bawdy, lusty, and strong willed, she refuses to allow men to control her existence and she takes measures to shape her own destiny. Although she is often viewed as an early precursor of feminist thought, some scholars argue that much of her *Prologue* can be viewed as anti-feminist rhetoric.

BIOGRAPHICAL INFORMATION

Chaucer was born in the 1340s into a family of London-based vintners. He spent most of his adult life as a civil servant, serving under three successive kings—Edward III, Richard II, and Henry IV—and much of what is known of his life is derived from various household records. In 1357 he served as a page to Elizabeth, the Countess of Ulster and wife of Prince Lionel, the third son of Edward III. In 1359, while serving in Edward's army in France, Chaucer was captured during the unsuccessful siege of Rheims. The king contributed to his ransom, and Chaucer shortly thereafter entered the king's service. By 1366 he had married Philippa Payne de Roet, a French noblewoman who had also been in the employment of the Countess of Ulster. Around this time Chaucer appears to have established a connection with John of Gaunt, Edward III's fourth son, who may have become Chaucer's patron; the fortunes of the two traced parallel courses over the next three decades, rising and falling in tandem. Chaucer traveled to Spain in 1366, on the first of a series of diplomatic missions throughout Europe. After a 1373 visit to Italy he returned to England and was appointed a customs official for the Port of London; he was given additional customs responsibilities in 1382. By 1385 he was living in Kent, where he was appointed a justice of the peace.

Although he became a member of Parliament in 1386, that year marked the beginning of a difficult period for Chaucer. He either resigned or was removed from his post as a customs official; additionally, he was not returned to Parliament. By 1387 his wife had died. Chaucer's fortunes rose again when John of Gaunt returned from the Continent in 1389, and the young King Richard II regained control of the government from the aristocracy, which had for a time been the dominant political force in England. Chaucer was appointed a clerk of the king's works but was removed from this office in 1391. Records suggest that by 1396 Chaucer had established a close relationship with John of Gaunt's son, the Earl of Derby, who as King Henry IV later confirmed Chaucer's grants from Richard and added an additional annuity in 1399. Chaucer then leased a house in the garden of Westminster Abbey where he lived for the rest of his life. He died on

October 25, 1400, and was buried in Westminster Abbey, an honor traditionally reserved for royalty. His tomb became the center of what is now known as Poet's Corner.

PLOT AND MAJOR CHARACTERS

The Canterbury Tales, the work generally regarded as Chaucer's masterpiece, was probably begun around 1386. The work is organized as a collection of stories told by a group of pilgrims on their way to the shrine of Thomas à Beckett in Canterbury. Within this overall framework are ten parts, which appear in different order in different manuscripts. Many critics therefore believe that Chaucer never realized his final plan for the work. The work opens with the *General Prologue,* introducing the pilgrims with short, vivid sketches. Twenty-four tales follow, interspersed with short dramatic "links" presenting lively exchanges among the pilgrims. The tales are highly diverse in style, subject matter, and theme; they include courtly romance, allegory, sermon, fable, and sometimes a mixture of genres. *The Wife of Bath's Tale* is one of only three tales by women, and the only tale offering insight into the life and passions of a woman in the secular world. The Wife's *Prologue* is layered with double entendres and witty wordplay, providing comic relief for the pilgrims and the readers.

In *The Wife of Bath's Tale* Alisoun offers a story of a Knight who, while walking in a field, spies a young maiden and rapes her. The Knight is tried before King Arthur for his crime and is sentenced to death. Queen Guenevere pleads on the Knight's behalf and King Arthur allows her to mete out the Knight's punishment. The Queen gives the Knight twelve months and a day to discover what women truly want. He is required to report back to the Queen at he end of this time and provide an answer. He scours the land asking the question of each woman he meets. Women give him different opinions in return: money, clothing, sexual satisfaction, but none can offer the definitive answer. His allotted time draws to a close, and he has not found an answer to this question. As he realizes that he has failed, he comes upon an old and ugly crone and asks her the question of what women truly desire above all. She agrees to provide him with the answer in return for his pledge that he will grant her wish—a wish that will be told to him at a later time. He travels back to the castle with the crone, and delivers his answer to the Queen: "'My lige lady, generally,' quod he, / 'Wommen desiren to have sovereynetee / As wel over his housbond as hir love, / And for to been in maistrie hym above. / This is youre mooste desir, thogh ye me kille. / Dooth as yow list; I am heer at youre wille'" (1037-42). The Queen allows the Knight to go free, but then the crone steps forward and claims the right to have the Knight fulfill his promise. The crone requires the Knight to marry her. The Knight is aghast but finally agrees. When they return to the crone's house for their wedding night, the crone discusses true gentility and charity with the Knight. He sees the error of his ways and reconciles himself to the marriage. The crone then offers him a choice: she can either remain old and ugly but an ever-faithful and obedient wife, or she can become young and beautiful but cannot promise that she will be obedient and faithful. The Knight allows the crone to decide, offering her sovereignty. Because the Knight has learned true humbleness and respect for his wife, she transforms into a beautiful young maiden and vows to be an obedient and faithful wife.

MAJOR THEMES

In the *The Wife of Bath's Prologue,* two themes are addressed. The first centers on marriage roles and power. Alisoun discusses her five marriages and her tactics for gaining power and financial independence through the use of her body. Her first marriage was at the age of twelve to a wealthy older man. With this husband and the next two, she was very pragmatic about the relationships. She used her body to control her husbands and to gain financial boons from them. She admitted that she had a healthy sexual appetite and alluded to the fact that she may quench those appetites outside of wedlock. Her fourth husband was young and lusty, and even kept a mistress. During this fourth marriage, Alisoun began courting Jankyn, a younger man without financial independence. After her fourth husband died (there has recently been speculation as to why this young man died and whether it was by natural causes), Alisoun broke her earlier rules of pragmatic marriage and wedded Jankyn for love. Ironically, now that the Wife was older and searching for love, Jankyn's position was parallel to that of Alison's with her first husbands—young Jankyn delighted in aggravating Alisoun and appeared to be in a position of power over her.

The second major theme in the *Prologue* is dissatisfaction with current religious thought. The Wife is a Christian and is undergoing a pilgrimage, but she doesn't blindly trust the religious authorities' interpretation of the Scriptures. Scholars in medieval Europe were seeking to understand the Bible more fully, and one common thought that was introduced during this time was that since the Bible depicts Jesus attending only one wedding, perhaps this is God's message that people should only marry once. Alisoun defends her right to remarry after being widowed (four times) by recounting the Biblical story of the Samaritan woman at the well who was living out of wedlock with a man after being widowed four times. Jesus commanded her to marry this fifth man. Alisoun uses this parable and the examples of Solomon, Abraham, and Jacob, all of whom had multiple wives. Alisoun also believes in God's command to be fruitful and multiply. She disagrees with the Church's teaching that chastity is preferable to second marriage; she believes that by sharing her bounty, she is closer to the real teachings of the Bible. Her bawdy description of the God-given tools used in this endeavor are thinly veiled double entendres, and she is interrupted by the Pardoner before she discusses the particulars of her five marriages. Throughout these descriptions the religious theme is intertwined with the marriage theme and Alisoun's desire for autonomy. Although true autonomy for women in medieval Europe is an impossibility, she outlines her strategies for control of self and the situations around her.

In the *Tale,* the Wife of Bath softens her views of charity and love but continues the theme of autonomy and power. Alisoun reworks the traditional story of the "Loathly Lady" with a decidedly feminist spin, putting the hag in a position of control and demoting the Knight to a position of submissiveness. Throughout the *Tale,* the Knight's fate is decided by women, first by Guenevere, then by the crone. Alisoun suggests that a man's true happiness can be realized when he allows his spouse to have some level of autonomy. Although the end of the *Tale* realigns the positions of power to more traditional gender roles, it is by the woman's own choice finally to be an obedient wife; therefore the *Tale* provides a milestone for women's quest for self-definition. The rehabilitation of the Knight is surprising, given the *Tale*'s beginning sentiment about the good nature of women in comparison to the base nature of men. Many commentators support the idea that in the *Tale* Alisoun is making a statement against prevailing beliefs that women are by nature base and sinful, yet men are capable of great nobility.

CRITICAL RECEPTION

Much of the scholarly debate concerning *The Wife of Bath's Prologue* and *Tale* focuses on Alisoun's role in feminist discourse. Many essayists address the misogynist views presented in *The Canterbury Tales* and attempt to determine whether Chaucer's use of Alisoun is meant to overthrow these views or reinforce them. Discussion on this topic is divided between those, such as H. Marshall Leicester, Jr., who see Alisoun as an early feminist striving for autonomy in an oppressive patriarchal society, and those, including Susan Crane and Catherine S. Cox, who view her as destined to fail in her search for equality, partly because she is trying to gain acceptance by emulating men instead of embracing her femininity, but mainly because she is a fictional character, written by a man. Several critics have investigated the religious dimensions of the *The Wife of Bath's Prologue* and *Tale.* James W. Cook has analyzed Alisoun's positions in relation to the sacraments, particularly marriage. Alcuin Blamires has explored the possibility that Chaucer uses Alisoun to challenge false teachings and wrongdoing by the clergy, comparing her views to those of the Lollards, a heretical sect that held the Bible as the sole authority on God's word and questioned the moral right of the clergy. Among the numerous other approaches to *The Wife of Bath's Prologue* and *Tale* are David S. Reed's examination of Alisoun's comic aspects, D. W. Robertson, Jr.'s analysis of her concern with status and wealth, and Susan Signe Morrison's and Elaine Treharne's investigations into how Chaucer uses and manipulates language in these works.

PRINCIPAL WORKS

Poetry

Romaunt of the Rose [translator; from Guillaume de Lorris's *Roman de la Rose*] c. 1360s
The Book of the Duchess c. 1368-69
The House of Fame c. 1378-81
The Parlement of Foules c. 1378-81
Troylus and Criseyde [adaptor; from Boccaccio's *Il Filostrato*] c. 1382-86
The Legend of Good Women c. 1386
The Canterbury Tales c. 1386-1400
Complaint of Mars; Complaint of Venus; Envoy to Bukton [printed by Julian Notary] 1499-1502
Chaucer's Lesser Poems Complete in Present-Day English [translated by James J. Donohue] 1974

Other Major Works

Boecius de consolacione philosophies [translator; from Boethius's *De consolatione philosophiae*] (prose) c. 1380s
The Equatorie of the Planetis (prose) c. 1391-92
Treatise on the Astrolabe (prose) c. 1391-92
*The Workes of Geffray Chaucer newly printed, with dyuers works which were neuer in print before [edited by William Thynne] (poetry and prose) 1532

The Complete Works of Geoffrey Chaucer. 7 vols. [edited by Walter W. Skeat] (poetry and prose) 1894-97

The Complete Poetry and Prose of Geoffrey Chaucer [edited by John H. Fisher] (poetry and prose) 1977; revised edition, 1989

The Riverside Chaucer [general editor Larry D. Benson] (poetry and prose) 1987

*This volume represents the first publication of *Romaunt of the Rose, The Book of the Duchess,* and *The Legend of Good Women.*

CRITICISM

David S. Reed (essay date 1970)

SOURCE: Reed, David S. "Crocodilian Humor: A Discussion of Chaucer's Wife of Bath." *Chaucer Review* 4, no. 2 (1970): 73-89.

[*In the following essay, Reed studies the negative characterization of the Wife of Bath and notes that her character is of low moral standards and amuses through her baseness and bad taste.*]

I

It is odd that many have found the Wife of Bath lifelike. If she is, it is not in a way that those who see her as a marvel of naturalistic invention would accept. In common sense human terms she is absurd and grotesque, a figment of that anti-feminist gallimaufry, the **Prologue** to her **Tale.** That many take her as a triumph of Chaucer's mellow and humane art tells us more about the place of women in our tradition than about the words before us. True, Chaucer was civilized: he shared the enjoyment of his courtly, humanist civilization in baiting women and the middle classes. But we are middle class, even if we think the middle classes ought to be baited; and women are not to be baited really, for their place has changed. In short our idea of civilization is different from Chaucer's. So it can hardly be that those who talk of the mellowness and humanity that went into the Wife really mean they wholeheartedly enjoy Chaucer's curmudgeonly and old-fashioned humor; or if they do, they are less than frank about it. It seems much more likely that they have found a way of misunderstanding Chaucer. And we have other ways as well, for our different ethos has not given us a detached view of the real nature of the Wife's comedy. It has made her an embarrassment, so that, fearing for Chaucer's good name, we misunderstand her elaborately.

Here are two ways of taking the Wife, both, to my mind, ways of mistaking her. The first is Walter C. Curry's:

Though one may not be entirely prepared to accept the opinion that she "is one of the most amazing characters . . . the brain of man has ever conceived," still she is so vividly feminine and human, so coarse and shameless in her discussion of the marital relations with her five husbands, and yet so imaginative and delicate in her story telling that one is fascinated against his will and beset with an irresistible impulse to analyze her dual personality with the view of locating, if possible, definite causes for the coexistence of more incongruent elements than are ordinarily found in human beings.[1]

The second is Bernard F. Huppé's:

In the **Wife's Prologue** Chaucer has constructed a subtle, dramatic monologue, which presents not only a woman of such reality that time has not withered her, but also a frame of judgment, stern as it is sympathetic. The comedy of the Wife's self-portrait has an underlying pathos because the reader understands—as she does not—that the vigor of her apology covers and contains the delusion which makes her life an empty lie.[2]

Clearly the attitudes of the two critics differ. One dallies with her; the other censures. But both agree in granting her character, implicitly at least, the elusive literary status of individuality. For, the first, in appreciating her complex vitality, must pretend to entertain her in her own right, and the reproaches of the second require a moral agent. However, to speak of a character having the pathos of individuality suits the case of one, like Criseyde, in a tragedy or, like Cavalcante, in Hell. Accordingly Curry is led to suggest Chaucer might have considered the Wife "his most tragic figure,"[3] and Huppé to see her unregenerate nature "confirmed on the way of damnation."[4]

But tragic or infernal subjectivity seem out of the question to me. I shall take the Wife as a stock figure in a varied sort of pantomime (I have no better word). And as for attitude or judgment, I shall not venture beyond the stock response such a figure and such comedy call for. This approach probably misses a lot, and it can scarcely be novel. I follow it to insist that what seems curiously antique, outworn, churlish even is the essence of the Wife's humor.

II

The Wife is a stock figure and an absurdity. If (as neither Curry nor Huppé are) we were consistent and thorough in our attempt to see the Wife in terms of higher modes of fiction, she would appear a monstrosity. But she belongs to low comedy or to pantomime, and within those modes she is lifelike. Here it is hard to speak of verisimilitude. What gives her life is the liveliness of pantomime: the stock figure of the Wife and the burlesque comedy of her **Prologue** and **Tale,** the masquerade of the world on pilgrimage, in which these are set, the narrator as impresario or master of ceremonies, all these conspire in a vivid illusion or invite our make believe.

In terms of pantomime, a figure like the Wife owes her liveliness to her being a stock absurdity. Simply because they are stock figures, the pilgrims have a perennial vitality and always seem lifelike. As Dryden put it in his "Preface to the Fables," "their general characters are still remaining in mankind, and even in England, though they are called by other names than those of Monks and Friars, and Canons, and Lady Abesses, and Nuns; for mankind is ever the same, and nothing lost out of nature, though everything is altered." Certainly this seems true of comic mankind. Dryden is of course praising Chaucer's comprehensive soul, yet it sounds almost as if he were talking of the shuffling of a pack of cards. Nor is this accidental. Probably a character has to be drawn from a highly conservative pack or stock to be recognizably comic. One finds the same figures in Jonson's comedy of humors and in Anthony Powell's social comedy. Even tricks are stock. Like Chaucer's Wife, Byron's Donna Julia, caught by her husband, overwhelms him with the tirade he has not had time to utter and shames him with his jealous suspicions of the truth. However, the Wife's vitality is not simply a matter of jokes' and comic figures' having long lives. Her absurdity works upon us to make her seem real. Outside fiction, when we call someone a "real character," it is a type we recognize, humorous and rather a card simply because typical. Such people may, in fact, strike us as unreal because they make play of the normal and everyday, so that we do not know whether to call them larger than life or smaller. But their very unreality makes them lively. It inveigles us into playing up to them, conspiring with them to make them real and lifelike. They are animated by the game we play with them, though we may indeed feel their life is a hoax like that of the bladders of wine Apuleius slew for thieves. Similarly in fiction, what lends such cartoon figures as the Wife their vitality is our willingness to play with them and be taken in by them. Whether demonic or genial, it is their distortion, or oddity, or exaggeration lays hold of us and makes us recognize them and endow them with life. The Wife is not a demonic figure. What is unnatural about her binds us all together in witness to her common humanity. Perhaps it is that a long comic tradition has given her standing in a rude and archaic folk sense of reality. At any rate, she is a genial humor.

Because we are involved in a comic displacement, the response she elicits from us is equivocal, and the question of how to take her becomes rather crocodilian. On the one hand we enjoy her jolly, hearty nature. On the other we know her to be, like Falstaff and Long John Silver, common and villainous. And yet, just because she is low and cunning, we find her jolly and call her human. She gains a sympathy as heartless as herself. She appeals to the Miller, Summoner, and Pardoner in us. So we like to hear of jealous old men tormented by a lively girl like her. But it also pleases us to see her done in in turn by age and nearly beaten at her own game by her last two husbands. At the same time, we are delighted to see her get off with it triumphantly.

The sympathy we accord her nature is licence, and licence was in the nature of pilgrimages. The host resembles a sort of prudent lord of misrule, and the *Wife's Prologue* is in the carnival spirit of the outing. Falstaff was rejected by the court and Bottom laughed out of it, both dismissed with the audience's sneaking sympathy or gratitude for the dance they led. Now obviously, since the pilgrimage was a journey to a shrine as well as a holiday and, moreover, a figure of "Thilke parfit glorious pilgrymage / That highte Jerusalem celestial" (I 50-51),[5] it would be fitting if Chaucer had brought such figures as the Wife to a reckoning, followed by repentance or rejection, in a grand anti-masque, or rather anti-pilgrimage, design. But nothing of the kind happens as far as her *Prologue* and *Tale* are concerned. Indeed, their happy endings are the inversion of such a proper conclusion, and misrule is left unshaken in that topsy-turvy.

Yet, if one reason for the Wife's being lifelike is that she is good fun, another is that she is a figure of execration. As a scandal she is butt as well as joker. Along with mothers-in-law, she belongs to a vulgar and perennial fund of anti-feminist jocularity. Hence Justinus in the *Merchant's Tale* and Chaucer in his *Envoi à Bukton* cite her as a dreadful warning against wives. She is a compendious type of the sort of woman-evil Dunbar, following Chaucer, treated with such sardonic relish in his *Tua Mariit Wemen and the Wedo*. Nor is she by any means a purely medieval literary sport: one finds the same sort of material brought together in Cleopatra, for instance, or Milton's Eve, or Molly Bloom. In short, the Wife is the "Archewyf," in the guise of comic shrew. She seems to have a superindividual lifelikeness because a type figure is meant to represent a class. But the class in the Wife's case is a pseudo-class since no such woman ever trod. It is this that makes her a lively fiction. Caricature works like synecdoche. It singles out and abstracts features in such a way that the most heterogeneous individuals are categorized together, and the very absence of likeness calls forth the most vigorous and lively distortion. The Wife seems to comprise all womanhood in one person, and yet all that apparently manifold nature is shrewish and can be reduced to a single formula or humor. Her type may not be obvious in the *General Prologue,* but what is implied by five husbands, gat teeth, and so on is exhaustively amplified in the *Prologue* to her *Tale.* There, in the spirit of a burlesque encyclopaedia, matter drawn from clerical, Romance, and probably popular traditions is crammed into a shrew's confession. With the same perverse learning her horoscope is cast as a formula for a shrew. The formula operates by the rules of distortion or disfigurement in the unfair way that "machinery" characterizes Arnold's "Philistines." So one misses the point if one imagines her case as a hard lot dealt her by fate. Because she is bourgeoise, everything can appear under the satirical aspect of botched and botching, and the wealth of a Venerean nature is disfigured under the influence of Mars to lecherousness, nagging, cheating, bickering, and misrule. The same formula covers her *Tale.* The romance is under Venus but Mars spoils it, as fits the teller. This is not tragedy but bathos. Part of what animates the Wife, then, is a sly and malicious elaboration of an idée fixe, which would indeed be an obsession if it were not a comic convention.

It is not her make-up that is subtle or complex but her presentation. It does not argue some complexity of fayness in the character of that other genial humor, Bottom, if Titania falls in love with him wearing an ass's head. It is a stock incongruity of pantomime deftly handled. Similarly, the Wife's character and the comic turns we expect of her are as conventionalized as the figure of a chessman and the sorts of moves it can make. It is to the play that is made of her and the wit and finesse with which she is handled we should look for any refinements of comedy.

The *General Prologue* is sophisticated pantomime, and it places the stock figure of the Wife on the kind of comic stage which gives her life. The pilgrimage itself, though it is also a pregnant metaphor for human life and the wayfaring of the masks of God, seems so beguilingly festive that the scene and the occasion become, as it were, the life and soul of the Wife along with the other pilgrims. It is a masquerade of the world, for the type figures, the Wife among them, are representative of the Estates of the Realm and of Christian pilgrims. They are disguised as a crowd of people in the Inn at Southwark. I think it is this disguise we delight in when we stress the individuality of the pilgrims. Their incognito constitutes their individuality. For us this is especially true since we do not think of the world in terms of its Estates. And, therefore, it does not automatically come to us that a merchant, a lawyer, and a wife "of beside Bath" are in fact Lawyer, Merchant, and Wife. But, quite apart from this accidental shift of interest, the figures are presented to us as if they each had an individual identity. The narrator meets them as a crowd of pilgrims, and the fiction is supported circumstantially. We are told when they meet and where, and in the links between the Tales we are given a fairly detailed itinerary. Formally, we are asked to take them as living and individual. For this reason the descriptions in the *General Prologue* appear to individuate pilgrims. Actually most of the detail is drawn from such sources as homiletic satire and physiognomic handbooks, and so really characterizes types. Yet, as in a dream allegory, those clues to what the persons are confront us enigmatically or transparently in the form of a mask. So, at the very moment the Wife's "hippes large" are meant to reveal her boisterous

and masterful disposition, they disguise her with such particularity that she seems to stand before us in the flesh. And Chaucer has accentuated the particularity of the figures by an apparent disregard for the rules of description. The seemingly unordered and casual jotting down of detail invests the pilgrims with the singularity of the picturesque. By contrast, the Theophrastan "character" creates no such illusion. That genre sets out to draw a general type of humanity—virtue, or vice, or foible, or mixture—belonging to no particular time or place. So we take even the most lifelike or circumstantial traits as illustrating a species rather than as characterizing an individual. Unlike the portraits of the *General Prologue,* "character" drawing does not attempt to use individual existence as a disguise for the type.[6]

The narrator gives the masquerade a courtly tone since his role is that of courteous master of ceremonies.[7] In the discussion of pleasantries in the second book of Castiglione's *The Courtier,* Federico Fregoso speaks of "festivity" or "urbanity" which "we see in the case of certain men who so gracefully and entertainingly narrate and describe something that has happened to them or that they have seen or heard, that with gestures and words they put it before our eyes and almost bring us to touch it with our hand."[8] Urbanity the narrator certainly has. With gentle folk he is respectful, with middle class persons laudatory but patronizing, and with low characters more forthright. One finds similar gradations of tone according to class in nineteenth century novels (Scott's for instance) and in the degrees of irony employed against "Barbarians," "Philistines," and "Populace" by Arnold. More than anything else, perhaps, it is such urbanity that satisfies us that the social scene is authentic, and one kind of observation that conjures up the reality of persons is the observation of the conventions of deference and condescension. In Langland's description of the people in the field full of folk where such urbanity is lacking it seems that his world is unworldly, though, in fact, many of his types are also Chaucer's. The urbanity of the *General Prologue,* on the other hand, immediately suggests a sense of the world and of what people are like. It also privileges us to view the sorts and conditions of men as a spectacle or entertainment. This is the narrator's "festivity": the urbane observation of the world is a courtly game. So with the Wife of Bath, the Merchant, the Lawyer, it is their respectability he singles out for praise; through their substance and status in their various callings they are presented as if they were worthy representatives of the commons. Their respectability is of course pinchbeck: as wife, parishioner, and, perhaps, weaver the Wife is a rogue. Here the malice belongs as much to courtly satire on middle class hypocrisy as to sermons and moralities. It is made apparent only through innuendo. Granted Chaucer's audience had no need to consult commentaries on what was implied by costly headwear on Sunday or by West Country weaving, still it would have interfered with their enjoyment of their inferior's vices if the point had been made in any other than a courteously bland manner.

Set in this higher pantomime is the comedy of the **Wife's Prologue** to her **Tale,** which is farce. It is not surprising that she becomes a problematic and bafflingly complex creature if one looks for psychological or moral ironies, or for the sort of higher comedy one expects in a novel. She is manipulated with an entire disregard for naturalistic conventions or psychological probability. She makes sense only in terms of burlesque and knockabout comedy.

In her **Prologue,** the Wife is her own impresario. Since what is put into her mouth as illustration of the "wo that is in mariage" is a farrago of anti-feminist lore, one might expect the comedy to be at her expense and women's. Yet, even if she exposed herself as a villain, she would gain the licence self-exposure gains. Her shrew's confession is, in fact, so enormous and put with such verve that it receives a comic absolution in her listeners' entertainment. Besides, the comedy is quite as much at the expense of husbands as of wives. By a sort of reflexive irony the Wife manages to be as much jester as jest. Her slippery womanhood is the bogey of the anti-feminist or "le jaloux," so that, at the very moment she is the object of his jibes, she is the source of his chagrin. An example is the farcical scene she sketches by way of illustrating how "Baar I stiffly myne olde housbondes in honde." To forestall a jealous husband, she recites his abuse as her injury. The joke against her is that she exposes herself to her listeners as the monster in his thought. But this is also a joke on her side since her being that monster is what makes her husbands ridiculous. If she is false, her effrontery mocks them. There is a similar point to be made about her marriage to Jankin. The cruel laughter against the widow hungry for youth and served by it as she had served her old husbands cannot stand up against her final triumph. And the Wife's getting the better of the mean and callow Jankin is a better joke than what he reads her from that boring misogynist's anthology of his. So satire against women dissolves in the farce of marriage, of which she is the master spirit.

If her confession is a sermon, as the Pardoner suggests, then it is a burlesque sermon in the spirit of the "sermon joyeux." In the first place, there is the joke about the preaching woman, on whom Dr. Johnson's comment doubtless speaks with the weight of conservative opinion. Had she been, like Melibeus' wife, a lady and an allegory, the case would have been different; but, since she is a low character, her learning is slapstick. Also belonging to the burlesque tradition of anti-order—like the women's sex strike in the *Lysistrata* or the annual marriages the first wife proposes in Dunbar's *The*

Tua Marriit Wemen and the Wedo—is the Wife's remedy for the woe in marriage, the rule of wives. Further, there are a number of pratfalls in the conduct of her sermon. Since her declared topic is "to speke of wo that is in mariage," one expects something of a "chanson de mal mariée" along the lines of "Oh the monotonous meanness of his lust . . . / It's the injustice . . . he is so unjust."[9] But, though the Wife utters complaints of this kind, it is herself, rather than her husbands, she shows to be the source of woe. Indeed, she boasts that she has been their whip and tribulation.

In the section before the Pardoner's interruption (D 1-162), she is made the mouthpiece of a clerical sort of buffoonery.[10] Whatever the excesses of the ascetic tradition in medieval Christianity, there was, of course, no question about the canonical status of marriage and remarriage. What the Wife does is simply to give Christian teaching a farcical twist. This is the reason for the inconsistency of the tone: sometimes a theologian seems to be speaking only to be overwhelmed by a cackle from the Wife. One need only consult I Cor. vii to see that her case is respectable in letter. But the ribald gloss she gives the letter subverts its spirit. Her treatment of her three main topics—remarriage, the states of marriage and virginity, love between husband and wife—parodies Christian edification. For, instead of rising soberly from the letter to the spirit, she gives the letter a gross and ludicrous interpretation. The result is a sort of sermon for carnival. Permission to remarry, for instance, has Paul's authority behind it. But the Wife multiplies the permission inordinately. She moves from a reasonable puzzlement over how many times Scripture seems to allow one to marry to citing Solomon's extravagant case:

> Lo, heere the wise kyng, daun Salomon:
> I trowe he hadde wyves mo than oon.
> As wolde God it were leveful unto me
> To be refresshed half so ofte as he!
>
> (D 35-38)

The allusions to Jerome's "Epistola Adversus Jovinianum" add a rather pedantic irony. The epistle contends for a rigorously spiritual ideal of marriage. The Wife, however, converts its higher pleading into most unspiritual liberties. For instance, Jerome heaps sarcasm on those unspiritual enough to remarry: certainly remarriage is better than having more than one husband simultaneously, and, since even a repentant fornicator can be forgiven, octogamy is not damned.[11] The Wife changes the grotesque word and sarcastic permission to a source of rejoicing. One cannot say that the Wife disagrees with Church teaching or Jerome; rather, she plays havoc with them. Again, in dealing with the exhortation to virginity and the permission to marry, her case is Pauline enough. Indeed, it seems that she is arguing with disarming modesty that, while virginity is perfection, marriage is also a state with its own excellences even if they are inferior:

> Virginitee is greet perfeccion,
> And continence eek with devocion,
> But Crist, that of perfeccion is welle,
> Bad nat every wight he sholde go selle
> Al that he hadde, and gyve it to the poore
> And in swich wise folwe hym and his foore.
> He spak to hem that wolde lyve parfitly. . . .

> (105-11)

Then the Wife adds her application of the teaching, and the edifying trend of her discussion collapses in the exuberance with which she embraces imperfection:

> And lordynges, by youre leve, that am nat I.
> I wol bistowe the flour of al myn age
> In the actes and in fruyt of mariage.

> (112-14)

In the same way, she gives Paul's treatment of the love between husband and wife a preposterous gloss. Paul spoke of the marriage debt, and the Wife will have her pound of flesh. The burlesque is not of course an early expression, disguised by being put in a bad mouth, of "the great sexual insurrection of our Anglo-Teutonic race" or of any other protest. What is behind the play being made of church teaching is a sort of goliardic scholasticism.

The Wife's *Tale* is also burlesque, though in a more subdued way. The opening broadside against the Friar makes it clear that a mock-romance is to follow. There are several points where the anti-feminist jocularity of her *Prologue* breaks in and romance lapses into bathos. Moreover, the *Tale* as a whole lends itself to a sly untuning. In skeleton it consists of two problems, the second being the consequence of solving the first. By promising to marry the beldame the knight learns the answer to the riddle the court of women have set him and saves his life. But fulfilling his promise means taking an undesirable wife, and that confronts him with a second problem. If one divides the story in two, each part containing a problem, then the second part is a mirror image of the first. In both parts there is a problem about women, and in both cases the solution is women's rule. In other respects the second part inverts the first. Whereas the knight rapes the maiden in the first part, the hag makes advances upon him in the second; and the fatal success of his answer to the first riddle is righted by the happy outcome of his answer to the dilemma the hag puts to him. This pattern invites structural analysis: it is figured upon polarities of masculine dominance (crudely featured in the knight's rape) and feminine (featured in the riddles as well as the beldame's compelling the knight to wed and take her in his arms). Through the miraculous transformation of the beldame the *Tale* resolves the polarity in favour

of women's mastery, which is a rather equivocal combination of Mars and Venus, male and female. The transformation mediates between other polarities such as age and youth, ugliness and beauty, and, presumably, low birth and high, and poverty and plenty as well. But this beautiful impossibility is an equivocal solution to the knight's dilemma.[12] The romance is sphinxlike: to fail to solve the problems would be disastrous, but the correct answer brings with it an ambiguous good fortune. This equivocal nature of the *Tale* is apt for burlesque and, as the Wife tells it, one senses that she is in ambush behind the beautiful impossibilities of romance. In her mouth, what is Cinderellalike in her *Tale* is gargoyled.

Clearly the *Tale* is a courtly one. The sovereignty of women is an article of courtly love, and the transformation of the beldame into a beautiful young woman makes her eligible for the love of a knight. But the Wife is not courtly, and the courtly game is garbled because she is let loose on it. Possibly Chaucer envisaged in her a fourteenth century Emma Bovary, whose imagination courtly romance had excited. The point had, after all, been made in the tag about Rome's being undone by romances. At any rate, it is clear from the portrait of the Prioress and from the *Franklin's Prologue* and *Tale* that Chaucer knew how to adapt courtly matter to the sort of comedy of manners in which uncourtly people aspire to courtly fashions. However, the Wife's imitation is closer to the kind of travesty one finds in Bottom's play, "Pyramus and Thisbe," and, as there, the courtly joke seems rather heartless. The burlesque intention would be clearer if some courtly version of the Wife's *Tale* had been current. Possibly Gower's "Tale of Florent" furnished the high analogue that the Wife brings to confusion. At any rate, the courtly doctrine of women's sovereignty, which the *Tale* illustrates, is also the Wife's peculiar concern. In her *Prologue* she made out that her supremacy was the law of love, and that under it her shrewishness was gentled. This might well be a domestic parody of the woman's place according to the conventions of courtly love. Remembering this, one finds in the part played by women in her *Tale* more of the rule of wive's than of ladies' grace; and her marriage to Jankin returns a quizzical echo to the happy ending of her *Tale*. What excludes the Wife from romance is represented in the beldame. Both are base born. The Wife is neither young nor beautiful; the beldame is old and ugly. The Wife may be well off as a burgher's widow, but surely she is not as rich as a lady; the beldame is poor. So it is hard not to spy the Wife behind the beldame's lecture and miraculous transformation. Indeed the lecture reminds one of the exegetical mischief of the Wife's *Prologue*. On "gentillesse," for instance, the beldame's argument is irreproachable. The theme "nobilitas sola est atque unica virtus" is a commonplace of the Romance tradition. And yet it is as if a game of croquet were being played with flamingoes and hedgehogs. The fine sentiments were never intended as a plea for a Loathly Lady. On the three other points (poverty, old age, and ugliness) her lecture is, I think, to be taken as comic gate crashing. Poverty, old age, and ugliness were banished from the garden of love, so arguments in favor of their admission, even the serious one on poverty, disconcert the rules. Finally, just as the Wife's glossing of authorities in her *Prologue* gave sober matter a ludicrous twist, so the envoy to her *Tale* sends romance widdershins.

> And thus they lyve unto hir lyves ende
> In parfit joye; and Jhesu Crist us sende
> Housbondes meeke, yonge, and fressh abedde,
> And grace t'overbyde hem that we wedde. . . .
>
> (1257-60)

III

Faced with antic comedy of the Wife's sort, one usually looks for a didactic purpose, either critical or edifying, to justify one's enjoyment. But I am at a loss to find any such moral strategy camouflaged in the *Wife's Prologue* or *Tale.*

The *Tale* is not a criticism of the standards of courtly love. Courtly love was a high and fantastic game, quite conscious of its being so. The Wife belongs to the game by making an anti-game of it. Whether one thinks of the game as a love game or a social game, the Wife's intrusion is confounding. But her parody is necessary to high manners, for they ask to be aped in order to establish their authority by laughing at the low imitation. And in the love game, itself a parody (of sacred love), played in scorn of marriage and in jeopardy of Reason and Nature, the Wife's role is like that of the Duenna of Jean de Meun. It is to blow the gaff on the game, not by being the mouth-piece of Reason or Nature, but by being a spectre of rogue womanhood, and so a remedy of love.[13]

As for the *Prologue* to her *Tale,* which is farce, its end is topsy-turvy and bathos. As a satire on women it simply lacks moral weight. Juvenal's "Sixth Satire," by contrast, apart from its sheer invective splendor, is concerned with the superfluities of the age; and Pope's "Epistle II" of the characters of women conveys a paradoxically generous recognition of their human nature. Further, the Wife's comedy also lacks anything that would pass for a serious discussion of marriage in more recent literature. To my mind, this is true of the other Tales of the so called Marriage Group as well. The Franklin's romance about "gentillesse" is really too slender to be a mirror for middle class marriages. Ethically, the *Parson's Tale* doubtless says all there is to be said on the subject. But to discover in the Wife's exposure of married vice an oblique lecture on married

virtue goes against the decorum of farce. Besides, it sounds like cant. However, it does not follow that, because the Wife's pantomime fails to be didactic or some high mode of imitation, it is anti-moral. A moral ethos is necessary if its inversions are to be funny. Similarly, like the Feasts of Fools and of Asses, the burlesque sermon depends on the decorum it overturns. It would be quite as absurd to find a heretic or immoral intention in such topsy-turvy as it would be to find an edifying one.

Comedy of the farcical mode, whose end is solely the preposterous conclusion, may leave one uneasy. The ridiculous as a form of imitation rather than of satire and the grotesque in which there is no allegory are attended by a kind of licence and by a primitive and undignified conviviality, which are disturbing. No doubt the study of literature is inherently priggish, but the Wife's world is crooked, the comedy of her marriages is as cruel and banal as those of a Punch and Judy show, and Chaucer's urbanity is a way of feasting upon the base and the ugly. And yet one cannot dismiss the Wife as unacceptable to modern taste, nor relegate her to the medieval world with the explanation that her pantomime belongs to an age of stricter hierarchies and more robust conventions. For one thing, if one rejects her in this way, one actually reinstates her as good fun, for the antic is only improved in the guise of the antique. For another, all comedy, in one form or another, involves the trite, the banal, and the indecorous; and, since the Wife incorporates these so generously, she can hardly go out of season. It is also simply in the nature of urbanity to play upon the gross, the distorted, and the cruel. Necessarily one's attitude to such comedy is ambivalent; that is what tickles one.

The comedy of the *Wife's Prologue* and *Tale* is a coarse joke and can and ought to be enjoyed on those terms. But is it nothing more? Antic comedy is, in fact, a mimetic mode in its own right, though one is used to finding it subservient to satire, or slander, or parable. In order to show one way in which it is an imitation, and not simply a revel or celebration of folly, I shall attempt to relate it to the courtly and religious ethos of Chaucer's age. In the most general terms, given a Realist and aristocratic frame of mind, whether we care to characterize the Wife by flesh, or womanhood, or Third Estate, she confronts us with a mischievous reality, or rather with the abortion of reality since she brings form to confusion. Like neoplatonic matter, which is mere privation of form or void stuff—the essentially grotesque as it were—antic comedy is naughty because it is naught, mischievous because envious of form and value, derisive because displaced. So the Wife's comedy of parody, inversion, and bathos is a mode of imitating the intractable and base anti-reality of the world and experience. And our genial and creaturely involvement with that anti-reality is expressed in our ambivalent attitude, and in the special licence antic comedy, like Erasmus' Folly, demands.

More specifically, one can relate the Wife's antic humor to religious attitudes. It is obvious from her *Prologue* that clerical satire had a share in shaping her bugbear womanhood. However, the scurrility and ridicule of the tradition, like Lear's madness, took in more than women. The usury of her bed is an image of the precious bane that rewards love of the flesh, and her misrule looks like an emblem of the fate of those who love the world. "So Bromyard, comparing Worldly Fortune to a contrary wife, reminds his hearers how 'sometimes it is literally depicted thus upon the walls in the form of a woman turning a wheel with her hands, who, as most often happens, shifts the wheel contrary to the wishes of him who is propelled on it or sits upon the top.'"[14] I do not, of course, wish to suggest Chaucer is contributing to De Contemptu Mundi satire, but he draws upon its pantomime possibilities. If the bouleversements of fortune, the illusions of the world, the deciduousness of the flesh are bathos and confusion, they can find expression in the farce of the "Archewyf."

At the same time, the material from clerical satire is placed in a context of courtly badinage against women and marriage. Here one can speak of the duplicity of tone that teases the earnest reader as part of courtly flyting. Flyting is part of courting, and, if the Wife is an image of the canker in the rose, she is also a kind of stalking horse.[15]

The Wife's comedy also belongs to another tradition of courtly flyting, in this case directed against the Third Estate. The Wife is both rogue and laughing stock because she is base; and the gross, the disgraceful, and the anarchic, unbound in the world of fabliaux and jig, are courtly entertainment. I suppose this might be an expression of class antagonism and a way of putting the disorderly commons in their place. And yet it is also a form of courting, for it calls for a pawky, bonhommous stance and for condescension to be entertained. Even if she is anti-pastoral, the Wife still calls for a version of pastoral attitudes. This is not simply because the comedy of her *Prologue* is placed in the low life of an old and famous provincial town, but also because, like Skelton's Elinour Rumming, the figure of the Wife and her sort of low comedy belong to popular, as much as to Romance or clerical, tradition. In Sir David Lindesay's *Ane Satyre of the Thrie Estatis,* Solace relates of his mother Bonnie Besse,

> Of twelf ʒeir auld sho learnit to swyfe:
> Thankit be the great God on lyue:
> Scho maid me fatheris four or fyue:
>   But dout, this is na mowis.
> Quhen ane was deid, sho gat ane vther:
> Was never man had sic ane mother.

> Of fatheris sho maid me ane futher,
>   Of lawit men and leirit.

(162-69)[16]

It is of course possible that both Chaucer and Lindesay drew on some folk heroine who began her career at twelve. But since Solace's lines closely resemble the Wife's

> For, lordynges, sith I twelve yeer was of age,
> Thonked be God that is eterne on lyve,
> Housbondes at chirche door I have had fyve,

(4-6)

it looks as if Lindesay was indebted to Chaucer. In that case, what is relevant is how naturally Chaucer's invention passes into Lindesay's popular farce of evil counsellors and misrule. Again, if one turns to the "Carols of Marriage" in Richard L. Greene, *The Early English Carols,*[17] one finds that all treat of the woe that is in marriage: of shrews, of widows, of wifely domination, expense, and unruly members. In particular *408* tells of an incident "at the townys end." Here it is the husband who is exasperated by the wife's tongue. He strikes her a blow on the ear of which, unlike Chaucer's Wife, she dies. Among the "Amorous Carols," *457* is possibly evidence of Chaucer's modifying popular tradition. At any rate, it seems to involve a Jankin and an Alysoun. The burden runs,

> "Kyrie, so kyrie,"
> Jankyn syngyt merie,
> With "aleyson."

Greene's note suggests that "aleyson" is probably a pun on the name of the girl. There is also a fleeting resemblance of situation to the Wife's admiring Jankin's pretty legs and feet at her fourth husband's funeral. In the carol the girl is at a Yule procession and there

> Jankyn at the Angnus beryot the paxbrede
> He twynkelid, but sayd nowt, and on myn fot he trede.

But it would be absurd to try to establish with a few such tenuous parallels that Chaucer actually drew on popular tradition for the Wife; nor is it important. What is important is that, as the comedy of shrews in farce, interlude, jig, ballad, and mystery play makes patent, the Wife's manifold comic femininity belongs to the humor of the people. In Chaucer the popular comedy becomes sophisticated. Part of that sophistication is simply that the comedy is seen as popular and so is attended by a courtly sense of distance from low life and low comedy, and by an urbane enjoyment of them.

There is a further reason for talking of the pastoral or popular nature of the *Wife's Prologue* and *Tale,* though it is a question, not of Chaucer's individual composition, but of the literary tradition in which it was formed.

That is the element of country matter, which, one might speculate, is a random survival of folk custom or of pagan belief. The provenance of the jealous husband and lusty wife, January and May, Winter's flyting with Summer is the May Game, and possibly the folk custom persisted in the comic tradition.[18] The transformation of the Loathly Lady looks like the harvest figure of crone and maiden, or the rejuvenation of the year, or some other seal of health and wealth; and what is rejected as superstition might be allowed to be a source of Romance.[19] Yet since both motifs crop up in inexhaustibly various shapes, the one for instance in George Eliot's Casaubon and Dorothea, the other in Mozart's Papagena, one might wonder if one can point to anything beyond their ubiquity. Still the medieval configurations of such matter are the grotesque and the marvellous, the farcical and the romantic. The anti-masque humor of the *Tale,* which makes a sophisticated play of the quaint that recalls *The Golden Ass* or *The Rape of the Lock,* in fact combines both. The *Wife's Prologue,* on the other hand, is purely farcical. Either mode, farce or romance, is attended by the ironies of rejection and condescension since either distances or repudiates and, at the same time, licenses what it shows.

One might class the Wife's comedy under the aspect of Hermes, the Trickster, in female garb, it is true. As agent of confusion and breaker of bounds her antic humor shares his sly buffoonery. The Trickster, like C. G. Jung's "shadow," is a type of the outcast and the base and, at the same time, "contains within it the seed of an enantiodromia, of a conversion into its opposite."[20] This paradox is latent in the Wife also, witness the comic reversals of her *Prologue* and the transformation in her *Tale.* Moreover, it is a hermetic cast in her nature that seems to ask for "transformation, through 'finding and thieving' . . . into riches, love, poetry, and all the ways of escape from the narrow confines of law, custom, circumstance, fate,"[21] for the Romantic transvaluation of all values, by which cupidity becomes the root of all morality, the eternal feminine draws us upwards, and the base is natural.

But, if one thing is clear about Chaucer's Wife, it is that she is fool's gold. So to say that she seems to ask for a hermetic transformation certainly does not mean one can talk about her as if her antic nature had been transformed. Nevertheless, it is only in terms of a historical revolution in literary values sympathetic to the sort of transformation she asks for that I can explain the surprising and elaborate judgments of the Wife and the enthusiastic press she has received in some post-Coleridgean criticism. I should say the transvaluation must be indeed hermetic if it can find redeeming, and more than redeeming, virtues in the Wife. Either it is an extravagant irony, or its values are somehow crooked. If irony, the account of the Wife must run in the following paradoxical way. She is a rogue, so she is spoken of as the incorrigibly vital. Except in her own terms, she is a scandal; therefore, she is extenuated as that epitome of the special case, the irreducibly individual. Her being becomes secret, and, therefore, Chaucer could only have divined it by a godlike act of creative imagination; and we, who read, can only approach her baffled and amazed. So she is enfranchised. Obviously a squinneying appraisal like this is sheer critical waggishness. It is as if the Wife's pantomime had invaded criticism and invested her with burlesque dignities. True, it is hard to speak of the Wife without duplicity, and some in the spirit of pantomime have written perceptively as well as entertainingly about her; nor would one wish to spoil the sport. But one should recognize the sport for what it is: a sort of condescending irony on the critics' part. Otherwise it becomes imposture on the Wife's, and her upside down world is taken seriously. To my mind, those values that so approve her roguery as fully human or find something excellent in her crookedness are askew.

To insist, on the other hand, on the penetration and seriousness of Chaucer's moral insight misses the point about the Wife. Obviously Chaucer meant her for a bad lot, and obviously he saw to it she set everything running counter-clockwise; so obviously, in fact, that insight is not in question. The Wife is blatant enough, and it requires a very special stare to evade recognizing her for what she is: a fashioning of the rogue figure of wife from a more than well worked vein of low comedy. What Chaucer's art added was range and suppleness of confusion. It is an urbane art. That, of course, does not mean that it is pander's art. Indeed, one can see the urbanity, amidst the festivity of the Pilgrimage, as a suspension of judgment against eternity. It does not presume to spy into that final unmasking of the masquerade of the world. But, since it is itself one of the masks, the urbanity expresses a sense of human finitude and of belonging to the pantomime of creaturely indignity. That, in a Christian as well as genial sense, is the human and worldly perspective of the *Canterbury Tales.*

Notes

1. *Chaucer and the Mediaeval Sciences,* 2nd ed. (New York, 1960), p. 91. Although I disagree with Professor Curry on the Wife's character, I have found his information most helpful for my discussion of the Wife as a type figure.

2. *A Reading of the Canterbury Tales* (State University of New York, 1964), p. 108.

3. Curry, p. 115.

4. Huppé, p. 123.

5. Citations from Chaucer in my text are to *The Complete Works,* ed. Fred N. Robinson, 2nd ed. (Boston, 1957).

6. See the discussion in Ralph Baldwin, *The Unity of the Canterbury Tales* (Copenhagen, 1955), pp. 35-57.

7. I put this view, for what it is worth, against that expressed by E. Talbot Donaldson, "Chaucer the Pilgrim," *PMLA,* LXIX (1954), 928-36, that the narrator is a buffoon. The tone is often falsely naive, but so is Pandarus', yet no one takes him for a simpleton. Buffoon and ironic man are akin, but the ironic man "lets you see all the while that he could enlighten you if he chose, and so makes a mock of you" (Francis M. Cornford, *The Origin of Attic Comedy,* ed. Theodore H. Gaster [New York, 1961,] p. 120). One recognizes that the ironic man's naiveté is put on; it is an affectation rather than an impersonation. Socrates's enemies resented it as an air of superiority; in the case of the narrator one takes it as part of his festivity and urbanity.

8. *The Book of the Courtier,* trans. Charles S. Singleton (New York, 1959), p. 141.

9. Robert Lowell, "To Speak of Woe that is in Marriage," *Life Studies* (New York, 1956), p. 82.

10. Cf. D. W. Robertson, Jr., *A Preface to Chaucer* (Princeton, 1962), pp. 317-31.

11. I. 14, 15 (*PL,* XXIII, 233, 234).

12. See Claude Lévi-Strauss, "The Structural Study of Myth," *Structural Anthropology* (New York, 1963), pp. 206-31, esp. n. 6 (pp. 230-31) on the Sphinx and the observations (pp. 225-26) on Cinderella. I shall take up the trickster theme later in this paper.

13. Cf. the ambiguous roles of Ovid's Dipsas (*Amores* I, "Elegy VIII") and of the nurse in the pseudo-Ovidian "De Vetula" (Edward K. Rand, *Ovid and his Influence* [New York, 1963], p. 130).

14. G. R. Owst, *Literature and Pulpit in Medieval England* (Oxford, 1961), p. 239.

15. See Francis L. Utley, *The Crooked Rib* (Columbus, 1944), pp. 30-34.

16. *Sir David Lindesay's Works,* Part IV, EETS, OS 37 (London, 1869).

17. (Oxford, 1935).

18. See E. K. Chambers, *The Mediaeval Stage* (London, 1903), I, 170.

19. See the chapter on "The Corn Mother and the Corn Maiden in Northern Europe," in Sir James G. Frazer, *The Golden Bough, Part V* (London, 1912), I, 131-70. Perhaps the enormous appetite of the hag in those analogues of the *Wife's Tale,* "King Henry" and "The Weddynge of Sir Gawen and Dame Ragnell," cited by G. H. Maynadier, *The Wife of Bath's Tale* (London, 1901), pp. 9-16, is an echo of the Famine of the Farm (Frazer, p. 140). On the rejuvenation of the year, compare the marriage of Mars to Anna Perenna (Ovid, *Fasti,* III, 675-96) and see Frazer's commentary in the *Fasti of Ovid* (London, 1929), III, pp. 121-27. See also Lévi-Strauss, pp. 230-31, n. 6 for another inviting line. This is, of course, the terrain of Shandyisms. What is important for my argument is that those elements should be recognized as "country." It does not matter whether they originate in the fertility myth and ritual of the Cambridge school. Indeed, the theories of that school might well illustrate the perennial vitality of such country matter as a source of romance and fancy.

20. "On the Psychology of the Trickster Figure" in Paul Radin, *The Trickster* (London, 1956), p. 211.

21. Karl Kerényi, "Trickster in Relation to Greek Mythology," Radin, p. 190.

James W. Cook (essay date summer 1978)

SOURCE: Cook, James W. "'That She Was Out of Alle Charitee':[1] Point-Counterpoint in the *Wife of Bath's Prologue* and *Tale.*" *Chaucer Review* 13, no. 1 (summer 1978): 51-65.

[*In the following essay, Cook uses religious doctrines of sacramental law to analyze the Wife of Bath's failure to comply with the spirit of the sacrament of marriage. Because Alisoun prefers to control her spouse rather than form a true union with him, she is the opposite of the hag she describes in her* Tale.]

In a provocative essay on Alice of Bath's narrative posture, Gloria K. Shapiro recently requested a more adequate treatment of the religious dimensions of the Wife of Bath's performance.[2] In the course of her discussion, Professor Shapiro observed: "The perfection in virtue through . . . the grace of God is the larger subject of Dame Alice's *Tale.*. . ."[3] And so I also think it to be.

Professor Shapiro, however, goes on to reach the ingenious conclusion that Alice, prompted by an almost "pathological insecurity,"[4] takes extraordinary pains to conceal her refined sensibilities and, with them, virtues so admirable and appreciative of purity that readers must henceforward regard the Wife as "partially beatified" by religious passion and as a more "convincing Christian" than is Chaucer's Prioress.[5]

In making this judgment, Professor Shapiro neither intends nor attempts to account systematically for the religious dimensions which interest her. In this essay, therefore, I propose to provide an overview of the major theological dimensions of the Wife's performance, especially those relevant to the theology of grace and of the sacraments. I shall also consider the relevant positions of a selection of influential churchmen with respect to those dimensions and shall suggest that, though Alice no doubt reveals more of herself than she intends in her portrait of the hag, religiously this revelation arises more from contrast than from identity of attitude. Finally, I shall insist that Alice cannot be counted among the Christian blessed—even partly, and I propose to examine the *Wife of Bath's Tale* as a medieval consideration of the sacramental efficacy of marriage.

In the *Summa Theologiae,* St. Thomas teaches: "Now the whole rite of the Christian religion is derived from the priesthood of Christ. It is clear, then, that the sacramental character is specifically the character of Christ, to whose priesthood the faithful are configured according to the sacramental characters, which are nothing else but certain participations of the priesthood of Christ, which are derived from Christ himself."[6] Established by Christ for the good of the Church, the sacraments were deemed by Augustine, by Thomas, by their followers, and finally by the Council of Trent to be true causes (*causa per se*) of grace.[7]

Though the Church considers matrimony least important among the sacraments, marriage is nevertheless Divinely ordained both to assist individuals in achieving spiritual perfection and to promulgate the growth of the Church. Accordingly, participation in each sacrament produces concomitant kinds and degrees of grace in the recipient and, also, certain observable benefits symptomatic of the grace which prepares human beings for the inspiration of the Holy Spirit, and for supernatural life.

St. Augustine specifies the sacramental benefits which flow from marriage. Among them, he lists the procreation of children, companionship between the sexes, the salubrious effect of matrimony in turning "carnal or youthful incontinence . . . to the honorable task of begetting children, so that marital intercourse makes something good out of the evil of lust," and finally, the benefit of parental affection for tempering the "concupiscence of the flesh."[8]

To these benefits St. Ambrose adds harmony (*armonia*)—a couple's peaceful enjoyment of one another's company. Where one does not find this harmony, the Saint assures us, "There is strife and dissention, which is not from God, for 'God is love'."[9]

But this harmony, which in a wedded couple can be taken to signify the efficacy of the sacrament, is by no means the automatic outcome of having participated in the marriage ceremony. For any sacrament to confer its special grace on the participants, a number of conditions must first be fulfilled. Some of these conditions arise from the nature of the sacraments themselves. Sacraments are constituted by three elements: "things (*res*), as the matter (*materia*), words (*verba*) as the form (*forma*), and the person of the minister conferring the sacrament with the intention of doing what the church does."[10] If all those elements are present, the church deems the sacrament valid. In the case of Alice's marriages, we have no reason to suppose the sacraments otherwise than valid in all respects.

Others of the conditions, however, depend upon the state of mind of the adult recipient. Thus the sacrament may be perfectly valid and yet prove productive of no grace for adults. This case obtains when the disposition of the recipient to receive the sacrament is marred either by an intention not to do what the church does, or by mortal sin. This view was fully developed by Chaucer's time and was later thus summarized by Bellarmine:

"Intention, faith and penitence are necessarily required in the adult recipient, not as active causes, for faith and penitence neither produce sacramental grace nor give the sacrament its efficacy, but rather they [can] only erect obstacles which indeed prevent the sacrament from being able to exercise its efficacy."[11]

It seems clear that Alice evidences in her behavior, her narrative posture, and her autobiographical *tour de force* a good many obstacles that prevent the sacrament from producing consequent grace. One of them, however, is not the issue Chaucer has her raise concerning the validity of her five marriages. Theologically speaking, the doubts she expresses on that score constitute a red herring dragged through her narrative to throw her auditors off the scent of her real heterodoxy. Her arguments in support of serial marriage—though they seem to contradict Christ and however they may have offended prevailing lay and clerical notions of good taste and propriety—are nevertheless perfectly doctrinal. Though the church and the fathers strongly preferred widowhood to remarriage, they never dared to countermand the scriptural authority for the latter. Augustine remarked: "Men are wont to raise the question concerning third and fourth and even a greater number of marriages. To answer them in a few words, I do not have the audacity to condemn any of these marriages nor to minimize the shame of their frequency."[12]

Alice's real heterodoxy appears, instead, in her obstinate refusal to subordinate her will to the Divine will as it is implicit in the marriage sacrament. This refusal reflects itself first in her defense of her sexual predilections, the willful origins of which she attempts to conceal under the guise of astrological compulsion:

> For certes, I am al Venerien
> In feelynge, and myn herte is Marcien.

Venus me yaf my lust, my likerousnesse,
And Mars yaf me my sturdy hardynesse;
Myn ascendent was Taur, and Mars therinne.
Allas! allas! that evere love was synne!
I folwed ay myn inclinacioun
By vertu of my constellacioun;
That made me I koude noght withdrawe
My chambre of Venus from a good felawe.

(D 609-18)

This essentially theatrical appeal for sympathy thinly disguises serious heresy. By citing her horoscope to excuse her behavior, Alice denies to her own will that degree of freedom which people require to be able to choose God's intention for their lives—the highest good—over their own preferences, which, flawed by original sin, necessarily constitute the lesser good.

Moreover, Alice's admission of her continuing concupiscence, one of the maladies sin causes, signifies the failure of the sacrament to prove efficacious and to produce, in her case, its consequent and curative grace. Had it done so, Alice would have displayed in her behavior the virtue of temperance—a sign of grace whose absence points directly to a defect in her will.[13]

Alice's willful heterodoxy also appears in the demand for mastery that she regularly imposes upon her husbands.

The church's insistence upon the husband's role as head of the family irks Alice—as it does some of her *Tale*'s critics. But in focusing argument on the pros and cons of the psychological justifications for Alice's militancy—justifications that arise from misguided clerical, lay, and societal antifeminism—critical discussion sometimes obscures the theological imperative for a unique mutuality in marriage. This mutuality must express itself not only in the spouses' physical union, but also and more importantly in the union of their wills and, beyond that, in the careful and caring maintenance of that union by cheerful, mutually supportive, and successful coping with the onerous round of daily tribulation which characterizes human life. According to St. Ambrose, the essence of marriage defines itself in the contract (*pactio*) which expresses the union of wills: "Thus when the marital union is begun, then the name of spouses is applied; for it is not the deflowering of virginity that makes the union, but the marital contract."[14]

As I shall argue below, in none of her marriages has Alice made a full commitment of her will to the sacrament, and from that reservation follow most unhappy religious consequences—sin, gracelessness, and loss of charity.

It seems, then, that critics who find in Alice of Bath the prototype of the twentieth century's liberated woman and who can sympathize with her as the victim of an ages-old antifeminist conspiracy spring a snare that Chaucer set for Alice herself.

In preferring experience over authority and in raising and answering to her own satisfaction the question "what do women most want?" Alice universalizes her limited and limiting experience; she perceives herself as Everywoman.

To the church, and I think to Chaucer, she represents instead Everyman, facing the bar of God's ultimate justice and stripped by her own tragic decisions of salvific grace and of true liberty.

The psychic stresses that appear in Chaucer's characterization of Alice—her selective appeals to authority, her need for public approval despite private viciousness; her concern with appearances, her continual discomfort in her marriages, the tension created by the ongoing warfare between her refined sensibilities, on the one hand, and her shrewishness, lust, and coarseness, on the other—are in themselves symptomatic of the uneasy state of her soul and of her bondage to her appetites.

Commenting on the works of St. Augustine, Henri Rondet observes that therein "Liberating grace . . . appears as a principle of unification, capable of restoring harmony among the divergent tendencies which are in the sinner's soul, which *are* the sinner himself precisely as sinner."[15] Thus the "pathological insecurity" to which Professor Shapiro has called our attention is itself indicative, not of beatitude, but of its opposite.

The theological universals that associate themselves with Alice's experience do not do so exclusively or even principally as a result of her woes in marriage with five husbands—though these are certainly relevant. The universals, rather, have essentially to do with Alice's self-selected misery as a human creature.

Thomas Aquinas offers elucidation here. Except for man, every creature has a divinely appointed end, a tendency to achieve it, and sufficient natural means to encompass it. Man, however, has been created a spirit for a spiritual end vastly disproportionate to his nature: "Although man is formed toward an ultimate end, he is unable to achieve that end naturally, but only through grace, and this is because of the eminence of that end."[16] Assisted by the gift of grace, man has the capacity actually to participate in the Divine nature—to achieve the beatific vision that is natural to no *creature*, but to the Creator only: "The gift of grace exceeds every faculty of the natural creature, for it is nothing other than a participation in the Divine nature . . . through participation in its likeness."[17]

But in this high distinction human misery originates. According to Thomas Aquinas and in the official view of the church, only God can make people fully happy, and people cannot reach God solely by their own efforts. They require God's freely offered help. Availing themselves of it, however, requires the exercise of will. People may accept God's grace; they may refuse it.

"God is the sun that gives the light, the soul is the eye that opens to the light, and sin is the opaque screen that comes between the soul and God."[18] Those who refuse grace blind themselves with sin and opt for the natural order at the expense of the beatific vision. The pragmatic consequence of that option is damnation, freely chosen.[19]

And there stands Alice. Despite her astrological disclaimer, she makes choices and knows it, and her speeches emphasize the conscious operation of her will:

> For sothe, I wol nat kepe me chaast in al.
> Whan myn housbonde is fro the world ygon,
> Som Cristen man shal wedde me anon. . . .
>
> I wol bistowe the flour of al myn age
> In the actes and in fruyt of mariage.
>
> I nyl envye no virginitee.
>
> I wol persevere; I nam nat precius.
> In wyfhood I wol use myn instrument
> As frely as my Makere hath it sent.
>
> An housbonde I wol have, I wol nat lette,
> Which shal be bothe my dettour and my thral,
> And have his tribulacion withal
> Upon his flessh, whil that I am his wyf.

(D 46-48, 113-14, 142, 148-50, 154-57)

These expressions of will follow an instructive pattern. Except for the last of them, each proceeds from a consideration of the position for which Alice has not opted: widowhood, virginity, and self-denial. Each one also involves a self-conscious rejection of its alternative despite lip service paid explicitly to virginity as a purer mode of conduct and, by implication perhaps, to the other two as well.

Given this pattern, we observe a curious and significant lacuna as well as a nasty shift in tone when Alice sets forth her expectations for her husbands.

With characteristic selectivity in choosing her authorities according to her tastes, Alice cites Paul in support of her power over her husband's body, but conveniently ignores that portion of the apostle's "*sentence*" that *liketh hir noght so weel*: namely, that husbands also have power over wives' bodies.[20]

As becomes abundantly clear in her account of her marriages, Alice reserves to herself authority over *both* bodies when she marries. Indeed, she reserves authority over her own body so that she can subsequently trade on it to gain opulent support and eventual control of her husbands' goods. This defect of intention on Alice's

part both reveals her misunderstanding of the sacramental nature of Christian marriage and creates a serious obstacle to the sacrament's efficacy in producing grace. Though she has often joined her body to another's, she has intentionally and regularly avoided the requisite union of wills.

Moreover, Alice does not intend in her marriages to strive after harmony nor after perennial mutual affection which requires "a positive and definite effort on the part of the spouses."[21] Instead, she elects to become the "*whippe.*" Her success in that role needs no special citation.

Yet another indication that Alice has never submitted to the sacrament nor committed to a husband appears in the way she hedges her bets against the future. Still married to her fourth husband, she dallies with Jankin, promises to become his wife—contingent upon her first becoming a widow—and assures her pilgrim listeners:

> Yet was I nevere withouten purveiance
> Of mariage, n'of othere thynges eek.
> I holde a mouses herte nat worth a leek
> That hath but oon hole for to sterte to,
> And if that faille, thanne is al ydo.

(570-74)

Theologically speaking, Alice's reservations as she approaches the sacrament of matrimony and her commitment to enjoy what she perceives as her own good at the expense both of the harmony of her unions and of sacramental efficacy place her in a most precarious situation: "In the case of those who have reached the age of reason, the reception of grace must be voluntary . . . ; there must be nothing in the soul which is an obstacle to the entry of sanctifying grace. Sanctifying grace cannot enter if the will still cleaves to some grave sin and refuses to renounce it. If a man should receive a sacrament in such a frame of mind, not merely does he receive no grace, but he is guilty of the sin of sacrilege."[22]

One is reluctant to pronounce with Huppé and Levy such a heavy judgment on Alice,[23] but her very devotion to self is, according to St. Thomas Aquinas, symptomatic of the sinner. In the sinner "there is a kind of spontaneous preference for one's own good in opposition to the universal good. The grace of God is necessary in order to correct this selfishness."[24]

Alice is caught. Five times she has had the opportunity to avail herself of the grace of the sacrament. Five times she has interposed her will and opted for the private good. Each time she does so, in the eyes of the church she sins mortally, becomes more obdurate in her chosen evil and more blind to the possibilities that sacramental grace offers, not only for temporal happiness, but also for eternal salvation.

One other point remains to be made in this connection. Mortal sin is of course so called because it has the power of destroying supernatural life. Says theologian G. H. Joyce:

> A fully deliberate violation of God's law in a grave matter involves the rejection of God as our last end. It is an act of formal rebellion against His authority. By such an act . . . the sinner of necessity forfeits the virtue of charity. Those who possess charity love God above all things: that is, they direct their lives to him as their last end. When a man shakes off the yoke of God's authority, he thereby makes self-gratification his end instead of God, and in so doing deprives himself of charity.[25]

If the theological pity of her performance is that she is damning herself, the psychological pity is that thereby she has rendered herself incapable of caring, of loving in the sense of *caritas* and *agape*. Her avowed motives in marrying, her treatment of her husbands, her incapacity for moral growth as it is reflected in her failure to learn from her experience, and her final curse, calling down early death upon husbands who reject wives' governance and invoking pestilence on those who spend too little, serve to confirm that view.

The pilgrim Chaucer gives us the key, after all, in the Wife's *General Prologue* portrait when he comments on her character:

> In al the parisshe wif ne was ther noon
> That to the offrynge bifore hire sholde goon;
> And if ther dide, certeyn so wrooth was she,
> That she was out of alle charitee.

> (A 449-52)

Being first in the offertory processional suggests a kind of mastery, and failure to achieve it produces frustration, anger, and a concomitant loss of charity that parallels the events in her autobiographical discourse.

One wonders, then, how, critics can argue for the moral identity of Alice and the morally beautiful hag of her *Tale.* Indeed, as John Ropollo noted years ago, the unregenerate knight of the early part of the story serves better than does the hag as Alice's moral surrogate.[26] The Wife's willfulness, compulsive sexuality, disregard for others, and the recourse to the force she used to impose her will on Jankin all reappear in the knight's rape of the peasant girl (D 886-88). Almost certainly Chaucer's innovation,[27] the rape underscores the moral similarity of the Wife and the knight of her *Tale* as a rapist, and Ropollo makes a convincing case for this identification and for the subsequent dissimilarity between Alice and her knight when, unlike her, he submits to discipline, receives his wife's instruction, and reforms. Heretofore unremarked, however, is a parallel between the knight's and Alice's reservation of their wills.

This correspondence occurs when the knight fulfills his freely given promise to perform the Hag's next request. Bound by his word, the chivalric code, the Queen's justice, the hag's determination, and the imperatives of the plot, the knight grudgingly marries the hag, thereby participating in the sacrament without the intention of doing what the church does. As Chaucer has Alice recount his demeanor:

> I seye ther nas no joye ne feeste at al;
> Ther nas but hevynesse and muche sorwe.
> For prively he wedded hire on the morwe,
> And al day after hidde hym as an owle,
> So wo was hym, his wyf looked so foule.

> (D 1078-82)

Just as the gentle persuasion of the pillow lecture on natural *gentilesse* overcomes the Knight's central objection to the social mis-matching implicit in this union, so, it seems, does his recognition of her moral beauty lessen the knight's objections to the hag's physical loathliness.[28] Thus the knight's reluctance to choose between the hag's proffered alternatives could mean one of two things. It could imply what Alice thinks it does—a choice between sensual gratification with the attendant risk of cuckoldry or secure reputation with sensual deprivation. For a more discriminating medieval person, however, it could also imply a fear that lost moral beauty was the price of improved physical appearance.

St. Ambrose raises the crucial question on this issue. In *De institutione virginis,* he asks husbands: "Why do you more require beauty of features in your spouse than moral beauty? Let a husband be pleased by integrity more than by pulchritude."[29] Elsewhere the Saint remarks: "For a woman's beauty does not delight a man as do her virtue and gravity. Who seeks the blessings of marriage should desire [a woman] not more wealthy or well dressed but [one] adorned with morality."[30] The hag displays real concern for her moral health. Discerning that another has found fault with her, the hag of the *Wife's Tale* immediately asks:

> What is my gilt? For Goddes love, tel me it,
> And it shal been amended, if I may.

> (D 1096-97)

Upon hearing the fault described, she proves by sweet reason that it is no fault at all, thereby keeping her word and amending it. Alice, however, displays no such concern for correcting her lapses. On the contrary, when Jankin attempts correction, he provokes immediate violent resistance, and the Wife's later observation upon her recollection of it:

> Ne I wolde nat of hym corrected be.
> I hate hym that me vices telleth me,
> And so doo mo, God woot, of us than I.

> (D 661-63)

Surely this is revelation through moral contrast rather than through identification.

In this connection, too, one must consider the Hag's implicit defense of the necessity for the operation of human freedom as support for her argument against hereditary gentility:

> Eek every wight woot this as wel as I,
> If gentillesse were planted natureelly
> Unto a certeyn lynage doun the lyne,
> Pryvee and apert, thanne wolde they nevere fyne
> To doon of gentillesse the faire office;
> They myghte do no vileynye or vice.
>
> (D 1133-38)

Neither the stars nor lineage determines gentility or viciousness; human beings choose good or evil for themselves. Again, Alice's theology is faulted by contrast.

As the *Wife's Tale* unravels, the sequence of events becomes important to the interpretation offered here. Convinced now by his wife's argument, the knight emblematically joins his will to hers when, without knowing what the outcome of her choice will be he addresses her as "My lady and my love, and wyf so deere . . ." (D 1230). These words echo the hag's from lines 1091-92, "I am youre owene love and eek youre wyf; / I am she which that saved hath youre lyf. . . ."

The knight's acknowledgment of the loathly lady as lady, love, and wife also signals that the moment has arrived when an already valid sacrament can also become efficacious. In his submission of his will to the sacrament, the knight becomes a full participant in the marriage and removes the obstacle to consequent grace.

The subsequent elation of the hag on being granted the mastery that *worldly* women most prize is a joy in which the knight can fully participate because her choice corresponds precisely to that which he would have made had it been among the proposed alternatives.

In exercising the mastery her husband cedes her, in contrast to Alice, the loathly lady *charitably* opts to obey him in everything "That myghte doon hym plesance or likyng" (D 1256), thereby acknowledging the mutuality of the relationship. This mutual cession confirms the union of wills that removes the obstacle of the knight's reservation and renders the sacrament efficacious and productive of grace.

The hag's transformation, no less miraculous than the knight's regeneration, and his response to her metamorphosis—"His herte bathed in a bath of blisse" (1253)—[31] symbolize the reception of grace as a result of sacramental efficacy.

Grace itself may be defined as adoption by God—as a state of divine sonship mutually exclusive with sin.[32] Moreover, as children of God, men and women are equally called to grace and are co-heirs of the supernatural life. Arguing against the contrast of the sexes in moral matters, St. Ambrose says: "Each one therefore ought to know himself, whether man or woman, because each is in the image and likeness of God."[33]

In her care for her husband's welfare, the hag has not only saved the knight's natural life, she has set him on the road to supernatural life as well. Indeed, the pillow lecture and the knight's conversion provide a practical example of a husband and wife's sharing together the life of grace. Along with mutual prayer and fasting, Dooley identifies mutual teaching and exhortation as signs of that life.[34]

A natural outcome of that grace is regeneration, by which is not meant merely a moral amelioration in a person's character—though certainly that occurs in the knight's progress from a willful, heedless rapist, to a subject bound by honor to become an unwilling bridegroom, to a committed husband, to one beatified by bliss. Regeneration properly signifies ". . . That a new nature has been conferred on us: that the humanity we received from our parents by natural generation has been transformed into something better. . . . The moral change which regeneration involves is the result of this far more fundamental renewing of the soul."[35]

Renewed by grace, the soul's faculties become elevated and receive appropriate gifts in the form of the three theological virtues: faith, hope, and charity. When grace resides in the soul, charity resides in the will and is "the virtue by which we love God above all things and our neighbor as ourselves for God's sake."[36] Charity, which is thus symptomatic of the receipt of grace, seems clearly evident in the mutual affection with which the knight and his no longer loathsome or loathed lady regard each other at the end of Alice's *Tale.*

Equally clearly, charity is absent from Alice's final curse, which mirrors those attitudes and practices that Alice learned at her old mother's knee,[37] and which she has not modified in the course of five marriages. One finds neither moral growth nor regeneration in Alice.

Just as a loss of charity implies a lack of grace, so a lack of wisdom symptomizes a loss of charity, for wisdom is that gift of the Holy Spirit which complements charity in those blessed with grace.

A momentary digression will recall that at baptism each person, justified for the first time, receives in that moment the whole range of supernatural virtues, both moral and theological, which render souls susceptible to the inspiration of the Holy Spirit.[38]

As I earlier noted, Thomas teaches that any mortal sin—like the knight's rape of the peasant girl, or Alice's infidelities and her reservations of her will in marriage—takes away charity.[39] Sin does not, however, also destroy faith and hope—though without charity those virtues remain misdirected.[40] Alice's misdirected faith appears again and again in her discomfort with her own situation. It also appears in her occasional prayers, and, negatively, in her curses. Her hope reveals itself in her unending search for yet another husband.

Even awash in sin, however, faith and hope remain virtues still and, speaking theologically, account for a portion of the Wife of Bath's unfailing attractive appetite for living and her optimism in spite of her experience of the woes of marriage. They account too, I think, for her concern about the opinions of others and for her theological rationalizing. Perhaps they also provide avenues for Alice's eventual, though unlikely, reformation.

Viewed in the light of issues relevant to a consideration of sacramental theology, the **Wife of Bath's Tale** raises and examines important questions which arise from the intersection of those issues with human life as it is lived in fact, in fantasy, and in feeling; in thought, in will, and in soul.[41]

Notes

1. *Canterbury Tales,* A 452. All line references are to F. N. Robinson, ed., *The Works of Geoffrey Chaucer,* 2nd ed. (Boston: Houghton Mifflin, 1957). The italics and conversion of a relative pronoun to a demonstrative are mine.

2. Gloria K. Shapiro, "Dame Alice as Deceptive Narrator," *ChauR,* 6 (1972), 130-41, hereafter cited as Shapiro.

3. Shapiro, p. 131.

4. Shapiro, p. 140.

5. Shapiro, p. 141.

6. St. Thomas Aquinas, *Summa Theologiae* 3.63.3. "Totus autem ritus christianae religionis derivatur a sacerdotio Christi. Et ideo manifestum est quod character sacramentalis specialiter est character Christi, cuius sacerdotio configurantur fideles secundum sacramentales characteres, qui nihil aliud sunt quam quaedam participationes sacerdotii Christi, ab ipso Christo derivatae."

7. See Paul Pourrat, *Theology of the Sacraments: A Study in Positive Theology* 6, 4th ed. (St. Louis: Herder, 1930), p. 190.

8. St. Augustine, "The Good of Marriage," *Treatises on Marriage and Other Subjects,* The Fathers of the Church 27 (New York: The Fathers of the Church, Inc., 1955), pp. 12-13.

9. St. Ambrose, *Expositionis in Lucam* 8, 3, (*PL* XV, 1856): "pugna atque dissensio est, quae non est a Deo, quia Deus charitas est."

10. Paul F. Palmer, *Sources of Christian Theology* (Westminster, Maryland: Darton, Longman, Todd, 1955), 1:97.

11. St. Robert Bellarmine, *De sacramentis in genere,* ed. Joseph Giuliano (Naples, 1858), 3:87: "Voluntas, fides et poenitentia in suscipiente adulto necessario requiruntur. Dispositiones ex parte subjecti, non ut caussae [*sic*] activae: non enim fides et poenitentia efficiunt gratiam sacramentalem, neque dant efficaciam sacramentis, sed solum tollunt obstacula, quae impedirent ne sacramenta suam efficaciam exercere possent."

12. St. Augustine, "The Excellence of Widowhood," trans. Sister M. Clement Eagan, in *The Fathers of the Church* 16 (New York: The Fathers of the Church, Inc., 1952), p. 295. For the scriptural authority upon which the Wife of Bath's position rests, see Matt. 22:24-30 and Luke 20:28-35.

13. See St. Bonaventure, *Breviloquium* 5.6.3: "Primo igitur ad integritatem perfectionis requiritur necessario perfectus recessus a malo, perfectus processus in bono et perfectus status in optimo. Quoniam autem malum aut procedit ex tumore superbiae, aut ex rancore malitiae, aut ex languore concupiscientiae." (First, therefore, [to achieve] the wholeness of perfection a perfect retreat from evil, a perfect progress toward the good, and a perfect attitude with respect to the highest good are necessarily required. Otherwise [spiritual] illness proceeds either from the swelling of pride, or from the rancour of ill will, or from the languor of concupiscence.) See also *Breviloquium* 6.13.1.

14. St. Ambrose, *De institutione virginis* 6, 41 (*PL* CCCXXXI, 41): "Cum enim initiatur coniugium tunc coniugii nomen adsciscitur; non enim defloratio virginitatis facit coniugium, sed pactio coniugialis." Not only does St. Ambrose insist on this point, the general practice of fourteenth-century ecclesiastical courts confirms that this doctrine was not an arcane theological nicety but a matter of popular consciousness. Karen A. Corsano in "Custom and Consent: A Study of Marriage in Fourteenth Century Paris and Normandy" (unpublished thesis, Pontifical Institute of Mediaeval Studies, Toronto, 1971), examines several cases in which the union of wills was the crucial point in the court's decisions concerning the validity of marriages. See also, William Joseph Dooley, *Marriage According to St. Ambrose* (Washington: Catholic University of America Press, 1948), p. 38.

15. Henri Rondet, *The Grace of Christ: A Brief History of the Theology of Grace,* trans. Tad W. Guzie

(New York: Newman Press, 1966), p. 97. Italics mine. See also St. Augustine, *Confessionum* 8,22 (*PL* XXXII, 759): "Nec plene volebam, nec plene nolebam. Ideo mecum contendebam, et dissipabar a me ipso." (Neither was I fully willing nor fully not willing. For that reason I was contending with myself and was destroying myself.)

16. St. Thomas Aquinas, *In Boethium de Trinitate* 6.4: "Quamvis homo inclinetur in finem ultimum, non potest naturaliter illum consequi, sed solum per gratiam, et hoc est propter eminentiam illius finis." See also *De Veritate* 10.11.7, and *Summa Theologiae* 1.62.6.

17. St. Thomas Aquinas, *Summa Theologiae* 1-2.112.1: "Donum gratiae excedit omnem facultatem naturae creatae, cum nihil aliud sit quam quaedam participatio divinae naturae . . . per quandam similitudinis participationem."

18. Rondet, *Grace*, p. 211. See also St. Thomas Aquinas, *Summa Theologiae* 1.48.4; 1-2.79.3; 2-2.2.3; 1-2.2.8; *Contra gentes* 3.159; and *De malo* 2.11.

19. See St. Thomas Aquinas, *Summa Theologiae* 1-2.5.2: "Peccatores autem qui non justificantur per gratiam non sunt electi culpam sed solum praesciti quod non sint gratiam habituri, sed suae naturae sint reliquendi." (Sinners, however, who are not justified by grace are not elected to guilt by the preordained will of God but it is only foreknown [to God] that they will not long for grace but will forsake their natures.)

20. See 1 Corinthians, 7:4. For a discussion of Chaucer's use of the Pauline *debitum,* see Joseph Mogan, "Chaucer and the *Bona Matrimonii,*" *ChauR,* 4 (1970), 123-41.

21. Dooley, *Marriage,* p. 38.

22. G. H. Joyce, *The Catholic Doctrine of Grace* (London: Burns, Oates and Washbourne, 1930), p. 183.

23. See Bernard F. Huppé, *A Reading of the Canterbury Tales* (Albany: State University of New York, 1964), p. 57. See also Bernard S. Levy, "The Wife of Bath's *Queynte Fantasye,*" *ChauR,* 4 (1970), 106-22.

24. Rondet, *Grace,* p. 27. Cf. St. Thomas Aquinas, *Summa Theologiae* 1-2. 109.3: "Sed in statu naturae corruptae homo ab hoc deficit secundum appetitum voluntatis rationalis, quae propter corruptionem naturae sequitur bonum privatum, nisi sanetur per gratiam Dei."

25. Joyce, *The Catholic Doctrine,* p. 202.

26. John P. Roppollo, "The Converted Knight in the Wife of Bath's Tale," *CE,* 12 (1951), 263-69. See also W. P. Albrecht, "The Sermon on *Gentilesse,*" *CE,* 12 (1951), 459.

27. The rape does not occur in any of the tale's extant analogues. See B. J. Whiting, "The Wife of Bath's Tale," in W. F. Bryan and Germaine Dempster, *Sources and Analogues of Chaucer's Canterbury Tales* (New York: Humanities Press, 1958), pp. 223-68. See also, G. H. Maynadier, *The Wife of Bath's Tale,* Grimm Library 13 (London, 1901), and Margaret Schlauch, "The Marital Dilemma in the *Wife of Bath's Tale,*" *PMLA,* 61 (1946), 416-30.

28. A tension worth noting arises between the primary emphasis the lady's foul appearance receives in Alice's interpolations, and the primary emphasis the knight places upon his own and his kin's being "*disparaged*"—mismatched—by the union.

29. St. Ambrose, *De institutione virginis* 4, 30 (*PL* XVI, 327): "Cur autem tu vultus decorem in coniuge magis quam morum requiris?" "Placeat uxor honestate magis quam pulchritudine."

30. St. Ambrose, *De Abraham* 1,2,6 (CSEL XXXII, i, 506): "Non enim tam pulchritudo mulieris quam virtus eius et gravitas delectat virum. Qui suavitatem quaerit coniugii non superiorem censu ambiat . . . non monilibus ornatam sed moribus."

31. Bernard S. Levy in "*Queynte Fantasye,*" pp. 109-10, has called attention to the baptismal quality of this image and to its sacramental implications.

32. See Joyce, *The Catholic Doctrine,* pp. 1-48.

33. St. Ambrose, *Exhortatio virginitatis* 10, 68 (*PL* XVI, 372): "Scire ergo se debet sive vir sive mulier, quia ad imaginem Dei est et similitudinem."

34. Dooley, *Marriage,* p. 30.

35. Joyce, p. 12. See also St. Thomas Aquinas, *Summa Theologiae* 1-2.110.4: "Gratia dicitur creari ex eo quod homines secundum ipsam creantur, id est in novo esse constituuntur ex nihilo."

36. Joyce, p. 82.

37. See *CT,* D 576.

38. See O. Lottin, "Les dons du Saint-Esprit chez les Théologiens depuis P. Lombard jusqu'à Thomas d'Aquin," in *Recherches de Théologie ancienne et médiévale* 1 (Louvain: Abbaye du Mont César, 1929), pp. 41-61. See also, Jean F. Bonnefoy, *Les dons du Saint-Esprit d'après Saint Bonaventure* (Paris: Vrin, 1929), and Rondet, *Grace,* p. 221.

39. *Summa Theologiae* 2-2.24.12.

40. See St. Thomas Aquinas, *De veritate* 14.7; and *Summa Theologiae* 2-2.4.4. Without charity, directed or formed faith (*fides formata*) becomes formless and misdirected (*fides informata*).

41. I am grateful to the Pontifical Institute of Mediaeval Studies at the University of Toronto for the
kind hospitality afforded me during my research
on this paper.

D. W. Robertson, Jr. (essay date spring 1980)

SOURCE: Robertson, D. W., Jr. "'And for My Land
thus Hastow Mordred Me?': Land Tenure, the Cloth
Industry, and the Wife of Bath."[1] *Chaucer Review* 14,
no. 4 (spring 1980): 403-20.

[*In the following essay, Robertson attempts to properly
define the Wife of Bath's financial and occupational
positions in regards to her landholdings, class standing,
education, and marriageability.*]

Embedded in the Wife's *Prologue* are various statements concerning transfers of land and wealth that may
be indicative of her legal status. She is sometimes
thought of as a freeholder under the common law, or,
alternatively, as a borough tenant. I should like to suggest here that she was probably thought of in Chaucer's
time as a rural clothier, and that her *Prologue* may
indicate further that she was a bondwoman. Although
the social distinction between freeholders and villeins
was disappearing in the later fourteenth century when
social status in rural communities depended on wealth
rather than on legal distinctions, and when increasing
numbers of villeins were more wealthy than some of
their neighboring freeholders, unfree status would have
been consistent with the iconographic overtones of the
Wife's character.[2] I believe that Chaucer was careful
about such matters and hope to demonstrate further
instances of this concern. Whether the conclusion
concerning status is found acceptable or not, however,
the following discussion should help to shed some light
for Chaucerians on the character of the late medieval
cloth industry, afford an explanation for the Wife's
concern about land, and suggest a reasonable explanation for her obvious and even ostentatious wealth.

With reference to her first three "good" husbands, who
were "riche and olde," she says, "They had me yeven
hir lond and hir tresoor" (204), so that she held these
husbands "hooly" in her hand, and pleased them only
for her "profit" and "ese" (211-224). Nevertheless she
complains, as if to all three of them in one person,

> "why hydestow, with sorwe,
> The keyes of thy chest awey fro me?
> It is my good as wel as thyn, pardee!"
>
> (308-310)

And she further asserts that her husband (*sc.* husbands)
cannot be "maister of my body and of my good," and
will forego one of them. Indeed, she charged for her

services, demanding "raunson" for them (411), and
endured their lust for "wynnyng" (406), thus converting
her Pauline "marriage debt" (153) into a means of
prostitution, apparently for the sake of ostentatious
dress, a common target for moral censure both in prose
and verse during the fourteenth century (cf. *ParsT*
[*Parson's Tale*], 932-34). There is a seeming inconsistency here, for if her husbands had given her their land
and wealth, why did she need access to their chests
(used to keep cash and documents, since there were no
banks)? Is her claim that the money is hers valid? Or is
she simply reflecting the "Theophrastian" opinion that a
wife will always claim "half part" of her husband's
goods (*MerchT* [*Merchant's Tale*], 1299-1300)?

Before seeking to answer these questions, we might
review very briefly a few points of English law. In the
first place, no one "owned" land. He or she held it of
someone else in some sort of tenure; and the person of
whom it was held, traditionally a "lord," although in
the complex tenurial relationships of the late Middle
Ages not necessarily a person of higher status, in turn
held it of someone else, the ultimate lord being the
king. Those who held directly of the king were called
"tenants in chief" of the crown. But the king did not
"own" land either, so that we can say that there was no
such thing as the "ownership" of land in medieval
England. In France there were "lordless" or "alodial"
lands, but not in England. An individual might be
"seised" of land, which meant that he occupied it either
in person or through someone else; or a manorial lord
might be "seised" of land occupied by his tenants, the
terms of whose occupancy and rights of inheritance
were governed by local custom, or, at times, by special
grant. Under the circumstances, unlike personal property
such as beds, robes, drapes, cups, silverware, gold and
silver, pots, pans, other kitchen utensils, kerchiefs,
stocks of wood, etc., land could not be devised or willed
to someone else. There were exceptions in burgage
tenure in some towns, where land could be devised
even to a person who was neither a direct nor a collateral heir, and among villeins on some manors.[3]

In spite of this situation, land was the most secure and
popular form of investment, and even merchants, after
accumulating cash from trade, often exchanged it for
land or purchased landed estates for retirement. Land
was then evaluated not for features like pleasant views,
flower gardens, proximity to beaches, schools, churches,
or markets, but for the annual income that might be
expected from it. That is, medieval documents do not
ordinarily evaluate land in terms of sale price, but
indicate that such and such land was worth so much a
year. And when sale prices were determined, they were
often awkwardly managed, although during the fifteenth
century a purchase price amounting to twenty years'
income became common.[4] During the fourteenth
century, tenants in need of cash might be expected to

make sacrifices, and there were land brokers in London, like Sir John Philpot, ready to arrange transactions.

Free land might be held in "fee simple," like the land acquired by the Sergeant of the Law (**GP** [*General Prologue*] 319), and such land had the advantage of liquidity because, with some exceptions on certain manors, it was freely alienable. But it was not highly suitable for the formation of estates, since collateral heirs could claim an interest in it, so that some landholders in the late Middle Ages sought to convert tenures in fee simple into tenures in fee tail, usually tail male, so that a male heir could not alienate it but was forced to retain it for his own male heir.[5] On the other hand, especially after the fifteenth century had begun to show its own economic peculiarities, there were those who sought to avoid the restrictions of entailments. Under the common law, primogeniture was the ordinary rule where male heirs were concerned except that in Kent and here and there elsewhere the custom of "gavelkind" prevailed, in accordance with which all sons shared equally in an inheritance. In some boroughs and in villein tenure on some manors "borough English" prevailed, in accordance with which the youngest son inherited.[6] Under the common law, females might inherit in instances where there was no male heir; and if there were more than one, land, or even a manor house,[7] and other tenurial rights, like the right to take the profits of a hundred courts,[8] were divided equally among them. If the land given to the Wife by her "good" husbands was land subject to the common law, it must not have been encumbered by reversions, remainders, or entailments, for the marriages were without issue and she says that she retained it after they died (630-31), in effect buying her fifth husband with it, just as her good husbands had purchased her when they were old; and then, finally, she implies that she recovered it. All this would have been a little awkward.

Under the common law, a principle of "Baron et Femme" (not completely abolished until 1935) operated,[9] in accordance with which all a wife's holdings both in land and personal property, including cash, vested in her husband. A husband could not rightfully alienate his wife's land without her consent, but he could dispose of personal property as he pleased. But the Wife of Bath must not have been subject to this rule, since the "tresoor" of her old husbands was attractive to her, and she managed, apparently without too much difficulty, to make extravagantly expensive pilgrimages (**GP** 463-67). That is, if their cash had vested in them immediately after their marriage, there would have been little point in their offering it to her in the first place. Moreover, she says that since they had given her their land she could govern them as she pleased, demanding "gaye thynges fro the fayre" (221) and chiding them unmercifully. Under the common law, she had no claim to any of the contents of any

husband's "chest." To continue for a moment with matters of common law, if a husband survived his wife, he was entitled to only half of her land during his lifetime "by Curtesy of England" (abolished as to fee simple in 1925), provided, as the old authorities said, that "a cry was heard within four walls," i.e., that a living child had been born of the union. It did not matter whether the child survived.[10] A widow, regardless of the dower specified "at church door," where in the Sarum Rite a husband endowed his wife with all his worldly goods, could claim only a third of her husband's holdings in land during her lifetime.[11] Meanwhile, under the common law a wife could incur debts only as an agent of her husband, not on her own behalf. The attitude of the royal courts was well expressed by Chief Justice Charleton of the Common Bench in 1388: "A writ of account was never maintainable against a woman, because a man would not have such a writ ensealed in the chancery against any woman, and it is the folly of a man that he should deliver any money to a woman for her to account for it."[12] But widows in burgage tenure sometimes (but not in all boroughs) inherited all their husband's holdings, including tenements, shops, and manufacturing facilities, and could be expected, with the aid of children, apprentices, and servants, to carry on the trade.[13] And widows in customary (servile or villein) tenure often entered the holdings of their deceased husbands, sometimes even alienating them on their own behalf after they had remarried.[14] In other words, there were some ways in which women in burgage or servile tenure enjoyed more freedom than their legal and (often but not always) social superiors. The evidence of the Wife's *Prologue* so far adduced makes one of these alternatives almost a certainty.

To continue with the *Prologue,* however, there are no references to land in connection with the fourth husband, the "revelour." Both he and the Wife were young, and their difficulties matters of jealousy rather than of tenure or of access to cash. We do know that she went on one of her costly pilgrimages to Jerusalem during this marriage, so that she must have had access to cash without selling her favors. In fact, her husband died at her return (495), an indication that he had managed the trade during her absence. She was happy to be rid of him and was niggardly with his funeral expenses, an indication, perhaps, that he had made no will or that he had little or nothing to dispose of in his own name. To her fifth husband, Jankyn, the Oxford student and parish clerk with legs and feet "clene and faire," she gave, as we have seen, "al the lond and fee" she had accumulated. Here "fee" probably means "heritable interest," and not simply "wealth." Under the common law, this gift would not have affected Jankyn's rights during her lifetime except his right to alienate without her consent. In any event, having grown old and having under some kind of jurisdiction guaranteed his inheritance, she naturally becomes suspicious that he may be awaiting her demise with some impatience in order to enjoy the profits of her land for himself and to attract a younger wife, perhaps with legs and feet like his own.[15] Hence her complaint,

"And for my land thus hastow mordred me?"

(801)

But since Jankyn lost his benefit of clergy when he married a widow,[16] her suspicions about his ultimate intentions if not of his murderous inclinations were probably correct. His clergy would not have protected him from being hanged or outlawed if he had indeed murdered her, and all his lands, held in any form of tenure, as well as his chattels, would have escheated to the crown, a fact that adds a certain sting to the complaint. He might have been able to purchase a royal pardon, but this procedure would have been risky unless he had an influential patron. However, the accusation worked, seasoned with a little sentimental appeal (802), and the Wife recovered her control over her land, presumably including the "fee," and wealth (814), as well as a kind of "maistrie" she had not quite succeeded in obtaining over her first four husbands, the first three of whom complained bitterly, while the fourth had a wandering eye. If the land was free land, or even if it was held in burgage tenure in some boroughs, Jankyn was left with the dubious prospect of "Curtesy of England," and this only if he was successful at literal "engendrure."

In so far as "engendrure" is concerned, there is no indication in her *Prologue* that the Wife had succeeded in literal obedience to the commandment to "wexe and multiplye," having in mind as she did her own gloss on this text,[17] as well as her own view of the nature of the "fruyt of mariage" (114). We may assume, therefore, that the Wife's recovery of her fee effectively removed any temptation Jankyn might have suffered. Perhaps a glance at the nature of land transfers under the common law will provide further clues as to the kind of tenure she enjoyed. Traditionally, seisin of land was transferred by a formal ceremony called "livery of seisin" in the presence of witnesses who could testify that the ceremony had been properly carried out. Since the testimony of witnesses was becoming subject to vicissitudes of one kind or another, livery was often supplemented by a written charter. Jankyn, a parish clerk like Absolon in the *Miller's Tale,* could probably make a "chartre of lond" (3327). Charters were more secure if they were indentured; that is, two copies were made on either half of a skin that was cut apart on a jagged line and a copy given to each party. If the two parts fit, the charter was considered valid. But charters could be stolen or forged, and the most secure method of transfer was by "fine" that involved a fictitious lawsuit and the inscription of a triple indenture, the one at the bottom of the skin, or the "foot," being left as a

court record. Surviving "feet of fines," as they are called, are important historical records.[18] In view of the Wife's adversary relationship with her husbands, only the last of these methods would have been completely safe. But it is difficult to imagine her undertaking the necessary legal procedures to acquire seisin from her first three husbands, to transfer such seisin to Jankyn, and finally to recover it, for under the common law a husband could not transfer land directly to his wife, nor a wife to a husband, and neither could be the heir of the other, since in this matter they were "one person." But there were ways of circumventing these restrictions. Thus the establishment of joint tenure between husband and wife through a final concord would insure a life estate to the survivor, although the Wife speaks of "gifts" rather than joint tenancies.

Possible explanations are available for the gifts or transfers. The first three husbands might well have enfeoffed the Wife with land or tenements of one kind or another, perhaps as a pre-condition of marriage, although if they took part in the trade, as the Wife's pilgrimages suggest that they did, and as the fourth husband almost certainly did, it is difficult to see how they lost control over their monetary wealth or tangible goods. Again, the Wife may have enfeoffed Jankyn with her tenements through a third party, and then later persuaded him to re-enfeoff her, again through a third party, perhaps this time with a final concord for security. No such procedures are mentioned in the text, but Chaucer may have thought that his audience would assume them. The assumption, sometimes made, that Jankyn's loss of control was simply an informal or personal arrangement does not account for the implications of "lond and fee," and hardly removes the tempting prospect that young man once had before him. And in all of the above instances in which the husband took part in the trade, a kind of joint tenure would have been implied during life with a strong social bias in favor of the husband. Again, if charters or other documents were involved in any of the land transactions mentioned in the *Prologue,* why does Chaucer fail to mention them? In the *Merchant's Tale,* where free holdings were involved, Januarie urges May to make charters granting her all his heritage (2171-75).

Boroughs varied enormously in character, administration, and custom. The tenements in a borough might be partly or entirely under manorial, baronial, ecclesiastical, or royal jurisdiction, and customs might vary in different parts of a single borough. In some, alienation was restricted by *retrait lignager,* or by the right of a kinsman to a kind of option to purchase.[19] Most boroughs contained adjacent arable lands that could be alienated separately, but ordinarily the most prosperous burgage tenants held little arable. Rents from burgage tenements could be traded in themselves, their value ranging from 6*d.* to £4, but on the average between 5*s.*

and 10s. Tenants held for life, by long lease, at will, remainder in fee, and "by Curtesy of England," the most common type of holding being by long lease.[20] It is unlikely that in a town near Bath rents would fall in the upper range of the above figures, and if the Wife depended on holdings such as these for three pilgrimages to Jerusalem, not to mention lesser journeys hardly undertaken with much penitential abstinence, her holdings must have been so extensive as to strain credulity. Her complaint, moreover, mentions "land," not tenements, messuages, shops, stalls, or rents. There is a reference to "hous and lond" (814) suggesting a single residence and holdings in land.

Finally, it has become conventional to assume that the Wife's place of origin "biside Bathe" implies the parish of St. Michael's "juxta Bathon," where there are said to have been weavers. But this is a conjecture, and Chaucer's phrase could just as well imply any village near Bath or simply a birthplace, as does the name "Alicia Bathe" in the records of Castle Combe mentioned below. E. M. Carus-Wilson indicated over twenty years ago that the Wife of Bath should be thought of as a "west-country clothier,"[21] participating in an industry that was expanding in the region using rural labor, mostly female,[22] and creating substantial wealth for its "managerial" participants, the clothiers. One of the most striking features of the rising cloth industry was its rural character. Thus R. A. Donkin tells us that "the most significant development was the gradual shift in the distribution of cloth-making away from the old-established towns and towards a much larger number of smaller places, many in fact mere villages. The gilds of textile workers in the older centres naturally tried to monopolise manufacture, but in the end they failed."[23] And R. E. Glasscock, writing specifically about the fourteenth century, says that "cloth-making was spreading rapidly in the rural areas made possible by the spread of the fulling mill, and encouraged by urban entrepreneurs who, free from the restrictions of town gilds, could produce cloth more cheaply in rural areas."[24] It should be added that gilds were becoming wary about women in the trade, and that they ordinarily enjoyed great power in town governments. It seems quite likely that Chaucer and his audience were well aware of these trends, and that most members of the audience would have concluded immediately that the Wife's prosperity was the result of her participation in the thriving rural cloth industry, not as a mere weaver, a proper companion for haberdashers, carpenters, dyers, and makers of tapestries in parish fraternities, but as a clothier, and certainly not as the holder of a large portion of the tenements in a suburb of Bath. But is what we are told about land transactions in the Wife's *Prologue* consistent with customary (unfree) tenure? Land in customary tenure, in which a holding did not involve seisin on the part of the tenant, was transferred in manorial courts,[25] where each transfer or entry might involve a fine set by

the court that was profitable for the lord. In many areas customary tenure had become in effect "copyhold" tenure, so named because the tenant kept a copy of the court record involving his land for himself. But copyhold tenure, which remained distinct from freehold tenure until 1925, did not alter the legal status of the copyholder in the Middle Ages. That is, a "native" or villein of his or her lord remained a native or villein. So long as the manorial steward, who presided over the court for his lord, maintained his rents, land transfers involving new entry fines were advantageous. An example will illustrate these principles more vividly than an abstract discussion.

Before we turn to the example, one more question that probably arose in the minds of Chaucer's audience, at least momentarily, should be considered. Why were the good old husbands willing to give up all their land and wealth in order to marry Alisoun? It is true that older men often find the prospect of fresh young wives attractive, as the *Tales* of the Miller and the Merchant sufficiently indicate, just as older women sometimes long for "Housbondes meeke, yonge, and fressh abedde." Perhaps the first of her husbands succumbed to a lure of this kind. But to account for two more in succession in this way, especially in a society in which a woman's treatment of her husband was likely to be well-known, and in which most persons were practical rather than romantic, is to strain the imagination. There were ways of satisfying "human needs," as we now like to call them, that did not demand the kind of sacrifice contemplated by young Aurelius in the *Franklin's Tale*. We should expect, therefore, that the Wife had something more profitable than her "propre yifte" (103, 608) to attract these old men, in spite of her obvious confidence in its powers. It did not, we notice, occupy the exclusive attention of her fourth husband, who "hadde a paramour" (454). But he married her nevertheless, probably to gain access to something else. That Chaucer does not tell us specifically what this "something else" was probably results from his very characteristic technique of indirection, allowing the audience just sufficient information to puzzle them a little before the answer dawns on them. The solution to this problem, as well as to the legal problems adduced above, may become apparent in our example.

The example in question is that of a native of her lord or bondwoman at Castle Combe in Wiltshire. First, by way of background, a rental of the manor in 1340 reveals the presence of a fulling mill on an acre of land held by a free tenant, John Daniel, who paid an annual rent of 20s. for it, but like all the other free tenants except one, a miller who held a virgate of land and a grain mill, he was a tenant "at the will of the lord," whose holding did not pass to his heirs.[26] In 1352 the lord abandoned the cultivation of his demesne for his own use and commuted the obligations of the customary tenants (villeins, natives, bondmen) to money rents.[27] In the seventies one Thomas Touker (a name meaning "fuller") took over the fulling mill and became one of the first clothiers in Castle Combe. The industry prospered in the area, and continued to do so in the fifteenth century.[28]

Our bondwoman, Margery Haynes, appears together with a list of her holdings in a manorial extent of 1454.[29] First, as the widow of Edward Walcote, known as Jones, she held a tenement and a virgate of land in customary tenure for which she owed a rent of 10*s.*, the obligation to serve as reeve or other official (or to pay a fine for not serving when elected by the court), and heriot (an obligation to the lord at the tenant's death, usually consisting of his best horse in servile tenure or a horse with trappings in free tenure, or in either instance a fine agreed upon between the tenant and the steward). Several virgates on the manor were said in the extent to contain 24 acres, so that we may assume that Margery's was of about this size, allowing for some flexibility in the meaning of *acre* and remembering that virgates might vary in area on a single manor. Margery is also listed, as the widow of William Haynes, her first husband, among the servile cottagers. In this category, ordinarily the most humble of all on agricultural manors, she held a cottage in South Street where she resided for 2*s.* In addition she held a close with a dovecote (probably the old manorial dovecote) and an adjacent "solo" or workshed for 4*s.* 6*d.*, a tenement in the gatehouse of the manor at the market with an adjacent curtilage or garden for 20*d.*, and a larger cottage near the cemetery for 4*s.* 10*d.* But her most important holding, still as a servile cottager, was a plot of three acres serving as a "milling-place." It contained three mills: a grain mill, a fulling mill, and a mill called a "Gyggemille" (a gig mill for teaseling cloth). As the extent puts it, "de eadem Margeria molendina sumptibus suis propriis sustentabit." Accompanying the mills was what must have been a large cottage in West Street, perhaps the original residence, valued at 5*s.* rent. For the mills and cottage together she paid 19*s.*10*d.*, since a milling place was rated at 14*s.*10*d.*, or about the equivalent of a virgate of land in accordance with manorial custom. In this respect manorial custom failed to account for industrial development, since the three mills, as we shall see, produced an income far greater than that from a virgate of agricultural land. It is of incidental interest that two other servile cottagers, both male, held fulling mills. One paid 20*s.* for a mill and a cottage; the other paid 21*s.* for his mill, a cottage, and a parcel of land.

Margery's first husband died in 1435, leaving at his death chattels valued by his friends and relatives appointed by the court to make an inquest at the enormous sum of 3,000 marks (£2,000), or twice what Aurelius in Chaucer's **Franklin's Tale** was worth. But the homage

of the manor (the men obliged to attend court)—as Scrope, the historian of Castle Combe and editor of its documents, suggests—"liable to similar imposts and naturally desirous to mitigate their rigour,"[30] testified that after debts, funeral expenses, and charitable bequests (like that of £20 for the fabric of the church and bell tower of Castle Combe) had been paid, the remainder would amount to only 200 marks. In any event, in 1436 the court imposed an entry fine of £40 so that Margery could retain the remainder of her husband's goods. Her son Thomas, apparently of age, was granted £43 12*s.* 4*d.* for his own use, £26 for his father's burial and anniversaries, and 60*s.* for the repair of a mill. This last grant suggests that he may have been associated with his mother in the trade. But it is noteworthy that the widow, not the son, was regarded as the heir to the business. Shortly thereafter Margery married Edward Jones, who brought his virgate and tenement with him, and she was fined what looks like a wildly extravagant merchet (fee for permission to marry, only 6*s.* 8*d.* elsewhere in the court rolls of Castle Combe, and often much less than this on agricultural manors in the fourteenth century), combined with an entrance fee, amounting altogether to £100. Scrope observes sagely that, in spite of these fines, "she appears to have offered a tempting prize." Indeed, Jones became fairly prosperous, for in 1439 we find him paying £10 5*s.* 7*d.* for some of the goods left in the confiscated estate of a deceased rector, including a silver gilt goblet, two silver cups, a dozen spoons, a silver belt, a feather bed, and other less luxurious items.[31]

However that may be, Jones did not gain immediate control of his new wife's holdings. In fact, he found it necessary to pay a fine of £60 in 1442 for a part of Margery's holdings, one of the cottages now being called a "shopa." And by this time the holdings included fishing rights at Gatecombe and Longbridge. Scrope and E. M. Carus-Wilson disagree on the nature of this fine, the latter stating that it was an addition to the £40 already paid to make up the £100 demanded at the time of the marriage.[32] But this is still a very large sum. The relationship between Margery and her husband was apparently satisfactory for a time, and the records suggest a form of joint tenancy. But in the following year we find Margery again paying £60 in the manorial court "ut possideat bona sua mobilia, pannos laneos, lanum [*sic*], mader pro tincturis, ac tenementa et molendina sua quae reputantur valere die obitus sui mille marcas."[33] Jones may have died, although his name appears in a court record of 1453.[34] It is noteworthy that the steward and his court had the usual difficulty in placing an evaluation on the holdings, but they were now once more firmly in Margery's hands, where they remained, as we have seen in the manorial extent of 1454. To conclude our story, Margery died in 1455. Her holdings passed to her son, Thomas Haynes, a reliable man who served as bailiff in 1457-58, for an entry fee of only £4.

Perhaps the court felt that the substantial fines already charged were almost enough. Happily, Thomas was manumitted in 1463 for £20.

Looking back over these events, we can see that Margery was a singularly wealthy woman, in spite of being a bondwoman. Her mills undoubtedly supplied a generous income, and the fulling mill and gig mill must have been especially profitable, since they would serve the needs of some of her fellow clothiers as well as her own. The documents indicate, as we have seen, that she had facilities for dyeing as well as for fulling and teaseling, and the further fact that she owned a stock of wool suggests that some of the tenements listed among her holdings were occupied by servants, mostly female, in addition to her two French man-servants, working at the various steps in cloth manufacture.³⁵ One can almost visualize the fulled red and white broadcloths, colors favored by her lord, Sir John Fastolf, who supplied cloth for uniforms, stretched out in strips four-and-a-half or six feet wide and seventy-two feet long on frames equipped with tenterhooks near the stream that ran through the village, which was situated in a narrow valley, awaiting their turn at the gig mill and the finishing ministrations of the shearers. Or we may imagine Margery standing before her cottage with one of her French servants chatting with the royal ulnager (an inspector of cloths) as cartloads of cloths folded and tacked by women make their way laboriously out of the village toward the highroad. The cloths of the Wife of Bath (at least in the imaginations of Chaucer's audience) would have been destined for Bristol, a thriving cloth port in the late fourteenth century. Chaucer, who was not a "realist," affords us no descriptions of the Wife's daily business concerns, but it is likely that most members of his audience needed no reminders and were thoroughly familiar with the sight of women sorting, carding, and spinning. They had seen weavers at their looms, heard the clatter of fulling mills, and experienced the unpleasant odors of dye vats. Through open doorways they had seen the look of concentration on the faces of shearers poising their long blades over cloths laid out on tables as they labored to create an even nap. To return to Castle Combe, it is likely that some of the women listed as cottagers in the manorial extent who were less fortunate than Margery, although one held a dyehouse, worked for Margery and other clothiers to pay their rents and sustain themselves. One of them, amusingly enough, called herself "Alicia Bathe." The dovecote probably provided food for Margery's table as well as profits substantially beyond its rent of 4*s.* 6*d.* And the fishing rights, much coveted in the Middle Ages when fish was an extremely popular food, not merely Lenten fare, had similar advantages. Castle Combe boasted good trout.

The example of Margery thus clarifies the probable nature of the Wife's land transactions and demonstrates the peculiar attractiveness of her land to her husbands. We are not told what facilities she had as a clothier. But the basic holding that made prosperity in cloth-making possible was ordinarily a fulling mill. Chaucer's audience might well have envisaged a dyehouse and other facilities, including work-sheds, but they may have spontaneously imagined also poor cottagers laboring at home, or even more substantial persons who preferred the daily wages of industry to the smaller and less certain monetary rewards of agricultural labor. A "milling-place" might be small in area, but the cash flow to be expected from it would have been far greater than that from many acres of agricultural land, or from a large number of borough tenements. It was probably this, rather than that other busy "milling-place" she mentions, that attracted her old husbands whose desire to increase their wealth made them willing to give their land and treasure to have access to it, and, where Jankyn was concerned, to fortify his patience with an elderly wife who was, to borrow a phrase, "ful of hoker and of bisemare." Whether the first husband brought her the cloth business or whether she inherited it we do not know, and the question is not important. The fact that the first three husbands were rich by country standards need not surprise us. Many villeins, especially those experienced as reeves, were able to take up holdings left vacant by the series of pestilences after 1349 and to manage them well, or to take over demesnes or parts of demesnes abandoned for rents by their lords. Throughout most of England, individual peasant holdings were growing larger. Thus there were bondmen who had more to offer than Edward Jones brought to Margery, and the general regard for land as an investment would have made these holdings tempting to the Wife. Finally, if the Wife's pilgrimages puzzle us, chevage, or the fine paid by a villein to leave the manor, was often light. It amounted to 20*d.* at the most at Castle Combe, where it was often less, and this would have been a very small preliminary expense for a trip to Cologne, Rome, or Jerusalem. Chaucer's picture of Alisoun's wealth, wandering, and intense interest in fleshly satisfaction is a caricature designed to exemplify certain concomitant trends in his society. In so far as wealth is concerned, the trend indicated is accurate, for by the early sixteenth century a clothier, like Thomas Spring of Lavenham, might be many times wealthier than either Margery Haynes or the fictitious Wife of Bath.³⁶

It is probably quite safe to conclude that Chaucer meant his audience to think of the Wife of Bath as a rural clothier from the west country and quite possibly as a bondwoman. The assumption that she was a free tenant either under the common law or under borough custom offers legal difficulties in explaining her land transactions and her ability to control her holdings after marriage. However, when we think of the Wife of Bath, we must resist the temptation that so often presents itself to literary historians to locate her in space and time rather than as something in the minds of Chaucer's audience. She is in effect a series of clues whose significance depends on the experience, the attitudes, the expectations, and the ideals of those who heard them. There is no real reason to think that either Chaucer or the members of his audience had any special prejudice against unfree tenants,[37] but in view of the nature of the Wife's **Prologue,** the first part of which is a kind of mock Lollard "lay sermon" in which she elevates the flesh and deprecates the spirit at the expense of the New Law and of St. Paul especially, the implication that she was a bondwoman would have been singularly appropriate in the light of Gal. 4, 22ff., where it is said, "But he who was of the bondwoman, was born according to the flesh," and "we are not the children of the bondwoman, but of the free: by the freedom wherewith Christ has made us free." This commonplace distinction, which would have been familiar to even the most unlettered among Chaucer's listeners, may indeed be the basis for the Clerk's figure of the "secte" of the Wife of Bath, whose adherents in avid pursuit of fleshly satisfactions flourish because the "gold" or wisdom in them is corrupted by the "brass" of Venus, so that they cannot like Griselda (originally a poor cottager) sustain the "sharpe scourges of adversitee" with which Christians were said to be providentially tested. Chaucer's portrait probably represents, as I have sought to show elsewhere,[38] a satire on the acquisitiveness of some of his contemporaries, the disruption of traditional hierarchies, the breakdown of established communities, and a concomitant decline in *mores,* all attributable in part, and especially in certain areas, to the rise of the cloth industry. In this connection, it may not be irrelevant to point out that the court at Castle Combe discovered bordellos in the village in 1416, 1419, and 1424,[39] a surprising multiplicity of such facilities in a small community, where some apparently shared the general outlook of the Wife of Bath. It cannot be emphasized too strongly that, although Chaucer's humorous satire is basically moral[40] and displays a learned use of traditional materials from a wide variety of sources, it is directed toward specific conditions and problems of his own time and place. Unless we come to understand more about these conditions, we can hardly appreciate the "relevance" of what he had to say to the immediate interests and concerns of his audience. We shall miss also the skill and agility with which he wields his satiric weapons.

Notes

1. I am grateful to Professor J. R. Strayer for reading this paper in an earlier form and making useful suggestions about legal matters. Any errors remaining are, however, my own. My colleague Gail Gibson also furnished valuable references and criticisms. Robinson's text of Chaucer is used in this article (*The Works of Geoffrey Chaucer,* ed. F. N. Robinson, 2nd ed. [Boston: Houghton Mifflin, 1957]).

2. For some of these overtones, see the present author's *A Preface to Chaucer* (Princeton Univ. Press, 1972), pp. 317-31, and the further observations in "Simple Signs from Everyday Life in Chaucer," to appear in *Signs and Symbols in Chaucer's Poetry,* ed. John P. Hermann and John J. Burke (Univ. of Alabama Press).

3. For the general principles in the paragraph above, see A. W. B. Simpson, *An Introduction to the History of the Land Law* (Oxford Univ. Press, 1961), and S. F. C. Milsom, *Historical Foundations of the Common Law* (London: Butterworth's, 1969). For wills of land in burgage tenure, see Simpson, *Introduction,* p. 14. Some idea of the variety of borough customs may be formed by glancing through Mary Bateson, *Borough Customs,* Selden Society 18 (1904) and 21 (1906). A few boroughs restricted devise. See M. de W. Hemmeon, "Burgage Tenure in Medieval England," *LQR,* 27 (1911), 44-46. Histories of individual towns sometimes contain more thorough information. For a good recent bibliography, see the list of works cited in Susan Reynolds, *An Introduction to the History of English Medieval Towns* (Oxford: Clarendon Press, 1977), pp. 202-23. For villein wills, see Cicely Howell, "Peasant Inheritance Customs in the Midlands 1280-1700," in *Family and Inheritance,* ed. Jack Goody, Joan Thirsk, and E. P. Thompson (Cambridge Univ. Press, 1976), p. 120.

4. Barbara Harvey, *Westminster Abbey and its Estates in the Middle Ages* (Oxford: Clarendon Press, 1977), pp. 197-98. Appendix IV of this work contains a record of the Abbey's purchases. During the second half of the fourteenth century, the price £66 13s. 4d. or 100 marks seems to have been curiously appropriate for a wide variety of holdings. See nos. 19, 20, 26, 27, 28, 30, 33, 36, 40, 43, 44. It was a convenient round sum, but it could purchase over 100 acres or a mill. Cf. the evaluations placed on the holdings of Margery Haynes, below. These, however, included chattels.

5. Kenneth B. McFarlane, *The Nobility of the Later Middle Ages* (Oxford: Clarendon Press, 1973), pp. 270-74.

6. On peasant inheritance customs, see Rosamond Jane Faith, "Peasant Families and Inheritance Customs in Medieval England," *AgHR,* 14 (1966), 77-95.

7. For a description of a manor house made necessary by the fact that it was to be divided equally between two daughters who inherited it, see

Marion K. Dale, *Court Rolls of Chalgrave Manor 1278-1313*, Bedfordshire Historical Record Society, 28 (1950), xxxi-xxxii. The house with its grounds and outbuildings to which Sir Nigel de Loring retired after many campaigns in the field still sounds attractive.

8. For a striking example, see Helen M. Cam, *Liberties and Communities in Medieval England* (New York: Barnes & Noble, 1963), p. 127.

9. J. H. Baker, *An Introduction to English Legal History* (London, 1971), pp. 258-59. The rule that a husband could not alienate his wife's lands was strictly enforced at Nottingham. See W. H. Stevenson, *Records of the Borough of Nottingham* (London: Her Majesty's Stationery Office, 1882), I, 83, 123-25. Under the common law, however, a wife could not act against her husband, so that if he did alienate her land she was obliged to wait until his death before she could seek to recover it in court. See Donald W. Sutherland, *The Assize of Novel Disseisin* (Oxford: Clarendon Press, 1973), p. 112.

10. Simpson, *Introduction*, p. 66. Professor Donald W. Sutherland, who generously read and commented on this article after it had been submitted, informs me that Simpson is here misleading, since husbands usually enjoyed all holdings of their deceased wives for life "by Curtesy."

11. *Ibid.*, p. 65, and Baker, *Introduction*, pp. 146-47. However, a widow received half in Kent and in the boroughs of Ipswich, Nottingham, and Torksey. The general limitation to a third makes the argument advanced by Cecile Margulies, *MS* (1962), 210-16, concerning the Wife's acquisitions from her first husbands, questionable. The Sarum ceremony is now conveniently available in R. P. Miller, *Chaucer: Sources and Backgrounds* (New York: Oxford Univ. Press, 1977), pp. 374-84.

12. *Year Books of Richard II: 12 R II*, ed. George F. Deiser (Ames Foundation, 1914), pp. 164-65.

13. For examples in the cloth industry, see Barbara McClenaghan, *The Springs of Lavenham* (Ipswich: W. E. Harrison, 1924), p. 18, and, in the fifteenth century, Gladys A. Thornton, *A History of Clare, Suffolk* (Cambridge Univ. Press, 1928), pp. 181-82.

14. Edward Britton, *The Community of the Vill* (Toronto: Macmillan of Canada, 1977), pp. 20-24.

15. Cf. M. M. Postan's "marriage fugue" as described by J. Z. Titow in *Essays in Agrarian History*, I (Newton Abbot, 1968), p. 45.

16. Pollock and Maitland, *The History of English Law*, 2nd ed. (Cambridge Univ. Press, 1952), I, 445.

17. Cf. *A Preface to Chaucer*, pp. 322-23.

18. Simpson, *Introduction*, pp. 112-17.

19. Hemmeon, "Burgage Tenure," *LQR*, 26 (1910), 344. This article appears in two sections of Vol. 26 and in one section of Vol. 27 of the *Review*.

20. *Ibid.*, 26 (1910), 336-40.

21. "Trends in the Export of English Woolens in the Fourteenth Century," *EcHR*, 2, ser. 3 (1950-51), 177. This is an extremely important article by the foremost authority on the late-medieval English cloth industry.

22. A good literary example of an ordinary worker from another region and a later period is afforded by Mak's wife in the Wakefield *Second Shepherd's Play*. The same play contains in the complaint of the Second Shepherd (ed. Cawley, lines 55-108) a picture of hierarchical inversion under the Old Law as it perennially manifests itself similar to that so strongly recommended by the Wife. The solution, implicit in the Wife's Scriptural citations and explicit in the play lines 710ff.) is the same in both instances.

23. In H. C. Darby, *A New Historical Geography of England before 1600* (1973; rpt., Cambridge Univ. Press, 1976), pp. 113-14. Cf. Edward Miller, "The Fortunes of the English Textile Industry during the Thirteenth Century," *EcHR*, 18 (1965), 64-82.

24. In Darby, *Historical Geography*, p. 170. Cf. McClenaghan, *Springs*, p. 6.

25. The observation of Thornton, *Clare*, p. 108, that "a great part of the business of the manorial court was in witnessing the transfer of unfree land" reflects a common situation, although on many manors minor temporary land transactions among servile tenants were often not recorded or even brought before the court if they did not interfere with rents and services.

26. For the rental, see G. Poulett Scrope, *History of the Manor and Ancient Barony of Castle Combe in the County of Wilts* (London, 1852), pp. 146-51. Oddly, one of the free tenants, a miller (p. 147), owed light agricultural services and a rooster and three hens on the Feast of St. Martin (11 Nov.) if he had a wife, or one rooster and one hen if he had no wife. He was also obliged to serve as reeve if elected, although this obligation, like the agricultural services and the chickens, was usually a villein obligation. But see Harvey, *Westminster Abbey*, p. 108.

27. Scrope, *Castle Combe*, pp. 81-82. For the benefit of students of literature unfamiliar with agricultural manors, it may be appropriate to explain that such

manors were frequently, but not always, divided into demesne lands cultivated for the benefit of the lord of the manor (who might be resident, resident occasionally, or non-resident), who might consume or sell their produce, or do both, and the lands of his tenants, free or servile, or both. Villein tenants traditionally owed "customary" services (determined by local manorial custom) on the lord's demesne, such as plowing, harrowing, sowing, weeding, reaping, harvesting, stacking hay, etc. Such services were usually divided into "works," each work consisting of one-half a day's labor, the number of works owed in a year being determined roughly by the size of the tenant's holding, although other factors might intervene. Tenants with large holdings sometimes employed workers, who might be local cottagers or itinerant laborers, to perform their works. Villeins also paid rents, ordinarily less than those paid by free tenants but ordinarily about the same if the value placed on their works was added to them. In addition to their work on demesne lands, villeins might be required to perform a variety of miscellaneous services, like carting, carrying messages, spreading straw in manor houses, providing horse shoes or plow irons (if they were smiths), etc. They paid for agistment (pasturing pigs in the lord's park), repaired roads, and took their grain to the lord's mill. Some owed gifts of eggs, chickens, honey, fish, rushes, or other produce at specified times of the year. They might be required to attend the manorial court (which met traditionally "from three weeks to three weeks," but often less frequently in practice) and to act, if elected by the court, as one of the manorial servants: as reeve, *messor* (an office that varied depending on the character of the manor), plowman, miller, butcher, ponder, baker, dairy maid, etc. The number and nature of such offices varied from place to place. Those from more prosperous families might serve as jurors or ale-tasters. The extent and nature of villein obligations depended on a number of factors: the difference in area between demesne land and customary land, climate, soil, proximity to the sea, to marshes, or to rivers, etc. Some free tenants owed minor services like mending park fences or supervising villein workers. The salient feature of late-medieval England was its diversity, and, after the middle of the fourteenth century, its propensity for change. It is very difficult to generalize about "the medieval English peasant" during the years of Chaucer's maturity.

Diversity extended to land measurements. The following observations are suggestive rather than definitive. A *knight's fee* contained four, five, or, at times, eight *hides* or *carucates* of anywhere from 120 to 160 acres. In the north, a *bovate* was one-eighth of a hide; in the south, a *yardland* or *virgate* was one-fourth of a hide. One-fourth of a yardland was called a *ferling*. The word *acre* originally meant almost any strip of arable land. A traditional acre (except in Cornwall) is four *perches* wide and forty perches long (or a strip of similar area but of different dimensions), but perches varied locally from the *King's perch* of sixteen-and-a-half feet. A quarter of an acre is a *rood*. On many manors the *virgate*, which actually ranged in size from ten to sixty-eight acres, was the standard by which holdings were measured; that is, tenants were said to hold one or more virgates, a half virgate, a quarter virgate, or a *cotland* consisting of five acres more or less, or combinations of these units. There is thus no way of "defining" a virgate, for even if we are told that on a certain manor it consisted of thirty acres (a common measurement), unless measured acres are specified we still do not know its size. Moreover, English soils varied in friability, productivity, and suitability for various crops, sometimes on a single manor and very markedly in different parts of the country.

After the Black Death, there was an increasing tendency on the part of many lords to abandon the cultivation of their demesne lands for their own use, leasing those lands and substituting money rents for customary services and obligations. There was a general desire, both on the part of lords and on the part of agricultural workers, for ready cash. Hence, the leasing of demesnes by the lords and the demand for wages by the day and better food allowances on the part of agricultural workers, who were stimulated by opportunities for day work in industries, like the cutlery trade at Thaxted in Essex, or, above all, by the cloth industry generally, but especially in the west country around Bristol, in Suffolk, in Essex, and in various towns like High Wycombe (Bucks) on the road between London and Oxford. For the last, see L. J. Ashford, *The History of the Borough of High Wycombe* (London, 1960), pp. 40-41. The results were a breakdown of traditional manorial communities, many of which had been closely knit cooperative groups, with a consequent decline in *mores*, rising wages and prices, and a largely unsuccessful effort to control them on the part of the government through the justices of the peace. Meanwhile, after about 1360, on many manors families whose ancestors had occupied the same land for many generations disappeared, replaced by new tenants with larger holdings, interested chiefly in profit, a development that hardly cemented community solidarity. It is probably impossible to understand Chaucer's characters very well without keeping these general trends in mind, as well as their specific consequences, which are still being explored by historians.

28. E. M. Carus-Wilson, "Evidences of Industrial Growth on Some Fifteenth-Century Manors," in her *Essays in Economic History* (London, 1962), II, 159-63. The account of Castle Combe in these pages, based on new research, supplements that of Scrope for the period in question.

29. Scrope, *Castle Combe*, pp. 203-21.

30. *Ibid.*, p. 223.

31. Pp. 224, 228.

32. *Loc. cit.*

33. *Castle Combe*, p. 225, note.

34. *Ibid.*, pp. 245-46. It is possible that this may have been the son of the original Edward Jones.

35. For the French manservants, see Carus-Wilson, *Essays*, II, 163. The process of cloth manufacture is described in her classic article, "The Woolen Industry," in *The Cambridge Economic History of Europe*, II (1952), 379-81.

36. McClenaghan, *Springs*, pp. 49, 73-78, 86-88. Thomas was lord of many manors in Suffolk and Norfolk, two in Essex, and one in Cambridgeshire. He also held other lands and tenements. His tomb still stands in Lavenham Church, and one may visit the Lady Chapel he provided and see the tower to which he made generous contributions.

37. Cf. my article, "Some Disputed Chaucerian Terminology," *Speculum*, 52 (1977), 571-81.

38. See note 1, above, and the article "Chaucer and the 'Commune Profit': The Manor," to appear in a *Festschrift*.

39. *Castle Combe*, pp. 235, 236, 237. The first of these is said to have been in operation for five years "ad grave nocumentum." The proprietor was fined only 20*d.*, but he was ordered to desist or pay a much larger fine.

40. Moral analysis of what we should call psychological, social, political, and economic problems is characteristic of the late Middle Ages, and is a Classical inheritance modified by specifically Christian ideals. I believe that a failure to recognize this fact and to face its implications has led to distortions and to stubborn misunderstandings, not to mention a neglect of much of Chaucer's humor, for the perception of the ridiculous depends on departures from accepted values. An illustration of the general principle is afforded by the list of books recommended to Charles VI by Philippe de Mézières. It emphasized the Scriptures and service books first, the *Ethics* and *Politics* of Aristotle, the *De regimine principum* of Aegidius Romanus, which was very popular in England, and included Augustine's *City of God* and the *Policraticus* of John of Salisbury, with which Chaucer was familiar and which stresses the need for community integrity based on virtue. It is very probable that Chaucer's audience was spontaneously responsive to concepts like the distinction between spiritual servitude among "sons of the bondwoman" and what they regarded as true freedom. Cf. Chaucer, *ParsT, 149*: ". . . wel oghte man have desdayn of synne, sith that thurgh synne, ther as he was free, now is he maked bonde." The Wife is appropriately followed in the Tales by the Friar and the Summoner, who, far from furnishing a mere interlude in "the marriage group," illustrate the corruption of the administration of God's mercy and justice through a literal-minded desire for wealth and fleshly satisfaction of exactly the kind advocated with inadvertent ludicrousness by the Wife. Philippe's Order of the Passion, based firmly on moral grounds, was very influential at the English court. See J. J. N. Palmer, *England, France and Christendom* (Chapel Hill: Univ. of North Carolina Press, 1972), pp. 187-90. Chaucer's own admiration for one of Philippe's "evangelists," Otto de Granson, is obvious and needs no comment.

H. Marshall Leicester, Jr. (essay date 1984)

SOURCE: Leicester, H. Marshall, Jr. "Of a Fire in the Dark: Public and Private Feminism in *The Wife of Bath's Tale*." *Women's Studies* 11, nos. 1-2 (1984): 157-78.

[*In the following essay, Leicester develops a theory of the outward feminism of* The Wife of Bath's Tale *and the private, insecure aspects of Alisoun's psyche that are unconsciously included in her female-empowered* Tale. *Leicester also asserts that Alisoun's* Tale *represents Chaucer's growing appreciation of feminist ideas.*]

The Wife of Bath's Tale is not only a text concerned with the position of women, it is a text whose speaker is a woman and a feminist—at least that is the fiction the text offers—and the body of this essay will concentrate on the Wife herself as the speaker of her ***Tale***. While my own prejudices, for better or for worse, will no doubt be evident from what follows, I do not claim here to define feminism or to say what women "are" or ought to do. My interest is in the Wife's feminism as it is evidenced in Chaucer's text, and I attempt to discriminate between two versions of feminism—two possible stances women may, in their own interest, adopt in the world—that the Wife seems to embody in the telling of her *Tale.* The first of these I call "public," and identify with a polemical, reactive, and necessarily "illiberal" position that women may take toward the male world and its institutions. The second, "private," form is less easy to classify in the nature of the case, but at least in Chaucer's practice here it is at once more humanist (in the sense of being interested in what individuals can make, positively, of the culture and institutions that precede and surround them) and more humane—or at any rate "nicer." This second form, because it is always dependent on individual situations, choices, and responses, always remains problematical and open to reinterpretation. It should be clear from the outset, however, that my aim is not, or not merely, to denigrate the first kind of feminism at the expense of the second. I am concerned to show that there is a difference between the two kinds, but also to show that these forms or modes are complementary as well as opposed, that there is a dialectical relationship at work in the Wife's situation and her responses.

Though the method I adopt here is largely a version of the time-honored one of "dramatic" analysis, I am aware that "the Wife of Bath" is a fiction, a construction made from the language of the *Tale,* and that that fiction is a male poet's impersonation of a female speaker. It appears that there is some relation for Chaucer between taking a position on women—about who they are, what they want, and how they should proceed—and taking a woman's position. Though I must insist that we take the fact of impersonation seriously (and therefore refrain from too hasty an ascription to "Chaucer" of features in the *Tale* that properly belong to the narrating Wife), I do not wish to lose sight, as I think Chaucer does not, of the issue of the poet's relation to his character, and if I begin with an examination of the Wife's feminism, I will end with some suggestions about Chaucer's.[1]

In this essay I will concentrate on the Wife's tale of the Loathly Lady, leaving her *Prologue* as far as possible in the background and in the shade. I do so partly for reasons of space, but also because I think the *Tale* deserves better than it usually gets. It often seems to be taken by critics as a mere appendage to the more brilliant *Prologue,* an appendage that restates the *Prologue*'s main argument about the value of feminine sovereignty or "maistrye" in marriage in a relatively mechanical form, marred (or enlivened, depending on the critic's taste) by some "characteristic" though irrelevant touches by the Wife, like the Midas exemplum; complicated perhaps by a windy and dull (or moving and serious) pillow-lecture on "gentilesse" that does not even sound much like her; but concluding straightforwardly enough with the QED of the Knight's submission and the magical transformation at the end.[2]

There is something to be said for an interpretation of this sort. It is not so much wrong as incomplete, a place to start in thinking about the *Tale* rather than the last word. In fact, a version of this interpretation is the place where the Wife of Bath starts, in the sense that it seems to be her advance plan for the *Tale.* We can assume, I think, that the Wife knows before she begins the story what she intends to do with it, and that she has already decided on the changes in the plot of the traditional version that will produce the polemical feminist moral she draws at the end. This moral and the feminist ideology that goes with it are what might be called the public meaning of the *Tale*—her word is "apert"—and this public meaning is backed, as public meanings always are, by Authority. In this case the authority in question is that of the Wife herself. One way of looking at her *Prologue*—and one way she herself presents it—is to see it as a process whereby the Wife's account of her own experiences in marriage leads to her thesis about marriage in general. In this reading, her experiences allow her to say "The necessity of feminine 'maistrye' is what my life proves, and so does the story I am about to tell." Such a reading constitutes the Wife's past *as* past, as something that is over and done with and therefore something that can be summed up, generalized from. Her life adds up to a final meaning which the *Tale* merely confirms. This reading is at least in accord with the Wife's explicit or public project in both the *Prologue* and the *Tale.* Not liking the exempla that are offered to her by the male world in the guise of "auctoritee," she turns to her own experience with the intention of becoming an authority herself. Like the Pardoner, she sets out to make an example of herself. Once this is accomplished, she offers the *Tale* as a counter-exemplum to set in opposition to those in Janekyn's book of wicked wives and the male misogynist tradition. The tale of the Loathly Lady is itself traditional, which is to say that it is public property, and to tell it is to go public, to move beyond a local and idiosyncratic personal history and take one's place in a larger world.

The public world, the past, and authority are thus the determinants of the "apert" project of the *Tale,* which is conceived by the Wife as a statement of counter-ideology, that is, a statement in *opposition* to the structures of male domination she has encountered and continues to encounter in her life. The form her counterattack takes is that of appropriating the instruments or institutions of masculine power. Both the public world of storytelling and the story itself are by definition male-dominated, and the Wife, as we know, has strong feelings about that. Combative and competitive as ever, she takes an aggressively feminist public position in structuring the world of the *Tale* and pointing its moral. She may be said to *womanhandle* the traditional story, which, as a chivalric romance, is in its original form an instrument of the dominant ideology and its values, such as loyalty and courtesy, that demonstrate male superiority. E. T. Donaldson's succinct summary of the analogues brings out this ideological bias—and the Wife's subversion of it—clearly:

> In the analogues the story is handled in a different style, its real point being to demonstrate the courtesy of the hero, who weds the hag uncomplainingly and treats her as if she were the fairest lady in the land; in two versions the knight is Sir Gawain, the most courteous of Arthur's followers, who promises to marry her not in order to save his own life but his king's. The lady's transformation is thus a reward of virtue. In Chaucer the polite knight becomes a convicted rapist who keeps his vow only under duress and in the sulkiest possible manner.[3]

As I have intimated, I take the differences between Chaucer's version of the tale and its analogues as evidence of the speaker's agency, evidence that the Wife knows the traditional version and deliberately alters it in a way that makes the feminist message more pointed and polemical. The fact that only in her version is the knight a rapist means that only in her version is the quest for what women most desire linked specifically and logically to the knight's character and to the question of male-female relations. Clearly this particular knight, as a surrogate for men in general, needs to learn more about women, and the plot becomes a device for forcing him to do so, putting him in a position more familiar to women, who have to cater to male desires, and giving power to women from the beginning of the *Tale.* This is one example of appropriation, of using what are normally masculine forms for feminine ends. Another example is the "gentilesse" speech, a form of argument that aims at breaking down the external hierarchies of power constituted by birth and possessions—"temporal thyng that man may hurte and mayme"—in favor of equality before God and individual responsibility for establishing worth and achieving salvation. This argument is traditionally egalitarian, but scarcely feminist. It is sometimes used to urge the right of lowborn men to love and woo noble ladies, but I do not recall it being used before the Wife to argue that ugly old women are good enough not only to go to the same heaven as knights but to marry them. Since in no other version of the tale does anything like this speech occur, its function as additional feminist propaganda in the altered tale is clear. Finally, of course, the sovereignty argument that is the point of the story, affirmed in open court halfway through and supplying the twist at the conclusion, is obviously a reversal of ordinary male-female power relations and an aggressively polemical appropriation of all those dreary (and nervous?) arguments about the proper hierarchical subordination of women to men in medieval discussions of the subject.

This reading I call the Straw Man version of the tale, both because as a critical interpretation it makes the tale easy to summarize and dismiss, and because I think the phrase describes the Wife's open public project in telling it.[4] She makes a straw man of the traditional tale and its hero, sets up the knight and the old story as images of masculine pretension in order to knock them over, and obviously she carries out this project. Along the way she takes advantage of the power of her temporary position as narrator or straw-stuffer to enjoy her work. She enjoys, no doubt about it, the satisfaction in fiction and fantasy of dominating the ill-bred knight and all his kind, and the pleasure of imagining herself, in the form of her surrogate the hag, magically young and beautiful again, though these pleasures are clearly marginal and incidental to the public message.

So far, I think, there will be little disagreement about the general character of the *Tale* and its "appropriateness" to the Wife. The problem, obviously, is what to do with the more anomalous features of it that do not seem to fit the public project, and that raise questions about the character of the speaker. It is very common to see such features, especially perhaps the "gentilesse" speech, as revealing things about the Wife of which she herself is unaware, and to use these slips or contradictions as a way of pinning down her character.[5] Such a proceeding puts the reader in possession of "facts" about the Wife that allow the assumption of a position superior to her from which she can be fixed and placed, understood and dismissed. We know "who she is" and can proceed to construct from that an account of her past and the probabilities of her future, though it is perhaps a matter for uneasiness that such characterizations and careers range in the literature from sociopathic murderess to tragic heroine to comic embodiment of the Life Force.[6]

It seems to me, however, that if the Wife does have a public feminist agenda in the *Tale,* she may also have conscious attitudes about the role she plays in order to carry it out, and that these attitudes are to be elicited precisely from her voicing of the message, from the ways she comments on, revises, ignores, or otherwise deploys the elements of the *Tale.* The matter of what else the Wife gets out of telling the story, whether fantasies of rejuvenation or of power, begins to touch on a set of themes and ideas that are at work in both the *Prologue* and the *Tale* in dialectical tension with their "apert" public and authoritative ones. I have so far reserved these issues, but it is obvious what they are, since the categories are those of the Wife herself: the private ("privy") world and Experience.[7] The Straw Man version of the tale, with its doctrinaire feminism and oppositional stance, has something a little too static and structural about it, something other critics besides myself have found a little uncomfortable. My real point, however, is that the Wife does too. Her public project does not really do justice to the complex and dynamic character of the *now* of speaking in both *Prologue* and

Tale, the sense of ongoing life and discovery that cannot be totally reduced to an order or an argument, cannot be shut up in forms or completely subjected to authority, even the Wife's own. In the *Tale* this set of concerns is registered first by the Wife's relative lack of interest in polemical closure: having set up the straw man, she is oddly dilatory in knocking him over, in getting on with the demonstration. She spends the first hundred and twenty lines, a good quarter of the *Tale,* not telling it. Instead she pursues what we might call her private interests.

The most famous example of this tendency is the Midas exemplum, in which the tale of the Loathly Lady vanishes utterly for thirty lines—more if you count the introductory matter—and we find ourselves in the middle of a completely different story about Midas's ass's ears and his wife's inability to keep them secret. The occasion of this digression is the knight's quest to discover what women most desire, and as the Wife lists the variety of opinions he encounters we can feel her losing interest in the *quest*—whose outcome is a foregone conclusion—and getting interested in the *question*. The old story and its old-time Arthurian world are simply dropped in favor of matters of more immediate interest. Just as it is more fun for the Wife at the beginning of the *Tale* to take a shot at the Friar's virility in retaliation for his disparagement of her *Prologue* than to linger over the romantic world of "fayerie," here it is more interesting to her to consider the variety of possible answers to the question than to give the "right" one. Her voice moves into the present tense, she includes herself among the women whose opinions are being solicited, she indicates that she finds some of them better than others: "Somme seyde that oure hertes been moost esed / Whan that we been yflatered and yplesed. / He gooth ful ny the sothe, I wol nat lye."[8]

The Midas exemplum itself, though superficially unflattering to women and apparently totally unconnected to the story, is actually a reflection of the Wife's impatience with masculine foolishness, and it has a certain relevance to the development of the romance. It is, after all, not just *any* secret that the wife of Midas finds herself unable to contain, but one that a great many women, including the Wife of Bath, have had occasion to notice: "Myn housbonde hath longe asses erys two!" Pope, who borrowed the Wife's revision of Ovid for the *Epistle to Arbuthnot,* saw quite clearly what the message was:

> Out with it *Dunciad*! let the secret pass,
> That secret to each fool, that he's an ass;
> The truth once told (and wherefore should we lie?)
> The queen of Midas slept, and so may I.

This is a secret women have to conceal all the time, especially about their nearest and dearest. The exemplum focuses strongly on the genuine anguish of Mi-

das's queen. She is a woman bound by ties of trust and affection—ties she herself acknowledges—to a man who loves her, and with whom her own reputation is involved. But he is still a fool:

> He loved hire moost, and trusted hire also;
> He preyede hire that to no creature
> She sholde tellen of his disfigure.
> She swoor him, "Nay," for al this world to wynne,
> She nolde do that vileynye or synne,
> To make hir housbonde han so foul a name.
> She nolde nat telle it for hir owene shame.
> But nathelees, hir thoughte that she dyde,
> That she so longe sholde a conseil hyde.

> (III 958-66)

This is not the sort of secret the Wife herself is used to concealing, as she points out in her *Prologue* (III 534-42), and we have only to replace Midas's wife with the Wife of Bath, and Midas himself with, say, husband number four, or with Janekyn at a moment when he is grinning at her over the top of his book of wicked wives (III 672), to see how graphically the exemplum records a realistic frustration and tension that the Wife knows well as a daily component of real marriages, even, or especially, good ones.[9] But it is equally interesting to replace the queen of Midas with the queen of Arthur, who has to proceed so tactfully to rescue the young rapist from vengeful masculine justice so she can set him on the right track. The Wife puts great stress on the careful courtesy, a style appropriate to a chivalric setting, with which the queen works to get her way. The line "The queene thanketh the kyng with al hir myght" (III 899), in particular, seems deliberately to overstress her courtesy in order to call attention to it. It seems to me that in the Midas exemplum the Wife evokes the real strains involved in feminine submission to and manipulation of masculine egos that the earlier scene leaves out, while reminding us that she herself is considerably less patient than either queen. She reacts to something she feels is missing in her original and supplies it, but she does so only outside the framework of the story.

Something similar happens with the issue of the quest itself. If the Wife gets involved in the question of what women most desire, and drops the story in order to pursue it, this suggests that the question is hardly settled for her except for polemical purposes. The "right" answer is always hedged. The hag remarks that there is no woman, however proud, "That *dar seye nay* of that I shal thee teche" (III 1019, emphasis added), and when the knight announces the answer the ladies who judge him are similarly cagey. They do not say he is right, they just don't say he is wrong: "In al the court ne was ther wyf, ne mayde, / Ne wydwe, that *contraried* that he sayde, / But seyden he was worthy han his lyf" (III 1043-45, emphasis added). In fact, the queen gets exactly what she asks for, "An answere suffisant in this mateere" (III 910), that is, an answer that suffices, one that will do rather than one that is definitive.[10] The reason for this is, as the Wife knows and demonstrates by her digressive interest in the "wrong" answer, that the question is an impossible one and the quest for a single answer is a fool's errand anywhere outside a story. In reality—in experience—different women want different things, and the same woman, like the Wife herself, may want different things at different times.

What we are seeing here is a developing tension between the public and authoritative functions of the *Tale* as polemical feminist propaganda and a more complex set of experiential interests that do not seem to fit the public plot very comfortably. The doctrinaire feminist argument of the *Tale* is acceptable as a position for women in general, and the Wife certainly does not disagree with it, but it is not very responsive to the detail and nuance of her own situation, and therefore it does not interest her very much. When she introduces herself into the *Tale* in the figure of the hag, she does so in a way that, while never losing sight of the public message and her status as an authority, focuses increasingly on a set of "privy" and experiential concerns of her own that come to constitute a subtext running underneath and in some tension with the "apert" surface.

The description that accompanies the entrance of the hag into the *Tale* is a compact portrayal of the Wife's sense of her own career as she has developed it in the *Prologue,* and makes most sense when it is read in reference to that development:

> And in his wey it happed hym to ryde,
> In al this care, under a forest syde,
> Wher as he saugh upon a daunce go
> Of ladyes foure and twenty, and yet mo;
> Toward the whiche daunce he drow ful yerne,
> In hope that som wysdom sholde he lerne.
> But certeinly, er he cam fully there,
> Vanysshed was this daunce, he nyste where.
> No creature saugh he that bar lyf,
> Save on the grene he saugh sittynge a wyf—
> A fouler wight ther may no man devyse.
>
> (III 989-99)

As I have already suggested, in order to constitute herself as an authority the Wife has to give her experience a definitive shape and meaning from which she can generalize, and this means that her past is behind her, over and done with. It disappears as experience in a way that makes her feel that her life is finished. Her famous lines on her youth, "But, Lord Christ! whan that it remembreth me," leading to the reflection "That I have had my world as in my tyme" (III 469-73), are followed immediately by a meditation that conveys her sharp awareness of the sad difference between now and then:

> But age, allas! that al wole envenyme,
> Hath me biraft my beautee and my pith.

> Lat go, farewel! the devel go therwith!
> The flour is goon, ther is namoore to telle;
> The bren, as I best kan, now moste I selle.
>
> (III 474-78)

This pattern, this set of feelings, is recapitulated in the description of the hag. The four and twenty dancing ladies are connected with the dance of feminine freedom from the "limitacioun" of friars and other masculine trammels, a freedom associated with the elf-queen and her "joly compaignye" at the dawn of time and the beginning of the *Tale.* But they are also associated with the Wife's youth—"How koude I daunce to an harpe smale" (III 457)—and with her richly variegated experience of life and love, the "olde daunce." Her memory swirls and dances with all the women she has been until they vanish away, she knows not where, and leave her all alone as she has become, as she is now. The analogues often spend time having fun with the comically grotesque ugliness of the hag: "Then there as shold haue stood her mouth, / then there was sett her eye,"[11] and so forth. The Wife's more reserved refusal to describe her is also more inward, suggesting not what can be seen but what is felt. I think her words here will bear the inflection: "A fouler wight ther may no *man* devyse," that is, "If you, the men who look at me as I speak, think that I am decayed, what must I feel, who know what I was—no mere description will do justice to that." It is no wonder that the hag tells the knight, "Sire knyght, heer forth ne lith no wey" (III 1001).[12]

Now in public terms this is a range of experience with which courtly romance does not deal, and the only answer the form has to the problems of the passing of the "flour," especially in a woman, is magic, that is, fantasy, like the transformation at the end of this story. Those problems are relegated to what happens after stories like this one are over, when, as we know, they lived happily ever after. The Wife does not believe in magic of this sort, any more than she believes that real men deal with the prospect of marrying old and ugly women with the courtesy and equanimity of a Sir Gawain, and part of what she is doing in her description of the wedding and the wedding night is to *confront* a genre that has no room for her and other women in her situation with the *fact of herself*. One can feel the glee with which she appropriates the rhetoric of courtesy, "smylynge everemo" (III 1086), and baiting the knight (and the self-gratulatory masculine conventions he stands for so shakily) with a blank-eyed rehearsal of official ideals:

> "Is this the lawe of kyng Arthures hous?
> Is every knyght of his so dangerous?
> I am youre owene love and eek youre wyf;
> I am she which that saved hath youre lyf,
> And, certes, yet ne dide I yow nevere unright;
> Why fare ye thus with me this firste nyght?
> Ye faren lyk a man had lost his wit.

What is my gilt? For Goddes love, tel me it,
And it shal been amended, if I may."

(III 1089-97)

The knight's heartfelt response shows how much the Wife thinks such chivalric courtesy is worth in the face of real-life decay: "'Amended?' quod this knyght, 'allas! nay, nay! . . . / Thou art so loothly, and so oold also'" (III 1098-1100).

The hag replies that she *could* amend all this, and in the story she can, since she has magical powers. If that were all the Wife was interested in, the **Tale** might now proceed to its conclusion in the assertion of mastery and the pleasures of fantasy. But because she does not believe in magic, the Wife *refuses* the temptation to fantasy that the **Tale** offers, puts it off to a brief moment at the very end, and proceeds to digress, that is, to *take over* the **Tale** and turn it forcibly toward what I see as a more tough-minded examination of her own situation and its potentialities. The speech on "gentilesse," "poverte," and "elde" is notable for the diminished image of human possibility it presents throughout, for its constant stress on the inadequacy of earthly hopes and earthly power:

Ful selde up riseth by his branches smale
Prowesse of man, for God, of his goodnesse,
Wole that of hym we clayme oure gentillesse;
For of oure eldres may we no thyng clayme
But temporel thyng, that man may hurte and mayme.

(III 1128-32)

In the face of all this human weakness, the speech consistently urges a stoic position. Boethius and Seneca are prominent in it. The burden especially of the account of poverty is "Stop striving for impossible goals and the fulfillment of petty human desires." "He that coveiteth is a povre wight, / For he wolde han that is nat in his myght" (III 1187-8). Instead, embrace your weakness, understand it, and make of it an occasion of virtue. True "gentilesse" lies not in human glory but in gentle deeds, and the hateful good of poverty leads a man to know his God. The Wife of Bath uses the mask of the hag, as an image of her own diminished powers and vanished "flour," to try out this rhetoric, to see what the bran is worth. As a version of herself, the hag functions as a kind of worst-case scenario for the Wife: "Suppose I never get married again, suppose I *am* old and ugly and my life *is* essentially over; suppose that the energy of my youth is gone forever and that there is nothing left from now on but the downward slope to death. What resources of self-respect and dignity remain to me?" If all she has left is her wisdom, she can at least use it to guide her into old age, where it may be necessary for her to adopt a more conventional style of life and attend to the needs of her soul.

If it feels like there is something a little disingenuous about this position, and if a less respectful paraphrase

of it might be "Well, I can always get religion," this is probably because we know the Wife too well by now to be entirely convinced by the more pious version. My real point, again, is that the same is true of her, and that the inadequacies for her of this passive, static, and renunciatory position are part of what she discovers in the very act of trying it out. The best evidence of this is the emergence of a counter-message in the "gentilesse" digression itself, a "privy" subtext that affirms something very different from its "apert" argument, and in fact subverts it. This first shows up in what I call the torchbearer simile, the rhetorical treatment of a formal argument that is in itself clear and easy to make. Boethius does it in a brief sentence: If "gentilesse" were a gift of nature it would always be the same everywhere, "sicut ignis ubique terrarum numquam tamen calere desistit," as fire is always and everywhere hot.[13] This is the Wife of Bath's version:

If gentillesse were planted natureely
Unto a certeyn lynage doun the lyne,
Pryvee and apert, thanne wolde they nevere fyne
To doon of gentilesse the faire office;
They myghte do no vileynye or vice.
Taak fyr, and ber it in the derkeste hous
Bitwix this and the mount of Kaukasous,
And lat men shette the dores and go thenne;
Yet wole the fyr as faire lye and brenne
As twenty thousand men myghte it biholde;
His office natureel ay wol it holde,
Up peril of my lyf, til that it dye.
Heere may ye se wel how that genterye
Is nat annexed to possessioun,
Sith folk ne doon hir operacioun
Alwey, as dooth the fyr, lo, in his kynde.

(III 1134-49)

The point to notice here is how the image of the fire is detached from the argument, slightly displaced from logical sequence, and foregrounded in a way that makes the argument itself hard to follow because the image is so detailed and so compelling, so much more developed than what surrounds it (or, I might add, than it is in any of its sources). This foregrounding makes the voice seem fascinated by the image of the fire flaming out in isolation and darkness, and this effect of fascination is independent of the place of the image in the argument. Its bright energy is affirmed over against all the conventional rhetoric of human weakness that surrounds it, and this is one key to its source and meaning.

Another key is the associations that fire has taken on in the Wife's **Prologue** and elsewhere in the **Tale,** which find their way into this image:

For peril is bothe fyr and tow t'assemble:
Ye knowe what this ensample may resemble.

(III, 89-90)

If fire is initially and fundamentally associated with sexuality for the Wife, it also acquires an aggressive dimension in the intimations of sexual threat that her free use of her sex sometimes takes on:

> He is to greet a nygard that wolde werne
> A man to lighte a candle at his lanterne;
> He shal have never the lasse light, pardee.
> Have thou ynogh, thee thar nat pleyne thee.
>
> (III 333-36)

> Thou liknest [women's love] also to wilde fyr;
> The moore it brenneth, the moore it hath desir
> To consume every thyng that brent wol be.
>
> (III 373-375)

As the second example here suggests, fire comes to be associated with what is *uncontrollable,* especially by masculine limits and standards. It is something that breaks through and consumes the oppressions of male decorum, as in the case of Midas's wife:

> Hir thoughte it swal so soore aboute hir herte
> That nedely som word hire moste asterte;
> And sith she dorste telle it to no man,
> Doun to a mareys faste by she ran—
> Til she cam there, hir herte was a-fyre.
>
> (III 967-71)

Fire has, then, for the Wife, far more than conventional connotations of inexhaustible energy, linked not only with sexuality but also with her self-assertion and sense of independence, with everything at the core of her that makes her aware of her own vitality. If that vitality is presented in more negative and destructive terms earlier in the poem, presented more as men see it when they try to smother it, here in its more inward manifestations it takes on a more positive sense as an image of the Wife's freedom even in the midst of constraint. Her private attraction to the image of the torch is an index of her *resistance* to the darkness, to the message of human weakness and decay that surrounds the fire and the woman. What is important about this upsurge of inner fire is that it happens spontaneously, and it happens *now,* in the act of speaking. The Wife rediscovers as she speaks that her resistance, her energy, her fire, is not gone at all, and has lasted beyond the decay of her youth and beauty. It is this awareness that lies behind the reservations she expresses when she comes to draw the moral consequences of the "gentilesse" argument:

> Yet may the hye God, and so hope I,
> Grante me grace to lyven vertuously.
> Thanne am I gentil, whan that I bigynne
> To lyven vertuously, and weyve synne.
>
> (III 1173-76)

The conditional mood in which this statement is cast calls attention to the fact that the speaker withholds herself from complete identification with the position

expressed: "I hope God grants me the grace to live virtuously when I decide to begin" carries the implication that that time is not yet.[14]

There is thus little point to the sort of critical objection that notes how the Wife of Bath cannot qualify as "gentil" under her own definition in the speech, and takes this circumstance as an "irony" of which she is unaware, since this is precisely the point the Wife is affirming triumphantly in her handling of the speech.[15] The content or *doctrine* here is neither "out of character" nor in it for the Wife. Rather, it is something that culture (masculine culture) makes available, and which the Wife is *using* for her own purposes—here perhaps as a kind of potential *remedia amoris* or "remedye of love." What the Wife reaps in this section of the *Tale* are the real fruits of her experience. External youth and beauty are and were, she discovers, just as deceptive as the traditional wisdom has always maintained them to be, because they worked to conceal from her the real inner sources of her vitality, the capacity for the enjoyment of life and the indomitable spirit that are still with her now that their conventional physical signs have passed. The external deprivation, the "poverte," is the condition that makes possible the discovery of inner richness. It is indeed a bringer-out of busyness and an amender of sapience, precisely because it "maketh [a man] his God *and eek hymself* to knowe."

By the time she gets to "elde," the hag is speaking out clearly for the Wife, in words we have heard before:

> Now, sire, of elde ye repreve me;
> And certes, sire, *thogh noon auctoritee*
> *Were in no book,* ye gentils of honour
> Seyn that men sholde an oold wight doon favour, . . .
> And auctours shal I fynden, as I gesse.
>
> (III 1207-12, emphasis added)

Elde is essentially dismissed, left for the future, because it is not yet time in the Wife's life—and that time may never come—for her to lapse into decorum, piety, and silence. No more than Janekyn with his book can those Church fathers and stoic philosophers—men, every Jack of them—tame her. As she moves into the ending of the *Tale,* the Wife asserts her vitality and her resistance to the deadening pressure of conventional proprieties in her treatment of the conclusion of the story. She does this, for instance, in the riddle, whose form in the analogues is a choice between having the hag fair by day and foul by night or vice-versa. The Wife of Bath's version—foul and obedient or fair and take your chances—reaffirms the sense of her own energy, independence, and impenitence that has been growing in her during the latter part of the *Tale*: "I'd do it all again, and I *will* if I get the chance."

> Or elles ye wol han me yong and fair,
> And take youre aventure of the repair

That shal be to youre hous by cause of me,
Or in som oother place, may wel be.

(III 1223-26)

The extent to which the concerns and the mood generated in the subtext of the "gentilesse" speech dominate the more conventional aspects of the story is further pointed up by the Wife's handling of the final lines of the *Tale,* in which she drops the happy ending in the middle of a line and goes out swinging:

And thus they lyve unto hir lyves ende
In parfit joye; and Jhesu Crist us sende
Housbondes meeke, yonge, and fressh abedde,
And grace t'overbyde hem that we wedde;
And eek I praye Jhesu shorte hir lyves
That wol nat be governed by hir wyves;
And olde and angry nygardes of dispence,
God sende hem soone verray pestilence!

(III 1257-64)

This concluding speech is a return to the public occasion of the *Tale* in the sense that it presents the Wife in the polemical and oppositional role that is appropriate to the general feminist message and her original battle plan for the *Tale,* But that public role, and even that message, are qualified by the private experience of the telling. The shrew of the end of the *Tale* is a straw woman, a role the Wife plays for tactical reasons that have to do precisely with the inadequacies of the public situation in which she speaks, with respect to the complexities of experience. It is clear from both the *Prologue* and the *Tale* that for the Wife "maistrye" is not really a simple mechanical reversal of male domination. In both cases, once the woman has been granted sovereignty she refrains from exercising it, and this suggests that it is primarily a tool for achieving feminine independence *within* marriage so that more satisfactory relations between the sexes can have a chance to develop.[16]

"Maistrye" is a way of making room for the possibility of love in the patriarchal world by giving women space to be responsible partners in a relationship. As only an "answere suffisaunt," it is where everything that is important about marriage begins, not where it ends. If anyone knows that "they lived happily ever after" is no way to talk about the experience of marriage, it is the Wife. Marriage is where things get harder, though potentially richer and more satisfying, not easier. But this aspect of marriage, the potential it offers for private fulfillment, is not really appropriate to the situation in which the Wife is performing. In the first place, the experience of real relationships is not something that can be conveyed in a story like this, and the Wife makes no effort to present the knight as someone who really learns something or changes his mind; he is simply coerced throughout the *Tale.*[17] In the second place, and more especially, the experience of real relationships is

not something that can be or that needs to be conveyed to a casually assembled group of strangers encountered on a pilgrimage, most of them males, with whom there is little likelihood of, and little reason for, intimacy. The man-eating monster of the end of the *Tale* and elsewhere may be a caricature of the real Wife of Bath, but as a role it is also a way of making sure that no one will try to take advantage of her—it asserts her independence and keeps it firmly in view, and it is in this sense that "maistrye" and the polemical feminism associated with it is dialectically necessary in the world as a woman finds it, as a precondition for the mutuality she might prefer. The conditions of the male-dominated public world may be said to force this position on the Wife, and its necessity shows just how unsatisfactory the public situation of women is in human terms. To make the male world into a straw man—to be forced to do so in order to fight its ubiquitous and dehumanizing public pressures—is to accept a logic of opposition and appropriation that can only drive one to constitute oneself as a straw woman.[18]

"But lordynges, by youre leve, that am nat I." Beyond and behind the public, necessarily caricatured feminism of the "apert" narration, there is a set of "privy" experiences that constitute, for Chaucer in the person of the Wife, a deeper and more existentially responsible feminism and a more searching critique of male domination. At this level, what the Wife responds to intuitively about the story is less what it includes than what it leaves out. One of the most notably sexist things about this particular story and the courtly romance genre of which it is a part is the assumption that women have no other consequential interests beyond courtship and marriage. Men may do battle and have adventures, but the stories of the women in romance are all love stories. As we have seen, such a story has no way of handling an ugly old woman—or even an attractive but not classically beautiful middle-aged one—except by magic, and no place at all for issues like a woman's experience of age and the prospect of death. Too narrowly feminist a reading of *The Wife of Bath's Tale*—or perhaps I should say, a reading of the Wife as too narrow, too exclusively polemical, a feminist—runs the danger of being itself anti-feminist because, like the masculine-conditioned romance, it confines the Wife of Bath too exclusively to issues of gender and sexual relations. These issues are very important to the Wife herself; they have dominated much of her life, and they are fully represented in her *Tale.* But to hold her exclusively to them, or for her to do so herself, does not allow her all the other things in her life and experience, including her personhood before age and death. In fact, in her *Tale* we see the speaker as a woman exercising her "purveyaunce," considering her options in line with her own philosophy: "I holde a mouses herte nat worth a leek / That hath but oon hole for to sterte to" (III 572-73). She may find her way back into marriage and the dance of relationship that has occupied and engaged her for so long, but she may not. In this open situation, she herself remains open. By the end of her *Tale* she has evoked her own energies in the face of what those energies have to contend with, and enacted a variety of possible responses to her situation and her unknown future. What she finds is that her experience has provided her with extensive resources for continuing to *woman-handel* with the authorities—with God the father, with the masculine world, and with Old Man Death—and that she need not commit or confine herself to any particular role or position except as a tactical move in whatever game she may have occasion to play. She does not need to define herself once and for all.

This lack of closure in the Wife's life and personality is, finally, an aspect of Chaucer's feminism, since of course there is no Wife of Bath. What there is is an impersonation, a man's attempt to think himself inside a woman's head and to speak from her point of view and with her voice. While I think from the evidence that Chaucer knew a lot about women, I am not in a position to speak with authority on this topic since, like the poet, I lack certain essential experiences. But I do see that in imagining what it might be like to be a woman, Chaucer felt it important to imagine one who remained in a final sense provisional and a mystery to herself—one who had not settled her own fate, and whose inability to predict for certain what would happen to her and who she might become kept her alive to herself and to him. This is still, no doubt, a masculine projection, since I do not think he knew these things about himself either, but in allowing the Wife of Bath to be as genuinely uncertain about these matters as he was himself, I think Chaucer was trying to sustain her mystery, her possibility and her independence—I think he was trying to respect her privacy.

Notes

1. For a more extended and theoretical account of some of these issues, see my "The Art of Impersonation: A General Prologue to the *Canterbury Tales,*" *PMLA,* 95 (1980), 213-24.

2. See, for example, George Lyman Kittredge, *Chaucer and His Poetry* (Cambridge, Mass.: Harvard University Press, 1915, rpt. 1972), p. 191; R. M. Lumiansky, *Of Sondry Folk: The Dramatic Principle in the Canterbury Tales* (Austin: University of Texas Press, 1955), pp. 117-129; Bernard F. Huppé, *A Reading of the Canterbury Tales,* rev. ed. (Albany: SUNY, 1967), pp. 107-135 (Huppé actually uses the phrase "QED," p. 134); Trevor Whittock, *A Reading of the Canterbury Tales* (Cambridge, England: Cambridge University Press, 1968), pp. 118-168.

3. *Chaucer's Poetry: An Anthology for the Modern Reader,* 2nd ed. (New York: The Ronald Press, 1975), p. 1077. On the Wife's changes in the

traditional story see also Meredith Cary, "Sovereignty and the Old Wife," *Papers on Language and Literature,* 5 (1969), 375-80.

4. This point has not been altogether lost on critics, though they seldom seem to give the Wife much credit for seeing it too. John P. McCall, *Chaucer Among the Gods* (University Park: Pennsylvania State University Press, 1979), uses the phrase "straw men" of the Wife's exempla, p. 139. Ellen Schauber and Ellen Spolsky, "The Consolation of Alison: The Speech Acts of the Wife of Bath," *Centrum,* 5 (1977), 20-34, have shown how the basis of all four of what they identify as the Wife's most common speech acts is the setting up of a proposition which is subsequently denied.

5. See, e.g., Lumiansky, *Sondry Folk,* pp. 126-29.

6. For the murderess and sociopath, see Beryl Rowland, "On the Timely Death of the Wife of Bath's Fourth Husband," *Archiv für das Studium der Neueren Sprachen und Literaturen,* 209 (1972), 273-82; Doris Palomo, "The Fate of the Wife of Bath's 'Bad Husbands,'" *ChauR,* 9 (1975), 303-319; and Donald B. Sands. "The Non-Comic, Non-Tragic Wife: Chaucer's Dame Alys as Sociopath," *ChauR,* 12 (1978), 171-82. For intimations of tragedy, see, among others, F. M. Salter, "The Tragic Figure of the Wife of Bath," *Transactions of the Royal Society of Canada,* 48, Series 3 (1954), 1-13. For the life force, see Rose A. Zimbardo, "Unity and Duality in the *Wife of Bath's Prologue* and *Tale,*" *TSL,* 11 (1966), 11-18.

7. So far as I can tell, the distinction between the public and private functions of the *Tale* was first made in Charles A. Owen's pioneering and still fundamental study, "The Crucial Passages in Five of the *Canterbury Tales,* A Study in Irony and Symbol," *JEGP,* 52 (1953), 294-311, rpt. in Edward Wagenknecht, ed., *Chaucer, Modern Essays in Criticism* (New York: Oxford University Press, 1959), p. 260. Owen is also one of the first to identify the element of fantasy or wish-fulfillment in the *Tale,* a perception that has become so common in discussions of it as to make specific citation pointless.

8. *Canterbury Tales,* III 929-31. Line references are to F. N. Robinson, ed., *The Works of Geoffrey Chaucer,* 2nd ed. (Boston: Houghton Mifflin, 1957).

9. Since I do not have space or occasion here for an analysis of the Wife's *Prologue,* I ought perhaps to say that I consider her fifth marriage a good one. The Wife's remark "And yet in bacon hadde I nevere delit" (III 418) refers not only to her dislike of old meat in a sexual sense but also to the

fact that she is not much interested in conventional marital harmony of the sort for which the Dunmow Flitch was awarded (see III 217-23). From this point of view, Janekyn and the Wife are a remarkably compatible couple: they both like to talk, they both like to fight, and they both like to make love.

10. See R. E. Kaske, "Chaucer's Marriage Group," in Jerome Mitchell and William Provost, eds., *Chaucer the Love Poet* (Athens: University of Georgia Press, 1973), p. 52.

11. *The Marriage of Sir Gawaine,* in Bartlett J. Whiting, "*The Wife of Bath's Tale,*" in W. F. Bryan and Germaine Dempster, eds., *Sources and Analogues of Chaucer's Canterbury Tales* (rpt. New York: Humanities Press, 1958), p. 237.

12. See P. Verdonk, "'Sire Knyght, Heer Forth Ne Lith No Wey': A Reading of Chaucer's *The Wife of Bath's Tale,*" *Neophilologus,* 60 (1976), 305-07.

13. *Consolatio Philosophiae,* III pr. 4.

14. Dorothy Colmer sees this, "Character and Class in the *Wife of Bath's Tale,*" *JEGP,* 72 (1973), 335.

15. E.g., Lumiansky, *Sondry Folk*; J. F. Ropollo, "The Converted Knight in Chaucer's 'Wife of Bath's Tale,'" *CE,* 12 (1951), 263-69; W. P. Albrecht, "The Sermon on 'Gentilesse,'" *CE,* 12 (1951), 459; Tony Slade, "Irony in *The Wife of Bath's Tale,*" *MLR,* 64 (1969), 241-47.

16. Once again a number of commentators have recognized the provisional and preliminary—what I would call the public—character of the idea of "maistrye," though once again the Wife herself has not been given much credit for understanding it. Owen, "Crucial Passages," was the first to note the importance of the hag's refusal to exercise domination. Of the several critics who have developed this perception and seen that what the Wife wants—what women want—is some form of mutuality in relationships, particularly fine accounts are given by Donald R. Howard, *The Idea of the Canterbury Tales* (Berkeley: University of California Press, 1976), pp. 254-55, and T. L. Burton, "The Wife of Bath's Fourth and Fifth Husbands and Her Ideal Sixth: The Growth of a Marital Philosophy," *ChauR,* 13 (1978), 34-50, esp. 46-47.

17. See Colmer, "Character and Class," p. 336, and Verdonk, "'Sire Knyght,'" 305 and 307.

18. David Aers, *Chaucer, Langland and the Creative Imagination* (London: Routledge and Kegan Paul, 1980), chapter 6, "Chaucer: Love, Sex and Marriage," pp. 143-73, sees this point as "Chaucer's"

message in the poem. See also Alfred David, *The Strumpet Muse* (Bloomington: University of Indiana Press, 1976), pp. 135-58.

Mary Carruthers (essay date March 1985)

SOURCE: Carruthers, Mary. "Clerk Jankyn *At Hom to Bord / With My Gossib.*" *English Language Notes* 22, no. 3 (March 1985): 11-20.

[*In the following essay, Carruthers refutes many commonly held assertions about the nature of the Wife of Bath's relationship with Jankyn. By analyzing fourteenth-century English usage, Carruthers identifies Jankyn as the relative of a close friend (one who is godparent to one of Alisoun's children), not as a stranger who merely boards in town. Through this interpretation, Carruthers argues, the Wife's change from manipulating spouse to manipulated spouse has richer irony.*]

In her fond description of past *jolitee,* the Wife of Bath recalls with particular pleasure her young fifth husband:

> He som tyme was a clerk of Oxenford,
> And hadde left scole, and wente at hom to bord
> With my gossib, dwellynge in oure toun;
> God have hir soule! hir name was Alisoun.
>
> (D. 527-530)[1]

Interpretive consensus concerning the circumstances of Jankyn's return would indicate that, having gone to Oxford for a few years, he came back to the region where he had been raised and boarded with a local lady, who was also Alisoun's dear friend and aide in idle talk and sexual exploits. The general misapprehension is reflected even by the editors of the *Middle English Dictionary,* who cite this particular use of the phrase *at hom* to illustrate the meaning "in or to one's native town" (s.v. *hom,* 3a [c]). Unfortunately, this paraphrase is based upon the modern meanings of the nouns in lines 528-9; full and thoughtful consideration of the lexicographical content of this description, and its historical context, will not support this interpretation of Chaucer's text, nor the meaning now commonly assigned to the clause "wente at hom to bord / With my gossib."

The Wife of Bath, we are told in *The General Prologue,* is not from Bath, but "of biside Bathe," that is from near (but not in) Bath.[2] Bath itself was a small town even by medieval standards; only forty-four acres were enclosed by the city walls, although a larger area around the city (known as *Bath forinsecum* or *forum*) was included in the revenue farm granted to the Bishop of Bath and Wells from the time of Edward I.[3] It is difficult, given the localization of the Wife's dwelling in the *Prologue* portrait, to account for the presence of a boarding-house or inn where Jankyn may be supposed to have been a boarder. We recall that the two clerks in *The Reeve's Tale* when marooned for the night in the village of Trumpington were unable to lodge at an inn and stayed (for payment) with the miller and his family, even though Trumpington was near (*biside*) Cambridge. Trumpington is of the order of magnitude of villages "biside Bathe." But the probable interpretation of this line does not depend (nor could it) upon speculation concerning the magnitude of Chaucer's fictional village. Better comprehension of what the words used in this phrase mean will clarify it; their mimetic status is directly reflective of lexicographical evidence.

In trying to determine historically the meaning of any word there is an inevitably large area of uncertainty involved, a philological variant of the Heisenberg principle, for in the very act of semantic reconstruction one must also partly misconstrue. We are forced to determine what most words meant in the past chiefly by a process of determining what they did not mean, with the attendant problems which such a method entails. And when we have delimited an area of possible meaning, we are then able only to map out a range of probability and likelihood within that often broad area, derived from a word's occurrences in evidence whose existence is due to the accidents of its transmission. As uncertain a process as historical philology is, however, the range of meaning which it restores is real, in the sense that one cannot simply disregard those probabilities in interpreting a text. The essay which follows seeks to restore a tiny fragment of the *Wife of Bath's Prologue* from too many readings which have done just that. What the clause under examination most probably means is that clerk Jankyn came back to his own house (not just his home-town) and ate his meals (i.e. lived) at home with his family, a member of which was a close friend of the Wife's and a baptismal sponsor for one of her children. This paraphrase expresses the commonest meanings in the fourteenth century of the three nouns I wish to examine in this essay: *hom, bord,* and *godsib* (*gossib*).

The phrase *at hom* means "at or to one's native house" as Chaucer uses it. *Hām* in Old English always means a dwelling, a particular place, best translated by Latin *domus, domicilium, villa, mansio, praedium* (Bosworth-Toller, *A Dictionary of Old English* and *Supplement,* s.v. *hām*; cf. s.v.—*hām, ham*). The gradual extension of the word's meaning from "one's native dwelling" to "native region" vaguely and generally conceived, and then to pure metaphor (as in "Home is where the heart is") is difficult to pinpoint within any period, as a note in the *Oxford English Dictionary* warns (*OED,* s.v. *home*). The phrase *at hom* is the Middle English development of the Old English adverbial accusative *hām* with verbs of motion. Perhaps especially in this

conservative phrase, therefore, ME. *hom* continued to carry its restricted, original meaning of "one's own house" (to which one was going).

Chaucer rarely uses the word *hom* in a context where it may refer to something besides one's native dwelling. The one apparent instance is in *Truth*: "Her is non hoom, her nis but wildernesse" (17). But the use of *hām* to refer to the dwellings of spirits has several precedents in Old English—indeed, the idea that both Heaven and Hell contain dwellings for souls is Biblical. The use of *hom* to establish the Christian teaching that one belongs in Heaven is well attested from Old English as a particular use in a strictly limited context. Indeed, such a paradoxical usage of the word depends upon and thus emphasizes its primary meaning of "one's native (earthly) house."

Two other occurrences in Chaucer are perhaps ambiguous. The Parson is praised in *The General Prologue* for not seeking advancement; he "dwelte at hoom, and kepte wel his folde" (A.512). Here the phrase probably refers to his whole native parish rather than simply his own house, although even in this instance the more restricted meaning is certainly included. Similarly, Criseyde praises Troilus because he "bereth hym here at hom so gentily" (*Troilus and Criseyde,* 2.187), including surely the whole area of Troy city, not just Troilus' own house, although her words also include that. It is interesting to note in this regard that -*hām* as a place-name element in Old English probably referred to a whole group of dwellings in an area, whereas *ham* (with a short vowel) referred to a single 'home.' To the extent that such a distinction existed in Old English, however, and the evidence, as Bosworth-Toller suggests, is not overwhelming, it was certainly lost by the Norman Conquest. But the conflation of these two meanings may be residually reflected in Chaucer's use of *hom* in these instances to refer both to a particular house and to it and those around it in a limited area (Troy, the Parson's parish).

Other than these instances, the one specialized, the other ambiguous, when Chaucer uses the word *hom* in the prepositional phrase *at hom,* he means "native dwelling." Three examples will suffice to make this point, although many others could be adduced. In *The Clerk's Tale,* Griselda vows to see the procession of the marquise, but first "wol I fonde / To doon at hoom" (E.283-284); in *Troilus and Criseyde,* Calchas bemoans his loss of "a doughter that I lefte, allas! / Slepyng at hom" (4.92-93); and earlier in the Wife's *Prologue,* she complains to her niggardly old husband, "I sitte at hoom, I have no thrifty clooth" (D.238).

But more trouble, I suspect, has been given to modern readers by the phrase *to bord* than by *at hom. Bord* is a word that has become restricted in its meaning in this type of context since Chaucer's time, even as *hom* has been extended. In the fourteenth century, *bord* was a noun meaning "meals," as in the phrase "bed and board," a transfer of the original meaning, "table," itself extended from "wooden plank (used as a table)." The meaning "pay money for meals at a fixed rate" had not yet arisen, nor had the word developed a verb form. *OED*'s earliest citations for this meaning (and for the verb) are from the sixteenth century. Such phrases as *maken bord* or *gon to bord* mean simply "to eat meals," as in this sentence from *The Book of Margery Kempe*: "he led hem wyth hym to þe place þer he went to boorde" (102/31),[4] or this from a fourteenth-century *Ancrene Riwle* (ms. Pepys 2498, Magdalene College, Cambridge):[5] "Summe ancres maken her boord wiþ her gestes" (183/7-8), both cited by *MED* (s.v. *bord,* 5[c]). John, the carpenter in *The Miller's Tale* "that gestes heeld to bord" (A.3188), probably collected money from them but that implication is made by the word *gestes* (and confirmed by the use fifteen lines later of *hostelrye* to refer to John's house) not by the word *bord*.[6] Chaucer uses *geste(s)* here in its original meaning of "stranger," as he does in *Troilus and Criseyde* 2.1111: "Ther is right now come into town a gest, / A Greek espie." That *gestes* also customarily paid is implied in the following lines from *The Canon's Yeoman's Tale* concerning the priest who was "so servysable / Unto the wyf, where as he was at table, / That she wolde suffre hym no thyng for to paye / For bord ne clothyng" (G.1014-1017). But that one can *bord* in one's own house (*at hom*) is indicated by many examples in Chaucer, among them this line from the *Wife's Prologue*: "I wolde nat spare hem at hir owene bord" (D.421). When Jankyn is said to have gone *to bord at hom,* the words mean that he lived with his family.

The least understood of the three nouns in the phrases used by Chaucer to place clerk Jankyn is *godsib,* perhaps just because it seems to us so evident. Every Chaucerian knows that the noun *godsib* (*gossip*) originally referred to some sort of relationship like that denoted now by *godparent* or *godchild,* but altered its meaning to what the *OED* defines as "a person, mostly a woman, of light and trifling character, esp. one who delights in idle talk" (s.v. *gossip,* 3), via the transitional meaning of "familiar acquaintance, friend, chum" (s.v. *gossip,* 2). But it is important to realize that the earliest citations in *OED* for the word's fully debased meanings are from the late sixteenth and seventeenth centuries. During the fourteenth century, the ordinary reference of *godsib* was still to a baptismal sponsor.

Moreover, Middle English *godsib* meant not "one's own godparent," but "the godparent of one's child." In the Middle English *Lai le Fraine,* two knights who are great friends each marry, and the lady of one gives birth to twin boys, whereupon her husband sends a messenger to his best friend to "say he schal mi gossibbe be" (42).[7]

Chaucer's Parson, defining the types of lechery, says that "certes, parentele is in two maneres, outher goostly or flesshly; goostly, as for to deelen with his godsibbes. For right so as he that engendreth a child is his flesshly fader, right so is his godfader his fader espiritueel. For which a womman may in no lasse synne assemblen with hire godsib than with hire owene flesshly brother" (I.907-908). The comparison adduced by the Parson to a "flesshly brother" makes clear what variety of spiritual relationship is being referred to; a *godsib* is one's contemporary, the generational relationship denoted by the element *-sib,* (*OED,* s.v. *sib*). Dame Alice has at least one male *godsib* as well:

> And if I have a gossib or a freend,
> Withoute gilt, thou chidest as a feend,
> If that I walke or pleye unto his hous!
>
> (D.243-245)

It is interesting that although the *Middle English Dictionary* gives "one's sponsor at baptism or confirmation, a godparent" (s.v. *godsib,* 1[a]) as a distinctive meaning of *godsib,* none of the citations given by the editors unambiguously supports this meaning. Indeed in several, including the lines we are studying from the *Wife's Prologue,* the reference is clearly to a contemporary person, rather than an elder or a child. Alisoun's "gossib" is not her own godmother, nor even just a friend, but a friend who is (as the lines cited from *Lai le Fraine* and *The Parson's Tale* indicate) a sponsor of her child.[8] The clue given by this word should at least give pause to those who confidently build interpretations based upon the Wife's "evident" childlessness. I have argued the danger of assuming this view before,[9] since Chaucer's text neither makes nor should be expected to make any statement one way or the other on the matter, but the lexicographical evidence of *godsib* adds cogent force to my earlier warning.

Sponsorship was defined doctrinally as a kind of binding kinship ritually granted through the sacrament of baptism, but as genuine as the kinship of blood. The medieval Church had severe strictures against marriage between individuals related in this way, extending, according to St. Thomas Aquinas, as far as marriage between children of godfathers and godmothers.[10] Canonically, however, only the sponsor and the person officiating contract the bond with the baptised person which constitutes an invalidating (diriment) impediment to marriage. Thus, *godsib,* like *godparent,* was considered to be a real form of kinship, regarded seriously as such by the Church, and serving to bind ties among medieval families. The relation of *godsib* could be used to cement profitable alliances as well as personal friendships (as in *Lai le Fraine*), and *godsibs* served a variety of useful functions performed also by blood-kin, including helping to arrange marriages. The *Paston Letters* reflect a careful choice and use of *godsibs* in a variety of matters.[11] Part of the irony in Alisoun's courtship of Jankyn "for love and no ricchesse," depends on our perceiving the expectation her neighbors would have had for Jankyn's future when his family became allied through the tie of *godsib* to the village's wealthiest widow. Alice implies that she had to use her wiles and snares to land Jankyn all by herself, but her *godsib*'s function during their meetings was more than just that of chaperone. Jankyn's family could hardly have hoped for a better result from their spiritual kinship; indeed the Wife's situation with respect to Jankyn, an ironic reversal of her earlier family-arranged marriages, makes all the more poignant and absurd her initial romantic hopes for this fifth alliance.

Thus, the relationship denoted by *godsib* in the fourteenth century, is an adult one, between friends of the same generation, who sponsor each others' children, a coparenting of spirit as well as blood. A godfather or godmother, by contrast, is called just that. The *MED* cites another manual of sins like *The Parson's Tale*, the fifteenth century allegorical treatise called *Jacob's Well*, which cautions against what it describes vividly as the seventh depth of the slime-pit (*wose*) of lechery, "betwen a man & his gossybe or between godfadyr & goddau ȝter or be[twen] a chyldren of godfadyr & godmodyr" (*Jacob's Well*, 162/6).[12] The *Middle English Dictionary* editors use this quotation as evidence for *godsib* meaning "godparent," but the relationship of "co-parent (in a spiritual bond)" is denoted, distinguished clearly in the quoted text from a "godparent/godchild" relationship.

The fact that close friends were often chosen to be one's children's sponsors is reflected by a secondary meaning of *godsib* in later Middle English, that of 'friend, pal,' especially as a word of address. Thus, Gluttony in *Piers Plowman* is greeted by Betty the brewster as "gossib" (B.5.302), and one of the cautionary tales in *The Book of the Knight of Latour-Landry* turns on the ability of a roper's deceitful wife to enlist her reliable "gossip" in duping her husband.[13] But neither of these instances clearly excludes the use of the word *godsib* to mean "baptismal sponsor for one's children." The best description of the role of gossips at a medieval baptism remains that of H. S. Bennett in *The Pastons and Their England*. Basing his account upon the conventionalized witnesses found in *post-mortem* inquests, Bennett describes how the midwife took the baby to church for christening, the godparents having been summoned, accompanied by the usual crowd of neighbors (like marriages and all processions, baptisms formed a standard part of parish entertainment), how the ceremony was described afterwards to the mother by the midwife and gossips upon their return from church, and how the remainder of the day was spent in feasting the gossips and neighbors.[14] The *post-mortem* inquests reflect the conventions

of the landed classes, since they were held to determine the age of an heir to a tenant-in-chief.[15] The majority from this period which I have examined and which name the baptismal sponsors, name three: two men (usually including a religious who is often the officiating cleric) and a woman in the case of a male child; and two women and a man in the case of a female.[16] The sacrament itself encouraged one sponsor, and allowed two, although several of the age-proofs mention only the priest who did the baptism (his spiritual kinship to the child was conferred by the sacrament). In a small village, the network of kinship formed through the *godsib* tie could have been quite extensive.

Let me summarize what lines 527-530 of the *Wife's Prologue* tell us about clerk Jankyn: he is from a local family "of biside Bathe," sent off to Oxford for a short time but now returned home to live with his family (and work for little reward as parish clerk). The Wife of Bath is closely connected through the tie of *godsib* with one of Jankyn's close female relatives, most likely his mother, since she is the female relative commonly found *at hom*. Furthermore, the mothers of medieval families customarily had charge of arranging the marriages for their offspring (with the father's final approval), and Alisoun's wealth, once the impediment of her fourth husband is removed, would make her a most attractive candidate. The very coziness and familiarity of the arrangements implied in lines 527-530 help to set up Alisoun's eventual comic fall when Jankyn proves to be less tractable than he at first seems. Our understanding of these arrangements is essential to our ability to interpret with some correctness what the text suggests the circumstances of Alisoun's fifth marriage to be, and the rich social context evoked by the *experience* recounted in her *Prologue.*

Notes

1. All textual references are to F. N. Robinson, ed. *The Works of Geoffrey Chaucer,* 2nd edition (Boston, 1957)

2. On the significance of this crucial detail of her portrait, see my article, "The Wife of Bath and the Painting of Lions," *PMLA* 94 (1979), 209-222.

3. J. Byrchmore, "Medieval and Elizabethan Bath," *The Book of Bath* (Bath, 1925), p. 59; see also Austin J. King and B. H. Watts, *The Municipal Records of Bath, 1189-1604* (London 1885), especially pp. 12-27, for an account of earliest charters and other records of the town. They note (p. 27) that Bath "was a very considerable centre of the West of England wollen trade," a weaver's shuttle forming part of the arms of the priory.

4. S. B. Meech and H. E. Allen, eds., *The Book of Margery Kempe,* EETS o.s. 212 (London, 1940).

5. A. Zettersten, ed., *The English Text of the Ancrene Riwle,* EETS o.s. 274 (London, 1976).

6. John's house is called both an *hostelrye* (A.3203) and an *in* (A.3622).

7. M. Wattie, ed., *The Middle English Lai le Fraine,* Smith College Studies in Modern Language, 10 (Northampton, Mass: Smith College, 1929); see also line 50.

8. The case of *godsib* affords a particularly clear instance of the philological uncertainty principle at work. Even after ruling out its evidently unmedieval meanings, as I have just done, there is still the uncertainty left in the fact that while the word *godsib* denotes a relationship of sponsorship among individuals of the same generation, it does not seem to refine further whether the relationship referred to in a given context is that of (a) two godparents of the same child; (b) the parent of a child one is sponsor to; or (c) the sponsor of one's own child. All three refinements are possible instances of *godsib*-hood. In glossing Alisoun's casual reference to "my gossib" as 'the sponsor of her child,' I give the most probable meaning of the word as used in the surviving evidence of the fourteenth century in contexts like this one, for while there are several instances of individuals addressing as *mi godsib* a person who is certainly a sponsor for one of their own children, there are none I have found in which either of the other two varieties of *godsib* is as certainly intended.

9. See my article, "The Wife of Bath and the Painting of Lions," 221, note 31.

10. St. Thomas Aquinas, *Summa theologica, Supplement* Q. 56; cf. the quotation from *Jacob's Well* which occurs later in this essay. The canonical status of the spiritual kinship conferred by baptismal sponsorship is defined in *The Catholic Encyclopedia,* s.v. *sponsors* (New York, 1967-74).

11. For example, in a 1475 petition to Edward IV begging his aid in recovering the manor of Caister, John Paston II refers to an earlier successful intercession by his "gossib þe Bisshop of Wynchestre"; Norman Davis, ed., *Paston Letters and Papers,* (London, 1971), I.488.

12. A. Brandeis, ed., *Jacob's Well, EETS* o.s. 115 (London, 1900).

13. References are to G. Kane and E. T. Donaldson, eds., *Piers Plowman: The B Version* (London, 1975), and to Thomas Wright, ed., *The Book of the Knight of Latour-Landry, EETS* o.s. 33 (London, 1906).

14. H. S. Bennett, *The Pastons and Their England* (1922; rpt. Cambridge, 1968), p. 194.

15. Edgar B. Graves, *A Bibliography of English History to 1485* (London, 1975), p. 627.

16. Of one representative group of 18 such proofs of age, fourteen list the heir's baptismal sponsors. All fourteen give three names; in the case of the thirteen males, the pattern is invariably two men and one woman, whereas in the case of the one female heir two women and a man are listed: William D. Cooper, ed., "Proofs of Age of Sussex Families, temp. Edw. II to Edw. IV," *Sussex Archaeological Collections* (Sussex Archaeological Society) 12 (1860), pp. 23-44. The form of these proofs was quote conventional in nature— see the separate notes by R. C. Fowler and M. T. Martin, *English Historical Review* 22 (1907), 101-103, 526-527; certainly the number of sponsors, their gender and social class would seem to have become conventional among the gentry subjects of the recorded inquests by the fifteenth century, for the earlier proofs display greater variation. The extent to which this change reflects the growth of a social convention or the development of an official formula cannot, of course, be exactly determined; undoubtedly some combination of the two factors is involved. A translation of most such proofs is to be found, *passim.,* in the *Calendar of Inquisitions Post-Mortem (Henry III-Richard II),* 15 vols. (London: H.M.S.O., 1904-70); by no means all list the baptismal sponsors, but of those which do, the pattern shown in the Sussex proofs prevails, although it is by no means universal. In about half the proofs from the early years of Edward III's reign, the fact of baptism is recorded with no sponsors' names given besides that of the priest; in several proofs for male heirs the two godfathers only are recorded, one being the officiating cleric who was always godfather (and thus *godsib* to the parents). In general, the later the date, the more apt one is to find the names of a full set of godparents listed in addition to the priest. Very few of these proofs from any period are for female children; fewer still list the names of their sponsors, but when they do the names are usually those of women. One can deduce from this pattern of evidence a custom of naming male sponsors for male children, females for females, and on occasion, the naming of a full set of godparents for children of both sexes, this last practice becoming more frequent in the documents as one moves into the fifteenth century.

Works Cited

Aers, David. *Chaucer, Langland, and the Creative Imagination.* London: Routledge, 1980.

Bloch, R. Howard. *Medieval French Literature and Law.* Berkeley: U of California P, 1977.

Bolton, Whitney. "The Wife of Bath: Narrator as Victim." *Women and Literature* ns 1 (1980): 54-65.

Carruthers, Mary. "The Wife of Bath and the Painting of Lions." *PMLA* 94 (1979): 209-22.

Chaucer, Geoffrey. *The Works of Geoffrey Chaucer.* Ed. F. N. Robinson. 2nd. ed. Boston: Houghton, 1957.

Christine de Pizan. *The Book of the City of Ladies.* Trans. Earl Jeffrey Richards. New York: Persea, 1982.

Colmer, Dorothy. "Character and Class in the *Wife of Bath's Tale.*" *Journal of English and Germanic Philology* 72 (1973): 329-39.

Crane, Susan. *Insular Romans: Politics, Faith, and Culture in Anglo-Norman and Middle English Literature.* Berkeley: U of California P, 1986.

Delany, Sheila. "Sexual Economics: Chaucer's Wife of Bath and the Book of Margery Kempe." *Minnesota Review* ns 5 (1975): 104-15.

Duby, Georges. *Medieval Marriage: Two Models from Twelfth-Century France.* Trans. Elborg Forster. Baltimore: Johns Hopkins UP, 1978.

———. *The Three Orders: Feudal Society Imagined.* Trans. Arthur Goldhammer. Chicago: Chicago UP, 1980.

Gallacher, Patrick J. "Dame Alice and the Nobility of Pleasure." *Viator* 13 (1982): 275-93.

Geoffroy de la Tour Landry. *The Book of the Knight of the Tower.* Trans. William Caxton. Ed. M. Y. Offord. EETS ss 2. London: Oxford UP, 1971.

———. *Le livre du Cevalier de la Tour Landry.* Ed. Anatole de Montaiglon. Paris: Jannet, 1854.

Green, Richard Firth. "The *Familia Regis* and the *Familia Cupidinis.*" *English Court Culture in the Later Middle Ages.* Ed. V. J. Scattergood and J. W. Sherbourne. New York: St. Martin's, 1983. 87-108.

Haller, Robert S. "The Wife of Bath and the Three Estates." *Annuale mediaevale* 6 (1965): 47-64.

Howard, Donald. *The Idea of the* Canterbury Tales. Berkeley: U of California P, 1976.

Jameson, Fredric. *The Political Unconscious: Narrative as a Socially Symbolic Act.* Ithaca: Cornell UP, 1981.

Jean de Meun and Guillaume de Lorris. *Le roman de la rose.* Ed. Félix Lecoy. 3 vols. CFMA 92, 95, 98. Paris: Champion, 1973-76.

———. *The Romance of the Rose.* Trans. Harry W. Robbins. New York: Dutton, 1962.

Jordan, Robert M. "The Question of Genre: Five Chaucerian Romances." *Chaucer at Albany.* Ed. R. H. Robbins. New York: Franklin, 1975. 77-103.

Kempe, Margery. *The Book of Margery Kempe.* Ed. Sanford Brown Meech. EETS os 212. London: Oxford UP, 1940.

Koban, Charles. "Hearing Chaucer Out: The Art of Persuasion in *Wife of Bath's Tale.*" *Chaucer Review* 5 (1970-71): 225-39.

Leicester, H. Marshall, Jr. "The Art of Impersonation: A General Prologue to the *Canterbury Tales.*" *PMLA* 95 (1980): 213-24.

———. "Of a Fire in the Dark: Public and Private Feminism in the *Wife of Bath's Tale.*" *Women's Studies* 11 (1984): 157-78.

The Letters of Abelard and Heloise. Trans. Betty Radice. Harmondsworth: Penguin, 1974.

Malone, Kemp. "*Wife of Bath's Tale.*" *Modern Language Review* 57 (1962): 481-91.

Mann, Jill. *Chaucer and Medieval Estates Satire.* Cambridge: Cambridge UP, 1973.

Margulies, Cecile Stoller. "The Marriages and the Wealth of the Wife of Bath." *Mediaeval Studies* 24 (1962): 210-16.

Monfrin, J. "Poème anglo-normand sur le marriage, les vices et les vertus, par Henri (XIIIe siecle)." *Mélanges de langue et de littérature du moyen-âge et de la renaissance offerts à Jean Frappier.* 2 vols. Geneva: Droz, 1970. 2: 845-66.

Murtaugh, Daniel M. "Women and Chaucer." *ELH* 38 (1971): 473-92.

Palomo, Dolores. "The Fate of the Wife of Bath's 'Bad Husbands.'" *Chaucer Review* 9 (1974-75): 303-19.

Parker, Patricia A. *Inescapable Romance: Studies in the Poetics of a Mode.* Princeton: Princeton UP, 1979.

Patterson, Lee. "'For the Wyves love of Bathe': Feminine Rhetoric and the Poetic Resolution in the *Roman de la rose* and the *Canterbury Tales.*" *Speculum* 58 (1983): 656-95.

Robertson, D. W., Jr. "'And for My Land Thus Hastow Mordred Me?': Land Tenure, the Cloth Industry, and the Wife of Bath." *Chaucer Review* 14 (1979-80): 403-20.

———. *A Preface to Chaucer: Studies in Medieval Perspectives.* Princeton: Princeton UP, 1962.

Rowland, Beryl. "Chaucer's Dame Alys: Critics in Blunderland?" *Neuphilolologische Mittellungen* 73 (1972): 381-95.

Ruggiers, Paul. *The Art of the* Canterbury Tales. Madison: U of Wisconsin P, 1965.

Sands, Donald B. "The Non-comic, Non-tragic Wife: Chaucer's Dame Alys as Sociopath." *Chaucer Review* 12 (1977-78): 171-82.

Shahar, Shulamith. *The Fourth Estate: A History of Women in the Middle Ages.* Trans. Chaya Galai. London: Methuen, 1983.

Specht, Henrik. *Chaucer's Franklin in the* Canterbury Tales. Copenhagen: Akademisk, 1981.

Vale, Malcolm. *War and Chivalry: Warfare and Aristocratic Culture in England, France, and Burgundy at the End of the Middle Ages.* London: Duckworth, 1981.

Vance, Eugene. "Le combat érotique chez Chrétien de Troyes." *Poétique* 12 (1972): 544-71.

Winney, James, ed. *The Wife of Bath's Prologue and Tale.* By Geoffrey Chaucer. Cambridge: Cambridge UP, 1965.

Susan Crane (essay date January 1987)

SOURCE: Crane, Susan. "Alison's Incapacity and Poetic Instability in *The Wife of Bath's Tale.*" PMLA 102, no. 1 (January 1987): 20-7.

[*In the following essay, Crane investigates the Wife of Bath's attempts to define her autonomy, and she observes that many of Alisoun's ideas conflict with one another, and her quest for women's independence is unsustainable.*]

Geoffrey Chaucer's *Wife of Bath's Tale* so closely illustrates the concerns of its *Prologue* that critics agree it can only be understood in relation to its assertive, female, marriage-minded narrator. But why does Alison's *Tale* resemble an Arthurian romance? Her *Prologue* is based on antifeminist tracts, marital satire, biblical exegesis—a clerical mixture from which Alison draws life and departs like the Eve of amphibians leaving the sea while carrying its salt in her veins. It would seem beyond this creature's ken to speak of ladies' gracious mercy, of quests and fairy knowledge. Only the Wife's idealizing nostalgia for her happily-ever-after with Jankyn anticipates the generic character of her *Tale.*

I argue that we can better understand the disjunction between the Wife's *Prologue* and *Tale,* and the peculiar generic makeup of the tale itself, by appealing to the works' historical situation. I am not referring to the recent critical trend that analyzes Alison as if she were a real, fully developed personality. So treated, she appears to be a "sociopath," homicidal, nymphomaniacal, a mass of bizarre symptoms (see, e.g., Rowland; Palomo; Sands). A second historicizing trend associates her trade and station with medieval land tenure laws, dower practices, and legal records, but these efforts, while valuable contextually, remove us from confronting Alison as she exists in her own language (see, e.g., Margulies; Colmer; Robertson, "'And'"). She is neither an individual (if she were, she would indeed be monstrous) nor a mirror for historical conditions but a fiction who tells a fiction.

Yet the history of cultural beliefs can contribute to an understanding of these fictions. Ideologies inform genres more directly than do economic and social conditions, and they can mediate for us between a literary text and its historical moment.[1] Romances, for example, shape ideals of chivalry and courtesy into narratives about how to interpret and assess those ideals. This is more fully what romances do than is representing the daily life of courts. Similarly, antifeminist satire tells us little about what actual marriages were like but much about how the clergy conceived of sexuality and femininity.

The Wife of Bath's Tale draws heavily on romance and antifeminist satire. Alison has no existence independent of her words, but her words in their generic formations allude to social and religious convictions that have extraliterary importance. Attending to those convictions can help us see why Alison draws on romance, why she draws on it imperfectly, and what the discourse on *gentillesse* has to do with the rest of her performance.

Two issues in particular—gender and sovereignty—are of concern to Alison. Both issues have intertextual subtleties of some depth, and both also have practical influence in the world. The Wife's *Tale* confronts the social belief that feminine power should be strictly limited, and it attempts to establish a defense of secular women's sovereignty that opposes the conventions available to Alison. She revels in the attractions of power and argues that her active desire for it is justified by the benefits she wins from it and the peace and happiness that yielding to it will bring to men. Yet her vaunted abilities as a "wys wyf" (D 231) are precisely those the satirists condemn, while her happy endings are patently illusory. The illogicalities and confusions in her narrative are commonly attributed to her error: she is a parodic or comic figure who inverts accepted morality, or a sinful one who denies Christian teaching, and therefore she cannot argue cogently. But whether or not she is comical or morally wrong, she is of substantial interest from other perspectives. Her attempt to redefine women's sovereignty is rhetorically and culturally significant, and from these perspectives Alison's apparent confusions propel her convictions beyond traditional discourses toward a realm of expression where there is as yet no language. In her narrative and logical ruptures themselves, in her destabilizations of genre, gender, *gentillesse,* and sovereignty, we can perceive something of what "wommen moost desiren" (D 905) as well as how inexpressible that desire is.

The kinds of power Alison designates as "sovereignty" vacillate contradictorily, in part because she confronts generic and ideological differences on the issue. Her *Tale* analyzes a belief that informs both antifeminist satire and romance: that gender sets limits on personal capability and social power. Both literatures develop conventions about feminine abilities, women's special knowledge in affairs of the heart and hearth, and the ways women exercise their capacity in those affairs. Chaucer's works often venture far from generic norms, but his poetry can still illustrate the conventions of these two genres regarding feminine power.

Heroines of romance tend to be more delicate emotionally and less capable intellectually than men (Dorigen's laments, Criseyde's fear, Theseus's subjection of Femenye), but their exceptional beauty inspires love and adumbrates a fineness of character that may not quite be fulfilled (Dorigen's rash promise, Criseyde's falseness). For men they are the arbiters of love, courtesy, and high sentiment. Their excellence in these matters reproduces in the emotional sphere the hierarchy of feudal relations, leading to a sublimation and refinement of passion that are metaphorically elevating (Arveragus's and Aurelius's courtships of Dorigen, the Man in Black's courtship of fair White). But the demanding standards of noble ladies, after inspiring men to improve, are complemented by the ultimate compliance that brings courtship to fruition. From the romance tradition at large it is clear that resourcefulness, sharp wit, and magical power are located in minor female figures or dangerous ones more than in heroines (La Vieille, Lunete, Morgan le Fay, Chaucer's Cassandra). The admirable women of romance wield their emotional sovereignty in ways beneficial to men and pleasurable to audiences, deferring stasis for a time but finally yielding in harmonious accord with male desire.

In contrast, antifeminist satire is nonnarrative, organized instead by an authoritative voice that rigidifies and fragments femaleness into a set of discrete exempla and negative topoi on nagging, mercenary dependence, overbearing sexuality, and so on:

> And if that she be foul, thou seist that she
> Coveiteth every man that she may se,
>
> . . . . .
>
> Thou liknest [wommenes love] also to wilde fyr;
> The moore it brenneth, the moore it hath desir
> To consume every thyng that brent wole be.
>
> . . . . .
>
> "Bet is," quod he, "thyn habitacioun
> Be with a leon or a foul dragoun
> Than with a womman usynge for to chyde."
>
> (D 265-66, 373-75, 775-77)[2]

Seeking to discourage clerics from cohabitation and sexual relations, the satirists mount an all-out attack on feminine emotional and domestic power. Significantly, romance poets and satirists agree in according women a potential for excellence in domesticity and love, but satirists make the failure of that potential a chief argument for avoiding women: contrary to what the suitor

expects, a woman will not delight or comfort him. Moreover, the qualities that in romance contribute to women's emotional excellence define their unworthiness in satire. Their greater fragility manifests itself in weeping and clinging, their capacity for love leads to torments of jealousy and sexual conflict, and their irrationality tyrannizes men like a child's or a badly trained animal's: "For as an hors I koude byte and whyne. / I koude pleyne, and yit was in the gilt, / Or elles often tyme hadde I been spilt" (D 386-88). Antifeminists thus argue that women's emotional sovereignty is harmful, aggressive, and falsely exercised instead of imagining with the romance poets that women's sovereignty derives from native feminine virtues.

Initially, the Wife of Bath addresses the issues of gender and power as they are formulated in anti-feminist satire. As readers have long noted with pleasure, her own origin in the very texts she disputes forces her to shadowbox with herself, receiving almost as many blows as she delivers. However cleverly Alison attempts to parry satiric convictions—by celebrating the less-than-perfect life rather than accepting admonishments to perfection, by claiming that the rational male should yield reasonably to the less rational female—still the notion that women's claims to sovereignty are unjustified is inextricably woven into the generic fabric of her *Prologue.* Alison's shift to romance is thus a strategic one, challenging antifeminist versions of the issue by confronting them with a genre that celebrates women's emotive power instead of undermining it. Romance is the "profeminist" literature, it would appear, that can combat the negative formulations of Theophrastus and Jerome.

But her tactic comes as a surprise in view of her own textual origins and of conventional rebuttals of the antifeminist version of women's sovereignty. The Wife's character is drawn from the gender conceptions of estates literature as well as from satire, and neither of these points of origin prepares us for her romance.

Alison's "Venerien" (D 609) femaleness is more firmly rooted, as Jill Mann has shown, in her estate than in her horoscope (see also Shahar; Monfrin). Estates literature distinguishes not only among ways of life (workers, nobles, clergy) but also between men and women. Secular women are assigned to a separate female estate. This fourth estate is subdivided according to women's social status in their relations to men rather than according to professions or work in the world: women are maidens or spouses or widows; they tempt, bear children, and so on. This formulation of social identity obviously makes women's significance dependent on their relations to men, providing little justification for Alison's claims to supremacy. Nor does the presentation of her trade offer her any better justification. Alison's cloth making, mentioned only in her *General Prologue* portrait, turns out to have no importance in her life. Little more than a version of the spinning proverbially assigned to women along with deceit and weeping (D 401-02) as secondary sex characteristics, cloth making is not what gives Alison some measure of dominance during and beyond her marriages. Rather, her "sexual economics" extract wealth from her husbands in exchange for domestic peace (Delany).[3] The effacement of the Wife's trade from her *Prologue* and *Tale* is a disenfranchising move that underlines her functional dependence. In keeping with estates ideology, her social identity is restricted to her wifehood, while her defense of "Marcien" hardiness and dominance (D 610) inverts antifeminist condemnations of the marital estate.

What history can show us about the Wife of Bath is less the daily working and living conditions of women than the ways men and women conceived their situations. The strong presence of antifeminist and estates ideology in the Wife's portrait and *Prologue* renders her claim to sovereignty intensely problematic, and a wider context of women's voices demonstrates her isolation even from her own fictive sex.[4] It is not only male writers who pervasively assert that women's sexuality defines their situation and that men should be sovereign over women. Heloise, who is anthologized in Jankyn's "book of wikked wyves" (D 685), portrays herself in her letters as the source and, from birth, nothing but the source of Abelard's misfortune: "What misery for me—born as I was to be the cause of such a crime! Is it the general lot of women to bring total ruin on great men? Hence the warning about women in Proverbs." Submissiveness offers her a way to minimize her sex's power to do harm, so Heloise represents her love's merits to have been the extraordinary sacrifices by which "I have carried out all your orders so implicitly that when I was powerless to oppose you in anything, I found strength at your command to destroy myself. . . . I believed that the more I humbled myself on your account, the more gratitude I should win from you" (*Letters* 130, 113).[5] Margery Kempe, who like Heloise takes uneasy refuge from marriage in celibacy and religious self-castigation, likens Mary and Joseph's wedding to her own spiritual marriage to God, praying that like a perfect wife she "myth han grace to obeyn hym, louyn & dredyn hym, worschepyn & preysyn hym, & no-thyng to louyn but þat he louyth, ne no-thyng to welyn but þat he wolde, & euyr to be redy to fulfillyn hys wil bothyn nyght & day wyth-owtyn grutchyng er heuynes" (199).[6]

That Margery speaks through two male amanuenses and that Heloise was educated in clerical orthodoxy by Abelard himself only begin to indicate the constraints on their self-presentation. Yet they concur, while Chaucer's Alison does not, that women should value submis-

sion and sacrifice and should watch vigilantly over their explosive sexuality. Christine de Pizan also chooses obedience as her touchstone when refuting the antimatrimonial satirists of Jankyn's book. Despite her argument in the *City of Ladies* that women are capable of independence, Christine counters the claims of Valerius and Theophrastus that women are domineering and unloving with examples of wives supreme in servitude—they follow their husbands to battle and exile, eat their cremated husbands' ashes or kiss the rotting corpses; they treat unfaithful husbands with love and respect; they are as constant as Griselda (117-34, 170-76).[7] From the unlettered Margery to the highly educated and original Christine, women writers defend their sex partly by accepting cultural models of female submission.

A story of Griselda, then, would be the widely expected rebuttal to the antifeminist challenge of *The Wife of Bath's Prologue*. But the *Clerk's Tale* comes later (and differently); the Wife's *Tale* is another kind of rebuttal altogether.

Initially, romance provides Alison with an argument to use against the satirists. In that her *Tale* lacks chivalric or military adventures and features a crucially knowledgeable and capable female character, it is not a standard romance. But it does answer to the phrase Chaucer uses, according to Donald Howard (52-53n), to designate his romances, "storial thyng that toucheth gentillesse" (A 3179).[8] True to the genre are the setting in "th'olde dayes of the Kyng Arthour" (D 857) and the educative knowledge by which women direct men's emotional development. Arthur's justice is tempered by Guinevere's mercy as is Theseus's by the "verray wommanhede" of weeping ladies who plead for Palamon and Arcite (A 1748-61).[9] The old hag, like other romance heroines, has special insight in matters of love and morality that leads the knight to change for the better and to achieve happiness in love.

Alison manipulates her romance with an eye to antifeminist assertions, using her new genre to attract validity to the version of women's sovereignty condemned by antifeminist writers. For that sovereignty is not identical in romance and in satire. Wives of satire seize tangible economic and physical terrain by force and subterfuge: "I have the power durynge al my lyf / Upon his propre body, and noght he"; "Atte ende I hadde the bettre in ech degre / By sleighte, or force, or by som maner thyng" (D 158-59, 404-05). Ladies of romance control men's devotion not by force or even by their own volition but by reason of their excellence (Dorigen, Criseyde). The Wife's *Tale,* in referring to romance conventions, implies an equivalence between the unjustified tyranny of satire's wives and the meritorious supremacy of romance heroines. Clearly, there is no Dorigen or Criseyde in her story. The hag is aggressive, manipulative, and sexually demanding in the best satiric vein, but her high and magical attributes—as queen of fairies, as goal of a quest for life, as moral guide, and finally as love object of the knightly hero—obscure her antifeminist connections and work to validate her active exercise of power.

But while romance dignifies the claim to women's sovereignty in this *Tale,* frequent antifeminist touches paradoxically vitiate the romantic elevation Alison seems to desire. The answers proposed to Guinevere's question catalog feminine weaknesses, from "Somme seyde wommen loven best richesse" to "we kan no conseil hyde" (D 925, 980). The violence of sexual relations through Alison's *Tale* and the animal metaphors for women (limed like birds, kicking like galled horses, booming like bitterns) answer to the satiric conviction that women are profoundly irrational, sensual creatures.

One explanation of this difficulty in the narration is that the Wife is incapable of sustaining the romance mode; she cannot help slipping back into the antifeminist attitudes from which she herself was drawn. For other critics, the "restrained idiom of the *Tale* proper . . . suggests that a courtly narrator has replaced the Wife" or that Chaucer speaks directly in some passages (Winney 23).[10] These explanations place Alison's *Tale* beyond her control and make its antifeminist elements no more than inopportune and debilitating interruptions of a standard romance. We would do better to accept that the Wife of Bath is the voice Chaucer assigns to *Prologue* and *Tale* alike and to hear her out. Alison is not a person constrained by plausibility but a fictional voice that knows and can perform whatever is useful to dramatizing the interests attributed to it. Her tendency to slip from the realm of satire into romance and back again is worth considering as her move, one suited to her concern with women's sovereignty.

Alison's transitions between satire and romance betray the incongruity of the two generic visions and, consequently, their shared inadequacy to her argument. The knight's trial culminates this process of recognition. Several shifts that may have seemed involuntary, from queenly power to proverbial foibles, from fairy illusion to all-too-solid flesh, are here recuperated in a full return to romantic sensibility. The hierarchical display of Guinevere's assembly of judgment evokes fictional love courts, with the "queene hirself sittynge as a justise" (D 1028), and the answer she and her ladies accept from the knight seems to tally with courtly conventions about women's superiority in matters of the heart. Yet the hag anticipates that the ladies will not gladly admit the knight's answer; even "the proudeste" will simply not "dar seye nay" (D 1017-19). Echoing her suspicion, the knight concludes his answer insistently: "This is your mooste desir, thogh ye me kille" (D 1041). The implication of resistance marks a disparity between satiric sovereignty, actively claimed and energetically wielded,

and the passive, apparently unwilled sovereignty of women in romance. To force the queen's ladies into accepting that "Wommen *desiren* to have sovereynetee" (D 1038) is to confront the romance vision that has dignified women's power with Alison's fiercer vision that women consciously seek and enjoy it.

The Wife's return to a satiric conviction at this point underlines the insufficiency of either conventional discourse for dramatizing a worthy sovereignty of secular women. Satire denies their worth. Romance seems a genre in which women's excellence brings power, but the appearance proves false. A heroine's strength lasts only for the temporal and fantastic space that delays her submission and demonstrates the capabilities of her suitor. Her mercy and compliance are the necessary closure to her aloof independence and her ability to command devotion. In a historical study of marriage practices, Georges Duby concludes that the Old French poetry of adultery and love service is based on a "fundamentally mysogenous" conception of woman as merely a means to male self-advancement: "Woman was an object and, as such, contemptible" (*Medieval* 14, 108).[11] Eugene Vance corroborates Duby's historical analysis by connecting early lyrics of adultery to romances of proud ladies: throughout, love's poetic expression is typically "le combat érotique," an aesthetic of antithesis recognizing the violence that is veiled by the mystified perfection of *fine amor* (548; see also Bloch 153-56).

These researches suggest that the violent sexual relations of the *Wife of Bath's Tale* do not depart from romance tradition so much as exaggerate it, while the *Tale*'s presentation from the knight's point of view, its evasion of punishment for the knight, and the queen's merely contingent authority (for which she "thanketh the kyng with al hir myght" [D 899]) offer a recognizably romantic, masculine imagining. The hag's power over her "walwing" knight is anomalous, more like the power of Morgan le Fay in *Sir Gawain and the Green Knight* than like that of a conventional heroine. But even the hag surrenders in the end. The joyful and thoroughly fanciful resolution that fulfills the knight's "worldly appetit" (D 1218) illustrates the most romance can render. Here, as in Alison's *Prologue,*, "her very verbalizations remain unavoidably dependent, feminine respeakings of a resolutely masculine idiom" (Patterson 682; see also Aers 143-51).

Heloise, Christine, and Margery Kempe similarly reiterate clerical wisdom about the failings and duties of their sex. One further female voice, taking a noble rather than a clerical perspective, demonstrates that modern critics are not the first to find misogyny and male violence in courtly conventions. Toward the end of his book of instruction for his daughters, Geoffroy de la Tour Landry writes at some length of his wife's opposition to his belief "that a lady or damoyselle myght loue peramours in certayne caas." According to Geoffroy, his wife objected that men's assertions about the value of love service "are but sport and esbatement of lordes and of felawes in a langage moche comyn." Men's conventional language (drawn from courtly tradition) has no relation to their feelings, says this wife, so their declarations of love should not be trusted. Her understanding that courtly speaking is masculine rather than feminine presages modern analyses of romance. Men use this discourse against women, to make conquests: "these wordes coste to them but lytyll to say for to gete the better and sooner the grace and good wylle of theyr peramours." Nor do they undertake tasks for love but "only for to enhaunce them self, and for to drawe vnto them the grace and vayne glory of the world" (*Book* 163, 164; *Livre* 246-48).[12] In her view, then, male power does not surrender to female excellence in courtly interaction. Consequently, her arguments on the subject support Geoffroy's instructions to their daughters to restrain their sexuality and to be humbly obedient in their relations with men.

If the elevation of women in romance was understood to be chimerical and if even noble writers concur with clerical ones on the importance of female submissiveness, how is the Wife of Bath to formulate (even fictionally) an argument in defense of women's desire for sovereignty? In many ways her *Tale* does not manage to transcend the categories of her age, and her argument remains partial, awkward, and illogical. For example, the curtain lecture urges the knight to rise above the worldly indulgences of wealth and station, but the lecturer then fulfills his sensual desires. She rejects the social hierarchy and nobility of blood in the same speech, yet she appeals to "my sovereyn lady queene" (D 1048) for the knight's hand and promises him to become as beautiful "As any lady, emperice, or queene" (D 1246; see Haller; Murtaugh; Bolton).

There are many such confusions in the Wife's *Prologue* and *Tale*; perhaps most elusive is what Alison means by sovereignty in the first place. The power it signifies seems constantly to vacillate, but three major contradictions can be distinguished. Alison sometimes associates sovereignty with economic gain, "wynnyng" (D 416), yet she seems to win nothing from her fourth husband, gives up her gains to Jankyn, and makes the hag speak eloquently against the significance of wealth. At other points, coercion, including physical domination, renders Alison's metaphor "myself have been the whippe" (D 175) very nearly literal, but she moves easily from coercion to accommodation with Jankyn as does the hag with her knight. And finally, her conception of sovereignty seems to demand the trust or the high opinion of her husbands. "Thou sholdest seye, 'Wyf, go wher thee liste . . . / I knowe yow for a trewe wyf, dame Alys'" (D 318-20), she instructs her old husbands,

and Jankyn fulfills her desire in acceding, "Myn owene trewe wyf, / Do as thee lust the terme of al thy lyf" (D 819-20). Nonetheless, the Wife cheerfully undermines her demand for trust and respect by asserting and demonstrating that women are untrustworthy: "half so boldely kan ther no man / Swere and lyen, as a womman kan" (D 227-28).

Why does Alison constantly alter and even cancel each of her versions of sovereignty? The solution is not that women's desire for power is nothing but a desire for love. Love is a relatively simple matter for her, something she often gets from men. In contrast, sovereignty vacillates confusingly even in love's presence: with the "daungerous" Jankyn and knight (D 514, 1090), it works to perpetuate love, as if it were analogous to integrity or merit, but in her four earlier marriages it tyrannizes or substitutes for love, as if it were mere self-interest. The Wife's casual manipulation of her old husbands' devotion—"They loved me so wel, by God above, / That I ne tolde no deyntee of hir love" (D 207-08)—suggests that the question of power precedes and subsumes the question of men's love: it is sovereignty that "worldly wommen loven best" (D 1033). The object of this fundamental love is elusive, and its elusiveness partly accounts for its desirability, in accordance with Alison's psychological principle "Forbede us thyng, and that desiren we" (D 519). Female power, in any form, is the most heretical of her desires (Howard 252; Aers 143-46), unsustained in any of the conventional discourses on which she draws. Looking beyond those discourses necessarily leaves the Wife inarticulate, even about the meaning of the sovereignty she imagines. She desires to validate the forbidden but can hardly formulate what it is.

Still, her very failures of articulation make gestures that indicate what the worth of female power might be. Alison signals the direction of her desire through a series of poetic transformations. The hag's physical metamorphosis is only the most dazzling of many mutations demonstrating that genres, genders, and words themselves are not fixed phenomena but fluid media through which new potential can be realized.

Romance is the appropriate form for confronting an unknowable desire. Its "strategy of delay" holds narrative "on the threshold before the promised end, still in the wilderness of wandering, 'error,' or 'trial'" (Parker 5, 4). This fantastic space permits traditional medieval romance to imagine, however contingently, a kind of female sovereignty that Alison manipulates, as we have seen, to justify the willed power condemned in antifeminist satire. But in that very manipulation, she recognizes the illusoriness of women's power in romance and cracks the *Tale*'s generic frame. Neither romance nor satire can answer Alison's longing, and her vacillation expresses her desire to pass beyond their limits.

Women also cross gender lines in the Wife's *Tale.* The barber in Midas's story becomes a wife; the ladies' court of judgment replaces Arthur's; and the hag comes to speak like a cleric, while her husband submits with wifely meekness to her "wise governance" (D 1231). These substitutions make women the active movers of plot, as they are not in conventional romance, where they may inspire chivalric activity but where that activity is itself the source of change and growth. Gender displacements extend to the fairy realm, as the "elf-queene with hir joly compaignye" (D 860), who are all feminine when the knight encounters them (D 992), seem to metamorphose during Alison's introduction from "joly" dancers to potent incubi threatening women in the Arthurian countryside. The knight-rapist and the king both move from having power to surrendering it, while women throughout the *Tale* move themselves into male purviews. Does this plot's exclusion of chivalric adventures echo and reverse the *Prologue*'s effacement of Alison's cloth-making profession, emphasizing the dependence of men on women in the *Tale*? Even the comic victory of friars over fairies in the *Tale*'s first lines is vitiated when the fairy wife's pillow sermon demonstrates her intimate knowledge of religious texts. Reassigning women to positions of authority traces the path of their transgression in the narrative itself. The power they exercise is not always benign or even admirable, since worthy female sovereignty is a concept Alison cannot fully articulate, but the gender shifts themselves loosen the bond between maleness and power that makes female sovereignty inconceivable.

In the lecture on *gentillesse* and *poverte,* we are taught that even words are unfixed, because the categories they designate can be reconceived from changed perspectives. *Gentillesse* is not, as the knight thinks, a question of "nacioun" and "kynde" (D 1068, 1101), of merit determined by blood alone. Rather, "he is gentil that dooth gentil dedis" (D 1170). This familiar clerical topos restricts and relativizes the second estate's claim to superiority by emphasizing the disjunction between supremacy of birth and the moral supremacy over which the church has special authority (see Duby, *Three*).[13] So alien does this argument seem to Alison's views on female sovereignty that some critics treat it as a mere interruption: "it is in fact addressed to the audience. Chaucer apparently wished to include such a discourse at this point" (Jordan 89).[14] But in that it challenges fixed categories, the speech on *gentillesse* and *poverte* is of a piece with the *Tale*'s other instances of transformation and is appropriate to an old hag who can so easily redefine herself as beautiful and young.

Beginning with the words themselves, the hag's speech subverts the conventional meanings of *gentillesse* and *poverte,* using paradox and oxymoron to emphasize the process of reversal: the sinner "nys nat gentil, be he duc or erl; / For vileyns synful dedes make a cherl" (D

1157-58); "Poverte is hateful good" (D 1195). The direction of these reversals moves away from the concept of nobility and poverty as objective states beyond individual control, asserting instead that conscious choices determine them: "Thanne am I gentil whan that I bigynne / To lyven vertuously" (D 1175-76); "he that noght hath, ne coveiteth have, / Is riche, although ye holde him but a knave" (D 1189-90). The two processes, the semantic destabilization and the assertion that individuals can define their situations, connect this speech to Alison's wider preoccupation with sovereignty: that is the most unstable of her terms and the one she seeks most persistently to reconceive. Without a culturally authoritative recourse for her half-imagined redefinition, Alison displaces the achievement to the hag's analogous transformations of *gentillesse* and *poverte.* Perfectly in consonance with recognized authorities, yet grounded in arguments for self-determination, the hag's definitions imply that *soverey-netee* may also be open to new and freely chosen meanings. Emphasizing the possibility, the hag's mutation into an authoritative expert enacts the claim that women can deserve power, and her husband recognizes that when he surrenders *marital* sovereignty to her on the basis of her *moral* excellence.[15] Like the elevation of romance, the morality of clerical exhortation is here appropriated (partially and not altogether fairly) to support Alison's defense of female sovereignty.

The hag's self-transformations culminate the various shifts and changes surrounding gender and power in the *Wife of Bath's Tale.* Perhaps we have not attended sufficiently to these instabilities because of Alison's air of tenacious assurance. She tackles her issue with such conviction that we expect her account to make sense, and so we resolve her inconsistencies by deciding that she is driven by nymphomania, or represents fallen willfulness, or conversely that she rises to philosophical wisdom through the experience of her *Tale.*[16] Critical conclusions about what Alison "wants" proliferate, yet it is meaningful that she does not provide a consistently readable answer.[17] If I were attempting to wrest coherence from the Wife's preoccupation with women's sovereignty, I would argue that sovereignty's associations with and dissociations from financial gain, domestic control, sexual aggressiveness, and love are all informed by a conviction that women should not strive for equality in marriage but should, rather, refuse to wield power that they have securely won. This tactic appears to resolve the battle of the sexes into blissful reciprocity, but the Wife's envoy reveals a still-polarized combativeness that denies transcendence.

But when we make the Wife of Bath coherent, she becomes too easy to dismiss. She inscribes something more complex in her inconsistencies themselves, and it is important to consider how they too comment on gender and power. They stress that the Wife's justification of sovereignty is inexpressible in that it cannot be sustained by any conventional discourse. Whatever is compelling in her self-defense does not finally come from the language of satire or romance or moral philosophy, all of which she misappropriates. The inadequacy of her arguments, the mutability of *gentillesse* and *sovereynetee,* the shifting genders, and the flow of genres in her *Tale* record the impossibility of Alison's undertaking. Her own restless metamorphoses, from antifeminist creation to romancer to clerical scholar and back to militant wife in her envoy, emphasize that each tradition on which she draws denies women sovereignty. In this context, that she and her old hag do not exercise their hardwon power intriguingly contradicts their persistent desire to win it. Is this a surrender to male fantasy? Or is Alison incapable of representing the full achievement of women's power? Or is sovereignty here again to be construed as trust, rather than as economic security or coercive domination? Can her envoy sustain any one of these explanations?

More important than Alison's failure to resolve such dilemmas is the elusive longing her many transformations betray. Her insatiable desire is more forceful and preoccupying than any of her illusory conclusions. Sovereignty's redefinitions are all provisional, each canceling another, because the most Alison can tell us about her ideal of female power is that it is not present. In her present, she can only tear the inert texts that have determined her, and wish for more.

Notes

1. I use the term *ideology* not to disparage but, rather, to describe a set of interrelated beliefs that informs a particular way of life and works to validate that way of life in its attempts to win and maintain a place for itself in the world. On relations between history, ideology, and romance see Jameson; Shahar; Crane.

2. Robinson's notes list the connections between such passages and the works of Theophrastus, Jean de Meun, Matheolus, Jerome, and others. In this discussion I am claiming a "clerical" and "satiric" sensibility for these writers and their works, even for those who were not themselves clerics (e.g., Ovid) and for works that are not satires in the full generic sense, because anti-feminist writing was so fully integrated into the medieval tradition of clerical satire. Some scholars prefer the term *anti-matrimonial* to *antifeminist,* but the strategy of the tradition is to speak against marriage by speaking against women. On the *WBP* [*Wife of Bath's Prologue*] and another kind of clerical satire, the *sermon joyeux,* see Patterson.

3. Many critics have noted Alison's conflation of sex and gain in her marriages. It is also important that, in the dynamic of these marriages, Alison

does not herself produce the wealth she deploys. Wealth is something inert that she wins from men by subterfuge and force, not something she generates by cloth making.

4. Her distance from models of womanhood may contribute to exegetical interpretations that her *Prologue* and *Tale* are not so much about femininity as about "the problem of willfulness" or "carnality": see Koban; Robertson, *Preface* 317-31. If the text has a tropological level on which the interactions of pure moral qualities can be analyzed, it nonetheless also makes literal statements with which I am concerned.

5. The ideas of Heloise anthologized in Jankyn's book are probably those against marriage that Abelard reports in the *Historia calamitatum* (*Letters* 70-74), adapted in Jean de Meun's *Roman de la rose* (vol. 2, lines 8729-58; *Romance,* pp. 177-78).

6. See also Margery's account of her own marriage to God (87).

7. For editions of Christine's French text in preparation, see Richards's introd. xxv.

8. On Chaucer's romances cf. Jordan; Ruggiers 151-246.

9. See also *The Legend of Good Women* G 317-444 (Alceste, "so charytable and trewe" [G 434], rescues Chaucer from the God of Love's punishment) and Ruggiers 208. In the following discussion I assume that Arthur's queen in *WBT* [*Wife of Bath's Tale*] may be called Guinevere and that the old hag is the "elf-queene" of line 860.

10. According to Malone, "If the tale befits her, it does so by contrast, not by likeness" (489). My argument owes much to Leicester, "Art."

11. See also 12-15, 105-10. Green draws a similar conclusion on the social implications of later courtly poetry.

12. Mary Carruthers proposes that *WBT* opposes "courtesy-books" like Geoffroy's.

13. Some scholars relate the speech on *gentillesse* to Alison's "social class, the new rich, resentful of the claims of the old rich" (Colmer 329; see also Carruthers; Howard 105-06), but her class and professional origins are suppressed so markedly in favor of her estate and sex that the latter categories should have more to do with the speech than the former. Nor is the topos "he is gentil that dooth gentil dedis" to my knowledge ever a bourgeois one for medieval writers; rather, when it appears outside clerical contexts, its use is to sustain the nobility's separateness by adding moral criteria to those of birth: see Vale 14-32; Specht 104-08.

14. According to Koban, the speech is one of the *CT*'s "crystallizing utterances" in which Chaucer educates us in "humanizing truths" (227-28; see also Winney 24).

15. Only by accepting that the knight has listened to his wife and been changed by her words can we explain the difference between "My love? . . . nay, my dampnacioun!" (D 1067) and "My lady and my love, and wyf so deere, / I put me in youre wise governance" (D 1230-31). Unless he is "glosing" her like Jankyn (D 509), which is unlikely in view of his thoughtful sigh (D 1228), the hag has talked him into loving and respecting her.

16. See Gallacher; see also Rowland; Palomo; Sands; and n. 4 above.

17. Chaucer's dramatization of an undecided Alison is remarkable not least in refraining from authorial judgment, a gesture Leicester attributes to Chaucer's own character: "This lack of closure in the Wife's life and personality is, finally, an aspect of Chaucer's feminism" ("Of a Fire" 175).

Susan Crane (essay date March 1988)

SOURCE: Crane, Susan. "Alison of Bath Accused of Murder: Case Dismissed." *English Language Notes* 25, no. 3 (March 1988): 10-15.

[*In the following essay, Crane provides a tongue-in-cheek look at the mysterious death of Alisoun's fourth husband and defends the Wife against the charge of murder.*]

"Professional scholars," said Sherlock Holmes, "like professional detectives, are not reasoning animals. If the murder in the **Wife of Bath's Prologue** has not been discovered before, it is because I had never read that part of the **Canterbury Tales** until a fortnight ago." Holmes would not find it surprising that his case against Alison, as reported by Vernon Hall in the third volume of *The Baker Street Journal,* has failed to convince most of our unreasoning profession.[1] However, the academic brief on the revelour's convenient death has grown fatter over the years, and it is now time to clear Alison's name and return her to those halcyon days when she stood accused of nothing worse than being an icon of fallen willfulness.

It would be an easy task to acquit Alison on the ground that the evidence against her is insubstantial and ambiguous. I could argue that Alison is proud of her flirtation with Jankyn because it illustrates her acquisitive "purveiance" (D 566, 570). "I holde a mouses herte nat worth a leek / That hath but oon hole for to sterte

to" (D 572-73): far from plotting to get rid of a husband, she boasts that she is lining up Jankyn behind number four, doubling rather than changing her options. Further, when Alison lets slip the narrative thread—"now, sire, lat me se what I shal seyn" (D 585)—her accusers hear a sinister evasion of just how "blood bitokeneth gold" (D 581) in this case. The argument cannot be accepted without complementary evidence on what crimes are being suppressed at the five other points when Alison's narrative restarts from a dead stop (D 480-81, 563, 627, 666-68, 711-12). Has she poisoned all the men "short, or long, or blak, or whit" (D 624) that she abandons with the sudden "What sholde I seye" (D 627)? Has she bludgeoned the old clerks whose habits she is describing just before her abrupt "But now to purpos" (D 711)? A much fatter brief than we see before us would be required to validate the charge that Alison's casual narration betrays a felonious nature. Finally, I could argue that while Jankyn does taunt Alison with examples of husband murder, it is not that but the book's testimony on women's chiding and sensuality that finally moves Alison to action. Alison recognizes the validity of *those* charges, and she has left us a vigorous defense of her ability to scold and to seduce. But there is little to suggest that either Jankyn or his wife perceives murder to be the most pertinent and painful of his book's antifeminist accusations.

Thus Alison could be acquitted simply for lack of evidence, but that would not satisfy her accusers, whose case is one of those instances of argument from absence: what is *not* there is crucial. I would like to make two observations about how these gaps are glossed by those who think the Wife of Bath murdered number four. First, critics sustain this accusation by assuming that Alison is not a literary character, a text, but rather a person who has a complete life that we can recover by conjecture. Second, the accusers refer their charge to antifeminist tracts such as Jankyn's book of wicked wives, in which the worst of the accusations against women is that they may be expected to murder their husbands. This Wife exemplifies fully what the satirical tradition tells us about wives.

Both of these components of the case against Alison are fraught with difficulties. To begin with her ontological status, imagining Alison to be capable of murder entails a naive confusion of the textual and the organic that has nothing to do with the ordinary recognition that literature strives to imitate life. Of course literary characters resemble living people, but the reality of fictional characters is enclosed in and determined by their texts. This seems so evident that I would hesitate to mention it, were it not a principle so frequently ignored in discussions of Alison of Bath: "We can easily imagine her when young. . . . In her formative years she read romantic stories of the Arthurian knights. . . . [But] the twelve year old bride, anticipating the realization of her girlish romantic dreams, finds herself bound in holy wedlock to an old man barely capable of making love."[2] This fabrication is launched from details in the text but soars rapidly into the ozone of readerly imagination. Why should we connect romances with Alison's formative years; why with private reading? Because the dreamy susceptibility we might then attribute to her might lead to a disappointment so great that she might later feel murderous. Such inventions derive from the tradition that brought us *The Girlhood of Shakespeare's Heroines* and conjectures about what Hamlet ate for breakfast. Or in Alison's case, "Why she married her fourth husband is not clear. Can it be that she was drunk at the time?"[3] In a court of law this would amount to inadmissible insinuation. In critical circles the work of Marshall Leicester, David Benson, and many others encourages us to acknowledge the textuality of literary characters by respecting the limits of their representation.[4] Alison does look lifelike, but to invent more of her life than Chaucer has already given us is to take ourselves for poets.

Yet Alison's accusers explain her crime by inventing for her an extratextual history and psychopathology whose slender relations to the text are attributed to Alison's guilty self-concealment. For Beryl Rowland, even the Wife's abrupt narrative transitions "suggest a pathological state"; concerning the "oother compaignye in youthe" (A 461), Rowland notes that "precocious sexual experience may create in a woman a trauma which makes her hate all men. . . . Hence the obvious satisfaction that Alys expresses at her winnings, and the contempt which she shows for men's desires."[5] Donald Sands, analyzing the Wife as a "psychiatric case," discovers that she suffers from "a disorder which recent psychiatric texts label a sociopathic personality disturbance, an illness characterized by antisocial reaction, dyssocial reaction, and usually addiction (in Alys's case, probably to alcohol)."[6] If the Wife of Bath were a living creature, she would indeed look bizarre, but the work of psychiatrists would not help us to handle her. Could we galvanize her into life, she would appear, like Frankenstein's monster, an alien being horrifically different from ourselves.[7] Refusing to notice the irreducible Otherness of art, Sands aligns Alison with Charles Manson while Rowland diagnoses her as a nymphomaniac. Taking Alison to be a real woman thus sustains an argument that she is disturbed enough to commit murder, just as can inventing for her a tragically disappointed girlhood. But these moves misapprehend the kind of reality that fictional characters enjoy. Alison does not have a complete existence "before" or "behind" the poetry. She exists as her spoken text calls her into being. However lifelike the poetry makes her, we should not imagine that she has a still deeper life that we can recover by any stretch of critical ingenuity.

Indeed, and ironically, taking the *Wife of Bath's Prologue* as an instance of "the human psyche responding to circumstance"[8] leads Alison's accusers to assessments as negative and extreme as those of the exegetical critics against whom they often define their endeavor. For D. W. Robertson and his followers, Alison has little or no relation to living women; she is instead an "iconographic figure" of carnality, "the mouthpiece of a clerical sort of buffoonery," "an allegorical figure representing human carnality."[9] The exegetical critics believe that Chaucer draws an iconic Alison to further a philosophical argument, whereas the critics who accuse her of murder believe we should think of her as a disturbed woman—"the emasculating bitch, the frigid nymphomaniac, the Sadistic swinger."[10] I would argue that pressing her into an iconic frame and inflating her to fully human proportions distort alike her fictional identity and deprive her of her true existence as a literary character.

This hidden affinity between exegetical critics and those who accuse Alison of murder raises my second objection to the accusation: It necessitates an impoverished account of what Chaucer is doing in the *Wife of Bath's Prologue.* As one who could countenance the murder of her husband, Alison would be not just guilty of a great crime, she would embody the worst of the antifeminist charges detailed in Jankyn's book. Her accusers share this conviction with those who call her an icon. Rowland defines Alison in terms of medieval commonplaces and asserts that Chaucer's task is to make the commonplace "credible." Sherlock Holmes assures us that it is "obvious that the Wife is one of Chaucer's contributions to those satires against women beloved of the Middle Ages. . . . If, then, Chaucer was holding the Wife up as an example of what a woman should not be, it should not surprise us if he made her willing to cause the death of a husband."[11] If D. W. Robertson's theory of iconographic figures did not forbid the invention of a romantic girlhood or a criminal psychopathology for Alison, he might well have agreed that she shares homicide with her sisters in the tradition of clerical satire. For both sets of critics, the Wife is another exemplum for Jankyn's book, a wicked wife indeed.

Is the *Wife of Bath's Prologue* a remotivation of medieval commonplaces, a contribution to the antifeminist canon? I believe this is a partial and distorted version of the text. On this point I would like to call to the bar two character witnesses, both disarmingly affable and both more subtle than they care to appear, Dr. Watson and Geoffrey Chaucer. Watson suggests with some delicacy that Holmes suspects Alison due to his "imperfect sympathy for the opposite sex," and that Alison expresses concern for Jankyn's soul not because he was her partner in crime but "because she loved him."[12] Watson's observation of affective states provides more reliable data than all the circumstantial evidence gathered by Alison's accusers. It is not important to my case, though it does provide evidence of a circumstantial kind, that neither Chaucer's Clerk, nor the Merchant, nor the **"Envoy to Bukton"** expresses the least suspicion that Alison is homicidal. It *is* important that Alison's accusers identify her fully with the misogynist tradition of clerical satire: she is "woman as her own worst enemy"; "an example of what a woman should not be."[13] Chaucer's presentation of Alison, I submit, is more subtle than that.

To close this case, Chaucer might well testify that he does not aspire to be anthologized in Jankyn's book. Rather, he has dramatized that book's inertness, pastness, and univocal flatness, by placing it in the home of a still-fictional but comparatively reflective character who responds to its assertions about marriage. Alison's argument is notoriously illogical; she is constructed from the very tradition she opposes, and must assemble her defense of women from the clerical case against them. Chaucer seems to be asking: How would antifeminist literature sound, if the wives it describes could listen? How would the clerical authors look from the viewpoint of their own targets? At first Chaucer may have conceived the *Wife of Bath's Prologue* as a literary joke in which the women of satire simply talk back to their authors, but as he worked through the *Prologue,* Chaucer seems to have reached for more: Alison acquires emotions and reflections that have no place in the tradition, detaching her from clerical discourse and allowing her a critical perspective on it. The reflective awareness with which she speaks of the antifeminist tradition makes her *Prologue* far more than a mere rerun of the clerical case against women. Her searching contradictoriness does not come to rest in a final authorial judgment, and according to Leicester, "this lack of closure in the Wife's life and personality is, finally, an aspect of Chaucer's feminism."[14] Any reading that collapses the *Wife of Bath's Prologue* back into the antifeminist vision of "what a woman should not be" is crucially reductive—yet the move is inherent to arguing that Alison should be suspected of murdering her revelour.

Women and men of the jury: The case against Alison rests on two false apprehensions about her *Prologue.* First, her accusers claim that she is essentially human in the dimensions of her life and the constitution of her psyche, so that we may conjecture about her childhood and measure her by the standards of clinical psychology. The evidence so collected is inadmissible. A second misapprehension is that Alison merely fulfills antifeminist expectations rather than reassessing the tradition. This reading is critically disingenuous. Chaucer here investigates the limits of a tradition in which "no womman of no clerk is preysed" (D 706). Let us not imitate those clerks whose first premise is that "womman was the los of al mankynde" (D 720), a homicide from the

start. Let us rather listen to how Alison shakes the foundations of that belief, questioning its origins in celibacy and contrasting its simplicity to her own complexity. Let us now conclude our deliberations with a resounding "case dismissed."

Notes

1. Vernon Hall, Jr., "Sherlock Holmes and the Wife of Bath," *The Baker Street Journal* 3 (1948): 84-93 (quotation p. 85). Other articles accusing the Wife are: Doris Palomo, "The Fate of the Wife of Bath's 'Bad Husbands,'" *Chaucer Review* 9 (1974-75): 303-19; Beryl Rowland, "Chaucer's Dame Alys: Critics in Blunderland?" *Neuphilologische Mitteilungen* 73 (1972): 381-95; and "On the Timely Death of the Wife of Bath's Fourth Husband," *Archiv für das Studium der neueren Sprachen und Literaturen* 209 (1972-73): 273-82; Donald B. Sands, "The Non-Comic, Non-Tragic Wife: Chaucer's Dame Alys as Sociopath," *Chaucer Review* 12 (1977-78): 171-82. Chaucer quotations are from *The Riverside Chaucer,* ed. Larry D. Benson et al. (Boston, 1987). This paper was read to the Chaucer Division of the MLA, December 1986.

2. Palomo, pp. 304-05; see also pp. 311-12 on the conjectural identification of Jankyn the clerk with Jankyn the apprentice: "Once a puppy trailing at [Alison's] heels with that stupefied adoration of the boy just discovering the stirrings of sexuality and the excitement of beauty in woman, Jankyn at twenty has become a not very scrupulous college graduate looking for an easy way to get ahead in the world, willing to exploit the aging woman he once idolized." C. David Benson discusses the methodological problems of what he calls the "dramatic theory" in *Chaucer's Drama of Style: Poetic Variation and Contrast in the "Canterbury Tales"* (Chapel Hill, 1986), pp. 3-19.

3. Rowland, "Chaucer's Dame Alys," p. 389.

4. See note 2 above and H. Marshall Leicester, Jr., "The Art of Impersonation: A General Prologue to the *Canterbury Tales,*" *PMLA* 95 (1980): 213-24.

5. Rowland, "Timely Death," p. 274; "Chaucer's Dame Alys," p. 391.

6. Sands, p. 171.

7. Cf. Daniel M. Murtaugh, "Women and Geoffrey Chaucer," *ELH* 38 (1971): 483: "Like Frankenstein's monster she stands up and terrorizes her male creators with a thwarted plea for love."

8. Palomo, p. 314.

9. D. W. Robertson, Jr., *A Preface to Chaucer: Studies in Medieval Perspectives* (Princeton, 1962), pp. 317-31 (quotation at p. 330); David S. Reid,

"Crocodilian Humor: A Discussion of Chaucer's Wife of Bath," *Chaucer Review* 4 (1969-70): 80; Sarah Disbrow, "The Wife of Bath's Old Wives' Tale," *Studies in the Age of Chaucer* 8 (1986): 60.

10. Sands, p. 173, connecting Rowland's articles and his own.

11. Rowland, "Chaucer's Dame Alys," p. 385; Hall, p. 90.

12. Hall, pp. 91, 87.

13. Palomo, p. 318; Hall, p. 90. Chaucer's references to the Wife of Bath are in the *Clerk's Tale* (E 1170-73), *Merchant's Tale* (E 1685-87), and "Lenvoy de Chaucer a Bukton" (lines 29-30).

14. "Of a Fire in the Dark: Public and Private Feminism in the *Wife of Bath's Tale*," *Women's Studies* 11 (1984): 157-78 (quotation at p. 175). I discuss this paragraph's assertions more fully in "Alison's Incapacity and Poetic Instability in *The Wife of Bath's Tale*," *PMLA* 102 (1987): 20-28.

Elaine Tuttle Hansen (essay date 1988)

SOURCE: Hansen, Elaine Tuttle. "The Wife of Bath and the Mark of Adam." *Women's Studies* 15, no. 4 (1988): 399-416.

[*In the following essay, Hansen argues against viewing* The Wife of Bath's Tale *and* Prologue *as early feminist writing, but proposes that the texts permit scholars to study the role of women in the fourteenth century and their attempts to claim a type of self-definition within the limitations of language and society.*]

> The wyf of Bathe take I for auctrice
> þat womman han no ioie ne deyntee
> þat men sholde vp-on hem putte any vice.
>
> (Hoccleve, *Dialogus cum Amico*, c. 1422)[1]

From the early fifteenth century to the late twentieth, at least one fact about the elusive Wife of Bath has never been disputed: where they agree on nothing else, her numerous commentators, like Hoccleve, take the Wife "for auctrice," as "a woman whose opinion is accepted as authoritative."[2] Controversy over the precise meaning and value of the Wife's opinion effectively ensures her authoritative status, and now perhaps more than ever before she is a figure to be reckoned with by anyone interested in the history, both factual and literary, of women. Faced with the problem of women's absence and silence in the past, recent feminist historians and literary critics turn with enthusiasm to the Wife as a rare instance of woman as agent, speaker, and (most recently) reader.[3] More than any other well-known literary character, she is frequently compared with histori-

cally real personages, from Christine de Pisan to Simone de Beauvoir.[4] Where treated as a fictive character, she is often read in a sociological and historical context, as a sign of Chaucer's empathy with real women, and as a realistic, historically plausible foil to the idealized views of femininity found in prescriptive texts of the period, possibly even "a truly practicing feminist," and indubitably a survivor and a spokeswoman.[5] A few protests have been lodged against the seemingly incurable tendency to overly lifelike readings of the Wife of Bath, as well as the related assessments of her power, autonomy, and energy as a woman.[6] But if the Wife of Bath is merely a fictional female character, and not an attractive or "free" or even representative woman, then what more does the twentieth-century feminist critic have to say about her?

I want to answer that clearly rhetorical question in two phases here, as I reaffirm the importance of the Wife of Bath to feminist criticism and theory at the same time that I argue that we must not so readily take her as "auctrice," as a female speaker or subject or as a straightforward mimetic representation of any arguably "real" female experience. In the first phase of this argument, I offer a relatively conventional close reading of the poem, treating the Wife and other characters as if they were psychologically verisimilar human beings from whose reported speech and actions the audience of this text identifies and interprets a living self in a social context. I read this self, however, in a way that emphasizes its powerlessness, self-destructiveness, and silencing, and I argue that the Wife's discourse in **Prologue** and **Tale** belies her apparent garrulity, autonomy, and dominance. Even at this level of interpretation she paradoxically represents, I conclude, not the full and remarkable presence we have normally invested her with, but a dramatic and important instance of woman's silence and suppression in history and in language. In the second phase of my argument, I consider the implications of my insistence on the Wife's negation for our understanding of the literary inscription of prominent cultural myths about male authors and about women, in fiction and in fact.

Part I

"But she was somdel deef, and that was scathe."[7]

It is hardly necessary to rehearse the reasons why the Wife of Bath might well be read as a woman who defies the stereotype of the passive, submissive, and fundamentally silent female, particularly as this ideal is celebrated in the antifeminist heroines who bracket her own performance, the Man of Law's long-suffering Constance and the Clerk's patient Griselda. Against the background they figure, the Wife stands out even more prominently as the chatterbox, the gossip, the obsessive prattler, a type prominent in medieval literature and given mythical stature in another of the *Canterbury Tales,* the Merchant's, when Proserpina debates the woman question with her husband Pluto and is made to proclaim: "I am a womman, nedes moot I speke, / Or elles swelle til myn herte breke" (IV. 2305-06). The Wife may also be viewed as the female storyteller, overtly challenging and at the same time emulating both male authority and the male author, and presenting us with one of our earliest literary images of the female as verbal artist. Sandra Gilbert and Susan Gubar's description of the wicked Queen in Snow White might serve equally well to characterize the Wife: "a plotter, a plot-maker, a schemer, a witch, an artist, an impersonator, a woman of almost infinite creative energy, witty, wily, and self-absorbed as all artists traditionally are."[8] In her *Prologue,* moreover, which is twice as long as her *Tale,* the Wife lays claim to the power of language to control the behavior of others. Through verbal attack, as she alleges and demonstrates, she gained and kept the upper hand in her first three marriages. She views words, like sex and money, as strategic weapons in the war between the sexes, and she presents her verbal tactics as repayment in kind against the men in her life: 'I quitte hem word for word . . . I ne owe hem nat a word that it nys quit" (III. 422-25). One might well argue that she successfully frees herself and repays the whole antifeminist tradition by turning the tables on male authority, parodying its rhetorical strategies and thus revealing its prejudice and absurdity by impersonating the male voice.[9]

But this view of the Wife as triumphant and powerful, often accompanied by the assumption that Chaucer intends to criticize or at least poke fun at antifeminist arguments, is only partially accurate, and needs to be qualified, as other readers have suggested, by a recognition of the Wife's limitations, which the *Prologue* and *Tale* make equally clear. Despite her ability and eagerness to speak, the Wife of Bath is not essentially more free or self-determined or able to "communicate" than the good, silent woman, like Griselda or Constance, and her own words help us to understand that this is so.

Throughout her *Prologue,* the Wife's language reflects precisely the power differential overtly dramatized in other of the *Tales,* especially the Clerk's. The first 170 lines of the *Prologue* consist mostly of direct and indirect quotation from both biblical and patristic texts, and so they are punctuated with tags that taken together underscore the gender of official speakers and critics: "quod he," "thus seyde he," "he speketh," "th'apostel seith," "Mark telle kan," etc. Although she begins to speak of her own "experience"—she has "had" five husbands—only nine lines into her speech she cites her first authority, and the terms in which she does are so particularly salient. "But me was toold, certeyn, nat longe agoon is . . ." (III. 9), she says, that biblical injunction forbids multiple marriage. The sudden ap-

pearance of the adversative at the beginning of line 9 immediately signals the oppugnant stance she takes throughout the rest of the *Prologue.* The use of the passive transformation, "me was told," puts the Wife first in the surface structure of the sentence; she is indeed self-absorbed and attempts to use her words, like her church offering, to affirm her preeminence. But in the deep structure of the sentence, "Someone told me," the Wife is the object of the verb, or in case grammar terms the "patient." Magically transformed, like the Old Hag in her *Tale,* the Wife takes a place in the surface structure of the sentence that disguises her fundamental status, seen only in the base sentence, as a person acted upon rather than acting, a human being whose behavior is subject to the criticism and correction of some higher authority. Furthermore, although later in the *Prologue* the Wife repeatedly identifies the "auctoritees" against whom she argues, the subject in the deep structure of this sentence remains unexpressed. As the audience would presumably know, the antifeminist argument that follows in the succeeding "that" clause comes from St. Jerome; but it is not clear whether the Wife has it directly from his writings or, as is more likely, from some male reader of Jerome like her fifth husband. All we learn from the *Prologue* is that someone, at some unspecified time in the relatively recent past ("nat longe agoon is"), told the Wife that her behavior was immoral, and she does not say who—perhaps she has forgotten or does not wish to identify a living critic, or perhaps she does not know exactly who, just as she cannot say quite when: no one told her, and everyone told her. The authority against which she rebels is not that of any single person; there is no tyrannical lord in her life as there is in Griselda's. The Wife is defending herself against a much vaguer and more mysterious force of social disapproval, powerfully unnamed and unnameable, and her later attempts to meet specific arguments are self-defeating efforts to pin down and triumph over that generalized, mystifying, and hence invincible hostility that she meets from all sides.

This crucial vagueness and uncertainty, this Orwellian mystification of the power behind language, is further reflected in the opening lines as the Wife claims that she does not fully understand the meaning, although she understands the hostility and disapproval, of the arguments against her. She goes on to cite the highest authority of "Jhesus, God and man": tellingly, the story of Jesus she relates is one that reveals not his loving-kindness, but his apparently gratuitous reproof of the Samaritan woman. The Wife's professed inability to understand the meaning of his rebuke serves both to challenge its authority and to reveal her own nebulous insecurity:

> What that he mente therby, I kan nat seyn;
> But that I axe, why that the fifthe man
> Was noon housbonde to the Samaritan?

How manye myghte she have in mariage?

(III. 20-23)

Note that she asks her bold questions of no one in particular, and of everyone. We see again that generalized feeling that someone out there knows more than she does. Immediately afterwards, instead of rejecting authority that she does not understand or that conflicts with her own experience (whatever that may be), she proceeds to choose another "gentil" text to support her argument: "God bad us for to wexe and multiplye" (III. 28). This is all, of course, strategic on her part and very funny. It also underlines a serious truth about the nature of power in her world: God's characteristic speech act is a command; created in His image, all men, even Christ, speak sharp words to women, for reasons that are purposefully obscure and obscured; and the Wife, along with all women, is "told" by received opinion that her behavior is wrong. She struggles to understand why, she seems to want both to subvert and to be right and "good,"[10] and so she asks questions and tries to find or make authorities that speak on her side, and those of us who are not horrified by her blasphemy will admire her resilience and persistence and courage. We also see, however, that as long as she accepts (or, what amounts to the same thing, attempts to invert) the basic power differential and the obfuscation of power reflected and supported by the language she uses, her struggles are in vain. This protofeminist, this "archewyf" and "auctrice" is not even as critical of her true masters, as awake to her less obvious but equally fundamental subjection, as patient Griselda.

The rest of the *Prologue* provides evidence that supports this reading. In telling us about her first three old husbands, the Wife quotes herself, demonstrating how she verbally attacked them and always won; but ironically, since her method was to accuse her husbands of standard antifeminist attitudes, for yet another 150 lines we are subjected (as she was) to a further deafening stream of misogynist platitudes, here from folk rather than learned tradition. The repeated "thou seist" tag again necessitated by the quotation within quotation emphasizes the fact that she is fighting against, and at some level knows she is fighting against, the power of male voices to control her own behavior. Again ironically, of course, all is false; her first three husbands were not bright enough to talk this much, but she is trying to pin down that invisible and omnipresent power that she knows will control her if she gives it a chance. And with her fifth husband the Wife herself is aptly repaid for all her earlier deceits. She undergoes a perverse version of wish-fulfillment—an experience she uses and revises when she tells her *Tale*—when the story she invented to control her first three husbands comes true. Jankyn really does attack her, that is, with antifeminist doctrine, this time of a learned and hence even more authoritative variety. In the final section of

her *Prologue,* as she describes the contents of his antifeminist miscellany by quoting from it at great length, the Wife again gives the stronger voice in the text, as in reality, to the opposition.

One might argue that all this quotation merely shows us what a woman is up against and therefore highlights the Wife's victory over it, but it is also essential to remember that throughout her performance the Wife, both consciously and unconsciously, endorses the antifeminist stereotypes she cites, proving again that, as Fredric Jameson claims, "transgressions, presupposing the laws or norms or taboos against which they function, thereby end up precisely reconfirming those laws."[11] She boasts, for instance, of her feminine powers to lie and deceive and manipulate men, and this unwitting self-deprecation, I suggest, is not very different from the idealized statements of victimization that "good" women, like Constance or Griselda, are willing and even eager to utter. Both the dumb woman and the wily, witty, creative woman live in a world where protest against received opinion is normally silenced and dialogue precluded; and so the patient and the impatient woman—the norm and the transgression—are two sides of the same coin, able to see themselves and speak for themselves only in terms provided by the dominant language and mythology of their culture. The Wife's loss of hearing is caused, or so we are told at the end of her *Prologue,* by her one silent action, her violent attempt to destroy Jankyn's book, the written word that has made her what she is. This cryptic, unsettling, and foreshortened drama of role reversal, mock murder, and humiliation discloses the mutual degradation that marital relations entail in her world; and the Wife's mutilation serves as a climactic symbol of the simultaneously dumbing and deafening effect of the dominant discourse and the social structure it enforces.

The Wife's *Tale* has been seen as an antidote to the use of male authority and endless quotation in the *Prologue,* but on closer examination things are not really very different. For a while, the tables do seem genuinely turned: the *Tale* begins with a casual rape, but the rapist is sentenced to death and the queen (thanks to the "grace" of the king) is granted power over his life. She gives him a twelve-month and a day to find out what women want most, and now the story sounds like the pronouns have been reversed. The Knight can save his neck if he finds out what the opposite sex really desires; the price he is asked to pay for the correct answer is one more often exacted from women: he is required to satisfy the lawful sexual appetites of someone old and physically repulsive to his suddenly refined sensibilities. The heroine of the *Tale,* an Elf Queen disguised as an Old Hag, is a powerful artist, able to transform herself and gain mastery over her husband through her wise and "gentil" (and thoroughly orthodox) speech. But the ending of the *Tale* safely returns us to a more familiar plot, and a more suitable alignment of the sexes. The rapist not only saves his life but is rewarded by the promise of an unfailingly beautiful, faithful, and obedient wife, as the Hag who gave him the answer, who had all the power, gives it up, and transforms herself into a Constance or Griselda. The denouement reveals that the Wife herself, at some level, has little confidence in the female's powers of speech. Although the Hag/Elf Queen, like the Queen in Snow White, has the creative drive of an artist, it is thwarted and used self-destructively to transform herself into what every man wants most, a woman "bothe fair and good" (III. 1241) who "obeyed hym in every thyng / That myghte doon hym plesance or likyng" (III. 1255-56). The Hag chooses that silent beauty which only in a fairy tale is anything but fleeting and dangerous, and with the "happy ending" the heroine relinquishes her power and dissolves into literal silence and alleged submission, the archetypal feminine transformation.

The Wife, of course, does not; she has the last word, and I think we can begin to see why that word must be a curse on men:

> And eek I praye Jhesu shorte hir lyves
> That wol nat be governed by hir wyves;
> And olde and angry nygardes of dispence,
> God sende hem soone verray pestilence!

(III. 1261-64)

The speaker who utters a curse assumes, as the Wife always does, the power of language, in a literal rather than a metaphorical sense. She wishes to injure the addressee, or the person or persons cursed, and reduces the object of her imprecation to linguistic powerlessness: there is nothing you should or can say in response to a curse, no way to ward it off, and in fact you do not even have to hear or know about it for it to be effective. Its efficaciousness depends not, however, on the speaker's power, but on the power of some external, presumably divine or supernatural force whose aid is invoked for the purposes of simply destroying the opposition and closing off communication. The curse, at once vague and all encompassing, is only a response in kind, then, to the hostility the Wife meets on all sides, and an application of the repressive training a patriarchal culture has given her in the power of language. It is by the same token not a response, but an involuntary, extraverbal cry of anger that implicitly denies the autonomy of both speaker and addressee and undercuts the Wife's putative attempt to speak of and for herself.[12]

PART II

> Who peyntede the leon, tel me who?
> By God! if wommen hadde written stories
> As clerkes han withinne hire oratories,
> They wolde han writen of men moore wikkednesse
> Than al the mark of Adam may redresse.

(III. 692-96)

In any discussion of the Wife of Bath as a speaking subject, the Wife's intriguing question—who painted the lion? from whose point of view is this story being told?—requires close attention. Here the character is made to allude self-reflexively to the problem that I have been arguing is most central to feminist interpretations of this text, to the actual silence and absence of the Wife and "woman." If women had ever authored stories, she points out, they would be very different ones (although actually, as she imagines it here, they would also be much the same—equally determined, that is, by the anxieties of gender difference and the resultant competition between men and women). We thus have a female character indirectly but unequivocally reminding us at the very center of her fictional narrative not only that an author's gender always colors the written (and spoken) word, but also that this text affords no exception to the rule that women have *not* written the story. A male author created the Wife, and "her" teasing, playful, characteristically hostile and arguably unconscious reference to this fact mirrors and confirms what we have seen in both the *Prologue* and the *Tale*: a feminine monstrosity who is the product of the patriarchal authority she ineffectively and only superficially rebels against. It is an apparently paradoxical but finally explicable and revealing fact that the one woman in the *Canterbury Tales* who is so often viewed, for good or bad, as a survivor is the one who reminds the attentive listener that "she," like every female character in the male-authored text, never existed at all; in an important sense the Wife is not only just as powerless and silent, but also just as unreal, just as unrepresentable, as a saintly Constance or a patient Griselda.

The passage on the painting of lions reminds us, in other words, that the Wife's actual *failure* to speak of and for herself or "woman" is a symptom of the *impossibility* of her doing so, by virtue of her gendered exclusion from the role of storyteller. This reminder ensures at every level the Wife's and woman's negation, as even the most wordy and verisimilar of female characters is (de)constructed by the text as that which is not actually speaking and not actually being represented, that which stands outside the bounds of language and literary convention altogether. And it is precisely this fact, I contend, that makes the Wife of Bath an important figure for feminist analysis. Understood as a construction of the text, the fact that, as Marshall Leicester has put it, "there is no Wife of Bath"[13] need not lead us to conclude that this character is another instance of woman's power *or* powerlessness, in history or in literature, or of the author's feminism *or* antifeminism. Instead, it can help us to read this complicated, convoluted text for the insights it affords us into the ways and means by which the literary tradition has maneuvered within, accounted for, and profited from the socio-gender system as we know it. In particular, I would stress the way in which my reading challenges two cultural myths: the myth of "Chaucer"'s special sympathy or empathy with women, and the myth of gender difference itself, to which Chaucer's works give such prominence.

To address the first point, the vexed question of Chaucer's apparent fellow-feeling for women, I want to consider two arguments that seem to support the notion that Chaucer sympathizes not merely with his female characters, but with the particular insights of late twentieth-century feminist criticism into the social construction of "woman." First, the position of the feminine exemplified by the Wife—a position finally outside the bounds, as we have seen, of the representable—may be viewed, like all marginal positions, as a potentially subversive one. Above all, the enforced silence of women and the impossibility of representing a "real" female speaker threatens both the author's control and the audience's ability to understand the character and the poem: the evanescence of the Wife and "woman"'s position marks the limits, in other words, of both representation and interpretation.[14] To argue that we can never know "who she is" because she is "not anyone" seems to state the obvious and beg the question, but it also calls into question the effectuality of precisely the kind of reading—or its opposite—that I have offered in the first part of this essay. Viewing the Wife as a psychologically verisimilar, speaking self, such readings allow us to assume a momentary, illusory power over the character and the world, to situate ourselves, as Leicester again puts it, in "a position superior to her from which she can be fixed and placed, understood and dismissed." And it may be argued that the text itself, by inscribing the silence of the Wife as / and "woman" in the many ways I have suggested, refuses to let us rest securely and comfortably in that dominant position, and hence that Chaucer at least tacitly advocates an anti-authoritarian stance that the modern feminist reader must value.[15]

A case might be made for Chaucer's allegedly feminist leanings, moreover, based on a related issue: the similarities between the position of women and the apparent position of the poet himself. As all readers of this poem know, the *Canterbury Tales* as a whole seems structured to highlight and even exaggerate a situation common to all (literary) texts: stories both reveal and create tellers; no tale can be interpreted except as the product of a human speaker, and yet that same human speaker behind each tale is also firmly identified as the fictional creation of yet another speaker. There is a possibility of infinite regression, a dramatization of the *mise en abyme,* and hence a fundamental and threatening absence of identifiable authority again in this situation that leads to a well-known interpretive problem: how do we know where "Chaucer the poet" (not to speak of "Chaucer the man") is at any moment? Or who, at any point, is speaking? The voice of the poet

creates, at best, a slippery, ironic persona who offers us—like the Wife of Bath—someone who is not really there, only "the traces of a presence that asserts its simultaneous absence."[16]

Like the Wife: the figure of the poet and the woman, then, are alike in many ways. At the level of historical realism, they may seem particularly homologous in their (in)subordinate position. Recent scholars have suggested that the medieval poet may well be understood in terms of the ambivalent, insecure, and inferior position that he held in the fourteenth-century court;[17] as marginalized and subordinated figures, poets and women alike may be simultaneously complicitous with and suspicious of both the ideology that tries but fails to define them and of the audience to and for whom they speak. Both the Wife and "Chaucer" tell lies that subvert the authority of the word to speak any truth at all, stories that threaten any correspondence between utterance and meaning and that undermine orthodox assumptions about the nature of intention and identity. In their silence and absence, both poet and woman stand together, by this reading, in the position of the limit of that which can be represented. And again as verisimilar selves they seem to share an ideologically sanctioned fantasy of silent submission and wordless transformation that their excessive fluency covers and belies: the "happy ending" of the Wife's *Tale,* although qualified by both her *Prologue* and her curse, seems oddly analogous to the poet's famous **"Retraction,"** problematized by its uncomfortable relation to all of the work that precedes it.

But here the provocative analogy between poet and "woman," "Chaucer" and Wife, may break down in a way I find particularly interesting, and the case for Chaucer's sympathy or empathy with women becomes at best moot. The Wife's curse once more is telling: it functions as a commentary on her own fantasy for which we find no counterpart following the **Retraction.** Chaucer's strategy in the *Canterbury Tales* seems to involve the displacement of the commitment that speaking entails onto other voices in an attempt to remain as free of the constraints of language, as powerfully muted and unnamed and unspoken as possible. The poet does exercise (to this day, one might argue) the power of silence, and the Retraction in a sense simply reinforces that silence without deconstructing the work it ostensively "retracts." The figure of the male poet constructed by the text as a whole, then, can only caution us against thinking we can know anything at all about the author— including his sexual politics.

The Wife's curse, on the other hand, reveals that the female character created by Chaucer retains a paradoxical and fatal faith in language itself that is in practice self-destructive: invoking the power of language to destroy rather than create, she at once discloses and betrays her own commitment to speaking, validates the patriarchal authority she seeks to resist, and renounces the power of silence that the poet seems more able to exploit. From this perspective, the Wife's performance demonstrates that Chaucer's "woman" suffers from a delusion that the implied author does not reproduce. Her curse in particular serves to distinguish her quite dramatically from the figure of the male poet, and more importantly to defuse the very threat of women's silence and unrepresentability that the poet both acknowledges and strategically counters. The lesson of the poem seems to be that a naive faith in language does not serve women well because language is, according to the ***Canterbury Tales,*** an instrument for reproducing the conventions that constrain and deny both the experience of women and the representation of that experience. But this is just the lesson that the Wife, unlike the poet, is not allowed to learn or profit from: as learned in "scole-matere" (III. 1272) as any clerk, she cannot escape the convention of the happy ending that legitimates the knight's originally illicit and violent desire by subordinating and silencing the Hag/Elf Queen, any more than she can escape the need to transgress and thus reinforce the laws of language and the myths of culture that at once condemn her to speak and silence her.

Like the more local myth of this male author's special sympathy with women, the larger (and apparently contradictory) myth of woman's difference, I suggest, is promoted by the ***Canterbury Tales*** and Chaucer's other works in order to counter another threat to the male poet and his male audience: the threat that men too may be constrained and even constituted by the socio-gender system and by their sexuality, the aspect of experience most overtly affected by notions of gender.[18] Through the creation of female caricatures like the Wife of Bath or her foils, Constance and Griselda, the text confirms women's difference from men and defines "woman" as a question, an issue, a conundrum. Women in Chaucer's poems, in other words, by virtue of the complexity and exaggeration of their culturally feminine traits, stand out as problems for the male characters, and for the audience interpreting the text. The chief difference I have focused on here, because it is so prominent in the text, is the constraint imposed by women's gendered position on speech itself: the fact that she is woman precedes and invalidates the possibility that the Wife or any other female character might be, like a man, a speaker. But closer inspection of the male characters in the poem reveals that they do not in fact have "free" access to speech, that they too are troubled by the issue of gender; and in fact the ***Tales*** as a whole dramatize the impossibility of constructing any self, female or male, prior to or apart from considerations of gender. I cannot begin to suggest in any detail how this claim is supported and amplified in specific cases, how it opens up, as I believe it does, interpretive space at the very center of every tale and its teller. But I ask you to think

of the ways in which, for figures like the clerk, the Knight, the Monk, the Nun's Priest, and the Pardoner, for example, the broad concept of gender serves as a locus of formative and irresolvable conflict: between the individual and the group, between wife and husband, self and other, private and public, freedom and imprisonment, tyranny and servitude, experience and authority. The pilgrims (and the characters in their tales) all reveal, I submit, what is more usually presented in western culture as a specifically feminine pathology. The Wife of Bath and "woman"'s foregrounded difference, a result of gender, gives way to a subground of sameness, as all of the speakers in the poem are constrained by their gender roles, suffer the anxiety of sexual difference, and have (or present) only an unstable sense of "self," riddled with contradiction. The varieties of *maistrie* that these fragmentary and elusive selves seek cover (more and less successfully) their unilateral and ideologically sanctioned desire to submit to someone or something that will define and recognize them and console them for their mortality.

And what I am calling, for the sake of this argument, the pilgrim's femininity is manifest, above all, in their problematic relation to language. Real and fictive women, this poem finally may suggest, are not excluded from some power of language to which men have access. As a donnée of the literary form of the ***Tales,*** pilgrims of either sex are both "speaker" and "spoken";[19] all human beings in the world of this text are, as a precondition of their existence, the "kind of fiction" usually associated in western culture with women "in that they are defined by others as components of the language and thought of others."[20] If the garrulous woman and the silent woman are, as I have argued, two sides of the same coin, it is the common medium of exchange in the pilgrim economy. Like the Wife, all of the pilgrims exhibit at some level an aggressive refusal to be silenced at the same time that they act out their communal fantasy of mute submission. From the outset, this essential contradiction in the human relation to language underlies the whole enterprise of the poem in ways that have not been adequately examined. Note, for example, how the Host's initial proposal of the story-telling game appeals to the pilgrims on two apparently incompatible counts: he offers relief for the life-threatening dis-ease of silence—"confort ne myrthe is noon / To ride by the weye doumb as a stoon" (I. 773-74; remember Constance, "doumb . . . as a tree," II. 1055); and at the same time his assumption of authority simultaneously delivers them from the burden of self-expression or self-determination and robs them of their voices. "Hoold up youre hondes, withouten moore speche" (I. 783), he commands, and they silently obey.

The Wife of Bath thus tells us a great deal about the power and tenacity of the myth of feminine difference, where this myth is successfully aligned with radical instability, indeterminacy, and internal contradiction, and above all with the impossibility of becoming a speaking subject who is not also spoken. Through the text's construction of this notorious female character, these essentially human problems and anxieties are effectively displaced onto "woman," and the feminine gender is what we may usefully term "marked," in various senses of the word. In the language of linguistics, "markedness" refers to the fact that one of a minimal pair may be more specifically characterized or delimited in its usage than the other; in the minimal pair constituted by masculine and feminine in our culture, the latter, in the text as in the world, bears an identifying "mark," a visible sign and even a predestined character, it seems, of sexual difference. This markedness by virtue of gender is inscribed in English in the prominent fact of the generic masculine, and linguists educe from their study of this and other features of the language precisely what we have found in the Wife's characterization and its subsequent interpretations: "a tendency, on the one hand, to equate humanity with the male sex and, on the other hand, to assume that femaleness defines women, whose individuality becomes submerged in categorizing principles that treat all women as identical."[21] "Femaleness defines women": so too females, marked by their gender in ways that males in western culture seem not to be, are kept within "marks," limits and boundaries that define and contain their "individuality," and the Wife turns out to be a reflection of "categorizing principles" rather than a speaking subject. Wearing and reproducing the "mark," the brand, the inscription, of the gender system as we know it, she, like any female, moreover, becomes the "mark" at which hostile forces aim, the object, the target of antifeminist attack.

An awareness of both the overt markedness and the covert universalization of the feminine in the *Canterbury Tales* may be helpful in explaining the obstacles that impede any search for what Arlyn Diamond aptly calls "Chaucer's Women and Women's Chaucer." On the one hand, as I have suggested, Chaucer's essentially anti-romantic conception of the engendered self and his understanding of the tyranny of linguistic and literary conventions may readily appear, especially when we are focusing on his portraits of women, like sympathy or even identification with the female characters and the feminine bind. So too the form of the *Canterbury Tales* (as "pluralized discourse") may seem to undermine a masculine teleology and even suggest the open-ended, plural, anti-authoritarian, "irrational" qualities of what in the late twentieth century has been called *écriture féminine*. And the poet's own self-dramatized and self-defensive refusal to take an authoritative stance (or any stance at all) may seem to subvert "the orthodoxies of literary and sexual authority,"[22] as Lee Patterson has recently argued, so that traditional criticism can continue to read Chaucer's invisibility, as Virginia

Woolf read Shakespeare's, as a sign of the great artist's "incandescence," his aloofness from polemic and prejudice: "his grudges and spites and antipathies are hidden from us . . . Therefore his poetry flows from him free and unimpeded."[23]

But what is "hidden" is precisely what still exists, and may be found; and a feminist perspective enables us to perceive that sympathy or identification with the position of women, in the case of the *Canterbury Tales,* need in no way actually depose or disrupt the unimpeded flow of a powerful misogynistic code. The complex and contradictory myths about women in western culture, enacted so prominently and successfully by the female characters in the poem, simultaneously manage and account for the suppression of the principle worked out by the position of the feminine and thus the "individuality" and humanity of any female. We cannot expect to find a woman speaking in the poem; how could she? Why would we? "There is no Wife of Bath," and a feminist criticism that seeks no more and no less than the "authoritative" voices of women will find itself excluded from a poem by, about, and for men. As Patterson again reminds us, "the manner and mode of the Wife of Bath's appearance is the crucial move in a self-reflexive examination that occupies the poet in Fragments II and III [and I would add IV, which includes the *Clerk's Tale*], a scrutiny that is directed towards precisely the maleness of his imagination—towards, that is, his career as a poet of women."[24] Women (the fact and the fiction) are central, indeed indispensable to the careers of male poets and their "efforts at poetic self-definition": this is not news. But when we focus on the centrality of the thematic of the feminine and interpret its textual manifestations as evidence of the female character's authoritative status or of the male poet's feminism or wise humanism, dispassion, or incandescence, we miss or dismiss too quickly what a feminist analysis of the *Canterbury Tales* discloses about the structures of antifeminism, about the displacement and usurpation of female silence, and about the hidden "mark of Adam," the fact that males are also constrained and constituted by gender.

Notes

1. Cited in Caroline F. E. Spurgeon, *Five Hundred Years of Chaucer Criticism and Allusion, 1357-1900* (London: Cambridge University Press, 1925), Vol. 1, p. 33.

2. *Middle English Dictionary,* B. 1, p. 515.

3. For discussion of the Wife as an "aural reader," see Susan Schibanoff, "Taking the Gold out of Egypt: The Art of Reading as a Woman," in *Gender and Reading,* ed. Elizabeth A. Flynn and Patrocinio P. Schweickart (Baltimore and London: John Hopkins Press, 1986), pp. 83-106.

4. Schibanoff actually compares the Wife with the quasi-autobiographical narrator "Christine" of the *Book of the City of Women.* Lawrence Lipking, "Aristotle's Sister: A Poetics of Abandonment," *Critical Inquiry,* 19 (1983), 61-81, puts the Wife in the company of women writers ranging from Sappho and Lady Murasaki to Virginia Woolf and de Beauvoir.

5. I oversimplify by grouping all of the following critics together, but the kind of recent scholarship I have in mind is exemplified in works such as: W. F. Bolton, "The Wife of Bath: Narrator as Victim," *Women and Literature,* 1 (1980), 54-65; Mary Carruthers, "The Wife of Bath and the Painting of Lions," *PMLA,* 94 (1979), 209-22; Arlyn Diamond, "Chaucer's Women and Women's Chaucer," in *The Authority of Experience,* ed. Diamond and Lee Edwards (Amherst: Univ. of Massachusetts Press, 1977), pp. 60-83; Robert W. Hanning, "From Eva and Ave to Eglentyne and Alisoun: Chaucer's Insight into the Roles Women Play," *Signs,* 2 (1977), 580-99; Kenneth Oberempt, "Chaucer's Anti-Misogynist Wife of Bath," *Chaucer Review,* 10 (1976), 287-302; and Hope Phyllis Weissman, "Antifeminism and Chaucer's Characterization of Women," in *Geoffrey Chaucer: A Collection of Original Articles,* ed. George D. Economou (NY: McGraw Hill, 1975), pp. 93-110. Maureen Fries refers to the Wife as "a truly practicing feminist" in "'Slydynge of Corage': Chaucer's Criseyde as Feminist and Victim," in *The Authority of Experience,* p. 59.

6. See, for instance, David S. Reid, "Crocodilian Humor: A Discussion of Chaucer's Wife of Bath," *Chaucer Review,* 4 (1970), 73-89; Ellen Schauber and Ellen Spolsky, "The Consolation of Alison: The Speech Acts of the Wife of Bath," *Centrum,* 5 (1977), 20-34; and Wayne Shumaker, "Alisoun in Wander-land: A Study in Chaucer's Mind and Literary Method," *ELH,* 18 (1961), 77-89.

7. "General Prologue," 446; all subsequent quotations from the *Canterbury Tales* are taken from F. N. Robinson, ed., *The Works of Geoffrey Chaucer,* (Boston: Houghton Mifflin, 1961), and cited parenthetically by part and line.

8. *The Madwoman in the Attic* (New Haven: Yale Univ. Press, 1979), p. 30.

9. For this view see Marjorie M. Malvern, "'Who peyntede the leon, tel me who?' Rhetorical and Didactic Roles Played by an Aesopic Fable in the *Wife of Bath's Prologue,*" *Studies in Philology,* 80 (1983), 238-52; Barry Sanders, "Chaucer's Dependence on Sermon Structure in the *Wife of Bath's Prologue* and *Tale.*" *Studies in Medieval Culture,* 4 (1974), 437-45; and James Spisak, "Antifemi-

nism Bridled: Two Rhetorical Contexts," *Neuphilologische Mitteilungen,* 81 (1980), 150-60.

10. Gloria K. Shapiro makes this point in "Dame Alice as Deceptive Narrator," *Chaucer Review,* 6 (1971), 130-41.

11. *The Political Unconscious* (Ithaca: Cornell Univ. Press, 1981), p. 68.

12. See Margaret Homans, "'Her Very Own Howl': The Ambiguities of Representation in Recent Women's Fiction," *Signs,* 9 (1983), 186-205, for an analogous discussion in a very different historical period of the question of women's relation to language and the specific issue of what happens (in literary texts, at least) when women fail or destroy themselves in their attempts to appropriate the dominant discourse and are left to utter a 'referentless' cry of rage that takes them outside discourse.

13. "Of a fire in the dark: Public and private feminism in the *Wife of Bath's Tale,*" *Women's Studies,* 11 (1984), 157-78.

14. Compare Shoshana Felman's discussion of Balzac's "The Girl with the Golden Eyes," in "Rereading Femininity," *Yale French Studies,* 62 (1981), 19-44: "It is thus not only the conventional authority of sovereign masculinity that Paquita's femininity threatens but the authority of any representative code as such, the smooth functioning of the very institution of representation" (32).

15. This is Marshall Leicester's reading of Chaucer's sexual politics in "Of a fire in the dark"; the quotation in the preceding sentence is found on pp. 161-62.

16. Leicester, "The Art of Impersonation: A General Prologue to the *Canterbury Tales,*" *PMLA,* 95 (1980), 220.

17. See R. F. Green, *Poets and Princepleasers* (Toronto: Univ. of Toronto Press, 1980); Richard Waswo, "The Narrator of *Troilus and Criseyde,*" *ELH,* 50 (1983), 1-25; and for a comparable argument based on a later continental situation, Paul Zumthor, "From (Hi)Story to Poem, or the Paths of Pun: The Grands Rhetoriqueurs of Fifteenth-Century France," *New Literary History,* 10 (1979) 231-62.

18. The understanding of "gender" and the "sociogender system" upon which my reading is based comes from Gayle Rubin, "The Traffic in Women: Notes on the 'Political Economy' of Sex," in *Towards an Anthropology of Women,* ed. Rayna R. Reiter (NY and London: Monthly Review Press, 1975), 157-210.

19. The contradiction of women that Levi-Strauss notes, cited by Rubin, p. 201.

20. Thus Myra Jehlen describes the situation that women writers must deal with as a "precondition" to their writing, in "Archimedes and the Paradox of Feminist Criticism." *Signs,* 6 (1981), 575-601.

21. Sally McConnell-Ginet, "Linguistics and the Feminist Challenge," in *Women and Language in Literature and Society,* ed. McConnell-Ginet, Ruth Borker, and Nelly Furman (NY: Praeger, 1980), p. 9. See also Monique Wittig, "The Mark of Gender," in *The Poetics of Gender,* ed. Nancy K. Miller (NY: Columbia Univ. Press, 1986), pp. 63-73.

22. Lee Patterson, "'For the Wyves Love of Bathe': Feminine Rhetoric and Poetic Resolution in the *Roman de la Rose* and the *Canterbury Tales,*" *Speculum,* 58 (1983), 656-95.

23. *A Room of One's Own,* (NY and London: Harcourt, Brace Jovanovitch, 1929), pp. 58-59.

24. Patterson, p. 687.

Alcuin Blamires (essay date 1989)

SOURCE: Blamires, Alcuin. "The Wife of Bath and Lollardy." *Medium Aevum* 58, no. 2 (1989): 224-42.

[*In the following essay, Blamires probes the similar themes in the anti-authority tirade in* The Wife of Bath's Prologue *and Lollardy, a religious movement that was often seen as anti-church and heretical.*]

I

'Re-readings' of Chaucer conducted according to radical socio-historical principles will characteristically maintain that **The Canterbury Tales** represents (as Stephen Knight puts it) 'a continuing and tense engagement with its period', and that individual tales are 'potent realizers' of conflicts within late fourteenth-century society.[1] However, in view of Chaucer's ostensible reluctance to offer direct comment on such upheavals as the Peasants' Revolt, interpretations offered by critics of that persuasion frequently strain credulity: they betray a programmatic urge to recruit both local detail and larger narrative as witnesses to an ideological preoccupation ascribed a priori to the poet.

Knight's own contention (drawing on an incidental remark by Robertson) that attitudes developed in the **Wife of Bath's Prologue** bear some relationship to those cultivated by the heretical movement known as Lollardy, may seem at first sight an example of ideological wish-fulfilment founded on nothing more concrete than sweepingly defined 'convergence'. Knight claims that since the Wife attacks clerical authority and makes 'a stand against an oppressive church with learning and vigour', her approach is therefore 'convergent with a major force of innovation [i.e. Lollardy], one that was not in the period readily distinguished from civil dissent'. From this alleged convergence we get quickly to the stirring—if indigestible—proposition that she is a 'dissenting female industrialist quasi-Lollard'.[2]

I take it that if Knight could have aligned the Wife with Lollardy less loosely than that, he would certainly have done so. Since such an alignment will be explored in this article, it is as well to acknowledge immediately that there are good reasons why she could never be supposed a comprehensive representative of Lollardy. For example she seems to approve of pilgrimages, which the sect condemned; and she is given to swearing, which Lollards also abhorred, as Chaucer reminds us in the tale-link known as the *Epilogue of the Man of Law's Tale*: here the Host smells a Lollard in the wind as soon as the Parson ventures to condemn one of his hearty oaths (II 1166-73). Incidentally this is Chaucer's only overt reference to Lollardy, though it has sometimes been held to confirm a hypothesis that the Parson is represented in the *General Prologue* as an adherent of the movement. It is prudent to recall the *Epilogue's* uncertain status. Since it appears neither in the Hengwrt nor in the Ellesmere MS, it is conceivably spurious. Among more plausible possibilities, it may represent a draft link which Chaucer abandoned—perhaps because, with the passage of time, outright jests concerning Lollardy no longer seemed to him amusing or prudent.[3]

Despite the Wife's counter-Lollard traits, the justification for locating key parts of her monologue in the context of Lollardy is by no means insubstantial. This can be asserted notwithstanding also the difficulty of establishing precisely what that context was during the period 1387/8-1400 to which the composition of the *Tales* is generally assigned.[4] The full rigour of ecclesiastical machinery against Lollard suspects was not geared up until the years following 1400: consequently recorded proceedings disclosing the extent and the tenets of the movement before then are patchy in comparison with those from the first thirty years of the fifteenth century. There are certain risks, sometimes necessarily taken during the present discussion, in attempting to supplement the incomplete picture of Lollardy in Chaucer's time by resorting to the subsequent evidence. For example, we should make allowance for ways in which the eventual campaign of repression resulted in a sharper definition of the movement's features, and made it less feasible for uncommitted people to associate themselves with principles espoused by Lollards, than would have been the case before the turn of the century.[5] Nevertheless it is safe to assert that by the time Wyclif died in 1384 he had stirred up a hornets' nest in the interlocking spheres of theology and politics; that his popularizing Lollard followers were causing profound official alarm during that decade and the next; and that the publication of their 'manifesto' in London in 1395 implies that these dissenters were by then a self-conscious force to be reckoned with.[6]

These remarks must suffice for the moment to indicate that what Gower called 'this newe secte of Lollardie' was a live public issue in the 1390s.[7] A Southwark tavern-keeper's knowledge of it, however reductive, would not be aberrant in that decade. Chaucer himself— even more than Gower—had reason to be sensitive to the controversy, given his connections both with John of Gaunt (a notable patron of Wyclif at first, and reputedly a champion of the Wycliffite call for a vernacular Bible) and with a group of men in Richard II's service nowadays dubbed 'the Lollard knights'.[8] But, what has the Wife of Bath to do with these considerations?

II

We might begin by noting some circumstantial factors which support, or are at least not inconsistent with, the arguments to be mooted here. These factors are the Wife's stated occupation and provenance. As an individual in the 'clooth-makyng' trade (I 447) and as a resident of the environs of Bath, she epitomizes the social background as well as one of the particular regions in which Lollardy flourished. In the words of one historian, Lollards initially 'found supporters among the trades-people of large towns'. Their movement 'became increasingly artisan', taking root 'in both rural and urban districts in the various branches of the woollen industry', though perhaps more because that industry was so predominant than because of any predisposition among its participants.[9] Although records of heretical activity at Bath itself (not then a very large town) are lacking, nearby Bristol was an early centre of Lollardy. Wyclif's associate John Purvey is said to have preached Lollard 'errors' in Bristol in the late 1380s. McFarlane claims that prosperous artisans in 'the hinterland of small cloth-weaving towns [such as Bath] to which Bristol served as port' proved 'sympathetic to the new ideas'.[10]

Of course these circumstances in themselves establish no case that the prospect of a Bath clothmaker would have put Chaucer's readers or auditors on the edge of their seats in tense expectation of heretical discourse. What they do establish is that *if* the Wife may otherwise be found to display some Lollard characteristics, Chaucer has provided her with a 'corroborative' background. The Lollard characteristic on which we shall first concentrate arises from her insistence, in the first part of her *Prologue,* on appealing directly to the Bible— and particularly from her use of one significant word as she does so.

The word in question is *expres,* which occurs three times in the text. First, when she observes that no mat-

ter how men may 'glosen' the Almighty's injunction, 'wel I woot, expres, withoute lye, / God bad us for to wexe and multiplye' (III 27-8); again, in her challenge

> Wher can ye seye, in any manere age,
> That hye God defended mariage
> By expres word?
>
> (III 59-62)

and once more when, summarizing Jankyn's nightly anti-feminist readings to her, she (I suppose, rather than he) says of Eve's responsibility for the Fall; 'Lo, heere expres of womman may ye fynde / That womman was the los of al mankynde' (III 719-20).[11]

Now, although scrupulous analysis of what St Paul or Christ said and did not say concerning celibacy and marriage is ubiquitous in the treatise *Adversus Jovinianum* by St Jerome, from which the first two of these three observations are adapted, it is less clear that Jerome's phraseology explicitly prompts the Wife's intensifier, *expres.* Perhaps this intensifier carries through the implications of debating-points which the Wife has borrowed (III 24-5, 61-7) from Jovinian. We are led to recall how Jerome grudgingly conceded Jovinian's point that Scripture does not 'define' the allowable quota of remarriages, and how he laconically observed that the Lord's natural reluctance to 'prescribe' virginity sent Jovinian wild with exultation.[12] Her use of *expres* also sustains the illusion that she has scoured Scripture for statements and silences on these matters which provoke a campaigning instinct in her. However, there may be lodged within the Wife's diction the clue to a specifically Lollard cast of mind. Not only did the sect persistently justify its beliefs by recourse to what Scripture explicitly authorized and did not authorize: there is also evidence for supposing that *expres* and its cognates featured within a 'sectarian' vocabulary. Let us consider these points in turn.

Characteristic statements about the primacy of scriptural authority were made by two notable Lollard defendants. One was an educated layman named Walter Brut, tried before the Bishop of Hereford in 1393. In the language of an official record, Brut stated that he would accept any refutations 'ex auctoritate scripture sacre aut probabili racione in scriptura sacra fundata'.[13] He was therefore adopting essentially the same Wycliffite criteria that we encounter in the case of the priest William Thorpe, who wrote an account of his own interrogation by Archbishop Arundel which took place in 1407. Thorpe tells us of his initial prayer: 'what euer þing þat I schulde speke, þat I miʒte haue þerto trewe autorite of scripture or open resoun' (f. 19ʳ).[14] Accordingly he parries his interrogators' arguments again and again by reference to Scripture. For example, in response to a test question, whether those who withhold tithes might be 'acursid' by the Church, he ventures surprise 'þat ony preest dar seie men to be acursid, *wiþouten grounde of goddis word*' and challenges any clerk to demonstrate 'where þis sentence, cursinge hem þat tiþen not now, is iwriten in goddis lawe' (f. 59ʳ; my emphasis).

Thorpe is addressing topics other than the Wife's, with more elaborate logic, but he strikes a similar chord in his fundamentalist approach to Scripture—one which he had apparently practised for at least twenty years, that is, from the 1380s.[15] He is closest to the Wife's idiom when, citing the gospels, he protests that since '*bi þe word of crist speciali*, þat is his voice, prestis ben comaundid to preche', they must do so, regardless of episcopal licensing procedures (f. 37ʳ⁻ᵛ, my emphasis). Moreover, Thorpe finds himself provoking in acute form the kind of expostulations, from an actual jury of ecclesiastical authorities, that the Wife expects her own fundamentalism to provoke in an imaginary one ('So that the clerkes be nat with me wrothe . . .', III 125). The Archbishop turns to three other clerks present and exclaims, according to Thorpe; 'Lo, seres, þis is þe bisinesse and þe maner of þis losel and siche oþer, to pike out scharpe sentencis of holy writ and of doctours for to maynteyne her sect and her loore aȝens þe ordenaunce of holi chirche' (f. 38ʳ).

So far we have seen several expressions by which Lollards articulated their adherence to what Thorpe at another point calls the 'pleyne tixt' of the Bible (f. 64ᵛ). Among these expressions, 'wiþouten *grounde* of goddis word' is one that particularly leads us into what Anne Hudson has identified as a 'sect vocabulary'.[16] She shows how the Lollards' predilection for *ground, grounded, ungrounded* etc., arises from their 'belief that the only true *ground* is scripture'. Her argument could be massively strengthened from Reginald Pecock's exhaustive syllogistic discussion of precisely this terminology (including an element of semantic discrimination) in the opening part of his anti-Lollard *Repressor of Over Much Blaming of the Clergy* (c. 1450). For our purposes it is admittedly a somewhat late text. But it was written by a man apparently intimate with Lollard discourse, which no doubt preserved for some considerable time that uniformity and distinctiveness which seemed so remarkable to Knighton at an earlier date.[17]

Since Pecock is a reliable witness to habitual Lollard diction in the elaborate attention he pays to the expression 'groundid in Holi Scripture', then it is likely also that he is reflecting another piece of recognized Lollard terminology when he engages at some length with the significance of 'express' scriptural injunction.[18] He does so because he is about to defend church images and pilgrimages from the condemnations heaped upon them by Lollards on the usual narrow basis of what the Bible categorically prescribed or failed to prescribe. Pecock's

first 'supposicioun' in this passage immediately reveals the greater latitude that he would wish to be exercised in the interpretation of scriptural precept. He asserts that whoever 'expresseli' bids any 'gouernaunce' to be carried out, therefore 'includingli' bids all those *further* (unspecified) things to be done which logically flow out of the said 'gouernaunce'.[19] Therefore one cannot rightly insist 'that needis ech gouernaunce of Goddis . . . lawe and seruise muste be groundid expresseli in Holi Scripture'.[20] Pecock is surely turning his opponents' vocabulary against them, rather than introducing terminology of his own. That explains why he proceeds to elaborate his point with an ostentatious display of sarcasm, which would be gratuitous unless recognizable sectarian cant were its target. Nowhere in Scripture, he goes on, 'is expresse mensioun mad' of *clocks*:[21] does this put clocks morally beyond the pale? Again, 'Where is it groundid expresseli in Scripture, that men mowe lete schaue her berdis?',[22] and so forth. It is a blatant attempt to discredit through mimicry the claim of 'tho erring persones . . . clepid Lollardis' that they can know all of 'Goddis lawe . . . bi her reeding and studiyng in the Bible oonli'.[23]

For a student of the Wife of Bath it is quite remarkable to discover in the midst of this discussion what reads very much like a caricature of her, assimilating not only her devotion to 'expres word' and her brash anticlericalism, but her 'coverchiefs' into the bargain:

> Wolde God thilk men and wommen (and namelich thilk wommen whiche maken hem silf so wise bi the Bible, that thei no deede wollen allowe to be vertuose and to be doon in mannis vertuose conuersacioun, saue what thei kunnen fynde expresseli in the Bible, and ben ful coppid of speche anentis clerkis, and avaunten and profren hem silf whanne thei ben in her iolite and in her owne housis forto argue and dispute aȝens clerkis), schulden not were couercheefs into tyme thei couthen schewe bi her Bible where it is expresseli bede, counselid, or witnessid in her Bible to be doon.
>
> (*Repressor*, I, 123)

It looks as if Pecock had encountered or heard tell of abrasive Lollard women no less formidable and voluble than Chaucer's 'dame Alys'.

Lollard texts confirm that *expres* and its cognates were indeed likely to be used at key points in the sect's arguments, though it is true that the incidence does not reach eye-catching levels. In a Lollard anti-mendicant sermon written before 1413 the author invokes God's law 'comaundinge expresli þat þer shulde on no wise be a nedi and a begger among þe peple'. The *Thirty-Seven Conclusions of the Lollards* (pre-1401?) include an attack on 'þe cumpanie of fleisly cardynals, whois office eiþer ordre is not founden expresly in holy writte'. Again, in an early fifteenth-century treatise orthodox eucharistic doctrine is spurned as a modern invention 'nouȝt tauȝt expresly in wordes in eny party of hooly writt'. And a sermon from the same period puts the view that 'bileeue seiþ priueli þing þat men nediþ not þus to trowe, and sum þing expresseli þat men schulden opunli trowe'.[24]

Since we are dealing with words current outside the sect as well as prominent within it, absolute proof regarding the elements of a distinctively 'Lollard' vocabulary ideally necessitates (as Hudson points out) a large word-search using a wide range of 'controls'.[25] Such a search would go beyond the scope of this preliminary exploration. I am reasonably persuaded that *expres/expressly* should be added to Hudson's list, and hence that the Wife of Bath, being a lay person determined to confute clerical lore on the basis of un-glossed scriptural evidence, is applying Lollard vocabulary in a Lollard manner. The evidence of usage elsewhere in Chaucer qualifies but does not sabotage that hypothesis. The Parson several times reproves be-haviour that is 'expres agayn' God's commandments;[26] but we have already observed that he himself has been thought to manifest some Lollard traits. Otherwise there are stray instances involving the eagle's obedience to Jove's 'expres commaundement' (*The House of Fame,* 2021) and an allegation that Virginius holds his daughter 'expres agayn the wyl' of Apius (**Physician's Tale,** C 182). If we look beyond Chaucer, we shall certainly find straightforward examples from orthodox sources to set beside those in Lollard texts. For instance, *MED* cites *Cleanness,* where the poet asserts a point that is 'proued expresse in [Daniel's] profecies'.[27] There is no tincture of subversion in this statement, or in the surgeon Guy de Chauliac's observation that 'Haly Ab-bas . . . seiþ expressely' that teeth have 'no felyng bi hem selfe'.[28] It is necessary to remember that the Lol-lards were not inventing language: rather, they were ap-propriating particular nuances within particular locu-tions which thereby became, as it were, their movement's slogans.

In assessing how far that appropriation might be opera-tive in the Wife of Bath's case, we should take account of the whole contemporary climate of opinion concern-ing lay discussion of religion in the vernacular. It had long been established ecclesiastical advice to the laity that 'it is inowȝþ to þe to beleuen as holychurche techeþ þe and lat þe clerkes alone with þe argumentes'.[29] By the latter part of the fourteenth century this attitude was increasingly unacceptable to reformers, including many who were far from 'Wycliffite' in their other opinions. However, before long the otherwise orthodox were un-able to go on advocating the dissemination of scriptural knowledge in the vernacular without attracting suspicion of heresy.[30] As early as 1382 it was being noted that the Lollards 'read the gospels and learn them by heart in the vernacular, and "mumble" the one to the other'.[31] The more the spread of the sect came to light, the more

repressive grew the campaign against scriptural matter propounded in English. It was chronicled that during 1388 'in pleno parliamento magnus rumor exuberavit' concerning Lollards and their preachings and their English books 'quasi per totam Angliam'.[32] To a Lollard writing (in this case in Latin) an Apocalypse com-mentary in prison during 1389/90, there was no doubt-ing a ruthless prelatical drive to extirpate all evangelical material written 'in lingwa materna'.[33]

In these circumstances (though how comprehensively they would affect writers across the country it is hard to say), to be seen to wrangle contrariously over points of Scripture in the mother tongue might be to court ecclesiastical opprobrium. Since the ground the Wife of Bath treads implies more acquaintance with vernacular Scripture than would at that juncture seem meet for a lay person, she would have struck some contemporaries as treading dangerously. The provocation doubles in that she is a woman; worse still, a woman aping preach-ing techniques. When the Pardoner butts in to compli-ment her as a 'noble prechour' (III 165), his jest takes us back to current controversy. The standard orthodox view of preaching held that 'no lay person or Religious, unless permitted by a Bishop or the Pope, and no woman, no matter how learned or saintly, ought to preach'.[34] Lollards, on the other hand, challenged the licensing restriction, gave preaching a special priority, and argued that any lay Christian had the power to preach. Walter Brut, whom we mentioned earlier, specifically championed also a woman's right to do so. In 1393 his submission that 'women have power and authority to preach and make the body of Christ' provoked elaborate refutation. Such controversy seems worth recalling, while we contemplate the Wife as a 'noble prechour' or (retrospectively in the **Friar's Pro-logue,** III 1272) as a dabbler in 'scole-matere'. The condescending tone contrived at these points, by pilgrims who are responding to the Wife as a prospec-tive competitor, is reminiscent of Knighton's mock-enthusiasm for the way in which, thanks to Lollardy, 'both men *and women* were suddenly transformed into doctors of evangelical doctrine by means of the vernacular'.[35]

The most strident response to this novelty was to tell women to go back to the distaff. Thus Hoccleve rebuked those women, thin of wit, who 'Wole argumentis make in holy writ':

> Lewde calates! sittith doun and spynne,
> And kakele of sumwhat elles . . .
>
> To Clerkes grete apparteneth þat aart
> The knowleche of þat, god hath fro yow shit.[36]

At about the same time it was a popular cry against Margery Kempe that she should abandon her unconven-tional lifestyle, and 'go spynne & carde as oþer women don'.[37] Margery found herself constantly mistaken for a Lollard. Among the chief reasons for this was her conspicuous command of the Bible. When she recounts 'a story of Scriptur' among some monks at Canterbury, one of them objects that this demonstrates a familiarity with Holy Writ that she could not (should not?) have acquired by herself, but only from the Holy Ghost or the devil. It is a short step from this to the chorus of taunts shouted at her—'þow xalt be brent, fals lollare'—as she makes a prudent retreat from the precincts.[38] At another point the Archbishop of York, though eventually satisfied as to her orthodoxy, requires her to stop 'teaching' and 'challenging' the people in his diocese. When she cites a Gospel passage in support of her right to 'spekyn of God', she generates further suspicion whose foundation (as noted by the editors) is 'probably that Margery would not be quoting Scripture if she had not been engaged in Lollard Bible studies', and she provokes a 'gret clerke' to quote 'Seynt Powyl . . . a-geyns hir þat no woman xulde prechyn'.[39]

Of course Lollardy and lay preaching had become much more highly fraught issues around the time of Oldcastle's Lollard rebellion in 1414 (which made Hoccleve and Margery's interlocutors so aggressive) than they probably were in the 1390s. Even making due allowance for that, we may reasonably conclude that the Wife of Bath's demotic and fundamentalist mode of 'preaching' was calculated to broach questions that were already a matter for nervous concern at the period of her creation. What may be more startling is to discover that the advent of Lollardy also caused nervousness about the very topic of marriage and celibacy which so exercises the Wife.

III

We are apt to assume that in creating the Wife of Bath Chaucer engages with a timeless textual world of anti-feminist and matrimonial polemic that reaches back across the centuries and for which it would be idle to seek a specific stimulus in late fourteenth-century England. Yet the Lollards turned celibacy into a newly contentious topic. This is apparent from certain emphases they added to Wyclif's latterly intense distaste for the religious orders. In their London publication, the *Twelve Conclusions* of 1395, the third conclusion

is þat þe lawe of continence annexyd to presthod, þat in preiudys of wimmen was first ordeynid, inducith sodomie in al holy chirche . . . þe correlary of þis conclusiun is þat þe priuat religions, begynneris of þis synne, were most worthi to ben anullid.

In addition the eleventh conclusion asserts:

þat a uow of continence mad in oure chirche of wommen, þe qwiche ben fekil and vnperfyth in kynde, is cause of bringging of most horrible synne [*viz.* lesbian-

ism and bestiality] . . . þe correlary is þat widuis, and qwiche as han takin þe mantil and þe ryng [i.e. a ritual vow of chastity such as Margery Kempe herself made] . . . we wolde þei were weddid, for we can nout excusin hem fro priue synnis.[40]

There are points here which one would wish to have seen more fully developed, notably the emotive assertion that priestly celibacy was instituted 'in preiudys of wimmen'. Does it insinuate an unfair restriction on women's sexual chances, because so many males were obliged by their orders to abjure contact with them? Or does it bespeak a female grievance against that anti-feminism which was assumed to derive from celibacy and which, in the Wife's phrase, made it 'impossible / That any clerk wol speke good of wyves' (III 688-9)? The former interpretation was among those canvassed by the Dominican Roger Dymmok when he compiled a systematic refutation of the *Twelve Conclusions* for Richard II, probably shortly after their publication. Since he was apparently not quite sure how to take the 'prejudice' claim, it may not have represented any thoroughly formulated Lollard tenet. *If,* wrote Dymmok, they meant that priestly celibacy took too many males out of matrimonial circulation, his instincts told him that there were nevertheless few women bent on marriage who could not find suitable partners.[41]

With *The Wife of Bath's Prologue* in mind, let us dwell a little upon two intertwined aspects of these *Conclusions.* One is the cynical estimate of human capacities for sexual restraint which they incorporate, and which Dymmok found deeply offensive. The other, most interesting in its specificity, is the correlative recommendation that widows should remarry.

The wider context for these opinions was Lollard contempt for *religiones privatae,* and the movement's general repudiation of vows. In a sense chastity became a casualty of polemic against vows *per se,* a point that is perhaps implicit even in an argument (ascribed to John Purvey) specifically querying vows of chastity. Did not Scripture say: 'Non possem esse continens nisi Deus det'? Was it not therefore irrational to vow chastity without being able to know God's inscrutable intentions towards oneself?[42] However, this proves to be less typical of recorded Lollard reservations about celibacy than is the argument which depends upon the natural force of sexual instinct and the dangers of disrupting it. Thus William White, a priest who scandalized the authorities by presuming to marry even after having once ostensibly abjured heresy, shared the London manifesto's view that a sexually repressed priesthood gave occasion for priestly vice.[43] His disciples in Norfolk were deeply indoctrinated with the idea that it was proper, indeed commendable, for priests and nuns to marry and hence (as two of them added, perhaps pointedly) 'bringe forth frute of here bodyes'.[44]

Further research is needed to determine whether the movement developed a consistent doctrine on sexuality. Some adherents may have set particular store by the duty of bringing forth fruit. Proceedings by the Bishop of Salisbury in 1389 in the case of a heretic named William Ramsbury exposed his belief—among a range of normal Lollard doctrines—not just that the religious should marry, but also that if a man's wife proved sterile it would be meritorious to dismiss her and take a fertile partner, and that it was proper for laymen or priests to have intercourse with many partners, 'hoc propter multiplicacionem generis humani'. Hudson thinks Ramsbury somehow derived these wilder notions from the continental sect of the Free Spirit. However, historians of heresy have begun to cast doubt upon the existence of that sect. Ramsbury's views have been attributed instead simply to 'dislike of clerical and monastic celibacy' allied with a practical emphasis on procreation.[45] Unless he was one of those freelance 'rogues of the Rasputin variety'—in Lambert's phrase—who speciously combine religion with libertinism,[46] he must represent an extreme form of the tendency in some Lollard circles to devalue celibacy by emphatically promoting (marital) heterosexuality and its *frute*. By the same token, suspicions about Lollardy rather than (as Hudson argues) about the shadowy sect of the Free Spirit, could have been the basis for a test question put to Margery Kempe at York: 'þes wordys how þei xuld ben vndirstondyn, "Crescite & multiplicamini"'.[47] Margery carefully answers that the words signify the increase of 'frute gostly' as well as of bodily procreation.

It is rather well known that the Wife of Bath *seems* to interpret the same 'gentil text' (III 28-9) as a warrant for unlimited remarriage. This interpretation engagingly modifies the more usual form of literal understanding (apparent in Ramsbury's case) which was quite often mocked by mediaeval satirists.[48] At the same time, her implied interpretation allows her attitude to procreation itself to remain as elusive here as it continues to be when she archly refers to the 'ese / Of engendrure' for which 'membres . . . of generacion' were wrought (III 127-8, 116). These are considerations which make it difficult to define her standpoint firmly as a 'Lollard' one, yet they do not lessen the topicality of that standpoint. Indeed, some interesting evidence exists to suggest that the 'Crescite et multiplicamini' text may have functioned as a touchstone for detecting Lollard 'error' well before Margery Kempe's time. If that were so, we might need to estimate afresh how seriously the Wife challenges the Church when she spurns the validity of any gloss (III 26) on the same text, or when she asserts a widow's right to bestow herself again 'In the actes and in fruyt [whatever fruit she means] of mariage' (III 113-14).

The evidence arises in Dymmok's refutation of the eleventh London Conclusion. He rehearses at some length what he alleges to be the typical propaganda of the Lollards against female vows of chastity. Sure enough, the 'wexe and multiplye' command is central. They argue, he says, that such vows directly contravene the *divina ordinacio* by which women are to replenish the earth, and that they oppose the instinctuality of sexual attraction:

> Et cum Deus eas [mulieres] ad prolem propagandam creauerit, atque precepto affirmatiuo easdem constrinxerit, ut terram sobolis multiplicacione replerent, ipsas eciam uiris in auxilium assignauerit ad generacionis actum, et easdem sub uiri potestate iugiter uoluerit permanere, 'Quecunque igitur,' inquiunt, 'uotum continencie emiserit, totam hanc diuinam ordinacionem, quantum in se est, frustrare conatur, quod nullomodo alicui creature licite poterit conuenire'. 'Qua eciam temeritatis', inquiunt, 'audacia presumis attemptare diuine disposicioni contrarium, naturali inclinacioni directe oppositum, qua quamlibet cogi oportet uirorum consorcia appetere, ut uno eodemque actu delectacionem naturalem atque ipsius purgacionem necessariam assequi ualeant, et sic opera peiora declinent. Si enim eas Deus uoluisset a uirorum consorciis penitus abstinere, ipsis feminis inclinaciones tales non indidisset, ut uiros appeterent, nec earum naturas materiis superfluis onerasset, quod talibus purgacionibus indigeret.' Et sic per hunc modum lasciuiam necessariam affirmant, continenciam impossibilem predicant, et contra diuinum preceptum illam esse allegant. Quibus uersutis argumentis plenis fallaciis et decepcionibus animas simplices et indoctas mulierum intendunt decipere ac terrere, ne continenciam perpetuam seruare quouismodo proponant, ut sic facilius eis abuti ualeant ad libitum eo, quod inter cetera docent non ipsis licere cuicunque poscenti intuitu caritatis et suam indigenciam pretendenti corpus suum denegare. Et sic cum Nicholaitis hereticis conueniunt, qui uoluerunt mulieres esse communes, quorum facta Deus maxime abhominatur.[49]

Dymmok goes on to confront his opponents with a Thomistic exegesis of the Genesis text. Admittedly, the extract I have presented need not be taken altogether at face value. Dymmok might be fabricating arguments presumed by anti-Lollards to underlie their Conclusion rather than reporting arguments seen or heard. The closing allegation that the sect's leaders cynically encourage female converts towards promiscuity smacks of a familiar charge whereby the orthodox have often—justly or unjustly—sought to ostracize unorthodox sects. Yet his representation of their case against repression of heterosexual *inclinacio* by vows that contravene God's *praeceptum affirmativum* may not have been too wide of the mark. Nor may Ramsbury have been the only Lollard who stretched that case in a libertarian direction.

In any case, it seems fair to state that chastity was hardly a neutral topic in the 1390s. The 1395 *Conclusions* ensured that the Church had to refurbish its arguments on behalf of religious celibacy and female vows of chastity. The Wife of Bath herself is cautious. She does not, like the compilers of the *Twelve Conclusions,* condemn wholesale 'þe lawe of continence annexyd to presthod'; she concedes that 'Virginitee is greet perfeccion, / And continence eek with devocion' (III 105-6). If she does share with those compilers a strong sense that 'weddyng in freletee' (III 92) is the appropriate course for those such as herself who (in the *Conclusions*' phrase) are 'vnperfyth in kynde', on the other hand she 'nyl envye no virginitee' (142) and therefore avoids the more extreme position held by Lollards, 'that chastite of monkes, chanons, freres, nonnes, prestes and of any other persones is not commendable ne meritorie'.[50] In other words Chaucer creates for the Wife a warily poised attitude, in which I would postulate that the element of wariness owes something to the fact that the topic had become problematic at the time of writing, as well as to his source material in Jerome.

IV

In a comprehensive investigation of the text's Lollard affiliations, we could dwell productively on later parts of the Wife's *Prologue* which acquire fresh colour once we are alerted to the topicality of her arguments in lines 1-162. For example, Jankyn's nightly readings to her from a 'book of wikked wyves' would amount to a parody of the practice in Lollard cells whereby heretical doctrine characteristically passed around 'through domestic, familial introductions'.[51] It is very typical of Chaucer's delight in irony that he should invert such a practice by exploring the notion of a domestic situation in which the 'dissenter' has to cope with *counter-*propaganda from her spouse instead of being gratified by a recital of radical views. I hardly need add that after an ensuing squabble, she obliges Jankyn to burn this book (III 816). Tearing pages from a book—as she has also done—is one thing; burning a book is quite another. It can signify that the book's contents have been officially judged heretical. Naturally enough, much Lollard literature went up in flames, as at a public burning in Oxford in 1410. Such rituals probably became more common after Archbishop Arundel's *Constitutions* (drafted 1407) toughened the establishment's campaign against Wycliffite literature. But there is earlier evidence for burnings, if we take at face value what is stated by the author of the *Opus Arduum* (1389/90) concerning a 'generalem mandatum prelatorum *ad comburendum,* destruendum et condemnandum' vernacular gospel writings.[52] I suspect that the burning of Jankyn's book completes Chaucer's cycle of Lollard allusions in the Wife's *Prologue.* The proponent of dissent mischievously inverts the very mechanisms by which dissent was supposed to be eradicated. The 'heretic' wins an outlandish victory by forcing her clerical opponent to destroy his words, not hers.

Rather than pursuing this reading in detail to encompass further factors such as the subsequent friction between

the Wife and the Friar (remembering that Lollards detested the friars, particularly for converting Scripture into 'scole-matere'), let us assimilate the implications of what has here been argued.

It may be objected that, while I have extensively elaborated the 'convergence' between the Wife and Lollardy, I have not decisively proved a connection. The paradoxical defence must be that however much Chaucer wished to gain a hearing for Lollard views via the Wife, he would not have deemed it prudent to advertise this too explicitly (even in the case of a speaker for whose words he could pretend to admit no responsibility). He was writing at a time when the risk attaching to lay polemic founded upon 'express' scriptural warrant, if difficult to quantify, could not have been minimal.[53] To me it appears that anxieties relating to that risk motivate the Wife's cautionary remark 'As taketh not agrief of that I seye' (III 191). Unfortunately this is a circular deduction. An equally circular response would have to be made against anyone who asks why the Wife's 'preaching' on celibacy and marriage is vested so largely in devious plunderings from such a staple text as *Adversus Jovinianum.* Chaucer is perforce using a defensive strategy, addressing Wycliffite controversies through a source safeguarded by its ancient pedigree. Indeed he may be imitating the Lollards' own guerrilla strategy whereby they frequently lodged their ideologically sensitive tenets within the beguiling confines of officially acceptable texts such as the *Ancrene Riwle.*[54]

If the foregoing evidence of Lollard tendencies in the Wife of Bath commands critical assent, what conclusions regarding either the Wife, or Chaucer's interest in Lollardy, might thence arise? One means of responding is to juxtapose our experience of the Wife with Pecock's diagnosis of what factors make women ready converts to Lollard fundamentalism. He suggests that all laypersons who cultivate vernacular Scripture in the Lollard way are misled into supposing that moral truth resides exclusively in the Bible, because the Bible is in parts so 'delectable' and devotion-inspiring, and because an excessive 'affeccioun or wil' (as against 'intelleccioun or resoun') predisposes them to find all-sustaining 'hony' there. Given women's proportionately stronger 'affeccioun' and proportionately weaker 'resoun', they in particular are susceptible to the fundamentalist approach.[55] In Chaucer, the gender-stereotyping thus displayed by Pecock is more often food for mirth (as the Wife herself intimates, III 434-42) than food for thought. Nor does the Wife hunger for *devotional* 'hony' in Scripture. Yet there is this much in common with Pecock's assessment: she does evince a powerful *wil,* not much slowed down by *intelleccioun,* to derive moral corroboration for her beliefs from the un-glossed Word. In the process she so manipulates citations from Scripture (for example, that concerning the marital 'debt', III 154-62) that we must fancy Chaucer to be laughing up his sleeve at her exegetical limitations. However, such mockery should not be taken to prove that the poet was out of sympathy with the Lollards' desire for straightforward biblical self-education. On the contrary, the Wife's stumblings serve to underline the predicament of the 'lewid puple' who 'crieþ aftir holi writ', while intolerant church officials 'stoppen holi writ as myche as þei moun'.[56]

V

The ambivalence of ***The Wife of Bath's Prologue*** will probably not be much qualified by a discovery of her Lollard 'dimension', except in that we shall be detecting new facets to that ambivalence. But there are, I think, two broad implications of some importance. One is that we ought to reconsider the extent of Chaucer's involvement with, and response to, principles stridently advanced by this controversial pressure-group that gathered strength as his literary career developed.[57] It may be that we shall then uncover more reinforcement of the radical critics' case for reading his work 'in a consciously sociohistorical light'[58] than many readers would hitherto have expected. There is no point in denying that Chaucer is temperamentally a 'bookish' poet. Yet we do not have to suppose him as indifferent to the world of current controversy as he sometimes pretends to be. If it remains true that he finds his greatest source of creative nourishment in a chest full of books, the constructs he fashions through the agency of 'these olde appreved stories' can nevertheless mediate the 'tydynges' of contemporary controversy. So far as Lollardy is concerned, we might fruitfully reflect, for example, on questions about image-worship which arise from the narrator's intense devotion to the daisy icon in the ***Prologue*** to ***The Legend of Good Women***. Is Chaucer there mediating a contentious debate about the legitimacy of venerating church images (triggered by Wycliffite polemic) through the disarming channel of marguerite conventions?[59]

The second broad implication, with which I shall conclude, concerns Chaucer's distinctive interest in how people quote, use, ply, and misappropriate or 'harass' written *auctoritee*. He developed something of an obsession with this, and modern discussion of it proceeds apace.[60] Into that discussion I should like to inject the following hypothesis. Among other things (possibly above all other things) Chaucer was drawn to become a connoisseur of the operations of *auctoritee* within spoken or literary argument by the furore surrounding that central feature of Lollardy which so dismayed the Lollards' opponents and which must therefore have affected a poet who moved in Lollard circles. This central feature was the methodology they applied when they sought to 'pike out scharpe sentencis of holy writ and of doctours for to maynteyne her sect

and her loore'. Not only the Wife of Bath, but Chaucer's whole work, may require fresh study with such features in mind.

Notes

1. Stephen Knight, *Geoffrey Chaucer* (Oxford, 1986), pp. 5-6. Some other socio-historical readings in this vein are: Stephen Knight, 'Chaucer and the sociology of literature', *SAC*, II (1980), 15-51; P. Strohm, 'Form and social statement in *Confessio Amantis* and *The Canterbury Tales*', *SAC*, I (1979), 17-40; and David Aers, *Chaucer* (Brighton, 1986).

2. Knight, *Geoffrey Chaucer*, pp. 98, 103. D. W. Robertson, Jr, speaks of the Wife's 'mock-Lollard sermon' in '"And for my land thus hastow mordred me?": land tenure, the cloth industry, and the Wife of Bath', *ChauR*, XIV (1980), 403-20 (p. 415). For information about the Lollards and their beliefs, I am heavily indebted to two volumes of collected essays: Margaret Aston, *Lollards and Reformers* (London, 1984); Anne Hudson, *Lollards and their Books* (London, 1985). Among other important studies are M. Deanesly, *The Lollard Bible* (Cambridge, 1920); K. B. McFarlane, *John Wycliffe and the Beginnings of English Nonconformity* (London, 1952). For discussion of Lollardy and English literary culture, see Janet Coleman, *English Literature in History 1350-1400* (London, 1981), ch. iv.

3. All Chaucer references are to *The Riverside Chaucer*, ed. by Larry D. Benson (Boston, Mass., 1987). On the Parson and Lollardy, see D. V. Ives, 'A man of religion', *MLR*, XXVII (1932), 144-8; and, more recently, David Lawton, 'Chaucer's two ways: the pilgrimage frame of *The Canterbury Tales*', *SAC*, IX (1987), 3-40 (pp. 36-40). The Epilogue is termed 'spurious' in *The Canterbury Tales,* ed. by N. F. Blake (London, 1980), p. 9, but is thought to have been 'abandoned' by Chaucer in *The Works of Geoffrey Chaucer*, ed. by F. N. Robinson, 2nd edn (Boston, Mass., 1957), p. 697; see also Derek Pearsall, *The Canterbury Tales* (London, 1985), p. 20.

4. One can only guess at the date of the Wife's *Prologue* itself. Robinson assigns 'the later *Canterbury Tales* (including the "Marriage Group")' to 1393-1400, but states that 'a reference to the Wife of Bath in the *Envoy to Bukton* fixes the composition of her *Prologue,* almost with certainty, before 1396' (*Works of Chaucer,* ed. Robinson, pp. xxix, 698).

5. See the example of the sermon-writer, thought to be a friar, who feared persecution because his policy regarding the use of the vernacular over-

lapped with that which was prohibited on account of the Lollards: Anne Hudson and H. L. Spencer, 'Old author, new work: the sermons of MS Longleat 4', *MÆ*, LIII (1984), 220-38. D. A. Lawton suggests, reasonably, that, whereas in the late 1370s and early 1380s one could have 'sympathized with Lollard aspirations . . . without regarding oneself as a Lollard', the situation in the later 1380s and 1390s was such that 'Lollard sympathizers would have had to make a choice whether to accept or reject an increasingly dangerous label': 'Lollardy and the "Piers Plowman" tradition', *MLR*, LXXVI (1981), 780-93 (p. 780).

6. On the evolution of anti-Lollard measures at this time, see H. G. Richardson, 'Heresy and the lay power under Richard II', *EHR*, LI (1936), 1-28. For a text of the 'manifesto', i.e. *Twelve Conclusions of the Lollards* (said to have been pinned up on the doors of Westminster Hall and St Paul's), see Anne Hudson, *Selections from English Wycliffite Writings* (Cambridge, 1978), pp. 24-9.

7. *Confessio Amantis,* Prologue, 346, (*The English Works of John Gower,* ed. by G. C. Macaulay, 2 vols., EETS, ES, 81-2 (1900-1), I, 14). A link between the Wife of Bath and Lollardy could be conjectured from the Clerk's punning expression 'al hire *secte*' (IV 1171); but the analogously witty application of the term 'sekte' to Jason's fraternity of heretical lovers (*LGW*, 1382) makes that doubtful. W. Matthews takes the term in a non-topical sense in 'The Wife of Bath and all her sect', *Viator,* V (1974), 413-43.

8. On Chaucer and John of Gaunt, see, e.g., George Kane, *Chaucer* (Oxford, 1984), pp. 22, 27-8, 67-8, 70-1. The nature of John of Gaunt's relationship with Wyclif is extensively discussed in J. H. Dahmus, *The Prosecution of John Wyclif* (New Haven, Conn., 1952), while his support for a vernacular Bible is asserted in the text edited by C. Bühler, 'A Lollard tract: on translating the Bible', *MÆ*, VII (1938), 167-87 (p. 178). K. B. McFarlane, *Lancastrian Kings and Lollard Knights* (Oxford, 1972), affirmed the 'Lollardy' of a group of courtiers known to Chaucer, but grounds for scepticism remain, according to J. Anthony Tuck, 'Carthusian monks and Lollard knights: religious attitudes at the court of Richard II', in *Reconstructing Chaucer,* ed. by Paul Strohm and Thomas J. Heffernan, SAC Proceedings, 1 (Knoxville, Tenn., 1985), pp. 149-61. See also David L. Jeffrey, 'Chaucer and Wyclif: biblical hermeneutic and literary theory in the XIVth century', in *Chaucer and Scriptural Tradition,* ed. by D. L. Jeffrey (Ottawa, 1984), pp. 109-40.

9. Margaret Aston, 'Lollardy and sedition, 1381-1431', *Past and Present,* XVII (1960), 1-44 (p. 15), repr. in her *Lollards and Reformers,* pp. 1-47 (p. 19).

10. Anne Hudson, 'John Purvey: a reconsideration of the evidence', *Viator,* XII (1981), 355-80 (pp. 359-60), repr. in her *Lollards and their Books,* pp. 85-110 (pp. 89-90); K. B. McFarlane, *John Wycliffe and the Beginnings of English Nonconformity,* pp. 112-13. A 'John of Bath' was interrogated in 1418: see Anne Hudson, 'Some aspects of Lollard book-production', *Studies in Church History,* IX (1972), 147-57 (p. 156), repr. in *Lollards and their Books,* 181-91 (p. 190); John A. F. Thomson, *The Later Lollards* (Oxford, 1965), pp. 26-7. William Ramsbury, who confessed in 1389 to having preached Lollard errors in the diocese of Salisbury, may have preached in the Bath and Wells diocese too: see Anne Hudson, 'A Lollard mass', *Journal of Theological Studies,* XXIII (1972), 407-19 (pp. 411-12), repr. in *Lollards and their Books,* pp. 111-23 (pp. 115-16).

11. A subsequent reappearance of the word in her *Tale,* where the 'olde wyf' declares that in Seneca or Boethius 'shul ye seen expres that it no drede is / That he is gentil that dooth gentil dedis' (III 1168-9) obliquely sustains the Wife of Bath's enthusiasm for explicit authorities.

12. See (PL, XXIII): '. . . ob hanc causam non esse uxorum numerum definitum' (col. 234) and context; also 'Hic adversarius tota exsultatione bacchatur: hoc velut fortissimo ariete, virginitatis murum quatiens: "Ecce, inquit, Apostolus profitetur de virginibus, Domini se non habere praeceptum: et qui cum auctoritate de maritis et uxoribus jusserat, non audet imperare quod Dominus non praecepit . . ."' (*ibid.,* col. 227). The couplet in which the Wife first uses *expres* is to be compared with: 'Quod autem ait: *Crescite et multiplicamini, et replete terram (Gen.* i, 28), necesse fuit prius plantare silvam et crescere, ut esset quod postea posset excidi. Simulque consideranda vis verbi, *replete terram.* Nuptiae terram replent, virginitas paradisum' (*ibid.,* col. 235).

13. Margaret Aston, 'Lollard women priests?', *Journal of Ecclesiastical History,* XXXI (1980), 441-61 (p. 447 n. 24), repr. in her *Lollards and Reformers,* pp. 49-70 (p. 55). See *ibid.,* pp. 444-51 (rpt, pp. 52-9) for her discussion of the Brut case. Wyclif himself wrote of his willingness to retract any of his conclusions which could be proved 'scripture sacre contrarias', and insisted on the supreme authority of holy writ: see *De Veritate Sacrae Scripturae,* ed. by R. Buddensieg, Wyclif Society, Vol. I (London, 1905), pp. 355-6, 394. Compare the Lollard formulation 'truþe þat God himsilf

seiþ and techiþ in þe gospel þat schulden men worschipe and take as bileeue, and oþir lawe of mennes fynding schulden men litil telle by' (Hudson, *Selections*, XV, 150-2 (p. 78)).

14. *The Examination of Master William Thorpe* can be consulted in *Fifteenth Century Prose and Verse*, ed. by A. W. Pollard (London, 1903), pp. 97-174. Pollard's text is based on an early printed version (*c.* 1530). Also now known are two Latin manuscript versions, and an English one in Oxford, Bodleian Library, MS Rawlinson c.208, ff. 1-91ᵛ, all fifteenth-century: see Hudson, *Selections*, p. 155. My quotations are taken from MS Rawl. c.208.

15. He is alleged to have travelled the north, preaching, 'þis twenti wyntir and more' (f. 8ᵛ), and protests that he will not forsake 'þe lore þat I haue bisied me fore þis þritti ʒeer and more' (f. 21ʳ).

16. Anne Hudson, 'A Lollard sect vocabulary?', in *So Many People Longages and Tonges: Philological Essays in Scots and Mediaeval English presented to Angus McIntosh*, ed. by Michael Benskin and M. L. Samuels (Edinburgh, 1981), pp. 15-30 (pp. 21-22), repr. in her *Lollards and their Books*, pp. 165-80 (pp. 171-2).

17. See C. Babington's edition of *The Repressor*, 2 vols., Rolls Series (London, 1860), where Pecock discusses the concept 'groundid in Holi Scripture' extensively (I, 1-130), and makes semantic distinctions (I, 26-7). His 'inside' knowledge of Lollard language is considered by Hudson in 'Sect vocabulary', pp. 17-18 (rpt., pp. 167-8); and Knighton's attribution of *unius loquelae* to members of the sect is reviewed *ibid.*, pp. 15-16 (rpt, pp. 165-6).

18. Pecock, *The Repressor*, ed. Babington, I, 110-30.

19. *Ibid.*, p. 111.

20. *Ibid.*, p. 117.

21. *Ibid.*, p. 118.

22. *Ibid.*, p. 119.

23. *Ibid.*, pp. 127-8.

24. Quoted from Hudson, *Selections*, XVII, 59-60 (p. 95); XXIV, 128-9 (p. 125); XXI A, 66-7 (p. 111); XV, 278-80 (p. 82), with dates as tentatively assigned in Hudson's notes. See further: 'expres contrarious to þe newe testament' (*ibid.*, III, 137 (p. 28); and 'syþen it is forbeden hym so expresse by þe forseyde heste of God' (*ibid.*, XIX, 182-3 (p. 101)).

25. Hudson, 'Sect vocabulary', p. 24 (rpt, p. 174). When the Oxford edition of *English Wycliffite Sermons* is complete, research on Lollard language will be much facilitated. The Latin work of the sect's Dominican opponent Roger Dymmok furnishes one contemporary 'control': see *Rogeri Dymmok: Liber Contra XII Errores et Hereses Lollardorum*, ed. by H. S. Cronin, Wyclif Society (London, 1922), in which are found locutions such as 'expresse contra' (pp. 281/5-6, 290-19); '. . . expresse castitatem est professa' (p. 72/26-7); and a citation of Aristotle, 'ubi ponit expresse . . .' (p. 82/10-12).

26. *Parson's Tale*, X 587, 795, 798.

27. *Cleanness*, ed. by J. J. Anderson (Manchester, 1977), l. 1158; the line is cited in *MED, s.v.* 'expres/se' *adv.*, (a).

28. *MED, s.v.* 'expres(se)li', *adv.*, (a).

29. *Middle English Sermons*, ed. by W. O. Ross, EETS, OS, 209 (London, 1940), p. 128.

30. See Hudson & Spencer, 'Old author, new work', pp. 228-33.

31. Coleman, *English Literature in History*, p. 209, quoting a sermon given by Henry Crump at St Mary's, Oxford. The Lollards' rote learning of the Bible is noted again *c.* 1450 by Pecock in *The Repressor* (ed. Babington, I, 129).

32. McFarlane, *Lancastrian Kings*, p. 193. For the full text, see *Polychronicon Ranulphi Higden*, Vol. IX, ed. by J. R. Lumby, Rolls Series, 41 (London, 1886), p. 171. Richardson, 'Heresy and the lay power', pp. 10-18, describes 1388 as a 'turning point' in official recognition of the threat posed by Lollardy.

33. Anne Hudson, 'A neglected Wycliffite text', *Journal of Ecclesiastical History*, XXIX (1978), 257-79 (p. 267), repr. in her *Lollards and their Books*, pp. 43-65 (p. 53), quoting from the *Opus Arduum*. On the same page Hudson notes that the authorities who examined William Smith in 1389 confiscated books 'quos in materna lingua de evangelio et de epistolis . . . conscripserat'. On the subject of Lollardy and the vernacular in general, see Anne Hudson, 'Lollardy: the English heresy?', *Studies in Church History*, XVIII (1982), 261-83, repr. in *Lollards and their Books*, pp. 141-63; Margaret Aston, 'Lollardy and literacy', *History*, LXII (1977), 347-71, repr. in her *Lollards and Reformers*, pp. 193-217; and again, Margaret Aston, 'Wyclif and the vernacular', in *From Ockham to Wyclif*, ed. by Anne Hudson and Michael Wilks, *Studies in Church History* Subsidia, 5 (Oxford, 1987), pp. 281-330. A supposition that Chaucer himself sympathized with the campaign for an English Bible could be derived from the way in which he justifies his use of the vernacular

in the Prologue to the *Treatise on the Astrolabe,* ll. 28-35 ('But natheles suffise to the these trewe conclusions in Englissh as wel as sufficith to these noble clerkes Grekes these same conclusions in Grek . . . and to Latyn folk in Latyn; whiche Latyn folk had hem first out of othere dyverse langages, and writen hem in her owne tunge'), thus recapitulating a major thread in Lollard polemic on behalf of Bible translation.

34. Robert of Basevorn's *Forma Praedicandi* (1322), ch. iv, trans. in J. J. Murphy, *Three Medieval Rhetorical Arts* (Berkeley, Calif., 1971), p. 124.

35. For Brut's arguments, see Aston, 'Lollard women priests?', pp. 444ff. (rpt, pp. 52ff.). Knighton is quoted *ibid.,* p. 442 (rpt, p. 50).

36. 'To Sir John Oldcastle' (dated 1415) (in *Hoccleve's Works: The Minor Poems,* ed. by F. J. Furnivall and I. Gollancz, EETS, ES, 61, 73, (London, 1892, 1925; rpt rev. by Jerome Mitchell and A. I. Doyle (London, 1970)), ll. 145-52.

37. *The Book of Margery Kempe,* ed. by S. B. Meech and H. E. Allen, EETS, OS, 212 (London, 1940), p. 129.

38. *Ibid.,* pp. 27-8.

39. *Ibid.,* pp. 125-6 and n. 14. See Clarissa W. Atkinson, *Mystic and Pilgrim* (Ithaca, NY, 1983), pp. 103-28 for a survey of Margery's relations with the Church. Margery herself mentions Master Aleyn, a White Friar, as one who 'enformyd hir in qwestyons of Scriptur whan sche wolde any askyn hym' (*Book of Margery Kempe,* ed. Meech & Allen, p. 168/7-9).

40. Hudson, *Selections,* III, 25-34, 154-62 (pp. 25, 28).

41. *Liber Contra XII Errores,* ed. Cronin, pp. 74-5. For Dymmok's full responses to the third and eleventh Conclusions, see *ibid.,* pp. 71-88, 272-91. If Lollards did object to priestly celibacy in the way he suggests, this train of thought was not peculiar to them, as is shown by its appearance in the Host's remarks on the Monk as a potential 'tredefowel' (VII 1943-53).

42. From a catalogue of John Purvey's heresies and errors 'extracti de libello suo haeretico', in *Fasciculi Zizaniorum,* ed. by W. W. Shirley, Rolls Series (London, 1858), pp. 383-99 (p. 392, Item VII.2). On the status of this catalogue, see Hudson, 'John Purvey', pp. 361-2 (rpt, pp. 91-2).

43. See the record of White's examination (1428) in *Fasciculi Zizaniorum,* ed. Shirley, pp. 420, 425-6. Although the Wife of Bath, too, hints broadly at sexual frustration and transgression among clerks (III 707-10), she would of course have much precedent for this in conventional anti-clerical satire.

44. N. P. Tanner, *Heresy Trials in the Diocese of Norwich, 1428-31,* Camden Society, 4th ser., 20 (London, 1977), pp. 148, 166; cf. statements *ibid.,* pp. 34, 57, 61, 73, 95, 158.

45. I draw on the text of Ramsbury's errors, and discussion of them, in Hudson, 'A Lollard mass', pp. 416-7, 408-10 (rpt, pp. 120-1, 113-14), but also on a sceptical response to the Free Spirit hypothesis in M. D. Lambert, *Medieval Heresy* (London, 1977), pp. 178, 239 n. 23.

46. Lambert, *Medieval Heresy,* p. 180.

47. *Book of Margery Kempe,* ed. Meech & Allen, p. 121; see also p. 121 nn. 2-3, p. 144 nn. 17-18; Hudson, 'Lollard Mass', p. 410 (rpt, p. 114). John Mahoney, 'Alice of Bath: her "secte" and "gentil text"', *Criticism,* VI (1964), 144-55, claims that the Brotherhood of the Free Spirit is relevant not only to Margery Kempe but also to the Wife of Bath.

48. Jerome's comment is given in n. 12 above. Margery's interpretation is consistent with one found in *Vox Clamantis,* III.27 (*The Major Latin Works of John Gower,* trans. by E. W. Stockton (Seattle, NY, 1962), pp. 161-2). Elsewhere in the *Vox* (III.17 and IV.13) Gower satirizes literal interpretation of the same text (*Major Latin Works,* trans. Stockton, pp. 148, 179). Further testimony to the attention the text was receiving is another discussion of it *c.* 1405-10 in *Dives and Pauper,* ed. by P. H. Barnum, I:2, EETS, OS, 280 (London, 1980), pp. 78-9.

49. *Liber Contra XII Errores,* ed. Cronin, p. 275. The argument beginning 'Si enim eas Deus uoluisset' compares interestingly with the Wife's 'to what conclusion / Were membres maad . . .' (III 115-16).

50. Tanner, *Heresy Trials,* p. 166. Although many of the Norwich defendants were charged with holding this view, it is sensible to note Tanner's caveat (p. 20) that 'the questionnaire on which the charges were based has made the defendants' beliefs appear more uniform than they were'.

51. Aston, 'Lollardy and literacy', p. 357 (rpt, p. 203), with particular reference to Margery Baxter of Norfolk, whose husband read Lollard texts to her at night. See also Claire Cross, '"Great reasoners in Scripture": the activities of women Lollards 1380-1530', in *Medieval Women,* ed. by Derek Baker, *Studies in Church History,* Subsidia, 1 (Oxford, 1978), pp. 359-80 (p. 363).

52. On the Oxford burning, see Anne Hudson, 'Contributions to a history of Wycliffite writings', *N & Q,* CCXVIII (1973), 443-53 (p. 445), repr. in

her *Lollards and their Books,* pp. 1-12 (p. 3); and for other instances, see Anne Hudson, 'A Lollard quaternion', *RES,* XXII (1971), 435-42 (p. 441 nn. 3 and 4), repr. in *Lollards and their Books,* pp. 193-200 (p. 199 nn. 3 and 4); and Thomson, *Later Lollards,* p. 27. On Arundel's Constitutions, see Hudson, 'Lollardy: the English heresy?', pp. 266-9 (rpt, pp. 146-9). *Opus Arduum* is quoted from Hudson, 'Neglected Wycliffite text', p. 267 (rpt, p. 53). An alternative view of the fate of Jankyn's book refers us to the fact that Jerome's friend Pammachius destroyed copies of *Adversus Jovinianum* when the treatise caused trouble after its initial circulation: see Mary Carruthers, 'The Wife of Bath and the painting of lions', *PMLA,* XCIV (1979), 209-22 (p. 211).

53. It is worth recalling that even the prospect of giving a perfectly innocuous rendering of the Dives-Lazarus story in *Confessio Amantis* prompts Gower to apologise for anglicizing that which the clergy 'In latin tunge . . . rede and singe', VI.975-6).

54. On this strategy, see Anne Hudson, 'The expurgation of a Lollard sermon-cycle', *Journal of Theological Studies,* XXII (1971), 451-65 (p. 453), repr. in her *Lollards and their Books,* pp. 201-15 (p. 203).

55. Pecock, *The Repressor,* ed. Babington, I, 66-7.

56. From the Wycliffite Bible (1395-7?) in Hudson, *Selections,* XIV, 20-3 (p. 67). The Wife has been much criticized for her 'abuse' of biblical quotation, from which the poet's disdain for literal exegesis *per se* is sometimes inferred. For a more judicious view, see Lawrence Besserman, '"Glosynge is a glorious thyng": Chaucer's biblical exegesis', in *Chaucer and Scriptural Tradition,* ed. Jeffrey, pp. 65-73.

57. The generally rather conservative scholarly estimate of Chaucer's Lollard affiliations is represented in F. R. H. Du Boulay, 'The historical Chaucer', in *Writers and their Backgrounds: Geoffrey Chaucer,* ed. by D. S. Brewer (London, 1974), pp. 33-57 (pp. 44-5).

58. Knight, *Geoffrey Chaucer,* p. 3.

59. In 'A Chaucer manifesto', forthcoming in *ChauR,* XXXIV (1989), I explore the comment on idolatry implicit in this text—though without specifically addressing the Lollard perspective now suggested.

60. 'Harass' is R. W. Hanning's apt expression in 'Roasting a friar, mis-taking a wife, and other acts of textual harassment in Chaucer's *Canterbury Tales*', *SAC,* VII (1985), 3-21. Among other studies, see Sheila Delany, *Chaucer's House of Fame:*

the *Poetics of Skeptical Fideism* (Chicago, 1972), *passim*; Stewart Justman, 'Medieval monism and abuse of authority in Chaucer', *ChauR,* XI (1976), 95-111; A. C. Spearing, 'Chaucerian authority and inheritance', in *Literature in Fourteenth Century England,* ed. by P. Boitani and A. Torti (Tübingen; Cambridge, 1983), pp. 185-202; Aers, *Chaucer,* pp. 7-13; A. Blamires, *The Canterbury Tales* (London, 1987), pp. 50-6; Jacqueline T. Miller, *Poetic License: Authority and Authorship in Medieval and Renaissance Contexts* (Oxford, 1987), chs. i and ii.

Colin A. Ireland (essay date January 1991)

SOURCE: Ireland, Colin A. "'A Coverchief or a Calle': The Ultimate End of the Wife of Bath's Search for Sovereignty." *Neophilologus* 75, no. 1 (January 1991): 150-59.

[*In the following essay, Ireland compares* The Wife of Bath's Tale *with an Irish story in which the country of Ireland is personified as a woman—sometimes young, beautiful, and fertile, sometimes old and worn—to symbolize the state of the nation.*]

The Wife of Bath's search for sovereignty in marriage is the central theme in both her ***Prologue*** and in the ***Tale*** she tells. Modern criticism tends to maintain a clear distinction between the Wife's ***Prologue*** and her ***Tale,*** noting specifically that the style of the ***Tale*** is more formal and less lively than her earthy ***Prologue.*** This stylistic difference is highlighted by the evidence that in some earlier arrangements of the ***Canterbury Tales*** the Wife of Bath was originally intended to relate the tale told by the Shipman. Although the ***Tale***'s concern with sovereignty in marriage suits well the Wife's own personal preoccupations, its courtly setting and sermon-like style are a bit incongruous for her less-than-idealistic approach to life. The Irish analogues of the 'loathly lady' theme in ***The Wife of Bath's Tale*** have long been acknowledged but the Irish parallels of the Wife of Bath herself have not received the notice they deserve. This paper will show that Irish parallels to the Wife of Bath herself are intimately related to the Irish 'loathly lady' analogues through the theme of sovereignty, though certainly not restricted to sovereignty in marriage.[1] Such evidence shows that Chaucer, in this case, had good precedents for his final arrangement of teller to tale.

Since the Irish literary works containing these analogues of the 'loathly lady' and the Wife of Bath are unlikely to be Chaucer's immediate sources their existence in his work suggest that, like his choice of English over French as his medium of expression, many motifs and themes employed in the *Canterbury Tales* had a common currency in fourteenth-century England. However, their manifestation would most consistently have been at a sub-literary level. In *The Wife of Bath's Tale* this is most suggestively reflected in Chaucer's use of the word *calle* 'headdress' (line 1018).[2] Although its etymology in English is doubtful, it is clearly the Irish word *caille* 'veil' from which is derived *caillech,* a word whose semantic development reverberates with meaning for the Wife of Bath and her *Tale.*

We must, first of all, understand the Irish versions of the 'loathly lady' stories in their full cultural context. One of the most consistently portrayed metaphors throughout Irish cultural history is that a king 'marries' his kingdom and that a royal ordination is actually a wedding feast (*banfheis*) between the monarch and his 'sovereignty'. In other words the kingdom itself, whether a small territory or the entire island of Ireland, is thought of as female and is espoused to the king. The 'sovereignty' displays her approval and acceptance of the monarch by dispensing a liquor, or an elixir. This may occur at the wedding feast, that is to say, at the ordination, itself. Or, as is typical in many medieval Irish political 'prophecies', the 'sovereignty' pours out liquor for a future monarch symbolizing her acceptance of him and his ascension to the throne.[3] The second element of the word *banfheis,* i.e. *feis,*[4] may mean 'spending the night with, sleeping with', or simply 'feast, banquet'. The two meanings are not necessarily mutually exclusive, and in this context at least, are not meant to be differentiated. This extended metaphor of portraying Ireland as a woman appears to have been well established since the pre-Christian era and to have survived into the present age, even among Anglo-Irish writers. The 'sovereignty' may be described in a full range of aspects from a fair young maiden; fresh, virginal and eager for the promises of nuptial pleasures with a vigorous new monarch. Or, she may be portrayed as a haggard, weary old woman, abandoned by an exiled king, or widowed at his death. The portrait of the 'sovereignty', then, often serves as a barometer revealing the state of the nation.

The Irish stories with the 'loathly lady' motif descend to us in two major versions, one might call them the 'southern' and 'northern' versions. Each has its own variants, some told in prose, others in verse, the intertextuality of this theme attesting to the richness of early Irish literary culture. Both versions are political allegories meant to explain, claim, or justify, the dominance of certain families in the kingship of their respective regions. Both versions utilize the established metaphor of 'sovereignty' as a female. The basic outline of both versions is that brothers, sons of a monarch, are continually being tested, usually in a manner unknown to themselves. After displaying in various ways their worthiness, they go out together on a hunt where they meet the 'loathly lady' whose detailed description is so grotesque and hideous that she nearly seems non-human. The hunt out in a wild, often forested, area is a common motif in both medieval Irish and Welsh narrative which signals that the characters are about to have an 'otherworldly' experience.[5]

In the first, or 'southern', version the sons of Dáire Doimthech compete to see whose descendants will dominate the kingship of Munster in the south of Ireland. In anticipation of a prophecy regarding who will attain the kingship, all of the brothers are named Lugaid. A prose variant, which was first noted by Whitley Stokes as an analogue of *The Wife of Bath's Tale,* is recorded in the *Cóir Anmann* (Fitness of Names).[6] The primary purpose of this text is to explain through medieval etymologies, like those of Isidore of Seville, the various appellatives or nicknames used to differentiate one Lugaid from another. A verse variant of this tale is found in the metrical *Dindshenchas,* a text which records the history and legends attached to eminent places throughout Ireland.[7] It is Lugaid Laígde who, in order to help his brothers, agrees to kiss the 'loathly lady' in return for food and shelter. She instantly turns into a beautiful and desirable young woman and reveals herself to be the 'sovereignty'. She says that she will 'sleep' with many of Lugaid's descendants, that is to say of course, that they will attain the kingship.

The second, or 'northern', version is the better known because it deals with the eponymous Níall, the fifth-century ancestor of the Uí Néill dynasts. The tale explains (or justifies) their subsequent domination of the symbolic high-kingship of Tara. A verse variant is attributed to the scholar-poet, Cuán Ó Lothcháin (obit c. 1024).[8] He is described by Eoin MacNeill as one of the 'synthetic historians', a term used by MacNeill, himself a historian, to describe those medieval scholars actively involved in 'synthesizing' Irish history and legend. Closely related prose variants are preserved in the Book of Ballymote[9] and the Yellow Book of Lecan.[10] In this version the five sons of Eochu Muigmedón compete for recognition. Four brothers are the sons of the queen, Mongfhind. The fifth brother, Níall, is the king's son by a slave-woman. In this version too, the sons go out together on a hunt which sets the scene for an 'otherwordly' encounter. In the evening after the camp is set up each brother goes out singly to fetch water. Each, in turn, comes to a well guarded by a hideous hag (i.e. the 'sovereignty') who demands a kiss in return for a drink.[11] Those who refuse are excluded from ever gaining the kingship. Those who comply ensure for themselves, and/or their descendants, the symbolic high-kingship of Tara. In one variant, Níall not only agrees to kiss the hag but willingly lies with her. While in his embrace she is transformed into a lovely, desirable maiden. The allegorical implications are fully disclosed when the maiden, after revealing herself as the 'sovereignty' (*flaithius*), tells Níall:

> 'Just as you saw me initially as hideous, beastly and terrifying, and subsequently as beautiful, so is the sovereignty; for it is seldom gained without battles and strife but ultimately for anyone it is beautiful and becoming'.[12]

The descendants of Níall, through the various branches of the kindred, became the most powerful and influential political family in Irish history. Many of its members were redoubtable Irish leaders during the Elizabethan wars in Ireland.

One of the most appealing, yet enigmatic, literary characters from Old Irish poetry is a figure who almost certainly derives from, or at least was modelled on, this metaphor of the 'sovereignty' of a region as a female. We encounter her in a poem which, based on the contrasting opinions of its various editors, one can assign to the ninth century. Although the poem has attracted the attention of several translators and anthologizers, no critical consensus has emerged on just how best to define this character. She is usually referred to as the 'Old Woman' or 'Hag' of Beare, a lonely peninsula in the southwest of Ireland which reaches out into the stormy Atlantic. In the poem she is depicted as having been the consort of kings in her youth, but is now withered with age:

> These arms, these scrawny things you see,
>   scarce merit now their little joy
> when lifted up in blessing
>   over sweet student boy
>
> These arms you see,
>   these bony scrawny things,
> had once more loving craft
>   embracing kings.
>
> When Maytime comes
>   the girls out there are glad,
> and I, old hag, old bones,
>   alone am sad.[13]

The reliance on the 'sovereignty' metaphor in explaining the character of the 'Old Woman of Beare' is strengthened by her insistence that, although she is ravaged by old age, she does not regret her youth and is jealous only of Femen 'whose crop is still gold'. Femen is the plain around Cashel in Co. Tipperary, the site of the kings of Munster.

A tradition that the 'Old Woman of Beare' had a succession of husbands is a feature that reminds us of the Wife of Bath. A prose preface in one of the five manuscript copies of the poem states:

> She passed into seven periods of youth, so that every husband used to pass from her to death of old age, so that her grandchildren and greatgrandchildren were peoples and races.[14]

It must be noted, however, that this is not specifically stated in the poem, but only in one prose preface.

Another Irish literary character who probably descends directly from the metaphor of the 'sovereignty' is Queen Medb (Maeve) of the *Táin Bó Cúailnge* (Cattle Raid of Cooley). Etymologically the name Medb is cognate with English 'mead'. Her name originally meant 'the one who intoxicates' signifying her function as dispenser of the 'liquor of sovereignty'.[15] When we meet her in the *Táin* she has evolved beyond metaphor into a fully developed character with her own clearly-defined personality, personal history and family (including genealogy).

The Book of Leinster version of the *Táin*, redacted in the mid-twelfth century, opens with the renowned 'Pillow Talk',[16] one of the most delightful scenes between a man and woman in Irish literature, and one redolent of a personality like the Wife of Bath. Medb contends with her husband, Ailill, over the value of their respective possessions which is shown to be equal in every particular except that Ailill possessed a fine bull, Findbennach, which Medb could not match. It is this perceived lack on Medb's part that sets in train the events of the *Táin* when she rallies the armies of Ireland to proceed against Ulster in order to capture the Donn Cúailnge, a bull to equal Findbennach.

But it is not merely Medb's acquisitive nature, nor her martial hardiness (making her the equal of any man) that remind us of the Wife of Bath. For Medb herself demanded an unusual bride-price the likes of which no other woman had demanded of the men of Ireland. Her husband must be without meanness, without jealousy and without fear. In the context of early medieval societies it is easy enough to understand the expectations that a king be generous and fearless. But in a male-dominated world it could hardly be expected that he would not be jealous. Yet Medb insists that it would not be suitable that she should have a jealous husband for as she states, 'I never had a man without another in his shadow'.[17] Medb's insistence on her own independence is remarkable. Some might argue that her series of lovers is proof that she, at least formerly, was a manifestation of the 'sovereignty'. Each lover would represent a future king. But it must be noted that during the course of the *Táin* she cuckolds Ailill with Fergus mac Róig, a warrior from Ulster in exile among her Connacht troops. Yet there is never any suggestion that Fergus is, therefore, the next in line for the kingship.[18] Medb, as we meet her in the *Táin,* is more appropriately treated as an invented literary character than as a demoted symbol of 'sovereignty'. Whatever early Irish literature inherited from pagan Celtic ideology we should expect it to play no greater role than that played by Classical pagan deities in other medieval literatures. Medb might well have said, along with the Wife of Bath:

Venus me yaf my lust, my likerousnesse,
and Mars yaf me my sturdy hardynesse

(lines 611-12)

Both of these robust, vigorous women characters have much in common regardless of the source of the literary allusions employed to describe them.

The social reality of early Ireland, particularly with regard to marriage and divorce, helps lend these literary characters their vitality. Despite the persistent, and in several respects accurate, stereotype of medieval Ireland as the 'Land of Saints and Scholars', many social customs and practices whose origins pre-date the Church's influence continued unabated. Polygamy, particularly among the higher social ranks, was an accepted practice, as was easy divorce and subsequent remarriage of either partner. These practices persisted, despite the best efforts of reforming clergy, until the collapse of the native Irish order, that is, well into the time of the Elizabethan conquest.[19] They are customs and practices which were frequently scorned and disparaged by the English in Ireland. Whatever about the orthodoxy of certain medieval Irish social practices, the deliberate syncretism of native Irish customs with those current on the Continent, usually introduced by the Church, is one of the features that makes the study of Irish literature and cultural history so fascinating. This blend is frequently demonstrated in the early law-tracts, most of which were redacted in the late seventh- to early eighth centuries. Early Irish law was 'customary law'. It does not record edicts and legislation but instead delineates social organization and outlines time-honoured practices.[20]

The law-tract *Bretha Crólige,* concerned primarily with rights and responsibilities in the maintenance of the sick and injured, offers a dramatic example of this syncretism on a matter relating to marriage. It states:

> For there is a dispute in Irish law as to which is more proper, whether many sexual unions or a single one: for the chosen [people] of God lived in plurality of unions, so that it is not easier to condemn it than to praise it.[21]

We have here early Irish lawyers, writing c. 700, who cite precedents from the Old Testament as justification for the continuation of the long established Irish practice of polygamy. One can almost hear the Wife of Bath, nearly seven hundred years later, disputing from the standpoint of her *experience* against the Church fathers in favour of multiple marriages. She cites scripture, specifically Solomon (line 35), Abraham (line 55) and Jacob (line 56) in justification of her views. Likewise, the commentator on the Irish law-tract cited above lists Solomon, David and Jacob as examples of polygamists.[22]

One must not over-romanticize the status and social independence of women in medieval Ireland. The early Irish law-tracts leave no doubt that a woman was always subordinate to some man: when young, to her father; when married, to her husband; when widowed, to a brother or her son. Nevertheless, a married woman of some social rank who acquired or controlled a fair amount of material wealth (excluding land, which she was not allowed to possess) could act with a degree of autonomy not available to her counterpart in a monogamous society.[23] Irish history provides the names of several such women, a noteworthy example being Gormlaith who died c. 946. She was herself the daughter of a king of Ireland and married in succession three kings: Cormac mac Cuilennáin, king-bishop of Cashel in Munster; Cerball, king of Leinster; and Níall Glúndub, king of Ireland and a member of the Uí Néill. There are several poems attributed to her, most of them are laments for her last husband, Níall. Since some of these poems are linguistically too late to have been composed by her it seems likely that they were attributed to her in order to increase the prestige of the Uí Néill. But it is entirely probable that she herself authored several of the poems. The title *Serc Gormlaithe do Níall*[24] 'The Love of Gormlaith for Níall', preserved from the tenth-century saga lists, in addition to the poems mentioned above, attests to the well-established tradition of her great love for Níall. She spent the waning years of her life in a convent.

Gormlaith represents only one historical example of many Irish women whose full lives and multiple husbands might remind us of the Wife of Bath. Many such women flourished during those centuries when Ireland was more completely bi-cultural, with the English customs practiced in the Pale and the native Irish order in force beyond.[25] But we need not confine ourselves to the native Irish for interesting parallels. For example, Dame Alice Kyteler from the English community in Kilkenny had four husbands. She was accused of witchcraft in 1324, perhaps for political reasons, and fled to England. It is often through the disapproving comments of the English in Ireland at the time that we gain insight into the social customs as practiced by the contemporary Irish who saw little need to comment on themselves in this way. For example, the statute of Kilkenny, promulgated in 1366, was an attempt by the English authorities in Ireland to halt the increasingly rapid assimilation of the English colony to Irish customs and manners, including use of the Irish language.[26] It provides a clear example of how Irish customs influenced the English in Ireland and, hence, suggests how Irish terms and customs could become known in the England of Chaucer's time.

It is this contact between English and Irish that brings us to the next point. *Calle* is a word found frequently in Middle English texts of the fourteenth century, and is used by Chaucer in the *The Wife of Bath's Tale* (line 1018). The new *Riverside Chaucer,* in the textual glosses at the bottom of the page, defines it as a 'hair-net worn as a headdress'. The second edition of the **Complete Works of Geoffrey Chaucer** by F. N. Robinson lists *calle* in its glossary as 'caul; hair-net; headdress'. The University of Michigan's *Middle English Dictionary* suggests that it might be derived from O.E. *cawl* 'basket, container, net, sieve', and rejects the suggestion made in the O.E.D. under *caul* that it is related to O.F. *cale* 'small cap; headdress', arguing that 'OF *cale* of the 15th c. is either a back-formation from *calotte* or a borrowing from English'.[27] Whatever about the etymology of the French word, the Middle English *calle* must be a borrowing from Irish *caille* 'veil'. This word is among the fifth century borrowings from Latin into Irish. Its Latin source is *pallium* 'covering; cloak, mantle', the substitution of the sound /k/ for /p/ proving its great age.[28] Once Irish *caille* became current in English usage its confusion with O.E. *cawl* would only be natural. Both the O.E. and Irish words suggest something woven and, hence, net-like. In the prose tale *Compert Conchubair* (The Conception of Conchobar) we find an example of *caille* suggesting 'net, web', certainly something woven, in the line 'she strained the water into the cup through her *caille*'.[29] This tale provides a particularly interesting context for this word because the characters and events of the tale belong to pagan prehistory. Nevertheless, the Middle Irish redactor understood a *caille* to be a typical article of clothing for a, in this case, young woman. It is perfectly clear that Mid.E. *calle* and Ir. *caille* both meant some type of head-covering or 'veil' commonly worn by women. With this overlap in the semantic fields of O.E. *cawl* and Irish *caille* it would naturally follow that the native English monosyllabic word would win out over the disyllabic Irish word, particularly with the tendency for Middle English words to lose final -*e*.

The semantic development in Irish of the derived word *caillech* has important ramifications for Chaucer's use of *calle* in **The Wife of Bath's Tale**. *Caillech* is literally 'a veiled one', i.e. a 'nun'. This meaning is well attested from the Old Irish period, that is before 900, in saints' lives and other religious writings. But already in the same period it had developed the meaning 'old woman', suggesting that many women who 'took the veil' in the early Middle Ages did so as their life options and alternatives were reduced in their later years. Perhaps the most famous example of a *caillech* in Old Irish literature is the *Caillech Bérri,* or the 'Old Woman of Beare', discussed previously. She calls herself the *caillech* in the second stanza of the poem, stating explicitly further on that she now wears the 'veil':

> No wedding wether killed for me,
>   an end to all coquetry;
> a pitiful veil (*caille*) I wear
>   on thin and faded hair.

> Well do I wear
>   plain veil (*caille*) on faded hair;

> many colours I wore
>   and we feasting before.[30]

One should keep in mind the historical example of Gormlaith, cited above, who eventually retired to a convent.

Perhaps the most striking use of the term *caillech,* and one attested in the Old Irish period as well, is as a 'hag, crone, witch'. In the Irish versions of the 'loathly lady' cited above, *caillech* is used interchangeably with *sentainne* 'old woman' for the grotesquely hideous women the kings-to-be were expected to kiss.[31] Thus for anyone familiar with these Irish analogues, Chaucer's lines resonate with deeper implications when his own variant of the 'loathly lady' says to the young knight:

> Lat se which is the proudeste of hem alle,
> That wereth on a coverchief or a calle,
> That dar seye nay of that I shall thee teche.

> (lines 1017-19)

Calle, when seen in a context informed by the Irish analogues, is more than just a woman's headdress. It may serve as a badge of her station in life and may imply those who have taken the veil as their years advanced, women for whom the Irish term *caillech* applies. In the Wife's **Tale** they are the women in the queen's court whose *experience* will verify the 'loathly lady's' advice to the young knight. As for the Wife of Bath herself, her own *experience* must have made her aware of the limitations of her search for sovereignty, for it could never allow her to gain *maistrye* over time and old age. Despite her lusty, and optimistic, 'welcome the sixte' husband (line 45) as she set out to Canterbury, a sadder and more resigned realization must also reside behind her motives for going on pilgrimage. But it is to our eternal pleasure that Chaucer chose to portray the Wife of Bath when he did, rather than wait until she had become the *Caillech* of Bath.

Notes

1. I do not present these Irish analogues as an example of source study. Given the style and setting of the *Tale* it is hardly likely that Chaucer himself was even remotely aware of the tale's Irish analogues. The best study of how this motif may have come into the purview of Chaucer's work is still Sigmund Eisner, *A Tale of Wonder, a Source Study of The Wife of Bath's Tale* (Wexford, 1957). However, the cultural context of the sovereignty theme and its various manifestations in Irish literature are very informative for an appreciation of the Wife's *Prologue* and her *Tale*. The social history of the period in England makes it quite likely that Chaucer was aware of many stereotypes entertained by the English about the Irish and their social practices.

2. All quotations and line citations from the *Prologue* and the *Tale* are from *The Riverside Chaucer,* Larry D. Benson, gen. ed. (Oxford, 1988).

3. Much has been written on this theme, among the more important articles are: T. F. O'Rahilly, 'The Names *Érainn* and *Ériu*', *Ériu* 14 (1946) 7-28, esp. 14-21; R. A. Breatnach, 'The Lady and the King, a Theme of Irish Literature', *Studies: An Irish Quarterly Review* 42 (1953) 321-36; Proinsias Mac Cana, 'Aspects of the Theme of King and Goddess in Irish Literature', *Études Celtiques* 7 (1955-7) 76-104, 356-413; ibid. 8 (1958) 59-65; Rachel Bromwich, 'Celtic Dynastic Themes and Breton Lays', *Études Celtiques* 9 (1961) 439-74.

4. For definitions of Irish words, see the Royal Irish Academy's *Dictionary of the Irish Language* (Dublin, 1913-76).

5. Notice that in the *Tale* the knight first sees the fairy women dance, and subsequently meets the 'loathly lady', as he is riding through a forest (lines 989-999).

6. Whitley Stokes, '*Cóir Anmann,* The Fitness of Names', *Irische Texte* iii (Leipzig, 1897) 316-23 §10.

7. Edward J. Gwynn, *Metrical Dindshenchas* iv, Todd Lecture Series xi (Dublin, 1924) 134-43.

8. Maud Joynt, 'Echtra Mac Echdach Mugmedóin', *Ériu* 4 (1910) 91-111.

9. Standish H. O'Grady, *Silva Gadelica* i-ii (London, 1892) i 326-30 (Irish), ii 368-73 (English).

10. Whitley Stokes, 'The Death of Chrimthann son of Fidach, and the Adventures of the Sons of Eochaid Muigmedón', *Revue Celtique* 24 (1903) 172-207; esp. pp. 190-203.

11. Although in this variant of the tale the brothers are only seeking water from the 'loathly lady' it is clearly meant as a parallel symbol for the 'liquor' dispensed to the future king by the 'sovereignty'.

12. Stokes, *Revue Celtique* 24 (1903) 200 §16.

13. The translation of these stanzas is from James Carney, *Medieval Irish Lyrics* (1967: Dublin, 1985) 31, 33. The most recent edition and translation of this poem is by Donncha Ó hAodha, 'The Lament of the Old Woman of Beare', in *Sages, Saints and Storytellers, Celtic Studies in Honour of Professor James Carney,* edd. Donnchadh Ó Corráin, Liam Breatnach, Kim McCone (Maynooth, 1989) 308-31. It gives a full bibliography of previous editions and translations and includes extensive textual notes.

14. Ó hAodha, 309. For a very engaging and insightful discussion of the place of the 'Old Woman of Beare' in Irish tradition, see the recent article by Tomás Ó Cathasaigh, 'The Eponym of Cnogba', *Éigse* 23 (1989) 27-38.

15. T. F. O'Rahilly, *Ériu* 14 (1946) 15.

16. Cecile O'Rahilly, ed. and trans., *Táin Bó Cúailnge from the Book of Leinster* (Dublin, 1967). Thomas Kinsella's more widely known translation does not follow the order of the tale as preserved in the Book of Leinster. The 'pillow talk' in his translation is found on pages 52-8; *The Tain* (Oxford, 1970).

17. The line in Irish reads, *dáig ní raba-sa ríam can fer ar scáth araile ocum*; C. O'Rahilly, 2 line 37.

18. Francis John Byrne notes that archaic genealogical poems, possibly as old as the seventh century, trace the origins of several Munster peoples to this union between Medb and Fergus mac Róig; *Irish Kings and High-Kings* (London, 1973) 171. Such evidence suggests the depth of tradition and relative age of the stories dealing with the *Táin.*

19. For articles treating marriage in medieval Ireland, see *Marriage in Ireland,* Art Cosgrove, ed. (Dublin, 1985), particularly the articles by Donnchadh Ó Corráin, 'Marriage in Early Ireland' 5-24, and Art Cosgrove, 'Marriage in Medieval Ireland, 25-50.

20. For a lucid introduction to early Irish law and social practice, see Fergus Kelly, *A Guide to Early Irish Law* (Dublin, 1988), particularly pp. 68-79 for marriage, divorce and the legal capacity of women.

21. Daniel A. Binchy, 'Bretha Crólige', *Ériu* 12 (1938) 1-77; p. 45 §57.

22. ibid. 47. Donnchadh Ó Corráin in his article 'Marriage in Early Ireland' makes it clear that the Irish lawyers drew on canon law in support of their views on marriage and were not merely defending pre-Christain Irish practices against the Church, art. cit. (note 19).

23. For a good overview, consult Katharine Simms, 'The Legal Position of Irishwomen in the Later Middle Ages', *The Irish Jurist* 10 new series (1975) 96-111.

24. The title of this tale is ambiguous. I have translated it on the basis of the tradition of the poems ascribed to Gormlaith which depict her great love for Níall. But according to early Irish grammar *do* may express the agent of a verbal noun so that a more accurate translation might be 'Níall's Love for Gormlaith'. The likely politoliterary context of this title is discussed by Proinsias Mac Cana, *The Learned Tales of Ireland*

(Dublin, 1980) 103-05. For some background on Gormlaith, see the editions of poems ascribed to her by Anne O'Sullivan, 'Triamhuim Ghormlaithe', *Ériu* 16 (1952) 189-99; and Osborn Bergin, *Irish Bardic Poetry* (Dublin, 1970) 202-15, 308-15.

25. Consult *Women in Irish Society, the Historical Dimension,* Margaret Mac Curtain and Donncha Ó Corráin, edd. (Dublin, 1978), specifically the articles by Ó Corráin, 'Women in Early Irish Society' 1-13, and Katharine Simms, 'Women in Norman Ireland' 14-25.

26. For insight into the literature of the English colony in Ireland, see *A New History of Ireland II 1169-1534,* Art Cosgrove, ed. (Oxford, 1987), particularly chapter 26 by Alan Bliss and Joseph Long, 'Literature in Norman French and English to 1534' 708-36.

27. *Middle English Dictionary* Part. C.1, ed. Hans Kurath (Ann Arbor, 1959) 21.

28. Damian McManus, 'A Chronology of the Latin Loan-words in Early Irish', *Ériu* 34 (1983) 21-71; p. 48 §59.

29. The line reads: *sithlais in uisci isin cuach tria chailli*; Kuno Meyer, 'Anecdota from the Stowe Ms. no. 992', *Revue Celtique* 6 (1883-85) 173-92; p. 175 line 42.

30. Carney, 33.

31. Note the shrew in the misericord depicted on the frontispiece in the edition by James Winny, *The Wife of Bath's Prologue and Tale* (Cambridge, 1965).

Catherine S. Cox (essay date March 1993)

SOURCE: Cox, Catherine S. "Holy Erotica and the Virgin Word: Promiscuous Glossing in *The Wife of Bath's Prologue*." *Exemplaria* 5, no. 1 (March 1993): 207-37.

[*In the following essay, Cox explores the sexual connotations of the term "glossing," highlights the double entendres in* The Wife of Bath's Prologue, *and investigates the link between sexual fulfillment and control of language. Cox maintains that although the Wife of Bath seeks to fight the patriarchal system, her lack of feminine discourse forces her to use male definitions, and ultimately she is unsuccessful in self-definition.*]

Although the Wife of Bath, in her *Prologue,* argues in a quasi-feminist voice for the validity of her own experience and authority,[2] her narrative seems ambiguously—

and ambivalently—both feminist and anti-feminist.[3] This sense of the narrative becomes clearer when we consider the Wife to be a textual "feminine"[4] representation, one constructed within the parameters of "masculine" discourse and articulated in masculine terms,[5] even as specific components of the construction may be identified as feminine. My interest in the textual feminine here corresponds not to any internal textual privileging of an *écriture féminine*[6] but to masculine and feminine components of an epistemological metaphor of paradigmatic distinction. The feminine may be understood as an engendered epistemological construct existing *within* the parameters of an ostensibly masculine discourse. The Wife, herself a textual construct, does not produce what could be described as a feminine discourse; rather, she is produced by and reiterates an ostensibly masculine discourse, though as I hope to demonstrate, her narrative calls attention to an ambivalent feminine poetics within those parameters.

As a character within a fictional frame, the Wife exists as words of narrative; her existence is a textual reality. And as a fictional voice articulated from moment to moment by narrative structures, the Wife does not control the agency of her own narrative, her "own" voice, even as the narrative voice constructs the illusion of character. As Marshall Leicester notes,

> What we call the Wife of Bath exists in the text as a set of unresolvable tensions between self-revelation and self-presentation, repentance and rebellion, determinism and freedom, the individual and the institution, Venus and Mars, past and present. In each of these cases the opposition is both necessary and unsustainable, and the terms ceaselessly turn into one another. Of course the Wife is a construction, an interpretation.[7]

The Wife may be read as both narrative construct and literary character, the former existing discursively, as a rhetorical construct, and the latter as a mimetic reality, having an imagined history and psychological profile. Although without the latter there would be no "Wife," Chaucer's concern lies more clearly with the former, and my own remarks attend primarily to the Wife as the narrative/discursive construct that Chaucer uses to delineate his own discovering of the limits of discourse. While the Wife ultimately does not replace or supplant the masculine with what could be construed as an *écriture féminine,* her characterization nonetheless challenges patriarchal orthodoxy in its evocation of the feminine component of epistemological dualism and the text's grappling with the tensions thereby introduced.

This said, I want to consider the linguistic, discursive, and sexual ambiguities of the Wife's attention to "glossing," which I shall eventually connect to the narrative's articulation of an ambivalent feminine poetics. This poetics in turn inscribes Chaucer's concern with his own glossing, his own sense of the equivocalness of discursive investiture. To gloss a word, phrase, or passage is to supply a new and more readily accessible interpretation or annotation, ostensibly for clarification or explanation. Owing to the word's etymology,[8] however, an underlying erotic sense informs its use in the Wife's discourse. For example, the Wife's description of glossing—"Men may devyne and glosen up and doun," "Glose whoso wole, and seye bothe up and doun" (III.26, 119)[9]—not only suggests a thorough attempt at interpretation, covering both ends and everything that is between them, but also hints at erotic activity, of the connotations of which the Wife is no doubt aware and in which, indeed, the character delights. It is important, too, to note the shift in gender identification: first, the Wife insists that "men" may gloss (III.26), using a noun which while signifying a general sense of "people" is nonetheless masculine; she then uses "whoso" (III.119), signifying "anyone," masculine or feminine.[10] What is initially described as a masculine activity is arguably subsequently assigned to—or appropriated by—the feminine. Both men and women may "gloss," be it sexually or textually; as the Wife clearly demonstrates in her own ambiguous "glossing," the tongue is, in effect, androgynous or bisexual,[11] belonging to and representative of both the masculine and the feminine.

Glossing informs the role of the text as mediation of desire, underscored throughout the *Prologue* by the Wife's articulation of sexualized language "pleye":

> But yet I praye to al this compaignye
> If that I speke after my fantasye,
> As taketh not agrief of that I seye;
> For myn entente nis but for to pleye
>
> III.190-92

claims the Wife, using a disclaimer typical of Chaucerian narrators (who remind us not to "make ernest of game" [I.3186], not to impart to the text with such seriousness that it is stripped of its wit and pleasure).[12] Glossing is connected to sexualized textuality[13] in the Wife's description of the episode involving Jankyn's "book of wikked wyves" (III.685), for example, an episode which demonstrates that this particular text serves as an instrument of seduction.[14] It is, after all, the book that prompts the confrontation that in turn leads to reconciliation (according to the Wife's narrative of events). Jankyn is described as preferring the book to his wife, substituting the eros of the text for the eros of the marital relationship; the Wife notes that he amuses himself with the book, reading it "gladly, nyght and day" (III.669). The confrontation between Jankyn and the Wife is provoked by the Wife's apparent jealousy over her husband's preferring to spend his evenings with his book rather than with her. Thus the book substitutes for desire (for Jankyn) and then effects desire's mediation, ultimately bringing together Jankyn

and the Wife. Indeed, the Wife notes that he gave her control "of his tonge and of his hond also" (III.815), again suggesting the correlation of eros and language in her controlling of his "tonge."[15] The Wife's narrative insists upon an alignment of the two, eros and language, and indeed her *Prologue* itself "glosses" one in terms of the other.

There is, then, a crucial connection between eros and language that the Wife draws upon throughout her narrative; her attention to sex may be understood as attention to language and vice versa, for her discourse on marriage is not only a commentary on marriage as institution, but also on the discourse of that institution and, indeed, on discourse itself. Further, as the Wife embodies the textuality of the framing narrative, her textuality is sexualized just as her body is textualized. The relationship of textuality and sexuality is underscored by attention to the abuse of each component in that abuse of eros—perversion—serves as a commentary upon or metaphor of the abuse of language. As Eugene Vance comments, "The equation between idolatry, including idolatry of the letter, and sexual perversion became a subtle force in medieval poetics,"[16] informing sexual metaphors that call attention to their own signification processes in addition to thematic considerations of the activities described. The Wife's inclusion of fairly explicit double entendres, then, provides an incessant, though erratic, reminder throughout her *Prologue* that the character is commenting on both medium and message, that the narrative addresses concerns of both textual representation and normative presuppositions in the narrative's moral dimension. Chaucer sets out the Wife as a kind of narrative decoy in order to confront normative/narrative presuppositions and to test the dangers of glossing in relation to his own poetic appropriation. He demonstrates the inevitability of discursive promiscuity—an inhering insistence upon the resistance of language to unmitigated subjection.

While moralizing readings that fault the Wife's behavior or find her wanting—conventional masculine readings—are clearly supported by the text's own emphases,[17] the Wife, as a narrative construct, as a textual representation of Woman, also supports a reading that challenges this perspective without ignoring the unfavorable details included in the Wife's construction. In other words, to find a feminine valorization inhering in the Wife's narrative is not—and need not be—to ignore the reality of the portrait.

The Wife delights in *talking* about sexuality;[18] the language of eros is, for her, apparently far more appealing than is any active participation itself. Indeed, with regard to her "olde houbondes" she notes,

> For wynning wolde I al his lust endure,
> And make me a feyned appetit;
> And yet in bacon hadde I nevere delit.
>
> III.416-18

She endures her husband's sexual demands in order to maintain her profit-making status as "wyf."[19] Moreover, she confesses outright that she feigns an appetite, that she fakes arousal and desire because she has no interest in nor derives enjoyment from "bacon." (She describes her husband[s] sexually as "bacon," old meat, aged and dry, while her own female anatomy she identifies as "*bele chose,*" beautiful thing [III.447, 510].) Her comment suggests that for all her sexually charged banter and erotic "pleye," language is the medium of eros for her, and the excitement she does not find any longer in active sexuality, she finds in language, its substitute. The Wife participates in an eroticization of the letter, for the erotic sense of language apparently holds for the Wife far greater appeal than does participation in the activities to which the language refers; her "*bele chose*" is her "pleye" of language, not the play of her female anatomy, and she apparently derives satisfaction from the response that her word-"pleye" elicits from her audience. To construct her "pleye," then, she imposes connotations not only according *to* her pleasure, but *for* her pleasure as well.[20]

The Wife's use of "appetyt" to describe her desire for sexual/textual pleasure—*jouissance*—is curious in its apparent inconsistency, for she claims first to feign an appetite, suggesting that none is present, and then to follow an appetite of her own natural desires: "And make me a feyned appetit" (III.417) and "evere folwede myn appetit" (III.622). "Appetit" is first described as absent, then present. Clearly, while the Wife desires to desire (to borrow the phrase made popular by Mary Anne Doane),[21] she apparently finds actual sexual desire lacking; in its place she not only constructs the illusion of its presence, but then claims to follow that very (feigned) desire as well. The apparent contradiction is reconciled, however, by the Wife's implicit core intention: to elicit a response from her predominantly male audience, even if her narrative/rhetorical performance demands inconsistencies in the narrative/rhetorical line. "Rhetorical" here suggests that "desire" is constructed by the discourse; it exists only as the rhetorical line suggests its existence; the rhetorical line is not informed by an a priori desire, but rather the line generates it simultaneously with its articulation even if the articulation contradicts itself. "Desire" is for the Wife rhetorical, for her desire to desire seems to be accompanied by a desire to be *recognized* as having desire; she seems to construct her narrative for the effect of eliciting approval from her audience and, as such, the narrative voice ventriloquizes, speaking their language—the language of the audience—rather than her "own." Hence her claims of sexual promiscuity ("I ne loved nevere by

no discrecioun"—III.622) and her impulse to talk about this alleged lack of discretion may be understood as an attempt to enhance the likelihood of acquiring this recognition from her audience. Indeed, the Wife's attempts to maintain audience interest render her a caricature, an exaggeration of a woman who not only desires to desire but who uses that desire as a rhetorical strategy, as a sexualized *captatio benevolentiae*. As a caricature of a feminine desire produced by the dominant masculine discourse, the Wife is not only made a spectacle, but is shown as a conspirator in her own objectification.[22] Hence too her own narrative of desire continues despite interruption ("Abyde! quod she"—III.169), while the subsequent telling of the formal *Tale* is contingent upon the audience's interest ("if ye wol heere"—III.828; "right as yow lest"—III.854; "If I have licence"—III.856). Her *Prologue,* which reports her own desire, is privileged over her *Tale,* which narrates the desire of wholly fictive others (themselves produced by a fictive construct).

Moreover, in calling attention to her "appetit," the Wife calls attention to her desire as a desire to consume, be it sexually, textually, or otherwise. In effect, as she "glosses," she consumes both partners and texts, appropriating them for her own use and deriving from them whatever satisfaction she can find. Her warning—"For peril is bothe fyr and tow t'assemble; / Ye knowe what this ensample may resemble" (III.89-90)—uses the consumption metaphor of fire and fuel that suggests, or "resembles," the consuming nature of sexuality.[23] In addition, her attention to consumption imagery calls attention to the twofold manifestation of her ambivalent desire: it represents both lack and surplus. Louise Fradenburg comments:

> The inability of the Wife's desire to find closure—the sense in which it is a desire for desire—is thus presented, on one level, as lack. But of course this characterization of her desire is meant to constrain the text's presentation, on another level, of desire as multiplicity, a supplement or surplus—*as always more than* its representations, and hence as always urged to remake the world.[24]

Her glossing suggests a kind of excess that calls attention to its own vicariousness. In Derridean terms, the Wife's excess may be understood as supplement:

> The supplement adds itself, it is a surplus, a plenitude enriching another plenitude, the *fullest measure* of presence. . . . But the supplement only supplements. It adds only to replace. It intervenes or insinuates itself *in-the-place-of-it*; if it fills, it is as if one fills a void.[25]

The process of consumption, as the Wife describes it, not only represents an attempt to fill in empty space, to satisfy some perceived lack, but also suggests the underlying almost paradoxical nature of desire as represented by the Wife: in her quest to fill the empty spaces, she is depicted as consuming far more than is needed but remaining necessarily unfulfilled by the vicariousness of her excessive supplementation. Thus Chaucer locates in the Wife his angst about his own measure of supplementation and appropriation; he constructs and embodies in the Wife his own concern with excess.

It is therefore quite fitting that the Wife should be initially described as having "hipes large" (I.472), as having excessive flesh or girth, for she apparently fails to respect any boundary or limit of consumption. (Overconsumption of food and drink[26] is obviously manifest in the kind of carnal evidence that cannot be negated through language alone.) Further, she aligns her excessive consumption of drink with other sumptuary interests: "And after wyn on Venus moste I thynke: / For al so siker as cold engendreth hayl, / A likerous mouth moste han a likerous tayl" (III.464-6), suggesting that perhaps she must ply herself with alcohol to trigger a minimum erotic response or, additionally, that in her mind activities of consumption—carnal behaviors—are locked together. Her comment, too, erotically aligns "mouth" and "tayl," noting that both may be described as "likerous," that is, lustful, greedy, eager; "likerous" suggests "gourmandizing—with food, drink, and licking," and its connotations extend to "lechery;" and here the Wife's alignment seems to emphasize the possible aural pun.[27] The Wife's "mouth" is as eager as her "tayl," indeed even more so, and calls attention to the Wife's carnal excesses, for the mouth is the point of intake for excesses of food and drink, and it is a vehicle for her excess of words, most of which are associated with her "tayl." Further, the "mouth" and "tayl" may be likened in sexual terms, an analogy articulated in contemporary feminist theory by Luce Irigaray and discussed at length in Jane Burns's recent analysis of fabliaux,[28] in that the mouth not only resembles the "tayl," but serves as its substitute as well. For the Wife the mouth is instrumental in effecting not merely consumption but *excessive* consumption, both sexually and textually. Hence she describes herself as "Gattothed" (III.603), again associating her mouth with her sexual behavior, and reiterating that consumption—effected by mouth—is, for the Wife, an erotic act.[29]

The mouth is the locus of sexuality for the Wife, for not only does it contain the teeth that apparently serve as a kind of beacon to her audience, affirming her erotic interests, but, more important, it houses the origin of speech—it is the location of the tongue of which the Wife seems so fond. Indeed, the tongue mediates the instrumentality of both textuality and sexuality. Flesh and text cleave through the instrumentality of the tongue, and the two are united through the metaphoricity of "glossing." The tongue both covers and consumes; for the Wife, to "gloss" a text is to sexualize it, and, in turn, the sexualized text elicits erotic excitement. The

tongue seduces as well, having potential use as an instrument of flattery and deception; the efficacy of flattery may be accorded to the tongue.[30] Along these lines the Wife notes that her husband could easily seduce her with his tongue: "And therwithal so wel koude he me glose / Whan that he wolde han my *bele chose*" (III.509-10). In this respect, "glossing" functions as erotic foreplay.[31]

The Wife exploits the etymology of "glossing" and the practice of glossing biblical texts to construct a sexual rhetoric. Her treatment of patristic authority in conjunction with her descriptions of her own experience results in a kind of "holy erotica," a scriptural glossing designed for titillation. Her quasi-holy erotic discourse represents a rhetorical mixing, for her sexual rhetoric comprises a mixing, or coupling, of two distinct registers, the theological and the erotic.[32] Erotica represents a "coupling" of textuality and sexuality, for it textualizes sex and sexualizes the text in its sexual instrumentality. Moreover, the instrumentality of erotica is an autoerotic one, for it serves the self and requires no other; it is narcissistic, an erotic exclusion of otherness manifest in self-affection.[33] Glossing the Bible and its concomitant patristic directives is, for the Wife, an erotic act; she derives a kind of erotic excitement and satisfaction from her glossing and in conveying—or exhibiting—her glossing to an audience. The autoeroticism of the glossing is extended further in that the body as *textus* becomes a target for her own glossing as well; she, in effect, glosses herself.

Moreover, this sexual rhetoric is again a substitution, interchanging textuality and sexuality in a blurring of the boundaries between the two. This substitution is of course not limited to the female alone, as the Wife notes, for Jankyn himself used the text as a substitute for eros (III.669-70). In addition, the Wife argues that such substitution by men is fairly commonplace:

> The clerk, whan he is oold, and may noght do
> Of Venus werkes worth his olde sho,
> Thanne sit he doun, and writ in his dotage
> That wommen kan nat kepe hir mariage!

> III.707-10

But the major difference between masculine and feminine substitution, according to the Wife's demonstration, is that while men read and write about eros, women *talk* about it. Speaking to an audience provides the kind of direct, immediate response not possible through writing; while men derive satisfaction from the solitary act of writing about eros, women, the Wife suggests, desire active appreciation and response from an audience, an "other." Erotic textuality is an active oral process for the Wife, delighting both speaker and audience through the instrumentality of the mouth and tongue.

Having identified the narrative's use of "gloss" as both a destabilizing erotic metaphor and a discursive operating feature of narrative errancy, I would now like to turn to the self-reflexive, or metatextual, "glossing" that underscores the narrative's attention to an en-gendered epistemology, beginning with the Wife's rambling treatise on the role of sex in marriage, wherein she argues in favor of unrestrained sexuality by suggesting that procreation justifies such behavior (though she acknowledges no offspring of her own):

> For hadde God comanded maydenhede,
> Thanne hadde He dampned weddyng with the dede.
> And certes, if ther were no seed ysowe,
> Virginitee, thanne wherof sholde it growe?
>
> III.69-72

By first aligning the image of seed and sowing to "virginitee" as the desired fruits of that labor, the Wife extends the metaphor not only to evoke the relationship of seed and sowing to sexual reproduction, but also to question the paradox inhering in what she has determined to be the scriptural privileging of virginity.[34] Human seed must be sown if procreation is to take place, and, according to widespread fourteenth-century explanations of physiology and reproduction, this sowing entails both male and female seed—the female contributes her own seed to the conception process even as she serves as the receptacle for the male seed.[35]

The Wife's exegetical glossing here is flawed by hyperbole, for she uses an extreme example and has lifted out of context the exegetical directives regarding marriage and procreation. One could of course argue that she is reacting to the views of Jerome, whose rigid and excessive advocation of virginity is coupled with an attack on marriage. To this end, the Wife fulfills Jerome's realistic recognition that his virginity directive could hardly be met with widespread acceptance or successful implementation.[36] Further, her ironic, satiric treatment of marriage doctrine calls attention to the flawed structure of such directives, suggesting that

> all pretensions to and regulations of marital affairs, all selective codes of behavior, are ludicrous because, as the Wife of Bath suggests, they come from precisely those people who know least about them;[37]

again the Wife privileges "experience" as "auctoritee." Her response to Jerome, however, is in part problematic because Jerome's views are hardly typical of the Wife's contemporary social context, and, moreover, the Augustinian argument that "Christian virginity could be praised without denigrating marriage"[38] marks a more realistic and acceptable stand for both the Church and those who follow the Church's directives.[39] Thus while the Wife shows off her knowledge of patriarchal "auctoritee," she simultaneously is shown to demonstrate her appropriation of anachronistic core issues, to avail

herself of patriarchal orthodoxy in the construction of her rhetorical lines even as she mis/represents them by omission or exaggeration. And because virginity is too rigid a directive, the Wife accepts no directive, no restraint; she rejects the notion of continence in its entirety, observing no balance or moderation within the parameters of sexual behavior. It is hardly surprising that she who delights so in talking of sexuality would be aghast at what she perceives to be the virginity directive's rigid constraints and at the implicit repression that such a decorum represents.

But by casting sexuality in the radical division of virginity/promiscuity, the Wife leaves no middle ground for women. Her dichotomizing imposes upon her social/political reality what might be described as patriarchal binary thought, "this endless series of hierarchical binary oppositions that always in the end come back to the fundamental 'couple' of male/female";[40] virginity, as the patriarchal ideal, is privileged within this schema as the positive, male component of the dual, while promiscuity serves as the negative complement, ultimately the target of scorn. Here, then, the Wife subverts her ostensibly assertive stance to an insidious and ultimately oppressive patriarchal context. And clearly, too, the Wife seems to invert the positive/negative valuation underlying her dichotomy—perhaps owing to her desire for audience approval—and identifies herself as promiscuous: "I ne loved nevere by no discrecioun" (III.622), she notes, boldly stating that she lacks discretion or discrimination in matters of "love"—love in its erotic, sexual sense, which the Wife herself equates with sin: "Allas, allas! That evere love was synne" (III.614), she exclaims, smugly identifying herself as a sinner. The either/or rigidity of the Wife's imposed identifications is as reductionistic and value-laden as the patriarchal "auctoritee" against which she ostensibly rails. Further, her identification calls attention to the problematic masculine nature of her stereotypical sexual boasting: she in effect speaks like a man about acting like a man, using a bullying sexuality to confront restrictive social and theological guidelines, yet seeming to sacrifice her femininity in the process of adhering to the masculine dichotomy that she herself introduces to the rhetorical line.

The Wife's sexualized dichotomizing is further problematized by engendered tropes of fertility and propagation. In terms of the Pauline sowing metaphor, "seed" must be "sown" if the word is to propagate, and unsown seed represents unused potential. with regard to the command "to wexe and multiplye" (III.28), the Wife notes, "that gentil text kan I wel understonde" (III.29). The pleasures of the text are propagated by multiplication, and, therefore, by extension, to deny multiplication is both to deny the pleasure of the text and to curtail further propagation. Following this analogy, "virginitee" may be understood not only as the physical state of sexual chastity, but also, as the Wife suggests, a state of unused capability, of wasted potential—of seed unsown. Literal and figurative manifestations of "seed" constitute a complex relationship of signification structures that underscores the Wife's *Prologue*'s attention to poetic language, specifically as the language of the *Prologue* explicates what may be described as its own figurative multiplicity, its awareness of the crucial relationship between polysemy and poetry. The sexual wordplay in the *Prologue* may be understood as a commentary on the necessity of polysemy if poetic language is to mean.[41] Through this garrulous, vulgar voice, Chaucer addresses his own concerns about the complex dangers of discursive fertility/promiscuity, the paradoxical necessity of the author's appropriations of language to his own task. Poetic language is necessarily polysemous, and no matter how the poet wishes to control his own words, to limit their fertility, he proves by that very desire that language is too fertile, promiscuous, beyond control. The Wife exploits the polysemy of language in order to construct her sexual wordplay; she insists that many seeds be sown, many shades of meaning inhere in the language of her discourse in order for the "pleye" to occur. The Wife as a representation of Woman is a caricature, an exaggeration that draws from an anti-feminist tradition even as it ostensibly attacks that tradition. The Wife is shown to delight in the entertainment value of the word-"pleye," yet at the same time she seems oblivious to the contradictions inhering in her self-revelatory discourse, making unclear just what, in fact, she is advocating, though clearly she couches her argument in sexual terms to an ostensibly feminist end.

The Wife seems similarly oblivious to the ramifications of those contradictions in terms of what many readers perceive to be the *Prologue*'s valorization of the feminine. To this end, the Wife's discourse calls attention to an apparent and problematic alignment of the "feminine" and the "carnal." The pairing of "flesh" and "female" suggests a correlation of the feminine and the carnal, in that the seductive threat of the female to the male finds epistemological representation in the seductive threat of the carnal to the spiritual (indeed, many well-known instances of medieval misogyny can be traced to this analogy).[42] And in a positive sense, just as the literal carnal is, in terms of signification, the base starting point from which further spiritual meaning may be conceived, so, too, the feminine represents positive potential.[43] But to suggest that the feminine be equated wholly with the carnal as the Wife embodies carnality is to suggest that the Wife's limiting, restrictive, and rather hostile generalizations—the either/or dichotomy of virginity and promiscuity—are valid. The crux here is the Wife's appropriation, that is, her attempting to take possession—"assertively" and "knowingly," as Carolyn Dinshaw argues[44]—of the patriarchal language of which she presumably recognizes the efficacy, or at least the necessity. The Wife would arguably not need

to appropriate patriarchal discourse if she had at her disposal an alternative discourse; nor would she appropriate the patriarchal if she were not confident of its efficacy and utility. In short, she usurps what she knows works—or, more accurately, what she knows should give the illusion of working—apparently hoping that the appropriation will supply her discourse with the authority, credibility, and efficacy that she herself finds lacking.

The Wife's appropriative glossing may be understood, in terms of medieval sign theory that designates language in terms of property, as a problematic dichotomizing of public and private (or, in Bakhtinian terms, as the public or social dimension rather than an authoritative or privileged system).[45] Medieval theologians, philosophers, and poets would have understood language in terms of the literal and figurative, proper and improper, as usurpative and polysemous: the literal sense is considered "proper," that is, the *signum proprium,* signifying the most immediate level of meaning, while the figurative sense is improper, the *signum translatum,* in the sense that meaning is transferred.[46] In dealing with "property," Augustine, for example, realizes that one must also deal with appropriation in the sense of usurpation: "metaphora est usurpata translatio," notes Augustine in *Contra mendacium,* identifying metaphor as a usurpative translation, a transferring of meaning that is not only arbitrary but pleasurable as well—"impositio ad placitum"—imposed according to the pleasure of the imposer;[47] the Wife, of course, is no stranger to the pleasures of textuality. To use language figuratively is thus to usurp meaning and transfer it; beyond the literal sense, language signifies according to usurpation and transfer, and transfer by usurpation allows for the Wife's bawdy and significant word-"pleye." Usurpative transfer, then, allows for public access to private appropriation.

Further, the public/private semantic implications of the Wife's attention to glossing are framed by the aforementioned patriarchal binary thought, manifest in the ubiquitous medieval "epistemology by contraries," which asserts that comparison is the basis for all understanding and that definition is contingent upon the difference identified by the process of comparison.[48] This epistemology likewise comments on poetic language itself, for poetic language—metaphor—may be understood as the comparison (or *ratio*) of differences. Jean de Meun's well-known commentary on this epistemology in *Le roman de la rose,* perhaps its best medieval articulation,[49] is informed by medieval commentaries on the polarities outlined in Aristotle's *Metaphysics,* which Aristotle himself attributes to Pythagoras, whereby polarities are used to construct an epistemology of contraries through a series of related opposites, including, among others, male and female, limited and unlimited, one and plural.[50] It is reasonable to argue, as does Toril Moi, that "it doesn't much matter which 'couple' one chooses to highlight: the hidden male/female opposition with its inevitable positive/negative evaluation can always be traced as the underlying paradigm";[51] therefore, associations may not only be traced between paired items but extended to the male/female implications of any duality as well.

Clearly, the epistemology by contraries, in its construction of oppositional binarisms, dichotomizes. The dichotomizing of contraries within the epistemology, however, is not the rigid, exclusive dichotomizing evident in the Wife's demonstration. For while the Wife uses dichotomy to construct a valuated identification strategy of patriarchal labels, the epistemology uses dichotomy to *establish* difference, not to condemn it, and to use that difference as a means of freeing or enhancing thought, not to constrict or reduce it. If the Wife's narrative is interpreted within a context of this epistemology, her use of sexual language takes on additional connotations. Significantly, the epistemology aligns "female" with "unlimited" and "plural," suggesting that that which is "female" may be understood as "unlimited" and "plural" as well. (This ancient connection between the feminine and the plural is articulated in contemporary feminist theory by Luce Irigaray, who argues that "women's speaking lips / *écriture-féminine* metonymically suggest plurality, multiplicity, and the dissolution of bounds."[52]) Although infinite limitlessness would ultimately call into question the very possibility of meaning, the "unlimited" taken in conjunction with "plural" connotes a sense of polysemy, that is, a choice of more than one even if some ultimate limit must be identified or assumed. In this sense, the table of polarities supplies a means of understanding the impact of gender polarities on medieval language and thought.[53]

But the usurpative appropriation demonstrated in the Wife's narrative is problematic owing to the ostensibly feminine agency of the appropriation in relation to private discourse.[54] On the one hand, the excess of the Wife's glossing—culturally marked as feminine—underscores the Wife's insistence that the restrictive, oppressive signifying practices of the patriarchal "auctoritee" be opened up; the Wife invites further glossing even as she herself glosses, thereby challenging patriarchal claims of interpretive closure. Additionally, one might situate the Wife's challenge in a context of Lollardy, specifically the Lollards' rejection of patriarchal interpretive exclusivity. Peggy Knapp, in her analysis of the Wife's glossing, convincingly argues,

> The "gospel glosen" associated with Lollardy did not, of course, immediately cause the patristic glosses to lose currency, but Wyclif's attack on the system's authority and attempted substitution of a "gloss" with different underpinnings made the ideology that sustained it *visible*. Ideology works best not when it is an idea being argued for but when it is the ground on

which other ideas are argued: it cannot become fully visible without losing some of its privilege.[55]

As such, the Wife may be seen as challenging the propriety of private, self-serving glossing by exposing its underlying ideological exclusivity.

And yet the Wife is herself shown as privatizing language. The Wife usurps patriarchal discourse, patriarchal "auctoritee," in an apparent attempt to challenge its dominance; and yet her usurpation effects an exclusivity not unlike that which she confronts. Just as she speaks like a man in challenging men's speech, so too she speaks the exclusive language of patriarchy in professing to speak out against patriarchal "auctoritee"; it is no less exclusive just because it intends to confront exclusivity. The Wife's struggle with exclusivity marks Chaucer's own anxiety about appropriation: How is he to effect the usurpation necessary for polysemous signification without himself risking a personal exclusivity? Can the poet use language effectively and poetically without claiming it as his own? To retain possession to the exclusion of other possibilities is to render language problematic in that the possessive usurper not only denies language its proper—and thus accessible and universal—sense, but also attempts to control how the language is understood. In short, exclusive appropriation denies language the very plurality that allows it to signify beyond the literal; attempting to privatize language renders the language meaningless to anyone except the private, possessive usurper.

The Wife professes to argue against virginity, the restricted sowing of seed, but in her attempt to usurp patriarchal language, she renders her language (as she possesses it) unisemous, not polysemous—in a sense, "virgin." In other words, in attempting to possess language that she cannot own, she harbors its meaning as a secret unto herself, attempting to control through possession the propriety of its signification. In fact, the Wife explicitly desires to mark her discourse as her "own," as having private meaning susceptible to misinterpretation by an audience: "If that I speke after my fantasye . . ." (III.190). Her discourse is a subjective external articulation of an internal narrative, private and inaccessible even if partially, and willfully, exposed; it is a "queynte fantasye" (III.516) not unlike that which she says belongs to "[w]e wommen" (III.515). In attempting to appropriate language—in effect, "re-virginizing" it—she denies it the polysemy it would otherwise entail; the "virgin" word is unisemous. Moreover, the unisemy of the "virgin" word may be likened to the unisemy of the autoerotic word; both represent private appropriation—or retention—of ultimately wasted potential. A significant feature of the Wife's autoerotic textuality is in her female-ness; although the metaphor of male auto-/homoeroticism (what R. Howard Bloch terms "sterile perversions")[56] representing delight in one's own language is treated by Alan of Lille, Dante, and others,[57] Chaucer's treatment of the metaphor is given an interesting—and significant—twist in that the Wife's autoeroticism is female. While masculine metaphors of auto-/homo-eroticism call attention to the *spilling* of seed/language, the Wife's own autoeroticism calls attention to the *retention,* or privatization, of seed/language. In short, the Wife harbors, hides, and covers her words, veiling them in her own autoerotic delight.[58] The Wife, then, usurps, or tries to usurp, from language its capacity to produce meaning outside of her own control, denying language its polysemous potential, rendering it tantamount to un-sown virgin seed.

If the "female" sense of language is "unlimited" and "plural," then virginity defeats that sense; virginity hinders language because just as the virgin female represents wasted potential (as the Wife suggests), so, too, the "virgin" word lacks the sense of unlimited, plural signification. And although, as Hélène Cixous has convincingly argued, the binary epistemology inevitably reduces anything aligned with the female to a negative, inferior status within the hierarchy,[59] in poetic terms the association of "feminine" and "plural" is significant. In attempting to deny the "unlimitedness" or "plurality" of language (that is, in attempting to control its signification), the Wife "re-virginizes" her language by denying its "unlimitedness" and "plurality"; she arguably denies it its "femaleness" as well. In short, the Wife reduces the unlimited to the limited, the plural to the one and, in essence, the female to the male even as she seemingly attempts to valorize a new sense of the feminine. Thus, while the Wife is sterile, "her" words are not; she wastes but all the same exploits and entertains potential. Chaucer's impulse to re-virginize words, to appropriate them to limited, private use, in fact foregrounds their resistance to such appropriation. Bakhtin might understand this as the public and social dimension of words, a "dialogically agitated and tension-filled environment of alien words, value judgments, and accents," where a word "weaves in and out of complex interrelationships, merges with some, recoils from others," and where it "cannot fail to brush up against thousands of living dialogic threads."[60] The Wife, with every attempt to control words, instead empowers them to escape her control. Through the Wife's narrative Chaucer suggests that this desire for re-virginizing is essentially unappeasable; it exists as a kind of wishful thinking, an index of e(xc)lusive desire: "*if* that I speke after my fantasye," "*if* wommen had writen stories" (III.190, 693, my emphasis).

But the Wife's appropriation of masculine discourse does not supply a newer "feminine" discourse; it merely supplies what could be labeled "the Wife of Bath's" discourse, an *écriture d'Alisoun* ("sounding other"—al-i-*soun*). The Wife's attempting to privatize—to possess privately—language not only denies it the plurality necessary if her argument is to work within the context of her discourse, but also provides commentary on the relationship between eros and language given attempts at privatization. Again, the Wife's attempt to make private that which is public may be understood in conjunction with her eroticization of the letter—her delight in talking about sexual issues—as an auto-erotic act. Not only does the Wife find pleasure in words, in glossing, she finds pleasure in her *own* words, her *own* glossing. As a lover of her own words she is, in effect, her own lover. Her autoerotic textuality is private and exclusive, and although she may evoke a laugh from her audience through her "pleye," that laughter serves less to corroborate her complaints than to reinforce the autoerotic motivation for her sexual rhetoric. She supplies the object of her own delight, and attempts to retain possession even as such possession effects a sense of wasted potential through its exclusion of plurality. (The ambivalent nature of the Wife's appropriation is illustrated by her own framework: because the Wife insists upon the rigid parameters of her own reductionistic dichotomizing—virgin/harlot, in particular—she effectively excludes even herself as *wyf.*)

To this end, the Wife's sexual representation is both paradoxical and ambivalent. As a harborer of the auto-erotic "virgin" word, the Wife represents a sexuality unwilling to participate within masculine parameters; it is, in a sense, uncorrupted by masculine seed yet corrupted by its own exclusiveness. In seeking satisfaction, the Wife instead generates it herself through autoerotic textuality—erotic glossing—and revels in the experience of her own delight. Ultimately, however, the narrative speaks to unrealized desire, for the Wife's "holy erotica" is not enough; the privatization of eros leaves her hungry for more, and she remains—both textually and sexually—isolated and constrained within the parameters of the masculine discourse. Hence her promiscuity: the Wife is depicted as continuously searching, grasping, mixing, seeking rhetorical satisfaction through a series of appropriations. Thus her self-proclaimed status of bullying sexuality, her own attempts to depict herself as an unattractively aggressive and indiscriminate woman, is balanced with the reality of her own frustration and unfulfillment; the apparent auto-/homo-erotic valorization is yet another cover or veil. The Wife thus inscribes ambivalently the paradox of "re-virginized" language, implicating her author: the more the poet strives for the "virgin" word, the more he confirms the promiscuity of discourse.

The Wife herself provides a concrete example of what happens when meaning is made personal:

> Who peyntede the leon, tel me who?
> By God, if wommen hadde writen stories,
> As clerkes han withinne hire oratories,

They wolde han writen of men moore wikkednesse
Than al the mark of Adam may redresse.

                                III.692-96

Her reference to Aesop's lion does call into question the subjectivity inhering in any artistic representation, and the Wife indeed uses the example effectively in this respect.[61] However, the bitter, angry words that follow the example undermine her apparent efforts to demonstrate a need for a feminine-sympathetic perspective by suggesting that she seeks to replicate the masculine crime of misrepresentation; the women's stories would merely supply an equally distorted view, framed by an opposing perspective. Hence she advocates that the hegemonic patriarchal discourse be replaced by an equally hegemonic feminine one. The Wife's narrative seems to claim that a feminine replication of masculine "wikkednesse" should be advocated and privileged simply because its perpetrators are feminine, so that somehow the feminine is inherently better than the masculine, though she usurps the masculine, thereby suggesting that she cannot offer any equally effective feminine counterpart and that she must take what is not hers and claim it for herself. But rejecting or usurping the masculine does not constitute a feminine even as the Wife's inversion challenges the hegemony of the masculine. Hence the ambivalence of her narrative: her ostensibly pro-feminist arguments are betrayed by an articulation that supports what it professes to subvert.[62]

Hence the Wife's narrative comes across as an anti-anti-feminist (rather than "feminist") misogamous discourse that may be read as a kind of anti-feminist feminism. It attempts to refute the conventions of anti-feminist textuality—laying the groundwork for ideological challenge—but supports those conventions through illustration that seems only to validate the stereotypes upon which the conventions are based. As Robert Hanning argues, "The Wife is lost in a world of words of which she is also a constituent. She exists as a literary creation of men, a system of texts and glosses which she repeatedly attacks but always ends up confirming."[63] Within the conventions of anti-feminist textuality, the Wife does fight back—or talks back—using the only weapon she knows, that with which she has been assaulted; as Deborah Ellis notes, "Indeed, women who verbally attack men most successfully use not their 'own' language but rather that of the men they resist."[64] Hence the Wife's appropriation of "men's" language serves to articulate her complaints but does little to effect a newer, "feminine" system of discourse.

The character of the Wife is associated with that of a weaver of fabric and, likewise, she is a weaver of texts, lifting and borrowing from even the most unlikely of sources to weave together a narrative web both self-promoting and self-incriminating; as she asserts specific argumentative points, she subsequently undermines them in a discourse that wanders from one idea to another, perhaps never really certain of its own purpose. And while the text of the *Prologue* is itself a fertile and provocative commentary on its own textual processes and the processes of engendered epistemological representation, the fictive character who voices those words is rendered oddly pathetic by her own role in the process. Unable to promote any single argument to any effective end, the Wife employs a sexual rhetoric that may indeed be described as promiscuous, that is, "mixed" or "confused" as well as "indiscriminate" (from the root *pro/miscere*). Just as the Wife cannot confine herself sexually to any single partner—"Welcome the sixte, whan that ever he shal!" (III.45)—so, too, she cannot find rhetorical satisfaction in any single argumentative line.

But the Wife is presented as caricature, and her quasi-feminist appropriation invites further consideration in its necessary resistance to closure. Since any personal usurpation of the masculine hardly suffices as a feminine, her ineffectual promiscuous narrative perhaps underscores a need for some alternative; at a minimum, her futile usurpation calls into question the role of the feminine in a masculine hermeneutics, even if her ambivalent sexual textuality frustrates the reader's attempts to identify any potential resolution. Peggy Knapp comments,

> Alisoun of Bath may become, then, a figure for the garrulous, incorrigible, inexplicable text, always *wandrynge by the weye,* always escaping from any centralizing authority that attempts to take over her story. She wants to be glossed and gives out a wealth of clues to reading her enigma, but no one reading will master the rest. And the glossing she invites is itself readable as the work of high intellect and spiritual insight, or the play of material forces and sexual cajolery, or both.[65]

Indeed, the Wife's narrative, through its attention to the feminine utility of poetic polysemy, asserts a feminine valorization, albeit a problematic one: an ambivalent, paradoxical, and unresolved anti-feminist feminism. If the Wife leaves us with these unresolved problematic relationships of gender, language, and society, it is perhaps because through her we see the poet discovering the limits of poetry; she is, after all, his writing, and we read him both in her and through her. Hence the unresolved issues are crucial to readers' appreciation of Chaucer's narrative construction because they *are* unresolved, and they invite further critical conversation and debate. Indeed, as the Wife notes, "Have thou ynogh, thee thar nat pleyne thee" (III.336).

Notes

1. An early draft of this paper was presented at the Seventh Citadel Conference on Medieval and Renaissance Literature, 1 March 1991. I would like to thank David Allen for inviting me to participate.

2. See, for instance, Mary Carruthers, "The Wife of Bath and the Painting of Lions," *PMLA* 94 (1979): 209-22, who reads Alisoun's argument as "triumphant"; Marjorie Malvern, "'Who peyntede the leon, tel me who?': Rhetorical and Didactic Roles Played by an Aesopic Fable in the *Wife of Bath's Prologue*," *SP* 80 (1983): 238-52, also reads the Wife as "triumphant" satire; Maureen Fries, "'Slydyng of Corage': Chaucer's Criseyde as Feminist and Victim," in *The Authority of Experience: Essays in Feminist Criticism,* ed. Arlyn Diamond and Lee Edwards (Amherst: University of Massachusetts Press, 1977), 45-59, comments in the conclusion to her analysis of Criseyde that Chaucer, through his depiction of the Wife, is a "truly practicing feminist" (59); Barrie Ruth Straus, "The Subversive Discourse of the Wife of Bath: Phallocentric Discourse and the Imprisonment of Criticism," *ELH* 55 (1988): 527-54, contrasts her own analysis with the conventionally "hostile" or "dismissive" readings of Donaldson, Robertson, Donald Sands, and Beryl Rowland.

3. Elaine Tuttle Hansen, "Fearing for Chaucer's Good Name," in *Reconceiving Chaucer: Literary Theory and Historical Interpretation,* ed. Thomas Hahn, *Exemplaria* 2 (1990): 23-36, provides an extensive overview of *Wife* criticism in relation to feminist perspectives; see also Arthur Lindley's recent overview, "'Vanysshed Was This Daunce, He Nyste Where': Alisoun's Absence in the *Wife of Bath's Prologue* and *Tale*," *ELH* 59 (1992): 1-21.

4. I use quotation marks initially to introduce terminology, e.g., "feminine," and while I omit them upon subsequent use, they should be understood throughout the text.

5. I use "masculine" and "feminine" to correspond to social/cultural perceptions of gender (gender = L. *gener-, genus,* of a kind, category, from *genare,* to beget; see Jacques Derrida, "The Law of Genre," tr. Avital Ronell, reprinted in *Critical Inquiry* 7.1 [Autumn 1980]: 55-81, on the interconnectedness of gender and genre), distinct from "male" and "female" in the strict biological sense, though as we shall see, "male" and "female" are used in Aristotelian/Pythagorean epistemologies to correspond to both gender and sex. (Eve Kosofsky Sedgwick has further demonstrated the slipperiness of these distinctions in relation to sex, gender, and sexuality in *Epistemology of the Closet* [Berkeley: University of California Press, 1990], 27-32, "Axiom 2.") See also Carolyn Dinshaw, *Chaucer's Sexual Poetics* (Madison: University of Wisconsin Press, 1989) on the "masculine" and "feminine" in Chaucerian poetics; it will be useful to note here that Chaucer's being male does not

necessarily indicate that his text is "masculine" or that the character of the Wife is constructed from a "masculine" perspective.

6. The possibility of an *écriture féminine* as a wholly feminine way of writing is theorized by Hélène Cixous and Luce Irigaray but rejected by Julia Kristeva; see Hélène Cixous, "The Laugh of the Medusa," trans. Keith Cohen and Paula Cohen (revised version of "Le rire de la Méduse," *L'Arc* 1975: 39-54), in *The Signs Reader: Women, Gender, and Scholarship,* ed. Elizabeth Abel and Emily K. Abel (Chicago: University of Chicago Press, 1983), 279-97; Luce Irigaray, *This Sex Which Is Not One,* trans. Catherine Porter with Carolyn Burke (Ithaca: Cornell University Press, 1985), esp. 28-32, 132-41; Julia Kristeva, "Women's Time," trans. Alice Jardine and Harry Blake, in *Feminist Theory: A Critique of Ideology,* ed. Nannerl O. Keohane, Michelle Z. Rosaldo, and Barbara C. Gelpi (Chicago: University of Chicago Press, 1982), 39-53.

7. H. Marshall Leicester, *The Disenchanted Self: Representing the Subject in the Canterbury Tales* (Berkeley: University of California Press, 1990), 138.

8. "Glose" derives from the Greek *glossa,* tongue; according to the MED, the word denotes commentary, interpretation, and explanation; further, the term is used to suggest blandishment, flattery, and cajolery. The word's origin, "tongue," isn't lost on the Wife, however, and this underlying erotic sense informs her carefully constructed double entendres. See also Robert W. Hanning, "'I Shal Finde It in a Maner Glose': Versions of Textual Harassment in Medieval Literature," in *Medieval Texts and Contemporary Readers,* ed. Laurie A. Finke and Martin B. Shichtman (Ithaca: Cornell University Press, 1987), 27-50; Lawrence Besserman, "Glosynge is a Glorious Thyng: Chaucer's Biblical Exegesis," in *Chaucer and Scriptural Tradition,* ed. David Lyle Jeffrey (Ottawa: University of Ottawa Press, 1984), 65-73; Peggy A. Knapp, "Wandrynge by the Weye: On Alisoun and Augustine," in *Medieval Texts and Contemporary Readers,* 142-57.

9. All citations of the *Canterbury Tales* refer to the *Riverside Chaucer,* general editor Larry D. Benson (Boston: Houghton Mifflin, 1987); fragment and line numbers supplied in text.

10. My analysis is based on Fernand Mossé, *A Handbook of Middle English* (Baltimore: Johns Hopkins University Press, 1952), and Norman Davis, et al., *A Chaucer Glossary* (Oxford: Oxford University Press, 1979); see also John M. Fyler, "Man, Men, and Women in Chaucer's Poetry," in

The Olde Daunce: Love, Friendship, Sex, and Marriage in the Medieval World, ed. Robert R. Edwards and Stephen Spector (Albany: State University of New York Press, 1991), 154-76, and Mary Nyquist, "Ever (wo)Man's Friend: A Response to John Fyler and Elaine Tuttle Hansen," in *Reconceiving Chaucer,* 37-47.

11. See Dinshaw, *Sexual Poetics,* 193n14; I agree with Dinshaw's assertion that "Chaucer has a deep and acute sense of the differences between the genders in Western patriarchal culture," and I use "androgynous" and "bisexual" to include both, not to blur the crucial distinctions—differences—between them even as they may likewise participate within identical textual parameters. (See also Leicester, *Disenchanted Self,* 414-17.) Hélène Cixous, in "Laugh of the Medusa" defines "bisexuality" as "the presence . . . of both sexes, nonexclusion either of the difference or of one sex, and, from this 'self-permission,' multiplication of the effects of the inscription of desire" (288).

12. Other Chaucerian disclaimers include the pilgrim-Chaucer's (I.727-44), the Miller's (I.3136-40), and the pilgrim-Chaucer's subsequent disclaimer of the Miller's disclaimer (3185-86). Barrie Straus, "Subversive Discourse," argues that the Wife's disclaimer "could be read as the Wife's acknowledgment of 'woman's place'—traditionally restricted to privacy, domesticity, and silence. . . . Under the guise of knowing her place, however, the Wife proceeds to transgress it" (529), but I read the Wife's disclaimer as mimicking the masculine disclaimers rather than as challenging them.

13. As Lisa J. Kiser comments, "It has become something of a truism among modern critics that the Wife of Bath's performance demonstrates the close relationship between narrative and personal desire" (*Truth and Textuality in Chaucer's Poetry* [Hanover: University Press of New England, 1991], 136). The connection between eros and language is ubiquitous in medieval poetics.

14. Dante's *Inferno* 5.137-8 supplies a textual model: "Galeotto fu 'l libro e chi lo scrisse: quel giorno più non vi leggemmo avante" ["A Gallehault indeed, that book and he / who wrote it, too; that day we read no more"]—ed. and trans. Allen Mandelbaum (1980; New York: Bantam, 1982); all further *Inferno* citations refer to this edition, with canto and line numbers supplied. See related commentary by R. A. Shoaf, *Dante, Chaucer, and the Currency of the Word: Money, Images, and Reference in Late Medieval Poetry* (Norman, OK: Pilgrim, 1984), 261n6; Giuseppe Mazzotta, *Dante, Poet of the Desert: History and Allegory in the Divine Comedy* (Princeton: Princeton University Press, 1979), 165-70; Karla Taylor, *Chaucer Reads "The Divine Comedy"* (Stanford: Stanford University Press, 1989), 59-63; Jesse M. Gellrich, *The Idea of the Book in the Middle Ages: Language Theory, Mythology, and Fiction* (Ithaca: Cornell University Press, 1985), 149-54.

15. Chaucer's alignment of "tongue" and "hand" is, I believe, a possible play on the Latin sexual pun of tongue and hand (*glossae tradere*). On "*glossae tradere*" and "*cunnum lingere*" in the Latin tradition, see Jan Ziolkowski, *Alan of Lille's Grammar of Sex: The Meaning of Grammar to a Twelfth-Century Intellectual* (Cambridge: The Medieval Academy of America, 1985), 55-56; and J. N. Adams, *The Latin Sexual Vocabulary* (London: Duckworth, 1982), 134-6.

16. Eugene Vance, "The Differing Seed: Dante's Brunetto Latini," reprinted in *Mervelous Signals: Poetics and Sign Theory in the Middle Ages* (Lincoln: University of Nebraska, 1986), 232.

17. On such "moralizing" readings, see commentary in the articles by Lindley, Straus, and Hansen, cited above.

18. Of course since the Wife is narrative, she can only talk; however, her apparent attitude toward her subject matter varies. Clearly she suggests delight when speaking of sexual matters, just as she clearly suggests anger when describing antifeminist stereotypes of women.

19. "Wyf" according to the OED, means not only "woman" in a general sense but "especially one engaged in the sale of some commodity," "the mate of a male animal," and "a woman joined to a man by marriage." The Wife evokes all four senses when she describes herself as "wyf," though she focuses on "wyf" in terms of marital status. See also Davis et al., *Glossary,* 171.

20. The correlation of pleasure and text is suggested by the ubiquitous medieval theory of signification used by St. Augustine, Dante, and others, *impositio ad placitum,* "[meaning] imposed according to the pleasure" [of the reader]; see Shoaf, *Currency,* 175: "For [the Wife], '*le plaisir du texte*' is '*le texte du plaisir*'—and that is her '*écriture*'." See also M. D. Chenu, O.P., "The Symbolist Mentality," in *Nature, Man, and Society in the Twelfth Century: Essays on Theological Perspectives in the Latin West,* trans. Jerome Taylor and Lester K. Little (Chicago: University of Chicago Press, 1968), 99-145.

In contemporary theory the relationship between pleasure and text is perhaps best articulated by Roland Barthes, *The Pleasure of the Text,* translated by Richard Miller (New York: Farrar, Straus and Giroux), esp. 17, 59. In Lacanian terms, this pleasure corresponds to *jouissance,* "the place of a hole in knowing, being and feeling [Lacan] called the place of desire" (Ellie Ragland-Sullivan, Introduction to *Lacan and the Subject of Language,* ed. Ellie Ragland-Sullivan and Mark Bracher [New York: Routledge, 1991], 2). In Julia Kristeva's words,

> our only chance to avoid being neither master nor slave of meaning lies in our ability to insure our mastery of it (through technique or knowledge) as well as our passage through it (through play or practice). In a word, *jouissance.*

See the Preface to *Desire in Language,* trans. Thomas Gora, Alice Jardine, and Leon S. Roudiez (New York: Columbia University Press, 1980), x.

21. Mary Anne Doane, *The Desire to Desire: The Woman's Film of the 1940's* (Bloomington: Indiana University Press, 1987).

22. Feminist film theory analyzes "spectacle" in relation to women and desire; see, for instance, Laura Mulvey's "Visual Pleasure and Narrative Cinema," *Screen* 16 (1975): 6-18, reprinted in *Women and Cinema,* ed. Karyn Kay and Gerald Peary (New York: Dutton, 1977), 412-28. "Spectacle" analyses derive from applications of the Lacanian "gaze"; see Jacques Lacan, "Of the Gaze as *Objet petit a,*" *The Four Fundamental Concepts of Psycho-Analysis,* ed. Jacques-Alain Miller and trans. Alan Sheridan (New York: Norton, 1978), 65-119. Sarah Stanbury has recently used feminist film theory in medieval "gaze studies"; see, for instance, "The Virgin's Gaze: Spectacle and Transgression in Middle English Lyrics of the Passion," *PMLA* 106 (1991): 1083-93.

23. The MED notes that "assemble" suggests, in addition to "come together, gather; join, blend," "[t]o have intercourse." On the use of "assemble" in conjunction with "fyr," see H. Marshall Leicester, Jr., "Of a Fire in the Dark: Public and Private Feminism in the *Wife of Bath's Tale,*" *Women in the Middle Ages,* ed. Hope Phyllis Weissman, *WS* 11 (1984): 157-78, especially 170-71.

24. Louise O. Fradenburg, "The Wife of Bath's Passing Fancy," *SAC* 8 (1986): 44.

25. Jacques Derrida, *Of Grammatology,* trans. Gayatri Chakravorty Spivak (Baltimore: Johns Hopkins University Press, 1976), 144-45.

26. Caroline Walker Bynum, *Holy Feast and Holy Fast: The Religious Significance of Food to Medieval Women* (Berkeley: University of California Press, 1987), comments on the "wide range of positive resonances for both physicality and food" among religious women of the period (300).

Bynum effectively demonstrates that the consumption of food was not regarded with the kind of fear and control that characterizes modern attitudes, but it is still important to acknowledge the attitude toward *excessive* food consumption, or gluttony—"intemperate or special appetite for food and/or drink . . . the sixth of the seven deadly sins" (MED). Dante, for example, places the gluttons in the Third Circle, "per la dannosa colpa de la gola" ("for the damning sin of gluttony"—*Inf.* 6.53). Langland, too, speaks harshly of gluttony, and links it to the mouth and tongue (*The Vision of Piers Plowman: A Complete Edition of the B-Text,* edited by A. V. C. Schmidt [London: Dent, 1978]): "'Shryve thee and be shamed therof, and shewe it with thi mouthe.' / 'I, Gloton,' quod the gome, 'gilty me yelde—/ That I have trespased with my tonge, I kan noght telle how ofte . . .'" (5.367-9).

27. Thomas W. Ross, "Taboo-Words in Fifteenth-Century England," in *Fifteenth Century Studies,* ed. Robert F. Yeager (New York: Archon, 1984), 150; see also Paull F. Baum, "Chaucer's Puns," *PMLA* 71 (1956): 240.

28. E. Jane Burns, "Knowing Women: Female Orifices in Old French Farce and Fabliau," in *Skirting the Texts: Feminisms' Re-readings of Medieval and Renaissance Texts,* ed. Barrie Ruth Straus, *Exemplaria* 4.1 (Spring 1992): 81-104. Burns analyzes a fabliau which uses anal descriptions to identify female genitals: "To call a vagina an asshole is to characterize woman's lower orifice in terms of man's own singular hole, obscuring the fact that women have two distinct openings in the lower body" (87); the Wife, in using the ambiguous word "tayl," would seem to evoke a similar confusing of the masculine and the feminine, reducing the feminine plural to the masculine singular.

Luce Irigaray suggests an extended analogy between oral and genital "lips" in "This Sex Which is Not One" and "When Our Lips Speak Together," both reprinted in *This Sex Which is Not One,* 23-33 and 205-18, respectively. Elizabeth Gross, "The Body of Signification," in *Abjection, Melancholia, and Love: The Work of Julia Kristeva,* edited by John Fletcher and Andrew Benjamin (New York: Routledge, 1990), comments (88),

> All sexual organs and erotigenic zones, Lacan claims, are structured in the form of the *rim,* which is the space between two corporeal surfaces, an interface between the inside and the outside of the body. . . . The erotogenic rim which locates the sexual drive in a particular bodily zone is a hole, or gap or lack seeking an object to satisfy it.

Medieval poets were themselves aware of the obvious similarities; see Evelyn Birge Vitz, *Medi-*

eval Narrative and Modern Narratology: Subjects and Objects of Desire (New York: New York University Press, 1989), especially 86-87, and Helen Lemay, "Women and the Literature of Obstetrics and Gynecology," in *Medieval Women and the Sources of History,* ed. Joel T. Rosenthal (Athens: University of Georgia Press, 1990), 189-209; Lemay's essay is particularly useful for its bibliography.

29. Caroline Bynum comments on medieval concepts of "erotic" in "The Body of Christ in the Later Middle Ages: A Reply to Leo Steinberg," reprinted in *Fragmentation and Redemption: Essays on Gender and the Human Body in Medieval Religion* (New York: Zone, 1991), 79-117, especially 86-87, suggesting that medieval perspectives on the body—and genitals in particular—as represented in art were not as sexually focused as are modern interpretations. Along these lines, see also Karma Lochrie, "The Language of Transgression: Body, Flesh, and Word in Mystical Discourse," in *Speaking Two Languages: Traditional Disciplines and Contemporary Theory in Medieval Studies,* ed. Allen J. Frantzen (Albany: State University of New York Press, 1991), 115-40, especially 119. John A. Nichols, "Female Nudity and Sexuality in Medieval Art," in *New Images of Medieval Women: Essays Toward a Cultural Anthropology,* ed. Edelgard E. DuBruck (Lewiston, NY: Edwin Mellon, 1989), 165-76, however, argues that there is an underlying eroticism that focuses negatively on women, a "medieval concept that the female nude is an unnatural and immoral state for a woman" (176). See also Elizabeth Robertson, "Medieval Views of Spirituality," in *Early English Devotional Prose and the Female Audience* (Knoxville: University of Tennessee Press, 1990), 32-43.

30. Dante, for instance, comments on the flatterer's "sufficiency of tongue" in *Inferno* 18. 109-136. See also related commentary in Douglas Radcliff-Umstead, "Erotic Sin in the *Divine Comedy,*" in *Human Sexuality in the Middle Ages and Renaissance,* ed. Douglas Radcliff-Umstead (Pittsburgh: University of Pittsburgh Center for Medieval and Renaissance Studies, 1978), especially 64-67.

31. Carolyn Dinshaw, "'Glose / bele chose': The Wife of Bath and Her Glossators," in *Sexual Poetics,* comments (125):

> But, curiously, it is the openly pejorated, carnal, ostentatiously masculine glossing by the clerk Jankyn that the Wife—the body of the text—finds so appealing, so effective, so irresistible. . . . Glossing here is unmistakably carnal, a masculine act performed on the feminine body, and it leads to pleasure for both husband and wife, both clerk and text.

While this particular instance of "glossing" represents a masculine act, the Wife's treatment of "glossing" here does not preclude the possibility of reciprocation; indeed, the Wife seems herself quite capable of "glossing"—one could argue that as the Wife usurps the masculine propriety of "glossing" in its textual sense, so too does she usurp its erotic sense as well.

32. Though secular rather than spiritual, the Wife's discourse is not unlike that of the mystics, who articulate spiritual experiences in vividly erotic language. On the mystics' erotic language, see Wolfgang Riehle, *The Middle English Mystics,* trans. Bernard Standring (London: Routledge and Kegan Paul, 1981), 24-103. The Wife's erotica, in particular, is "feminine," that is, aural rather than visual; on visual/masculine/religious pornography, see Margaret R. Miles, *Carnal Knowing: Female Nakedness and Religious Meaning in the Christian West* (Boston: Beacon Press, 1989), 117-68. See also the review article by J. Giles Milhaven, "A Medieval Lesson on Bodily Knowing: Women's Experience and Men's Thought," *JAAR* 57 (1989): 341-72.

33. On autoeroticism as a good, see Luce Irigaray, "This Sex Which is Not One" and "When Our Lips Speak Together," in *This Sex Which Is Not One.* The present argument, I should emphasize, identifies autoeroticism as it is depicted in medieval poetry and poetics, where it is clearly negative in suggesting wasted potential, a point to which I shall return.

34. Here the Wife evokes a medieval commonplace of fertility imagery based on seed and sowing used by Alan of Lille, Jean de Meun, Dante, and others, to suggest fertility, regeneration, and fruition. "Seed" in this sense corresponds to the "seed" of conception—with biblical origins—and, by extension, to "seed" as "word," informed in part by Pauline sowing metaphor. For Pauline "virginity" directives, see 1 Cor 7.25-40. On "virginity" as a cultural and literary aesthetic informed by theological dicta, see R. Howard Bloch, *Medieval Misogyny and the Invention of Western Romantic Love* (Chicago: University of Chicago Press, 1991), esp. 93-112.

35. See James A. Brundage, *Law, Sex, and Christian Society in Medieval Europe* (Chicago: University of Chicago Press, 1987), 450-51, on physiological connotations of "seed" with regard to conception.

36. Elizabeth A. Clark, "'Adam's Only Companion': Augustine and the Early Christian Debate on Marriage," in *The Olde Daunce,* 18; see also Erik Kooper, "Loving the Unequal Equal: Medieval Theologians and Marital Affection," in the same volume, 44-56.

37. Katharine M. Wilson and Elizabeth M. Makowski, *Wykked Wyves and the Woes of Marriage: Misogamous Literature from Juvenal to Chaucer* (Albany: State University of New York Press, 1990), 161.

38. Clark, "Christian Debate," 19; see also Judith Ferster, *Chaucer on Interpretation* (Cambridge: Cambridge University Press, 1985), 124-25, on the relationship between Jerome and St. Paul with regard to permitted behaviors.

39. See Peter Brown, *The Body and Society: Men, Women, and Sexual Renunciation in Early Christianity* (New York: Columbia University Press, 1988), 410.

40. Toril Moi, *Sexual/Textual Politics: Feminist Literary Theory* (New York: Methuen, 1985), 104, commenting on Hélène Cixous; see Cixous's "Sorties: Out and Out: Attacks/Ways Out/Forays," in *The Newly Born Woman,* translated by Betsy Wing (Minneapolis: University of Minnesota Press, 1986), 63:

   > Man
   > _____
   > Woman
   >
   > Always the same metaphor: we follow it, it carries us, beneath all figures, wherever discourse is organized. If we read or speak, the same thread or double braid is leading us through-out literature, philosophy, criticism, centuries of representation and reflections.
   >
   > Thought has always worked through opposition . . .

41. "Polysemy" corresponds to the "many senses" of language, the crucial plurality or multiplicity of figurative language. Chenu, *Nature, Man, and Society,* notes, "So essential a characteristic was [polysemy] that to constrict its meaning for the sake of clarity would have been to sterilize it, to kill its vitality" (136).

42. On examples of medieval misogyny and their patristic origins, see R. Howard Bloch, "Medieval Misogyny," in *Misogyny, Misandry, and Misanthropy,* ed. R. Howard Bloch and Frances Ferguson (Berkeley: University of California Press, 1989), 1-24.

43. The Wife embodies the ambivalence of the "carnal" in terms of the body; on the one hand, the carnal, as grotesque and vulgar as it may be, *is* the human state, yet the carnal is simultaneously condemned in theological discourse. Mark C. Taylor comments in *Erring: A Postmodern A/theology* (Ithaca: Cornell University Press, 1985), that (172)

   > The body as grotesque is the body that eats, drinks, shits, pisses, and fucks. The boundary between bodies is a permeable membrane; it has gaps and holes to let the inside out and the outside in. . . . When inside is only inside and outside is only outside, when eating, drinking, pissing, shitting, and fucking stop or are stopped, vital current no longer flows and the body truly dies.

   This necessary carnality is acknowledged within medieval theology; Julia Kristeva comments (*Tales of Love,* trans. Leon Roudiez [New York: Columbia University Press, 1987], 167, citing Bernard of Clairvaux, *Oeuvres complètes* 4.69):

   > Let us recall one of the many expressions of that ambivalence: "We also love our spirit in carnal fashion when we break it through prayer, with tears, sighs, and moans. We love our flesh with a spiritual love when, after we have subjected it to the spirit, we exercise it spiritually for the good and watch with judgment over its conservation."

   The validity of "carnal" as a starting point of interpretation is suggested by Langland throughout *Piers Plowman B,* particularly Passus 1, where Holi Chirche offers Will the "mesure" directive of moderation with regard to carnality. Similarly, Henryson explores metaphors of carnality in the *Testament of Cresseid,* especially in the opening stanzas, lines 22-40.

   Robertsonianism has insightfully—if excessively—explored "carnality"; see D. W. Robertson, Jr., *A Preface to Chaucer: Studies in Medieval Perspectives* (Princeton: Princeton University Press, 1962), 318-36.

44. *Sexual Poetics,* 120.

45. Bakhtin argues that these dimensions are not necessarily dichotomized, that they need not be mutually exclusive. See "Discourse in the Novel," in *The Dialogic Imagination,* edited by Michael Holquist and translated by Caryl Emerson and Michael Holquist (Austin: University of Texas Press, 1981), 342ff.

46. Marcia Colish, *The Mirror of Language: A Study in the Medieval Theory of Knowledge,* revised edition (Lincoln: University of Nebraska Press, 1983), 42; see also Shoaf, *Currency,* 33-34:

   > In the Middle Ages "proper" denoted what we mean by the word "literal"—the first, the primary sense of a word. This sense is the "property" of the word. Extraliteral or metaphoric senses of a word were indicated, most suggestively, by terms like "usurpata translatio." These senses are "improper": they are not the property of the word; they are brought to the word, added to it, imposed upon it.

47. Eugene Vance, "Augustine's *Confessions* and the Poetics of the Law," reprinted in *Mervelous Signals,* 9.

48. It is important to note that the pairing exists within the parameters of an epistemology. Outside the epistemology, valuation necessarily obtains; Mark

C. Taylor notes, "Invariably one term is privileged through the divestment of its relative. The resultant economy of privilege sustains an asymmetrical hierarchy" (*Erring,* 9). There is then an epistemologically contingent value relationship articulated by the dual, without necessarily a coincidence of internal and external valuation.

R. A. Shoaf has articulated a methodology of "juxtology," whereby a critical utility of difference is made accessible by the coincidence of opposites. See "Medieval Studies After Derrida After Heidegger," in *Sign, Sentence, Discourse: Language in Medieval Thought and Literature,* ed. Julian N. Wasserman and Lois Roney (Syracuse: Syracuse University Press, 1989), 9-30, esp. 23-24, and, in connection with Renaissance poetics, "'For There Is Figures in All Things': Juxtology in Shakespeare, Spenser, and Milton," in *The Work of Dissimilitude: Essays from the Sixth Citadel Conference on Medieval and Renaissance Literature,* ed. David G. Allen and Robert A. White (Newark: University of Delaware Press, 1992), 266-85, esp. 272-73.

49. See Guillaume de Lorris and Jean de Meun, *Le roman de la rose,* ed. Félix Lecoy, 3 vols. (Paris: Champion, 1966-74): 21543-52. Jon Whitman discusses the Aristotelian origins of Jean's comment on definition, in "Dislocations: The Crisis of Allegory in the *Romance of the Rose,*" in *Languages of the Unsayable: The Play of Negativity in Literature and Literary Theory,* ed. Sanford Budick and Wolfgang Iser (New York: Columbia University Press, 1989), 259-79, esp. 275-76.

50. Aristotle in *Metaphysics* comments on the construction of contraries by the Pythagoreans Alcmaion of Croton, Parmenides, and Melissus; the Pythagorean contraries are listed (in *Aristotle: Selected Works,* trans. Hippocrates G. Apostle and Lloyd P. Gerson [Grinnell, Iowa: Peripatetic Press, 1982], A.5):

Finite-Infinite	Resting-Moving
Odd-Even	Straight-Curved
One-Many	Light-Darkness
Right-Left	Good-Bad
Male-Female	Square-Rectangle

Genevieve Lloyd, *The Man of Reason: "Male" and "Female" in Western Philosophy* (Minneapolis: University of Minnesota Press, 1984), comments on the gender-specific implications of the ancient polarities; see especially 2-9.

See also Prudence Allen, R.S.M., *The Concept of Woman: The Aristotelian Revolution (750 B.C.-1250 A.D.)* (London: Eden, 1985); Thelma S. Fenster, Introduction, *Gender and the Moral Order in Medieval Society,* ed. Thelma S. Fenster, *Thought* 64 (1989): 201-7; Ian Maclean, *The Renaissance Notion of Woman: A Study in the Fortunes of Scholasticism and Medical Science in European Intellectual Life* (Cambridge: Cambridge University Press, 1980), 2-3; Bynum, "'. . . And Woman His Humanity': Female Imagery in the Religious Writing of the Later Middle Ages," reprinted in *Fragmentation and Redemption,* 151, and "The Female Body and Religious Practice," in the same volume, 200-22, on the Aristotelian dualities manifest in medieval thought. (As the present essay was being readied for print, I read Sheila Delany's "Anatomy of the Resisting Reader: Some Implications of Resistance to Sexual Word-play in Medieval Literature," in *Skirting the Texts,* 7-34, which makes a connection between the epistemological "female" and poetic "polysemy" similar to the argument that I present here.)

51. *Sexual/Textual Politics,* 105.

52. Anna Anapoulous, "Writing the Mystic Body: Sexuality and Textuality in the *écriture-féminine* of Saint Catherine of Genoa," in *Feminism and the Body,* ed. Elizabeth Grose, *Hypatia* 6 (1991), 204n12, commenting on Irigaray's "When Our Lips Speak Together."

53. Caroline Bynum comments (". . . And Woman," 151),

> Male and female were contrasted and asymmetrically valued as intellect/body, active/passive, rational/irrational, reason/emotion, self-control/lust, judgment/mercy, and order/disorder. In the devotional writing of the later Middle Ages, they were even contrasted in the image of God—Father or Bridegroom—and soul (anima)—child or bride.

54. See Leicester, *Disenchanted Self,* on the Wife's "private" construction that "do not produce a single, 'true' private self revealed behind the facade of the public performance" (99).

55. "Wandrynge by the Weye," 153; Knapp continues,

> The Lollards accused users of patristic glosses of obscuring the truth of the Bible, and ecclesiastical authorities accused Lollards of the same thing. . . . In short, "gloss" had become by the fourteenth century, in Bakhtin's phrase, "an active participant in social dialogue."

(276)

56. R. Howard Bloch, *Etymologies and Genealogies: A Literary Anthropology of the French Middle Ages* (Chicago: University of Chicago Press, 1983), 136. "Sterile" identifies *wasted,* as distinct from *deficient,* potential. Apparently, forbidden (sterile) sexual activities involving women together were considered far less sinful and had far less dire consequences than did sexual sins involving

men, though female "solitary vice" was considered equivalent to a woman's "vice with a woman." Medieval penitential handbooks identify the penitential obligations incurred by specific acts and thus provide some basis for comparison. For example, Patrick Geary, *Readings in Medieval History* (Lewiston, NY: Broadview, 1989), cites the penitential code of Theodore (ca. 668-690), noting that (278) a man who "defiles himself" does penance for forty days, while a woman does penance for three years; a man who commits sodomy with a man does seven years ("this is the worst of evils"), while a woman who "practices vice with a woman" does penance for three years, the same as for "solitary vice." See also Brundage, *Law, Sex, and Christian Society*, 398-400, 472-4, and Bernadette J. Brooten, "Paul's Views on the Nature of Women and Female Homoeroticism," in *Immaculate and Powerful: The Female in Sacred Image and Social Reality*, ed. Clarissa W. Atkinson, Constance H. Buchanan, and Margaret R. Miles (Boston: Beacon, 1985), 61-87.

57. See, for example, the conversation between Dante and Brunetto Latini in the realm of the sodomites (*Inferno* 15) and the description of sterile grammar in *De planctu naturae* (Meter 1). See also commentary in Vance, "Differing Seed," and Joseph Pequigney, "Sodomy in Dante's *Inferno* and *Purgatorio*," *Representations* 36 (1991): 22-42.

58. With regard to the relationship between "female" and "hidden," Irigaray attacks Freud's equation of the hidden and nothingness in terms of female sexuality in "This Sex Which Is Not One" (26):

> While [a woman's] body finds itself thus eroticized, and called to a double movement of exhibition and of chaste retreat in order to stimulate the drives of the "subject," her sexual organ represents *the horror of nothing to see*. . . . This organ which has nothing to show for itself also lacks a form of its own.

Irigaray correctly distinguishes between *nothing to see* (the hidden) and *nothing* (absence or lack); the former denotes existence, even if removed from sight and therefore mysterious and unknown.

59. Cixous notes, "Traditionally, the question of sexual difference is treated by coupling it with the opposition: activity/passivity. . . . It is even possible not to notice that there is no place whatsoever for woman in the calculations" ("Sorties," 64).

60. "Discourse," 276.

61. See also Sheila Delany, "Strategies of Silence in the Wife of Bath's Recital," in *Reconceiving Chaucer*, 49-69; Delany notes (54),

To return to the painting of lions: If we interpret the fable consistently, we find that its narrative line forces the conclusion that woman's best hope is to work within the controlling sphere of a superior (presumably male) intelligence. In this way, the Wife of Bath, like the lion she quotes, also speaks against herself, and can only do so in citing this story whose givens—animal versus human—already constrain interpretation, already load the dice.

62. Laura Kendrick, *Chaucerian Play: Comedy and Control in the Canterbury Tales* (Berkeley: University of California Press, 1988), notes (126):

> The Wife both tempts and masters us, making us identify with repressive *female* authority, which knows what is best for us. Even so, the Wife of Bath's and woman's ascendancy is temporary after all; it occurs in the unreal play time and space of the Wife's stories.

63. Hanning, "Maner Glose," 45-46. See also Ferster, *Chaucer on Interpretation* (124):

> But she claims not to be merely the antifeminists' nightmare, but their creation, and she attacks their language because it demeans and limits women. By describing women as monsters of sensuality, greed, and deceit, they produce monstrously sensual, greedy, and deceitful women.

64. Deborah Ellis, "The Merchant's Wife's Tale: Language, Sex, and Commerce in Margery Kempe and in Chaucer," *Exemplaria* 2 (Fall 1990): 601.

65. "Wandrynge by the Weye," 157.

Susan Signe Morrison (essay date spring 1996)

SOURCE: Morrison, Susan Signe. "Don't Ask, Don't Tell: The Wife of Bath and Vernacular Translations." *Exemplaria* 8, no. 1 (spring 1996): 97-123.

[*In the following essay, Morrison asserts that, through* The Wife of Bath's Prologue *and* Tale, *Chaucer is seeking to authenticate the use of English vernacular as a legitimate language for writing, maintaining that they "can be read as addressing the issues of the vernacular and the role female audiences play in receiving and passing on translations of authoritative texts, as well as vindicating Chaucer's authority as a vernacular author."*]

The Friar in his **Prologue** scolds the Wife of Bath, accusing her of preaching, and exhorting her to let the proper authorities, like himself, carry out an activity which is natural to them. Although he admits that she says "muche thyng right wel" (1273),[1] he denies her permission to carry on:

> "But, dame, heere as we ryde by the weye,
> Us nedeth nat to speken but of game,

And lete auctoritees, on Goddes name,
To prechyng and to scoles of clergye."

                                        1274-77

The Friar's position in the established Church allows him to comment on the potentially threatening activities of a perceived female preacher. While it was a long-established custom for mothers and midwives to baptize in "cases of necessity" and for women to instruct other women and children privately in matters of religion, the Church took a firm stand against women publicly teaching men.[2] Late fourteenth-century Lollardly activities provide a possible subtext for the Friar's criticism on the Wife's public declarations; his comments read as a reaction to the Wife's words which threaten the established monopoly of authorized men on religious interpretation.

A major threat to this monopoly was universal accessibility to the texts which constituted authority. The translation of authoritative texts into the vernacular, thereby making them available to new audiences, could allow the abuses—or self-interested readings—of traditional authorities to come to light. While vernacular translations were not an innovation of the late fourteenth century,[3] the late Middle Ages witnessed the shattering of the monopoly on authoritative knowledge exercised by university-educated, Latin-literate males, due to the increasing abundance of vernacular religious and medical literature.[4] Chaucer's endorsement of vernacular translations of authoritative texts is, I will argue, a unifying subtext to the **Wife of Bath's Prologue** and **Tale**.[5]

Two authors of texts translated into the vernacular are alluded to towards the end of the Wife's **Prologue**. The Wife regrets that there are no women writers to counteract the abuses of clerkly writers:

By God, if wommen hadde writen stories,
As clerkes han withinne hire oratories,
They wolde han writen of men moore wikkednesse
Than al the mark of Adam may redresse.

                                        693-96

But women *had* "writen stories." The Wife herself mentions two of them several lines prior to the above-mentioned speech in describing Jankyn's "book of wikked wyves" (685):

And eek ther was somtyme a clerk at Rome,
A cardinal, that highte Seint Jerome,
That made a book agayn Jovinian;
In which book eek ther was Tertulan,
Crisippus, Trotula, and Helowys,
That was abbesse nat fer from Parys,
And eek the Parables of Salomon,

Illustration by Walter Appleton Clark, from a 1907 edition of The Canterbury Tales, *edited by Percy Wallace Mackay.*

Ovides Art, and bookes many on,
And alle thise were bounden in o volume.

                                        673-81

Texts by Heloise and those ascribed to Trotula[6] were translated into the vernacular. The significance of the Abelard-Heloise correspondence, translated by Jean de Meun and called *La vie et les epistres de maistre Pierre Abelart et Heloïs sa fame,*[7] for the Wife's **Prologue** will be addressed later in this paper. Medical texts proliferated in the late Middle Ages, including those ascribed to Trotula, who was reputed to be a woman physician practicing medicine in Salerno, Italy, in the late eleventh or early twelfth century.[8] The goals of vernacular translators tend to be similar, despite the diverse context and content of texts. The proclaimed intent of the translator of a Trotula text, *The Knowing of Woman's Kind in Childing,* reads as follows:

I thynke to do myn ententyffe bysynes forto drau oute of Latyn into Englysch dyverse causis of here maladyes, the synes that they schall knou hem by, and the curys helpynge to hem, afture the tretys of dyverse mastrys that have translatyde hem out of Grek into Latyn. And because whomen of oure tonge cunne bettyre rede and undyrstande thys langage than eny other, and every whoman lettyrde may rede hit to other unlettyrd and help hem and conceyle hem in here maledyes, withowtyn scheuynge here dysese to man, I have thys drauyn and wryttyn in Englysch.

And yf hit fall any man to rede hit, I pray hym and scharge hym in Oure Lady behalve that he rede hit not in no dyspyte ne sclaundure of no women, ne for no cause but for the hele and helpe of hem, dredynge that vengauns myht fall to hym as hit hath do to other that have scheuyd here prevytees in sclaundyr of hem; undyr-stondynge in certyne that they have no other evylys that nou be alyue than thoo women hade that nou be seyntys in hevyn.[9]

Compare this to the introduction of the Wycliffite Bible:

þis trett[yse] þat folewþ proueþ þat eche nacioun may lefully haue holy writ in here moder tunge.

Siþen þat þe trouþe of God stondiþ not in oo langage more þan in anoþer, but who so lyueþ best and techiþ best plesiþ moost God, of what language þat euere it be, þerfore þe lawe of God writen and tauȝt in Englisch may edifie þe commen pepel, as it doiþ clerkis in Latyn, siþen it is þe sustynance to soulis þat schulden be saued. . . . And herfore Crist in þe houre of his assencioun comaundid to hise diciplis to preche it to alle pepelis—but, we be siker, neiþer only in Frensch ne in Latyn, but in þat langage þat þe pepel vsed to speke, for þus he tauȝt hymself. And here is a rule to cristyne folke of what langage so euere þei be: it is an hiȝe sacrifi[c]e to God to knowe holy writ and to do þeraftur, wher it be tauȝt or writen to hem in Latyn or in Englisch, in Frensche or in Duche, or in ony oþer langage after þe pepel haþ vnderstondynge.[10]

Both introductions acknowledge that English is the medium through which information can be communicated to those groups marginalized from the language of privileged scholars and masters, either common people and/or women. Just as women reading the vernacular medical text have an obligation to share the information they learn with their fellow women, so do Lollard texts express a duty for the literate: "whoso kan rede bookis *in his langage,* and so knoweþ þe better Goddis law, he is bounden to spended þat kunnynge and þat grace to þe worschipe of God and to helpe of his euene cristen."[11] Just as men should not use the information they learn about women to defame women, so should learned clerks not keep the true word of God from men and women, but share it openly. Only evil clerks pervert God's truth: "But þe kynrede of Caym, of Daton and Abiron wolden þat þe gospel slepe sage, for þei ben clepid cristyne of manye: þei prechen somwhat of þe gospel, and gloson it as hem likeþ."[12] These vernacular texts, religious and medical, are careful to announce why the translation has been undertaken—to make more widely accessible information which can heal body and soul—and to warn against misuse of the text.

Clearly some readers felt anxiety concerning women's access to texts, which can be seen in existing glosses on the Wife of Bath's words. Glosses in manuscripts Ellesmere and Egerton 2864 bear witness to a conflict in the late fourteenth and early fifteenth centuries between what has been called the "old" reader and the "new" reader. The Ellesmere glosses on the Wife's *Prologue*

endorse the new reader, the private and "non-traditional" (that is to say, not necessarily male or clerkly) reader of vernacular texts, while the glossator of the Egerton 2864 manuscript clearly privileges the traditional Latin-literate reader. Susan Schibanoff sees the two glossators as reacting in opposite ways to "Alison's 'bookishness'—a woman's literal and metaphorical taking of texts into her own hands—[which] dramatizes an extreme act of new reading."[13] *The Canterbury Tales,* with its textual professional rivals, such as the Friar and Summoner, and the rivalries witnessed in the glossators of the texts associated with the Wife, demonstrates "a much larger social and religious controversy over another kind of 'new' reading that had already begun in Chaucer's time and would continue far beyond it: lay reading of the vernacular Bible."[14] Since the learning of Latin constituted the entry into an exclusive male realm, separate from the lower-status female home,[15] any attempt to translate and disseminate information from Latin would be seen by educated men as potentially threatening.

But how threatening is the Wife of Bath? She certainly reinterprets authoritative texts. One text she treats has already undergone clerkly attention: her own body, which she tells us Jankyn has glossed "so wel" (509). In her reglossing of that text, her body, the sexual organ functions metonymically as the female body, the generator or source of her authority of experience. Numerous critics have commented on the Wife's predilection for sexual glossing. Lee Patterson has written about the importance of the rhetorical device of *dilatio* for the Wife's discourse, a strategy which is sexual in implication.[16] Catherine S. Cox reads the Wife's glossing as an erotic activity in itself: "her *'bele chose'* is her *'pleye'* of language, not the play of her female anatomy." Glossing constitutes a kind of erotic foreplay in this argument and the Wife constructs "a sexual rhetoric. . . . The autoeroticism of the glossing is extended further in that the body as *textus* becomes a target for her own glossing as well; she, in effect, glosses herself."[17]

Significantly, the Wife translates her sexual instrument using three different phrases: the Middle English *queynte,* the French *bele chose* and the Latin *quoniam.* Why does she use these three languages? This use of three languages for the same signified constitutes more than just the cuteness or obscenity of which she has been charged.[18] While the Wife's *Prologue* has been read in the context of numerous source texts, such as *sermons joyeux,* sermons concerning the marriage at Cana, polemical sermonizing in general, and deportment books,[19] another textual antecedent has not yet been thoroughly explored: that of vernacular works, including medical treatises such as those attributed to Trotula. A group of manuscripts labeled "Trotula Translation

A"[20] converges with issues present in *The Wife of Bath's Prologue.* The translator of one of these Trotula manuscripts, MS Additional 12195, writes

> Wherfor in worchep of ower lady and of all þe seynts I thynke to do myn intent and bessynes for to schew after the french and latyn þe diveris of þe maladis and þe signes þat ye schall know theme by and þe cures helpyng to theme after the tretys of diveris masteris.[21]

This passage shows the tri-lingual nature of translation in late fourteenth-century England, from Latin and/or French into the vernacular, English. The Wife's chosen signifiers for her genitalia coincide with the three languages[22] circulating in fourteenth-century England: Latin, the language of the church and the law; French, the language of the nobility, law and commerce; and English, the vernacular and potentially subversive tongue.[23] The Wife glosses her sexual organ in Latin and French, the languages of intellectual and authoritative discourse, and in English, the vernacular which permits transmission of privileged discourse to a larger and lay audience.[24] Is it any wonder that the Wife refers to the sexual organ in three different languages, the three languages which were in use in England at the time she is given voice and the three languages which either represent power or threaten established power? The heteroglossia of the Wife's speech is literal in that she uses three languages to justify and authorize her statements. She translates her source of authority, her text of the sexual organ, into the three languages which constitute aspects of authority and power.

But her discourse remains problematic, as Lee Patterson suggests:

> Try as she (and Chaucer) might, she remains confined within the prison house of masculine language; she brilliantly rearranges and deforms her authorities to enable them to disclose new areas of experience, but she remains dependent on them for her voice.[25]

Catherine S. Cox agrees, arguing that the Wife "is produced by and reiterates an ostensibly masculine discourse." She concludes that in using "male discourse" the Wife fails to establish anything other than an equally repressive "feminine discourse."[26] Andrew Galloway reads the Wife as briefly occupying the authoritative position of preachers on marriage, but concurs with Patterson and Cox that "[w]hat the Wife steals from the authority of preachers whose discourse she invokes she also robs from her own authority."[27] R. W. Hanning suggests that her appeal to experience is largely bogus "since texts keep invading the Wife's monologue and setting the terms for her argument." Ultimately, he argues, she is "beten for a book," beaten *by* a book.[28] These critical viewpoints agree that by utilizing masculine strategies of power, such as glossing, the Wife simply weakens her own stance.

The Wife provides Latin, French and English versions of her text. But this multilingual action is not simple translation; the word for word literal transcription of *bele chose* is "beautiful thing," not *queynte* or *quoniam.* The Prologue to the Wycliffite Bible, chapter 15, explicitly discusses the problems of translating from one language to another and the inevitable *interpretation* which the translator stamps on the text.

> First it is to knowe þat þe beste translating is, out of Latyn into English, to translate aftir þe sentence and not oneli aftir þe wordis . . . and go not fer fro þe lettre; and if þe lettre mai not be suid in þe translating, let þe sentence euere be hool and open, for þe wordis owen to serue to þe entent and sentence, and ellis þe wordis ben superflu eiþer false. . . . But in translating of wordis equiuok, þat is þat haþ manie significacions vndur oo lettre, mai liʒtli be pereil. For Austyn seiþ in þe secounde book of *Cristene Teching* þat, if equiuok wordis be not translatid into þe sense eiþer vndurstonding of þe autour, it is errour.[29]

Meaning and intent must be conveyed for a translation to be true or accurate. The very difficulty of translating *sentence* was in fact the basis for resistance to a translation of the Bible. Typically, vernacular translations provided both a paraphrase of a text and exegetical glossing.[30] Translation and interpretation, then, came to be virtually indistinguishable. *Translatio,* for the late medieval writer, would necessarily involve *inventio.*[31] Using the example of Chaucer's *Boece* translation, Rita Copeland cites the use of doublets, different glosses on one word which stem from various source texts (i.e., Boethius and then commentators on Boethius).[32] Offering readers more than one word signals verbal differences among the sources; the discrepancies among the words function then like glosses, and thus implicit interpretations.[33]

Reading the Wife's use of three terms for her sexual organ following this model suggests she is interpreting the concept of her sexual organ through the differences among its variant signifiers and their variant sources. Her words for her sexual organ come from various traditions, both the Latin and, as we will see, a vernacular version of a medical text. If Copeland's model of medieval vernacular translation holds true and we apply it to the Wife's own translation work, then we can see that the Wife is not simply slavishly replicating masculine strategies and texts. In fact,

> medieval vernacular translations can radically differentiate themselves from the original texts. . . . [P]aradoxically, medieval translations can achieve the status of primary texts within their vernacular literary traditions, as they substitute themselves, through interpretative refiguration, for the original text.[34]

As R. A. Shoaf suggests, "[t]o translate is to violate an authority."[35] The Wife's translation of the sexual organ, then, while drawing on source material from other traditions, texts and authors, creates her own unique interpretation. She opens up meaning by suggesting alternatives for the signified, her sexual organ. Rather than being trapped by male discourse, she transcends it.[36] Furthermore, we, as readers or listeners, are ourselves forced into the position of glossators.[37] We are given the various translations of a text, here the sexual organ or female body, and must interpret for ourselves. We are empowered by her vernacularizing of the text, by her multiple glossing. Chaucer, through the Wife, promotes autonomy in interpretation by the reader.

Power to interpret disturbs those specialists who previously had exclusive access to material, hence the controversy over the vernacular translation of the Bible.[38] This controversy resembled issues concerning vernacular translations of medical texts,[39] like those ascribed to Trotula, whose intended audience included

> not only literate women but also unlettered women, who can have the book read aloud for their edification. Although men are not categorically forbidden to read the treatise (a prohibition that would have been unenforceable in any case), they are warned not to use the book for 'slandering' women, despising them for their diseases.[40]

One such audience member is Jankyn, whose "book of wikked wives" includes selections from Trotula (677).[41] One Trotula manuscript, Oxford Bodley MS Douce 37, on the *Knowing of Woman's Kind in Childing*, discusses the *Differences between Men and Women*. The fourth of such differences

> ys bytuene here leggis, for ther have men a yerde [penis] with other portynauns [appurtenances] and ther hathe women an opynynge wyche ys calde in Frenche a "bele chose," or ellys a wykket of the wombe.[42]

Why this coincidence of terms in Chaucer and a medical text? Perhaps "bele chose" was simply a well-known term, current and available to lay readers of English. It's possible Chaucer read this medical treatise or one similar to it and therefore used the term.[43] Or the Trotula translator might have read Chaucer and subsequently used the Wife's term for sexual organ. There is no way we can determine the origin of the term in Chaucer for sure, although it seems to me that the first two possibilities are the more likely. In fact, a closely related phrase, "prive chose," was in common currency during Chaucer's time. The *Great Surgery* of Guy of Chauliac (d. 1368) describes a hermaphrodite in the following way: "In a womman forsothe there is another in the whiche a yerde [penis] and prive stones [testicles] apperen above the prive chose [vulva]."[44] Another example in the same context, the "priue chose of woman," appears in John de Trevisa's translation of Bartholemeus Anglicus's *De proprietatibus rerum* which dates from 1398.[45] The use of "prive chose" for the vulva in medi-

cal texts in the late fourteenth century indicates that Chaucer's utilization of "chose" would not be unusual for his contemporary readers and listeners. Furthermore, the currency of "prive chose" means that "bele chose" would probably be understood even by a non-French literate audience.

This coincidence of "bele chose" with a vernacular medical tract is suggestive for the Wife's agenda in the *Prologue* as a whole. In a sense, the Wife is offering an alternative medical text in the vernacular by which women can validate not only their peculiar biological experiences, but their experiences in marriage. Just as vernacular medical texts disturb the monopoly which university- or Latin-trained men had in medical practice, so too does her marriage tract undermine the male monopoly over describing or discussing marital experience. The Wife's *Prologue* and *Tale* should be seen in the larger context of vernacular writings and translations in the late Middle Ages. Disempowered classes— male or female—could enter the discourse of power through access to authoritative texts increasingly available in the vernacular. The Wife's translation of the source of her power into three languages is suggestive of lay medical tracts and the larger web of vernacular texts in the late Middle Ages. This suggests that Chaucer intends for us to read the Wife's *Prologue* as critical of monolithic authority itself and as validating a new, previously disempowered, audience.

The recognition and validation of a new audience is what connects Heloise to this discussion. Commentators suggest Chaucer knew of Heloise from Jean de Meun's *Roman de la rose* and most simply assume that Jankyn's book (677-78) refers to Peter Abelard's quoting of her letter in which she argues him out of marriage.[46] Superficial similarities exist between the Wife and Heloise. Both want something from their respective spouses which they aren't getting: whether marital debt or correspondence.[47] Both insist on being heard and presenting their own side of the story.[48] Jean, in his summation of the story of Abelard and Heloise, writes that

> [s]he asked him to love her but not to claim any right of her except those of grace and freedom, without lordship or mastery, so that he might study, entirely his own man, quite free, without tying himself down, and that she might also devote herself to study, for she was not empty of knowledge.[49]

Perhaps this passage is echoed in both the *Prologue* and the *Tale* where this issue of mastery comes up. The Wife admits she has gotten "By maistrie, al the soveraynetee" (818) from Jankyn. The rapist-knight tells the queen in answer to her question

> "Wommen desiren to have sovereynetee
> As wel over hir housbond as hir love,
> And for to been in maistrie hym above."

1038-40

The Wife endorses the concept of mastery while Heloise rejects it. The automatic assumption that Jankyn's Heloise allusion refers to misogynist and misogamous arguments is not incorrect.

But what if, in fact, the equation of Heloise with anti-marriage views is too limiting an analysis of the Wife's allusion to Heloise? Jill Mann points out that medieval commentators rejected Heloise's own anti-feminist interpretation of her role in the affair and write virtually unanimously in sympathy for her.[50] Heloise is important for more ideas than simply the arguments Abelard ventriloquizes for her. "Helowys" is referred to as an "abbesse nat fer fro Parys," rather than as Abelard's lover or wife. Surely this reference to her being an abbess as opposed to (mere) lover has some significance. In Letter 5, one of the so-called "Letters of Direction," Heloise asks Abelard to sketch out a version of the Rule of St. Benedict appropriate for women, since these rules did not take into consideration the peculiarities of women's physique and emotions. In fact, her criticism suggests that the Rule was "inadequate to the requirements of women."[51] Her asking Abelard for new rules could be read as nothing revolutionary. After all, she's going to the same old source—a Latin educated male of the Church. But Heloise's request also suggests that no single truth exists. The notion of a handbook for women which Abelard must create in response to Heloise's letter is not unlike the one the Wife offers us in her *Prologue* and the vernacular medical and religious texts which swirl in the subtext of the *Canterbury Tales*. Rules change depending on the recipients or audience of those rules. Truth *is* different for women. The references to Trotula and Heloise in *The Wife of Bath's Prologue* suggest the necessity for texts designed for female audiences, which must be translated into the vernacular. The Wife's realm is not the cloistered and strictly female audience of the Paraclete, but a mixed—in terms both of gender and religious status—audience of pilgrims on the open road. While Heloise wrote in Latin, the Wife speaks in the vernacular, thus expanding the field of her potential audience. The Wife's translation of the source of her authority into three languages draws on issues which vernacular translations explicitly lay out. By presenting us with three versions (*queynte, bele chose,* and *quoniam*) for the same text (sexual organ), Chaucer through the Wife forces us to play the role of glossator ourselves and forces, if not endorses, our glossing.

To conclude, let us return to *The Wife of Bath's Prologue* and *Tale* to read them in light of the argument above. Critics have oscillated between two poles concerning the *Prologue,* either seeing the Wife as the personification of carnality and misogynist fears and stereotypes and/or admiring the Wife for her energy and *joie de vivre.* The *Tale,* on the other hand, is simply troubling. The raped maiden is violated in terms not only of the plot, but also of the text, in that she is forgotten once the knight comes to court. The women at the court intervene on behalf of the rapist, who is ultimately rewarded with a beautiful young wife for his transgression against a woman. Additionally, the choice of the romance genre for the Wife has long been a puzzle for critics, many of whom find it more in character for her to tell a fabliau.[52] I hope to show how reading both the *Prologue* and *Tale* in terms of issues of vernacular and Latin usage and related concerns of authority and audience can illuminate the place of the Wife of Bath and her texts in the Chaucer canon.

The Wife welcomes a female audience throughout her discourse by using metaphors which the average woman, an unlettered wife, could easily understand. Her metaphoric exercises invoke bread and bread-making, an activity with which women undoubtedly would be familiar. When she contrasts virgins and wives, the Wife says,

> Lat hem be breed of pured whete-seed,
> And lat us wyves hoten barly-breed;
> And yet with barly-breed, Mark telle kan,
> Oure Lord Jhesu refresshed many a man.

> 143-46

When she describes how she would complain to her husbands in order not to be reprimanded herself, she comments, "Whoso that first to mille comth, first grynt" (389). In talking of her relatively advanced age, she says,

> The flour is goon; ther is namoore to telle;
> The bren, as I best kan, now moste I selle.

> 477-78

Although she addresses only men and religious women within the context of the *Tales* as a whole, her homely metaphors, while drawing on Jerome and possibly Paul,[53] open up possibilities for other audiences, such as lay-women, to understand her arguments more easily. How could such a wife succeed in reaching other wives? Don't husbands and celibate men have a monopoly on private and public preaching to women? After all, even the Wife admits that husbands preach.[54] She tells how Jankyn "often tymes wolde preche, / And me of olde Romayn geestes teche" (641-42). Yet the Wife also teaches,[55] admitting she has her own "lawe" (219) for controlling her husbands. Her own experiences with her husbands function as a kind of pedagogical text for "Ye wise wyves" (225) to follow and use in their own marriages.

Isn't she giving her trade secrets away to the enemy? In the Wife's essentialist view of women, women are doomed to reveal such secrets even to their own detriment. Women can't help but pass on private information. The Wife herself admits that her own marriages were far from a household affair. Her best friend heard all.

> Hir name was Alisoun.
> She knew myn herte, and eek my privetee,
> Bet than oure parisshe preest, so moot I thee!
> To hire biwreyed I my conseil al.
> For hadde myn housbonde pissed on a wal,
> Or doon a thyng that sholde han cost his lyf,
> To hire, and to another worthy wyf,
> And to my nece, which that I loved weel,
> I wolde han toold his conseil every deel.
> And so I dide ful often, God it woot,
> That made his face often reed and hoot
> For verray shame, and blamed hymself for he
> Had toold to me so greet a pryvetee.
>
> 530-42

The female audience the Wife addresses gets increasingly larger, until three other women know the innermost secrets of her marriage. In fact, this female audience knows more than the one member of society sanctioned to hear such confessions, a male priest; and the privileged male on the edge of this gossiping group will become the Wife's fifth husband, Jankyn himself. The anxiety the Wife's husband feels reflects the anxiety felt among those men who opposed vernacular translations; once privileged men no longer maintained exclusive access to knowledge, society itself would be threatened with subversion. Think of the hope expressed by the translator of the Trotula text quoted above that reading women would pass information along and that men would not use this information against women; think also of the comparable passage in the introduction to the Wycliffite Bible. The Wife's *Prologue* addresses these issues of vernacular translations and audience and the anxiety produced when secrets are made common knowledge.

The *Tale* reinforces the Wife's view that women are incapable of keeping secrets. The Wife's rewriting of the Ovidian Midas legend maintains "we wommen konne no thyng hele" (950). Midas's wife cannot refrain from passing on, even to the watery marsh, the information that Midas has ass's ears:[56] "hir thoughte that she dyde / That she so longe sholde a conseil hyde" (965-66). The Wife glosses this text by commenting,

> Heere may ye se, thogh we a tyme abyde,
> Yet out it moot; we kan no conseil hyde.
>
> 979-80

Just as the Wife and Midas's wife reveal male confidences, so too does the availability of vernacular texts disturb the status quo and the control learned men have had on information. The audience of vernacular texts was frequently singled out as a female one; hence part of the cause for the anxiety the Lollards aroused. This passage in the *Tale,* however misogynist, is also empowering; the ability or tendency for women to reveal secrets only heightens their own power. Those who possess secrets in common create a community of power. When the Wife in her *Prologue* tells her girlfriends her husband's secrets, those women create a privileged group, knowledgeable about a man. Midas's wife discloses her husband's shame, thus leaving him open to ridicule. Just as vernacular texts disrupt the power of the Latin tradition, so too women threaten male power by revealing men's secrets.

The *Tale* shows what happens when strictly female groups allow a man access to their communal knowledge. Female audiences abound in the *Tale*. The "queene and other ladyes mo" (894) intervene to test the rapist. They ask him to figure out the answer to a female secret. The rapist encounters "ladyes foure and twenty, and yet mo" (992) dancing while on his travels and thus encounters the old woman. Back in the palace

> Ful many a noble wyf, and many a mayde,
> And many a wydwe, for that they been wise,
> The queene hirself sittynge as a justise,
> Assembled been, his answere for to heere.
>
> 1026-29

When he reveals the secret desire of women,

> In al the court ne was ther wyf, ne mayde,
> Ne wydwe that contraried that he sayde.
>
> 1043-44

While an exchange takes place repeatedly between groups of women and one man, the women all fully expect that once a secret is revealed, good faith will be maintained. Access to matters formerly secret gives power, hence the warning to men reading the Trotula Middle English translation not to abuse women with private information about their gynecology. The status of truth changes once hidden confidences are exposed to previously uninformed audiences. No longer to be used simply to exert power over others, exchange of secrets in good faith necessitates the maintenance of respect by the recipient of a confidence. Therefore in the *Tale,* despite all his curses, the rapist knight must marry the old woman since she revealed the secret of women to him.

The knight complains that the hag is not only ugly, but "of so lough a kynde" (1101), whereupon the famous "gentilesse" speech commences. The hag points out that lords do not always perform "gentil dedes" (1115), arguing "he is gentil that dooth gentil dedis" (1170). If we read this as a metatextual comment on the vernacular, we could understand her view that, just as lords don't always act in a noble way, so too the Latin tradition does not always act nobly, specifically in misogynist writings. She cites traditional (males writing in Latin) *auctoritees* to endorse her view that nobility is not an accident of birth.

> "Thenketh hou noble, as seith Valerius,
> Was thilke Tullius Hostillius,
> That out of poverte roos to heigh noblesse."
>
>   1165-67

While vernacular texts might have been despised for not being Latin and authoritative, as the old woman argues about herself,

> "Al were it that myne auncestres were rude,
> Yet may the hye God, and so hope I,
> Grante me grace to lyven vertuously.
> Thanne am I gentil, whan that I bigynne
> To lyven vertuously and weyve synne."
>
>   1172-76

Vernacular texts were seen as "rude," yet the old hag, the Wife, and Chaucer argue for the potential nobility of the vernacular verse. The hag is old, like the English language, and neither is accorded proper respect—yet. The Wife's *Tale* speaks to the resistance by powerful men to the loss of their authority in the dissemination of vernacular translations to female audiences. In accepting her argument, the knight is rewarded; or, in this metatextual reading, acceptance of the vernacular is rewarded. The old woman is transformed into a beauty, or, as the Clerk describes Griselda's transformation upon putting on noble clothes, she is "translated" (385).[57] This beauty comes when her authority is recognized and accepted by the knight/Latin tradition who has resisted the old hag/vernacular. Now the vernacular is seen as beautiful, "fair" and "yong" (1251).

The whole question of the Latin tradition, authority, and the vernacular boils down to the question of who's in and who's out, who's excluded and who's included. The *Tale*'s structure bases itself on the figure of limitation and boundary. The initial fairyland the Wife describes (857-63) is in a pre-lapsarian state, replete with images of fullness: "fulfild of fayerye" (859), when fairies "[d]aunced ful ofte" (861). The time she harks back to is spoken of in terms of proliferation: "manye hundred yeres ago" (863). But the multiplicity of the past has ended. Three times in eleven lines she uses the word "lymytour[s]" or "lymytacioun" (866, 874, 877), which refers to the friars licensed to beg in a given district and which mocks the pilgrim Friar who also is a "lymytour" (1.209, 1.269, III. 1265). Though a "lymytour" in the sense of "one who or that which limits" was not used until the late fifteenth century, "lymytacioun" is used in the sense of "the action of limiting" as early as 1380 by Wyclif.[58] I would suggest that not only the religious connotation for these words is being suggested in this early part of the Wife's *Tale.* The fact

that the words are used three times within a few lines suggests we are to pay attention to them. Limitations are set up in this opening passage before the rape occurs. We are told that the "lymytours" bless

> halles, chambres, kichenes, boures,
> Citees, burghes, castels, hye toures,
> Thropes, bernes, shipnes, dayeryes. . . .
>
>   869-71

The places described are locations which are limited, structures of defined spaces, quite unlike the "grene mede" (861) where the elf-queen dances with her company in fairyland. These "lymytours" infect spaces where all classes and both genders dwell, city folk and country folk: castles and barns, kitchens and ships. The entire society is hemmed in and constricted by the actions of these limiters. In the metatextual reading of the *Tale,* the "lymytour" lies in wait to dishonor women (874-81), just as authoritative texts, such as those misogynist ones cited in Jankyn's book, lie in wait to dishonor and limit women who are denied the opportunity and authority to retaliate or defend themselves. The most extreme instance of this limitation is seen in the raped maiden. It is crucial that she is cut out of the rest of the *Tale*—nothing can bring back the voices of women from the past who have been violated and denied a voice.

Only through the rapist-knight's acceptance of the ugly hag can a world of openness and fullness return. The qualifiers in the closing passage of the *Tale* suggest abundance and shade off into hyperbole. The hag is now "so" fair and "so" young (1251). He kisses her "[a] thousand tyme" (1254) and she obeys him in "every" thing (1255). They live "unto hir lyves ende / In parfit joye" (1257-58). Most embroidered of all is the happiness of the rapist-knight whose heart is "bathed in a bath of blisse" (1253). The use of "bath" twice in one line for the conclusion of the Wife's *Tale,* plus the uncommon use of alliteration to reinforce the impact of these words, suggests both the Wife's emphasis on this sense of plenitude and her direct association with such plenitude, in that she comes from Bath.

By the late fourteenth century, England had witnessed traumatizing events and dire disruptions in its social hierarchy and control, the most obvious example being the revolt of 1381.[59] The limitations and hierarchies which the culture engendered and replicated were no longer functioning. The Wife suggests that the only recourse for a society to heal itself from disruptions is, in fact, to restructure itself. In the terms of her *Prologue* and *Tale,* this means providing access to all of things formerly kept secret and exclusive. These revelations constitute a two-way street: men's knowledge must becomes available to women just as women's secrets become available to men.[60] Only the expansion of truth beyond the limits of a specific group can lead to understanding and, ultimately, reconciliation and healing.

This potential for reconciliation of various groups with their separate interests raises issues of the vernacular. The liminal position of a vernacular writer as author in the late fourteenth century is alluded to obliquely in the *Tale.* The old woman assures the knight,

> "And certes, sire, thogh noon auctoritee
> Were in no book, ye gentils of honour
> Seyn that men sholde an oold wight doon favour
> And clepe hym fader, for youre gentillesse;
> And auctours shal I fynden, as I gesse."
>
> 1208-12

Of course, she won't necessarily *find* authoritative writers, as she suggests, but perhaps *invent* them, as *fynden* ambiguously suggests. She'll invent authority and authorities to support her ambiguous position who'll necessarily write in the vernacular. Chaucer's concern about the vernacular and the role of translation is not restricted to the Wife's *Prologue* and *Tale.* This issue comes up repeatedly throughout his corpus.

Chaucer's own role as author is questionable since he writes not in Latin, but in the vernacular. Within thirty lines (43-63) of *A Treatise on the Astrolabe,* Chaucer refers to his activities and himself with the following words: "endityng" (43, 45), "writen" (48), "compilator" (61-62), and "translatid" (63). These words constitute similar if not identical activities in Chaucer's eyes, and the seemingly indiscriminate use of these words for his writing activities hints at an anxiety concerning his artistic achievement. He must do this well, fashioning his own authority as a writer in the vernacular by playing with the role of author and the words connected to the writing act. As a vernacular writer, considering the ambiguous position of vernacular texts in the late Middle Ages, the very achievement of his work could be in doubt. As Tim Machan points out

> [T]he tension between his cultural status as a vernacular writer and his recognition of his authorial achievement is both expressed and resolved in Chaucer's conception of translation, and . . . it is this tension which underlies the conceptual and procedural overlap between Chaucer the translator and Chaucer the original writer. For by medieval standards Chaucer was a paradox—a "vernacular author."[61]

But the introduction to *A Treatise on the Astrolabe* explicitly endorses the legitimacy of diverse languages for expressing similar conclusions, including his "lighte Englissh" (51).[62]

Chaucer's narrator in various poems recurrently denies responsibility for his text, arguing that he is simply translating or transcribing. In actuality, of course, the work is original and unique due to Chaucer's revisions of his source material.[63] Concepts such as writing, *endityng, makyng,* translation, and *compilatio* recur in his various works and *translacioun* and *endityng* were indistinguishable for a writer like Chaucer. That is to say, *inventio* and compilation were an integral part of the act of original composition no matter how he designated the task.[64]

The Wife of Bath functions as Chaucer's counterpart in her writerly activities. Her defense of the vernacular, thinly veiled in both her *Prologue* and *Tale,* is both Chaucer's defense and a defense of Chaucer. The Wife's *Tale* can be read as addressing the issues of the vernacular and the role female audiences play in receiving and passing on translations of authoritative texts, as well as vindicating Chaucer's authority as a vernacular author. The Wife of Bath's *Prologue* and *Tale* are suggestive of a larger web of vernacular works in the late Middle Ages, works directed at new and previously ignored audiences. The *Prologue* and *Tale* should be read in the context of increased vernacular writings and translations in the late Middle Ages since the way disempowered classes—women or non-aristocrats—can enter the discourse of power is through access to authoritative texts, available in the vernacular. Chaucer, in citing Trotula and Heloise in Jankyn's book which otherwise lists exclusively male authors, recognizes the validity of a new audience and a different truth for women.

Notes

1. Unless otherwise indicated, all references to the text are according to line number from fragment III, *Riverside Chaucer,* 3rd edition, gen. ed. Larry D. Benson (Boston: Houghton Mifflin Company, 1987).

2. Margaret Aston, *Lollards and Reformers: Images and Literacy in Late Medieval Religion* (London: Hambledon Press, 1984), 53, 58. See Andrew Galloway, "Marriage Sermons, Polemical Sermons, and *The Wife of Bath's Prologue*: A Generic Excursus," *SAC* 14 (1992): 1-30, for a further discussion of polemics against preaching, especially 24ff. Arguments both for and against female preaching relied on Biblical passages and subsequent glosses. See Aston, 55.

3. Bella Millett, "Women in No Man's Land: English recluses and the development of vernacular literature in the twelfth and thirteenth centuries," in *Women and Literature in Britain, 1150-1500,* ed. Carol M. Meale (Cambridge: Cambridge University Press, 1993): 86-103.

4. Joanne Jasin, "The Transmission of Learned Medical Literature in the Middle English *Liber Uricrisiarum,*" *Medical History* 37 (1993): 313-29,

especially 328. Linda E. Voigts and Michael R. McVaugh discuss how phlebotomy texts extended their influence from academically-trained physicians and surgeons to empirically experienced surgeons and barbers after 1300 in *A Latin Technical Phlebotomy and Its Middle English Translation,* Transactions of the American Philosophical Society 74 (Philadelphia: American Philosophical Society, 1984), 7. See also Russell Hope Robbins, "Medical Manuscripts in Middle English," *Speculum* 45 (1970): 393-415. R. A. Shoaf points out how the "Latin tradition was becoming increasingly alien to a rising bourgeoisie that clamored for translations into the vernacular," in "Notes towards Chaucer's Poetics of Translation," *SAC* 1 (1979): 59.

5. This in turn implies that Chaucer was sympathetic to certain Lollard beliefs that upheld the dissemination and reception of vernacular texts. David Lyle Jeffrey argues more generally that "we can see close correspondence between Chaucer's apparent thinking and Wyclif's expressed opinions and convictions on a number of quite controversial subjects" in "Chaucer and Wyclif: Biblical Hermeneutic and Literary Theory in the XIVth Century," *Chaucer and the Scriptural Tradition,* ed. Jeffrey (Ottawa: University of Ottawa Press, 1984), 114. Aston writes, "It was as a vernacular literate movement that Lollardy had gathered momentum and it was as a vernacular literate movement that it was suspected and persecuted" (*Lollards and Reformers,* 27).

6. Granted, there have been scholarly questions as to the authorship of these texts. All the so-called Trotula texts may not be properly ascribed to her, if she even existed. The debate about Heloise's authorship has been put to rest by Peter Dronke, *Women Writers of the Middle Ages* (Cambridge: Cambridge University Press, 1991), 140-43.

7. Dronke, 108. Benson acknowledges the existence of this translation but suggests "Chaucer probably did not know the letters directly," (*Riverside Chaucer,* 871 n677). However, D. W. Robertson, Jr., *Abelard and Heloise* (New York: Dial Press, 1972), 154, presumes Chaucer used another Jean de Meun text, his French version of Boethius, for his own translation of *The Consolation of Philosophy.* David F. Hult, "Language and Dismemberment: Abelard, Origen, and the *Romance of the Rose,*" in *Rethinking the Romance of the Rose: Text, Image, Reception,* ed. Kevin Brownlee and Sylvia Huot (Philadelphia: University of Pennsylvania Press, 1992), 120-21, argues that a number of puns in the *Roman de la rose* are interlingual, stemming from the translation of the *Historia calamitatum* into French. Jill Mann, *Geoffrey Chau-*

cer (Atlantic Highlands, N.J.: Humanities Press International, Inc., 1991), 54, 199 n10, suggests that Chaucer knew the Latin originals of the Heloise-Abelard correspondence.

8. Alexandra Barratt, ed., *Women's Writing in Middle English* (London: Longman, 1992), 27. See also John F. Benton, "Trotula, Women's Problems, and the Professionalization of Medicine in the Middle Ages," *Bulletin of the History of Medicine* 59 (1985): 30-53.

9. Quoted in Barratt, *Women's Writing,* 30-31. See also Audrey Eccles, "The Early Use of English for Midwiferies," *NM* 78 (1971): 377-85.

10. Anne Hudson, ed., *Selections From English Wycliffite Writings* (Cambridge: Cambridge University Press, 1978), 107-8. Hudson also discusses the Wycliffite language of the Wife of Bath in her *The Premature Revolution: Wycliffite Texts and Lollard History* (Oxford: Clarendon, 1988), 393. See also Curt Buhler, "A Lollard tract: On Translating the Bible into English," *MÆ* 7 (1938): 167-83.

11. Quoted in Hudson, *The Premature Revolution,* 185 n64, my italics. See also A. J. Minnis's work on authorial intention in translation, both "'Authorial Intention' and 'Literal Sense' in the Exegetical Theories of Richard Fitzralph and John Wyclif: An Essay in the Medieval History of Biblical Hermeneutics," *Proceedings of the Royal Irish Academy* 75, section C (1975): 1-31, and also his *Medieval Theory of Authorship: Scholastic Literary Attitudes in the later Middle Ages* (London: Scolar Press, 1984). Jeffrey also discusses "intention" and the reader ("Chaucer and Wyclif," 115ff).

12. Hudson, *Selections from English Wycliffite Writings,* 107.

13. Susan Schibanoff, "The New Reader and Female Textuality in Two Early Commentaries on Chaucer," *SAC* 10 (1988): 77.

14. Schibanoff, "The New Reader and Female Textuality," 84. Janet Coleman connects the problems which an increasingly literate public created for the status quo in the fourteenth century to Plato's *Phaedrus,* wherein he warns that "writing would turn men into public nuisances," *Medieval Readers and Writers 1350-1400* (New York: Columbia University Press, 1981), 157-58.

15. Walter J. Ong, S. J., "Latin Language Study as a Renaissance Puberty Rite," *SP* 56 (1959): 103-24. Ong goes on to discuss the vernacular as metonymic for the home, childhood and women.

16. Lee Patterson, "'For the Wyves love of Bathe': Feminine Rhetoric and Poetic Resolution in the *Roman de la rose* and the *Canterbury Tales,*" *Speculum* 58 (1983): 656-95.

17. Catherine S. Cox, "Holy Erotica and the Virgin Word: Promiscuous Glossing in *The Wife of Bath's Prologue,*" *Exemplaria* 5 (1993): 214, 219, 220.

18. This paper does not concern itself with some critics' disgust at the vulgarity of the Wife's "euphemisms." Maureen Quilligan comments "not surprisingly, Alisoun is a figure who uses many full-blown, dirty words, made all the more wonderfully vulgar by her fake French euphemisms: she is a character, however, whose speech Chaucer claims he merely records," *The Allegory of Female Authority: Christine de Pizan's Cité des Dames* (Ithaca, N.Y.: Cornell University Press, 1991), 35-36. I myself chose to use "sexual organ" throughout this essay after it was pointed out, at the Philological Association of the Pacific Coast "Chaucer and Related Topics" session, where I first presented this paper as a talk (November 1993), that my own use of *pudendum* was in itself a euphemism, is coy or "quaint," and replicates the very culture which stigmatizes female sexuality both by using Latin and by implying that female sexual parts are "shameful" ("pudendum"). Larry Benson argues that *queynte* is etymologically distinct from "cunt" and was not considered obscene in Middle English, stating that "[q]ueynte is not the forerunner of the modern obscenity; it was not the normal word for 'vagina'; and it was not considered vulgar or obscene," "The 'Queynte' Punnings of Chaucer's Critics," in *Reconstructing Chaucer,* SAC Proceedings 1, ed. Paul Strohm and Thomas J. Heffernan (Knoxville: University of Tennessee Press, 1985), 33. Benson argues that "queynte" is equivalent to "elegant, pleasing thing" and that she is "talking cute" when she is speaking to her old husband (447). He concludes that "given the Wife of Bath's propensity for euphemism and periphrasis, a direct obscenity is the last thing we would expect from her" (43-45). The overall success of Benson's argument is undermined by the not-so-subtle misogynistic asides he makes (30, 31). Susan Crane criticizes Benson's conclusions by taking his own rhetoric to task in "Medieval Romance and Feminine Difference in *The Knight's Tale,*" *SAC* 12 (1990): 55-56. It is worth noting Augustine's view of obscene words and euphemisms in *De dialectica* 7.100-103:

> [The chastity of the ears] would be offended if the private part of the body were called by a low or vulgar name, though the thing with a different name is the same. If the shamefulness of the thing signified were not covered over by the propriety of the signifying word, then the base character of both would affect both sense and mind.

Quoted by Hult, "Language and Dismemberment," 114, from the translation of B. Darrell Jackson

(Dordrecht, Holland: D. Reidel, 1975). While the signified is the same, the signifier is what can cause offense. The Wife also calls genitalia "membres" (116), "thynges" (121), "instrument" (132, 149), "chambre of Venus" (618) and "privee place" (620). But *queynte* has aroused the most critical debate and anger. Thomas Hahn, "Teaching the Resistant Woman: The Wife of Bath and the Academy," *Exemplaria* 4 (1992): 440, suggests "that verbal profusion [calls] to account the clerkly view that these 'thinges' are not signifieds at all, but signs marked on the body 'to knowe a female from a male' (III.122)."

19. Mary Carruthers sees Alisoun attacking the body of marital lore articulated in deportment books "written to foster 'gentilesse'" such as *The Book of the Knight of LaTour-Landry,* "The Wife of Bath and the Painting of Lions," *PMLA* 94 (1979): 209-22.

20. Monica H. Green, "Obstetrical and Gynecological Texts in Middle English" in *SAC* 14 (1992): 53-88, discusses Middle English translations of Latin gynecological texts and their audiences. Elsewhere Green has discussed the spurious assignment of Trota's name to various texts circulated in the Middle Ages. See "Women's Medical Practice and Health Care in Medieval Europe," in *Sisters and Workers in the Middle Ages,* ed. Judith M. Bennett, Elizabeth A. Clark, Jean F. O'Barr, B. Anne Vilen, and Sarah Westphal-Wihl (Chicago: University of Chicago Press, 1989), 39-78.

21. Green, "Obstetrical," 65. Green further notes that "MSS Sloane 421A, Douce 37, and Bodley 483 claim only Latin as their source language" (n34).

22. Law in particular necessitated expertise in three languages in the fourteenth century.

> The Rolls of Parliament were regularly in Latin and French, but occasional entries indicate that the discussion was in English. . . . In 1362 the clerks admitted for the first time that Parliament was addressed in English, and in the same year Parliament decreed that all legal proceedings had to be carried on in English because the litigants could not understand French. . . . Evidently by the 1360s most oral exchange in commerce and government must have been carried on in English, but the records were still kept in Latin and French. Formal education was in Latin, and the writing masters who taught English clerks the secretarial skills of *ars dictaminis* taught them in Latin and French. Virtually all religious and cultural writings intended for any kind of circulation were in Latin or French.

John H. Fisher, "A Language Policy for Lancastrian England," *PMLA* 107 (1992): 1169-70. See also Albert C. Baugh and Thomas Cable, *A History of the English Language,* 4th ed. (Englewood Cliffs, N.J.: Prentice Hall, 1993), chapter 6, and J. D. Burnley, "Late Medieval English Translation:

Types and Reflections," in *The Medieval Translator: The Theory and Practice of Translation in the Middle Ages,* ed. Roger Ellis (Cambridge, England: D. S. Brewer, 1989), 40-41.

23. See the discussion of this issue in Anne Hudson, *Lollards and Their Books* (London: Hambledon Press, 1985), chapter 9.

24. Carol Meale cautions against a "rigid association" of women with a particular language, citing Alice West's casual reference to owning books in Latin, French and English; see her article "'. . . alle the bokes that I haue of latyn, englisch, and frensch': Laywomen and Their Books in Late Medieval England," in *Women and Literature,* 128-58, especially 138.

25. Patterson, "For the Wyves Love," 682. See also Ralph Hanna III, "*Compilatio* and the Wife of Bath," in *Latin and Vernacular: Studies in Late-Medieval Texts and Manuscripts,* ed. A. J. Minnis (Cambridge, England: D. S. Brewer, 1989), 7, who sees her "entrapped in the language of her enslavement."

26. Cox, "Holy Erotica and the Virgin Word," 208.

27. Galloway, "Marriage Sermons," 13, 18.

28. R. W. Hanning, "Roasting a Friar, Mis-taking a Wife, and Other Acts of Textual Harassment in Chaucer's *Canterbury Tales,*" *SAC* 7 (1985): 19, 20.

29. Hudson, *Selections from English Wycliffite Writings,* 68, 71.

30. Rita Copeland points out that

> For the medieval author, translation is no less than an act of *translatio,* of metaphor or troping, for translation refigures, through interpretative reception and transference, what has previously been known in a different textual condition.

"Rhetoric and Vernacular Translation in the Middle Ages," *SAC* 9 (1987): 43, 51.

31. Burnley, "Late Medieval English Translation," 41.

32. The use of doublets can also be seen in Jean de Meun's translation of the Abelard and Heloise letters. "The commonest form of expansion is that represented by the translation of one Latin term or expression by two synonymous or near-synonymous ones in the French," writes Leslie C. Brook in "Synonymic and Near-Synonymic Pairs in Jean de Meun's Translation of the Letters of Abelard and Heloise," *NM* 87 (1986): 17. For Jean de Meun's translation theory as presented in his translation of Boethius's *Consolation,* see Brook, "Comment évaluer une traduction du treizième siècle? Quelques considérations sur la traduction

des lettres d'Abélard et d'Héloïse faite par Jean de Meun," *The Spirit of the Court: Selected Proceedings of the Fourth Congress of the International Courtly Literature Society,* ed. Glyn S. Burgess, et al. (Woodbridge, Suffolk: D. S. Brewer, 1985), 66.

33. Copeland, "Rhetoric and Vernacular Translation," 61-62. Hult cites *Roman de la rose* 21543-52, in which glosses are discussed:

> Thus things go by contraries; one is the gloss of the other. If one wants to define one of the pair, he must remember the other, or he will never, by any intention, assign a definition to it; for he who has no understanding of the two will never understand the difference between them, and without this difference no definition that one can make can come to anything.

Hult, "Language and Dismemberment," 135; trans. Charles Dahlberg, *Romance of the Rose* (Princeton: Princeton University Press, 1971), 135.

34. Copeland, "Rhetoric and Vernacular Translation," 74.

35. "A translation, in one sense, is literally a missaying. . . . It violates the original. A translation violates a prior intention or purpose" (Shoaf, "Notes towards Chaucer's Poetics," 58). Carolyn Dinshaw, *Chaucer's Sexual Poetics* (Madison: University of Wisconsin Press, 1989), 122, argues that glossing "is a gesture of appropriation."

36. Lesley Kordecki writes,

> Surely dogmatic univalent glossing is integral to patristic power maintenance, but texts that imbed contrary interpretive interjections . . . open up meaning—what Dinshaw calls "reading like a woman." . . . Chaucer's famous indirect method, his open-ended conclusions, his oxymoronic quality all are a result of conflicting imbedded glosses which pit one answer or interpretation against another.

"Let Me 'telle yow what I mente': The *Glossa Ordinaria* and the *Nun's Priest's Tale,*" *Exemplaria* 4 (1992): 374, 383. Dinshaw's argument that the Wife "*mimics* the operations of patriarchal discourse" likewise reads the Wife's discourse as an affirmation and not as trapped by patriarchal discourse (*Chaucer's Sexual Poetics,* 115).

37. Hanning points out that the Wife "refers to her sexual organ by a French euphemism which *we* must 'gloss'—thus putting the concept of interpretation, in a sexual context, at the forefront of our activity as readers at that moment" ("Roasting a Friar," 20).

38. As Hanna puts it ("*Compilatio,*" 11):

> Perhaps most distressing for the conservative, Englished Latin had been cut free from the Latin tradition and its learned practice of reading. It had become

"open." Englished texts were now consultable and interpretable, perhaps in ways unforeseen, seditious and dangerous. They had lost the support provided by that system of control and indoctrination by which Latin had always been approached—the grammatical education which made "fit" and trained readers. Such Englished texts, like the compiling activities by which the Wife constructs her *Prologue,* were now part of a more general discourse where they might be abused.

Aston remarks (*Lollards and Reformers,* 206):

> This Master John Wycliffe, the chronicler Henry Knighton wrote accusingly some years after his death, translated the Gospel from Latin into English so that it was more open to laymen and ignorant people, including "women who know how to read," whereas previously it had been the preserve of well-read clerks of good understanding.

39. C. H. Talbot, *Medicine in Medieval England* (London: Oldbourne, 1967), 196-97, discusses the proliferation of vernacular medical texts in the late Middle Ages and the anxiety it caused among university-trained males who attempted, but failed, to have Parliament pass a bill in 1421 which would prevent and punish non-university-trained medical practitioners, including, of course, women. He also speculates on "the probability that the vernacular texts dealing with gynaecology, written expressly for women so that they need not have recourse to male practitioners, may have been written or translated by [women]." Also see Elaine E. Whitaker, "Reading the Paston Letters Medically," *ELN* 31 (1993): 19-27.

40. Green, "Obstetrical and Gynecological Texts," 58. Elsewhere, Green offers the intriguing theory that the appeal to modesty of such introductions might in fact be a strategy to ensure that women's health remain in the domain of women health practitioners to "ensure them a field of practice where men could neither claim competence nor offer competition" ("Women's Medical Practice," 74).

Benton writes that many such vernacular texts "differ from the Latin *Trotula* and pay more attention to the practical obstetrical problems which concerned female practitioners" ("Trotula," 48). Benton goes on to assert that Trotula's name was mentioned often and intentionally in these medical treatises because she was a woman, and thus an authority in a realm men could know nothing about (50-51); at the same time, Latin medical treatises containing Trotula texts were not in the possession of female readers, by and large:

> By including in their medical compendia these [Latin] treatises falsely attributed to Trota, medieval physicians . . . unwittingly excluded women even further from participation in their own medicine. Though the treatises of "Trotula" bear a woman's name, they were the central texts of the gynecological medicine practiced and taught by men.

(52)

41. Some critics have seen this reference to Trotula as exemplary of the Wife as purveyor of "old wives' tales." Thomas J. Garbáty, "Chaucer's Weaving Wife," *JAP* 81 (1968): 342-46, sees the Wife as an "old Bawd" in the tradition of Ovid's Dispas. And of course La Vieille in *Roman de la rose* has also been seen as her foremother. Sarah Disbrow, "The Wife of Bath's Old Wives' Tale," *SAC* 8 (1986): 59-71, investigates the history of the "old wives' tale" tradition which stands as a subtext for the Wife's *Prologue* and *Tale.* Lorrayne Baird-Lange contends that Trotula "serves as a *type* of the Wife of Bath, as personification of medieval misogyny, both clerical and medical," from "Trotula's Fourteenth-Century Reputation, Jankyn's Book, and Chaucer's Trot," in *Reconstructing Chaucer,* ed. Strohm and Heffernan, 246. Accusations of prostitution also have been tied to this theme. See Rodney Delasanta, "Alisoun and the Saved Harlots," *ChauR* 12 (1978): 218-35; Hope Phyllis Weissman, "Why Chaucer's Wife is from Bath," *ChauR* 15 (1980): 11-36; and Edgar S. Laird, "Mars in Taurus at the Nativity of the Wife of Bath," *ELN* 28 (1990): 16.

42. Barratt, *Women's Writing,* 32.

43. Baird-Lange writes, "No evidence in his writings suggests that Chaucer was well versed in either the gynecological-obstetric treatises or the cosmetic and beauty regimens ascribed to Trotula" ("Trotula's Fourteenth-Century Reputation," 255). While she may be right that Chaucer never studied this subject intensely, he certainly could have looked through a few of these texts and picked up the terminology. I do not wish to argue that he knew of or used one particular version.

44. Quoted in Danielle Jacquart and Claude Thomasset, *Sexuality and Medicine in the Middle Ages,* trans. Matthew Adamson (Princeton: Princeton University Press, 1988), 171, 141.

45. Cited in the *OED,* 2nd. ed., s.v. "chose." This quote comes from the Tollemache MS. The text has been edited by M. C. Seymour, *On the Properties of Things: John Trevisa's Translation of Bartholomaeus Anglicus "De proprietatibus rerum": A Critical Text* (Oxford: Clarendon Press, 1975).

46. For example, the notes in the *Riverside Chaucer* and Robert P. Miller, ed., *Chaucer: Sources and Backgrounds* (New York: Oxford University Press, 1977), 447-51. See also Baird-Lange for a summary of explanations for Heloise's inclusion in Jankyn's book, "Trotula's Fourteenth-Century Reputation," 245-46. Peggy Kamuf, *Fictions of Feminine Desire: Disclosures of Heloise* (Lincoln: University of Nebraska Press, 1982), 4, suggests how Abelard appropriated Heloise's anti-marriage argument.

47. See Kamuf, *Fictions,* 11-12 and III.633.

48. See Miller, *Chaucer,* 447, and *Riverside Chaucer,* 871 n677. Heloise is mentioned in *Roman de la rose* 8759-8832.

49. Translated in Miller, *Chaucer,* 458.

50. Mann, *Geoffrey Chaucer,* 52-55. Mann goes on to read Heloise's argument "dialogically," that is, the framework for Heloise's anti-marriage and misogynist argument transforms it into her defense. Chaucer uses this technique for the Wife of Bath so that her *Prologue* can be read against itself (70, 77ff). "Her tirade thus functions simultaneously as a demonstration of female bullying and a witness to masculine oppression" (79). Katharina M. Wilson and Elizabeth M. Makowski, *Wykked Wyves and the Woes of Marriages: Misogamous Literature from Juvenal to Chaucer* (Albany: State University of New York Press, 1990), 152, argue that the Wife's *dissuasio* from marriage is "disguised as a *persuasio.*"

51. Dronke, *Women Writers,* 130.

52. See, for example, Robert J. Meyer, "Chaucer's Tandem Romance: A Generic Approach to the *Wife of Bath's Tale* as Palinode," *ChauR* 18 (1984): 221-38, and Louise O. Fradenburg, "The Wife of Bath's Passing Fancy," *SAC* 8 (1986): 31-58.

53. Russell A. Peck, "Biblical Interpretation: St. Paul and *The Canterbury Tales,*" in Jeffrey, *Chaucer and the Scriptural Tradition,* 145. John Gardner also points out that "grinding meal" was slang in the fourteenth century for sexual intercourse; see *The Poetry of Chaucer* (Carbondale: Southern Illinois University Press, 1977), 261.

54. See "[Thou] seist . . ." speeches, lines 248, 254, 257, 263, 265, 270, 271, 273, 278, 282, 285, 292, 293, 302, 337, 348, 362, 366, 376.

55. Compare her activities to those of Margery Kempe, who tells the clerics questioning her, "I do not preach, sir; I do not go into any pulpit. I use only conversation and good words," in *The Book of Margery Kempe,* translated by B. A. Windeatt (Harmondsworth: Penguin, 1985), 164.

56. See Patterson "For the Wyves Love," especially 656-58, for his argument that this Midas digression problematizes men's listening.

57. David Wallace, in a fascinating article, "'Whan She Translated Was': A Chaucerian Critique of the Petrarchan Academy," in *Literary Practice and Social Change in Britain, 1380-1530,* ed. Lee Patterson (Berkeley: University of California Press, 1990), 194, argues that Chaucer deliberately uses the verb *translaten* to emphasize "Walter's power as both ruler and rhetor." Wallace equates Walter with Petrarch in terms of the dichotomies village/court and vernacular/Latin. "Both Walter and Petrarch, who gaze with a court-trained eye, know that village or vernacular virtue is blind to itself. Such virtue can only be made visible if it is translated to court space in court language." Petrarch's translation of Boccaccio's vernacular text into Latin is undermined by Chaucer's rejection of that Latin version, in that "Chaucer chooses to restore this text to the vernacular" (196). Also see Dinshaw, *Chaucer's Sexual Poetics,* 132-55, for a discussion of the gender politics of translation.

58. See *OED,* 2nd ed., under the entries "limit," "limitation," and "limiter."

59. For more on the social situation in the late fourteenth century, see Patterson, *Chaucer and the Subject of History* (Madison: University of Wisconsin Press, 1991); Janet Coleman, *Medieval Readers and Writers*; and Paul Strohm, *Social Chaucer* (Cambridge: Harvard University Press, 1989).

60. As Patterson puts it, "[I]f men are really committed to a disinterested quest for truth they will avoid a surface misogyny in favor of the wisdom offered by the full story" (*Chaucer and the Subject of History,* 288).

61. Machan continues,

> If posing as a translator in the *Troilus* enabled Chaucer to act as an author, it is perhaps to be expected that even when writing in a way which most closely resembles modern conceptions of translation he should perform many apparently authorial operations, such as combining and rearranging texts. . . . To be simply a vernacular writer precluded Chaucer from exercising his unique literary genius; but to be an author was a cultural impossibility. By conceiving literary production in general as translation to a greater or lesser extent, Chaucer enabled himself to act as that paradoxical creature, the vernacular author.

"Chaucer as Translator," in *The Medieval Translator,* ed. R. Ellis, 64-66.

62. Wallace argues that Chaucer "shares Dante's profound conviction that the vernacular is uniquely adequate to human experience" ("Whan She Translated Was," 199).

63. "Not one of Chaucer's translations consists simply of the grammatical and lexical transference of a text in one language to another; they all involve, though in various ways, the incorporation of material from other texts or the inclusion of original and significant Chaucerian additions," writes Tim Machan, "Chaucer as Translator," 60-62. Wallace points out that "[t]ranslation in Chaucer is a term that is customarily hedged with nervous qualifica-

tions: it is an activity that calls for some sort of apology or explanation" ("Whan She Translated Was," 197).

64. Machan, "Chaucer as Translator," 64, and Burnley, "Late Medieval English Translation," 44. Burnley goes on to write that "whether [the poet] regards himself as an author, enditer, compiler, or translator probably has more to do with the particular posture of humility or self-enhancement which he chooses to adopt than with any sharp distinctions in his actual mode of procedure" (48). The Wife, too, is no mere "*compilator,*" or citer and quoter of authoritative texts. Hanna points out that the compiler "seeks to become a transparent vehicle—merely an arranger of statements. The statements themselves are presented without qualification, as if purely descriptive" ("*Compilatio,*" 6). The Wife's compilations expose the rhetorical fiction of the depersonalized *compilator.*

Susanne Sara Thomas (essay date 1997)

SOURCE: Thomas, Susanne Sara. "What the Man of Law Can't Say: The Buried Legal Argument of *The Wife of Bath's Prologue." Chaucer Review* 31, no. 3 (1997): 256-71.

[*In the following essay, Thomas draws a correlation between Alisoun's adamant defense of her rights concerning her body and a mock legal case.*]

In the **Prologue** to her **Tale** the Wife of Bath argues that Paul gave wives authority over their husbands. She summarizes her argument thus:

> I have the power durynge al my lyf
> Upon his propre body, and noght he.
> Right thus the Apostel tolde it unto me,
> And bad oure housbondes for to love us weel.
> Al this sentence me liketh every deel.
>
> (D 158-62)[1]

There is some ambiguity in the Wife's reference to Paul's words as a "sentence," a term which in Middle English has a number of meanings, including an opinion, a doctrine, a judgment rendered by God or by a court, a punishment imposed by a court, a statute or law, and a practice or custom (*MED*). Immediately following the above-quoted lines, the Pardoner responds to the Wife's remarks by exclaiming: "Now, dame, . . . by God and by Seint John! / Ye been a noble prechour in this cas" (164-65). Like "sentence," the word "cas" has a variety of meanings, such as a state of affairs, an event, an action or deed, an instance or example, a civil or criminal question contested before a court of law, an

accusation or charge (*MED*). In both quotations there is a disjunction between legal and religious terminology. Is, for instance, the "sentence" of Paul, in the Wife's use of the term, a religious doctrine, a judgment rendered by God; or a legal doctrine, a judgment rendered by a court? The Pardoner calls the Wife a "prechour," which suggests that in his view she is arguing religious doctrine; and yet, the Pardoner conjoins this label with the statement that the Wife is arguing a "cas," a word which has legal, but not religious connotations. The Pardoner suggests that the Wife is presenting a legal issue for the listeners' judgment. I will argue that the Wife is not delivering a mock sermon, as critics such as Lee Patterson[2] and Charles E. Shain[3] have argued, but is, rather, delivering a mock legal case.

While I agree with Patterson and Shain that the Wife is in control of her rhetoric rather than powerless before it, and does not suffer from what one critic has called "a certain mental blindness,"[4] I differ about what type of rhetoric it is that she is in control *of.* While Patterson argues that the Wife offers a *sermon joyeux* in the **Prologue,** he bolsters his argument with some points which, in fact, undermine his assessment of her rhetorical strategy. He claims that the Wife "preempts the very language of accusation" in her "mastery of masculine modes of argument."[5] However, is a *sermon joyeux* the embodiment of "the language of accusation"? Or does this not sound, again, like a disjunction between legal and religious terminology? And what could more embody a masculine mode of argument than the rhetoric of the courtroom, stemming as it does from the agonistic tradition of the Greeks and Romans, and replacing in medieval society, or perhaps merely embodying another form of, the trial by battle? Furthermore, the Wife's strategy of turning other people's words against them is surely more appropriate to the cross-examination strategy of the courtroom than to the pulpit.

Like Patterson, Shain is convinced that the Wife's **Prologue** results from the fact that Chaucer, like all of his contemporaries, "was steeped in the lore of pulpit rhetoric."[6] Shain goes so far as to posit that "Chaucer had *inevitably* to make use of that powerful and pervasive instrument of medieval culture, the sermon" [italics mine].[7] However, the trial, in both the ecclesiastical and secular courts, was increasingly becoming another "powerful and pervasive instrument of medieval culture," and it is inevitable, as well, that Chaucer, having performed the functions of magistrate and civil servant, would also have been steeped in this powerful cultural form.

Derek Persall has noted that Chaucer's lifetime saw "the increasing use of litigation and the increasing sophistication of legal procedure."[8] He concludes, "[T]he law, which had once functioned and been thought of as a last resort when all means of reconciling disputes had failed, was now becoming a first resort."⁹ The Wife may be mocking the newly evolving forms of legal procedure and argumentation, and their practitioners. Furthermore, this interpretation can explain the Wife's use of legal terminology which critics in the "sermonist" camp must ignore. Some of the terminology of the *Prologue* can only be fully understood in the context of fourteenth-century legal practices; however, Shain and Patterson overlook disjunctions between legal and theological terminology.

The form of the Wife of Bath's rhetoric closely follows certain Common Law practices of presenting a case. These legal echoes create an unwritten text behind the garrulousness of her *Prologue.* However, some legal background and definitions are necessary to facilitate this discussion. Sir Matthew Hale's *History of the Common Law* serves well to define what the Common Law is: "The Laws of England may aptly enough be divided into two kinds, *viz. Lex Scripta,* the written Law; and *Lex non Scripta,* the unwritten Law: For although . . . all the Laws of this Kingdom have some Monuments or Memorials thereof in Writing, yet all of them have not their Original in Writing; for some of those Laws have obtained their Force by immemorial Usage or Custom, and such Laws are properly call'd *Leges non Scriptae,* or unwritten Laws or Customs."¹⁰ The Common Law of England is unique in its use of unwritten law; unlike legal systems which are derived from the Roman tradition, it is not completely codified. As Henry Sumner Maine explains, "The theoretical descent of Roman jurisprudence from a code, the theoretical ascription of English law to immemorial unwritten tradition, were the chief reasons why the development of their system differed from the development of ours."¹¹ The *Leges non Scriptae* create an indeterminate quality in the English Law, as well as an instability, which in its positive aspect is an adaptability to changing social and political circumstances.

The *lex non scripta* is determined and decisions are made by examining prior cases and thereby establishing the "custom of the courts." A modern legal writer explains: "The idea of looking back to prior cases for guidance is as old as our professional courts. . . . During the Middle Ages . . . prior cases were also inspected, but rarely revered. Law was not found in a single case; rather, a group of cases illustrated the true law. Law, in this sense, was the total custom of the courts."¹² However, it has been established by legal historians that the citation of cases in medieval courts took a necessarily vague form. Arthur R. Hogue explains:

> In the Middle Ages the courts were unquestionably guided by traditions and customs built up in the handling of case after case. But there was not the cita-

tion of cases in the modern fashion. Rather, citation took the form of professional memory and ultimately the only authority cognizable by the court was the record of the case. But this record, it must be remembered, might be buried under several hundred pounds of parchment rolls and consequently be very difficult to find; to "search the record" was a serious task which the court would not lightly assign to anyone.¹³

Thus, the case record from which the *lex non scripta* was determined was "buried," even though it did exist in written form. Oral recitation of the record was necessary, and one of the tasks of the professional lawyer was to memorize this inaccessible case record.

The movement towards literacy, which created the written case record, also created the *need* for a new profession, one which then sought to expand its role. The legal profession has from its very inception incited suspicion and hostility. May McKisack, for instance, notes how during the Peasants' Revolt on June 13, 1381, "prisons were opened and in Cheapside a number of lawyers, Flemings and other unpopular persons . . . were summarily beheaded."¹⁴ The unpopularity of the profession may be related to the form of oral argumentation it uses, and to the profession's alignment with rhetoric, *not* with either writing or literacy.

The form of legal argumentation in the fourteenth century was fundamentally similar to that practiced at present.¹⁵ Legal reasoning, which depends upon a balancing of findings on both the law which applies in a case and the facts which apply (or can be proven), has always been problematic to logicians. For instance, in "A Semiotics of Legal Argument" Duncan Kennedy discusses the logical problem inherent in the conventions of legal argumentation: "From the great mass of facts, the lawyer selects those that he or she thinks can be cast as 'relevant' to one of the preexisting rule formulae that together compose the *corpus juris.* Then the lawyer works to recast both facts and formula so that the desired outcome will appear compelled by mere rule application."¹⁶ A further convention of legal argumentation described by Kennedy is that "argument and counterargument are presented as simply 'correct' as applied to the general question, without this presentation binding the arguer in any way on the nested subquestion."¹⁷ Kennedy concludes his dissection of legal argumentation by asserting:

> Legal argument has a certain mechanical quality, once one begins to identify its characteristic operations. Language seems to be "speaking the subject," rather than the reverse. It is hard to imagine that an argument so firmly channeled into bites could reflect the full complexity either of the fact situation or the decision-maker's ethical stance toward it. It is hard to imagine doing this kind of argument in utter good faith, that is, to imagine doing it without some cynical strategy in fitting foot to shoe.¹⁸

The Wife of Bath is aligned with the legal profession through her use of similar rhetorical strategies. John Manly has pointed out how highly rhetorical the *Wife of Bath's Prologue* and *Tale* are. He claims that about fifty percent of their content consists of rhetorical devices, with only the *Monk's Tale* and the *Manciple's Tale* showing a higher incidence.[19] John A. Alford has demonstrated that the rhetorical Wife is the philosophical Clerk's direct counterpart. He states: "The Clerk has not merely gone 'unto logyk'; he is Logic personified. The Wife is not only one of the most rhetorical of the storytellers; she is Dame Rhetoric herself. . . . [A]nd their performances stand out as examples of (and commentaries upon) the two disciplines they represent."[20] In Alford's interpretation, the conflict between the Wife and the Clerk "is rooted in the recurrent tension between two modes of discourse, rhetorical and philosophical."[21] We see in this opposition a tension between oral and written traditions, although Alford does not address this dichotomy in his article.

In Platonic thought the opposition between rhetoric and logic/dialectic is essentially a moral one. Alford explains: "In contrast to dialectic, whose object is truth, rhetoric is morally indifferent. Its only guide is self-interest. Its practitioners may side with the true but they may just as easily side with the false—to deceive, to have the guilty judged innocent, to make the worse cause seem the better. . . . Their object, in a word, is not truth but *power*."[22] We can see from the examples which Alford uses the obvious connection between rhetoric and the legal profession, and by an extension which Alford does *not* make, between the Wife of Bath and the lawyer. The objections to and anxiety caused by the legal profession seem to be related to its professional practice of undermining what Douglas Canfield has termed "the chivalric code of the word as bond." He says of the Wife: "Her most dangerous weapon is not so much her 'queinte' . . . but her tongue, with which she subverts not only Scripture, . . . but the entire Code."[23]

Essentially, for the medieval audience, the lawyer is aligned with speech, not written language. It is what lawyers *orally* do to *texts* which causes the most suspicion and anxiety, just as what the Wife of Bath does to texts in her narrative arouses suspicions about, and objections to, her. The Wife wields rhetorical power over the written word which lies "buried" in her argument just as the case records do in their heaps of parchment scrolls. It is not easy to "search the record" in the Wife's case either, as one must have considerable memory of Scripture to be able to recall extemporaneously the "buried" halves of her Scriptural quotations.

The same vagueness of citation common to the fourteenth-century judicial system is notable in reference to the Wife's use of citation in the first part of her *Prologue.* The "cas" she argues is founded upon doctrine which is proven by reference to the writings of St. Paul, but typically the Wife cites only one half of a "sentence" and ignores the other. In lines 158-62, quoted in the opening paragraph above, the Wife uses two statements of Paul as her authority. The first reads, "The wife has not the power of her own body, but the husband; and likewise also he hath not power of his own body, but the wife" (I Cor 7:4). She uses this passage to affirm the "sentence:" "I have the power duryinge al my lyf / Upon his propre body, and noght he" (158-59). Similarly, she makes use of Paul's commandment, "Husbands, love your wives" (Eph 5:25), while suppressing the fact that this "sentence" is embedded in a text which also commands, "Wives, submit yourselves unto your own husbands, as unto the Lord" (Eph 5:22). The Wife exploits the "buried" nature of the scriptural case record she cites in her effort to establish her own laws of marriage which are based upon "custom," not the text of the New Testament. She establishes the *lex non scripta* of marriage, which then takes precedence over the *lex scripta* of Paul. From the point of view of English jurisprudence, this is correct procedure.

The Wife mediates between the written laws of marriage found in the New Testament and the "custom" of marriage established by experience. She finds the "custom of marriage" by examining a group of "cases": her five marriages. We can make an alignment between her use of "experience" and the legal use of "custom." In her determination of the "custom of marriage" the Wife also uses the legal strategy of combining a rule formula with a body of facts. She applies her rule to her marriages, but the marriages are recast in a manner that proves her rule.

The Wife presents her argument without addressing the counter-argument, thereby following a standard form of legal argumentation. "I quitte hem word for word" (422) she says, proclaiming that she is presenting one side of a battle of words, not dialectically balancing the sides of a logical argument. Like a barrister, she engages in a verbal contest which has distinctly well-drawn lines of demarcation. Verbal ammunition, and not fairness, is the primary consideration in the formulation of her argument. As a sermon, the Wife's speech would be absurd; however, as an example of legal reasoning it is quite typical of the rhetorical strategy of the courtroom.

The Wife's use of Paul involves channeling him into "bites" which automatically become rules which are then presented as simply "correct" as applied to the general question of a wife's authority over her husband. The other halves of the quotations do not *have* to be addressed, as her assertions do not have to be binding on "the nested sub-questions." The Wife applies her bites of law to her facts, which are taken from the history of her marriages, and proves that her definition of the custom of marriage is correct. She recounts the stories of her marriages in such a way that her authority over her husbands is proven. However, her rule has been cast in such a way that her stories will prove it, and the facts presented in the narratives are limited to those that prove her rule. Whether or not the Wife is found to be "misquoting" or "misusing" Scripture depends upon whether one considers her to be using a dialectical strategy or a rhetorical one. The agonistic form of trial law, by this period fully established, does not compel barristers to give a fair and balanced description of the other side's position; in fact, procedure compels them to do the opposite. Lawyers, like all rhetoricians, must continually play to an audience, and cannot follow the motive of fair play. As Alford states of the rhetoricians: "To achieve 'the maistre,' to manipulate other people into believing or behaving according to one's own wishes is 'what *orators* most desire.'"[24]

At the conclusion of the "Thou seist" passages in the *Prologue,* the Wife explains, in summary, "Under that colour hadde I many a myrthe" (399). While "colour" contains the meaning of "pretense," it also refers to a legal practice called "pleading colour" which was invented in the fourteenth century. D. W. Sutherland explains this peculiar practice:

> It is odd that the defendant should have to describe not only his own claim but also the plaintiff's. . . . But this description of the plaintiff's claim by the defendant was the specific element of "color," and the law insisted that the defendant include it if he wanted any discussion of the parties' rights in court before the case went to a jury. And if this seems strange, it is surely much stranger that what the defendant said about the plaintiff's claim was not true and not expected to be true, but pure sham, pure fiction.[25]

Sutherland claims that colour was "a product of the early fourteenth century. . . . Fourteenth century barristers could give fictitious color if they wanted to, and sometimes they did."[26] It became by the fifteenth century necessary to ascribe false claims to one's legal opponents in order to facilitate judgment and mediation of a case.[27]

The "Thou seist" passages in the *Prologue* are clearly meant to be seen as instances of pleading colour, for not only does the Wife specifically refer to her ploys as "colour", the Wife concludes this section of the poem by saying:

> Lordynges, right thus, as ye have understonde,
> Baar I stifly myne olde housbondes on honde
> That thus they seyden in his dronkenesse;
> And al was fals, but that I took witnesse
> On Janekyn, and on my nece also.
>
> (379-83)

In this passage the Wife openly admits that she ascribed false arguments to her husbands, and invented fictional claims which she used against them. It seems that in the Wife's use of "colour" there is a buried reference to a developing legal practice, one whose ironies and, perhaps we could even say, moral subversiveness, Chaucer could not have failed to notice.

It is the rhetorical nature of the legal profession which makes it dangerous and highly unpopular. What lawyers orally do to a buried case record in the fourteenth century gives room for abuse in the legal system. It seems that it was not in their function as *writers* of documents that lawyers were attacked by the peasants during the Revolt, but in their role as rhetorical *speakers* about *hidden documents*. It is "hidden writing" and those who have control and mastery over it which appear to pose the greatest threat to the "word as bond."

If the Wife is, as Canfield argues, "subversive to the chivalric code of the word as bond,"[28] it is not as "subversive female," but in her appropriation of the barrister's rhetoric that she poses a serious threat to the "code." Michael Clanchy has noted that the increased dependence upon litigation and the increasing sophistication of legal procedures toward the end of the medieval period had the effect of "weakening and straining the bonds of affection in feudal lordship."[29] The courtroom undermined the chivalric code of the oral oath as much as any other force at work to bring about the demise of feudal society. As a "mock lawyer" the Wife is much more dangerous to the chivalric code than she is as a "resistant woman."[30] In the face of a growing bureaucracy, the personal, feudal ties of the oral oath were fast disappearing. The agonistic approach of trial procedure was antithetical to the idea of personal allegiance contained in feudal bonds.

Jean Sire de Joinville, in his "Histoire de St. Louis" describes King Louis as the ideal feudal king who settles disputes between his subjects in person. Joinville describes the king not as a judge who makes rulings, but rather as one who presides over the making of bargains and compromises.[31] On the other hand, the bureaucratic system now in place in England was devoid of the personal attention of the king as arbitrator, and replaced bargaining with hostile litigation. M. T. Clanchy explains:

> Henry II devised an automated system of justice emphasizing speed and decisiveness. The plaintiff obtained a writ in standardized form . . . instructing a jury to be summoned, the jury gave a verdict of 'Yes' or 'No,' and judgement and execution then followed. The system stopped people rambling on about their grievances by compelling them to confine their statements within prescribed forms. . . . Like Frederick II's system, the common law penalized people for making agreements. To compromise with the defendant was to insult the king, whose aid had been given to the plaintiff to prosecute a wrongdoer. . . . Henry II's automated system of law made it easier—and more necessary—for neighbors to sue each other in the king's court.[32]

In Clanchy's assessment it is legal procedure itself which is pulling society apart. The bureaucratic system is disintegrating feudal ties and replacing them with increasingly necessary disputes.

Carolyn Dinshaw has said, "The Wife is everything the Man of Law can't say."[33] Dinshaw argues that the Wife is exposing the techniques of the "clerkly *glossatores*," "exposing techniques that they would rather keep invisible,"[34] yet the Wife's rhetorical techniques go far beyond mere glossing. She is herself a product of uncertainty; her contradictions and antagonism are an embodied depiction of the new bureaucratic system itself. As Dame Barrister, the Wife represents the agonism and contorted logic of the new bureaucratic order of society. However, like the Man of Law, good bureaucrats are always possessively secretive as bureaucracy works best when it and its procedures are kept the most invisible. A modern writer has noted that in contemporary American society few people have any understanding of even their basic legal rights.[35] This problem stems from the occulted nature of the procedures of all bureaucratic systems.

From an historical perspective there are a number of significant factors underlying the Wife's attitude toward texts and documents. She uses texts in a manipulative fashion and also attacks them, tearing "thre leves" out of one and tossing another in the fire. The increasing bureaucratic dependence upon documents in the fourteenth century caused concern about their proper use and function, and about the nature of what constituted a "valid document." As M. T. Clanchy states, "Documents did not immediately inspire trust."[36] The Peasant's Revolt of 1381 reveals anxiety about legal documents in the rebel's inconsistent use of them. The peasants burned legal documents and then turned around and asked for other documents as proof, usually within a remarkably brief period of time, suggesting a naive attitude towards what constitutes proof of an agreement. For if proof can be burned and the agreement cancelled, of what value is any document as proof?

May McKisack relates how in their attack on the Abbey of St. Albans on June 15, 1381, the rebels burned the charters of the Abbot "by virtue of which he enjoyed his manorial rights, and, displaying the king's charter, forced him to seal a deed of manumission concocted by themselves."[37] Just two days earlier, the peasants had rejected the King's offer of a charter of pardon, calling it "a mockery and some of them, returning to the city, ordered the execution of all lawyers."[38] A further instance of the rebels' attitude toward legal documents occurred during their attack on Cambridge. The peasants, McKisack relates,

> entered St. Mary's during mass and seized the chest containing the university archives . . . ; another chest full of parchments was taken from the house of the Carmelites. Both chests (containing documents of priceless value to the historian of the medieval university) were publicly burned in Market Square, an old woman named Margery Starre crying, 'Away with the learning of clerks, away with it!' as she flung parchments on the fire. The rebels then drew up a document whereby the university formally surrendered its privileges to the town and agreed to be governed by the municipal authorities.[39]

It appears that it is not writing and literacy which the peasants are objecting to, as they are willing to use documents to their advantage. However, the peasants place too much faith in the power of the document in and of itself, when it is only proof of a preceding agreement. The document is not the actual agreement, and can only be offered in court as *evidence* of an agreement. Once in the courtroom, as we see in the Wife of Bath's performance, rhetoric seizes a manipulative power over the documentary evidence.

During the Revolt the peasants demonstrate a belief in the magical power of the document itself. This is illustrated in their attitude that if it is burned it has no power, and if it is in hand it is all-powerful. They are naively unaware of the ascendant power of the legal profession and its ability to manipulate documentary evidence. Legal procedures are much more complex than the peasants are admitting to in their actions. They attempt to override the bureaucracy, but ultimately cannot. To do the peasants justice, however, we must acknowledge that legal naiveté remains a problem in modern, democratic societies. One legal author recently asked: "Is it really the case that it is the fault of lawyers that no one understands the law but lawyers?"[40]

The autumn Parliament of 1381 confirmed "the king's revocation of his charters of manumission to the rebels,"[41] demonstrating the fundamental worthlessness of the documents which the peasants had demanded and received. The rebels' initial skepticism about the power of a written charter had within days given way to an almost magical belief in it. Too late did they discover that the documents had no magical power, nor any real power at all, as power did not rest in the written charters but in those with the power to manipulate and interpret them. It is through interpretation and application that the legal document assumes meaning as proof of an agreement.

In an examination of the peasants' actions in the Revolt of 1381 we can see a crippling legal confusion. While I am in agreement with Steven Justice's assertion that the peasants did have a degree of literacy and legal knowledge, Justice ignores the fact that the peasants' legal demands and legal ideology were somewhat confused.[42] During the Revolt, they frequently demanded documents which did not exist. As in their previous belief in the legal value of the Domesday Book,[43] the peasants exhibited a mythical belief in the existence of ancient legal documents which were supposed to promote their freedom from bondage. The peasants believed in a chivalric legal past where words held true. They longed, essentially, for a mythic legal past, not as it *was,* but as they nostalgically imagined it to have been. The peasants believed in the value of the "word as bond," whereas in the new legal bureaucracy this bond was routinely subverted. It was, in fact, the bureaucratic legal system itself which undermined the written documents which formed the only remaining evidence of those ancient oral oaths.

The peasants were looking back to an Edenic past—a time when the oral word was the bond, and the written document was a recording of what was spoken, not merely negotiable evidence, as it had now become. In Jesse Gellrich's interpretation of the events of 1381, what incited the anger of the peasants toward legal documents was "the theft of spoken promise—what peasants took to be their natural right—out of the venerated symbol of it on the inscribed page."[44] That spoken promises and legal contracts appear to be two separate and distinct things is at the heart of the peasants' legal anxieties and confusion. They wanted the oral promises given to be put in writing as proof, but discovered that the new "proofs" were worthless. The peasants could not create by themselves legally valid documents.

In the Revolt the peasants looked for and attempted to create the equivalent of what we could oxymoronically call "written oaths," documents which would constitute evidence of the oral ties which once bound them to their land. They *believed* that the original documentary evidence surviving from the oral past offered them legal redress, when in reality this is extremely unlikely. They also believed that they could create new charters, not realizing that these documents could easily be subverted or ignored. The peasants addressed their complaints to the king personally, wanting to see in him a king similar to Joinville's portrait of St. Louis. They wanted to see the king as their seignorial protector and arbitrator; however, this direct contact between king and subjects had been replaced by a bureaucracy which now oversaw the complex procedures embodied in what one scholar refers to as "the extraordinary formalism of medieval common law."[45] The peasants rebelled against the mediation of these bureaucratic officiaries who now blocked their access to their lord, the King.

M. T. Clanchy has demonstrated that "lay literacy grew out of bureaucracy,"[46] and in this sense literacy and bureaucracy worked together to block the peasants from obtaining the mediating function of their king as feudal lord. If the peasants were opposed to literacy it was in this context that it appeared most hostile to their customary rights: law now equalled bureaucracy. Feudal law was personal and based on oral oaths which did not require the function of intermediaries, but now law was a complex bureaucratic system. It had become the modern definition of "law," that is, "everything to do with the administration of justice in a society, such as the law or laws, the lawyers, the judges, and every system, office, and functionary concerned with the enactment, application, determination, and enforcement of the laws."[47]

Bruce Lyon explains that "the last two centuries of medieval England witnessed the elaboration of the machinery of process and of the rules of pleadings and a refinement of legal principles previously established. No longer was the law dominated and molded by legislation but by a skilled, learned, proud, and jealous legal profession."[48] He explains further:

> It was during the fourteenth and fifteenth centuries that the legal profession became highly organized and obtained a monopoly over the law. . . . It was this learned, skilled, and tough legal profession that molded and practiced a tough common law that withstood all competition and attempts to weaken it and emerged triumphant under the legal principle that the law of the realm is the supreme master, above both king and parliament.[49]

So, while the king, parliament, and peasants try to wrest control of the law, the battle is about to be won by the legal profession, and this profession is instrumental in bringing about the ascendancy of a bureaucratic system over a feudal one. The lawyers' powers lie in the indeterminacy of the unwritten rules and customs which control the application and interpretation of the written laws. In the fourteenth century their power also lay in the occulted nature of the buried case record.

The Wife's argument in the *Prologue* is ostensibly about the authority of the wife over the husband in marriage; however, the buried legal argument is about the legal authority of the oral over the written. This aspect of the *Prologue* reflects the social tensions in the background of the literary performance. There is, in fact, a battle going on outside the poem for control of the law, a battle which will be won by "a skilled, learned, proud, and jealous legal profession" with which the Wife is subtly aligned through her appropriation of legal rhetoric. There is also a buried accusation against the misuse of documents by those in power, including both king and parliament. The Wife covertly exposes the tortuous logic by which the courts are making their rulings, bringing up the question of who is ruling whom, or what is being ruled by what. Is law ruling or is rhetoric? And what form of law has precedence, if law indeed is ruling—the written or the unwritten?

The authority of the *lex non scripta* over the *lex scripta* forms not only a backdrop to the Wife's *Prologue,* it *is* her *Prologue.* The Wife's fifth husband reads her a case history of wicked wives, and she quites him by tearing "thre leves" out of the book and making him later "brenne his book" (D 816), an action which echoes that of the defiant peasant Margery Starre who cried, "Away with the learning of clerks, away with it!" However, unlike the rebel peasants, the Wife asks not for a new *lex scripta,* but creates for herself a *lex non scripta.* Her "lawe" of marriage is an oral argument which quites the written word. She proves through wily argumentation that wives were given authority over their husbands, and that she has *had* authority over her own. Doubtless her argumentation throughout makes the foot fit the shoe, but this form of rhetoric is about to become a powerful force in society. Furthermore, the Wife's *Prologue* leads to a tale about a legal case, its sentencing, and the commuting of that sentence, giving further justification for the legal undertones of her *Prologue.*

Chaucer aligns the Wife of Bath with the practitioners of a form of oral argumentation which uses a particular form of logic and rule application. In the tension between *lex scripta* and *lex non scripta,* the Wife is on the side of the unwritten law. She "proves" her authority in her *Prologue*; and, as one who is aligned with the *lex non scripta,* she does have authority. The courts have the power to interpret the *lex scripta,* and through rhetoric and rule application they make it say what they want it to say. Likewise, the Wife assumes the power of oral interpretation over the written texts of both Paul and her husbands. There is buried in her *Prologue* an alignment between the hatred toward lawyers (and their power of interpretation) demonstrated by the peasants' attacks upon them, and the hatred toward women (whose rhetoric is necessarily oral) in written texts of the period. The Wife is aligned in her *Prologue* with interpretation, the unwritten law, and legal rhetoric, and most significantly with the mediation between written and unwritten.

At his coronation ceremony Richard II "swore on the cross to confirm the laws and customs of the people."[50] However, just what exactly constituted "the laws and customs" was not that easy to determine. For instance, a historian notes that in the coronation ceremony, "especially noteworthy were the pains taken to remove any doubt that the laws which the king swore to confirm were those which had been established in the reign of Edward the Confessor, not those which had been ordained by the legislation of Edward I," and further, an alteration was made to the coronation oath established in 1308 for Edward II, "whereby the king swore to uphold whatever laws the people might elect for the glory of God. For these phrases there was substituted in the coronation oath of 1377 an ambiguous reference to the laws of the church."[51] From the very opening of his reign, those close to Richard attempted to escape from being bound by the laws and customs of the people; however, the underlying problem is the uncertainty of

what constituted the laws and customs. Were they established by Parliament's spoken word and by the written laws which it established; or, was the law established by the decisions of the Judges whom Richard consulted on his rights and obligations; or by immemorial custom filtered down through the established case record; or by the word of the King himself? At the heart of this confusion is the dichotomy inherent in the common law between the supposed certainty of codified law, and the flexibility and apparent uncertainty of the unwritten law determined by custom.

The Wife of Bath reinforces rule by law (a written/oral negotiation) rather than by oath and sovereignty. She is aligned with the new order of things which will not be bound by the sovereignty of the king, but takes the power of interpretation and negotiation unto itself. Neither the written laws nor the sovereign oath rule; what now rules is the professional, bureaucratic negotiation between *lex scripta* and *lex non scripta.* The buried argument of the Wife's *Prologue* is that those who are professionally assuming the power of legal interpretation are an emerging political force destined to become "the supreme master, above both king and parliament."

Notes

1. All references to the text of Chaucer are to Larry D. Benson, et al., eds., *The Riverside Chaucer* (Boston, 1987), and they will be included within the text as line citations.

2. See, Lee Patterson, "The Wife of Bath and the Triumph of the Subject," *Chaucer and the Subject of History* (Madison, 1991), 280-321; and, "For the Wyves Love of Bath; Feminine Rhetoric and Poetic Resolution in the *Roman de la Rose* and the *Canterbury Tales*," *Speculum* 58 (1983): 656-95.

3. See Charles E. Shain, "Pulpit Rhetoric in Three Canterbury Tales," *MLN* 70 (1955): 235-45.

4. Chauncey Wood, *Chaucer and the Country of the Stars* (Princeton, 1970), 174.

5. Patterson, "For the Wyves Love," 678,

6. Shain, "Pulpit Rhetoric," 235.

7. Shain, "Pulpit Rhetoric," 236.

8. Derek Pearsall, *The Life of Geoffrey Chaucer: A Critical Biography* (Cambridge, Mass., 1992), 248.

9. Pearsall, *The Life,* 248.

10. Sir Matthew Hale, *The History of the Common Law of England,* ed. Charles M. Gray (Chicago, 1971), 3.

11. Henry Sumner Maine, *Ancient Law* (Tucson, 1986), 7.

12. Frederick G. Kempin, Jr., *An Historical Introduction to Anglo-American Law* (St. Paul, 1990), 103.

13. Arthur R. Hogue, *Origins of the Common Law* (Hamden, 1974), 190.

14. May McKisack, *The Fourteenth Century 1307-1399* (Oxford, 1959), 410.

15. See Donald W. Sutherland, "Legal Reasoning in the Fourteenth Century: The Invention of 'Color' in Pleading," *On The Laws and Customs of England: Essays in Honor of Samuel E. Thorne,* ed. Morris S. Arnold et al. (Chapel Hill, 1981), 182.

16. Duncan Kennedy, "A Semiotics of Legal Argument," *Law and Semiotics,* ed. Roberta Kevelson (New York, 1989), 184.

17. Ibid., 190.

18. Ibid., 192.

19. John Matthews Manly, "Chaucer and the Rhetoricians," *Proceedings of the British Academy* 12 (1926): 95-113; rpt. *Chaucer Criticism: The Canterbury Tales,* ed. Richard Schoeck and Jerome Taylor (Notre Dame, 1960), 268-90.

20. John A. Alford, "The Wife of Bath versus the Clerk of Oxford: What Their Rivalry Means," *ChauR* 21 (1986): 110.

21. Ibid., 109.

22. Ibid., 110.

23. Douglas Canfield, *Word as Bond in English Literature from the Middle Ages to the Restoration* (Philadelphia, 1989), 122.

24. Alford, 124.

25. Sutherland, "Legal Reasoning," 184.

26. Ibid., 186.

27. Although it is no longer necessary to "plead colour," the term remains part of the legal lexicon and is understood as a common tactic. The term was used, for instance, in Milo Gayelin, "Their Own Petard: Many Lawyers Find Malpractice Suits Aren't Fun After All," *The Wall Street Journal,* July 6, 1995, A1, A6. A defense lawyer explaining the nature of the growing number of legal malpractice suits states: "In many cases where conflicts [of interest between the lawyer and the opposite side] are alleged, the conflicts really do not cause anyone any harm. They're in there for color."

28. Canfield, *Word as Bond,* 118.

29. M. T. Clanchy, "Law and Love in the Middle Ages," *Disputes and Settlements: Law and Human Relations in the West,* ed. John Bossy (Cambridge, 1983), 62.

30. This is Thomas Hahn's label for her in "Teaching the Resistant Woman: The Wife of Bath and the Academy," *Exemplaria* 4 (1992): 431-40.

31. See N. L. Corbett, ed., *La vie de St Louis: Texte de XIVe siècle* (Quebec, 1977), 95.

32. Clanchy, "Law and Love," 62.

33. Carolyn Dinshaw, *Chaucer's Sexual Poetics* (Madison, 1989), 115.

34. Ibid., 120.

35. Fredric G. Gale, *Political Literacy* (New York, 1994), passim.

36. M. T. Clanchy, *From Memory to Written Record: England 1066-1307,* 2nd ed. (Cambridge, Mass., 1993), 294.

37. McKisack, 415.

38. McKisack, 411.

39. McKisack, 416-17.

40. Gale, *Political Literacy,* 11.

41. McKisack, 419.

42. Steven Justice, *Writing and Rebellion: England in 1381* (Berkeley, 1994).

43. Rosamond Faith, "The 'Great Rumour' of 1377 and Peasant Ideology," *The English Rising of 1381,* ed. R. H. Hilton and T. H. Aston (Cambridge, Engl., 1984), 43-73. She states of this early revolt, "its legitimizing ideas seem not to have come from egalitarian hopes of a better future but from views of an idealized past. It was conservative to the point of archaism, and the book that largely inspired it was not the Bible, but the Domesday Book."

44. Jesse Gellrich, *Discourse and Dominion in the Fourteenth Century* (Princeton, 1995), 161.

45. Richard Firth Green, "Chaucer's Man of Law and Collusive Recovery," *N & Q* 40 (1993): 303-05.

46. Clanchy, *From Memory,* 19 and passim.

47. Gale, *Political Literacy,* 6.

48. Bruce Lyon, *A Constitutional and Legal History of Medieval England,* 2nd ed. (New York, 1980), 613.

49. Ibid., 625.

50. Richard H. Jones, *The Royal Policy of Richard II* (Oxford, 1968), 14.

51. Ibid., 14-15.

Charles W. M. Henebry (essay date 1997)

SOURCE: Henebry, Charles W. M. "Apprentice Janekyn/Clerk Jankyn: Discrete Phases in Chaucer's

Developing Conception of the Wife of Bath." *Chaucer Review* 32, no. 2 (1997): 146-61.

[*In the following essay, Henebry further develops the theory that Chaucer rewrote and revised the Wife of Bath's character repeatedly. He contends that Chaucer changed Alisoun's views on marriage, fidelity, and autonomy throughout the writing process and eventually blended these ideas together to form a multidimensional character.*]

The idea that the Wife of Bath did not spring forth fully fledged from the mind of her creator is not a new one. Her character is in conception both original and complex. For this reason, the thesis that she underwent a process of reconception and revision is attractive— not simply to critics who are inclined to believe that something cannot come out of nothing, but also to those who would like to know more about the way in which something often *does* do just that in the creation of great art. However, as Sidney noted (echoing Horace), art is that which conceals its own artifice; without access to the working manuscript, we can only hope to detect the poet's developmental process in the fissures where the poem does not quite hang together. Just such a fissure has been detected by some critics between the portrait of the Wife of Bath in the *General Prologue* and the story she tells in the *Prologue* to her own *Tale,* for she seems in the one to have made herself financially independent of her husbands by means of a thriving business in the manufacture of cloth, while in the other she makes no explicit reference to this trade, but tells instead how she attained independence through sheer shrewishness. I plan, however, in this essay to consider the Wife's *Prologue* in isolation from her portrait, her *Tale,* and from her appearances in the tales told by the Clerk and Merchant. To the extent that I am successful in tracing a pattern of development through her *Prologue,* it will remain for others to show how this process may be understood within the larger context of the *Canterbury Tales.*

The *Prologue* is a good candidate for close analysis in terms of development and reconception because, as R. F. Jones and Robert F. Pratt have shown, it is an intricate patch-work of different sources and styles which can be roughly divided into three main sections.[1] The Wife opens with a defense of matrimony against the claims of St. Jerome on behalf of virginity. In seeming contradiction of her initial claim that experience alone is sufficient grounds for a discussion of marriage, she relies extensively in this first section on biblical authority, St. Paul in particular. Her closely-argued discourse is written in the style of a theological tract or sermon, drawing on arguments both for and against marriage which are found in Jerome's *Adversus Jovinianum.* Having shown the viability, if not the superiority, of marriage in comparison with virginity, the Wife describes

marriage in terms of raw sexuality, placing her emphasis on the marital debt:

> In wyfhod I wol use myn instrument
> As frely as my Makere hath it sent.
> If I be daungerous, God yeve me sorwe!
> Myn housbonde shal it have bothe eve and morwe,
> Whan that hym list come forth and paye his dette.
> An housbonde wol I have—I wol nat lette—
> Which shal be bothe my dettour and my thral,
> And have his tribulacion withal
> Upon his flessh, whil that I am his wyf.
>
> (D 149-57)[2]

This picture of the marital state contrasts sharply with the one that follows in the next section, in which the Wife describes in detail how she harassed her first three husbands, withholding sex from them in order to get the upper hand. Her emphasis shifts from marriage as sexual thralldom to marriage as a struggle for psychological and economic dominion. Sex is no longer the mutual duty of husband and wife, but rather a favor which is offered by the wife only for monetary reward: "I wolde no lenger in the bed abyde, / If that I felte his arm over my syde, / Til he had maad his raunson unto me; / Thanne wolde I suffre hym do his nycetee" (409-12). I do not deny that the transition between these two sections is handled well; the Pardoner (no doubt the one of the few marriageable men on the pilgrimage who would have been alarmed at the prospect of having to "paye his dette") is made to interrupt the Wife by remarking that if he would have to "bye it on my flessh so deere," he would avoid getting married. This brings up the subject of hardship in marriage (the subject which the Wife had initially proposed to discuss), and she replies that if he wishes to speak of hardship, she can show him real tribulation. The deftness of this transition, however, is really a testament to the degree of difference between the two sections. Here, in speaking of her first three husbands, all of whom were much older and richer than she, the Wife relies entirely on experience rather than authority. Her experiences, moreover, are drawn by Chaucer out of a different collection of sources: the *Miroir de mariage* of Eustace Deschamps, the self-portrait of La Vieille in Jean de Meun's *Roman de la rose,* and the *Liber aureolus de nuptiis* of Theophrastus. True, the *Liber aureolus* forms part of the same anti-matrimonial tradition with the *Adversus Jovinianum* (indeed, the *Liber aureolus* was preserved from classical times as a chapter within Jerome's epistle), but the emphasis in Chaucer's selections from Theophrastus is less anti-matrimonial than misogynist. In place of arguments against the state of marriage, we have disparaging remarks as to the capacity of women to satisfy their husbands intellectually.

Passing over the story of the Wife's fourth husband for the moment (the "revelour" who keeps a mistress on the side), we come upon the third and last major section of the *Prologue.* It describes the Wife's travails at the hands of her fifth husband, the violent-tempered Jankyn, a clerk who habitually reads aloud to her from an anthology of anti-matrimonial and misogynist writings. This section is especially remarked for its narrative sequences. Two scenes in particular are rendered by Chaucer with a vivacity and color worthy of the best of the tales and not present elsewhere in the *Prologue*: that of the Wife's first meeting and courtship with Jankyn out in the fields during Lent and that in which she precipitates their climactic battle by ripping three pages from his book in the middle of one of his nightly readings. Anthologies such as Jankyn's were actively promoted by the Church in the fourteenth century in a campaign "to promote clerical celibacy and to encourage young men to embrace celibacy with eagerness and thanksgiving."[3] Part of the irony, of course, is that Jankyn is woefully misusing the book when, having chosen to ignore its admonitions and marry, he goes on to apply it as an instrument of torture to his wife. But of equal interest, as many critics have noted, is the appearance of the book as a text *within* the narrative. For its contents, listed by the Wife, include many of Chaucer's anti-matrimonial and anti-feminist sources for the earlier sections of the Wife's *Prologue.* As such, the book provides a sort of ironic commentary to cap the story of the Wife's apparently lifelong struggle with the "authority" of these writers. This serves in a sense to unify the disparate sections of the Wife's *Prologue,* but it also serves to set the narrative of her fifth marriage apart from the story of her earlier marriages. Up to this point, Jankyn's book (or one very like it in Chaucer's possession) has served as a reservoir from which proverbial arguments are silently drawn and placed in the mouths of characters. Now Chaucer begins, through Jankyn, to quote directly from their source and, in doing so, shifts his focus away from proverbs to concentrate on exemplary narratives of "wykked wives." As a result, this third section is as distinct from the second as the second is from the first.

These differences of style, source, and focus suggest that the three sections of the Wife's *Prologue* may well have been conceived and written at different times. We are ultimately concerned, however, with developmental process; mere difference cannot of itself enable determination of the order of conception and composition. Nor is difference in itself even sufficient evidence that the various sections of the *Prologue* were conceived and written at different times, for as N. F. Blake has pointed out in this connection, difference can also arise from a complex original idea incorporating a variety of sources:

> As for the composition of the WBP it has been claimed that it consists of several parts and that these witness to various stages in the *Prologue*'s growth, which in turn reflect Chaucer's continued interest and involvement in the Wife herself. The *Prologue* may for critical

purposes be divided into two parts, the "sermon" on marriage and virginity on the one hand, and the description of the Wife's marriages on the other. This does not mean that the two parts were necessarily composed at different times. No manuscript contains only the one or other part, and so the only support for this idea of a serial-type composition is individual scholars' subjective reactions. Yet the *Prologue* relies on several different sources, and the differences in tone and approach may reflect those sources. This is something that happens frequently in the poem.[4]

Blake's devotion to manuscript evidence can run to excess, but it provides us here with a useful check on speculation and purely subjective reactions. Evidence of Chaucer's changing conception of the Wife must be sought, if it is to be sought at all, in the text of *Prologue* itself.

It is my contention that evidence of precisely this sort is to be found in the varied presentation which Jankyn receives from the Wife over the course of her narrative. Jankyn does not seem to have been originally conceived by Chaucer as a clerk, for the Wife refers to him at one point in her description of her first three marriages as "oure apprentice Janekyn" (D 303). This gives the impression of an unlearned, probably unlettered apprentice in the Wife's cloth-making trade. He could not have been the owner, much less the devoted reader, of a "book of wykked wives," nor could he logically have participated in the famous Lenten courtship scene, for he seems already to be intimately acquainted with the Wife and stands therefore in no need of an introduction via her gossib. This impression of household intimacy is confirmed when Janekyn puts in his next appearance:

> Baar I stifly myne olde housbondes on honde
> That thus they seyden in hir dronkenesse;
> And al was fals, but that I took witnesse
> On Janekyn, and on my nece also.
>
> (D 380-83)

If Janekyn is to be considered a plausible corroborating witness to such goings-on, he (along with the niece) must be living in the same house with the Wife and her husband(s), whether as a relative, as an apprentice, or as some sort of boarder. It is, of course, possible that this Janekyn is a different individual from the Jankyn who later becomes her fifth husband. After all, the Wife has the same name as her gossib, "dame Alys' (D 548). Her name, though, is far more common in Chaucer, and in Middle English generally, than Jankyn. The Riverside editors agree with me in treating Janekyn and Jankyn as the same person (enjoining the reader to use the trisyllabic Janekyn even where Jankyn is written) though they do not go on to comment upon or explain his mysterious change of profession.[5] Another possible explanation might be found in the word "apprentice" if in some circumstances it could be used to denote a scholar or clerk. In this case, "oure apprentice Janekyn" would be a scholar who, since he is considered a plausible witness to her husband(s)' bouts with drunkenness, must be boarding with them. This would not explain the story of how the Wife meets and courts Jankyn in a field during Lent two hundred lines later, but it would at least remove the obstacle of his sudden change from apprentice to clerk. A search of the MED, however, indicates that while the word "apprentice" was occasionally used as a synonym for "disciple" in the fields of law and theology, its use in these circumstances required clarification in the surrounding context: "Many trewe men, boþe apprentis and avocatis" (Wycliffe, *Sermons,* 1.382); "The witte of justices or of serivantis, or of famose kunnyng apprentises in the kingis lawe" (Pecock, *Faith,* 228); "Whereby I made the so wys, That thow be-kam myn aprentys" (Lydgate, *Pilgr,* 5684).[6] In each of these cases, the writer has been careful to indicate by the context that he means not an apprentice to a manual trade, but rather a disciple of law or theology. The context in the Wife's speech proves quite opposite in its implication: "And yet of oure apprentice Janekyn . . . hastow caught a fals suspecioun." Her use of the word "oure" in this statement to her husband(s) can be taken to mean nothing other than that Janekyn is *their* apprentice, presumably in their cloth-making business. This, in fact, is the interpretation which the editors of the MED give to this phrase, classifying it with quite a number of other instances of the use of "apprentice" under the main definition: "One bound by legal agreement for a certain number of years to serve a craftsman or tradesman in return for instruction in the craft or trade." It therefore seems more than likely that the discrepancy we have observed between apprentice Janekyn and clerk Jankyn represents neither distinct characters nor an unusual application of "apprentice," but rather two stages in Chaucer's conception of Jankyn's character and, by implication, in his conception of the Wife's autobiographical narrative.

This is precisely the light in which Robert A. Pratt sees this discrepancy in his essay, "The Development of the Wife of Bath": he uses Jankyn's transformation from apprentice to scholar to bolster his claim that the differences we have noted of theme and source material between the second and third sections of the *Prologue* represent different stages in the *Prologue*'s conception. This is the one aspect of Pratt's argument which Blake's rebuttal fails to overturn—indeed, fails even to address. Having noticed the discrepancy between apprentice Janekyn and clerk Jankyn independently of Pratt, I hope to supplement his argument with insights of my own.[7] This will enable us to construct a coherent picture of Chaucer's developing conception of the Wife in the process of writing her *Prologue.*

That apprentice Janekyn was indeed intended to be Alys's fifth husband is suggested by the circumstances in which he is introduced in a speech of the Wife to one of her earlier husbands:

> And yet of oure apprentice Janekyn,
> For his crispe heer, shynynge as gold so fyn,
> And for he squiereth me bothe up and doun,
> Yet hastow caught a fals suspecioun.
> I wol hym noght, togh thou were deed tomorwe!
>
> (D 303-07)

Her doting description of his hair and of his behavior towards her belies the emphatic denial she makes at the end of the passage. That, however, is the ingenious method of her railing, as she explains it to her fellow pilgrims. She would habitually preempt her husband(s)'s legitimate complaints about her behavior by complaining loudly that he was always criticizing her. In this passage she accuses her husband(s) of thinking Janekyn handsome and of suspecting her motives with respect to their young apprentice, and by doing so she is trying to force him not simply to disavow his suspicions, but to positively avow that he has no reason for being suspicious: that Janekyn is *not* handsome and that his behavior is *perfectly* honorable. But because she has given to us the key with which to decipher all this double-talk, we know that Jankyn must indeed be quite handsome, his hair fine gold, and that her husband(s) probably has every reason to suspect that were he to die, she would soon wed again. Chaucer goes out of his way to suggest in this passage an erotic tension within the household between the Wife and her apprentice, a tension no doubt destined to end in marriage upon the death of her current husband.

As things turn out, though, she marries someone else instead. This fourth husband is not, however, distinctly different in character or behavior from what we might have imagined the apprentice Janekyn to have turned out like had he not been transformed into a clerk. Apprentice Janekyn was to be the young and randy colt whom the Wife would marry at the end of her long career of fleecing tired old men; he was to be the one who would turn the tables on her, subjecting her to all the tortures of shrewishness, teasing sexuality, and jealousy to which she had subjected each of her old husbands. Had this theme of turnabout been fully developed, it would have added point and irony to the *Merchant's Tale,* for, growing old, the Wife's May would recapitulate January's mistake: she would be the one with money and young Janekyn the one with ambition and good looks. This early theme remains visible in the introduction which the Wife gives of her fifth husband:

> I trowe I loved hym best, for that he
> Was of his love daungerous to me.
> We wommen han, if that I shal nat lye,

In this matere a queynte fantasye;
Wayte what thyng we may nat lightly have,
Therafter wol we crie al day and crave.

(D 513-18)

I would go so far as to argue that the passage from which this quotation is drawn (D 503-24) is an artifact of Chaucer's initial conception of the Wife's marriage to apprentice Janekyn. No mention is made here of Clerk Jankyn's studies or of his love for anti-feminist literature. Instead, the emphasis falls upon turnabout and role-reversal. In the context of this passage, he is "daungerous" with his love not in the sense of physical brutality, but rather in the sense of playing hard to get—a role which is ordinarily that of the woman and one which we have seen the Wife practice adeptly upon her old husbands. Alison has made the mistake of giving her love to him outright, just as each of her old husbands did with her, and now she finds, as they did, that she has to buy affection back with coin of a different color. This thoroughgoing reversal of her early marriages leaves no room for the fourth husband whom we meet in lines D 453-502, for his distinguishing characteristic of a "revelour" would certainly have been an aspect of apprentice Janekyn's personality: she had been wont to wander and make her husbands jealous, so too would he have done the same to her. It seems likely to me, therefore, that Janekyn was originally conceived as her one "bad" husband, a "revelour" who drove the Wife to distraction with jealousy.

What I think happened to this plan was that Chaucer suddenly saw the possibility of having the Wife confront directly the literary exponents of anti-matrimonial and misogynist diatribe by making her fifth husband a clerk. Because he still wanted to have the Wife deal with the problem of jealousy, though, he split off a new fourth husband from his original plan. This theory is corroborated by the fact that Chaucer's primary literary models for the character of the Wife, Jean de Meun's La Vieille and Villon's La Belle Heulmière, both fall for only a single "bad" lover late in life.[8] This does not necessarily mean, however, that Chaucer originally planned only four husbands for the Wife. Robert F. Fleissner has argued that Chaucer chose five as the number of the Wife's husbands for not-insignificant numerological reasons.[9] This presents little difficulty, for, as Pratt points out, the Wife's collective portrait of her elderly husbands is so undifferentiated that it might easily have once described four men rather than just three.[10]

Of greater interest is the question of what led Chaucer to have the Wife directly address the anti-matrimonial, misogynist tradition. Our brief survey of his sources in the *Prologue* has shown that in the second section he drew primarily on de Meun and Theophrastus for a collection of anti-feminist proverbs which he has the Wife accuse her husband(s) of uttering while in his cups. Chaucer may well have been reading Theophrastus from an anthology of anti-matrimonial literature like the book owned by Jankyn. Proverbial misogyny could, of course, sound plausible in the mouths of unlearned husbands, but anti-feminist anthologies also contained a great number of stories of evil wives culled from Scripture, myth, and history which could only be introduced by a scholarly character. Clerk Jankyn offered just such a plausible solution and, as I have already suggested, a way to comment explicitly upon the anti-matrimonial tradition and its perverse effects on marriage. Once a clerk-husband had been invented, it was then possible to conceive the first section of the *Prologue,* for without the Wife's long exposure to his never-ending readings of Jerome's *Adversus Jovinianum,* she could never have plausibly defended marriage so ably, matching authority with authority. This is the argument made by Pratt, who further notes that if the Wife's defense of marriage is removed along with the Pardoner's interruption, the first six lines of her *Prologue* (which declare that she will rely on experience rather than authority, and promise to speak of "wo that is in mariage") will make a much nicer fit with the section which then follows directly after, the story of her first three marriages.[11] Thus, it seems likely that the Wife's account of her fifth husband was composed after her account of her first three husbands, perhaps after some work had arleady been done on the Wife's experiences while married to the revelour, apprentice Janekyn. And then at the very end, Chaucer probably inserted the Wife's defense of matrimony into the beginning of her *Prologue.*

Thus far we have treated the Wife's account of her stormy fifth marriage as having been conceived and written as a single unit, some time after the account of her first three marriages, and (probably) some time before the defense of marriage which opens her *Prologue.* In doing so, we have followed in Pratt's footsteps, endeavoring to repeat and even amplify his successes and to avoid the pitfalls of his analysis. There is reason to believe, however, that the Wife's fifth marriage was not conceived as a unit, but was, rather, reconceived in a process similar to the one we have observed in the development of the *Prologue* as a whole. The clue is an easy one to overlook and is, unfortunately, not so unambiguous in its interpretation as the one we have been following up to now. It is, however, profound in its implications. What it shares in common with "oure apprentice," ironically enough, is that it is also a reference to Jankyn. After telling the story of their first meeting and rapid courtship in a field during Lent, the Wife goes on to describe how, during the funeral of her fourth husband, she was struck by the handsomeness of Jankyn's legs and feet:

To chirche was myn housbonde born a-morwe
With neighebores, that for hym maden sorwe
And Jankyn, oure clerk, was oon of tho.
As help me God, whan that I saugh hym go
After the beere, me thoughte he hadde a paire
Of legges and of feet so clene and faire
That al myn herte I yaf unto his hoold.

(D 593-99)

There are a number of things in this passage which cry out for explanation, but chief among them is the Wife's use of the pronoun "oure" to modify "clerk". Surely, if Jankyn is her new lover, with whom she has already made arrangements in case something happens to her fourth husband, the appropriate pronoun would have been "my". And if he is her lover already, then why does Chaucer place such an emphasis on his legs and feet, as if this were the moment at which she fell in love, or at any rate made up her mind that she was in love with him? It also seems strange that Jankyn would walk so close behind the bier if he is a secret lover and a stranger to her husband (and until recently, to the Wife herself). Finally, the Wife uses "oure" only two lines after and within the same sentence as she refers to her deceased husband. All these odd instances lead me to suspect that at the time Chaucer wrote this passage, he was still thinking of Jankyn as a member of the Wife's household—most likely a clerk boarding with her and her husband, like Nicholas in the **Miller's Tale.** These lines would, then, seem to represent an intermediary stage in the process of Jankyn's development: from an apprentice who lives in the same house with the Wife, to a scholar who boards with her, and finally to a scholar boarding with one of her intimate friends whom she meets in the fields during Lent.

Before we further investigate the implications of such a model, however, we need to be sure of our foundation. For a great deal is riding on the assumption that the word "oure" cannot in this instance be taken to mean "my". Here the MED gives us pause, for its editors list, under the seventh of nine meanings for "oure": "our, my: often used with a singular referent, indicating familiarity, endearment, or domestic intimacy, sometimes with pejorative connotations."[12] If "oure" could be used for "my" in intimate situations, we would be able to account for "oure clerk" quite simply, without the necessity of postulating that it represents some sort of intermediate stage in Jankyn's development. Upon closer examination, however, none of the eight textual citations listed in the MED fits the case of the Wife and her lover with any degree of accuracy. Citations from the *Ancrene Riwle* and from Gower's *Confessio Amantis* refer, respectively, to friars and to a prelate with the collective "our" in what seems primarily a gesture of speaking in the first place for an institution and in the second for the people in general. Neither is connected to the situation here at hand or even, with apologies to

the editors at the MED, to the definition under consideration. In the remaining six citations the precise meaning of the pronoun is ambiguous, but in each case its use carries a strong connotation of the domestic sphere: "Oure syre bradys lyke a dere" (Leve Lystynes p. 31); "Colle oure dogge' (CT NP B² 4573); "my lord don Juan, Oure deere cosyn" (CT Sh B² 1259); "Oure dame" (Sum D 1797 and WBP D 311); "Our wurthi werwolf" (W Pal 2306). The strangest in this collection is that taken from the alliterative romance *William of Palerne,* also known as *William and the Werewolf.* The use of "oure" here, though, is not substantially different from its use in "oure dogge," as the werewolf in this passage has just been seen in a dream by William's lover, Melior, acting the part of a guard dog by protecting the rock quarry where she and William are hiding from a lion and a crowd of other wild beasts.

This consistency of application implies that the peculiar use of "oure" to mean "my" arose from its customary application within a family in the identification of collective kinship (our mother, our father, our dog, etc.), becoming gradually associated with the family as a unit—the household. Thus the Wife of Bath in a clarifying instance missed by the editors of the MED calls her husband(s) affectionately "oure sheep" (D 432), even though they are the only two persons present, because she means that he is figuratively the sheep of the household, of their family unit. Here, and I think elsewhere as well, "oure" does not translate simply as "my" but rather denotes household intimacy and a close familial relationship. This may seem an overly complex interpretation, but it is necessary if we are to adequately explain the Wife's use of "oure" in line D 311: "What," she says, arguing with her husband(s), "wenestow make an ydiot of oure dame?" Here "oure" *cannot* mean "my", for she is referring to herself. Rather, as before, "oure dame" means the "the lady of our house." This, in fact, is precisely the gloss offered by the Riverside Edition.[13] Similarly, when the Nun's Priest tells us, as narrator, that along with the widow and her daughters ran "Colle oure dogge, and Talbot, and Gerland," he does not mean to imply that Colle is his own dog, or that he was himself a member of the widow's household, but simply (and with an engaging intimacy) that Colle, the household dog, ran with the others after Reynard the fox.

This clarification of the MED definition has its immediate bearing upon the Wife's reference to Jankyn as "oure clerk." It would seem to preclude the possibility that Jankyn is not a member of her household, and that the Wife means simply "my clerk" as in "my lover." Some might insist that she is using "oure" as a special sign of intimacy because they have just plighted troth in the Lenten fields. But while this is conceivable, it does not fit the pattern we have established in our survey of Middle English usage. Every one of our examples has made use of "oure" in a context of domestic rather than erotic intimacy, and we cannot simply speculate as to the possible meanings of Middle English words, but must endeavor to stick as closely as possible to the range of their contemporary usage.

Clerk Jankyn, then, is referred to here as though he were a member of the Wife's household, quite possibly a boarder. This interpretation is, as we have seen already, consistent with the immediate context of a funeral procession in which Jankyn appears as a prominent mourner. It is, however, entirely inconsistent with the story the Wife has just finished telling of her meeting and courtship with Jankyn, according to which they were introduced by the Wife's "gossyb dame Alys," in whose house Jankyn was a boarder.[14] That Lent, the Wife's fourth husband happened to be away in London on business, and this left her free to range about, "for to se, and eek for to be seye" (D 552). The three of them attended various vigils, processions, miracle plays, and marriages, and one day the Wife found herself walking in the fields with Jankyn. It was here that she proposed marriage to him, telling him of a marvelous dream she had had of him. Because this scene is so much more detailed an account of the process through which they became lovers than that of the funeral scene, we may safely assume that it was written afterwards as a modification and further elaboration. On the other hand, the story of the Wife's tempestuous marriage with this clerk was almost certainly conceived and written concurrently with the funeral. The story of their marriage was, after all, the whole reason Jankyn became a clerk, and the funeral scene is really nothing more than a simple account of how Alys came to meet and marry such a man: he was a boarder at her house, and during the funeral of her husband she noticed—probably not for the first time, but it was the first time she could act on the impulse— just how handsome he was. The funeral scene, then, was conceived and written as part of the original narrative of the Wife's marriage to clerk Jankyn, and both scene and narrative together represent a stage in the story's conception prior to the Lenten courtship. Both of these suppositions are corroborated by the Wife's account of her wedding with Jankyn. If we ignore the astrological digression of lines D 609-26 (almost certainly added in revision as portions of the argument are missing from some manuscripts) the wedding scene links the funeral scene organically to the marriage narrative which follows:

> What sholde I seye but, at the monthes ende,
> This joly clerk, Jankyn, that was so hende,
> Hath wedded me with greet solempnytee.
>
> (D 627-29)

Why, after all, would the Wife apologize in this manner for offering an inadequate account of her brief mourning and rapid courtship of Jankyn when she has more than adequately explained both in the Lenten scene? Why indeed, if not because the Lenten scene had not yet been conceived when these lines were written?

Having established that the funeral scene was almost certainly conceived and written before the famous scene of the Wife's courtship of Jankyn which it follows, the next logical step would be to piece together a reconstruction of the narrative's initial form. I suspect, however, that while Chaucer probably saved much of his earlier work (and indeed seems to have missed correcting certain minor discrepancies which we have employed here as clues), he must certainly have canceled key passages and transitions. Thus, while it is easy to imagine the death of her fourth husband (D 495-502: "Lat hym fare wel; God gyve his soule reste! / He is now in his grave and in his cheste") being followed directly by the funeral scene (D 593ff.: "To chirche was myn hous-bonde born a-morwe / With neighebores, that for hym maden sorwe"), it is difficult to figure out how the Wife's introductory comments about her fifth marriage might be made to fit between these two passages: D 502-24: "Now of my fifthe housbonde wol I telle, / God lete his soule nevere come in helle! / And yet was he to me the mooste shrewe; / That feele I on my ribbes al by rewe / . . . / Greet prees at market maketh deere ware, / And to greet cheep is holde at litel prys: / This knoweth every womman that is wys." This is confusing because, as I have noted above, these lines may well have been written for apprentice Janekyn rather than clerk Jankyn, and probably predate all the rest. Of course, it is possible that they were written for apprentice Janekyn, set aside when Chaucer first altered his conception, and then re-integrated when the Lenten courtship scene was introduced. But it is also possible that we are now missing the transition sequence which used to link the Wife's introduction of her fifth husband to the funeral scene at which we learn how she became stricken with love for him. In the midst of such uncertainties, I wish to concentrate upon what can be concluded with confidence on the basis of the available evidence.

Jankyn, then, seems at first to have been conceived as an apprentice, then as a clerk boarding in the Wife's house, and finally as a clerk boarding with the Wife's gossip. In thinking about the importance of this second change, we need first to realize what the first alteration left unchanged. For while changing Jankyn from apprentice to clerk utterly transformed the possibilities for their married life, it did not substantially change how they were to meet and fall in love: in both cases they are thrown together by circumstance, by the accident of living together in the same house. Few details are provided by Chaucer, and few are needed: the apprentice is handsome and often squires the Wife gallantly about town on her errands; the boarder is handsome and she takes special note of this at her last husband's funeral—her hour both of opportunity and need. These simple plots require no further explanation or adumbration because they are the stuff of fabliau, a genre noted for simplicity both of conception and execution. Beryl Rowland summarizes the critical consensus as follows:

> The [fabliau] plot itself is single and clear-cut with a dénouement that seems inevitable; it makes a steady progression usually involving some kind of sexual conflict whereby one character or group of characters is outwitted by another; it exploits stock types and keeps the attention focused on action rather than character by employing certain conventions of behavior which the audience can readily anticipate and accept. The wife is inevitably lecherous, and also cunning enough to outsmart her menfolk. . . . [D]escription, like characterization, is minimal and never allowed to impede the movement of the action.[15]

What is important for us here is the premium which the fabliau places on rapidity and movement. The use of conventional characters enables the writer to quickly place each one in relation to the others, and then let this initial configuration play itself out by way of stratagem, betrayal, revenge, and counter-revenge. This was taken over by Chaucer in his first two conceptions of the Wife's fifth husband, Jankyn. But some time after writing the story of Alys and Jankyn's epic battle of the book, or perhaps in the process of writing it, Chaucer seems to have become dissatisfied with this simplistic conception of how they met and fell in love. She herself had said that Jankyn was the great love of her life, and after the writing the touching story of their reconciliation—a rapprochement worked out in despite of years of bitter hatred, hatred which existed in direct proportion to their love—I think Chaucer must have come to believe her. Such a love was not simply the material of farce, though it certainly had farcical qualities. Such a love, imperfect and yet profound as it was, could not be conceived as the product of a simplistic configuration of stock characters—widow and apprentice, widow and boarder clerk—but had instead to be given a more explicit, individuated foundation:

> I seye that in the feeldes walked we,
> Til trewely we hadde swich daliance,
> This clerk and I, that of my purveiance
> I spak to hym and seyde hym how that he,
> If I were widwe, sholde wedde me.

> (D 564-68)

The result was an original conception which, it seems, Chaucer was still working on in the last years of his life. Unsatisfied, perhaps, with this account of how a forty-year-old woman could manage to charm a twenty-year-old into marriage, he added the dream passage, in which the Wife lets Jankyn know, in an enchantingly poetic manner, that their life together will be satisfying both sexually and economically:[16]

> I seyde I mette of hym al nyght,
> He wolde han slayn me as I lay upright,
> And al my bed was ful of verray blood;
> "But yet I hope that ye shal do me good,
> For blood bitokeneth gold, as me was taught."

> (D 577-81)

This dream continues the process of trying to find adequate means to explain the origin of the deep and yet quite tawdry passion which binds the Wife and her clerk together. Her dream is, of course, all a lie, and yet we cannot doubt but that Jankyn *had* enchanted her, and that she managed in this way to enchant him. Such is the seed, half-lie, half-truth, from which their passionate, conflicted love grew, blossomed, and, at the very last, bore fruit.

We have located two discrepancies in Chaucer's presentation of Jankyn and have used them as clues in tracing the development of the **Wife of Bath's Prologue.** While superficially similar in wording and in their immediate implication, they are artifacts of two quite different changes in Chaucer's initial conception. The first had certainly the more profound impact, for the introduction of clerk Jankyn made possible the Wife's first-hand encounter and confrontation with the anti-matrimonial, misogynist literary tradition, and also—in all likelihood—made possible the scholarly defense of marriage against virginity with which she begins the **Prologue.** The second discrepancy points, however, to a change of plans which is equally original in conception, for it represents a turn away from the conventionalities of character formation in the fabliau (and, for that matter, in the *Roman de la rose*), pointing in the direction of more modern notions of a character as a fully-realized individual. It is hazardous, of course, to project modern biases upon Chaucer, whether they are of the moral or literary sort, but the rich complexity which is the Wife of Bath invites such a response: "[De Meun's la Vieille] is a demonstration that women out of order are out of reason, and that freedom breeds unbridled lust and desire to dominate. The Wife of Bath's monologue is not so transparent: it demands to be looked *into*, puzzles and intrigues the observer, offers opportunities for contrary responses, creates, though itself a monologue, the effect of a dialogue, within the speaker and also within the reader."[17] The complexity and rich texture to which Derek Pearsall testifies in this passage are in large part the result of the process of conception and reconception which we have been studying. Chaucer's multiple additions and revisions give the **Prologue** a layered effect, like the rich build-up of paint on a canvas. If we wish to understand his striking originality, we must first appreciate the creative process through which his portrait came into being.

Notes

1. On the basis of thematic and stylistic differences as well as differences of source material, Jones

divided the Wife's *Prologue* into two main sections—her defense of matrimony and the story of her five marriages—and claimed that these differences pointed to a modification of Chaucer's original conception of the Wife (Richard F. Jones, "A Conjecture on the *Wife of Bath's Prologue*," *JEGP* 24 (1925): 519-20). Pratt modified Jones's model, subdividing the Wife's marriages between the first three "good" husbands and the two "bad" ones, once again on the basis of differences of source material and theme (Robert A. Pratt, "The Development of the Wife of Bath," in *Studies in Medieval Literature in Honor of Professor Albert Carol Baugh,* ed. MacEdward Leach [Philadelphia, 1961], 45-79, see esp. 50-51). In the brief outline of the structure of the Wife's *Prologue* which follows, I am indebted to Pratt for the basic outlines of my tripartite division (although I make some minor modifications). I owe my summary of Chaucer's sources to Bartlett J. Whiting, "*The Wife of Bath's Prologue*," in *Sources and Analogues of Chaucer's "Canterbury Tales,"* ed. W. F. Bryan and Germaine Dempster (Chicago, 1941), 207-22; to Robert P. Miller, ed., *Chaucer: Sources and Backgrounds* (New York, 1977), 399-402; and to Dean Spruill Fansler, *Chaucer and the Roman de la Rose* (Gloucester, 1965), 168-69.

2. All references to the *Canterbury Tales* are from *The Riverside Chaucer,* ed. Larry D. Benson (Boston, 1987) and appear parenthetically in the text.

3. Chaucer, *The Tales of Canterbury,* ed. R. A. Pratt (Boston, 1966), 268n.

4. N. F. Blake, "The Wife of Bath and Her Tale," *Leeds Studies in English* n.s. 13 (1982), 45.

5. *Riverside,* note to line 303, p. 1126.

6. MED, "apprentice" (sense b).

7. One weakness of Pratt's argument is its reliance on the notion that Chaucer originally intended for the Wife to tell what is now the *Shipman's Tale.* Hazel Sullivan has examined this idea thoroughly, finding little evidence in favor and a number of compelling arguments against ("A Chaucerian puzzle," in *A Chaucerian Puzzle and Other Medieval Essays,* ed. Natalie Grimes Lawrence and Jack A. Reynolds, *University of Miami Publications in English and American Literature* 5 (1961), 1-46).

8. William Matthews, "The Wife of Bath and All Her Sect," *Viator* 5 (1974): 436, 442.

9. Robert F. Fleissner, "The Wife of Bath's Five," *ChauR* 8 (1973): 128-32.

10. Pratt, 55-56.

11. Pratt, 53-56.

12. MED, "our(e)" (sense 7.a).

13. *The Riverside Chaucer,* note to line 311.

14. Mary Carruthers has suggested that Jankyn's relationship to the Wife's gossib was not that of a stranger paying rent, but of a close relative ("Clerk Jankyn *at Hom to Bord / With My Gossib*," *ELN* 22:3 [1985]: 11-20):

> He som tyme was a clerk of Oxenford,
> And hadde left scole, and wente at hom to bord
> With my gossib, dwellinge in oure toun.
>
> (D 527-29)

"At hom", Carruthers points out, did not have the same metonymic range it has now, and could not refer to one's home town, but only to one's physical home. Moreover, "bord" still referred in Middle English to meals taken in any context, not just that of an "individual paying rent for board and bed." Carruthers further argues that the small town in which the Wife dwelled, "biside Bathe," was too small to have had facilities for boarders. After all, the students in the *Reeve's Tale* are forced to lodge overnight with their enemy the Miller when the sun goes down in the town of Trumpington, "biside" Cambridge. All this may be thought to throw doubt upon the idea that Chaucer initially envisioned clerk Jankyn as a boarder in the Wife's house, for she certainly could not have married a relative boarding with her. However, the evidence of the *Reeve's Tale* speaks only to the difficulties of finding lodging in a small town on short notice. That more permanent lodging could be arranged is clear enough from the *Miller's Tale.*

15. Beryl Rowland, "What Chaucer Did To the Fabliau," *Studia Neophilologica* 51:1 (1979): 205.

16. Because this passage, among others, is not present in many manuscripts (including the Hengwrt), Manly and Rickert believe that it and the others were added by Chaucer at a late date, after early manuscript editions had been made and circulated among friends (John M. Manly and Edith Rickert, *The Text of "The Canterbury Tales" Studied on the Basis of All Known Manuscripts* [Chicago, 1940], 3: 454). Blake, however, argues that the absence of these passages from the Hengwrt is a sign of their illegitimacy (N. F. Blake, "The Relationship between the Hengwrt and the Ellesmere Manuscripts of the 'Canterbury Tales'," *Essays and Studies* 32 [1979]: 1-18). The idea that a mere scribe or editor inserted these passages into the *Wife of Bath's Prologue,* however, seems to me unlikely. Each of them is lyrically beautiful

and imaginatively original; the dream-vision which the Wife invents for her lover is particularly striking for how well it fits into the process we have traced in Chaucer's development of her narrative.

17. Derek Pearsall, *The Canterbury Tales* (London, 1985), 76.

Alcuin Blamires (essay date 2002)

SOURCE: Blamires, Alcuin. "Refiguring the 'Scandalous Excess' of Medieval Woman: The Wife of Bath and Liberality." In *Gender in Debate from the Early Middle Ages to the Renaissance,* edited by Thelma S. Fenster and Clare A. Lees, pp. 57-78. New York: Palgrave, 2002.

[*In the following essay, Blamires contrasts the Wife of Bath to Blanche from* The Book of the Duchess, *studies Christine de Pizan's theories on the masculine and feminine definitions of largesse and liberality, and uncovers the stereotype common in Chaucer's time that women were miserly and selfish.*]

Medieval defenses of women can seem strangely heterogeneous: Bizarre conglomerations of biblical observation, judicial logic, physiology, anecdote, exemplum, moral polemic, topped off with a colorful froth of psychoanalytical speculation about the motives of detractors. Yet there is an underlying continuity, which is to be found in the moral or ethical dimension of the debate. This is explicitly so, of course, where a writer tries to claim particular virtues for one sex and to demonize the other sex by ascribing contrary vices, as in the case of wrangling over whether men or women are more sexually depraved. The moral preoccupation is sustained with regard to the contentious crux of the relative guilt of Adam or Eve. Gender issues remain moral issues when exempla of all sorts are invoked in defense of women or against them. The present essay will show that although moral implications may not always be very apparent to us, medieval gender discourse invokes particular "vices and virtues" categories in nuanced ways. We shall enhance our understanding even of such heavily discussed works as *The Wife of Bath's Prologue* and *Tale* if we retrieve the strategies of moral dialectic that they incorporate.[1]

The element of moral dialectic within the gender debate that may yet prove most interesting—for there are discoveries to be made—is the strategy whereby medieval defenders of women translated alleged moral deficits of women into moral credits. Since from our perspective medieval constructions of women appear generated and sustained through persistent indoctrination, it might be apt to use the term *redoctrination* to designate the strategy that reverses normative paradigms

of deficits and credits. Of course, these reversals could readily be referred to as "paradoxes." The disadvantage of thinking in terms of paradox is that commentary on early gender polemic often reads paradox as a self-mocking trope, one that draws skeptical attention to the sheer brazenness with which it switches traditional weaknesses into strengths.[2] Interpreted thus, paradox used in defense of women dwindles into an intellectual juggling act, or what Helen Solterer calls a "two-timing discourse" for the entertainment of the cognoscenti.[3] That it was occasionally so should not forestall inquiry into the serious (though not necessarily solemn) revisionary moves that the rhetoric of reversal could accomplish. Adoption of the fresh term "redoctrination" may encourage us to appreciate afresh the radical intervention in gender prejudice that proponents of reversal sometimes sought to achieve.

Specimen medieval examples of this redoctrination, deriving profeminine hypotheses (of a sort) from various misogynistic notions of feminine deficiency, would be: That the ascribed "weakness" or "fragility" of women fosters a peace-loving disposition, as against the violence that masculine "hardness" induces;[4] and that the imputed "inferiority" of woman's judgment logically implies that Adam must be held more guilty in the Fall than Eve.[5]

I should like to investigate here another, quite drastic instance of redoctrination, one that discloses a fascinating collision of moral impulses lurking within misogyny, near the heart (even) of gender debate in the Middle Ages. The justification for claiming so much would be that the instance I have in mind focuses on excess. The expression "scandalous excess" in the title of this paper is borrowed from Howard Bloch's 1987 article on medieval misogyny.[6] By "scandalous excess" Bloch means extravagance in dress and ornament such as misogyny anciently pilloried in women—an excess characterized as "surplus," and which he identifies as a corollary of the secondariness of woman in Creation.[7] For in woman's status as "supplement" to Adam, Bloch detects the core of a misogynous paradigm that holds women supplementary, literally an "excess," in all respects. (Actually Bloch is too mesmerized by this paradigm of supplementarity; he elides the difference between "supplementary" and "second." After all, to the argument that the male had prime position in Creation, there was from early times the ready retort that woman was created second to an improved formula;[8] or, in the bibliographic analogy delightfully proposed by Constantia Munda in 1617, woman was the "second edition" of God's best creation—presumably with the import that second editions remove the defects found in the first.)[9]

Yet "scandalous excess" is a resonant expression for quite other reasons than Bloch indicates. Excess, in the ethical tradition that the Middle Ages received from antiquity, was the malfunction of a given virtue in one direction; deficiency was the malfunction in the other direction. The principle was Aristotelian, but the Middle Ages did not have to wait for the complete translation of Aristotle's *Ethics* in the thirteenth century to know of it, for it percolated through other channels, such as the *sententia* voiced in Chaucer's *Canon's Yeoman's Tale*: "That that is overdoon, it wol nat preeve / Aright . . . it is a vice" (VIII.645-6).[10]

Now innumerable readers have come across the sort of dyspeptic rhetoric produced by medieval writers about alleged vices of excess and deficiency in women. There are notorious and shrill examples in the last part of Andreas Capellanus's *De amore*. Women are there held to be driven by *rapacitas*, addicted to gain, to the extent that they consider it a virtue to hoard whatever they get [*omnia reservare*] and to give it to none [*nemini largiri*].[11] As against the deficiency of generosity shown in this material avarice, they are also held to display a contrary excess of sexual generosity, for they are driven by lust and "unable to deny" their bodies [*neque sui corporis solatia denegare*], so no man could satisfy their libido.[12] A further classic allegation of excess in Andreas concerns speech. It is the complaint that women can't keep quiet. Secrets burn them up inside; women cannot restrain their tongues from talking.[13]

Familiarity with this material breeds neglect, but what happens if we delve into the categories of excess and deficiency here glimpsed in Andreas, and into their relations to gender stereotypes? We shall focus on the virtue of liberality, or largesse—*liberalitas* and *largitas* being, it must be emphasized, interchangeable names in the Middle Ages for the virtue of generosity: "Another word for liberality [*liberalitas*] is bountifulness [*largitas*]."[14]

In certain crucial ways, of course, the chief medieval womanly virtue was guarding or keeping, not giving. It was a social hypothesis of ancient origin, still urged by Christine de Pizan in *Le Livre des trois vertus,* that while a man's role is to acquire goods for the household, a woman's is to "conserve" such goods through prudent domestic management (Latin *conservare,* Middle English *kepen*).[15] She should steer prudently between parsimony and wastefulness, for, as *The Merchant's Tale* hypothesizes, she "kepeth his good, and wasteth never a deel" (IV.1343). This arrangement tended to reserve to males the prerogative of conspicuous material liberality[16] and therefore the charisma of what was often reckoned a particularly fine virtue of humanity.[17] That *largesse* "makes" the noble man was a medieval maxim, as one could read on the authority of Boethius.[18] Conversely, in Lydgate's *Fall of Princes* it is axiomatic that in the case of a lord who abandons "largesse," "negardship exilith ientilesse."[19] The classic medieval story of competitive *liberalità* (taken up by

Chaucer in *The Franklin's Tale*) explores the magnanimity of three males. The woman in the story, the Dorigen figure, apparently has no claim in the competition.[20]

Since some readers of courtly literature will primarily be aware of largesse as a defining feature of social class, it is important to observe at this point that largesse/liberality was not a concept discussed only with reference to class (i.e., the nobility, who clearly could afford to be generous). Rather, as this study seeks to show, it had a wider scope, which derived in part from biblical advice; it also had an asymmetrical gender application. Even the world of literary courtship, where generosity served to distinguish noble from *vilein* behavior, tended to reinforce an insinuation that largesse was masculine. The *Romance of the Rose* commands male lovers to give "largement."[21] The lover in Gower's *Confessio amantis* fanatically complies—he would shower his lady with gifts if she would let him—"Als freliche as god hath it yive, / It schal ben hires"[22] (V.4769-70). Giving as lavishly as God has given: It is a significant formulation, as we shall see.

How much did the patterns of thought we are following *exclude* women from the prerogative of practicing liberality? Christine de Pizan, repudiating misogynous suppositions of female greed, pointedly asserts in her *City of Ladies* that she could dwell on the endless *largesces* and *liberalités* of women, who are only too happy to see money used with wise generosity rather than hoarded away in some chest by a miser.[23] In this respect, Christine makes the classic reactive move in the debate about women: She recovers for women a virtue that the other side alleges they lack. But equally, as the passage implicitly discloses, Christine is aware that many women are not in a position to practice the virtue of liberality because they are kept on a tight rein financially by miserly husbands.[24] They "guard the little that they can have" for the sake of the household, she suggests, but their reward is perverse—they acquire a reputation for graspingness.[25] Unwittingly echoing Christine, Andrée Blumstein deduces that historically there is a social causation for stereotypes of womanly "greed" in the structured financial dependence of women on men, which fixed women in the position of petitioning males for money.[26] Christine herself would have found the stereotype rehearsed in one of her sources, the *De mulieribus claris* of Boccaccio, who confirms an assumption that women are innately parsimonious even as he expresses enthusiasm over exceptions.[27] Christine protests that this imputed vice should be revised into a virtue: Using the other classic debating move, which I have dubbed redoctrination, she proves the alleged "avarice" to be "prudence" instead. Such behavior "is not at all avarice or greed, but is a sign of great prudence."[28]

Small wonder that wives are heard in **The Canterbury Tales** insisting that one of the top seven qualities women want in husbands is generosity: They should be *free, and no nygard.*[29] But however generous a husband might be, a wife was supposed to "conserve" her husband's goods on his behalf just as she conserved her body on his behalf, since her body constituted another category of his "goods." A kind of wordplay reinforced the principle of double conservation. In Boccaccio's Latin, it is a matter of being both *servatrix pudicitiae* [guardian of her sexual modesty] and *servatrix thesaurum* [guardian of the family treasures].[30] In English, it is a matter of the wife "*keeping* goods": In Chaucer's **Shipman's Tale,** a merchant urges his wife to "kepe oure good" scrupulously, just when she has in fact decided to offer a sexual part of it elsewhere (VII.241-3). Generosity in a woman might carry a certain danger. There should be some keeping in a lady's giving.[31]

However, if some cultural impulses favored a feminine generosity that was scrupulously calibrated, other cultural impulses constructed the feminine to be a beneficent, abundant source of bounty and radiance. One such cultural impulse that is pertinent here linked the feminine with the dissemination of goodness. It came through medieval lyric tradition and was of a Neo-Platonist kind, derived from sources such as Pseudo-Dionysius. Pseudo-Dionysius offers the following definition of divine goodness: "The Essential Good, by the very fact of its existence, extends goodness into all things." Like the sun, which "gives light to whatever is able to partake of its light," the originary principle of Good "sends the rays of its undivided goodness to everything with the capacity . . . to receive it."[32]

The significance of this in the present context is that it contributes powerfully to a concept of liberality that Chaucer reaches for when he wants to memorialize a woman, Duchess Blanche, in his elegiac poem **The Book of the Duchess.** In this text, the Black Knight eventually describes his dead wife as a paradigm of abundance. True, he has to accommodate the proprieties of more inhibiting feminine virtues before winning through to that thought. We are assured that her charismatic and magnetic look was consistent with "mesure"; it was never "foly sprad" (line 874), and it bespoke a "brotherly" love for decent folk. In *this* sort of love "she was wonder large" [marvellously generous, ll.891-3].

Yet Chaucer finally allows the discourses of Neo-Platonism and liberality to triumph over the discourse of decorum. When Blanche relaxed, he says,

> . . . she was lyk to torche bryght
> That every man may take of lyght
> Ynogh, and hyt hath never the lesse.
> Of maner and of comlynesse

> Ryght so ferde my lady dere;
> For every wight of hire manere
> Myght cacche ynogh, yif that he wolde,
> Yif he had eyen hir to biholde.

(ll.961-70)

Here is the familiar Neo-Platonic concept of rays of goodness (in Blanche's case, her "manere"), which can be "caught" by every person with the capacity to do so ["Yf he had eyen . . ."]. But here also is a simile powerfully associated with liberality: The simile of a distribution of fire or light from a source (in this case, a torch) that remains unimpoverished by such distribution.

The locus classicus for this analogy is Cicero's ethical treatise, the *De officiis* I.16. Cicero finds the elementary principle of *liberalitas*—what he calls *vulgaris liberalitas*—enshrined in the offering of common property for the common benefit. He exemplifies this through a quotation from Ennius: "To give directions to another who's lost, is to light another's lamp by one's own: No less shines one's own lamp after lighting another's." The principle is reiterated in the maxim "let anyone who will, take fire from fire." Other maxims reinforcing the point are that water should be freely given from a flowing source, and (something to note in relation to **The Wife of Bath's Tale**) that one should give good advice to anyone in doubt. Cicero argues that ideal liberality with private property actually conforms to the same principle, that is, it does not seriously deplete one's means—otherwise liberality consumes the basis for further liberality.[33]

In ethical literature, accordingly, liberality is always delicately poised between parsimony (deficient liberality) on one hand, and prodigality (excess liberality) on the other:

> Tak Avarice and tak also
> The vice of Prodegalite;
> Between hem Liberalite,
> Which is the vertu of Largesse,
> Stant and governeth his noblesse.[34]

True, Christian moral treatises tirelessly repeated that if you had much, you should give lavishly, mindful of the *largesse* of God to humanity[35]—a divine abundance that is itself memorably imagined by the writer of the Middle English *Pearl* in terms of water poured out of a bottomless gulf.[36] God's largesse was a model of *un*calculating charity—and definitions of largesse overlapped considerably, albeit a little uncomfortably, with those of charity. The ethic of giving uncalculatingly might be said to have been always in tension with the received reverence for moderation. "In Charity," as Sir Francis Bacon was to assert, "there is no Excesse."[37]

Sometimes in medieval discussion there lurks a beguiling hypothesis that if you emulate unrestrained divine abundance, God will enhance your resources to sustain such generosity. When the personification of Largesse is described in *The Romance of the Rose,* Guillaume de Lorris writes that "God caused her wealth to multiply, so that however much she gave away, she always had more."[38] But if human generosity here fortunately accelerates, as it were, the divine supply, it was more normal to urge, unlike Sir Francis Bacon, that liberality be moderated according to the Ciceronian (and Aristotelian) golden mean. The right use of riches meant avoiding excess or *fool-largesse* on one side and parsimony on the other.[39] The crux was the first of these: A self-impoverishing generosity was not largesse—it was prodigality.

The wonder of Chaucer's Blanche is that her personality is a torchlike phenomenon that is at once private yet *undepletable.* She herself, or her radiant personality, is (in modern idiom) an infinitely "sustainable resource." What the remainder of this paper will argue is that the Wife of Bath models herself, or is modeled, in much the same way.

Chaucer's Wife of Bath carries out a policy of bodily *largesse.* She formulates this in the terms appropriate to the moral discourse of liberality. Liberality, after all, is about the right *use* of riches. Everyone, she recalls from Scripture, has some special gift from God (III.103-4). She proposes to utilize whatever bountiful sexual resources she has received. It is precisely the sort of argument found in moral exhortations to generosity and charity. "So bids St Peter [as *The Book of Vices and Virtues* puts it] that the graces that God hath lent us, that we should deal forth to our neighbours" in the interests of "common profit."[40] The underlying ethical principle was that whatever superabundance some people have, they have in order to gain the merit of "dispensing it well" [*bona dispensatio*].[41]

It is in this spirit that the Wife of Bath sees herself as using her "instrument" as "frely" as God has given it (ll.149-50)—indeed, she says she uses it free of pedantic calculations about her partner's size, color, degree of poverty, or humble social status (ll.622-6). In the same spirit, she represents herself bestowing her body as refreshment, so as to emulate the Lord's own miracle of supplying five undepletable barley loaves that could feed five thousand.

All of which is brought to a sensational focus in Alisoun's own adoption of the old Ciceronian liberality topos. Declaring women's desire to be free and expansive, ["at oure large," l.322], she argues that husbands should be contented with a sufficiency from wives, and generous-minded about any surplus:

> Ye shul have queynte right ynogh at eve.
> He is to greet a nygard that wolde werne
> A man to lighte a candle at his lanterne;

He shal have never the lasse light, pardee.
Have thou ynogh, thee that nat pleyne thee.

(ll.332-6)

Chaucer may have picked up this knowingly sexual application of the "torch" image from one of his favorite authors, Ovid, in *Ars Amatoria,* or from Jean de Meun, who, in the *Romance of the Rose,* suggests that such an application is notorious.[42] One's first thought may be that it is a spurious travesty of the social imperative of generosity, or of what was admired in Blanche.[43] Blanche, of course, radiates her charisma unselfconsciously, in a stringently *involuntary* way,[44] which corresponds rather precisely with the Pseudo-Dionysian notion of goodness as a source exerting raylike beneficence by virtue of its sheer existence, not as a matter of active choice. By contrast, the Wife flaunts her bounty self-consciously, laced with a mischievous nuance of threat ["ye *shul* have ynogh"]. Small wonder that this is the side of *The Wife of Bath's Prologue* that prompts even well-disposed critics to splutter censoriously about the Wife's "theatrical exaggeration of female sexuality," her "licentious charity," and her "false analogies" that "pervert" orthodox positions.[45]

Must that be our response? Might not Chaucer have become genuinely interested in asking why personal physical "superabundance" should not come under the rubric of liberality? When Boccaccio does almost the same thing in a story in the *Decameron,* the fictional audience, albeit at first amused, concludes unanimously that the point is accurately made. Again the context presents a spirited woman protesting her moral obligation to give away whatever sexual surplus her husband is unable to respond to. This is the tale of Madonna Filippa, who is arrested for adultery but resolves to defend herself with "the truth." Her defense is that the law on adultery bears inequitably on women, who in any case can satisfy more male partners than vice versa. Thus, having satisfied her husband sexually, "What is she to do with what is left over?" Is it not better for her to "present it to a gentleman who loves her" rather than "throw it to the dogs" or let it "turn bad or go to waste"?[46] Implicitly invoked here as the opposite of good practice in liberality is a stereotype of niggardliness—the skinflint who hoards food only for it to go off.[47] Such hoarding amounts in medieval moral discourse to a defrauding of those who might otherwise have benefited from it.[48]

Technically it might be easy to puncture the moral delight of both Madonna Filippa and Alisoun in their sustainable bodily largesse. For one thing, although liberality did not consist only in material goods, but in other forms of assistance too, sexual favors are not a medium of generosity that the discourse of liberality normally contemplates. For another, according to strict doctrine, Alisoun's body is not hers to give: The lantern owner in her analogy is her husband.[49] Ethical discourse insists, moreover, that liberality is to be applied in the "right way" to the "right recipients,"[50] whereas Alisoun confesses to observing "no discrecioun" in her choice of recipients (ll.622-6). Above all, there is the catch that moralists knew that the characteristic trick of prodigality was to pass itself off as liberality. Each vice can be masked as a virtue, and so, according to Alan of Lille, "a harlotlike relationship with Prodigality lyingly advertises itself as a tribute to Generosity."[51] Alisoun's generosity certainly sounds more like prodigality when she later associates herself with Venus's love of "ryot and dispence" (III.700).

Even if it were conceded, however, that the Wife of Bath is disguising prodigality as generosity, she would retain more sympathy in terms of ethical discourse than the miser. Aristotle had already noted that prodigality resembles liberality, that actually the prodigal has the natural inclination toward liberality, and even that a prodigal is distinctly preferable to a miser because "he benefits a number of people," whereas the niggard "benefits nobody" (a concession echoed by Aquinas).[52] This is rather crucial because the Wife of Bath is representing tightfisted lantern owners (her husbands) as "niggards," as part of her overall campaign to project men as a miserly species intent on locking all women and cash away in the safe. At least her natural bent toward liberality benefits somebody.

It is not just that the Wife's prodigality *resembles* largesse. Her attitude conforms in another important respect with that virtue, in that she thinks in terms of "not withholding." Witness her famous suggestion that she "koude noght withdrawe" her "chambre of Venus from a good felawe" (III.617-18). A characteristic of largesse, though one that always took it riskily near prodigality, was that true generosity makes it hard to hold back one's goods. Vernacular writers were aware of this, but the point is formally and etymologically made by Aquinas, who explains that *largitas* and *liberalitas* are synonyms because both signify a "letting go" rather than a "retention."[53]

Such evidence may not of itself remove skepticism. It might be felt that this exploration of the liberality discourse merely confirms that the Wife's *Prologue* is a lurid parody of (or at least a joke about) these ethical issues—and that at the end of the day Chaucer does no more than highlight with a snigger a disproportion between female and male sexual capacities. Yet a reason for tempering skepticism arises if we recall that the Ciceronian passage that is a matrix for the torch/lantern figure links it with other gestures of liberality: In particular, with giving directions to someone lost, or giving good advice to someone in doubt. It was not necessary to go back to Cicero to know that liberality encompassed kind advice. "Largesse does not consist only in material gifts, as a wise man has said, but also in comforting words," as Christine de Pizan generalizes.[54] Moreover, an association of the torch figure with freely given counsel was especially conspicuous in the Middle Ages at a high point of the ubiquitous Alexander narrative: Alexander, having heard that the abstemious King Dindimus frowns on his own lifestyle, somewhat rashly invites Dindimus to counsel him about it. Alexander adds that by giving such counsel Dindimus will not diminish his own wisdom any more than a "blazing brand" or "bright candle" is diminished by igniting other lights.[55]

The availability of such a connection in the late Middle Ages opens the possibility, at a stroke, of a new way of understanding the relation between the sexual liberality banteringly mooted in the Wife's *Prologue,* and the liberality of counsel that is offered at two points by the old woman of *The Wife of Bath's Tale*: First when she whispers a secret answer to the despairing knight (who is indeed "lost") in order to save his life; and second when she counsels him about his prejudices after he has been obliged to marry her. Readers often wonder whether in disclosing the secret she epitomizes medieval stereotypes of women as "incontinent of speech," as "overflowing mouths."[56] Alisoun tempts us with that stereotype by introducing a story of Midas's wife, who could not contain the secret that Midas had grown ass's ears.[57] Yet the point of this much-discussed allusion, I suggest, is that Midas was a byword for *avarice*.[58] Mrs. Midas epitomizes the antithesis of that avarice: To her it seemed that her knowledge "swal so soore aboute hir herte / That nedely som word hire moste asterte," and Alisoun comments: "out it moot" (III.967-8, 980). This un-withholdability should not be written off as sheer indiscipline. It further articulates liberality's "letting go" as opposed to "retention." So too the old woman's liberality with her counsel in the *Tale* deploys the non-diminishing resource of words to save a life, and such liberality is to be associated with Alisoun's bodily generosity.[59]

Counsel was certainly associated with generosity in medieval moral literature, however unexpected that link may be to us.[60] In *The Book of Vices and Virtues* it is the spiritual Gift of Counsel, vested particularly in the elderly, that is held to dispel the sin of avarice and to promote the virtue of mercy or *pitee,* which people can primarily enact by being *large and curteis* to each other, as opposed to keeping shut purses like covetous men.[61] As it happens, this is quite a good description of the efficacy of the elderly woman's counseling of the knight in the *Wife of Bath's Tale.*

Miserliness, not largesse, is gendered masculine by Alisoun. Through her is expressed an idea that women stand against masculine miserliness in three of life's most important departments: money, sex, and speech.

The ethic of largesse is here decisively regendered feminine. The sensual largesse in Alisoun is unrestrained, but a woman's unrestraint is what saves the knight's life in the ***Tale***. Admittedly there is a contradictory current in Alisoun's self-presentation—her ***Prologue*** speaks of "winning" and "selling" and even "ransom."[62] This is a reminder that her ***Prologue*** discourse produces emphases of such inconsistency as to build what Arthur Lindley calls a "haystack of contradictions," and the disconcerting oscillation between generous and mercantile impulses is one of its facets.[63] But whereas the intermittently mercantile impulse has been widely noted, neither the full extent of Alisoun's impulse of liberality nor its subtle continuity between ***Prologue*** and ***Tale*** has been well understood. Besides, her tough trade talk constitutes at least in part a survival tactic adopted in reaction to masculine oppression. The trigger that can switch off feminine reactiveness and *enable men to understand women's liberality* is a change in men's own perception of women, a removal of the scales from the eyes: "Cast up the curtyn, looke how that it is," to quote the old woman at the end (III.1249).[64] To reach this stage, it seems that feminine largesse has to save men from themselves.

If the exploration of these ideas in ***The Wife of Bath's Prologue*** and ***Tale*** gives grounds, hitherto unnoticed, for a positive ethical interpretation worth pondering in itself, such exploration also raises some wider questions touching on gender and essentialism. In particular, we might ask whether the refiguring, or redoctrination, of female "excess" as "liberality" escapes the frying pan of one misogynistic stereotype only to fall into the fire of another kind of essentialism; and more broadly, there is the problem of whether the whole notion of appropriating moral attributes seriously advanced any pro-feminine position in medieval debate about women.

It is as well to begin by heading off one sinister possibility. What we have seen are two male writers, Chaucer and Boccaccio, redefining an untamable sexual impetus, something that misogyny fears in women, as a form of admirable generosity. The whole thing could be interpreted as the misogynous trick of the male author: What men cannot own of women's sexuality through conventional doctrines of chastity, they seek to gain "on the side" by invoking an alternative doctrine of liberality that authorizes women to distribute their surplus urges freely (blissfully oblivious, meanwhile, to outcomes such as pregnancy).

The catch here is that male writers are joined by female in this project. Marie de France writes a whole *lai* (*Lanval*) in which a woman's material and sexual bounty pointedly shows up deficiencies in Arthurian society. In this story a mysterious woman offers Lanval her love when he has been neglected by the court. She becomes a source that emulates the undiminishable

quality of God's abundance; for when Lanval commits himself to her, she gives a double boon that "however generously [*largement*] he gave or spent, she would still find enough for him"; and wherever love might be made, there he would find her, ready.[65] When he fails the sole condition she places on this bounty, and discloses this secret love, her generosity still extends to saving him from the wrath of Arthur and Guinevere. She transports him out of society altogether. Although this tale raises questions about male sexual fantasy, and although it hints that the woman's liberality is a phenomenon somehow incompatible with the cynical state of normative society (it is an ideal unattained even by so elevated a woman as Arthur's queen), the impression that nevertheless Marie deliberately locates the principle of largesse of all sorts in a woman remains hard to resist. As Regula Evitt puts it, "The woman's 'giving gift' establishes a paradigm of concatenating, reproductive generosity: one that Marie associates with the feminine autonomy that Celtic myth regularly ascribes to the otherworld. The woman gives so that Lanval can give; she, in turn, will give more if Lanval will give more as well."[66]

Of course, any suggestion that generosity might be a special virtue of women would nowadays strike many readers as an essentializing move, and one liable, moreover, to essentialize that virtue in ways convenient to men. Doubtless the same risk attaches to the much more recent, and extremely pertinent, discussion of "giving" by Hélène Cixous in her well-known piece entitled "Sorties." Cixous suggests that what men want out of their giving is to prove something, to gain "plus-value of virility, authority, power," and that men can't help this because that is "how society is made." But where a woman is concerned, "How does *she* give?"

> She too gives *for.* She too, with open hands, gives herself—pleasure, happiness, increased value, and enhanced self-image. But she doesn't try to "recover her expenses." She is able not to return to herself, never settling down, pouring out, going everywhere to the other. She does not flee extremes; she is not the being-of-the-end (the goal), but she is how-far-being—reaches.

A paragraph later, Cixous is developing a similar view of libido, arguing that a woman does not "create a monarchy of her body or her desire"; hers is not a "party dictatorship." "Her libido is cosmic, just as her unconscious is worldwide."[67] A few lines further on, Cixous adds a familiar *verbal* dimension to this vision of liberality: "Her tongue doesn't hold back but holds forth, doesn't keep in but keeps on enabling." Obviously what is provocative here in relation to what we have discussed is both the convergence of certain liberational drives that are held to constitute something centrally "feminine," and the consciously insurrectionist, patriarchy-subverting tonality with which they are asserted.

The presence of these emphases in Cixous's writing demonstrates that the redoctrination that refutes the misogynous charge of feminine excess by self-consciously celebrating that excess as liberality articulates a defense of the feminine that is having a long history. And just as Cixous worries some feminists by seeming to "run the risk of constructing a universal model of femininity,"[68] so the medieval profeminine alternative to the alleged female vice of "excess" leans distinctly toward an essentializing version of woman as icon of sexual and material sustenance.

Notwithstanding that, there is a case for saying that in the context of a culture in which Andreas and others could wield their bullying rhetoric with impunity, any challenge to misogyny is nevertheless worth hearing about. The redoctrination strategy had, I suppose, a kind of disconcerting or destabilizing efficacy. The same can be said of Christine de Pizan's assertion that what men stereotyped as women's tightfistedness was really prudence—a necessity for women who didn't want households to be ruined by their husbands' self-indulgences. Not only does the "vice" become a "virtue," it becomes a virtue that bracingly exposes a latent masculine complacency.

Redoctrination is not, therefore, a negligible instrument of moral dialectic in medieval gender debate. Modern readers who are sensitized to feminism feel uncomfortable with most of the moral wrangling in the medieval debate about women. It smells of a patriarchal and priestly methodology for consigning women to passive or emasculating virtues that keep them under control: In other words, it threatens women with virtues they do not want. And yet, moral discourse was not only an unavoidable "master" discourse, the general terrain across which medieval debate of all sorts, including gender debate, was inevitably conducted. It was sometimes a democratic weapon too, always capable of sudden levelings, sudden challenges to the patriarchal cast of mind. As Christine de Pizan realized, women might ultimately benefit more from a complete cessation in the use of gendered moral labeling. Nevertheless she, and other profeminine voices before her (and if I am right, Chaucer too), also realized that in a climate saturated by moral analysis, valuable structures of argument lay close at hand in the "vices and virtues" field, which was culture's most massively disseminated instrument of analytical discourse.

The moral argument went on anyway. The virtue of liberality was still being enigmatically appropriated for women by a writer calling herself (or himself) Jane Anger in the treatise *Protection of Women* in 1589, and with this I close. "That we are liberal, men will not deny since many of them have received more kindness in one day at our hands, than they can repay in a whole yeare." So far, that is not enigmatic: but then Anger adds, with a mischievous Wife-of-Bathly gleam in the eye, "Some have so glutted themselves with our liberality as they cry, No more."[69]

Notes

1. The present essay originated as a paper developed through conferences of the New Chaucer Society (Sorbonne, 1998) and Fordham University (New York, 1999), and was presented also as a Lansdowne lecture (University of Victoria, 2000). I should like to thank Norm Klassen, Thelma Fenster, and Elizabeth Archibald for providing these opportunities.

2. See, for example, Ian Maclean, *The Renaissance Notion of Woman* (Cambridge: Cambridge University Press, 1980), p. 91, and Linda Woodridge, *Women and the English Renaissance: Literature and the Nature of Womankind, 1540-1620* (Urbana: University of Illinois Press, 1984), p. 59. For further reflections on the balance of facetiousness and seriousness in the debate, see Alcuin Blamires, *The Case for Women in Medieval Culture* (Oxford: Clarendon Press, 1997), pp. 5-7, 36-7, and 124.

3. Helen Solterer, *The Master and Minerva: Disputing Women in French Medieval Culture* (Berkeley and Los Angeles: University of California Press, 1995), p. 148.

4. Blamires, *The Case for Women,* pp. 83-9.

5. Blamires, *The Case for Women,* pp. 32, 114-19.

6. R. Howard Bloch, "Medieval Misogyny," *Representations* 20 (1987): 1-14.

7. Ibid., 13.

8. Blamires, *The Case for Women,* pp. 96-8, 105. For other critical discussions of Bloch's essay, see Elizabeth A. Clark and others, "Commentary on Bloch, 'Medieval Misogyny'," *Medieval Feminist Newsletter* 7 (1989): 2-16.

9. Constantia describes woman as the "second edition of the Epitome of the whole world," and the "second Tome of that goodly volume compiled by God"; *The Worming of a Mad Dogge,* in *The Early Modern Englishwoman,* pt. 1, vol. 4, *Defences of Women,* introduced by Susan G. O'Malley (Aldershot: Scolar; Vermont: Ashgate, 1996), p. 2.

10. All Chaucer quotations are from *The Riverside Chaucer,* ed. Larry D. Benson (Boston: Houghton Mifflin, 1987); *The Canterbury Tales* are cited by Roman numeral and line number in the body of

my text. The *Riverside* note to VIII.645-6 cites a manuscript gloss supplying the common proverb "Omne quod est nimium vertitur in vitium"; though a specific *Ethics* reference is not impossible—cf. "Vertu is the mene, / As Etik seith," *Prologue to the Legend of Good Women,* "F" 165-6. See Aristotle, *Ethics,* II. vi, trans. J. A. K. Thomson (Harmondsworth: Penguin, 1953), pp. 100-2. Jill Mann cites the partial medieval Latin translation circulating in the thirteenth century, ed. R.-A. Gauthier, *Ethica Nichomachea, Aristoteles Latinus* (Leiden and Brussels: E. J. Brill and Desclée de Brouwer, 1972): "Medietas autem, duarum maliciarum, huius quidem secundum superfluitatem, huius vero indigenciam. Et adhuc, quoniam hee quidem deficiunt, hee autem superhabundant, eius quod oportet, et in passionibus et in operacionibus, virtus autem medium et invenit et vult," in "Satisfaction and Payment in Middle English Literature," *Studies in the Age of Chaucer* 5 (1983): 17-48 (pp. 18-19).

11. *Andreas Capellanus on Love,* ed. and trans. P. G. Walsh (London: Duckworth, 1982), pp. 310-11.

12. Walsh, pp. 318-21. Andreas thus articulates a view that women "exhaust male substance" both in the financial and physiological domains. Physiologically women's sexual demands "weaken" men's bodies by intercourse (Walsh pp. 304-5), and cf. Chaucer's *Parson's Tale,* X.147, and D. Jacquart and C. Thomasset, *Sexuality and Medicine in the Middle Ages,* trans. M. Adamson (Cambridge: Polity Press, 1988), p. 56.

13. Walsh, pp. 316-19.

14. "Unde et alio nomine liberalitas largitas nominatur," St. Thomas Aquinas, *Summa theologiae,* IIa IIae q. 117 on Liberality, in *Summa theologiae,* gen. ed. Thomas Gilby, O.P., 60 vols., vol. 41, *Virtues of Justice in the Human Community,* ed. and trans. T. C. O'Brien (London: Blackfriars, in conjunction with Eyre and Spottiswoode; and New York: McGraw-Hill, 1972), pp. 224-5. See also Chaucer, *Parson's Tale,* X.464, where among signs of *gentillesse* listed by the Parson is "to be liberal, that is to seyn, large."

15. "Vous devez mettre grant peine [. . .] de mettre a proufit les biens et la chevance que vos mariz, par leur labour [. . .] ameinent ou pourchacent. Et est l'office de l'omme d'acquerre et faire venir ens les provisions; et la femme les doit ordonner et dispenser par bonne discrecion [. . .] sans trop grant escharceté, et aussi bien se garder de fole largece [. . .]. Et doit bien aviser en toutes choses que gast n'en puist estre fait, ne s'en attendre du tout a la meisgnee; ains elle meismes doit etre dessus et s'en prendre souvent garde, et de ses choses vouloir avoir le compte" [You ought to devote very great care (. . .) to using to the best advantage all the goods and provisions that your husbands by their labor (. . .) obtain for the home. It is the duty of the man to acquire all the necessary provisions (. . .). Likewise the woman ought to manage and allocate them with good discretion (. . .) without too much parsimoniousness, and equally she ought to guard against foolish generosity (. . .). She should understand that nothing must be wasted, and she should expect all her household to be frugal. She herself must be in overall charge and always watchful]; *Le Livre des trois vertus,* ed. Charity Cannon Willard and Eric Hicks (Paris: Champion, 1989), III.1, p. 173, and *The Treasure of the City of Ladies,* trans. Sarah Lawson (Harmondsworth: Penguin, 1985), p. 146. For further discussion of this topos, see Blamires, *Case for Women,* pp. 91-3.

16. In *The Shipman's Tale,* the merchant "heeld a worthy hous, / For which he hadde alday so greet repair / For his largesse" (VII.20-22); and "Free was daun John, and manly [so *Riverside,* though "namely" in the earlier Robinson edition] of dispence" (VII.43).

17. "Dear son (. . .) generosity [*largesce*] is the mistress and queen that gives lustre to every virtue," *Cligés* 188-90, ed. Alexandre Micha (Paris: Champion, 1978); and *Chretien de Troyes, Arthurian Romances,* trans. D. D. R. Owen (London: Dent, 1987), p. 95; Alan of Lille's Natura sees *largitas* as the means whereby the human mind becomes "a palace of virtues" and whereby people "bind themselves together" in love; *The Plaint of Nature* XVIII, trans. James J. Sheridan (Toronto: Pontifical Institute of Mediaeval Studies, 1980), p. 213. Andreas writes that "omnis sine largitate virtus nulla putatur" [every virtue without generosity is regarded as nothing] (Walsh, pp. 304-5).

18. "Largitas maxime claros facit," Boethius *De consolatione philosophiae,* II. pr. 5 ("largesse maketh folk cleer of renoun" in Chaucer's *Boece,* II. pr. 5, 10). See also *Cligés* (197), "Par soi fet prodome largesce" [Liberality on its own makes a worthy man]. Sir Gawain describes *larges* as one of the attributes "þat longez to kny3tes," *Sir Gawain and the Green Knight,* line 2381, ed. J. R. R. Tolkien and E. V. Gordon, 2nd ed. by Norman Davis (Oxford: Clarendon Press, 1967).

19. Part of a protest by "Glad Pouert" against Fortune in John Lydgate, *The Fall of Princes,* III.372-5,

ed. Henry Bergen (pt. ii), Early English Text Society. Extra Series 122 (London: Oxford University Press, 1924).

20. Boccaccio's discussion of *liberalità* in his two versions of this narrative (the *Filocolo* IV.4 and *Decameron* X.5) is expertly reviewed in N. S. Thompson, *Chaucer, Boccaccio, and the Debate of Love* (Oxford: Clarendon Press, 1996), pp. 251-7.

21. "Li amant / Doignent du lor plus largement / Que cil vilain"; Guillaume de Lorris and Jean de Meun, *Le Roman de la Rose,* ed. Daniel Poirion (Paris: Garnier-Flammarion, 1974), l. 2214; all further quotations are from this edition. Cf. "Resoun wole that a lover be / In his yiftes more large and fre / Than cherles that can not of lovyng"; in the Chaucerian *Romaunt of the Rose,* ll. 2331-3.

22. *Confessio,* V.4769-70, in *The English Works of John Gower,* ed. G. C. Macaulay, Early English Text Society, Extra Series 81-2 (London: Oxford University Press, 1900-1).

23. Christine says to Droitture that she has seen "de femmes moult hommourables en discrete largesce de ce que elles povoyent" and knows women joyful over money "bien employé, que nul aver ne pourroit avoir de tirer a soy et mettre en coffre," in *Le Livre de la cité des dames,* ed. Maureen Curnow, Ph.D dissertation, Vanderbilt University (1975), Xerox University Microfilms (Ann Arbor), II.66.2, pp. 963-4; see also *The Book of the City of Ladies,* trans. Earl Jeffrey Richards (London: Pan Books, 1983), p. 210; and Droitture responds, "de inffinies largesces, courtoysies et liberalités de femmes te pourroye dire," II.67.2 (Curnow p. 965, trans. Richards p. 211).

24. So in the *Livre des trois vertus* Christine suggests that some wives "si ne pourroient ycelles par effect, quelque bon vouloir que elles eussent, user de celle vertu de largesce" [cannot practice this virtue of generosity, even though they may have good will], ed. Willard and Hicks I.21, p. 81, trans. Lawson I.20, p. 80.

25. "On les reppute avaires [. . .] je te promet qu'il est assez de femmes [. . .] que, se elles aveyent de quoy, ne seoyent pas escharces ne averes en honneurs faire et donner largement . . . On les tient communement si a destroit d'argent que ce pou que elles en pueent avoir le gardent [. . .]." They have to complain about the wastefulness of husbands who are "larges gasteurs de biens," *Cité,* II.66.1 (ed. Curnow pp. 962-3, trans. Richards p. 209).

26. Andrée K. Blumstein, *Misogyny and Idealization in the Courtly Romance* (Bonn: Bouvier, 1977), p. 7.

27. See remarks in *De mulieribus claris,* ed. Vittoria Zaccaria, in *Tutte le opere,* vol. X (Verona: Mondadori, 1970), pp. 274-8 and 314-19; *Concerning Famous Women,* trans. Guido A. Guarino (New Brunswick, N.J.: Rutgers University Press, 1963), pp. 150-1 and 173-5.

28. "Sy n'est mie tel chose avarice ne escharceté, ains est signe de tres grant prudence," *Cité,* II.66.1 (ed. Curnow pp. 962-3, trans. Richards p. 209).

29. "We alle desiren . . . To han housbondes hardy, wise, and free, / And secree, and no nygard, ne no fool, / Ne hym that is agast of every tool, / Ne noon avauntour," says Pertelote in the *Nun's Priest's Tale* (VII.2913-17); and "yet me greveth moost his nygardye, / And wel ye woot that wommen naturelly / . . . wolde that hir housbondes sholde be / Hardy, wise, and riche, and therto free, / And buxom unto his wyf, and fresshe abedde," says the wife in *The Shipman's Tale* (VII.172-7).

30. Boccaccio discusses the relationship between Zenobia's munificence and her caution as servatrix in *De mulieribus claris,* ed. Zaccaria, pp. 410-12; trans. Guarino, p. 228. In *The Monk's Tale* Chaucer abbreviates into one descriptive phrase, "large with mesure" (VII.2299).

31. Gower's Amans labors to articulate the complicated generosity that the ideal lady discreetly shows toward others: "Sche takth and yifth in such degre, / That as be weie of friendlihiede / Sche can so kepe hir wommanhiede / That every man spekth of hir wel," *Confessio Amantis,* V.4753-7.

32. Pseudo-Dionysius, *The Divine Names,* in *The Complete Works,* trans. Colm Luibheid (London: 1987), pp. 71-2.

33. Cicero, *De Officiis,* I.16, ed. and trans. Walter Miller (London: Heinemann; and New York: Macmillan, 1913), pp. 52-6.

34. Gower, *Confessio,* V.7644-48.

35. In a discussion of Mercy, *The Book of Vices and Virtues* notes the "grete largenesse" of God who gives generously to all "after þat þei ben, as seynt Iame seiþ, & makeþ his sonne schyne vpon þe goode and vpon þe schrewen, as he seiþ in the gospel." Since God is so "large" to us, giving us "alle þe goodes þat we haue, we schulde be large and curteis eche of vs to oþer," as urged in the Gospel: "Beþ merciable, as ȝoure fadre is merciable"; ed. W. Nelson Francis, Early English Text Society, Ordinary Series 217 (London: Oxford University Press, 1942), p. 193. Under "De cupiditate" in *Jacob's Well* there is a discussion of *nygardschippe* that cites Tobit 4.7 ("Ex substantia tua fac eleemosynam, et noli avertere faciem tuam

ab ullo paupere"), and urges "ȝif þou haue myche, ȝyue þou plentyvously; ȝyf þou haue lytel, gladly ȝeue þou part therof to þe poore": see also ch. 50, "De paupertate spiritus, & de largitate," which cites Christ as exemplar of generosity, his arms symbolically open on the cross; ed. Arthur Brandeis, Early English Text Society, Ordinary Series 115 (London: Kegan Paul, Trench, Trübner, 1900), pp. 121-2, and pp. 307-11.

36. "For þe gentyl Cheuentayn is no chyche, [. . . He] laueȝ his gyfteȝ as water of dyche, / Oþer goteȝ of golf þat neuer charde. / Hys fraunchyse is large"; *Pearl* (ll. 605-9), ed. E. V. Gordon (Oxford: Clarendon Press, 1953).

37. See Essay XIII, "Of Goodnesse, and Goodnesse of Nature," in Sir Francis Bacon, *The Essayes or Counsels,* ed. Michael Kiernan (Oxford: Clarendon, 1985), p. 39: "*Goodnesse* answers to the *Theologicall Vertue Charitie,* and admits no Excesse, but Errour. The desire of Power in Excesse, caused the Angels to fall; The desire of Knowledge in Excesse, caused Man to fall; But in *Charity,* there is no Excesse; Neither can Angell, or Man, come in danger by it."

38. Trans. Frances Horgan, *The Romance of the Rose* (Oxford: Oxford University Press, 1994), p. 18 [Et Diex li fesoit foisonner / Ses biens, si qu'ele ne savoit / Tant donner cum el plus avoit; ed. Poirion, ll. 1136-8].

39. The point is elaborated in Chaucer's *Tale of Melibee,* which urges that riches are to be used "in swich a manere that men holde yow nat to scars, ne to sparynge, ne to fool-large—that is to seyen, over-large a spendere. / For right as men blamen an avaricious man by cause of his scarsetee and chyncherie, / in the same wise is he to blame that spendeth over-largely" (VII.1596-1600). This exposition of the use of riches derives from a brief hint in chapters 43 and 45 of Albertano's treatise, and takes up his invitation to draw on a chapter, "De acquirendis et conservandis opibus," in his *De amore et dilectione dei et proximi et aliarum rerum et de forma vitae.* See *Albertani Brixiensis Liber consolationis et consilii,* ed. Thor Sundby, Chaucer Society, 2nd ser. Viii (London: Trubner, 1873); and *Sources and Analogues of Chaucer's* Canterbury Tales, ed. W. F. Bryan and Germaine Dempster (Chicago: University of Chicago Press, 1941), p. 563.

40. *Vices and Virtues,* p. 146; see also the treatise's further discussion of "largenesse" on pp. 193 and 212-16.

41. Aquinas invokes Ambrose on the point that *superabundantia* is bestowed upon some so that they can gain the merit of *bona dispensatio* [good stewardship] whereby the *liberalis* spends on others more than self; *Summa theologiae* 2a 2ae q. 117, art. 1, on "whether liberality is a virtue." For similar statements, see Chaucer, *Boece,* II. pr. 5; *Dives and Pauper,* VII.12, ed. Priscilla Barnum, I, pt. 2, Early English Text Society, Ordinary Series 280 (Oxford: Oxford University Press, 1980), p. 160. For a survey of the doctrine of wealth as stewardship, see Miri Rubin, *Charity and Community in Medieval Cambridge* (Cambridge: Cambridge University Press, 1987), ch. 3, "The Idea of Charity Between the Twelfth and Fifteenth Centuries," pp. 54-98.

42. Poirion, ll. 7405-14. Jealousy is berated for greediness: "It is foolish to hoard such a thing, for it is the candle in the lantern, and if you gave its light to a thousand people, you would not find its flame smaller" (trans. Horgan, pp. 113-14). A moderately wide dissemination of the figure is attested in Bartlett J. and Helen W. Whiting, *Proverbs, Sentences, and Proverbial Phrases from English Writings Mainly Before 1500* (Cambridge, Mass.: Harvard University Press, 1968), C24, "One Candle can light many." The antecedent in Ovid is: "Sufficit et damni pars caret illa metu. / Quis vetet adposito lumen de lumine sumi? / Quisve cavo vastas in mare servet aquas?" [That part endures, and has no fear of loss. What forbids to take light from a light that is set before you? or who would guard vast waters upon the cavernous deep?]; *Ars amatoria,* III.88ff, in *Ovid II: The Art of Love, and Other Poems,* ed. and trans. J. H. Mozley, 2nd ed. revised by G. P. Goold (Cambridge, Mass.: Harvard University Press; and London: Heinemann, 1979), pp. 124-5. For an extended discussion of the Ovidian link, see Michael Calabrese, *Chaucer's Ovidian Arts of Love* (Gainesville: University Press of Florida, 1994), pp. 81-111.

43. For manipulation of ethical commonplaces elsewhere in Chaucer, see e.g., *The Miller's Tale,* I.3530.

44. This aspect of Blanche's representation is well elicited by Priscilla Martin, *Chaucer's Women: Nuns, Wives and Amazons* (Basingstoke: Macmillan, 1990), p. 25.

45. Lee Patterson, "'For the Wyves love of Bathe': Feminine Rhetoric and Poetic Resolution in the *Roman de la Rose* and the *Canterbury Tales,*" *Speculum* 58 (1983): 656-94 (p. 680); Martin, *Chaucer's Women,* pp. 70, 96. However, an alternative view links the Wife's sexual generosity with the philosophy of "plenitude" promoted by the school of Chartres; Paul G. Ruggiers, *The Art of the Canterbury Tales* (Madison: University of Wisconsin Press, 1965), pp. 198-200.

46. *The Decameron,* trans. G. H. McWilliam (Harmondsworth: Penguin, 1972), pp. 499-500 [Le done . . . le quali molto meglio che gli uomini potrebbero a molti sodisfare; . . . domando io voi, io che doveva fare o debbo di quel che gli avanza? Debbolo io gittare ai cani? Non è egli molto meglio servirne un gentile uomo che piú che sé m'ama, che lasciarlo perdere o guastare?], *Decameron* VI.7, ed. Cesare Segre (Milan: Mursia, 1984), pp. 398-9.

47. Keeping food like this is cited under *nygardschippe,* a subcategory of *Cupiditas,* in *Jacob's Well,* p. 121. Christine de Pizan urges that prudential vigilance in the household entails care that no food goes bad (so nothing is wasted that could have helped the poor), *Livre des trois vertus,* ed. Willard and Hicks, III.1, p. 176, trans. Lawson, p. 148.

48. "For al that þe ryche man hat pasynge hys nedful lyuynge aftir þe stat of his dispensacion it is þe pore mannys;" *Dives and Pauper* VII.12, ed. Barnum, p. 160.

49. The woman who gives her body to someone other than her husband therefore commits "theft"; see *Parson's Tale,* X.876-77. Cicero points out that giving as a result of robbing another is not liberality (*De Officiis,* I.14, pp. 47-9).

50. Aristotle, *Ethics,* IV.i, trans. Thomson, p. 110.

51. *Plaint of Nature,* XVIII; trans. J. J. Sheridan, p. 214. The fourteenth-century English treatise *Speculum Christiani* explains that "wast ouerspens is called largys and fredam of hert;" see Thomas Bestul, *Satire and Allegory in* Wynnere and Wastoure (Lincoln: University of Nebraska Press, 1974), p. 21, citing *Speculum Christiani,* ed. Gustaf Holmstedt, Early English Text Society, Ordinary Series 182 (London: Oxford University Press, 1933), p. 232. Bestul also cites Isidore, *Sententiae* 2.35 1-3, PL 83.636-7.

52. *Ethics,* IV.1, trans. Thomson p. 146; Aquinas, *Summa theologiae* IIa IIae 119.3, Responsio, trans. O'Brien, pp. 273-5.

53. "[. . .]the bountiful do not hold back but let go" [quod largum est, non est retentivum sed est emissivum], and "when someone lets something go [emittit] he liberates it [liberat] from his care and control"; *Summa theologiae* IIa IIae 117.2, Responsio, trans. O'Brien, p. 225. See also a passage from Wace, *Brut* (ll. 3685-9), cited by David Burnley in *Courtliness and Literature* (Harlow, Essex: Addison Wesley Longman, 1998), p. 71: "Bledudo was more generous than his father" [plus larges fu de duner] and "did not know how to refuse or retain anything of his own" [Nule rien ne saveit veer / Ne a suen ués rien retenir].

54. [. . . largece ne s'estant mie tant seulement en dons, come dit un sage, mais aussi en reconfort de parole], *Livre des trois vertus,* ed. Willard and Hicks, I.20, p. 78, trans. Lawson, I.19, p. 78. Christine elsewhere reports her father's view that learning was a treasure that one could keep giving away, without losing any; *Le Livre de la Mutacion de Fortune,* I.3, trans. Kevin Brownlee in *The Selected Writings of Christine de Pizan,* ed. Renate Blumenfeld-Kosinski and Kevin Brownlee (New York: W. W. Norton, 1997), p. 91. I am grateful to Renate Blumenfeld-Kosinski for bringing this detail to my attention.

55. Alexander writes to Dindimus, King of the Brahmans, that he understands that Dindimus frowns on his own laws and lifestyle, and that the Brahmans' *manars* differ profoundly from those of other people: "Bott deyned it ȝour doctryne bedene vs to write, / ȝoure customes & ȝoure conscience & of ȝour clene thewis, / We miȝt sum connynge, per ca, chach of ȝoure wordis, / And ȝour lare of a leke suld neuire þe les worth. / Slike similitude of science is sett, as of kynde, / As of a blesand brand or of a briȝt candill. / For many liȝtis of a liȝt is liȝtid othirequile, / And ȝit the liȝt at þam liȝtis is liȝtid as before," *The Wars of Alexander,* ll. 4354-61, ed. Hoyt N. Duggan and Thorlac Turville-Petre, Early English Text Society, Special Series 10 (Oxford: Oxford University Press, 1989). This and most other Middle English translations closely follow at this juncture the Latin of the *Historia de preliis,* a late-twelfth-century interpolated version of a narrative going back to Greek romance.

56. So Sheila Delany, "Strategies of Silence in the Wife of Bath's Recital," *Exemplaria* 2 (1990): 49-69 (p. 51); and Calabrese, *Chaucer's Ovidian Arts of Love,* p. 108.

57. "[. . .] hir thoughte that she dyde, / That she so longe sholde a conseil hyde" (III.965-6).

58. Midas appears in Gower's section *de avaricia,* in the *Confessio Amantis* beginning at V.141. Keats (Sonnet 17) bids poets be "Misers of sound and syllable, no less / Than Midas of his coinage." It has been customary to derive negative readings of the Wife of Bath from the interpolated episode of Midas's wife, as does R. L. Hoffman, *Ovid and the Canterbury Tales* (Philadelphia: University of Pennsylvania Press, 1966), pp. 145-9, though more ambiguous possibilities are glimpsed in Patterson, "'For the Wyves love of Bathe'," pp. 657-8.

59. Women's divulgence of secrets in the *Tale* has not I think been seen in this light before, though it has been held by Susan Signe Morrison to herald "a community of power"; "Don't Ask, Don't Tell:

The Wife of Bath and Vernacular Translations," *Exemplaria* 8 (1996): 97-123 (p. 117); and see Karma Lochrie's important analysis of "gossip" in the Wife of Bath's performance, in *Covert Operations: The Medieval Uses of Secrecy* (Philadelphia: University of Pennsylvania Press, 1999), pp. 56-61.

60. The connection was consolidated through commentary on the Beatitudes, which from Augustine onward had forged links between the "spirits" listed in Isaiah 11.2-3 and the Beatitudes in the Sermon on the Mount (Matt. 5.3-10). *Beati misericordes* (Matt. 5.7) was conventionally linked with *spiritus consilii* (Isa. 11.2).

61. *Vices & Virtues,* pp. 188-93; and see p. 145 for *conseil* as an aspect of *charite.* In *Jacob's Well,* ch. 50, "De paupertate spiritus, & de largitate, & elemosina, & misericordia, & dono consilii," *largenesse* is said to embrace the gift of "counseyl," which itself prompts and inspires one how best to be generous, p. 311.

62. Paralleling the generous motives already discussed is Alisoun's impulsive gift of all her property to her young fifth husband (III.630-1); but a contradictory mercantile thread is exemplified in her prior eagerness to obtain her elderly husbands' land and treasure, claiming to have endured their desire because "al is for to selle" as a "raunson" (ll. 411, 414)—even the bran that succeeds her flour with age (l. 478). Such brash engagement in marketability needs to be read, of course, in the context of a society acutely attuned to dowry negotiation.

63. "'Vanysshed Was This Daunce, He Nyste Where': Alisoun's Absence in the *Wife of Bath's Prologue and Tale,*" *English Literary History* 59 (1992): 1-21 (p. 9) repr. in *Chaucer: The Canterbury Tales,* Longman Critical Reader, ed. Steve Ellis (Harlow: Addison Wesley Longman, 1998), pp. 100-120 (p. 108).

64. Perception is an important concept in the *Tale*: fire remains fire unseen in a dark room (III.1139-43); poverty is a "spectacle" enabling one to see friends (ll. 1203-4); and, after the casting up of the curtain, the "knyght saugh verraily," ll. 1249-50.

65. "Ja cele rien ne vudra mes / Quë il nen ait a sun talent; / Doinst e despende largement, / Ele li troverat asez" (ll. 136-9), and "Ja ne savrez cel liu penser. . . . Que jeo ne vus seie en present / A fere tut vostre talent" (l. 163), *Lais,* ed. A Ewert (Oxford: Blackwell, 1978); *The Lais of Marie de France,* trans. Glyn Burgess (Harmondsworth: Penguin, 1986), pp. 74-5.

66. "When Echo Speaks: Marie de France and the Poetics of Remembrance," in *Minding the Body:* *Women and Literature in the Middle Ages, 800-1500,* ed. Monica Brzezinski Potkay and Regula Meyer Evitt (New York: Twayne, 1997), pp. 77-101 (pp. 95-6). Although it would be a simplification to attribute a systematic female gendering of liberality to the *lais,* the evidence of *Lanval* is supplemented by conspicuous acts of generosity by women in *Le Fresne* and *Eliduc.*

67. "Sorties: Out and Out: Attacks/Ways Out/Forays," in *The Feminist Reader,* 2nd ed., ed. Catherine Belsey and Jane Moore (Basingstoke: Macmillan, 1997), pp. 91-116 (pp. 95-7).

68. Belsey and Moore, p. 11.

69. Jane Anger, *Her Protection for Women* (London: 1589), in *The Early Modern Englishwoman,* pt. 1. vol. 4, *Defences of Women,* introduced O'Malley, fol. Cv.

Elaine Treharne (essay date 2002)

SOURCE: Treharne, Elaine. "The Stereotype Confirmed? Chaucer's Wife of Bath." In *Writing Gender and Genre in Medieval Literature: Approaches to Old and Middle English Texts,* edited by Elaine Treharne, pp. 93-115. Cambridge: D. S. Brewer, 2002.

[*In the following essay, Treharne contends that in* The Wife of Bath's Prologue, *Chaucer reinforces many misconceptions of women's ability to manipulate and claim language.*]

'I write woman: woman must write woman. And man, man'[1]

INTRODUCTION: METHODS OF ANALYSIS

This essay will focus on one of the most memorable English literary characters: Chaucer's Wife of Bath. I shall be taking a primarily sociolinguistic approach in interpreting her: drawing out interactions between language and gender, language and power that are as relevant now as they always have been in male-female relations, and in engendering and maintaining the powerful ideologies that drive both the social construction of identity and academic discourses of character and morality.

The complexity of interpreting Chaucer's *Canterbury Tales* arguably forms a major impetus for continuing to study the poet and his most famous work. As well as bringing to life his cast of pilgrims on their journey to Canterbury, Chaucer provides us with a multiplicity of generically and stylistically varied tales to entertain and engage us. The polyphony of the author, narrator, tale-tellers, and characters within the tales leads to a layered narrative in which the least distinguishable voice is that of the author. When readers seek to determine what the meanings of the text might be, both within its contemporary context, and to the modern reader, this obscurity of the author inevitably problematises any act of interpretation.

So it is that there is little that can be definitive in reading and interpreting Chaucer. This, naturally, is ideal fodder for critics, and among Chaucer's many controversial characters, one of the most ultimately indefinable is the Wife of Bath.

CRITICAL RESPONSE TO THE WIFE OF BATH

Critical response to the Wife of Bath has been as diverse as it has been emotive. Early commentators such as William Blake found her to be 'a scourge and a blight'. He went on to comment that he 'shall say no more of her, nor expose what Chaucer has left hidden; let the young reader study what he has said of her: it is useful as a scare-crow. There are of such characters born too many for the peace of the world.'[2] Of the Wife's *Prologue* itself, Dryden comments that: 'I translated *Chaucer* first [before Boccaccio], and among the rest pitch'd on *The Wife of Bath's Tale*; not daring, as I have said, to adventure on her *Prologue*; because 'tis too licentious.'[3]

From these early, slightly prudish comments, twentieth-century criticism emerged to illustrate a continuing controversy in scholarly response, particularly to the Wife of Bath as a character. Kittredge's famous article on 'Chaucer's Discussion of Marriage' reveals (under the guise of the Clerk's anticipated response) that 'The woman was an heresiarch, or at best a schismatic. She set up, and aimed to establish, a new and dangerous sect, whose principle was that the wife should rule the husband . . . She had garnished her sermon with scraps of Holy Writ and rags and tatters of erudition, caught up, we may infer, from her last husband.'[4]

More recently, Tony Slade reaches a similarly critical judgement, claiming that 'The Wife's character has already been exposed in some detail in her *Prologue,* which rambles around the theme of "sovereynetee" in marriage; her tone is coarse and garrulous, and there is little evidence of that sort of delicate poetic beauty which some critics have professed to find in the *Tale* itself.'[5]

Notably, these unfavourable readings are by male critics. One of the most significant developments in the interpretation of the Wife of Bath has come from those women (and some male) critics seeking to appropriate the Wife for feminist scholarship in the last three decades. These responses have extended across the full range of critical approaches, incorporating the psycho-

analytic, the New Historicist or Cultural Materialist, to deconstructive affective stylistic and reader-response theory.[6] Such methodologies have yielded readings of the Wife that see her as a shrewd businesswoman[7] in an emergent bourgeoisie, a 'master of parody'[8] providing a corrective to the 'truths' of conventional authorities; or a 'proto-feminist',[9] an early independently minded woman seeking to reject oppressive patriarchy.

In discussing the manner in which the Wife engages with the writings of the anti-feminists cited throughout her *Prologue,* and takes issue with the ways in which women in contemporary medieval society are portrayed, Jill Mann comments that:

> The double structure of the Wife's speech thus has a meaning of far wider import than its role in the Wife's individual experience. And yet it plays a crucial role in creating our sense of the Wife as a living individual. For what it demonstrates is her *interaction* with the stereotypes of her sex, and it is in this interaction that we feel the three-dimensionality of her existence. That is, she does not live in the insulated laboratory world of literature, where she is no more than a literary object, unconscious of the interpretations foisted upon her; she is conceived as a woman who lives in the real world, in full awareness of the anti-feminist literature that purports to describe and criticise her behaviour, and she has an attitude to *it* just as it has an attitude to her.[10]

Further, citing Patterson's phrase, Mann comments that 'Chaucer could not invent a new "female language", and sensibly did not try to do so . . . but . . . the Wife's *Prologue* is designed precisely to make the reader conscious of the confining nature of "the prison house of masculine language".'[11]

While there is a good deal of truth in these statements, I would suggest that Chaucer does nonetheless attempt to 'invent a new female language' inasmuch as he provides a voice for the Wife that deliberately attempts to emulate aspects of a woman's language, albeit from an entirely stereotypically conceived basis. Moreover, the textual dissemination of the authorities against which she speaks was such that the access she has had to them can only have come through an interpretative mediator—her fifth husband Jankyn with his impromptu evenings spent vernacularising the Latin *auctoritas* contained within the anti-feminist writings. Not only, then, does the Wife internalise the interpreted words of the Church Fathers, but she re-interprets them, uttering them in a language—English—that was itself marginalised, Other: in so doing, she further marginalises herself even as she seeks to situate herself within the realm of the authoritative.

Problematising the issue of verbal and social intercourse, the Wife is interpreted by Barrie Ruth Straus from a psychoanalytic perspective as 'participating in a homosexual exchange with the Pardoner' in the course of her *Prologue,* following the Pardoner's interruption. 'Under the guise of sharing with men the secret of the feigned appetite as one of women's ways of handling men, the Wife articulates the homoerotic nature of phallocentric sexuality: that it is masculine desire seeking only itself. When she makes the Pardoner her accomplice in betraying her husbands' secrets, she in effect puts the Pardoner in bed with her and her husbands.'[12]

While this reading is puzzling, Straus's overall evaluation of the Wife is one that foregrounds the opacity of the text: that 'The Wife of Bath is the uncontrollable voice that eludes interpretative truth. The ultimate secret she reveals is that all who think they can control, penetrate, and master such texts as she represents are deluded. All the critics can do is create interpretations that double their own desire.'[13] It surely is the case that the crucial aspect of Chaucer's work is the demands made on the readers' own interpretation and moral response. As Chauncey Wood succinctly puts it: 'it is not the text that produces readings but the readings that produce the text.'[14] But here, certainly in Straus's argument, and elsewhere in other scholarly comments, the critic appears to perceive the Wife as the shaper of her own *Prologue* and *Tale,* as a 'voice' that effectively propagandises a new 'truth'. Lynne Dickson, for example, argues that:

> Despite textual signals that Alison tries to control and disempower the antifeminist topos, it ultimately overwhelms her. The sheer length of her *Prologue* and the fact that she loses her train of thought six times support the reading that Alison experiences considerable discomfort with her speaking situation. One of the *Prologue*'s strategies, then, seems to be to expose the tyranny of masculine discourse: it oppresses even a figure like Alison. This revelation is complemented by the text's method of hailing its reader as more complicated and open than the oppressively monolithic audience that Alison cannot escape.[15]

And it is this that strikes me as most problematic: to read the Wife as if she were anything other than a fiction masterfully created by Chaucer is to fall into the trap of 'truth' that he sets through his vivid, realistic depictions.

There is no doubt that Chaucer ventriloquises his female fiction effectively. The Wife's is a voice that resonates loudly in Middle English literature, and that assists in making her stand out as one of the most memorable of all female literary characters. It is precisely this multi-layered speech-act that permits for a sociolinguistic analysis employing theories of language and power, and language and gender to determine the possible nature of the characterisation of the Wife, and the potential acuity of and purpose in Chaucer's depiction.

FOLKLINGUISTIC STEREOTYPES OF WOMEN'S LANGUAGE

Sociolinguistics is the modern study of the ways in which language operates within society. It emerged, in part, from Saussure's analyses of language in the earlier part of the twentieth century, and the movement away from more historical modes of language analysis such as philology, dominant in the nineteenth century. Through sociolinguistic experiment, it has proven possible to determine, for example, the use by particular groups of speakers of variant forms of language. Where this usage correlates to a social, economical, or gendered group, relationships between language and power, language and class, and language and gender can be determined and analysed. The discipline, in principle, is not a judgemental one: no values are notionally placed on the results; rather, it collects and collates empirical data about variability within language and possible determining features.[16]

There is no question about Chaucer's own language awareness. In *The Reeve's Tale,* the two students, John and Aleyn, are of Northern origin. Their speech is peppered with Northernisms that are interpreted by the editors of *The Riverside Chaucer* as 'apparently the first case of this kind of joking imitation of a dialect recorded in English literature'.[17] Chaucer thus attempts, with relative success, the phonetic representation of variant forms of English within his text. Taking a wider linguistic perspective, Chaucer demonstrates himself to be very conscious of his role as a transmitter of the vernacular, at a time when its prestige as a vehicle for literary production had yet to be firmly established. In his lengthy Romance, *Troilus and Criseyde,* Chaucer's narrator comments:

> And for ther is so gret diversite
> In Englissh and in writyng of oure tonge,
> So prey I God that non myswrite the,
> Ne the mysmetre for defaute of tonge;
> And red wherso thow be, or elles songe,
> That thow be understonde, God I biseche![18]

Furthermore, Chaucer's awareness of literary form is not only evident from his manipulation of it within *The Canterbury Tales*' variety and versatility, but also from his comments through the voice of the Parson of the associations of alliterative verse in contemporary England:

> But trusteth wel, I am a Southren man;
> I kan nat geeste 'rum, ram, ruf', by letter,
> Ne, God woot, rym holde I but litel better;
> And therefore, if yow list—I wol nat glose—
> I wol yow telle a myrie tale in prose[19]

Chaucer's mockery of this poetic form in the mouth of the prose-telling, truth-telling Parson illustrates clearly the author's own linguistic acuity and observation.

The demands of ostensibly telling the truth by repeating the (fictional) words of the characters in his writing result in Chaucer's creation of a variety of realistic voices, each of which is suited in varying degrees to a particular pilgrim narrator. In the case of the majority of the pilgrims, the men, Chaucer's main concern may have been the representation of a register appropriate to each narrator; for example, in the choice of doctrinaire prose for the Parson; the courtly language and rhyme royal versification of the Knight in his philosophical romance; the classically-infused religious register of the Monk throughout his episodic tragedy; and the bawdy language and frequent colloquialisms uttered by the Miller in his complex fabliau. In the case of the three women who tell tales, however, the Wife of Bath, the Prioress, and the Second Nun, Chaucer has not only to find a register and style suitable to their respective status, but also an appropriate means of imitating the language usage of women.

It has long been the case that the perceived differences between men's use of language and women's have been thought worthy of judgemental comment, especially by male scholars and writers. These differences have until very recently been noted in order to indicate women's irritating habits, their deviancy or inadequacy in language usage in comparison to the norm—that is, men's language usage.[20] This 'inferior' use by women of language is, of course, part of the paradigm of the social and familial subjugation of women, for perceived inequality in language usage reflects and contributes to actual inequality in society. Such attitudes to women's speech—that women are not as adept at language usage, or that there are particular forms of language use more appropriate to women—persist, however, in phrases such as 'girls' talk', or 'women talk too much', or 'ladies shouldn't swear'.

The myths surrounding women's use of language are ancient in origin, and their constancy and ubiquity is testimony to the stability of a social order which has undoubtedly been, until relatively recently, patriarchal, institutionally controlled, and exclusive. Chaucer's linguistic awareness yields interesting results in terms of his use of then-current (and in many cases still current), folklinguistic or anecdotal accounts of women as speakers. His ventriloquism as the Wife of Bath, and indeed as the Prioress and Second Nun, offers ideal material for analysis using socio-linguistic theory, and leads to the conclusion that he was very much immersed in, and quite content to perpetuate, the stereotypes of women's language use prevalent in late medieval academic (and therefore male) culture. An evaluation of the female pilgrims becomes, consequently, not so much a matter of what they say, but of how they say it.

Although Chaucer himself has been regarded by some scholars as a proto-feminist writer, this seems akin to anachronistic wishful thinking. Better, it seems, if one wants to regard him as proto-anything, is the conception of Chaucer as a proto-sociolinguist, or more properly perhaps, proto-folklinguist. He is a writer whose fictional creations deliberately raise issues of the relationship between language and social structures, and who question implicitly the status quo in crucial cultural relationships such as language and gender.

Before I outline the major aspects of mythical language use by women incorporated by Chaucer into his depiction of the Wife of Bath, I should like to offer a word of caution to allay any suspicions that my focus on this methodology may have prompted. First, sociolinguistic analysis focuses mostly on *parole,* that is the actual *spoken* utterance, and here, I will be applying it to written language, and moreover, a fairly formal versified language. Even so, it is a relevant approach, since Chaucer the author through his pilgrim narrator is claiming to be repeating the actual spoken words of his subject, the Wife of Bath. Second, sociolinguistics often analyses language synchronically. However, as it assists in explaining relations between language users and society, it can most fruitfully be used diachronically in order to illustrate and elucidate power relations in society at any given point in social evolution.

Perhaps the primary linguistic determinants of women's language, and it should be noted that these are also folklinguistic,[21] are that women gossip, nag, verbally harass, give bad advice, cannot be trusted, and talk uncontrollably. This myth could be evinced by very considerable numbers of quotations from texts, both ancient and modern. The twelfth-century *Proverbs of Alfred,* numbers fifteen and sixteen,[22] for example, reveal that:

> Þus queþ Alvred:
> 'Ne wurþ þu never so wod
> Ne so wyn-drunke,
> Þat evere segge þine wife
> Alle þine wille.
> For if þu iseye þe bivore
> Þine ivo alle,
> And þu hi myd worde
> Iwreþþed hevedest,
> Ne scholde heo hit lete
> For þing lyvyinde,
> Þat heo ne scholde þe forþ upbreyde
> Of þine baleusyþes.
> Wymmon is word-wod,
> And haveþ tunge to swift;
> Þeyh heo wel wolde,
> Ne may heo hi nowiht welde.'
> . . . Þe mon þat let wymmon
> His mayster iwurþe,
> Ne schal he never beon ihurd
> His wordes loverd;
> Ac heo hine schal steorne
> Totrayen and toteone,
> And selde wurþ he blyþe and gled
> Þe mon þat is his wives qued.

Mony appel is bryht wiþute
And bitter wiþinne;
So is many wymmon
On hyre fader bure
Schene under schete,
And þeyh heo is schendful.

In these proverbs, erroneously ascribed to King Alfred, and surviving in a number of thirteenth-century manuscripts, oft-repeated criticisms of women's language usage are iterated. Women are 'word-wod' ('word-mad' or 'wild in speech') and cannot be trusted to hold their tongue; an infuriated wife's prolixity will inevitably result in her public reprimanding of the unfortunate husband in front of even his worst enemies; and women in general simply cannot control their verbosity, even if they try to. Such commonplace and stereotypical myths about women's language usage are entirely bound up, from the male perspective, with a woman's trustworthiness, her discretion, and her overall demeanour and appearance.

Such proverbial derogations of women's language, and the inevitable allying of 'shrewishness' with a more general female proclivity to unfortunate and unacceptable habits, are explicit in Chaucer. The Merchant, for example, tells his (clearly male) audience to: 'Suffre thy wyves tonge, as Catoun bit; / She shal comande, and thou shal suffren it';[23] and the host adds to *The Merchant's Tale,* that:

I have a wyf, though she povre be,
But of hir tonge a labbyng shrewe is she,
And yet she hath an heep of vices mo;[24]

Women's loquaciousness thus becomes symptomatic of their general urge to 'comande' with the consequence that the male recipient—usually the husband—must endure excessive torment as a result. This insidious stereotyping of women,[25] and wives in particular, is endemic in the writings of medieval male authors. Elements of this folklinguistic myth to which women have been subject are ancient, and develop in part from the most authoritative of sources, the Bible. In I Timothy 2.11-14, for instance, St Paul asserts: 'Let the woman learn in silence, with all subjection. But I suffer not a woman to teach, nor to usurp authority over the man; but to be in silence. For Adam was first formed; then Eve. And Adam was not seduced, but the woman, being seduced, was in the transgressions.' From such scripture and subsequent exegesis, therefore, emerges the ideal woman: a silent one.[26] 'It is possible to go even further and to suggest that when women are supposed to be quiet, a talkative woman is one who talks at all.'[27]

This is the easiest myth to evidence as replicated by Chaucer in his creation. The Wife has by far the longest *Prologue* in the *Tales,* and one where the narratorial subjectivity is more pronounced than elsewhere, other than the feminised *Pardoner's Prologue.* Moreover, confirming the stereotype of the verbose woman are the speeches within the speech by which the Wife recalls her own words to her husbands, condemning the successive husbands' anti-feminist commonplaces, while simultaneously confirming them. The myths of women's inability to maintain privacy, their tendency to gossip, and to speak of 'trivial' matters—such as love and relationships—are shown to be part of the operative mode of the Wife. When she discusses Jankyn, who went to board with her friend Alison, we learn that the Wife tells Alison everything:

She knew myn herte, and eek my privetee,
Bet that oure parrisshe preest, so moot I thee!
To hire biwreyed I my conseil al.
For hadde myn housbonde pissed on a wal,
Or doon a thing that sholde han cost his lyf,
To hire, and to another worthy wyf,
And to my nece, which that I loved weel,
I wolde han toold his conseil every deel.
And so I did ful often, God it woot,
That made his face often reed and hoot
For verray shame, and blamed himself for he
Had toold to me so greet a pryvetee.[28]

Here, the Wife takes obvious pride in recounting her indiscretions that occur 'ful often', not only to her best friend, but also to another woman, and to her niece. These intimate news reports include the revelation of secrets told to her by her husband, even those where disclosure would have cost him dearly. Her delight in these activities, no matter how positively they can be read,[29] serves to confirm the stereotype of the 'gossiping' woman, incapable of remaining discreet, incapable of earning trust. The Wife's pleasure and self-approval in these activities, the lack of censure she appears to receive, reinforces those proverbs and myths that warn men of the danger of telling women their secrets, and then subsequently blame the same men for the foolishness they show in trusting their wives. Such confirmation of the 'truths' about women (and, one might add here, too-trusting men) perpetuated by male authors like Chaucer actually weakens the Wife's position, and stereotypes her even as she tries to throw the anti-feminist stereotyping back at her husbands. And, while the length of the *Prologue* itself is the most obvious evidence of the woman's mythical inability to be brief, Chaucer invites us to look more closely at the Wife's language through the ample amount of evidence he provides for her in mimicking the voice of the late fourteenth-century widow. Her *Prologue,* in effect, becomes a handbook to observations on women's language, some five hundred years before a sustained thesis was advanced.

LANGUAGE AND GENDER

When Otto Jespersen wrote his famous book on language and its origins in 1922,[30] he ostensibly presented empirical evidence to validate his work. In his chapter entitled 'Woman' (with, significantly, as pointed out by various later twentieth-century linguists, no comparable chapter for 'Man'),[31] he signalled that women's language requires its own discussion and set of comments, because it is not the norm; rather, it is to be measured against the normative language usage of the white, middle-class male. Chaucer's lengthy characterisation of the Wife of Bath similarly marks her out as beyond the norm. While this positively questions social roles, it also highlights the manner in which the Wife is outside; in providing the Wife with an opportunity to talk about herself at a length and in a manner not afforded to any other pilgrim, Chaucer marks her out as 'unusual' or 'remarkable' (in a positive reading) and as 'deviant' (in a negative). As she is representative of the non-standard, it is almost inevitable that she can be read as being depicted derogatorily in comparison with the norm,[32] particularly within the fourteenth-century cultural and social contexts of male dominance and female subordination.

Jespersen and Chaucer have a good deal in common as proponents of folklinguistic stereotyping of women's language: Jespersen provides a list of the folklinguistic myths to which sociolinguists in the 1970s and 1980s felt compelled to reply, and not always with a rebuttal. Much of Jespersen's 'evidence' is based on anecdote rather than objective and empirical observation, but it is cited as (his) truth because of the permeation of long-held derogatory views about women's language usage. Similarly, Chaucer is able to manipulate stereotypical facets of women's language usage through his creation, and he, to a significant extent, pre-empts in a literary framework what Jespersen would go on to write within a linguistic structure some five hundred and more years later.

Jespersen's account of women's language provides a blueprint for the promulgation of folklinguistic stereotyping, iterating commonplaces about women's particular characteristics of language usage that owe more to the medieval proverb than they do to the objective collation of data. Among the key features he notes are the divergences between the 'lower and higher registers of language':

> The difference between the two 'languages' is one of degree only: they are two strata of the same language, one higher, more solemn, stiff and archaic, and another lower, more natural and familiar, and this easy, or perhaps we should say slipshod, style is the only one recognized for ordinary women.[33]

He goes on to discuss the use of hyperbolic lexis and intonation in women's speech:

> Another tendency noticed in the language of . . . women is pretty widely spread among French and English women, namely, the excessive use of intensive words and the exaggeration of stress and tone-accent to mark emphasis.[34]

This he expands upon with the remarkable series of examples and explanations:

> the fondness of women for hyperbole will very often lead the fashion with regard to adverbs of intensity, and these are very often used with disregard of their proper meaning . . . There is another intensive which has something of the eternally feminine about it, namely *so* . . . The explanation of this characteristic feminine usage is, I think, that women much more often than men break off without finishing their sentences, because they start talking without having thought out what they are going to say.[35]

This hyperbole of intensifiers helps assist, perhaps, in making more emphatic and startling the woman's subject of discourse, because, according to Jespersen, women are incapable of what might be loosely termed 'straight-talking'; hence, their preference for euphemism:

> But when . . . we come to . . . vocabulary and style, we shall find a much greater number of differences . . . There is certainly no doubt, however, that women in all countries are shy of mentioning certain parts of the human body and certain natural functions by the direct and often rude denominations which men, and especially young men, prefer when among themselves. Women will therefore invent innocent and euphemistic words and paraphrases, which sometimes may in the long run come to be looked upon as the plain or blunt names, and therefore in their turn have to be avoided and replaced by more decent words.[36]

Considering that women are so innovative in language, having to 'invent innocent . . . words and phrases', it comes as something of a surprise to discover that:

> the vocabulary of a woman as a rule is much less extensive than that of a man . . . Woman as a rule follows the main road of language, where man is often inclined to turn aside into a narrow footpath or even to strike out a new path for himself . . . Those who want to learn a foreign language will therefore always do well at the first stage to read many ladies' novels, because there they will continually meet with just those everyday words and combinations which the foreigner is above all in need of, what may be termed the indispensable small-change of a language.[37]

The fact that women are adept at the 'small change' of language, that they talk before they have thought through what they are going to say, and that they pepper their speech with intensifiers and phatic words, is summarised by Jespersen's general explanation:

> The volubility of women has been the subject of innumerable jests: it has given rise to popular proverbs in many countries . . . The superior readiness of speech of women is a concomitant of the fact that their vocabulary is smaller and more central than that of men. But this again is connected with another indubitable fact, that women do not reach the same extreme points as men, but are nearer the average in most

respects . . . Genius is more common among men by virtue of the same general tendency by which idiocy is more common among men. The two facts are but two aspects of a larger zoological fact—the greater variability of the male.[38]

And the causes for the major linguistic distinctions evinced between the sexes are:

mainly dependent on the division of labour enjoined in primitive tribes and to a great extent also among more civilized peoples. For thousands of years the work that especially fell to men was such as demanded an intense display of energy for a comparatively short period, mainly in war and in hunting. Here, however, there was not much occasion to talk, nay, in many circumstances talk might even be fraught with danger. And when that rough work was over, the man would either sleep or idle his time away, inert and torpid, more or less in silence. Woman on the other hand, had a number of domestic occupations which did not claim such an enormous output of spasmodic energy. To her was at first left not only agriculture, and a great deal of other work which in more peaceful times was taken over by men; but also much that has been till quite recently her almost exclusive concern—the care of children, cooking, brewing, baking, sewing, washing, etc.—things which for the most part demanded no deep thought, which were performed in company and could well be accompanied with a lively chatter.[39]

While it is easy enough to dismiss Jespersen out of hand for his subjective descriptions of women's language usage and domestic habits particularly in the light of more recent sociolinguistic theory, it is the case that his analyses, anecdotal as they may be, reflect commonly held beliefs about the way women use language—not only in 1922 when his book was published, but also in the present day. It is precisely because these folklinguistic myths about women's language have a millennia-old history, and are ubiquitous, that it is possible to ascertain Chaucer's own use of them in the depiction of, arguably, his greatest literary fiction, the Wife of Bath.

MAN WRITES WOMAN

If repetition, euphemism, hyperbole, unfinished sentences (and illogicality), limited vocabulary, volubility, and a contextual focus on domestic issues are characteristic of the deviant speech of women, and any indication of the limited nature of one's language, then certainly Alison is made a chief exemplar.[40] Throughout the ***Prologue,*** she is ventriloquised using hyperbole and phatic fillers: empty phrases such as 'by my fey' (line 203) and 'God woot' (used six times in a variety of combinations).[41] Such phrases are generally not only phatic, in that they add little to the semantic context, but they are, cumulatively, hyperbolic, giving an exaggerated effect to her various points. In its most positive interpretation, the Wife's apparent insistence on placing

considerable emphasis on 'truth', and the witness of God's testimony in her text through the use of 'God woot', acts ironically to undermine the authority that she claims here for herself.

Hyperbole and the use of intensifying adverbs are well illustrated throughout the ***Prologue.*** I have already mentioned the use of 'God woot', but a different kind of hyperbole is yielded by the frequent use of the adverbs 'wel', 'ful', 'verray', 'so' (alone, 49 times) and 'ofte(n)'. These intensifiers are used throughout the ***Prologue***—one hundred times, every eight lines or so, a percentage that is higher than other ***Prologues,*** such as that of the Pardoner (one every 15 lines), or the Miller (one every 10). The receptive consequences of using intensifiers in speech is to add to the exaggerative, emotive, and individuated nature of the discourse; judged against the 'norm' of language usage, the result is that the authority of the speaker is weakened. The following sample quotation from lines 27-30 illustrates this use of intensifiers (in the repetition and insistence on the truth of her personal knowledge in line 27, in particular):

'But wel I woot, expres, withoute lye,
God bad us for to wexe and multiplye;
That gentil text kan I wel understonde.
Eek wel I woot, he seyde myn housbonde . . .'

Alison is here made to emphasise the veracity of her experience, but in a manner that is less declarative and assertive than defensive and exaggerative. Chaucer's mimicry of the stereotypical features of a woman's speech, then, renders the content of that speech less authoritative, more subjective and less effective than it might otherwise have been.

From this brief survey, Chaucer's encapsulation of stereotypical aspects of women's speech pre-empts many of the same elements described in Jespersen's account of the variation between the sexes' use of language in his chapter. To these folklinguistic characteristics can be added others that have been proposed by more modern socio-linguists in the last few decades. Robin Lakoff, in *Language and Woman's Place,*[42] for example, asserts that adjectives such as 'adorable', 'charming', 'sweet', 'lovely', and 'divine' belong to women's speech. These adjectives are 'terms that denote approval of the trivial, the personal; that express approbation in terms of one's own personal emotional reaction, rather than by gauging the likely general reaction.'[43] In terms of syntax too, according to Lakoff, 'women's speech is peculiar'.[44] Women use tag-questions: 'used when the speaker is stating a claim, but lacks full confidence in the truth of that claim'.[45] Other characteristics would include the tendency of women to being open to interruption by men in mixed sex conversations.[46] Each of these so-called traits of women's language have been shown to be questionable, measured as they were against the norm of male 'standard' patterns of language usage.[47] These conclusions by Lakoff and other linguists have rightly been the focus of corrective criticism by subsequent empirical research, particularly because the conclusions drawn from these early observations was that women's language use was inferior to that of men: less assertive, less convincing, less credible.[48]

It is only the recent late twentieth-century corrective criticism of feminist linguists that has succeeded in beginning to reposition women's speech as different from but equal to that of men. Thus Chaucer's fourteenth-century replication of stereotypical features of women's speech in his portrait of the Wife of Bath succeeds in producing—for him and for his contemporary audience—a fictional woman who is ultimately 'deficient' in her discourse in comparison to the norm of the male pilgrims. He fundamentally accomplishes the depiction of a woman who is undermined by her own prolixity and hyperbole, and who, furthermore, exhibits virtually all the major elements of women's stereotypical language usage in her *Prologue.*

In this respect, in addition to the features noted above, the Wife's discourse frequently demonstrates the use of tag questions, rhetorical questions, and questions that are answered intratextually—39 times in all: when she tells her audience that she often went to vigils, processions and the like (lines 555-8), and wore her scarlet robes (559), 'Thise wormes, ne thise motthes, ne thise mytes, / Upon my peril, frete hem never a deel; / And wostow why? For they were used weel' (lines 560-2); or, again, 'What rekketh me', she says, 'though folk sete vileynye / Of shrewed Lameth and his bigamye?' (lines 53-4), showing here both colloquial language as well as rhetorical questioning, seeking approval or co-operation from her audience in the claim of her often-married status. In relation to the declamation by Jespersen[49] and others that women avoid language that directly pertains to taboo subjects such as sex or parts of the body, the Wife engages in euphemism, as well as underlining her point with a rhetorical question, ultimately seeking agreement from her audience:

> Of uryne, and oure bothe thynges smale
> Were eek to knowe a femele from a male,
> And for noon oother cause,—say ye no?
> The experience woot wel it is noght so.[50]

The number of such questions within this text[51] contrasts with one question in the *Pardoner's Prologue,* and one in the *Parson's Prologue,* each of them a shorter text than the Wife's *Prologue*; the proportional disparity is evident enough.

As regards interruption, the Wife of Bath is interrupted twice: once by the laudatory Pardoner at lines 163-92, and once by the Friar's laughter at line 829. The first of these interruptions is worth citing in context:

> Up stirte the pardoner, and that anon:
> 'Now, dame,' quod he, 'by God and by seint John!
> Ye been a noble prechour in this cas.
> I was aboute to wedde a wyf; allas!
> What sholde I bye it on my flessh so deere?
> Yet hadde I levere wedde no wyf to-yeere!'
> 'Abyde!' quod she, 'my tale is nat bigonne.
> Nay, thou shalt drynken of another tonne,
> Er that I go, shal savoure wors than ale.
> And whan that I have toold thee forth my tale
> Of tribulacion in mariage,
> Of which I am expert in al myn age,
> This is to seyn, myself have been the whippe,—
> Than maystow chese wheither thou wolt sippe
> Of thilke tonne that I shal abroche.
> Be war of it, er thou to ny approche;
> For I shal telle ensamples mo than ten.
> —Whoso that nyl be war by othere men,
> By hym shul othere men corrected be.—
> The same wordes writeth Ptholomee;
> Rede in his Almageste, and take it there.'
> 'Dame, I wolde praye yow, if youre wyl it were,'
> Seyde this pardoner, 'as ye bigan,
> Telle forth youre tale, spareth for no man,
> And teche us yonge men of youre praktike.'
> 'Gladly', quod she, 'sith it may yow like;
> But that I praye to al this compaignye,
> If that I speke after my fantasye,
> As taketh not agrief of that I seye;
> For myn entente is nat but for to pleye.'[52]

In this particular excerpt, many of the facets of the stereotypical woman's language usage are exemplified. Not only is the Wife interrupted (albeit to be asked to give advice), but she does not hold her train of thought (demonstrating the lack of logicality or sequenced thought so often attributed to women); she cites authority to lend weight to her argument but attributes the proverb wrongly to Ptolemy; and she exaggerates for effect in declaring that she will tell more than ten examples of, presumably, tribulation in marriage. While other pilgrims are interrupted—Chaucer the pilgrim, for example, in the telling of *The Tale of Sir Thopas*—and while other pilgrims use hyperbole, such as the Physician in his formulaic description of Virginia, for instance, it is the bringing together of all these features in the *Wife of Bath's Prologue* that marks her character out as employing, to a considerable extent, the stereotypical characteristics of women's speech labelled (until recently, that is) 'deficient' or 'deviant' in relation to the norm of male language usage. Through these characteristics, Chaucer effectually renders his literary creation 'powerless' in the face of masculine oppression: an oppression filtered through judgements about language use, reflecting and contributing to patriarchal social and cultural paradigms.

'Experience, though noon auctoritee'—the opening gambit of the Wife—is, then, precisely the point; she has no authority, either through her inability to read and interpret the authoritative texts she cites, or through her teaching and preaching in the manner Chaucer permits her. But any pretence at authority that Chaucer allows, and which is seized upon by positivist readings of the Wife, is undermined conclusively by Chaucer's stereotypical and perceptibly inferior forms of women's speech recorded and employed by him.

The emphasis on the Wife and her spoken language is most clearly pointed up by the semioclastic act in which she engages when she literally and deliberately destroys the written word contained in Jankyn's book. This act privileges metaphorically the Wife's reliance on the spoken word for authority as well as symbolising her derision of everything Jankyn's book represents. This foregrounding of the vocal, the supposed domain of women, extends to the gendered aspect of actual spoken discourse: that is that women are reliant on the uttered word—theirs primarily by virtue of exclusion from formal education—but that it can never be superior to, or more authoritative than, men's reliance on the written word, on traditional *auctoritee.*

Moreover, the Wife, in contrast to the other female tellers, is not 'literate': the level of traditional literacy she attains, she attains through hearing, not reading the Latin texts. Whereas the Prioress and Second Nun have access to (at the very least in the vernacular), and repeat, traditional tales in a manner very much according both with their positions and their stereotypical gendered roles, the Wife is ostensibly free of these ideologically imposed constraints. Although at times the Wife immerses herself in the discourse of patriarchy, presumably to be heard—to sound authoritative—she is ultimately unable to overcome this discourse[53] because of her verbal powerlessness: the way in which, through Chaucer, her words render the argument ineffectual.

Illustrating this most effectively is the analysis of that spoken word within the framework of sociolinguistics or, more appropriately, folklinguistics. It is here, within that analysis, that the nexus of her power is located, for it is here that Chaucer is operating at his most indefinable level: one might wonder what it is that he intended in ventriloquising so effectively the voice of the woman. Depending on how one interprets the text, the author has either created a female fiction whose power is defined by *what* she says,[54] or a female fiction who becomes powerless through the manner in which she speaks, no matter what she actually says.

Chaucer's awareness of language usage and the power of language is everywhere evident. He creates an opaque text through his multi-layered approach, breaking many of the rules of conversation between reader and writer that demand clarity of meaning, a process of implicature where the relationship between what is stated and what is implicit is clear, and where there is explicit co-operation. The lack of explicitness in the creation of the Wife has led inevitably to the problema-

tising of what she is meant to stand for, and what Chaucer intended through her depiction. She has been labelled as the worst of women, as a proto-feminist, appropriated by scholars to meet their own requirements. The same, of course, is true of Chaucer. What is certain is that as author he questions issues of language and power, of typical fourteenth-century gender roles and social relationships in a way that is itself didactic. Ironically, perhaps, the ultimate powerlessness of the female voice is that, in reality, it does not exist, for this is not a woman speaking here giving voice to the concerns of female experience, it is a male author enacting the role of woman, silencing her as effectively as the female audience of texts such as *Hali Meiðhad* and *Ancrene Wisse* are silenced.[55]

Chaucer has the opportunity to subvert social expectation, to undermine stereotype, but it is not an opportunity he exploits here, though he may appear to be doing so at the surface level. On the contrary, as a man of his day, he confirms the stereotypes of women, but also indirectly raises issues about the validity of ideological norms that he subsequently refuses to clarify. No matter how much or how little Chaucer and subsequent critics sympathise with the character of the Wife of Bath, may celebrate her creation as a wonderfully independent, free-thinking woman or might condemn her as the harridan of the anti-feminist diatribes she so joyously appropriates, she is ultimately powerless: powerless not so much through what she says, but through *how* she says it. And that makes her a fourteenth-century victim of patriarchal ideology, no matter what our own view of her might be.

In the **Envoy to Bukton,** the Wife is presented as a humorous case study against the recipient's imminent marriage, and against women like her in general.[56] While we may be meant to laugh at her, even find her a joyous and exuberant creation, she is, in the final analysis, a stereotype. It is precisely because Chaucer adopts, with considerable success, the stratagem of replicating women's speech that critics and students are so frequently momentarily beguiled into believing they are reading the real words of a real woman. Chaucer's linguistic acuity and his ability to deceive—despite the formal restraints of the written verse form—are what make his observations, not only of social *mores* and culture in late fourteenth-century England, but also of social and communicative interaction so interesting. Aspects of gendered language use are brought to the fore in the Wife's *Prologue* that would not be the focus of sustained scholarly research for another five hundred years, and in this, as in so many other things, Chaucer's innovation is remarkable.[57]

Notes

1. Hélène Cixous, 'The Laugh of the Medusa: New French Feminisms' (1976), trans. Keith Cohen and

Paula Cohen, cited in *Feminist Literary Theory: A Reader,* ed. by Mary Eagleton, 2nd ed. (Oxford: Blackwell, 1996), p. 322.

2. William Blake, *A Descriptive Catalogue of Pictures, Poetical and Historical Inventions, Painted by William Blake* (1809), cited in 'Early Appreciations', in *Chaucer: The Canterbury Tales,* ed. by J. J. Anderson, Casebook Series (London: Macmillan, 1974), p. 39.

3. John Dryden, Preface to *Fables Ancient and Modern* (1700), in 'Early Appreciations', in *Chaucer: The Canterbury Tales,* p. 31.

4. G. L. Kittredge, 'Chaucer's Discussion of Marriage', repr. in *Chaucer: The Canterbury Tales,* pp. 61-92, at p. 66.

5. Tony Slade, 'Irony in the *Wife of Bath's Tale*', repr. in *Chaucer: The Canterbury Tales,* pp. 160-71, at p. 162.

6. Many of these perspectives are well exemplified in Ruth Evans and Lesley Johnson, ed., *Feminist Readings in Middle English Literature: The Wife of Bath and All Her Sect* (London: Routledge, 1994). The editors' Introduction (pp. 1-21), in particular, situates recent scholarship within the overall context of feminist criticism.

7. Mary Carruthers, 'The Wife of Bath and the Painting of Lions', repr. with a new 'Afterword' in *Feminist Readings,* pp. 22-53.

8. Carruthers, 'The Wife of Bath', p. 26.

9. See, for example, Marion Wynne-Davies, '"The Elf-Queen with Hir Joly Compaignye": Chaucer's *Wife of Bath's Tale*', in *Women and Arthurian Literature: Seizing the Sword,* ed. by Marion Wynne-Davies (New York: St Martin's Press, 1996), pp. 14-35.

10. Jill Mann, *Geoffrey Chaucer* (London: Harvester Wheatsheaf, 1991), p. 79.

11. Mann, *Chaucer,* p. 80.

12. Barrie Ruth Straus, 'Subversive Discourse of the Wife of Bath: Phallocentric Discourse and the Imprisonment of Criticism', repr. in *Chaucer: Contemporary Critical Essays,* ed. by Valerie Allen and Aers Axiotis, New Casebooks (London: Macmillan, 1997), pp. 126-44 (at p. 133).

13. Straus, 'Subversive Discourse of the Wife of Bath', p. 142.

14. Chauncey Wood, 'Affective Stylistics and the Study of Chaucer', *Studies in the Age of Chaucer* 6 (1984), 21-40 (at p. 39).

15. Lynne Dickson, 'Deflection in the Mirror: Feminine Discourse in *The Wife of Bath's Prologue and Tale*', *Studies in the Age of Chaucer* 15

(1993), p. 79. Dickson does go on to say that 'Drawing lines between the fictional and the actual in *The Wife's Prologue* is problematic because Alison herself is not an actual speaking woman but a fictional construct' (p.85, n.50). There should not, of course, be any difficulty 'drawing lines between the fictional and the actual' since the entire *Prologue* is a fiction however realistically the fiction might be portrayed.

16. See, for example, Ronald Wardhaugh, *An Introduction to Sociolinguistics,* 2nd ed. (Oxford: Blackwell, 1992).

17. *The Reeve's Tale,* lines 4084-9, for example, illustrate a multitude of Northern spellings [in small capitals] in the quotation below:

> "Allas," quod John, "Aleyn, for Cristes peyne
> Lay doun thy swerd, and I wil myn ALSWA.
> I is ful WIGHT, God WAAT, as is a RAA;
> By Goddes herte, he SAL nat scape us BATHE!
> Why ne had thow PIT the capul in the LATHE?
> Ilhayl! By God, Alayn, thou is a fonne!"

All quotations are taken from Larry D. Benson, ed., *Riverside Chaucer,* 3rd ed. (Oxford: Oxford University Press, 1987), unless otherwise stated. The quotation commenting on dialect in *The Reeve's Tale* is from the *Riverside Chaucer,* p. 850b.

18. *Troilus and Criseyde,* lines 1792-9.

19. *The Parson's Tale,* lines 42-6.

20. The derogatory comments of male commentators on women's language subsequently led to the proposition that women's language is powerless, indicative of women's inferiority in verbal communication. In recent years, this 'powerlessness' has been reappraised and shown to be demonstrative of women's communicative strengths of co-operation, lucidity, and solidarity. See, for example, Dale Spender, *Man Made Language* (London: Routledge, 1980), Deborah Cameron, *Feminism and Linguistic Theory* (London: Macmillan, 1985), and Jennifer Coates, *Women, Men and Language,* 2nd ed. (London: Macmillan, 1993).

21. That is, long perpetuated myths, which are still highly visible in social interaction and communication today, and to which this author does not, in any way, subscribe.

22. Elaine Treharne, ed., *Old and Middle English: An Anthology* (Oxford: Blackwell, 2000), pp. 364-5.

23. *The Merchant's Tale,* lines 1377-8.

24. The Epilogue to *The Merchant's Tale,* lines 2427-9.

25. In Passus V of *Piers Plowman,* for example, the sin of Wrath tells his audience that he has encouraged the malicious gossip and 'wicked words' of nuns while employed as their cook. See A. V. C. Schmidt, ed., *William Langland: A Critical Edition of the B-Text* (London: Dent Everyman, 1978), Passus V, lines 151-63.

26. As discussed by Jennifer Coates, *Women, Men and Language,* pp. 33-6, illustrated by a number of medieval and Renaissance literary sources.

27. Spender, *Man Made Language,* p. 43.

28. *The Wife of Bath's Prologue,* lines 531-42.

29. Some critics have read this narration of the Wife's network of female friends as demonstrating the close and powerful communities that women formed in this period. This may well, indirectly, be the case, but it remains that Chaucer is depicting here a less-than-positive picture of women's volubility as the norm. Susan Signe Morrison, 'Don't Ask, Don't Tell: The Wife of Bath and Vernacular Translations', *Exemplaria* 8 (1996), 97-123, discusses this same passage at pp. 115-16, and suggests at p. 116 that: 'The anxiety the Wife's husband feels reflects the anxiety felt among those men who opposed vernacular translations; once privileged men no longer maintained exclusive access to knowledge, society itself would be threatened with subversion'; and at p. 117, 'the ability or tendency for women to reveal secrets only heightens their own power'.

30. Otto Jespersen, *Language, Its Nature, Development, and Origin* (London: Allen and Unwin, 1922). Chapter XIII is devoted to 'The Woman'.

31. See, for example, Coates, *Women, Men and Language,* pp. 18-20; Dale Spender, *Man Made Language,* pp. 10-11.

32. As Jenkins and Kramarae state: 'Both the theory and the methodology [of the stratification approach taken by sociolinguists] are based on the implicit assumption that the communicative experience of white middle class males is prototypical . . . the experience of women, other ethnic groups and classes are treated as deviations', cited in *Feminist Linguistic Theory,* ed. by Deborah Cameron (London: Macmillan, 1985), p. 45, from Mercilee Jenkins and Cheris Kramarae, 'A Thief in the House: The Case of Women and Language', in *Men's Studies Modified,* ed. Dale Spender (London: Pergamon, 1981), p. 16.

33. Jespersen, *Language, Its Nature, Development, and Origin,* p. 242.

34. Ibid., p. 243.

35. Ibid., p. 250.

36. Ibid., p. 245. Elaborating on this characteristic (which he labels 'affectation'), Jespersen goes on to say at p. 246: 'There can be no doubt that women exercise a great and universal influence on linguistic development through their instinctive shrinking from coarse and gross expressions and their preference for refined and (in certain spheres) veiled and indirect expressions.'

37. Ibid., p. 248.

38. Jespersen, *Language, Its Nature, Development, and Origin,* p. 253.

39. Ibid., p. 254.

40. As a model of the non-standard, the ab-norm-al, deviating from the norm (the powerful male hegemony), the Wife is a fictional example of the powerless mode of discourse.

41. The analysis of fillers is made more complex by the verse form, which by virtue of the couplets occasionally demands phatic phrases to complete the scansion and rhyme.

42. *Language and Woman's Place* (New York: Harper & Row, 1975), p. 226.

43. Ibid., p. 227.

44. Ibid., p. 228.

45. Ibid., p. 229.

46. For a critique of which see Spender, *Man Made Language,* pp. 43-5.

47. See, for example, Spender, *Man Made Language,* pp. 8-9; Cameron, *Feminism and Linguistic Theory,* 33-4.

48. Lakoff 'states that women lack authority and seriousness, they lack conviction and confidence. In her view, in comparison with the (ostensibly) forceful and effective language of men, women are tentative, hesitant, even trivial, and are therefore "deficient"': Spender, *Man Made Language,* p. 8.

49. See above, page 107.

50. *Wife's Prologue,* lines 121-4.

51. The number of interrogative structures, whether rhetorical or direct, will, to an extent, depend on the editorial process. The majority of them are unequivocally provided by the syntax.

52. *Wife's Prologue,* lines 163-92.

53. A point made by Morrison in 'Don't Ask, Don't Tell: The Wife of Bath and Vernacular Translations', pp. 122-23.

54. Which would be Carruthers' reading in 'The Wife of Bath and the Painting of Lions'.

55. In both these earlier texts, the authors imagine their audiences' responses and questions in a series of indirectly reported questions framed by 'You ask . . .', and in rhetorical questions seeking the audiences' approbation. See B. Millett and J. Wogan-Browne, ed., *Medieval English Prose for Women from the Katherine Group and 'Ancrene Wisse'* (Oxford: Oxford University Press, 1992).

56.   This lytel writ, proverbes, or figure
        I sende yow; take kepe of yt, I rede;
        Unwys is he that kan no wele endure.
        If thou be siker, put the nat in drede.
        The Wyf of Bathe I pray yow that ye rede
        Of this matere that we have on honde.
        God graunte yow your lyf frely to lede
        In fredam, for ful hard is to be bonde.

    Lenvoy de Chaucer a Bukton, in the *Riverside Chaucer,* pp. 655-6, lines 25-32.

57. I should like to thank Professors Greg Walker, David F. Johnson and Roy M. Liuzza for their helpful comments on an early draft of this paper.

FURTHER READING

Criticism

Amsler, Mark. "The Wife of Bath and Women's Power." *Assays* 4 (1987): 67-83.

Examines the issues of class standing, wealth, and self-sufficiency for women in Chaucer's *The Canterbury Tales,* using the Wife of Bath as an example.

Beidler, Peter G. "Transformations in Gower's *Tale of Florent* and Chaucer's *Wife of Bath's Tale*." In *Chaucer and Gower: Difference, Mutuality, Exchange,* edited by R. F. Yeager, pp. 100-14. Victoria, British Colombia: University of Victoria, 1991.

Studies the differences and similarities between John Gower's *Tale of Florent* and Chaucer's *Wife of Bath's Tale.*

Blanch, Robert J. "'Al was this land fulfild of fayerye': The Thematic Employment of Force, Willfulness, and Legal Conventions in Chaucer's *Wife of Bath's Tale*." *Studia Neophilologica* 57, no. 1 (1985): 41-51.

Focuses on the legal consequences of rape in Chaucer's era and examines Chaucer's many references to laws and contracts in *The Wife of Bath's Tale.*

Cooper, Helen. "The Shape Shiftings of the Wife of Bath." In *Chaucer Traditions: Studies in Honour of Derek Brewer,* edited by Ruth Morse and Barry Windeatt, pp. 168-84. Cambridge: Cambridge University, 1990.

Explores the various facets of the Wife of Bath's personality and examines certain interpretations of her words and actions.

Delany, Sheila. "Strategies of Silence in the Wife of Bath's Recital." *Exemplaria* 2, no. 1 (spring 1990): 49-69.

Probes the silences and the omissions of *The Wife of Bath's Prologue* and *Tale* and how these gaps relay information about Chaucer the man and the poet.

Dickson, Lynne. "Deflection in the Mirror: Feminine Discourse in *The Wife of Bath's Prologue* and *Tale.*" *Studies in the Age of Chaucer* 15 (1993): 61-90.

Defines the Wife of Bath's attempts to claim language and self-definition as temporary and not fully developed, yet recognizes Chaucer's nontraditional attempt to explore feminine discourse.

Hagen, Susan K. "The Wife of Bath: Chaucer's Inchoate Experiment in Feminist Hermeneutics." In *Rebels and Rivals: The Contestive Spirit in* The Canterbury Tales, edited by Susanna Greer Fein, David Raybin, and Peter C. Braeger, pp. 105-24. Kalamazoo, Mich.: Medieval Institute Publications, 1991.

Asserts that Chaucer's attempts to establish feminine discourse in *The Wife of Bath's Prologue* are unsuccessful owing to Chaucer's masculine-centered viewpoint.

Knapp, Peggy A. "Alisoun Weaves a Text." *Philological Quarterly* 65, no. 3 (summer 1986): 387-401.

Uses the analogy of weaving to characterize the Wife of Bath's multi-layered viewpoints, ideologies, and willfulness in an era of female submissiveness.

Lee, Brian S. "Exploitation and Excommunication in *The Wife of Bath's Tale.*" *Philological Quarterly* 74, no. 1 (winter 1995): 17-35.

Questions the lack of moral outrage over the rape of the maiden in *The Wife of Bath's Tale* and investigates the steps taken to bring about justice.

Leicester, H. Marshall, Jr. "Retrospective Revision and the Emergence of the Subject in *The Wife of Bath's Prologue.*" In *The Disenchanted Self: Representing the Subject in the Canterbury Tales,* pp. 82-113. Berkeley: University of California Press, 1990.

Provides an in-depth overview of *The Wife of Bath's Prologue* and focuses on Alisoun's sense of self during her lengthy discourse.

Longsworth, Robert. "The Wife of Bath and the Samaritan Woman." *Chaucer Review* 34, no. 4 (2000): 372-87.

Evaluates the Wife of Bath's wariness of trusting authoritative biblical interpretations of God's will over common sense, experience, and the actual text of the Bible.

Puhvel, Martin. "*The Wife of Bath's Tale*: Mirror of Her Mind." *Neuphilologische Mitteilungen* 100, no. 3 (1999): 291-300.

Establishes that "the Wife's *Tale* largely mirrors and in some ways amplifies the portrait she paints of herself through the lengthy self-revelation in her *Prologue*."

Richman, Gerald. "Rape and Desire in *The Wife of Bath's Tale*." *Studia Neophilologica* 61, no. 2 (1989): 161-65.

Recounts the ironies in the Knight's crime and penance in *The Wife of Bath's Tale* and traces the underlying theme of freely given love, observing: "We all desire not the sterile domination of rape and the marriage debt but true love."

Rigby, S. H. "The Wife of Bath, Christine De Pizan, and the Medieval Case for Women." *Chaucer Review* 35, no. 2 (2000): 133-65.

Uses *The Wife of Bath's Prologue* and works by medieval writer Christine de Pizan to illustrate a woman's life in medieval England, and investigates early literary instances of women's self-definition, self-determination, and discourse.

Additional coverage of Chaucer's life and career is contained in the following sources published by Thomson Gale: *British Writers*, **Vol. 1;** *British Writers: The Classics*, **Vol. 1;** *British Writers Retrospective Supplement*, **Vol. 2;** *Concise Dictionary of British Literary Biography, Before 1660*; *Dictionary of Literary Biography*, **Vol. 146;** *DISCovering Authors*; *DISCovering Authors 3.0*; *DIS-Covering Authors: British Edition*; *DISCovering Authors: Canadian Edition*; *DISCovering Authors Modules: Most-studied Authors* **and** *Poets*; *Literature and Its Times*, **Vol. 1;** *Literature Criticism from 1400 to 1800*, **Vols. 17, 56;** *Literature Resource Center*; *Poetry Criticism*, **Vol. 19;** *Poetry for Students*, **Vol. 14;** *Poets: American and British*; *Reference Guide to English Literature*, **Ed. 2;** *Twayne's English Authors*; *World Literature and Its Times*, **Vol. 3;** *World Literature Criticism Supplement*; **and** *World Poets*.

How to Use This Index

Calvino, Italo
  1923-1985 .... CLC 5, 8, 11, 22, 33, 39,
                                    73; SSC 3, 48

list all author entries in the following Gale Literary Criticism series:

AAL = Asian American Literature
BG = The Beat Generation: A Gale Critical Companion
BLC = Black Literature Criticism
BLCS = Black Literature Criticism Supplement
CLC = Contemporary Literary Criticism
CLR = Children's Literature Review
CMLC = Classical and Medieval Literature Criticism
DC = Drama Criticism
HLC = Hispanic Literature Criticism
HLCS = Hispanic Literature Criticism Supplement
HR = Harlem Renaissance: A Gale Critical Companion
LC = Literature Criticism from 1400 to 1800
NCLC = Nineteenth-Century Literature Criticism
NNAL = Native North American Literature
PC = Poetry Criticism
SSC = Short Story Criticism
TCLC = Twentieth-Century Literary Criticism
WLC = World Literature Criticism, 1500 to the Present
WLCS = World Literature Criticism Supplement

The cross-references

See also CA 85-88, 116; CANR 23, 61;
DAM NOV; DLB 196; EW 13; MTCW 1, 2;
RGSF 2; RGWL 2; SFW 4; SSFS 12

list all author entries in the following Gale biographical and literary sources:

AAYA = Authors & Artists for Young Adults
AFAW = African American Writers
AFW = African Writers
AITN = Authors in the News
AMW = American Writers
AMWR = American Writers Retrospective Supplement
AMWS = American Writers Supplement
ANW = American Nature Writers
AW = Ancient Writers
BEST = Bestsellers
BPFB = Beacham's Encyclopedia of Popular Fiction: Biography and Resources
BRW = British Writers
BRWS = British Writers Supplement
BW = Black Writers
BYA = Beacham's Guide to Literature for Young Adults
CA = Contemporary Authors
CAAS = Contemporary Authors Autobiography Series
CABS = Contemporary Authors Bibliographical Series
CAD = Contemporary American Dramatists
CANR = Contemporary Authors New Revision Series
CAP = Contemporary Authors Permanent Series
CBD = Contemporary British Dramatists
CCA = Contemporary Canadian Authors
CD = Contemporary Dramatists
CDALB = Concise Dictionary of American Literary Biography
CDALBS = Concise Dictionary of American Literary Biography Supplement
CDBLB = Concise Dictionary of British Literary Biography

CMW = *St. James Guide to Crime & Mystery Writers*
CN = *Contemporary Novelists*
CP = *Contemporary Poets*
CPW = *Contemporary Popular Writers*
CSW = *Contemporary Southern Writers*
CWD = *Contemporary Women Dramatists*
CWP = *Contemporary Women Poets*
CWRI = *St. James Guide to Children's Writers*
CWW = *Contemporary World Writers*
DA = *DISCovering Authors*
DA3 = *DISCovering Authors 3.0*
DAB = *DISCovering Authors: British Edition*
DAC = *DISCovering Authors: Canadian Edition*
DAM = *DISCovering Authors: Modules*
   DRAM: *Dramatists Module;* **MST:** *Most-studied Authors Module;*
   MULT: *Multicultural Authors Module;* **NOV:** *Novelists Module;*
   POET: *Poets Module;* **POP:** *Popular Fiction and Genre Authors Module*
DFS = *Drama for Students*
DLB = *Dictionary of Literary Biography*
DLBD = *Dictionary of Literary Biography Documentary Series*
DLBY = *Dictionary of Literary Biography Yearbook*
DNFS = *Literature of Developing Nations for Students*
EFS = *Epics for Students*
EXPN = *Exploring Novels*
EXPP = *Exploring Poetry*
EXPS = *Exploring Short Stories*
EW = *European Writers*
FANT = *St. James Guide to Fantasy Writers*
FW = *Feminist Writers*
GFL = *Guide to French Literature,* Beginnings to 1789, 1798 to the Present
GLL = *Gay and Lesbian Literature*
HGG = *St. James Guide to Horror, Ghost & Gothic Writers*
HW = *Hispanic Writers*
IDFW = *International Dictionary of Films and Filmmakers: Writers and Production Artists*
IDTP = *International Dictionary of Theatre: Playwrights*
LAIT = *Literature and Its Times*
LAW = *Latin American Writers*
JRDA = *Junior DISCovering Authors*
MAICYA = *Major Authors and Illustrators for Children and Young Adults*
MAICYAS = *Major Authors and Illustrators for Children and Young Adults Supplement*
MAWW = *Modern American Women Writers*
MJW = *Modern Japanese Writers*
MTCW = *Major 20th-Century Writers*
NCFS = *Nonfiction Classics for Students*
NFS = *Novels for Students*
PAB = *Poets: American and British*
PFS = *Poetry for Students*
RGAL = *Reference Guide to American Literature*
RGEL = *Reference Guide to English Literature*
RGSF = *Reference Guide to Short Fiction*
RGWL = *Reference Guide to World Literature*
RHW = *Twentieth-Century Romance and Historical Writers*
SAAS = *Something about the Author Autobiography Series*
SATA = *Something about the Author*
SFW = *St. James Guide to Science Fiction Writers*
SSFS = *Short Stories for Students*
TCWW = *Twentieth-Century Western Writers*
WLIT = *World Literature and Its Times*
WP = *World Poets*
YABC = *Yesterday's Authors of Books for Children*
YAW = *St. James Guide to Young Adult Writers*

Literary Criticism Series
Cumulative Author Index

Andreas Capellanus fl. c. 1185- .... **CMLC 45**
See also DLB 208
Andreas-Salome, Lou 1861-1937 ... **TCLC 56**
See also CA 178; DLB 66
Andreev, Leonid
See Andreyev, Leonid (Nikolaevich)
See also DLB 295; EWL 3
Andress, Lesley
See Sanders, Lawrence
Andrewes, Lancelot 1555-1626 .... **LC 5**
See also DLB 151, 172
Andrews, Cicily Fairfield
See West, Rebecca
Andrews, Elton V.
See Pohl, Frederik
Andreyev, Leonid (Nikolaevich)
1871-1919 .... **TCLC 3**
See Andreev, Leonid
See also CA 104; 185
Andric, Ivo 1892-1975 .... **CLC 8; SSC 36;**
TCLC 135
See also CA 81-84; 57-60; CANR 43, 60;
CDWLB 4; DLB 147; EW 11; EWL 3;
MTCW 1; RGSF 2; RGWL 2, 3
Androvar
See Prado (Calvo), Pedro
Angelique, Pierre
See Bataille, Georges
Angell, Roger 1920- .... **CLC 26**
See also CA 57-60; CANR 13, 44, 70; DLB
171, 185
Angelou, Maya 1928- ... **BLC 1; CLC 12, 35,**
64, 77, 155; PC 32; WLCS
See also AAYA 7, 20; AMWS 4; BPFB 1;
BW 2, 3; BYA 2; CA 65-68; CANR 19,
42, 65, 111; CDALBS; CLR 53; CP 7;
CPW; CSW; CWP; DA; DA3; DAB;
DAC; DAM MST, MULT, POET, POP;
DLB 38; EWL 3; EXPN; EXPP; LAIT 4;
MAICYA 2; MAICYAS 1; MAWW;
MTCW 1, 2; NCFS 2; NFS 2; PFS 2, 3;
RGAL 4; SATA 49, 136; WYA; YAW
Angouleme, Marguerite d'
See de Navarre, Marguerite
Anna Comnena 1083-1153 .... **CMLC 25**
Annensky, Innokentii Fedorovich
See Annensky, Innokenty (Fyodorovich)
See also DLB 295
Annensky, Innokenty (Fyodorovich)
1856-1909 .... **TCLC 14**
See also CA 110; 155; EWL 3
Annunzio, Gabriele d'
See D'Annunzio, Gabriele
Anodos
See Coleridge, Mary E(lizabeth)
Anon, Charles Robert
See Pessoa, Fernando (Antonio Nogueira)
Anouilh, Jean (Marie Lucien Pierre)
1910-1987 . **CLC 1, 3, 8, 13, 40, 50; DC**
8, 21
See also CA 17-20R; 123; CANR 32; DAM
DRAM; DFS 9, 10, 19; EW 13; EWL 3;
GFL 1789 to the Present; MTCW 1, 2;
RGWL 2, 3; TWA
Anselm of Canterbury
1033(?)-1109 .... **CMLC 67**
See also DLB 115
Anthony, Florence
See Ai
Anthony, John
See Ciardi, John (Anthony)
Anthony, Peter
See Shaffer, Anthony (Joshua); Shaffer,
Peter (Levin)

Anthony, Piers 1934- .... **CLC 35**
See also AAYA 11, 48; BYA 7; CA 200;
CAAE 200; CANR 28, 56, 73, 102; CPW;
DAM POP; DLB 8; FANT; MAICYA 2;
MAICYAS 1; MTCW 1, 2; SAAS 22;
SATA 84, 129; SATA-Essay 129; SFW 4;
SUFW 1, 2; YAW
Anthony, Susan B(rownell)
1820-1906 .... **TCLC 84**
See also CA 211; FW
Antiphon c. 480B.C.-c. 411B.C. .... **CMLC 55**
Antoine, Marc
See Proust, (Valentin-Louis-George-Eugene)
Marcel
Antoninus, Brother
See Everson, William (Oliver)
Antonioni, Michelangelo 1912- .... **CLC 20,**
144
See also CA 73-76; CANR 45, 77
Antschel, Paul 1920-1970
See Celan, Paul
See also CA 85-88; CANR 33, 61; MTCW
1
Anwar, Chairil 1922-1949 .... **TCLC 22**
See Chairil Anwar
See also CA 121; 219; RGWL 3
Anzaldua, Gloria (Evanjelina)
1942- .... **HLCS 1**
See also CA 175; CWP; DLB 122;
FW; LLW 1; RGAL 4
Apess, William 1798-1839(?) .... **NCLC 73;**
NNAL
See also DAM MULT; DLB 175, 243
Apollinaire, Guillaume 1880-1918 .... **PC 7;**
TCLC 3, 8, 51
See Kostrowitzki, Wilhelm Apollinaris de
See also CA 152; DAM POET; DLB 258;
EW 9; EWL 3; GFL 1789 to the Present;
MTCW 1; RGWL 2, 3; TWA; WP
Apollonius of Rhodes
See Apollonius Rhodius
See also AW 1; RGWL 2, 3
Apollonius Rhodius c. 300B.C.-c.
220B.C. .... **CMLC 28**
See Apollonius of Rhodes
See also DLB 176
Appelfeld, Aharon 1932- ... **CLC 23, 47; SSC**
42
See also CA 112; 133; CANR 86; CWW 2;
DLB 299; EWL 3; RGSF 2
Apple, Max (Isaac) 1941- .... **CLC 9, 33; SSC**
50
See also CA 81-84; CANR 19, 54; DLB
130
Appleman, Philip (Dean) 1926- .... **CLC 51**
See also CA 13-16R; CAAS 18; CANR 6,
29, 56
Appleton, Lawrence
See Lovecraft, H(oward) P(hillips)
Apteryx
See Eliot, T(homas) S(tearns)
Apuleius, (Lucius Madaurensis)
125(?)-175(?) .... **CMLC 1**
See also AW 2; CDWLB 1; DLB 211;
RGWL 2, 3; SUFW
Aquin, Hubert 1929-1977 .... **CLC 15**
See also CA 105; DLB 53; EWL 3
Aquinas, Thomas 1224(?)-1274 ..... **CMLC 33**
See also DLB 115; EW 1; TWA
Aragon, Louis 1897-1982 .... **CLC 3, 22;**
TCLC 123
See also CA 69-72; 108; CANR 28, 71;
DAM NOV, POET; DLB 72, 258; EW 11;
EWL 3; GFL 1789 to the Present; GLL 2;
LMFS 2; MTCW 1, 2; RGWL 2, 3
Arany, Janos 1817-1882 .... **NCLC 34**
Aranyos, Kakay 1847-1910
See Mikszath, Kalman

Aratus of Soli c. 315B.C.-c.
240B.C. .... **CMLC 64**
See also DLB 176
Arbuthnot, John 1667-1735 .... **LC 1**
See also DLB 101
Archer, Herbert Winslow
See Mencken, H(enry) L(ouis)
Archer, Jeffrey (Howard) 1940- .... **CLC 28**
See also AAYA 16; BEST 89:3; BPFB 1;
CA 77-80; CANR 22, 52, 95; CPW; DA3;
DAM POP; INT CANR-22
Archer, Jules 1915- .... **CLC 12**
See also CA 9-12R; CANR 6, 69; SAAS 5;
SATA 4, 85
Archer, Lee
See Ellison, Harlan (Jay)
Archilochus c. 7th cent. B.C.- .... **CMLC 44**
See also DLB 176
Arden, John 1930- .... **CLC 6, 13, 15**
See also BRWS 2; CA 13-16R; CAAS 4;
CANR 31, 65, 67, 124; CBD; CD 5;
DAM DRAM; DFS 9; DLB 13, 245;
EWL 3; MTCW 1
Arenas, Reinaldo 1943-1990 .. **CLC 41; HLC**
1
See also CA 124; 128; 133; CANR 73, 106;
DAM MULT; DLB 145; EWL 3; GLL 2;
HW 1; LAW; LAWS 1; MTCW 1; RGSF
2; RGWL 3; WLIT 1
Arendt, Hannah 1906-1975 .... **CLC 66, 98**
See also CA 17-20R; 61-64; CANR 26, 60;
DLB 242; MTCW 1, 2
Aretino, Pietro 1492-1556 .... **LC 12**
See also RGWL 2, 3
Arghezi, Tudor .... **CLC 80**
See Theodorescu, Ion N.
See also CA 167; CDWLB 4; DLB 220;
EWL 3
Arguedas, Jose Maria 1911-1969 .... **CLC 10,**
18; HLCS 1; TCLC 147
See also CA 89-92; CANR 73; DLB 113;
EWL 3; HW 1; LAW; RGWL 2, 3; WLIT
1
Argueta, Manlio 1936- .... **CLC 31**
See also CA 131; CANR 73; CWW 2; DLB
145; EWL 3; HW 1; RGWL 3
Arias, Ron(ald Francis) 1941- .... **HLC 1**
See also CA 131; CANR 81; DAM MULT;
DLB 82; HW 1, 2; MTCW 2
Ariosto, Ludovico 1474-1533 ... **LC 6, 87; PC**
42
See also EW 2; RGWL 2, 3
Aristides
See Epstein, Joseph
Aristophanes 450B.C.-385B.C. .... **CMLC 4,**
51; DC 2; WLCS
See also AW 1; CDWLB 1; DA; DA3;
DAB; DAC; DAM DRAM, MST; DFS
10; DLB 176; LMFS 1; RGWL 2, 3; TWA
Aristotle 384B.C.-322B.C. .... **CMLC 31;**
WLCS
See also AW 1; CDWLB 1; DA; DA3;
DAB; DAC; DAM MST; DLB 176;
RGWL 2, 3; TWA
Arlt, Roberto (Godofredo Christophersen)
1900-1942 .... **HLC 1; TCLC 29**
See also CA 123; 131; CANR 67; DAM
MULT; EWL 3; HW 1, 2; LAW
Armah, Ayi Kwei 1939- . **BLC 1; CLC 5, 33,**
136
See also AFW; BW 1; CA 61-64; CANR
21, 64; CDWLB 3; CN 7; DAM MULT,
POET; DLB 117; EWL 3; MTCW 1;
WLIT 2
Armatrading, Joan 1950- .... **CLC 17**
See also CA 114; 186
Armitage, Frank
See Carpenter, John (Howard)

Armstrong, Jeannette (C.) 1948- .... **NNAL**
 See also CA 149; CCA 1; CN 7; DAC;
 SATA 102
Arnette, Robert
 See Silverberg, Robert
**Arnim, Achim von (Ludwig Joachim von
 Arnim)** 1781-1831 ..... **NCLC 5; SSC 29**
 See also DLB 90
Arnim, Bettina von 1785-1859 ...... **NCLC 38,
 123**
 See also DLB 90; RGWL 2, 3
Arnold, Matthew 1822-1888 ..... **NCLC 6, 29,
 89, 126; PC 5; WLC**
 See also BRW 5; CDBLB 1832-1890; DA;
 DAB; DAC; DAM MST, POET; DLB 32,
 57; EXPP; PAB; PFS 2; TEA; WP
Arnold, Thomas 1795-1842 .... **NCLC 18**
 See also DLB 55
Arnow, Harriette (Louisa) Simpson
 1908-1986 .... **CLC 2, 7, 18**
 See also BPFB 1; CA 9-12R; 118; CANR
 14; DLB 6; FW; MTCW 1, 2; RHW;
 SATA 42; SATA-Obit 47
Arouet, Francois-Marie
 See Voltaire
Arp, Hans
 See Arp, Jean
Arp, Jean 1887-1966 .... **CLC 5; TCLC 115**
 See also CA 81-84; 25-28R; CANR 42, 77;
 EW 10
Arrabal
 See Arrabal, Fernando
Arrabal, Fernando 1932- ... **CLC 2, 9, 18, 58**
 See Arrabal (Teran), Fernando
 See also CA 9-12R; CANR 15; EWL 3;
 LMFS 2
Arrabal (Teran), Fernando 1932-
 See Arrabal, Fernando
 See also CWW 2
Arreola, Juan Jose 1918-2001 .... **CLC 147;
 HLC 1; SSC 38**
 See also CA 113; 131; 200; CANR 81;
 CWW 2; DAM MULT; DLB 113; DNFS
 2; EWL 3; HW 1, 2; LAW; RGSF 2
Arrian c. 89(?)-c. 155(?) .... **CMLC 43**
 See also DLB 176
Arrick, Fran .... **CLC 30**
 See Gaberman, Judie Angell
 See also BYA 6
Arrley, Richmond
 See Delany, Samuel R(ay), Jr.
Artaud, Antonin (Marie Joseph)
 1896-1948 .... **DC 14; TCLC 3, 36**
 See also CA 104; 149; DA3; DAM DRAM;
 DLB 258; EW 11; EWL 3; GFL 1789 to
 the Present; MTCW 1; RGWL 2, 3
Arthur, Ruth M(abel) 1905-1979 ..... **CLC 12**
 See also CA 9-12R; 85-88; CANR 4; CWRI
 5; SATA 7, 26
Artsybashev, Mikhail (Petrovich)
 1878-1927 .... **TCLC 31**
 See also CA 170; DLB 295
Arundel, Honor (Morfydd)
 1919-1973 .... **CLC 17**
 See also CA 21-22; 41-44R; CAP 2; CLR
 35; CWRI 5; SATA 4; SATA-Obit 24
Arzner, Dorothy 1900-1979 .... **CLC 98**
Asch, Sholem 1880-1957 .... **TCLC 3**
 See also CA 105; EWL 3; GLL 2
Ascham, Roger 1516(?)-1568 .... **LC 101**
 See also DLB 236
Ash, Shalom
 See Asch, Sholem
Ashbery, John (Lawrence) 1927- .. **CLC 2, 3,
 4, 6, 9, 13, 15, 25, 41, 77, 125; PC 26**
 See Berry, Jonas
 See also AMWS 3; CA 5-8R; CANR 9, 37,
 66, 102; CP 7; DA3; DAM POET; DLB
 5, 165; DLBY 1981; EWL 3; INT
 CANR-9; MTCW 1, 2; PAB; PFS 11;
 RGAL 4; WP

Ashdown, Clifford
 See Freeman, R(ichard) Austin
Ashe, Gordon
 See Creasey, John
Ashton-Warner, Sylvia (Constance)
 1908-1984 .... **CLC 19**
 See also CA 69-72; 112; CANR 29; MTCW
 1, 2
Asimov, Isaac 1920-1992 ..... **CLC 1, 3, 9, 19,
 26, 76, 92**
 See also AAYA 13; BEST 90:2; BPFB 1;
 BYA 4, 6, 7, 9; CA 1-4R; 137; CANR 2,
 19, 36, 60, 125; CLR 12, 79; CMW 4;
 CPW; DA3; DAM POP; DLB 8; DLBY
 1992; INT CANR-19; JRDA; LAIT 5;
 LMFS 2; MAICYA 1, 2; MTCW 1, 2;
 RGAL 4; SATA 1, 26, 74; SCFW 2; SFW
 4; SSFS 17; TUS; YAW
Askew, Anne 1521(?)-1546 .... **LC 81**
 See also DLB 136
Assis, Joaquim Maria Machado de
 See Machado de Assis, Joaquim Maria
Astell, Mary 1666-1731 .... **LC 68**
 See also DLB 252; FW
Astley, Thea (Beatrice May) 1925- ... **CLC 41**
 See also CA 65-68; CANR 11, 43, 78; CN
 7; DLB 289; EWL 3
Astley, William 1855-1911
 See Warung, Price
Aston, James
 See White, T(erence) H(anbury)
Asturias, Miguel Angel 1899-1974 .... **CLC 3,
 8, 13; HLC 1**
 See also CA 25-28; 49-52; CANR 32; CAP
 2; CDWLB 3; DA3; DAM MULT, NOV;
 DLB 113, 290; EWL 3; HW 1; LAW;
 LMFS 2; MTCW 1, 2; RGWL 2, 3; WLIT
 1
Atares, Carlos Saura
 See Saura (Atares), Carlos
Athanasius c. 295-c. 373 .... **CMLC 48**
Atheling, William
 See Pound, Ezra (Weston Loomis)
Atheling, William, Jr.
 See Blish, James (Benjamin)
Atherton, Gertrude (Franklin Horn)
 1857-1948 .... **TCLC 2**
 See also CA 104; 155; DLB 9, 78, 186;
 HGG; RGAL 4; SUFW 1; TCWW 2
Atherton, Lucius
 See Masters, Edgar Lee
Atkins, Jack
 See Harris, Mark
Atkinson, Kate 1951- .... **CLC 99**
 See also CA 166; CANR 101; DLB 267
Attaway, William (Alexander)
 1911-1986 .... **BLC 1; CLC 92**
 See also BW 2, 3; CA 143; CANR 82;
 DAM MULT; DLB 76
Atticus
 See Fleming, Ian (Lancaster); Wilson,
 (Thomas) Woodrow
Atwood, Margaret (Eleanor) 1939- ... **CLC 2,
 3, 4, 8, 13, 15, 25, 44, 84, 135; PC 8;
 SSC 2, 46; WLC**
 See also AAYA 12, 47; AMWS 13; BEST
 89:2; BPFB 1; CA 49-52; CANR 3, 24,
 33, 59, 95; CN 7; CP 7; CPW; CWP; DA;
 DA3; DAB; DAC; DAM MST, NOV,
 POET; DLB 53, 251; EWL 3; EXPN; FW;
 INT CANR-24; LAIT 5; MTCW 1, 2;
 NFS 4, 12, 13, 14, 19; PFS 7; RGSF 2;
 SATA 50; SSFS 3, 13; TWA; WWE 1;
 YAW
Aubigny, Pierre d'
 See Mencken, H(enry) L(ouis)
Aubin, Penelope 1685-1731(?) .... **LC 9**
 See also DLB 39

Auchincloss, Louis (Stanton) 1917- .. **CLC 4,
 6, 9, 18, 45; SSC 22**
 See also AMWS 4; CA 1-4R; CANR 6, 29,
 55, 87, 130; CN 7; DLB 2,
 244; DLBY 1980; EWL 3; INT CANR-
 29; MTCW 1; RGAL 4
Auden, W(ystan) H(ugh) 1907-1973 . **CLC 1,
 2, 3, 4, 6, 9, 11, 14, 43, 123; PC 1;
 WLC**
 See also AAYA 18; AMWS 2; BRW 7;
 BRWR 1; CA 9-12R; 45-48; CANR 5, 61,
 105; CDBLB 1914-1945; DA; DA3;
 DAB; DAC; DAM DRAM, MST, POET;
 DLB 10, 20; EWL 3; EXPP; MTCW 1, 2;
 PAB; PFS 1, 3, 4, 10; TUS; WP
Audiberti, Jacques 1900-1965 .... **CLC 38**
 See also CA 25-28R; DAM DRAM; EWL 3
Audubon, John James 1785-1851 . **NCLC 47**
 See also ANW; DLB 248
Auel, Jean M(arie) 1936- .... **CLC 31, 107**
 See also AAYA 7, 51; BEST 90:4; BPFB 1;
 CA 103; CANR 21, 64, 115; CPW; DA3;
 DAM POP; INT CANR-21; NFS 11;
 RHW; SATA 91
Auerbach, Erich 1892-1957 .... **TCLC 43**
 See also CA 118; 155; EWL 3
Augier, Emile 1820-1889 .... **NCLC 31**
 See also DLB 192; GFL 1789 to the Present
August, John
 See De Voto, Bernard (Augustine)
Augustine, St. 354-430 .... **CMLC 6; WLCS**
 See also DA; DA3; DAB; DAC; DAM
 MST; DLB 115; EW 1; RGWL 2, 3
Aunt Belinda
 See Braddon, Mary Elizabeth
Aunt Weedy
 See Alcott, Louisa May
Aurelius
 See Bourne, Randolph S(illiman)
Aurelius, Marcus 121-180 .... **CMLC 45**
 See Marcus Aurelius
 See also RGWL 2, 3
Aurobindo, Sri
 See Ghose, Aurabinda
Aurobindo Ghose
 See Ghose, Aurabinda
Austen, Jane 1775-1817 ...... **NCLC 1, 13, 19,
 33, 51, 81, 95, 119; WLC**
 See also AAYA 19; BRW 4; BRWC 1;
 BRWR 2; BYA 3; CDBLB 1789-1832;
 DA; DA3; DAB; DAC; DAM MST, NOV;
 DLB 116; EXPN; LAIT 2; LATS 1; LMFS
 1; NFS 1, 14, 18; TEA; WLIT 3; WYAS
 1
Auster, Paul 1947- .... **CLC 47, 131**
 See also AMWS 12; CA 69-72; CANR 23,
 52, 75, 129; CMW 4; CN 7; DA3; DLB
 227; MTCW 1; SUFW 2
Austin, Frank
 See Faust, Frederick (Schiller)
 See also TCWW 2
Austin, Mary (Hunter) 1868-1934 . **TCLC 25**
 See Stairs, Gordon
 See also ANW; CA 109; 178; DLB 9, 78,
 206, 221, 275; FW; TCWW 2
Averroes 1126-1198 .... **CMLC 7**
 See also DLB 115
Avicenna 980-1037 .... **CMLC 16**
 See also DLB 115
Avison, Margaret 1918- .... **CLC 2, 4, 97**
 See also CA 17-20R; CP 7; DAC; DAM
 POET; DLB 53; MTCW 1
Axton, David
 See Koontz, Dean R(ay)

Barbellion, W. N. P. .... **TCLC 24**
See Cummings, Bruce F(rederick)
Barber, Benjamin R. 1939- .... **CLC 141**
See also CA 29-32R; CANR 12, 32, 64, 119
Barbera, Jack (Vincent) 1945- .... **CLC 44**
See also CA 110; CANR 45
Barbey d'Aurevilly, Jules-Amedee
1808-1889 .... **NCLC 1; SSC 17**
See also DLB 119; GFL 1789 to the Present
Barbour, John c. 1316-1395 .... **CMLC 33**
See also DLB 146
Barbusse, Henri 1873-1935 .... **TCLC 5**
See also CA 105; 154; DLB 65; EWL 3;
RGWL 2, 3
Barclay, Bill
See Moorcock, Michael (John)
Barclay, William Ewert
See Moorcock, Michael (John)
Barea, Arturo 1897-1957 .... **TCLC 14**
See also CA 111; 201
Barfoot, Joan 1946- .... **CLC 18**
See also CA 105
Barham, Richard Harris
1788-1845 .... **NCLC 77**
See also DLB 159
Baring, Maurice 1874-1945 .... **TCLC 8**
See also CA 105; 168; DLB 34; HGG
Baring-Gould, Sabine 1834-1924 ... **TCLC 88**
See also DLB 156, 190
Barker, Clive 1952- .... **CLC 52; SSC 53**
See also AAYA 10, 54; BEST 90:3; BPFB
1; CA 121; 129; CANR 71, 111; CPW;
DA3; DAM POP; DLB 261; HGG; INT
CA-129; MTCW 1, 2; SUFW 2
Barker, George Granville
1913-1991 .... **CLC 8, 48**
See also CA 9-12R; 135; CANR 7, 38;
DAM POET; DLB 20; EWL 3; MTCW 1
Barker, Harley Granville
See Granville-Barker, Harley
See also DLB 10
Barker, Howard 1946- .... **CLC 37**
See also CA 102; CBD; CD 5; DLB 13,
233
Barker, Jane 1652-1732 .... **LC 42, 82**
See also DLB 39, 131
Barker, Pat(ricia) 1943- ...... **CLC 32, 94, 146**
See also BRWS 4; CA 117; 122; CANR 50,
101; CN 7; DLB 271; INT CA-122
Barlach, Ernst (Heinrich)
1870-1938 .... **TCLC 84**
See also CA 178; DLB 56, 118; EWL 3
Barlow, Joel 1754-1812 .... **NCLC 23**
See also AMWS 2; DLB 37; RGAL 4
Barnard, Mary (Ethel) 1909- .... **CLC 48**
See also CA 21-22; CAP 2
Barnes, Djuna 1892-1982 .... **CLC 3, 4, 8, 11,
29, 127; SSC 3**
See Steptoe, Lydia
See also AMWS 3; CA 9-12R; 107; CAD;
CANR 16, 55; CWD; DLB 4, 9, 45; EWL
3; GLL 1; MTCW 1, 2; RGAL 4; TUS
Barnes, Jim 1933- .... **NNAL**
See also CA 108; 175; CAAE 175; CAAS
28; DLB 175
Barnes, Julian (Patrick) 1946- . **CLC 42, 141**
See also BRWS 4; CA 102; CANR 19, 54,
115; CN 7; DAB; DLB 194; DLBY 1993;
EWL 3; MTCW 1
Barnes, Peter 1931-2004 .... **CLC 5, 56**
See also CA 65-68; CAAS 12; CANR 33,
34, 64, 113; CBD; CD 5; DFS 6; DLB
13, 233; MTCW 1
Barnes, William 1801-1886 .... **NCLC 75**
See also DLB 32
Baroja (y Nessi), Pio 1872-1956 .... **HLC 1;
TCLC 8**
See also CA 104; EW 9

Baron, David
See Pinter, Harold
Baron Corvo
See Rolfe, Frederick (William Serafino
Austin Lewis Mary)
Barondess, Sue K(aufman)
1926-1977 .... **CLC 8**
See Kaufman, Sue
See also CA 1-4R; 69-72; CANR 1
Baron de Teive
See Pessoa, Fernando (Antonio Nogueira)
Baroness Von S.
See Zangwill, Israel
Barres, (Auguste-)Maurice
1862-1923 .... **TCLC 47**
See also CA 164; DLB 123; GFL 1789 to
the Present
Barreto, Afonso Henrique de Lima
See Lima Barreto, Afonso Henrique de
Barrett, Andrea 1954- .... **CLC 150**
See also CA 156; CANR 92
Barrett, Michele .... **CLC 65**
Barrett, (Roger) Syd 1946- .... **CLC 35**
Barrett, William (Christopher)
1913-1992 .... **CLC 27**
See also CA 13-16R; 139; CANR 11, 67;
INT CANR-11
Barrie, J(ames) M(atthew)
1860-1937 .... **TCLC 2**
See also BRWS 3; BYA 4, 5; CA 104; 136;
CANR 77; CDBLB 1890-1914; CLR 16;
CWRI 5; DA3; DAB; DAM DRAM; DFS
7; DLB 10, 141, 156; EWL 3; FANT;
MAICYA 1, 2; MTCW 1; SATA 100;
SUFW; WCH; WLIT 4; YABC 1
Barrington, Michael
See Moorcock, Michael (John)
Barrol, Grady
See Bograd, Larry
Barry, Mike
See Malzberg, Barry N(athaniel)
Barry, Philip 1896-1949 .... **TCLC 11**
See also CA 109; 199; DFS 9; DLB 7, 228;
RGAL 4
Bart, Andre Schwarz
See Schwarz-Bart, Andre
Barth, John (Simmons) 1930- ... **CLC 1, 2, 3,
5, 7, 9, 10, 14, 27, 51, 89; SSC 10**
See also AITN 1, 2; AMW; BPFB 1; CA
1-4R; CABS 1; CANR 5, 23, 49, 64, 113;
CN 7; DAM NOV; DLB 2, 227; EWL 3;
FANT; MTCW 1; RGAL 4; RGSF 2;
RHW; SSFS 6; TUS
Barthelme, Donald 1931-1989 ... **CLC 1, 2, 3,
5, 6, 8, 13, 23, 46, 59, 115; SSC 2, 55**
See also AMWS 4; BPFB 1; CA 21-24R;
129; CANR 20, 58; DA3; DAM NOV;
DLB 2, 234; DLBY 1980, 1989; EWL 3;
FANT; LMFS 2; MTCW 1, 2; RGAL 4;
RGSF 2; SATA 7; SATA-Obit 62; SSFS
17
Barthelme, Frederick 1943- ...... **CLC 36, 117**
See also AMWS 11; CA 114; 122; CANR
77; CN 7; CSW; DLB 244; DLBY 1985;
EWL 3; INT CA-122
Barthes, Roland (Gerard)
1915-1980 .... **CLC 24, 83; TCLC 135**
See also CA 130; 97-100; CANR 66; DLB
296; EW 13; EWL 3; GFL 1789 to the
Present; MTCW 1, 2; TWA
Barzun, Jacques (Martin) 1907- ..... **CLC 51,
145**
See also CA 61-64; CANR 22, 95
Bashevis, Isaac
See Singer, Isaac Bashevis
Bashkirtseff, Marie 1859-1884 .... **NCLC 27**
Basho, Matsuo
See Matsuo Basho
See also PFS 18; RGWL 2, 3; WP

Basil of Caesaria c. 330-379 .... **CMLC 35**
Basket, Raney
See Edgerton, Clyde (Carlyle)
Bass, Kingsley B., Jr.
See Bullins, Ed
Bass, Rick 1958- .... **CLC 79, 143; SSC 60**
See also ANW; CA 126; CANR 53, 93;
CSW; DLB 212, 275
Bassani, Giorgio 1916-2000 .... **CLC 9**
See also CA 65-68; 190; CANR 33; CWW
2; DLB 128, 177, 299; EWL 3; MTCW 1;
RGWL 2, 3
Bastian, Ann .... **CLC 70**
Bastos, Augusto (Antonio) Roa
See Roa Bastos, Augusto (Antonio)
Bataille, Georges 1897-1962 .... **CLC 29**
See also CA 101; 89-92; EWL 3
Bates, H(erbert) E(rnest)
1905-1974 .... **CLC 46; SSC 10**
See also CA 93-96; 45-48; CANR 34; DA3;
DAB; DAM POP; DLB 162, 191; EWL
3; EXPS; MTCW 1, 2; RGSF 2; SSFS 7
Bauchart
See Camus, Albert
Baudelaire, Charles 1821-1867 . **NCLC 6, 29,
55; PC 1; SSC 18; WLC**
See also DA; DA3; DAB; DAC; DAM
MST, POET; DLB 217; EW 7; GFL 1789
to the Present; LMFS 2; RGWL 2, 3;
TWA
Baudouin, Marcel
See Peguy, Charles (Pierre)
Baudouin, Pierre
See Peguy, Charles (Pierre)
Baudrillard, Jean 1929- .... **CLC 60**
See also DLB 296
Baum, L(yman) Frank 1856-1919 .. **TCLC 7,
132**
See also AAYA 46; BYA 16; CA 108; 133;
CLR 15; CWRI 5; DLB 22; FANT; JRDA;
MAICYA 1, 2; MTCW 1, 2; NFS 13;
RGAL 4; SATA 18, 100; WCH
Baum, Louis F.
See Baum, L(yman) Frank
Baumbach, Jonathan 1933- .... **CLC 6, 23**
See also CA 13-16R; CAAS 5; CANR 12,
66; CN 7; DLBY 1980; INT CANR-12;
MTCW 1
Bausch, Richard (Carl) 1945- .... **CLC 51**
See also AMWS 7; CA 101; CAAS 14;
CANR 43, 61, 87; CSW; DLB 130
Baxter, Charles (Morley) 1947- . **CLC 45, 78**
See also CA 57-60; CANR 40, 64, 104;
CPW; DAM POP; DLB 130; MTCW 2
Baxter, George Owen
See Faust, Frederick (Schiller)
Baxter, James K(eir) 1926-1972 .... **CLC 14**
See also CA 77-80; EWL 3
Baxter, John
See Hunt, E(verette) Howard, (Jr.)
Bayer, Sylvia
See Glassco, John
Baynton, Barbara 1857-1929 .... **TCLC 57**
See also DLB 230; RGSF 2
Beagle, Peter S(oyer) 1939- .... **CLC 7, 104**
See also AAYA 47; BPFB 1; BYA 9, 10,
16; CA 9-12R; CANR 4, 51, 73, 110;
DA3; DLBY 1980; FANT; INT CANR-4;
MTCW 1; SATA 60, 130; SUFW 1, 2;
YAW
Bean, Normal
See Burroughs, Edgar Rice
Beard, Charles A(ustin)
1874-1948 .... **TCLC 15**
See also CA 115; 189; DLB 17; SATA 18

Benford, Gregory (Albert) 1941- ..... **CLC 52**
See also BPFB 1; CA 69-72, 175; CAAE 175; CAAS 27; CANR 12, 24, 49, 95; CSW; DLBY 1982; SCFW 2; SFW 4

Bengtsson, Frans (Gunnar) 1894-1954 .... **TCLC 48**
See also CA 170; EWL 3

Benjamin, David
See Slavitt, David R(ytman)

Benjamin, Lois
See Gould, Lois

Benjamin, Walter 1892-1940 .... **TCLC 39**
See also CA 164; DLB 242; EW 11; EWL 3

Ben Jelloun, Tahar 1944-
See Jelloun, Tahar ben
See also CA 135; CWW 2; EWL 3; RGWL 3; WLIT 2

Benn, Gottfried 1886-1956 .. **PC 35; TCLC 3**
See also CA 106; 153; DLB 56; EWL 3; RGWL 2, 3

Bennett, Alan 1934- .... **CLC 45, 77**
See also BRWS 8; CA 103; CANR 35, 55, 106; CBD; CD 5; DAB; DAM MST; MTCW 1, 2

Bennett, (Enoch) Arnold 1867-1931 .... **TCLC 5, 20**
See also BRW 6; CA 106; 155; CDBLB 1890-1914; DLB 10, 34, 98, 135; EWL 3; MTCW 2

Bennett, Elizabeth
See Mitchell, Margaret (Munnerlyn)

Bennett, George Harold 1930-
See Bennett, Hal
See also BW 1; CA 97-100; CANR 87

Bennett, Gwendolyn B. 1902-1981 .... **HR 2**
See also BW 1; CA 125; DLB 51; WP

Bennett, Hal .... **CLC 5**
See Bennett, George Harold
See also DLB 33

Bennett, Jay 1912- .... **CLC 35**
See also AAYA 10; CA 69-72; CANR 11, 42, 79; JRDA; SAAS 4; SATA 41, 87; SATA-Brief 27; WYA; YAW

Bennett, Louise (Simone) 1919- .... **BLC 1; CLC 28**
See also BW 2, 3; CA 151; CDWLB 3; CP 7; DAM MULT; DLB 117; EWL 3

Benson, A. C. 1862-1925 .... **TCLC 123**
See also DLB 98

Benson, E(dward) F(rederic) 1867-1940 .... **TCLC 27**
See also CA 114; 157; DLB 135, 153; HGG; SUFW 1

Benson, Jackson J. 1930- .... **CLC 34**
See also CA 25-28R; DLB 111

Benson, Sally 1900-1972 .... **CLC 17**
See also CA 19-20; 37-40R; CAP 1; SATA 1, 35; SATA-Obit 27

Benson, Stella 1892-1933 .... **TCLC 17**
See also CA 117; 154, 155; DLB 36, 162; FANT; TEA

Bentham, Jeremy 1748-1832 .... **NCLC 38**
See also DLB 107, 158, 252

Bentley, E(dmund) C(lerihew) 1875-1956 .... **TCLC 12**
See also CA 108; DLB 70; MSW

Bentley, Eric (Russell) 1916- .... **CLC 24**
See also CA 5-8R; CAD; CANR 6, 67; CBD; CD 5; INT CANR-6

ben Uzair, Salem
See Horne, Richard Henry Hengist

Beranger, Pierre Jean de 1780-1857 .... **NCLC 34**

Berdyaev, Nicolas
See Berdyaev, Nikolai (Aleksandrovich)

Berdyaev, Nikolai (Aleksandrovich) 1874-1948 .... **TCLC 67**
See also CA 120; 157

Berdyayev, Nikolai (Aleksandrovich)
See Berdyaev, Nikolai (Aleksandrovich)

Berendt, John (Lawrence) 1939- ...... **CLC 86**
See also CA 146; CANR 75, 93; DA3; MTCW 1

Beresford, J(ohn) D(avys) 1873-1947 .... **TCLC 81**
See also CA 112; 155; DLB 162, 178, 197; SFW 4; SUFW 1

Bergelson, David (Rafailovich) 1884-1952 .... **TCLC 81**
See Bergelson, Dovid
See also CA 220

Bergelson, Dovid
See Bergelson, David (Rafailovich)
See also EWL 3

Berger, Colonel
See Malraux, (Georges-)Andre

Berger, John (Peter) 1926- .... **CLC 2, 19**
See also BRWS 4; CA 81-84; CANR 51, 78, 117; CN 7; DLB 14, 207

Berger, Melvin H. 1927- .... **CLC 12**
See also CA 5-8R; CANR 4; CLR 32; SAAS 2; SATA 5, 88; SATA-Essay 124

Berger, Thomas (Louis) 1924- .. **CLC 3, 5, 8, 11, 18, 38**
See also BPFB 1; CA 1-4R; CANR 5, 28, 51, 128; CN 7; DAM NOV; DLB 2; DLBY 1980; EWL 3; FANT; INT CANR-28; MTCW 1, 2; RHW; TCWW 2

Bergman, (Ernst) Ingmar 1918- ...... **CLC 16, 72**
See also CA 81-84; CANR 33, 70; CWW 2; DLB 257; MTCW 2

Bergson, Henri(-Louis) 1859-1941 . **TCLC 32**
See also CA 164; EW 8; EWL 3; GFL 1789 to the Present

Bergstein, Eleanor 1938- .... **CLC 4**
See also CA 53-56; CANR 5

Berkeley, George 1685-1753 .... **LC 65**
See also DLB 31, 101, 252

Berkoff, Steven 1937- .... **CLC 56**
See also CA 104; CANR 72; CBD; CD 5

Berlin, Isaiah 1909-1997 .... **TCLC 105**
See also CA 85-88; 162

Bermant, Chaim (Icyk) 1929-1998 ... **CLC 40**
See also CA 57-60; CANR 6, 31, 57, 105; CN 7

Bern, Victoria
See Fisher, M(ary) F(rances) K(ennedy)

Bernanos, (Paul Louis) Georges 1888-1948 .... **TCLC 3**
See also CA 104; 130; CANR 94; DLB 72; EWL 3; GFL 1789 to the Present; RGWL 2, 3

Bernard, April 1956- .... **CLC 59**
See also CA 131

Berne, Victoria
See Fisher, M(ary) F(rances) K(ennedy)

Bernhard, Thomas 1931-1989 ..... **CLC 3, 32, 61; DC 14**
See also CA 85-88; 127; CANR 32, 57; CDWLB 2; DLB 85, 124; EWL 3; MTCW 1; RGWL 2, 3

Bernhardt, Sarah (Henriette Rosine) 1844-1923 .... **TCLC 75**
See also CA 157

Bernstein, Charles 1950- .... **CLC 142**
See also CA 129; CAAS 24; CANR 90; CP 7; DLB 169

Bernstein, Ingrid
See Kirsch, Sarah

Berriault, Gina 1926-1999 .... **CLC 54, 109; SSC 30**
See also CA 116; 129; 185; CANR 66; DLB 130; SSFS 7, 11

Berrigan, Daniel 1921- .... **CLC 4**
See also CA 33-36R, 187; CAAE 187; CAAS 1; CANR 11, 43, 78; CP 7; DLB 5

Berrigan, Edmund Joseph Michael, Jr. 1934-1983
See Berrigan, Ted
See also CA 61-64; 110; CANR 14, 102

Berrigan, Ted .... **CLC 37**
See Berrigan, Edmund Joseph Michael, Jr.
See also DLB 5, 169; WP

Berry, Charles Edward Anderson 1931-
See Berry, Chuck
See also CA 115

Berry, Chuck .... **CLC 17**
See Berry, Charles Edward Anderson

Berry, Jonas
See Ashbery, John (Lawrence)
See also GLL 1

Berry, Wendell (Erdman) 1934- ... **CLC 4, 6, 8, 27, 46; PC 28**
See also AITN 1; AMWS 10; ANW; CA 73-76; CANR 50, 73, 101; CP 7; CSW; DAM POET; DLB 5, 6, 234, 275; MTCW 1

Berryman, John 1914-1972 ... **CLC 1, 2, 3, 4, 6, 8, 10, 13, 25, 62**
See also AMW; CA 13-16; 33-36R; CABS 2; CANR 35; CAP 1; CDALB 1941-1968; DAM POET; DLB 48; EWL 3; MTCW 1, 2; PAB; RGAL 4; WP

Bertolucci, Bernardo 1940- ..... **CLC 16, 157**
See also CA 106; CANR 125

Berton, Pierre (Francis Demarigny) 1920- .... **CLC 104**
See also CA 1-4R; CANR 2, 56; CPW; DLB 68; SATA 99

Bertrand, Aloysius 1807-1841 .... **NCLC 31**
See Bertrand, Louis oAloysiusc

Bertrand, Louis oAloysiusc
See Bertrand, Aloysius
See also DLB 217

Bertran de Born c. 1140-1215 .... **CMLC 5**

Besant, Annie (Wood) 1847-1933 ..... **TCLC 9**
See also CA 105; 185

Bessie, Alvah 1904-1985 .... **CLC 23**
See also CA 5-8R; 116; CANR 2, 80; DLB 26

Bestuzhev, Aleksandr Aleksandrovich 1797-1837 .... **NCLC 131**
See also DLB 198

Bethlen, T. D.
See Silverberg, Robert

Beti, Mongo .... **BLC 1; CLC 27**
See Biyidi, Alexandre
See also AFW; CANR 79; DAM MULT; EWL 3; WLIT 2

Betjeman, John 1906-1984 ...... **CLC 2, 6, 10, 34, 43**
See also BRW 7; CA 9-12R; 112; CANR 33, 56; CDBLB 1945-1960; DA3; DAB; DAM MST, POET; DLB 20; DLBY 1984; EWL 3; MTCW 1, 2

Bettelheim, Bruno 1903-1990 .... **CLC 79; TCLC 143**
See also CA 81-84; 131; CANR 23, 61; DA3; MTCW 1, 2

Betti, Ugo 1892-1953 .... **TCLC 5**
See also CA 104; 155; EWL 3; RGWL 2, 3

Betts, Doris (Waugh) 1932- ..... **CLC 3, 6, 28; SSC 45**
See also CA 13-16R; CANR 9, 66, 77; CN 7; CSW; DLB 218; DLBY 1982; INT CANR-9; RGAL 4

Bevan, Alistair
See Roberts, Keith (John Kingston)

Bey, Pilaff
See Douglas, (George) Norman

Bialik, Chaim Nachman 1873-1934 .... **TCLC 25**
See also CA 170; EWL 3

Bickerstaff, Isaac
See Swift, Jonathan

Boyle, T. C.
See Boyle, T(homas) Coraghessan
See also AMWS 8

Boyle, T(homas) Coraghessan
1948- .... **CLC 36, 55, 90; SSC 16**
See Boyle, T. C.
See also AAYA 47; BEST 90:4; BPFB 1;
CA 120; CANR 44, 76, 89; CN 7; CPW;
DA3; DAM POP; DLB 218, 278; DLBY
1986; EWL 3; MTCW 2; SSFS 13, 19

Boz
See Dickens, Charles (John Huffam)

Brackenridge, Hugh Henry
1748-1816 .... **NCLC 7**
See also DLB 11, 37; RGAL 4

Bradbury, Edward P.
See Moorcock, Michael (John)
See also MTCW 2

Bradbury, Malcolm (Stanley)
1932-2000 .... **CLC 32, 61**
See also CA 1-4R; CANR 1, 33, 91, 98;
CN 7; DA3; DAM NOV; DLB 14, 207;
EWL 3; MTCW 1, 2

Bradbury, Ray (Douglas) 1920- .... **CLC 1, 3,
10, 15, 42, 98; SSC 29, 53; WLC**
See also AAYA 15; AITN 1, 2; AMWS 4;
BPFB 1; BYA 4, 5, 11; CA 1-4R; CANR
2, 30, 75, 125; CDALB 1968-1988; CN
7; CPW; DA; DA3; DAB; DAC; DAM
MST, NOV, POP; DLB 2, 8; EXPN;
EXPS; HGG; LAIT 3, 5; LATS 1; LMFS
2; MTCW 1, 2; NFS 1; RGAL 4; RGSF
2; SATA 11, 64, 123; SCFW 2; SFW 4;
SSFS 1; SUFW 1, 2; TUS; YAW

Braddon, Mary Elizabeth
1837-1915 .... **TCLC 111**
See also BRWS 8; CA 108; 179; CMW 4;
DLB 18, 70, 156; HGG

Bradfield, Scott (Michael) 1955- .... **SSC 65**
See also CA 147; CANR 90; HGG; SUFW
2

Bradford, Gamaliel 1863-1932 .... **TCLC 36**
See also CA 160; DLB 17

Bradford, William 1590-1657 .... **LC 64**
See also DLB 24, 30; RGAL 4

Bradley, David (Henry), Jr. 1950- .... **BLC 1;
CLC 23, 118**
See also BW 1, 3; CA 104; CANR 26, 81;
CN 7; DAM MULT; DLB 33

Bradley, John Ed(mund, Jr.) 1958- . **CLC 55**
See also CA 139; CANR 99; CN 7; CSW

Bradley, Marion Zimmer
1930-1999 .... **CLC 30**
See Chapman, Lee; Dexter, John; Gardner,
Miriam; Ives, Morgan; Rivers, Elfrida
See also AAYA 40; BPFB 1; CA 57-60; 185;
CAAS 10; CANR 7, 31, 51, 75, 107;
CPW; DA3; DAM POP; DLB 8; FANT;
FW; MTCW 1, 2; SATA 90, 139; SATA-
Obit 116; SFW 4; SUFW 2; YAW

Bradshaw, John 1933- .... **CLC 70**
See also CA 138; CANR 61

Bradstreet, Anne 1612(?)-1672 ...... **LC 4, 30;
PC 10**
See also AMWS 1; CDALB 1640-1865;
DA; DA3; DAC; DAM MST, POET; DLB
24; EXPP; FW; PFS 6; RGAL 4; TUS;
WP

Brady, Joan 1939- .... **CLC 86**
See also CA 141

Bragg, Melvyn 1939- .... **CLC 10**
See also BEST 89:3; CA 57-60; CANR 10,
48, 89; CN 7; DLB 14, 271; RHW

Brahe, Tycho 1546-1601 .... **LC 45**
See also DLB 300

Braine, John (Gerard) 1922-1986 . **CLC 1, 3,
41**
See also CA 1-4R; 120; CANR 1, 33; CD-
BLB 1945-1960; DLB 15; DLBY 1986;
EWL 3; MTCW 1

Braithwaite, William Stanley (Beaumont)
1878-1962 .... **BLC 1; HR 2; PC 52**
See also BW 1; CA 125; DAM MULT; DLB
50, 54

Bramah, Ernest 1868-1942 .... **TCLC 72**
See also CA 156; CMW 4; DLB 70; FANT

Brammer, William 1930(?)-1978 ...... **CLC 31**
See also CA 77-80

Brancati, Vitaliano 1907-1954 .... **TCLC 12**
See also CA 109; DLB 264; EWL 3

Brancato, Robin F(idler) 1936- .... **CLC 35**
See also AAYA 9; BYA 6; CA 69-72; CANR
11, 45; CLR 32; JRDA; MAICYA 2;
MAICYAS 1; SAAS 9; SATA 97; WYA;
YAW

Brand, Dionne 1953- .... **CLC 192**
See also BW 2; CA 143; CWP

Brand, Max
See Faust, Frederick (Schiller)
See also BPFB 1; TCWW 2

Brand, Millen 1906-1980 .... **CLC 7**
See also CA 21-24R; 97-100; CANR 72

Branden, Barbara .... **CLC 44**
See also CA 148

Brandes, Georg (Morris Cohen)
1842-1927 .... **TCLC 10**
See also CA 105; 189; DLB 300

Brandys, Kazimierz 1916-2000 .... **CLC 62**
See also EWL 3

Branley, Franklyn M(ansfield)
1915-2002 .... **CLC 21**
See also CA 33-36R; 207; CANR 14, 39;
CLR 13; MAICYA 1, 2; SAAS 16; SATA
4, 68, 136

Brant, Beth (E.) 1941- .... **NNAL**
See also CA 144; FW

Brathwaite, Edward Kamau
1930- .... **BLCS; CLC 11; PC 56**
See also BW 2, 3; CA 25-28R; CANR 11,
26, 47, 107; CDWLB 3; CP 7; DAM
POET; DLB 125; EWL 3

Brathwaite, Kamau
See Brathwaite, Edward Kamau

Brautigan, Richard (Gary)
1935-1984 .... **CLC 1, 3, 5, 9, 12, 34, 42;
TCLC 133**
See also BPFB 1; CA 53-56; 113; CANR
34; DA3; DAM NOV; DLB 2, 5, 206;
DLBY 1980, 1984; FANT; MTCW 1;
RGAL 4; SATA 56

Brave Bird, Mary .... **NNAL**
See Crow Dog, Mary (Ellen)

Braverman, Kate 1950- .... **CLC 67**
See also CA 89-92

Brecht, (Eugen) Bertolt (Friedrich)
1898-1956 ..... **DC 3; TCLC 1, 6, 13, 35;
WLC**
See also CA 104; 133; CANR 62; CDWLB
2; DA; DA3; DAB; DAC; DAM DRAM,
MST; DFS 4, 5, 9; DLB 56, 124; EW 11;
EWL 3; IDTP; MTCW 1, 2; RGWL 2, 3;
TWA

Brecht, Eugen Berthold Friedrich
See Brecht, (Eugen) Bertolt (Friedrich)

Bremer, Fredrika 1801-1865 .... **NCLC 11**
See also DLB 254

Brennan, Christopher John
1870-1932 .... **TCLC 17**
See also CA 117; 188; DLB 230; EWL 3

Brennan, Maeve 1917-1993 ... **CLC 5; TCLC
124**
See also CA 81-84; CANR 72, 100

Brent, Linda
See Jacobs, Harriet A(nn)

Brentano, Clemens (Maria)
1778-1842 .... **NCLC 1**
See also DLB 90; RGWL 2, 3

Brent of Bin Bin
See Franklin, (Stella Maria Sarah) Miles
(Lampe)

Brenton, Howard 1942- .... **CLC 31**
See also CA 69-72; CANR 33, 67; CBD;
CD 5; DLB 13; MTCW 1

Breslin, James 1930-
See Breslin, Jimmy
See also CA 73-76; CANR 31, 75; DAM
NOV; MTCW 1, 2

Breslin, Jimmy .... **CLC 4, 43**
See Breslin, James
See also AITN 1; DLB 185; MTCW 2

Bresson, Robert 1901(?)-1999 .... **CLC 16**
See also CA 110; 187; CANR 49

Breton, Andre 1896-1966 .. **CLC 2, 9, 15, 54;
PC 15**
See also CA 19-20; 25-28R; CANR 40, 60;
CAP 2; DLB 65, 258; EW 11; EWL 3;
GFL 1789 to the Present; LMFS 2;
MTCW 1, 2; RGWL 2, 3; TWA; WP

Breytenbach, Breyten 1939(?)- .. **CLC 23, 37,
126**
See also CA 113; 129; CANR 61, 122;
CWW 2; DAM POET; DLB 225; EWL 3

Bridgers, Sue Ellen 1942- .... **CLC 26**
See also AAYA 8, 49; BYA 7, 8; CA 65-68;
CANR 11, 36; CLR 18; DLB 52; JRDA;
MAICYA 1, 2; SAAS 1; SATA 22, 90;
SATA-Essay 109; WYA; YAW

Bridges, Robert (Seymour)
1844-1930 .... **PC 28; TCLC 1**
See also BRW 6; CA 104; 152; CDBLB
1890-1914; DAM POET; DLB 19, 98

Bridie, James .... **TCLC 3**
See Mavor, Osborne Henry
See also DLB 10; EWL 3

Brin, David 1950- .... **CLC 34**
See also AAYA 21; CA 102; CANR 24, 70,
125, 127; INT CANR-24; SATA 65;
SCFW 2; SFW 4

Brink, Andre (Philippus) 1935- . **CLC 18, 36,
106**
See also AFW; BRWS 6; CA 104; CANR
39, 62, 109; CN 7; DLB 225; EWL 3; INT
CA-103; LATS 1; MTCW 1, 2; WLIT 2

Brinsmead, H. F(ay)
See Brinsmead, H(esba) F(ay)

Brinsmead, H. F.
See Brinsmead, H(esba) F(ay)

Brinsmead, H(esba) F(ay) 1922- ...... **CLC 21**
See also CA 21-24R; CANR 10; CLR 47;
CWRI 5; MAICYA 1, 2; SAAS 5; SATA
18, 78

Brittain, Vera (Mary) 1893(?)-1970 . **CLC 23**
See also CA 13-16; 25-28R; CANR 58;
CAP 1; DLB 191; FW; MTCW 1, 2

Broch, Hermann 1886-1951 .... **TCLC 20**
See also CA 117; 211; CDWLB 2; DLB 85,
124; EW 10; EWL 3; RGWL 2, 3

Brock, Rose
See Hansen, Joseph
See also GLL 1

Brod, Max 1884-1968 .... **TCLC 115**
See also CA 5-8R; 25-28R; CANR 7; DLB
81; EWL 3

Brodkey, Harold (Roy) 1930-1996 .. **CLC 56;
TCLC 123**
See also CA 111; 151; CANR 71; CN 7;
DLB 130

Brodsky, Iosif Alexandrovich 1940-1996
See Brodsky, Joseph
See also AITN 1; CA 41-44R; 151; CANR
37, 106; DA3; DAM POET; MTCW 1, 2;
RGWL 2, 3

Butts, Mary 1890(?)-1937 .... **TCLC 77**
See also CA 148; DLB 240

Buxton, Ralph
See Silverstein, Alvin; Silverstein, Virginia B(arbara Opshelor)

Buzo, Alex
See Buzo, Alexander (John)
See also DLB 289

Buzo, Alexander (John) 1944- .... **CLC 61**
See also CA 97-100; CANR 17, 39, 69; CD 5

Buzzati, Dino 1906-1972 .... **CLC 36**
See also CA 160; 33-36R; DLB 177; RGWL 2, 3; SFW 4

Byars, Betsy (Cromer) 1928- .... **CLC 35**
See also AAYA 19; BYA 3; CA 33-36R, 183; CAAE 183; CANR 18, 36, 57, 102; CLR 1, 16, 72; DLB 52; INT CANR-18; JRDA; MAICYA 1, 2; MAICYAS 1; MTCW 1; SAAS 1; SATA 4, 46, 80; SATA-Essay 108; WYA; YAW

Byatt, A(ntonia) S(usan Drabble)
1936- .... **CLC 19, 65, 136**
See also BPFB 1; BRWC 2; BRWS 4; CA 13-16R; CANR 13, 33, 50, 75, 96; DA3; DAM NOV, POP; DLB 14, 194; EWL 3; MTCW 1, 2; RGSF 2; RHW; TEA

Byrne, David 1952- .... **CLC 26**
See also CA 127

Byrne, John Keyes 1926-
See Leonard, Hugh
See also CA 102; CANR 78; INT CA-102

Byron, George Gordon (Noel)
1788-1824 ..... **NCLC 2, 12, 109; PC 16; WLC**
See also BRW 4; BRWC 2; CDBLB 1789-1832; DA; DA3; DAB; DAC; DAM MST, POET; DLB 96, 110; EXPP; LMFS 1; PAB; PFS 1, 14; RGEL 2; TEA; WLIT 3; WP

Byron, Robert 1905-1941 .... **TCLC 67**
See also CA 160; DLB 195

C. 3. 3.
See Wilde, Oscar (Fingal O'Flahertie Wills)

Caballero, Fernan 1796-1877 .... **NCLC 10**

Cabell, Branch
See Cabell, James Branch

Cabell, James Branch 1879-1958 .... **TCLC 6**
See also CA 105; 152; DLB 9, 78; FANT; MTCW 1; RGAL 4; SUFW 1

Cabeza de Vaca, Alvar Nunez
1490-1557(?) .... **LC 61**

Cable, George Washington
1844-1925 .... **SSC 4; TCLC 4**
See also CA 104; 155; DLB 12, 74; DLBD 13; RGAL 4; TUS

Cabral de Melo Neto, Joao
1920-1999 .... **CLC 76**
See Melo Neto, Joao Cabral de
See also CA 151; DAM MULT; LAW; LAWS 1

Cabrera Infante, G(uillermo) 1929- . **CLC 5, 25, 45, 120; HLC 1; SSC 39**
See also CA 85-88; CANR 29, 65, 110; CDWLB 3; CWW 2; DA3; DAM MULT; DLB 113; EWL 3; HW 1, 2; LAW; LAWS 1; MTCW 1, 2; RGSF 2; WLIT 1

Cade, Toni
See Bambara, Toni Cade

Cadmus and Harmonia
See Buchan, John

Caedmon fl. 658-680 .... **CMLC 7**
See also DLB 146

Caeiro, Alberto
See Pessoa, Fernando (Antonio Nogueira)

Caesar, Julius .... **CMLC 47**
See Julius Caesar
See also AW 1; RGWL 2, 3

Cage, John (Milton, Jr.)
1912-1992 .... **CLC 41; PC 58**
See also CA 13-16R; 169; CANR 9, 78; DLB 193; INT CANR-9

Cahan, Abraham 1860-1951 .... **TCLC 71**
See also CA 108; 154; DLB 9, 25, 28; RGAL 4

Cain, G.
See Cabrera Infante, G(uillermo)

Cain, Guillermo
See Cabrera Infante, G(uillermo)

Cain, James M(allahan) 1892-1977 .. **CLC 3, 11, 28**
See also AITN 1; BPFB 1; CA 17-20R; 73-76; CANR 8, 34, 61; CMW 4; DLB 226; EWL 3; MSW; MTCW 1; RGAL 4

Caine, Hall 1853-1931 .... **TCLC 97**
See also RHW

Caine, Mark
See Raphael, Frederic (Michael)

Calasso, Roberto 1941- .... **CLC 81**
See also CA 143; CANR 89

Calderon de la Barca, Pedro
1600-1681 .... **DC 3; HLCS 1; LC 23**
See also EW 2; RGWL 2, 3; TWA

Caldwell, Erskine (Preston)
1903-1987 .... **CLC 1, 8, 14, 50, 60; SSC 19; TCLC 117**
See also AITN 1; AMW; BPFB 1; CA 1-4R; 121; CAAS 1; CANR 2, 33; DA3; DAM NOV; DLB 9, 86; EWL 3; MTCW 1, 2; RGAL 4; RGSF 2; TUS

Caldwell, (Janet Miriam) Taylor (Holland)
1900-1985 .... **CLC 2, 28, 39**
See also BPFB 1; CA 5-8R; 116; CANR 5; DA3; DAM NOV, POP; DLBD 17; RHW

Calhoun, John Caldwell
1782-1850 .... **NCLC 15**
See also DLB 3, 248

Calisher, Hortense 1911- ..... **CLC 2, 4, 8, 38, 134; SSC 15**
See also CA 1-4R; CANR 1, 22, 117; CN 7; DA3; DAM NOV; DLB 2, 218; INT CANR-22; MTCW 1, 2; RGAL 4; RGSF 2

Callaghan, Morley Edward
1903-1990 ..... **CLC 3, 14, 41, 65; TCLC 145**
See also CA 9-12R; 132; CANR 33, 73; DAC; DAM MST; DLB 68; EWL 3; MTCW 1, 2; RGEL 2; RGSF 2; SSFS 19

Callimachus c. 305B.C.-c. 240B.C. .... **CMLC 18**
See also AW 1; DLB 176; RGWL 2, 3

Calvin, Jean
See Calvin, John
See also GFL Beginnings to 1789

Calvin, John 1509-1564 .... **LC 37**
See Calvin, Jean

Calvino, Italo 1923-1985 .... **CLC 5, 8, 11, 22, 33, 39, 73; SSC 3, 48**
See also CA 85-88; 116; CANR 23, 61; DAM NOV; DLB 196; EW 13; EWL 3; MTCW 1, 2; RGSF 2; RGWL 2, 3; SFW 4; SSFS 12

Camara Laye
See Laye, Camara
See also EWL 3

Camden, William 1551-1623 .... **LC 77**
See also DLB 172

Cameron, Carey 1952- .... **CLC 59**
See also CA 135

Cameron, Peter 1959- .... **CLC 44**
See also AMWS 12; CA 125; CANR 50, 117; DLB 234; GLL 2

Camoens, Luis Vaz de 1524(?)-1580
See Camoes, Luis de
See also EW 2

Camoes, Luis de 1524(?)-1580 . **HLCS 1; LC 62; PC 31**
See Camoens, Luis Vaz de
See also DLB 287; RGWL 2, 3

Campana, Dino 1885-1932 .... **TCLC 20**
See also CA 117; DLB 114; EWL 3

Campanella, Tommaso 1568-1639 .... **LC 32**
See also RGWL 2, 3

Campbell, John W(ood, Jr.)
1910-1971 .... **CLC 32**
See also CA 21-22; 29-32R; CANR 34; CAP 2; DLB 8; MTCW 1; SCFW; SFW 4

Campbell, Joseph 1904-1987 .... **CLC 69; TCLC 140**
See also AAYA 3; BEST 89:2; CA 1-4R; 124; CANR 3, 28, 61, 107; DA3; MTCW 1, 2

Campbell, Maria 1940- .... **CLC 85; NNAL**
See also CA 102; CANR 54; CCA 1; DAC

Campbell, (John) Ramsey 1946- ..... **CLC 42; SSC 19**
See also AAYA 51; CA 57-60; CANR 7, 102; DLB 261; HGG; INT CANR-7; SUFW 1, 2

Campbell, (Ignatius) Roy (Dunnachie)
1901-1957 .... **TCLC 5**
See also AFW; CA 104; 155; DLB 20, 225; EWL 3; MTCW 2; RGEL 2

Campbell, Thomas 1777-1844 .... **NCLC 19**
See also DLB 93, 144; RGEL 2

Campbell, Wilfred .... **TCLC 9**
See Campbell, William

Campbell, William 1858(?)-1918
See Campbell, Wilfred
See also CA 106; DLB 92

Campion, Jane 1954- .... **CLC 95**
See also AAYA 33; CA 138; CANR 87

Campion, Thomas 1567-1620 .... **LC 78**
See also CDBLB Before 1660; DAM POET; DLB 58, 172; RGEL 2

Camus, Albert 1913-1960 ...... **CLC 1, 2, 4, 9, 11, 14, 32, 63, 69, 124; DC 2; SSC 9; WLC**
See also AAYA 36; AFW; BPFB 1; CA 89-92; CANR 131; DA; DA3; DAB; DAC; DAM DRAM, MST, NOV; DLB 72; EW 13; EWL 3; EXPN; EXPS; GFL 1789 to the Present; LATS 1; LMFS 2; MTCW 1, 2; NFS 6, 16; RGSF 2; RGWL 2, 3; SSFS 4; TWA

Canby, Vincent 1924-2000 .... **CLC 13**
See also CA 81-84; 191

Cancale
See Desnos, Robert

Canetti, Elias 1905-1994 .. **CLC 3, 14, 25, 75, 86**
See also CA 21-24R; 146; CANR 23, 61, 79; CDWLB 2; CWW 2; DA3; DLB 85, 124; EW 12; EWL 3; MTCW 1, 2; RGWL 2, 3; TWA

Canfield, Dorothea F.
See Fisher, Dorothy (Frances) Canfield

Canfield, Dorothea Frances
See Fisher, Dorothy (Frances) Canfield

Canfield, Dorothy
See Fisher, Dorothy (Frances) Canfield

Canin, Ethan 1960- .... **CLC 55; SSC 70**
See also CA 131; 135

Cankar, Ivan 1876-1918 .... **TCLC 105**
See also CDWLB 4; DLB 147; EWL 3

Cannon, Curt
See Hunter, Evan

Cao, Lan 1961- .... **CLC 109**
See also CA 165

Cape, Judith
See Page, P(atricia) K(athleen)
See also CCA 1

Corcoran, Barbara (Asenath)
1911- .... **CLC 17**
See also AAYA 14; CA 21-24R, 191; CAAE 191; CAAS 2; CANR 11, 28, 48; CLR 50; DLB 52; JRDA; MAICYA 2; MAICYAS 1; RHW; SAAS 20; SATA 3, 77; SATA-Essay 125

Cordelier, Maurice
See Giraudoux, Jean(-Hippolyte)

Corelli, Marie .... **TCLC 51**
See Mackay, Mary
See also DLB 34, 156; RGEL 2; SUFW 1

Corman, Cid .... **CLC 9**
See Corman, Sidney
See also CAAS 2; DLB 5, 193

Corman, Sidney 1924-2004
See Corman, Cid
See also CA 85-88; 225; CANR 44; CP 7; DAM POET

Cormier, Robert (Edmund)
1925-2000 .... **CLC 12, 30**
See also AAYA 3, 19; BYA 1, 2, 6, 8, 9; CA 1-4R; CANR 5, 23, 76, 93; CDALB 1968-1988; CLR 12, 55; DA; DAB; DAC; DAM MST, NOV; DLB 52; EXPN; INT CANR-23; JRDA; LAIT 5; MAICYA 1, 2; MTCW 1, 2; NFS 2, 18; SATA 10, 45, 83; SATA-Obit 122; WYA; YAW

Corn, Alfred (DeWitt III) 1943- .... **CLC 33**
See also CA 179; CAAE 179; CAAS 25; CANR 44; CP 7; CSW; DLB 120, 282; DLBY 1980

Corneille, Pierre 1606-1684 ... **DC 21; LC 28**
See also DAB; DAM MST; DLB 268; EW 3; GFL Beginnings to 1789; RGWL 2, 3; TWA

Cornwell, David (John Moore)
1931- .... **CLC 9, 15**
See le Carre, John
See also CA 5-8R; CANR 13, 33, 59, 107; DA3; DAM POP; MTCW 1, 2

Cornwell, Patricia (Daniels) 1956- . **CLC 155**
See also AAYA 16; BPFB 1; CA 134; CANR 53, 131; CMW 4; CPW; CSW; DAM POP; MSW; MTCW 1

Corso, (Nunzio) Gregory 1930-2001 . **CLC 1, 11; PC 33**
See also AMWS 12; BG 2; CA 5-8R; 193; CANR 41, 76; CP 7; DA3; DLB 5, 16, 237; LMFS 2; MTCW 1, 2; WP

Cortazar, Julio 1914-1984 ... **CLC 2, 3, 5, 10, 13, 15, 33, 34, 92; HLC 1; SSC 7**
See also BPFB 1; CA 21-24R; CANR 12, 32, 81; CDWLB 3; DA3; DAM MULT, NOV; DLB 113; EWL 3; EXPS; HW 1, 2; LAW; MTCW 1, 2; RGSF 2; RGWL 2, 3; SSFS 3; TWA; WLIT 1

Cortes, Hernan 1485-1547 .... **LC 31**

Corvinus, Jakob
See Raabe, Wilhelm (Karl)

Corwin, Cecil
See Kornbluth, C(yril) M.

Cosic, Dobrica 1921- .... **CLC 14**
See also CA 122; 138; CDWLB 4; CWW 2; DLB 181; EWL 3

Costain, Thomas B(ertram)
1885-1965 .... **CLC 30**
See also BYA 3; CA 5-8R; 25-28R; DLB 9; RHW

Costantini, Humberto 1924(?)-1987 . **CLC 49**
See also CA 131; 122; EWL 3; HW 1

Costello, Elvis 1954- .... **CLC 21**
See also CA 204

Costenoble, Philostene
See Ghelderode, Michel de

Cotes, Cecil V.
See Duncan, Sara Jeannette

Cotter, Joseph Seamon Sr.
1861-1949 .... **BLC 1; TCLC 28**
See also BW 1; CA 124; DAM MULT; DLB 50

Couch, Arthur Thomas Quiller
See Quiller-Couch, Sir Arthur (Thomas)

Coulton, James
See Hansen, Joseph

Couperus, Louis (Marie Anne)
1863-1923 .... **TCLC 15**
See also CA 115; EWL 3; RGWL 2, 3

Coupland, Douglas 1961- .... **CLC 85, 133**
See also AAYA 34; CA 142; CANR 57, 90, 130; CCA 1; CPW; DAC; DAM POP

Court, Wesli
See Turco, Lewis (Putnam)

Courtenay, Bryce 1933- .... **CLC 59**
See also CA 138; CPW

Courtney, Robert
See Ellison, Harlan (Jay)

Cousteau, Jacques-Yves 1910-1997 .. **CLC 30**
See also CA 65-68; 159; CANR 15, 67; MTCW 1; SATA 38, 98

Coventry, Francis 1725-1754 .... **LC 46**

Coverdale, Miles c. 1487-1569 .... **LC 77**
See also DLB 167

Cowan, Peter (Walkinshaw)
1914-2002 .... **SSC 28**
See also CA 21-24R; CANR 9, 25, 50, 83; CN 7; DLB 260; RGSF 2

Coward, Noel (Peirce) 1899-1973 . **CLC 1, 9, 29, 51**
See also AITN 1; BRWS 2; CA 17-18; 41-44R; CANR 35; CAP 2; CDBLB 1914-1945; DA3; DAM DRAM; DFS 3, 6; DLB 10, 245; EWL 3; IDFW 3, 4; MTCW 1, 2; RGEL 2; TEA

Cowley, Abraham 1618-1667 .... **LC 43**
See also BRW 2; DLB 131, 151; PAB; RGEL 2

Cowley, Malcolm 1898-1989 .... **CLC 39**
See also AMWS 2; CA 5-8R; 128; CANR 3, 55; DLB 4, 48; DLBY 1981, 1989; EWL 3; MTCW 1, 2

Cowper, William 1731-1800 ..... **NCLC 8, 94; PC 40**
See also BRW 3; DA3; DAM POET; DLB 104, 109; RGEL 2

Cox, William Trevor 1928-
See Trevor, William
See also CA 9-12R; CANR 4, 37, 55, 76, 102; DAM NOV; INT CANR-37; MTCW 1, 2; TEA

Coyne, P. J.
See Masters, Hilary

Cozzens, James Gould 1903-1978 . **CLC 1, 4, 11, 92**
See also AMW; BPFB 1; CA 9-12R; 81-84; CANR 19; CDALB 1941-1968; DLB 9, 294; DLBD 2; DLBY 1984, 1997; EWL 3; MTCW 1, 2; RGAL 4

Crabbe, George 1754-1832 .... **NCLC 26, 121**
See also BRW 3; DLB 93; RGEL 2

Crace, Jim 1946- .... **CLC 157; SSC 61**
See also CA 128; 135; CANR 55, 70, 123; CN 7; DLB 231; INT CA-135

Craddock, Charles Egbert
See Murfree, Mary Noailles

Craig, A. A.
See Anderson, Poul (William)

Craik, Mrs.
See Craik, Dinah Maria (Mulock)
See also RGEL 2

Craik, Dinah Maria (Mulock)
1826-1887 .... **NCLC 38**
See also Craik, Mrs.; Mulock, Dinah Maria
See also DLB 35, 163; MAICYA 1, 2; SATA 34

Cram, Ralph Adams 1863-1942 ..... **TCLC 45**
See also CA 160

Cranch, Christopher Pearse
1813-1892 .... **NCLC 115**
See also DLB 1, 42, 243

Crane, (Harold) Hart 1899-1932 .... **PC 3; TCLC 2, 5, 80; WLC**
See also AMW; AMWR 2; CA 104; 127; CDALB 1917-1929; DA; DA3; DAB; DAC; DAM MST, POET; DLB 4, 48; EWL 3; MTCW 1, 2; RGAL 4; TUS

Crane, R(onald) S(almon)
1886-1967 .... **CLC 27**
See also CA 85-88; DLB 63

Crane, Stephen (Townley)
1871-1900 ...... **SSC 7, 56, 70; TCLC 11, 17, 32; WLC**
See also AAYA 21; AMW; AMWC 1; BPFB 1; BYA 3; CA 109; 140; CANR 84; CDALB 1865-1917; DA; DA3; DAB; DAC; DAM MST, NOV; DLB 12, 54, 78; EXPN; EXPS; LAIT 2; LMFS 2; NFS 4; PFS 9; RGAL 4; RGSF 2; SSFS 4; TUS; WYA; YABC 2

Cranmer, Thomas 1489-1556 .... **LC 95**
See also DLB 132, 213

Cranshaw, Stanley
See Fisher, Dorothy (Frances) Canfield

Crase, Douglas 1944- .... **CLC 58**
See also CA 106

Crashaw, Richard 1612(?)-1649 .... **LC 24**
See also BRW 2; DLB 126; PAB; RGEL 2

Cratinus c. 519B.C.-c. 422B.C. ..... **CMLC 54**
See also LMFS 1

Craven, Margaret 1901-1980 .... **CLC 17**
See also BYA 2; CA 103; CCA 1; DAC; LAIT 5

Crawford, F(rancis) Marion
1854-1909 .... **TCLC 10**
See also CA 107; 168; DLB 71; HGG; RGAL 4; SUFW 1

Crawford, Isabella Valancy
1850-1887 .... **NCLC 12, 127**
See also DLB 92; RGEL 2

Crayon, Geoffrey
See Irving, Washington

Creasey, John 1908-1973 .... **CLC 11**
See Marric, J. J.
See also CA 5-8R; 41-44R; CANR 8, 59; CMW 4; DLB 77; MTCW 1

Crebillon, Claude Prosper Jolyot de (fils)
1707-1777 .... **LC 1, 28**
See also GFL Beginnings to 1789

Credo
See Creasey, John

Credo, Alvaro J. de
See Prado (Calvo), Pedro

Creeley, Robert (White) 1926- .. **CLC 1, 2, 4, 8, 11, 15, 36, 78**
See also AMWS 4; CA 1-4R; CAAS 10; CANR 23, 43, 89; CP 7; DA3; DAM POET; DLB 5, 16, 169; DLBD 17; EWL 3; MTCW 1, 2; RGAL 4; WP

Crevecoeur, Hector St. John de
See Crevecoeur, Michel Guillaume Jean de
See also ANW

Crevecoeur, Michel Guillaume Jean de
1735-1813 .... **NCLC 105**
See Crevecoeur, Hector St. John de
See also AMWS 1; DLB 37

Crevel, Rene 1900-1935 .... **TCLC 112**
See also GLL 2

Crews, Harry (Eugene) 1935- ..... **CLC 6, 23, 49**
See also AITN 1; AMWS 11; BPFB 1; CA 25-28R; CANR 20, 57; CN 7; CSW; DA3; DLB 6, 143, 185; MTCW 1, 2; RGAL 4

DLB 2, 76, 227; DLBY 1994; EWL 3; EXPN; EXPS; LAIT 4; MTCW 1, 2; NCFS 3; NFS 2; RGAL 4; RGSF 2; SSFS 1, 11; YAW

Ellmann, Lucy (Elizabeth) 1956- ..... **CLC 61**
See also CA 128

Ellmann, Richard (David)
1918-1987 .... **CLC 50**
See also BEST 89:2; CA 1-4R; 122; CANR 2, 28, 61; DLB 103; DLBY 1987; MTCW 1, 2

Elman, Richard (Martin)
1934-1997 .... **CLC 19**
See also CA 17-20R; 163; CAAS 3; CANR 47

Elron
See Hubbard, L(afayette) Ron(ald)

Eluard, Paul .... **PC 38; TCLC 7, 41**
See Grindel, Eugene
See also EWL 3; GFL 1789 to the Present; RGWL 2, 3

Elyot, Thomas 1490(?)-1546 .... **LC 11**
See also DLB 136; RGEL 2

Elytis, Odysseus 1911-1996 .... **CLC 15, 49, 100; PC 21**
See Alepoudelis, Odysseus
See also CA 102; 151; CANR 94; CWW 2; DAM POET; EW 13; EWL 3; MTCW 1, 2; RGWL 2, 3

Emecheta, (Florence Onye) Buchi
1944- .... **BLC 2; CLC 14, 48, 128**
See also AFW; BW 2, 3; CA 81-84; CANR 27, 81, 126; CDWLB 3; CN 7; CWRI 5; DA3; DAM MULT; DLB 117; EWL 3; FW; MTCW 1, 2; NFS 12, 14; SATA 66; WLIT 2

Emerson, Mary Moody
1774-1863 .... **NCLC 66**

Emerson, Ralph Waldo 1803-1882 . **NCLC 1, 38, 98; PC 18; WLC**
See also AMW; ANW; CDALB 1640-1865; DA; DA3; DAB; DAC; DAM MST, POET; DLB 1, 59, 73, 183, 223, 270; EXPP; LAIT 2; LMFS 1; NCFS 3; PFS 4, 17; RGAL 4; TUS; WP

Eminescu, Mihail 1850-1889 .. **NCLC 33, 131**

Empedocles 5th cent. B.C.- .... **CMLC 50**
See also DLB 176

Empson, William 1906-1984 ... **CLC 3, 8, 19, 33, 34**
See also BRWS 2; CA 17-20R; 112; CANR 31, 61; DLB 20; EWL 3; MTCW 1, 2; RGEL 2

Enchi, Fumiko (Ueda) 1905-1986 ..... **CLC 31**
See Enchi Fumiko
See also CA 129; 121; FW; MJW

Enchi Fumiko
See Enchi, Fumiko (Ueda)
See also DLB 182; EWL 3

Ende, Michael (Andreas Helmuth)
1929-1995 .... **CLC 31**
See also BYA 5; CA 118; 124; 149; CANR 36, 110; CLR 14; DLB 75; MAICYA 1, 2; MAICYAS 1; SATA 61, 130; SATA-Brief 42; SATA-Obit 86

Endo, Shusaku 1923-1996 ..... **CLC 7, 14, 19, 54, 99; SSC 48; TCLC 152**
See Endo Shusaku
See also CA 29-32R; 153; CANR 21, 54, 131; DA3; DAM NOV; MTCW 1, 2; RGSF 2; RGWL 2, 3

Endo Shusaku
See Endo, Shusaku
See also DLB 182; EWL 3

Engel, Marian 1933-1985 .... **CLC 36; TCLC 137**
See also CA 25-28R; CANR 12; DLB 53; FW; INT CANR-12

Engelhardt, Frederick
See Hubbard, L(afayette) Ron(ald)

Engels, Friedrich 1820-1895 .. **NCLC 85, 114**
See also DLB 129; LATS 1

Enright, D(ennis) J(oseph)
1920-2002 .... **CLC 4, 8, 31**
See also CA 1-4R; 211; CANR 1, 42, 83; CP 7; DLB 27; EWL 3; SATA 25; SATA-Obit 140

Enzensberger, Hans Magnus
1929- .... **CLC 43; PC 28**
See also CA 116; 119; CANR 103; EWL 3

Ephron, Nora 1941- .... **CLC 17, 31**
See also AAYA 35; AITN 2; CA 65-68; CANR 12, 39, 83

Epicurus 341B.C.-270B.C. .... **CMLC 21**
See also DLB 176

Epsilon
See Betjeman, John

Epstein, Daniel Mark 1948- .... **CLC 7**
See also CA 49-52; CANR 2, 53, 90

Epstein, Jacob 1956- .... **CLC 19**
See also CA 114

Epstein, Jean 1897-1953 .... **TCLC 92**

Epstein, Joseph 1937- .... **CLC 39**
See also CA 112; 119; CANR 50, 65, 117

Epstein, Leslie 1938- .... **CLC 27**
See also AMWS 12; CA 73-76; 215; CAAE 215; CAAS 12; CANR 23, 69; DLB 299

Equiano, Olaudah 1745(?)-1797 . **BLC 2; LC 16**
See also AFAW 1, 2; CDWLB 3; DAM MULT; DLB 37, 50; WLIT 2

Erasmus, Desiderius 1469(?)-1536 ..... **LC 16, 93**
See also DLB 136; EW 2; LMFS 1; RGWL 2, 3; TWA

Erdman, Paul E(mil) 1932- .... **CLC 25**
See also AITN 1; CA 61-64; CANR 13, 43, 84

Erdrich, Louise 1954- .... **CLC 39, 54, 120, 176; NNAL; PC 52**
See also AAYA 10, 47; AMWS 4; BEST 89:1; BPFB 1; CA 114; CANR 41, 62, 118; CDALBS; CN 7; CP 7; CPW; CWP; DA3; DAM MULT, NOV, POP; DLB 152, 175, 206; EWL 3; EXPP; LAIT 5; LATS 1; MTCW 1; NFS 5; PFS 14; RGAL 4; SATA 94, 141; SSFS 14; TCWW 2

Erenburg, Ilya (Grigoryevich)
See Ehrenburg, Ilya (Grigoryevich)

Erickson, Stephen Michael 1950-
See Erickson, Steve
See also CA 129; SFW 4

Erickson, Steve .... **CLC 64**
See Erickson, Stephen Michael
See also CANR 60, 68; SUFW 2

Erickson, Walter
See Fast, Howard (Melvin)

Ericson, Walter
See Fast, Howard (Melvin)

Eriksson, Buntel
See Bergman, (Ernst) Ingmar

Eriugena, John Scottus c.
810-877 .... **CMLC 65**
See also DLB 115

Ernaux, Annie 1940- .... **CLC 88, 184**
See also CA 147; CANR 93; NCFS 3, 5

Erskine, John 1879-1951 .... **TCLC 84**
See also CA 112; 159; DLB 9, 102; FANT

Eschenbach, Wolfram von
See Wolfram von Eschenbach
See also RGWL 3

Eseki, Bruno
See Mphahlele, Ezekiel

Esenin, Sergei (Alexandrovich)
1895-1925 .... **TCLC 4**
See Yesenin, Sergey
See also CA 104; RGWL 2, 3

Eshleman, Clayton 1935- .... **CLC 7**
See also CA 33-36R; 212; CAAE 212; CAAS 6; CANR 93; CP 7; DLB 5

Espriella, Don Manuel Alvarez
See Southey, Robert

Espriu, Salvador 1913-1985 .... **CLC 9**
See also CA 154; 115; DLB 134; EWL 3

Espronceda, Jose de 1808-1842 ..... **NCLC 39**

Esquivel, Laura 1951(?)- ... **CLC 141; HLCS 1**
See also AAYA 29; CA 143; CANR 68, 113; DA3; DNFS 2; LAIT 3; LMFS 2; MTCW 1; NFS 5; WLIT 1

Esse, James
See Stephens, James

Esterbrook, Tom
See Hubbard, L(afayette) Ron(ald)

Estleman, Loren D. 1952- .... **CLC 48**
See also AAYA 27; CA 85-88; CANR 27, 74; CMW 4; CPW; DA3; DAM NOV, POP; DLB 226; INT CANR-27; MTCW 1, 2

Etherege, Sir George 1636-1692 . **DC 23; LC 78**
See also BRW 2; DAM DRAM; DLB 80; PAB; RGEL 2

Etheria fl. 4th cent. - .... **CMLC 70**

Euclid 306B.C.-283B.C. .... **CMLC 25**

Eugenides, Jeffrey 1960(?)- .... **CLC 81**
See also AAYA 51; CA 144; CANR 120

Euripides c. 484B.C.-406B.C. .... **CMLC 23, 51; DC 4; WLCS**
See also AW 1; CDWLB 1; DA; DA3; DAB; DAC; DAM DRAM, MST; DFS 1, 4, 6; DLB 176; LAIT 1; LMFS 1; RGWL 2, 3

Evan, Evin
See Faust, Frederick (Schiller)

Evans, Caradoc 1878-1945 ... **SSC 43; TCLC 85**
See also DLB 162

Evans, Evan
See Faust, Frederick (Schiller)
See also TCWW 2

Evans, Marian
See Eliot, George

Evans, Mary Ann
See Eliot, George

Evarts, Esther
See Benson, Sally

Everett, Percival
See Everett, Percival L.
See also CSW

Everett, Percival L. 1956- .... **CLC 57**
See Everett, Percival
See also BW 2; CA 129; CANR 94

Everson, R(onald) G(ilmour)
1903-1992 .... **CLC 27**
See also CA 17-20R; DLB 88

Everson, William (Oliver)
1912-1994 .... **CLC 1, 5, 14**
See also BG 2; CA 9-12R; 145; CANR 20; DLB 5, 16, 212; MTCW 1

Evtushenko, Evgenii Aleksandrovich
See Yevtushenko, Yevgeny (Alexandrovich)
See also RGWL 2, 3

Ewart, Gavin (Buchanan)
1916-1995 .... **CLC 13, 46**
See also BRWS 7; CA 89-92; 150; CANR 17, 46; CP 7; DLB 40; MTCW 1

Ewers, Hanns Heinz 1871-1943 ..... **TCLC 12**
See also CA 109; 149

Ewing, Frederick R.
See Sturgeon, Theodore (Hamilton)

Exley, Frederick (Earl) 1929-1992 .... **CLC 6, 11**
See also AITN 2; BPFB 1; CA 81-84; 138; CANR 117; DLB 143; DLBY 1981

Eynhardt, Guillermo
　See Quiroga, Horacio (Sylvestre)
Ezekiel, Nissim (Moses) 1924-2004 .. **CLC 61**
　See also CA 61-64; 223; CP 7; EWL 3
Ezekiel, Tish O'Dowd 1943- .... **CLC 34**
　See also CA 129
Fadeev, Aleksandr Aleksandrovich
　See Bulgya, Alexander Alexandrovich
　See also DLB 272
Fadeev, Alexandr Alexandrovich
　See Bulgya, Alexander Alexandrovich
　See also EWL 3
Fadeyev, A.
　See Bulgya, Alexander Alexandrovich
Fadeyev, Alexander .... **TCLC 53**
　See Bulgya, Alexander Alexandrovich
Fagen, Donald 1948- .... **CLC 26**
Fainzilberg, Ilya Arnoldovich 1897-1937
　See Ilf, Ilya
　See also CA 120; 165
Fair, Ronald L. 1932- .... **CLC 18**
　See also BW 1; CA 69-72; CANR 25; DLB
　33
Fairbairn, Roger
　See Carr, John Dickson
Fairbairns, Zoe (Ann) 1948- .... **CLC 32**
　See also CA 103; CANR 21, 85; CN 7
Fairfield, Flora
　See Alcott, Louisa May
Fairman, Paul W. 1916-1977
　See Queen, Ellery
　See also CA 114; SFW 4
Falco, Gian
　See Papini, Giovanni
Falconer, James
　See Kirkup, James
Falconer, Kenneth
　See Kornbluth, C(yril) M.
Falkland, Samuel
　See Heijermans, Herman
Fallaci, Oriana 1930- .... **CLC 11, 110**
　See also CA 77-80; CANR 15, 58; FW;
　MTCW 1
Faludi, Susan 1959- .... **CLC 140**
　See also CA 138; CANR 126; FW; MTCW
　1; NCFS 3
Faludy, George 1913- .... **CLC 42**
　See also CA 21-24R
Faludy, Gyoergy
　See Faludy, George
Fanon, Frantz 1925-1961 .... **BLC 2; CLC 74**
　See also BW 1; CA 116; 89-92; DAM
　MULT; DLB 296; LMFS 2; WLIT 2
Fanshawe, Ann 1625-1680 .... **LC 11**
Fante, John (Thomas) 1911-1983 .... **CLC 60;
　SSC 65**
　See also AMWS 11; CA 69-72; 109; CANR
　23, 104; DLB 130; DLBY 1983
Far, Sui Sin .... **SSC 62**
　See Eaton, Edith Maude
　See also SSFS 4
Farah, Nuruddin 1945- ...... **BLC 2; CLC 53,
　137**
　See also AFW; BW 2, 3; CA 106; CANR
　81; CDWLB 3; CN 7; DAM MULT; DLB
　125; EWL 3; WLIT 2
Fargue, Leon-Paul 1876(?)-1947 .... **TCLC 11**
　See also CA 109; CANR 107; DLB 258;
　EWL 3
Farigoule, Louis
　See Romains, Jules
Farina, Richard 1936(?)-1966 .... **CLC 9**
　See also CA 81-84; 25-28R
Farley, Walter (Lorimer)
　1915-1989 .... **CLC 17**
　See also BYA 14; CA 17-20R; CANR 8,
　29, 84; DLB 22; JRDA; MAICYA 1, 2;
　SATA 2, 43, 132; YAW

Farmer, Philip Jose 1918- .... **CLC 1, 19**
　See also AAYA 28; BPFB 1; CA 1-4R;
　CANR 4, 35, 111; DLB 8; MTCW 1;
　SATA 93; SCFW 2; SFW 4
Farquhar, George 1677-1707 .... **LC 21**
　See also BRW 2; DAM DRAM; DLB 84;
　RGEL 2
Farrell, J(ames) G(ordon)
　1935-1979 .... **CLC 6**
　See also CA 73-76; 89-92; CANR 36; DLB
　14, 271; MTCW 1; RGEL 2; RHW; WLIT
　4
Farrell, James T(homas) 1904-1979 . **CLC 1,
　4, 8, 11, 66; SSC 28**
　See also AMW; BPFB 1; CA 5-8R; 89-92;
　CANR 9, 61; DLB 4, 9, 86; DLBD 2;
　EWL 3; MTCW 1, 2; RGAL 4
Farrell, Warren (Thomas) 1943- ...... **CLC 70**
　See also CA 146; CANR 120
Farren, Richard J.
　See Betjeman, John
Farren, Richard M.
　See Betjeman, John
Fassbinder, Rainer Werner
　1946-1982 .... **CLC 20**
　See also CA 93-96; 106; CANR 31
Fast, Howard (Melvin) 1914-2003 .. **CLC 23,
　131**
　See also AAYA 16; BPFB 1; CA 1-4R, 181;
　214; CAAE 181; CAAS 18; CANR 1, 33,
　54, 75, 98; CMW 4; CN 7; CPW; DAM
　NOV; DLB 9; INT CANR-33; LATS 1;
　MTCW 1; RHW; SATA 7; SATA-Essay
　107; TCWW 2; YAW
Faulcon, Robert
　See Holdstock, Robert P.
Faulkner, William (Cuthbert)
　1897-1962 .... **CLC 1, 3, 6, 8, 9, 11, 14,
　18, 28, 52, 68; SSC 1, 35, 42; TCLC
　141; WLC**
　See also AAYA 7; AMW; AMWR 1; BPFB
　1; BYA 5, 15; CA 81-84; CANR 33;
　CDALB 1929-1941; DA; DA3; DAB;
　DAC; DAM MST, NOV; DLB 9, 11, 44,
　102; DLBD 2; DLBY 1986, 1997; EWL
　3; EXPN; EXPS; LAIT 2; LATS 1; LMFS
　2; MTCW 1, 2; NFS 4, 8, 13; RGAL 4;
　RGSF 2; SSFS 2, 5, 6, 12; TUS
Fauset, Jessie Redmon
　1882(?)-1961 .. **BLC 2; CLC 19, 54; HR
　2**
　See also AFAW 2; BW 1; CA 109; CANR
　83; DAM MULT; DLB 51; FW; LMFS 2;
　MAWW
Faust, Frederick (Schiller)
　1892-1944(?) .... **TCLC 49**
　See Austin, Frank; Brand, Max; Challis,
　George; Dawson, Peter; Dexter, Martin;
　Evans, Evan; Frederick, John; Frost, Fred-
　erick; Manning, David; Silver, Nicholas
　See also CA 108; 152; DAM POP; DLB
　256; TUS
Faust, Irvin 1924- .... **CLC 8**
　See also CA 33-36R; CANR 28, 67; CN 7;
　DLB 2, 28, 218, 278; DLBY 1980
Faustino, Domingo 1811-1888 ...... **NCLC 123**
Fawkes, Guy
　See Benchley, Robert (Charles)
Fearing, Kenneth (Flexner)
　1902-1961 .... **CLC 51**
　See also CA 93-96; CANR 59; CMW 4;
　DLB 9; RGAL 4
Fecamps, Elise
　See Creasey, John
Federman, Raymond 1928- .... **CLC 6, 47**
　See also CA 17-20R, 208; CAAE 208;
　CAAS 8; CANR 10, 43, 83, 108; CN 7;
　DLBY 1980
Federspiel, J(uerg) F. 1931- .... **CLC 42**
　See also CA 146

Feiffer, Jules (Ralph) 1929- ...... **CLC 2, 8, 64**
　See also AAYA 3; CA 17-20R; CAD; CANR
　30, 59, 129; CD 5; DAM DRAM; DLB 7,
　44; INT CANR-30; MTCW 1; SATA 8,
　61, 111
Feige, Hermann Albert Otto Maximilian
　See Traven, B.
Feinberg, David B. 1956-1994 .... **CLC 59**
　See also CA 135; 147
Feinstein, Elaine 1930- .... **CLC 36**
　See also CA 69-72; CAAS 1; CANR 31,
　68, 121; CN 7; CP 7; CWP; DLB 14, 40;
　MTCW 1
Feke, Gilbert David .... **CLC 65**
Feldman, Irving (Mordecai) 1928- ..... **CLC 7**
　See also CA 1-4R; CANR 1; CP 7; DLB
　169
Felix-Tchicaya, Gerald
　See Tchicaya, Gerald Felix
Fellini, Federico 1920-1993 .... **CLC 16, 85**
　See also CA 65-68; 143; CANR 33
Felltham, Owen 1602(?)-1668 .... **LC 92**
　See also DLB 126, 151
Felsen, Henry Gregor 1916-1995 ..... **CLC 17**
　See also CA 1-4R; 180; CANR 1; SAAS 2;
　SATA 1
Felski, Rita .... **CLC 65**
Fenno, Jack
　See Calisher, Hortense
Fenollosa, Ernest (Francisco)
　1853-1908 .... **TCLC 91**
Fenton, James Martin 1949- .... **CLC 32**
　See also CA 102; CANR 108; CP 7; DLB
　40; PFS 11
Ferber, Edna 1887-1968 .... **CLC 18, 93**
　See also AITN 1; CA 5-8R; 25-28R; CANR
　68, 105; DLB 9, 28, 86, 266; MTCW 1,
　2; RGAL 4; RHW; SATA 7; TCWW 2
Ferdowsi, Abu'l Qasem 940-1020 . **CMLC 43**
　See also RGWL 2, 3
Ferguson, Helen
　See Kavan, Anna
Ferguson, Niall 1964- .... **CLC 134**
　See also CA 190
Ferguson, Samuel 1810-1886 .... **NCLC 33**
　See also DLB 32; RGEL 2
Fergusson, Robert 1750-1774 .... **LC 29**
　See also DLB 109; RGEL 2
Ferling, Lawrence
　See Ferlinghetti, Lawrence (Monsanto)
Ferlinghetti, Lawrence (Monsanto)
　1919(?)- ..... **CLC 2, 6, 10, 27, 111; PC 1**
　See also CA 5-8R; CANR 3, 41, 73, 125;
　CDALB 1941-1968; CP 7; DA3; DAM
　POET; DLB 5, 16; MTCW 1, 2; RGAL 4;
　WP
Fern, Fanny
　See Parton, Sara Payson Willis
Fernandez, Vicente Garcia Huidobro
　See Huidobro Fernandez, Vicente Garcia
Fernandez-Armesto, Felipe .... **CLC 70**
Fernandez de Lizardi, Jose Joaquin
　See Lizardi, Jose Joaquin Fernandez de
Ferre, Rosario 1938- ...... **CLC 139; HLCS 1;
　SSC 36**
　See also CA 131; CANR 55, 81; CWW 2;
　DLB 145; EWL 3; HW 1, 2; LAWS 1;
　MTCW 1; WLIT 1
Ferrer, Gabriel (Francisco Victor) Miro
　See Miro (Ferrer), Gabriel (Francisco
　Victor)
Ferrier, Susan (Edmonstone)
　1782-1854 .... **NCLC 8**
　See also DLB 116; RGEL 2
Ferrigno, Robert 1948(?)- .... **CLC 65**
　See also CA 140; CANR 125

Gertler, T. .... **CLC 34**
See also CA 116; 121
Gertsen, Aleksandr Ivanovich
See Herzen, Aleksandr Ivanovich
Ghalib .... **NCLC 39, 78**
See Ghalib, Asadullah Khan
Ghalib, Asadullah Khan 1797-1869
See Ghalib
See also DAM POET; RGWL 2, 3
Ghelderode, Michel de 1898-1962 ..... **CLC 6,
11; DC 15**
See also CA 85-88; CANR 40, 77; DAM
DRAM; EW 11; EWL 3; TWA
Ghiselin, Brewster 1903-2001 .... **CLC 23**
See also CA 13-16R; CAAS 10; CANR 13;
CP 7
Ghose, Aurabinda 1872-1950 .... **TCLC 63**
See Ghose, Aurobindo
See also CA 163
Ghose, Aurobindo
See Ghose, Aurabinda
See also EWL 3
Ghose, Zulfikar 1935- .... **CLC 42**
See also CA 65-68; CANR 67; CN 7; CP 7;
EWL 3
Ghosh, Amitav 1956- .... **CLC 44, 153**
See also CA 147; CANR 80; CN 7; WWE
1
Giacosa, Giuseppe 1847-1906 .... **TCLC 7**
See also CA 104
Gibb, Lee
See Waterhouse, Keith (Spencer)
Gibbon, Edward 1737-1794 .... **LC 97**
See also BRW 3; DLB 104; RGEL 2
Gibbon, Lewis Grassic .... **TCLC 4**
See Mitchell, James Leslie
See also RGEL 2
Gibbons, Kaye 1960- .... **CLC 50, 88, 145**
See also AAYA 34; AMWS 10; CA 151;
CANR 75, 127; CSW; DA3; DAM POP;
DLB 292; MTCW 1; NFS 3; RGAL 4;
SATA 117
Gibran, Kahlil 1883-1931 . **PC 9; TCLC 1, 9**
See also CA 104; 150; DA3; DAM POET,
POP; EWL 3; MTCW 2
Gibran, Khalil
See Gibran, Kahlil
Gibson, William 1914- .... **CLC 23**
See also CA 9-12R; CAD 2; CANR 9, 42,
75, 125; CD 5; DA; DAB; DAC; DAM
DRAM, MST; DFS 2; DLB 7; LAIT 2;
MTCW 2; SATA 66; YAW
Gibson, William (Ford) 1948- ... **CLC 39, 63,
186, 192; SSC 52**
See also AAYA 12; BPFB 2; CA 126; 133;
CANR 52, 90, 106; CN 7; CPW; DA3;
DAM POP; DLB 251; MTCW 2; SCFW
2; SFW 4
Gide, Andre (Paul Guillaume)
1869-1951 ..... **SSC 13; TCLC 5, 12, 36;
WLC**
See also CA 104; 124; DA; DA3; DAB;
DAC; DAM MST, NOV; DLB 65; EW 8;
EWL 3; GFL 1789 to the Present; MTCW
1, 2; RGSF 2; RGWL 2, 3; TWA
Gifford, Barry (Colby) 1946- .... **CLC 34**
See also CA 65-68; CANR 9, 30, 40, 90
Gilbert, Frank
See De Voto, Bernard (Augustine)
Gilbert, W(illiam) S(chwenck)
1836-1911 .... **TCLC 3**
See also CA 104; 173; DAM DRAM, POET;
RGEL 2; SATA 36
Gilbreth, Frank B(unker), Jr.
1911-2001 .... **CLC 17**
See also CA 9-12R; SATA 2

Gilchrist, Ellen (Louise) 1935- .. **CLC 34, 48,
143; SSC 14, 63**
See also BPFB 2; CA 113; 116; CANR 41,
61, 104; CN 7; CPW; CSW; DAM POP;
DLB 130; EWL 3; EXPS; MTCW 1, 2;
RGAL 4; RGSF 2; SSFS 9
Giles, Molly 1942- .... **CLC 39**
See also CA 126; CANR 98
Gill, Eric 1882-1940 .... **TCLC 85**
See Gill, (Arthur) Eric (Rowton Peter
Joseph)
Gill, (Arthur) Eric (Rowton Peter Joseph)
1882-1940
See Gill, Eric
See also CA 120; DLB 98
Gill, Patrick
See Creasey, John
Gillette, Douglas .... **CLC 70**
Gilliam, Terry (Vance) 1940- .... **CLC 21, 141**
See Monty Python
See also AAYA 19; CA 108; 113; CANR
35; INT CA-113
Gillian, Jerry
See Gilliam, Terry (Vance)
Gilliatt, Penelope (Ann Douglass)
1932-1993 .... **CLC 2, 10, 13, 53**
See also AITN 2; CA 13-16R; 141; CANR
49; DLB 14
Gilman, Charlotte (Anna) Perkins (Stetson)
1860-1935 ...... **SSC 13, 62; TCLC 9, 37,
117**
See also AMWS 11; BYA 11; CA 106; 150;
DLB 221; EXPS; FW; HGG; LAIT 2;
MAWW; MTCW 1; RGAL 4; RGSF 2;
SFW 4; SSFS 1, 18
Gilmour, David 1946- .... **CLC 35**
Gilpin, William 1724-1804 .... **NCLC 30**
Gilray, J. D.
See Mencken, H(enry) L(ouis)
Gilroy, Frank D(aniel) 1925- .... **CLC 2**
See also CA 81-84; CAD; CANR 32, 64,
86; CD 5; DFS 17; DLB 7
Gilstrap, John 1957(?)- .... **CLC 99**
See also CA 160; CANR 101
Ginsberg, Allen 1926-1997 .... **CLC 1, 2, 3, 4,
6, 13, 36, 69, 109; PC 4, 47; TCLC
120; WLC**
See also AAYA 33; AITN 1; AMWC 1;
AMWS 2; BG 2; CA 1-4R; 157; CANR
2, 41, 63, 95; CDALB 1941-1968; CP 7;
DA; DA3; DAB; DAC; DAM MST,
POET; DLB 5, 16, 169, 237; EWL 3; GLL
1; LMFS 2; MTCW 1, 2; PAB; PFS 5;
RGAL 4; TUS; WP
Ginzburg, Eugenia .... **CLC 59**
Ginzburg, Natalia 1916-1991 .... **CLC 5, 11,
54, 70; SSC 65**
See also CA 85-88; 135; CANR 33; DFS
14; DLB 177; EW 13; EWL 3; MTCW 1,
2; RGWL 2, 3
Giono, Jean 1895-1970 .... **CLC 4, 11; TCLC
124**
See also CA 45-48; 29-32R; CANR 2, 35;
DLB 72; EWL 3; GFL 1789 to the
Present; MTCW 1; RGWL 2, 3
Giovanni, Nikki 1943- ...... **BLC 2; CLC 2, 4,
19, 64, 117; PC 19; WLCS**
See also AAYA 22; AITN 1; BW 2, 3; CA
29-32R; CAAS 6; CANR 18, 41, 60, 91,
130; CDALBS; CLR 6, 73; CP 7; CSW;
CWP; CWRI 5; DA; DA3; DAB; DAC;
DAM MST, MULT, POET; DLB 5, 41;
EWL 3; EXPP; INT CANR-18; MAICYA
1, 2; MTCW 1, 2; PFS 17; RGAL 4;
SATA 24, 107; TUS; YAW
Giovene, Andrea 1904-1998 .... **CLC 7**
See also CA 85-88

Gippius, Zinaida (Nikolaevna) 1869-1945
See Hippius, Zinaida (Nikolaevna)
See also CA 106; 212
Giraudoux, Jean(-Hippolyte)
1882-1944 .... **TCLC 2, 7**
See also CA 104; 196; DAM DRAM; DLB
65; EW 9; EWL 3; GFL 1789 to the
Present; RGWL 2, 3; TWA
Gironella, Jose Maria (Pous)
1917-2003 .... **CLC 11**
See also CA 101; 212; EWL 3; RGWL 2, 3
Gissing, George (Robert)
1857-1903 .... **SSC 37; TCLC 3, 24, 47**
See also BRW 5; CA 105; 167; DLB 18,
135, 184; RGEL 2; TEA
Giurlani, Aldo
See Palazzeschi, Aldo
Gladkov, Fedor Vasil'evich
See Gladkov, Fyodor (Vasilyevich)
See also DLB 272
Gladkov, Fyodor (Vasilyevich)
1883-1958 .... **TCLC 27**
See Gladkov, Fedor Vasil'evich
See also CA 170; EWL 3
Glancy, Diane 1941- .... **NNAL**
See also CA 136, 225; CAAE 225; CAAS
24; CANR 87; DLB 175
Glanville, Brian (Lester) 1931- .... **CLC 6**
See also CA 5-8R; CAAS 9; CANR 3, 70;
CN 7; DLB 15, 139; SATA 42
Glasgow, Ellen (Anderson Gholson)
1873-1945 .... **SSC 34; TCLC 2, 7**
See also AMW; CA 104; 164; DLB 9, 12;
MAWW; MTCW 2; RGAL 4; RHW;
SSFS 9; TUS
Glaspell, Susan 1882(?)-1948 ..... **DC 10; SSC
41; TCLC 55**
See also AMWS 3; CA 110; 154; DFS 8,
18; DLB 7, 9, 78, 228; MAWW; RGAL
4; SSFS 3; TCWW 2; TUS; YABC 2
Glassco, John 1909-1981 .... **CLC 9**
See also CA 13-16R; 102; CANR 15; DLB
68
Glasscock, Amnesia
See Steinbeck, John (Ernst)
Glasser, Ronald J. 1940(?)- .... **CLC 37**
See also CA 209
Glassman, Joyce
See Johnson, Joyce
Gleick, James (W.) 1954- .... **CLC 147**
See also CA 131; 137; CANR 97; INT CA-
137
Glendinning, Victoria 1937- .... **CLC 50**
See also CA 120; 127; CANR 59, 89; DLB
155
Glissant, Edouard (Mathieu)
1928- .... **CLC 10, 68**
See also CA 153; CANR 111; CWW 2;
DAM MULT; EWL 3; RGWL 3
Gloag, Julian 1930- .... **CLC 40**
See also AITN 1; CA 65-68; CANR 10, 70;
CN 7
Glowacki, Aleksander
See Prus, Boleslaw
Gluck, Louise (Elisabeth) 1943- .. **CLC 7, 22,
44, 81, 160; PC 16**
See also AMWS 5; CA 33-36R; CANR 40,
69, 108; CP 7; CWP; DA3; DAM POET;
DLB 5; MTCW 2; PFS 5, 15; RGAL 4
Glyn, Elinor 1864-1943 .... **TCLC 72**
See also DLB 153; RHW
Gobineau, Joseph-Arthur
1816-1882 .... **NCLC 17**
See also DLB 123; GFL 1789 to the Present
Godard, Jean-Luc 1930- .... **CLC 20**
See also CA 93-96

Gozzano, Guido 1883-1916 .... **PC 10**
See also CA 154; DLB 114; EWL 3

Gozzi, (Conte) Carlo 1720-1806 .... **NCLC 23**

Grabbe, Christian Dietrich
1801-1836 .... **NCLC 2**
See also DLB 133; RGWL 2, 3

Grace, Patricia Frances 1937- .... **CLC 56**
See also CA 176; CANR 118; CN 7; EWL
3; RGSF 2

Gracian y Morales, Baltasar
1601-1658 .... **LC 15**

Gracq, Julien .... **CLC 11, 48**
See Poirier, Louis
See also CWW 2; DLB 83; GFL 1789 to
the Present

Grade, Chaim 1910-1982 .... **CLC 10**
See also CA 93-96; 107; EWL 3

Graduate of Oxford, A
See Ruskin, John

Grafton, Garth
See Duncan, Sara Jeannette

Grafton, Sue 1940- .... **CLC 163**
See also AAYA 11, 49; BEST 90:3; CA 108;
CANR 31, 55, 111; CMW 4; CPW; CSW;
DA3; DAM POP; DLB 226; FW; MSW

Graham, John
See Phillips, David Graham

Graham, Jorie 1950- .... **CLC 48, 118**
See also CA 111; CANR 63, 118; CP 7;
CWP; DLB 120; EWL 3; PFS 10, 17

Graham, R(obert) B(ontine) Cunninghame
See Cunninghame Graham, Robert
(Gallnigad) Bontine
See also DLB 98, 135, 174; RGEL 2; RGSF
2

Graham, Robert
See Haldeman, Joe (William)

Graham, Tom
See Lewis, (Harry) Sinclair

Graham, W(illiam) S(idney)
1918-1986 .... **CLC 29**
See also BRWS 7; CA 73-76; 118; DLB 20;
RGEL 2

Graham, Winston (Mawdsley)
1910-2003 .... **CLC 23**
See also CA 49-52; 218; CANR 2, 22, 45,
66; CMW 4; CN 7; DLB 77; RHW

Grahame, Kenneth 1859-1932 ...... **TCLC 64,
136**
See also BYA 5; CA 108; 136; CANR 80;
CLR 5; CWRI 5; DA3; DAB; DLB 34,
141, 178; FANT; MAICYA 1, 2; MTCW
2; RGEL 2; SATA 100; TEA; WCH;
YABC 1

Granger, Darius John
See Marlowe, Stephen

Granin, Daniil .... **CLC 59**

Granovsky, Timofei Nikolaevich
1813-1855 .... **NCLC 75**
See also DLB 198

Grant, Skeeter
See Spiegelman, Art

Granville-Barker, Harley
1877-1946 .... **TCLC 2**
See Barker, Harley Granville
See also CA 104; 204; DAM DRAM;
RGEL 2

Granzotto, Gianni
See Granzotto, Giovanni Battista

Granzotto, Giovanni Battista
1914-1985 .... **CLC 70**
See also CA 166

Grass, Guenter (Wilhelm) 1927- ... **CLC 1, 2,
4, 6, 11, 15, 22, 32, 49, 88; WLC**
See also BPFB 2; CA 13-16R; CANR 20,
75, 93; CDWLB 2; DA; DA3; DAB;
DAC; DAM MST, NOV; DLB 75, 124;
EW 13; EWL 3; MTCW 1, 2; RGWL 2,
3; TWA

Gratton, Thomas
See Hulme, T(homas) E(rnest)

Grau, Shirley Ann 1929- .... **CLC 4, 9, 146;
SSC 15**
See also CA 89-92; CANR 22, 69; CN 7;
CSW; DLB 2, 218; INT CA-89-92,
CANR-22; MTCW 1

Gravel, Fern
See Hall, James Norman

Graver, Elizabeth 1964- .... **CLC 70**
See also CA 135; CANR 71, 129

Graves, Richard Perceval
1895-1985 .... **CLC 44**
See also CA 65-68; CANR 9, 26, 51

Graves, Robert (von Ranke)
1895-1985 .. **CLC 1, 2, 6, 11, 39, 44, 45;
PC 6**
See also BPFB 2; BRW 7; BYA 4; CA 5-8R;
117; CANR 5, 36; CDBLB 1914-1945;
DA3; DAB; DAC; DAM MST, POET;
DLB 20, 100, 191; DLBD 18; DLBY
1985; EWL 3; LATS 1; MTCW 1, 2;
NCFS 2; RGEL 2; RHW; SATA 45; TEA

Graves, Valerie
See Bradley, Marion Zimmer

Gray, Alasdair (James) 1934- .... **CLC 41**
See also BRWS 9; CA 126; CANR 47, 69,
106; CN 7; DLB 194, 261; HGG; INT
CA-126; MTCW 1, 2; RGSF 2; SUFW 2

Gray, Amlin 1946- .... **CLC 29**
See also CA 138

Gray, Francine du Plessix 1930- ..... **CLC 22,
153**
See also BEST 90:3; CA 61-64; CAAS 2;
CANR 11, 33, 75, 81; DAM NOV; INT
CANR-11; MTCW 1, 2

Gray, John (Henry) 1866-1934 ...... **TCLC 19**
See also CA 119; 162; RGEL 2

Gray, Simon (James Holliday)
1936- .... **CLC 9, 14, 36**
See also AITN 1; CA 21-24R; CAAS 3;
CANR 32, 69; CD 5; DLB 13; EWL 3;
MTCW 1; RGEL 2

Gray, Spalding 1941-2004 .... **CLC 49, 112;
DC 7**
See also CA 128; 225; CAD; CANR 74;
CD 5; CPW; DAM POP; MTCW 2

Gray, Thomas 1716-1771 .... **LC 4, 40; PC 2;
WLC**
See also BRW 3; CDBLB 1660-1789; DA;
DA3; DAB; DAC; DAM MST; DLB 109;
EXPP; PAB; PFS 9; RGEL 2; TEA; WP

Grayson, David
See Baker, Ray Stannard

Grayson, Richard (A.) 1951- .... **CLC 38**
See also CA 85-88, 210; CAAE 210; CANR
14, 31, 57; DLB 234

Greeley, Andrew M(oran) 1928- ...... **CLC 28**
See also BPFB 2; CA 5-8R; CAAS 7;
CANR 7, 43, 69, 104; CMW 4; CPW;
DA3; DAM POP; MTCW 1, 2

Green, Anna Katharine
1846-1935 .... **TCLC 63**
See also CA 112; 159; CMW 4; DLB 202,
221; MSW

Green, Brian
See Card, Orson Scott

Green, Hannah
See Greenberg, Joanne (Goldenberg)

Green, Hannah 1927(?)-1996 .... **CLC 3**
See also CA 73-76; CANR 59, 93; NFS 10

Green, Henry .... **CLC 2, 13, 97**
See Yorke, Henry Vincent
See also BRWS 2; CA 175; DLB 15; EWL
3; RGEL 2

Green, Julian (Hartridge) 1900-1998
See Green, Julien
See also CA 21-24R; 169; CANR 33, 87;
DLB 4, 72; MTCW 1

Green, Julien .... **CLC 3, 11, 77**
See Green, Julian (Hartridge)
See also EWL 3; GFL 1789 to the Present;
MTCW 2

Green, Paul (Eliot) 1894-1981 .... **CLC 25**
See also AITN 1; CA 5-8R; 103; CANR 3;
DAM DRAM; DLB 7, 9, 249; DLBY
1981; RGAL 4

Greenaway, Peter 1942- .... **CLC 159**
See also CA 127

Greenberg, Ivan 1908-1973
See Rahv, Philip
See also CA 85-88

Greenberg, Joanne (Goldenberg)
1932- .... **CLC 7, 30**
See also AAYA 12; CA 5-8R; CANR 14,
32, 69; CN 7; SATA 25; YAW

Greenberg, Richard 1959(?)- .... **CLC 57**
See also CA 138; CAD; CD 5

Greenblatt, Stephen J(ay) 1943- ...... **CLC 70**
See also CA 49-52; CANR 115

Greene, Bette 1934- .... **CLC 30**
See also AAYA 7; BYA 3; CA 53-56; CANR
4; CLR 2; CWRI 5; JRDA; LAIT 4; MAI-
CYA 1, 2; NFS 10; SAAS 16; SATA 8,
102; WYA; YAW

Greene, Gael .... **CLC 8**
See also CA 13-16R; CANR 10

Greene, Graham (Henry)
1904-1991 .... **CLC 1, 3, 6, 9, 14, 18, 27,
37, 70, 72, 125; SSC 29**
See also AITN 2; BPFB 2; BRWR 2; BRWS
1; BYA 3; CA 13-16R; 133; CANR 35,
61, 131; CBD; CDBLB 1945-1960; CMW
4; DA; DA3; DAB; DAC; DAM MST,
NOV; DLB 13, 15, 77, 100, 162, 201,
204; DLBY 1991; EWL 3; MSW; MTCW
1, 2; NFS 16; RGEL 2; SATA 20; SSFS
14; TEA; WLIT 4

Greene, Robert 1558-1592 .... **LC 41**
See also BRWS 8; DLB 62, 167; IDTP;
RGEL 2; TEA

Greer, Germaine 1939- .... **CLC 131**
See also AITN 1; CA 81-84; CANR 33, 70,
115; FW; MTCW 1, 2

Greer, Richard
See Silverberg, Robert

Gregor, Arthur 1923- .... **CLC 9**
See also CA 25-28R; CAAS 10; CANR 11;
CP 7; SATA 36

Gregor, Lee
See Pohl, Frederik

Gregory, Lady Isabella Augusta (Persse)
1852-1932 .... **TCLC 1**
See also BRW 6; CA 104; 184; DLB 10;
IDTP; RGEL 2

Gregory, J. Dennis
See Williams, John A(lfred)

Grekova, I. .... **CLC 59**
See Ventsel, Elena Sergeevna
See also CWW 2

Grendon, Stephen
See Derleth, August (William)

Grenville, Kate 1950- .... **CLC 61**
See also CA 118; CANR 53, 93

Grenville, Pelham
See Wodehouse, P(elham) G(renville)

Greve, Felix Paul (Berthold Friedrich)
1879-1948
See Grove, Frederick Philip
See also CA 104; 141, 175; CANR 79;
DAC; DAM MST

Greville, Fulke 1554-1628 .... **LC 79**
See also DLB 62, 172; RGEL 2

Grey, Lady Jane 1537-1554 .... **LC 93**
See also DLB 132

Hawthorne, Nathaniel 1804-1864 ... **NCLC 2, 10, 17, 23, 39, 79, 95; SSC 3, 29, 39; WLC**
See also AAYA 18; AMW; AMWC 1; AMWR 1; BPFB 2; BYA 3; CDALB 1640-1865; DA; DA3; DAB; DAC; DAM MST, NOV; DLB 1, 74, 183, 223, 269; EXPN; EXPS; HGG; LAIT 1; NFS 1; RGAL 4; RGSF 2; SSFS 1, 7, 11, 15; SUFW 1; TUS; WCH; YABC 2

Haxton, Josephine Ayres 1921-
See Douglas, Ellen
See also CA 115; CANR 41, 83

Hayaseca y Eizaguirre, Jorge
See Echegaray (y Eizaguirre), Jose (Maria Waldo)

Hayashi, Fumiko 1904-1951 .... **TCLC 27**
See Hayashi Fumiko
See also CA 161

Hayashi Fumiko
See Hayashi, Fumiko
See also DLB 180; EWL 3

Haycraft, Anna (Margaret) 1932-
See Ellis, Alice Thomas
See also CA 122; CANR 85, 90; MTCW 2

Hayden, Robert E(arl) 1913-1980 ..... **BLC 2; CLC 5, 9, 14, 37; PC 6**
See also AFAW 1, 2; AMWS 2; BW 1, 3; CA 69-72; 97-100; CABS 2; CANR 24, 75, 82; CDALB 1941-1968; DA; DAC; DAM MST, MULT, POET; DLB 5, 76; EWL 3; EXPP; MTCW 1, 2; PFS 1; RGAL 4; SATA 19; SATA-Obit 26; WP

Hayek, F(riedrich) A(ugust von) 1899-1992 .... **TCLC 109**
See also CA 93-96; 137; CANR 20; MTCW 1, 2

Hayford, J(oseph) E(phraim) Casely
See Casely-Hayford, J(oseph) E(phraim)

Hayman, Ronald 1932- .... **CLC 44**
See also CA 25-28R; CANR 18, 50, 88; CD 5; DLB 155

Hayne, Paul Hamilton 1830-1886 . **NCLC 94**
See also DLB 3, 64, 79, 248; RGAL 4

Hays, Mary 1760-1843 .... **NCLC 114**
See also DLB 142, 158; RGEL 2

Haywood, Eliza (Fowler) 1693(?)-1756 .... **LC 1, 44**
See also DLB 39; RGEL 2

Hazlitt, William 1778-1830 ...... **NCLC 29, 82**
See also BRW 4; DLB 110, 158; RGEL 2; TEA

Hazzard, Shirley 1931- .... **CLC 18**
See also CA 9-12R; CANR 4, 70, 127; CN 7; DLB 289; DLBY 1982; MTCW 1

Head, Bessie 1937-1986 ...... **BLC 2; CLC 25, 67; SSC 52**
See also AFW; BW 2, 3; CA 29-32R; 119; CANR 25, 82; CDWLB 3; DA3; DAM MULT; DLB 117, 225; EWL 3; EXPS; FW; MTCW 1, 2; RGSF 2; SSFS 5, 13; WLIT 2; WWE 1

Headon, (Nicky) Topper 1956(?)- ..... **CLC 30**

Heaney, Seamus (Justin) 1939- ..... **CLC 5, 7, 14, 25, 37, 74, 91, 171; PC 18; WLCS**
See also BRWR 1; BRWS 2; CA 85-88; CANR 25, 48, 75, 91, 128; CDBLB 1960 to Present; CP 7; DA3; DAB; DAM POET; DLB 40; DLBY 1995; EWL 3; EXPP; MTCW 1, 2; PAB; PFS 2, 5, 8, 17; RGEL 2; TEA; WLIT 4

Hearn, (Patricio) Lafcadio (Tessima Carlos) 1850-1904 .... **TCLC 9**
See also CA 105; 166; DLB 12, 78, 189; HGG; RGAL 4

Hearne, Samuel 1745-1792 .... **LC 95**
See also DLB 99

Hearne, Vicki 1946-2001 .... **CLC 56**
See also CA 139; 201

Hearon, Shelby 1931- .... **CLC 63**
See also AITN 2; AMWS 8; CA 25-28R; CANR 18, 48, 103; CSW

Heat-Moon, William Least .... **CLC 29**
See Trogdon, William (Lewis)
See also AAYA 9

Hebbel, Friedrich 1813-1863 . **DC 21; NCLC 43**
See also CDWLB 2; DAM DRAM; DLB 129; EW 6; RGWL 2, 3

Hebert, Anne 1916-2000 .... **CLC 4, 13, 29**
See also CA 85-88; 187; CANR 69, 126; CCA 1; CWP; CWW 2; DA3; DAC; DAM MST, POET; DLB 68; EWL 3; GFL 1789 to the Present; MTCW 1, 2; PFS 20

Hecht, Anthony (Evan) 1923- ...... **CLC 8, 13, 19**
See also AMWS 10; CA 9-12R; CANR 6, 108; CP 7; DAM POET; DLB 5, 169; EWL 3; PFS 6; WP

Hecht, Ben 1894-1964 ..... **CLC 8; TCLC 101**
See also CA 85-88; DFS 9; DLB 7, 9, 25, 26, 28, 86; FANT; IDFW 3, 4; RGAL 4

Hedayat, Sadeq 1903-1951 .... **TCLC 21**
See also CA 120; EWL 3; RGSF 2

Hegel, Georg Wilhelm Friedrich 1770-1831 .... **NCLC 46**
See also DLB 90; TWA

Heidegger, Martin 1889-1976 .... **CLC 24**
See also CA 81-84; 65-68; CANR 34; DLB 296; MTCW 1, 2

Heidenstam, (Carl Gustaf) Verner von 1859-1940 .... **TCLC 5**
See also CA 104

Heidi Louise
See Erdrich, Louise

Heifner, Jack 1946- .... **CLC 11**
See also CA 105; CANR 47

Heijermans, Herman 1864-1924 .... **TCLC 24**
See also CA 123; EWL 3

Heilbrun, Carolyn G(old) 1926-2003 .... **CLC 25, 173**
See Cross, Amanda
See also CA 45-48; 220; CANR 1, 28, 58, 94; FW

Hein, Christoph 1944- .... **CLC 154**
See also CA 158; CANR 108; CDWLB 2; CWW 2; DLB 124

Heine, Heinrich 1797-1856 .... **NCLC 4, 54; PC 25**
See also CDWLB 2; DLB 90; EW 5; RGWL 2, 3; TWA

Heinemann, Larry (Curtiss) 1944- .. **CLC 50**
See also CA 110; CAAS 21; CANR 31, 81; DLBD 9; INT CANR-31

Heiney, Donald (William) 1921-1993
See Harris, MacDonald
See also CA 1-4R; 142; CANR 3, 58; FANT

Heinlein, Robert A(nson) 1907-1988 . **CLC 1, 3, 8, 14, 26, 55; SSC 55**
See also AAYA 17; BPFB 2; BYA 4, 13; CA 1-4R; 125; CANR 1, 20, 53; CLR 75; CPW; DA3; DAM POP; DLB 8; EXPS; JRDA; LAIT 5; LMFS 2; MAICYA 1, 2; MTCW 1, 2; RGAL 4; SATA 9, 69; SATA-Obit 56; SCFW; SFW 4; SSFS 7; YAW

Helforth, John
See Doolittle, Hilda

Heliodorus fl. 3rd cent. - .... **CMLC 52**

Hellenhofferu, Vojtech Kapristian z
See Hasek, Jaroslav (Matej Frantisek)

Heller, Joseph 1923-1999 . **CLC 1, 3, 5, 8, 11, 36, 63; TCLC 131, 151; WLC**
See also AAYA 24; AITN 1; AMWS 4; BPFB 2; BYA 1; CA 5-8R; 187; CABS 1; CANR 8, 42, 66, 126; CN 7; CPW; DA; DA3; DAB; DAC; DAM MST, NOV, POP; DLB 2, 28, 227; DLBY 1980, 2002; EWL 3; EXPN; INT CANR-8; LAIT 4; MTCW 1, 2; NFS 1; RGAL 4; TUS; YAW

Hellman, Lillian (Florence) 1906-1984 .. **CLC 2, 4, 8, 14, 18, 34, 44, 52; DC 1; TCLC 119**
See also AAYA 47; AITN 1, 2; AMWS 1; CA 13-16R; 112; CAD; CANR 33; CWD; DA3; DAM DRAM; DFS 1, 3, 14; DLB 7, 228; DLBY 1984; EWL 3; FW; LAIT 3; MAWW; MTCW 1, 2; RGAL 4; TUS

Helprin, Mark 1947- .... **CLC 7, 10, 22, 32**
See also CA 81-84; CANR 47, 64, 124; CDALBS; CPW; DA3; DAM NOV, POP; DLBY 1985; FANT; MTCW 1, 2; SUFW 2

Helvetius, Claude-Adrien 1715-1771 .. **LC 26**

Helyar, Jane Penelope Josephine 1933-
See Poole, Josephine
See also CA 21-24R; CANR 10, 26; CWRI 5; SATA 82, 138; SATA-Essay 138

Hemans, Felicia 1793-1835 ...... **NCLC 29, 71**
See also DLB 96; RGEL 2

Hemingway, Ernest (Miller) 1899-1961 ... **CLC 1, 3, 6, 8, 10, 13, 19, 30, 34, 39, 41, 44, 50, 61, 80; SSC 1, 25, 36, 40, 63; TCLC 115; WLC**
See also AAYA 19; AMW; AMWC 1; AMWR 1; BPFB 2; BYA 2, 3, 13, 15; CA 77-80; CANR 34; CDALB 1917-1929; DA; DA3; DAB; DAC; DAM MST, NOV; DLB 4, 9, 102, 210; DLBD 1, 15, 16; DLBY 1981, 1987, 1996, 1998; EWL 3; EXPN; EXPS; LAIT 3, 4; LATS 1; MTCW 1, 2; NFS 1, 5, 6, 14; RGAL 4; RGSF 2; SSFS 17; TUS; WYA

Hempel, Amy 1951- .... **CLC 39**
See also CA 118; 137; CANR 70; DA3; DLB 218; EXPS; MTCW 2; SSFS 2

Henderson, F. C.
See Mencken, H(enry) L(ouis)

Henderson, Sylvia
See Ashton-Warner, Sylvia (Constance)

Henderson, Zenna (Chlarson) 1917-1983 .... **SSC 29**
See also CA 1-4R; 133; CANR 1, 84; DLB 8; SATA 5; SFW 4

Henkin, Joshua .... **CLC 119**
See also CA 161

Henley, Beth .... **CLC 23; DC 6, 14**
See Henley, Elizabeth Becker
See also CABS 3; CAD; CD 5; CSW; CWD; DFS 2; DLBY 1986; FW

Henley, Elizabeth Becker 1952-
See Henley, Beth
See also CA 107; CANR 32, 73; DA3; DAM DRAM, MST; MTCW 1, 2

Henley, William Ernest 1849-1903 .. **TCLC 8**
See also CA 105; DLB 19; RGEL 2

Hennissart, Martha
See Lathen, Emma
See also CA 85-88; CANR 64

Henry VIII 1491-1547 .... **LC 10**
See also DLB 132

Henry, O. ..... **SSC 5, 49; TCLC 1, 19; WLC**
See Porter, William Sydney
See also AAYA 41; AMWS 2; EXPS; RGAL 4; RGSF 2; SSFS 2, 18

Henry, Patrick 1736-1799 .... **LC 25**
See also LAIT 1

Henryson, Robert 1430(?)-1506(?) ...... **LC 20**
See also BRWS 7; DLB 146; RGEL 2

Henschke, Alfred
See Klabund

Henson, Lance 1944- .... **NNAL**
See also CA 146; DLB 175

Hiraoka, Kimitake 1925-1970
See Mishima, Yukio
See also CA 97-100; 29-32R; DA3; DAM DRAM; GLL 1; MTCW 1, 2

Hirsch, E(ric) D(onald), Jr. 1928- .... **CLC 79**
See also CA 25-28R; CANR 27, 51; DLB 67; INT CANR-27; MTCW 1

Hirsch, Edward 1950- .... **CLC 31, 50**
See also CA 104; CANR 20, 42, 102; CP 7; DLB 120

Hitchcock, Alfred (Joseph)
1899-1980 .... **CLC 16**
See also AAYA 22; CA 159; 97-100; SATA 27; SATA-Obit 24

Hitchens, Christopher (Eric)
1949- .... **CLC 157**
See also CA 152; CANR 89

Hitler, Adolf 1889-1945 .... **TCLC 53**
See also CA 117; 147

Hoagland, Edward 1932- .... **CLC 28**
See also ANW; CA 1-4R; CANR 2, 31, 57, 107; CN 7; DLB 6; SATA 51; TCWW 2

Hoban, Russell (Conwell) 1925- ... **CLC 7, 25**
See also BPFB 2; CA 5-8R; CANR 23, 37, 66, 114; CLR 3, 69; CN 7; CWRI 5; DAM NOV; DLB 52; FANT; MAICYA 1, 2; MTCW 1, 2; SATA 1, 40, 78, 136; SFW 4; SUFW 2

Hobbes, Thomas 1588-1679 .... **LC 36**
See also DLB 151, 252, 281; RGEL 2

Hobbs, Perry
See Blackmur, R(ichard) P(almer)

Hobson, Laura Z(ametkin)
1900-1986 .... **CLC 7, 25**
See Field, Peter
See also BPFB 2; CA 17-20R; 118; CANR 55; DLB 28; SATA 52

Hoccleve, Thomas c. 1368-c. 1437 ...... **LC 75**
See also DLB 146; RGEL 2

Hoch, Edward D(entinger) 1930-
See Queen, Ellery
See also CA 29-32R; CANR 11, 27, 51, 97; CMW 4; SFW 4

Hochhuth, Rolf 1931- .... **CLC 4, 11, 18**
See also CA 5-8R; CANR 33, 75; CWW 2; DAM DRAM; DLB 124; EWL 3; MTCW 1, 2

Hochman, Sandra 1936- .... **CLC 3, 8**
See also CA 5-8R; DLB 5

Hochwaelder, Fritz 1911-1986 .... **CLC 36**
See Hochwalder, Fritz
See also CA 29-32R; 120; CANR 42; DAM DRAM; MTCW 1; RGWL 3

Hochwalder, Fritz
See Hochwaelder, Fritz
See also EWL 3; RGWL 2

Hocking, Mary (Eunice) 1921- .... **CLC 13**
See also CA 101; CANR 18, 40

Hodgins, Jack 1938- .... **CLC 23**
See also CA 93-96; CN 7; DLB 60

Hodgson, William Hope
1877(?)-1918 .... **TCLC 13**
See also CA 111; 164; CMW 4; DLB 70, 153, 156, 178; HGG; MTCW 2; SFW 4; SUFW 1

Hoeg, Peter 1957- .... **CLC 95, 156**
See also CA 151; CANR 75; CMW 4; DA3; DLB 214; EWL 3; MTCW 2; NFS 17; RGWL 3; SSFS 18

Hoffman, Alice 1952- .... **CLC 51**
See also AAYA 37; AMWS 10; CA 77-80; CANR 34, 66, 100; CN 7; CPW; DAM NOV; DLB 292; MTCW 1, 2

Hoffman, Daniel (Gerard) 1923- . **CLC 6, 13, 23**
See also CA 1-4R; CANR 4; CP 7; DLB 5

Hoffman, Eva 1945- .... **CLC 182**
See also CA 132

Hoffman, Stanley 1944- .... **CLC 5**
See also CA 77-80

Hoffman, William 1925- .... **CLC 141**
See also CA 21-24R; CANR 9, 103; CSW; DLB 234

Hoffman, William M(oses) 1939- ..... **CLC 40**
See Hoffman, William M.
See also CA 57-60; CANR 11, 71

Hoffmann, E(rnst) T(heodor) A(madeus)
1776-1822 .... **NCLC 2; SSC 13**
See also CDWLB 2; DLB 90; EW 5; RGSF 2; RGWL 2, 3; SATA 27; SUFW 1; WCH

Hofmann, Gert 1931- .... **CLC 54**
See also CA 128; EWL 3

Hofmannsthal, Hugo von 1874-1929 ... **DC 4; TCLC 11**
See also CA 106; 153; CDWLB 2; DAM DRAM; DFS 17; DLB 81, 118; EW 9; EWL 3; RGWL 2, 3

Hogan, Linda 1947- ..... **CLC 73; NNAL; PC 35**
See also AMWS 4; ANW; BYA 12; CA 120; CANR 45, 73, 129; CWP; DAM MULT; DLB 175; SATA 132; TCWW 2

Hogarth, Charles
See Creasey, John

Hogarth, Emmett
See Polonsky, Abraham (Lincoln)

Hogg, James 1770-1835 .... **NCLC 4, 109**
See also DLB 93, 116, 159; HGG; RGEL 2; SUFW 1

Holbach, Paul Henri Thiry Baron
1723-1789 .... **LC 14**

Holberg, Ludvig 1684-1754 .... **LC 6**
See also DLB 300; RGWL 2, 3

Holcroft, Thomas 1745-1809 .... **NCLC 85**
See also DLB 39, 89, 158; RGEL 2

Holden, Ursula 1921- .... **CLC 18**
See also CA 101; CAAS 8; CANR 22

Holderlin, (Johann Christian) Friedrich
1770-1843 .... **NCLC 16; PC 4**
See also CDWLB 2; DLB 90; EW 5; RGWL 2, 3

Holdstock, Robert
See Holdstock, Robert P.

Holdstock, Robert P. 1948- .... **CLC 39**
See also CA 131; CANR 81; DLB 261; FANT; HGG; SFW 4; SUFW 2

Holinshed, Raphael fl. 1580- .... **LC 69**
See also DLB 167; RGEL 2

Holland, Isabelle (Christian)
1920-2002 .... **CLC 21**
See also AAYA 11; CA 21-24R; 205; CAAE 181; CANR 10, 25, 47; CLR 57; CWRI 5; JRDA; LAIT 4; MAICYA 1, 2; SATA 8, 70; SATA-Essay 103; SATA-Obit 132; WYA

Holland, Marcus
See Caldwell, (Janet Miriam) Taylor (Holland)

Hollander, John 1929- .... **CLC 2, 5, 8, 14**
See also CA 1-4R; CANR 1, 52; CP 7; DLB 5; SATA 13

Hollander, Paul
See Silverberg, Robert

Holleran, Andrew 1943(?)- .... **CLC 38**
See Garber, Eric
See also CA 144; GLL 1

Holley, Marietta 1836(?)-1926 .... **TCLC 99**
See also CA 118; DLB 11

Hollinghurst, Alan 1954- .... **CLC 55, 91**
See also CA 114; CN 7; DLB 207; GLL 1

Hollis, Jim
See Summers, Hollis (Spurgeon, Jr.)

Holly, Buddy 1936-1959 .... **TCLC 65**
See also CA 213

Holmes, Gordon
See Shiel, M(atthew) P(hipps)

Holmes, John
See Souster, (Holmes) Raymond

Holmes, John Clellon 1926-1988 ...... **CLC 56**
See also BG 2; CA 9-12R; 125; CANR 4; DLB 16, 237

Holmes, Oliver Wendell, Jr.
1841-1935 .... **TCLC 77**
See also CA 114; 186

Holmes, Oliver Wendell
1809-1894 .... **NCLC 14, 81**
See also AMWS 1; CDALB 1640-1865; DLB 1, 189, 235; EXPP; RGAL 4; SATA 34

Holmes, Raymond
See Souster, (Holmes) Raymond

Holt, Victoria
See Hibbert, Eleanor Alice Burford
See also BPFB 2

Holub, Miroslav 1923-1998 .... **CLC 4**
See also CA 21-24R; 169; CANR 10; CDWLB 4; CWW 2; DLB 232; EWL 3; RGWL 3

Holz, Detlev
See Benjamin, Walter

Homer c. 8th cent. B.C.- .... **CMLC 1, 16, 61; PC 23; WLCS**
See also AW 1; CDWLB 1; DA; DA3; DAB; DAC; DAM MST, POET; DLB 176; EFS 1; LAIT 1; LMFS 1; RGWL 2, 3; TWA; WP

Hongo, Garrett Kaoru 1951- .... **PC 23**
See also CA 133; CAAS 22; CP 7; DLB 120; EWL 3; EXPP; RGAL 4

Honig, Edwin 1919- .... **CLC 33**
See also CA 5-8R; CAAS 8; CANR 4, 45; CP 7; DLB 5

Hood, Hugh (John Blagdon) 1928- . **CLC 15, 28; SSC 42**
See also CA 49-52; CAAS 17; CANR 1, 33, 87; CN 7; DLB 53; RGSF 2

Hood, Thomas 1799-1845 .... **NCLC 16**
See also BRW 4; DLB 96; RGEL 2

Hooker, (Peter) Jeremy 1941- .... **CLC 43**
See also CA 77-80; CANR 22; CP 7; DLB 40

Hooker, Richard 1554-1600 .... **LC 95**
See also BRW 1; DLB 132; RGEL 2

hooks, bell
See Watkins, Gloria Jean

Hope, A(lec) D(erwent) 1907-2000 .... **CLC 3, 51; PC 56**
See also BRWS 7; CA 21-24R; 188; CANR 33, 74; DLB 289; EWL 3; MTCW 1, 2; PFS 8; RGEL 2

Hope, Anthony 1863-1933 .... **TCLC 83**
See also CA 157; DLB 153, 156; RGEL 2; RHW

Hope, Brian
See Creasey, John

Hope, Christopher (David Tully)
1944- .... **CLC 52**
See also AFW; CA 106; CANR 47, 101; CN 7; DLB 225; SATA 62

Hopkins, Gerard Manley
1844-1889 .... **NCLC 17; PC 15; WLC**
See also BRW 5; BRWR 2; CDBLB 1890-1914; DA; DA3; DAB; DAC; DAM MST, POET; DLB 35, 57; EXPP; PAB; RGEL 2; TEA; WP

Hopkins, John (Richard) 1931-1998 .. **CLC 4**
See also CA 85-88; 169; CBD; CD 5

Hopkins, Pauline Elizabeth
1859-1930 .... **BLC 2; TCLC 28**
See also AFAW 2; BW 2, 3; CA 141; CANR 82; DAM MULT; DLB 50

Hopkinson, Francis 1737-1791 .... **LC 25**
See also DLB 31; RGAL 4

Hopley-Woolrich, Cornell George 1903-1968
See Woolrich, Cornell
See also CA 13-14; CANR 58; CAP 1;
CMW 4; DLB 226; MTCW 2

Horace 65B.C.-8B.C. .... **CMLC 39; PC 46**
See also AW 2; CDWLB 1; DLB 211;
RGWL 2, 3

Horatio
See Proust, (Valentin-Louis-George-Eugene)
Marcel

Horgan, Paul (George Vincent
O'Shaughnessy) 1903-1995 .. **CLC 9, 53**
See also BPFB 2; CA 13-16R; 147; CANR
9, 35; DAM NOV; DLB 102, 212; DLBY
1985; INT CANR-9; MTCW 1, 2; SATA
13; SATA-Obit 84; TCWW 2

Horkheimer, Max 1895-1973 .... **TCLC 132**
See also CA 216; 41-44R; DLB 296

Horn, Peter
See Kuttner, Henry

Horne, Frank (Smith) 1899-1974 .... **HR 2**
See also BW 1; CA 125; 53-56; DLB 51;
WP

Horne, Richard Henry Hengist
1802(?)-1884 .... **NCLC 127**
See also DLB 32; SATA 29

Hornem, Horace Esq.
See Byron, George Gordon (Noel)

Horney, Karen (Clementine Theodore
Danielsen) 1885-1952 .... **TCLC 71**
See also CA 114; 165; DLB 246; FW

Hornung, E(rnest) W(illiam)
1866-1921 .... **TCLC 59**
See also CA 108; 160; CMW 4; DLB 70

Horovitz, Israel (Arthur) 1939- .... **CLC 56**
See also CA 33-36R; CAD; CANR 46, 59;
CD 5; DAM DRAM; DLB 7

Horton, George Moses
1797(?)-1883(?) .... **NCLC 87**
See also DLB 50

Horvath, odon von 1901-1938
See von Horvath, Odon
See also EWL 3

Horvath, Oedoen von -1938
See von Horvath, Odon

Horwitz, Julius 1920-1986 .... **CLC 14**
See also CA 9-12R; 119; CANR 12

Hospital, Janette Turner 1942- .... **CLC 42,
145**
See also CA 108; CANR 48; CN 7; DLBY
2002; RGSF 2

Hostos, E. M. de
See Hostos (y Bonilla), Eugenio Maria de

Hostos, Eugenio M. de
See Hostos (y Bonilla), Eugenio Maria de

Hostos, Eugenio Maria
See Hostos (y Bonilla), Eugenio Maria de

Hostos (y Bonilla), Eugenio Maria de
1839-1903 .... **TCLC 24**
See also CA 123; 131; HW 1

Houdini
See Lovecraft, H(oward) P(hillips)

Houellebecq, Michel 1958- .... **CLC 179**
See also CA 185

Hougan, Carolyn 1943- .... **CLC 34**
See also CA 139

Household, Geoffrey (Edward West)
1900-1988 .... **CLC 11**
See also CA 77-80; 126; CANR 58; CMW
4; DLB 87; SATA 14; SATA-Obit 59

Housman, A(lfred) E(dward)
1859-1936 .... **PC 2, 43; TCLC 1, 10;
WLCS**
See also BRW 6; CA 104; 125; DA; DA3;
DAB; DAC; DAM MST, POET; DLB 19,
284; EWL 3; EXPP; MTCW 1, 2; PAB;
PFS 4, 7; RGEL 2; TEA; WP

Housman, Laurence 1865-1959 .... **TCLC 7**
See also CA 106; 155; DLB 10; FANT;
RGEL 2; SATA 25

Houston, Jeanne (Toyo) Wakatsuki
1934- .... **AAL**
See also AAYA 49; CA 103; CAAS 16;
CANR 29, 123; LAIT 4; SATA 78

Howard, Elizabeth Jane 1923- ..... **CLC 7, 29**
See also CA 5-8R; CANR 8, 62; CN 7

Howard, Maureen 1930- .... **CLC 5, 14, 46,
151**
See also CA 53-56; CANR 31, 75; CN 7;
DLBY 1983; INT CANR-31; MTCW 1, 2

Howard, Richard 1929- .... **CLC 7, 10, 47**
See also AITN 1; CA 85-88; CANR 25, 80;
CP 7; DLB 5; INT CANR-25

Howard, Robert E(rvin)
1906-1936 .... **TCLC 8**
See also BPFB 2; BYA 5; CA 105; 157;
FANT; SUFW 1

Howard, Warren F.
See Pohl, Frederik

Howe, Fanny (Quincy) 1940- .... **CLC 47**
See also CA 117, 187; CAAE 187; CAAS
27; CANR 70, 116; CP 7; CWP; SATA-
Brief 52

Howe, Irving 1920-1993 .... **CLC 85**
See also AMWS 6; CA 9-12R; 141; CANR
21, 50; DLB 67; EWL 3; MTCW 1, 2

Howe, Julia Ward 1819-1910 .... **TCLC 21**
See also CA 117; 191; DLB 1, 189, 235;
FW

Howe, Susan 1937- .... **CLC 72, 152; PC 54**
See also AMWS 4; CA 160; CP 7; CWP;
DLB 120; FW; RGAL 4

Howe, Tina 1937- .... **CLC 48**
See also CA 109; CAD; CANR 125; CD 5;
CWD

Howell, James 1594(?)-1666 .... **LC 13**
See also DLB 151

Howells, W. D.
See Howells, William Dean

Howells, William D.
See Howells, William Dean

Howells, William Dean 1837-1920 ... **SSC 36;
TCLC 7, 17, 41**
See also AMW; CA 104; 134; CDALB
1865-1917; DLB 12, 64, 74, 79, 189;
LMFS 1; MTCW 2; RGAL 4; TUS

Howes, Barbara 1914-1996 .... **CLC 15**
See also CA 9-12R; 151; CAAS 3; CANR
53; CP 7; SATA 5

Hrabal, Bohumil 1914-1997 .... **CLC 13, 67**
See also CA 106; 156; CAAS 12; CANR
57; CWW 2; DLB 232; EWL 3; RGSF 2

Hrotsvit of Gandersheim c. 935-c.
1000 .... **CMLC 29**
See also DLB 148

Hsi, Chu 1130-1200 .... **CMLC 42**

Hsun, Lu
See Lu Hsun

Hubbard, L(afayette) Ron(ald)
1911-1986 .... **CLC 43**
See also CA 77-80; 118; CANR 52; CPW;
DA3; DAM POP; FANT; MTCW 2; SFW
4

Huch, Ricarda (Octavia)
1864-1947 .... **TCLC 13**
See also CA 111; 189; DLB 66; EWL 3

Huddle, David 1942- .... **CLC 49**
See also CA 57-60; CAAS 20; CANR 89;
DLB 130

Hudson, Jeffrey
See Crichton, (John) Michael

Hudson, W(illiam) H(enry)
1841-1922 .... **TCLC 29**
See also CA 115; 190; DLB 98, 153, 174;
RGEL 2; SATA 35

Hueffer, Ford Madox
See Ford, Ford Madox

Hughart, Barry 1934- .... **CLC 39**
See also CA 137; FANT; SFW 4; SUFW 2

Hughes, Colin
See Creasey, John

Hughes, David (John) 1930- .... **CLC 48**
See also CA 116; 129; CN 7; DLB 14

Hughes, Edward James
See Hughes, Ted
See also DA3; DAM MST, POET

Hughes, (James Mercer) Langston
1902-1967 ..... **BLC 2; CLC 1, 5, 10, 15,
35, 44, 108; DC 3; HR 2; PC 1, 53;
SSC 6; WLC**
See also AAYA 12; AFAW 1, 2; AMWR 1;
AMWS 1; BW 1, 3; CA 1-4R; 25-28R;
CANR 1, 34, 82; CDALB 1929-1941;
CLR 17; DA; DA3; DAB; DAC; DAM
DRAM, MST, MULT, POET; DFS 6, 18;
DLB 4, 7, 48, 51, 86, 228; EWL 3; EXPP;
EXPS; JRDA; LAIT 3; LMFS 2; MAI-
CYA 1, 2; MTCW 1, 2; PAB; PFS 1, 3, 6,
10, 15; RGAL 4; RGSF 2; SATA 4, 33;
SSFS 4, 7; TUS; WCH; WP; YAW

Hughes, Richard (Arthur Warren)
1900-1976 .... **CLC 1, 11**
See also CA 5-8R; 65-68; CANR 4; DAM
NOV; DLB 15, 161; MTCW 1;
RGEL 2; SATA 8; SATA-Obit 25

Hughes, Ted 1930-1998 . **CLC 2, 4, 9, 14, 37,
119; PC 7**
See Hughes, Edward James
See also BRWC 2; BRWR 2; BRWS 1; CA
1-4R; 171; CANR 1, 33, 66, 108; CLR 3;
CP 7; DAB; DAC; DLB 40, 161; EWL 3;
EXPP; MAICYA 1, 2; MTCW 1, 2; PAB;
PFS 4, 19; RGEL 2; SATA 49; SATA-
Brief 27; SATA-Obit 107; TEA; YAW

Hugo, Richard
See Huch, Ricarda (Octavia)

Hugo, Richard F(ranklin)
1923-1982 .... **CLC 6, 18, 32**
See also AMWS 6; CA 49-52; 108; CANR
3; DAM POET; DLB 5, 206; EWL 3; PFS
17; RGAL 4

Hugo, Victor (Marie) 1802-1885 .... **NCLC 3,
10, 21; PC 17; WLC**
See also AAYA 28; DA; DA3; DAB; DAC;
DAM DRAM, MST, NOV, POET; DLB
119, 192, 217; EFS 2; EW 6; EXPN; GFL
1789 to the Present; LAIT 1, 2; NFS 5;
RGWL 2, 3; SATA 47; TWA

Huidobro, Vicente
See Huidobro Fernandez, Vicente Garcia
See also DLB 283; EWL 3; LAW

Huidobro Fernandez, Vicente Garcia
1893-1948 .... **TCLC 31**
See Huidobro, Vicente
See also CA 131; HW 1

Hulme, Keri 1947- .... **CLC 39, 130**
See also CA 125; CANR 69; CN 7; CP 7;
CWP; EWL 3; FW; INT CA-125

Hulme, T(homas) E(rnest)
1883-1917 .... **TCLC 21**
See also BRWS 6; CA 117; 203; DLB 19

Humboldt, Wilhelm von
1767-1835 .... **NCLC 134**
See also DLB 90

Hume, David 1711-1776 .... **LC 7, 56**
See also BRWS 3; DLB 104, 252; LMFS 1;
TEA

Humphrey, William 1924-1997 .... **CLC 45**
See also AMWS 9; CA 77-80; 160; CANR
68; CN 7; CSW; DLB 6, 212, 234, 278;
TCWW 2

Humphreys, Emyr Owen 1919- .... **CLC 47**
See also CA 5-8R; CANR 3, 24; CN 7;
DLB 15

Humphreys, Josephine 1945- ..... CLC 34, 57
See also CA 121; 127; CANR 97; CSW;
DLB 292; INT CA-127

Huneker, James Gibbons
1860-1921 .... TCLC 65
See also CA 193; DLB 71; RGAL 4

Hungerford, Hesba Fay
See Brinsmead, H(esba) F(ay)

Hungerford, Pixie
See Brinsmead, H(esba) F(ay)

Hunt, E(verette) Howard, (Jr.)
1918- .... CLC 3
See also AITN 1; CA 45-48; CANR 2, 47,
103; CMW 4

Hunt, Francesca
See Holland, Isabelle (Christian)

Hunt, Howard
See Hunt, E(verette) Howard, (Jr.)

Hunt, Kyle
See Creasey, John

Hunt, (James Henry) Leigh
1784-1859 .... NCLC 1, 70
See also DAM POET; DLB 96, 110, 144;
RGEL 2; TEA

Hunt, Marsha 1946- .... CLC 70
See also BW 2, 3; CA 143; CANR 79

Hunt, Violet 1866(?)-1942 .... TCLC 53
See also CA 184; DLB 162, 197

Hunter, E. Waldo
See Sturgeon, Theodore (Hamilton)

Hunter, Evan 1926- .... CLC 11, 31
See McBain, Ed
See also AAYA 39; BPFB 2; CA 5-8R;
CANR 5, 38, 62, 97; CMW 4; CN 7;
CPW; DAM POP; DLBY 1982; INT
CANR-5; MSW; MTCW 1; SATA 25;
SFW 4

Hunter, Kristin 1931-
See Lattany, Kristin (Elaine Eggleston)
Hunter

Hunter, Mary
See Austin, Mary (Hunter)

Hunter, Mollie 1922- .... CLC 21
See McIlwraith, Maureen Mollie Hunter
See also AAYA 13; BYA 6; CANR 37, 78;
CLR 25; DLB 161; JRDA; MAICYA 1,
2; SAAS 7; SATA 54, 106, 139; SATA-
Essay 139; WYA; YAW

Hunter, Robert (?)-1734 .... LC 7

Hurston, Zora Neale 1891-1960 .... BLC 2;
CLC 7, 30, 61; DC 12; HR 2; SSC 4;
TCLC 121, 131; WLCS
See also AAYA 15; AFAW 1, 2; AMWS 6;
BW 1, 3; BYA 12; CA 85-88; CANR 61;
CDALBS; DA; DA3; DAC; DAM MST,
MULT, NOV; DFS 6; DLB 51, 86; EWL
3; EXPN; EXPS; FW; LAIT 3; LATS 1;
LMFS 2; MAWW; MTCW 1; NFS 3;
RGAL 4; RGSF 2; SSFS 1, 6, 11, 19;
TUS; YAW

Husserl, E. G.
See Husserl, Edmund (Gustav Albrecht)

Husserl, Edmund (Gustav Albrecht)
1859-1938 .... TCLC 100
See also CA 116; 133; DLB 296

Huston, John (Marcellus)
1906-1987 .... CLC 20
See also CA 73-76; 123; CANR 34; DLB
26

Hustvedt, Siri 1955- .... CLC 76
See also CA 137

Hutten, Ulrich von 1488-1523 .... LC 16
See also DLB 179

Huxley, Aldous (Leonard)
1894-1963 .... CLC 1, 3, 4, 5, 8, 11, 18,
35, 79; SSC 39; WLC
See also AAYA 11; BPFB 2; BRW 7; CA
85-88; CANR 44, 99; CDBLB 1914-1945;
DA; DA3; DAB; DAC; DAM MST, NOV;
DLB 36, 100, 162, 195, 255; EWL 3;
EXPN; LAIT 5; LMFS 2; MTCW 1, 2;
NFS 6; RGEL 2; SATA 63; SCFW 2;
SFW 4; TEA; YAW

Huxley, T(homas) H(enry)
1825-1895 .... NCLC 67
See also DLB 57; TEA

Huysmans, Joris-Karl 1848-1907 ... TCLC 7,
69
See also CA 104; 165; DLB 123; EW 7;
GFL 1789 to the Present; LMFS 2; RGWL
2, 3

Hwang, David Henry 1957- . CLC 55; DC 4,
23
See also CA 127; 132; CAD; CANR 76,
124; CD 5; DA3; DAM DRAM; DFS 11,
18; DLB 212, 228; INT CA-132; MTCW
2; RGAL 4

Hyde, Anthony 1946- .... CLC 42
See Chase, Nicholas
See also CA 136; CCA 1

Hyde, Margaret O(ldroyd) 1917- ..... CLC 21
See also CA 1-4R; CANR 1, 36; CLR 23;
JRDA; MAICYA 1, 2; SAAS 8; SATA 1,
42, 76, 139

Hynes, James 1956(?)- .... CLC 65
See also CA 164; CANR 105

Hypatia c. 370-415 .... CMLC 35

Ian, Janis 1951- .... CLC 21
See also CA 105; 187

Ibanez, Vicente Blasco
See Blasco Ibanez, Vicente

Ibarbourou, Juana de 1895-1979 ..... HLCS 2
See also DLB 290; HW 1; LAW

Ibarguengoitia, Jorge 1928-1983 ..... CLC 37;
TCLC 148
See also CA 124; 113; EWL 3; HW 1

Ibn Battuta, Abu Abdalla
1304-1368(?) .... CMLC 57
See also WLIT 2

Ibn Hazm 994-1064 .... CMLC 64

Ibsen, Henrik (Johan) 1828-1906 .... DC 2;
TCLC 2, 8, 16, 37, 52; WLC
See also AAYA 46; CA 104; 141; DA; DA3;
DAB; DAC; DAM DRAM, MST; DFS 1,
6, 8, 10, 11, 15, 16; EW 7; LAIT 2; LATS
1; RGWL 2, 3

Ibuse, Masuji 1898-1993 .... CLC 22
See Ibuse Masuji
See also CA 127; 141; MJW; RGWL 3

Ibuse Masuji
See Ibuse, Masuji
See also DLB 180; EWL 3

Ichikawa, Kon 1915- .... CLC 20
See also CA 121

Ichiyo, Higuchi 1872-1896 .... NCLC 49
See also MJW

Idle, Eric 1943- .... CLC 21
See Monty Python
See also CA 116; CANR 35, 91

Ignatow, David 1914-1997 .... CLC 4, 7, 14,
40; PC 34
See also CA 9-12R; 162; CAAS 3; CANR
31, 57, 96; CP 7; DLB 5; EWL 3

Ignotus
See Strachey, (Giles) Lytton

Ihimaera, Witi (Tame) 1944- .... CLC 46
See also CA 77-80; CANR 130; CN 7;
RGSF 2; SATA 148

Ilf, Ilya .... TCLC 21
See Fainzilberg, Ilya Arnoldovich
See also EWL 3

Illyes, Gyula 1902-1983 .... PC 16
See also CA 114; 109; CDWLB 4; DLB
215; EWL 3; RGWL 2, 3

Imalayen, Fatima-Zohra
See Djebar, Assia

Immermann, Karl (Lebrecht)
1796-1840 .... NCLC 4, 49
See also DLB 133

Ince, Thomas H. 1882-1924 .... TCLC 89
See also IDFW 3, 4

Inchbald, Elizabeth 1753-1821 ...... NCLC 62
See also DLB 39, 89; RGEL 2

Inclan, Ramon (Maria) del Valle
See Valle-Inclan, Ramon (Maria) del

Infante, G(uillermo) Cabrera
See Cabrera Infante, G(uillermo)

Ingalls, Rachel (Holmes) 1940- .... CLC 42
See also CA 123; 127

Ingamells, Reginald Charles
See Ingamells, Rex

Ingamells, Rex 1913-1955 .... TCLC 35
See also CA 167; DLB 260

Inge, William (Motter) 1913-1973 ..... CLC 1,
8, 19
See also CA 9-12R; CDALB 1941-1968;
DA3; DAM DRAM; DFS 1, 3, 5, 8; DLB
7, 249; EWL 3; MTCW 1, 2; RGAL 4;
TUS

Ingelow, Jean 1820-1897 .... NCLC 39, 107
See also DLB 35, 163; FANT; SATA 33

Ingram, Willis J.
See Harris, Mark

Innaurato, Albert (F.) 1948(?)- ... CLC 21, 60
See also CA 115; 122; CAD; CANR 78;
CD 5; INT CA-122

Innes, Michael
See Stewart, J(ohn) I(nnes) M(ackintosh)
See also DLB 276; MSW

Innis, Harold Adams 1894-1952 .... TCLC 77
See also CA 181; DLB 88

Insluis, Alanus de
See Alain de Lille

Iola
See Wells-Barnett, Ida B(ell)

Ionesco, Eugene 1912-1994 ... CLC 1, 4, 6, 9,
11, 15, 41, 86; DC 12; WLC
See also AAYA 46; CA 9-12R; 144; CANR 55; CWW
2; DA; DA3; DAB; DAC; DAM DRAM,
MST; DFS 4, 9; EW 13; EWL 3; GFL
1789 to the Present; LMFS 2; MTCW 1,
2; RGWL 2, 3; SATA 7; SATA-Obit 79;
TWA

Iqbal, Muhammad 1877-1938 .... TCLC 28
See also CA 215; EWL 3

Ireland, Patrick
See O'Doherty, Brian

Irenaeus St. 130- .... CMLC 42

Irigaray, Luce 1930- .... CLC 164
See also CA 154; CANR 121; FW

Iron, Ralph
See Schreiner, Olive (Emilie Albertina)

Irving, John (Winslow) 1942- ... CLC 13, 23,
38, 112, 175
See also AAYA 8; AMWS 6; BEST 89:3;
BPFB 2; CA 25-28R; CANR 28, 73, 112;
CN 7; CPW; DA3; DAM NOV, POP;
DLB 6, 278; DLBY 1982; EWL 3;
MTCW 1, 2; NFS 12, 14; RGAL 4; TUS

Irving, Washington 1783-1859 . NCLC 2, 19,
95; SSC 2, 37; WLC
See also AMW; CDALB 1640-1865; CLR
97; DA; DA3; DAB; DAC; DAM MST;
DLB 3, 11, 30, 59, 73, 74, 183, 186, 250,
254; EXPS; LAIT 1; RGAL 4; RGSF 2;
SSFS 1, 8, 16; SUFW 1; TUS; WCH;
YABC 2

Irwin, P. K.
See Page, P(atricia) K(athleen)

Isaacs, Jorge Ricardo 1837-1895 ... NCLC 70
See also LAW

Isaacs, Susan 1943- .... CLC 32
See also BEST 89:1; BPFB 2; CA 89-92;
CANR 20, 41, 65, 112; CPW; DA3; DAM
POP; INT CANR-20; MTCW 1, 2

Koestler, Arthur 1905-1983 ... **CLC 1, 3, 6, 8, 15, 33**
See also BRWS 1; CA 1-4R; 109; CANR 1, 33; CDBLB 1945-1960; DLBY 1983; EWL 3; MTCW 1, 2; NFS 19; RGEL 2

Kogawa, Joy Nozomi 1935- .... **CLC 78, 129**
See also AAYA 47; CA 101; CANR 19, 62, 126; CN 7; CWP; DAC; DAM MST, MULT; FW; MTCW 2; NFS 3; SATA 99

Kohout, Pavel 1928- .... **CLC 13**
See also CA 45-48; CANR 3

Koizumi, Yakumo
See Hearn, (Patricio) Lafcadio (Tessima Carlos)

Kolmar, Gertrud 1894-1943 .... **TCLC 40**
See also CA 167; EWL 3

Komunyakaa, Yusef 1947- .. **BLCS; CLC 86, 94; PC 51**
See also AFAW 2; AMWS 13; CA 147; CANR 83; CP 7; CSW; DLB 120; EWL 3; PFS 5, 20; RGAL 4

Konrad, George
See Konrad, Gyorgy
See also CWW 2

Konrad, Gyorgy 1933- .... **CLC 4, 10, 73**
See Konrad, George
See also CA 85-88; CANR 97; CDWLB 4; CWW 2; DLB 232; EWL 3

Konwicki, Tadeusz 1926- .... **CLC 8, 28, 54, 117**
See also CA 101; CAAS 9; CANR 39, 59; CWW 2; DLB 232; EWL 3; IDFW 3; MTCW 1

Koontz, Dean R(ay) 1945- .... **CLC 78**
See also AAYA 9, 31; BEST 89:3, 90:2; CA 108; CANR 19, 36, 52, 95; CMW 4; CPW; DA3; DAM NOV, POP; DLB 292; HGG; MTCW 1; SATA 92; SFW 4; SUFW 2; YAW

Kopernik, Mikolaj
See Copernicus, Nicolaus

Kopit, Arthur (Lee) 1937- ...... **CLC 1, 18, 33**
See also AITN 1; CA 81-84; CABS 3; CD 5; DAM DRAM; DFS 7, 14; DLB 7; MTCW 1; RGAL 4

Kopitar, Jernej (Bartholomaus)
1780-1844 .... **NCLC 117**

Kops, Bernard 1926- .... **CLC 4**
See also CA 5-8R; CANR 84; CBD; CN 7; CP 7; DLB 13

Kornbluth, C(yril) M. 1923-1958 .... **TCLC 8**
See also CA 105; 160; DLB 8; SFW 4

Korolenko, V. G.
See Korolenko, Vladimir Galaktionovich

Korolenko, Vladimir
See Korolenko, Vladimir Galaktionovich

Korolenko, Vladimir G.
See Korolenko, Vladimir Galaktionovich

Korolenko, Vladimir Galaktionovich
1853-1921 .... **TCLC 22**
See also CA 121; DLB 277

Korzybski, Alfred (Habdank Skarbek)
1879-1950 .... **TCLC 61**
See also CA 123; 160

Kosinski, Jerzy (Nikodem)
1933-1991 .... **CLC 1, 2, 3, 6, 10, 15, 53, 70**
See also AMWS 7; BPFB 2; CA 17-20R; 134; CANR 9, 46; DA3; DAM NOV; DLB 2, 299; DLBY 1982; EWL 3; HGG; MTCW 1, 2; NFS 12; RGAL 4; TUS

Kostelanetz, Richard (Cory) 1940- .. **CLC 28**
See also CA 13-16R; CAAS 8; CANR 38, 77; CN 7; CP 7

Kostrowitzki, Wilhelm Apollinaris de
1880-1918
See Apollinaire, Guillaume
See also CA 104

Kotlowitz, Robert 1924- .... **CLC 4**
See also CA 33-36R; CANR 36

Kotzebue, August (Friedrich Ferdinand) von
1761-1819 .... **NCLC 25**
See also DLB 94

Kotzwinkle, William 1938- ..... **CLC 5, 14, 35**
See also BPFB 2; CA 45-48; CANR 3, 44, 84, 129; CLR 6; DLB 173; FANT; MAICYA 1, 2; SATA 24, 70, 146; SFW 4; SUFW 2; YAW

Kowna, Stancy
See Szymborska, Wislawa

Kozol, Jonathan 1936- .... **CLC 17**
See also AAYA 46; CA 61-64; CANR 16, 45, 96

Kozoll, Michael 1940(?)- .... **CLC 35**

Kramer, Kathryn 19(?)- .... **CLC 34**

Kramer, Larry 1935- .... **CLC 42; DC 8**
See also CA 124; 126; CANR 60; DAM POP; DLB 249; GLL 1

Krasicki, Ignacy 1735-1801 .... **NCLC 8**

Krasinski, Zygmunt 1812-1859 .... **NCLC 4**
See also RGWL 2, 3

Kraus, Karl 1874-1936 .... **TCLC 5**
See also CA 104; 216; DLB 118; EWL 3

Kreve (Mickevicius), Vincas
1882-1954 .... **TCLC 27**
See also CA 170; DLB 220; EWL 3

Kristeva, Julia 1941- .... **CLC 77, 140**
See also CA 154; CANR 99; DLB 242; EWL 3; FW; LMFS 2

Kristofferson, Kris 1936- .... **CLC 26**
See also CA 104

Krizanc, John 1956- .... **CLC 57**
See also CA 187

Krleza, Miroslav 1893-1981 .... **CLC 8, 114**
See also CA 97-100; 105; CANR 50; CDWLB 4; DLB 147; EW 11; RGWL 2, 3

Kroetsch, Robert 1927- .. **CLC 5, 23, 57, 132**
See also CA 17-20R; CANR 8, 38; CCA 1; CN 7; CP 7; DAC; DAM POET; DLB 53; MTCW 1

Kroetz, Franz
See Kroetz, Franz Xaver

Kroetz, Franz Xaver 1946- .... **CLC 41**
See also CA 130; EWL 3

Kroker, Arthur (W.) 1945- .... **CLC 77**
See also CA 161

Kropotkin, Peter (Aleksieevich)
1842-1921 .... **TCLC 36**
See Kropotkin, Petr Alekseevich
See also CA 119; 219

Kropotkin, Petr Alekseevich
See Kropotkin, Peter (Aleksieevich)
See also DLB 277

Krotkov, Yuri 1917-1981 .... **CLC 19**
See also CA 102

Krumb
See Crumb, R(obert)

Krumgold, Joseph (Quincy)
1908-1980 .... **CLC 12**
See also BYA 1, 2; CA 9-12R; 101; CANR 7; MAICYA 1, 2; SATA 1, 48; SATA-Obit 23; YAW

Krumwitz
See Crumb, R(obert)

Krutch, Joseph Wood 1893-1970 ..... **CLC 24**
See also ANW; CA 1-4R; 25-28R; CANR 4; DLB 63, 206, 275

Krutzch, Gus
See Eliot, T(homas) S(tearns)

Krylov, Ivan Andreevich
1768(?)-1844 .... **NCLC 1**
See also DLB 150

Kubin, Alfred (Leopold Isidor)
1877-1959 .... **TCLC 23**
See also CA 112; 149; CANR 104; DLB 81

Kubrick, Stanley 1928-1999 .... **CLC 16; TCLC 112**
See also AAYA 30; CA 81-84; 177; CANR 33; DLB 26

Kumin, Maxine (Winokur) 1925- ..... **CLC 5, 13, 28, 164; PC 15**
See also AITN 2; AMWS 4; ANW; CA 1-4R; CAAS 8; CANR 1, 21, 69, 115; CP 7; CWP; DA3; DAM POET; DLB 5; EWL 3; EXPP; MTCW 1, 2; PAB; PFS 18; SATA 12

Kundera, Milan 1929- . **CLC 4, 9, 19, 32, 68, 115, 135; SSC 24**
See also AAYA 2; BPFB 2; CA 85-88; CANR 19, 52, 74; CDWLB 4; CWW 2; DA3; DAM NOV; DLB 232; EW 13; EWL 3; MTCW 1, 2; NFS 18; RGSF 2; RGWL 3; SSFS 10

Kunene, Mazisi (Raymond) 1930- ... **CLC 85**
See also BW 1, 3; CA 125; CANR 81; CP 7; DLB 117

Kung, Hans .... **CLC 130**
See Kung, Hans

Kung, Hans 1928-
See Kung, Hans
See also CA 53-56; CANR 66; MTCW 1, 2

Kunikida Doppo 1869(?)-1908
See Doppo, Kunikida
See also DLB 180; EWL 3

Kunitz, Stanley (Jasspon) 1905- .. **CLC 6, 11, 14, 148; PC 19**
See also AMWS 3; CA 41-44R; CANR 26, 57, 98; CP 7; DA3; DLB 48; INT CANR-26; MTCW 1, 2; PFS 11; RGAL 4

Kunze, Reiner 1933- .... **CLC 10**
See also CA 93-96; CWW 2; DLB 75; EWL 3

Kuprin, Aleksander Ivanovich
1870-1938 .... **TCLC 5**
See Kuprin, Aleksandr Ivanovich; Kuprin, Alexandr Ivanovich
See also CA 104; 182

Kuprin, Aleksandr Ivanovich
See Kuprin, Aleksander Ivanovich
See also DLB 295

Kuprin, Alexandr Ivanovich
See Kuprin, Aleksander Ivanovich
See also EWL 3

Kureishi, Hanif 1954(?)- .... **CLC 64, 135**
See also CA 139; CANR 113; CBD; CD 5; CN 7; DLB 194, 245; GLL 2; IDFW 4; WLIT 4; WWE 1

Kurosawa, Akira 1910-1998 ..... **CLC 16, 119**
See also AAYA 11; CA 101; 170; CANR 46; DAM MULT

Kushner, Tony 1956(?)- .... **CLC 81; DC 10**
See also AMWS 9; CA 144; CAD; CANR 74, 130; CD 5; DA3; DAM DRAM; DFS 5; DLB 228; EWL 3; GLL 1; LAIT 5; MTCW 2; RGAL 4

Kuttner, Henry 1915-1958 .... **TCLC 10**
See also CA 107; 157; DLB 8; FANT; SCFW 2; SFW 4

Kutty, Madhavi
See Das, Kamala

Kuzma, Greg 1944- .... **CLC 7**
See also CA 33-36R; CANR 70

Kuzmin, Mikhail (Alekseevich)
1872(?)-1936 .... **TCLC 40**
See also CA 170; DLB 295; EWL 3

Kyd, Thomas 1558-1594 .... **DC 3; LC 22**
See also BRW 1; DAM DRAM; DLB 62; IDTP; LMFS 1; RGEL 2; TEA; WLIT 3

Kyprianos, Iossif
See Samarakis, Antonis

L. S.
See Stephen, Sir Leslie

Lewis, Alun 1915-1944 .... **SSC 40; TCLC 3**
See also BRW 7; CA 104; 188; DLB 20, 162; PAB; RGEL 2

Lewis, C. Day
See Day Lewis, C(ecil)

Lewis, C(live) S(taples) 1898-1963 .... **CLC 1, 3, 6, 14, 27, 124; WLC**
See also AAYA 3, 39; BPFB 2; BRWS 3; BYA 15, 16; CA 81-84; CANR 33, 71; CDBLB 1945-1960; CLR 3, 27; CWRI 5; DA; DA3; DAB; DAC; DAM MST, NOV, POP; DLB 15, 100, 160, 255; EWL 3; FANT; JRDA; LMFS 2; MAICYA 1, 2; MTCW 1, 2; RGEL 2; SATA 13, 100; SCFW; SFW 4; SUFW 1; TEA; WCH; WYA; YAW

Lewis, Cecil Day
See Day Lewis, C(ecil)

Lewis, Janet 1899-1998 .... **CLC 41**
See Winters, Janet Lewis
See also CA 9-12R; 172; CANR 29, 63; CAP 1; CN 7; DLBY 1987; RHW; TCWW 2

Lewis, Matthew Gregory
1775-1818 .... **NCLC 11, 62**
See also DLB 39, 158, 178; HGG; LMFS 1; RGEL 2; SUFW

Lewis, (Harry) Sinclair 1885-1951 . **TCLC 4, 13, 23, 39; WLC**
See also AMW; AMWC 1; BPFB 2; CA 104; 133; CDALB 1917-1929; DA; DA3; DAB; DAC; DAM MST, NOV; DLB 9, 102, 284; DLBD 1; EWL 3; LAIT 3; MTCW 1, 2; NFS 15, 19; RGAL 4; TUS

Lewisohn, Ludwig 1883-1955 .... **TCLC 19**
See also CA 107; 203; DLB 4, 9, 28, 102

Lewton, Val 1904-1951 .... **TCLC 76**
See also CA 199; IDFW 3, 4

Leyner, Mark 1956- .... **CLC 92**
See also CA 110; CANR 28, 53; DA3; DLB 292; MTCW 2

Lezama Lima, Jose 1910-1976 .... **CLC 4, 10, 101; HLCS 2**
See also CA 77-80; CANR 71; DAM MULT; DLB 113, 283; EWL 3; HW 1, 2; LAW; RGWL 2, 3

L'Heureux, John (Clarke) 1934- ...... **CLC 52**
See also CA 13-16R; CANR 23, 45, 88; DLB 244

Liddell, C. H.
See Kuttner, Henry

Lie, Jonas (Lauritz Idemil)
1833-1908(?) .... **TCLC 5**
See also CA 115

Lieber, Joel 1937-1971 .... **CLC 6**
See also CA 73-76; 29-32R

Lieber, Stanley Martin
See Lee, Stan

Lieberman, Laurence (James)
1935- .... **CLC 4, 36**
See also CA 17-20R; CANR 8, 36, 89; CP 7

Lieh Tzu fl. 7th cent. B.C.-5th cent.
B.C. .... **CMLC 27**

Lieksman, Anders
See Haavikko, Paavo Juhani

Li Fei-kan 1904-
See Pa Chin
See also CA 105; TWA

Lifton, Robert Jay 1926- .... **CLC 67**
See also CA 17-20R; CANR 27, 78; INT CANR-27; SATA 66

Lightfoot, Gordon 1938- .... **CLC 26**
See also CA 109

Lightman, Alan P(aige) 1948- .... **CLC 81**
See also CA 141; CANR 63, 105

Ligotti, Thomas (Robert) 1953- ...... **CLC 44; SSC 16**
See also CA 123; CANR 49; HGG; SUFW 2

Li Ho 791-817 .... **PC 13**

Li Ju-chen c. 1763-c. 1830 .... **NCLC 137**

Liliencron, (Friedrich Adolf Axel) Detlev von 1844-1909 .... **TCLC 18**
See also CA 117

Lille, Alain de
See Alain de Lille

Lilly, William 1602-1681 .... **LC 27**

Lima, Jose Lezama
See Lezama Lima, Jose

Lima Barreto, Afonso Henrique de
1881-1922 .... **TCLC 23**
See also CA 117; 181; LAW

Lima Barreto, Afonso Henriques de
See Lima Barreto, Afonso Henrique de

Limonov, Edward 1944- .... **CLC 67**
See also CA 137

Lin, Frank
See Atherton, Gertrude (Franklin Horn)

Lin, Yutang 1895-1976 .... **TCLC 149**
See also CA 45-48; 65-68; CANR 2; RGAL 4

Lincoln, Abraham 1809-1865 .... **NCLC 18**
See also LAIT 2

Lind, Jakov .... **CLC 1, 2, 4, 27, 82**
See Landwirth, Heinz
See also CAAS 4; DLB 299; EWL 3

Lindbergh, Anne (Spencer) Morrow
1906-2001 .... **CLC 82**
See also BPFB 2; CA 17-20R; 193; CANR 16, 73; DAM NOV; MTCW 1, 2; SATA 33; SATA-Obit 125; TUS

Lindsay, David 1878(?)-1945 .... **TCLC 15**
See also CA 113; 187; DLB 255; FANT; SFW 1; SUFW 1

Lindsay, (Nicholas) Vachel
1879-1931 .... **PC 23; TCLC 17; WLC**
See also AMWS 1; CA 114; 135; CANR 79; CDALB 1865-1917; DA; DA3; DAC; DAM MST, POET; DLB 54; EWL 3; EXPP; RGAL 4; SATA 40; WP

Linke-Poot
See Doeblin, Alfred

Linney, Romulus 1930- .... **CLC 51**
See also CA 1-4R; CAD; CANR 40, 44, 79; CD 5; CSW; RGAL 4

Linton, Eliza Lynn 1822-1898 .... **NCLC 41**
See also DLB 18

Li Po 701-763 .... **CMLC 2; PC 29**
See also PFS 20; WP

Lipsius, Justus 1547-1606 .... **LC 16**

Lipsyte, Robert (Michael) 1938- ...... **CLC 21**
See also AAYA 7, 45; CA 17-20R; CANR 8, 57; CLR 23, 76; DA; DAC; DAM MST, NOV; JRDA; LAIT 5; MAICYA 1, 2; SATA 5, 68, 113; WYA; YAW

Lish, Gordon (Jay) 1934- ... **CLC 45; SSC 18**
See also CA 113; 117; CANR 79; DLB 130; INT CA-117

Lispector, Clarice 1925(?)-1977 .... **CLC 43; HLCS 2; SSC 34**
See also CA 139; 116; CANR 71; CDWLB 3; DLB 113; DNFS 1; EWL 3; FW; HW 2; LAW; RGSF 2; RGWL 2, 3; WLIT 1

Littell, Robert 1935(?)- .... **CLC 42**
See also CA 109; 112; CANR 64, 115; CMW 4

Little, Malcolm 1925-1965
See Malcolm X
See also BW 1, 3; CA 125; 111; CANR 82; DA; DA3; DAB; DAC; DAM MST, MULT; MTCW 1, 2

Littlewit, Humphrey Gent.
See Lovecraft, H(oward) P(hillips)

Litwos
See Sienkiewicz, Henryk (Adam Alexander Pius)

Liu, E. 1857-1909 .... **TCLC 15**
See also CA 115; 190

Lively, Penelope (Margaret) 1933- .. **CLC 32, 50**
See also BPFB 2; CA 41-44R; CANR 29, 67, 79, 131; CLR 7; CN 7; CWRI 5; DAM NOV; DLB 14, 161, 207; FANT; JRDA; MAICYA 1, 2; MTCW 1, 2; SATA 7, 60, 101; TEA

Livesay, Dorothy (Kathleen)
1909-1996 .... **CLC 4, 15, 79**
See also AITN 2; CA 25-28R; CAAS 8; CANR 36, 67; DAC; DAM MST, POET; DLB 68; FW; MTCW 1; RGEL 2; TWA

Livy c. 59B.C.-c. 12 .... **CMLC 11**
See also AW 2; CDWLB 1; DLB 211; RGWL 2, 3

Lizardi, Jose Joaquin Fernandez de
1776-1827 .... **NCLC 30**
See also LAW

Llewellyn, Richard
See Llewellyn Lloyd, Richard Dafydd Vivian
See also DLB 15

Llewellyn Lloyd, Richard Dafydd Vivian
1906-1983 .... **CLC 7, 80**
See Llewellyn, Richard
See also CA 53-56; 111; CANR 7, 71; SATA 11; SATA-Obit 37

Llosa, (Jorge) Mario (Pedro) Vargas
See Vargas Llosa, (Jorge) Mario (Pedro)
See also RGWL 3

Llosa, Mario Vargas
See Vargas Llosa, (Jorge) Mario (Pedro)

Lloyd, Manda
See Mander, (Mary) Jane

Lloyd Webber, Andrew 1948-
See Webber, Andrew Lloyd
See also AAYA 1, 38; CA 116; 149; DAM DRAM; SATA 56

Llull, Ramon c. 1235-c. 1316 .... **CMLC 12**

Lobb, Ebenezer
See Upward, Allen

Locke, Alain (Le Roy)
1886-1954 .... **BLCS; HR 3; TCLC 43**
See also BW 1, 3; CA 106; 124; CANR 79; DLB 51; LMFS 2; RGAL 4

Locke, John 1632-1704 .... **LC 7, 35**
See also DLB 31, 101, 213, 252; RGEL 2; WLIT 3

Locke-Elliott, Sumner
See Elliott, Sumner Locke

Lockhart, John Gibson 1794-1854 .. **NCLC 6**
See also DLB 110, 116, 144

Lockridge, Ross (Franklin), Jr.
1914-1948 .... **TCLC 111**
See also CA 108; 145; CANR 79; DLB 143; DLBY 1980; RGAL 4; RHW

Lockwood, Robert
See Johnson, Robert

Lodge, David (John) 1935- .... **CLC 36, 141**
See also BEST 90:1; BRWS 4; CA 17-20R; CANR 19, 53, 92; CN 7; CPW; DAM POP; DLB 14, 194; EWL 3; INT CANR-19; MTCW 1, 2

Lodge, Thomas 1558-1625 .... **LC 41**
See also DLB 172; RGEL 2

Loewinsohn, Ron(ald William)
1937- .... **CLC 52**
See also CA 25-28R; CANR 71

Logan, Jake
See Smith, Martin Cruz

Logan, John (Burton) 1923-1987 .... **CLC 5**
See also CA 77-80; 124; CANR 45; DLB 5

Mariner, Scott
See Pohl, Frederik
Marinetti, Filippo Tommaso
1876-1944 .... **TCLC 10**
See also CA 107; DLB 114, 264; EW 9;
EWL 3
Marivaux, Pierre Carlet de Chamblain de
1688-1763 .... **DC 7; LC 4**
See also GFL Beginnings to 1789; RGWL
2, 3; TWA
Markandaya, Kamala .... **CLC 8, 38**
See Taylor, Kamala (Purnaiya)
See also BYA 13; CN 7; EWL 3
Markfield, Wallace 1926-2002 .... **CLC 8**
See also CA 69-72; 208; CAAS 3; CN 7;
DLB 2, 28; DLBY 2002
Markham, Edwin 1852-1940 .... **TCLC 47**
See also CA 160; DLB 54, 186; RGAL 4
Markham, Robert
See Amis, Kingsley (William)
Markoosie .... **NNAL**
See Patsauq, Markoosie
See also CLR 23; DAM MULT
Marks, J
See Highwater, Jamake (Mamake)
Marks, J.
See Highwater, Jamake (Mamake)
Marks-Highwater, J
See Highwater, Jamake (Mamake)
Marks-Highwater, J.
See Highwater, Jamake (Mamake)
Markson, David M(errill) 1927- .... **CLC 67**
See also CA 49-52; CANR 1, 91; CN 7
Marlatt, Daphne (Buckle) 1942- .... **CLC 168**
See also CA 25-28R; CANR 17, 39; CN 7;
CP 7; CWP; DLB 60; FW
Marley, Bob .... **CLC 17**
See Marley, Robert Nesta
Marley, Robert Nesta 1945-1981
See Marley, Bob
See also CA 107; 103
Marlowe, Christopher 1564-1593 . **DC 1; LC 22, 47; PC 57; WLC**
See also BRW 1; BRWR 1; CDBLB Before
1660; DA; DA3; DAB; DAC; DAM
DRAM, MST; DFS 1, 5, 13; DLB 62;
EXPP; LMFS 1; RGEL 2; TEA; WLIT 3
Marlowe, Stephen 1928- .... **CLC 70**
See Queen, Ellery
See also CA 13-16R; CANR 6, 55; CMW
4; SFW 4
Marmion, Shakerley 1603-1639 .... **LC 89**
See also DLB 58; RGEL 2
Marmontel, Jean-Francois 1723-1799 .. **LC 2**
Maron, Monika 1941- .... **CLC 165**
See also CA 201
Marquand, John P(hillips)
1893-1960 .... **CLC 2, 10**
See also AMW; BPFB 2; CA 85-88; CANR
73; CMW 4; DLB 9, 102; EWL 3; MTCW
2; RGAL 4
Marques, Rene 1919-1979 .. **CLC 96; HLC 2**
See also CA 97-100; 85-88; CANR 78;
DAM MULT; DLB 113; EWL 3; HW 1,
2; LAW; RGSF 2
Marquez, Gabriel (Jose) Garcia
See Garcia Marquez, Gabriel (Jose)
Marquis, Don(ald Robert Perry)
1878-1937 .... **TCLC 7**
See also CA 104; 166; DLB 11, 25; RGAL
4
Marquis de Sade
See Sade, Donatien Alphonse Francois
Marric, J. J.
See Creasey, John
See also MSW
Marryat, Frederick 1792-1848 .... **NCLC 3**
See also DLB 21, 163; RGEL 2; WCH

Marsden, James
See Creasey, John
Marsh, Edward 1872-1953 .... **TCLC 99**
Marsh, (Edith) Ngaio 1895-1982 .. **CLC 7, 53**
See also CA 9-12R; CANR 6, 58; CMW 4;
CPW; DAM POP; DLB 77; MSW;
MTCW 1, 2; RGEL 2; TEA
Marshall, Garry 1934- .... **CLC 17**
See also AAYA 3; CA 111; SATA 60
Marshall, Paule 1929- .. **BLC 3; CLC 27, 72; SSC 3**
See also AFAW 1, 2; AMWS 11; BPFB 2;
BW 2, 3; CA 77-80; CANR 25, 73, 129;
CN 7; DA3; DAM MULT; DLB 33, 157,
227; EWL 3; LATS 1; MTCW 1, 2;
RGAL 4; SSFS 15
Marshallik
See Zangwill, Israel
Marsten, Richard
See Hunter, Evan
Marston, John 1576-1634 .... **LC 33**
See also BRW 2; DAM DRAM; DLB 58,
172; RGEL 2
Martel, Yann 1963- .... **CLC 192**
See also CA 146; CANR 114
Martha, Henry
See Harris, Mark
Marti, Jose
See Marti (y Perez), Jose (Julian)
See also DLB 290
Marti (y Perez), Jose (Julian)
1853-1895 .... **HLC 2; NCLC 63**
See Marti, Jose
See also DAM MULT; HW 2; LAW; RGWL
2, 3; WLIT 1
Martial c. 40-c. 104 .... **CMLC 35; PC 10**
See also AW 2; CDWLB 1; DLB 211;
RGWL 2, 3
Martin, Ken
See Hubbard, L(afayette) Ron(ald)
Martin, Richard
See Creasey, John
Martin, Steve 1945- .... **CLC 30**
See also AAYA 53; CA 97-100; CANR 30,
100; DFS 19; MTCW 1
Martin, Valerie 1948- .... **CLC 89**
See also BEST 90:2; CA 85-88; CANR 49,
89
Martin, Violet Florence 1862-1915 .. **SSC 56; TCLC 51**
Martin, Webber
See Silverberg, Robert
Martindale, Patrick Victor
See White, Patrick (Victor Martindale)
Martin du Gard, Roger
1881-1958 .... **TCLC 24**
See also CA 118; CANR 94; DLB 65; EWL
3; GFL 1789 to the Present; RGWL 2, 3
Martineau, Harriet 1802-1876 ...... **NCLC 26, 137**
See also DLB 21, 55, 159, 163, 166, 190;
FW; RGEL 2; YABC 2
Martines, Julia
See O'Faolain, Julia
Martinez, Enrique Gonzalez
See Gonzalez Martinez, Enrique
Martinez, Jacinto Benavente y
See Benavente (y Martinez), Jacinto
Martinez de la Rosa, Francisco de Paula
1787-1862 .... **NCLC 102**
See also TWA
Martinez Ruiz, Jose 1873-1967
See Azorin; Ruiz, Jose Martinez
See also CA 93-96; HW 1
Martinez Sierra, Gregorio
1881-1947 .... **TCLC 6**
See also CA 115; EWL 3

Martinez Sierra, Maria (de la O'LeJarraga)
1874-1974 .... **TCLC 6**
See also CA 115; EWL 3
Martinsen, Martin
See Follett, Ken(neth Martin)
Martinson, Harry (Edmund)
1904-1978 .... **CLC 14**
See also CA 77-80; CANR 34, 130; DLB
259; EWL 3
Martyn, Edward 1859-1923 .... **TCLC 131**
See also CA 179; DLB 10; RGEL 2
Marut, Ret
See Traven, B.
Marut, Robert
See Traven, B.
Marvell, Andrew 1621-1678 .... **LC 4, 43; PC 10; WLC**
See also BRW 2; BRWR 2; CDBLB 1660-
1789; DA; DAB; DAC; DAM MST,
POET; DLB 131; EXPP; PFS 5; RGEL 2;
TEA; WP
Marx, Karl (Heinrich)
1818-1883 .... **NCLC 17, 114**
See also DLB 129; LATS 1; TWA
Masaoka, Shiki -1902 .... **TCLC 18**
See Masaoka, Tsunenori
See also RGWL 3
Masaoka, Tsunenori 1867-1902
See Masaoka, Shiki
See also CA 117; 191; TWA
Masefield, John (Edward)
1878-1967 .... **CLC 11, 47**
See also CA 19-20; 25-28R; CANR 33;
CAP 2; CDBLB 1890-1914; DAM POET;
DLB 10, 19, 153, 160; EWL 3; EXPP;
FANT; MTCW 1, 2; PFS 5; RGEL 2;
SATA 19
Maso, Carole 19(?)- .... **CLC 44**
See also CA 170; GLL 2; RGAL 4
Mason, Bobbie Ann 1940- ... **CLC 28, 43, 82, 154; SSC 4**
See also AAYA 5, 42; AMWS 8; BPFB 2;
CA 53-56; CANR 11, 31, 58, 83, 125;
CDALBS; CN 7; CSW; DA3; DLB 173;
DLBY 1987; EWL 3; EXPS; INT CANR-
31; MTCW 1, 2; NFS 4; RGAL 4; RGSF
2; SSFS 3,8; YAW
Mason, Ernst
See Pohl, Frederik
Mason, Hunni B.
See Sternheim, (William Adolf) Carl
Mason, Lee W.
See Malzberg, Barry N(athaniel)
Mason, Nick 1945- .... **CLC 35**
Mason, Tally
See Derleth, August (William)
Mass, Anna .... **CLC 59**
Mass, William
See Gibson, William
Massinger, Philip 1583-1640 .... **LC 70**
See also DLB 58; RGEL 2
Master Lao
See Lao Tzu
Masters, Edgar Lee 1868-1950 ...... **PC 1, 36; TCLC 2, 25; WLCS**
See also AMWS 1; CA 104; 133; CDALB
1865-1917; DA; DAC; DAM MST,
POET; DLB 54; EWL 3; EXPP; MTCW
1, 2; RGAL 4; TUS; WP
Masters, Hilary 1928- .... **CLC 48**
See also CA 25-28R, 217; CAAE 217;
CANR 13, 47, 97; CN 7; DLB 244
Mastrosimone, William 19(?)- .... **CLC 36**
See also CA 186; CAD; CD 5
Mathe, Albert
See Camus, Albert
Mather, Cotton 1663-1728 .... **LC 38**
See also AMWS 2; CDALB 1640-1865;
DLB 24, 30, 140; RGAL 4; TUS

McFadden, David 1940- .... **CLC 48**
   See also CA 104; CP 7; DLB 60; INT CA-
   104
McFarland, Dennis 1950- .... **CLC 65**
   See also CA 165; CANR 110
McGahern, John 1934- ... **CLC 5, 9, 48, 156;**
   SSC 17
   See also CA 17-20R; CANR 29, 68, 113;
   CN 7; DLB 14, 231; MTCW 1
McGinley, Patrick (Anthony) 1937- . **CLC 41**
   See also CA 120; 127; CANR 56; INT CA-
   127
McGinley, Phyllis 1905-1978 .... **CLC 14**
   See also CA 9-12R; 77-80; CANR 19;
   CWRI 5; DLB 11, 48; PFS 9, 13; SATA
   2, 44; SATA-Obit 24
McGinniss, Joe 1942- .... **CLC 32**
   See also AITN 2; BEST 89:2; CA 25-28R;
   CANR 26, 70; CPW; DLB 185; INT
   CANR-26
McGivern, Maureen Daly
   See Daly, Maureen
McGrath, Patrick 1950- .... **CLC 55**
   See also CA 136; CANR 65; CN 7; DLB
   231; HGG; SUFW 2
McGrath, Thomas (Matthew)
   1916-1990 .... **CLC 28, 59**
   See also AMWS 10; CA 9-12R; 132; CANR
   6, 33, 95; DAM POET; MTCW 1; SATA
   41; SATA-Obit 66
McGuane, Thomas (Francis III)
   1939- .... **CLC 3, 7, 18, 45, 127**
   See also AITN 2; BPFB 2; CA 49-52;
   CANR 5, 24, 49, 94; CN 7; DLB 2, 212;
   DLBY 1980; EWL 3; INT CANR-24;
   MTCW 1; TCWW 2
McGuckian, Medbh 1950- .... **CLC 48, 174;**
   PC 27
   See also BRWS 5; CA 143; CP 7; CWP;
   DAM POET; DLB 40
McHale, Tom 1942(?)-1982 .... **CLC 3, 5**
   See also AITN 1; CA 77-80; 106
McIlvanney, William 1936- .... **CLC 42**
   See also CA 25-28R; CANR 61; CMW 4;
   DLB 14, 207
McIlwraith, Maureen Mollie Hunter
   See Hunter, Mollie
   See also SATA 2
McInerney, Jay 1955- .... **CLC 34, 112**
   See also AAYA 18; BPFB 2; CA 116; 123;
   CANR 45, 68, 116; CN 7; CPW; DA3;
   DAM POP; DLB 292; INT CA-123;
   MTCW 2
McIntyre, Vonda N(eel) 1948- .... **CLC 18**
   See also CA 81-84; CANR 17, 34, 69;
   MTCW 1; SFW 4; YAW
McKay, Claude .... **BLC 3; HR 3; PC 2;**
   TCLC 7, 41; WLC
   See McKay, Festus Claudius
   See also AFAW 1, 2; AMWS 10; DAB;
   DLB 4, 45, 51, 117; EWL 3; EXPP; GLL
   2; LAIT 3; LMFS 2; PAB; PFS 4; RGAL
   4; WP
McKay, Festus Claudius 1889-1948
   See McKay, Claude
   See also BW 1, 3; CA 104; 124; CANR 73;
   DA; DAC; DAM MST, MULT, NOV,
   POET; MTCW 1, 2; TUS
McKuen, Rod 1933- .... **CLC 1, 3**
   See also AITN 1; CA 41-44R; CANR 40
McLoughlin, R. B.
   See Mencken, H(enry) L(ouis)
McLuhan, (Herbert) Marshall
   1911-1980 .... **CLC 37, 83**
   See also CA 9-12R; 102; CANR 12, 34, 61;
   DLB 88; INT CANR-12; MTCW 1, 2
McManus, Declan Patrick Aloysius
   See Costello, Elvis

McMillan, Terry (L.) 1951- . **BLCS; CLC 50,**
   61, 112
   See also AAYA 21; AMWS 13; BPFB 2;
   BW 2, 3; CA 140; CANR 60, 104, 131;
   CPW; DA3; DAM MULT, NOV, POP;
   MTCW 2; RGAL 4; YAW
McMurtry, Larry (Jeff) 1936- .. **CLC 2, 3, 7,**
   11, 27, 44, 127
   See also AAYA 15; AITN 2; AMWS 5;
   BEST 89:2; BPFB 2; CA 5-8R; CANR
   19, 43, 64, 103; CDALB 1968-1988; CN
   7; CPW; CSW; DA3; DAM NOV, POP;
   DLB 2, 143, 256; DLBY 1980, 1987;
   EWL 3; MTCW 1, 2; RGAL 4; TCWW 2
McNally, T. M. 1961- .... **CLC 82**
McNally, Terrence 1939- .... **CLC 4, 7, 41, 91**
   See also AMWS 13; CA 45-48; CAD;
   CANR 2, 56, 116; CD 5; DA3; DAM
   DRAM; DFS 16, 19; DLB 7, 249; EWL
   3; GLL 1; MTCW 2
McNamer, Deirdre 1950- .... **CLC 70**
McNeal, Tom .... **CLC 119**
McNeile, Herman Cyril 1888-1937
   See Sapper
   See also CA 184; CMW 4; DLB 77
McNickle, (William) D'Arcy
   1904-1977 .... **CLC 89; NNAL**
   See also CA 9-12R; 85-88; CANR 5, 45;
   DAM MULT; DLB 175, 212; RGAL 4;
   SATA-Obit 22
McPhee, John (Angus) 1931- .... **CLC 36**
   See also AMWS 3; ANW; BEST 90:1; CA
   65-68; CANR 20, 46, 64, 69, 121; CPW;
   DLB 185, 275; MTCW 1, 2; TUS
McPherson, James Alan 1943- . **BLCS; CLC**
   19, 77
   See also BW 1, 3; CA 25-28R; CAAS 17;
   CANR 24, 74; CN 7; CSW; DLB 38, 244;
   EWL 3; MTCW 1, 2; RGAL 4; RGSF 2
McPherson, William (Alexander)
   1933- .... **CLC 34**
   See also CA 69-72; CANR 28; INT
   CANR-28
McTaggart, J. McT. Ellis
   See McTaggart, John McTaggart Ellis
McTaggart, John McTaggart Ellis
   1866-1925 .... **TCLC 105**
   See also CA 120; DLB 262
Mead, George Herbert 1863-1931 . **TCLC 89**
   See also CA 212; DLB 270
Mead, Margaret 1901-1978 .... **CLC 37**
   See also AITN 1; CA 1-4R; 81-84; CANR
   4; DA3; FW; MTCW 1, 2; SATA-Obit 20
Meaker, Marijane (Agnes) 1927-
   See Kerr, M. E.
   See also CA 107; CANR 37, 63; INT CA-
   107; JRDA; MAICYA 1, 2; MAICYAS 1;
   MTCW 1; SATA 20, 61, 99; SATA-Essay
   111; YAW
Medoff, Mark (Howard) 1940- .... **CLC 6, 23**
   See also AITN 1; CA 53-56; CAD; CANR
   5; CD 5; DAM DRAM; DFS 4; DLB 7;
   INT CANR-5
Medvedev, P. N.
   See Bakhtin, Mikhail Mikhailovich
Meged, Aharon
   See Megged, Aharon
Meged, Aron
   See Megged, Aharon
Megged, Aharon 1920- .... **CLC 9**
   See also CA 49-52; CAAS 13; CANR 1;
   EWL 3
Mehta, Gita 1943- .... **CLC 179**
   See also CA 225; DNFS 2
Mehta, Ved (Parkash) 1934- .... **CLC 37**
   See also CA 1-4R; 212; CAAE 212; CANR
   2, 23, 69; MTCW 1
Melanchthon, Philipp 1497-1560 .... **LC 90**
   See also DLB 179

Melanter
   See Blackmore, R(ichard) D(oddridge)
Meleager c. 140B.C.-c. 70B.C. ...... **CMLC 53**
Melies, Georges 1861-1938 .... **TCLC 81**
Melikow, Loris
   See Hofmannsthal, Hugo von
Melmoth, Sebastian
   See Wilde, Oscar (Fingal O'Flahertie Wills)
Melo Neto, Joao Cabral de
   See Cabral de Melo Neto, Joao
   See also CWW 2; EWL 3
Meltzer, Milton 1915- .... **CLC 26**
   See also AAYA 8, 45; BYA 2, 6; CA 13-
   16R; CANR 38, 92, 107; CLR 13; DLB
   61; JRDA; MAICYA 1, 2; SAAS 1; SATA
   1, 50, 80, 128; SATA-Essay 124; WYA;
   YAW
Melville, Herman 1819-1891 ..... **NCLC 3, 12,**
   29, 45, 49, 91, 93, 123; SSC 1, 17, 46;
   WLC
   See also AAYA 25; AMW; AMWR 1;
   CDALB 1640-1865; DA; DA3; DAB;
   DAC; DAM MST, NOV; DLB 3, 74, 250,
   254; EXPN; EXPS; LAIT 1, 2; NFS 7, 9;
   RGAL 4; RGSF 2; SATA 59; SSFS 3;
   TUS
Members, Mark
   See Powell, Anthony (Dymoke)
Membreno, Alejandro .... **CLC 59**
Menander c. 342B.C.-c. 293B.C. .... **CMLC 9,**
   51; DC 3
   See also AW 1; CDWLB 1; DAM DRAM;
   DLB 176; LMFS 1; RGWL 2, 3
Menchu, Rigoberta 1959- .. **CLC 160; HLCS**
   2
   See also CA 175; DNFS 1; WLIT 1
Mencken, H(enry) L(ouis)
   1880-1956 .... **TCLC 13**
   See also AMW; CA 105; 125; CDALB
   1917-1929; DLB 11, 29, 63, 137, 222;
   EWL 3; MTCW 1, 2; NCFS 4; RGAL 4;
   TUS
Mendelsohn, Jane 1965- .... **CLC 99**
   See also CA 154; CANR 94
Menton, Francisco de
   See Chin, Frank (Chew, Jr.)
Mercer, David 1928-1980 .... **CLC 5**
   See also CA 9-12R; 102; CANR 23; CBD;
   DAM DRAM; DLB 13; MTCW 1; RGEL
   2
Merchant, Paul
   See Ellison, Harlan (Jay)
Meredith, George 1828-1909 ... **TCLC 17, 43**
   See also CA 117; 153; CANR 80; CDBLB
   1832-1890; DAM POET; DLB 18, 35, 57,
   159; RGEL 2; TEA
Meredith, William (Morris) 1919- .... **CLC 4,**
   13, 22, 55; PC 28
   See also CA 9-12R; CAAS 14; CANR 6,
   40, 129; CP 7; DAM POET; DLB 5
Merezhkovsky, Dmitrii Sergeevich
   See Merezhkovsky, Dmitry Sergeyevich
   See also DLB 295
Merezhkovsky, Dmitry Sergeevich
   See Merezhkovsky, Dmitry Sergeyevich
   See also EWL 3
Merezhkovsky, Dmitry Sergeyevich
   1865-1941 .... **TCLC 29**
   See Merezhkovsky, Dmitrii Sergeevich;
   Merezhkovsky, Dmitry Sergeevich
   See also CA 169
Merimee, Prosper 1803-1870 ... **NCLC 6, 65;**
   SSC 7
   See also DLB 119, 192; EW 6; EXPS; GFL
   1789 to the Present; RGSF 2; RGWL 2,
   3; SSFS 8; SUFW
Merkin, Daphne 1954- .... **CLC 44**
   See also CA 123

Misharin, Alexandr .... **CLC 59**

Mishima, Yukio ... **CLC 2, 4, 6, 9, 27; DC 1; SSC 4**
See Hiraoka, Kimitake
See also AAYA 50; BPFB 2; GLL 1; MJW; MTCW 2; RGSF 2; RGWL 2, 3; SSFS 5, 12

Mistral, Frederic 1830-1914 .... **TCLC 51**
See also CA 122; 213; GFL 1789 to the Present

Mistral, Gabriela
See Godoy Alcayaga, Lucila
See also DLB 283; DNFS 1; EWL 3; LAW; RGWL 2, 3; WP

Mistry, Rohinton 1952- ...... **CLC 71; SSC 73**
See also CA 141; CANR 86, 114; CCA 1; CN 7; DAC; SSFS 6

Mitchell, Clyde
See Ellison, Harlan (Jay)

Mitchell, Emerson Blackhorse Barney
1945- .... **NNAL**
See also CA 45-48

Mitchell, James Leslie 1901-1935
See Gibbon, Lewis Grassic
See also CA 104; 188; DLB 15

Mitchell, Joni 1943- .... **CLC 12**
See also CA 112; CCA 1

Mitchell, Joseph (Quincy)
1908-1996 .... **CLC 98**
See also CA 77-80; 152; CANR 69; CN 7; CSW; DLB 185; DLBY 1996

Mitchell, Margaret (Munnerlyn)
1900-1949 .... **TCLC 11**
See also AAYA 23; BPFB 2; BYA 1; CA 109; 125; CANR 55, 94; CDALBS; DA3; DAM NOV, POP; DLB 9; LAIT 2; MTCW 1, 2; NFS 9; RGAL 4; RHW; TUS; WYAS 1; YAW

Mitchell, Peggy
See Mitchell, Margaret (Munnerlyn)

Mitchell, S(ilas) Weir 1829-1914 .... **TCLC 36**
See also CA 165; DLB 202; RGAL 4

Mitchell, W(illiam) O(rmond)
1914-1998 .... **CLC 25**
See also CA 77-80; 165; CANR 15, 43; CN 7; DAC; DAM MST; DLB 88

Mitchell, William (Lendrum)
1879-1936 .... **TCLC 81**
See also CA 213

Mitford, Mary Russell 1787-1855 ... **NCLC 4**
See also DLB 110, 116; RGEL 2

Mitford, Nancy 1904-1973 .... **CLC 44**
See also CA 9-12R; DLB 191; RGEL 2

Miyamoto, (Chujo) Yuriko
1899-1951 .... **TCLC 37**
See Miyamoto Yuriko
See also CA 170, 174

Miyamoto Yuriko
See Miyamoto, (Chujo) Yuriko
See also DLB 180

Miyazawa, Kenji 1896-1933 .... **TCLC 76**
See Miyazawa Kenji
See also CA 157; RGWL 3

Miyazawa Kenji
See Miyazawa, Kenji
See also EWL 3

Mizoguchi, Kenji 1898-1956 .... **TCLC 72**
See also CA 167

Mo, Timothy (Peter) 1950(?)- ... **CLC 46, 134**
See also CA 117; CANR 128; CN 7; DLB 194; MTCW 1; WLIT 4; WWE 1

Modarressi, Taghi (M.) 1931-1997 ... **CLC 44**
See also CA 121; 134; INT CA-134

Modiano, Patrick (Jean) 1945- .... **CLC 18**
See also CA 85-88; CANR 17, 40, 115; CWW 2; DLB 83, 299; EWL 3

Mofolo, Thomas (Mokopu)
1875(?)-1948 .... **BLC 3; TCLC 22**
See also AFW; CA 121; 153; CANR 83; DAM MULT; DLB 225; EWL 3; MTCW 2; WLIT 2

Mohr, Nicholasa 1938- .... **CLC 12; HLC 2**
See also AAYA 8, 46; CA 49-52; CANR 1, 32, 64; CLR 22; DAM MULT; DLB 145; HW 1, 2; JRDA; LAIT 5; LLW 1; MAICYA 2; MAICYAS 1; RGAL 4; SAAS 8; SATA 8, 97; SATA-Essay 113; WYA; YAW

Moi, Toril 1953- .... **CLC 172**
See also CA 154; CANR 102; FW

Mojtabai, A(nn) G(race) 1938- ..... **CLC 5, 9, 15, 29**
See also CA 85-88; CANR 88

Moliere 1622-1673 ..... **DC 13; LC 10, 28, 64; WLC**
See also DA; DA3; DAB; DAC; DAM DRAM, MST; DFS 13, 18; DLB 268; EW 3; GFL Beginnings to 1789; LATS 1; RGWL 2, 3; TWA

Molin, Charles
See Mayne, William (James Carter)

Molnar, Ferenc 1878-1952 .... **TCLC 20**
See also CA 109; 153; CANR 83; CDWLB 4; DAM DRAM; DLB 215; EWL 3; RGWL 2, 3

Momaday, N(avarre) Scott 1934- ...... **CLC 2, 19, 85, 95, 160; NNAL; PC 25; WLCS**
See also AAYA 11; AMWS 4; ANW; BPFB 2; BYA 12; CA 25-28R; CANR 14, 34, 68; CDALBS; CN 7; CPW; DA; DA3; DAB; DAC; DAM MST, MULT, NOV, POP; DLB 143, 175, 256; EWL 3; EXPP; INT CANR-14; LAIT 4; LATS 1; MTCW 1, 2; NFS 10; PFS 2, 11; RGAL 4; SATA 48; SATA-Brief 30; WP; YAW

Monette, Paul 1945-1995 .... **CLC 82**
See also AMWS 10; CA 139; 147; CN 7; GLL 1

Monroe, Harriet 1860-1936 .... **TCLC 12**
See also CA 109; 204; DLB 54, 91

Monroe, Lyle
See Heinlein, Robert A(nson)

Montagu, Elizabeth 1720-1800 .... **NCLC 7, 117**
See also FW

Montagu, Mary (Pierrepont) Wortley
1689-1762 .... **LC 9, 57; PC 16**
See also DLB 95, 101; RGEL 2

Montagu, W. H.
See Coleridge, Samuel Taylor

Montague, John (Patrick) 1929- ..... **CLC 13, 46**
See also CA 9-12R; CANR 9, 69, 121; CP 7; DLB 40; EWL 3; MTCW 1; PFS 12; RGEL 2

Montaigne, Michel (Eyquem) de
1533-1592 .... **LC 8; WLC**
See also DA; DAB; DAC; DAM MST; EW 2; GFL Beginnings to 1789; LMFS 1; RGWL 2, 3; TWA

Montale, Eugenio 1896-1981 ... **CLC 7, 9, 18; PC 13**
See also CA 17-20R; 104; CANR 30; DLB 114; EW 11; EWL 3; MTCW 1; RGWL 2, 3; TWA

Montesquieu, Charles-Louis de Secondat
1689-1755 .... **LC 7, 69**
See also EW 3; GFL Beginnings to 1789; TWA

Montessori, Maria 1870-1952 ...... **TCLC 103**
See also CA 115; 147

Montgomery, (Robert) Bruce 1921(?)-1978
See Crispin, Edmund
See also CA 179; 104; CMW 4

Montgomery, L(ucy) M(aud)
1874-1942 .... **TCLC 51, 140**
See also AAYA 12; BYA 1; CA 108; 137; CLR 8, 91; DA3; DAC; DAM MST; DLB 92; DLBD 14; JRDA; MAICYA 1, 2; MTCW 2; RGEL 2; SATA 100; TWA; WCH; WYA; YABC 1

Montgomery, Marion H., Jr. 1925- .... **CLC 7**
See also AITN 1; CA 1-4R; CANR 3, 48; CSW; DLB 6

Montgomery, Max
See Davenport, Guy (Mattison, Jr.)

Montherlant, Henry (Milon) de
1896-1972 .... **CLC 8, 19**
See also CA 85-88; 37-40R; DAM DRAM; DLB 72; EW 11; EWL 3; GFL 1789 to the Present; MTCW 1

Monty Python
See Chapman, Graham; Cleese, John (Marwood); Gilliam, Terry (Vance); Idle, Eric; Jones, Terence Graham Parry; Palin, Michael (Edward)
See also AAYA 7

Moodie, Susanna (Strickland)
1803-1885 .... **NCLC 14, 113**
See also DLB 99

Moody, Hiram (F. III) 1961-
See Moody, Rick
See also CA 138; CANR 64, 112

Moody, Minerva
See Alcott, Louisa May

Moody, Rick .... **CLC 147**
See Moody, Hiram (F. III)

Moody, William Vaughan
1869-1910 .... **TCLC 105**
See also CA 110; 178; DLB 7, 54; RGAL 4

Mooney, Edward 1951-
See Mooney, Ted
See also CA 130

Mooney, Ted .... **CLC 25**
See Mooney, Edward

Moorcock, Michael (John) 1939- ...... **CLC 5, 27, 58**
See Bradbury, Edward P.
See also AAYA 26; CA 45-48; CAAS 5; CANR 2, 17, 38, 64, 122; CN 7; DLB 14, 231, 261; FANT; MTCW 1, 2; SATA 93; SCFW 2; SFW 4; SUFW 1, 2

Moore, Brian 1921-1999 ... **CLC 1, 3, 5, 7, 8, 19, 32, 90**
See Bryan, Michael
See also BRWS 9; CA 1-4R; 174; CANR 1, 25, 42, 63; CCA 1; CN 7; DAB; DAC; DAM MST; DLB 251; EWL 3; FANT; MTCW 1, 2; RGEL 2

Moore, Edward
See Muir, Edwin
See also RGEL 2

Moore, G. E. 1873-1958 .... **TCLC 89**
See also DLB 262

Moore, George Augustus
1852-1933 .... **SSC 19; TCLC 7**
See also BRW 6; CA 104; 177; DLB 10, 18, 57, 135; EWL 3; RGEL 2; RGSF 2

Moore, Lorrie .... **CLC 39, 45, 68**
See Moore, Marie Lorena
See also AMWS 10; DLB 234; SSFS 19

Moore, Marianne (Craig)
1887-1972 .... **CLC 1, 2, 4, 8, 10, 13, 19, 47; PC 4, 49; WLCS**
See also AMW; CA 1-4R; 33-36R; CANR 3, 61; CDALB 1929-1941; DA; DA3; DAB; DAC; DAM MST, POET; DLB 45; DLBD 7; EWL 3; EXPP; MAWW; MTCW 1, 2; PAB; PFS 14, 17; RGAL 4; SATA 20; TUS; WP

Moore, Marie Lorena 1957- .... **CLC 165**
See Moore, Lorrie
See also CA 116; CANR 39, 83; CN 7; DLB 234

Mujica Lainez, Manuel 1910-1984 ... **CLC 31**
See Lainez, Manuel Mujica
See also CA 81-84; 112; CANR 32; EWL 3; HW 1

Mukherjee, Bharati 1940- ..... **AAL; CLC 53, 115; SSC 38**
See also AAYA 46; BEST 89:2; CA 107; CANR 45, 72, 128; CN 7; DAM NOV; DLB 60, 218; DNFS 1, 2; EWL 3; FW; MTCW 1, 2; RGAL 4; RGSF 2; SSFS 7; TUS; WWE 1

Muldoon, Paul 1951- .... **CLC 32, 72, 166**
See also BRWS 4; CA 113; 129; CANR 52, 91; CP 7; DAM POET; DLB 40; INT CA-129; PFS 7

Mulisch, Harry 1927- .... **CLC 42**
See also CA 9-12R; CANR 6, 26, 56, 110; DLB 299; EWL 3

Mull, Martin 1943- .... **CLC 17**
See also CA 105

Muller, Wilhelm .... **NCLC 73**

Mulock, Dinah Maria
See Craik, Dinah Maria (Mulock)
See also RGEL 2

Munday, Anthony 1560-1633 .... **LC 87**
See also DLB 62, 172; RGEL 2

Munford, Robert 1737(?)-1783 .... **LC 5**
See also DLB 31

Mungo, Raymond 1946- .... **CLC 72**
See also CA 49-52; CANR 2

Munro, Alice 1931- .... **CLC 6, 10, 19, 50, 95; SSC 3; WLCS**
See also AITN 2; BPFB 2; CA 33-36R; CANR 33, 53, 75, 114; CCA 1; CN 7; DA3; DAC; DAM MST, NOV; DLB 53; EWL 3; MTCW 1, 2; RGEL 2; RGSF 2; SATA 29; SSFS 5, 13, 19; WWE 1

Munro, H(ector) H(ugh) 1870-1916 .... **WLC**
See Saki
See also CA 104; 130; CANR 104; CDBLB 1890-1914; DA; DA3; DAB; DAC; DAM MST, NOV; DLB 34, 162; EXPS; MTCW 1, 2; RGEL 2; SSFS 15

Murakami, Haruki 1949- .... **CLC 150**
See Murakami Haruki
See also CA 165; CANR 102; MJW; RGWL 3; SFW 4

Murakami Haruki
See Murakami, Haruki
See also DLB 182; EWL 3

Murasaki, Lady
See Murasaki Shikibu

Murasaki Shikibu 978(?)-1026(?) ... **CMLC 1**
See also EFS 2; LATS 1; RGWL 2, 3

Murdoch, (Jean) Iris 1919-1999 ... **CLC 1, 2, 3, 4, 6, 8, 11, 15, 22, 31, 51**
See also BRWS 1; CA 13-16R; 179; CANR 8, 43, 68, 103; CDBLB 1960 to Present; CN 7; CWD; DA3; DAB; DAC; DAM MST, NOV; DLB 14, 194, 233; EWL 3; INT CANR-8; MTCW 1, 2; NFS 18; RGEL 2; TEA; WLIT 4

Murfree, Mary Noailles 1850-1922 .. **SSC 22; TCLC 135**
See also CA 122; 176; DLB 12, 74; RGAL 4

Murnau, Friedrich Wilhelm
See Plumpe, Friedrich Wilhelm

Murphy, Richard 1927- .... **CLC 41**
See also BRWS 5; CA 29-32R; CP 7; DLB 40; EWL 3

Murphy, Sylvia 1937- .... **CLC 34**
See also CA 121

Murphy, Thomas (Bernard) 1935- ... **CLC 51**
See also CA 101

Murray, Albert L. 1916- .... **CLC 73**
See also BW 2; CA 49-52; CANR 26, 52, 78; CSW; DLB 38

Murray, James Augustus Henry
1837-1915 .... **TCLC 117**

Murray, Judith Sargent
1751-1820 .... **NCLC 63**
See also DLB 37, 200

Murray, Les(lie Allan) 1938- .... **CLC 40**
See also BRWS 7; CA 21-24R; CANR 11, 27, 56, 103; CP 7; DAM POET; DLB 289; DLBY 2001; EWL 3; RGEL 2

Murry, J. Middleton
See Murry, John Middleton

Murry, John Middleton
1889-1957 .... **TCLC 16**
See also CA 118; 217; DLB 149

Musgrave, Susan 1951- .... **CLC 13, 54**
See also CA 69-72; CANR 45, 84; CCA 1; CP 7; CWP

Musil, Robert (Edler von)
1880-1942 .... **SSC 18; TCLC 12, 68**
See also CA 109; CANR 55, 84; CDWLB 2; DLB 81, 124; EW 9; EWL 3; MTCW 2; RGSF 2; RGWL 2, 3

Muske, Carol .... **CLC 90**
See Muske-Dukes, Carol (Anne)

Muske-Dukes, Carol (Anne) 1945-
See Muske, Carol
See also CA 65-68, 203; CAAE 203; CANR 32, 70; CWP

Musset, (Louis Charles) Alfred de
1810-1857 .... **NCLC 7**
See also DLB 192, 217; EW 6; GFL 1789 to the Present; RGWL 2, 3; TWA

Mussolini, Benito (Amilcare Andrea)
1883-1945 .... **TCLC 96**
See also CA 116

Mutanabbi, Al-
See al-Mutanabbi, Ahmad ibn al-Husayn Abu al-Tayyib al-Jufi al-Kindi

My Brother's Brother
See Chekhov, Anton (Pavlovich)

Myers, L(eopold) H(amilton)
1881-1944 .... **TCLC 59**
See also CA 157; DLB 15; EWL 3; RGEL 2

Myers, Walter Dean 1937- .. **BLC 3; CLC 35**
See also AAYA 4, 23; BW 2; BYA 6, 8, 11; CA 33-36R; CANR 20, 42, 67, 108; CLR 4, 16, 35; DAM MULT, NOV; DLB 33; INT CANR-20; JRDA; LAIT 5; MAICYA 1, 2; MAICYAS 1; MTCW 2; SAAS 2; SATA 41, 71, 109; SATA-Brief 27; WYA; YAW

Myers, Walter M.
See Myers, Walter Dean

Myles, Symon
See Follett, Ken(neth Martin)

Nabokov, Vladimir (Vladimirovich)
1899-1977 .... **CLC 1, 2, 3, 6, 8, 11, 15, 23, 44, 46, 64; SSC 11; TCLC 108; WLC**
See also AAYA 45; AMW; AMWC 1; AMWR 1; BPFB 2; CA 5-8R; 69-72; CANR 20, 102; CDALB 1941-1968; DA; DA3; DAB; DAC; DAM MST, NOV; DLB 2, 244, 278; DLBD 3; DLBY 1980, 1991; EWL 3; EXPS; LATS 1; MTCW 1, 2; NCFS 4; NFS 9; RGAL 4; RGSF 2; SSFS 6, 15; TUS

Naevius c. 265B.C.-201B.C. .... **CMLC 37**
See also DLB 211

Nagai, Kafu .... **TCLC 51**
See Nagai, Sokichi
See also DLB 180

Nagai, Sokichi 1879-1959
See Nagai, Kafu
See also CA 117

Nagy, Laszlo 1925-1978 .... **CLC 7**
See also CA 129; 112

Naidu, Sarojini 1879-1949 .... **TCLC 80**
See also EWL 3; RGEL 2

Naipaul, Shiva(dhar Srinivasa)
1945-1985 .... **CLC 32, 39; TCLC 153**
See also CA 110; 112; 116; CANR 33; DA3; DAM NOV; DLB 157; DLBY 1985; EWL 3; MTCW 1, 2

Naipaul, V(idiadhar) S(urajprasad)
1932- .... **CLC 4, 7, 9, 13, 18, 37, 105; SSC 38**
See also BPFB 2; BRWS 1; CA 1-4R; CANR 1, 33, 51, 91, 126; CDBLB 1960 to Present; CDWLB 3; CN 7; DA3; DAB; DAC; DAM MST, NOV; DLB 125, 204, 207; DLBY 1985, 2001; EWL 3; LATS 1; MTCW 1, 2; RGEL 2; RGSF 2; TWA; WLIT 4; WWE 1

Nakos, Lilika 1903(?)-1989 .... **CLC 29**

Napoleon
See Yamamoto, Hisaye

Narayan, R(asipuram) K(rishnaswami)
1906-2001 . **CLC 7, 28, 47, 121; SSC 25**
See also BPFB 2; CA 81-84; 196; CANR 33, 61, 112; CN 7; DA3; DAM NOV; DNFS 1; EWL 3; MTCW 1, 2; RGEL 2; RGSF 2; SATA 62; SSFS 5; WWE 1

Nash, (Frediric) Ogden 1902-1971 . **CLC 23; PC 21; TCLC 109**
See also CA 13-14; 29-32R; CANR 34, 61; CAP 1; DAM POET; DLB 11; MAICYA 1, 2; MTCW 1, 2; RGAL 4; SATA 2, 46; WP

Nashe, Thomas 1567-1601(?) .... **LC 41, 89**
See also DLB 167; RGEL 2

Nathan, Daniel
See Dannay, Frederic

Nathan, George Jean 1882-1958 .... **TCLC 18**
See Hatteras, Owen
See also CA 114; 169; DLB 137

Natsume, Kinnosuke
See Natsume, Soseki

Natsume, Soseki 1867-1916 .... **TCLC 2, 10**
See Natsume Soseki; Soseki
See also CA 104; 195; RGWL 2, 3; TWA

Natsume Soseki
See Natsume, Soseki
See also DLB 180; EWL 3

Natti, (Mary) Lee 1919-
See Kingman, Lee
See also CA 5-8R; CANR 2

Navarre, Marguerite de
See de Navarre, Marguerite

Naylor, Gloria 1950- ..... **BLC 3; CLC 28, 52, 156; WLCS**
See also AAYA 6, 39; AFAW 1, 2; AMWS 8; BW 2, 3; CA 107; CANR 27, 51, 74, 130; CN 7; CPW; DA; DA3; DAC; DAM MST, MULT, NOV, POP; DLB 173; EWL 3; FW; MTCW 1, 2; NFS 4, 7; RGAL 4; TUS

Neff, Debra .... **CLC 59**

Neihardt, John Gneisenau
1881-1973 .... **CLC 32**
See also CA 13-14; CANR 65; CAP 1; DLB 9, 54, 256; LAIT 2

Nekrasov, Nikolai Alekseevich
1821-1878 .... **NCLC 11**
See also DLB 277

Nelligan, Emile 1879-1941 .... **TCLC 14**
See also CA 114; 204; DLB 92; EWL 3

Nelson, Willie 1933- .... **CLC 17**
See also CA 107; CANR 114

Nemerov, Howard (Stanley)
1920-1991 .... **CLC 2, 6, 9, 36; PC 24; TCLC 124**
See also AMW; CA 1-4R; 134; CABS 2; CANR 1, 27, 53; DAM POET; DLB 5, 6; DLBY 1983; EWL 3; INT CANR-27; MTCW 1, 2; PFS 10, 14; RGAL 4

Norway, Nevil Shute 1899-1960
See Shute, Nevil
See also CA 102; 93-96; CANR 85; MTCW 2

Norwid, Cyprian Kamil
1821-1883 .... **NCLC 17**
See also RGWL 3

Nosille, Nabrah
See Ellison, Harlan (Jay)

Nossack, Hans Erich 1901-1978 .... **CLC 6**
See also CA 93-96; 85-88; DLB 69; EWL 3

Nostradamus 1503-1566 .... **LC 27**

Nosu, Chuji
See Ozu, Yasujiro

Notenburg, Eleanora (Genrikhovna) von
See Guro, Elena (Genrikhovna)

Nova, Craig 1945- .... **CLC 7, 31**
See also CA 45-48; CANR 2, 53, 127

Novak, Joseph
See Kosinski, Jerzy (Nikodem)

Novalis 1772-1801 .... **NCLC 13**
See also CDWLB 2; DLB 90; EW 5; RGWL 2, 3

Novick, Peter 1934- .... **CLC 164**
See also CA 188

Novis, Emile
See Weil, Simone (Adolphine)

Nowlan, Alden (Albert) 1933-1983 ... **CLC 15**
See also CA 9-12R; CANR 5; DAC; DAM MST; DLB 53; PFS 12

Noyes, Alfred 1880-1958 ...... **PC 27; TCLC 7**
See also CA 104; 188; DLB 20; EXPP; FANT; PFS 4; RGEL 2

Nugent, Richard Bruce 1906(?)-1987 ... **HR 3**
See also BW 1; CA 125; DLB 51; GLL 2

Nunn, Kem .... **CLC 34**
See also CA 159

Nwapa, Flora (Nwanzuruaha)
1931-1993 .... **BLCS; CLC 133**
See also BW 2; CA 143; CANR 83; CDWLB 3; CWRI 5; DLB 125; EWL 3; WLIT 2

Nye, Robert 1939- .... **CLC 13, 42**
See also CA 33-36R; CANR 29, 67, 107; CN 7; CP 7; CWRI 5; DAM NOV; DLB 14, 271; FANT; HGG; MTCW 1; RHW; SATA 6

Nyro, Laura 1947-1997 .... **CLC 17**
See also CA 194

Oates, Joyce Carol 1938- .. **CLC 1, 2, 3, 6, 9, 11, 15, 19, 33, 52, 108, 134; SSC 6, 70; WLC**
See also AAYA 15, 52; AITN 1; AMWS 2; BEST 89:2; BPFB 2; BYA 11; CA 5-8R; CANR 25, 45, 74, 113, 129; CDALB 1968-1988; CN 7; CP 7; CPW; CWP; DA; DA3; DAB; DAC; DAM MST, NOV, POP; DLB 2, 5, 130; DLBY 1981; EWL 3; EXPS; FW; HGG; INT CANR-25; LAIT 4; MAWW; MTCW 1, 2; NFS 8; RGAL 4; RGSF 2; SSFS 17; SUFW 2; TUS

O'Brian, E. G.
See Clarke, Arthur C(harles)

O'Brian, Patrick 1914-2000 .... **CLC 152**
See also AAYA 55; CA 144; 187; CANR 74; CPW; MTCW 2; RHW

O'Brien, Darcy 1939-1998 .... **CLC 11**
See also CA 21-24R; 167; CANR 8, 59

O'Brien, Edna 1936- ..... **CLC 3, 5, 8, 13, 36, 65, 116; SSC 10**
See also BRWS 5; CA 1-4R; CANR 6, 41, 65, 102; CDBLB 1960 to Present; CN 7; DA3; DAM NOV; DLB 14, 231; EWL 3; FW; MTCW 1, 2; RGSF 2; WLIT 4

O'Brien, Fitz-James 1828-1862 ..... **NCLC 21**
See also DLB 74; RGAL 4; SUFW

O'Brien, Flann .... **CLC 1, 4, 5, 7, 10, 47**
See O Nuallain, Brian
See also BRWS 2; DLB 231; EWL 3; RGEL 2

O'Brien, Richard 1942- .... **CLC 17**
See also CA 124

O'Brien, (William) Tim(othy) 1946- . **CLC 7, 19, 40, 103**
See also AAYA 16; AMWS 5; CA 85-88; CANR 40, 58; CDALBS; CN 7; CPW; DA3; DAM POP; DLB 152; DLBD 9; DLBY 1980; MTCW 2; RGAL 4; SSFS 5, 15

Obstfelder, Sigbjoern 1866-1900 .... **TCLC 23**
See also CA 123

O'Casey, Sean 1880-1964 .... **CLC 1, 5, 9, 11, 15, 88; DC 12; WLCS**
See also BRW 7; CA 89-92; CANR 62; CBD; CDBLB 1914-1945; DA3; DAB; DAC; DAM DRAM, MST; DFS 19; DLB 10; EWL 3; MTCW 1, 2; RGEL 2; TEA; WLIT 4

O'Cathasaigh, Sean
See O'Casey, Sean

Occom, Samson 1723-1792 .... **LC 60; NNAL**
See also DLB 175

Ochs, Phil(ip David) 1940-1976 .... **CLC 17**
See also CA 185; 65-68

O'Connor, Edwin (Greene)
1918-1968 .... **CLC 14**
See also CA 93-96; 25-28R

O'Connor, (Mary) Flannery
1925-1964 .... **CLC 1, 2, 3, 6, 10, 13, 15, 21, 66, 104; SSC 1, 23, 61; TCLC 132; WLC**
See also AAYA 7; AMW; AMWR 2; BPFB 3; BYA 16; CA 1-4R; CANR 3, 41; CDALB 1941-1968; DA; DA3; DAB; DAC; DAM MST, NOV; DLB 2, 152; DLBD 12; DLBY 1980; EWL 3; EXPS; LAIT 5; MAWW; MTCW 1, 2; NFS 3; RGAL 4; RGSF 2; SSFS 2, 7, 10, 19; TUS

O'Connor, Frank .... **CLC 23; SSC 5**
See O'Donovan, Michael Francis
See also DLB 162; EWL 3; RGSF 2; SSFS 5

O'Dell, Scott 1898-1989 .... **CLC 30**
See also AAYA 3, 44; BPFB 3; BYA 1, 2, 3, 5; CA 61-64; 129; CANR 12, 30, 112; CLR 1, 16; DLB 52; JRDA; MAICYA 1, 2; SATA 12, 60, 134; WYA; YAW

Odets, Clifford 1906-1963 ..... **CLC 2, 28, 98; DC 6**
See also AMWS 2; CA 85-88; CAD; CANR 62; DAM DRAM; DFS 3, 17; DLB 7, 26; EWL 3; MTCW 1, 2; RGAL 4; TUS

O'Doherty, Brian 1928- .... **CLC 76**
See also CA 105; CANR 108

O'Donnell, K. M.
See Malzberg, Barry N(athaniel)

O'Donnell, Lawrence
See Kuttner, Henry

O'Donovan, Michael Francis
1903-1966 .... **CLC 14**
See O'Connor, Frank
See also CA 93-96; CANR 84

Oe, Kenzaburo 1935- .. **CLC 10, 36, 86, 187; SSC 20**
See Oe Kenzaburo
See also CA 97-100; CANR 36, 50, 74, 126; CWW 2; DA3; DAM NOV; DLB 182; DLBY 1994; EWL 3; LATS 1; MJW; MTCW 1, 2; RGSF 2; RGWL 2, 3

Oe Kenzaburo
See Oe, Kenzaburo
See also EWL 3

O'Faolain, Julia 1932- .... **CLC 6, 19, 47, 108**
See also CA 81-84; CAAS 2; CANR 12, 61; CN 7; DLB 14, 231; FW; MTCW 1; RHW

O'Faolain, Sean 1900-1991 ...... **CLC 1, 7, 14, 32, 70; SSC 13; TCLC 143**
See also CA 61-64; 134; CANR 12, 66; DLB 15, 162; MTCW 1, 2; RGEL 2; RGSF 2

O'Flaherty, Liam 1896-1984 .... **CLC 5, 34; SSC 6**
See also CA 101; 113; CANR 35; DLB 36, 162; DLBY 1984; MTCW 1, 2; RGEL 2; RGSF 2; SSFS 5

Ogai
See Mori Ogai
See also MJW

Ogilvy, Gavin
See Barrie, J(ames) M(atthew)

O'Grady, Standish (James)
1846-1928 .... **TCLC 5**
See also CA 104; 157

O'Grady, Timothy 1951- .... **CLC 59**
See also CA 138

O'Hara, Frank 1926-1966 .... **CLC 2, 5, 13, 78; PC 45**
See also CA 9-12R; 25-28R; CANR 33; DA3; DAM POET; DLB 5, 16, 193; EWL 3; MTCW 1, 2; PFS 8; 12; RGAL 4; WP

O'Hara, John (Henry) 1905-1970 . **CLC 1, 2, 3, 6, 11, 42; SSC 15**
See also AMW; BPFB 3; CA 5-8R; 25-28R; CANR 31, 60; CDALB 1929-1941; DAM NOV; DLB 9, 86; DLBD 2; EWL 3; MTCW 1, 2; NFS 11; RGAL 4; RGSF 2

O Hehir, Diana 1922- .... **CLC 41**
See also CA 93-96

Ohiyesa
See Eastman, Charles A(lexander)

Okada, John 1923-1971 .... **AAL**
See also BYA 14; CA 212

Okigbo, Christopher (Ifenayichukwu)
1932-1967 .... **BLC 3; CLC 25, 84; PC 7**
See also AFW; BW 1, 3; CA 77-80; CANR 74; CDWLB 3; DAM MULT, POET; DLB 125; EWL 3; MTCW 1, 2; RGEL 2

Okri, Ben 1959- .... **CLC 87**
See also AFW; BRWS 5; BW 2, 3; CA 130; 138; CANR 65, 128; CN 7; DLB 157, 231; EWL 3; INT CA-138; MTCW 2; RGSF 2; WLIT 2; WWE 1

Olds, Sharon 1942- .. **CLC 32, 39, 85; PC 22**
See also AMWS 10; CA 101; CANR 18, 41, 66, 98; CP 7; CPW; CWP; DAM POET; DLB 120; MTCW 2; PFS 17

Oldstyle, Jonathan
See Irving, Washington

Olesha, Iurii
See Olesha, Yuri (Karlovich)
See also RGWL 2

Olesha, Iurii Karlovich
See Olesha, Yuri (Karlovich)
See also DLB 272

Olesha, Yuri (Karlovich) 1899-1960 . **CLC 8; SSC 69; TCLC 136**
See Olesha, Iurii; Olesha, Iurii Karlovich; Olesha, Yury Karlovich
See also CA 85-88; EW 11; RGWL 3

Olesha, Yury Karlovich
See Olesha, Yuri (Karlovich)
See also EWL 3

Oliphant, Mrs.
See Oliphant, Margaret (Oliphant Wilson)
See also SUFW

Oliphant, Laurence 1829(?)-1888 .. **NCLC 47**
See also DLB 18, 166

Page, Thomas Nelson 1853-1922 .... **SSC 23**
See also CA 118; 177; DLB 12, 78; DLBD
13; RGAL 4

Pagels, Elaine Hiesey 1943- .... **CLC 104**
See also CA 45-48; CANR 2, 24, 51; FW;
NCFS 4

Paget, Violet 1856-1935
See Lee, Vernon
See also CA 104; 166; GLL 1; HGG

Paget-Lowe, Henry
See Lovecraft, H(oward) P(hillips)

Paglia, Camille (Anna) 1947- .... **CLC 68**
See also CA 140; CANR 72; CPW; FW;
GLL 2; MTCW 2

Paige, Richard
See Koontz, Dean R(ay)

Paine, Thomas 1737-1809 .... **NCLC 62**
See also AMWS 1; CDALB 1640-1865;
DLB 31, 43, 73, 158; LAIT 1; RGAL 4;
RGEL 2; TUS

Pakenham, Antonia
See Fraser, Antonia (Pakenham)

Palamas, Costis
See Palamas, Kostes

Palamas, Kostes 1859-1943 .... **TCLC 5**
See Palamas, Kostis
See also CA 105; 190; RGWL 2, 3

Palamas, Kostis
See Palamas, Kostes
See also EWL 3

Palazzeschi, Aldo 1885-1974 .... **CLC 11**
See also CA 89-92; 53-56; DLB 114, 264;
EWL 3

Pales Matos, Luis 1898-1959 .... **HLCS 2**
See Pales Matos, Luis
See also DLB 290; HW 1; LAW

Paley, Grace 1922- .. **CLC 4, 6, 37, 140; SSC 8**
See also AMWS 6; CA 25-28R; CANR 13,
46, 74, 118; CN 7; CPW; DA3; DAM
POP; DLB 28, 218; EWL 3; EXPS; FW;
INT CANR-13; MAWW; MTCW 1, 2;
RGAL 4; RGSF 2; SSFS 3

Palin, Michael (Edward) 1943- .... **CLC 21**
See Monty Python
See also CA 107; CANR 35, 109; SATA 67

Palliser, Charles 1947- .... **CLC 65**
See also CA 136; CANR 76; CN 7

Palma, Ricardo 1833-1919 .... **TCLC 29**
See also CA 168; LAW

Pamuk, Orhan 1952- .... **CLC 185**
See also CA 142; CANR 75, 127; CWW 2

Pancake, Breece Dexter 1952-1979
See Pancake, Breece D'J
See also CA 123; 109

Pancake, Breece D'J .... **CLC 29; SSC 61**
See Pancake, Breece Dexter
See also DLB 130

Panchenko, Nikolai .... **CLC 59**

Pankhurst, Emmeline (Goulden)
1858-1928 .... **TCLC 100**
See also CA 116; FW

Panko, Rudy
See Gogol, Nikolai (Vasilyevich)

Papadiamantis, Alexandros
1851-1911 .... **TCLC 29**
See also CA 168; EWL 3

Papadiamantopoulos, Johannes 1856-1910
See Moreas, Jean
See also CA 117

Papini, Giovanni 1881-1956 .... **TCLC 22**
See also CA 121; 180; DLB 264

Paracelsus 1493-1541 .... **LC 14**
See also DLB 179

Parasol, Peter
See Stevens, Wallace

Pardo Bazan, Emilia 1851-1921 .... **SSC 30**
See also EWL 3; FW; RGSF 2; RGWL 2, 3

Pareto, Vilfredo 1848-1923 .... **TCLC 69**
See also CA 175

Paretsky, Sara 1947- .... **CLC 135**
See also AAYA 30; BEST 90:3; CA 125;
129; CANR 59, 95; CMW 4; CPW; DA3;
DAM POP; INT CA-129; MSW; RGAL 4

Parfenie, Maria
See Codrescu, Andrei

Parini, Jay (Lee) 1948- .... **CLC 54, 133**
See also CA 97-100; CAAS 16; CANR 32,
87

Park, Jordan
See Kornbluth, C(yril) M.; Pohl, Frederik

Park, Robert E(zra) 1864-1944 ..... **TCLC 73**
See also CA 122; 165

Parker, Bert
See Ellison, Harlan (Jay)

Parker, Dorothy (Rothschild)
1893-1967 . **CLC 15, 68; PC 28; SSC 2;
TCLC 143**
See also AMWS 9; CA 19-20; 25-28R; CAP
2; DA3; DAM POET; DLB 11, 45, 86;
EXPP; FW; MAWW; MTCW 1, 2; PFS
18; RGAL 4; RGSF 2; TUS

Parker, Robert B(rown) 1932- .... **CLC 27**
See also AAYA 28; BEST 89:4; BPFB 3;
CA 49-52; CANR 1, 26, 52, 89, 128;
CMW 4; CPW; DAM NOV, POP; INT
CANR-26; MSW; MTCW 1

Parkin, Frank 1940- .... **CLC 43**
See also CA 147

Parkman, Francis, Jr. 1823-1893 .. **NCLC 12**
See also AMWS 2; DLB 1, 30, 183, 186,
235; RGAL 4

Parks, Gordon (Alexander Buchanan)
1912- .... **BLC 3; CLC 1, 16**
See also AAYA 36; AITN 2; BW 2, 3; CA
41-44R; CANR 26, 66; DA3; DAM
MULT; DLB 33; MTCW 2; SATA 8, 108

Parks, Suzan-Lori 1964(?)- .... **DC 23**
See also AAYA 55; CA 201; CAD; CD 5;
CWD; RGAL 4

Parks, Tim(othy Harold) 1954- ...... **CLC 147**
See also CA 126; 131; CANR 77; DLB 231;
INT CA-131

Parmenides c. 515B.C.-c.
450B.C. .... **CMLC 22**
See also DLB 176

Parnell, Thomas 1679-1718 .... **LC 3**
See also DLB 95; RGEL 2

Parr, Catherine c. 1513(?)-1548 .... **LC 86**
See also DLB 136

Parra, Nicanor 1914- ... **CLC 2, 102; HLC 2;
PC 39**
See also CA 85-88; CANR 32; CWW 2;
DAM MULT; DLB 283; EWL 3; HW 1;
LAW; MTCW 1

Parra Sanojo, Ana Teresa de la
1890-1936 .... **HLCS 2**
See de la Parra, (Ana) Teresa (Sonojo)
See also LAW

Parrish, Mary Frances
See Fisher, M(ary) F(rances) K(ennedy)

Parshchikov, Aleksei 1954- .... **CLC 59**
See Parshchikov, Aleksei Maksimovich

Parshchikov, Aleksei Maksimovich
See Parshchikov, Aleksei
See also DLB 285

Parson, Professor
See Coleridge, Samuel Taylor

Parson Lot
See Kingsley, Charles

Parton, Sara Payson Willis
1811-1872 .... **NCLC 86**
See also DLB 43, 74, 239

Partridge, Anthony
See Oppenheim, E(dward) Phillips

Pascal, Blaise 1623-1662 .... **LC 35**
See also DLB 268; EW 3; GFL Beginnings
to 1789; RGWL 2, 3; TWA

Pascoli, Giovanni 1855-1912 .... **TCLC 45**
See also CA 170; EW 7; EWL 3

Pasolini, Pier Paolo 1922-1975 .. **CLC 20, 37,
106; PC 17**
See also CA 93-96; 61-64; CANR 63; DLB
128, 177; EWL 3; MTCW 1; RGWL 2, 3

Pasquini
See Silone, Ignazio

Pastan, Linda (Olenik) 1932- .... **CLC 27**
See also CA 61-64; CANR 18, 40, 61, 113;
CP 7; CSW; CWP; DAM POET; DLB 5;
PFS 8

Pasternak, Boris (Leonidovich)
1890-1960 ...... **CLC 7, 10, 18, 63; PC 6;
SSC 31; WLC**
See also BPFB 3; CA 127; 116; DA; DA3;
DAB; DAC; DAM MST, NOV, POET;
EW 10; MTCW 1, 2; RGSF 2; RGWL 2,
3; TWA; WP

Patchen, Kenneth 1911-1972 .... **CLC 1, 2, 18**
See also BG 3; CA 1-4R; 33-36R; CANR
3, 35; DAM POET; DLB 16, 48; EWL 3;
MTCW 1; RGAL 4

Pater, Walter (Horatio) 1839-1894 . **NCLC 7,
90**
See also BRW 5; CDBLB 1832-1890; DLB
57, 156; RGEL 2; TEA

Paterson, A(ndrew) B(arton)
1864-1941 .... **TCLC 32**
See also CA 155; DLB 230; RGEL 2; SATA
97

Paterson, Banjo
See Paterson, A(ndrew) B(arton)

Paterson, Katherine (Womeldorf)
1932- .... **CLC 12, 30**
See also AAYA 1, 31; BYA 1, 2, 7; CA 21-
24R; CANR 28, 59, 111; CLR 7, 50;
CWRI 5; DLB 52; JRDA; LAIT 4; MAI-
CYA 1, 2; MAICYAS 1; MTCW 1; SATA
13, 53, 92, 133; WYA; YAW

Patmore, Coventry Kersey Dighton
1823-1896 .... **NCLC 9**
See also DLB 35, 98; RGEL 2; TEA

Paton, Alan (Stewart) 1903-1988 ...... **CLC 4,
10, 25, 55, 106; WLC**
See also AAYA 26; AFW; BPFB 3; BRWS
2; BYA 1; CA 13-16; 125; CANR 22;
CAP 1; DA; DA3; DAB; DAC; DAM
MST, NOV; DLB 225; DLBD 17; EWL
3; EXPN; LAIT 4; MTCW 1, 2; NFS 3,
12; RGEL 2; SATA 11; SATA-Obit 56;
TWA; WLIT 2; WWE 1

Paton Walsh, Gillian 1937- .... **CLC 35**
See Paton Walsh, Jill; Walsh, Jill Paton
See also AAYA 11; CANR 38, 83; CLR 2,
65; DLB 161; JRDA; MAICYA 1, 2;
SAAS 3; SATA 4, 72, 109; YAW

Paton Walsh, Jill
See Paton Walsh, Gillian
See also AAYA 47; BYA 1, 8

Patterson, (Horace) Orlando (Lloyd)
1940- .... **BLCS**
See also BW 1; CA 65-68; CANR 27, 84;
CN 7

Patton, George S(mith), Jr.
1885-1945 .... **TCLC 79**
See also CA 189

Paulding, James Kirke 1778-1860 ... **NCLC 2**
See also DLB 3, 59, 74, 250; RGAL 4

Paulin, Thomas Neilson 1949-
See Paulin, Tom
See also CA 123; 128; CANR 98; CP 7

Paulin, Tom .... **CLC 37, 177**
See Paulin, Thomas Neilson
See also DLB 40

Pausanias c. 1st cent. - .... **CMLC 36**
Paustovsky, Konstantin (Georgievich)
1892-1968 .... **CLC 40**
See also CA 93-96; 25-28R; DLB 272;
EWL 3
Pavese, Cesare 1908-1950 .... **PC 13; SSC 19;**
TCLC 3
See also CA 104; 169; DLB 128, 177; EW
12; EWL 3; PFS 20; RGSF 2; RGWL 2,
3; TWA
Pavic, Milorad 1929- .... **CLC 60**
See also CA 136; CDWLB 4; CWW 2; DLB
181; EWL 3; RGWL 3
Pavlov, Ivan Petrovich 1849-1936 . **TCLC 91**
See also CA 118; 180
Pavlova, Karolina Karlovna
1807-1893 .... **NCLC 138**
See also DLB 205
Payne, Alan
See Jakes, John (William)
Paz, Gil
See Lugones, Leopoldo
Paz, Octavio 1914-1998 . **CLC 3, 4, 6, 10, 19,**
51, 65, 119; HLC 2; PC 1, 48; WLC
See also AAYA 50; CA 73-76; 165; CANR
32, 65, 104; CWW 2; DA; DA3; DAB;
DAC; DAM MST, MULT, POET; DLB
290; DLBY 1990, 1998; DNFS 1; EWL
3; HW 1, 2; LAW; LAWS 1; MTCW 1, 2;
PFS 18; RGWL 2, 3; SSFS 13; TWA;
WLIT 1
p'Bitek, Okot 1931-1982 .... **BLC 3; CLC 96;**
TCLC 149
See also AFW; BW 2, 3; CA 124; 107;
CANR 82; DAM MULT; DLB 125; EWL
3; MTCW 1, 2; RGEL 2; WLIT 2
Peacock, Molly 1947- .... **CLC 60**
See also CA 103; CAAS 21; CANR 52, 84;
CP 7; CWP; DLB 120, 282
Peacock, Thomas Love
1785-1866 .... **NCLC 22**
See also BRW 4; DLB 96, 116; RGEL 2;
RGSF 2
Peake, Mervyn 1911-1968 .... **CLC 7, 54**
See also CA 5-8R; 25-28R; CANR 3; DLB
15, 160, 255; FANT; MTCW 1; RGEL 2;
SATA 23; SFW 4
Pearce, Philippa
See Christie, Philippa
See also CA 5-8R; CANR 4, 109; CWRI 5;
FANT; MAICYA 2
Pearl, Eric
See Elman, Richard (Martin)
Pearson, T(homas) R(eid) 1956- .... **CLC 39**
See also CA 120; 130; CANR 97; CSW;
INT CA-130
Peck, Dale 1967- .... **CLC 81**
See also CA 146; CANR 72, 127; GLL 2
Peck, John (Frederick) 1941- .... **CLC 3**
See also CA 49-52; CANR 3, 100; CP 7
Peck, Richard (Wayne) 1934- .... **CLC 21**
See also AAYA 1, 24; BYA 1, 6, 8, 11; CA
85-88; CANR 19, 38, 129; CLR 15; INT
CANR-19; JRDA; MAICYA 1, 2; SAAS
2; SATA 18, 55, 97; SATA-Essay 110;
WYA; YAW
Peck, Robert Newton 1928- .... **CLC 17**
See also AAYA 3, 43; BYA 1, 6; CA 81-84,
182; CAAE 182; CANR 31, 63, 127; CLR
45; DA; DAC; DAM MST; JRDA; LAIT
3; MAICYA 1, 2; SAAS 1; SATA 21, 62,
111; SATA-Essay 108; WYA; YAW
Peckinpah, (David) Sam(uel)
1925-1984 .... **CLC 20**
See also CA 109; 114; CANR 82
Pedersen, Knut 1859-1952
See Hamsun, Knut
See also CA 104; 119; CANR 63; MTCW
1, 2

Peeslake, Gaffer
See Durrell, Lawrence (George)
Peguy, Charles (Pierre)
1873-1914 .... **TCLC 10**
See also CA 107; 193; DLB 258; EWL 3;
GFL 1789 to the Present
Peirce, Charles Sanders
1839-1914 .... **TCLC 81**
See also CA 194; DLB 270
Pellicer, Carlos 1900(?)-1977 .... **HLCS 2**
See also CA 153; 69-72; DLB 290; EWL 3;
HW 1
Pena, Ramon del Valle y
See Valle-Inclan, Ramon (Maria) del
Pendennis, Arthur Esquir
See Thackeray, William Makepeace
Penn, William 1644-1718 .... **LC 25**
See also DLB 24
PEPECE
See Prado (Calvo), Pedro
Pepys, Samuel 1633-1703 ... **LC 11, 58; WLC**
See also BRW 2; CDBLB 1660-1789; DA;
DA3; DAB; DAC; DAM MST; DLB 101,
213; NCFS 4; RGEL 2; TEA; WLIT 3
Percy, Thomas 1729-1811 .... **NCLC 95**
See also DLB 104
Percy, Walker 1916-1990 .... **CLC 2, 3, 6, 8,**
14, 18, 47, 65
See also AMWS 3; BPFB 3; CA 1-4R; 131;
CANR 1, 23, 64; CPW; CSW; DA3;
DAM NOV, POP; DLB 2; DLBY 1980,
1990; EWL 3; MTCW 1, 2; RGAL 4;
TUS
Percy, William Alexander
1885-1942 .... **TCLC 84**
See also CA 163; MTCW 2
Perec, Georges 1936-1982 .... **CLC 56, 116**
See also CA 141; DLB 83, 299; EWL 3;
GFL 1789 to the Present; RGWL 3
Pereda (y Sanchez de Porrua), Jose Maria
de 1833-1906 .... **TCLC 16**
See also CA 117
Pereda y Porrua, Jose Maria de
See Pereda (y Sanchez de Porrua), Jose
Maria de
Peregoy, George Weems
See Mencken, H(enry) L(ouis)
Perelman, S(idney) J(oseph)
1904-1979 .. **CLC 3, 5, 9, 15, 23, 44, 49;**
SSC 32
See also AITN 1, 2; BPFB 3; CA 73-76;
89-92; CANR 18; DAM DRAM; DLB 11,
44; MTCW 1, 2; RGAL 4
Peret, Benjamin 1899-1959 .... **PC 33; TCLC**
20
See also CA 117; 186; GFL 1789 to the
Present
Peretz, Isaac Leib 1851(?)-1915
See Peretz, Isaac Loeb
See also CA 201
Peretz, Isaac Loeb 1851(?)-1915 ...... **SSC 26;**
TCLC 16
See Peretz, Isaac Leib
See also CA 109
Peretz, Yitzkhok Leibush
See Peretz, Isaac Loeb
Perez Galdos, Benito 1843-1920 ..... **HLCS 2;**
TCLC 27
See Galdos, Benito Perez
See also CA 125; 153; EWL 3; HW 1;
RGWL 2, 3
Peri Rossi, Cristina 1941- .. **CLC 156; HLCS**
2
See also CA 131; CANR 59, 81; DLB 145,
290; EWL 3; HW 1, 2
Perlata
See Peret, Benjamin

Perloff, Marjorie G(abrielle)
1931- .... **CLC 137**
See also CA 57-60; CANR 7, 22, 49, 104
Perrault, Charles 1628-1703 ... **DC 12; LC 2,**
56
See also BYA 4; CLR 79; DLB 268; GFL
Beginnings to 1789; MAICYA 1, 2;
RGWL 2, 3; SATA 25; WCH
Perry, Anne 1938- .... **CLC 126**
See also CA 101; CANR 22, 50, 84; CMW
4; CN 7; CPW; DLB 276
Perry, Brighton
See Sherwood, Robert E(mmet)
Perse, St.-John
See Leger, (Marie-Rene Auguste) Alexis
Saint-Leger
Perse, Saint-John
See Leger, (Marie-Rene Auguste) Alexis
Saint-Leger
See also DLB 258; RGWL 3
Perutz, Leo(pold) 1882-1957 .... **TCLC 60**
See also CA 147; DLB 81
Peseenz, Tulio F.
See Lopez y Fuentes, Gregorio
Pesetsky, Bette 1932- .... **CLC 28**
See also CA 133; DLB 130
Peshkov, Alexei Maximovich 1868-1936
See Gorky, Maxim
See also CA 105; 141; CANR 83; DA;
DAC; DAM DRAM, MST, NOV; MTCW
2
Pessoa, Fernando (Antonio Nogueira)
1888-1935 ..... **HLC 2; PC 20; TCLC 27**
See also CA 125; 183; DAM MULT; DLB
287; EW 10; EWL 3; RGWL 2, 3; WP
Peterkin, Julia Mood 1880-1961 ...... **CLC 31**
See also CA 102; DLB 9
Peters, Joan K(aren) 1945- .... **CLC 39**
See also CA 158; CANR 109
Peters, Robert L(ouis) 1924- .... **CLC 7**
See also CA 13-16R; CAAS 8; CP 7; DLB
105
Petofi, Sandor 1823-1849 .... **NCLC 21**
See also RGWL 2, 3
Petrakis, Harry Mark 1923- .... **CLC 3**
See also CA 9-12R; CANR 4, 30, 85; CN 7
Petrarch 1304-1374 .... **CMLC 20; PC 8**
See also DA3; DAM POET; EW 2; LMFS
1; RGWL 2. 3
Petronius c. 20-66 .... **CMLC 34**
See also AW 2; CDWLB 1; DLB 211;
RGWL 2, 3
Petrov, Evgeny .... **TCLC 21**
See Kataev, Evgeny Petrovich
Petry, Ann (Lane) 1908-1997 .. **CLC 1, 7, 18;**
TCLC 112
See also AFAW 1, 2; BPFB 3; BW 1, 3;
BYA 2; CA 5-8R; 157; CAAS 6; CANR
4, 46; CLR 12; CN 7; DLB 76; EWL 3;
JRDA; LAIT 1; MAICYA 1, 2; MAIC-
YAS 1; MTCW 1; RGAL 4; SATA 5;
SATA-Obit 94; TUS
Petursson, Halligrimur 1614-1674 .... **LC 8**
Peychinovich
See Vazov, Ivan (Minchov)
Phaedrus c. 15B.C.-c. 50 .... **CMLC 25**
See also DLB 211
Phelps (Ward), Elizabeth Stuart
See Phelps, Elizabeth Stuart
See also FW
Phelps, Elizabeth Stuart
1844-1911 .... **TCLC 113**
See Phelps (Ward), Elizabeth Stuart
See also DLB 74
Philips, Katherine 1632-1664 . **LC 30; PC 40**
See also DLB 131; RGEL 2
Philipson, Morris H. 1926- .... **CLC 53**
See also CA 1-4R; CANR 4

Phillips, Caryl 1958- .... **BLCS; CLC 96**
　　See also BRWS 5; BW 2; CA 141; CANR
　　63, 104; CBD; CD 5; CN 7; DA3; DAM
　　MULT; DLB 157; EWL 3; MTCW 2;
　　WLIT 4; WWE 1

Phillips, David Graham
　　1867-1911 .... **TCLC 44**
　　See also CA 108; 176; DLB 9, 12; RGAL 4

Phillips, Jack
　　See Sandburg, Carl (August)

Phillips, Jayne Anne 1952- .... **CLC 15, 33,**
　　139; SSC 16
　　See also BPFB 3; CA 101; CANR 24, 50,
　　96; CN 7; CSW; DLBY 1980; INT
　　CANR-24; MTCW 1, 2; RGAL 4; RGSF
　　2; SSFS 4

Phillips, Richard
　　See Dick, Philip K(indred)

Phillips, Robert (Schaeffer) 1938- .... **CLC 28**
　　See also CA 17-20R; CAAS 13; CANR 8;
　　DLB 105

Phillips, Ward
　　See Lovecraft, H(oward) P(hillips)

Philostratus, Flavius c. 179-c.
　　244 .... **CMLC 62**

Piccolo, Lucio 1901-1969 .... **CLC 13**
　　See also CA 97-100; DLB 114; EWL 3

Pickthall, Marjorie L(owry) C(hristie)
　　1883-1922 .... **TCLC 21**
　　See also CA 107; DLB 92

Pico della Mirandola, Giovanni
　　1463-1494 .... **LC 15**
　　See also LMFS 1

Piercy, Marge 1936- .... **CLC 3, 6, 14, 18, 27,**
　　62, 128; PC 29
　　See also BPFB 3; CA 21-24R; 187; CAAE
　　187; CAAS 1; CANR 13, 43, 66, 111; CN
　　7; CP 7; CWP; DLB 120, 227; EXPP;
　　FW; MTCW 1, 2; PFS 9; SFW 4

Piers, Robert
　　See Anthony, Piers

Pieyre de Mandiargues, Andre 1909-1991
　　See Mandiargues, Andre Pieyre de
　　See also CA 103; 136; CANR 22, 82; EWL
　　3; GFL 1789 to the Present

Pilnyak, Boris 1894-1938 . **SSC 48; TCLC 23**
　　See Vogau, Boris Andreyevich
　　See also EWL 3

Pinchback, Eugene
　　See Toomer, Jean

Pincherle, Alberto 1907-1990 ...... **CLC 11, 18**
　　See Moravia, Alberto
　　See also CA 25-28R; 132; CANR 33, 63;
　　DAM NOV; MTCW 1

Pinckney, Darryl 1953- .... **CLC 76**
　　See also BW 2, 3; CA 143; CANR 79

Pindar 518(?)B.C.-438(?)B.C. .... **CMLC 12;**
　　PC 19
　　See also AW 1; CDWLB 1; DLB 176;
　　RGWL 2

Pineda, Cecile 1942- .... **CLC 39**
　　See also CA 118; DLB 209

Pinero, Arthur Wing 1855-1934 .... **TCLC 32**
　　See also CA 110; 153; DAM DRAM; DLB
　　10; RGEL 2

Pinero, Miguel (Antonio Gomez)
　　1946-1988 .... **CLC 4, 55**
　　See also CA 61-64; 125; CAD; CANR 29,
　　90; DLB 266; HW 1; LLW 1

Pinget, Robert 1919-1997 .... **CLC 7, 13, 37**
　　See also CA 85-88; 160; CWW 2; DLB 83;
　　EWL 3; GFL 1789 to the Present

Pink Floyd
　　See Barrett, (Roger) Syd; Gilmour, David;
　　Mason, Nick; Waters, Roger; Wright, Rick

Pinkney, Edward 1802-1828 .... **NCLC 31**
　　See also DLB 248

Pinkwater, Daniel
　　See Pinkwater, Daniel Manus

Pinkwater, Daniel Manus 1941- .... **CLC 35**
　　See also AAYA 1, 46; BYA 9; CA 29-32R;
　　CANR 12, 38, 89; CLR 4; CSW; FANT;
　　JRDA; MAICYA 1; PC 27
　　See also CA 104; 153; CANR 103; DA;
　　46, 76, 114; SFW 4; YAW

Pinkwater, Manus
　　See Pinkwater, Daniel Manus

Pinsky, Robert 1940- .... **CLC 9, 19, 38, 94,**
　　121; PC 27
　　See also AMWS 6; CA 29-32R; CAAS 4;
　　CANR 58, 97; CP 7; DA3; DAM POET;
　　DLBY 1982, 1998; MTCW 2; PFS 18;
　　RGAL 4

Pinta, Harold
　　See Pinter, Harold

Pinter, Harold 1930- .. **CLC 1, 3, 6, 9, 11, 15,**
　　27, 58, 73; DC 15; WLC
　　See also BRWR 1; BRWS 1; CA 5-8R;
　　CANR 33, 65, 112; CBD; CD 5; CDBLB
　　1960 to Present; DA; DA3; DAB; DAC;
　　DAM DRAM, MST; DFS 3, 5, 7, 14;
　　DLB 13; EWL 3; IDFW 3, 4; LMFS 2;
　　MTCW 1, 2; RGEL 2; TEA

Piozzi, Hester Lynch (Thrale)
　　1741-1821 .... **NCLC 57**
　　See also DLB 104, 142

Pirandello, Luigi 1867-1936 .. **DC 5; SSC 22;**
　　TCLC 4, 29; WLC
　　See also CA 104; 153; CANR 103; DA;
　　DA3; DAB; DAC; DAM DRAM, MST;
　　DFS 4, 9; DLB 264; EW 8; EWL 3;
　　MTCW 2; RGSF 2; RGWL 2, 3

Pirsig, Robert M(aynard) 1928- ... **CLC 4, 6,**
　　73
　　See also CA 53-56; CANR 42, 74; CPW 1;
　　DA3; DAM POP; MTCW 1, 2; SATA 39

Pisarev, Dmitrii Ivanovich
　　See Pisarev, Dmitry Ivanovich
　　See also DLB 277

Pisarev, Dmitry Ivanovich
　　1840-1868 .... **NCLC 25**
　　See Pisarev, Dmitrii Ivanovich

Pix, Mary (Griffith) 1666-1709 .... **LC 8**
　　See also DLB 80

Pixerecourt, (Rene Charles) Guilbert de
　　1773-1844 .... **NCLC 39**
　　See also DLB 192; GFL 1789 to the Present

Plaatje, Sol(omon) T(shekisho)
　　1878-1932 .... **BLCS; TCLC 73**
　　See also BW 2, 3; CA 141; CANR 79; DLB
　　125, 225

Plaidy, Jean
　　See Hibbert, Eleanor Alice Burford

Planche, James Robinson
　　1796-1880 .... **NCLC 42**
　　See also RGEL 2

Plant, Robert 1948- .... **CLC 12**

Plante, David (Robert) 1940- . **CLC 7, 23, 38**
　　See also CA 37-40R; CANR 12, 36, 58, 82;
　　CN 7; DAM NOV; DLBY 1983; INT
　　CANR-12; MTCW 1

Plath, Sylvia 1932-1963 ..... **CLC 1, 2, 3, 5, 9,**
　　11, 14, 17, 50, 51, 62, 111; PC 1, 37;
　　WLC
　　See also AAYA 13; AMWR 2; AMWS 1;
　　BPFB 3; CA 19-20; CANR 34, 101; CAP
　　2; CDALB 1941-1968; DA; DA3; DAB;
　　DAC; DAM MST, POET; DLB 5, 6, 152;
　　EWL 3; EXPN; EXPP; FW; LAIT 4;
　　MAWW; MTCW 1, 2; NFS 1; PAB; PFS
　　1, 15; RGAL 4; SATA 96; TUS; WP;
　　YAW

Plato c. 428B.C.-347B.C. ... **CMLC 8; WLCS**
　　See also AW 1; CDWLB 1; DA; DA3;
　　DAB; DAC; DAM MST; DLB 176; LAIT
　　1; LATS 1; RGWL 2, 3

Platonov, Andrei
　　See Klimentov, Andrei Platonovich

Platonov, Andrei Platonovich
　　See Klimentov, Andrei Platonovich
　　See also DLB 272

Platonov, Andrey Platonovich
　　See Klimentov, Andrei Platonovich
　　See also EWL 3

Platt, Kin 1911- .... **CLC 26**
　　See also AAYA 11; CA 17-20R; CANR 11;
　　JRDA; SAAS 17; SATA 21, 86; WYA

Plautus c. 254B.C.-c. 184B.C. ...... **CMLC 24;**
　　DC 6
　　See also AW 1; CDWLB 1; DLB 211;
　　RGWL 2, 3

Plick et Plock
　　See Simenon, Georges (Jacques Christian)

Plieksans, Janis
　　See Rainis, Janis

Plimpton, George (Ames)
　　1927-2003 .... **CLC 36**
　　See also AITN 1; CA 21-24R; 224; CANR
　　32, 70, 103; DLB 185, 241; MTCW 1, 2;
　　SATA 10; SATA-Obit 150

Pliny the Elder c. 23-79 .... **CMLC 23**
　　See also DLB 211

Pliny the Younger c. 61-c. 112 ...... **CMLC 62**
　　See also AW 2; DLB 211

Plomer, William Charles Franklin
　　1903-1973 .... **CLC 4, 8**
　　See also AFW; CA 21-22; CANR 34; CAP
　　2; DLB 20, 162, 191, 225; EWL 3;
　　MTCW 1; RGEL 2; RGSF 2; SATA 24

Plotinus 204-270 .... **CMLC 46**
　　See also CDWLB 1; DLB 176

Plowman, Piers
　　See Kavanagh, Patrick (Joseph)

Plum, J.
　　See Wodehouse, P(elham) G(renville)

Plumly, Stanley (Ross) 1939- .... **CLC 33**
　　See also CA 108; 110; CANR 97; CP 7;
　　DLB 5, 193; INT CA-110

Plumpe, Friedrich Wilhelm
　　1888-1931 .... **TCLC 53**
　　See also CA 112

Plutarch c. 46-c. 120 .... **CMLC 60**
　　See also AW 2; CDWLB 1; DLB 176;
　　RGWL 2, 3; TWA

Po Chu-i 772-846 .... **CMLC 24**

Podhoretz, Norman 1930- .... **CLC 189**
　　See also AMWS 8; CA 9-12R; CANR 7, 78

Poe, Edgar Allan 1809-1849 ..... **NCLC 1, 16,**
　　55, 78, 94, 97, 117; PC 1, 54; SSC 1,
　　22, 34, 35, 54; WLC
　　See also AAYA 14; AMW; AMWC 1;
　　AMWR 2; BPFB 3; BYA 5, 11; CDALB
　　1640-1865; CMW 4; DA; DA3; DAB;
　　DAC; DAM MST, POET; DLB 3, 59, 73,
　　74, 248, 254; EXPP; EXPS; HGG; LAIT
　　2; LATS 1; LMFS 1; MSW; PAB; PFS 1,
　　3, 9; RGAL 4; RGSF 2; SATA 23; SCFW
　　2; SFW 4; SSFS 2, 4, 7, 8, 16; SUFW;
　　TUS; WP; WYA

Poet of Titchfield Street, The
　　See Pound, Ezra (Weston Loomis)

Pohl, Frederik 1919- .... **CLC 18; SSC 25**
　　See also AAYA 24; CA 61-64; 188; CAAE
　　188; CAAS 1; CANR 11, 37, 81; CN 7;
　　DLB 8; INT CANR-11; MTCW 1, 2;
　　SATA 24; SCFW 2; SFW 4

Poirier, Louis 1910-
　　See Gracq, Julien
　　See also CA 122; 126; CWW 2

Poitier, Sidney 1927- .... **CLC 26**
　　See also BW 1; CA 117; CANR 94

Pokagon, Simon 1830-1899 .... **NNAL**
　　See also DAM MULT

Polanski, Roman 1933- .... **CLC 16, 178**
　　See also CA 77-80

Pritchett, V(ictor) S(awdon)
1900-1997 ... **CLC 5, 13, 15, 41; SSC 14**
See also BPFB 3; BRWS 3; CA 61-64; 157;
CANR 31, 63; CN 7; DA3; DAM NOV;
DLB 15, 139; EWL 3; MTCW 1, 2;
RGEL 2; RGSF 2; TEA

Private 19022
See Manning, Frederic

Probst, Mark 1925- .... **CLC 59**
See also CA 130

Prokosch, Frederic 1908-1989 ...... **CLC 4, 48**
See also CA 73-76; 128; CANR 82; DLB
48; MTCW 2

Propertius, Sextus c. 50B.C.-c.
16B.C. .... **CMLC 32**
See also AW 2; CDWLB 1; DLB 211;
RGWL 2, 3

Prophet, The
See Dreiser, Theodore (Herman Albert)

Prose, Francine 1947- .... **CLC 45**
See also CA 109; 112; CANR 46, 95; DLB
234; SATA 101, 149

Proudhon
See Cunha, Euclides (Rodrigues Pimenta)
da

Proulx, Annie
See Proulx, E(dna) Annie

Proulx, E(dna) Annie 1935- ...... **CLC 81, 158**
See also AMWS 7; BPFB 3; CA 145;
CANR 65, 110; CN 7; CPW 1; DA3;
DAM POP; MTCW 2; SSFS 18

**Proust, (Valentin-Louis-George-Eugene)
Marcel** 1871-1922 .... **TCLC 7, 13, 33;
WLC**
See also BPFB 3; CA 104; 120; CANR 110;
DA; DA3; DAB; DAC; DAM MST, NOV;
DLB 65; EW 8; EWL 3; GFL 1789 to the
Present; MTCW 1, 2; RGWL 2, 3; TWA

Prowler, Harley
See Masters, Edgar Lee

Prus, Boleslaw 1845-1912 .... **TCLC 48**
See also RGWL 2, 3

Pryor, Richard (Franklin Lenox Thomas)
1940- .... **CLC 26**
See also CA 122; 152

Przybyszewski, Stanislaw
1868-1927 .... **TCLC 36**
See also CA 160; DLB 66; EWL 3

Pteleon
See Grieve, C(hristopher) M(urray)
See also DAM POET

Puckett, Lute
See Masters, Edgar Lee

Puig, Manuel 1932-1990 .... **CLC 3, 5, 10, 28,
65, 133; HLC 2**
See also BPFB 3; CA 45-48; CANR 2, 32,
63; CDWLB 3; DA3; DAM MULT; DLB
113; DNFS 1; EWL 3; GLL 1; HW 1, 2;
LAW; MTCW 1, 2; RGWL 2, 3; TWA;
WLIT 1

Pulitzer, Joseph 1847-1911 .... **TCLC 76**
See also CA 114; DLB 23

Purchas, Samuel 1577(?)-1626 .... **LC 70**
See also DLB 151

Purdy, A(lfred) W(ellington)
1918-2000 .... **CLC 3, 6, 14, 50**
See also CA 81-84; 189; CAAS 17; CANR
42, 66; CP 7; DAC; DAM MST, POET;
DLB 88; PFS 5; RGEL 2

Purdy, James (Amos) 1923- .... **CLC 2, 4, 10,
28, 52**
See also AMWS 7; CA 33-36R; CAAS 1;
CANR 19, 51; CN 7; DLB 2, 218; EWL
3; INT CANR-19; MTCW 1; RGAL 4

Pure, Simon
See Swinnerton, Frank Arthur

Pushkin, Aleksandr Sergeevich
See Pushkin, Alexander (Sergeyevich)
See also DLB 205

Pushkin, Alexander (Sergeyevich)
1799-1837 .... **NCLC 3, 27, 83; PC 10;
SSC 27, 55; WLC**
See Pushkin, Aleksandr Sergeevich
See also DA; DA3; DAB; DAC; DAM
DRAM, MST, POET; EW 5; EXPS; RGSF
2; RGWL 2, 3; SATA 61; SSFS 9; TWA

P'u Sung-ling 1640-1715 .... **LC 49; SSC 31**

Putnam, Arthur Lee
See Alger, Horatio, Jr.

Puzo, Mario 1920-1999 .... **CLC 1, 2, 6, 36,
107**
See also BPFB 3; CA 65-68; 185; CANR 4,
42, 65, 99, 131; CN 7; CPW; DA3; DAM
NOV, POP; DLB 6; MTCW 1, 2; NFS 16;
RGAL 4

Pygge, Edward
See Barnes, Julian (Patrick)

Pyle, Ernest Taylor 1900-1945
See Pyle, Ernie
See also CA 115; 160

Pyle, Ernie .... **TCLC 75**
See Pyle, Ernest Taylor
See also DLB 29; MTCW 2

Pyle, Howard 1853-1911 .... **TCLC 81**
See also BYA 2, 4; CA 109; 137; CLR 22;
DLB 42, 188; DLBD 13; LAIT 1; MAI-
CYA 1, 2; SATA 16, 100; WCH; YAW

Pym, Barbara (Mary Crampton)
1913-1980 .... **CLC 13, 19, 37, 111**
See also BPFB 3; BRWS 2; CA 13-14; 97-
100; CANR 13, 34; CAP 1; DLB 14, 207;
DLBY 1987; EWL 3; MTCW 1, 2; RGEL
2; TEA

Pynchon, Thomas (Ruggles, Jr.)
1937- ...... **CLC 2, 3, 6, 9, 11, 18, 33, 62,
72, 123, 192; SSC 14; WLC**
See also AMWS 2; BEST 90:2; BPFB 3;
CA 17-20R; CANR 22, 46, 73; CN 7;
CPW 1; DA; DA3; DAB; DAC; DAM
MST, NOV, POP; DLB 2, 173; EWL 3;
MTCW 1, 2; RGAL 4; SFW 4; TUS

Pythagoras c. 582B.C.-c. 507B.C. . **CMLC 22**
See also DLB 176

Q
See Quiller-Couch, Sir Arthur (Thomas)

Qian, Chongzhu
See Ch'ien, Chung-shu

Qian Zhongshu
See Ch'ien, Chung-shu
See also CWW 2

Qroll
See Dagerman, Stig (Halvard)

Quarrington, Paul (Lewis) 1953- ..... **CLC 65**
See also CA 129; CANR 62, 95

Quasimodo, Salvatore 1901-1968 .... **CLC 10;
PC 47**
See also CA 13-16; 25-28R; CAP 1; DLB
114; EW 12; EWL 3; MTCW 1; RGWL
2, 3

Quatermass, Martin
See Carpenter, John (Howard)

Quay, Stephen 1947- .... **CLC 95**
See also CA 189

Quay, Timothy 1947- .... **CLC 95**
See also CA 189

Queen, Ellery .... **CLC 3, 11**
See Dannay, Frederic; Davidson, Avram
(James); Deming, Richard; Fairman, Paul
W.; Flora, Fletcher; Hoch, Edward
D(entinger); Kane, Henry; Lee, Manfred
B(ennington); Marlowe, Stephen; Powell,
(Oval) Talmage; Sheldon, Walter J(ames);
Sturgeon, Theodore (Hamilton); Tracy,
Don(ald Fiske); Vance, John Holbrook
See also BPFB 3; CMW 4; MSW; RGAL 4

Queen, Ellery, Jr.
See Dannay, Frederic; Lee, Manfred
B(ennington)

Queneau, Raymond 1903-1976 ..... **CLC 2, 5,
10, 42**
See also CA 77-80; 69-72; CANR 32; DLB
72, 258; EW 12; EWL 3; GFL 1789 to
the Present; MTCW 1, 2; RGWL 2, 3

Quevedo, Francisco de 1580-1645 .... **LC 23**

Quiller-Couch, Sir Arthur (Thomas)
1863-1944 .... **TCLC 53**
See also CA 118; 166; DLB 135, 153, 190;
HGG; RGEL 2; SUFW 1

Quin, Ann (Marie) 1936-1973 .... **CLC 6**
See also CA 9-12R; 45-48; DLB 14, 231

Quincey, Thomas de
See De Quincey, Thomas

Quindlen, Anna 1953- .... **CLC 191**
See also AAYA 35; CA 138; CANR 73, 126;
DA3; DLB 292; MTCW 2

Quinn, Martin
See Smith, Martin Cruz

Quinn, Peter 1947- .... **CLC 91**
See also CA 197

Quinn, Simon
See Smith, Martin Cruz

Quintana, Leroy V. 1944- ...... **HLC 2; PC 36**
See also CA 131; CANR 65; DAM MULT;
DLB 82; HW 1, 2

Quiroga, Horacio (Sylvestre)
1878-1937 .... **HLC 2; TCLC 20**
See also CA 117; 131; DAM MULT; EWL
3; HW 1; LAW; MTCW 1; RGSF 2;
WLIT 1

Quoirez, Francoise 1935- .... **CLC 9**
See Sagan, Francoise
See also CA 49-52; CANR 6, 39, 73; CWW
2; MTCW 1, 2; TWA

Raabe, Wilhelm (Karl) 1831-1910 . **TCLC 45**
See also CA 167; DLB 129

Rabe, David (William) 1940- .. **CLC 4, 8, 33;
DC 16**
See also CA 85-88; CABS 3; CAD; CANR
59, 129; CD 5; DAM DRAM; DFS 3, 8,
13; DLB 7, 228; EWL 3

Rabelais, Francois 1494-1553 .... **LC 5, 60;
WLC**
See also DA; DAB; DAC; DAM MST; EW
2; GFL Beginnings to 1789; LMFS 1;
RGWL 2, 3; TWA

Rabinovitch, Sholem 1859-1916
See Aleichem, Sholom
See also CA 104

Rabinyan, Dorit 1972- .... **CLC 119**
See also CA 170

Rachilde
See Vallette, Marguerite Eymery; Vallette,
Marguerite Eymery
See also EWL 3

Racine, Jean 1639-1699 .... **LC 28**
See also DA3; DAB; DAM MST; DLB 268;
EW 3; GFL Beginnings to 1789; LMFS
1; RGWL 2, 3; TWA

Radcliffe, Ann (Ward) 1764-1823 ... **NCLC 6,
55, 106**
See also DLB 39, 178; HGG; LMFS 1;
RGEL 2; SUFW; WLIT 3

Radclyffe-Hall, Marguerite
See Hall, (Marguerite) Radclyffe

Radiguet, Raymond 1903-1923 ...... **TCLC 29**
See also CA 162; DLB 65; EWL 3; GFL
1789 to the Present; RGWL 2, 3

Radnoti, Miklos 1909-1944 .... **TCLC 16**
See also CA 118; 212; CDWLB 4; DLB
215; EWL 3; RGWL 2, 3

Rado, James 1939- .... **CLC 17**
See also CA 105

Radvanyi, Netty 1900-1983
See Seghers, Anna
See also CA 85-88; 110; CANR 82

Rae, Ben
See Griffiths, Trevor

Ross, Martin 1862-1915
See Martin, Violet Florence
See also DLB 135; GLL 2; RGEL 2; RGSF 2

Ross, (James) Sinclair 1908-1996 ... **CLC 13; SSC 24**
See also CA 73-76; CANR 81; CN 7; DAC; DAM MST; DLB 88; RGEL 2; RGSF 2; TCWW 2

Rossetti, Christina (Georgina) 1830-1894 .... **NCLC 2, 50, 66; PC 7; WLC**
See also AAYA 51; BRW 5; BYA 4; DA; DA3; DAB; DAC; DAM MST, POET; DLB 35, 163, 240; EXPP; LATS 1; MAICYA 1, 2; PFS 10, 14; RGEL 2; SATA 20; TEA; WCH

Rossetti, Dante Gabriel 1828-1882 . **NCLC 4, 77; PC 44; WLC**
See also AAYA 51; BRW 5; CDBLB 1832-1890; DA; DAB; DAC; DAM MST, POET; DLB 35; EXPP; RGEL 2; TEA

Rossi, Cristina Peri
See Peri Rossi, Cristina

Rossi, Jean-Baptiste 1931-2003
See Japrisot, Sebastien
See also CA 201; 215

Rossner, Judith (Perelman) 1935- . **CLC 6, 9, 29**
See also AITN 2; BEST 90:3; BPFB 3; CA 17-20R; CANR 18, 51, 73; CN 7; DLB 6; INT CANR-18; MTCW 1, 2

Rostand, Edmond (Eugene Alexis) 1868-1918 .... **DC 10; TCLC 6, 37**
See also CA 104; 126; DA; DA3; DAB; DAC; DAM DRAM, MST; DFS 1; DLB 192; LAIT 1; MTCW 1; RGWL 2, 3; TWA

Roth, Henry 1906-1995 ..... **CLC 2, 6, 11, 104**
See also AMWS 9; CA 11-12; 149; CANR 38, 63; CAP 1; CN 7; DA3; DLB 28; EWL 3; MTCW 1, 2; RGAL 4

Roth, (Moses) Joseph 1894-1939 ... **TCLC 33**
See also CA 160; DLB 85; EWL 3; RGWL 2, 3

Roth, Philip (Milton) 1933- ... **CLC 1, 2, 3, 4, 6, 9, 15, 22, 31, 47, 66, 86, 119; SSC 26; WLC**
See also AMWR 2; AMWS 3; BEST 90:3; BPFB 3; CA 1-4R; CANR 1, 22, 36, 55, 89; CDALB 1968-1988; CN 7; CPW 1; DA; DA3; DAB; DAC; DAM MST, NOV, POP; DLB 2, 28, 173; DLBY 1982; EWL 3; MTCW 1, 2; RGAL 4; RGSF 2; SSFS 12, 18; TUS

Rothenberg, Jerome 1931- .... **CLC 6, 57**
See also CA 45-48; CANR 1, 106; CP 7; DLB 5, 193

Rotter, Pat ed. .... **CLC 65**

Roumain, Jacques (Jean Baptiste) 1907-1944 .... **BLC 3; TCLC 19**
See also BW 1; CA 117; 125; DAM MULT; EWL 3

Rourke, Constance Mayfield 1885-1941 .... **TCLC 12**
See also CA 107; 200; YABC 1

Rousseau, Jean-Baptiste 1671-1741 ...... **LC 9**

Rousseau, Jean-Jacques 1712-1778 .... **LC 14, 36; WLC**
See also DA; DA3; DAB; DAC; DAM MST; EW 4; GFL Beginnings to 1789; LMFS 1; RGWL 2, 3; TWA

Roussel, Raymond 1877-1933 .... **TCLC 20**
See also CA 117; 201; EWL 3; GFL 1789 to the Present

Rovit, Earl (Herbert) 1927- .... **CLC 7**
See also CA 5-8R; CANR 12

Rowe, Elizabeth Singer 1674-1737 ..... **LC 44**
See also DLB 39, 95

Rowe, Nicholas 1674-1718 .... **LC 8**
See also DLB 84; RGEL 2

Rowlandson, Mary 1637(?)-1678 .... **LC 66**
See also DLB 24, 200; RGAL 4

Rowley, Ames Dorrance
See Lovecraft, H(oward) P(hillips)

Rowley, William 1585(?)-1626 .... **LC 100**
See also DLB 58; RGEL 2

Rowling, J(oanne) K(athleen) 1966- .... **CLC 137**
See also AAYA 34; BYA 11, 13, 14; CA 173; CANR 128; CLR 66, 80; MAICYA 2; SATA 109; SUFW 2

Rowson, Susanna Haswell 1762(?)-1824 .... **NCLC 5, 69**
See also DLB 37, 200; RGAL 4

Roy, Arundhati 1960(?)- .... **CLC 109**
See also CA 163; CANR 90, 126; DLBY 1997; EWL 3; LATS 1; WWE 1

Roy, Gabrielle 1909-1983 .... **CLC 10, 14**
See also CA 53-56; 110; CANR 5, 61; CCA 1; DAB; DAC; DAM MST; DLB 68; EWL 3; MTCW 1; RGWL 2, 3; SATA 104

Royko, Mike 1932-1997 .... **CLC 109**
See also CA 89-92; 157; CANR 26, 111; CPW

Rozanov, Vasilii Vasil'evich
See Rozanov, Vassili
See also DLB 295

Rozanov, Vasily Vasilyevich
See Rozanov, Vassili
See also EWL 3

Rozanov, Vassili 1856-1919 .... **TCLC 104**
See Rozanov, Vasilii Vasil'evich; Rozanov, Vasily Vasilyevich

Rozewicz, Tadeusz 1921- ...... **CLC 9, 23, 139**
See also CA 108; CANR 36, 66; CWW 2; DA3; DAM POET; DLB 232; EWL 3; MTCW 1, 2; RGWL 3

Ruark, Gibbons 1941- .... **CLC 3**
See also CA 33-36R; CAAS 23; CANR 14, 31, 57; DLB 120

Rubens, Bernice (Ruth) 1923- ... **CLC 19, 31**
See also CA 25-28R; CANR 33, 65, 128; CN 7; DLB 14, 207; MTCW 1

Rubin, Harold
See Robbins, Harold

Rudkin, (James) David 1936- .... **CLC 14**
See also CA 89-92; CBD; CD 5; DLB 13

Rudnik, Raphael 1933- .... **CLC 7**
See also CA 29-32R

Ruffian, M.
See Hasek, Jaroslav (Matej Frantisek)

Ruiz, Jose Martinez .... **CLC 11**
See Martinez Ruiz, Jose

Ruiz, Juan c. 1283-c. 1350 .... **CMLC 66**

Rukeyser, Muriel 1913-1980 . **CLC 6, 10, 15, 27; PC 12**
See also AMWS 6; CA 5-8R; 93-96; CANR 26, 60; DA3; DAM POET; DLB 48; EWL 3; FW; GLL 2; MTCW 1, 2; PFS 10; RGAL 4; SATA-Obit 22

Rule, Jane (Vance) 1931- .... **CLC 27**
See also CA 25-28R; CAAS 18; CANR 12, 87; CN 7; DLB 60; FW

Rulfo, Juan 1918-1986 .. **CLC 8, 80; HLC 2; SSC 25**
See also CA 85-88; 118; CANR 26; CDWLB 3; DAM MULT; DLB 113; EWL 3; HW 1, 2; LAW; MTCW 1, 2; RGSF 2; RGWL 2, 3; WLIT 1

Rumi, Jalal al-Din 1207-1273 ...... **CMLC 20; PC 45**
See also RGWL 2, 3; WP

Runeberg, Johan 1804-1877 .... **NCLC 41**

Runyon, (Alfred) Damon 1884(?)-1946 .... **TCLC 10**
See also CA 107; 165; DLB 11, 86, 171; MTCW 2; RGAL 4

Rush, Norman 1933- .... **CLC 44**
See also CA 121; 126; CANR 130; INT CA-126

Rushdie, (Ahmed) Salman 1947- .... **CLC 23, 31, 55, 100, 191; WLCS**
See also BEST 89:3; BPFB 3; BRWS 4; CA 108; 111; CANR 33, 56, 108; CN 7; CPW 1; DA3; DAB; DAC; DAM MST, NOV, POP; DLB 194; EWL 3; FANT; INT CA-111; LATS 1; LMFS 2; MTCW 1, 2; RGEL 2; RGSF 2; TEA; WLIT 4; WWE 1

Rushforth, Peter (Scott) 1945- .... **CLC 19**
See also CA 101

Ruskin, John 1819-1900 .... **TCLC 63**
See also BRW 5; BYA 5; CA 114; 129; CDBLB 1832-1890; DLB 55, 163, 190; RGEL 2; SATA 24; TEA; WCH

Russ, Joanna 1937- .... **CLC 15**
See also BPFB 3; CA 5-28R; CANR 11, 31, 65; CN 7; DLB 8; FW; GLL 1; MTCW 1; SCFW 2; SFW 4

Russ, Richard Patrick
See O'Brian, Patrick

Russell, George William 1867-1935
See A.E.; Baker, Jean H.
See also BRW 8; CA 104; 153; CDBLB 1890-1914; DAM POET; EWL 3; RGEL 2

Russell, Jeffrey Burton 1934- .... **CLC 70**
See also CA 25-28R; CANR 11, 28, 52

Russell, (Henry) Ken(neth Alfred) 1927- .... **CLC 16**
See also CA 105

Russell, William Martin 1947-
See Russell, Willy
See also CA 164; CANR 107

Russell, Willy .... **CLC 60**
See Russell, William Martin
See also CBD; CD 5; DLB 233

Russo, Richard 1949- .... **CLC 181**
See also AMWS 12; CA 127; 133; CANR 87, 114

Rutherford, Mark .... **TCLC 25**
See White, William Hale
See also DLB 18; RGEL 2

Ruyslinck, Ward .... **CLC 14**
See Belser, Reimond Karel Maria de

Ryan, Cornelius (John) 1920-1974 ..... **CLC 7**
See also CA 69-72; 53-56; CANR 38

Ryan, Michael 1946- .... **CLC 65**
See also CA 49-52; CANR 109; DLBY 1982

Ryan, Tim
See Dent, Lester

Rybakov, Anatoli (Naumovich) 1911-1998 .... **CLC 23, 53**
See also CA 126; 135; 172; SATA 79; SATA-Obit 108

Ryder, Jonathan
See Ludlum, Robert

Ryga, George 1932-1987 .... **CLC 14**
See also CA 101; 124; CANR 43, 90; CCA 1; DAC; DAM MST; DLB 60

S. H.
See Hartmann, Sadakichi

S. S.
See Sassoon, Siegfried (Lorraine)

Saba, Umberto 1883-1957 .... **TCLC 33**
See also CA 144; CANR 79; DLB 114; EWL 3; RGWL 2, 3

Sabatini, Rafael 1875-1950 .... **TCLC 47**
See also BPFB 3; CA 162; RHW

Sabato, Ernesto (R.) 1911- .... **CLC 10, 23; HLC 2**
See also CA 97-100; CANR 32, 65; CDWLB 3; DAM MULT; DLB 145; EWL 3; HW 1, 2; LAW; MTCW 1, 2

Schwartz, Delmore (David)
1913-1966 ... CLC **2, 4, 10, 45, 87; PC 8**
See also AMWS 2; CA 17-18; 25-28R;
CANR 35; CAP 2; DLB 28, 48; EWL 3;
MTCW 1, 2; PAB; RGAL 4; TUS

Schwartz, Ernst
See Ozu, Yasujiro

Schwartz, John Burnham 1965- .... CLC **59**
See also CA 132; CANR 116

Schwartz, Lynne Sharon 1939- .... CLC **31**
See also CA 103; CANR 44, 89; DLB 218;
MTCW 2

Schwartz, Muriel A.
See Eliot, T(homas) S(tearns)

Schwarz-Bart, Andre 1928- .... CLC **2, 4**
See also CA 89-92; CANR 109; DLB 299

Schwarz-Bart, Simone 1938- . **BLCS; CLC 7**
See also BW 2; CA 97-100; CANR 117;
EWL 3

Schwerner, Armand 1927-1999 .... PC **42**
See also CA 9-12R; 179; CANR 50, 85; CP
7; DLB 165

**Schwitters, Kurt (Hermann Edward Karl
Julius)** 1887-1948 .... TCLC **95**
See also CA 158

Schwob, Marcel (Mayer Andre)
1867-1905 .... TCLC **20**
See also CA 117; 168; DLB 123; GFL 1789
to the Present

Sciascia, Leonardo 1921-1989 .. CLC **8, 9, 41**
See also CA 85-88; 130; CANR 35; DLB
177; EWL 3; MTCW 1; RGWL 2, 3

Scoppettone, Sandra 1936- .... CLC **26**
See Early, Jack
See also AAYA 11; BYA 8; CA 5-8R;
CANR 41, 73; GLL 1; MAICYA 2; MAI-
CYAS 1; SATA 9, 92; WYA; YAW

Scorsese, Martin 1942- .... CLC **20, 89**
See also AAYA 38; CA 110; 114; CANR
46, 85

Scotland, Jay
See Jakes, John (William)

Scott, Duncan Campbell
1862-1947 .... TCLC **6**
See also CA 104; 153; DAC; DLB 92;
RGEL 2

Scott, Evelyn 1893-1963 .... CLC **43**
See also CA 104; 112; CANR 64; DLB 9,
48; RHW

Scott, F(rancis) R(eginald)
1899-1985 .... CLC **22**
See also CA 101; 114; CANR 87; DLB 88;
INT CA-101; RGEL 2

Scott, Frank
See Scott, F(rancis) R(eginald)

Scott, Joan .... CLC **65**

Scott, Joanna 1960- .... CLC **50**
See also CA 126; CANR 53, 92

Scott, Paul (Mark) 1920-1978 ...... CLC **9, 60**
See also BRWS 1; CA 81-84; 77-80; CANR
33; DLB 14, 207; EWL 3; MTCW 1;
RGEL 2; RHW; WWE 1

Scott, Ridley 1937- .... CLC **183**
See also AAYA 13, 43

Scott, Sarah 1723-1795 .... LC **44**
See also DLB 39

Scott, Sir Walter 1771-1832 .... NCLC **15, 69,
110; PC 13; SSC 32; WLC**
See also AAYA 22; BRW 4; BYA 2; CD-
BLB 1789-1832; DA; DAB; DAC; DAM
MST, NOV, POET; DLB 93, 107, 116,
144, 159; HGG; LAIT 1; RGEL 2; RGSF
2; SSFS 10; SUFW 1; TEA; WLIT 3;
YABC 2

Scribe, (Augustin) Eugene 1791-1861 . **DC 5;
NCLC 16**
See also DAM DRAM; DLB 192; GFL
1789 to the Present; RGWL 2, 3

Scrum, R.
See Crumb, R(obert)

Scudery, Georges de 1601-1667 .... LC **75**
See also GFL Beginnings to 1789

Scudery, Madeleine de 1607-1701 .. LC **2, 58**
See also DLB 268; GFL Beginnings to 1789

Scum
See Crumb, R(obert)

Scumbag, Little Bobby
See Crumb, R(obert)

Seabrook, John
See Hubbard, L(afayette) Ron(ald)

Sealy, I(rwin) Allan 1951- .... CLC **55**
See also CA 136; CN 7

Search, Alexander
See Pessoa, Fernando (Antonio Nogueira)

Sebastian, Lee
See Silverberg, Robert

Sebastian Owl
See Thompson, Hunter S(tockton)

Sebestyen, Igen
See Sebestyen, Ouida

Sebestyen, Ouida 1924- .... CLC **30**
See also AAYA 8; BYA 7; CA 107; CANR
40, 114; CLR 17; JRDA; MAICYA 1, 2;
SAAS 10; SATA 39, 140; WYA; YAW

Sebold, Alice 1963(?)- .... CLC **193**
See also CA 203

Secundus, H. Scriblerus
See Fielding, Henry

Sedges, John
See Buck, Pearl S(ydenstricker)

Sedgwick, Catharine Maria
1789-1867 .... NCLC **19, 98**
See also DLB 1, 74, 183, 239, 243, 254;
RGAL 4

Seelye, John (Douglas) 1931- .... CLC **7**
See also CA 97-100; CANR 70; INT CA-
97-100; TCWW 2

Seferiades, Giorgos Stylianou 1900-1971
See Seferis, George
See also CA 5-8R; 33-36R; CANR 5, 36;
MTCW 1

Seferis, George .... CLC **5, 11**
See Seferiades, Giorgos Stylianou
See also EW 12; EWL 3; RGWL 2, 3

Segal, Erich (Wolf) 1937- .... CLC **3, 10**
See also BEST 89:1; BPFB 3; CA 25-28R;
CANR 20, 36, 65, 113; CPW; DAM POP;
DLBY 1986; INT CANR-20; MTCW 1

Seger, Bob 1945- .... CLC **35**

Seghers, Anna .... CLC **7**
See Radvanyi, Netty
See also CDWLB 2; DLB 69; EWL 3

Seidel, Frederick (Lewis) 1936- .... CLC **18**
See also CA 13-16R; CANR 8, 99; CP 7;
DLBY 1984

Seifert, Jaroslav 1901-1986 . CLC **34, 44, 93;
PC 47**
See also CA 127; CDWLB 4; DLB 215;
EWL 3; MTCW 1, 2

Sei Shonagon c. 966-1017(?) .... CMLC **6**

Sejour, Victor 1817-1874 .... DC **10**
See also DLB 50

Sejour Marcou et Ferrand, Juan Victor
See Sejour, Victor

Selby, Hubert, Jr. 1928-2004 ..... CLC **1, 2, 4,
8; SSC 20**
See also CA 13-16R; CANR 33, 85; CN 7;
DLB 2, 227

Selzer, Richard 1928- .... CLC **74**
See also CA 65-68; CANR 14, 106

Sembene, Ousmane
See Ousmane, Sembene
See also AFW; CWW 2; EWL 3; WLIT 2

Senancour, Etienne Pivert de
1770-1846 .... NCLC **16**
See also DLB 119; GFL 1789 to the Present

Sender, Ramon (Jose) 1902-1982 ...... CLC **8;
HLC 2; TCLC 136**
See also CA 5-8R; 105; CANR 8; DAM
MULT; EWL 3; HW 1; MTCW 1; RGWL
2, 3

Seneca, Lucius Annaeus c. 4B.C.-c.
65 .... CMLC **6; DC 5**
See also AW 2; CDWLB 1; DAM DRAM;
DLB 211; RGWL 2, 3; TWA

Senghor, Leopold Sedar 1906-2001 ... BLC **3;
CLC 54, 130; PC 25**
See also AFW; BW 2; CA 116; 125; 203;
CANR 47, 74; DAM MULT, POET;
DNFS 2; EWL 3; GFL 1789 to the
Present; MTCW 1, 2; TWA

Senna, Danzy 1970- .... CLC **119**
See also CA 169; CANR 130

Serling, (Edward) Rod(man)
1924-1975 .... CLC **30**
See also AAYA 14; AITN 1; CA 162; 57-
60; DLB 26; SFW 4

Serna, Ramon Gomez de la
See Gomez de la Serna, Ramon

Serpieres
See Guillevic, (Eugene)

Service, Robert
See Service, Robert W(illiam)
See also BYA 4; DAB; DLB 92

Service, Robert W(illiam)
1874(?)-1958 .... TCLC **15; WLC**
See Service, Robert
See also CA 115; 140; CANR 84; DA;
DAC; DAM MST, POET; PFS 10; RGEL
2; SATA 20

Seth, Vikram 1952- .... CLC **43, 90**
See also CA 121; 127; CANR 50, 74, 131;
CN 7; CP 7; DA3; DAM MULT; DLB
120, 271, 282; EWL 3; INT CA-127;
MTCW 2; WWE 1

Seton, Cynthia Propper 1926-1982 .. CLC **27**
See also CA 5-8R; 108; CANR 7

Seton, Ernest (Evan) Thompson
1860-1946 .... TCLC **31**
See also ANW; BYA 3; CA 109; 204; CLR
59; DLB 92; DLBD 13; JRDA; SATA 18

Seton-Thompson, Ernest
See Seton, Ernest (Evan) Thompson

Settle, Mary Lee 1918- .... CLC **19, 61**
See also BPFB 3; CA 89-92; CAAS 1;
CANR 44, 126; CN 7; CSW; DLB 6;
INT CA-89-92

Seuphor, Michel
See Arp, Jean

Sevigne, Marie (de Rabutin-Chantal)
1626-1696 .... LC **11**
See Sevigne, Marie de Rabutin Chantal
See also GFL Beginnings to 1789; TWA

Sevigne, Marie de Rabutin Chantal
See Sevigne, Marie (de Rabutin-Chantal)
See also DLB 268

Sewall, Samuel 1652-1730 .... LC **38**
See also DLB 24; RGAL 4

Sexton, Anne (Harvey) 1928-1974 ..... CLC **2,
4, 6, 8, 10, 15, 53, 123; PC 2; WLC**
See also AMWS 2; CA 1-4R; 53-56; CABS
2; CANR 3, 36; CDALB 1941-1968; DA;
DA3; DAB; DAC; DAM MST, POET;
DLB 5, 169; EWL 3; EXPP; FW;
MAWW; MTCW 1, 2; PAB; PFS 4, 14;
RGAL 4; SATA 10; TUS

Shaara, Jeff 1952- .... CLC **119**
See also CA 163; CANR 109

Shaara, Michael (Joseph, Jr.)
1929-1988 .... CLC **15**
See also AITN 1; BPFB 3; CA 102; 125;
CANR 52, 85; DAM POP; DLBY 1983

Shackleton, C. C.
See Aldiss, Brian W(ilson)

Singleton, Ann
See Benedict, Ruth (Fulton)

Singleton, John 1968(?)- .... **CLC 156**
See also AAYA 50; BW 2, 3; CA 138;
CANR 67, 82; DAM MULT

Sinjohn, John
See Galsworthy, John

Sinyavsky, Andrei (Donatevich)
1925-1997 .... **CLC 8**
See Sinyavsky, Andrey Donatovich; Tertz,
Abram
See also CA 85-88; 159

Sinyavsky, Andrey Donatovich
See Sinyavsky, Andrei (Donatevich)
See also EWL 3

Sirin, V.
See Nabokov, Vladimir (Vladimirovich)

Sissman, L(ouis) E(dward)
1928-1976 .... **CLC 9, 18**
See also CA 21-24R; 65-68; CANR 13;
DLB 5

Sisson, C(harles) H(ubert)
1914-2003 .... **CLC 8**
See also CA 1-4R; 220; CAAS 3; CANR 3,
48, 84; CP 7; DLB 27

Sitting Bull 1831(?)-1890 .... **NNAL**
See also DA3; DAM MULT

Sitwell, Dame Edith 1887-1964 ..... **CLC 2, 9,
67; PC 3**
See also BRW 7; CA 9-12R; CANR 35;
CDBLB 1945-1960; DAM POET; DLB
20; EWL 3; MTCW 1, 2; RGEL 2; TEA

Siwaarmill, H. P.
See Sharp, William

Sjoewall, Maj 1935- .... **CLC 7**
See Sjowall, Maj
See also CA 65-68; CANR 73

Sjowall, Maj
See Sjoewall, Maj
See also BPFB 3; CMW 4; MSW

Skelton, John 1460(?)-1529 ..... **LC 71; PC 25**
See also BRW 1; DLB 136; RGEL 2

Skelton, Robin 1925-1997 .... **CLC 13**
See Zuk, Georges
See also AITN 2; CA 5-8R; 160; CAAS 5;
CANR 28, 89; CCA 1; CP 7; DLB 27, 53

Skolimowski, Jerzy 1938- .... **CLC 20**
See also CA 128

Skram, Amalie (Bertha)
1847-1905 .... **TCLC 25**
See also CA 165

Skvorecky, Josef (Vaclav) 1924- ...... **CLC 15,
39, 69, 152**
See also CA 61-64; CAAS 1; CANR 10,
34, 63, 108; CDWLB 4; DA3; DAC;
DAM NOV; DLB 232; EWL 3; MTCW
1, 2

Slade, Bernard .... **CLC 11, 46**
See Newbound, Bernard Slade
See also CAAS 9; CCA 1; DLB 53

Slaughter, Carolyn 1946- .... **CLC 56**
See also CA 85-88; CANR 85; CN 7

Slaughter, Frank G(ill) 1908-2001 ... **CLC 29**
See also AITN 2; CA 5-8R; 197; CANR 5,
85; INT CANR-5; RHW

Slavitt, David R(ytman) 1935- ..... **CLC 5, 14**
See also CA 21-24R; CAAS 3; CANR 41,
83; CP 7; DLB 5, 6

Slesinger, Tess 1905-1945 .... **TCLC 10**
See also CA 107; 199; DLB 102

Slessor, Kenneth 1901-1971 .... **CLC 14**
See also CA 102; 89-92; DLB 260; RGEL
2

Slowacki, Juliusz 1809-1849 .... **NCLC 15**
See also RGWL 3

Smart, Christopher 1722-1771 . **LC 3; PC 13**
See also DAM POET; DLB 109; RGEL 2

Smart, Elizabeth 1913-1986 .... **CLC 54**
See also CA 81-84; 118; DLB 88

Smiley, Jane (Graves) 1949- ...... **CLC 53, 76,
144**
See also AMWS 6; BPFB 3; CA 104;
CANR 30, 50, 74, 96; CN 7; CPW 1;
DA3; DAM POP; DLB 227, 234; EWL 3;
INT CANR-30; SSFS 19

Smith, A(rthur) J(ames) M(arshall)
1902-1980 .... **CLC 15**
See also CA 1-4R; 102; CANR 4; DAC;
DLB 88; RGEL 2

Smith, Adam 1723(?)-1790 .... **LC 36**
See also DLB 104, 252; RGEL 2

Smith, Alexander 1829-1867 .... **NCLC 59**
See also DLB 32, 55

Smith, Anna Deavere 1950- .... **CLC 86**
See also CA 133; CANR 103; CD 5; DFS 2

Smith, Betty (Wehner) 1904-1972 .... **CLC 19**
See also BPFB 3; BYA 3; CA 5-8R; 33-
36R; DLBY 1982; LAIT 3; RGAL 4;
SATA 6

Smith, Charlotte (Turner)
1749-1806 .... **NCLC 23, 115**
See also DLB 39, 109; RGEL 2; TEA

Smith, Clark Ashton 1893-1961 .... **CLC 43**
See also CA 143; CANR 81; FANT; HGG;
MTCW 2; SCFW 2; SFW 4; SUFW

Smith, Dave .... **CLC 22, 42**
See Smith, David (Jeddie)
See also CAAS 7; DLB 5

Smith, David (Jeddie) 1942-
See Smith, Dave
See also CA 49-52; CANR 1, 59, 120; CP
7; CSW; DAM POET

Smith, Florence Margaret 1902-1971
See Smith, Stevie
See also CA 17-18; 29-32R; CANR 35;
CAP 2; DAM POET; MTCW 1, 2; TEA

Smith, Iain Crichton 1928-1998 .... **CLC 64**
See also BRWS 9; CA 21-24R; 171; CN 7;
CP 7; DLB 40, 139; RGSF 2

Smith, John 1580(?)-1631 .... **LC 9**
See also DLB 24, 30; TUS

Smith, Johnston
See Crane, Stephen (Townley)

Smith, Joseph, Jr. 1805-1844 .... **NCLC 53**

Smith, Lee 1944- .... **CLC 25, 73**
See also CA 114; 119; CANR 46, 118;
CSW; DLB 143; DLBY 1983; EWL 3;
INT CA-119; RGAL 4

Smith, Martin
See Smith, Martin Cruz

Smith, Martin Cruz 1942- .. **CLC 25; NNAL**
See also BEST 89:4; BPFB 3; CA 85-88;
CANR 6, 23, 43, 65, 119; CMW 4; CPW;
DAM MULT, POP; HGG; INT CANR-
23; MTCW 2; RGAL 4

Smith, Patti 1946- .... **CLC 12**
See also CA 93-96; CANR 63

Smith, Pauline (Urmson)
1882-1959 .... **TCLC 25**
See also DLB 225; EWL 3

Smith, Rosamond
See Oates, Joyce Carol

Smith, Sheila Kaye
See Kaye-Smith, Sheila

Smith, Stevie .... **CLC 3, 8, 25, 44; PC 12**
See Smith, Florence Margaret
See also BRWS 2; DLB 20; EWL 3; MTCW
2; PAB; PFS 3; RGEL 2

Smith, Wilbur (Addison) 1933- .... **CLC 33**
See also CA 13-16R; CANR 7, 46, 66;
CPW; MTCW 1, 2

Smith, William Jay 1918- .... **CLC 6**
See also AMWS 13; CA 5-8R; CANR 44,
106; CP 7; CSW; CWRI 5; DLB 5; MAI-
CYA 1, 2; SAAS 22; SATA 2, 68

Smith, Woodrow Wilson
See Kuttner, Henry

Smith, Zadie 1976- .... **CLC 158**
See also AAYA 50; CA 193

Smolenskin, Peretz 1842-1885 .... **NCLC 30**

Smollett, Tobias (George) 1721-1771 ... **LC 2,
46**
See also BRW 3; CDBLB 1660-1789; DLB
39, 104; RGEL 2; TEA

Snodgrass, W(illiam) D(e Witt)
1926- .... **CLC 2, 6, 10, 18, 68**
See also AMWS 6; CA 1-4R; CANR 6, 36,
65, 85; CP 7; DAM POET; DLB 5;
MTCW 1, 2; RGAL 4

Snorri Sturluson 1179-1241 .... **CMLC 56**
See also RGWL 2, 3

Snow, C(harles) P(ercy) 1905-1980 ... **CLC 1,
4, 6, 9, 13, 19**
See also BRW 7; CA 5-8R; 101; CANR 28;
CDBLB 1945-1960; DAM NOV; DLB 15,
77; DLBD 17; EWL 3; MTCW 1, 2;
RGEL 2; TEA

Snow, Frances Compton
See Adams, Henry (Brooks)

Snyder, Gary (Sherman) 1930- . **CLC 1, 2, 5,
9, 32, 120; PC 21**
See also AMWS 8; ANW; BG 3; CA 17-
20R; CANR 30, 60, 125; CP 7; DA3;
DAM POET; DLB 5, 16, 165, 212, 237,
275; EWL 3; MTCW 2; PFS 9, 19; RGAL
4; WP

Snyder, Zilpha Keatley 1927- .... **CLC 17**
See also AAYA 15; BYA 1; CA 9-12R;
CANR 38; CLR 31; JRDA; MAICYA 1,
2; SAAS 2; SATA 1, 28, 75, 110; SATA-
Essay 112; YAW

Soares, Bernardo
See Pessoa, Fernando (Antonio Nogueira)

Sobh, A.
See Shamlu, Ahmad

Sobh, Alef
See Shamlu, Ahmad

Sobol, Joshua 1939- .... **CLC 60**
See Sobol, Yehoshua
See also CA 200; CWW 2

Sobol, Yehoshua 1939-
See Sobol, Joshua
See also CWW 2

Socrates 470B.C.-399B.C. .... **CMLC 27**

Soderberg, Hjalmar 1869-1941 ...... **TCLC 39**
See also DLB 259; EWL 3; RGSF 2

Soderbergh, Steven 1963- .... **CLC 154**
See also AAYA 43

Sodergran, Edith (Irene) 1892-1923
See Soedergran, Edith (Irene)
See also CA 202; DLB 259; EW 11; EWL
3; RGWL 2, 3

Soedergran, Edith (Irene)
1892-1923 .... **TCLC 31**
See Sodergran, Edith (Irene)

Softly, Edgar
See Lovecraft, H(oward) P(hillips)

Softly, Edward
See Lovecraft, H(oward) P(hillips)

Sokolov, Alexander V(sevolodovich) 1943-
See Sokolov, Sasha
See also CA 73-76

Sokolov, Raymond 1941- .... **CLC 7**
See also CA 85-88

Sokolov, Sasha .... **CLC 59**
See Sokolov, Alexander V(sevolodovich)
See also CWW 2; DLB 285; EWL 3; RGWL
2, 3

Sokolov, Sasha .... **CLC 59**

Solo, Jay
See Ellison, Harlan (Jay)

Sologub, Fyodor .... **TCLC 9**
See Teternikov, Fyodor Kuzmich
See also EWL 3

Solomons, Ikey Esquir
See Thackeray, William Makepeace

Solomos, Dionysios 1798-1857 .... NCLC 15

Solwoska, Mara
See French, Marilyn

Solzhenitsyn, Aleksandr I(sayevich)
1918- .. **CLC 1, 2, 4, 7, 9, 10, 18, 26, 34, 78, 134; SSC 32; WLC**
See Solzhenitsyn, Aleksandr Isaevich
See also AAYA 49; AITN 1; BPFB 3; CA 69-72; CANR 40, 65, 116; DA; DA3; DAB; DAC; DAM MST, NOV; EW 13; EXPS; LAIT 4; MTCW 1, 2; NFS 6; RGSF 2; RGWL 2, 3; SSFS 9; TWA

Solzhenitsyn, Aleksandr Isaevich
See Solzhenitsyn, Aleksandr I(sayevich)
See also EWL 3

Somers, Jane
See Lessing, Doris (May)

Somerville, Edith Oenone
1858-1949 .... SSC 56; TCLC 51
See also CA 196; DLB 135; RGEL 2; RGSF 2

Somerville & Ross
See Martin, Violet Florence; Somerville, Edith Oenone

Sommer, Scott 1951- .... CLC 25
See also CA 106

Sondheim, Stephen (Joshua) 1930- . CLC 30, 39, 147; DC 22
See also AAYA 11; CA 103; CANR 47, 67, 125; DAM DRAM; LAIT 4

Sone, Monica 1919- .... AAL

Song, Cathy 1955- .... AAL; PC 21
See also CA 154; CANR 118; CWP; DLB 169; EXPP; FW; PFS 5

Sontag, Susan 1933- .... CLC 1, 2, 10, 13, 31, 105
See also AMWS 3; CA 17-20R; CANR 25, 51, 74, 97; CN 7; CPW; DA3; DAM POP; DLB 2, 67; EWL 3; MAWW; MTCW 1, 2; RGAL 4; RHW; SSFS 10

Sophocles 496(?)B.C.-406(?)B.C. .... CMLC 2, 47, 51; DC 1; WLCS
See also AW 1; CDWLB 1; DA; DA3; DAB; DAC; DAM DRAM, MST; DFS 1, 4, 8; DLB 176; LAIT 1; LATS 1; LMFS 1; RGWL 2, 3; TWA

Sordello 1189-1269 .... CMLC 15

Sorel, Georges 1847-1922 .... TCLC 91
See also CA 118; 188

Sorel, Julia
See Drexler, Rosalyn

Sorokin, Vladimir .... CLC 59
See Sorokin, Vladimir Georgievich

Sorokin, Vladimir Georgievich
See Sorokin, Vladimir
See also DLB 285

Sorrentino, Gilbert 1929- .. CLC 3, 7, 14, 22, 40
See also CA 77-80; CANR 14, 33, 115; CN 7; CP 7; DLB 5, 173; DLBY 1980; INT CANR-14

Soseki
See Natsume, Soseki
See also MJW

Soto, Gary 1952- ... CLC 32, 80; HLC 2; PC 28
See also AAYA 10, 37; BYA 11; CA 119; 125; CANR 50, 74, 107; CLR 38; CP 7; DAM MULT; DLB 82; EWL 3; EXPP; HW 1, 2; INT CA-125; JRDA; LLW 1; MAICYA 2; MAICYAS 1; MTCW 2; PFS 7; RGAL 4; SATA 80, 120; WYA; YAW

Soupault, Philippe 1897-1990 .... CLC 68
See also CA 116; 147; 131; EWL 3; GFL 1789 to the Present; LMFS 2

Souster, (Holmes) Raymond 1921- .... CLC 5, 14
See also CA 13-16R; CAAS 14; CANR 13, 29, 53; CP 7; DA3; DAC; DAM POET; DLB 88; RGEL 2; SATA 63

Southern, Terry 1924(?)-1995 .... CLC 7
See also AMWS 11; BPFB 3; CA 1-4R; 150; CANR 1, 55, 107; CN 7; DLB 2; IDFW 3, 4

Southerne, Thomas 1660-1746 .... LC 99
See also DLB 80; RGEL 2

Southey, Robert 1774-1843 .... NCLC 8, 97
See also BRW 4; DLB 93, 107, 142; RGEL 2; SATA 54

Southworth, Emma Dorothy Eliza Nevitte
1819-1899 .... NCLC 26
See also DLB 239

Souza, Ernest
See Scott, Evelyn

Soyinka, Wole 1934- .. BLC 3; CLC 3, 5, 14, 36, 44, 179; DC 2; WLC
See also AFW; BW 2, 3; CA 13-16R; CANR 27, 39, 82; CD 5; CDWLB 3; CN 7; CP 7; DA; DA3; DAB; DAC; DAM DRAM, MST, MULT; DFS 10; DLB 125; EWL 3; MTCW 1, 2; RGEL 2; TWA; WLIT 2; WWE 1

Spackman, W(illiam) M(ode)
1905-1990 .... CLC 46
See also CA 81-84; 132

Spacks, Barry (Bernard) 1931- .... CLC 14
See also CA 154; CANR 33, 109; CP 7; DLB 105

Spanidou, Irini 1946- .... CLC 44
See also CA 185

Spark, Muriel (Sarah) 1918- ..... CLC 2, 3, 5, 8, 13, 18, 40, 94; SSC 10
See also BRWS 1; CA 5-8R; CANR 12, 36, 76, 89, 131; CDBLB 1945-1960; CN 7; CP 7; DA3; DAB; DAC; DAM MST, NOV; DLB 15, 139; EWL 3; FW; INT CANR-12; LAIT 4; MTCW 1, 2; RGEL 2; TEA; WLIT 4; YAW

Spaulding, Douglas
See Bradbury, Ray (Douglas)

Spaulding, Leonard
See Bradbury, Ray (Douglas)

Speght, Rachel 1597-c. 1630 .... LC 97
See also DLB 126

Spelman, Elizabeth .... CLC 65

Spence, J. A. D.
See Eliot, T(homas) S(tearns)

Spencer, Anne 1882-1975 .... HR 3
See also BW 2; CA 161; DLB 51, 54

Spencer, Elizabeth 1921- .... CLC 22; SSC 57
See also CA 13-16R; CANR 32, 65, 87; CN 7; CSW; DLB 6, 218; EWL 3; MTCW 1; RGAL 4; SATA 14

Spencer, Leonard G.
See Silverberg, Robert

Spencer, Scott 1945- .... CLC 30
See also CA 113; CANR 51; DLBY 1986

Spender, Stephen (Harold)
1909-1995 .... CLC 1, 2, 5, 10, 41, 91
See also BRWS 2; CA 9-12R; 149; CANR 31, 54; CDBLB 1945-1960; CP 7; DA3; DAM POET; DLB 20; EWL 3; MTCW 1, 2; PAB; RGEL 2; TEA

Spengler, Oswald (Arnold Gottfried)
1880-1936 .... TCLC 25
See also CA 118; 189

Spenser, Edmund 1552(?)-1599 ..... LC 5, 39; PC 8, 42; WLC
See also BRW 1; CDBLB Before 1660; DA; DA3; DAB; DAC; DAM MST, POET; DLB 167; EFS 2; EXPP; PAB; RGEL 2; TEA; WLIT 3; WP

Spicer, Jack 1925-1965 .... CLC 8, 18, 72
See also BG 3; CA 85-88; DAM POET; DLB 5, 16, 193; GLL 1; WP

Spiegelman, Art 1948- .... CLC 76, 178
See also AAYA 10, 46; CA 125; CANR 41, 55, 74, 124; DLB 299; MTCW 2; SATA 109; YAW

Spielberg, Peter 1929- .... CLC 6
See also CA 5-8R; CANR 4, 48; DLBY 1981

Spielberg, Steven 1947- .... CLC 20, 188
See also AAYA 8, 24; CA 77-80; CANR 32; SATA 32

Spillane, Frank Morrison 1918-
See Spillane, Mickey
See also CA 25-28R; CANR 28, 63, 125; DA3; MTCW 1, 2; SATA 66

Spillane, Mickey .... CLC 3, 13
See Spillane, Frank Morrison
See also BPFB 3; CMW 4; DLB 226; MSW; MTCW 2

Spinoza, Benedictus de 1632-1677 .. LC 9, 58

Spinrad, Norman (Richard) 1940- ... CLC 46
See also BPFB 3; CA 37-40R; CAAS 19; CANR 20, 91; DLB 8; INT CANR-20; SFW 4

Spitteler, Carl (Friedrich Georg)
1845-1924 .... TCLC 12
See also CA 109; DLB 129; EWL 3

Spivack, Kathleen (Romola Drucker)
1938- .... CLC 6
See also CA 49-52

Spoto, Donald 1941- .... CLC 39
See also CA 65-68; CANR 11, 57, 93

Springsteen, Bruce (F.) 1949- .... CLC 17
See also CA 111

Spurling, (Susan) Hilary 1940- .... CLC 34
See also CA 104; CANR 25, 52, 94

Spyker, John Howland
See Elman, Richard (Martin)

Squared, A.
See Abbott, Edwin A.

Squires, (James) Radcliffe
1917-1993 .... CLC 51
See also CA 1-4R; 140; CANR 6, 21

Srivastava, Dhanpat Rai 1880(?)-1936
See Premchand
See also CA 118; 197

Stacy, Donald
See Pohl, Frederik

Stael
See Stael-Holstein, Anne Louise Germaine Necker
See also EW 5; RGWL 2, 3

Stael, Germaine de
See Stael-Holstein, Anne Louise Germaine Necker
See also DLB 119, 192; FW; GFL 1789 to the Present; TWA

Stael-Holstein, Anne Louise Germaine
Necker 1766-1817 .... NCLC 3, 91
See Stael; Stael, Germaine de

Stafford, Jean 1915-1979 .. CLC 4, 7, 19, 68; SSC 26
See also CA 1-4R; 85-88; CANR 3, 65; DLB 2, 173; MTCW 1, 2; RGAL 4; RGSF 2; SATA-Obit 22; TCWW 2; TUS

Stafford, William (Edgar)
1914-1993 .... CLC 4, 7, 29
See also AMWS 11; CA 5-8R; 142; CAAS 3; CANR 5, 22; DAM POET; DLB 5, 206; EXPP; INT CANR-22; PFS 2, 8, 16; RGAL 4; WP

Stagnelius, Eric Johan 1793-1823 . NCLC 61

Staines, Trevor
See Brunner, John (Kilian Houston)

Stairs, Gordon
See Austin, Mary (Hunter)
See also TCWW 2

Stalin, Joseph 1879-1953 .... **TCLC 92**

Stampa, Gaspara c. 1524-1554 .... **PC 43**
See also RGWL 2, 3

Stampflinger, K. A.
See Benjamin, Walter

Stancykowna
See Szymborska, Wislawa

Standing Bear, Luther
1868(?)-1939(?) .... **NNAL**
See also CA 113; 144; DAM MULT

Stannard, Martin 1947- .... **CLC 44**
See also CA 142; DLB 155

Stanton, Elizabeth Cady
1815-1902 .... **TCLC 73**
See also CA 171; DLB 79; FW

Stanton, Maura 1946- .... **CLC 9**
See also CA 89-92; CANR 15, 123; DLB
120

Stanton, Schuyler
See Baum, L(yman) Frank

Stapledon, (William) Olaf
1886-1950 .... **TCLC 22**
See also CA 111; 162; DLB 15, 255; SFW
4

Starbuck, George (Edwin)
1931-1996 .... **CLC 53**
See also CA 21-24R; 153; CANR 23; DAM
POET

Stark, Richard
See Westlake, Donald E(dwin)

Staunton, Schuyler
See Baum, L(yman) Frank

Stead, Christina (Ellen) 1902-1983 ... **CLC 2,
5, 8, 32, 80**
See also BRWS 4; CA 13-16R; 109; CANR
33, 40; DLB 260; EWL 3; FW; MTCW 1,
2; RGEL 2; RGSF 2; WWE 1

Stead, William Thomas
1849-1912 .... **TCLC 48**
See also CA 167

Stebnitsky, M.
See Leskov, Nikolai (Semyonovich)

Steele, Sir Richard 1672-1729 .... **LC 18**
See also BRW 3; CDBLB 1660-1789; DLB
84, 101; RGEL 2; WLIT 3

Steele, Timothy (Reid) 1948- .... **CLC 45**
See also CA 93-96; CANR 16, 50, 92; CP
7; DLB 120, 282

Steffens, (Joseph) Lincoln
1866-1936 .... **TCLC 20**
See also CA 117; 198

Stegner, Wallace (Earle) 1909-1993 .. **CLC 9,
49, 81; SSC 27**
See also AITN 1; AMWS 4; ANW; BEST
90:3; BPFB 3; CA 1-4R; 141; CAAS 9;
CANR 1, 21, 46; DAM NOV; DLB 9,
206, 275; DLBY 1993; EWL 3; MTCW
1, 2; RGAL 4; TCWW 2; TUS

Stein, Gertrude 1874-1946 .... **DC 19; PC 18;
SSC 42; TCLC 1, 6, 28, 48; WLC**
See also AMW; AMWC 2; CA 104; 132;
CANR 108; CDALB 1917-1929; DA;
DA3; DAB; DAC; DAM MST, NOV,
POET; DLB 4, 54, 86, 228; DLBD 15;
EWL 3; EXPS; GLL 1; MAWW; MTCW
1, 2; NCFS 4; RGAL 4; RGSF 2; SSFS 5;
TUS; WP

Steinbeck, John (Ernst) 1902-1968 ... **CLC 1,
5, 9, 13, 21, 34, 45, 75, 124; SSC 11,
37; TCLC 135; WLC**
See also AAYA 12; AMW; BPFB 3; BYA 2,
3, 13; CA 1-4R; 25-28R; CANR 1, 35;
CDALB 1929-1941; DA; DA3; DAB;
DAC; DAM DRAM, MST, NOV; DLB 7,
9, 212, 275; DLBD 2; EWL 3; EXPS;
LAIT 3; MTCW 1, 2; NFS 1, 5, 7, 17,
19; RGAL 4; RGSF 2; RHW; SATA 9;
SSFS 3, 6; TCWW 2; TUS; WYA; YAW

Steinem, Gloria 1934- .... **CLC 63**
See also CA 53-56; CANR 28, 51; DLB
246; FW; MTCW 1, 2

Steiner, George 1929- .... **CLC 24**
See also CA 73-76; CANR 31, 67, 108;
DAM NOV; DLB 67, 299; EWL 3;
MTCW 1, 2; SATA 62

Steiner, K. Leslie
See Delany, Samuel R(ay), Jr.

Steiner, Rudolf 1861-1925 .... **TCLC 13**
See also CA 107

Stendhal 1783-1842 .. **NCLC 23, 46; SSC 27;
WLC**
See also DA; DA3; DAB; DAC; DAM
MST, NOV; DLB 119; EW 5; GFL 1789
to the Present; RGWL 2, 3; TWA

Stephen, Adeline Virginia
See Woolf, (Adeline) Virginia

Stephen, Sir Leslie 1832-1904 .... **TCLC 23**
See also BRW 5; CA 123; DLB 57, 144,
190

Stephen, Sir Leslie
See Stephen, Sir Leslie

Stephen, Virginia
See Woolf, (Adeline) Virginia

Stephens, James 1882(?)-1950 .... **SSC 50;
TCLC 4**
See also CA 104; 192; DLB 19, 153, 162;
EWL 3; FANT; RGEL 2; SUFW

Stephens, Reed
See Donaldson, Stephen R(eeder)

Steptoe, Lydia
See Barnes, Djuna
See also GLL 1

Sterchi, Beat 1949- .... **CLC 65**
See also CA 203

Sterling, Brett
See Bradbury, Ray (Douglas); Hamilton,
Edmond

Sterling, Bruce 1954- .... **CLC 72**
See also CA 119; CANR 44; SCFW 2; SFW
4

Sterling, George 1869-1926 .... **TCLC 20**
See also CA 117; 165; DLB 54

Stern, Gerald 1925- .... **CLC 40, 100**
See also AMWS 9; CA 81-84; CANR 28,
94; CP 7; DLB 105; RGAL 4

Stern, Richard (Gustave) 1928- ... **CLC 4, 39**
See also CA 1-4R; CANR 1, 25, 52, 120;
CN 7; DLB 218; DLBY 1987; INT
CANR-25

Sternberg, Josef von 1894-1969 .... **CLC 20**
See also CA 81-84

Sterne, Laurence 1713-1768 .... **LC 2, 48;
WLC**
See also BRW 3; BRWC 1; CDBLB 1660-
1789; DA; DAB; DAC; DAM MST, NOV;
DLB 39; RGEL 2; TEA

Sternheim, (William Adolf) Carl
1878-1942 .... **TCLC 8**
See also CA 105; 193; DLB 56, 118; EWL
3; RGWL 2, 3

Stevens, Mark 1951- .... **CLC 34**
See also CA 122

Stevens, Wallace 1879-1955 . **PC 6; TCLC 3,
12, 45; WLC**
See also AMW; AMWR 1; CA 104; 124;
CDALB 1929-1941; DA; DA3; DAB;
DAC; DAM MST, POET; DLB 54; EWL
3; EXPP; MTCW 1, 2; PAB; PFS 13, 16;
RGAL 4; TUS; WP

Stevenson, Anne (Katharine) 1933- .. **CLC 7,
33**
See also BRWS 6; CA 17-20R; CAAS 9;
CANR 9, 33, 123; CP 7; CWP; DLB 40;
MTCW 1; RHW

Stevenson, Robert Louis (Balfour)
1850-1894 ...... **NCLC 5, 14, 63; SSC 11,
51; WLC**
See also AAYA 24; BPFB 3; BRW 5;
BRWC 1; BRWR 1; BYA 1, 2, 4, 13; CD-
BLB 1890-1914; CLR 10, 11; DA; DA3;
DAB; DAC; DAM MST, NOV; DLB 18,
57, 141, 156, 174; DLBD 13; HGG;
JRDA; LAIT 1, 3; MAICYA 1, 2; NFS
11; RGEL 2; RGSF 2; SATA 100; SUFW;
TEA; WCH; WLIT 4; WYA; YABC 2;
YAW

Stewart, J(ohn) I(nnes) M(ackintosh)
1906-1994 .... **CLC 7, 14, 32**
See Innes, Michael
See also CA 85-88; 147; CAAS 3; CANR
47; CMW 4; MTCW 1, 2

Stewart, Mary (Florence Elinor)
1916- .... **CLC 7, 35, 117**
See also AAYA 29; BPFB 3; CA 1-4R;
CANR 1, 59, 130; CMW 4; CPW; DAB;
FANT; RHW; SATA 12; YAW

Stewart, Mary Rainbow
See Stewart, Mary (Florence Elinor)

Stifle, June
See Campbell, Maria

Stifter, Adalbert 1805-1868 .. **NCLC 41; SSC
28**
See also CDWLB 2; DLB 133; RGSF 2;
RGWL 2, 3

Still, James 1906-2001 .... **CLC 49**
See also CA 65-68; 195; CAAS 17; CANR
10, 26; CSW; DLB 9; DLBY 01; SATA
29; SATA-Obit 127

Sting 1951-
See Sumner, Gordon Matthew
See also CA 167

Stirling, Arthur
See Sinclair, Upton (Beall)

Stitt, Milan 1941- .... **CLC 29**
See also CA 69-72

Stockton, Francis Richard 1834-1902
See Stockton, Frank R.
See also CA 108; 137; MAICYA 1, 2; SATA
44; SFW 4

Stockton, Frank R. .... **TCLC 47**
See Stockton, Francis Richard
See also BYA 4, 13; DLB 42, 74; DLBD
13; EXPS; SATA-Brief 32; SSFS 3;
SUFW; WCH

Stoddard, Charles
See Kuttner, Henry

Stoker, Abraham 1847-1912
See Stoker, Bram
See also CA 105; 150; DA; DA3; DAC;
DAM MST, NOV; HGG; SATA 29

Stoker, Bram . **SSC 62; TCLC 8, 144; WLC**
See Stoker, Abraham
See also AAYA 23; BPFB 3; BRWS 3; BYA
5; CDBLB 1890-1914; DAB; DLB 36, 70,
178; LATS 1; NFS 18; RGEL 2; SUFW;
TEA; WLIT 4

Stolz, Mary (Slattery) 1920- .... **CLC 12**
See also AAYA 8; AITN 1; CA 5-8R;
CANR 13, 41, 112; JRDA; MAICYA 1,
2; SAAS 3; SATA 10, 71, 133; YAW

Stone, Irving 1903-1989 .... **CLC 7**
See also AITN 1; BPFB 3; CA 1-4R; 129;
CAAS 3; CANR 1, 23; CPW; DA3; DAM
POP; INT CANR-23; MTCW 1, 2; RHW;
SATA 3; SATA-Obit 64

Stone, Oliver (William) 1946- .... **CLC 73**
See also AAYA 15; CA 110; CANR 55, 125

Stone, Robert (Anthony) 1937- ... **CLC 5, 23,
42, 175**
See also AMWS 5; BPFB 3; CA 85-88;
CANR 23, 66, 95; CN 7; DLB 152; EWL
3; INT CANR-23; MTCW 1

Swanson, Logan
See Matheson, Richard (Burton)

Swarthout, Glendon (Fred)
1918-1992 .... **CLC 35**
See also AAYA 55; CA 1-4R; 139; CANR
1, 47; LAIT 5; SATA 26; TCWW 2; YAW

Sweet, Sarah C.
See Jewett, (Theodora) Sarah Orne

Swenson, May 1919-1989 ...... **CLC 4, 14, 61,**
106; PC 14
See also AMWS 4; CA 5-8R; 130; CANR
36, 61, 131; DA; DAB; DAC; DAM MST,
POET; DLB 5; EXPP; GLL 2; MTCW 1,
2; PFS 16; SATA 15; WP

Swift, Augustus
See Lovecraft, H(oward) P(hillips)

Swift, Graham (Colin) 1949- ...... **CLC 41, 88**
See also BRWC 2; BRWS 5; CA 117; 122;
CANR 46, 71, 128; CN 7; DLB 194;
MTCW 2; NFS 18; RGSF 2

Swift, Jonathan 1667-1745 ..... **LC 1, 42, 101;**
PC 9; WLC
See also AAYA 41; BRW 3; BRWC 1;
BRWR 1; BYA 5, 14; CDBLB 1660-1789;
CLR 53; DA; DA3; DAB; DAC; DAM
MST, NOV, POET; DLB 39, 95, 101;
EXPN; LAIT 1; NFS 6; RGEL 2; SATA
19; TEA; WCH; WLIT 3

Swinburne, Algernon Charles
1837-1909 ... **PC 24; TCLC 8, 36; WLC**
See also BRW 5; CA 105; 140; CDBLB
1832-1890; DA; DA3; DAB; DAC; DAM
MST, POET; DLB 35, 57; PAB; RGEL 2;
TEA

Swinfen, Ann .... **CLC 34**
See also CA 202

Swinnerton, Frank Arthur
1884-1982 .... **CLC 31**
See also CA 108; DLB 34

Swithen, John
See King, Stephen (Edwin)

Sylvia
See Ashton-Warner, Sylvia (Constance)

Symmes, Robert Edward
See Duncan, Robert (Edward)

Symonds, John Addington
1840-1893 .... **NCLC 34**
See also DLB 57, 144

Symons, Arthur 1865-1945 .... **TCLC 11**
See also CA 107; 189; DLB 19, 57, 149;
RGEL 2

Symons, Julian (Gustave)
1912-1994 .... **CLC 2, 14, 32**
See also CA 49-52; 147; CAAS 3; CANR
3, 33, 59; CMW 4; DLB 87, 155; DLBY
1992; MSW; MTCW 1

Synge, (Edmund) J(ohn) M(illington)
1871-1909 .... **DC 2; TCLC 6, 37**
See also BRW 6; BRWR 1; CA 104; 141;
CDBLB 1890-1914; DAM DRAM; DFS
18; DLB 10, 19; EWL 3; RGEL 2; TEA;
WLIT 4

Syruc, J.
See Milosz, Czeslaw

Szirtes, George 1948- .... **CLC 46; PC 51**
See also CA 109; CANR 27, 61, 117; CP 7

Szymborska, Wislawa 1923- ... **CLC 99, 190;**
PC 44
See also CA 154; CANR 91; CDWLB 4;
CWP; CWW 2; DA3; DLB 232; DLBY
1996; EWL 3; MTCW 2; PFS 15; RGWL
3

T. O., Nik
See Annensky, Innokenty (Fyodorovich)

Tabori, George 1914- .... **CLC 19**
See also CA 49-52; CANR 4, 69; CBD; CD
5; DLB 245

Tacitus c. 55-c. 117 .... **CMLC 56**
See also AW 2; CDWLB 1; DLB 211;
RGWL 2, 3

Tagore, Rabindranath 1861-1941 .... **PC 8;**
SSC 48; TCLC 3, 53
See also CA 104; 120; DA3; DAM DRAM,
POET; EWL 3; MTCW 1, 2; PFS 18;
RGEL 2; RGSF 2; RGWL 2, 3; TWA

Taine, Hippolyte Adolphe
1828-1893 .... **NCLC 15**
See also EW 7; GFL 1789 to the Present

Talayesva, Don C. 1890-(?) .... **NNAL**

Talese, Gay 1932- .... **CLC 37**
See also AITN 1; CA 1-4R; CANR 9, 58;
DLB 185; INT CANR-9; MTCW 1, 2

Tallent, Elizabeth (Ann) 1954- .... **CLC 45**
See also CA 117; CANR 72; DLB 130

Tallmountain, Mary 1918-1997 .... **NNAL**
See also CA 146; 161; DLB 193

Tally, Ted 1952- .... **CLC 42**
See also CA 120; 124; CAD; CANR 125;
CD 5; INT CA-124

Talvik, Heiti 1904-1947 .... **TCLC 87**
See also EWL 3

Tamayo y Baus, Manuel
1829-1898 .... **NCLC 1**

Tammsaare, A(nton) H(ansen)
1878-1940 .... **TCLC 27**
See also CA 164; CDWLB 4; DLB 220;
EWL 3

Tam'si, Tchicaya U
See Tchicaya, Gerald Felix

Tan, Amy (Ruth) 1952- . **AAL; CLC 59, 120,**
151
See also AAYA 9, 48; AMWS 10; BEST
89:3; BPFB 3; CA 136; CANR 54, 105;
CDALBS; CN 7; CPW 1; DA3; DAM
MULT, NOV, POP; DLB 173; EXPN;
FW; LAIT 3, 5; MTCW 2; NFS 1, 13, 16;
RGAL 4; SATA 75; SSFS 9; YAW

Tandem, Felix
See Spitteler, Carl (Friedrich Georg)

Tanizaki, Jun'ichiro 1886-1965 ... **CLC 8, 14,**
28; SSC 21
See Tanizaki Jun'ichiro
See also CA 93-96; 25-28R; MJW; MTCW
2; RGSF 2; RGWL 2

Tanizaki Jun'ichiro
See Tanizaki, Jun'ichiro
See also DLB 180; EWL 3

Tanner, William
See Amis, Kingsley (William)

Tao Lao
See Storni, Alfonsina

Tapahonso, Luci 1953- .... **NNAL**
See also CA 145; CANR 72, 127; DLB 175

Tarantino, Quentin (Jerome)
1963- .... **CLC 125**
See also CA 171; CANR 125

Tarassoff, Lev
See Troyat, Henri

Tarbell, Ida M(inerva) 1857-1944 . **TCLC 40**
See also CA 122; 181; DLB 47

Tarkington, (Newton) Booth
1869-1946 .... **TCLC 9**
See also BPFB 3; BYA 3; CA 110; 143;
CWRI 5; DLB 9, 102; MTCW 2; RGAL
4; SATA 17

Tarkovskii, Andrei Arsen'evich
See Tarkovsky, Andrei (Arsenyevich)

Tarkovsky, Andrei (Arsenyevich)
1932-1986 .... **CLC 75**
See also CA 127

Tartt, Donna 1963- .... **CLC 76**
See also CA 142

Tasso, Torquato 1544-1595 .... **LC 5, 94**
See also EFS 2; EW 2; RGWL 2, 3

Tate, (John Orley) Allen 1899-1979 .. **CLC 2,**
4, 6, 9, 11, 14, 24; PC 50
See also AMW; CA 5-8R; 85-88; CANR
32, 108; DLB 4, 45, 63; DLBD 17; EWL
3; MTCW 1, 2; RGAL 4; RHW

Tate, Ellalice
See Hibbert, Eleanor Alice Burford

Tate, James (Vincent) 1943- ..... **CLC 2, 6, 25**
See also CA 21-24R; CANR 29, 57, 114;
CP 7; DLB 5, 169; EWL 3; PFS 10, 15;
RGAL 4; WP

Tauler, Johannes c. 1300-1361 ...... **CMLC 37**
See also DLB 179; LMFS 1

Tavel, Ronald 1940- .... **CLC 6**
See also CA 21-24R; CAD; CANR 33; CD
5

Taviani, Paolo 1931- .... **CLC 70**
See also CA 153

Taylor, Bayard 1825-1878 .... **NCLC 89**
See also DLB 3, 189, 250, 254; RGAL 4

Taylor, C(ecil) P(hilip) 1929-1981 ... **CLC 27**
See also CA 25-28R; 105; CANR 47; CBD

Taylor, Edward 1642(?)-1729 .... **LC 11**
See also AMW; DA; DAB; DAC; DAM
MST, POET; DLB 24; EXPP; RGAL 4;
TUS

Taylor, Eleanor Ross 1920- .... **CLC 5**
See also CA 81-84; CANR 70

Taylor, Elizabeth 1932-1975 ..... **CLC 2, 4, 29**
See also CA 13-16R; CANR 9, 70; DLB
139; MTCW 1; RGEL 2; SATA 13

Taylor, Frederick Winslow
1856-1915 .... **TCLC 76**
See also CA 188

Taylor, Henry (Splawn) 1942- .... **CLC 44**
See also CA 33-36R; CAAS 7; CANR 31;
CP 7; DLB 5; PFS 10

Taylor, Kamala (Purnaiya) 1924-2004
See Markandaya, Kamala
See also CA 77-80; NFS 13

Taylor, Mildred D(elois) 1943- .... **CLC 21**
See also AAYA 10, 47; BW 1; BYA 3, 8;
CA 85-88; CANR 25, 115; CLR 9, 59,
90; CSW; DLB 52; JRDA; LAIT 3; MAI-
CYA 1, 2; SAAS 5; SATA 135; WYA;
YAW

Taylor, Peter (Hillsman) 1917-1994 .. **CLC 1,**
4, 18, 37, 44, 50, 71; SSC 10
See also AMWS 5; BPFB 3; CA 13-16R;
147; CANR 9, 50; CSW; DLB 218, 278;
DLBY 1981, 1994; EWL 3; EXPS; INT
CANR-9; MTCW 1, 2; RGSF 2; SSFS 9;
TUS

Taylor, Robert Lewis 1912-1998 .... **CLC 14**
See also CA 1-4R; 170; CANR 3, 64; SATA
10

Tchekhov, Anton
See Chekhov, Anton (Pavlovich)

Tchicaya, Gerald Felix 1931-1988 .. **CLC 101**
See Tchicaya U Tam'si
See also CA 129; 125; CANR 81

Tchicaya U Tam'si
See Tchicaya, Gerald Felix
See also EWL 3

Teasdale, Sara 1884-1933 .... **PC 31; TCLC 4**
See also CA 104; 163; DLB 45; GLL 1;
PFS 14; RGAL 4; SATA 32; TUS

Tecumseh 1768-1813 .... **NNAL**
See also DAM MULT

Tegner, Esaias 1782-1846 .... **NCLC 2**

Teilhard de Chardin, (Marie Joseph) Pierre
1881-1955 .... **TCLC 9**
See also CA 105; 210; GFL 1789 to the
Present

Temple, Ann
See Mortimer, Penelope (Ruth)

Urquhart, Jane 1949- .... **CLC 90**
See also CA 113; CANR 32, 68, 116; CCA
1; DAC

Usigli, Rodolfo 1905-1979 .... **HLCS 1**
See also CA 131; EWL 3; HW 1; LAW

Ustinov, Peter (Alexander)
1921-2004 .... **CLC 1**
See also AITN 1; CA 13-16R; 225; CANR
25, 51; CBD; CD 5; DLB 13; MTCW 2

U Tam'si, Gerald Felix Tchicaya
See Tchicaya, Gerald Felix

U Tam'si, Tchicaya
See Tchicaya, Gerald Felix

Vachss, Andrew (Henry) 1942- .... **CLC 106**
See also CA 118, 214; CAAE 214; CANR
44, 95; CMW 4

Vachss, Andrew H.
See Vachss, Andrew (Henry)

Vaculik, Ludvik 1926- .... **CLC 7**
See also CA 53-56; CANR 72; CWW 2;
DLB 232; EWL 3

Vaihinger, Hans 1852-1933 .... **TCLC 71**
See also CA 116; 166

Valdez, Luis (Miguel) 1940- ..... **CLC 84; DC**
10; HLC 2
See also CA 101; CAD; CANR 32, 81; CD
5; DAM MULT; DFS 5; DLB 122; EWL
3; HW 1; LAIT 4; LLW 1

Valenzuela, Luisa 1938- .... **CLC 31, 104;**
HLCS 2; SSC 14
See also CA 101; CANR 32, 65, 123; CD-
WLB 3; CWW 2; DAM MULT; DLB 113;
EWL 3; FW; HW 1, 2; LAW; RGSF 2;
RGWL 3

Valera y Alcala-Galiano, Juan
1824-1905 .... **TCLC 10**
See also CA 106

Valerius Maximus fl. 20- .... **CMLC 64**
See also DLB 211

Valery, (Ambroise) Paul (Toussaint Jules)
1871-1945 .... **PC 9; TCLC 4, 15**
See also CA 104; 122; DA3; DAM POET;
DLB 258; EW 8; EWL 3; GFL 1789 to
the Present; MTCW 1, 2; RGWL 2, 3;
TWA

Valle-Inclan, Ramon (Maria) del
1866-1936 .... **HLC 2; TCLC 5**
See also CA 106; 153; CANR 80; DAM
MULT; DLB 134; EW 8; EWL 3; HW 2;
RGSF 2; RGWL 2, 3

Vallejo, Antonio Buero
See Buero Vallejo, Antonio

Vallejo, Cesar (Abraham)
1892-1938 .... **HLC 2; TCLC 3, 56**
See also CA 105; 153; DAM MULT; DLB
290; EWL 3; HW 1; LAW; RGWL 2, 3

Valles, Jules 1832-1885 .... **NCLC 71**
See also DLB 123; GFL 1789 to the Present

Vallette, Marguerite Eymery
1860-1953 .... **TCLC 67**
See Rachilde
See also CA 182; DLB 123, 192

Valle Y Pena, Ramon del
See Valle-Inclan, Ramon (Maria) del

Van Ash, Cay 1918-1994 .... **CLC 34**
See also CA 220

Vanbrugh, Sir John 1664-1726 .... **LC 21**
See also BRW 2; DAM DRAM; DLB 80;
IDTP; RGEL 2

Van Campen, Karl
See Campbell, John W(ood, Jr.)

Vance, Gerald
See Silverberg, Robert

Vance, Jack .... **CLC 35**
See Vance, John Holbrook
See also DLB 8; FANT; SCFW 2; SFW 4;
SUFW 1, 2

Vance, John Holbrook 1916-
See Queen, Ellery; Vance, Jack
See also CA 29-32R; CANR 17, 65; CMW
4; MTCW 1

Van Den Bogarde, Derek Jules Gaspard
Ulric Niven 1921-1999 .... **CLC 14**
See Bogarde, Dirk
See also CA 77-80; 179

Vandenburgh, Jane .... **CLC 59**
See also CA 168

Vanderhaeghe, Guy 1951- .... **CLC 41**
See also BPFB 3; CA 113; CANR 72

van der Post, Laurens (Jan)
1906-1996 .... **CLC 5**
See also AFW; CA 5-8R; 155; CANR 35;
CN 7; DLB 204; RGEL 2

van de Wetering, Janwillem 1931- ... **CLC 47**
See also CA 49-52; CANR 4, 62, 90; CMW
4

Van Dine, S. S. .... **TCLC 23**
See Wright, Willard Huntington
See also MSW

Van Doren, Carl (Clinton)
1885-1950 .... **TCLC 18**
See also CA 111; 168

Van Doren, Mark 1894-1972 .... **CLC 6, 10**
See also CA 1-4R; 37-40R; CANR 3; DLB
45, 284; MTCW 1, 2; RGAL 4

Van Druten, John (William)
1901-1957 .... **TCLC 2**
See also CA 104; 161; DLB 10; RGAL 4

Van Duyn, Mona (Jane) 1921- ...... **CLC 3, 7,**
63, 116
See also CA 9-12R; CANR 7, 38, 60, 116;
CP 7; CWP; DAM POET; DLB 5; PFS
20

Van Dyne, Edith
See Baum, L(yman) Frank

van Itallie, Jean-Claude 1936- .... **CLC 3**
See also CA 45-48; CAAS 2; CAD; CANR
1, 48; CD 5; DLB 7

Van Loot, Cornelius Obenchain
See Roberts, Kenneth (Lewis)

van Ostaijen, Paul 1896-1928 .... **TCLC 33**
See also CA 163

Van Peebles, Melvin 1932- .... **CLC 2, 20**
See also BW 2, 3; CA 85-88; CANR 27,
67, 82; DAM MULT

van Schendel, Arthur(-Francois-Emile)
1874-1946 .... **TCLC 56**
See also EWL 3

Vansittart, Peter 1920- .... **CLC 42**
See also CA 1-4R; CANR 3, 49, 90; CN 7;
RHW

Van Vechten, Carl 1880-1964 ... **CLC 33; HR**
3
See also AMWS 2; CA 183; 89-92; DLB 4,
9, 51; RGAL 4

van Vogt, A(lfred) E(lton) 1912-2000 . **CLC 1**
See also BPFB 3; BYA 13, 14; CA 21-24R;
190; CANR 28; DLB 8, 251; SATA 14;
SATA-Obit 124; SCFW; SFW 4

Vara, Madeleine
See Jackson, Laura (Riding)

Varda, Agnes 1928- .... **CLC 16**
See also CA 116; 122

Vargas Llosa, (Jorge) Mario (Pedro)
1939- .... **CLC 3, 6, 9, 10, 15, 31, 42, 85,**
181; HLC 2
See Llosa, (Jorge) Mario (Pedro) Vargas
See also BPFB 3; CA 73-76; CANR 18, 32,
42, 67, 116; CDWLB 3; DA; DA3; DAB;
DAC; DAM MST, MULT, NOV; DLB
145; DNFS 2; EWL 3; HW 1, 2; LAIT 5;
LATS 1; LAW; LAWS 1; MTCW 1, 2;
RGWL 2; SSFS 14; TWA; WLIT 1

Varnhagen von Ense, Rahel
1771-1833 .... **NCLC 130**
See also DLB 90

Vasiliu, George
See Bacovia, George

Vasiliu, Gheorghe
See Bacovia, George
See also CA 123; 189

Vassa, Gustavus
See Equiano, Olaudah

Vassilikos, Vassilis 1933- .... **CLC 4, 8**
See also CA 81-84; CANR 75; EWL 3

Vaughan, Henry 1621-1695 .... **LC 27**
See also BRW 2; DLB 131; PAB; RGEL 2

Vaughn, Stephanie .... **CLC 62**

Vazov, Ivan (Minchov) 1850-1921 . **TCLC 25**
See also CA 121; 167; CDWLB 4; DLB
147

Veblen, Thorstein B(unde)
1857-1929 .... **TCLC 31**
See also AMWS 1; CA 115; 165; DLB 246

Vega, Lope de 1562-1635 .... **HLCS 2; LC 23**
See also EW 2; RGWL 2, 3

Vendler, Helen (Hennessy) 1933- ... **CLC 138**
See also CA 41-44R; CANR 25, 72; MTCW
1, 2

Venison, Alfred
See Pound, Ezra (Weston Loomis)

Ventsel, Elena Sergeevna 1907-
See Grekova, I.
See also CA 154

Verdi, Marie de
See Mencken, H(enry) L(ouis)

Verdu, Matilde
See Cela, Camilo Jose

Verga, Giovanni (Carmelo)
1840-1922 .... **SSC 21; TCLC 3**
See also CA 104; 123; CANR 101; EW 7;
EWL 3; RGSF 2; RGWL 2, 3

Vergil 70B.C.-19B.C. ... **CMLC 9, 40; PC 12;**
WLCS
See Virgil
See also AW 2; DA; DA3; DAB; DAC;
DAM MST, POET; EFS 1; LMFS 1

Verhaeren, Emile (Adolphe Gustave)
1855-1916 .... **TCLC 12**
See also CA 109; EWL 3; GFL 1789 to the
Present

Verlaine, Paul (Marie) 1844-1896 .. **NCLC 2,**
51; PC 2, 32
See also DAM POET; DLB 217; EW 7;
GFL 1789 to the Present; LMFS 2; RGWL
2, 3; TWA

Verne, Jules (Gabriel) 1828-1905 ... **TCLC 6,**
52
See also AAYA 16; BYA 4; CA 110; 131;
CLR 88; DA3; DLB 123; GFL 1789 to
the Present; JRDA; LAIT 2; LMFS 2;
MAICYA 1, 2; RGWL 2, 3; SATA 21;
SCFW; SFW 4; TWA; WCH

Verus, Marcus Annius
See Aurelius, Marcus

Very, Jones 1813-1880 .... **NCLC 9**
See also DLB 1, 243; RGAL 4

Vesaas, Tarjei 1897-1970 .... **CLC 48**
See also CA 190; 29-32R; DLB 297; EW
11; EWL 3; RGWL 3

Vialis, Gaston
See Simenon, Georges (Jacques Christian)

Vian, Boris 1920-1959(?) .... **TCLC 9**
See also CA 106; 164; CANR 111; DLB
72; EWL 3; GFL 1789 to the Present;
MTCW 2; RGWL 2, 3

Viaud, (Louis Marie) Julien 1850-1923
See Loti, Pierre
See also CA 107

Vicar, Henry
See Felsen, Henry Gregor

Vicente, Gil 1465-c. 1536 .... **LC 99**
See also DLB 287; RGWL 2, 3

Vicker, Angus
See Felsen, Henry Gregor

Waldman, Anne (Lesley) 1945- .... **CLC 7**
See also BG 3; CA 37-40R; CAAS 17;
CANR 34, 69, 116; CP 7; CWP; DLB 16

Waldo, E. Hunter
See Sturgeon, Theodore (Hamilton)

Waldo, Edward Hamilton
See Sturgeon, Theodore (Hamilton)

Walker, Alice (Malsenior) 1944- .... **BLC 3;**
CLC 5, 6, 9, 19, 27, 46, 58, 103, 167;
PC 30; SSC 5; WLCS
See also AAYA 3, 33; AFAW 1, 2; AMWS
3; BEST 89:4; BPFB 3; BW 2, 3; CA 37-
40R; CANR 9, 27, 49, 66, 82, 131;
CDALB 1968-1988; CN 7; CPW; CSW;
DA; DA3; DAB; DAC; DAM MST,
MULT, NOV, POET, POP; DLB 6, 33,
143; EWL 3; EXPN; EXPS; FW; INT
CANR-27; LAIT 3; MAWW; MTCW 1,
2; NFS 5; RGAL 4; RGSF 2; SATA 31;
SSFS 2, 11; TUS; YAW

Walker, David Harry 1911-1992 ...... **CLC 14**
See also CA 1-4R; 137; CANR 1; CWRI 5;
SATA 8; SATA-Obit 71

Walker, Edward Joseph 1934-2004
See Walker, Ted
See also CA 21-24R; CANR 12, 28, 53; CP
7

Walker, George F. 1947- .... **CLC 44, 61**
See also CA 103; CANR 21, 43, 59; CD 5;
DAB; DAC; DAM MST; DLB 60

Walker, Joseph A. 1935- .... **CLC 19**
See also BW 1, 3; CA 89-92; CAD; CANR
26; CD 5; DAM DRAM, MST; DFS 12;
DLB 38

Walker, Margaret (Abigail)
1915-1998 .... **BLC; CLC 1, 6; PC 20;**
TCLC 129
See also AFAW 1, 2; BW 2, 3; CA 73-76;
172; CANR 26, 54, 76; CN 7; CP 7;
CSW; DAM MULT; DLB 76, 152; EXPP;
FW; MTCW 1, 2; RGAL 4; RHW

Walker, Ted .... **CLC 13**
See Walker, Edward Joseph
See also DLB 40

Wallace, David Foster 1962- ... **CLC 50, 114;**
SSC 68
See also AAYA 50; AMWS 10; CA 132;
CANR 59; DA3; MTCW 2

Wallace, Dexter
See Masters, Edgar Lee

Wallace, (Richard Horatio) Edgar
1875-1932 .... **TCLC 57**
See also CA 115; 218; CMW 4; DLB 70;
MSW; RGEL 2

Wallace, Irving 1916-1990 .... **CLC 7, 13**
See also AITN 1; BPFB 3; CA 1-4R; 132;
CAAS 1; CANR 1, 27; CPW; DAM NOV,
POP; INT CANR-27; MTCW 1, 2

Wallant, Edward Lewis 1926-1962 ... **CLC 5,**
10
See also CA 1-4R; CANR 22; DLB 2, 28,
143, 299; EWL 3; MTCW 1, 2; RGAL 4

Wallas, Graham 1858-1932 .... **TCLC 91**

Waller, Edmund 1606-1687 .... **LC 86**
See also BRW 2; DAM POET; DLB 126;
PAB; RGEL 2

Walley, Byron
See Card, Orson Scott

Walpole, Horace 1717-1797 .... **LC 2, 49**
See also BRW 3; DLB 39, 104, 213; HGG;
LMFS 1; RGEL 2; SUFW 1; TEA

Walpole, Hugh (Seymour)
1884-1941 .... **TCLC 5**
See also CA 104; 165; DLB 34; HGG;
MTCW 2; RGEL 2; RHW

Walrond, Eric (Derwent) 1898-1966 .... **HR 3**
See also BW 1; CA 125; DLB 51

Walser, Martin 1927- .... **CLC 27, 183**
See also CA 57-60; CANR 8, 46; CWW 2;
DLB 75, 124; EWL 3

Walser, Robert 1878-1956 ..... **SSC 20; TCLC**
18
See also CA 118; 165; CANR 100; DLB
66; EWL 3

Walsh, Gillian Paton
See Paton Walsh, Gillian

Walsh, Jill Paton .... **CLC 35**
See Paton Walsh, Gillian
See also CLR 2, 65; WYA

Walter, Villiam Christian
See Andersen, Hans Christian

Walters, Anna L(ee) 1946- .... **NNAL**
See also CA 73-76

Walther von der Vogelweide c.
1170-1228 .... **CMLC 56**

Walton, Izaak 1593-1683 .... **LC 72**
See also BRW 2; CDBLB Before 1660;
DLB 151, 213; RGEL 2

Wambaugh, Joseph (Aloysius), Jr.
1937- .... **CLC 3, 18**
See also AITN 1; BEST 89:3; BPFB 3; CA
33-36R; CANR 42, 65, 115; CMW 4;
CPW 1; DA3; DAM NOV, POP; DLB 6;
DLBY 1983; MSW; MTCW 1, 2

Wang Wei 699(?)-761(?) .... **PC 18**
See also TWA

Warburton, William 1698-1779 .... **LC 97**
See also DLB 104

Ward, Arthur Henry Sarsfield 1883-1959
See Rohmer, Sax
See also CA 108; 173; CMW 4; HGG

Ward, Douglas Turner 1930- .... **CLC 19**
See also BW 1; CA 81-84; CAD; CANR
27; CD 5; DLB 7, 38

Ward, E. D.
See Lucas, E(dward) V(errall)

Ward, Mrs. Humphry 1851-1920
See Ward, Mary Augusta
See also RGEL 2

Ward, Mary Augusta 1851-1920 ... **TCLC 55**
See Ward, Mrs. Humphry
See also DLB 18

Ward, Peter
See Faust, Frederick (Schiller)

Warhol, Andy 1928(?)-1987 .... **CLC 20**
See also AAYA 12; BEST 89:4; CA 89-92;
121; CANR 34

Warner, Francis (Robert le Plastrier)
1937- .... **CLC 14**
See also CA 53-56; CANR 11

Warner, Marina 1946- .... **CLC 59**
See also CA 65-68; CANR 21, 55, 118; CN
7; DLB 194

Warner, Rex (Ernest) 1905-1986 ...... **CLC 45**
See also CA 89-92; 119; DLB 15; RGEL 2;
RHW

Warner, Susan (Bogert)
1819-1885 .... **NCLC 31**
See also DLB 3, 42, 239, 250, 254

Warner, Sylvia (Constance) Ashton
See Ashton-Warner, Sylvia (Constance)

Warner, Sylvia Townsend
1893-1978 .. **CLC 7, 19; SSC 23; TCLC**
131
See also BRWS 7; CA 61-64; 77-80; CANR
16, 60, 104; DLB 34, 139; EWL 3; FANT;
FW; MTCW 1, 2; RGEL 2; RGSF 2;
RHW

Warren, Mercy Otis 1728-1814 ..... **NCLC 13**
See also DLB 31, 200; RGAL 4; TUS

Warren, Robert Penn 1905-1989 .. **CLC 1, 4,**
6, 8, 10, 13, 18, 39, 53, 59; PC 37; SSC
4, 58; WLC
See also AITN 1; AMW; AMWC 2; BPFB
3; BYA 1; CA 13-16R; 129; CANR 10,
47; CDALB 1968-1988; DA; DA3; DAB;

DAC; DAM MST, NOV, POET; DLB 2,
48, 152; DLBY 1980, 1989; EWL 3; INT
CANR-10; MTCW 1, 2; NFS 13; RGAL
4; RGSF 2; RHW; SATA 46; SATA-Obit
63; SSFS 8; TUS

Warrigal, Jack
See Furphy, Joseph

Warshofsky, Isaac
See Singer, Isaac Bashevis

Warton, Joseph 1722-1800 .... **NCLC 118**
See also DLB 104, 109; RGEL 2

Warton, Thomas 1728-1790 .... **LC 15, 82**
See also DAM POET; DLB 104, 109;
RGEL 2

Waruk, Kona
See Harris, (Theodore) Wilson

Warung, Price .... **TCLC 45**
See Astley, William
See also DLB 230; RGEL 2

Warwick, Jarvis
See Garner, Hugh
See also CCA 1

Washington, Alex
See Harris, Mark

Washington, Booker T(aliaferro)
1856-1915 .... **BLC 3; TCLC 10**
See also BW 1; CA 114; 125; DA3; DAM
MULT; LAIT 2; RGAL 4; SATA 28

Washington, George 1732-1799 .... **LC 25**
See also DLB 31

Wassermann, (Karl) Jakob
1873-1934 .... **TCLC 6**
See also CA 104; 163; DLB 66; EWL 3

Wasserstein, Wendy 1950- ... **CLC 32, 59, 90,**
183; DC 4
See also CA 121; 129; CABS 3; CAD;
CANR 53, 75, 128; CD 5; CWD; DA3;
DAM DRAM; DFS 5, 17; DLB 228;
EWL 3; FW; INT CA-129; MTCW 2;
SATA 94

Waterhouse, Keith (Spencer) 1929- . **CLC 47**
See also CA 5-8R; CANR 38, 67, 109;
CBD; CN 7; DLB 13, 15; MTCW 1, 2

Waters, Frank (Joseph) 1902-1995 .. **CLC 88**
See also CA 5-8R; 149; CAAS 13; CANR
3, 18, 63, 121; DLB 212; DLBY 1986;
RGAL 4; TCWW 2

Waters, Mary C. .... **CLC 70**

Waters, Roger 1944- .... **CLC 35**

Watkins, Frances Ellen
See Harper, Frances Ellen Watkins

Watkins, Gerrold
See Malzberg, Barry N(athaniel)

Watkins, Gloria Jean 1952(?)- .... **CLC 94**
See also BW 2; CA 143; CANR 87, 126;
DLB 246; MTCW 2; SATA 115

Watkins, Paul 1964- .... **CLC 55**
See also CA 132; CANR 62, 98

Watkins, Vernon Phillips
1906-1967 .... **CLC 43**
See also CA 9-10; 25-28R; CAP 1; DLB
20; EWL 3; RGEL 2

Watson, Irving S.
See Mencken, H(enry) L(ouis)

Watson, John H.
See Farmer, Philip Jose

Watson, Richard F.
See Silverberg, Robert

Watts, Ephraim
See Horne, Richard Henry Hengist

Watts, Isaac 1674-1748 .... **LC 98**
See also DLB 95; RGEL 2; SATA 52

Waugh, Auberon (Alexander)
1939-2001 .... **CLC 7**
See also CA 45-48; 192; CANR 6, 22, 92;
DLB 14, 194

Westermarck, Edward 1862-1939 . **TCLC 87**

Westlake, Donald E(dwin) 1933- . **CLC 7, 33**
See also BPFB 3; CA 17-20R; CAAS 13; CANR 16, 44, 65, 94; CMW 4; CPW; DAM POP; INT CANR-16; MSW; MTCW 2

Westmacott, Mary
See Christie, Agatha (Mary Clarissa)

Weston, Allen
See Norton, Andre

Wetcheek, J. L.
See Feuchtwanger, Lion

Wetering, Janwillem van de
See van de Wetering, Janwillem

Wetherald, Agnes Ethelwyn
1857-1940 .... **TCLC 81**
See also CA 202; DLB 99

Wetherell, Elizabeth
See Warner, Susan (Bogert)

Whale, James 1889-1957 .... **TCLC 63**

Whalen, Philip (Glenn) 1923-2002 .... **CLC 6, 29**
See also BG 3; CA 9-12R; 209; CANR 5, 39; CP 7; DLB 16; WP

Wharton, Edith (Newbold Jones)
1862-1937 ... **SSC 6; TCLC 3, 9, 27, 53, 129, 149; WLC**
See also AAYA 25; AMW; AMWC 2; AMWR 1; BPFB 3; CA 104; 132; CDALB 1865-1917; DA; DA3; DAB; DAC; DAM MST, NOV; DLB 4, 9, 12, 78, 189; DLBD 13; EWL 3; EXPS; HGG; LAIT 2, 3; LATS 1; MAWW; MTCW 1, 2; NFS 5, 11, 15; RGAL 4; RGSF 2; RHW; SSFS 6, 7; SUFW; TUS

Wharton, James
See Mencken, H(enry) L(ouis)

Wharton, William (a pseudonym) . **CLC 18, 37**
See also CA 93-96; DLBY 1980; INT CA-93-96

Wheatley (Peters), Phillis
1753(?)-1784 ... **BLC 3; LC 3, 50; PC 3; WLC**
See also AFAW 1, 2; CDALB 1640-1865; DA; DA3; DAC; DAM MST, MULT, POET; DLB 31, 50; EXPP; PFS 13; RGAL 4

Wheelock, John Hall 1886-1978 .... **CLC 14**
See also CA 13-16R; 77-80; CANR 14; DLB 45

Whim-Wham
See Curnow, (Thomas) Allen (Monro)

White, Babington
See Braddon, Mary Elizabeth

White, E(lwyn) B(rooks)
1899-1985 .... **CLC 10, 34, 39**
See also AITN 2; AMWS 1; CA 13-16R; 116; CANR 16, 37; CDALBS; CLR 1, 21; CPW; DA3; DAM POP; DLB 11, 22; EWL 3; FANT; MAICYA 1, 2; MTCW 1, 2; NCFS 5; RGAL 4; SATA 2, 29, 100; SATA-Obit 44; TUS

White, Edmund (Valentine III)
1940- .... **CLC 27, 110**
See also AAYA 7; CA 45-48; CANR 3, 19, 36, 62, 107; CN 7; DA3; DAM POP; DLB 227; MTCW 1, 2

White, Hayden V. 1928- .... **CLC 148**
See also CA 128; DLB 246

White, Patrick (Victor Martindale)
1912-1990 ...... **CLC 3, 4, 5, 7, 9, 18, 65, 69; SSC 39**
See also BRWS 1; CA 81-84; 132; CANR 43; DLB 260; EWL 3; MTCW 1; RGEL 2; RGSF 2; RHW; TWA; WWE 1

White, Phyllis Dorothy James 1920-
See James, P. D.
See also CA 21-24R; CANR 17, 43, 65, 112; CMW 4; CN 7; CPW; DA3; DAM POP; MTCW 1, 2; TEA

White, T(erence) H(anbury)
1906-1964 .... **CLC 30**
See also AAYA 22; BPFB 3; BYA 4, 5; CA 73-76; CANR 37; DLB 160; FANT; JRDA; LAIT 1; MAICYA 1, 2; RGEL 2; SATA 12; SUFW 1; YAW

White, Terence de Vere 1912-1994 ... **CLC 49**
See also CA 49-52; 145; CANR 3

White, Walter
See White, Walter F(rancis)

White, Walter F(rancis) 1893-1955 ... **BLC 3; HR 3; TCLC 15**
See also BW 1; CA 115; 124; DAM MULT; DLB 51

White, William Hale 1831-1913
See Rutherford, Mark
See also CA 121; 189

Whitehead, Alfred North
1861-1947 .... **TCLC 97**
See also CA 117; 165; DLB 100, 262

Whitehead, E(dward) A(nthony)
1933- .... **CLC 5**
See also CA 65-68; CANR 58, 118; CBD; CD 5

Whitehead, Ted
See Whitehead, E(dward) A(nthony)

Whiteman, Roberta J. Hill 1947- ...... **NNAL**
See also CA 146

Whitemore, Hugh (John) 1936- .... **CLC 37**
See also CA 132; CANR 77; CBD; CD 5; INT CA-132

Whitman, Sarah Helen (Power)
1803-1878 .... **NCLC 19**
See also DLB 1, 243

Whitman, Walt(er) 1819-1892 .. **NCLC 4, 31, 81; PC 3; WLC**
See also AAYA 42; AMW; AMWR 1; CDALB 1640-1865; DA; DA3; DAB; DAC; DAM MST, POET; DLB 3, 64, 224, 250; EXPP; LAIT 2; LMFS 1; PAB; PFS 2, 3, 13; RGAL 4; SATA 20; TUS; WP; WYAS 1

Whitney, Phyllis A(yame) 1903- .... **CLC 42**
See also AAYA 36; AITN 2; BEST 90:3; CA 1-4R; CANR 3, 25, 38, 60; CLR 59; CMW 4; CPW; DA3; DAM POP; JRDA; MAICYA 1, 2; MTCW 2; RHW; SATA 1, 30; YAW

Whittemore, (Edward) Reed, Jr.
1919- .... **CLC 4**
See also CA 9-12R; 219; CAAE 219; CAAS 8; CANR 4, 119; CP 7; DLB 5

Whittier, John Greenleaf
1807-1892 .... **NCLC 8, 59**
See also AMWS 1; DLB 1, 243; RGAL 4

Whittlebot, Hernia
See Coward, Noel (Peirce)

Wicker, Thomas Grey 1926-
See Wicker, Tom
See also CA 65-68; CANR 21, 46

Wicker, Tom .... **CLC 7**
See Wicker, Thomas Grey

Wideman, John Edgar 1941- ... **BLC 3; CLC 5, 34, 36, 67, 122; SSC 62**
See also AFAW 1, 2; AMWS 10; BPFB 4; BW 2, 3; CA 85-88; CANR 14, 42, 67, 109; CN 7; DAM MULT; DLB 33, 143; MTCW 2; RGAL 4; RGSF 2; SSFS 6, 12

Wiebe, Rudy (Henry) 1934- .. **CLC 6, 11, 14, 138**
See also CA 37-40R; CANR 42, 67, 123; CN 7; DAC; DAM MST; DLB 60; RHW

Wieland, Christoph Martin
1733-1813 .... **NCLC 17**
See also DLB 97; EW 4; LMFS 1; RGWL 2, 3

Wiene, Robert 1881-1938 .... **TCLC 56**

Wieners, John 1934- .... **CLC 7**
See also BG 3; CA 13-16R; CP 7; DLB 16; WP

Wiesel, Elie(zer) 1928- .... **CLC 3, 5, 11, 37, 165; WLCS**
See also AAYA 7, 54; AITN 1; CA 5-8R; CAAS 4; CANR 8, 40, 65, 125; CDALBS; DA; DA3; DAB; DAC; DAM MST, NOV; DLB 83, 299; DLBY 1987; EWL 3; INT CANR-8; LAIT 4; MTCW 1, 2; NCFS 4; NFS 4; RGWL 3; SATA 56; YAW

Wiggins, Marianne 1947- .... **CLC 57**
See also BEST 89:3; CA 130; CANR 60

Wiggs, Susan .... **CLC 70**
See also CA 201

Wight, James Alfred 1916-1995
See Herriot, James
See also CA 77-80; SATA 55; SATA-Brief 44

Wilbur, Richard (Purdy) 1921- ..... **CLC 3, 6, 9, 14, 53, 110; PC 51**
See also AMWS 3; CA 1-4R; CABS 2; CANR 2, 29, 76, 93; CDALBS; CP 7; DA; DAB; DAC; DAM MST, POET; DLB 5, 169; EWL 3; EXPP; INT CANR-29; MTCW 1, 2; PAB; PFS 11, 12, 16; RGAL 4; SATA 9, 108; WP

Wild, Peter 1940- .... **CLC 14**
See also CA 37-40R; CP 7; DLB 5

Wilde, Oscar (Fingal O'Flahertie Wills)
1854(?)-1900 ..... **DC 17; SSC 11; TCLC 1, 8, 23, 41; WLC**
See also AAYA 49; BRW 5; BRWC 1, 2; BRWR 2; BYA 15; CA 104; 119; CANR 112; CDBLB 1890-1914; DA; DA3; DAB; DAC; DAM DRAM, MST, NOV; DFS 4, 8, 9; DLB 10, 19, 34, 57, 141, 156, 190; EXPS; FANT; LATS 1; RGEL 2; RGSF 2; SATA 24; SSFS 7; SUFW; TEA; WCH; WLIT 4

Wilder, Billy .... **CLC 20**
See Wilder, Samuel
See also DLB 26

Wilder, Samuel 1906-2002
See Wilder, Billy
See also CA 89-92; 205

Wilder, Stephen
See Marlowe, Stephen

Wilder, Thornton (Niven)
1897-1975 .. **CLC 1, 5, 6, 10, 15, 35, 82; DC 1; WLC**
See also AAYA 29; AITN 2; AMW; CA 13-16R; 61-64; CAD; CANR 40; CDALBS; DA; DA3; DAB; DAC; DAM DRAM, MST, NOV; DFS 1, 4, 16; DLB 4, 7, 9, 228; DLBY 1997; EWL 3; LAIT 3; MTCW 1, 2; RGAL 4; RHW; WYAS 1

Wilding, Michael 1942- ...... **CLC 73; SSC 50**
See also CA 104; CANR 24, 49, 106; CN 7; RGSF 2

Wiley, Richard 1944- .... **CLC 44**
See also CA 121; 129; CANR 71

Wilhelm, Kate .... **CLC 7**
See Wilhelm, Katie (Gertrude)
See also AAYA 20; BYA 16; CAAS 5; DLB 8; INT CANR-17; SCFW 2

Wilhelm, Katie (Gertrude) 1928-
See Wilhelm, Kate
See also CA 37-40R; CANR 17, 36, 60, 94; MTCW 1; SFW 4

Wilkins, Mary
See Freeman, Mary E(leanor) Wilkins

Yanez, Jose Donoso
See Donoso (Yanez), Jose
Yanovsky, Basile S.
See Yanovsky, V(assily) S(emenovich)
Yanovsky, V(assily) S(emenovich)
1906-1989 .... CLC 2, 18
See also CA 97-100; 129
Yates, Richard 1926-1992 .... CLC 7, 8, 23
See also AMWS 11; CA 5-8R; 139; CANR
10, 43; DLB 2, 234; DLBY 1981, 1992;
INT CANR-10
Yeats, W. B.
See Yeats, William Butler
Yeats, William Butler 1865-1939 . PC 20, 51;
TCLC 1, 11, 18, 31, 93, 116; WLC
See also AAYA 48; BRW 6; BRWR 1; CA
104; 127; CANR 45; CDBLB 1890-1914;
DA; DA3; DAB; DAC; DAM DRAM,
MST, POET; DLB 10, 19, 98, 156; EWL
3; EXPP; MTCW 1, 2; NCFS 3; PAB;
PFS 1, 2, 5, 7, 13, 15; RGEL 2; TEA;
WLIT 4; WP
Yehoshua, A(braham) B. 1936- .. CLC 13, 31
See also CA 33-36R; CANR 43, 90; EWL
3; RGSF 2; RGWL 3
Yellow Bird
See Ridge, John Rollin
Yep, Laurence Michael 1948- .... CLC 35
See also AAYA 5, 31; BYA 7; CA 49-52;
CANR 1, 46, 92; CLR 3, 17, 54; DLB 52;
FANT; JRDA; MAICYA 1, 2; MAICYAS
1; SATA 7, 69, 123; WYA; YAW
Yerby, Frank G(arvin) 1916-1991 ..... BLC 3;
CLC 1, 7, 22
See also BPFB 3; BW 1, 3; CA 9-12R; 136;
CANR 16, 52; DLB 76; DAM MULT; DLB 76;
INT CANR-16; MTCW 1; RGAL 4; RHW
Yesenin, Sergei Alexandrovich
See Esenin, Sergei (Alexandrovich)
Yesenin, Sergey
See Esenin, Sergei (Alexandrovich)
See also EWL 3
Yevtushenko, Yevgeny (Alexandrovich)
1933- ...... CLC 1, 3, 13, 26, 51, 126; PC
40
See Evtushenko, Evgenii Aleksandrovich
See also CA 81-84; CANR 33, 54; CWW
2; DAM POET; EWL 3; MTCW 1
Yezierska, Anzia 1885(?)-1970 .... CLC 46
See also CA 126; 89-92; DLB 28, 221; FW;
MTCW 1; RGAL 4; SSFS 15
Yglesias, Helen 1915- .... CLC 7, 22
See also CA 37-40R; CAAS 20; CANR 15,
65, 95; CN 7; INT CANR-15; MTCW 1
Yokomitsu, Riichi 1898-1947 .... TCLC 47
See also CA 170; EWL 3
Yonge, Charlotte (Mary)
1823-1901 .... TCLC 48
See also CA 109; 163; DLB 18, 163; RGEL
2; SATA 17; WCH
York, Jeremy
See Creasey, John
York, Simon
See Heinlein, Robert A(nson)
Yorke, Henry Vincent 1905-1974 ..... CLC 13
See Green, Henry
See also CA 85-88; 49-52
Yosano Akiko 1878-1942 .... PC 11; TCLC 59
See also CA 161; EWL 3; RGWL 3
Yoshimoto, Banana .... CLC 84
See Yoshimoto, Mahoko
See also AAYA 50; NFS 7

Yoshimoto, Mahoko 1964-
See Yoshimoto, Banana
See also CA 144; CANR 98; SSFS 16
Young, Al(bert James) 1939- ... BLC 3; CLC
19
See also BW 2, 3; CA 29-32R; CANR 26,
65, 109; CN 7; CP 7; DAM MULT; DLB
33
Young, Andrew (John) 1885-1971 ...... CLC 5
See also CA 5-8R; CANR 7, 29; RGEL 2
Young, Collier
See Bloch, Robert (Albert)
Young, Edward 1683-1765 .... LC 3, 40
See also DLB 95; RGEL 2
Young, Marguerite (Vivian)
1909-1995 .... CLC 82
See also CA 13-16; 150; CAP 1; CN 7
Young, Neil 1945- .... CLC 17
See also CA 110; CCA 1
Young Bear, Ray A. 1950- ... CLC 94; NNAL
See also CA 146; DAM MULT; DLB 175
Yourcenar, Marguerite 1903-1987 ... CLC 19,
38, 50, 87
See also BPFB 3; CA 69-72; CANR 23, 60,
93; DAM NOV; DLB 72; DLBY 1988;
EW 12; EWL 3; GFL 1789 to the Present;
GLL 1; MTCW 1, 2; RGWL 2, 3
Yuan, Chu 340(?)B.C.-278(?)B.C. .. CMLC 36
Yurick, Sol 1925- .... CLC 6
See also CA 13-16R; CANR 25; CN 7
Zabolotsky, Nikolai Alekseevich
1903-1958 .... TCLC 52
See Zabolotsky, Nikolay Alekseevich
See also CA 116; 164
Zabolotsky, Nikolay Alekseevich
See Zabolotsky, Nikolai Alekseevich
See also EWL 3
Zagajewski, Adam 1945- .... PC 27
See also CA 186; DLB 232; EWL 3
Zalygin, Sergei -2000 .... CLC 59
Zamiatin, Evgenii
See Zamyatin, Evgeny Ivanovich
See also RGSF 2; RGWL 2, 3
Zamiatin, Evgenii Ivanovich
See Zamyatin, Evgeny Ivanovich
See also DLB 272
Zamiatin, Yevgenii
See Zamyatin, Evgeny Ivanovich
Zamora, Bernice (B. Ortiz) 1938- .. CLC 89;
HLC 2
See also CA 151; CANR 80; DAM MULT;
DLB 82; HW 1, 2
Zamyatin, Evgeny Ivanovich
1884-1937 .... TCLC 8, 37
See Zamiatin, Evgenii; Zamiatin, Evgenii
Ivanovich; Zamyatin, Yevgeny Ivanovich
See also CA 105; 166; EW 10; SFW 4
Zamyatin, Yevgeny Ivanovich
See Zamyatin, Evgeny Ivanovich
See also EWL 3
Zangwill, Israel 1864-1926 ... SSC 44; TCLC
16
See also CA 109; 167; CMW 4; DLB 10,
135, 197; RGEL 2
Zappa, Francis Vincent, Jr. 1940-1993
See Zappa, Frank
See also CA 108; 143; CANR 57
Zappa, Frank .... CLC 17
See Zappa, Francis Vincent, Jr.
Zaturenska, Marya 1902-1982 ..... CLC 6, 11
See also CA 13-16R; 105; CANR 22
Zayas y Sotomayor, Maria de 1590-c.
1661 .... LC 102
See also RGSF 2

Zeami 1363-1443 .... DC 7; LC 86
See also DLB 203; RGWL 2, 3
Zelazny, Roger (Joseph) 1937-1995 . CLC 21
See also AAYA 7; BPFB 3; CA 21-24R;
148; CANR 26, 60; CN 7; DLB 8; FANT;
MTCW 1, 2; SATA 57; SATA-Brief 39;
SCFW; SFW 4; SUFW 1, 2
Zhang Ailing 1920(?)-1995
See Chang, Eileen
See also CWW 2; RGSF 2
Zhdanov, Andrei Alexandrovich
1896-1948 .... TCLC 18
See also CA 117; 167
Zhukovsky, Vasilii Andreevich
See Zhukovsky, Vasily (Andreevich)
See also DLB 205
Zhukovsky, Vasily (Andreevich)
1783-1852 .... NCLC 35
See Zhukovsky, Vasilii Andreevich
Ziegenhagen, Eric .... CLC 55
Zimmer, Jill Schary
See Robinson, Jill
Zimmerman, Robert
See Dylan, Bob
Zindel, Paul 1936-2003 ...... CLC 6, 26; DC 5
See also AAYA 2, 37; BYA 2, 3, 8, 11, 14;
CA 73-76; 213; CAD; CANR 31, 65, 108;
CD 5; CDALBS; CLR 3, 45, 85; DA;
DA3; DAB; DAC; DAM DRAM, MST,
NOV; DFS 12; DLB 7, 52; JRDA; LAIT
5; MAICYA 1, 2; MTCW 1, 2; NFS 14;
SATA 16, 58, 102; SATA-Obit 142; WYA;
YAW
Zinov'Ev, A. A.
See Zinoviev, Alexander (Aleksandrovich)
Zinoviev, Alexander (Aleksandrovich)
1922- .... CLC 19
See also CA 116; 133; CAAS 10
Zizek, Slavoj 1949- .... CLC 188
See also CA 201
Zoilus
See Lovecraft, H(oward) P(hillips)
Zola, Emile (Edouard Charles Antoine)
1840-1902 ...... TCLC 1, 6, 21, 41; WLC
See also CA 104; 138; DA; DA3; DAB;
DAC; DAM MST, NOV; DLB 123; EW
7; GFL 1789 to the Present; IDTP; LMFS
1, 2; RGWL 1, 2; TWA
Zoline, Pamela 1941- .... CLC 62
See also CA 161; SFW 4
Zoroaster 628(?)B.C.-551(?)B.C. ... CMLC 40
Zorrilla y Moral, Jose 1817-1893 .... NCLC 6
Zoshchenko, Mikhail (Mikhailovich)
1895-1958 .... SSC 15; TCLC 15
See also CA 115; 160; EWL 3; RGSF 2;
RGWL 3
Zuckmayer, Carl 1896-1977 .... CLC 18
See also CA 69-72; DLB 56, 124; EWL 3;
RGWL 2, 3
Zuk, Georges
See Skelton, Robin
See also CCA 1
Zukofsky, Louis 1904-1978 ... CLC 1, 2, 4, 7,
11, 18; PC 11
See also AMWS 3; CA 9-12R; 77-80;
CANR 39; DAM POET; DLB 5, 165;
EWL 3; MTCW 1; RGAL 4
Zweig, Paul 1935-1984 .... CLC 34, 42
See also CA 85-88; 113
Zweig, Stefan 1881-1942 .... TCLC 17
See also CA 112; 170; DLB 81, 118; EWL
3
Zwingli, Huldreich 1484-1531 .... LC 37
See also DLB 179

PC Cumulative Nationality Index

AMERICAN

Aiken, Conrad (Potter) **26**
Alexie, Sherman **53**
Ammons, A(rchie) R(andolph) **16**
Angelou, Maya **32**
Ashbery, John (Lawrence) **26**
Auden, W(ystan) H(ugh) **1**
Baca, Jimmy Santiago **41**
Baraka, Amiri **4**
Berry, Wendell (Erdman) **28**
Bishop, Elizabeth **3, 34**
Bly, Robert (Elwood) **39**
Bogan, Louise **12**
Bradstreet, Anne **10**
Braithwaite, William **52**
Brodsky, Joseph **9**
Brooks, Gwendolyn (Elizabeth) **7**
Brown, Sterling Allen **55**
Bryant, William Cullen **20**
Bukowski, Charles **18**
Cage, John **58**
Carruth, Hayden **10**
Carver, Raymond **54**
Cervantes, Lorna Dee **35**
Chin, Marilyn (Mei Ling) **40**
Cisneros, Sandra **52**
Clampitt, Amy **19**
Clifton, (Thelma) Lucille **17**
Corso, (Nunzio) Gregory **33**
Crane, (Harold) Hart **3**
Cullen, Countée **20**
Cummings, E(dward) E(stlin) **5**
Dickey, James (Lafayette) **40**
Dickinson, Emily (Elizabeth) **1**
Doolittle, Hilda **5**
Doty, Mark **53**
Dove, Rita (Frances) **6**
Dunbar, Paul Laurence **5**
Duncan, Robert (Edward) **2**
Dylan, Bob **37**
Eliot, T(homas) S(tearns) **5, 31**
Emerson, Ralph Waldo **18**
Erdrich, Louise **52**
Ferlinghetti, Lawrence (Monsanto) **1**
Forché, Carolyn (Louise) **10**
Francis, Robert (Churchill) **34**
Frost, Robert (Lee) **1, 39**
Gallagher, Tess **9**
Ginsberg, Allen **4, 47**
Giovanni, Nikki **19**
Glück, Louise (Elisabeth) **16**
Guest, Barbara **55**
Hacker, Marilyn **47**
Hammon, Jupiter **16**
Harjo, Joy **27**
Harper, Frances Ellen Watkins **21**

Hass, Robert **16**
Hayden, Robert E(arl) **6**
H. D. **5**
Hogan, Linda **35**
Hongo, Garrett Kaoru **23**
Howe, Susan **54**
Hughes, (James) Langston **1, 53**
Ignatow, David **34**
Jackson, Laura (Riding) **44**
Jarrell, Randall **41**
Jeffers, (John) Robinson **17**
Johnson, James Weldon **24**
Jordan, June **38**
Kenyon, Jane **57**
Kinnell, Galway **26**
Knight, Etheridge **14**
Komunyakaa, Yusef **51**
Kumin, Maxine (Winokur) **15**
Kunitz, Stanley (Jasspon) **19**
Lanier, Sidney **50**
Levertov, Denise **11**
Levine, Philip **22**
Lindsay, (Nicholas) Vachel **23**
Longfellow, Henry Wadsworth **30**
Lorde, Audre (Geraldine) **12**
Lowell, Amy **13**
Lowell, Robert (Traill Spence Jr.) **3**
Loy, Mina **16**
MacLeish, Archibald **47**
Mackey, Nathaniel **49**
Madhubuti, Haki R. **5**
Masters, Edgar Lee **1, 36**
Meredith, William (Morris) **28**
Merrill, James (Ingram) **28**
Merton, Thomas **10**
Merwin, W. S. **45**
Millay, Edna St. Vincent **6**
Momaday, N(avarre) Scott **25**
Moore, Marianne (Craig) **4, 49**
Mueller, Lisel **33**
Nash, (Frediric) Ogden **21**
Nemerov, Howard (Stanley) **24**
Niedecker, Lorine **42**
O'Hara, Frank **45**
Olds, Sharon **22**
Olson, Charles (John) **19**
Oppen, George **35**
Ortiz, Simon J(oseph) **17**
Parker, Dorothy (Rothschild) **28**
Piercy, Marge **29**
Pinsky, Robert **27**
Plath, Sylvia **1, 37**
Poe, Edgar Allan **1, 54**
Pound, Ezra (Weston Loomis) **4**
Quintana, Leroy V. **36**
Reese, Lizette Woodworth **29**

Rexroth, Kenneth **20**
Rich, Adrienne (Cecile) **5**
Riley, James Whitcomb **48**
Ríos, Alberto **57**
Robinson, Edwin Arlington **1, 35**
Roethke, Theodore (Huebner) **15**
Rose, Wendy **13**
Rukeyser, Muriel **12**
Sanchez, Sonia **9**
Sandburg, Carl (August) **2, 41**
Sarton, (Eleanor) May **39**
Schwartz, Delmore (David) **8**
Schnackenberg, Gjertrud **45**
Schwerner, Armand **42**
Sexton, Anne (Harvey) **2**
Shapiro, Karl (Jay) **25**
Silverstein, Shel **49**
Snyder, Gary (Sherman) **21**
Song, Cathy **21**
Soto, Gary **28**
Stein, Gertrude **18**
Stevens, Wallace **6**
Stone, Ruth **53**
Stryk, Lucien **27**
Swenson, May **14**
Tate, Allen **50**
Teasdale, Sara **31**
Thoreau, Henry David **30**
Toomer, Jean **7**
Urista, Alberto H. **34**
Viereck, Peter (Robert Edwin) **27**
Wagoner, David (Russell) **33**
Wakoski, Diane **15**
Walker, Alice (Malsenior) **30**
Walker, Margaret (Abigail) **20**
Warren, Robert Penn **37**
Wheatley (Peters), Phillis **3**
Whitman, Walt(er) **3**
Wilbur, Richard **51**
Williams, William Carlos **7**
Wright, James (Arlington) **36**
Wylie, Elinor (Morton Hoyt) **23**
Yamada, Mitsuye **44**
Zukofsky, Louis **11**

ARGENTINIAN

Borges, Jorge Luis **22, 32**
Storni, Alfonsina **33**

AUSTRALIAN

Hope, A. D. **56**
Wright, Judith (Arundell) **14**

AUSTRIAN

Trakl, Georg **20**

Nationality Index